H A

D0106394

SPAIN

CANDY LEE LaBALLE

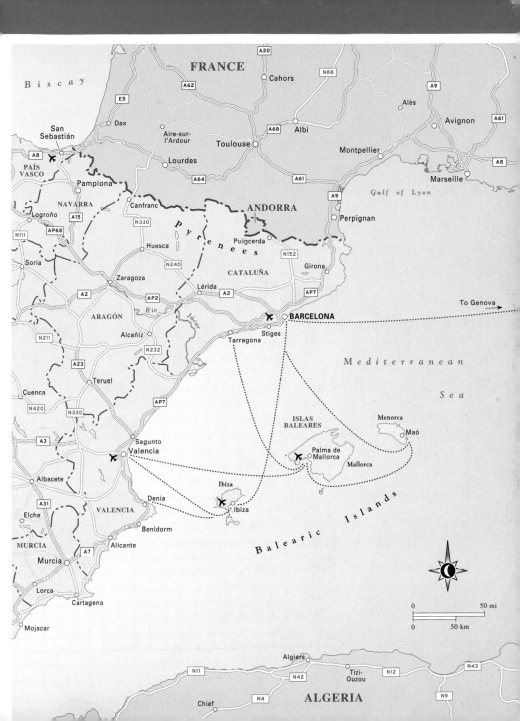

DISCOVER SPAIN

There is no single Spain to speak of. Even the
Spaniards themselves refer to this dizzyingly diverse land as "Las
Españas" ("the Spains"). Beyond its glittering Mediterranean
beaches, the most geographically diverse country in Europe
unfolds. It is a land criss-crossed by rivers and mountain ranges,
from the majestic Pyrenees to the dramatic Picos de Europa.
The lush green valleys all around give rise to fertile areas such
as La Rioja, famed worldwide for its velvety red wines. In the
center of the country, the dusky brown plains of the central Meseta
unfurl – home to both the country's vibrant capital city of Madrid
and the old stomping grounds of literature's most famous Spanish
son, Don Quixote. Even in Andalucía, where the sun shines in
copious amounts and the beaches are nearly mythical, the
land still surprises, offering both Spain's highest rainfall and its
only desert.

the colorful, curvy bench of Gaudí's Parc Güell

Over history, this geographic variety has given rise to a nation of plurality. Differing cultures, cuisine, and customs co-exist under the red and yellow flag of Spain. Though Castellano (Castilian Spanish) is the national language, several regional tongues are just as important including Catalan in Cataluña, Euskara in the País Vasco, and Gallego in Galicia. On the table, the diversity takes a tasty turn in "typically Spanish" dishes that include meaty Asturian stews, fish fried in olive oil from Andalucía, sophisticated Catalan sauces, and, of course, fragrant Valencian paella. Spanish architecture too is a feast of variety: with whitewashed villages in Andalucía; medieval castles in Castille y León; thousand-year-old Moorish palaces in Sevilla, Córdoba, and Granada; Gaudí's whimsical buildings in Barcelona; and the delirious titanium-skinned Guggenheim in Bilbao.

This diversity also translates into a dazzling year-round roster

Plaza Mayor, Madrid

of festivals, from horse shows in Jerez to mammoth bonfires in Valencia to the infamous running of the bulls in Pamplona. There are solemn Easter Week processions in Andalucía, elaborate mock battles between Christians and Moors in Alicante, human castle-building in Tarragona, fire-breathing dancing dragons in Cataluña, tomato fights in Buñol, and wine battles in La Rioja. Meanwhile, every town in the country, no matter how small, has its own home-grown festival that brings out the locals from grannies to tots for late-night dancing in the streets followed by an early-morning breakfast of *churros y chocolate* (fried dough and hot chocolate) at an open-air stand. There is a party going on somewhere in Spain most every day of the year.

Within this national obsession with fiesta is the thread that weaves together the myriad pieces of the Spanish cultural fabric – the Spaniard's immense gusto for life. There may not be a single Spain, but from Ávila to Aínsa, Salamanca to Segovia, Zaragoza to Zafra, the Spanish – no matter their social, economic,

whitewashed houses in the Costa Brava village of Calella

or political background – jump head, heart, and soul first into life. Meals are leisurely, wine-fueled affairs that always end in *sobremesa*, a lively post-meal conversation; vacations are long and the calendar is liberally sprinkled with holidays; family and friends are paramount, always trumping professional careers; going out is so much a part of the national consciousness that it has its own noun, *la marcha*; tapas, those savory little dishes so popular in modern gastronomy and *el tapeo*, or "going for tapas," are an essential part of life. It is this passion for the daily pleasures of life that is at the heart of what makes Spain, Spain. As any Spaniard will tell you, *En España se vive muy bien* – "In Spain you live very well."

The bottom line is that no matter your interests, Spain will meet them. Art lovers can luxuriate in the world-famous Museo del Prado. History buffs can view 20,000-year-old cave paintings in Cantabria. Adrenaline junkies can kite-surf in Tarifa, hike in the Pyrenees, or party the night away in Ibiza. Urbanites can find full-time stimulation

Fiestas del Pilar, Zaragoza

in Spain's best cities – Madrid, Barcelona, and Valencia – while those seeking a slower pace can get way off the beaten path in Galicia, Aragón, or Extremadura. Whatever you choose, wherever you go, one thing is sure: The "classic Spain" that enticed visitors like Ernest Hemingway – flowing wine, cobbled streets, flamenco, fiesta – will be there. For throughout Spain, from the Pyrenees to the Mediterranean, there is always a sunny spot available at a sidewalk café where the tacka-tak of flamenco pours out of the radio, wine is drawn from a barrel, and the laughter of locals fills the air. When you find this place – and you will – savor it. This is the real Spain and, for however briefly, it will let you too live very well. *¡Aproveche!*

charming downtown Pontevedra, Galicia

© TURGALICIA

Contents

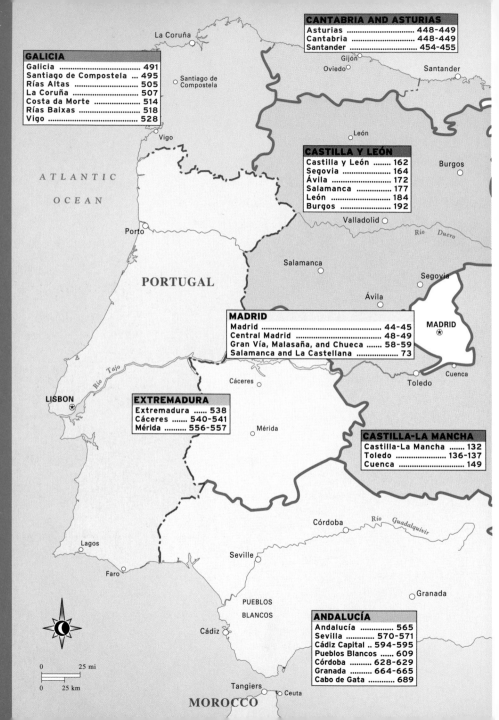

14

GALICIA

CANTABRIA AND ASTURIAS

CASTILLA Y LEÓN

MADRID

EXTREMADURA

CASTILLA-LA MANCHA

ANDALUCÍA

ATLANTIC
OCEAN

La Coruña

Santiago de
Compostela

Vigo

Porto

PORTUGAL

Río Tajo

LISBON

Lagos

Faro

Gijón

Oviedo

León

Valladolid

Salamanca

Ávila

Cáceres

Mérida

Seville

Cádiz

PUEBLOS
BLANCOS

Santander

Burgos

Segovia

Río Duero

MADRID

Cuenca

Toledo

Córdoba

Río Guadalquivir

Granada

Tangiers

Ceuta

MOROCCO

0   25 mi
0   25 km

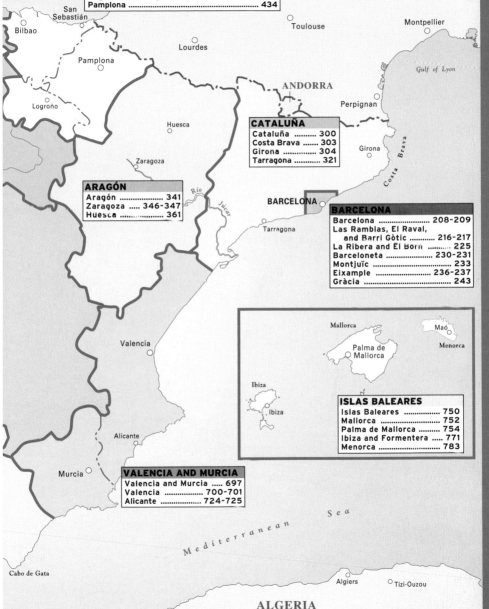

MAP CONTENTS

FRANCE

ANDORRA

Gulf of Lyon

BARCELONA

Mediterranean Sea

ALGERIA

© AVALON TRAVEL PUBLISHING, INC.

The Lay of the Land

MADRID

Located in the very center of the country, Madrid is the geographic heart of Spain. As the capital, it is also the social and cultural hub offering a dizzying variety of sights, sounds, and sensations spread across a handful of charming barrios. The historic core teems with sights from the world-famous **Museo del Prado** to the grand **Palacio Real.** The elegant **Plaza Mayor** anchors **La Latina,** one of Madrid's oldest barrios, full of 16th- and 17th-century buildings that house some of Spain's best tapas and wine bars. Trendy **Chueca** is home to one of Europe's most vibrant gay and lesbian communities. Working-class **Lavapiés** nurtures both centuries-old Madrid customs and the city's most international community. If you like nightlife, Madrid complies with a world-famous scene that starts late and goes until dawn. Afterwards, join the locals for a traditional breakfast of churros and hot chocolate.

CASTILLA-LA MANCHA

The great plateau Castilla-La Mancha is the most homogenous of Spain's provinces, rolling out in a dusky, mottled plain for some 77,700 square kilometers (30,000 square miles), the horizon broken only by groves of olive trees, a smattering of windmills, and stone-colored villages that seem as if time marched right by them. If it sounds familiar, it should. This is **Don Quixote** land, where the world's most famous literary figure stomped around looking for knightly glory and getting himself into hilarious trouble along the way. It is also home to the glorious city of **Toledo,** a UNESCO world treasure that houses one of the most atmospheric medieval quarters in the world. Its hive of twisting streets gives evidence of a glorious past when Toledo was one of the most cultured and sophisticated cities in Europe with Moors, Christians, and Jews living productively and peacefully side by side.

CASTILLA Y LEÓN

Castilla y León is the old stomping grounds of Isabel and Fernando, the Catholic Kings who forged a single nation out of dozens of fractious fiefdoms. The rambling, mountainous landscape bears witness to this era with hundreds of imposing medieval castles and brooding cathedrals, including the **Catedral de Burgos,** one of the world's most magnificent Gothic buildings. The city of **León** has its own astonishing cathedral with nearly 1,900 square meters (20,000 square feet) of stained glass. **Salamanca** offers a wealth of shimmering Renaissance buildings including the **Plaza Mayor,** the largest and most elegant main square in Spain. Stoic **Ávila** boasts nearly 2.5 kilometers (1.5 miles) of medieval walls that are among the best preserved in Europe. Perhaps the star city in Castilla y León's dazzling constellation is **Segovia,** with its Roman aqueduct, fairytale castle, and maze of 12th-century Romanesque churches.

BARCELONA

The most cosmopolitan of Spain's cities, Barcelona is a vibrant, vivacious, visionary place. Sitting on the Mediterranean Sea, this is where Antoni Gaudí found inspiration and built the world's most whimsical structures, including **La Sagrada Família.** Picasso spent his youth here and the **Museu Picasso** offers a brilliant look at his artistic development. Meanwhile, each barrio offers its own charms. **Barri Gòtic** seduces with a brooding jungle of medieval lanes. **Barceloneta** offers neighborly tapas bars, excellent seafood, and a boisterous stretch of beach. **El Born** bristles with boutiques, art galleries, and restaurants where the food is turned into art. **El Raval** offers bohemian hip and a whole lot of grit. **Gràcia** is still very much an old-fashioned barrio, with a good mix of expats and artists sharing the sidewalks with *abuelas* (grandmothers) pushing their carts to market.

CATALUÑA

Comprising the northeastern corner of Spain, Cataluña is tucked between the Mediterranean and the Pyrenees. While Barcelona is its jewel, Cataluña offers many other gems including **Girona,** with its impressive medieval Jewish barrio; **Figueres,** Salvador Dalí's hometown and site of his amazing **Teatre-Museu Dalí;** and **Tarragona,** a former Roman capital and home to some of Spain's best Roman ruins. Along the coast, the dramatic, almost surreal **Costa Brava** boasts several lovely fishing villages including **Cadaqués** and **Roses,** the tiny town that serves as ground zero for Ferran Adrià, the most famous chef in the world. The **Catalan Pyrenees** offers an abundance of natural riches from the low-lying volcanic wonderland of **La Garrotxa** to the spectacular peaks and world-class skiing of **Vall d'Aran.**

ARAGÓN

Aragón stretches north from the jagged ocher plains of **Teruel** through the verdant green valley of **Zaragoza** and straight up into **Huesca** where the soaring Pyrenees are at their most dramatic. In the south, Teruel is home to some spectacular sights, including the **Mudejar towers** of Teruel city and the medieval wonderland of **Albarracín,** one of the most evocative villages in Spain. Zaragoza, the capital of the region of the same name, offers the monumental **Basílica del Pilar,** some truly impressive Roman ruins, and the Moorish palace **La Aljafería.** Up north, Huesca is home to the **Somontano** wine region, the perfectly preserved medieval town of **Aínsa,** and the **Aragonese Pyrenees.** The wildest and steepest area of the Pyrenees, it offers world-class climbing and extreme sports as well as the captivating, accessible beauty of the **Parque Nacional de Ordesa y Monte Perdido.**

PAÍS VASCO, LA RIOJA, AND NAVARRA

Even clustered together, the three regions of País Vasco, La Rioja, and Navarra comprise one of the smallest corners of Spain. Dominated by the Pyrenees to the east and the Cantabrian Sea to the north, this area makes up for in culture, food, and fiesta what it lacks in size. On the Basque coast, **San Sebastián** glitters like a jewel on the steely blue sea. It is a mecca for foodies who flock to its acclaimed restaurants and gourmet tapas bars. Nearby **Bilbao** is home to the titanium delirium of the **Museo Guggenheim,** one of the most famous buildings in the world. La Rioja, traversed by the Ebro, one of Spain's mightiest rivers, is the source of Spain's most famous wine. All along the rolling green valleys are rustic vineyards dotted with bodegas open for visits. Navarra is home to **Pamplona** and the infamous running of the bulls.

CANTABRIA AND ASTURIAS

Snaking along the Cantabrian Sea, Cantabria and Asturias comprise a colorful ribbon of nature's exuberance. The cobalt-blue sea laps pristine white beaches backed by deep-green forests that crawl up steely gray mountains topped by frilly white peaks. It is a place truly worthy of the word awesome. At the center stands the **Picos de Europa,** rising suddenly to nearly 2,750 meters (9,000 feet) just a few kilometers from the shore. The Picos offer clear glacial lakes, ancient Romanesque churches, and tiny villages famed for their potent Cabrales blue cheese. Meanwhile, the coast is dotted with picturesque villages, such as **Santillana del Mar,** with its preserved 16th-century medieval core; the ancient fishing village of **San Vicente de la Barquera; Comillas,** with its sunflower-covered Gaudí house; and wild, pristine beaches, including the **Playa del Silencio** and **Playa de las Cuevas del Mar.**

GALICIA

Deep green and very wet, Galicia comprises the northwest corner of Spain. Its northern coast, lapped by the cold waters of the Cantabrian Sea, is dotted with secluded coves and beaches. The Atlantic coast to the west is wilder, especially along the **Costa da Morte** where land meets sea in a tumultuous clash of nature. Further south, the coast is distinguished by estuaries reaching deep into the land. They house fishing villages, colorful ports, and lively towns such as **Vigo** where you can eat freshly shucked oysters right on the street. Inland Galicia is most famed for the city of **Santiago de Compostela** and its monumental Catedral, one of the loveliest Gothic buildings in Spain. Beyond Santiago, inner Galicia is misty, often inaccessible land. Mountainous and threaded with rivers, it is dotted with ancient stone churches and postage-sized farms plowed by mules.

EXTREMADURA

Extremadura is Spain's Wild West. Sparsely populated, its lands roll out in fields of wheat and groves of olive trees. Herds of fat, black pigs nuzzle the ground feasting on acorns. *Toros* (bulls) scratch the dusty earth with their forelegs. Giant storks fly above, long sticks in their beaks, on their way to build the giant nests that top the region's buildings. Extremadura was also home to the world's original cowboys—conquistadors like Cortés and Pizarro who conquered the Americas and carved their names in history books. They brought back vast wealth and built the elegant cities of **Cáceres and Trujillo,** which shimmer today with a hushed medieval charm. Down south, **Mérida** glittered way before the rest of Spain even existed. Founded in 25 B.C., it was one of the most important cities in the Roman Empire, as evidenced by the city's amazing wealth of Roman ruins.

ANDALUCÍA

Stretching across Southern Spain, Andalucía comprises some of the most varied geography in Europe with mountain ranges, deserts, and a glorious stretch of coast bathed by two bodies of water—the cold, churning Atlantic and the warm, tranquil Mediterranean. The former offers the gorgeous, wind-swept beaches of **Costa de la Luz** while the latter laps the protected coves of **Cabo de Gata.** History and culture are just as varied. The Alhambra in **Granada,** the Alcázar in **Sevilla,** and the Mezquita in **Córdoba** are legacies of Andalucía's Moorish past. Flamenco and bullfighting are more recent legacies that have come to define Spanish culture. **Cádiz, Jerez, Ronda,** and every town in between explode each year in week-long *ferias* (fairs) that attempt to redefine bacchanalia with all-night dancing, parading horses, and free-flowing *jerez* (sherry).

VALENCIA AND MURCIA

Hugging the southern Mediterranean coast, the regions of Valencia and Murcia are known jointly as Levante, or "from the east." Inland, the landscape is dominated by mountains and fertile farmland including vast groves of the famed Valencian oranges. Near the coast, the land is riddled with wetlands such as **Albufera,** a bio-reserve just outside of Valencia city that also offers the best paella in the region. The coast, particularly the shimmering **Costa Blanca,** is blessed with some of the longest, finest, whitest beaches in all of the Mediterranean. Though some of it has been "resorted" to death, tiny towns like **Altea** and **Dénia** are still dreamy Mediterranean escapes. Meanwhile, the biggest city in the region, **Valencia,** is cosmopolitan, cultured, and, during its **Las Fallas festival,** absolutely crazy.

ISLAS BALEARES

The four islands of the Islas Baleares shimmer in the Mediterranean Sea just off the coast of Valencia. **Mallorca,** the largest of the four, offers both the buzzing capital city of **Palma de Mallorca** and a rugged, mountainous coast of verdant valleys and dramatic cliffs that is a paradise for hikers and bikers. **Ibiza,** besides being the most notorious party capital in the world, is edged in some of the dreamiest coves imaginable. **Formentera,** the tiniest of the islands, is the least developed. Mostly flat, it has a very low, very green ridge running along its center and miles of beautiful wild beaches. **Menorca** is the most remote and, in many ways, the wildest of the islands. In addition to dramatic rocky coasts, remote coves, and brilliantly white, fine sand beaches, it is dotted with prehistoric monuments from the Talaiot culture.

Planning Your Trip

If you have the luxury of time and money, the best way to enjoy Spain is slowly—the way you would savor a meal at a world-famous Spanish restaurant such as El Bulli. However, even if you take it city by city, a week at a time, over the course of years, you'll still barely scratch the surface. If your time is limited, deciding what to see can be overwhelming. Many travelers are afraid that they might miss something. However, the flip side of all that variety is that you are guaranteed to have an amazing time wherever you go. In just a few blocks in Madrid you can see world-class art, have tapas, see a flamenco performance, and then dance until dawn. That is also true of Barcelona, Valencia, Sevilla, and even off-the-beaten-path places like Zaragoza, Girona, and Cáceres. The bottom line: Don't try to rush around seeing and doing everything in a short amount of time. Wherever you go, for whatever amount of time, Spain will come to you. If you have five days or less, you can get in two big cities at the most. With a week, you have more options. Two weeks and you can see the best of Spain. Let your itinerary be led by your interests. If you are fascinated by the romantic Spain of *Carmen* and flamenco, head to Andalucía. If you like art and architecture, it has to be Barcelona. For a buzzing city vibe with nightlife to match, head to Madrid. Foodies should aim their forks at Cataluña and País Vasco. Wine lovers, head to La Rioja, Ribera del Duero, or Somontano. And 24-hour party people, Ibiza is for you.

WHEN TO GO

Your decision of when to travel to Spain should be based on the seasons and what each offers in terms of weather, services, prices, and festivals.

Asturias mist

vineyards, La Rioja

Overall, Spain's climate is Mediterranean with dry, hot summers, moderate winters, and a well-deserved reputation for ample sunshine. However, because of Spain's geographical diversity, climate and temperatures vary widely. Galicia is similar to Seattle with its misty skies and long, cold, rainy winters. Almería is a desert with the hot temperatures and dryness to prove it. The Pyrenees are cold and snowy all winter and only really thaw out in the depths of summer. Almost all the main touristic cities—Barcelona, Madrid, Sevilla, Valencia—get very hot in summer, reaching unbearable temperatures by July and August. Conversely, winter is chilly in each of them, including sunny Sevilla. The vast interior *meseta* (plateau) is cold-to-the-bone during winter.

Spring and fall are the ideal times for almost every region of Spain. Temperatures are moderate throughout the country and on the Mediterranean coasts the waters are warm enough for swimming. Spring is particularly wonderful in both Madrid and Barcelona. After the gray days of winter, both cities burst into bloom, not only with colorful blossoms and flowering trees but with an incredible sense of optimism and promise. Excitement is in the air as cafés put out their sidewalk tables, street musicians emerge with their accordions, and couples (young and old) take to kissing on sidewalk benches. In Galicia and along the Cantabrian coast into País Vasco, spring and fall will still be a bit chilly—you'll need a light jacket to stroll along the beach and rain will be common enough that you'll have to travel with an umbrella. Fall can be spectacular in La Rioja when the vineyards turn bright red in anticipation of the *vendimia* (harvest)—one of the most exciting times to be in the region. Spring and fall are okay times for visiting the Pyrenees if your plan is hiking and climbing, but snow and ice can still be a problem well into April and starting up again by September.

Except in summer havens like the Islas Baleares, most everything in Spain will be open in spring and fall, and prices will be a bit lower than the summertime highs. In theory, you can expect fewer tourists, though as every guidebook and magazine article touts the glories of spring and fall, that is changing—notably in Barcelona, Madrid, and Sevilla. Of the two seasons, fall tends to be less busy as so many people are starting school and getting back to their regular post-summer lives. However, fall also has fewer festivals, while spring teems with them—Semana Santa throughout Andalucía, the Feria de Abril in Sevilla, the Horse Festival in Jerez, Moros y Cristianos in Alicante and Valencia, and San Isidro in Madrid are just a few.

Winter offers cold temperatures inland, particularly on the plains of Castile, of which Madrid is a part. In the mountainous regions, snow and ice are common. Rain can pummel the northern coasts. Meanwhile, the Mediterranean coasts and the Islas Baleares remain sunny,

the crescent beach of Roses, Cataluña

though the waters might be too chilly for swimming and you'll probably want a sweater for the evenings. However, the cities make up for what the weather withholds. Fewer tourists venture to Spain in winter. Lines are gone (or a lot shorter) at top sights like museums and monuments. Restaurants aren't crowded, hotels have more availability, and tourist offices are a lot less busy. Plummeting prices are another plus. Hotel rates can reduce by as much as a third—especially in Andalucía, on the coasts, and in Barcelona. Madrid's rates fluctuate less. The downside of this is that hours are often reduced in winter—always check the opening and closing times before planning your day. In the Islas Baleares, many places shut down altogether. Several of Spain's liveliest festivals are held in winter—Carnival reaches riotous proportions in both Sitges and Cádiz in February. Las Fallas, one of the world's greatest parties, takes over Valencia in March.

Summer is a victim of its own beautiful excess. Temperatures are glorious along the coasts. The Mediterranean and Atlantic beaches are simply sizzling, and not just because of the temperatures. This is peak tourist season—prices are at their highest, rooms are at their scarcest, and sights, restaurants, bars, and clubs are packed every day and night of the week. If you want to visit the coasts during this time, book ahead and consider having your vacation in June or July. August is the traditional Spanish vacation month and entire inland villages seem to pack up and plop themselves at the beach. The Pyrenees and Picos de Europa are green and warm in summer, while the northern coasts are at their most inviting. You'll still need reservations wherever you go, but the northern regions don't reach the same touristic heights as the southern coasts do.

The least attractive of sights in summer are the cities. Madrid, Barcelona, and Sevilla are positively seething with tourists, temperatures are viciously hot, and hotels are scarce (when you do book make sure your room has air-conditioning). Come August, when the Spaniards head for vacations, these vibrant cities become ghost towns as stores, restaurants, and bars close up for the month. Of course, there are still places to shop, eat, and dance—just a lot fewer of them than usual. Still, summer brings with it Spain's best, or at least most notorious, festivals including San Fermín in Pamplona, Tomatina in Buñol, Valencia, the Sonar Music Festival in Barcelona, the Batalla del Vino (wine fight) in Haro, La Rioja, and the wild club parties of Ibiza.

WHAT TO TAKE

You could show up to Spain with only a credit card and the clothes on your back and in a matter of hours outfit yourself completely for your vacation. Spain is a modern, commercial hub and there is nothing you can't get here. That said, your best bet is a **mid-sized bag** with wheels both for navigating the long passages in Madrid's and Barcelona's airports and for tugging around as you hunt for your hotel. Backpacks are really only appropriate for backpackers, who will often be carrying sleeping and camping gear for a long trek across Europe. If you do plan to do some treks in nature while you are here, pack a smaller daypack or backpack within your suitcase. For sightseeing, an across-the-shoulder bag is preferable to a backpack both because you can access its contents much easier when walking and because it makes you less of a target for the pickpockets in the cities. You might also want to buy a **money belt** to wear under your clothing.

Spanish pharmacies are easy to find on the street. Just look for the flashing green cross.

When packing **clothing,** try to stick to light, mix-and-match items that don't need ironing. Larger hotels will be able to offer you an iron, but smaller, cheaper places may not. Keep in mind that Spain is both more fashionable and formal than the United States. Though shorts, jeans, and T-shirts are now commonplace, especially among younger Spaniards, track suits are worn only in gyms. That said, the most important thing is that you are comfortable—this is your vacation after all. If you want to wear shorts and sandals, do so. However, keep in mind that sleeveless tops are forbidden in some cathedrals and religious monuments, particularly in smaller towns. Have a light shirt or sweater to throw over your shoulders if you are visiting such places. Unless you are traveling in the dog-heat of summer, be prepared to layer with a few light sweaters and maybe a jacket. If you will be going out to a big club, the same kind of club-wear you'd expect in the States is fine here. For upscale restaurants and events, bring upscale clothing—nice slacks and a collared shirt for men, a dressy outfit for women. However, shops are plentiful and if you suddenly score tickets to the opera, you can easily pick up something nice to wear. Very few places will require men to wear a jacket and tie.

In summer, keep in mind that you will sweat a lot. You should have enough light shirts so that you can change a couple times per day. Bring your own swimsuit; bathing wear is inordinately expensive in Spain. In winter, bring gloves, hat, and coat if you are going anywhere but the Mediterranean coast. Finally, if you wear XXL sizes, do bring everything you will need. Spain's clothing stores tend to only stock smaller sizes. One exception is the super-chain H&M.

You will be walking a lot, so bring **comfortable shoes.** Though some older guide books say tennis shoes are not acceptable, that is no longer true. However, you will need something dressier for some nightclubs, high-end restaurants, and upscale cultural events. Also, keep in mind that Spain is a major producer of footwear, so you might want to have a little extra cash worked into your budget for a new pair or three. Items such as **accessories, sunglasses, and jewelry** are completely up to you and what you want to carry (but it is never a good idea to travel with expensive jewels).

Personal items should be kept to a minimum if you will be moving around a lot. You'll want your hygiene and beauty items, especially if you use particular products for skin conditions. Anything else can be bought here, including shampoos, toothpaste, and other hygiene items, and nicer hotels usually provide such toiletries. Sunscreens tend to be a bit more expensive in Spain, but they are readily available. If you really need to bring a **hairdryer,** make sure it is small and adaptable to Spain's 220 voltage. However, bigger hotels will always have a hairdryer in the bathroom. At smaller hotels, check with the front desk, they often have one on hand.

If you take **prescription drugs,** be sure to bring enough to last the length of your trip. Have a copy of the prescription or a photocopy of the drug's label in case you need a refill. Spanish pharmacies will fill most prescriptions with the exception of narcotics

(but even that depends on the pharmacist). Also, you might check with a pharmacy about the cost of a refill whether you need it or not. Spain's drug costs are much lower than those in the United States. You may find that the cost here is even lower than your co-pay in the United States.

If you bring any rechargeable items such as **cameras, video recorders, laptops,** or **Blackberrys,** double-check to make sure the charger can handle 220 voltage and pick up a **European plug converter.** Spain's outlets feature two round holes about an inch apart. Converters cost less than €1 at any hardware or department store in Spain.

Finally, be sure to bring all the necessary documents such as your **passport,** a **copy of your passport** in case yours should get stolen or lost, and your **state driver's license** if you will be renting a car. An **international driving license** is technically not needed, but depending on the car rental agency, it may be requested. You can get one at any AAA office for less than $20. For **credit card numbers,** the safest option is to email yourself a copy of your credit card numbers and the appropriate customer service telephone numbers for reporting a stolen or missing card.

Explore Spain

THE 14-DAY BEST OF SPAIN

In a land as dramatically diverse as Spain, is it possible to see the best that the country offers during a standard two-week vacation? If you plan carefully, pack lightly, and follow this strategy, the answer is a resounding *sí!* This itinerary will take you from the bustling cities of Madrid and Barcelona to the seductive charms of San Sebastián and Bilbao in the País Vasco with a detour through the magnificent Moorish past of Andalucía along the way. The strategy starts in Madrid, where most North American travelers land. It is created for non-drivers, but you can easily do it by car if you want to motor down roads less traveled. This intense itinerary can easily be stretched out by adding a few days to your favorite city or taking off on a side-trip. Reduce it by cutting out a city or a few days here and there. Either way, you are sure to explore the very best of this amazing country, a feat made even more intriguing when you realize that this journey still only barely scratches the surface of Spain.

Day 1

After landing in **Madrid,** plan on an easy day to recover from the flight. Take a siesta and then visit the **Plaza Mayor,** quite possibly the most wonderful introduction to Spain you could wish for. Next, head to nearby **Calle Cava Baja** and the **tapas bars of La Latina** for a light dinner Spanish-style!

Day 2

Visit the **Palacio Real** and the **Prado Museum.** If the weather is nice, take a walk through the lovely **El Retiro** park. In the evening, have dinner at the ancient **Casa Alberto** near Huertas and then follow up with a fine glass of sherry at **La Venencia.** If you are feeling energetic, head to **Plaza Santa Ana** and environs for a taste of Madrid's famed nightlife. Just remember, most bars don't get going until well after midnight.

Day 3

Take the morning AVE high-speed train to **Toledo** or the bus to **Segovia.** Both cities offer Spanish history, mystery, and excellent food. In the evening, back in Madrid, have a walk down

the buzzing **Gran Vía** before heading into trendy **Chueca** for the famed wild-mushroom tapas at **Cisne Azul.**

Day 4

Take an early AVE to **Sevilla.** Spend the morning at the **Real Alcázar,** the **Catedral,**

Palacio Real, Madrid

La Mezquita, Córdoba

and **La Giralda.** Have lunch and then take a siesta—you will need it. Around 6 P.M., head to the **Barrio Santa Cruz,** one of Spain's most magical quarters. For dinner, graze the tapas bars along **Calle Mateos Gago,** not missing the wonderful **Bar Giralda.** Around midnight, head to **Triana** and **Casa Anselma** for an authentic, passionate night of flamenco. If you don't have that sort of energy, try **El Arenal** for a show at 8:30 P.M. If time is flexible, add another night in Sevilla. Check with the tourist office to see if there is a bullfight on at **Plaza de Toros de la Real Maestranza,** one of the most famous bullrings in the world.

Day 5

In the morning, take in whatever sights you didn't yet see (or just sleep off the night before), then catch the noon AVE to **Córdoba.** Spend the early afternoon in **La Mezquita** (remembering that it closes early in fall and winter). To save time, consider staying close to the Mezquita in a hotel such as **Maimónides** or **Hotel Mezquita.** Spend dinner tapas-hopping. Tapas are a religion in Córdoba and a night in the tapas bars is one you'll never forget. The tourist office offers a handy tapas map.

Day 6

Head to **Granada** via bus (there is no direct train). In the afternoon, head to your pre-booked reservation at the **Alhambra,** a 13th-century Moorish palace and one of the loveliest

buildings in the world. Spend the late afternoon exploring the labyrinthine streets of the **Albaicín** and enjoying tapas. In the evening, see a flamenco show at a cave in **Sacromonte,** or head straight to **Barcelona** on the overnight train. If you choose to do this, you'll have to store your luggage in Granada during the day. The best bet is to go directly from your morning bus to the train station where you can pick up your ticket and lock down your goods.

Day 7

If you haven't chosen the overnight train, take an early flight to **Barcelona** (though if time is not a worry, renting a car and spending a few days following the Mediterranean coast up through Valencia is a pleasant option). By the time you settle in, it will be lunchtime. Head to **Mercat de la Boqueria** and the world-famous **Bar Pinotxo.** After lunch, ramble up **Las Ramblas** and into **Eixample** to see the Gaudí buildings—**Casa Batlló, La Sagrada Família, La Pedrera,** and **Parc Güell.** Spend the evening in lively **El Born** for tapas and drinks.

Day 8

Head first thing to **Museu Picasso** (it will be packed by noon). Afterwards, get lost in the alleys of **Barri Gòtic,** visiting the **Catedral de Barcelona** and the **Museu d'Història de la Ciutat** along the way. For lunch, head to buzzing **Barceloneta** for seafood. Afterwards, stroll along the **beach** then catch the

Museo Guggenheim, Bilbao

cable car to **Montjuïc** where you can visit **Fundació Joan Miró,** a fascinating museum of this modern master's art. Come evening, try to catch a concert at the **Palau de la Música Catalana** or go gourmet with a meal at one of Barcelona's many temples of haute cuisine.

Day 9

Today, explore working-class **Gràcia** or bohemian **El Raval.** If you feel the need to escape the city madness, train out to the mountaintop monastery of **Montserrat** or head to the fine beaches of **Sitges.** Back in Barcelona, spend the evening exploring the bars and cafés of **Barri Gòtic** and finish the night with a drink in the fairy forest of **Bosc de les Fades.** If you want something heavier, hit one of the dance clubs down on **Port Olímpic.** You can also opt for the overnight train to **San Sebastián.**

Day 10

If you didn't take the train, catch a morning flight to **San Sebastián.** (If you have the time, the drive is quite dramatic, skirting the foothills of the majestic Pyrenees.) Take a stroll along the elegant **Paseo de la Concha,** visit the moody open-air sculptures **El Peine del Viento,** or take a dip in the bay. Come evening, prepare for a night of gastronomic indulgence in the **world-famous *pintxos* bars** of the **Parte Vieja.**

Day 11

Catch the bus (or a cab) to the seaside town of **Hondarribia** (Fuenterrabía in Spanish). One of the most picturesque fishing villages in **País Vasco,** tiny Hondarribia also offers a fairy-tale 15th-century medieval center. Have lunch at the boisterous seafood house **Hermandad de Pescadores.** Either spend the night here at the moody and magnificent **Palacio de Carlos V,** a medieval palace with suits of armor lining its walls, or head back to San Sebastián.

Day 12

Bright and early catch the bus to **Bilbao.** In the morning, visit the **Museo Guggenheim,** one of the world's most exuberant displays of architecture. Afterwards, take the **Funicular de Artxanda** uphill for an amazing view. Have lunch in the beautiful old **Café Iruña** in the Abando district. After a siesta, stroll the atmospheric streets of the **Casco Viejo,** having tapas and wine along the way.

Day 13

Enjoy a leisurely breakfast in Bilbao, then catch a flight back to **Madrid.** Take the day easy with souvenir shopping in **Sol** and then a leisurely lunch of paella at **Arrocería Gala.** In the evening, head to **Medina Mayrit** for a luxurious two-hour float in the Arabic baths—the perfect place to relax after your trip and reflect on all the wonders you've just seen.

Day 14

Leave your luggage at the hotel, and start your last morning in Spain with a Madrid breakfast of *churros y chocolate* at **El Brillante.** Then head next door to the **Museo Reina Sofía** for a gaze on Picasso's masterpiece *Guernica,* one of the most important paintings in the world. Afterwards, collect your luggage and head to Barajas airport.

TAPAS, PAELLA, AND RIOJA: A REGIONAL FOOD AND WINE ODYSSEY

In the last decade, Spain has surpassed France as the food world's most revered culinary destination. Cataluña and the País Vasco (Basque Country) have led the revolution. This strategy will take you to some of those regions' top dining destinations with side trips to the vineyards of La Rioja and Somontano. Keep in mind that most bodegas (wineries) will require at least one-day advance notice of your visit and that most of the restaurants listed here require reservations. Though it is possible to do much of this trip by public transport, you'll be able to see and do more by renting a car.

Day 1

Your culinary journey starts in Madrid. After a short siesta to recover from the long flight, visit **Sol and Plaza Mayor** in the early evening. Plan dinner at **La Broche,** the showcase restaurant of superstar Spanish chef Sergi Arola. The all-white dining room is the backdrop for the exquisite, adventurous food that has earned Arola accolades from far and wide. After dinner, head to the sophisticated **Del Diego** for the best cocktails in town.

Day 2

Spend the morning at the **Museo del Prado,** then head to the nearby **Viridiana** for lunch, one of Spain's first culinary-groundbreaking restaurants. Foodies worldwide agree that the sublime cuisine of chef Abraham García more than merits its rave reviews. In the evening, stroll through **La Latina,** enjoying the city's best tapas bars, being sure not to miss the rustic **El Tempranillo** with its extensive list of fine Spanish wines.

Day 3

Catch the first-class coach to **Logroño,** arriving mid-afternoon. Spend the early evening wandering the historic district, **Casco Antiguo.** Around 9 P.M., head to **Calle Laurel,** a tiny pedestrian street that teems with lively *pinchos* bars. Be sure to seek out trendy **La Gota del Vino** for award-winning *pinchos* and excellent rioja by the glass.

Day 4

Rent a car in Logroño and head west just out of town to **Bodega Marques de Arviza,** run by dynamic young winemaker Elsa Ubis. Continue to the hilltop town of **Briones,** home to the **Dinastía Vivanco Museo de la Cultura del Vino,** a spacious, modern wine interpretation center. Have a gourmet lunch overlooking the vineyards or cross the road to the unassuming gas station for a hearty meal of local favorites. After lunch, drive to **Haro,** the "wine capital" of La Rioja and home to several bodegas, including the not-to-be-missed **Bodegas Muga.** Spend the night in **Hotel Los**

pimientos de piquillo drying on balcony, Laguardia

Agustinos, a 14th-century convent. Dine either at the hotel's ultra-modern restaurant **Las Duelas,** which features sophisticated cuisine, or rustic **Casa Terete,** which has served succulent wood-roasted lamb for over a century.

Day 5

In the morning, head for the sleepy medieval village of **Briñas** and the bodega of **Heredad Baños Bezares.** Next, amble through the countryside with **Elciego** as your goal. There visit the **Marqués de Riscal Ciudad del Vino,** a titanium-skinned wine center, museum, and bodega created by mega-architect Frank Gehry. Have lunch in its gourmet restaurant run by chef Francis Paniego. Next, head to the walled village of **Laguardia,** one of the most magical places in Spain. Visit the atmospheric **Bodega El Fabulista** with its wine caves dug deep below the town. Stay at the 17th-century **Posada Mayor de Migueloa,** which also houses a top-rated dining room. Be sure to have an evening glass of rioja in the atmospheric **Plaza Mayor.**

Day 6

The Laguardia tourist office offers an informative booklet on the bodegas in the valley below the town. Start with **Ysois Bodegas,** designed by famed Spanish architect Santiago Calatrava. **Bodegas Palacio** is more traditional and has a rustic restaurant perfect for lunch. Afterwards, head to **Vitoria.** Enjoy a leisurely evening stroll through the city's medieval quarter, then head to the award-winning **Sagartoki** for sublime *pintxos.* If you'd like a fuller meal, try the highly acclaimed **Zaldiarán** for an exquisite taste of New Basque Cuisine.

Day 7

Get an early start for the two-hour drive to **San Sebastián** or catch an early bus or train. Spend the early afternoon exploring the medieval **Parte Vieja** and grazing its famed *pintxos* bars. Don't miss **Ganbara** for wild mushrooms and the acclaimed **La Cuchara de San Telmo** for foie gras. After a siesta and maybe a dip in the bay, head to dinner at one of the several world-famous restaurants in the vicinity, such as **Arzak, Martín Berasategui,** or **Mugaritz.** Remember, reservations are imperative.

Day 8

After a morning stroll along the **Paseo de la Concha,** stopping for a brioche and *café con leche,* make the three-hour drive to **Zaragoza,** the capital of **Aragón.** Spend the afternoon visiting the monumental **Basílica del Pilar,** the **La Seo** cathedral, and the city's extensive Roman ruins, and then prepare for a gourmet meal in the romantic **Montal,** located inside the gorgeous stone cloister of a 16th-century palace.

Days 9 and 10

After breakfast at the belle epoque **Gran Café Zaragoza,** drive to **Barbastro,** the capital of the **Somontano wine region,** one of Spain's most exciting up-and-coming D.O.s (appellations). Plan your tour of the bodegas at the wine center **Complejo de San Julián y Santa Lucía.** Have dinner at the top-rated **Flor** and set off early the next day for a tour of the area's best bodegas, including **Bodegas Pirineos, Viñas del Vero,** and **Enate.**

Day 11

Make your way to **Barcelona.** (Consider dropping off your car here as the rest of this itinerary is easiest by public transport.) Spend the afternoon wandering the medieval **Barri Gòtic.** For dinner, try either the inventive **Espai Sucre,** where chef Jordi Butrón brings a sweet touch to main courses, or **Comerç 24,**

where chef Carles Abellan creates astonishingly inventive gourmet tapas. Finish up with cocktails at **Espai Barroc,** an ornate 14th-century palace.

Day 12

In the morning, visit the **Museu Picasso** and then wander through **El Born** to **Abac,** one of Spain's most acclaimed restaurants, for a lunch of chef Xavier Pellicer's fanciful cuisine. In the afternoon, catch the **Bus Turistic** for a tour through Gaudí's whimsical world in Eixample. Give yourself time to have coffee under the spires of **La Sagrada Família.** For dinner, stimulate your senses at the buzz-worthy **Cinc Sentits.**

Day 13

After breakfast at one of the lively stands in the **Mercat de la Boqueria,** catch a train to **Girona.** Spend the afternoon exploring moody, medieval **El Call,** the old Jewish quarter, and be sure to stop for a tapas at **Boira** in the elegant **Plaça de l'Indepèndencia.** In the evening, catch a cab to **El Celler de Can Roca.** Located just outside of town, it has a reputation as one of the best restaurants in the world. Advance reservations are essential.

Day 14

Take an early flight or train to **Madrid.** Have your last meal in the atmospheric **Sobrino del Botín.** Opened in 1725, it is the world's oldest restaurant and was the setting for the last meal in Hemingway's *The Sun Also Rises.* It also makes the perfect last meal for your gastronomic tour of Spain.

A TOUR THROUGH OLD SPAIN

Way before flamenco, bullfighting, and tapas, there was Old Spain—a contentious land of fractious kingdoms, where knights such as El Cid tramped around in war-weary armor, fairy-tale castles dotted the landscape, and cavernous cathedrals took centuries to build. It was a land that gave birth to Isabel and Fernando, the powerful Catholic Kings who pushed the Moors out of Spain, united the country under one flag, unleashed the Spanish Inquisition, and sent Columbus on his merry way to the New World. The conquistadors who followed in his footsteps claimed the Americas for the Spanish crown and pumped massive wealth back into Spain. This long, legendary history has left behind castles, cathedrals, and towns, many of which are UNESCO World Heritage Sites. This itinerary takes you to some of the most evocative regions of Old Spain. It is still possible in many of these places to find yourself alone among the ruins. The main towns on this tour can be traveled to by public transport, but for maximum flexibility, as well as the chance to explore abandoned castles and dusky little villages, a rental car is the best option.

Day 1

From Madrid, head to **Ávila** where you can walk atop an impressive ring of **11th-century medieval walls.** This was the home of famed Catholic mystic Santa Teresa and you shouldn't miss the **church of Santa Teresa,** where a finger from the long-dead saint sits under glass. If that is not appetizing, buy some sweets from a convent where nuns follow recipes said to be handed down from the saint herself.

Day 2

Set off early for the evocative stone city of **Trujillo,** one of Spain's most beautiful cities. After lunch in the lively **Plaza Mayor,** get lost in **La Villa,** the walled medieval core that shimmers with 15th- and 16th-century mansions built by conquistadors who found their fortunes in the New World. Stay the night in a sumptuous 16th-century convent at the **Parador de Trujillo.**

Days 3 and 4

In the morning, head to **Cáceres,** another town the conquistadors built. Wander through the golden-hued buildings of the **Ciudad Monumental** and have a lunch of

local specialties at the rustically charming **El Figón de Eustaquio.** Afterwards, set off on the three-hour drive north to **Salamanca,** arriving just before sunset—which must be witnessed from the city's pink-hued **Plaza Mayor,** one of the most magnificent main squares in Spain. Check in for the night at any of the hotels that open up right onto the plaza. The next morning, hunt for the hidden frog on the 15th-century facade of the **University of Salamanca** and take a walk across the 1st-century **Roman bridge.**

Days 5 and 6

Head north to **León,** maybe stopping along the way to visit the **bodegas of Toro.** In León, awe at the **cathedral,** which boasts 125 stained-glass windows, and the opulent 16th-century **Convento de San Marcos.** At night, enjoy the boisterous atmosphere of the tapas bars in **Barrio Húmedo.** The next day, take a detour out of León to the tiny village of **Astorga** with its medieval walls, Roman ruins, Gaudí architecture, and chocolate factory.

Catedral de Burgos

Day 7

Aim to arrive in **Burgos** around 2 P.M. for lunch at **Mesón del Cid,** a 16th-century house looking over the **Catedral de Burgos,** the largest Gothic cathedral in the world and final burial place of the legendary knight El Cid. The restaurant also runs a cozy hotel. In the evening, join lively locals for tapas along **Calle Sombrería** and **Calle San Lorenzo.**

Day 8

Enjoy breakfast on the elegant **Paseo del Espolón** before heading south to the perfectly preserved medieval village of **Covarrubias.** After lunch at **De Galo,** continue south to **Santo Domingo** to see the world-famous Gregorian chanting monks perform at the 10th-century **Santo Domingo de Silos monastery.** The mass is at 7 P.M. so take this opportunity to just relax. Stay the night at **Tres Coronas,** which also houses the village's best restaurant.

Day 9

Spend the day in the wine region of **Ribera del Duero,** home to some of Spain's most famous bodegas. Base yourself in **Peñafiel** at the **Hotel Ribera del Duero** and be sure to visit that town's well-preserved 14th-century fortified castle.

Day 10

Bright and early, head south to **Segovia** and spend the day exploring its architectural and historic wonders including the **Roman aqueduct,** the fairy-tale castle **Alcázar** where Isabel first met Fernando, and the half-dozen 12th-century **Romanesque churches.** Be sure to enjoy the city's famed roast suckling pig at **José María.** In the evening, take a walk through the ancient stone plazas and see the **Cathedral of Segovia** dramatically lit at night.

Day 11

Continue southeast towards **Cuenca** and check into the gorgeous **Posada de San José.** After a leisurely lunch at any of the restaurants overlooking the town's dramatic gorges, wander the medieval streets and see the *casas colgadas,* the ancient hanging houses that cling to the cliffs high above the gorge.

Have an evening cocktail at the 16th-century **Convento de San Pablo,** which now houses a modern and luxurious parador.

Days 12 and 13

Drive east to **Valencia,** where you should turn in your car. Conquered by El Cid in the 11th century, Valencia teems with medieval sights, including the atmospheric streets that make up **Barrio del Carmen** and the Gothic splendor of the **Lonja de la Seda.** On your second day in Valencia, take a break from the Old World with a visit to the gleaming arts and science complex **La Ciutat,** home to one of the world's greatest aquariums. Have a traditional Valencian paella lunch on the beach and spend the evening relaxing by the Mediterranean Sea.

Day 14

Fly or catch a train to **Madrid** first thing in the morning. Spend your last day visiting the **Palacio Real,** one of Europe's largest palaces. Tour its **Royal Armory** to see suits of armor and weaponry worn throughout the battles of Old Spain. After your tour through Old Spain, you'll really be able to appreciate this monumental collection.

LA COSTA VERDE ROUTE

The rain in Spain does not fall mainly on the plain—it falls in the Costa Verde, the "Green Coast," leaving in its wake one of the most dramatic, melancholic, breathtaking landscapes in all of Spain. Though green dominates the regions of País Vasco, Cantabria, Asturias, and Galicia, there is a whole lot more to the palette—deep blue seas and steely blue skies, white frothy waves and golden white beaches, stone gray churches and dark cliffs. Bound by the Cantabrian Sea and a soaring ridge of mountains—including the spectacular Picos de Europa—the Costa Verde feeds the senses and soothes the soul. While not unknown to tourists, particularly Spanish and French, it is just far enough off the beaten path to feel undiscovered and wild. There are a few must-see big cities along the way, but the bulk of the trip takes you through wild beaches, pint-sized fishing villages, and ancient ruins. You can hit a lot by bus and the wonderfully creaky FEVE train, but the best way to enjoy this area is by car. The best time weather-wise for this trip is summer, though you will have to book ahead for accommodations. The shoulder months of June and September are just a smidgen chillier, but less crowded. Avoid this region in winter unless you are attracted to cold, wind, and rain.

Day 1

From Madrid, fly into **Bilbao,** where you can rent a car. Take time to see the glorious **Guggenheim,** designed by Frank Gehry. After hitting the road, your first stop is **Lekeitio,** a fishing town that offers little more than a picturesque harbor bobbing with tiny boats and wonderful seafood. Check into the rustic, yet elegant **Hotel Zubieta** and have an early meal at one of the boisterous seafood shacks along the harbor.

Day 2

Head to the lovely fishing village of **Castro-Urdiales,** just over the border in Cantabria. Have lunch on the wharf at **Asador Perla,** a raggedy tent with an outdoor grill that serves some of the best grilled sardines in the world. Next, amble westward towards **Santander,** stopping at whatever wild beach captures your interest. Take a stroll along the elegant **Paseo de Pereda** then head up to the **Palacio de**

la Magdalena for a stunning sunset view over the sea. Bed down for the night in the beachside **Hotel Las Brisas.**

Day 3

After breakfast, head to the inland town of **Santillana del Mar,** a perfectly preserved medieval city with cobbled lanes and a 7th-century church. Nearby, visit the 20,000-year-old cave paintings of **Altamira.** After lunch in the walled gardens of **Meson de los Villa**, head to the elegant seaside resort of **Comillas,** home to the whimsical **El Capricho,** a house designed by Antoni Gaudí. Stay at the romantic **Hotel Marina de Campíos.**

Days 4 and 5

After a leisurely breakfast, head towards the romantically tattered fishing village of **San Vicente de la Barquera,** one of the loveliest on the Cantabrian coast. Have lunch at the popular portside restaurant **El Marinero.** Across the Asturian border, the resort town of **Llanes** is surrounded by ooh-and-aah-worthy scenery and dozens of secluded beaches. Using

Llanes as your base, spend the next two days exploring this area, not missing the breathtaking **Playa de las Cuevas del Mar.** Be sure to prepare a picnic of local cheeses and sausages.

Day 6

Head to **Oviedo** to see some of the world's most intriguing **pre-Romanesque architecture**. Check into the quirky and luxurious **Libretto Hotel** for a few modern perks. Have dinner on **Calle Gascona,** where the cider flows from giant self-serve barrels and the thick steaks are grilled just right.

Days 7 and 8

Head back to the coast and visit the wild, cliff-lined **Playa del Silencio,** the charming seaside resort of **Luarca,** and the quaint little town of **Castropol,** where you can sleep in the **Palacete de Peñalba,** a fanciful Catalan art nouveau mansion designed by a student of Gaudí.

Day 9

After a morning stroll on the beach, drive inland to Galicia and the city of **Lugo** with its impressive set of 2nd-century **Roman walls.** After a lunch of tapas in the **Praza del Campo,** take the speedy A-6 to **La Coruña,** a bustling port city battered by the wild waves of the Atlantic. Take in the view from the **Torre de Hércules,** a 2nd-century Roman lighthouse, then have a late-afternoon stroll along the waterfront lined with *galerías,* distinctive white-framed glass balconies. Try Galician-style octopus for dinner at the rustic **A Lanchiña.**

Days 10 and 11

Catch the coastal road south and explore the dramatic **Costa da Morte.** In **Corme,** catch the dramatic sunset from the cliffs high above the Atlantic. Visit **Muxía** where "nets" of eels are hung to dry out in the sun. In **Finisterre,** walk out past the lighthouse, where for centuries pilgrims on the Camino de Santiago collected scallop shells

Costa da Morte

as proof of their pilgrimage. Use either the cozy **Hotel Rústico Muxía** or luxurious farmhouse **Insula Finisterrae** as your base.

Day 12

Head inland to **Santiago de Compostela** and check into the **Hostal dos Reis Católicos,** a magical 15th-century hospital turned luxury lodging. Wander the well-worn stone streets of Santiago, taking in the imposing **Catedral del Apósto,** where millions of faithfuls have flocked for more than 800 years. Have rustic Gallego fare at **O dezaseis.**

Day 13

Start your day with a stroll through the atmospheric **Mercado de Abastos** and have a slice of delicious almond *torta de Santiago* with *café con leche* for breakfast. Fly back to **Madrid** in the afternoon. That night, dine at the raucous **Maceiras.**

Day 14

Before flying home, visit the **Museo del Prado,** then finish up with a lunch of Asturian tapas and cider at the barrio favorite, **El Ñeru.**

ALTERNATIVE ANDALUCÍA

Andalucía is the place Spanish dream vacations are made of and every visitor should have Sevilla, Granada, and Córdoba on their checklist—but there is so much more to explore in Andalucía. None of the places listed here are so far off the path as to be unknown; they are just a lot less traveled than the big three and yet still offer the best of Andalucía—from sherry bodegas to windswept beaches to tiny white villages glistening high above the sea. A car is the best way to enjoy this area, but you can easily pick and choose a few places to explore via public transportation. The easiest way to start if you have arrived in Spain via Madrid, is to take the AVE (high-speed train) to Sevilla and rent a car there, first taking time out to see the city. Before you go, be sure to check out the *Andalucía* chapter to see if your visit will correspond with one of the region's many vibrant festivals.

Day 1

From Sevilla, head to the elegant town of **Jerez de la Frontera,** the sherry capital of the world. Visit traditional bodegas such as **González Byass, Domecq,** and **Sandeman,** then go see the famous Andalusian dancing horses. Stay the night with locals at the homey **Riad** or choose luxury at **Hotel Villa Jerez.** In the evening, enjoy tapas and flamenco at the boisterous **La Moderna.**

Day 2

Bright and early head towards the **Sierra de Grazalema,** home to the tiny sparkling-white villages known as the **Pueblos Blancos.** Your first stop is **Arcos de la Frontera,** where you can get lost in the maze of medieval streets that make up the Casco Viejo. Have lunch in the atmospheric **El Patio** before driving east towards **Zahara de la Sierra,** which sits high above a turquoise lake. After touring the town, check into **El Vínculo,** a 17th-century olive oil *molino* (mill) just outside of town that has been converted into a cozy inn.

Day 3

Continue west to the ancient village of **Olvera,** watched over by a crumbling 12th-century Moorish castle. Either have lunch at the rustic **Mesón Fuente del Pino** or pack a picnic and hit the **Vía Verde** hiking path, a converted rail path. Mesón Fuente del Pino is attached to a rustic hotel that makes a charming overnight option.

Day 4

Head to **Setenil de las Bodegas,** where the ancient white houses are built right into the cliffs. Have lunch overlooking the valley at **Restaurante Terraza El Mirador,** then continue on to **Ronda** and check into either the **Parador de Ronda** with its expansive views or the quirky, bohemian hideout of **Hotel Enfrente Arte.** Spend the rest of

sunset, Costa de la Luz

seafood, Cádiz

the day and evening enjoying the breathtaking vistas from Ronda's **Puente Nuevo,** a 17th-century bridge spanning a 120-meter-deep (400-foot) gorge, and wandering the old Moorish center, **La Ciudad.** Treat yourself to a gourmet meal at **Restaurante Tragabuches,** one of the best restaurants in Andalucía.

Days 5 and 6

Head down the coast to **Tarifa,** the southernmost tip of Europe. This elegant seaside city is also one of the windsurfing and kite-surfing capitals of the world. If you'd like to try either, check into the **100 Percent Fun Hotel** and stay awhile. If not, head west along the glistening **Costa de la Luz,** a stretch of fine beaches dotted with tiny resorts and even tinier fishing villages. Not to miss is

Bolonia, where Roman ruins sit among the sandy dunes, and **Zahara de los Atunes,** a charming laid-back beach town where you can stay in a traditional white-washed Andalusian hotel, **Doña Lola.**

Day 7

Continue up the coast to **Cádiz,** the oldest continuously inhabited city in Europe. Small and atmospheric, it will captivate you with its simple charms such as fresh fried fish from a stand in the lively **Plaza de los Flores,** the romantically tattered 18th-century mansions in the **Barrio del Mentidero,** and the seaside ruins of a **Roman theater.** Spend the night at the 18th-century palace of **Hospedería Las Cortes de Cádiz** and in the morning, take the train back to Sevilla.

MADRID

If Barcelona is the architect of cutting-edge Spain, Madrid is the seamstress, stitching together past and present, grandeur and grunge, pomp and simplicity, all without batting an eye. Walking from the worn cobblestones of Plaza Mayor to the screaming glitz of Gran Vía, it is hard not to be dazzled by the contrasts. The city built Europe's largest Royal Palace and adopted a peasant farmer as its patron saint. Three of the world's greatest art museums—the Prado, the Reina Sofía, and the Thyssen—are clustered on one of its grandest streets—Paseo del Prado. A few blocks away cloistered nuns bake sweets following a 16th-century recipe. Every year Madrid throws one of Europe's most audacious gay pride parades and a few months later it herds sheep down the same streets.

By day the city sizzles with activity—home to more than four million people (nearly six million including the suburbs), the seat of the Spanish government, and the center of Spain's financial world—traffic is thick and the noise incessant. Come evening, not much changes: Whole families spill out into the plazas, restaurants fill to bursting, and *madrileños* (as Madrid residents are called) take to the streets. World famous for its raucous nightlife, with one bar for every 100 residents, Madrid is as vibrant at 3 A.M. as it is at 3 P.M.

The result is a city that never bores. Gaze on *Las Meninas* (arguably the world's most important painting) by morning, dine in a 300-year-old tavern for lunch, stroll the lush walkways of the Retiro in early evening, try dozens of tapas on a dinnertime walk

HIGHLIGHTS

◖ **Plaza Mayor:** This jewel of 16th-century Hapsburg architecture is the lively heart and living history of old Madrid (page 51).

◖ **Palacio Real:** The largest palace in Europe, this marvel of 18th-century construction offers an up-close look at the sumptuous lifestyle of Spain's monarchy, past and present (page 54).

◖ **Gran Vía:** An explosive jumble of shops, restaurants, and jaw-dropping architecture, this truly grand avenue is the throbbing commercial vein of the city (page 56).

◖ **Museo del Prado:** Housing the largest – and arguably the most prestigious – collection of artistic masterpieces in the world, the Prado is essential must-see Madrid. No visit to the Spanish capital is complete without gazing upon Velázquez's famed *Las Meninas* (page 61).

◖ **Barrio de las Letras:** The haunt of Cervantes and his contemporaries back in the 16th century, this charming quarter is now home to some of Madrid's hottest nightlife. Take a daytime walk through literary history and come back after nightfall for a dose of modern frivolity (page 64).

◖ **El Retiro:** Do like the locals and escape the rush of the city with a leisurely stroll through this lush park. Hidden among the verdant paths are architectural treasures like the gorgeous *Palacio de Cristal* (page 64).

◖ **Museo Reina Sofía:** One word: *Guernica.* Picasso's unflinching commentary on the personal tragedies unleashed by war is as emotionally charged now as it was when it was painted in 1937 (page 67).

◖ **Madrid de los Austrias:** In this delightful maze of 16th- and 17th-century cobblestone streets at the heart of La Latina barrio, the full force of the famous Madrid passion for life is unleashed every Sunday as thousands descend upon the neighborhood to while away the afternoon with *cañas*, tapas, and laughter (page 68).

◖ **Paseo de la Castellana:** The best way to enjoy the opulent elegance of this majestic boulevard is by hopping a bus and heading straight north. The half-hour ride will take you past gardened walkways, stately palaces, and monumental public art (page 72).

LOOK FOR ◖ TO FIND RECOMMENDED SIGHTS, ACTIVITIES, NIGHTLIFE, DINING, AND LODGING.

through the ancient plazas of La Latina, join locals sipping wines at sidewalk cafés, and dance to world-famous DJs at packed clubs until dawn.

Most European capitals are more beautiful, more historic, or more stately. They sit on grand rivers, overlook seas, house ancient monuments. Not Madrid. Plucked down in the middle of the Iberian Peninsula, far from the sea, on a dusty mesa prone to harsh winters and searing summers, the Spanish capital seems strangely misplaced. For centuries it was a rural outpost of hard-scrabble peasants and long-toiling farmers. All that changed on the whim of a monastic 16th-century king who decided to set down his royal roots in this rural land. An old refrain goes *"de Madrid al cielo"* ("from Madrid to heaven"). Perched more than 610 meters (2,000 feet) above sea level, it is certainly closer to heaven than any other capital city in Europe. The high air has a clarity and shimmer that produces an achingly beautiful sky. Each evening it falls into a splendor of deep pink, orange, and magenta that has inspired writers and artists for centuries. Modest Madrid, thrust into the royal limelight, has more than lived up to its status as Spain's capital city. How could it not? The next step up is heaven.

PLANNING YOUR TIME

In two jam-packed days you can graze the Goyas, taste the tapas, and mingle just a bit with the *madrileños*. If you are really energetic, you can even squeeze in a half-day trip to **Toledo** or **El Escorial.** (See sidebar, *Two Days in Madrid.*) For a more leisurely pace, and a chance to get a real feel for the vibrancy of the city, you'll need at least three days, and one of those should be decidedly low-key so that you will have energy to try a little of Madrid's world-famous nightlife.

If you are flying into Madrid, touring Spain, and then flying back out of Madrid, try to schedule your monument hopping when you first arrive, particularly the **Prado** and the **Royal Palace.** The overload of culture can be draining, so it is best to hit them when you are at your freshest. Then, on your way back, schedule one or two days to casually soak in *la vida madrileña* with a walk in the **Retiro** or a tapas tour of **La Latina.**

The best time in Madrid is spring, when the weather warms up and both the flowers and sidewalk terraces bloom. The energy is dizzying, as winter-weary residents take giddily to the streets for evening paseos and al fresco dining. This is also the season for some of the city's best festivals—**San Isidro** and **Dos de Mayo.** Spring also kicks off Madrid's bullfighting season. If you are in town on a Sunday, an evening at the bullring is a must. The only drawback is that everyone wants to come to Madrid in spring. Hotels shift into high-season rates and rooms book fast.

Fall is another good time of year to visit. The weather is still balmy and the city is at its most vibrant, back in full swing after the long months of summer vacation. Winter has its charms, though it can be bitterly cold. The plus is that there are fewer tourists to contend with. Christmas is particularly gorgeous with the whole city decorated in festive lights. Summer is what you make of it. On the one hand it is searingly hot. Walking from museum to monument can feel like a slog through a furnace. A hotel with air-conditioning is a must. Sights tend to close earlier and many of the smaller ones shut down altogether in August. The upside to this is fewer tourists, lower hotel prices, and a chance to see locals at their most laid-back. Work in the morning or not, summertime finds *madrileños* sipping *cañas* under the stars until way late. August also features the city's most explosive barrio festival—**La Paloma.**

HISTORY

Near the end of the 9th century, Emir Mohamed I of Córdoba ordered a fortress built on the ground where Madrid's Palacio Real stands today. He named this outpost Mayrit from the Arabic word *magerit,* meaning "source of water," referring to the many streams that ran through the area at that time. The Emir built walls extending as far back as the current barrio of La Latina.

MADRID

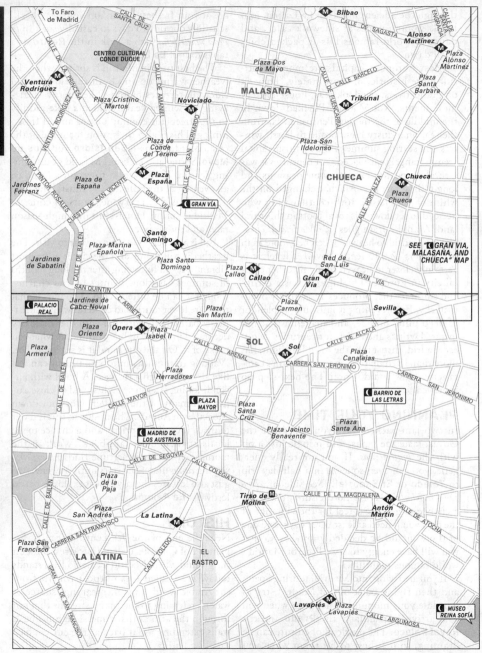

To Faro
de Madrid

CALLE DE SANTA CRUZ

CALLE DE LA PRINCESA

CENTRO CULTURAL
CONDE DUQUE

**Ventura
Rodríguez**

Plaza Cristino
Martos

Noviciado

Plaza Dos
de Mayo

MALASAÑA

CALLE DE SAGASTA

Bilbao

**Alonso
Martínez**

Plaza
Alonso
Martínez

CALLE DE SANTA ENGRACIA

CALLE DE AMANIEL

CALLE DE SAN BERNARDO

Plaza de
Conde
del Tereno

CALLE BARCELÓ

CALLE DE FUENCARRAL

Plaza San
Ildelonso

Tribunal

Plaza
Santa
Barbara

CHUECA

VENTURA RODRÍGUEZ

PASEO PINTOR ROSALES

Jardines
Ferranz

Plaza de
España

**Plaza
España**

GRAN VÍA

GRAN VÍA

Chueca

Plaza
Chueca

CALLE HORTALEZA

CUESTA DE SAN VICENTE

Jardines
de Sabatini

Plaza Marina
Epañola

CALLE DE BAILÉN

**Santo
Domingo**

Plaza Santo
Domingo

Plaza
Callao

Callao

Red de
San Luis

**Gran
Vía**

GRAN VÍA

**SEE "GRAN VÍA,
MALASAÑA, AND
CHUECA" MAP**

SAN QUINTÍN

**PALACIO
REAL**

Jardines de
Cabo Noval

C. ARRIETA

Plaza
San Martín

Plaza
Carmen

Sevilla

Ópera

Plaza
Oriente

Plaza
Isabel II

CALLE DEL ARENAL

SOL

Sol

CALLE DE ALCALÁ

CARRERA SAN JERÓNIMO

Plaza
Canalejas

CARRERA SAN JERÓNIMO

Plaza
Armería

CALLE DE BAILÉN

Plaza
Herradores

CALLE MAYOR

**PLAZA
MAYOR**

Plaza
Santa
Cruz

Plaza Jacinto
Benavente

**BARRIO DE
LAS LETRAS**

Plaza
Santa Ana

**MADRID DE
LOS AUSTRIAS**

CALLE DE SEGOVIA

CALLE COLEGIATA

Plaza
de la
Paja

Plaza
San Andrés

La Latina

**Tirso de
Molina**

CALLE DE LA MAGDALENA

**Antón
Martín**

CALLE DE ATOCHA

Plaza San
Francisco

CARRERA SAN FRANCISCO

GRAN VÍA DE SAN FRANCISCO

CALLE DE BAILÉN

LA LATINA

CALLE DE TOLEDO

EL
RASTRO

Lavapiés

Plaza
Lavapiés

CALLE ARGUMOSA

**MUSEO
REINA SOFÍA**

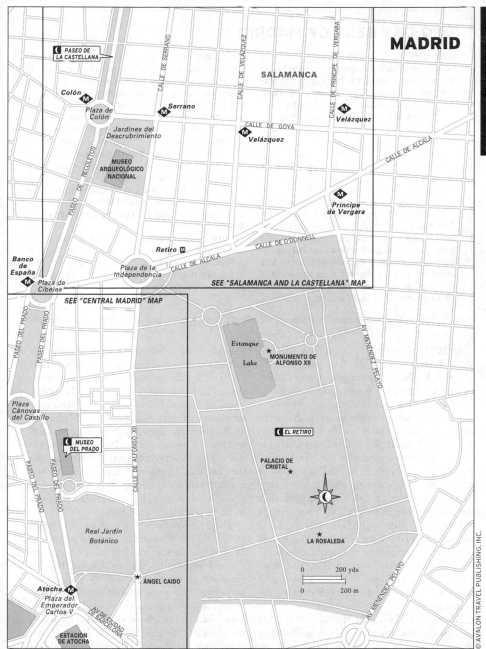

MADRID

SALAMANCA

PASEO DE LA CASTELLANA

Colón M

Plaza de Colón

Serrano M

Jardines del Descrubrimiento

CALLE DE SERRANO

CALLE DE VELÁZQUEZ

CALLE DE PRÍNCIPE DE VERGARA

CALLE DE GOYA

Velázquez M

Velázquez M

CALLE DE ALCALÁ

MUSEO ARQUEOLÓGICO NACIONAL

PASEO DE RECOLETOS

Príncipe de Vergara M

Banco de España

Retiro M

Plaza de la Independencia

CALLE DE ALCALÁ

CALLE DE O'DONNELL

M Plaza de Cibeles

SEE "SALAMANCA AND LA CASTELLANA" MAP

SEE "CENTRAL MADRID" MAP

PASEO DEL PRADO

PASEO DEL PRADO

Estanque
Lake

MONUMENTO DE ALFONSO XII

AV. MENÉNDEZ PELAYO

Plaza Cánovas del Castillo

MUSEO DEL PRADO

CALLE DE ALFONSO XII

EL RETIRO

PALACIO DE CRISTAL ★

PASEO DEL PRADO

Real Jardín Botánico

LA ROSALEDA ★

| 0 | | 200 yds |
| 0 | | 200 m |

Atocha M

Plaza del Emperador Carlos V

ÁNGEL CAIDO ★

AV. DE CIUDAD DE BARCELONA

AV. MENÉNDEZ PELAYO

ESTACIÓN DE ATOCHA

TWO-DAY BEST OF MADRID

DAY ONE

On day one, head straight to the **Puerta del Sol** and have a light breakfast upstairs at **Mallorquina**. No later than 10 A.M., start working your way to the **Plaza Mayor** and then on to the **Palacio Real,** arriving by noon. Skip the guided tour and make your own pace through the palace. By 2 P.M., start thinking about lunch (you're on Spanish time!). A lovely option is to get a terrace table right on the **Plaza Oriente** at **La Botillería**. After lunch, take a rest in the **Retiro,** or head back to your hotel for a nice siesta. You'll need it. Around 6:30 P.M., make your way to the **Reina Sofía** and head straight for *Guernica* (but remember the museum is closed on Tuesday). Afterwards, cross Calle Atocha and work your way to the **Barrio de las Letras.** Do some tapas-hopping around **Plaza Santa Ana** and don't miss the sherry bar **La Venencia.** If you've got energy to burn, join the *marcha* madness that starts to kick off around midnight.

DAY TWO

On day two, head over to **Plaza España** around 10 A.M. for an invigorating walk up **Gran Vía.** Get in some shopping and then head to Calle Alcalá for an early lunch at **Círculo de Bellas Artes.** Try to get a window seat. Around 2 P.M. head over to the **Museo del Prado** when it is at its slowest. Afterwards, stroll through **Barrio Lavapiés** and have a coffee at one of the terraces on Calle Argumosa. After a much-deserved siesta, head over to **La Latina** and catch the sunset over the **Jardines de las Vistillas.** Finish the evening with a **tapas crawl** along **Calle Cava Baja** in La Latina.

Optional itinerary: Either of the above mornings could be traded for a day trip to **Toledo** (see *Castilla-La Mancha*). The AVE trains can get you there in 35 minutes and the round-trip ticket is around €17.

In 1083, Mayrit was captured by Alfonso VI of Castile during the Christian Reconquest of the Iberian Peninsula. A year earlier, San Isidro, Madrid's patron saint, was born. During their attack on Mayrit, Alfonso's troops climbed the walls earning the nickname *gatos* (cats). Today, native-born *madrileños* are still called *gatos.* The Emir's fortress was turned into a residence for visiting royalty. Muslim soldiers attempted to regain the city several times during the 12th century. In 1115, they set up camp in the park that sits beneath the Royal Palace. That park is still called Campo del Moro (Camp of the Moors). Mayrit stayed firmly in the hands of the Christian kings of Castile. Medieval Madrid was a rural town made up of Christians, Moors, and Jews. The latter built and occupied the barrio Lavapiés before being expelled in 1492.

After Carlos I bestowed Madrid with the title of "crowned and imperial," the city really began to expand. When his son Felipe II moved the Spanish court to Madrid in 1561, he instantly turned the scruffy village into the capital of the country. Royalty, aristocrats, and businessmen poured into the area. The working classes followed and soon Madrid was buzzing with construction, commerce, and culture. Madrid de los Austrias (also known as Hapsburg Madrid) was born. Throughout the 16th and 17th centuries, gold obtained by Spanish expansion into the New World pumped riches into the city and sparked a building boom. Plaza Mayor is one example. El Escorial, Felipe II's colossal monument outside the city, is another.

The first Bourbon king took over the reign of Spain in 1700 and contributed greatly to Madrid's landscape, building museums, libraries, and hospitals in the city. Carlos III, who ascended to the throne in 1759, earned the nickname "Mayor of Madrid" because of the dozens of public works he installed in the city, from roads and canals to monuments including the Casa de Correos in Sol, the hospital that now houses the Museo Reina Sofía, the building that houses the Prado, and the Botanical Gardens right next to it.

Bourbon rule was interrupted when Napoleon marched into Madrid in 1808. On May 2 of that year, Madrid's citizenry rose up against the French troops whose brutal response was to massacre the protesters and execute the survivors the following day. Goya captured it all in his somber paintings *El dos de mayo* and *El tres de mayo,* both of which hang in the Museo del Prado. The War of Independence, also known as the Peninsular War, put Spain back into Spanish hands.

When the Spanish Civil War broke out in 1936, *madrileños* (much like their ancestors in 1808) resisted the advance of Franco's nationalist troops and Madrid became an international symbol of the fight against fascism. Franco's nationalist army settled in the Casa de Campo and unleashed a siege on the city that would last until 1939 when the General finally wrested control of the country, and the war ended. During Franco's long dictatorship, Madrid became more industrialized and millions of Spaniards migrated there from their impoverished villages. After his death, and the country's subsequent turn to democracy, Madrid flourished, becoming the country's leading economic and educational center—a role that continues today with no signs of letting up.

Sights

Depending on the map you consult or the person you ask, Madrid has dozens of differing barrios. The old part of Madrid is made up of the Sol, Plaza Mayor, Opera, and Paseo del Prado neighborhoods. To the south lie the colorful working-class barrios of La Latina, Lavapiés, and Atocha. To the north runs the grand boulevard of Gran Vía, a lively area full of shops, theaters, hotels, and excellent people-watching. Above that are the barrios of Malasaña and Chueca. Further north lies Madrid's most elegant barrio, Salamanca, a precise grid of graceful streets lined with very posh shops. Running west of Salamanca from Paseo del Prado all the way to the northernmost reaches of the city is the Paseo de la Castellana, Madrid's most emblematic boulevard, lined with parks, gardens, and sidewalk cafés. The following barrios and sights can be used as the basis of a walking tour or you can just hop the Metro (subway) to any of these barrios and start exploring.

SOL AND PLAZA MAYOR

Sometimes called the Centro Histórico, or the historic center, the tangle of centuries-old streets radiating out from the **Puerta del Sol** is the heart and soul of the capital. Sol, as it's locally known, is a pulsating hive of heavy-flowing traffic, exhaust-spewing buses, whistle-blowing policemen, bag-toting shoppers, backpack-lugging tourists, and business-minded locals. Overlooking the action is **Tío Pepe,** a massive neon billboard that has advertised Andalusian sherry for over 100 years. Be sure and pass through Sol at night, when Uncle Pepe is lit up in colorful glory.

The southern edge of Sol is dominated by the **Casa de Correos,** a monastic red-brick building built in the 1760s by Carlos III as a post office. During Franco's regime, the building housed military police and a basement prison where political prisoners regularly died of "suicide." Today, it is the seat of the regional government of Madrid and the site of Spain's New Year's Eve countdown. Thousands of people descend upon Sol each December 31 to greet the New Year beneath the giant clock on top of the building. As the clock strikes midnight, 12 gongs ring out. If you want good luck in the coming year, you have to eat a grape with each chime. To make it easier, grapes are sold skinless and seedless in cans of 12.

On the sidewalk in front of the Casa de Correos lies **Kilómetro Cero,** a scuffed-up plaque marking the absolute center of Spain. From this point, six major highways radiating

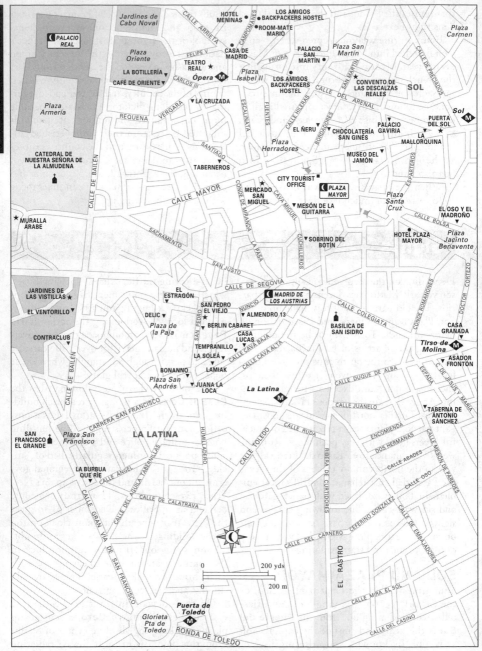

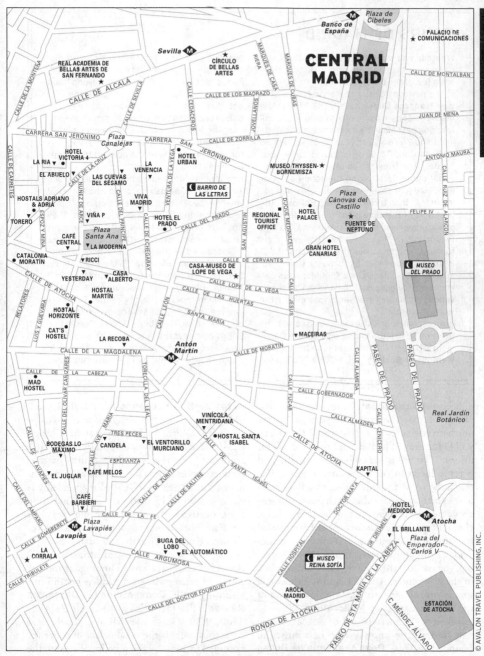

CENTRAL MADRID

TOURS OF MADRID

Whether you want to walk or ride, there are several sightseeing options in Madrid. Here are a few of the best.

The newest way to see Madrid is on a Segway. **Madsegs Glides** (tel. 91/542-2715, info@madsegs.com, www.madsegs.com, €60) will take you past Madrid's most emblematic spots including Plaza Mayor, Plaza España, Templo de Debod, and Barrio de las Letras during your "glide." The trips are an absolute blast, and you'll appreciate saving the strain on your legs. Madsegs covers about six hours of walking in less than three hours of gliding. However, the best part of the glide is the reaction from the public, especially senior citizens who just love to stop you to chat about the Segway. Things to know: You must weigh 70-250 pounds; 15 is the minimum age; if you must carry a bag, make it a backpack since shoulder bags can knock novice gliders off-balance; make reservations online well in advance for a glide in the warmer months.

An eccentric British expat obsessed with the Duke of Wellington (who helped crush Napoleon), Stephen Drake Jones founded the **The Wellington Society** (tel. 60/914-3203, www.wellsoc.org) to promote research and history of the Duke's military exploits in Spain. To support the society he offers walking tours through Madrid. A one-year €30 membership gets you the introductory two-hour tour and he does a brisk trade with over-50 American tourists. The walk is as notable for Stephen's informative and entertaining commentary as it is for the amount of wines he quaffs during stops at several Madrid taverns. Don't misperceive him, though. Stephen is a highly respected and sought-after Spanish historian who knows of what he speaks. He also offers a series of other tours from Bullfights to Bloody Madrid. They are a bit pricey, but legions of fans swear his charming company is worth it.

Sponsored by the Madrid Chamber of Commerce, **Descubre Madrid** (Pl. Mayor 27, Metro: Sol, tel. 91/588-2906, descubremadrid@munimadrid.es, www.esmadrid.com) is a series of walking tours in the city center. The tours change monthly but standards include Medieval Madrid, Hapsburg Madrid, Traditional Shops and Taverns, and Legends of Old Madrid. On Sundays, they team up with Bike in Spain to offer a tour by bike (bike rental fee

---

out through the country measure their distances. Across the busy intersection, on the northern edge of Sol, is the statue of the **El Oso y el Madroño** ("The Bear and the Tree"). This unusual symbol is the emblem of Madrid and is reproduced in the city's coat of arms. The reasons why are shrouded in legend, but a popular explanation says that both bears and *madroño* trees were plentiful around the medieval city, and since the *madroño,* a red berry used for jams and liqueurs, sounds similar to Madrid, a symbol was born. Whatever the meaning, the statue is the number-one meeting place in the city center. Another landmark meeting spot is on the western edge of Sol in front of the famed pastry shop **Mallorquina.**

Just a few doorsteps off of Sol, art lovers will find a little-known jewel of a museum. Founded in 1744, **Real Academia de Bellas Artes de San Fernando** (C/ Alcalá 13, tel. 91/524-0864, http://rabasf.insde.es, 9 A.M.–7 P.M. Tues.–Fri., 9 A.M.–2:30 P.M. Sat.–Mon., €2.40, free Wed.) was originally a fine arts academy. Over the centuries, wealthy patrons donated works of arts for the benefit of the students. Today, the highlight of the academy is its collection of 13 works by Goya, including the evocative carnival painting *Entierro de la Sardina.* The museum also holds works by Velázquez, Rubens, Picasso, and Juan Gris.

Just a bit north in the pedestrian zone between Sol and Plaza Santa Domingo is another clutch of outstanding art hidden behind unassuming walls. **Convento de las Descalzas Reales** (Pl. Descalzas, s/n, tel. 91/454-8800, 9:30 A.M.–5 P.M. Mon.–Sat., 9 A.M.–2 P.M. Sun., €5) is the royal palace of convents. Founded in 1560 by King Felipe II's sister, the

extra). Most tours run around two hours and cost under €4 and a few are free. An updated list can be found at the main tourist office in Plaza Mayor. Guides don't speak the best English, but they are true locals who pepper their tours with amusing anecdotes.

The best way to get a quick overview of the city is with **Madrid Vision** (tel. 91/779-1888, www.madridvision.es, 10 A.M.-9 P.M. spring and fall, 9:30 A.M.-midnight summer, 10 A.M.-7 P.M. winter, €14.50 per day, €19 for two days, €8 for seniors and children, free for under 6). You'll see their red double-decker, open-topped buses crawling all over town following three comprehensive routes: historical, modern, and monumental Madrid. A day pass lets you transfer among them. Tours lasts 45-75 minutes provided you don't get off the bus, but half the fun is hopping on and off. Buses run every 10-20 minutes. The accompanying audio tour comes in eight languages, but the quality is sketchy. Check out a few seats before settling in. Be sure to take a seat up top for the best photos. Tickets can be purchased at hotels, travel agents, the Madrid Vision office on Carrer Felipe IV between the Prado

and the Ritz, or easiest of all, right on the bus. Route 2, Modern Madrid, is the best bet for seeing sights beyond the city center including the majestic Paseo de la Castellana and Santiago Bernabéu stadium.

If you are not a DIY tourist, pop over to **Pullmantur** (Pl. Oriente 8, Metro: Ópera, tel. 91/541-1805, www.pullmantur-spain.com). Their basic packages are pretty standard tours that you could easily do on your own such as the Palacio Real and the Museo del Prado. However, there are some good options here. In winter, particularly at Christmastime when the city's grand avenues are lavishly decorated, check out the nightly Illuminations tour (8:30 P.M. daily except Sun., €12). You might also want to book with them for day trips to El Escorial, Valle de los Caidos, or Alcalá de Henares. If you choose their Toledo tour, stick with the half-day option (€34) leaving either at 8:45 A.M. or 3 P.M. There is also a decent day-long tour that takes in Ávila and Segovia. Skip the optional lunch and use the time to explore a little on your own. All tours depart from Plaza de Oriente and reservations are not necessary, just show up 20 minutes early.

Convent of the Royal Barefoot Nuns became a monastic retreat for aristocratic women who brought with them substantial dowries. The result was a convent dripping in riches, particularly art. By the 20th century the barefoot nuns had fallen on hard times. A special intervention by the Pope allowed the sisters to open the convent for tours, bringing in much needed revenue. Today visitors can see paintings from Titian and Rubens, elaborate tapestries, and curiosities like bits of wood that are said to come from Christ's cross.

If you head west on Calle Arenal, you'll come to **Pasadizo San Ginés,** a tiny alleyway on the left. It runs alongside the **Iglesia de San Ginés** (C/ Arenal 13, open only for mass), which has housed a church since the 1500s. At the end of the alley is the belle epoque **Chocolatería San Ginés.** Take a quick

left onto Calle Coloreros, a tiny alley lined with cafés and bars. It ends at Calle Mayor, just across from the Plaza Mayor.

◖ Plaza Mayor

Plaza Mayor has been Madrid's main square for centuries. In the 15th century it was the sight of a ramshackle market where craftspeople hawked their trade. All around the plaza, street names still bear evidence of these commercial origins: Tintoreros (dyers), Herradores (blacksmiths), Botoneros (button makers), Bordadores (embroiderers), and Latoneros (tinsmiths). After he made Madrid the capital of Spain in 1561, Felipe II ordered the square rebuilt. He's the one on the horse in the plaza's center. The first structure completed was the **Casa de Panadería** (the bread maker's house), which spans the north side of the square. The

© CANDY LEE LA BALLE

Catedral de Nuestra Señora de la Almudena looms over old Madrid.

colorful murals were added in the late 1990s, much to the horror of art and history buffs. Today, the building houses the **main tourist office.** The rest of the plaza was completed in 1619. For the next few centuries, the plaza retained its market nature, but also hosted bullfights, royal events, and religious ceremonies. This was also the site of public executions held under the Inquisition.

In 1854, after several devastating fires, the plaza was reconstructed to its current neoclassical facade, including 114 arches and 377 balconies, most of which belong to apartment dwellers. Plaza Mayor is once again the center of Madrid cultural life, hosting concerts, fairs, parades, and religious events. Every May, during San Isidro, the plaza hosts a giant *cocido madrileño* (a traditional chickpea and meat stew) cook-off and whole families line up early, Tupperware in tow, to fill up on the free portions. On January 6, the Reyes Magos (three wise kings), arrive in the plaza with a parade of clowns, acrobats, stiltwalkers, and marching bands.

There is no bad time to visit Plaza Mayor, but you'll catch it at its quietest in the early morning. As the day heats up, sun-tanning teens, accordion players, human statues, portrait painters, and buskers of all talent levels descend en masse. Pickpockets are among them, so be vigilant. Most guidebooks suggest avoiding the overpriced terraces that line the plaza. I agree in part. It is true, the food and drinks are near double what you'd pay elsewhere, but the ambience is priceless. Though I wouldn't recommend dining here, a simple breakfast or afternoon wine break at any of the terraces in the plaza makes for a wonderful moment in old Madrid.

If you step out of Plaza Mayor at the southeast corner onto Calle Girona you'll come to the Plaza Santa Cruz and the imposing **Palacio de Santa Cruz,** a magnificent example of 17th-century Hapsburg architecture. Originally it housed a prison where unfortunate souls accused of heresy by the Inquisition were held before being executed. It is closed to the public but if you are an architecture buff it is worth a look.

Back in Plaza Mayor, head to the southwest corner and the crooked stone steps leading out under the **Arco de Cuchilleros** (the knife makers' arch). If you continue straight onto Calle Cuchilleros you'll run into the world's oldest restaurant, **Sobrino del Botín.** Make a u-turn and head down **Calle Cava San Miguel** instead. On your right, the street is lined with *mesones.* These narrow cave-like bars reaching under Plaza Mayor have been around for centuries and are still a great way to kick off a night. Continue down the street and on the left you'll see the quaint **Mercado San Miguel** (Pl. San Miguel, s/n, 9 A.M.–2 P.M. and 5–8 P.M. Mon.–Fri., 9 A.M.–2 P.M. Sat.), a renovated 19th-century glass and wrought-iron market.

Plaza de la Villa

In the tidy Plaza de la Villa, midway between Plaza Mayor and Almudena Cathedral, three centuries of evolving Spanish architecture stand side by side. On the east of the plaza is **Torre de Los Lujanes,** an excellent example of Mudejar architecture, which combined Islamic, Christian, and Jewish building styles and was common throughout 15th century Spain. King Francis I of France was held prisoner here after losing in battle to Carlos I (also known as Charles V). Rumor has it that the French king swore he'd never bow down in front of Carlos. Charlie, being a clever one, had the side door of Lujanes (located on the corner of Calle Codo) closed in from the top to about halfway down. When the French king arrived for imprisonment, he had no choice but to bow upon entering. On the other side of the door King Carlos stood to receive his royal prisoner.

The next building is the **Casa de Cisneros,** built in 1537. Walk up to the carriage way and peer in at the exquisite ceiling and floor work. Next door is the **Casa de la Villa.** Completed in 1640 to serve as the town hall, the structure is a standard Hapsburg design with notable baroque doorways.

In the narrow den of streets across Calle Mayor from Plaza de la Villa is one of Madrid's oldest churches, **San Nicolás de los Servitas** (Pl. San Nicolás 8, tel. 91/559-4064). Its Mudejar tower dates from the 12th century and is a national monument.

ÓPERA

West of Sol is the area known as Ópera, called such because it is home to Madrid's opera house and a metro stop of the same name. The area oozes old-world style with cobbled streets lined by elegant buildings boasting broad marble entryways. At its southern edge looms the **Catedral de Nuestra Señora de la Almudena** (C/ Bailén 8–10, tel. 91/542-2200, 10 A.M.–1:30 P.M. and 6–7:30 P.M. Mon.–Sat., 10 A.M.–2:30 P.M. and 6–7:30 P.M. Sun.), Madrid's main cathedral. Construction of La Almudena, as it is locally known, was started in 1879 on the very ground where Madrid's oldest mosque had been demolished nine years earlier. The building project spanned more than 100 years and was stopped altogether during the Civil War. When it finally opened in 1993, the Pope showed up for its inauguration. Check out the colorful, psychedelic ceilings. They are

loathed by many *madrileños* who would have preferred a more traditional religious fresco.

Behind La Almudena, to the south, are the largest remains of the **Muralla Árabe,** the original walls of Muslim Madrid. They sit in a forlorn little park named for Emir Mohammed I who founded Mayrit (the city's original Muslim name) around 860. Shamefully neglected, the walls are littered with beer bottles. Despite this negligence, the city has been actively trying to unearth additional walls right under the apartment buildings on Calle Cava Baja. If the excavations go through, many tenants will lose their homes.

Plaza de Oriente

The spacious Plaza de Oriente is one of Madrid's most beloved plazas, with manicured gardens, grand statues, and a magnificent view of the Palacio Real. The city has the reviled Joseph Bonaparte to thank for it. During his brief reign as ruler of Spain, he ordered the plaza built. However, in order to do so several buildings had to be razed, including the church where Velázquez was buried. The loss of his remains is still considered a national tragedy and during the 1990s when the city undertook a plan to build a massive car park under the plaza, a desperate (and very politically charged) attempt was made to find the painter's remains. It didn't happen. The car park was built and Velázquez's bones remain lost. Fortunately, his artistic influence is still evident. At the center of the plaza is an equestrian statue of King Felipe IV based on a drawing by Velázquez. And over at Plaza de Oriente, 3, the house where he completed his masterpiece *Las Meninas* still stands.

The gardens of the plaza are lined by towering statues of Spain's early kings. They were meant to line the roof of the palace, but proved to be too heavy. Standing to the east of the plaza is the **Teatro Real,** one of Europe's grandest opera houses. Planned in 1818, it took over 30 years to build and the first opera was not performed there until 1850. The music didn't last long. Built over a series of underground streams, by 1925, the whole structure threatened to collapse. During the Civil War it

A FAIRY TALE COME TRUE

Letizia Ortiz Rocasolano was born in 1972 in the industrious little town of Oviedo in the northwest of Spain. Her grandfather was a taxi driver, her mother was a nurse, and her father was a journalist. Like all girls of that era, Letizia grew up with the vast possibilities offered to women after Franco's death. She decided to follow in her father's footsteps and studied journalism. After a brief marriage to one of her literature professors, she focused on her career and by 2002 had become a news anchor at a national television station. She was a model of the modern Spanish woman – hardworking, dedicated, smart, independent. Then she met the prince.

For over a decade, the love life of Prince Felipe de Borbón y Grecia, heir to the Spanish throne, had fueled heated debate in the popular press. Impossibly tall, dark, and handsome, the prince was widely considered Europe's most eligible bachelor. He had been romantically linked to statuesque blondes for years, including a lingerie model from Norway and a socialite from New York. Those relationships had riled a Spanish public who longed to see the future king married to a Spanish woman. As he approached 35, the press was relentless in pursuing leads into the prince's love life. In response, he publicly stated several times that he would marry only for love.

In November of 2002, Letizia traveled to Galicia to cover the sinking of the *Prestige* oil tanker off the coast of Spain. Prince Felipe was there, too, assessing the damage. They met, and in a coup worthy of a spy novel, managed to begin dating without the press or the public catching on. Letizia's father later said that even her family had no idea. In September of 2003, Letizia gave some college friends a tour of the television station where she worked. When one asked about her love life, Letizia confessed that was dating someone she might marry. Her friend said, "Well, if you get married and I don't find out about it I hope you're very happy." Letizia replied, "Don't worry. You'll find out."

On October 31, 2003, Letizia gave her last on-air report. She then went to her Madrid apartment, packed up her bags, and moved into the guest wing of the royal residence. The next day the Royal Family sent out a press release announcing the engagement of Felipe and Letizia. Spain went wild. The press couldn't believe they had been duped and scoured photographs for evidence of the relationship. All they could find was a single photo of the prince greeting a line of report-

housed soldiers and was damaged by an explosion. In the lean years of Franco's rule it was neglected and finally shut down permanently in 1988. In 1991, an ambitious renovation project began and the opera house reopened to its original splendor (but with better foundations) in 1997.

Built in 1611, the **Real Monasterio de la Encarnación** (Pl. Encarnación 1, Metro: Ópera, tel. 91/454-8803, 10:30 A.M.– 12:45 P.M. and 4–5:45 P.M. Tues., Thurs., and Sat., 10:30 A.M.–12:45 P.M. Fri., 11 A.M.– 1:45 P.M. Sun., €4), to the northeast of Plaza de Oriente, is best known as the home of a vial of the dried blood of St. Pantaleón. Legend has it that on July 27, the anniversary of

the saint's death, the vial's contents liquefy. If this miracle doesn't happen, calamity will follow. Originally built by the same architect who built the Plaza Mayor, the monastery was devastated by a fire and rebuilt in 1767 by Ventura Rodríguez.

◖ Palacio Real

When Felipe V, Spain's first Bourbon king, moved from France to Madrid in the early 1700s the royal residence was the Alcázar, a Moorish-style castle that stood on the same spot where the city's 9th-century Muslim fortress once stood. Felipe V, who had grown up in Versailles, was not impressed, and in 1734, he ordered the building of a royal residence

ers, including Letizia, at an awards ceremony the month before. Though there was some rumbling over Letizia's divorce and her commoner background, the public overwhelmingly accepted her. She was a face they knew and trusted, and a home-grown girl to boot. Felipe's official title is Prince of Asturias, and the public liked that Letizia was from Asturias. Even the segment of the population that opposes the monarchy system couldn't help being moved by the romance of it all. The Catholic Church, so powerful in this country, also gave its consent, as Letizia's first wedding had not occurred in a church.

The couple chose Madrid's La Almudena Cathedral as the sight of their royal nuptials, marking the first time in a century that a royal wedding would be held in the city. At the 1906 wedding of King Alfonso XIII and Scottish Princess Victoria Eugenie, an anarchist rebel threw a bomb at the royal procession as it wound through Madrid. The royals survived, but 20 bystanders were killed. Terrorism was not far from the minds of Felipe and Letizia as they planned their May 2004 wedding. In March of that year, terrorists had bombed four commuter trains in Madrid, resulting in 192 deaths and the worst crime of terrorism ever committed on Spanish soil. Security for the wedding

was tight, airspace was cleared overhead, and thousands of troops were stationed in the city. The couple cancelled bachelor and bachelorette parties and a city-planned firework show out of respect for the victims, instead directing the money into a fund for the victims. They also dedicated their wedding ceremony to the victims.

Despite torrential rain on the day of the wedding, Madrid glowed with joy. Thousands of flowers, colorful banners, and lights decorated the city. Tens of thousands of well-wishers lined the streets. Over 1,000 dignitaries, from Prince Charles to Nelson Mandela, attended the wedding. In a bow to Spanish royal tradition, just before Prince Felipe said "I do," he looked over to his father for approval. The King nodded his consent and Letizia, a career-minded commoner, became the Princess of Asturias and the future Queen of Spain. At the wedding banquet, the prince said, "I imagine it is obvious to all, because I can neither hide it, nor wish to: I am a happy man. And this is because I have the feeling of taking part in a dream come true; I have married the woman I love. Our union will last forever, and we offer it to our families and, above all, to our Destiny, intimately linked to the future of Spaniards."

that he hoped would rival his childhood home. Though he was long dead by the time the palace was finished in 1755, Felipe did achieve his goal. Madrid's Palacio Real is the largest palace in Western Europe and one of the most lavish in the world.

The Palacio Real (C/ Bailén, s/n, tel. 91/454-8800, www.patrimonionacional.es, 9:30 A.M.–5 P.M. Mon.–Sat., 9 A.M.–2 P.M. Sun., hours extended slightly in spring and summer, €8, €9 with guided tour, €3.50 for armory only) rivals the Museo del Prado as Madrid's top sight, drawing thousands of visitors daily. You won't catch the actual royal family among the hordes. The last royal resident was Alfonso XIII and the current royals live north of the

city in the Palacio de la Zarzuela. They only come to the Palacio Real for ceremonial events and on those occasions the palace is closed to the public.

Composed of granite and white stone from the nearby town of Colmenar, the exterior of the palace is both solemn and grandiose. Over an expanse of 134,710 square meters (1,450,000 square feet), the palace boasts 2,800 rooms, 870 windows, 270 balconies, and 44 staircases. Within is priceless artwork from masters such as Goya, Velázquez, and Caravaggio; miles of Spanish and Belgian tapestries; sheer tons of solid crystal chandeliers; hundreds of clocks (former resident Carlos IV was a passionate collector); and

Madrid's Palacio Real

enough antiques to furnish a small country. The decor is a sumptuous mix of styles from baroque to rococo to Asian opium den, reflecting the changing tastes of the royals who lived here for nearly two centuries.

Guided tours do not follow a set schedule, instead forming when there is a need. Usually this occurs every 20 minutes. The tour is not bad, but the amount of detail spewed by the no-nonsense guides can be mind-numbing. If you'd rather linger in the lavish surroundings, daydreaming about what it must have been like to actually live in a place like this, go on your own. The English-language pamphlet is comprehensive, plus each room features plaques with specific details.

Highlights include the lavish red and gold **Throne Room** with its gorgeous Titian ceiling fresco depicting the glory of Spain's history. King Juan Carlos and Queen Sofía still greet guests in this room for official functions. The private quarters of Carlos III, the palace's first resident, include the **Gasparini Room,** the king's opulent rococo dressing room, and

the **Porcelain Room,** which is completely covered in ornate porcelain plates. Whether or not you are into weaponry, you must cross the esplanade to the **Royal Armory,** which houses an unrivaled collection of arms dating back to the 13th century. Also pop into the **Royal Pharmacy,** an alchemist's wonderland of colored bottles and vials of various potions designed to cure what ailed the royal family.

If you are around on the first Wednesday of the month, look for the **changing of the guard.** However, Wednesday is not the best day to visit the palace. It is free for citizens of the European Union, which means crowds are heavier than usual. On the northern side of the palace are the **Jardines de Sabatini,** a serene maze of emerald greenery and elegant fountains.

GRAN VÍA

The tranquil refinement of Ópera is hemmed in by the shimmering buzz of Gran Vía, Madrid's main commercial zone and one of its most vibrant areas. The area is anchored on the west by **Plaza de España,** one of the larg-

© JEREMY REINES/WWW.MULTIMADRID.COM

est squares in Madrid. The plaza is ringed by shady trees towering over plentiful benches. The greenery is further ringed by a mass of tall buildings, including the imposing bulk of the 26-floor **Edificio de España** to the east, which was ostentatiously built by Franco between 1947 and 1953 at a time when Spain was being politically and financially ostracized by the world for its sympathy with Nazi Germany during World War II. The plaza sits on a plot of land that was once a meadow called Leganitos, which appears in a scene in *Don Quixote*. Fittingly, at the center of the plaza is the **Monumento de Cervantes.** It features a tall obelisk carved with characters and scenes from the ingenious Don's adventures. At its base is a statue of the writer looming over Don Quixote on his horse with Sancho Panza on his donkey. This is a favorite photo stop and even though it is forbidden, tourists regularly climb the horse to snap a close-up with their favorite fiction hero. The wide-open center of the plaza draws hordes of tourists and the hustlers who love them. If you decide to sit down for a spell, don't let your valuables detach for a second from your firm grip.

The best sight in **Gran Vía** is the grand, sweeping avenue itself. Cutting a swathe east—west just north of Sol, Madrid's "Great Way" is an architectural buff's delight lined with an extraordinary variety of early 20th-century buildings. As you walk along, be sure to look up once in a while to take in these lavish *edificios*. The avenue is also a dizzying buzz of commercial activity lined with retail shops and hotels for all budgets, massive city cinemas, and eateries from ice cream shops to tapas bars (including loads of fast-food places). Up top are some of Madrid's most exclusive apartments, plus the city's best open-air swimming pool. Of course there are thousands of beeping cars, roaring buses, and people, people, people. This is the perfect place to get a heady whiff of the city's cosmopolitan air.

Walking west from Plaza de España, you come to **Plaza Callao** on the edge of Sol's pedestrian shopping zone. All around the plaza are grand cinemas that host red-carpet premieres for top Spanish and Hollywood films. Looming over the western edge of the plaza is the **Allianz Building** (Gran Vía 39), a jewel of art deco achievement. The next stretch of Gran Vía continues west until **Red de San Luis,** where the Gran Vía metro stop is located. Calle Montera, leading south to Sol, is one of Madrid's most notorious red-light districts. Though it is safe to walk, you might feel uncomfortable. On the northern side of Gran Vía at the corner of Calle Fuencarral is the **Telefónica Building,** one of Madrid's earliest skyscrapers. The giant red clock at the top of the building is a fixture of the city's skyline. During the Civil War, Franco's troops bunkered in the Casa de Campo used the clock as a guide to send bombs and bullets down Gran Vía. The volley prompted war correspondents to nickname the avenue "Shell Alley." The ground floor of the building houses **Fundación Telefónica** (Gran Vía 28, tel. 90/011-0707, www.fundacion.telefonica.com, 10 A.M.–2 P.M. and 5–10 P.M. Tues.–Fri., 11 A.M.–10 P.M. Sat., 11 A.M.–2 P.M. Sun., free), a tranquil complement to Madrid's major art galleries. It houses an extensive modern art collection and offers rotating exhibitions, particularly retrospectives of art movements. Continuing along the north side of the avenue, you'll come to the famed **Museo Chicote** (Gran Vía 12). This classic cocktail bar, favored by Ernest Hemingway and Ava Gardner back in the 1930s, was one of the few businesses that stayed open throughout the Civil War. As bullets whizzed by, the brave and the wealthy sipped martinis here.

Calle Alcalá

Gran Vía merges into Calle Alcalá amid an explosion of stunning architecture. Right at the junction is the much-photographed **Metropolis Building** (C/ Alcalá 39). Completed in 1911, this Madrid landmark is a whimsy of French inspiration topped by a black slate dome trimmed in gold. **Iglesia de San José** (C/ Alcalá 43), an exuberant example of Madrid's baroque. Across the street, the **Círculo de Bellas Artes** (C/ Alcalá 42), a modernist six-floor building boasting broad

GRAN VÍA, MALASAÑA, AND CHUECA

Argülles

CALLE ALBERTO AGUILERA

MARQUES DE URQUIJO

BALTASAR GRACIAN

VALLEHERMOSO

CALLE DE SANTA CRUZ

CALLE ACUERDO

CALLE SAN DIMAS

SAN HERMENGILDO

MONTSERRAT

CALLE QUIÑONES

CALLE MARTIRES DE ALCALA

0   200 yds

0   200 m

CENTRO CULTURAL CONDE DUQUE

CAFÉ LA PALMA

CALLE DE CONDE DUQUE

CALLE DEL LIMON

CALLE DE AMANIEL

CALLE NORTE

Ventura Rodríguez

DUQUE DE LIRIA

CALLE DE LA PRINCESA

TRAVESIA DEL CONDE DUQUE

NOVICIADO

Noviciado

CALLE DE TUTOR

CALLE MARTIN DE LOS HEROS

CALLE JUAN ALVAREZ MENDIZABAL

VENTURA RODRIGUEZ

Plaza Cristino Martos

SAN BERNARDINO

SAN LEONARDO

REYES

Plaza de Conde del Tereno

MANZANA

GRILO

CALLE DE SAN BERNARDO

CALLE CRUZ VERDE

Parque Templo Debod

PASEO PINTOR ROSALES

★ TEMPLO DE DEBOD

Jardines Ferranz

★ MUSEO CERRALBO

Plaza de España

Plaza España

GRAN VÍA

GRAN VÍA

Parque de la Montaña

To Ermita de Santa Antonia de la Florida and Casa Mingo

CALLE DE IRUN

CADARSO

ARRIAZA

ILUSTRACIÓN

CUESTA DE SAN VICENTE

Jardines de Sabatini

CALLE RIO

CALLE DEL RELOT

CALLE DE BAILEN

CALLE DEL FOMENTO

CALLE LEGANITOS

FLOR ALTA

HOTEL EMPERADOR

Santo Domingo

Plaza Santo Domingo

Plaza Marina Epañola

Plaza Española

REAL MONASTERIO DE LA ENCARNACIÓN ★

SAN QUINTIN

CALLE DE LA BOLA

CALLE ARRIETA

Jardines del Palacio Real

PALACIO REAL

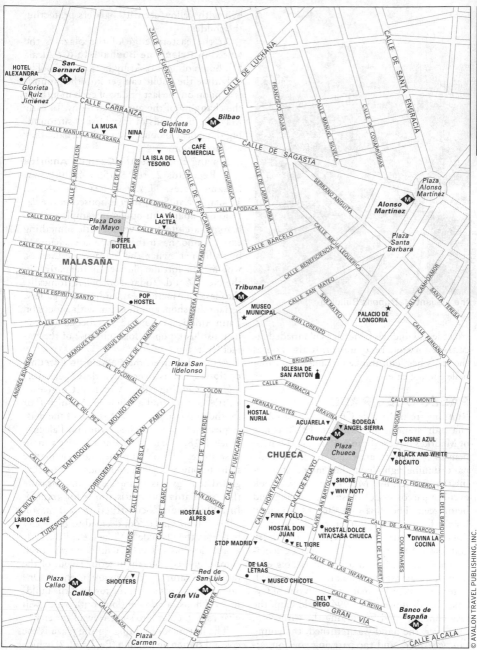

© CANDY LEE LABALLE

the elegant Metropolis Building

street-level windows beneath a colonnaded facade, is a national monument. It also houses the city's best cultural center and a stunning belle epoque café.

PASEO DEL PRADO

Running from Plaza de Cibeles south to Atocha train station, the Paseo del Prado is one of Madrid's busiest thoroughfares. It also happens to be spectacular, with a tree-lined shady park running right down the center of it. During the 19th century, Madrid's aristocrats took evening paseos under these trees, seeing and being seen. The **Plaza de Cibeles** is named for the fountain at its center, which features a lion-drawn chariot bearing Cybele, the Greek goddess of fertility. The fountain is a celebration point for Real Madrid fans after a big win. The crowd gets so thick that traffic is stopped. After a drunken fan made off with one of Cybele's hands during the 1994 World Cup, the city contemplated forbidding the gathering. However, the hand was returned, the young fan was fined, and the partying goes on, albeit with yellow security barriers protecting the goddess.

At the eastern edge of the plaza is the fenced-in **Palacio de Buenavista** (C/ Alcalá 51), home of Spain's Army headquarters. The only time the public can get into the grounds is at noon on the last Friday of each month for the changing of the guard ceremony. In early May, the hundreds of rose bushes surrounding the palace bloom. Even behind bars, they are spectacular.

Moving clockwise, the **Casa de America** (Po. Recoletos 2, tel. 91/595-4800, www.casamerica.es, 11 A.M.–8 P.M. Tues.–Sat., 11 A.M.–2 P.M. Sun., free) is housed in the Palacio de Linares, an opulent example of neobaroque architecture, with a little something extra. Rumor has it that the palace is haunted by its former owner, the Marqués de Linares, who made a fortune plundering the natives in the New World. Today, somewhat ironically, the Casa de America is an auditorium, gallery, restaurant, shop, and museum with a focus on Latin America. If you are into rococo decor at its most lush, pop in for a glimpse of the former ballroom.

Across the street, the **Palacio de Comunicaciones** looms over Plaza de Cibeles like a giant wedding cake. A little art nouveau, a little Gothic, and a whole lot Spanish flair for the dramatic, the Palace is one of the masterpieces of royal architect Antonio Palacios. Since 1918, it had served as the city's main post office. Climbing up the dramatic marble stairs to buy a single stamp under the soaring gilded ceilings was a simple everyday pleasure that Spaniards and tourists took for granted. In 2006, Madrid's construction-mad mayor, Alberto Ruiz Gallardón, decided to move city hall from the Plaza de la Villa to the Palacio de Comunicaciones. The €270 million project will completely redesign the interior layout of the building. Naturally, citizens are incensed. One bonus for visitors is that the tower of the building will house a *mirador* (look-out), which will give a spectacular bird's-eye view of the city.

The last major building on the plaza is the colossal **Banco de España** (Po. Prado 2), which houses the country's gold, as well as a fortune in artwork including a large selection of Goyas. Unfortunately, it is closed to the public. Further south along the Paseo del Prado, the pokey **Museo Naval** (Po. Prado 5, tel. 91/379-5842, www.museonavalmadrid.com, 10 A.M.–2 P.M. Tues.–Sun., closed Mon. and Aug., free) covers the breadth of Spain's seafaring history from the voyages of Columbus to the exploits of the Spanish Armada. Check out the first-ever map of the New World, etched by the first mate of the *Santa María*. It is all in Spanish, but if you are a naval/historical buff, you'll be fine.

Midway down the Paseo, **Plaza de Cánovas del Castillo,** better known as "Neptuno" after the Ventura Rodríguez–designed fountain at its center, is the stomping ground of Atlético Madrid fans after their big wins. The famed **Palace Hotel** stands here and just across the way, is its main rival, the **Ritz Hotel.** The plaza is also home to two of the musuems that make up Madrid's **Triángulo del Arte:** the Museo del Prado and the Museo Thyssen-Bornemisza. The third point in the "Triangle of Art" is the Reina Sofía, which lies a bit south in the neighborhood of Lavapiés.

◖ Museo del Prado

Arguably one of the world's most important fine art musuems, the Museo del Prado (Po. Prado, s/n, Metro: Banco de España, tel. 91/330-2800, www.museoprado.es, 9 A.M.– 8 P.M. Tues.–Sun., closed Mon., €6, free Sun.) holds the most extensive collection of any museum including over 8,600 paintings. Due to space limitations, only about 15 percent of the work can be displayed at any one time. A €92 million expansion project expected to finish in spring of 2007 should change that.

The bulk of the work on view reflects the changing tastes of Spanish royalty, with a heavy emphasis on religion, warfare, and mysticism. Masterpieces by court painters Francisco Goya and Diego Velázquez figure large in the collection, as do numerous examples of Flemish and Italian Renaissance works. It could take you days to see it all, however, in just about

two hours you can take in the museum's most interesting works. The names you need to add to your Prado checklist are Goya, Velázquez, Bosch, and El Greco. Be sure to grab one of the free **English-language guides** on your way in. The museum is known for re-arranging its works, so the guide is the indispensable latest word on what's where. However, in general the art is grouped by painter. You can also opt for the comprehensive **audio-guide** for €3.

So many guidebooks suggest one door or the other as the fastest way in, that both are equally crowded by now. A good bet is to head for the **Puerta de Goya,** the northern door on Calle Felipe IV, as the southern door at Plaza Murillo is favored by student groups. To best **avoid crowds,** go at opening on a weekday or during the Spanish lunch hour (2–4 P.M.) when the school groups have gone home to eat. Late evening, after 6 P.M. is another slow period, however you won't have time to linger. Also, unless you are on the strictest of budgets, avoid the Sunday free day when backpackers, students, and young lovers descend on the Prado en masse.

If you were to only see one painting in the entire museum, or even in all of Spain, *Las Meninas* by Velázquez would have to be it. Lauded in art and Spanish classes worldwide, this work is an incredible achievement of complex perspective and realistic atmosphere. Officially named *La Familia de Felipe IV,* the painting has at its center the young Princess Margarita, heir to the Spanish throne. Around her are her female attendants, known in the court as *meninas,* as well as one of the princess's royal dwarves. To the right we see the artist himself looking out of the picture and at the viewer. He is painting the portraits of King Felipe IV and Mariana of Austria, whose images are reflected in a mirror just behind the princess's head. Another great Velázquez to seek out is his atmospheric *Los Borrachos (The Drunkards),* featuring a group of ruddy-faced men drinking around an angelic boy sitting on a wine barrel.

Next up, Goya. Works by this Spanish genius are on display throughout the museum and scan the breadth of his career. Perhaps

MAKING THE MOST OF MADRID'S MUSEUMS

If you want to take in the three jeweled points of the **Triángulo del Arte,** Madrid's golden triangle of art – the Prado, the Thyssen, and the Reina Sofía – you'll need a day and a half. The cheapest way to go is by buying the **Abono de Paseo del Arte,** an art pass that allows you to view all three museums once in a calendar year. It costs €12. Regular admission to all three museums would come out to €15, so the savings is worth at least two *cafés con leche.* The pass is not well advertised at any of the museums so you will have to ask for it specifically. Generally, lines are shorter at the Thyssen, so you could start there. Also, keep in mind that the Prado and the Thyssen are closed on Mondays and the Reina Sofía is closed on Tuesday. To get the best of each museum, schedule two hours for

each, though keep in mind that you could easily spend a day in any of them – the quantity of art is that staggering.

Touring the museums is easy on your own with either the audio-guides or the printed guides offered at the museums. It is also easy enough to tag on to any of the dozens of tours that sweep through the museums daily. However, if you prefer a more personalized artistic experience, you can contract a private guide either at the museums or on your own. Madrid artist Susan Sartarelli (tel. 91/527-8967) offers tours to individuals and groups at any of the three museums. Originally from the United States, Susan has had a painting studio in Madrid for 15 years. She is an art-history buff and offers tours in English, Spanish, or Italian.

Diego Velázquez welcomes you to the Museo del Prado.

the best-known are *La Maja Desnuda* and the *La Maja Vestida,* twin paintings of a reclining woman rumored to be his young mistress. The nude painting was completed first, and only after public outcry, did Goya take action. Instead of clothing the original painting, he painted a second one. Notice how the clothed woman seems more "naked" than the nude one. For an important part of Madrid's history, seek out *El dos de mayo* and *El tres de mayo,* which commemorate the ill-fated uprising of Madrid's citizens against French armed forces. Save Goya's *Saturno Devorando a Su Hijo* for last. This horrific painting of Saturn chewing the head off his child is from Goya's *pinturas negras,* a series of dark, nightmarish works done near the end of the painter's life.

The works of Hieronymus Bosch, El Bosco in Spanish, are usually on the lower level. Give yourself some time to take in *The Garden of Earthly Delights,* the most acclaimed of this Dutch master's works. A triptych painted on wood, its three panels chronicle the fate of man from the paradise of the Eden to the misery of Hell. The painting is full of symbolism including satirical representations of the Catholic Church, such as a pig in a nun's habit and priests feasting in Hell. He also turned his critical paintbrush on himself—look behind the tree trunk in the panel of Hell to see El Bosco's self-portrait.

Also look out for the 16th-century master Dominikos Theotokópoulos, better known as El Greco. The Prado gives a nice overview of his changing style, starting with one of his early works *The Trinity* and finishing with *The Adoration of the Shepherds,* painted 35 years later. The latter is a brilliant example of El Greco's command of mannerism, a style characterized by exaggeration, contorted body positions, unrealistic proportions, and dark religious themes. It was painted, eerily enough, to hang in his own funeral chapel.

Another must-see is *Bacchanal* by the 16th-century Italian painter Titian. The work depicts mythological drunken debauchery at a festival of wine, and is an excellent example of Italian Renaissance painting. The reclining female nude in the bottom corner recalls classical Greek sculpture. Titian is best known in Spain for being the court painter for Carlos V and Felipe II. As a result, the Prado houses several notable works by this Venetian-born artist.

The museum has a café near the southern (Murillo) entrance. Go here only if you are dying for a drink. Water bottles are not allowed in the museum. You can bring in your camera, but flashes and tripods are not allowed. The guards are serious about this, so don't even think about it.

Next door to the Prado is the lovely **Real Jardín Botánico** (Pl. Murillo 2, tel. 91/420-0438, www.rjb.csic.es, 10 A.M.–sunset daily, €2). Built as a nursery for Carlos III, it is a city oasis of over 30,000 species of flowers, plants, and trees.

Museo Thyssen-Bornemisza

The wealthy family of the Baron Hans-Heinrich Thyssen-Bornemisza began collecting art in the 1920s with the goal of amassing an overview of Western painting. By the 1990s, the collection had grown to nearly 800 works and the Baron began searching for a public showcase for it. The United States, Great Britain, Germany, and Spain all vied for what was widely considered the most important private art collection in the world. Spain won the bid by offering to complete an extensive renovation of the 19th-century Palacio de Villahermosa to house the works. The location, across the street from the Prado, was another deciding factor. The fact that the Baron's fourth wife was Carmen Tita Cervera, a former Miss Spain, probably didn't hurt.

The Museo Thyssen-Bornemisza (Po. Prado 8, Metro: Banco de España, tel. 91/369-0151, www.museothyssen.org, 10 A.M.–7 P.M. Tues.–Sun., closed Mon., €6, €5 for temporary exhibits, €9 for a combined ticket including the main Thyssen, the Carmen collection, and the temporary exhibit) opened in 1992. With the addition of Señora Carmen's own impressive collection in 2004, it now houses over 1,000 works with examples from every major art movement since the 13th century.

One of the joys of this museum is the straightforward chronological layout. If you begin on the top floor of the building and wind your way down, you can literally walk through art history starting with the early birth of the Italian Renaissance, passing through the schools of Impressionism, German Expressionism, and Russian Constructivism, and then striding right back to the modern day with 20th-century geometric abstractions and pop art on the ground floor. A **self-guided tour** can be done in just about two hours.

What makes the Thyssen (TEE-sun), as it is called, stand out in Spain and in Europe, is its eclectic mix of well-known artists and lesser-known works. While the Prado holds their major works, art giants such as El Greco, Goya, Rembrandt, Titian, and Rubens all make an appearance here. There are also exemplary works from heavy-hitters such as Chagall, Degas, Gauguin, Hockney, Hopper, Miró, Lichtenstein, Picasso, Pollock, and Van Gogh. Throughout are brilliant works by artists that only art scholars might know, including painter Lucian Freud, grandson of the legendary psychoanalyst. His works just beg to be analyzed.

Parque del Buen Retiro

© CANDY-LEE LABALLE

❰ Barrio de las Letras

Just east of the Paseo del Prado and south of the Carrera San Gerónimo, is a charming barrio of crumbling old buildings, wrought-iron balconies overflowing with flowers, traditional *tabernas,* brash bars, restaurants, shops, and churches. Sometimes it is called "Huertas," after the pedestrian street that runs clear from the Paseo del Prado until just past Plaza Santa Ana. Huertas is also synonymous with nightlife due to the crush of bars on this street. By day, it is full of strolling tourists, old ladies lugging groceries, and young locals jogging by. If you look down, you'll see gold-lettered quotes from some of Spain's most acclaimed writers etched into the pavement. These give a clue to the area's other name, Barrio de las Letras (the Literary Quarter).

During the 16th and 17th centuries, this barrio was the center of literary life and the stomping grounds of Spain's most famous literary son, Miguel de Cervantes. The **house where Cervantes lived** (C/ Cervantes 2) is marked by a plaque. Ironically, this street also houses the **Casa-Museo de Lope de Vega** (C/ Cervantes 11, 91/429-9216, 10 A.M.–2 P.M. Tues.–Sat., closed Sun. and Mon., €1), which features a lovely garden where the prolific playwright spent most of his time. The two writers were contemporaries and great rivals. On the next street over, the **Convento de las Trinitarias Descalzas** (C/ Lope de Vega 18) is where Cervantes and his wife were buried. Unfortunately, after a 17th-century refurbishment of the convent, their remains were lost and remain so to this day. Whether or not you are interested in literary history, a daytime stroll through this atmospheric old barrio is a must. Make sure to stop off before or after in **Plaza Santa Ana** for a break.

❰ El Retiro

Sprawling for 300 lush acres just behind the Museo del Prado, the **Parque del Buen Retiro** is a gorgeous breath of fresh, fragrant air. Originally built in the 1600s as a private retreat for royals, the park was fully opened to the public in 1868. Since then it has drawn *madrileños* by the millions. Every Sunday, multi-generational families can be found strolling its broad promenades and shady lanes. They are joined by joggers, inline skaters, puppeteers, musicians, and soccer players. The park also has several monuments worth seeking out. There are "Usted está aquí" (you are here) signs posted throughout and most maps highlight the parks main thoroughfares.

El Retiro's largest feature is the artificial lake bordering the imposing **Monumento Alfonso XII.** Canoes can be rented at the boathouse on the northern end of the lake. Also look out for the breathtaking **Palacio de Cristal.** This wrought iron and glass palace was built in 1887 as a greenhouse for exotic plants. Today it serves as an extension gallery of the Reina Sofía. Try to get a photo of the palace reflected in the pond right in front. At the southern end of the park is the **Ángel Caído,** a statue of Lucifer falling from the sky. It is said to be the only public statue of Satan in the world. Just to the east of the Devil is **La Rosaleda,** a rose garden that is spectacular in full bloom. The latest addition to the park's monuments is its most moving. On the southwestern edge of the park, the **Bosque de los Ausentes** (Forest of the Departed) was planted in 2005 with 192 cypress and olive trees. Each tree represents one of the victims of the March 11, 2004 terrorist attack on commuter trains heading into nearby Atocha train station. (See sidebar, *We Were All Riding on Those Trains.*) At the complete opposite end of the Retiro, there is an entrance leading off of the **Puerta de Alcalá,** a truly majestic city gate built for Carlos III in the late 1700s. To the north of the gate, Barrio Salamanca unfolds.

Be aware that El Retiro is a natural draw for thieves looking to relieve dozing tourists of their goods. If you take a lie-down in the sun, make sure your things are tightly secured to your body—slip your foot through a strap on your backpack and keep your arm through

El Retiro's Ángel Caído

© CANDY LEE LABALLE

the handle of your purse. It is also best to avoid the park at night, unless you are interested in a little gay cruising. The southwestern corner of the park, particularly by the Chopera fitness center and the statue of the Ángel Caído, are popular hook-up spots for gay men.

ATOCHA AND LAVAPIÉS

The area to the south of Paseo del Prado and Sol is home to Madrid's traditional working-class neighborhoods. At the eastern edge is one of Spain's busiest train stations, **Estación de Atocha.** Even if you are neither coming nor going, it is worth a look for its gorgeous 19th-century wrought-iron and glass atrium, which shelters a lush tropical mini-forest complete with exotic plants, soaring tropical trees, and lazy turtles. Having a sandwich under this balmy canopy is a favorite lunchtime retreat during winter.

If you leave the Reina Sofía through the Restaurant Arola, turn right onto Calle Argumosa and start walking down, you'll enter one of Madrid's oldest working-class barrios and

WE WERE ALL RIDING ON THOSE TRAINS

At 7:39 A.M., I heard a long, scraping rumble, too loud to be a normal city noise. A few seconds later, another. Then the sirens began. They wailed continuously until late afternoon, and every time I checked the news, it was worse.

On March 11, 2004, 10 bombs blew up in four packed commuter trains, two trains at Atocha station near my home, the other trains at El Pozo and Santa Eugenia stations. They killed 177 people at the scene, and 15 more died under medical care. Another 2,062 were injured, some horribly maimed. The trains came from poorer parts of the Madrid area, and the dead included immigrants from 13 countries.

People wept in the streets and lined up for hours to give blood for the injured. Taxi drivers gave free rides to hospitals and to the makeshift morgue set up at the convention center near the airport. Morgue workers said the saddest thing was to hear mobile telephones ring in the handbags and backpacks of the dead, calls from people looking for their loved ones.

The next day, radio announcers were saying *saludos* (greetings) instead of the usual *buenos días* (good day) because it wasn't going to be a good day. Spontaneous shrines to the victims sprang up at the train stations. Black ribbons of mourning appeared in windows and on flags hung on balconies. That evening, 11,400,000 people, 28 percent of Spain's population, took to the streets to protest in every part of the country. Madrid's protest was the largest: two million people despite cold, pouring rain.

My husband sometimes took those commuter trains, so we had to go. It took us three hours to cover three kilometers, past Plaza de Colón to Atocha. Although the weather grew steadily worse and the pavement streamed with water, the mood remained determined and positive: We were there for peace, freedom, democracy, and the victims.

Young people came especially energized, with decorated umbrellas, face paint, and chants. At the end of the march in front of Atocha train station, they built an amazing shrine on the huge fountain in the middle of the traffic circle with flowers, signs, and candles, which they relit as fast as the raindrops put them out, though they themselves were drenched. We joined with them as they chanted: "It's not raining. Madrid is weeping."

But who had done it? At first the government insisted it was ETA, the Basque terrorist

---

the heart of the city's *castizo* identity, **Barrio Lavapiés.** From a word that means "pure-blooded," *castizo* evolved in 19th-century Madrid to mean authentic, to-the-bone, hard-working *madrileños*. Today, Lavapiés is just as hard-working, but a lot less *castizo*. Run down for years, property prices here fell massively compared to the rest of the city, opening up cheap apartments to a wave of immigrants, artists, and bohemian young couples. Walking through its steep mesh of streets, you'll pass Indian restaurants, Lebanese kabob shops, North African tea houses, Asian food stores, South American bars, Senegalese drum shops, alternative galleries, one-room art theaters, dozens of grungy bars, and more and more often, hip eateries launched by entrepreneurs with gentrification on their minds. Woven right through the multicultural fabric are traditional *tabernas*, hundred-year-old butcher shops, and a dizzying assortment of tiny storefronts specializing in anything from screws to springs. But be aware, Lavapiés is tattered around the edges. Its benches draw as many drunks as they do cigar-smoking old men in berets. That said, the locals are inviting, and everyone from shopkeepers to barkeeps will gladly welcome you into the mix. To the intrepid visitor, Lavapiés offers a fascinating glimpse into the global pulse of the city.

Calle Argumosa is lined with cafés and restaurants. During warm weather, they all put tables on the sidewalk, turning the length of the street into one massive terrace. Over on **Calle Doctor Fourquet,** there is a smattering of alternative galleries and independent clothing shops.

group. However, the evidence, including three unexploded bombs, pointed to an Islamic terrorist group with ties to Al Qaeda. The attack came three days before national elections. The incumbent People's Party had made Spain a U.S. ally in its war in Iraq, a move almost unanimously opposed by the Spanish population. The challenger, the Socialist Party, vowed to take Spanish troops out of Iraq. Indignation mounted as the government spin became clear. While there is still debate about how the bombing affected the election, the turnout was unusually high, 77.2 percent, and the Socialist Party won.

Police continued their investigations. They began to make arrests two days after the bombing, and on April 3 they moved in to arrest five suspects in an apartment in Leganés, a suburb of Madrid. The five blew themselves up rather than be taken, killing one police officer and injuring 11 others. One of the suspects was later described as the ringleader of the group. Police investigations and arrests have continued, and more than 100 suspects have been identified.

Meanwhile, the shrines for the victims at train stations grew, especially at Atocha.

Thousands and thousands of candles, along with bouquets of flowers, messages in many languages, photos, and remembrances, filled a floor inside the building and spilled out onto the sidewalk around the entrance. It remained there for months, and was finally replaced by a computerized gallery, *Más Cercanos* (Near and Dear), where visitors can leave a handprint and a message.

On the first anniversary of the bombing, the King and Queen inaugurated a memorial near Atocha in Retiro Park: the *Bosque de los Ausentes* (Forest of the Departed). It is a hill surrounded by a stream, since water is the symbol of life. A spiral path up the hill takes visitors past 192 cypress and olive trees, one for each of the victims.

I visited on Mother's Day, May 2, almost 14 months after the attack. In one of the cypress trees, someone had threaded white and red carnations – the traditional Mother's Day gift in Madrid. "We were all riding on those trains," was one of the chants at the protests. The victims included someone's mother. We also chanted, "We will not forget." How can we?

(Contributed by Sue Burke, a Madrid-based writer originally from Milwaukee, Wisconsin.)

Plaza Lavapiés itself is probably the least attractive part of the barrio; however, with the 2006 opening of the **Teatro Valle-Inclán,** a national playhouse, expectations are that full-scale gentrification is but a few years off.

Head west off of the plaza onto Calle Sombrerere to Calle Mesón de Paredes. On the square in front are the ruins of an 18th-century church destroyed in the Civil War. It has been artfully incorporated into a modern educational center. To the left, overlooking an empty corner is the barrio's most famous *corrala,* a structure common throughout working-class Madrid, it is a type of tenement building built around a central patio. In the case of this *corrala,* the surrounding walls are gone (hence the open corner). In the summer, it serves as the background for open-air *zarzuelas,* the light

operatic form that celebrates *castizo* life. Head north uphill on Calle Mesón de Paredes until you come to what many claim is Madrid's most authentic drinking hole, **Taberna de Antonio Sánchez.** Just west of here, at Plaza Cascorro and running down Calle Ribera de Curtidores, Madrid's 500-year-old flea market **El Rastro** sets up every Sunday.

◖ Museo Reina Sofía

At the southern tip of the Madrid's Art Triangle, Museo Reina Sofía (C/ Santa Isabel 52, tel. 91/774-1000, www.museoreinasofia.es, 10 A.M.–9 P.M. Mon. and Wed.–Sat., 10 A.M.–2:30 P.M. Sun., closed Tues., €3, free Sat. P.M. and Sun.) is one of Spain's most important modern art museums. Originally an 18th-century hospital, the part of the Reina Sofía

© JEREMY REINES/WWW.MULTIMADRID.COM

The Museo Reina Sofía houses Picasso's *Guernica*.

that opens up onto Santa Isabel is notable for its two futuristic glass elevators climbing up the side of the building. In 2005, the museum grew by over 50 percent with the addition of three stark red tile and glass buildings set under a single black slab roof. The extension includes an ultra-modern restaurant run by Spain's heartthrob celebrity chef Sergi Arola.

The collection is heavy with Spanish modern masters like Salvador Dalí, Eduardo Chillida, and Joan Miró, however the star of the show is Pablo Picasso's **Guernica,** one of the 20th century's most famous paintings. Picasso painted his 1937 black-and-white masterpiece in reaction to a horrific bombing attack on the small Basque town of Guernika-Lumo. Nazi fighter planes carried out the attack as a favor to Franco, who wanted to punish Basque separatists. Picasso refused to let the painting enter Spain while Franco was alive. When the painting finally arrived in Spain, it took up residency in the Prado. In the 1990s, against the wishes of Picasso's family, *Guernica* was moved to the Reina Sofía, where a room had been spe-

cially constructed for it. There are some who believe it should be moved back to the Prado, and a small faction of Basque art lovers who think it should reside in the País Vasco; however, no one who has ever seen it hanging at the center of Gallery 6 of the Reina Sofía can deny that the stark space is the perfect setting for the work. Leading up to the painting are several of the sketches Picasso made in preparation for the painting. They give an interesting insight into how this massive work was put together.

LA LATINA

The area bounded by Lavapiés to the east and Plaza Mayor and Sol to the north is generally referred to as La Latina. Its southern edge, like Lavapiés, has a strong affinity with Madrid's *castizo* culture and the streets are lined with scruffy shops, corner bars, and laundry hanging from balconies.

◖ Madrid de los Austrias
The northern part of La Latina, especially around **Plaza San Andrés** and **Plaza de la**

Paja, is quite arguably the most impressive old barrio in all of Madrid. Locally it is called "Madrid de los Austrias," referring to the 16th and 17th centuries when the Hapsburg dynasty ruled Spain. At that time, the city didn't extend much beyond this barrio, and many of the nobles lived along these very streets. Plaza Mayor and Plaza de la Villa are also legacies of the Hapsburg era. If you dug even deeper beneath these cobblestones, you'd find the remains of the Arabic walls that surrounded Mayrit during the 9th and 10th centuries. Be sure to spend time wandering around here, especially along **Calle Cava Baja** and **Calle Cava Alta,** which have the added bonus of being lined with the best tapas bars in the city.

Los Austrias also houses a fair bit of Madrid's religious history. The Mudejar tower of **San Pedro el Viejo** (Costanilla de San Pedro, tel. 91/365-1284) dates from before the 14th century. **Iglesia San Andrés** (Pl. San Andrés 1) and the attached **Capilla del Obispo** (Pl. de la Paja 9) soars majestically between the Plazas San Andrés and Paja. The Capilla, built in 1535,

© CANDY LEE LABALLE

Iglesia San Andrés in La Latina

is Madrid's only Gothic temple. The building is only open during mass, however the most memorable views can be had at nighttime when the dramatic lighting casts intricate shadows across the church's facade. Next to the church is **Museo de San Isidro** (Pl. San Andrés 2, tel. 91/366-7415, 9:30 A.M.–8 P.M. Tues.–Fri., 10 A.M.–2 P.M. Sat.–Sun., free), which honors the life and times of San Isidro, the 16th-century peasant and farmer who went on to become the patron saint of Madrid. The museum is set in a palace where San Isidro's much more humble abode once stood. Be sure to visit the well where San Isidro performed his greatest miracle. When his young son fell down into the well, San Isidro and his wife María de la Cabeza prayed and soon the water in the well rose, bringing the child safely back to dry ground. San Isidro's remains rest a few blocks away at the 17th-century **Basilica de San Isidro** (C/ Toledo 37, tel. 91/369-2037, 7:30 A.M.–1 P.M. and 6:30–8:30 P.M. Mon.–Sat., 7:15 A.M.–8:30 P.M. Sun.), a colossal example of Madrid's baroque architecture. During the **Fiestas de San Isidro,** the church becomes a pilgrimage point for Madrid's faithful.

San Francisco El Grande

On the western edge of La Latina, at the intersection of Carrera San Francisco and Calle Bailén, is the imposing 18th-century **San Francisco El Grande.** Not called El Grande for nothing, the church boasts an incredibly expansive dome. With a diameter of 33 meters (108 feet), it is larger than that of St. Paul's in London. Unfortunately, its size has endangered the rest of the church and long-term renovations are underway to make it steadier. The best view of the church is at night from the top of Carrera San Francisco when the dome is lit up.

Las Vistillas

If you continue north on Calle Bailén until Calle Morería, you reach the best view in the city. **Jardines de las Vistillas,** the steep, green park near this corner looks out over the city clear to the Sierra Guadarrama mountains. The sunset from here is breathtaking. At night, the spectacularly lit La Almudena cathedral dominates the view. Have an impromptu picnic or grab a table at the corner terrace, **El Ventorrillo.** The bridge to the right is the **Viaducto de Segovia.** This gorgeously arched structure has a gruesome history. For years it was a favorite place to commit suicide. The city put a stop to that by installing thick glass walls on either side of the bridge. Since then, only one death has occurred, but it is rumored to have been an unlucky bungee jumper.

ARGÜELLES

Northwest of the city center, Argüelles is a sprawling area that encompasses several barrios including Príncipe Pío and Moncloa. Mainly residential, the district boasts a few interesting sights. **Ermita de San Antonio de la Florida** (Gta. San Antonio de la Florida 5, tel. 91/542-0722, 10 A.M.–2 P.M. and 4–8 P.M. Tues.–Fri., 10 A.M.–2 P.M. Sat. and Sun., closed Mon.) is a must-see for Goya lovers as well as would-be lovers. The church, which *Newsweek* once called the Sistine Chapel of Madrid, contains one of Goya's most magnificent frescos, beneath which lies the artist's tomb. If you're a single woman and would rather not be, do like thousands of *señoritas* do and visit the church on June 13. Place 13 pins in the baptismal font, and then press your thumb into the bottom of the bowl. The number of pins that stick in your flesh is the number of beaus you'll have that year. Ouch! Be sure to combine your visit to the church with a meal at the famous Asturian cider house **Casa Mingo** just next door.

On the opposite side of Príncipe Pío train station is the **Templo de Debod** (Po. Pintor Rosales, s/n, Metro: Ventura Rodríguez, tel. 91/366-7415, 10 A.M.–2 P.M. and 6–8 P.M. Tues.–Fri., 10 A.M.–2 P.M. Sat.–Sun., closed Mon., €1.80, free Wed. and Sun.), a 2nd-century B.C. Egyptian temple. It was a gift from the Egyptian government after Spain helped rescue ancient monuments during the building of the Aswam Dam. It sits at the southern end of the tranquil **Parque del Oeste** and **La Rosaleda.** Not far from the temple, the **Museo Cerralbo** (C/ Ventura Rodríguez 17, Metro: Ventura

Templo de Debod

© JEREMY REINES/WWW.MULTIMADRID.COM

Rodríguez, tel. 91/547-3646, 9:30 A.M.–3 P.M. Tues.–Sat., 10 A.M.–3 P.M. Sun., closed Mon., €2.40) offers not only a glimpse of what one man collected in his lifetime, but also a glimpse of what that lifetime was like. The Marqués de Cerralbo bought this mansion specifically to display his collections of furniture, artifacts, and paintings, including works by El Greco and Titian. When he died in 1922, he donated the house to be used as a museum, provided it remain untouched. This act of generosity (or vanity) allows visitors to get a taste of aristocratic life. The ballroom and extravagant main stairway are breathtaking.

A bit to the north is the university area of Moncloa, home to the **Museo del Traje** (Av. de Juan de Herrera 2, Metro: Moncloa, tel. 91/550-4700, http://museodeltraje.mcu.es, 9:30 A.M.–7 P.M. Tues.–Sat., 10 A.M.–3 P.M. Sun., closed Mon., €3, free Sat. after 2:30 P.M. and Sun.). Amid screens running fashion film moments such as Marilyn's coquettish attempts to hold down the rising billows of her halter dress, an extensive display of clothing is displayed, from Spanish folk dress to haute couture, including several costumes from the 18th century. An added bonus is the chance to try on a piece. If you've ever wondered what it felt like to wear a bustle, this is your chance. Another Moncloa site is the **Faro de Madrid** (Av. de los Reyes Católicos, s/n, tel. 91/544-8104, 10 A.M.–1:45 P.M. and 5–8:45 P.M. Tues.–Sun., closed Mon., €1.75). Most of the world's major cities have their tourist-clamoring observation spots. London has the Eye. New York has the Empire State Building. Madrid has this dopey little tower, long in need of an overhaul. It does offer amazing views, and is worth the ride up if you are in this neighborhood.

Moving east, this district takes on the local name of **Argüelles** after the closest metro stop. It is a tranquil, middle-class neighborhood rife with residential apartments, retail shops, and restful park benches. Of most interest to the visitor is the imposing baroque complex housing the **Centro Cultural Conde Duque** (C/ Conde Duque 9–11, tel. 91/588-5834, 10 A.M.–9 P.M. Tues.–Sat., 11 A.M.–2:30 P.M. Sun., closed Mon.). Built in the early 1800s to house the Royal Guard, it was later used as both a military academy and an observatory. Today it is one of the city's most active cultural centers.

MALASAÑA AND CHUECA

North of Gran Vía is a maze of streets and plazas that make up Madrid's liveliest barrios. To the west of Calle Fuencarral, clear up to the bustling **Glorieta de Bilbao** is the barrio of Malasaña; to the east lies Chueca. Traditionally, these two neighborhoods have a lot in common—narrow streets lined with ancient shops, vegetable markets, and neighbors of all ages going about their daily bustle. Throughout both you'll find writers lingering at marble tables in belle epoque cafés, house-coated *señoras* mopping stoops, and blue-jumpered construction workers tucking into fat slices of *tortilla* at corner bars. More recently, distinctive personalities have emerged. Malasaña is a bit gruff, with a tough-kid attitude, albeit a kid with a skateboard, an addiction to techno,

and a ridiculous amount of money to spend on upscale street clothes. Chueca is not only the center of Madrid's gay and lesbian life, it is also achingly hip, brimming with trendy shops, exclusive salons, and daring restaurants. Of most interest to a visitor are the barrios themselves and they are best enjoyed in the early evening, when street life is at its liveliest.

Over in Malasaña, be sure to take a break in **Plaza Dos de Mayo**, a sandy, tree-lined plaza rimmed by cafés and restaurants. The central arch is the only remnant of the Monteleón barracks that stood here in the early 19th century. It was one of the main gathering points for the rebellious *madrileños* who rose up to fight French troops on May 2, 1808. During the 1980s, it was a focus of the *movida,* the creative movement that exploded after the death of Franco. The Chueca counterpoint is **Plaza Chueca**, a rather dingy square surrounded by apartment blocks. What it lacks in charm, it more than makes up for in people watching. Grab a plaza-side seat and enjoy the show.

As you walk down the alternative shopping paradise that is **Calle Fuencarral**, take a moment to check out the extravagant doorway of the **Museo Municipal** (C/ Fuencarral 78, Metro: Tribunal). Created by Pedro de Ribera, one of Madrid's official architects in the 18th century, it is arguably the best example of baroque architecture in the city. The museum itself is devoted to city history and will be closed for renovations until at least 2009.

As you wind your way through Chueca, pass by the **Palacio de Longoria** (Fernando VI 4, Metro: Alonso Martínez), a stunning example of art nouveau frivolity. Its spectacular facade of undulating lines and icing-like floral flourishes is a luscious contrast to its more staid neighbors. Currently, it is a den of literary activity as the headquarters of the Sociedad General de los Autores and is closed to the public. For a decidedly more macabre turn, pop into **Iglesia de San Antón** (C/ Hortaleza 63, Metro: Chueca, tel. 91/521-7473), a baroque edifice that has seen much better days. Inside are a few notable works including a Goya.

© CANDY LEE LABALLE

Madrid's best baroque doorway on the Museo Municipal

However, the treasure to seek out are the bones of Saint Valentine. Legend has it that the remains of the love-promoting Saint were sent to San Antón in the 18th century straight from the Vatican. If you go, show up after 6:30 P.M. and ask for the *huesos de san valentin* (WAY-sos de san bal-in-TEEN). In a glass-fronted box labeled *patron de los enamorados,* patron saint of the lovers, is a yellowing skull framed by a gruesome ring of bones—not very romantic. If you are in town on January 17, pass by the church to see the annual blessing of the pets. San Antón is the patron saint of animals, and each year thousands of *madrileños* line up with dogs, cats, birds, and iguanas to participate in this 17th-century tradition. Afterwards there is a boisterous animal parade around the barrio.

SALAMANCA AND LA CASTELLANA

The posh **Barrio Salamanca** unfurls north of the Retiro in an orderly grid of elegant streets and upscale shops. At its base is the **Plaza de Colón,** a wide, sunny esplanade ringed with benches and trees. It is home to the **Jardines del Descubrimiento,** a dirt-colored series of hulking carved stones that are supposed to pay homage to the Spain's discovery of the New World. Just south of the plaza is a much better monument to Spain's illustrious role in world history. The **Museo Arqueológico Nacional** (C/ Serrano 13, Metro: Colón, tel. 91/577-7912, www.man.es, 9:30 A.M.–8:30 P.M. Tues.–Sat., 9:30 A.M.–2:30 P.M. Sun., closed Mon., €3) holds an impressive variety of artifacts from prehistory onwards. On the back side of the museum is the **Biblioteca Nacional** (Po. Recoletos 22). Spain's national library is an impressive structure, but it is off-limits to all but pre-approved students and scholars, except for occasional exhibits.

At the northern end of Salamanca is the **Museo Lázaro Galdiano** (C/ Serrano 122, Metro: Gregorio Marañon, tel. 91/561-6084, www.flg.es, 10 A.M.–4:30 P.M. Wed.–Mon., closed Tues., €4). During the 19th century, Lázaro Galdiano, an author, editor, and very rich man, amassed Spain's most important private art collection. After his death, his 37-room mansion was turned into the museum. It houses several noteworthy Goyas, however the most spectacular painting is undoubtedly *El Salvador,* a hypnotic black and green painting of a young Jesus, attributed to Leonardo da Vinci. Though the original mansion has been outfitted as a gallery, each room features a photo from back when Galdiano was in residence. Don't forget to look up; the ceilings are inspiring. Though it is not really worth the detour unless you are an art fanatic, the museum makes a nice stop if you are traveling on the Madrid Vision bus.

◖ Paseo de la Castellana

Running through the heart of Madrid, north to south, is the city's loveliest boulevard, the Paseo de la Castellana. At its southern end, it begins life as the Paseo del Prado, becoming the Paseo de Recoletos at Plaza Cibeles, and finally La Castellana, as it's locally known, at Plaza de Colón. Though it is a major thoroughfare, holding up to eight lanes of traffic at its widest,

MADRID

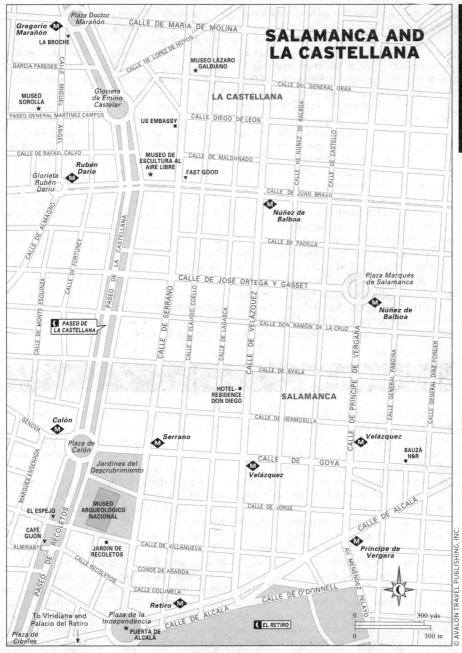

SALAMANCA AND LA CASTELLANA

Plaza Doctor Marañón
CALLE DE MARIA DE MOLINA
Gregorio Marañón
LA BROCHE
GARCIA PAREDES
CALLE DE LOPEZ DE HOYOS
MUSEO LÁZARO GALDIANO
CALLE DEL GENERAL ORÁA
CALLE MIGUEL ANGEL
Glorieta de Emilio Castelar
LA CASTELLANA
MUSEO SOROLLA
PASEO GENERAL MARTINEZ CAMPOS
US EMBASSY
CALLE DIEGO DE LEÓN
CALLE DE NÚÑEZ DE BALBOA
CALLE DE CASTELLO
CALLE DE RAFAEL CALVO
Rubén Darío
MUSEO DE ESCULTURA AL AIRE LIBRE
CALLE DE MALDONADO
Glorieta Rubén Darío
FAST GOOD
CALLE DE JUAN BRAVO
Núñez de Balboa
CALLE DE ALMAGRO
CALLE DE FORTUNEY
PASEO DE LA CASTELLANA
CALLE DE PADILLA
CALLE DE MONTE ESQUINZA
CALLE DE JOSÉ ORTEGA Y GASSET
Plaza Marqués de Salamanca
CALLE DE SERRANO
CALLE DE CLAUDIO COELLO
CALLE DE LAGASCA
CALLE DE VELÁZQUEZ
Núñez de Balboa
CALLE DON RAMÓN DE LA CRUZ
CALLE DE PRINCIPE DE VERGARA
PASEO DE LA CASTELLANA
CALLE DE AYALA
CALLE GENERAL PARDINA
CALLE GENERAL DIAZ PORLIER
HOTEL-RESIDENCE DON DIEGO
SALAMANCA
CALLE DE HERMOSILLA
GENOVA
Colón
Velázquez
Plaza de Colón
Serrano
BAUZÁ H&R
Jardines del Descrubrimiento
CALLE DE GOYA
Velázquez
MARQUÉS ENSENADA
CALLE DE JORGE
EL ESPEJO
PASEO DE RECOLETOS
MUSEO ARQUEOLÓGICO NACIONAL
CALLE DE ALCALÁ
CAFÉ GIJÓN
CALLE DE VILLANUEVA
Príncipe de Vergara
ALMIRANTE
JARDÍN DE RECOLETOS
AV MENÉNDEZ PELAYO
CALLE RECOLETOS
CONDE DE ARANDA
CALLE COLUMELA
Retiro
CALLE DE O'DONNELL
To Viridiana and Palacio del Retiro
Plaza de la Independencia
CALLE DE ALCALÁ
EL RETIRO
Plaza de Cibeles
PUERTA DE ALCALÁ

0   300 yds
0   300 m

it is bordered for most of its length with tree-lined walkways, vibrant little gardens, wooden benches, and playgrounds. The best way to get a view of this grand avenue is to catch **Bus 27** on the eastern side of the street and ride all the way to the last stop at **Plaza de Castilla,** a rather depressing massive traffic circle surrounded by office towers. You'll have to get off the bus here, and pay again to get back on. While you are waiting to board again, look up at the gravity-defying twin towers leaning over the bus station. The ride should take about 20 minutes each way, except during rush hours when it could be more than an hour.

Just south of Plaza de Castilla is the monumental **Estadio Santiago Bernabéu** (Av. Concha Espina 1, Metro: Santiago Bernabéu, tel. 91/398-4300, www.realmadrid.es). Home of the world-famous team Real Madrid, the 80,000-seat stadium was also the site of the 1982 World Cup. Best of all, Bernabéu (ber-na-BAY-oo), offers a unique tour that lets you get up close and personal with the stadium. For €9, you get practically unlimited access to the facilities—sit on the players' benches, visit the trophy room, or even check out the dressing rooms. The only thing you cannot do is step onto the playing field.

At the juncture where the Castellana passes under the Paseo de Eduardo Dato, the **Museo de Escultura al Aire Libre** is an open-air collection of sculptures tucked under the overpass. Notable works are those by Spanish sculptors Eduardo Chillida and Joan Miró. The stairs to the east of the garden go up to Calle Serrano, right alongside the **U.S. Embassy.** On the other side of the Castellana is one of Madrid's most charming museums, the **Museo Sorolla** (C/ General Martínez Campos 37, tel. 91/310-1584, www.museosorolla .mcu.es, 9:30 A.M.–3 P.M. Tues.–Sat., 10 A.M.–3 P.M. Sun., closed Mon., €3, free Sun.) is the former home and studio of modernist Spanish painter Joaquín Sorolla. His cheerful works are displayed in abundance throughout the museum, but the real treat is the house itself, which has been left exactly the way it was when he lived here at the turn of the 20th century. Even his studio still holds his paint-encrusted brushes.

Nightlife

In general, there are three main **nightlife zones** in Madrid's city center: **Huertas,** which is loosely the area running from the Paseo del Prado to Plaza Santa Ana and up to Sol; **Malasaña,** which spreads out in all directions from Plaza Dos de Mayo and draws a younger, rowdier crowd and lots of grungy bars and cheap drinks; and **Chueca,** which is the locus of gay and lesbian life in Madrid but also figures large in anyone's going-out plans, as many of the best bars are mixed. Other areas include La Latina, where the focus is on tapas and casual bars; Atocha, where you'll find several commercial megadiscos; Lavapiés, with a glut of arty bars and seedy hang-outs; and Gran Vía between Callao and Calle Alcalá, which is full of techno clubs and trendy cocktail lounges. Of course, since Madrid has the most bars of any city in the world, wherever you are in the city, you'll find thumping nightlife—just ask at your hotel or at the bar where you have your morning coffee.

Compared to other Spanish cities, drinking in Madrid is expensive. Compared to the United States, it is dirt cheap. Beers and wine will cost between €1.50 and €3, higher in big clubs and after-hours bars. *Copas* (mixed drinks) run from €4–7 in most places. Upscale and late-night bars charge more. Remember that most dance clubs will charge an *entrada* (cover charge) of anywhere from €5–20. In exchange you'll receive a slip of paper. Don't toss it out! It is valid for your first drink, whether you choose a cheap beer or a pricey cocktail. (See sidebar, *A Nightlife Survival Guide,* in the *Essentials* chapter.)

VAMOS A MARCHAR: A NIGHTLIFE ROUTE OF MADRID

© CANDY LEE LABALLE

Start your night at a wine bar.

Madrid is as famous for its nightlife as it is for its Goyas. With bars far outweighing the painter's masterpieces, there is no denying that *la marcha*, the march from bar to bar, is a vital part of Madrid's cultural landscape. Unfortunately, many visitors miss out on it. Those famed 4 A.M. traffic jams on Gran Vía and all-day Sunday dance parties remain myths to the casual tourist. The result is that the night belongs to the locals. If you want to join them, you'll need to do like they do and follow three simple rules. One, start late. If you head out anytime before 11 P.M. you'll be all alone with hundreds of tourists wondering where the action is. Two, go slow. Despite their passion for partying, *madrileños* don't believe in getting falling-down drunk. They'd miss out on the party that way. Remember that alcohol pours are three times what you'd get in the United States, so if you are a light drinker, one cocktail might do you in. Pace your drinking; you have a long night ahead. And three, keep moving. That is the whole point of *la marcha*. The fresh air and walking will keep you energized.

If you spend the day soaking up art, treading the streets, and grazing on tapas, you will need a siesta to make it out Madrid-style. A perfect time is around 6 P.M. in the lull between lunchtime and dinner hour. Grab two or three hours snooze time, and head out for a light dinner of tapas around 9:00 P.M. Around 10:30 P.M. follow this *marcha* route.

Start off at one of the *mesones* beneath Plaza Mayor on Calle Cava de San Miguel. **Mesón de la Guitarra** (No. 13) is a good bet to see men in tights strumming mandolins. Have some sangria and then stroll through Plaza Mayor (spectacularly lit-up at night), and towards Plaza Santa Ana. The streets should be filling up by then. You'll feel the energy – a happy buzz that foretells a really good time. Stop in at **La Venencia** (C/ Echegaray 7) for a glass of sherry and a dose of atmosphere. Head up the street to **Cardamomo** (C/ Echegaray 15) for a little upscale flamenco nightclubbing. Next head around the corner to **Viva Madrid.** Have one drink and dance it off upstairs.

Around 2 A.M., the bars start to close up and the *discobares* get going. Head back past Plaza Santa Ana to **Torero** (C/ Cruz 26), a packed-out locals' favorite. Next head to the other side of Sol and **Palacio Gaviria** (C/ Arenal 9) to do some late-night dancing under 19th-century chandeliers.

With your head swimming, your back sweaty, and your dancing shoes scuffed, do like the locals and head around the corner to **Chocolatería San Ginés** (Pasadizo de San Ginés 5) for a *chocolate y churros* fix. Lift your cup of bubbling chocolate in toast to yourself. You've just lived *la marcha* like a true *madrileño!*

SOL AND PLAZA MAYOR

The clutch of streets behind Sol down to Plaza Santa Ana blur into the nearby *marcha* zone of Huertas, bound by Paseo del Prado. Your best nightlife bet is to wander around any of them. Closer to Plaza Mayor, the nightlife pickings are slimmer, but you will always find something going on somewhere.

Bars

Along Cava de San Miguel there are several *mesones,* narrow bars that burrow back underneath Plaza Mayor. These traditional watering holes have been around for hundreds of years and still pack in a raucous crowd of locals, tourists, students, and the wacky wonderful minstrels called *la tuna,* groups of college boys dressed in Renaissance costumes complete with tights and wielding ukuleles. Each *mesón* specializes in something. At Champiñones, it's mushrooms, at Boquerones it is marinated anchovies, at Tortilla, it is the ubiquitous Spanish omelette. The best for a rollicking good time is ◖€ **Mesón de la Guitarra** (C/ Cava de San Miguel 13, Metro: Sol, tel. 91/599-9531, 7 P.M.–2 A.M. daily), which is a home base for the *tuna* who stop by around midnight most nights. An escape from all things Spanish is right across the street from Plaza Mayor at **El Imperfecto** (C/ Coloreros 5, Metro: Sol, 3 P.M.–2 A.M. daily), a cave-like space, cluttered with second-hand furniture. Attracting a youngish crowd of expats and *madrileños* but few tourists, the bar offers dozens of teas, fresh juices, homemade cakes, and an extensive list of cocktails for €6.50 each.

Over by Sol, another option to start the night is **Bodegas Melibea** (C/ Espoz y Mina 9, Metro: Sol, 7 P.M.–1:15 A.M. daily). Behind a tiled facade of Rubenesque nudes, this is a classic Spanish *taberna*— creaking wooden floor, aged barrels for tables, legs of *jamón* on the wall. Order *vermut de grifo* (sweet red vermouth served on tap), grab a table in the window, and watch the tourists go by gaping at the lusty tiles.

Dance Clubs

Built in 1850, the Italian Renaissance **Palacio**

Gaviria (C/ Arenal 9, Metro: Sol, tel. 91/526-6069, www.palaciogaviria.com, 9 P.M.–3 A.M. Mon.–Fri., 9 P.M.–5 A.M. Sat.–Sun., €8–10) is the kind of place you'd expect to house a museum. Instead, you'll find go-go dancers and club-goers of all ages grooving under frescoed ceilings and gilded chandeliers. Different salons host distinctly different music from Latin beats to hard house. Thursday night is international student night. Even if you are not a clubber, make an effort to visit one early evening just to take in the spectacular surroundings.

A few blocks to the east, **Sala Stella** (C/ Arlabán 7, Metro: Sevilla, noon–6 A.M. Thurs.–Sat., €10–12) is the best club in the center for the latest and greatest in electronic music. Running different parties on different nights, it attracts a loyal following of party people worshipping at the DJ booth of top spin-masters from around the world. Mondo is one of the best parties with an alternative mash of funky house. The Room is a night of classic hard house. Gets crowded, goes late. If you prefer something a bit more Spanish, go to **Torero** (C/ Cruz 26, Metro: Sol/Sevilla, tel. 91/523-1129, 11 P.M.–6 A.M. Tues.–Sat., €8–11), behind Sol. This is a favorite of young (and not so young) enthusiastic locals looking for a good time in close quarters. Upstairs features a playlist of Spanish pop favorites (everyone sings along), while downstairs is more mainstream dance. The best perch for people watching is the bleacher-style seating to the right of the door. Expect to wait in line to get in after 3 A.M. and dress smart (or at least leave the tennies in the hotel). Like most Madrid hot spots, it fills to bursting on weekends.

Jazz and Live Music

An institution in Madrid, **Café Central** (Pl. del Angel 10, Metro: Sol, tel. 91/369-4143, www.cafecentralmadrid.com, 1 P.M.–2:30 A.M. daily, cover varies) is an elegant café by day, intimate jazz club by night. The belle epoque room, complete with soaring ceilings and marble tables, draws top names in the international jazz scene. Shows start around 10:30 and if you are already in the café, you will be asked (very nicely) to pay the cover or leave.

PASEO DEL PRADO

If you only have one night in Madrid and want to experience a slice of the city's famed *marcha*, you can't go wrong wandering the tangle of streets from the Paseo del Prado up to Santa Ana. This area is usually referred to as "Huertas" due to the dense concentration of nightlife on the pedestrian street of the same name.

Bars

[**La Venencia** (C/ Echegaray 7, Metro: Sol, tel. 91/429-7313, 1–3:30 P.M. and 7:30 P.M.– 1:30 A.M. daily) is a must-see. Under peeling sherry posters, dusty vats, and acres of bottles, the wood-topped bar serves up nothing but sherry from the dry, pale *manzanilla* to the sweet, amber *oloroso*. Bartenders chalk your order onto the bar and serve you a side of the most savory olives you'll ever taste. If you go on a slow night and sit out back, don't be surprised if the house cat jumps into your lap. Another slow way to start the evening is at **Yesterday** (C/ Huertas 10, Metro: Sol, 9:30 P.M.–2 A.M. Mon.–Sat.). Run by American Nicole and flamenco dancer Antonio (they met when she left Maine to study flamenco with him over a decade ago), this is a cozy bar with dim lights, battered wicker furniture, and yellowing walls. The effect (along with the old jazz on the stereo) feels a lot like a New Orleans speakeasy, and in fact Antonio lived in the Crescent City for several years. The cocktails are perfectly rendered.

Around since forever, **Las Cuevas del Sésamo** (C/ Príncipe 7, Metro: Sol, tel. 91/429-6524, 7:30 P.M.–2 A.M. daily) is a Madrid favorite that draws tourists in the know. Look for the red and white neon sign hanging above the door. Entrance is through a hallway and down the stairs. When you get down to the cave, request a table and order a pitcher of sangria. Under walls painted in literary quotes (great way to practice your Spanish), a grandfatherly piano man plays feel-good Spanish tunes. Around the block, in a stunning setting that in the United States might end up as a

museum, **Viva Madrid** (C/ Manuel Fernández y González 7, Metro: Sol, tel. 91/429-3640, 1 P.M.–2 A.M. daily) is a quiet café by day, raucous club by night. The tiled exterior will coax the camera out of your pocket. The intricate wood ceiling in the first room will drop your jaw. The awe continues with the zinc bar, goose-mouthed taps, ornate mirrors, and Andalusian tiled walls. Back in the 1930s, this was a brothel and you can see that history reflected in the paintings throughout. At night, the bar serves up a musical cocktail of classic rock, salsa, and a bit of disco to a 35-plus crowd.

Flamenco Bars

Cardamomo (C/ Echergay 15, Metro: Sevilla, tel. 91/420-2184, www.cardamomo.net, 7 P.M.–3 A.M. daily) takes flamenco out of the *tablaos* and puts it on the dance floor where an appreciative crowd twirls, claps, and stomps all night. During the week there are occasional live performances. It is popular with up-and-coming flamenco singers and dancers letting loose on their nights off.

Jazz and Live Music

If you can ignore the mamie-faced jazz man on the door, you'll find one of Madrid's most intimate jazz clubs at **Café Populart** (C/ Huertas 22, Metro: Antón Martin, tel. 91/429-8407, www.populart.es, 6 P.M.–2:30 A.M. daily, shows at 11 P.M. and 12:30 A.M.). Local and touring jazz and blues acts are featured most nights of the week. The high-ceiling room is narrow and space tight so get there early if you want a table. No cover charge but expect a surcharge added to your drinks.

ATOCHA AND LAVAPIÉS

The steep streets leading down from Sol into Atocha and Lavapiés are riddled with dive bars, ancient *tabernas,* and hipper-than-thou bohemian bodegas. One note about safety, this area has a bad reputation (though the city is making valiant efforts to fix that). Especially in the Plaza Lavapiés you'll run into young drug dealers. They'll call out "costo" to you, the street slang for hash. Just keep walking. That said, you'll also notice the streets are full of young party-goers, older couples taking a stroll, kids kicking soccer balls, and a United Nations of ethnicities chatting on the street corners. As it gets late and the crowds thin out, stick to main streets such as Olivar, Argumosa, and Ave María. To catch a cab from the area, head uphill on Olivar to Calle Magdalena and turn right. Walk past Plaza Antón Martín and you should be able to hail a taxi on Calle Atocha.

Bars

There are several great spots in this area that straddle the border between café and bar. Try them during the day for a relaxed refuge or at night for a slow evening. A favorite of guidebook writers, **Taberna de Antonio Sánchez** (C/ Mesón de Paredes 13, Metro: Tirso de Molina, tel. 91/539-7826, noon–5 p.m. and 8 p.m.–midnight Mon.–Sat., noon–4 p.m. Sun.) more than deserves the accolades. The original Antonio was a bullfighter and the spirit of *la corrida* is heavy within these antiquated walls. Sánchez family members killed the bulls whose heads hang on the walls. Despite its fame, the *taberna* is just far enough off the tourist track to keep it refreshingly local. Sunday afternoons are the busiest.

The romantically tattered **Café Barbieri** (C/ Ave María 45, Metro: Lavapiés, tel. 91/527-3658, 3 p.m.–2 a.m. Sun.–Thurs., 3 p.m.–2:30 a.m. Fri.–Sat.) with faded red velvet benches, foggy mirrored walls, creaky marble tables, and even creakier floors is a favorite retreat for writers, students, and intellectuals, as well as a spattering of Lavapiés crazies. Coffees and cocktails are the specialties. Grab one or the other and a pen, and let your inner Hemingway loose. A few blocks uphill, **Vinícola Mentridana** (C/ San Eugenio 9, Metro: Antón Martín, tel. 91/527-8760, 1:30 p.m.–1:30 a.m. daily) is an antiquated wine bar complete with dusty bottles lining the walls and a creaky well-worn floor. For decades it has been a favorite retreat for locals both young and old, and lately it has become a boho-hip place to have a glass of wine, particularly on Sunday afternoons.

The blue-tiled **Bodegas lo Máximo** (C/ San Carlos 6, Metro: Lavapiés, tel. 91/539-0070, 7:30 p.m.–1:45 a.m. Mon.–Thurs., 2 p.m.–2:30 a.m. Fri.–Sat., 2 p.m.–2 a.m. Sun.) is a favorite among the arty denizens of Lavapiés. Trendy without trying, this women-run bar serves cheap beers and wines under swirly psychedelic lights. There are also a few simple tapas available until they run out. It is a must-stop on a *marcha* crawl of Lavapiés.

Dance Clubs

El Juglar (C/ Lavapiés 37, Metro: Lavapiés, tel. 91/528-4381, www.salajuglar.com, 9:30 p.m.–3 a.m. Sun.–Thurs., 9:30 p.m.–3:30 a.m. Fri.–Sat.) is the locus of all things hip in Lavapiés. The front room features a curved metal bar, brick walls, cheap drinks, and loud talk. The back room hosts acts from Detroit rock bands to flamenco fusion to belly dancers. After the show a DJ lets loose with a pumping mix of funk and soul. It gets packed from 1 a.m. on.

For two of the city's most notorious megadiscos, head uphill towards Atocha station. Tucked down between the Renfe and the AVE stations, **Ananda** (Av. Ciudad de Barcelona, s/n, Metro: Atocha Renfe, tel. 91/524-1144, www.ananda.es, midnight–5:30 a.m. Fri.–Sat., €10–15) feels a bit like Alice in Wonderland's acid tea party, with a clutter of flowing fabrics, swinging seats, jewel-colored pillows, glowing mini-Hindu shrines, candles, and incense set against the backdrop of solid dance music. The crowd is coifed and fit (body fat apparently checked at the door). During warmer months, a massive outdoor terrace nearly doubles the size of the place. Check the website for free passes to enter. Up the street is the obscenely grandiose **Kapital** (C/ Atocha 125, Metro: Atocha, www.grupo-kapital.com, midnight–6 a.m. Thurs.–Sun., €12–15), a one-stop super club for all your nightclub needs. Each of the seven floors has a different atmosphere from mainstream pop to fist-pumping house, jiggling salsa to Spanish pop. Locals swear they stay away, but there is no way the all-night long, sidewalk-snaking lines are just made of tourists. Drinks are pricey, but if you are even

PARTY ALL MORNING LONG

Madrid is world famous for its late-night scene: 4 A.M. traffic jams and early morning cafés jammed with club crawlers chowing on churros. Just about every night of the week, somewhere in the city, there is a party going on until dawn. That is when most people go home. But not all. For the really hard-core clubber, Madrid offers a few dance clubs that are so after-hours, they happen the next day. Where and when is constantly in flux. Clubs change names often. They shut down and move across town. They are really hot one night and the next, suddenly not. To find the latest and greatest, pick up a copy of In Madrid, the English-language monthly, and go to the Night Life section. It has candid reviews along with addresses, hours, and metro stops. Also check their website at www.in-madrid.com. Another way to get a handle on the scene is to visit Calle Fuencarral and pop into the clothing stores. You'll find tons of flyers, many with discount offers. Here are a few of the long-time legends on the daytime scene.

Once a month the macro-disco Fabrik is turned into a high-energy, free-for-all fest of house, trance, and techno called **Goa** (Av. Industria 82, Humanes, www.tripfamily.com, 10 A.M.–midnight Sun., €15). The club holds thousands and by lunchtime, the dance floor is a sea of humanity. There are five bars, a snack area, and a massive terrace where you can get a bit of rest in the sun before heading back inside for more. The only drawback is the location outside of town. To make it easier, free buses leave from in front of the club Ohm (Pl. Callao 4) starting at 9:30A.M. Bring cash. There are money machines but there is

a commission and they have been known to break down.

The world-famous **Space of Sound (Sala Macumba)** (Pl. Chamartín, s/n, Metro: Chamartín, www.comunidadspaceofsound .com, 10 A.M.–7 P.M. Sun., €20) is the ultimate party all Sunday long. Forget the Rastro, forget La Latina, forget sun, sangria, and snapping photos; if you crave hard house spun by top DJs, come to Space. With 1,600 square meters of dance floor, a galaxy of go-go dancers, and a euphoric crowd (refreshingly a bit older than the standard 20-something club kids), you could easily dance your day away. Lines form by noon, so go early. Also, for the first hour, entrance is deeply discounted. To get there, take Metro line 10 to Chamartín, follow the signs to the train station, take the escalators to the right up and out, then follow the thud of the deep bass line.

People (Sala Maxime) (Pt. Toledo 1, Metro: Puerta de Toledo, 7:30 P.M.–1 A.M. Sun., €8-12) is the party that ends it all. Though it doesn't start until Sunday evening, most hardcore Madrid clubbers consider this the last stop on a Saturday night out. Like Space, this Sunday-only event draws an exuberant crowd. The house DJs are nothing short of brilliant and really know how to keep the crowd frenzied. Expect enthusiastic whistling and cheering throughout the energetic set. If Oscar de Rivera is spinning, consider yourself blessed. You can get in free for the first hour, but it doesn't include a drink. Whether you do like the locals and make this your last call, or just go in fresh after a day at the Rastro, an experience at People is one you won't forget.

remotely into club culture, you have to see Kapital just once.

Flamenco Bars

Candela (C/ Olmo 3, Metro: Lavapiés, tel. 91/467-3382, 11 P.M.–5:30 A.M. Sun.–Thurs., 11 P.M.–6 A.M. Fri.–Sat.) is legendary among flamenco fans. Around 3:30 A.M., the crowds pour in, mostly Spanish with a good bit of ex-

pats in the mix. Squeeze in, start clapping, and make friends. Be sure to hold onto your wallets as local thieves take advantage of the frivolity to pick pockets. Rumor has it that flamenco legend Camarón de la Isla once gave an impromptu performance that lasted till dawn. Down the back hall by the bathrooms is a storage room where would-be Camaróns sometimes give their own performances. Ask someone if you can enter and then pull up a milk crate.

Terraces

Having a drink on a terrace on a warm summer night is as Spanish as sangria, bullfighting, and *tortilla española*. Almost any bar with a bit of sidewalk space will prop up tables outside the moment the air warms up. One of the most bohemian and least expensive *terraza* experiences runs along **Calle Argumosa** from the Reina Sofía to the Plaza Lavapiés as every bar from the dankest dive to the nicest eatery sets up tables along this tree-lined street. Getting a coveted seat is a combination of luck and pluck, but once situated you can stay all day watching the artier-than-thou set strut by with their mohawks, piercings, and impossibly large dogs. Some best bets along the street are **Heladeria Yoli** (no. 7) for the *granizada de café*, **El Económico** (no. 9) for great coffee, and **Achuri** (no. 21) for cheap eats and cheaper beer.

LA LATINA

The maze of streets and plazas in La Latina are best known for their wine bars and upscale *tabernas*. Most of the tapas places turn their focus to less eating and more drinking as the night wears on. When the bar culture really heats up here is on Sunday after the Rastro. From about 4–9 P.M. the entire barrio becomes a massive block party as crowds pour out onto the streets using the nearest cars as tabletops.

Bars

Dominated by a massive rectangular bar that leaves little room for standing, let alone drinking, **Bonanno** (Pl. del Humilladero 4, Metro: La Latina, tel. 91/366-6886, noon–2 A.M. daily) is perpetually crowded. Drawing a film industry crowd, the bar is loaded with creative types in black-framed glasses. Around the corner **Lamiak** (C/ Cava Baja 42, Metro: La Latina, tel. 91/365-5212, 1 P.M.–2 A.M. Tues.–Sat., 1–11 P.M. Sun., closed Mon.) is one of those places that is always fun. Under bright yellow walls, an animated crowd of 30-somethings quaff endless *cañas* and *tostas* piled high with crab salad, *tortilla, jamón,* and whatever else the kitchen feels like putting out. This place is absolutely wild on Sunday afternoons, just short of swinging from the ceilings. If you go, be ready to stay all day and night, the vibe here is addictive.

Dance Clubs

A bit sleazy, the way a good cabaret club should be, **Berlin Cabaret** (C/ Costanilla de San Pedro 11, Metro: La Latina, tel. 91/366-2034, www .berlincabaret.com, 11 P.M.–5 A.M. Mon.–Sat., closed Sun., €8–10) offers a hodge-podge of performances all week long, from magic to comedy, drag queens to show girls. Shows are all in Spanish, but for the dancing that goes on all night long afterwards, no language is required. Watch for the sinking floor! Throughout the night, the stage floor lowers to pick up a few dancers and a drag queen or two. They perform a quick number and then sink back down again. Lots of fun, but gets wildly crowded. For a hipper dance experience, head over to **ContraClub** (C/ Bailén 16, Metro: La Latina, tel. 91/365-5545, www.contraclub.com, 10 P.M.–5:30 A.M. Sun.–Thurs., 10 P.M.–6 A.M. Fri.–Sat., €6–8). Run by a Madrid film director, this maze-like space combines live music, independent films, and late-night dancing into one raucous club. Frequented by members of Madrid's incestuous film industry, it seems everybody knows everybody else at this under-the-radar house of cool. As the night wears on, it doesn't matter; everyone just wants to dance. Expect long lines on weekends after most bars close at 3 A.M.

Flamenco Bars

You never know what you'll get at 【 **La Soleá** (C/ Cava Baja 34, Metro: La Latina, tel. 91/366-0534, 10 P.M.–5 A.M. Tues.–Thurs., 10 P.M.–6 A.M. Fri.–Sat., closed Sun.–Mon.). In the two tiled rooms of this intimate bar, a house guitarist strums out classic flamenco riffs while members of the audience break into song. The lazy-eyed man squeezed next to you on the wrap-around bench could be a top singer waiting for the bottom of his whiskey glass to break into heart-wrenching wails. Some nights the singing is extraordinary, others less so, but it is always passionate. If both rooms are packed, stand close to one of the doors and wait, the crowd will eventually shift and you'll get a seat. Since there is no cover and drinks are not too pricey, you are expected to tip a few euros when the pot gets passed around.

Terraces

If you are in town between April and October, schedule an evening drink on the terrace of **El Ventorrillo** (C/ Bailén 14, Metro: La Latina, tel. 91/366-3578, noon–1 A.M. daily). Run by the charming Señora Pura (she of the black beehive hairdo), this is your run-of-the-mill café/bar with homemade Spanish goodies from *croquetas* to *tortilla*. But then there is the view. Situated on the corner of Bailén and Morería, at the opposite end of the Segovia viaduct from the Palacio Real, the terrace looks out over the Las Vistillas Park and the western edge of the city clear out to the blue rise of the Sierra Guadarrama mountains. The sunset will leave you speechless. If you visit Velázquez in the Prado, you'll see the same eternal sky in several of his works.

GRAN VÍA
Bars

℗ Del Diego (C/ Reina 12, Metro: Gran Vía, tel. 91/523-3106, 7 P.M.–3 A.M. Mon.–Thurs., 7 P.M.–3:30 A.M. Fri.–Sat., closed Sun.) has attracted both Hollywood royalty (George Clooney quaffed gin and tonics) and real Spanish royalty (before he wed, Prince Felipe was a regular). It's no wonder why. The blonde wood, white leather seats, and frosted glass walls create an oasis of sophistication that is decidedly non-pretentious. But the real draw is the cocktail menu featuring over 70 concoctions from classic to trendy. Each is prepared strictly to the specifications of proprietor Fernando del Diego. He is the one in the suit behind the bar elegantly brandishing a cocktail shaker over his head. Skip the seating area and finagle a spot at the bar to watch him work. And yes, the two waiters who look a lot like him are his

sons. If you aren't afraid of the hard stuff, Sr. del Diego makes the best Old Fashioned in Spain. For something lighter try the Agua de Valencia (cava and fresh orange juice). Another classic *coctelería* is **Museo Chicote** (Gran Vía 12, Metro: Gran Vía, tel. 91/532-6737, www .museo-chicote.com, 7 A.M.–3 A.M. Mon.–Sat., closed Sun.). Since 1931, this art deco gem has brought fine cocktails to a glittering clientele including Frank Sinatra, Sophia Loren, Ava Gardner, and Pedro Almodóvar. And, yes this is the same Chicote that appears in Hemingway's *The Fifth Column*. Papa was a regular here in the 1930s. The decor hasn't changed much since and sipping a drink in one of the curvy green booths is a delicious slip back in time. Come nighttime things fast forward and take on a techno glow. Voted Europe's "Best Bar in 2004" by MTV Europe, Chicote now hosts a roster of top Spanish and European DJs.

For a little less glamour and a little more action try **Shooters** (Gran Vía 31, enter on C/ Mesonero Romanos, Metro: Callao, tel. 91/522-4010, 3:30 P.M.–late Mon.–Sat., 4:30 P.M.–late Sun.). Half upscale sports bar, half pool hall, it is popular with a young international crowd and packs out during major sporting events. Start your evening with a game of pool on one of nine tables, and finish up vibing to house music as resident DJs pump it up until way late.

Dance Clubs

Larios Café (C/ Silva 4, Metro: Santo Domingo, tel. 91/547-9394, www.larioscafe.com, 8 P.M.–5 A.M. Sun.–Thurs., 8 P.M.–6 A.M. Fri.–Sat.) is a three-in-one den of Cuban cool, sleek settings, and gorgeous people-watching. Early evening, the New York loft–style upper floor serves up a modern take on Cuban cuisine. Later on a Latin jazz band kicks up and the focus turns to cocktails with *mojitos* and *caipirinhas* in the starring roles. Step downstairs and you'll find one of Madrid's trendier discos pumping a crowd-pleasing mix of Latin and house. For something louder and edgier, head over to **Ohm** (Pl. Callao 4, Metro: Callao, www.tripfamily.com, midnight–6 A.M. Fri.

and Sat., €10–15). Featuring only the latest and greatest house and dance tracks spun out by a roster of DJ superstars, and an exuberant crowd of Madrid's trendiest party people, this is the hottest party in town and shows no signs of letting up.

MALASAÑA AND CHUECA

Though divided by busy Calle Fuencarral, by day these bordering barrios blend into each other. At night the line is clearer with **Malasaña** nightlife west of Fuencarral dominated by grungy dance bars and roving teens drinking in the plazas. To the east, **Chueca** is home to Madrid's gay and lesbian nightlife along with the attendant trendy cafés, hip little restaurants, and raucous dance clubs. You'll also find hardcore gay clubs with strict (un)dress codes and dark rooms where anything goes standing right next to traditional *tabernas* and tapas bars frequented by elderly Spanish couples. For a complete listing of gay and lesbian bars and events, look for the free *Shangay* magazine. You can also just take a walk around the barrio and ask if a bar has *ambiente,* the Spanish term for gay and lesbian friendly.

Bars

In Malasaña, right on the Plaza Dos de Mayo, the chilled-out **Pepe Botella** (C/ San Andrés 12, Metro: Tribunal, tel. 91/522-4309, 11 A.M.–11 P.M. daily) is a great place to while away a few afternoon hours. The worn red velvet couches, tobacco-stained walls, and antiquated photos lend the café a writerly feel. Coffees and teas are top notch, but the cocktails at €5 are a steal. Pepe Botella was the nickname of Joseph Bonaparte, Napoleon's brother, who briefly ruled Madrid. Much loathed by the Spaniards, Joseph earned the nickname, which means Joe Bottles, not only for his penchant for drinking, but also for his effort to quell the masses by lowering taxes on cheap wine. It didn't work, and in the plaza right outside the window, the Spanish citizenry rose up in arms against the French in the famed battle of Dos de Mayo in 1808. Another great café/bar is **Café La Palma** (C/ Palma 62, Metro: Tribu-

nal, tel. 91/522-5031, www.cafelapalma.com, 4 P.M.–3 A.M. daily). You'll feel like a chameleon as you move through the maze of spaces from a straight-up café to a chilled down Arabic den to an overflowing dance floor/concert hall. Indie acts from around the world hit the stage most nights. Later on house DJs take the crowd from ambient to acid jazz to throwdown funk.

Keep the groove going at the kitschy **Tupperware** (C/ Corredera Alta de San Pablo 26, Metro: Tribunal, 9 P.M.–3:30 A.M. daily). Billed as a "pop bar museum," the music complies, with the DJs serving up a frothy mix of punk, pop, and indie-anything. The crowd is a mix of expat and local, with an anything-goes attitude. On the website for the band Sloan, one group member writes about being accidentally clocked on the head with a barstool at Tupperware. It's that kind of place. For a bit of historical partying, head over to **La Vía Lactea** (C/ Velarde 18, Metro: Tribunal, tel. 91/446-7581, 9 P.M.–3 A.M. Sun.–Wed., 9 P.M.–3:30 A.M. Thurs.–Sat.). In the 1980s, it was a focal point of the *movida,* the explosive avant-arts and nightlife movement of Madrid. It still retains the original funky decor complete with circa-1970s booths, grimy walls papered in rock posters, and cartoonish panels above the bar. During the week, older neighborhood folks hang here shooting pool to a background of Lou Reed. On the weekends, a 20-something crowd crams in, dancing to a mixture of old punk and new funk with a bit of rockabilly thrown in for fun.

◖ **Bodega Ángel Sierra** (C/ Gravina 11, Metro: Chueca, tel. 91/531-0126, noon–2:30 A.M. Mon.–Sat., noon–2 A.M. Sun.) is a bit of traditional Madrid in the heart of trendy Chueca. Check out the yellowing frescoes on the ceiling, the elaborately tiled walls, the zinc-topped bar flowing with water, and the ages-old dusty sherry bottles. The vibe here on Sunday afternoons is insane when both straight and gay, buttoned-up and punked-out, spill into the street with their drinks. A few blocks away, **Libertad 8** (C/ Libertad 8, Metro: Chueca, tel. 91/532-1150, 4 P.M.–

2:30 A.M. daily) has been packing in locals for decades. Under lights made of copper pans, the bar serves basic tapas of the *tortilla* type and cheap beers. Most nights the back room features a singer-songwriter or a storyteller (all in Spanish, I'm afraid).

Dance Clubs

Why Not? (C/ San Bartolomé 7, Metro: Chueca, 11 A.M.–5 A.M. daily) is a narrow underground tunnel that is insanely fun. An energetic crowd (gay, straight, young, old) sings along to an upbeat mix of old disco and Spanish hits from the *movida* while some incredibly agile waiters maneuver through the crowd saving you the trauma of working your way to the bar. But beware, this slip of a bar gets vacuum-packed with hundreds of dancing, drinking bodies. If you don't like the subway at rush hour, you'll hate this place.

Gay and Lesbian

Acuarela (C/ Gravina 10, Metro: Chueca, tel. 91/522-2143, noon–2:30 A.M. Mon.–Sat., noon–2 A.M. Sun.) feels more like the den of a well-traveled eccentric gay uncle than a bar. This is a favorite chill-out (and make-out) stop for both straight and gay couples. You'll recognize it by its wrap-around windows. Order anything from a *batido* (milkshake) to a scotch and settle into a big comfy chair. If the well-endowed nude angel hanging over the seating area makes you feel the need for a fig leaf, just look the other way and keep sipping. Another fun café/bar is **XXX** (C/ Clavel 4, Metro: Gran Vía, 3:30 P.M.–2 A.M. daily, €6). Though it sounds like a peep show, this laid-back café is equal parts kitsch and comfort. Grab a table at the wrap-around windows and watch the world go by on this lively corner. Come night, the music picks up, beautiful boys move in, and major flirting kicks in.

While the majority of the bars in Chueca are mixed or gay, there are very few that are lesbian. **Smoke** (C/ San Bartolomé 7, Metro: Chueca,

10 P.M.–2 A.M. Thurs.–Sun.) is an exception. This is a no-frills, laid-back space where 30-something women come to relax. There is a pool table out back and a friendly bar serving everything from coffees to cocktails. The most raucous dancing in Chueca has got to be at **Black and White** (C/ Libertad 34, Metro: Chueca, 10 P.M.–5 A.M. daily), a legend on the Chueca scene, which packs in a celebratory crowd of all ages. Expect drag shows, cabaret acts, thumping disco, and yes, the occasional hustler looking for a date. Another sizzling contender is **Rick's** (C/ Clavel 8, Metro: Gran Vía, 11 P.M.–6 A.M. daily), a pack-'em-tight, dance-'em-all-night kinda place. Decorated with memorabilia from the film *Casablanca,* which inspired the bar's name, Rick's is a bit battered around the edges, but is still a classic stop on a night crawl through Chueca. Though the music is pumped full of cheesy disco (English and Spanish), the dance floor (and hallways and anywhere else a body can fit) stays hopping. It is open to all, but few women, and even fewer straight men, dare to enter. **Truco** (C/ Gravina 10, Metro: Chueca, tel. 91/532-8921, 8 P.M.–2:30 A.M. Wed.–Sun.) is a lesbian mecca that draws gay men and straight couples, too. With no decor to speak of, a tiny bar and tired tracks of Spanish pop on replay, there is nothing fancy about this place. Yet it is wildly fun. Frenzied dancing starts up around midnight and goes on until closing.

Jazz and Live Music

One of the latest clubs on Madrid's jazz scene, **Bogui** (C/ Barquillo 29, Metro: Chueca, tel. 91/521-1568, www.boguijazz.com, 10 P.M.–6 A.M. daily, cover varies) is a modern space dominated by a baby grand piano. Music is mainly jazz with forays into blues and funk. Shows at 10:30 and midnight feature local and international acts, ranging from traditional bebop and swing to avant garde. Late nights feature DJs spinning electronica with jazzy touches.

Entertainment and Events

THE ARTS
Cultural Centers

Run by a nonprofit arts organization founded in 1880, **Círculo de Bellas Artes** (C/ Alcalá 42, enter on side street, Metro: Sevilla, tel. 91/360-5400, 9:30 A.M.–midnight daily) features top-tier contemporary art exhibits, theater productions, classic cinema, and literary events and lectures. Some nights, it shakes off its highbrow airs and takes on a get-down attitude, hosting some of Madrid's best late-night dance parties complete with world famous DJs. Of all the cultural centers in Madrid, and there are many, this is perhaps the most important and definitely the most invigorating.

The imposing building that is the **Conde Duque** (C/ Conde Duque 11, Metro: San Bernardo, tel. 91/588-5926, 10 A.M.–2 P.M. and 5:30–9 P.M. Tues.–Sat., 10:30 A.M.–2 P.M. Sun., closed Mon.) was originally built as barracks for royal soldiers in the 18th century. Now it is a multi-purpose arts center hosting top international rock, jazz, and blues acts. Especially interesting are the series of concerts following themes such as classical, flamenco, or gospel. It also houses several art spaces as well as the city-run **Museo Municipal de Arte Contemporáneo,** which has a decent permanent collection of modern art.

A multi-purpose space focusing on vanguard artistic expressions, **La Casa Encendida** (Ronda de Valencia 2, Metro: Lavapiés, tel. 91/602-4641, www.lacasaencendida.com, 10 A.M.–10 P.M. daily) supports a heavy roster of events, seminars, and expositions in mediums from experimental techno music and digital animation to modern dance and sculpture. The rooftop terrace is a great escape from the grit of nearby Atocha, though there is no bar nor café. Look out for the **Festival Flamenco** in late January when Casa Encendida hosts performances by the newest stars of the flamenco world. For information, it is best to visit the center. The website is confusing and only in Spanish.

Dance

Madrid offers a dazzling array of dance performances. The best modern troupe is the **Compañía Nacional de Danza** (tel. 91/354-5053, http://cndanza.mcu.es) and its younger, edgier sibling **CND2,** both under the artistic direction of Spanish dance master Nacho Duato. The internationally renowned **Ballet Nacional de España** (http://balletnacional .mcu.es) presents moving works that blend ballet with Spanish dance. All three of these troupes are on the road year-round. If you are lucky to be in Madrid for one of their performances, consider it a loving wink from fate and go. They often perform at the Teatro Real and the Teatro de La Zarzuela.

Several theaters regularly host modern dance performances. Two of the best are **Teatro de Madrid** (Av. Ilustración, s/n, 91/730-1750, www.teatromadrid.com, Metro: Barrio del Pilar) which features crowd-pleasing shows, and **Teatro Pradillo** (C/ Pradillo 12, 91/416-9011, www.teatropradillo.com, Metro: Concha Espina), which focuses on more cutting-edge works.

Film

The majority of Spain's movie houses show films dubbed in Spanish, including all the fancy movie palaces along Gran Vía. For a movie in its original language, look for "versión original" (V.O.) in the listing. A great source of film listings is the *Guía del Ocio,* available at newsstands for €1. Like theaters, Spanish cinemas come with assigned seating and an usher will show you to your seat. Films run €6–8. Featured in Almodóvar's *Talk to Her,* **Cine Dore** (C/ Santa Isabel 3, Metro: Antón Martín, tel. 91/369-1125, 4 P.M.–12:30 A.M. Tues.–Sun., closed Mon.) is the official cinema of Filmoteca Española, the Spanish film society. Each month features a roster of classic and modern masterpieces in V.O. shown in the restored art deco theater. During summer, a rooftop bar opens up where light-hearted films

Filmoteca Española shows classic films in the art deco Cine Dore.

are shown under the stars. Tickets are €1.35 and an *abono* of 10 films costs €10.22. For popular films (Hitchcock, John Cassavetes, anything with Audrey Hepburn), seats sell out fast, so arrive an hour early to get your ticket. While waiting, have a drink in the beautiful café. For more mainstream films in English, head for **Yelmo Cine Ideal** (C/ Doctor Cortezo 6, Metro: Tirso de Molina). This central cinema gets packed on weekends, so show up early to buy your tickets.

Flamenco
Like many Spanish cities, Madrid is full of flamenco *tablaos* (bars with a stage for performances). Some are authentic, some are pure touristic hype. Most fall somewhere in between. In general, avoid the dinner/show combos that are pushed at all hotels. Food is generally mediocre and overpriced and the crowds 100 percent tourists. Does this affect the performance? Many aficionados say yes, but the truth is unless you are a devout fan who knows your *copla* from your *cajón,* you will still

have a good time. The places listed below get high marks from both fans and tourists. A memorable flamenco fiesta would begin with tapas or dinner at **Casa Alberto** (see *Food*), then a show at **Casa Patas,** followed by a late night of listening at **La Soleá** (see *Nightlife*). Also be sure to check the Madrid tourist office website, www.esmadrid.com, for special performances. Several major flamenco productions appear year-round in Madrid's top theaters. In late January look for the **Flamenco Festival** sponsored by Caja Madrid.

Despite being an absolute must-see for tourists from around the world, **Casa Patas** (C/ Cañizares 10, Metro: Tirso de Molina, tel. 91/369-0496, www.casapatas.com, 10:30 P.M. Mon.–Thurs., 9 P.M. and midnight Fri.–Sat., no shows on Sun., €20 and up, reservations required) retains a respectable authenticity in the flamenco world. Shows feature traditional performers as well as young upstarts. The performance room is at the back of a traditional tiled *taberna.* With your entrance ticket, you get one drink. If you can't get a reservation, or would rather not pay the entrance fee, hang out at the bar up front. The vibe is still authentic, flamenco plays over the stereo, and performers (real and would-be) often congregate at the bar before and after the shows, occasionally breaking into song.

Despite couching their advertisement in terms of which famous people have visited their *tablao,* **Corral de la Morería** (C/ Morería 17, Metro: La Latina, tel. 91/365-8446, www .corraldelamoreria.com, 10 P.M. and midnight daily, €32 show with one drink, €75 show with dinner, reservations required) is the real deal and it also one of the few *tablaos* open on Sunday. Under the artistic direction of Blanca del Rey, one of the world's top flamenco dancers, the shows are vibrant, colorful, and passionate. The setting also has a nice Andalusian feel. Even if you can't understand a word of Spanish, expect to be moved. If you can't make the reservations, ask your hotel reception they can often get you in. If the weather is warm, before the early show, try to get a table for tapas and a spectacular sunset at **El Ventorrillo** (see *Nightlife).*

Owned by flamenco performers, **Las Carboneras** (Pl. Conde de Miranda 1, Metro: Sol, tel. 91/542-8677, www.tablaolascarboneras .com, 9 and 10:30 P.M. Mon.–Thurs., 9 and 11 P.M. Fri.–Sat., closed Sun., €22 with drink, show free with dinner from €45, reservations suggested) regularly pulls in top known and unknown talent to this modern *tablao* just around the corner from the Plaza Mayor. If you go here, start with dinner at nearby **Taberneros** (see *Food*).

The newest flamenco venue in town, **Las Tablas** (Pl. España 9, Metro: Plaza de España, tel. 91/542-0520, www.lastablasmadrid.com, 10:30 P.M. daily, €20 with drink, reservations suggested) was opened by two flamenco dancers frustrated with the frilly costumes and same old shows of the tourist *tablaos*. They created a contemporary space right on the Plaza de España that offers lesser known flamenco styles as well as modern takes on tradition. It lets dancers really let loose and if the dancers are happy, you can bet the guests are too. Tapas and dinner are available, but you'd be better off with an early dinner near Plaza de Oriente beforehand or, on the weekends, a La Latina tapas crawl afterwards.

Opera and Classical Music

Teatro de la Zarzuela (C/ Jovellanos 4, Metro: Sevilla, tel. 91/524-5400, http://teatrodela zarzuela.mcu.es, box office noon–6 P.M. daily, on show days until performance starts, €12–40) is the home of the light-hearted operatic form known as *zarzuela*. As *madrileño* as the Rastro, these musicals have a heavy emphasis on the *castizo* culture of working-class Madrid with lusty lads in capes strumming guitars and flirty lasses twirling fans. Even if your Spanish is up to par, the insider jokes and local slang makes it near impenetrable for tourists; but don't worry, the exuberant songs coax the crowds into a hand-clapping frenzy that goes beyond language. A real treat you won't soon forget.

One of Europe's premier opera houses, **Teatro Real** (Pl. Oriente, s/n, Metro: Ópera, tel. 91/516-0660, www.teatro-real.com, box office 10 A.M.–1:30 P.M. and 5:30–8 P.M. Mon.–Sat.) hosts world-class operatic favorites such

as *La Boheme* and *Don Giovanni* as well as an ongoing series of dance, Shakespearean theater, and classical music. As expected from a building with "royal" in the title, the theater is lushly appointed, with a horseshoe-shaped main area that seats over 1,600 spectators. An elaborate staging system allows several immense designs to be built onto swinging floors that can then rotate into place for show time. It also features an advanced acoustical design that ensures all seats are good seats. If you are under 26, head to any show about an hour beforehand to score massively discounted tickets.

Home to both the Spanish National Orchestra and the National Chorus, the ultra-modern **Auditorio Nacional de Música** (C/ Príncipe de Vergara 146, Metro: Cruz del Rayo, www .auditorionacional.mcu.es, tel. 91/337-0100, box office 4–6 P.M. Mon., 10 A.M.–5 P.M. Tues.–Fri., 11 A.M.–1 P.M. Sat.) hosts an invigorating program of classical music year-round. Expect anything from classic composers to avant-garde performances.

Theater and Musicals

As with any major city, Madrid's theater scene is exhaustive, running the gamut from mainstream Broadway fare to off-off-really-off art house productions. Check the tourist office's free magazine *Es Madrid* for the current listings. But take note, Madrid believes in presenting its theater in Spanish. For the small offering of theater in English, look for the free English-language monthly *In Madrid*. Hulking over the Plaza Jacinto Benavente, the **Teatro Calderón** (C/ Atocha 18, Metro: Sol, tel. 91/420-3797, www.teatrocalderon.com, box office 11:30 A.M.–2 P.M. and 5:30–7 P.M. Tues.–Sun., closed Mon.) hosts musicals with mass appeal such as *Fame, We Will Rock You,* and *Carmen*. Shows are in Spanish, including the theme songs you know so well. Founded as a theater in 1583, the building housing **Teatro Español** (C/ Príncipe 25, in Pl. Santa Ana, Metro: Sol, tel. 91/360-1480, box office 11:30 A.M.–1:30 P.M. and 5–7 P.M. Tues.–Sun.) is Madrid's oldest theater. Cervantes and Lope de Vega debuted works here in the 16th century. Today it is a stunning throwback to a more elegant era with ornate golden ceilings and plush red velvet everywhere. Its specialties are classical Spanish works presented straight-up and serious. The attached café is a nice respite before or after a show. In the most traditional of all Madrid barrios, the **Teatro Valle Inclán** (Pl. Lavapiés, s/n, Metro: Lavapiés, tel. 91/505-8800, box office noon–6 P.M. Tues.–Sun.) looms over the Plaza Lavapiés like a glass and cement cube dropped from space. Whatever the neighborhood's opinion of the architecture, there is total agreement that the theater, which houses Spain's Centro Dramático Nacional, has helped clean up the seedier aspects of the plaza and brought new life to the areas bars and restaurants. It hosts serious Spanish drama by renowned Spanish playwrights. And yes, it is all in Spanish.

FESTIVALS

The Madrid calendar is chock full of festivals, from wild free-for-alls with all-night dancing and drinking to solemn religious affairs to international arts events. Check the tourism office, particularly their publication *Es Madrid,* for a complete listing. There are also several religious and political holidays that you should be aware of, as many sights and shops will close on those days. The main art museums normally remain open, but you should check their websites to be sure. The dates are January 6; May 1, 2, and 15; August 15; October 12; November 1; and December 6, 8, 25, and 31. Also, expect closures on the Thursday and Friday before Easter.

Spring

The **Fiestas del Dos de Mayo** (Malasaña, May 1–2) celebrate the bold uprising of *madrileños* against Napoleon's forces in 1808. They lost miserably, but are forever immortalized for their bravery with Goya's paintings and this lively festival. The day begins with a military parade starting in Puerta del Sol. Later that evening, the Royal Guard takes to the streets, marching in period costumes from 1808. Meanwhile, on the other side of town, things

Rebaño Trashumante, the herding of sheep through Madrid in November

kick up in Malasaña (a neighborhood named for Manuela Malasaña, a seamstress who attacked the French troops with her scissors and was killed in the battle). Expect food stalls, live bands (flamenco to rock), and all-night dancing in the Plaza Dos de Mayo. Due to a governmental crackdown on noise, the fiesta is not as wild as it used to be, but it is still a good time and a great way to party with the locals.

The fiestas of **San Isidro** (all over Madrid but centered in Plaza Mayor and La Latina, throughout May, fiesta day is May 15) celebrate the life of San Isidro Labrador, the patron saint of peasants and laborers. Despite its capital status, Madrid has always taken pride in its reputation as a city of hard-working people of the land, so it is no surprise that San Isidro is also the patron saint of Madrid. To celebrate, the city throws parties for nearly a month. Expect everything from solemn religious pilgrimages around the Catedral de San Isidro to boisterous all-night *verbenas* (street fairs). Locals don *chulapo* outfits, which include checkered vests and berets for men, polka-dotted gowns, veils, and carnations in the hair for women. You'll see them dancing the *chotis* to polka-like music. Also look for fireworks over Las Vistillas. The fiestas of San Isidro coincide with Spain's most prestigious bullfighting event, the **Feria Taurina de San Isidro** at Las Ventas. See www .las-ventas.com for details (in Spanish) or ask at the tourist office.

If you are a fan of modern dance, **Madrid en Danza** (May–June) is for you. The city-sponsored festival draws dozens of top dance troupes from around the world, running the gamut from traditional native performances to the latest avant-garde companies. Of course, you can also expect ballet and flamenco.

Summer

If you are in Madrid in the dog heat of August, you'll discover many bars and shops closed and the nightly vibe a bit slower as so many *madrileños* have headed off for vacation. Don't let the lull fool you, the *madrileños* left behind really know how to throw a party and the **Fiestas de San Lorenzo, San Cayetano,** and **la Virgen de la Paloma** (La Latina and Lavapiés, mid–Aug.) are the wildest events in the city. Yes, there are solemn religious parades in which broad-backed men carry statues of the Virgin through the street, as well as traditional concerts and performances. But it is the *verbenas* where the Madrid penchant for partying shines through. First up are the parties of San Lorenzo and San Cayetano (around Aug. 7). The parties for the latter focus on Calle Argumosa in Lavapiés. The street turns into a massive outdoor café with live bands at either end. La Paloma (around Aug. 15) is next and is considered by locals to be the best party in town. La Latina turns into a massive street fest. Plaza Paja features a wacky mix of traditional groups and cover bands. Over on Calle Almendro, expect DJ action with an emphasis on dance. It is a wild time that is also very friendly. You'll see people of all ages, including kids, dancing crazily until the wee hours.

During International Gay Pride Day, cities around the world throw parties, but few can top the intense audacity of Madrid's **Orgullo Gay** (last weekend of June). Chueca turns into a huge street party and the plaza hosts top-name DJs all night long. Thousands turn out for the Saturday afternoon parade, which features marching drag queens, rolling DJ booths, and outrageous floats. Be aware, the boys (and girls) riding along are unafraid to bare all.

Summertime also brings two important arts festivals to the city. Since 1998, **Photo España** (www.phedigital.com, June–July) has focused on Spanish art photography. There are exhibitions throughout town including several clever street displays. **Veranos de la Villa** (throughout the city, July–Sept.) is the mother of all Madrid arts events. City-sponsored, it features dozens of performances from dance to theater, art to music. Many of the biggest performances happen at the **Conde Duque Cultural Center** (C/ Conde Duque 9, tel. 91/588-5834). Look out for events in public spaces such as flamenco in the Sabatini Gardens next to the Royal Palace or theater performances by the remains of the city's Arabic walls.

Fall

A more restrained counterpart to the Veranos de la Villa festival, the **Festival de Otoño** (throughout the city, Oct.–Dec.) is another city-wide presentation of theater, dance, and musical performance that draws top international acts to the city.

If you are in Madrid the first Sunday of November, get down to the center of the city to see an incredible sight—thousands of sheep being herded through the city streets. **Rebaño Trashumante** (sheep crossing) is an ancient tradition that continues to this day. It starts around 9 A.M. from the Casa de Campo, goes through Plaza Mayor and Sol, up to the Plaza de la Independencía and back. It is an event that makes for some amazing photos. Just be careful where you step!

Winter

Madrid doesn't celebrate **Carnival** (Feb.–Mar.) with the unbridled passion of other towns, but it is still a good party. Expect parades, costumed events, and concerts. The best party (and the most exclusive) is the elaborate masked ball at the **Círculo de Bellas Artes.** The fun ends on Ash Wednesday with the **Entierro de la Sardina** (the burial of the sardine), when a giant fish, starting from the Ermita de San Antonio de la Florida, is paraded through the streets with a marching band, and then finally buried at the Fuente de San Isidro.

The international art world descends on Madrid every February for the **Feria** **Internacional de Arte Contemporáneo** (Feria de Madrid, Metro: Campo de las Naciones, www.arco.ifema.es). Better known as ARCO, this contemporary art fair draws thousands of gallery owners, artists, dealers, and buyers. Each year an invited country sends a large contingent from its art community. The first few days are open only to those in the trade, but the weekend is open to the public. Tickets are expensive, but if you are a lover of contemporary art, don't miss it.

Shopping

SHOPPING DISTRICTS
Around Sol
Just north of Sol is a pedestrian shopping zone that webs off of two main streets, **Calle Preciados** and **Calle Carmen.** It is like a giant outdoor mall with dozens of fashion chains, souvenir shops, perfumeries, and a few mega-stores. There are also sidewalk cafés, buskers, and a little old lady with an organ grinder selling sweets. During Christmas the whole area turns into a mass of shopping-frenzied humanity. Spain's favorite department store, **El Corte Inglés** (C/ Preciados 2, 3, and 9, Metro: Sol, 10 A.M.–10 P.M. Mon.–Sat.), is the ultimate one-stop shop for everything from toiletries to Toledo swords. There are several locations in Madrid, but those on Calle Preciados are the most central. **FNAC** (C/ Preciados 28, Metro: Sol) offers five floors of books, films, and music. The Spanish music section is exhaustive and features a massive flamenco section. The periodicals section on the ground floor has the best selection of English-language newspapers and magazines in Madrid. There is more fashion shopping in Puerta del Sol, especially shoe shops, and on the streets leading to the west, **Calle Mayor** and **Calle Arenal.** Just be careful as you shop here. Pickpockets are rampant. Finally, leading south out of Sol, **Calle Carretas** is lined with clothing and shoe shops for men and women.

Gran Vía and North
Originally built as a showcase for Madrid high life, from shopping to hotels, the elegant Gran Vía, from Plaza Callao to Calle Alcalá, still bustles with clothing shops from luxury leather goods giant **Loewe** (Gran Vía 8, tel. 91/522-6815) to mass-appeal fashion chains such as **H&M** (Gran Vía 32). You'll also find Spain's answer to the super-bookstore. **Casa del Libro** (Gran Vía 29, Metro: Gran Vía, tel. 91/522-7758, 9:30 A.M.–9:30 P.M. Mon.–Sat., 11 A.M.–9 P.M. Sun.). There is a decent English-language section and a good choice of travel books and maps.

Calle Fuencarral leading north off of Gran Vía is the definitive den of all things trendy. Dozens of independent shops and a few boutiques like **Custo** offer the types of clothes that are freaky today, fashion tomorrow. About midway up the street is **Mercado de Fuencarral** (C/ Fuencarral 45, Metro: Tribunal, tel. 91/521-4152, 11 A.M.–9 P.M. Mon.–Sat.), the funky street-side mall that revolutionized Madrid's staid shopping scene. Independent clothing labels, tattoo artists, astrologers, and DJs create a young, fun vibe that makes forking over your hard-exchanged euros a pleasure.

Moving west of Fuencarral and into the streets surrounding **Plaza Chueca** you'll enter Madrid's version of Soho, with dozens of trendy boutiques, many dedicated to men's clothing. You'll also find the city's most innovative

SPANISH STYLE FROM A TO Z

With the international success of Spain's bi-annual fashion show Pasarela Cibeles, the world growth of super-chains like Zara, and the media frenzy sparked by hipster labels like Custo, Spanish fashion has definitely arrived on the world's catwalk. Here's a rundown of who's who and what they do.

Adolfo Dominguez (www.adolfodominguez.com), whose lines traditionally relied on a somber palette of classic looks, has diversified his style in the past few years to embrace more modern pieces. This is the place young up-and-comers go for conservative yet stylish clothing.

With a palette of poster-paint fabrics splashed with hearts and flowers, **Agatha Ruiz de la Prada** (www.agatharuizdelaprada.com) makes kids' clothing for adults. She also designs watches, beach towels, notebooks, pens, wallpaper, and yes, actual kids' clothes.

The young designer **Amaya Arzuaga** (www.amayaarzuaga.com) creates clothes that are both practical and stylish with an emphasis on asymmetrical cuts and classic materials. With her designs gaining fame in the United States and Europe, she is considered one of the next big things. Her family also owns one of the country's best bodegas, Bodegas Arzuaga Navarro.

Before going into business for himself, **Antonio Miró** (www.antoniomiro.com) was the brains behind Barcelona's Groc boutiques, where the rich and avant-garde bought their duds in the 1970s. These days, Miró's fashions straddle the border between fashion-forward and immensely wearable. He also has his hand in several different fields of design, including jeans, leather goods, and even bathroom faucets.

For footwear, it's got to be **Camper** (www.camper.com), the internationally renowned Mallorcan shoe company that churns out casual styles in bright colors by the boatload. You won't find ankle-whipping stilettos here, just high-quality fashionable comfort.

Founded by two brothers who started out designing cool T-shirts, **Custo Barcelona** (www.custo-barcelona.com) has grown into an international phenomenon that has sparked its own word in the fashion press – *Customania*. Combining bold designs, screaming colors, and unexpected fabrics, the Custo look is bright, sexy, and indispensable for any serious fashion slave.

David Delfín (www.davidelfin.com) is definitely the bad boy of Spanish fashion. Taking his inspiration from sources such as Nazi Ger-

housewares stores here. Shoe addicts feel they've died and gone to heaven when they stumble onto Chueca's **Calle Augusto Figueroa,** which runs south of the Plaza. The street is lined with *muestrarios,* storefront shops offering the latest samples from Spanish shoe manufacturers. The best part is that these one-of-a-kind designer shoes sell for run-of-the-mill prices. Visiting them could take hours; you may want to send your non-shoe-loving travel companions to nearby **Bodega Angel Sierra** to wait (see *Nightlife*).

Barrio Salamanca

Just north of the Retiro and east of Paseo de la Castellana is Madrid's swankiest shopping zone. Along Calles Serrano, Velázquez, José

Ortega y Gasset, and Goya, you'll find Rolls Royces waiting curbside and top-hatted ushers opening doors. All the usual haute suspects have their shops here. It is also home to **ABC Serrano** (Po. Castellana 34, Metro: Rubén Darío, tel. 91/577-5031, www.abcserrano.com, 10 A.M.–9 P.M. Mon.–Sat.), an upscale mall housed in a historic tiled building connecting the Castellana with Calle Serrano. The fourth floor café offers a nice respite from an intense day of credit card swiping. During the summer, the massive rooftop terrace becomes a late night hot spot peopled with Madrid's pampered see-and-be-seen set.

El Rastro

Spain's super flea market, **El Rastro** (C/ Rimany and the Taliban, Delfín has made a huge splash, both for his clothing and his audacity. The clothes aren't always wearable, but Delfín has a nose for publicity that is bound to make him an international name.

Opulent elegance for the ultra-confident women is the hallmark of **Josep Font's** fashions (www.josepfont.com). Using rich fabrics and exquisite tailoring, Font is one of the top couture designers in the country.

Synonymous with luxury, **Loewe** (www.loewe.com) has been producing soft-as-silk leather goods since 1846. They got their start right in the middle of Madrid on Calle Echegaray. Today, as part of the international mega-label LVMH, Loewe is a worldwide phenomenon, with perfumes, couture, and of course, their famous leather bags.

Loreak Mendian (www.loreakmendian.com). Is it a clothing line? A record label? Avant-garde art? The answer is all of the above. The clothes have a street punk meets surfer meets Bauhaus look and are a favorite among club kids. The company can be found sponsoring many alternative music events.

Lydia Delgado (www.lydiadelgado.es) designs elegant, sensual dresses for women who aren't afraid of their femininity. Expect close cuts, delicate detailing, and confident sexuality.

One of the fastest-growing designers among style-conscious Spaniards, **Purificación García** (www.purificaciongarcia.es) produces sophisticated, modern clothes in subdued colors. Her garments well outlast the fashion seasons in which they're produced.

Victorio y Lucchino (www.victorioyluc chino.com) are two Sevilla-based designers heavily inspired by the city's flamenco history, creating flouncy clothes in bright Mediterranean colors. As wedding dress designers, they are the current darlings of jet-set daughters who want to get married in a distinctly feminine gown.

Zara (www.zara.com), with nearly 1,000 stores around the world, is Spain's best-known mass-fashion export. Just as soon as the latest fashions hit the catwalk, Zara is pumping out inexpensive imitations. Prices are lower than you'd find at U.S. branches and the collection is larger and sleeker. It is best for stylish basics in mix-and-match colors. Affordable, trendy suits are also a staple.

To find out more about Spanish fashion and designers, check out the comprehensive website www.fashionfromspain.com.

---

bera de Curtidores and around, Metro: Tirso de Molina or La Latina, 7 A.M.–2 P.M. Sun.) has been going strong for over 500 years. From used screws to screeching parrots to pirated DVDs, if it can be sold, vendors at the Rastro will sell it. Giving church a hard run for its money, the Sunday-morning market draws thousands every week. Locals, tourists, children, and thieves meld into a lava flow of humanity spreading down from Plaza Cascorro. Some are looking for a bargain, a few are looking to lift wallets, the majority are here for the atmosphere.

Vendors begin setting up before dawn and the market reaches maximum capacity around 11 A.M. If you like your feet to touch the ground when you walk, aim to arrive around 1:30 P.M. when the hordes start to thin out.

Your best bets for real deals are used clothes, especially leather jackets, batik cloths, leather belts, purses, and basic souvenir goodies. Haggling is fine, but your Spanish better be up for it.

It can't be emphasized enough that if you go to El Rastro, you need to be extra-vigilant. Thieves thrive in the crowd, taking advantage of the crush of people to stick their slippery fingers in unsuspecting pockets and purses. Keep nothing in your back pockets, hold your purse to your chest, and make sure your camera strap is wrapped tightly around your wrist. And don't bring a backpack if you can help it. The crowd is just too tight.

About midway down Calle Ribera de Curtidores is a massive gray building that used to house a dance school. It is central beating grounds for dozens of dread-headed drummers. It is also a great perch for photos and getting an overview of the market.

As the market packs up, the plazas of La Latina just to the north fill up. Head on over and join the fun. (See sidebar, *La Latina Sunday Brunch*.)

TYPICALLY SPANISH SHOPS
Accessories

There is nothing more sensual than a woman wielding a fan and in the dog-heat of Spanish summers, there is also nothing more practical. Pick one up anywhere in town for just a few euros, but if you want the real deal visit **Casa de Diego** (Pt. del Sol 12, Metro: Sol, tel. 91/522-6643, 9:30 A.M.–8 P.M. Mon.–Sat.). With fans from €8 to over €500, this specialty shop has been putting *abanicos* into the hands of everyone from royalty to sweaty *señoras* for over a century. Another classic gift can be found around the corner at **Casa Jiménez** (C/ Preciados 42, Metro: Sol, tel. 91/548-0526, 10 A.M.–1:30 P.M. and 5–8 P.M. Mon.–Sat.). Since 1923, this family-run shop has been providing gorgeous, hand-embroidered silk shawls for everyone from Spanish aristocracy to Japanese tourists. Prices start around €30 and zoom up. If you want something a bit warmer, head over to **Capas Seseña** (C/ de la Cruz 23, Metro: Sol, tel. 91/531-6840, www.sesena.com, 10 A.M.–2 P.M. and 4:30–8 P.M. Mon.–Fri., 10 A.M.–2 P.M. Sat.), which has been making capes since 1901. A handmade cape has been a status symbol in Spain for centuries. A 1767 crackdown by the government to ban capes led to rioting in the streets. Rumor has it that Picasso insisted on being buried in his. Today you're more likely to glimpse one on an old-school businessman or a high-powered politician—even Hillary Clinton picked one up during a visit to Madrid. Classic style doesn't come cheap and capes cost €250–650.

Bullfighting Suits

For something really different, visit **Justo Algaba** (C/ Paz 4, Metro: Sol, tel. 91/523-3595, www.justoalgaba.com, 10 A.M.–2 P.M. and 5–8 P.M. Mon.–Fri.). This famed tailor has been making *trajes de luz* (suits of lights) for decades and counts among his clients the top matadors of the world. He also dressed the female matador in *Talk to Her*. A suit will set you back over €2,000 but considering it takes a team of tailors sewing for over a month to make just one, the price is cheap. A matador may need several for just one season; yours should last a lifetime. If you don't want to buy, at least pop in for a look-see.

Ceramics

Many people think ceramics when they think Spanish souvenirs. Since 1953, **Lladró** (Gran Vía 46, Metro: Gran Vía, tel. 91/701-0472, www.lladro.com, 10 A.M.–8 P.M. Mon.–Sat.) has been producing high-quality porcelain figurines that drive collectors crazy. If this is your thing, a visit to this shop is in order. Prices are marginally less than stateside and the tax is rebatable. For homier pieces, go to **Antigua Casa Talavera** (C/ Isabel la Católica 2, Metro: Santo Domingo, tel. 91/547-3417, 10 A.M.–1 P.M. and 5–8 P.M. Mon.–Fri., 10 A.M.–1 P.M. Sat.). This family-run shop offering a spectrum of Spanish ceramic styles has been in business for over 40 years; looking at their cluttered shop, you might think they haven't thrown out anything since then. Items are not priced, but expect reasonable values on smaller items. Larger pieces can be pricey, but the quality is worth it.

If you are a budding chef you know that the most important tool in the kitchen is a good knife and that prices for a top blade can be stratospheric. Fortunately you are in Spain and the region of Albacete is one of the world's top two producers of fine cutlery (Germany is the other). An excellent kitchen knife can cost as little as €15. To stock up, visit the wacky shop **Viñas Comercial** (C/ Atocha 62, Metro: Antón Martín, tel. 91/369-3495, 9:30 A.M.–2 P.M. and 5–8 P.M. Mon.–Fri., 9:30 A.M.–2 P.M. Sat.). Barely as wide as an elevator, this bright-red shop on the corner of Mercado Antón Martín sells all types of blades, and, in an only-in-Spain way, old-fashioned perfumes as well.

The elderly couple that runs the place couldn't be nicer. They don't speak English, but they are experts in sign language. They'll show you knives in all price ranges, but the best (and priciest) are those by Ramon Hermanos. Just don't forget to pack them in your checked luggage for the flight home.

Espadrilles

Another classic Spanish item is the espadrille. Dirt cheap and insanely comfy, this lowly slipper also occasionally makes the fashion catwalk. **Casa Hernanz** (C/ Toledo 18, Metro: Sol, tel. 91/366-5450, 9 A.M.–1:30 P.M. and 4:30–8 P.M., Mon.–Fri.,9 A.M.–1:30 P.M. Sat.), right behind the Plaza Mayor, has been making espadrilles by hand for decades. You might walk right past the dingy shop, but if you go inside, you'll find a worn wooden counter in front of boxes piled ceiling high. All you need to do is give them your size and the color you want and you'll score a basic pair for around €5. The high-heel versions with rhinestone trim are sexy and a steal for around €40. During the summer, expect long lines snaking out the door.

Flamenco

The physical shop of the comprehensive website **Flamenco-World.com** (C/ Huertas 62, Metro: Sol, tel. 91/360-0865, www .flamenco-world.com, 11 A.M.–2:30 P.M. and 5–8:30 P.M. Mon.–Sat.) offers everything a flamenco aficionado could want, from CDs to DVDs, books to postcards, dancing shoes to *cajones* (the boxed drum that a musician sits on to play).

Guitars

Founded in 1882, **Guitarras José Ramírez** (C/ Paz 8, Metro: Sol, tel. 91/531-4229, www .guitarrasramirez.com) produces some of the most sought-after Spanish guitars in the world. The shop is still run by the family and these days you'll find fourth and fifth generation Ramírez members tending to customers. Check out their mini-museum of antique guitars while you are there.

Souvenirs

Souvenir shops are like weeds all around the city's best monuments. One is not better than another and if you are just after t-shirts, magnets, and an apron done up like a flamenco gown, head in the vicinity of the Prado, the Plaza Mayor, or Sol. If you'd rather spend your time sightseeing and sipping vino under bulls' heads, contact American Nancy Brown at **At Spain** (Gran Vía 57, 10, Metro: Gran Vía, tel. 91/547-5091, www.atspain.com, by appointment). A longtime expat, Nancy founded this specialty gift shop with discriminating tourists in mind. She scours Spain to find the most unique gifts from olivewood salad bowls to charming Basque tablecloths. She also arranges gift packages and helps with shipping.

CIGARS, FOOD, AND WINE
Cigars

If you are a fan of fine cigars, you'll be happy to learn that Spain is a big supporter of Cuba's tobacco farms. As a result Cuban cigars are both inexpensive and plentiful. Most any corner tobacco shop will have a few top smokes on offer. However, **Cava de Puros** (C/ Barquillo 22, Metro: Chueca, tel. 91/522-0222, 9 A.M.–2 P.M. and 5–8 P.M. Mon.–Fri., 9 A.M.–2 P.M. Sat.) is the best store in town for Cuban cigars. English-speaking owner José Carlos is happy to help you make a selection from the vast walk-in humidor. However, he can't help you overcome U.S. customs restrictions against *habanas*. So you best smoke 'em while you got 'em, preferably on a nice terrace overlooking a sunset in Spain.

Olive Oil

Run by a non-profit organization dedicated to the promotion of Spanish olive oil, **Patrimonio Comunal Olivarero** (C/ Mejía Lequerica 1, Metro: Alonso Martínez, tel. 91/308-0505, www.pco.es, 10 A.M.–2 P.M. and 5–8 P.M. Mon.–Fri., 10 A.M.–2 P.M. Sat.) boasts over 100 extra virgin oils divided by olive type and price (see sidebar, *Liquid Gold* in the *Andalucía* chapter). Gorgeous bottles of all sizes and colors line the rustic green shelves and make unique (and tasty) souvenirs. Little English is spoken, but the staff will go out of their way to help you choose a good bottle. You're on your own with shipping.

Savories

Ferpal (C/ Arenal 7, Metro: Sol, tel. 91/532-3899, www.ferpalmadrid.com, 9:45 A.M.–8:45 P.M. daily) is a Madrid institution selling all things delectably Spanish. Despite its central location, prices are competitive and you'll see Spaniards lining up to buy *jamón,* sausages, smoked salmon, pâtés, cheeses, prepared sandwiches, cookies, and *conservas* (gourmet canned foods). While you are there, try their gorgeous *té de azafran* (saffron tea) at the corner bar. For something decidedly more upscale, visit **Cuenllas** (C/ Ferraz 3, Metro: Ventura Rodríguez, tel. 91/547-3133, www.cuenllas .com, 9 A.M.–2:30 P.M. and 5A.M.–8:30 P.M. Mon.–Fri., 9 A.M.–2:30 P.M. Sat., closed Sun.) on the eastern side of Plaza de España. They have a superb selection of cheeses, pâtés, and olive oils, as well as an extensive wine selection. An added bonus is the elegant wine bar/restaurant next door.

Sweets

Candied violets are a Madrid tradition and make a unique gift. **La Violeta** (Pl. Canalejas 6, Metro: Sol, tel. 91/522-5522, 10 A.M.–2 P.M. and 4:30–8:30 P.M., Mon.–Sat.) has been selling them from this hole-in-the-wall shop since 1915. The violet packaging is gorgeous and prices range from €1.20 to over €20. Over in La Latina, **Caramelos Paco** (C/ Toledo 55, Metro: La Latina, tel. 91/365-4258, www.caramelospaco.com, 9 A.M.–2 P.M. and 5–8:30 P.M. Mon.–Sat.), founded in 1936, is jammed floor to ceiling with candies of all flavors and shapes. Can't get a leg of *jamón* through customs? Paco's has one made out of sugar. Candies are sold by the kilo, just point to what you want and say *"un puñado"* (poo-NYA-do) for a handful.

Another way to get a sugar fix is to head to a convent. Throughout Spain cloistered nuns whip up traditional sweets as a way to make a little money for their order. Over near Plaza Mayor, **Convento de las Carboneras** (Pl.

Conde de Miranda 3, Metro: Sol, tel. 91/548-3701, 9:30 A.M.–1 P.M. and 4–6:30 P.M. daily until they run out), built in 1607, still houses a small group of elderly cloistered nuns. To buy, buzz the *Vente de Dulces* sign. Once inside, go to the *turno* and order your sweets through the elaborate lazy susan. Try a medio-kilo of *yemas,* candied yolks that were favored by Saint Teresa back in the 16th century.

Wine

Get an overview of Spanish wines at the bright, modern shop **Cata y Reserva** (C/ Conde de Xiquena 13, Metro: Chueca, tel. 91/319-0401, www.reservaycata.com, 11 A.M.–3 P.M. and 5–9 P.M. Mon.–Fri., 11 A.M.–3 P.M. Sat.). English-speaking owner Ezequiel Mateos is a walking encyclopedia about *vino* and an incredibly friendly guy to boot. If you'd prefer an little old-world charm with your purchase, visit **María Cabello** (C/ Echegaray 19, Metro: Sol, tel. 91/429-6088, 10 A.M.–2 P.M. and 5–8 P.M. Mon.–Fri., 10 A.M.–2 P.M. Sat.), a tiny shop with an ancient wooden counter and walls of dusty bottles crawling right up to the muralled ceiling. Run for 150 years by the same family, the current crop of attendants are extremely friendly and don't blink twice if you ask for a €2 table wine or a €100 rioja. Right around the corner from Plaza Santa Ana, it is also very accessible.

MERCADOS

For a glimpse of Spanish life *en vivo,* visit one of the city's traditional markets. The most photogenic is **San Miguel** (Pl. San Miguel, s/n, Metro: Sol, 9 A.M.–2 P.M. and 5–8 P.M. Mon.–Fri., 9 A.M.–2 P.M. Sat.) next to the Plaza Mayor. Within its elaborate 19th-century wrought-iron and glass facade is a nice selection of meat, cheese, and produce stalls, including the best wild mushroom stall in Madrid. Pop in for an apple at least. Many stalls are indefinitely closed as the market is in the long process of being bought out by a single investor who plans to build a world-class gourmet market here. **Antón Martín** (C/ Santa Isabel 5, Metro: Antón Martín, 9 A.M.–2 P.M. and 5–

8 P.M. Mon.–Fri., 9 A.M.–2 P.M. Sat.) is a colorful neighborhood market that makes up in liveliness for what it lacks in physical charm. Traditional meat and vegetable stalls stand next to health food booths and Asian counters serving rice balls. The art deco Cine Dore (see *Arts and Entertainment*) is on the edge of the market and the world-famous flamenco dance school Amor de Dios is upstairs. Go before lunch to see it in full action. Photos are allowed, but you should ask the individual stall owner out of respect. Over in Barrio Salamanca, **La Paz** (C/ Ayala 28, Metro: Serrano, 9 A.M.–2 P.M. and 5–8 P.M. Mon.–Fri., 9 A.M.–2 P.M. Sat.) is your basic *mercado* gone upscale. This is where well-heeled *madrileños* come for top-quality products. Look for the cheese stall **Boulette** with hundreds of Spanish cheeses on offer.

ENGLISH-LANGUAGE BOOKS

Run by Californian Jamie Poole and hubby Javi Sanz, **J&J Books and Coffee** (C/ Espíritu Santo 47, Metro: Noviciado, tel. 91/521-8576, www.jandjbooksandcoffee.net, 11 A.M.–midnight Mon.–Thurs., 11 A.M.–2 A.M. Fri.–Sat., 2–10 P.M. Sun.) is the only bookstore in Madrid where you can curl up in a comfy chair with a good book and a *café con leche*. The store's tiny bar boasting €1 beers also makes it a favorite among English teachers in Madrid. Check their website for poetry readings, language exchanges, and writing workshops. Across town, **Petra's International Bookshop** (C/ Campomanes 13, Metro: Ópera, tel. 91/541-7291, 11 A.M.–9 P.M. Mon.–Sat.) is a great funky-'round-the-edges used-book store. The English book selection is large and there is a good choice of Spanish travel and art books. Petra was the name of the original owner's long-gone cat, but there is always a book-loving feline hanging around coaxing pets out of weary travelers who miss their furry friends back home.

SPANISH FASHION

While not as cutting-edge as Barcelona in fashion, Madrid is a style-obsessed town. *Las españolas* believe that looking good is one of the basic needs in life, and most women over 30 wouldn't even think of stepping out to buy a loaf of bread without getting done up. As a result, the city's streets are crammed with clothing shops.

Chains

On the cheap-and-chic end of things, **Zara** (Gran Vía 34, Metro: Gran Vía) is ubiquitous in the capital, but this Gran Vía location is the biggest. Men are catered for on the top floor. A few doors down, **Leftie's** (Gran Vía 40), the Zara outlet store, is a dizzying display of clothes piled everywhere. Major bargains can be found here if you dig, but be careful: Many of the products are irreparable—gashed material, destroyed zippers, massive stains. If you hate crowds, do not even think of hitting Leftie's on a Saturday. The line to check out can be more than a half-hour long.

Mango (C/ Fuencarral 70, Metro: Tribunal) is another omnipresent chain in Spain and this is the best location in Madrid. Clothes are fashionable without being freaky. Upstairs is **Mango Outlet,** another bargain hunter's dream. Clothes are not as shoddy as at Leftie's, but do check the zippers, seams, and buttons before you buy. Also, even though the shops are connected by a stairwell, you must pay for the item on the floor from which it came. For a dose of flashy party wear in the latest cuts go to **Blanco** (C/ Mayor 14, Metro: Sol).

Men can do their own mass spending at **Springfield** (Gran Vía 76, Metro: Gran Vía) for smart, casual style. There is also **Pull and Bear** (C/ Carretas 23) for sporty clothes. For something more upscale try **Massimo Dutti** (C/ Serrano 17, Metro: Serrano).

For shoes, men, women, and kids need head no further than **Camper** (C/ Preciados 23, Metro: Sol) for their funky, comfortable wares. If it is leather bags you're after and Loewe is out of your budget, head over to **Salvador Bachiller** (C/ Velázquez 24, Metro: Serrano) for leather goods in a rainbow of colors.

Designer Shops

The majority of Spain's designers have shops in Madrid and almost all of them can be found in Barrio Salamanca. (See sidebar, *Spanish Style from A to Z.*) Or you could just wander down Calle Serrano where you'll find **Adolfo Domínguez** at No. 18; **Agatha Ruiz de la Prada** at 27; and **Purificación Garcia** at 28. You should seek out **Amaya Arzuaga** (C/ Lagasca 50, Metro: Serrano, tel. 91/426-2815, 10:30 A.M.–8:30 P.M. Mon.–Sat.), a major up-and-comer on the international catwalk. Her Madrid shop is her only outlet in Spain. If you need something a bit more funky, there are loads of small designers set up in the **Mercado Fuencarral** and around. One of the most exciting is **Divina Providencia** (C/ Fuencarral 42, Metro: Chueca, tel. 91/521-1095, www.divina providencia.com, 11 A.M.–9 P.M. Mon.–Sat.), which sells the exclusive line of young designer Esther Penélope. Her colorful styles are already popping up on the backs of Spain's latest crop of *famosos*. If you go near winter, check out Esther's extensive line of coats. Prices are very reasonable for the quality and originality.

Sports and Recreation

Bullfighting

Facing a bull in Madrid's Las Ventas bullring is akin to performing a solo at Carnegie Hall. A matador cannot get to the top of the bullfighting world without proving his (or her) mettle in the majestic **Plaza de Toros de las Ventas** (C/ Alcalá 237, Metro: Ventas, tel. 91/356-2200, www.las-ventas.com, box office open 10 A.M.–2 P.M. and 5–8 P.M. Fri. only). Inaugurated in 1931, Las Ventas, as it is commonly called, can hold nearly 24,000 spectators. During important bullfighting seasons, it sells out nightly. Madrid crowds are notoriously fickle, made up of die-hard aficionados. The *corrida* may look fine to you. But if you hear the crowd whistling, they are angry. And don't be surprised to see a sedately dressed grandmother loudly berate the matador. On the other hand, when this crowd is happy, it is electric. The *olés* will come in rhythmic waves, getting louder with each artful pass of the matador. At the end, if the crowd is very pleased people will wave white handkerchiefs, often in a bid to entice the president of the bullfight to award the matador an ear. For a particularly noble fight, the matador may win two ears and the tail. After a successful *corrida,* the matador struts proudly around the arena as the crowd (old men in particular) throw their hats in his path in the hope that he will pick it up and return it to them.

Ticket prices depend on where you sit, and can run from €4 to over €100 (much higher during San Isidro). Las Ventas is divided into 10 pie-shaped sections. The president's box is in section 10 and a skilled matador will coax the bull closest to this section so that the president can better see the *corrida*; therefore the best sections for viewing are 9, 10, and 1. Like any stadium, the closer you are to the action, the higher the cost of the ticket. The levels are called *tendidos. Baja* is ground level, *alta* is the next section up, and *gradas* are above that, recessed under an overhang. Above those you find *andanada,* the nosebleed section. Seats are further defined by *sol,* a seat in the sun; *sombra,* a seat in the shade; or *sol y sombra,* which has a bit of both as the sun moves across the ring. Shaded seats are the most expensive. There are really no bad viewing areas in the ring. If price is your main concern, it's up to the *andanada* for you, but be aware that it is steep and you may want to bring binoculars. For an excellent mid-range seat go for *tendido alto, sol y sombra,* section 3 or 8. If it is San Isidro, just be thankful if you get a seat at all.

Outside of major *ferias* (bullfighting fairs), you can **buy tickets** easily right at the bullring's *taquilla* (ticket office) on the Friday before that Sunday's bullfight (10 A.M.–2 P.M. and 5–8 P.M.). By law, the bullring must also release 1,000 tickets at 10 A.M. on the day of the bullfight. During Madrid's Feria Taurina de San Isidro in May these lines can snake

© KATIE PETRILLO

Plaza de Toros de las Ventas

around the building well before 9 A.M. There are several outlets where you can buy tickets, but they do add surcharges. The friendliest is **Localidades Galicia** (Pl. Carmen 1, 91/531-9131, 9:30 A.M.–1 P.M. and 4:30–7 P.M. Mon.–Sat., 9:30 A.M.–1 P.M. Sun.), located midway between the metros of Sol and Gran Vía. There are also ticket booths on Calle Victoria, between Sol and Plaza Santa Ana. Try **La Taurina** at the corner of the Pasaje Matheu, but take note that these agents add a very hefty surcharge of up to 20 percent. If you are in a nicer hotel, the concierge can usually arrange tickets for you for a fee. Finally, if you just don't want the hassle, tour operators like **Pullmantur** (see sidebar, *Tours of Madrid*) offer standard bullfight packages that are pretty pricey, but do include a bus tour of the city. There are a couple of online ticket sellers. The most notable one is **www.ticketstoros .com,** but if you order online you will have to go pick up the tickets in person on the day of the fight (C/ Goya 5, 1–4 P.M. only).

To really enjoy a bullfight at Ventas, remember a few **cultural rules.** Get there on time as the *corridas* are extremely punctual. You can enter through any door and then walk to your seat. The attendants don't speak English, but they are friendly pointers. Be sure and rent an *almohadilla* (cushion) for €1 (loose change please!). There are several bars throughout the ring and unlike in American stadiums, the prices are standard. If you have a drink, make sure you finish before starting time. Once the bullfight begins, the heavy doors to the seats are shut and you will not be allowed to enter until the first fight has ended, about 20 minutes. You'll see that your seat is nothing more than a very narrow space on the cement ledges (hence the need for the cushion!). In between the six fights, hawkers sell soft drinks, whiskey, and beer. Again, correct change is much appreciated. You are allowed to bring your own food and drink, but don't go overboard. Sandwiches would be out of place. Also remember you are in very tight quarters here, any crumbs you make will land on the person in front of you. There are short breaks between each fight, but remember if you dash out to the bathroom, you might run the risk of getting locked out for the next fight. If that happens, don't worry. The bars have huge televisions covering all the action up-close. One last note: Though there is no dress code, *madrileños* tend to dress well for an afternoon with the bulls. Dress "casual Friday" and you'll be just fine. (For more information, see sidebar *Bullfighting,* in the *Background* chapter.)

The **Plaza de Toros de las Ventas** is located on the eastern edge of the city. The easiest way to get there is by taking metro line 2 (red) or line 5 (green) to Ventas. The ring is at the top of the exits. For a colorful trip home, catch Bus 53 on Alcalá, on the same side as the ring. It follows a lovely 20-minute route through the city and finishes in Sol. Before you head to your hotel, you should stop in one of the many bars surrounding the ring. They come alive with aficionados detailing every aspect of that evening's bullfight. The best is **Los Timbales** (C/ Alcalá 225) with great tiled walls and bullfighting memorabilia.

Tauro Tour (C/ Alcalá 237, Metro: Ventas, tel. 91/556-9237, www.las-ventas.com/prensa/taurotour/ingles.pdf, 10 A.M.–2 P.M. and 5–8 P.M. Tues.–Sat., evening tours cancelled on bullfight days, €5 adults, €3 under 12) offers 40-minute guided visits of Las Ventas. The English/Spanish tour will give you near-total access to the bullring, including a chance to step out onto the same arena where all the death in the afternoon takes place. Call ahead to reserve a place.

At the back of Las Ventas near the Patio de Caballos, **Museo Taurino** (C/ Alcalá 237, Metro: Ventas, 9:30 A.M.–2:30 P.M. Tues.–Fri., 10 A.M.–1 P.M. Sun. Mar.–Oct., 9:30 A.M.–2:30 P.M. Mon.–Fri. Nov.–Feb., free) is a tidy museum of bullfighting memorabilia and art. Under the heads of several bulls who died nobly in Ventas, you'll also find the bloody suit of Manolete, one of Spain's most revered fighters, who was gored to death in 1947.

Health and Well-Being

Originally from Wales, **massage therapist oeth Williams** (tel. 69/921-2774) has called Madrid home for over a decade. Specializing in Swedish massage and Shiatsu, Elspeth can travel to your hotel or you can visit her central studio. Her prices are very competitive, plus as a Madrid enthusiast, she can give you a few tips on *la vida madrileña* while she kneads the kinks out of your travel-weary body.

One of the sleekest wellness centers in Madrid, **MasVital Zenter** (C/ Cruz 28, Metro: Sol, tel. 90/210-8910, www.masvital.org, 10 A.M.–10 P.M. Mon.–Sat., noon–6 P.M. Sun.) is also the most central. The specialty is massage and it comes in many styles: relaxing, invigorating, Thai, or the famous anti-cellulite (a necessity after days of grazing on *jamón*). A 50-minute rub-down runs just under €40.

Revive body and mind with a visit to **Medina Mayrit** (C/ Atocha, 14, Metro: Sol, tel. 90/233-3334, www.medinamayrit.com, 10 A.M.–midnight daily, €21–34). Under a cave of cinnamon walls and candlelight, three pools of water (hot, warm, and cold) provide a sensual escape. Floating along to the soft trance of Arabic music, it is hard to believe that Madrid is roaring along just above you. Baths last 1.5 hours and commence every two hours. Maximum capacity is 36 and on weekends it fills up. Late-night baths can be a bit risqué as amorous couples get carried away by the romantic environment. Reservations are a must and can be made on the phone (though English speakers are not always available). The website reservation system is sketchy. Best to make a visit there in person a couple of days before your bath. You have to pay 50 percent up front. You can have a bath with massage or bath only. Opt for the latter as the brief massage is half-hearted at best and takes away from your time in the water. The dressing rooms have lockers (bring a loose euro for the key), showers, soap (no shampoo), towels, and hair dryers. Swimsuits (not shorts, not underwear) are mandatory. If you don't have one, don't worry. Simple black suits for males and females are on sale for just €11.

Soccer

From September to May, Madrid goes soccer crazy as the Spanish *fútbol* season heats up.

Games are held most Sundays at about 6 P.M. The royal soccer experience is to be had at a Real match on their home turf at Bernabéu stadium. Get a more local (but just as exciting) perspective at an Atlético match. If you can't make it to either, pop into any corner bar during a game and you'll find half the neighborhood enthusiastically following every move on television. For English commentary and big-screen TVs, hit an Irish bar.

Real Madrid (Estadio Santiago Bernabéu, Po. Castellana, 144, Metro: Santiago Bernabéu, www.realmadrid.com) is the most famous *fútbol* club in the world. With three world cups, nine European cups, and countless other trophies, it is also one of the best. Nicknamed *los blancos* for their white uniforms, Real has been a member of the 1st division of *La Liga* (the Spanish soccer league) since 1928. From 2000 on, Real took on the nickname *Los Galácticos* (the galactic stars), as the team began signing top-level (very expensive) players, including Zidane, Ronaldo, and David Beckham. A game at Bernabéu is an experience you won't forget. Tickets can be had by calling Real agents (90/232-4324) or by visiting **Localidades Galicia** (Pl. Carmen, 1, 91/531-9131, 9:30 A.M.–1 P.M. and 4:30–7 P.M. Mon.–Sat., 9:30 A.M.–1 P.M. Sun.). Tickets for big games, especially between arch-enemy FC Barcelona and local rivals Atlético Madrid, can be hard to come across and very expensive.

Atlético de Madrid (Estadio Vicente Calderón, Po. Melancólicos, s/n, Metro: Pirámides, box office tel. 90/253-0500, www.clubatleti codemadrid.com), nicknamed *los rojiblancos* for their red and white striped uniforms, is Madrid's favorite underdog and is considered the team of the working classes. Atlético is third in the all-time Spanish rankings behind Real and Barcelona, but from 1999 to 2000, its ranking fell and the team landed in the second division. Back on top of their game, Atlético continues to evoke fierce loyalty in their fans. Attending a home game is an electrifying experience. Get tickets through Atlético's website or by calling the box office. You can also visit the stadium box office 11 A.M.–2 P.M.

and 5–8 P.M. the day before a game and from 11 A.M. the day of the game.

Swimming

The loveliest city-run pools are at **Casa de Campo** (Metro: Lago, €5). Set in the park, the complex features several pools including one for kids. There is also a snack bar and plenty of tree-shaded picnic spots. The best private pool is on the roof of the **Hotel Emperador** (Gran Vía 53, Metro: Santo Domingo, tel. 91/547-2800, 11 A.M.–9 P.M. daily, May–Sept., €25–35). It's a pricey place to swim but worth it for the stunning views. Prices on the weekend are €10 higher than during the week and it can get crowded. The best bet to enjoy the pool is to come mid-afternoon after the sun's harshest rays have passed and stay until sunset. A poolside bar offers snacks and drinks.

Parks

Sprawling for nearly 4,500 acres on the western edge of the city, **Casa de Campo** is a favorite day escape for city-dwellers. A tourist with just a few days in Madrid might skip it. If you go, take the metro to Lago; you'll get dropped off right near the park's artificial lake. You can rent rowboats or have a drink at one of the cafés along the water's edge. The park also houses a small, ill-kept zoo, **Zoo-Aquarium** (Metro: Batán, 91/512-3770, www.zooma drid.com, €15 adults, €13 under eight) and a pokey, yet expensive, amusement park, **Parque de Atracciones** (Metro: Batán, 91/463-2900, www.parquedeatracciones.es, €25 adults, €14 under six).

Running along the eastern side of Casa de Campo are two of Madrid's favorite strolling parks, **La Rosaleda** and the **Parque del Oeste** (Metro: Moncloa). Several sandy paths wind through the landscaped trees of these adjacent parks, which include a children's play area. La Rosaleda also boasts gorgeous rose gardens and hosts a rose competition in May. This part of the park runs along Paseo Pintor Rosales, which is full of sidewalk cafés perfect for taking in the view. Where the Paseo meets Calle Marqués del Urquijo, catch Madrid's cable car, the **Teleférico** (€5 adults, €3 under seven), which travels to the center of the Casa de Campo. The views are spectacular, particularly on the return trip, but if you have kids, you might not want to let them look straight down. In an effort to combat prostitution in the city center, the city has all but encouraged it in the Casa de Campo. All along the road from Lago to the zoo, ladies who believe in baring all to the constant stream of cars that go past are quite visible from the cable car.

To experience a 19th-century English-style garden, visit **Campo del Moro** (Metro: Príncipe Pío, 10 A.M.–sunset). Named for the Muslim troops who used this area as a staging ground to attack the medieval fortress that once stood where the Palacio Real is today, the park is a lovely escape complete with tailored greenery, graceful curving paths, and romantic shady spots. Though it is adjacent to the Palacio Real, you can only access the park from Calle Virgen del Puerto, which means a long, long walk around or a metro ride. If you do visit it, be sure to stop off at the adjacent **Parque de Atenas** afterwards. There is a lively open-air terrace serving up cool drinks and hot music to crowds of *madrileños* until the wee hours.

Accommodations

Even though Madrid is jam-packed with accommodations, demand is high, especially from April to July, and during the year-end holidays. It is highly recommended that you book ahead of time, either through an online booker or directly with the hotel. If you arrive without a reservation, head to one of the four main hotel areas of Madrid, and cross your fingers. Throughout the center from the **Paseo del Prado to Sol,** you'll find everything from backpacker's bunks to high-end luxury, though the majority of the places fall in the €50–100 category. Walk along Calles Huertas, Lope de Vega, and Prado and look up. Many *hostales* have their signs on the same floor as their accommodations. Along the Paseo del Prado you'll find higher-end places. Around **Atocha station** you'll find a lot of big hotels. Cheaper places can be found if you walk up Calle Atocha (a heavy uphill climb with luggage). A third hotel zone is found along **Gran Vía from Plaza Callao to Calle Alcalá.** Prices run the gamut. Keep your eyes focused at door level as most places have their plaques posted right above the building's buzzers. Finally, most of the high-priced luxury and business class hotels are located along the **Castellana** and in **Barrio Salamanca.**

There are two hotel booking agencies worth trying out. **Brújula** (91/315-7894) is located in the Atocha and Chamartín train stations and charges €2.50 per booking. **Viajes Aira** (91/305-4224) is located in terminals 1, 2, and 4 at Barajas airport and books mid-range and higher hotels for no fee.

When booking a hotel, ask if the price includes IVA (EE-vah), the hotel tax. Also check to see if breakfast is included. If it is not, don't spring for the hotel spread. Walk in any direction from any hotel in the city, and within minutes you'll find a neighborhood café with a great breakfast deal. In summer, inquire about air-conditioning. Even in the middle of the night, Madrid summers are brutal. Lastly, a note about noise. Madrid has been declared one of Europe's noisiest cities. In the early morning you'll hear delivery trucks, blaring horns, and the grating shudder of storefront metal gates being rolled up. At night, there are late-night revelers and the screeching whine of the garbage trucks, which seem scheduled to arrive under your window just as you begin to doze off. The noise is inside too, as many hotels, including some famed five-stars, have paper-thin walls, poor insulation, and creaky floors. If you are a light sleeper, you should bring a pair of earplugs. Even when the hotel swears their room is noise proof, there is no guarantee.

The prices listed below are for doubles in the high season. Through Internet bookers, you will no doubt pay less.

SOL AND PLAZA MAYOR
€50-100

Right behind the famous plaza from which it takes its name, the family-owned **⟨ Hotel Plaza Mayor** (C/ Atocha 2, Metro: Sol, tel. 91/360-0606, www.h-plazamayor.com, €85 d) is a great, inexpensive hotel. Rooms are colorful and modern while still being comfortable. Upgrade to a superior for about a dozen euros more and you'll get an exterior room with excellent views. However, the best of the best is the rooftop *Palomar* suite, a modern loft with a large bed, a massive bath, and a private terrace, which faces the west and Madrid's famous sunsets, all for around €140.

Closer to Sol, **Hostals Adriano and Adriá** (C/ Cruz 26, 4, Metro: Sol, tel. 91/521-1339 or 91/521-5612, hostaladriano@terra.es, www.adrianohostal.com, €63 d) are a sweet deal for the budget-minded. The 22 brightly colored rooms in these sister *hostales* offer large closets, ample bathroom space, and fridges in every room. The accommodating staff speak English.

€100-200

Hotel Victoria 4 (C/ Victoria 4, Metro: Sol, tel. 91/523-8430, reservas@hotelvictoria4.com, www.hotelvictoria4.com, €140 d, breakfast included) is a tasteful independent hotel with all the amenities you'd expect from a chain (Internet, room service, bar, restaurant, English-speaking staff). An added bonus is the large terrace overlooking a pedestrian walkway. In the tangle of pedestrian streets north of Sol, you'll come to Plaza San Martin, home to the Convento de las Descalzas Reales and the elegant **Palacio San Martín** (Pl. San Martín 5, Metro: Plaza Mayor, tel. 91/701-5000, info@hotelinturpalacio.com, www.hotelinturpalacio.com, €150 d). The rooms have high ceilings and large windows (ask for a view), the furnishings are classical, and the beds come piled with pillows. An added plus is the double-glazed

windows making this a quiet sleep. Skip the expensive buffet breakfast, but do go up to the rooftop restaurant to take in the lovely view of old Madrid. In the alley to the side of the hotel, a group of young buskers with mohawks and toy flutes spend the day dancing and begging. Just keep walking, they are harmless and the area is well traveled.

Back over by the Plaza Mayor, is the **Posada del Peine** (C/ Postas 17, Metro: Sol, tel. 91/523-8151, posada@hthoteles.com, www.hthoteles.com, €120 d). Part of the pitch of this small property is that it is housed in a 17th-century building. Unfortunately, you won't feel any of that antiquated charm as this is a High Tech hotel, meaning ultra-modern and, well, high tech. The rooms are tiny even by European standards and there are no baths, only showers (though they do feature hydro-massage heads). Nonetheless, it is always fully booked. Why? The great location in the winding streets next to Plaza Mayor.

ÓPERA
Under €50

Run by backpackers for backpackers, **Los Amigos Backpackers Hostel** (C/ Arenal 26, 4; C/ Campomanes 6, 4, Metro: Ópera, tel. 91/559-2472; 91/547-2472, reservas@losamigoshostel.com, www.losamigoshostel.com, €16–22 for a dorm bed, breakfast included) features bright rooms, friendly English-speaking staff, and all the usual amenities (linen, lockers, lounge area). Rooms range from doubles (at a fairly steep price of €45 per night with bunk beds and shared baths) to dormitories for 4–12 people. Prices increase for fewer beds. The two locations are very close to each other, and while they differ in their services (Wi-Fi at Arenal, laundry at Campomanes), the same fun vibe is evident at both.

€100-200

Room-Mate Mario (C/ Campomanes 4, Metro: Ópera, tel. 91/548-8548, mario@room-mate hoteles.com, www.room-matehoteles.com, €120 d, breakfast included) is your basic ultra-modern boutique hotel. Rooms are black and white with recessed light. Those on the street tend to be a bit noisy while those in the interior look out on a small inner courtyard. The staff is very friendly, and the standard continental breakfast that other hotels in this price range charge a fortune for is graciously included in the price. Other Room-Mates are due to open throughout the city by mid-2007. Look for Alicia (C/ Prado 2, alicia@room-matehoteles .com), which will feature a deluxe suite with private pool and terrace overlooking Plaza Santa Ana.

Just across the street from Mario is **Hotel Meninas** (C/ Campomanes 7, Metro: Ópera, tel. 91/541-2805, reservas@hotelmeninas.com, www.hotelmeninas.com, €185 d), another boutique hotel boom offering above-average service in an elegantly contemporary setting. Rooms are white retreats with fluffy down pillows and all the modern amenities.

Over €200

Just around the corner from the Royal Palace, the intimate **Casa de Madrid** (C/ Arrieta 2, Metro: Ópera, tel. 91/559-5791, infomadrid@ casademadrid.com, www.casademadrid.com, €260 d, breakfast included) will make you feel like the guest of royalty. And in a way, you are. This luxury B&B is the home of aristocrat and art dealer Marta Medina. Each of the seven rooms has its own theme (Indian, Spanish, Zen) and is decorated with Marta's personal collections. Prices are the same for all, so you might want to request the Greek room with its dramatic columns, starry painted ceiling, and large whirlpool tub. If you stay here, expect highly personalized service, and if Marta is in town, a little bit of aristocratic chat. Breakfast and evening wine in the lavish salon is included. The casa is marked on the street by a tiny gold plaque.

GRAN VÍA
Under €50

Hidden within a drab building above Madrid's hippest shopping street, **Hostal Los Alpes** (C/ Fuencarrel 17, 4, Metro: Gran Vía, tel. 91/531-7071, hostallosalpes@telefonica.net, www

.hostallosalpes.com, €40 d) is spic-and-span and refreshingly spacious. Wi-Fi is available to all, but air-conditioning is not. If booking in summer, be sure to request a room with it (adding €3 to the nightly price).

€50-100

Situated smack center in the bustle of Gran Vía, **Hostal Splendid** (Gran Vía 15, 5A, Metro: Gran Vía, tel. 91/522-4737, hostal-splendid@terra.es, www.hostalsplendid.com, €50 d) is not your typical cheap sleep. Richly decorated with Oriental-style carpets and dark hardwood floors, this *hostal* feels more like a relative's home than a hotel. English is not spoken, but with years in the business, they can manage to get you what you want.

About a 10 minute walk north of Gran Vía, **Hotel Alexandra** (C/ San Bernardo 29–31, Metro: San Bernardo, tel. 91/542-0400, ha lexandra@halexandra.com, www.halexandra .com, €88 d) is a solid hotel with all your basic amenities. Just far enough off the tourist path, you'll feel like you are staying in a real Spanish neighborhood. You are. Be sure to take a stroll down nearby Calle Manuela Malasaña, which is full of great restaurants, cozy bars, and hip shops. The metro stop San Bernardo is right at the front door of the hotel so you can be anywhere in the city in minutes. Another bonus is the consistently friendly staff.

€100-200

De Las Letras (Gran Vía 11, Metro: Gran Vía, tel. 91/523-7980, info@hoteldelasletras .com, www.hoteldelasletras.com, €160 d), owned by the hipster chain Habitat, is a luxe boutique hotel tucked into an 1817 building. Rooms offer sleek lines punctuated by decadent comfort. Down pillows are standard, as are Wi-Fi, in-room stereos, and a CD/book library for your use. The romper room–esque ground floor bar (complete with bright red rockers) is popular with locals as well as guests, and prices are refreshingly not over-inflated. Further up Gran Vía, you'll find a Madrid classic, the **Hotel Emperador** (Gran Vía 53, Metro: Santo Domingo, tel. 91/547-2800, comercial@

emperadorhotel.com, www.emperadorhotel
.com, €115 d). Though boasting four stars, the
hotel seems to have left at least two of them back
in the era of its early 1980s decor. Still, if you are
in town between May and September, the rooftop pool makes this an unbeatable place to stay.
With sweeping views of Madrid's skyline, it has
become a popular backdrop for Spanish films
and fashion shoots. An evening spent lounging
there, cocktail in hand, will make you feel pretty
famous yourself. One bit of advice: If you stay
here, request a room with a view.

PASEO DEL PRADO
Under €50
For convenience and price, you can't beat
Hostal López (C/ Huertas 54, Metro: Antón
Martín, tel. 91/429-4349, hostallopez@tele
fonica.net, www.hostallopez.com, €47 d).
Rooms are adorned with worn bedspreads, fluorescent lighting, and peeling plasterboard furniture, but they are kept clean and most stream
with sunlight from ceiling-high windows. Unlike many places twice the price, López has installed double doors on the street-side rooms to
keep noise out. All but one room have en suite
baths. Owner Nuria speaks perfect English and
is an encyclopedia of information for the budget traveler. If it is booked, take a walk around
the surrounding streets. This area just west of
the Paseo del Prado is full of cheap lodging.

€50-100
Closer to Plaza Santa Ana, you'll find one of
Madrid's quirkiest *hostales*. Each room at gay-
friendly **7 Colors Rooms** (C/ Huertas 14,
Metro: Sol, tel. 91/429-6935, 7colorsrooms@
7colorsrooms.com, www.7colorsrooms.com,
€85 for "superior double," breakfast included)
is decorated according to chromotherapy, the
art of using color to balance mind, body, and
spirit. Recessed lighting and a variety of control knobs let you make the color as intense or
as pale as your mood dictates. A great idea in a
great location, but with one great problem: All
your balance will go out of whack due to the
screeching noise from one of Madrid's busiest
nightlife streets. A calming solution is to re-

quest the Pink or Black and White room, both
well away from the street. "Standard doubles"
are available at €10 less, but they are barely bigger than a closet.

€100-200
Hotel El Prado (C/ Prado 11, Metro: Sol,
tel. 91/369-0234, hotelprado@pradohotel.com,
www.pradohotel.com, €170 d, €105 on weekends) is a classic three-star hotel right in the
center of the action. Originally built as a four-
star, the rooms are the largest you'll find in this
price range and feature all the amenities you
could want. Each is named for a Spanish wine
region and guests receive a booklet explaining
Spanish wine. Oddly though, you can't get any
wine here. All rooms are the same price, so ask
for one with a terrace on the 6th floor—the
views over old Madrid at night are spectacular.
If fully booked, inquire about their sister property **Hotel Lope de Vega,** just around the corner at C/ Lope de Vega 49. Staff at both places
receive raves for their friendliness.

Gran Hotel Canarias (Pl. Canovas
del Castillo 4, Metro: Banco de España, tel.
91/360-0799, reservas@granhotelcanarias
.com, www.granhotelcanarias.com, €164 d)
has a prime location, across the street from
the Prado. The views from the upper rooms
are spectacular, looking out over the Neptuno
fountain, with the green expanse of the Retiro
in the distance. Rooms have all the amenities
and the green marble bathrooms are over-the-
top luxe. Breakfast is sometimes included, depending on the rate you secure. Check to make
sure. If it is, you'll enjoy a lovely spread. If it
isn't, do like the locals do and hit any café.

Over €200
Built on the order of King Alfonso XIII, who
wanted a hotel in Madrid worthy of housing
visiting royalty, **Hotel Palace** (Pl. Cortes 7,
Metro: Banco de España, tel. 91/360-8000,
reservations.palacemadrid@westin.com, www
.westinpalacemadrid.com, €280 d, breakfast
included) was inaugurated in 1912 and has
been synonymous with refinement ever since.
Rooms are sumptuously appointed, though a

bit frayed with age. Request a room on the 4th floor, preferably with a balcony. Unless you are on an expense account, avoid dining in the hotel. Right around the corner on Calle Jesús are some of the best tapas bars in the center. However, make the splurge for a coffee in the spectacular Rotunda bar under the hotel's famed stained-glass dome.

Just a few blocks away, you will find a modern version of refinement. Combining sleek style with ethnic antiquities, **Hotel Urban** (Carrera de San Jerónimo 34, Metro: Sol, tel. 91/787-7770, urban@derbyhotels.com, www.derbyhotels.com, €245 d) is perfectly located midway between the Prado and Sol. The earth-toned rooms are a mix of contemporary design and ancient artifacts, courtesy of the hotel's owner who is an avid collector. The rooftop pool is hanky-sized but is a posh way to cool off after a day of sightseeing. Be sure to check out the mini-museum of Egyptian artifacts below the lobby. Expect all the best five-star amenities, including excellent front desk service in flawless English. However, skip both the bar and the restaurant. Prices are insane, guests strictly tourists, and service shamefully snotty.

ATOCHA AND LAVAPIÉS
Under €50

Architect Ricardo and graphic designer Ana inherited 【 **Hostal Santa Isabel** (C/ Santa Isabel 15, 4, Metro: Antón Martín, tel. 91/528-0063, info@hostalsantaisabel.com, www.hostal santaisabel.com, €50 d) from her father. The designing duo redid the 11 rooms in soothing off-white, added new showers, and hung contemporary art to create Madrid's best *hostal* in this price category. Be sure to request a streetside room, which includes spectacular views of the sunset over old Madrid. It is located just blocks from the Reina Sofía, on a working-class street that runs parallel with Calle Atocha. A few blocks away is **Hostal Martín** (C/ Atocha 43, Metro: Antón Martín, tel. 91/429-9579, info@hostalmartin.com, www.hostalmartin.com, €49 d). In addition to his namesake property, Jesús Martín runs several *hostales* at this

location. Like most places in this price category, decor is a dismal palette of 1970s brown florals, but the rooms are exceptionally airy and clean. President of a Madrid *hostal* association, Martín runs his properties according to the highest standards and hires staff who speak English.

The area between Atocha and Lavapiés also houses two of the city's best backpacker hostels. **Mad Hostel** (C/ Cabeza 24, Metro: Tirso de Molina, tel. 91/506-4840, info@madhostel.com, www.madhostel.com, €16 for a dorm bed, breakfast included) is set in a traditional Madrid building with a *corrala* (inner courtyard). Amenities include a bar with occasional live flamenco, Wi-Fi, Internet, a gym, and a small kitchen. However, the best feature is the large rooftop terrace overlooking the orange-tiled roofs of Lavapiés. Rooms sleep 4–6 in bunk beds and bathrooms are shared by the entire floor. For more privacy, a bunk in a room for four with private bath is €18 a person. Cross Calle Magdelena to get to the very popular **Cat's Hostel** (C/ Cañizares 6, Metro: Tirso de Molina, tel. 91/369-2807, info@catshostel.com, www.catshostel.com, €17 for a dorm bed, breakfast included). Set in an 18th-century palace, the hostel features bunk-bedded dormitories sleeping 4–12 set around a spectacularly tiled Moorish courtyard complete with burbling fountain. All modern amenities from Wi-Fi to wide-screen TVs in the popular bar are included. Bathrooms are shared, but four double rooms are available with private baths for €22 per person.

€50-100

Just around the corner from Plaza Santa Ana, **Hostal Horizonte** (Atocha 28, 2B, Metro: Antón Martín, tel. 91/369-0996, info@hostal horizonte.com, www.hostalhorizonte.com, €55 d) is a funky alternative to the standard budget *hostales*. Yes, the rooms are small, the noise from the streets (and the night staff) constant, and there is no air-conditioning. However, owner Julio has a flair for style and the decor throughout is a mix of Arabic influences and carnival colors edged in gold. If you are counting pennies, you can opt for a room without bath for €40. Reservations should be made early by Internet and you'll have to pay a deposit. Cancellation policies are harsh, so be sure before your book.

Closer to the train station, **Mediodía** (Pl. Emperador Carlos V 8, Metro: Atocha, tel. 91/527-3060, info@mediodiahotel.com, www.mediodiahotel.com, €65 d, breakfast included) is a classic Madrid hotel. The location couldn't be better—next to a metro stop, across from Atocha train station, and a stone's throw from Madrid's top sights. The 19th-century building has a certain run-down charm, but the rooms are cheerful, especially the upper rooms with a view over the busy plaza in front of the train station. The biggest drawback is that the hotel serves as a base for student travel groups. Teens run rampant. As a result the frazzled staff is considerably less than friendly.

€100-200

It doesn't look like much from the outside, but enter the old carriage way of **Catalonia Moratín** (C/ Atocha 23, Metro: Sol, tel. 91/369-7171, www.hoteles-catalonia.com, €135 d) and you'll be surprised. The builders did a great job of mixing details of this 18th-century palace (check out the impressive stairwell!) with modern design. Rooms are larger than normal for this price range and tastefully done in burgundy and yellow. Some face the soothing inner courtyard while others take on the street. If you choose the latter, ask for the 4th floor for a view. Overall, it is a great value, even though Wi-Fi and breakfast cost extra.

On the opposite end of Atocha, right across from the train station, **NH Sur** (Po. Infanta Isabel 9, Metro: Atocha, tel. 91/539-9400, nhsur@nh-hoteles.com, www.nh-hotels.com, €137 d) could not be a better hotel for those who want to do Madrid as well as day trips to nearby cities. As part of the highly regarded NH chain, services are top-notch and rooms are modern and comfortable, albeit very small. Be sure to ask for one on an upper floor so the view will at least compensate. During off-season (winter, dead-heat of summer) rooms have been known to go for as little as €50. Check Internet search engines for deals.

MALASAÑA AND CHUECA
Under €50
Hostal Don Juan (Pl. Vázquez de Mella 1, Metro: Gran Vía, tel. 91/522-7746, €48 d) is proof that a cheap *hostal* doesn't have to mean dank and dreary. Luxuriously decorated with dark wood antiques, original oil paintings, and silver tea sets, the rooms rival those of hotels charging three times as much. The doubles are spacious and feature newly renovated baths. The location is prime, on the edge of Chueca, just a block from Gran Vía. A bit further north and deeper into Chueca, a stay at gay-friendly **Hostal Dolce Vita** (C/ San Bartolomé 4, 3, Metro: Chueca, tel. 91/522-4018, info@hospedajedolcevita.com, www.hospedajedolcevita.com, €45 d, breakfast included) is like crashing in the kid's room of your trendiest friend. While the lobby and halls boast savoir faire, the play school–colored rooms with heart- and star-shaped lights just ooze pre-teen. But, it beats the drab dorms that dominate this price category. Plus, if you are on a budget and you don't mind sharing a bath, the price drops to €36 for a double.

A few blocks west, on the funky shopping street Calle Fuencarral, you'll find **Hostal Nuria** (C/ Fuencarral 52, Metro: Tribunal, tel. 91/531-9208, hsnuria@arrakis.es, www.hostalnuria.com, €39–45 d). Though the decor seems to be left over from Franco's reign (lots of olive green and nubby gold fabrics), this *hostal* is cheap and cheerful. With over 100 rooms in two buildings, its large size also means you get hotel amenities not usual in most *hostales*, including a multi-lingual staff and full restaurant (breakfast is under €3). Rooms with a tub cost more than those sporting only a shower. If visiting in summer, stay here only if you can get an air-conditioned room.

This neighborhood is also home to Madrid's newest crop of backpacker hostels. **Pop Hostel** (C/ Espíritu Santo 18, Metro: Noviciado, tel. 91/522-8663, reservas@pophostel.com, www.pophostel.com, €16–18 for a dorm bed, breakfast included) is located in the heart of Malasaña's *marcha* zone. Rooms sleep 4–10, and each has a private bath. The larger rooms also have

MADRID

private kitchens. Staff take their cue from the vivacious owner Facundo and are accommodating and super friendly. On the weekends they will gladly hook you up with free entry to hot nightspots. If booked, ask about their sister hostel **Olé** (C/ Manuela Malasaña 23). The rooms are more crowded than Pop, but the friendly vibe carries on.

€50-100
From a driving philosophy that posits, "to visit Madrid is to construct Madrid," the folks at ◖ **Casa Chueca** (C/ San Bartolomé 4, 2, Metro: Chueca, tel. 91/523-8127, info@casa chueca.com, www.casachueca.com, €55) have created a fresh take on the *hostal* experiences. Each room is an oasis of deep, soothing colors, and stylish furnishings. As you might expect from its location in the heart of Chueca, this friendly casa is also gay-friendly. It is in the same building as Hostal Dolce Vita.

€100-200
Like all of the hotels in the High Tech chain, the **Petit Palace Ducal** (C/ Hortaleza 3, Metro: Gran Vía, tel. 91/521-1043, ducal@ hotelpetitpalaceducal.com, www.hotelpetit palaceducal.com, €120 d) offers the latest electronic goodies while not foregoing feel-good touches like hydromassage showers and plush bed linens. Rooms are modern and modular and done up in black, red, and white, but they are on the small side. The location on the edge of Chueca has made it a favorite among trendy gay and lesbian travelers.

SALAMANCA AND LA CASTELLANA
€50-100
There are not many hotels in this price category in this part of town. **Hotel-Residencia Don Diego** (C/ Velázquez 45, Metro: Velázquez, tel. 91/435-0760, www.hostaldondiego.com, €91 d), which boasts simple rooms with updated baths, is an exception. This place is perfect if you've come to Madrid to spend your money on shopping, not sleeping, as the city's best high-end stores lie at the hotel's doorstep. It is

also out of the tourist rush of the center, so evening strolls will be with Spanish neighbors.

€100-200
At **Bauzá H&R** (C/ Goya 79, Metro: Goya, tel. 91/435-7545, info@hotelbauza.com, www .hotelbauza.com, €158 d), minimalism is the theme yet the dark wooden floors and low lighting give it a comfy glow. Luxurious zillion-count linens are standard on the beds and high-tech gadgets (plasma televisions, sound systems) are included in most rooms. The suites have wonderful terraces.

This area also houses a lovely apartment-hotel with luxe aspirations. The **Jardín de Recoletos** (C/ Gil de Santivañes 4, Metro: Banco de España, tel. 91/781-1640, info@ jardinderecoletos.com, www.jardinderecole tos.com, €195 d) is a great retreat if you plan on spending more than a few days in Madrid. Situated on a quiet residential street just steps from the Paseo de Recoletos, the complex's spacious apartments include a sitting area, mini-kitchen, and views of the street or garden. Opt for the latter.

Over €200
Just off the beaten track, **Hotel Orfila** (C/ Orfila 6, Metro: Alonso Martínez, tel. 91/702-7770, www.hotelorfila.com, €310 d) is a luxurious boutique hotel tucked into a 19th-century mansion. All the palatial fittings are intact, from the elegant carriage entranceway to the dramatic staircase. The furnishings are antiques, the amenities high-tech (Wi-Fi, satellite television), and the English-speaking service impeccable. The tranquil garden is the perfect refuge from the madness of Madrid. It is very close to the Castellana and Barrio Salamanca, and you must take an evening stroll down the Paseo Recoletos. The €25 breakfast is free on the weekends.

Just south of Barrio Salamanca, overlooking the lush greenery of the Retiro park, **Palacio del Retiro** (C/ Alfonso XII 14, Metro: Retiro, tel. 91/523-7460, pretiro@ac-hotels.com, www .ac-hotels.com, €250–315 d), opened at the end of 2004, has become Madrid's luxury hotel of choice. With all the amenities you'd expect in a five-star, the Palacio also offers a stunning setting in a 19th-century palace with a grand swirling staircase and majestic stained glass windows. The 51 rooms maintain their old-world charm with the addition of modern touches like plasma televisions and contemporary furniture.

Superior rooms and suites (no. 201 in the former palatial dining room is stunning) feature breathtaking views over the park. The neighborhood is one of the city's most exclusive and it is very quiet. A walk to the Prado will take five minutes, to Sol, 15. At night opt for a taxi as the walk back is uphill and deserted.

Food

Madrid's native cuisine doesn't extend much beyond *cocido madrileño* (a meaty broth thick with chickpeas); however as a melting pot of Spain, the city is teeming with regional Spanish restaurants serving excellent traditional foods from Valencian paella to Asturian *fabada*. To the delight of the country's growing legion of hard-core foodies, Madrid has taken the hint from its Catalan brethren and is getting bolder and brasher in the kitchen. The result is a host of upscale eateries. Of course, tapas are a classic and can be as simple as a few fat olives glistening in a slick of garlic-scented oil or elaborately prepared gourmet mini-dishes.

Unless otherwise noted, Madrid eateries keep standard Spanish dining hours, 1:30–4 p.m. for lunch and 8 p.m.–midnight for dinner. On the weekends, those hours may start later and go longer. Most eateries close at least one day a week, and take month-long vacations in August. If you go to any of the places below and find it closed, don't fret. Madrid is teeming with good eats. Walk around the corner, up the street, ask a pedestrian. Within minutes you'll find a great alternative. If a restaurant requires reservations, note that most of the more prestigious places will speak English.

SOL AND PLAZA MAYOR
Cafés and Desserts
It'd be a sin to pass through Sol and not visit **La Mallorquina** (C/ Mayor 2, Metro: Sol, tel. 91/521-1201, 9 a.m.–9:15 p.m. daily, €4). Founded in 1894, this bustling café stays busy all day. At the horseshoe-shaped counter in

the back, amiable white-coated barmen serve dozens of different pastries. Just point to what you like. Your best bet is to head here first thing in the morning, take an upstairs table in the window, and enjoy a *café con leche* and a *palmera de chocolate* (a thin, crunchy pastry dipped in chocolate) while watching Sol buzz awake. Around the corner **Chocolatería San Ginés** (Pasadizo de San Ginés 5, Metro: Sol, 6 p.m.–6 a.m. daily, €5) has been serving *chocolate y churros* for over 100 years. If you want to enjoy the marble-walled, old-world ambience, go in the early evening. After 4 a.m. the place packs with sweaty young things getting a sugar fix after a night of dancing.

Local Cuisine
Opened in 1725, **Sobrino del Botín** (C/ Cuchilleros 17, Metro: Sol, tel. 91/366-4217, www.botin.es, €35) is the world's oldest restaurant. Goya washed dishes there as a boy. Two centuries later, Hemingway was a regular. Add to this illustrious history the restaurant's rustic setting (beamed ceilings, ancient cast-iron ovens, copper pots on hooks) and you have a major tourist destination. Don't let that put you off. The food and the service are consistently top-notch and prices are not as inflated as you might expect. The house speciality, *cuchinillo* (suckling pig), is famed worldwide and is also the last supper in Hemingway's *The Sun Also Rises*.

Quick Bites
If you must have fast food, at least try it Spanish style. **Pan's and Company** has outlets all over

MADRID

ADVENTURES IN FOOD AND WINE

Some of the best pleasures of Madrid are the most flavorful. If you'd like a little education (or maybe just a bit of company) while you indulge your tastiest senses, check out these culinary gurus.

TAKE A WALK ON THE TAPAS SIDE

Madrileño Andrés Jarabo offers a tapas and wine tour through **Walks of Madrid** (tel. 65/391-2879, info@walksofspain.com, www.walksofmadrid .com, €49). A member of the Spanish Wine Tasting Association, the charming Andrés knows his vino and loves sharing it with guests from around the world. The three-hour walk goes through the heart of Old Madrid and stops at three secret spots for wine and food pairings. Along the way you'll get a bit of history too. Limited to eight, this intimate tour is a great way to meet likeminded travelers while seeing a bit of Madrid normally reserved for locals. Oh, and be sure to come hungry. Though the food is called tapas, you'll end up with enough for a hearty dinner.

OF GRAPES AND OLIVES

First American Mary O'Connor fell in love with wine, then she fell in love with Spain. Her double dose of bliss led to the founding of Madrid's only English-language wine-tasting school. Going way beyond rioja, **Planeta Vino** (tel. 91/310-2855, info@planetavino.net, www.planetavino .net, classes starting at €30) offers a variety of courses on Spanish wine. An evening's event might cover dessert wines, sherries, or *cavas*, Spanish sparkling wines. The most popular course is "Introduction to Spanish Wines" with tastings of the country's top pours. (See sidebar, *Spanish Wine: Beyond Rioja,* in the *Castilla y León* chapter.) Almost as varied as wine is Spain's other favorite liquid, olive oil. In a highly interesting and very tasty evening you'll learn how to choose, store, and use olive oil. You'll also taste several varieties from the pungent *picual* to the aromatic *arbequina*. And finally, you'll learn why it is so important to be a virgin. The oil, that is.

LUXURY GOURMET WEEKEND

For dedicated epicureans, it doesn't get more decadent than a culinary weekend in Madrid

© CANDY LEE LABALLE

Olives are the classic tapa served with wine.

with **Cellar Tours** (tel. 91/521-3939, info@cel lartours.com, www.cellartours.com). Native Californian Genevieve McCarthy offers highly personalized luxury wine tours throughout Spain, Italy, and Portugal. Within Madrid, she also offers this once-in-a-lifetime weekend package that includes a private cooking class in the home of a widely acclaimed Spanish chef (followed by dinner and reserve wines, of course); a personal guided tour of the Prado; a gourmet tapas tour of the city's top wine bars; five-star accommodations; luxury car service; and personalized attention from the affable Gen and her impeccable staff. This is a pricey package, but sated guests swear it is worth every delicious cent. Similar weekend packages are available throughout Spain.

COOKING THE SPANISH WAY

If your Spanish is up to par, you can try a cooking class at **Alambique** (Pl. Encarnación 2, Metro: Ópera, tel. 91/547-4220, info@alam bique.com, www.alambique.com). One of the city's first gourmet kitchen outlets, this shop also offers short and long cooking courses on everything from making gazpacho to frying fish Andalusian-style. Go to the website and click *cursos* to see what's cooking.

the center, including one in Sol, near the start of Calle Alcalá. Open all day, it offers sandwiches, salads, and very tasty fries. A few blocks up the street, the modern coffee house **Faborit** (C/ Alcalá 21, Metro: Sevilla, tel. 91/522-1106, 7:30 A.M.–midnight Mon.–Thurs., 7:30 A.M.–2 A.M. Fri., 9 A.M.–2 A.M. Sat., 9 A.M.–10 P.M. Sun., €6.50) offers a speedy lunchtime selection of panini and salads. The coffee and house-blended teas are also excellent. Wi-Fi is available, but only in the evening.

Another favorite spot for a quick something-something is the Spanish chain **Museo del Jamón** (C/ Mayor 7, Metro: Sol, tel. 91/531-2367, www.museodeljamon.es, 8:30 A.M.–1 A.M. daily, €10). What Velázquez is to the Prado, *jamón* is to the Museo del Jamón. Under walls covered in legs of ham hanging by their hooves (hard-core veggies might want to skip this), a mix of old men in berets and tourists clutching cameras sample the savory Spanish treat a zillion different ways. For just a bite, try a *montadito* (a roll-sized sandwich). For something more substantial, choose *pan tumaca* (a thick slice of rustic bread toasted, rubbed with fresh tomato, and topped with *jamón*). The quickest way to dine is at the stand-up bar. But beware, thieves prey on tourists here. Keep an eye on your things.

Tapas

Patatas Bravas (cubed, fried potatoes smothered in a spicy tomato sauce) is a typical tapa throughout Spain, but **Las Bravas** (C/ Cruz, corner of C/ Alvarez Gato, Metro: Sol, 12:30–4 P.M. and 7:30 P.M.–midnight daily, €8, no credit cards) claims to have created the eponymous dressing. Though there are several locations, this one in a glass-fronted corner makes for great people watching. Of course, you must have a *ración de bravas*, which arrives in minutes, steaming hot and delicious. Just around the corner is the historic **(El Abuelo** (C/ Victoria 12, Metro: Sol, noon–midnight Sun.–Thurs., noon–1 A.M., Fri.–Sat., €8). If you are allergic to shellfish, stay away; the only eating here is shrimp and more shrimp. Try *al ajillo* (sizzling with garlic), *a la plancha* (grilled and

salted), or *gabardina* (battered and fried). Show you're in the know by tossing your shells on the floor and washing your shrimp down with a *chato* of the house sweet red wine. Despite the absolute crush of tourists, this place is the real deal (and yes, if you ask nicely, you can get a photo of yourself behind the bar).

Vegetarian

One of the newest vegetarian restaurants in town, **Yerbabuena** (C/ Bordadores 3, tel. 91/548-0811, 1–4 P.M. and 8–11 P.M. daily, €17) is also one of the best. Serving ample portions of fresh fare, the chef/owner of Yerbabuena puts a gourmet touch on his creations. The interior is a soothing blend of pale lemon walls, leather chairs, and oversized light fixtures—making this veggie place a romantic spot for dinner.

ÓPERA
Cafés and Desserts

Grab an outside table at **La Botillería** (Pl. Oriente 4, Metro: Ópera, tel. 91/548-4620, 8:30 A.M.–1:30 A.M. Mon.–Thurs., 8:30 A.M.–2:30 A.M. Sat.–Sun., €15) for a gorgeous view of the Palacio Real. Despite the prime location, prices aren't as high as you'd expect. A couple of nice tapas (smoked salmon with smoked fish pâté is delish!) and a glass or two of wine will run around €15. If it is too chilly or the accordion-playing buskers are driving you crazy, pop into the café's elegant belle epoque dining room. The more crowded **Café de Oriente** next door has the same owner and the menu and prices are pretty similar. Right between them at number 3 is the building where Velázquez painted *Las Meninas*.

Tapas

The boisterous **El Ñeru** (C/ Bordadores 5, Metro: Ópera, tel. 91/548-1977, noon–midnight daily, €10) is a favorite stop on a Saturday afternoon. Under hanging racks of Asturian chorizo, friendly bartenders serve up gallons of cider. Each drink scores you a snack of *tortilla,* chorizo, or a spread of Cabrales (Asturian blue cheese) and they will ask you which you want, so be ready. Even though tipping is not required, go ahead and leave a few coins just to watch the bartender ring the cowbell over the bar.

The area between Plaza Mayor and Plaza de Oriente is home to several gourmet tapas bars including **Taberneros** (C/ Santiago 9, Metro: Ópera, tel. 91/542-2160, closed Mon., €20), a sexy wine bar with deep red walls and intimate tables. Dishes like *ceviche de salmón con lima* (salmon cured with lime) and *pulpo con miso* (octopus with miso) have Madrid foodies going wild, but be sure to ask for the specials of the day. A few blocks away, the elegant **La Cruzada** (C/ Amnistía 8, Metro: Ópera, tel. 91/548-0131, closed Sun. P.M., €20) offers exquisite dishes prepared with Spanish ingredients. Try the *pâté de perdiz* (wild partridge) or *crujiente de setas* (fried wild mushrooms with aioli sauce). The *menú del dia* is an economic introduction to the menu. Run by wine-lovers, there are over 100 bottles on the list and at least a dozen by the glass.

PASEO DEL PRADO
Cafés and Desserts
Nicknamed La Pecera (The Fishbowl), **(Café del Círculo de Bellas Artes** (C/ Alcalá 42, enter on side street, Metro: Sevilla, tel. 91/360-5400, 9:30 A.M.–midnight daily, €8), with soaring marble columns, frescoed ceilings, oil paintings, and sculptures throughout, is an elegant retreat from the rush of the city. Sipping a *café con leche* while overlooking buzzing Calle Alcalá from the massive windows is a highlight of a trip to Madrid. They also offer a basic *menú del dia* for €10, but you can stop in anytime for a wedge of *tortilla* or a pastry. You'll have to pay a €1 fee to enter the building but it goes to support the amazing arts programs at Círculo. Forget the summertime terrace. Prices go up pretty much proportionately to the amount of car exhaust you'll inhale.

Closer to the Prado, **La Platería** (C/ Moratín 49, Metro: Antón Martín, tel. 91/429-1722, 7:30 A.M.–1 A.M. Sun.–Thurs., 7:30 A.M.–2 A.M. Fri., 9 A.M.–2 A.M. Sat., €8), along with two nearby sister cafés, **El Hecho** (C/ Huertas 56) and **La Esquina del Café** (C/ Huertas 70), make up a trio of cozy escapes from sightseeing. Go for breakfast, a coffee break, or a light lunch of tapas or salads.

For a chilly treat, there is nothing more delectable on a sizzling afternoon than visiting **Ricci** (C/ Huertas 9, Metro: Sol, tel. 91/429-3345, 11 A.M.–midnight daily, €5) and getting a double scoop of *avellana* (hazelnut) ice cream to lick slowly as you take a paseo down Calle Huertas. Or if you prefer, there is banana, peach, tiramisu, chocolate, and on and on for a dozen flavors. Check out the artful displays of ice cream and if you see one you like, ask for a *prueba* (a little taste). In winter, the *helados* are still scooped, but there are coffees, hot chocolates, and crepes, too.

Local Cuisine
Since 1827, **(Casa Alberto** (C/ Huertas 18, Metro: Sol, tel. 91/429-9356, www.casaalberto.es, noon–1 A.M. Tues.–Sat., noon–4:30 P.M. Sun., closed Mon., €25) has been attracting a *madrileño* clientele from local *señores* to politicians, soccer stars to bullfighters. Around 400 years ago, Cervantes stayed in this building while writing *Don Quixote*. During the day, step up to the antique zinc bar and have a *vermut del grifo* (red vermouth on tap). It is pulled from an ancient tap in the wall, right above the dog-headed water fountain. The constantly flowing water was used in days long gone to keep the wine chilled. At night, make ressies to dine in the charming old-world dining room. House specialties are Spanish standards including *rabo de buey* (ox-tail stew) and *besugo* (sea bream). On weekend nights, there is often a guitar player serenading diners. He works on tips, so be sure to give him a couple of euros.

Regional Spanish Cuisine
Under poster-painted green walls hung with photos of rural life, **Maceiras** (C/ Jesús 7, Metro: Sol, tel. 91/429-1584, €15) brings a bit of Galicia to Huertas. To the strains of authentic Galician music (if it sounds Irish it is because the Galicians have Celtic roots), locals and tourists dive into plates of *pulpo* (octopus),

lacón (ham with paprika), or empanada (tuna pastry). The shellfish (especially the clams) is also divine, especially *marinera* (in a savory tomato-based broth). The *albariño,* a semi-sweet Galician white wine is served in tiny ceramic bowls. Unless you arrive before 9 P.M. expect a wait. Work your way to the bar in the back, and ask for the *lista* (the waiting list). Once seated, don't be surprised if you are closer to your neighbor than your dining companion, as there is no space between tables. A second location around the corner (C/ Huertas 66) is slightly larger, but just as packed.

For an inexpensive paella in a lovely setting, pay a visit to **Arrocería Gala** (C/ Moratín 22, Metro: Sol, tel. 91/429-2562, €20, no credit cards). Over 20 paellas are made to order and the house favorite is *marinera* chock full of seafood. Tables come set with bowls of aioli and romesco sauces, bread for dipping, and olives. The total price is a rock-bottom €13 per person. But beware, Gala is very serious about their house rules. One, tables of four or less must share one flavor of paella. Two, reservations are required, and do not dare turn up late. Three, unless they are stroller-age, kids pay full price. Four, come with cash as credit cards are not accepted. And five, don't sing "Happy Birthday"; for whatever reason, it is forbidden. If you can live with all that, you'll have a delicious time. When making reservations be sure to request the *jardín,* the gorgeous back-room garden under an antique glass roof. The house red is a surprisingly good drink at only €6 per bottle, but skip the forgettable desserts; there is no coffee to go along with them, anyway. Last note, for Saturday and Sunday lunch there are two seatings at 1:30 and 3:30 P.M. Saturday evening there are also only two seatings at 9 and 11 P.M.

Romantic

La Cueva del Gato (C/ Moratín 19, Metro: Sol, tel. 91/360-0943, €30, reservations suggested) is an intimate retreat in the midst of Huertas madness. The constantly changing menu focuses on traditional Spanish ingredients with sophisticated touches. The homemade pâté is simply luscious. Ask to sit in the

elegant upstairs dining room as the restaurant's namesake basement *cueva* (cave) is claustrophobic. A fine choice of Spanish wines are also available. The restaurant doubles as a gallery for Madrid artists and everything on the walls is for sale. If you don't want a full meal, check out the adjacent tapas bar where many of the restaurant's items come tapa-sized.

Tapas

Plaza Santa Ana is synonymous with *tapeando.* During the summer the plaza fills with *terrazas.* You'll have a good time at just about all of them. A temple to all things bull, **Viña P** (Pl. Santa Ana, 3, Metro: Sol, tel. 91/531-8111, €12) is a classic stop for those enamored by the world of bullfighting. The bar also features a nice selection of Spanish wines by the glass and grilled asparagus with aioli that is to die for. Right across the plaza you'll find **La Moderna** (Pl. Santa Ana, 12, Metro: Sol, tel. 91/420-1582, €12). A favorite among both locals and tourists, this bright spot serves tasty tapas and big-enough-to-share salads along with a good selection of wine by the glass. Try the *ave ahumado* (smoked capon with celery dressing). Just to the east of the plaza, you'll find **La Trucha** (C/ Manuel Fernández González 3, Metro: Sol, tel. 91/429-5833, €15). Tucked into a tiny alley with an improbably long name, "The Trout" specializes in fish. The house favorite is *pescadito frito* (fried fish). The decor is all Andalusian charm with ham legs and blue tiles and the older crowd is downright boisterous. Reservations are not accepted, so go early to snag a spot at the bar or a table out back. A second location is at Núñez de Arce 6.

ATOCHA AND LAVAPIÉS
After Hours

Despite being just a few blocks from Madrid's biggest *marcha* zone, few Spaniards even know about **La Recoba** (C/ Magdalena 27, Metro: Antón Martín, tel. 91/369-3988, 9:30 P.M.–6 A.M. daily, €12). One of the few places in town where you can eat very late, this lively bar serves Italian standards to a ravenous post-nightclub crowd. The pizzas

MADRID

are pretty blah, but the Chilean empanada with a savory mix of ground beef and raisins is delicious. Then again, at this time of the morning, who cares about the food? You'll be too amused by the live band and the various older gentlemen who really get down to some Argentinean-style karaoke.

Fusion Cuisine

Run by a local denizen of the Madrid alterna-arts scene, **Buga del Lobo** (C/ Argumosa 11, Metro: Lavapiés, tel. 91/467-6151, €15) is a den of upscale cool on a stretch of street populated by bohemian bodegas and dive bars. At the bar, the vibe is boisterous as the nightly crowds quaff wine under colorful murals of half-naked hula girls. Head upstairs and back to have a sit-down meal (avoid the weirdly painted brown room all the way at the back). The menu changes frequently, but be sure to try the *setas temporadas* (seasonal wild mushrooms). Other top dishes include the *bacalao* (cod) topped with a silken egg poached in truffle oil. Heavenly. The daily menu is a steal at just €10, making it the perfect place for lunch after visiting the nearby Reina Sofía.

Local Cuisine

Don't come to **Asador Frontón** (Pl. Tirso de Molina 7, Metro: Tirso de Molina, tel. 91/369-1617, closed Sun. P.M., €25, reservations recommended) expecting glamour. This simple dining room has been serving simple food for decades (and the decor shows it), but oh how delicious simple can be. The house specialty is *chuletón,* a massive T-bone steak grilled slowly and basted with sea salt. No garnish, no side dish, just a massive hunk of meat. *Madrileños* swear it's the best in town. But beware, even the heartiest of eaters will have trouble finishing it. Your best bet is to share with a friend. Start your meal with *pimientos asados* (roasted peppers).

Regional Spanish Cuisine

Considered by foodies worldwide to be one of the best *arrocerías* (rice houses) in Madrid, the tiny **El Ventorrillo Murciano** (C/ Tres Peces

20, Metro: Antón Martín, tel. 91/528-8309, closed Mon. and Tues. P.M., €35), on a side street just off the beaten path, offers several tasty versions of the famed rice dishes of Murcia. Under rustic brick walls, amid piles of fresh vegetables, tuck into *arroz negro* (a seafood paella tinted black with squid ink) or *arroz con verduras y conejo* (vegetables and rabbit).

Tapas

Casa Granada (C/ Doctor Cortezo, 17, Metro: Tirso de Molina, tel. 91/420-0825, noon–midnight Mon.–Sat., noon–10 P.M. Sun., €10) is your typical Spanish tapas bar. Cheap beer on tap, basic food, forgettable decor. Of course take all that and sit it on the 6th floor of a building overlooking southern Madrid, add a wrap-around terrace, and bam!, you've got an amazing destination. During the day a doorman will let you in, off-hours ring the buzzer to the right of the door. At peak times there is a wait for the few terrace tables, but once you snag one, you can stay all day. Best bet for tapas are the *sepia* (grilled squid with lemon) and *pimientos del Padrón.*

Back on the ground, **Café Melos** (C/ Ave María 44, Metro: Lavapiés, tel. 91/527-5054, 9 P.M.–2 A.M. Tues.–Sat., closed Sun.–Mon., €8, no credit cards) is a tiny, fluorescent-lit bar serving up heaps of Galician tapas to clamoring crowds. Get there early if you want any chance of being served. Grab a spot at the bar, and don't let go. The massive *croquetas* are some of the best you'll ever try. If you are really hungry try the *zapatilla,* a massive ham sandwich smothered in melting cheese. Wash it down with the house white, a crisp *ribeiro* served in traditional ceramic saucers. A few blocks away is another great tapas bar. **El Automático** (C/ Argumosa 17, Metro: Lavapiés, 6 P.M.–1:30 A.M. Mon.–Fri., noon–1:30 A.M. Sat.–Sun., €8) is a Lavapiés meeting point for artists, bohemians, and local blue-collar types. They are drawn by the eclectic music (New Orleans funk to big band), cheap drinks, and delicious homemade tapas. *Pastel de pollo* (chicken terrine studded with pistachio) is the house specialty. Unless you are at the terrace, there is no table service; order at the bar and keep track of what you have, they'll ask you when it is time to pay.

Over by Atocha, and open all day long, **El Brillante** (Gta. del Emperador Carlos V 8, Metro: Atocha, tel. 91/528-6966, 7 A.M.–3:30 P.M. daily, €8) is the perfect place for a midday break. Expect to see little old men in berets snugged up against backpackers in dreadlocks. Tapas are cheap and huge, and all the Spanish classics are done just right. In warmer weather be sure to grab a table on the terrace out back, facing the Reina Sofía.

Vegetarian
El Granero de Lavapiés (C/ Argumosa, 10, Metro: Lavapiés, tel. 91/467-7611, 1–4 P.M. daily, plus 8:30–11 P.M. Fri., €15) is a lunchtime favorite even among carnivores. Best bets are the meatless takes on meat-based dishes. The veggie hamburger and empanada are cases in point, both savory and satisfying. For dessert don't miss the chocolate-walnut brownie. The dining room is a little worn, but the service is serene and the prices paltry.

LA LATINA
Cafés and Desserts
Delic (Costanilla de San Andrés 14, Metro: La Latina, tel. 91/364-5450, 11 A.M.–2 A.M. daily, €6, no credit cards) is a very popular, laid-back café. Stop in during the day for their famed carrot cake or a Moroccan mint tea. Magazines in all languages are available for reading, but the people-watching is really too good to miss. At night, lights go down and *copas* flow. It gets wildly crowded, especially on Sunday afternoons.

LA LATINA SUNDAY BRUNCH

In the warmer months, right as the Sunday morning Rastro is winding down, the plazas and streets of La Latina start plumping up with hordes of laid-back *madrileños* looking for a few beers, a few snacks, and a really good time. For decades, this impromptu Sunday-afternoon street party has been a neighborhood phenomenon. In the last few years, as La Latina has become the address of choice for Madrid's creative community, especially film, the crowds have become hipper, edgier, and much, much bigger. It is not uncommon to see actors like Javier Bardem or directors like Pedro Almodóvar weaving through the crowds.

The action is centered on the sprawling Plaza San Andrés right in front of the Iglesia de San Andrés. If the sun is out, hundreds of people will be sprawled about in designer sunglasses sharing beers right from liter-sized bottles. They used to be accompanied by hippie drummers and the occasional drag-queen flamenco singer, but the church priest put a stop to all that. Seems all the hand-clapping was disrupting the services.

The tiny Plaza Humilladero, just next door, is the place to see and be seen. The truly cool set up at bar El Bonanno, a miniscule place that is unfathomably popular. The no-name tapas bar on the corner of Calle Cava Baja is also famous for its large, free tapas. The other main stomping zones are Calle Almendro and Plaza de la Paja, though all of La Latina's bars and restaurants will be packed from about 2 P.M. to sunset. Do like the locals and go from bar to bar, having one *caña* here, one vino there. Just be sure to graze on tapas as you go along.

In 2003, Madrid city government made it technically illegal to drink in public streets and the bars all have signs to that effect. It doesn't hold back these crowds, though. The bars don't seem too worried either. One aspect of the revelry that strikes visitors from abroad is its absolute civility. People go out of their way to return glasses and plates to the bars. Another thing that will surprise you is how they turn the closest car into an improvised tabletop. If the driver comes along, there are no harsh words or altercations. People just pick up their glasses, and wait for the next "table" to pull up. What's a little beer-glass ring in the face of barrio-wide frivolity?

Tapas

There are some very good restaurants in La Latina, including the famed **Casa Lucio** (C/ Cava Baja 35, tel. 91/365-3252, €30), where kings and celebrities dine on Spanish classics; the elegant **Julián de Tolosa** (C/ Cava Baja 18, tel. 91/365-8210, €45), which many claim serve the best steaks in the country; and the brilliantly tiled **La Chata** (C/ Cava Baja 24, tel. 91/366-1458, €20) serving roasted pig and lamb. But the best ways to dine in La Latina is *tapeando*. Over the last decade, the barrio has emerged as a destination for wine bars and creative tapas. Calles Cava Baja, Cava Alta, Nuncio, and all around Plaza San Andrés are full of them. Some are chic and über-trendy, but the best stick to the tried-and-true *taberna* culture of rustic environs, good wine, and high-quality food. Take a walk around and check out the menus posted on the street. Look inside, if it is crowded with laughing locals, it's probably a good bet. Have a tapa and enjoy, but remember to keep moving, that is the point of *el tapeo!* The places mentioned here are some of the best.

Hidden in the crook of a tiny street, the atmospheric sherry bar **Almendro, 13** (C/ Almendro 13, Metro: La Latina, tel. 91/365-4252, €12) is worth seeking out. Step up to the hole in the wall on the right and order the house specialty, *huevos rotos,* a decadent mix of fried potatoes topped with eggs and *jamón.* While your food is prepared, step over to the bar at the left and order a *manzanilla* (dry white sherry). Unlike most places, you pay when served here. If there are no open sherry barrels for sitting, do like the locals and eat standing up. On Sundays, the crowd often spills out into the street using the closest car as a table. Whatever you do, avoid the dark, depressing dining room downstairs. On the next street over, ◖ **Tempranillo** (C/ Cava Baja 38, Metro: La Latina, tel. 91/364-1532, €15) looks a lot like a place that should be preserved in sepia-toned photos. It is a favorite of both guidebook writers and locals. If you want to experience a bit of the latter, go on a weeknight. Under a wall of wine bottles and lazy ceiling fans,

wine-lovers sip up to 20 choice pours by the glass. Keep the *vino* company with a tapa of *rebanada de setas* (wild mushrooms with aioli) or *cordoníz con salmorejo* (cornish hen with a savory tomato spread). The savory *magret de pato* (duck breast served sizzling with a side of marinated baby onions) is made for sharing. A few doors away is **Casa Lucas** (C/ Cava Baja 30, Metro: La Latina, tel. 91/365-0804, closed Wed. A.M., €15), another place known for its excellent selection of wines by the glass. The list of imaginative tapas changes frequently, so be adventurous. With only six tables, it fills up fast, but if you don't mind standing you can eat at the bar. More culinary creativity is at **Juana la Loca** (Pl. Puerta de Moros, 4, Metro: La Latina, tel. 91/364-0525, 1 P.M.–1 A.M. daily, €15, no credit cards). Low lighting, deep blue walls, and antique mirrors provide a sophisticated backdrop for tasty favorites like *tortilla* stuffed with caramelized onions and *confit de pato con miel* (shredded duck in honey). This place is very popular, so if you want one of the few tables surrounding the bar, visit during the week or get there early on the weekend. They also have a great-value *menú del día* for just €12.

Vegetarian

One of the most elegant vegetarian restaurants in Madrid, **El Estragón** (Pl. Paja 10, Metro: La Latina, tel. 91/365-8982, €12) takes pride in offering innovative vegetarian fare with exotic touches from Asia, Morocco, and Italy. The *menú del día* is a great deal at €11 and includes a scrumptious homemade dessert and wine. At night, the lights are lowered, and candles set out, making this a romantic destination.

MALASAÑA AND CHUECA
Cafés and Desserts

For over a century the **Café Comercial** (Gta. Bilbao 7, Metro: Bilbao, 8 A.M.–1 A.M. daily, €6) has served as a focus of Madrid literary life. Splendidly tattered, it features soaring ceilings, marble tabletops, and massive windows. Coffees are a bit more expensive here than elsewhere, but you can linger all day over a magazine. The kiosk out front carries several in English. Internet access is available upstairs. A bit further south and well into Chueca, you'll find **Mamá Ínes** (C/ Hortaleza 22, Metro: Gran Vía, 10 A.M.–2 A.M. daily, €6), a sophisticated café with a solid menu of light fare and heavenly desserts. This is also a good bet for breakfast if you are staying in this area. By nightfall, the gay and trendy pour in, the *copas* start to flow, and the vibe gets more clubby.

Fusion Cuisine

Nina (C/ Manuela Malasaña, 10, Metro: Bilbao, tel. 91/591-0046, €25), with its loft-high ceilings, exposed brick, and industrial touches, made quite a splash when it opened in Malasaña, home to rock clubs, cozy tapas bars, and traditional bodegas. Food is billed as "creative Mediterranean" and the *berenjenas con leche y miel* (eggplant fritters with milk and honey) are to die for. Among Madrid's expat community, Nina is famous for its Saturday and Sunday brunch (€18), a concept little known in Spain. Reservations are a must.

Over on the edge of Chueca, you can find a more religious dining experience at **La Sacristía** (C/ Infantas 28, Metro: Chueca or Gran Vía, tel. 91/522-0945, closed Sun., €30). With heavy furniture under the gaze of medieval angels, the restaurant has a monastic, old-world vibe with a staff as surly as grade school nuns. But the food—classic Spanish with a creative spin—is truly heavenly. The house specialty is *bacalao* (cod) served 10 different ways.

Gourmet

Run by American Chad Kenyon, **Divina La Cocina** (C/ Colmenares 13, Metro: Chueca, tel. 91/531-3765, www.divinalacocina.com, €50, reservations suggested) has been tempting diners with daring dishes for over a decade. In an elegantly sexy setting under terra-cotta walls and candlelight, acclaimed chef José Luis de Castenedo offers surprising dishes that marry traditional Spanish ingredients like *bacalao, calamares,* and *cecina del ciervo* (cured venison) with partners such as cashews, lychees, and curry. His creativity has kept Madrid's most discriminating palates pleased, and Divina's seats full. If you need a change from Spanish dining of the tiled-wall and *jamón*-hanging variety, but don't want to mortgage your house with a meal at one of the city's foam-frenzied places, Divina is for you.

Quick Bites

Putting the kitsch into the kitchen, **Pink Pollo** (C/ Infantas 18, Metro: Gran Vía, €10) propels the lowly roast chicken into fast-food overdrive. Everything from the tables to the garbage bins to the plasticware comes in varying shades of pink from prom night sweet to strip club neon. If you can stomach the visual assault, you'll find lip-smacking good taste in a variety of plates. The *flamingo* is the classic roasted. There are also nuggets, fingers, wings, and a few interesting salads. Wash it all down with a mojito or a Pink Daquiri. Your best bet is to put on your shades, get your order to go, and eat in the plaza across the street. For a more traditional carry-out, visit **Horno San Onofre** (C/ Onofre, 3, Metro: Gran Vía, tel. 91/532-9060, 8 A.M.–9 P.M. Mon.–Sat., 9 A.M.–8 P.M. Sun.). Famed for their window displays (cathedrals, buildings, and streets all rendered in sweets), this traditional bakery offers a wide-selection of fresh-from-the-*horno* cakes and pastries and a savory selection of quiches and empanadas, perfect for an impromptu picnic in the sun. There is another branch around the corner (C/ Hortaleza 9) and one near Plaza Mayor (C/ Mayor 73). Expect long lines just before lunch.

Tapas

La Musa (C/ Manuela Malasaña, 18, Metro: Bilbao, tel. 91/448-7558, €12) is a cheerful tapas bar with simple decor, a good selection of wines by the glass, and yummy tapas with a twist. Try the *bomba* (a puff of potato stuffed with ground beef) or the *jabalí glaseado* (wild boar cooked in honey). Best bet? Order one of the tapas or salad samplers. The latter includes a yummy fried green tomato topped with goat cheese. They make a perfect meal for one or a great snack for two. There is a second location in La Latina (Costanilla de San Andrés 12). No ressies accepted, so arrive early for a table or be prepared to wait at the lively bar. Across the street, **Albur** (C/ Manuela Malasaña 15, Metro: Bilbao, tel. 91/594-2733, 1 P.M.–1 A.M. daily, €15) is the kind of place you wish you could call your corner bar—casual and comfy. Though once hailed in the *New York Times,* it is still very much a local's place. The food is Spanish peasant and your best bets are *revueltas* (scrambled eggs) or a *tosta de jamón* (thick grilled toast rubbed with tomato and topped with *jamón*). It is worth seeking out at lunchtime to try one of their *arroces del día* (a variety of paellas) for just €11.

Moving closer to Chueca, **Stop Madrid** (C/ Hortaleza 11, Metro: Gran Vía, tel. 91/521-8887, noon–1 A.M. Sun.–Wed., noon–2:30 A.M. Thurs.–Sat., €8) is housed in a 1920s *jamonería* (ham shop). The original marble counter serves as the bar and the display windows are jammed with dusty wine bottles. Fittingly, *jamón* is the most popular tapa and platefuls of it are washed down with a choice of dozens of imported beers. The traditional feel is amped up with trendy masses making a tapas stop before hitting the bars of nearby Chueca. Rumor has it that Pedro Almodóvar called **Bocaíto** (C/ Libertad 4–6, Metro: Chueca, tel. 91/532-1219, www.bocaito.com, closed Sat. A.M., Sun., and Aug., €15) "one of the best anti-depressants I know." Drawing an enthusiastic crowd of 30-somethings nightly, "The Little Mouth" is pure Spanish, from the hanging hams to the tiled walls to the bottles of wine piled to the ceiling. Over 100 types of *tostas* are offered. Skip the maze of dining rooms out back, where the waiters are grumpy and the prices plumped up.

Cisne Azul (C/ Gravina 19, Metro: Chueca, tel. 91/521-3799, €15) defies categorization. Julián Pulido Vega has been running this hole-in-the-wall, on the edge of Plaza Chueca, for over 30 years and seems bemused by the international press it has received, including a recent plug in *Food & Wine.* The bar is a classic Spanish dive right down to the litter-covered linoleum floor, glaring fluorescent lighting, and circa-1970s television set. Julián insists it is nothing more than a tapas bar. But it is the tapas that draw all the attention. Specializing in *setas silvestres* (wild mushrooms), Cisne Azul offers up to 10 different species daily from chanterelles to black trumpets, including Spanish favorites like *níscalo.* Take a look at what is on offer in the cooler to the right of the door. The waiter can give you the Latin names and the charts on the wall can help as well, but if you are not sure what to order, ask for a *mezcla* (a mix of different types). Prices depend on the season and availability. Preparation is simply extra virgin olive oil and a sprinkling of coarse salt. There are only nine tables and reservations are not taken, so arrive early to secure a table. Of course, you can always eat at the bar.

Vegetarian

With netting on the ceiling, bamboo-lined walls, colorful paintings, and primitive art, the romantic **La Isla del Tesoro** (C/ Manuela Malasaña 3, Metro: Bilbao, tel. 91/593-1440, €12, reservations suggested) feels like a bohemian Tahitian paradise tucked indoors. It is also just about the best vegetarian restaurant in the city. The menu is a wild mix of international influences—Asian, Morocco, Italian. At night, entrées rarely top €10, but the best bet is to come for lunch. The four-course menu is set for the day (no choices, no substitutions) and follows a theme (Tuesday Thai, Wednesday Russian, etc.). At €10 including wine, it is a steal. Food is prepped that morning so serving time is fast-food fast.

ARGÜELLES

If you visit Goya's resting place at the Ermita de San Antonio de Florida, be sure to make a stop afterwards at **Casa Mingo** (Po. Florida 2, Metro: Príncipe Pio, tel. 91/547-7918, 11 A.M.–midnight daily, €10). Though it appears in most guidebooks, this classic Asturian cider house is just far enough off the tourist path to be solidly Spanish. Under massive wooden cider kegs and exposed beam ceilings, multi-generational families cram into the long wooden tables and tuck into *pollo asado* (roasted chicken) and *chorizo a la sidra* (cooked in cider). If it is packed when you arrive, just stand by the door and make eye contact with a waiter, and you'll soon get seated. Then, do like the locals and order the chicken and a bottle of cider (natural is dry and un-carbonated, the waiter can show you how to pour it from up high to add bubbles to it). The lively atmosphere is priceless. Bring your camera and an empty stomach.

SALAMANCA AND LA CASTELLANA
Cafés and Desserts
In the middle of the delightful walking path of the Paseo de Recoletos, **El Espejo** (Po. Recoletos 31, Metro: Banco de España, tel. 91/319-1122, 10:30 A.M.–2:30 A.M. daily, €12) is an oasis of Parisian sophistication. Have breakfast under the gorgeous belle epoque glass pavilion. During warmer weather, enjoy a coffee on the terrace. Skip the food, though. It is just okay and doesn't merit the price. Just down the street is another wonderful café with a celebrated history. **Café Gijón** (Po. Recoletos 21, Metro: Banco de España, tel. 91/521-5425, 7 A.M.–1:30 A.M. daily, €14) has been a literary fixture in the city since 1888. Even though the terrace may beckon, you should have your coffee inside just to take in the antiquated charm of the place. Take note, that charm doesn't extend to the staff.

Quick Bites
If you are even remotely a fan of fine dining you've no doubt heard of Ferran Adrià, the Catalan chef famous for his foams and the impossibility of getting reservations at his restaurant El Bulli. (See *El Bulli:The Most Sought-After Reservation in the World* in the *Cataluña*

chapter.) Well, **Fast Good** (C/ Juan Bravo 3, Metro: Núñez de Balboa, www.fast-good .com, noon–midnight daily, €15) is his foray into fast food. If you are a true all-American beef burger lover, skip these prissy interpretations and go for a savory panini or one of the yummy roasted chickens. A plus to this place is that the kitchen is open all day, but to avoid long lines it is best to go well before or after the lunch rush.

Gourmet
Located in the posh environs of Hotel Miguel Ángel, **La Broche** (C/ Miguel Ángel 29, Metro: Gregorio Marañón, tel. 91/399-3437, www .labroche.com, closed Sat. and Sun., €150) is the home turf of Spanish superstar chef Sergi Arola. The dining room is all white so as not to distract from the food. Dishes like foamed hazelnuts with gelatin of white asparagus, peach confit with amaretto and crunchy leeks, and gazpacho of foie gras with white garlic ice cream, have earned La Broche world-wide acclaim. Reserve early online and confirm your reservation a few days before. Best bet is the *degustación* (tasting) menu.

Named for the 1961 Luis Buñuel classic, **Viridiana** (C/ Juan de Mena 14, Metro: Banco de España, tel. 91/531-1039, closed Sun., €80) is decorated with stills from the movie. However, it is the food that is the star here. Self-taught chef/owner Abraham García is nothing short of a genius, creating magical fusions of traditional Spanish cooking with any influence you can imagine. And unlike a lot of celebrated chefs, he turns them out in generous portions. The menu changes constantly and your best bet is the tasting menu for a delicious idea of what this master chef is capable of.

Information and Services

Tourist and Travel Information

The **main city tourist office** (Pl. Mayor 27, 91/588-2906, www.esmadrid.com, 9:30 A.M.–8:30 P.M. daily) is located under the Casa de Panadería in Plaza Mayor. In addition to information and maps, the office also distributes the free magazine *Es Madrid,* a monthly English/Spanish listing of events. This is also the meeting point for most of the **Descubre Madrid** walking tours. (See sidebar, *Tours of Madrid.*) The city runs three **information kiosks:** Plaza Cibeles, across from the Prado; Plaza Callao off of Gran Vía; and Plaza Felipe II in Barrio Salamanca. Before you head to Madrid, spend some time on their excellent website. Finally, you can **dial 010** for toll-free information. If you ask for an English-speaker, expect to wait on hold.

The **main regional tourist office** (C/ Duque de Medinaceli 2, 91/329-3951, 8 A.M.–8 P.M. Mon.–Sat., 9 A.M.–2 P.M. Sun.) is located behind the Palace Hotel, and offers Madrid city information as well as details on events in the greater Madrid community including destinations such as El Escorial. Their local and regional public transportation maps are excellent. You can find additional offices in Terminals 1 and 2 at Barajas airport, in the AVE arrivals lounge at Atocha train station, and near platform 20 in Chamartín train station.

Several **local publications** deliver information about events in the city. *In Madrid* is a hip English-language monthly aimed at the expat community. It features an overview of current events from arts to theater including an extensive clubs listing. Pick it up at Irish bars, English-language bookstores, some hotels, and the tourist office at Barajas Airport. Their website **www.in-madrid.com** is excellent. The best Spanish guide is the weekly *Guía del Ocio,* found at all news kiosks.

There are several **online information sources** that you should visit before coming to Madrid. For exhaustive lists of general information see **www.madridinsider.com,** an up-to-date database of everything from airport transfers to laundry services. If you want a more personal view of Madrid life and culture, spend time in the forums and boards at **www.multimadrid.com.** Run by longtime resident Jer Reines, "mm" as it is called, can give you insight on everything from where to find a late-night flamenco bar to the best way to get from the airport to the city center. It is also a great place to contact Madrid residents and visitors looking to meet up for a night of tapas-hopping. At **www.madaboutmadrid.com** you can find a hodge-podge of information on life and living in the city.

Free maps can be found all over town, including at the tourist office and **El Corte Inglés** stores, however the **best free maps** are those by the marketing firm **El Dibuk.** They focus on different areas of the city and give detailed street information. You will find them all over the center in shops, bars, and restaurants. Be sure to pick up one for each region. If you will spend time in Madrid, or are planning a road trip through the country, visit **Desnivel** (Pl. Matute 6, Metro: Sol, tel. 902/248-848, 10 A.M.–2 P.M. and 4:30–8:30 P.M. Mon.–Sat.). Dedicated to all things adventure, from mountain trekking to back-road exploring, this quaint shop stocks thousands of maps.

Banks and Currency Exchange

There are several **ATMs** in Barajas airport. Upon arrival, take out enough money to pay for your airport transfer. Taxi drivers frown on bills larger than a €20, so be sure to request an amount in a multiple of 20. Barajas has a problem with thieves who disguise themselves as tourists (often complete with luggage). These crooks specialize in taking advantage of travel-bleary tourists fresh off the plane. Keep your luggage between you and the ATM and cover your hand as you punch in your PIN. Once you arc in town, you can get larger amounts of cash.

The center of Madrid is teeming with banks and ATMs. During banking hours (9 A.M.–

2 P.M. Mon.–Sat.), the safest bet is to use the machines located inside the bank. On the street, practice common sense security. Of all the ATMs, those of **La Caixa** tend to work the best and allow the largest withdrawals.

You can **exchange U.S. dollars** at several sites in Barajas, but you'll find better rates at any of the *bancos* in the center, particularly around Sol. **BBVA** and **Banco Santander** are two of the larger ones. The **La Caixa** (C/ Arenal 24, Metro: Sol, tel. 91/559-2292) has a friendly staff that is used to dealing with foreigners. Rates do vary, but not by enough to make it worthwhile to shop around. Smaller branches in the barrio often refuse to exchange money, even if it is their bank's policy. Also, you will have to show your passport to exchange money, not a photocopy. Do not change money at one of the independent *cambios* unless you are in an absolute emergency. The rates are criminal.

If you have brought **travelers checks** as a back-up, the same major banks as above will change them. The former American Express office has changed to an **Interchange** (Pl. Cortes 2, Metro: Sevilla, 91/322-5500, 9 A.M.–7:30 P.M. Mon.–Fri., 9 A.M.–2 P.M. Sat.) and it will change all U.S.-dollar travelers checks (Visa, MasterCard, or American Express); again, you must bring your physical passport. The office is located just behind the Thyssen Museum.

If you need to have money wired, **Western Union** in the United States has an agreement with **Change Express** (Gran Vía 44–46, tel. 90/063-3633, 10 A.M.–10 P.M. daily). You'll have to coordinate the exchange with someone stateside and if you do not have a passport to receive the money, you will have to create a question and answer pass code with your contact. The staff speaks English. The larger post offices in Madrid also work with Western Union, but the hours are limited and the English even more so.

As throughout Spain, Madrid businesses accept **American Express, Visa,** and **MasterCard,** whether credit or debit. Other cards are not accepted, so leave them at home. Again, it is advisable to use your cards to pay for big-ticket items like your hotel bill, a splurge at a top restaurant, or a purchase in a major store. Do not use your credit card for smaller shops and stores. It is not the practice in Spain to obscure credit card numbers from sales receipts, and you are more likely to run into problems with a smaller business.

Communications

To buy stamps, head to any *estanco* (tobacco shop). They are throughout the city and easily identified by a brown-and-yellow sign that says "Tabacos." In the center, **Filatelia 2000** (C/ de la Cruz 1, Metro: Sevilla) is a friendly shop selling stamps and postcards. For full postal services head to Sol and the **El Corte Inglés** (C/ Preciados 1–4); the post office is in the basement.

Many hotels now offer Internet access, as do *locutorios* which are multi-functional phone, fax, photocopying, and Internet providers. **Easy Internet** (C/ Montera 10 Metro: Sol) 8 A.M.–1 A.M. daily) has dozens of terminals. Be aware that it is located on a street frequented by prostitutes. Another good bet is **BBiGG** (C/ Mayor 1, Metro: Sol), which is cheap, big, and clean. **Workcenter** (Pl. Canalejas, s/n, Metro: Sol, tel. 91/360-1395, 8 A.M.–11 P.M. daily) is a full-service office with Internet plus a host of other software. Buy a card at the copy desk downstairs, then go upstairs to use the computers. Thieves prey on Internet café users. Keep your bag on your lap or on the floor in front of you. If you have your laptop and want a little Wi-Fi in the sun, you can't beat **Plaza Wi-Fi** (www.plazawifi.com) for atmosphere. Their node is based right in the Plaza Mayor. Contact them to sign up before you go.

If you'd like to **rent a cell phone** or buy a SIM card for your phone to use in all of Spain, see **Onspanishtime** (C/ Correo 4, tel. 65/626-6844, Metro: Sol, www.onspanishtime.com). Reserve a rental or buy before you leave the United States by visiting their website or calling their U.S./Canada toll-free number, 800/240-6993. Run by an American expat, this office can help you with any cell- or phone-related question about American or Spanish phones.

The office also sells phone cards with very low rates to the States. More about the cards can be found at **www.europhonecards.org**.

The **area code** for Madrid is 91. See *Communications and Media* in *Essentials* for more on calling to and from Spain.

Emergency Services

In Madrid, you can call the **24-hour emergency helpline at 112** for police and fire. English is sometimes available. If you are the victim of a crime, you must report to it the *comisaría* (police station). The **main police station** (C/ Leganitos 19, Metro: Sol) is open 24 hours a day. The police hotline for English-speakers is 90/210-2112, but you'll have to wait to be attended.

For emergency medical service, **dial 061 for an ambulance** or head to the *urgencias* (emergency) of any major hospital. The nicest central hospital is **Hospital General Gregorio Marañón** (C/ Doctor Esquerdo 46) in Barrio Salamanca. For **non-emergency medical** needs you can go to the free Spanish-speaking clinic **Casa de Socorro** (C/ Navas de Toloso, 10, Metro: Gran Vía, tel. 91/521-0025, open 24 hours), but it is not the nicest facility. During normal working hours, **Unidad Medica** (C/ Conde de Aranda, 1, Metro: Retiro, tel. 91/435-1823, 9 A.M.–8 P.M. Mon.–Fri., 10 A.M.–1 P.M. Sat., in Aug. by appt. only) has a full staff of English-speaking doctors. Appointments can usually be made for the day you call. At €120 a visit, it is expensive, but it is the closest to an American-style medical provider you will find. If you have a dental need while in town, **British Dentist Richard Klein** (Po. Castellana, 15, Metro: Colón, tel. 91/310-5152) can take patients on short notice. A basic visit is about €90.

There are several *farmacias de guardia* (24-hour pharmacies) in the center. In Sol, they are located at **Calle Mayor 13** and **Calle Preciados 14.**

The **American Embassy** (C/ Serrano 75, Metro: Rubén Darío, tel. 91/587-2200) can assist with many emergencies. A duty officer takes calls after hours. The embassy website **www.embusa.es** also provides a wealth of information; click on U.S. Citizen Services.

Laundry Services

If you've been on the road a while and your clothes are smelling it, head to one of the city's coin laundries. The most basic, with two central locations is **Lavamatic** (C/ Cruz 35, Metro: Sol, 8 A.M.–9 P.M. daily, and C/ Válgame Dios 2, Metro: Chueca, 8 A.M.–9 P.M. daily). **Onda Blue** (C/ León 3, Metro: Antón Martín and C/ Hortaleza 84, Metro: Alonso Martínez, both open 8 A.M.–10:30 P.M. daily) has Internet terminals at its locations.

Luggage Storage

An American expat runs **Spain Storage** (C/ Correo 4, Metro: Sol, tel. 91/521-7934 or 66/980-4530, info@spainstorage.com, www.spainstorage.com) and will hold luggage for the short or long term at the cheapest prices in town. There are also lockers at Barajas airport; Atocha (in the AVE station) and Chamartín train stations; and Méndez Alvaro bus terminal. Prices run €1–5 per day. Look for *Consigna* or *almacenaje de equipaje* and check prices and hours. You don't want to miss a plane because the luggage center is closed.

Getting There

Air

Madrid's **Barajas airport** (tel. 90/240-4704, press 9 for English, www.aena.es), located about 16 kilometers (10 miles) northeast of the city center, is Spain's largest airport and the third most important in Europe. It has four terminals, including the architectural wonder of Terminal 4 (T4), which opened in 2006. Most international flights coming from the United States will land at T1 or T4. The other terminals are for national flights, as well as flights to European Union countries. The terminals are connected by a shuttle bus that runs about every five minutes. The airport's English website has extensive information about flights, terminals, and which airlines land where. You'll find the usual ATMs, money exchange, shops, and restaurants throughout Barajas, though the bulk are in T4 and T1. Also, you'll notice when picking up your luggage that the carts are free. Push down on the handle to make them move.

There are several ways to **transfer to the city center.** The easiest is by **taxi.** Exit the terminal and the taxis will be lined up. You have to go to the taxi at the front of the line. Usually there is an airport worker directing passengers to taxis. There is an airport departure fee of €4.20 and luggage is free. Prices are clearly marked in English in the taxi. To avoid getting ripped off, tell the taxi driver right away that you need a *una factura* (a receipt). Total cost to the center should be about €20 euros, a bit more on holidays or at night. Tipping is not required nor expected, though many Spaniards round up the bill to the nearest euro. The ride takes about 25 minutes with no traffic and up to 40 with traffic. Do not accept a taxi ride from anyone in the airport. Official taxis are white with a red diagonal stripe and wait outside. Anyone inside is a hustler.

Another option is airport shuttle. **Aerocity** (tel. 90/071-3583, press 2 for English, or 91/571-9696, info@aerocity.com, www.aerocity.com). Cost is around €16 euros for one person, €19 for two people. One piece of luggage is included per person, extra luggage costs €1 per piece. You can book ahead of time through their website or go directly to their office in T1, open 7:30 A.M.–midnight daily. If you are in T4 or arrive after the office is closed, dial the 900 number; it's attended 24 hours a day in English. You'll share the shuttle with other passengers, so expect two to three stops.

If you are not carrying too much luggage, Madrid's **metro** is the cheapest way into the city. It is also the most cumbersome. The *boca* (entrance) of the metro is in T2, a 20-minute walk from T1. From T4 you'll have to take the shuttle or walk even further. The ticket is €1 euro, though you may want to go ahead and buy a 10-trip ticket for €6.15, especially if you will be in Madrid a few days. From the Barajas metro stop, you take line 8 (pink) to Metro: Nuevos Ministerios. From there, you should transfer to the line that will take you to your hotel. Again, if you have large or heavy luggage, this is probably not your best bet.

Train

Madrid has two major train stations, Chamartín and Atocha. Trains for both stations are run by **Renfe** (tel. 90/224-0202, www.renfe.es). Both train stations are accessible by metro, however be sure to take Metro: Atocha-Renfe to arrive at Atocha station (Metro: Atocha is for the street of the same name). The stations are connected by the **Cercanías,** a regional commuter train that whizzes between the two every 10 minutes (€1.20).

Located in the north of Madrid, **Chamartín** serves northern Spain and international routes. Station hours are 5:30 A.M.–midnight daily and ticket sales are 6:35 A.M.–10:35 P.M. daily. The station has all the usual amenities, plus a tourist office and hotel bookers. To get to the city center from here, take metro line 10 (dark blue) or catch a taxi outside the station. A €2.20 fee is added for station pick-ups.

Right in the center of town **Atocha** serves

© CANDY LEE LABALLE

Enjoy a tropical rainforest while waiting for your train in Atocha station.

southern Spain and houses the AVE high-speed trains. The station can be confusing as it is a hobbled together from two distinct buildings. The AVE part, near the restored glass and iron atrium and next to the gorgeous botanical gardens, is where you will catch all your long-distance trains. Just follow the blue-and-yellow *Puerta de Atocha* signs. Catch the Cercanías trains on the other side (where the Metro: Atoche-Renfe is located). Look for the red circle with the yellow letter C. Station hours are 5 A.M.–1 A.M. daily with ticket sales 6:30 A.M.–10:25 P.M. daily. Be sure to arrive early when buying tickets, as the office is always crowded with waits up to 30 minutes. To avoid the lines, buy your Renfe train tickets at **El Cortes Inglés** (C/ Preciados 3, 1st and 7th floors); the €2 surcharge is more than worth it.

Bus

There are two main bus stations in Madrid. **Estación Sur de Autobuses** (C/ Méndez Alvaro 83, Metro: Méndez Alvaro, tel. 91/468-4200, www.estaciondeautobuses.com) will take you almost anywhere you want to go within Spain and beyond. **Estación de Conde de Casal** (C/ Fernández Shaw 1, Metro: Conde de Casal, www.auto-res.es, tel. 91/551-5601) travels to fewer places, though among them is Chinchón, a great day trip.

Car

Though driving in Madrid is strongly not recommended, if you must arrive to the city by car, you will find it easy to access from almost any point in Spain. The six major national roads (A-1–6) all begin in Madrid. As you get closer to the city, it is encircled by ring roads; the M-40 is the outer ring, hitting most of the major suburbs, while the M-30 hugs the city and provides access to its main thoroughfares. Parking in Madrid is very expensive, up to €30 per day. On the street, you'll be hard-pressed to find a spot. If you do, you must determine if it is a blue visitor's zone or a green resident's zone—indicated by the colored stripes on the ground. Time in the latter is limited. For both, buy a ticket from the *parquimetro,* which will be located somewhere on the block where you are parking. It must be displayed in your car window. To avoid all of this hassle, choose a hotel with parking and leave the car there while you do your sightseeing.

Getting Around

Metro

Madrid is compact and most sights are easily covered by foot. Half the fun of the city is wandering through the old streets. However, if you want to give your feet a rest, the Spanish capital also has one the most efficient and inexpensive subway systems (metro) in Europe. Madrid's **Metro** (tel. 90/244-4403, www.metromadrid.es) has 11 main lines crisscrossing the city. They are identified both by color and number on all maps and stations. Hotels, restaurants, and shops all generally tack the closest metro stop onto their advertisements and the stops are also used as reference points when moving around the city. If you don't know an address, you can always tell a taxi driver the name of the closest metro stop to your destination. The trick to finding your way through the system is knowing the destination of the line you will take. Lines are named by their final point. So line 3 (yellow) is called Moncloa-Legazpi for its two end points.

The cost is a flat €1 regardless of how many times you transfer within the system. The only additional fees arise if you leave Zone A, which as a tourist, there is no reason to do so. However, if you will be in Madrid more than a couple of days, you should pick up the **Metrobús** (€6.15), which gives you 10 journeys on metro or bus. Tickets can be bought from attendants or machines at the entrance to all stations.

The metro is open 6 A.M.–2 A.M. and trains run every 3–8 minutes. Beware of rush hours (7:30 A.M.–9:30 A.M. and 7:30 P.M.–9 P.M.) when the metro is packed with commuters. It is easier to just walk during those time. If you are heading home late and have to switch lines, be sure to catch the metro before 1:30 A.M. to avoid missing your transfer. And of course, be aware of your belongings. The metro is ripe pickings for thieves who take advantage of sleepy commuters and distracted tourists.

Bus

Like the metro, Madrid's **city buses** are well-run and cheap, costing just €1 per ride. Managing them is a bit trickier, as you need to know the city pretty well. The bus stops are labeled and the buses themselves feature scrolling red signs announcing the next stop. The website **www.emtmadrid.es** can offer more clarification. Buses run 6 A.M.– 11:30 P.M. each day and run every 10–15 minutes at the most.

Night buses called *buhos* (owls) take over 11:30 P.M.–5 A.M. There are 24 lines and they all originate at Plaza de Cibeles. Pronounced BOO-oh, the buses are identified by an N before the line number. They run every half-hour until 3 A.M., every hour after that.

Commuter Train

The **Cercanías** (www.renfe.es/cercanias/ Madrid) are 12 commuter trains that zip through the city and the surrounding regions. The main hub is at Atocha. They are an easy and inexpensive way of getting to El Escorial, Aranjuez, or Alcalá de Henares for a day trip. Ticket prices vary depending on how far you travel but range from €1.10–3.40 for a one-way trip. Buy tickets at the station from a coin-operated machine. Just punch in the name of your destination. *Ida y vuelta* is round-trip. Trains run 6 A.M.–11 P.M. every 10–30 minutes.

Tourist Passes

If you plan on using public transportation a lot during your stay in Madrid, the city offers *abonos turísticos*. The "A" pass allows unlimited trips on the metro, city buses, and Cercanías within the central city, called Zone A. If you head out of the city, you'll need to buy an extra ticket. For one day the cost is €3.50, five days costs €13.20, and seven days is €18.40.

Taxi

Madrid taxis are white with a red diagonal stripe across the front doors. A green light on top means the taxi is free, just hold out your hand to hail it. It is almost always easy to catch a taxi, just make your way to any sizeable street and they will be everywhere. The one time that they run really scarce is after 3 A.M., especially on weekends, when bars start to close and the masses hit the street. Many a club-goer has sobered up over a 30-minute walk home. Rates come in two fares, "A" which is weekday, and "B" which is evenings, holidays, and weekends. Fares are clearly marked in English on the window of the cab. A 10-minute cab ride through the center will cost around €6. Remember that there are supplements added at the airport, bus stations, and train stations, and there is no charge for luggage or pets. Be sure to have cash on hand, as credit cards are not accepted. Also don't bring a bill larger than a 20 as the driver won't be able to (or won't want to) break it. Though there are always tales of drivers try-ing to rip off tourists, the majority are friendly, hard-working, honest people.

Car Rental

Though driving in Madrid falls just short of a nightmare, renting a car is a must to drive through Spain's back roads. If you haven't booked through your travel agent back home or an online booker, head to the airport. You can rent in Atocha station, but that means deal-ing with the horrid traffic surrounding it. **Avis** (tel. 91/348-0100, www.avis.com, 7 A.M.–3 A.M. daily) and **Hertz** (91/509-7300, www.hertz.com, 7 A.M.–midnight daily) have offices in Barajas at T1, T2, and T4. They also both have offices in the Nuevos Ministerios metro station. You find the best rates online by visiting a broker such as www.carbookers.com or www.easycar.com.

Vicinity of Madrid

Two of the best day trips from Madrid will take you out of the Madrid community. **Segovia,** home to one of the best-preserved Roman aq-ueducts in the world, as well as the castle that inspired Walt Disney, is in Castilla y León. **Toledo,** a museum disguised as a medieval city, is in Castilla-La Mancha. Check those respec-tive chapters for more information. Within the community of Madrid, you can visit the fol-lowing towns.

EL ESCORIAL

Just 45 kilometers (28 miles) northwest of Ma-drid, the bedroom community of El Escorial is a suburb of chalets and luxury apartment buildings tucked into the lush green foothills of the Sierra de Guadarrama mountain range. It would be completely missable were it not for the immense palace, monastery, and mu-seum complex built by King Felipe II in the 16th century.

Sights

Felipe II was an obsessive monarch—obses-sively Catholic, obsessively mystical, obses-sively extravagant, and obsessively concerned with his own legacy. The colossal **Monasterio de San Lorenzo El Escorial** (tel. 91/890-5902, 10 A.M.–5 P.M. Tues.–Sun. Oct.–Mar., 10 A.M.–6 P.M. Tues.–Sun. Apr.–Sept., closed Mon. year-round, €9 with guided tour, €7 without) is where all his obsessions were wrought together in a granite edifice that has been called every-thing from a world wonder to a megalomania-cal monstrosity. Whatever the opinion, the fact remains that the monastery, with a 700-foot-wide facade, 2,675 windows, 1,200 doors, and over 16 kilometers (10 miles) of hallways, is an impressive feat of 16th-century architecture. It is also a UNESCO World Heritage Site.

The building commenced in 1563 and fin-ished in 1584. The main architect, Juan Her-rera, created a grid-like structure said to be based on the rack that Saint Lorenzo was burned to death on back in Roman times. The edifice is a stripped-down version of Renaissance design, and perfectly reflected the austerity of the age in which it was built. It was anything but austere in price, however, and the building dipped deeply into Spain's coffers. Within its stark walls, the monastery is a bit more palatial, filled with artworks by the usual suspects (Greco, Titian, and the like), miles of tapestries, libraries of books, and thousands of other royal and religious artifacts. It also houses the royal bones of nearly every monarch since Carlos V.

The **guided tour** is a great way to make sure you don't miss any details, but if you are short on time, you should opt for the **audio guide,** which will let you make your own pace. In about two hours you can see just about everything. If you decide to wing it on your own, it may seem overwhelming. Get a grip by focusing on a few must-sees. There are signs everywhere pointing you in the right direction, and the rooms all have English explanations. The **Museo de Arquitectura,** with models of the monastery, is a good place to get an overall feel of the building.

In the **Palacio de Felipe II** are the king's austere living quarters. The highlight is the pair of gorgeous inlaid wooden doors covered in fantastical imagery that lead into the throne room. In the bedroom, Felipe's sad little bed was placed so that he could view mass in the basilica below. He died from gout in this bed in 1598.

The **Panteón de los Reyes** is the ornate mausoleum originally built to house the bodies of Felipe II's parents Carlos V and Isabel. All but two royal leaders have joined them. In a bit of monarch machismo, only the queens who gave birth to kings are allowed to rest here. Next door, the **Panteón de los Infantes** is a marble tomb shaped like a wedding cake. It holds the remains of royal children who died before the age of seven. In contrast to the severe exterior of the monastery, both mausoleums are excessive symbols of the wealth and power of the Spanish regime in the time of King Felipe II.

The **Salas Capitulares** were meeting rooms for church leaders and are hung with paintings by El Greco, Titian, and Velázquez. The **Basilica,** the monastery's huge, square church emits an air of sanctity and down-right eeriness. It is also the coldest room in the building. The highlight is the lovely statue of *Christ's*

Crucifixion, carved of Carrera marble in 1576 by Benvenuto Cellini. The church opens onto the massive **Patio de los Reyes,** the monastery's main courtyard. The last room to look out for is the **Biblioteca,** Felipe's royal library. It houses over 40,000 volumes and rumor has it that the books are in such fine shape because the monks entrusted with watching over them throughout the 18th century were illiterate. The colorful fresco that covers the ceiling was completed in 1592 by Tibaldi and is a celebration of philosophy and art.

Food

The most popular spot for both locals and tourists is the lovely terrace café of **Hotel Miranda & Suizo** (C/ Floridablanca 18–20, tel. 91/890-4711) with light fare and decadent desserts. The art nouveau **Cafetín Croché** (C/ San Lorenzo 6) is a relaxed place for simple tapas. If you are looking for a cheap *menú del día,* try **La Chistera** (Pl. Jacinto Benevente 3, tel. 91/890-0160, €8.50), a basic eatery with Spanish food done right. For something a lot nicer, head uphill to **Horizontal** (C/ Horizontal, s/n, tel. 91/890-3811, www.restauran tehorizontal.com, 9:30 A.M.–midnight daily summer, 9:30 A.M.–8 P.M. Mon.–Wed. and 9:30 A.M.–midnight Fri.–Sun. winter, €20). A 20-minute walk will take you past some of the towns poshest homes. During the 16th and 17th centuries, this is where the nobility lived in modest palaces. The food is excellent and the forest setting serene.

Information

The **Oficina de Turismo** (C/ Grimaldi, 2) will have information on both the monastery, the **Valle de los Caídos,** and the town of El Escorial. For specific details on the monastery, see www.patrimonionacional.es/en/escorial/esco rial.htm, a comprehensive, if confusing, website run by the state organization that manages Spain's royal buildings.

Getting There and Around

The easiest way to El Escorial is by taking the **Autocares Herranz** bus number 661 or 664 from the Moncloa bus station (Metro: Moncloa). It leaves about every 15 minutes during the week, but is much less frequent on the weekend. The journey is about one hour long. The bus drops you off about 10 minutes walking from the monastery. You can also go by **Cercanías** regional train (less than €7 round-trip, about 1 hour). Be sure to take train C8A, not C8. They leave about every hour on the half-hour. Check www.renfe.es/cercanias/ Madrid for specifics. You arrive in El Escorial Abajo, the lower half of town. The monastery is a little over 1.5 kilometers (one mile) uphill. The **Herranz** shuttle bus leaves from the station every half-hour.

VALLE DE LOS CAÍDOS

In 1940, Franco stilling lapping in the recent victory of his nationalist troops in the Civil War and his own subsequent installment as dictator, proposed construction of his very own monument just 9.6 kilometers (six miles) from El Escorial. Valle de los Caídos (tel. 91/890-5611, www.patrimonionacional .es/infprac/visitas/valles.htm, 10 A.M.–5 P.M. Tues.–Sun. Oct.–Mar, 10 A.M.–6 P.M. Tues.–Sun. Apr.–Sept., closed Mon. year-round, €5), the Valley of the Fallen, was proposed as a way to commemorate those who died in the Spanish Civil War. Living victims of the war were not the intended honorees, a fact borne out by the forced use of imprisoned Republican troops to build the massive granite edifice. Controversial, then and now, the general consensus is that the monument is Franco's personal tribute to his own power and victory.

Politics aside, the building is an imposing feat of architecture. Over 220,000 tons of granite were carved out of the mountain to create the vast underground basilica and burial chambers. The rock was then used to build a 500-foot cross looming over the structure. The overall feel is stark, authoritarian, and stunningly grandiose. Within, Franco lays buried at the far end of the basilica, which at an astonishing 265 meters (870 feet), is larger than St. Peter's in Rome. José Antonio Primo de Rivera,

who founded the Falange party, the forerunner to the Nationalist party, lies near Franco. Beyond their bodies, over 50,000 soldiers from both sides of the war are interred.

There is a **funicular** (11 A.M.–4:30 P.M. Tues.–Sun. Oct.–Mar., 11 A.M.–7 P.M. Tues.–Sun. Apr.–Sept., closed Mon. year-round, €2.50) that runs from the monument to the base of the cross and offers spectacular views. It's a good option if you have time to kill before the return bus.

If you are really into Spanish history, this trip is interesting. However, for most visitors, it is not worth the hassle.

Getting There

Most people tack a trip to Valle de los Caídos onto a visit to El Escorial. There is only one bus per day. **Autocars Herranz** (Pl. Virgen de Gracia) bus number 660 leaves El Escorial at 3:15 P.M. and returns at 5:30 PM. The €7.80 ticket includes admission to the sight, so don't bother buying a combination ticket at El Escorial. It is only convenient for those who are driving.

ALCALÁ DE HENARES

Originally founded by the Romans as Complutum, modern Alcalá de Henares is a tidy town rich with intellectual history. It was Spain's first university town, built to support Universidad Complutense founded by Cardinal Cisneros in 1496. When Complutense moved to Madrid in 1836 it left the town downtrodden. Things picked up with the founding of the Universidad de Alcalá de Henares in 1977. Today, it is haven for exchange students and scholars, particularly those with a thing for Spain's favorite literary son. Miguel de Cervantes was born here in 1547 and the city celebrates this fact with tours, trains, and cultural events. The best of them is the **Semana Cervantina,** a weeklong party commemorating his birth on October 9. The old center of the city is gussied up to look as it did in the 16th century, costumed actors take to the streets, and a market selling traditional foods and crafts sets up in the Plaza Cervantes.

Sights

Head to the center of town and **Calle Mayor,** a shady pedestrian walkway through the city's old Jewish quarter. Today, it is lined by tapas bars and cafés. At about its midpoint, where it meets another charming street, **Calle Libreros,** is **Plaza de Cervantes,** a broad square rimmed with flowering trees and, of course, a statue of the beloved scribe. Whether he was born at that spot is up for debate, but **Casa Natal de Cervantes** (C/ Mayor 48, tel. 91/889-9654, 10 A.M.–6 P.M. Tues.–Sat., free) makes for a nice visit, decorated as it might have been when Cervantes was alive. It also houses a second edition of *Don Quixote.* Two doors down is Europe's oldest charity hospital, **Hospital de Antezana** (C/ Mayor 46), founded in 1484 and still going strong.

Throughout this neighborhood the streets are lined with **Colegio Mayores,** 16th-century student residences. The most famous is **Colegio Mayor de San Ildefonso** (Pl. de San Diego). The regal facade of this building is an example of Plateresque architecture, which imitates the look of hammered silver. Within are Gothic patios that have invited intellectual contemplation for over 500 years. You can wander through on your own or take a **guided tour** (every 30–45 minutes daily, €2.50). Though it is in Spanish, it will take you into many beautiful nooks that you wouldn't find on your own.

If you come into the city by train, pop over to the eccentrically lush **Palacio Laredo** (Po. de la Estación 10, www.alcalaturismo.com/edificios/laredo.html, 10 A.M.–2 P.M. and 5–8 P.M. Tues.–Fri., 11 A.M.–2 P.M. and 5–8 P.M. Sat. and Sun., closed Mon., €3). Architect Manuel José de Laredo planned the palace as a living overview of all styles of Spanish architecture and painting. The exterior is a riot of gothic, Mudejar, Renaissance, and modern dotted with courtyards, gardens, and towers. The interior sports murals, frescos, geometric mosaics, and Plateresque treatments.

Food

Like fun with your food? Visit the boisterous **El Índalo** (C/ Libreros 9, tel. 91/882-4415, 9:30 A.M.–1:30 P.M. Tues.–Sun., closed Mon.). Featuring classic Spanish food in a classic dining room with a massive wood bar, this unassuming spot is the social hub of Alcalá. Everyone in town makes their way there at least once a week, but on Sundays it really rocks, when families line up to get in. The draw is good food, done right. And the trick to getting your fill is to stick to the bar. For each beer you order, you are offered a very large snack, from fried calamari to a pork cutlet sandwich. For a more refined experience, head to **Hostería del Estudiante** (C/ Colegios 3, tel. 91/888-0330, €20, 1–4 P.M. and 9–11 P.M. daily, closed Aug.) for classic Castilian cooking in a gorgeous 16th-century Mudejar building.

Information

The **Oficina de Turismo** (Pl. de Cervantes, tel. 91/889-2694, summer hours 10 A.M.–2 P.M. and 5–7:30 P.M. Tues.–Sun., closed Mon., winter hours 10 A.M.–2 P.M. and 4–6:30 P.M. daily) can provide maps and information as well as guided tours. If you want a tour with a little literary flavor, opt for the **Quijote Tour** led by costumed characters from the novel. It only operates sporadically, so call the office to check the schedule. English speakers are sometimes available. For complete information about the city and its events, visit www.lacallemayor.net. Even though the website is in Spanish, it is fairly easy to navigate.

Getting There

The easiest way to Alcalá is by the **Cercanías** regional train (less than €5 round-trip, about 30 min.) from Atocha. You can buy your ticket from the automated machines (just punch in Alcalá de Henares) or from the usually grumpy attendants at the ticket booth. From the Alcalá de Henares station, walk down Paseo del la Estación, about 10 minutes to the center.

The **Tren de Cervantes** (www.renfe.es/tren_cervantes, Sat. and Sun., Mar.–Dec., €17 adult, €12 under 11) is a fun way to see Alcalá. A costumed crew acts out scenes from *Don Quixote* and hands out sweets. It includes a guided tour of the city. The only catch is the schedule. It leaves Atocha station at 11 A.M. and doesn't leave Alcalá until 7 P.M. Plus, the plays and the tour are in Spanish.

ARANJUEZ

Barely 48 kilometers (30 miles) south of Madrid's rush and roar, Aranjuez is an oasis of serenity and refinement in a lush valley along the River Tajo. From the 17th to the 19th century it served as the springtime residence of the Spain's royal family. Today, it is a favorite Sunday trip for Madrid families who picnic in its many parks. The best time to come is in late spring or summer when the landscape is at its most verdant. The palaces and the gardens of Aranjuez were declared a UNESCO World Heritage Site in 2001. The gardens also inspired the classical composition *Concierto de Aranjuez* and in the summer the royal gardens host free classical concerts. You could spend the whole day here wandering the gardens and parks, but if it is sights you are after, you can easily tackle them all and still have time for a nice lunch in just half a day.

Sights

For both kings and tourists, the gleaming white **Palacio Real** (Pl. de Parejas, s/n, tel. 91/891-1344, www.patrimonionacional.es/en/aranj/aranjuez.htm, winter hours 10 A.M.–5:15 P.M. Tues.–Sun., summer hours 10 A.M.–6:15 P.M. Tues.–Sun., closed Mon. year-round, €4.50 without guide, €5 with guide) is the reason to travel to Aranjuez. Built about the same time as El Escorial and by the same architects, the Palace has a similar austerity to the monument, but is much more palatial. Rooms of note include the **Porcelain Room,** which features elaborate walls made of pure porcelain; the dramatic **Hall of Mirrors;** and the **Queen's Room,** where you can catch a glimpse of how the royal ladies lived.

Surrounding the Palacio Real are the **Jardines de Aranjuez** (winter hours 8 A.M.–6:30 P.M. daily, summer hours 8 A.M.–8:30 P.M. daily, free). Each of the gardens has its own charms, but they all feature beautiful landscaping, chirpings bird, acres of flowers, majestic trees, and ornate fountains. The **Jardín de la Isla** is located on a man-made island across from the palace. The **Jardín del Príncipe** also houses a museum of royal barges as well as the **Casa del Labrador,** the "Farmer's Cottage." This is a gross misnomer as the building is actually another royal palace constructed by Carlos IV as a miniature party palace. It is filled with the royal requisite of art, jewels, and priceless furnishings.

Food

Aranjuez is nationally renowned for its local produce, particularly its strawberries and asparagus. During peak season (spring and summer), you can pick up a box of *fresones,* extra-large strawberries to enjoy in the gardens. For something more substantial, try **Casa Pablete** (C/ Stuart 108, tel. 91/891-0381, €15) a traditional tapas bar near the center of town complete with wood paneling, red-tiled floors, and checkered tablecloths. The fried calamari is a house specialty. For something more upscale, try **Casa José** (C/ Abastos 32, tel. 91/891-1488, 1–4 P.M. and 9 P.M.–midnight Tues.–Sat., 1–4 P.M. Sun., closed Mon. and Aug., 40€), often hailed as Aranjuez's finest culinary destination. Try the honey-grilled lamb to start and coconut *croquetas* for dessert. The restaurant, situated in one of the neighborhood's older houses, was recently renovated. Even so, it remains on the smallish side, so it would be best to reserve in advance.

Information

In addition to the standard maps and restaurant flyers, the **Oficina de Turismo** (Pl. San Antonio 9, tel. 91/891-0427) has an interactive display on the history and development of Aranjuez. They also send *Chicos de Amarillo,* a force of yellow-shirted ambassadors, into the streets to help tourists. The city's Spanish-language website is **www.aranjuez.es.**

Getting There

About every 20 minutes, a **Cercanías** regional train (less than €5 round-trip, about 40 min.) from Atocha station departs to Aranjuez. Buy your ticket before boarding. Another option is the much-touted **Tren de la Fresa** (departs from Atocha station, tel. 90/224-0202, www .museodelferrocarril.org/tren_fresa/informacion.html, Sat. and Sun., Apr.–June, €24 adults, €16 under 12). An antique steam train takes you along one of Spain's oldest railway lines to Aranjuez. During the 50-minute voyage, attendants in period costume offer guests strawberries. It includes a guided tour of the palace (in Spanish). The train leaves Atocha at 10:05 A.M. and leaves Aranjuez at 6 P.M. Note, the train is not air-conditioned and can get hot.

CHINCHÓN

Big city Madrid can sometimes feels like it's lacking old-world charm. Luckily, the postcard-perfect town of Chinchón, with its arcaded plaza mayor and tiny winding streets, serves up charm by the plaza load. The main sight is the town itself and the heart of it all is **Plaza Mayor.** Wide and oval-shaped, the plaza dates from the 15th century and is hemmed in by old buildings that sport 234 balconies. Achingly picturesque, it has been featured in films and television commercials. In July and August, the plaza is cleared of people and cafés and filled with bulls and matadors, becoming the town's impromptu *plaza de toros.* Easter Saturday, the plaza hosts one of Spain's most elaborate religious celebrations, the **Pasion de Chinchón,** which includes a reenactment of the Last Supper, Christ's walk to the crucifixion, and the crucifixion itself. Hundreds of costumed participants take place including legions of Roman soldiers and peasant-robed Christians. Overlooking the plaza is the 15th-century **Iglesia De Nuestra Señora De La Asunción,** a rambling baroque church that boasts its very own Goya, the magnificent *La Asunción de la Virgen.*

For information on the services offered in the area, visit the **Oficina de Turismo** in the Plaza Mayor and which offers guided tours of the town. You can also visit the website **www .turismochinchon.nopanic.com** for more comprehensive information about the area in both English and Spanish.

Food and Accommodations

Plaza Mayor is ringed by dozens of restaurants specializing in *cordero* (lamb) roasted in wood-burning ovens. Though you can't go wrong at just about any of them, a gourmet-approved winner is **Meson de la Virreina** (Pl. Mayor 28, tel. 91/894-0015, www.mesonvirreyna .com, €30), a rustic tavern full of medieval history and lots of flavor. Start with the garlic soup, another local dish. Another atmospheric dining option is an underground *cueva* (cellar). **Mesón Cuevas del Vino** (C/ Benito Hortelano 13, tel. 91/894-0285, €25) is a local favorite with an extensive wine cellar to complement the traditional Castilian fare.

If you get lulled in by Chinchón's charm, stay the night at the **Parador** (C/ Huertos 1, tel. 91/894-0836, €120) set in a 17th-century convent. Closer to Plaza Mayor is the 200-year-old **La Posada del Arco** (C/ Morata 5–7, www.laposadadelarco.com, tel. 91/894-0581, €60).

Getting There

Your best bet into Chinchón is by bus. Head to the **Le Veloz bus company** (Av. Mediterráneo 49, Metro: Conde de Casal, tel. 91/409-7602). Look for the green Le Veloz buses on the left side of the street. They generally leave every hour on the hour. There will be two stops in Chinchón; be sure to get off at the second one, then just ask your way to Plaza Mayor.

CASTILLA-LA MANCHA

Surrounding Madrid on three sides and rolling out in vast sunburned fields in all directions, Castilla-La Mancha is both Spain's most famous landscape and its least known. The fame comes from literature's favorite daft Don. As any high school English student knows, Don Quixote (Quijote in Spanish) and his faithful sidekick Sancho Panza attacked windmills, fought sheep, and bravely defended the honor of the not-so-lovely Dulcinea all in the desolate backward land of La Mancha. Not much has changed since Cervantes penned the masterpiece in 1605. The land is still vast and brown, a monotonous spread of olive groves, vineyards, and wheat fields. Ancient windmills still stand on grassy rises, sundering an infinite sky. A scattering of dusty villages still move slowly, watching centuries go by. This is exactly why the region is unknown—there just

isn't much to see. Most tourists slice through La Mancha at top speed, headed for Valencia or Andalucía. The intrepid few who do stop, find a Spain caught in time—a peaceful, rustic land punctuated by some of the country's most important cultural heritage sights.

Outside of Cervantes's errant knight, the region's most important claim to fame is the medieval city of Toledo, which has served as a capital for Visigoths, Arabs, and Christians during more than 2,000 years of tumultuous history. Some hundred-plus kilometers to the east, where La Mancha rises into a disheveled mess of low hills, the medieval fortressed village of Cuenca is dramatically carved into the side of an ancient gorge. Both towns have been declared World Heritage Sites.

Like the land itself, the cuisine of Casti-

© BRANDON LANE FERGUSON

HIGHLIGHTS

◖ Catedral de Toledo: Falling just short of a world wonder, Toledo's cathedral is a monumental achievement of Gothic and medieval architecture. Take it in slowly and savor the chills it will give you (page 138).

◖ Judería: Toledo's atmospheric Jewish quarter is full of ancient alleyways, centuries-old synagogues, and gorgeous views over the gorge of the River Tagus. It is also home to El Greco's masterpiece *El Entierro del Conde de Orgaz* (page 139).

◖ Casas Colgadas: The medieval town of Cuenca has hung precariously on an outcropping of rock above two deep river gorges for more than 1,000 years. Its gravity-defying hanging houses are the town's most emblematic features (page 150).

◖ Consuegra: Straight out of a scene from Cervantes' *Don Quixote*, this tiny Manchego town sprawls beneath a row of 16th-century windmills and a rambling 13th-century castle — it is easily the most picturesque village in Castilla-La Mancha (page 155).

◖ Almagro: Thanks to the presence of royal bankers who made this tiny town their headquarters in the 17th century, Almagro boasts some of the most lavish architecture in the barren plains of Castilla-La Mancha. The Plaza Mayor and the Corral de Comedias should not be missed (page 155).

◖ El Toboso: As the only town to actually be named in *Don Quixote*, charming El Toboso – home of the mythical Dulcinea – is a must-visit for true fans of the world's most famous errant knight (page 158).

LOOK FOR ◖ TO FIND RECOMMENDED SIGHTS, ACTIVITIES, DINING, AND LODGING.

---

lla-La Mancha seems medieval—earthenware pots bubbling with thick soups, whole roasted game, hearty meat stews. Local agricultural products also figure large in the diet especially eggplants, artichokes, garlic, and saffron. If you get a chance try *pisto manchego,* a vegetable stew of tomatoes, red peppers, and garlic often topped with a fried quail's egg. *Gazpacho manchego* is nothing like the world-famous cold tomato soup of the same name. This simmering stew of rabbit, partridge, tomatoes, and garlic is served atop unleavened bread.

The region's most famous gastronomic export is the cheese known the world over as *queso manchego.* (*Manchego* is the adjective used for products or people from Castilla-La Mancha). Made from the milk of sheep that graze only on local farms, the cheese has been a staple of the region for centuries—and yes, the cheese does pop up in *Don Quixote.*

PLANNING YOUR TIME

A visit to Toledo is perhaps the most popular day trip from Madrid. However, it is a town

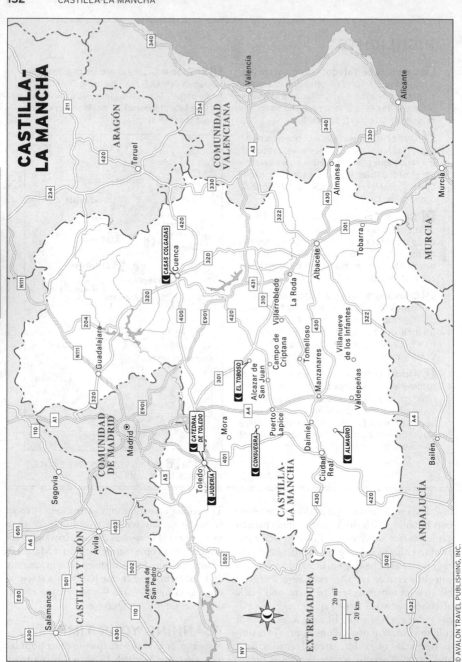

CASTILLA-LA MANCHA

© MARK DAGLISH

windmills and castles in Castilla-La Mancha

CASTILLA-LA MANCHA

best explored in the evening, after the hordes of bussed-in tourists have bussed back out. Consider spending the night. Head to Toledo after lunch, take in the sights before sunset, then return after dinner to see the medieval town dramatically lit up at night. The next morning you can be on a train to Madrid as early as 6 A.M. Just remember that many of Toledo's sights are closed on Mondays. If you have an extra day, Cuenca's dramatic hanging houses and tiny, twisting streets are a must-see. Whether you train, bus, or drive, the trip from Madrid runs about 2.5 hours each way, so it would be a hard pace for a day trip. Spend the night.

If you have two to three days to spare, rent a car in Toledo and take off in the footsteps of Don Quixote through tiny whitewashed villages, olive groves, and barren hills dotted with windmills—quite possibly the same ones that the daffy knight mistook for giants. This would be a trip into the real Spain, far from the *costa*-loving tourists and bussed-in day-trippers. It would be you, your car, and your

imagination let loose in a land seemingly untouched by either time or tourism.

HISTORY

Archaeological evidence indicates the Iber-Celts had camps throughout Castilla-La Mancha. The Romans later built a rather large settlement called Toletum on the site of present-day Toledo. When the Visigoths moved into the region in the 6th century, they also built their capital on present-day Toledo. Two centuries later when the Muslims rushed through Iberia, they too established a capital in Toledo. It is from this period that the region earned its current name. Mancha is derived from the Arabic word *al ansha,* which means "parched earth." The Muslim *taifa* (kingdom) of Toledo extended as far as the current boundaries of Castilla-La Mancha.

With the Christian Reconquista heating up throughout the 11th and 12th centuries, Castilla-La Mancha became a battlefront between the Christians and the Moors. Toledo fell to Christian forces in 1085. The fighting kept up until the famous 1212 Battle of Navas de Tolosa when Muslim forces were finally pushed out of Castilla-La Mancha. Following this victory, the region was lumped together with Madrid and named *Nueva Castilla,* New Castile. Old Castile was north of Madrid, roughly corresponding with the current region of Castilla y León.

Throughout the next few centuries, Nueva Castilla remained a land of warfare and peasantry. Forces tramped mercilessly through the land on their way to attack the Moors then entrenched in Andalucía. Meanwhile, smaller Christian fiefdoms fought each other for political power. Medieval fortresses throughout the region attest to this violent history. By the 1500s, Spain had been unified under one reign, and Toledo served as one of the kingdom's capital cities and the seat of the Catholic church in Spain.

When the king moved the capital permanently to Madrid in 1561, Toledo fell on hard times and there was a mass exodus out of the city. Over the next few centuries, famine throughout Castilla-La Mancha caused the region to become one of the most backward of the country.

During the Spanish Civil War, more despair fell on the region. Toledo was the sight of vicious fighting based at the Alcázar and many rural villages were devastated by the war. The poverty that gripped the country after the war also affected Castilla-La Mancha and again there was a mass exodus out of the countryside. In 1982, the region received status as one of Spain's autonomous regions and its current boundaries were drawn. Today, apart from Toledo and Cuenca, Castilla-La Mancha remains one of the least populated—and least visited—in Spain.

Toledo

The tiny town of Toledo packs a triple-whammy of culture. At its medieval height, Toledo was a center of literature, science, and language. Three cultures—Christian, Muslim, and Jewish—lived side by side, imprinting the town with their individual art and architecture. Two thousand years later, their remnants, including churches, synagogues, and medieval buildings, have turned Toledo into a living museum. Yet, despite the onslaught of daily visitors, the town maintains an elegant, proud air. For the tourist, there is no better place to experience such a wealth of Spanish history. Spanish poet Gregorio Marañón wrote, "Toledo is one of the few places in the world where it is no effort to dream." Tuck your map into your backpack and get lost in Toledo's magical streets and you'll understand what he meant.

SIGHTS
Whether you enter Toledo Monumental by foot or bus, you'll pass through the **Puerta de Bisagra,** which seems more like a palace than a gate with its coat of arms and stone towers.

It was built by Carlos I as an entrance to the town in 1550. Today, it still serves as the emblematic entryway to old Toledo. Further uphill, the **Puerta del Sol** is an 8th-century gate that once led to the Muslim medina.

Plaza Zocodóver
The name of this plaza derives from the Arabic word *souk* which means market, and for centuries this wedge-shaped square has been the commercial heart of old Toledo. East of the plaza is the **Museo Santa Cruz** (C/ Cervantes 3, tel. 92/522-1036, 10 A.M.–6:30 P.M. Mon.–Sat., 10 A.M.–2 P.M. Sun., free), a joyous Plateresque structure full of arches, echoing stone walkways, and meditative cloisters. Built at the beginning of the 16th century as a hospital, it now houses a haphazard collection of all things Toledo, from El Grecos to swords, religious artifacts to battle trophies. Seek out the spectacular *Asunción de la Virgen*. One of El Greco's most famed works, it shows Mary being swept up into heaven as medieval Toledo sleeps below.

THE SIEGE OF THE ALCÁZAR

At the time the Spanish Civil War broke out, Toledo's Alcázar was a military academy under the command of Colonel Jose Moscardó, a prominent Nationalist leader in the region. After receiving word that Francisco Franco had ordered a revolt by his military forces in a Nationalist bid to gain control of the country, the colonel called for all Civil Guard members in the region to amass at the Alcázar. After a State of War proclamation was read in Toledo on July 21, 1936, the town quickly fell into the hands of the Republican forces, who greatly outweighed Moscardó's troops. The colonel's motley crew included some 600 civil guards, 300 military cadets, and 100 right-wing civilian militia members. They were accompanied by over 600 civilians – mostly women and children – including the families of many of the Civil Guard troops.

The Alcázar was a potent symbol of Spain's military and a former royal residence. Capturing it would be a moral and symbolic victory for the Republicans who wanted both the military and the monarchy out of governmental affairs. The Nationalists viewed the Alcázar as a defense of their ideals and needed the victory to symbolize the strength and dominance of military Spain. Hence, the brutal fighting that followed was fueled by idealistic fervor and deep-rooted moral beliefs.

For over two months, the Republicans laid near-constant siege to the Alcázar. Bombs were dropped from the air, fires were set, grenades were launched, and food and supplies were cut off. The Nationalist troops managed to ward off each attack with a volley of rifle fire. Their resilience was due more to the solid construction of the Alcázar itself, rather than to the skill of the troops. By August, the Republicans, realizing that the building was impenetrable, began tunneling beneath it in order to attempt to bring it down with bombs. The explosions on September 18 greatly damaged the southwest tower but did not bring down the walls as the Republicans had hoped – an embarrassing fact caught by the journalists who had been invited by the Republicans to witness the event.

Less than 10 days later, Franco diverted Nationalist troops on their way to Madrid, into Toledo. They quickly took over the town and ended the siege. A few days later, Franco was declared *Generalissimo*, commander-in-chief of the military. The journalists were finally allowed to enter the Alcázar – at the invitation of the Nationalists. For the rest of the Civil War, and throughout Franco's nearly 40 years of dictatorship, the Alcázar was converted into a shrine to Nationalist bravery and heroism. Moscardó was lauded as a hero.

However, history is a slippery thing, especially when politics and passions are involved. Many of the Alcázar's most important moments are up for historical debate. In the first few days after the Nationalists entrenched themselves in the Alcázar, Moscardó is reported to have received a phone call from the Republican leader who promised to kill Moscardó's teenage son if the Alcázar was not immediately surrendered. Moscardó asked to speak with his son and then famously told him, "Commend your soul to God, shout 'Viva España,' and die like a hero." Some accounts claim the boy was shot immediately, others claim he was shot months later with a group of Nationalist prisoners, and still others claim the boy survived the war and moved to Madrid. True or not, the story became a powerful moment in Nationalist history, though quite coincidentally, the Christian soldier Guzmán El Bueno is reported to have said pretty much the same thing to his son during a 13th-century battle against Muslim forces in Tarifa.

Other inconsistencies in the history of the siege involve hostages. Republican historians have claimed that hundreds of innocent hostages were murdered inside the Alcázar. Nationalist sources give little account of hostages and attribute the few deaths among civilians in the Alcázar to natural causes.

Regardless of the facts, the Alcázar continues to be an imposing symbol of Spain's military history, even more so with the relocation of Spain's Army Museum to the Alcázar in 2007.

CASTILLA-LA MANCHA

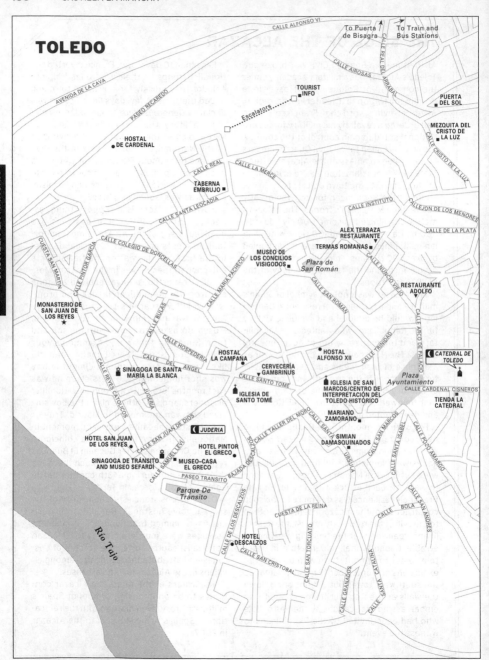

TOLEDO

CALLE ALFONSO VI

To Puerta de Bisagra

To Train and Bus Stations

CALLE AIROSAS

CALLE REAL DEL ARRABAL

AVENIDA DE LA CAVA

PASEO RECAREDO

TOURIST INFO

Escalators

PUERTA DEL SOL

HOSTAL DE CARDENAL

MEZQUITA DEL CRISTO DE LA LUZ

CALLE CHISTO DE LA LUZ

CALLE REAL

CALLE LA MERCE

TABERNA EMBRUJO

CALLE SANTA LEOCADIA

CALLE INSTITUTO

CALLEJON DE LOS MENORES

CALLE DE LA PLATA

ALEX TERRAZA RESTAURANTE

CALLE PINTOR GARCIA

CALLE COLEGIO DE DONCELLAS

TERMAS ROMANAS

MUSEO DE LOS CONCILIOS VISIGODOS

Plaza de San Román

CUESTA SAN MARTIN

CALLE MARIA PACHECO

CALLE NUNCIO VIEJO

RESTAURANTE ADOLFO

CALLE SAN ROMAN

MONASTERIO DE SAN JUAN DE LOS REYES

CALLE BULAS

CALLE TRINIDAD

CALLE ARCO DE PALACIO

CALLE HOSPEDERIA

HOSTAL LA CAMPANA

HOSTAL ALFONSO XII

CATEDRAL DE TOLEDO

CALLE DEL ANGEL

CERVECERÍA GAMBRINUS

CALLE SANTO TOME

Plaza Ayuntamiento

CALLE REYES CATOLICOS

C. JUDERIA

SINAGOGA DE SANTA MARÍA LA BLANCA

IGLESIA DE SANTO TOMÉ

IGLESIA DE SAN MARCOS/CENTRO DE INTERPRETACIÓN DEL TOLEDO HISTÓRICO

CALLE CARDENAL CISNEROS

TIENDA LA CATEDRAL

MARIANO ZAMORANO

SIMIAN DAMASQUINADOS

CALLE SAN MARCOS

CALLE SANTA ISABEL

CALLE POZO AMARGO

HOTEL SAN JUAN DE LOS REYES

CALLE SAN JUAN DE DIOS

JUDERIA

CALLE TALLER DEL MORO

CALLE SANTA URSULA

SINAGOGA DE TRÁNSITO AND MUSEO SEFARDI

HOTEL PINTOR EL GRECO

MUSEO-CASA EL GRECO

CALLE SAMUEL LEVI

BAJADA DESCALZOS

PASEO TRANSITO

Parque De Tránsito

CALLE SAN ANDRES

CALLE SAN GRANADOS

CALLE SANTA CATALINA

CALLE BOLA

CUESTA DE LA REINA

Río Tajo

HOTEL DESCALZOS

CALLE DE LOS DESCALZOS

CALLE SAN CRISTOBAL

CALLE SAN TORCUATO

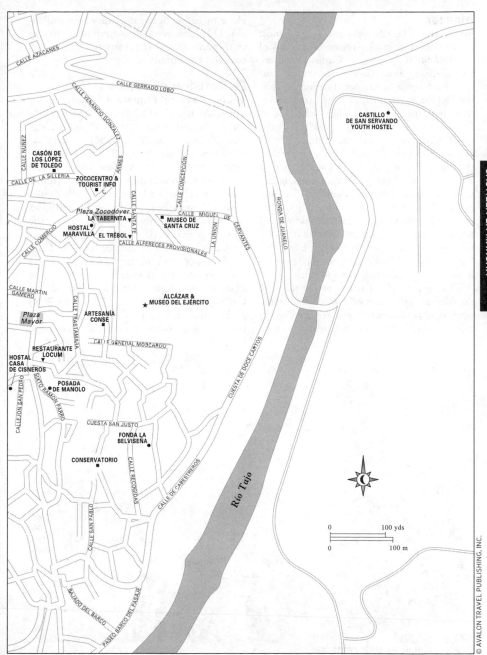

© AVALON TRAVEL PUBLISHING, INC.

CASTILLA-LA MANCHA

CALLE AZACANES

CALLE GERRADO LOBO

CALLE VENANCIO GONZALEZ

CALLE NUÑEZ

CASÓN DE
LOS LÓPEZ
DE TOLEDO

CALLE DE LA SILLERÍA

ZOCOCENTRO &
TOURIST INFO

ARMES

CALLE CONCEPCIÓN

CASTILLO
DE SAN SERVANDO
YOUTH HOSTEL

RONDA DE JUANELO

Plaza Zocodóver
LA TABERNITA

CALLE SANTA FE

CALLE MIGUEL DE CERVANTES

MUSEO DE
SANTA CRUZ

HOSTAL
MARAVILLA   EL TRÉBOL

CALLE COMERCIO

LA UNIÓN

CALLE ALFERECES PROVISIONALES

CALLE MARTIN
GAMERO

Plaza
Mayor

CALLE TRASTAMARA

ARTESANÍA
CONSE

ALCÁZAR &
MUSEO DEL EJÉRCITO

CUESTA DE DOCE CANTOS

RESTAURANTE
LOCUM

CALLE GENERAL MOSCARDU

HOSTAL
CASA
DE CISNEROS

CALLEJON SAN PEDRO

SIXTO RAMON PARRO

POSADA
DE MANOLO

CUESTA SAN JUSTO

FONDA LA
BELVISEÑA

CONSERVATORIO

CALLE RECOGIDAS

CALLE DE CABESTREROS

Río Tajo

CALLE SAN PABLO

0   100 yds

0   100 m

BAJADO DEL BARCO

PASEO BARCO DEL PASAJE

Alcázar

Just south of Plaza Zocodóver is Toledo's most recognizable landmark—the imposing hulk of the **Alcázar** (C/ Cuesta de Carlos V, s/n, tel. 92/522-1673). Since Roman rule, there has always been some sort of fortification on this, the highest point in the city. Its current form took shape under Carlos I when he had it outfitted as his royal residence in 1535. After the court moved to Madrid, the building served as a military barracks and a prison. It reached the pinnacle of its infamy during the Spanish Civil War when a group of Franco's Republican troops barricaded themselves inside. (See sidebar *The Siege of the Alcázar.*) Since 2005, it has been undergoing massive renovations to house Spain's extensive **Museo del Ejército** (military museum) and is expected to open late 2007. Check www.t-descubre.com for the latest information on opening hours and prices.

The steep tangle of streets to the south of the Alcázar is the heart of Toledo's traditional working-class district. If you are tired of the crowds, head here and in moments you'll be alone in streets nearly unchanged for millennia. There are several dirt-cheap places to stay in this area as well as a smattering of low-key bars and restaurants.

◖ Catedral de Toledo

Toledo's **Catedral Primada** (C/ Cardenal Cisneros, s/n, tel. 92/522-2241, www.architoledo.org/cathedral, 10:30 A.M.–6:30 P.M. Mon.–Sat., 10 A.M.–2 P.M. Sun., €5.50) achieves the miraculous by out-awing all of the other jaw-dropping sights in Toledo. Built between 1226 and 1492, it is one of the world's largest Gothic structures, about 1.5 kilometers (nearly a mile) long. Get your bearings by walking around the building first. You'll be amazed how the massive structure fits so snugly into the surrounding streets. The exterior is a riot of flying buttresses and soaring spires topped by a 300-foot tower. Get your best photos at the Plaza Ayuntamiento. On the north side on Calle Chapinería, look for the **Puerta de Reloj** tucked into a courtyard. Built in the 13th century, this is the oldest of the cathedral's doors.

Toledo's looming Gothic cathedral

© CANDY LEE LABALLE

On the opposite side of the building, check out the **Puerta de los Leones,** an exquisite entryway guarded by stone lions carved in 1460. Before heading inside, you'll have to buy a ticket at the **Tienda la Catedral,** across from the main tourist entrance on Calle Cardenal Cisneros. There is a long line most days, though Wednesday evenings, when it is free for Spanish citizens, tend to be the worst.

Once inside you'll be hit by the sheer grandiosity of the lofty space rising nearly 50 yards and held up by 88 stone columns. The main cathedral is dominated by the exquisitely carved wooden *coro* (choir stalls). A testament to the church's shared past with warfare, the seats of the lower choir depict the long battle to wrest control of Spain from the Moors. Each seat is emblazoned with the name of the towns conquered by Christian forces culminating in the 1492 conquest of Granada. The upper choir is carved with scenes of the gospels of Christ. The railing was built in the 1540s and is considered one of the world's finest examples of Renaissance ironwork. Across from the *coro* is the **Capilla Mayor** which houses the main altar, a 15th-century feast of gold and religious artwork rising to the ceiling. The most intriguing feature was added some 200 years later. Church leaders decided the cathedral was too gloomy during mass and that what was needed was a ray of sunshine. Baroque architect Narciso Tomé was brought in and two holes were cut—one in the Capilla Mayor and another in the cathedral's roof. Tomé and his four sons turned the gaping holes into the artistic masterpiece now called the *transparente.* Finished in 1732, it is a whimsical wreath of angels, sunbursts, and flourishes that capture the imagination. At least it did for one long-dead cardinal. Before dying, a Spanish cardinal is allowed to choose the final resting spot for his red hat. The bit of cloth hanging near the *transparente* belonged to just such a cardinal. There are several more hats in the cathedral, but this one has the best location.

The *sacristía* houses works by El Greco, Rubens, Michelangelo, and Goya. The highlight is El Greco's 1577 *El Expolio,* which depicts Christ being stripped of his regal red robe before the crucifixion. Over in the tesoro (treasury), also called the Capilla de la Torre, gape at the 400-plus pound monstrance, a vessel specifically designed to display the consecrated Host (communion wafers) before the faithful. This monstrance, made of solid gold, silver, diamonds, emeralds, and rubies, could rightly be called a monstrosity of religious opulence. During the celebration of Corpus Christi, it is paraded through Toledo on a special cart that keeps it from falling over despite the medieval twists and dips of the town's streets.

After leaving the Catedral, make a beeline for the nearby Iglesia de San Marcos which houses the **Centro de Interpretación del Toledo Histórico** (C/ Trinidad 7, tel. 92/522-1616, 10 A.M.–7 P.M. Tues.–Sat., 10:30 A.M.–1:30 P.M. Sun., €4). The excellent program "Keys to Toledo" gives a comprehensive overview of Toledo's cultural history with three-dozen interactive displays.

Judería

Located in the southwestern corner of the town, the Jewish Quarter is a lovely mess of twisting streets barely wide enough for cars, let alone the horses and donkeys that once clapped along its cobblestones. At the height of Toledo's famed tolerance for its three cultures, this barrio was a lively zone with nearly a dozen synagogues. After the forced expulsion of the Jews in 1492, they were destroyed or converted into Catholic churches.

The two most-visited sights in the Judería are memorials to Toledo's most famous adopted son—El Greco. (See sidebar, *The Greek in Toledo.*) The painter created his most famous works in Toledo, not the least of these is the 1586 masterpiece *El Entierro del Conde de Orgaz,* which depicts the 1312 burial of the Count of Orgaz. In the top half of the painting, the heavens open up to receive the count's soul. Across the center, in attendance is a row of Spanish nobility from the time that El Greco painted the work. The artist himself is included, seventh from the left, looking directly at the viewer. At the center of the work, Saint

THE GREEK IN TOLEDO

El Greco was born Dominikos Theotokópulos in 1541 in Crete. In the 1560s, he trained in Renaissance techniques in Venice under the famous Spanish court painter Titian. Some of his earliest works are strongly influenced by the Venetian master. After a few years in Rome studying the works of Michelangelo, among others, he moved to Toledo in 1577. There he became known as El Greco, Spanish for "the Greek."

El Greco received his first Spanish commission almost upon landing in Spain – the sumptuous 1577 *Asunción de la Virgen*, now housed in Toledo's Museo Santa Cruz. The work marks the beginning of El Greco's departure from the Italianate schools and the emergence of his own distinctive style. Despite his local success, he desperately wanted to land a commission for El Escorial, the massive retreat that Felipe II was building outside of Madrid. El Greco sent the king two paintings, but the king rejected them, and the painter remained in Toledo.

El Greco had friends in the Catholic church in Toledo and soon landed a commission to paint *El Expolio* for the cathedral. Though his painting was accepted, the high price he demanded for it caused church leaders to haul El Greco to court. Throughout his career, El Greco was sued for overcharging for his work. This did not seem to dampen the demand for his painting, and it definitely did not hurt El Greco's lavish lifestyle. He and his Toledo-born wife lived in a palace near the Paseo del Tránsito and regularly entertained the region's most highbrow citizens, including politicians, nobles, and writers.

In 1586, El Greco completed the work that he is most famous for, *El Entierro del Conde de Orgaz*, which has hung in its current spot in Iglesia Santo Tomé for over 400 years. In it, some of El Greco's most distinctive painterly traits are obvious – elongated figures, tightly filled spaces, a hint of mysticism, and a move away from the realism that so obsessed his contemporaries.

El Greco was enamored of his adopted hometown and repeatedly painted it, both as a landscape and as a backdrop to other scenes – he once painted the crucifixion of Christ against the Toledo skyline. One of his most famous paintings – instantly recognizable to Art History 101 students – is the moody *View of Toledo*, which hangs in the Metropolitan Museum of Art in New York. Under a tumultuous sky, Toledo slumbers as only El Greco could see it, with the cathedral magically moved to the left of the Alcázar.

During El Greco's last years, he continued to develop his style, focusing more on religious paintings with an aim to portray the spiritual emotion of the images rather than realistic representations. One of the most famous examples is *La Adoración de los Pastores*, completed in 1614, the year of his death. Painted for his burial chamber, the painting has an eerie shimmer that seems to emanate from within. It is now resident in Madrid's Museo del Prado, while the painter rests his eternal bones in Toledo's Monasterio de Santo Domingo el Antiguo.

Augustine and Saint Stephen carry the dead count to his grave. The boy pointing at the miraculous event is El Greco's son. The painting is located in the antechamber of the 14th-century **Iglesia de Santo Tomé** (Pl. Conde, s/n, tel. 92/525-6098, 10 A.M.–5:45 P.M. daily, €1.90). The only other notable feature of the church is its exquisite Mudejar tower. A few steps away is the **Museo-Casa El Greco** (C/ Samuel Leví, s/n, tel. 92/522-4405, 10 A.M.–2 P.M. and 4–6 P.M. Tues.–Sat., 10 A.M.–2 P.M. Sun., €2.40). Though the artist never resided here, the house recreates the era in which he lived. It also houses several of his works.

Next door to the El Greco museum is the **Sinagoga de Tránsito** (C/ Samuel Leví, s/n, tel. 92/522-3665, 10 A.M.–2 P.M. and 4–6 P.M. Tues.–Sat., extended hours in summer, €2.40). The synagogue is a perfect example of Toledo's mix of cultures. It was built in 1366 under special order of the Castilian King Pedro I, a Christian Monarch. The builders were Muslims and their imprint is visible in the main chamber of the synagogue, particularly in the exquisitely carved ceiling and walls. The attached **Museo Sefardí** (the name Sefardí comes from Sepharad, the Hebrew word for Spain) demonstrates in artifacts and art the long history of Jews in Spain. Be sure to take a break in the **Parque de Tránsito** just across the street from the synagogue. It sits on a rocky gorge overlooking a deep bend in the River Tagus. A few blocks away is another surviving synagogue, the 12th-century **Sinagoga Santa María Blanca** (C/ Reyes Católicos 4, tel. 92/522-7257, 10 A.M.–6 P.M. daily, €1.90). It is an intimate space delineated by a series of intricately carved Moorish arches. In 1405, it was converted into a Christian temple. The wooden altar dating from the mid-14th century depicts the story of John the Baptist.

The Jewish Quarter also houses one of Toledo's most magnificent Christian buildings, the **Monasterio de San Juan de los Reyes** (C/ San Juan de los Reyes 2, tel. 92/522-3802, 10 A.M.–6 P.M. daily, €1.90). Built in 1476, it is a gorgeous example of Gothic perfection. The star-shaped interior dome is notable, but the true joy lies in wandering the elaborately carved cloisters that surround a garden sporting a lone orange tree. The northern wall of the church is covered in the shackles that held Christian prisoners liberated from the Moors in the battle for Granada.

Northwest Toledo

In the streets to the north of the Judería and west of the Cathedral, you'll find a Toledo a bit less tourist trampled. Punctuated by Renaissance churches, this area is your best bet for getting lost among the locals. It is also a good place to learn about Toledo's earliest history. The **Museo de los Concilios Visigodos** (Pl. San Román, s/n, tel. 92/522-7872, 10 A.M.–2 P.M. and 3:30–6:15 P.M. Tues.–Sat., 10 A.M.–2 P.M. Sun., €0.60) recounts Toledo's Visigothic past through artifacts and interactive displays. A few blocks away, the **Termas Romanas** (Pl. Amador de los Ríos, tel. 92/525-3080, 10 A.M.–2 P.M. and 5–9 P.M. Tues.–Sat., 10 A.M.–2 P.M. Sun.) houses a cultural center on the sight of Roman ruins. It also organizes

tours of Toledo's archaeological sites. For a bit of Muslim culture, work your way north to the **Mezquita del Cristo de la Luz** (C/ Cuesta de Carmelitas Descalzos 10, tel. 92/525-4191, 10 A.M.–2 P.M. and 3:30–6 P.M. daily, €1.90), a 10th-century mosque with grand marble columns and Visigothic architectural details.

Sightseeing in Toledo

To arrange a private tour of Toledo, contact a guide through www.guiasdetoledo.es. Prices begin at €130 for three hours and do not include entrance fees for monuments. There are several companies offering thematic tours of Toledo and its surroundings; you'll see their colored flyers all over town. One of the best is **Entorno Toledo** (C/ Cuesta de la Ciudad 5, tel. 92/525-4125, info@entornotoledo.com, www .entornotoledo.com, 10 A.M.–10 P.M. daily). The charming Julián Baños has put together a team of official tour guides, historians, and researchers to create everything from the standard tour through the three cultures of Toledo to specialized walks that mine the town's rich

an ancient alleyway snakes through Toledo

© CANDY LEE LABALLE

history from the Visigoths to the Inquisition, the medieval to the mystical. Their night tours are highly recommended, but be sure to take the later one that runs well after sunset. Tours cost €15–25 per person.

Design your own self-guided tour by visiting www.t-descubre.com and clicking on "t-routes." These routes can also be found in the free magazine *T-Descubre,* available at hotels, restaurants, and tourist offices throughout the city.

The newest way to see Toledo is on a **Segway** (www.e-tur.es, tel.66/774-4494, €35). The 1.5 hour "glide" leaves from Plaza Zocodóver and includes a 15-minute training session. Minimum age is 12 and groups are limited to seven people. English is spoken, but take note—under Toledo's strict tour guide regulations, this is not considered a tour and very little information on sights is given.

For a good overview of the town, including spectacular views from the other side of the river, hop on the **Zocotren** (C/ Sillería 14, tel. 92/522-0300, www.zocotren.com, 11 A.M.–midnight daily, €3.45, children €2.10) for a mini-train tour of the town. Yes, it is goofy-looking, but it is worth chucking your vanity down your backpack and grabbing a seat. Try this at the start of your day to get your bearings, or do a nighttime tour when your feet just can't take the cobblestones anymore.

ENTERTAINMENT AND EVENTS
Nightlife
Toledo's nightlife is scattered throughout the old town. Ask your hotel receptionist or just go wandering. For a pleasant early evening try **Bar Enebro** (Pl. Santiago de los Caballeros 1, 9 A.M.–12:30 A.M. Mon.–Fri., 11 A.M.–1 A.M. Sat.–Sun.). This friendly spot draws as many locals as tourists. Its motto is "you don't drink, you don't eat," and each beer comes with a massive free tapa. A sister location, **Enebro 2** (Pl. San Justo 9), is a bit more low-key with a large terrace.

Things heat up in a trio of über-cool clubs. **Café Teatro Pícaro** (C/ Cadenas 6, 3 P.M.–4 A.M. daily) starts out as a laid-back cof-

fee house and segues into a late-night dance club. As the name implies, there are also live performances from theater to jazz. The sleek **Garcilaso Club** (C/ Rojas 5, 3 P.M.–1 A.M. Sun.–Wed., 3 P.M.–6 A.M. Thurs.–Sat.) hosts top-notch DJs and up-and-coming Spanish indie rockers. **Círculo del Arte** (Pl. San Vicente 3, tel. 92/521-2981, 10 A.M.–2:30 A.M. Mon.–Wed., 10 A.M.–6 A.M. Thurs.–Sat., noon–3 A.M. Sun.) is a striking example of modern pleasures mixed with antique treasures. This coffee house/art gallery/disco is set in a 13th-century Mudejar temple. You couldn't pick a more atmospheric setting for breakfast or dancing until dawn.

Festivals and Events
Toledo's most famous festival is the magical **Corpus Christi** held the ninth Sunday after Easter, which usually falls near the end of May, or the beginning of June. The festival's origins lie in the 13th century and it has been going strong in Toledo since then. The main event is the parading of the elaborate monstrance from the cathedral through the streets. In the days leading up to this religious display, the town is decked out in flowers, streets are covered with white awnings, balconies are draped in tapestries, and miles of twinkling lights are strung. The day before the event, the ground is covered in flower petals and fragrant herbs. On Corpus Christi Sunday, hundreds of costumed marchers precede the monstrance through crowds burning incense and chanting ancient hymns.

Closely following Corpus Christi in religious significance is the annual **Semana Santa** processions. (See sidebar *All About Semana Santa* in the *Andalucía* chapter.) As in most towns throughout Spain, robed penitents march through the streets each night in the week leading up to Easter. As they solemnly wind through the darkened town, carrying heavy wooden crosses, candles, and incense, Toledo is eerily transported back to the medieval ages.

Mid-August ushers in the festivals of the **Virgen del Sagrario,** celebrating the patron saint of Toledo with a week of street parties, concerts, and religious events. The cathedral opens up its well to the public and lines snake for blocks with Toledanos hoping for a swig of the miraculous water.

SHOPPING

Walking around Toledo, it is hard not to bump into a centuries-old monument. When you do, you'll ricochet right onto a souvenir shop. They are everywhere and prices range from a few centimos to thousands of euros, with quality just as broad. The best bet for a unique purchase is a piece of *damasquinado* (damascene) metalwork. Popular in the 15th century, the art has Arabic origins and consists in hammering threads of gold or silver into iron, creating intricate patterns. Pieces can be as large as shields or as small as lapel pins. Try **Simian Damasquinados** (C/ Santa Úrsula 6, tel. 92/525-1054) where there are sometimes craftspeople on hand to demonstrate the technique. Another favorite purchase is a fabled Toledo sword. For centuries, warriors throughout Europe sought to own a Toledo sword. Nowadays, they are produced mainly for collectors, tourists, and film productions. A good place to buy is **Mariano Zamorano** C/ Ciudad 19, tel. 92/522-2634), a family-owned shop that is a museum in itself. Since the 16th century, the nearby town of Talavera de la Reina has been making rustic pottery distinguished by its bright blues and yellows. A good source is **Artesanía Conse** (C/ Horno de los Bizcochos 7, tel. 92/522-7678), which does a nice job in reproducing antique designs.

If you are in town on a Tuesday, be sure to visit the bustling **flea market** that unfurls on Paseo de Marchen not far from the Puerta de Bisagra.

ACCOMMODATIONS
Under €50

◖ **Hotel Descalzos** (C/ Descalzos 30, tel. 92/522-2888, descalzo@hostaldescalzos.com www.hostaldescalzos.com, €48) is an unassuming gem. It doesn't look like much upon entry—a fluorescent-lit lobby, black leather furniture. Spirits don't pick up much with the plain Jane room fittings. However, if you score

a room with a view, your window will overlook a bend in the Tagus river where it is crossed by the 14th-century San Martín bridge. When it is lit up at night, it is stunning. Even if you don't get a room with a view, this tiny hotel makes up for it with the only pool in the old center. Full of whirlpool jets and set in a charming terracotta terrace, this is the perfect place to relax after a day of sightseeing. **Hostal Maravilla** (Pl. Barrio Rey 7, tel. 92/522-8582, informacion@ hotel-maravilla.com, www.hotel-maravilla .com, €44) is a cheap charmer right off of Plaza Zocodóver on a pedestrian alleyway. It features all the basic amenities at basic prices. Set in a 10th-century castle first built by the Moors, **Castillo de San Servando** (tel. 92/522-4554, alberguesclm@jccm.es, www.reaj.com, €11 per bunk) is one of the most lavish accommodations you'll find in Toledo. As a member of Hostelling International (HI), it is also one of the cheapest. You must be an HI member to stay here, but you can get buy your card from reception. You don't need to be under 26 to stay here, but if you are, your nightly rate will be less than €10. Rooms are spacious, bathrooms are immaculate, the pool is refreshing, and the views are jaw-dropping. It is about a 15-minute uphill hike out of the city center, but you can take local bus 11. If you prefer to be in town and still want to stick to a strict budget, the **Fonda La Belviseña** (C/ Cuesta del Can 5, tel. 92/522-0067, €20) is an ancient warren of bare-bones rooms with lumpy beds. Sinks are included, but showers and toilets are shared down the hall. It is very popular with students. If you are lugging a heavy backpack, be aware, the Fonda is up a steep alley south of the Alcázar that taxis can't access.

€50-100

◖ **Posada de Manolo** (C/ Sixto Ramón Parro 8, tel. 92/528-2250, toledo@laposadade manolo.com, www.laposadademanolo.com, €70, breakfast included) is one of those places you never forget. Heart-achingly charming, this tiny inn of 14 rooms is just a few blocks from the cathedral. Each of the three floors takes its decorating cue from the three cultures of Toledo—Arabic, Christian, and Jewish. On the first floor, the Arabic room "Los Curtidores" boasts its own tiled patio. Upper floors look out onto the street. The best view is to be had from the top-floor dining room where you look over the roof of the cathedral while sipping your morning coffee. **Hostal Casa de Cisneros** (C/ Cardenal Cisneros 1, tel. 92/522-8828, marjo@hostal-casa-de-cisneros.com, www.hostal-casa-de-cisneros.com, €80) is a 10-room inn tucked into a 16th-century townhouse just steps from the cathedral. The ground floor features a glass floor looking into the basement of the 9th-century Muslim structure that once stood here. Rooms are small, but location and ambience can't be beat. **Hostal Alfonso XII** (C/ Alfonso XII 18, tel. 92/525-2509, info@hostal-alfonso12.com, www.hostal-alfonso12.com, €60, breakfast included) is tucked inside a traditional Toledo home in the Judería. With only six cozy rooms, this family-run inn features personal attention and lovely balconies overlooking an ancient alleyway. Another inexpensive option is **La Campana** (C/ La Campana 10–12, tel. 92/522-1659, reservas@hostalcampana.com, www.hostalcampana.com, €60), located right across from the Iglesia de Santo Tomé. Rooms are nicely furnished and the restaurant is quite good.

Over €100

Hotel Pintor El Greco (C/ Alamillos del Tránsito, 13, tel. 92/528-5191, info@hotelpintorelgreco.com, www.hotelpintorelgreco.com, €115) is a charming 40-room hotel set in a 17th-century building that once housed a bakery. Located on the edge of the Judería, the hotel seems more like a furnishing store cluttered with local pottery, thick-knotted carpets, and cushy sofas. The spacious rooms are pure rustic comfort with excellent mattresses. Located close to the Puerta de Bisagra, **Hostal del Cardenal** (Po. Recaredo 24, tel. 92/522-4900, cardenal@hostaldelcardenal.com, www.hostaldelcardenal.com, €106) is an atmo-

spheric hotel tucked into an 18th-century mansion that was built for a former archbishop of Toledo. While the rooms are nice enough, the real draw is the elegant courtyard and gardens. The stately restaurant, featuring classic Castilian dishes, has long been synonymous with upscale dining in Toledo. Though below the city walls, the hotel is just yards away from the base of the escalators that go up into the old town. **Hotel San Juan de los Reyes** (C/ Reyes Católicos, 5, tel. 92/528-3535, info@hotel-sanjuandelosreyes.com, www.hotel-sanjuandelosreyes.com, €150) is a gorgeous new hotel that elegantly combines its antiquated facade with modern touches. Located on the edge of the Judería in a building that once housed a sword factory, it features tastefully appointed rooms—be sure to ask for one with a view—and an extremely accommodating staff.

The **Parador de Toledo** (Cerro de Emperador, s/n, tel. 92/522-1850, toledo@parador.es, €150) is one of the most famous paradors (state-run, luxury hotels in reformed palaces) in Spain. The rooms are exquisitely appointed, however the real draw is the spectacular view of old Toledo over the river. Insist on a room with a view. This is said to be the point where El Greco painted his famous landscape of the city. The restaurant is lovely, but the food is so-so at best and quite overpriced. Have breakfast here and meals in town. The Parador is located about 3.2 kilometers (two miles) outside of the old city, which means a €7 cab or a quick bus ride. The Parador will be undergoing renovations into 2008, during which time rooms will be limited and the pool closed. If it is booked, try the **Best Western Hotel Domenico** (Cerro del Emperador, s/n, tel. 92/528-0101, http://bestwestern.worldexecutive.com, €123) right next door. Again, be sure to request a room with a view over old Toledo.

FOOD

Toledo's cuisine is inextricably entwined with the surrounding land—wild game and fresh produce combined with local flavorings such

AN ANCIENT TASTE OF TOLEDO

Throughout Toledo, you'll see signs hawking *mazapán*. Marzipan, as it's known in English, is a deceptively simple treat made from just two ingredients – sugar and almonds. Spanish law dictates that premium-quality marzipan consist of at least 50 percent almonds. With over 50 species of almond grown in Spain, and dozens of producers dedicated to marzipan production, the varieties are endless. A "love it or hate it" sweet, marzipan is traditionally eaten Christmas day. It is often molded into shapes and figures and then painted with edible coloring. Leonardo da Vinci often used marzipan to create sculptures and models. Unfortunately, his royal employers found the artworks irresistible and promptly devoured anything the great artist made.

In addition to Spain, top world producers are Italy, Germany, Cyprus, and Iraq, though true marzipan aficionados swear that Toledo produces the best. But where does marzipan come from? If you ask around Toledo, you'll be pointed to the local order of San Clemente nuns. Legend has it that back in the Middle Ages when famines where whipping through Castilla-La Mancha, the clever nuns concocted a dough by crushing almonds and mixing them with sugar. This nutritional manna not only helped them survive, but also gave them a way to make a little money on the side. It has also fueled the Toledo marzipan trade. Today, convents throughout Toledo still churn out tons of the chewy sweets all year long.

Of course, reality is long-removed from legend. Historical documents indicate that marzipan was made in the Arab world as far back as the 700s. The Muslim rulers who took up residence in Spain in the 8th century brought with them sugarcane and almond trees. It is most likely from them that the tradition of marzipan arrived in Toledo. By the 11th century, Toledo's *mozarabes* (Christians who lived under Muslim rule in Spain) wrote of eating marzipan at Christmas time. It is true that the nuns of various convents, including San Clemente, began to make marzipan in the Middle Ages – they just didn't invent it.

Today, Toledo imports hundreds of tons of almonds from Valencia each year to produce their world-quality marzipan. Variations to try are: *huesos de santos* (literally, saint's bones), thin tubes of marzipan filled with a paste made from sweetened pumpkin; *empiñonadas*, small logs of marzipan rolled in pine nuts and baked; and *delicias de mazapán*, crescent shapes filled with a creamy egg-yolk center.

The most famous place to buy marzipan is **Santo Tomé** (C/ Santo Tomé 3, tel. 92/522-3763), run by the same family since 1856. There are two other locations in town, including one right on Plaza Zocodóver. Check out their window displays, which feature Toledo monuments rendered completely in marzipan. You can also visit any one of the convents scattered throughout the northwest part of the city. Try **Convento de Santa Rita** (C/ Santa Úrsula). Pick your choice from the display window, then press the buzzer under the sign that says *venta aquí*. A nun will appear behind the lazy susan. Tell her what you want and put your money down. She'll spin your treats right out to you. When you take your first taste, remember that you are biting into a thousand-year-old taste of Toledo tradition.

as saffron, garlic, and almonds. Many dishes seem straight out of the Middle Ages. The most popular local offering is *perdiz* (partridge), often served *estofada* (stewed) or with *pochas* (large white beans). *Carcamusas,* a stew of venison and tomatoes, and *cochifrito,* stewed lamb with tomatoes, saffron, and white wine, are also local standards. Vegetarians can stick to locally raised artichokes and roasted red peppers.

Cafés and Desserts
Café-Bar Toledo (Pl. Zocodóver 11, tel. 92/522-5557, 7:30 A.M.–2 A.M. daily, €8) is located right on Plaza Zocodóver. Despite the absolute crush of tourists, this bar still very much caters to locals with €3 breakfasts and basic tapas and sandwiches served all day. The terrace out front is a perfect place to watch the town bustle by. **Café Bar Osiris** (Pl. Barrio

Nuevo 2, tel. 92/525-4400, 8 A.M.–midnight daily, €8) is a no-nonsense breakfast or coffee stop over in the Judería.

Local Cuisine

Adolfo (C/ Granada 6, tel. 92/522-7321, 1–4 P.M. and 8 P.M.–midnight Tues.–Sat., 8 P.M.–midnight Sun., closed Mon., €60) has been Toledo's most famous dining room for decades. Consistently rated at the top of the Campsa scale (Spain's version of Michelin), Adolfo features classic Toledano fare in a lovingly restored 14th-century home. The wine cellar boasts over 17,000 bottles, but don't worry, the impeccable staff will help you narrow it down. Their stellar dish is *perdiz en dos vinos* (partridge in two wines). For dessert you have to try their marzipan selection, hand-made by the pastry chef. Devotees of this almond treat swear that Adolfo's are the best. (See sidebar, *An Ancient Taste of Toledo.*)

In recent years, several newcomers have risen up to challenge Adolfo as the city's top dining destination. The best of the lot is **Casón de los López de Toledo** (C/ Sillería 3, tel. 92/525-4774, 1:30–4:30 P.M. and 8:30–11 P.M. Mon.–Sat., 1:30–4:30 P.M. Sun., €40). Set in a gorgeously reformed home, the dining room offers classic local fare with modern touches—roasted lamb with a vinaigrette of fennel, chocolate cake with saffron ice cream. The setting rivals the food. Each floor has been done to reflect the three cultures of Toledo and is packed with art and antiques (all for sale by the way). The ground floor opens onto an inner courtyard and features a café that is open 9 A.M.–midnight daily. At night, the basement cave turns into a lively dance club (9 P.M.–2 A.M. Mon.–Sat., closed Sun.). Another good bet for upscale local fare is **Locum** (C/ Locum 6, tel. 92/522-0334, 1:30–4 P.M. Mon., 1:30–4 P.M. and 8:30–11 P.M. Wed.–Sun., closed Tues., €35), a rustic dining room with sophisticated taste right behind the cathedral. Try the lamb caramelized with Pedro Ximénez sherry. If you want local flavor without biting into your budget, you can't do better than **Alex Terraza Restaurante** (Pl. Amador de los Ríos 10, tel.

92/522-3963, 9 A.M.–midnight Tues.–Sun., closed Mon.), particularly at lunchtime (1:30–4 P.M.) when a three-course meal costs just €9. The bulk of the dining takes place on the large terrace set on a very peaceful tree-lined plaza. If you go in the evening, ask to sit in the dining room built into an ancient cave beneath the restaurant.

Tapas

Near the top of the city escalators, **Taberna Embrujo** (C/ Santa Leocadia 6, tel. 92/521-0706, 8 A.M.–4 P.M. and 8 P.M.–midnight Wed.–Fri., noon–midnight Sat.–Sun., 8 A.M.–4 P.M. Mon.–Tues., €15) is an upscale tapas bar with a fantastic wine list. It is popular with local professionals and the lucky tourists who stumble upon it. Just behind Plaza Zocodóver are two more good bets for tapas. **La Tabernita 10** (C/ Santa Fé 10, tel. 92/521-3006, 10:30 A.M.–4 P.M. and 8 P.M.–midnight daily, €10) is a traditional Spanish tavern. Try the *huevos rotos,* fried eggs with potatoes. **El Trébol** (C/ Santa Fé 2, tel. 92/521-3702, 10 A.M.–4 P.M. and 8 P.M.–midnight daily, €12) is a boisterous favorite. The terrace, butted up against the walls of the Convento Santa Fé, is a lovely spot to take a break. Near El Greco's house, try **Cervecería Gambrinus** (C/ Santo Tomé 10, tel. 92/521-4440, 11 A.M.–2 A.M. daily, €12) for solid tapas and good beer. The real draw is the shady terrace right on bustling Santo Tomé—which despite being miniscule by American standards, is the widest street in all of old Toledo!

INFORMATION

The regional Castilla-La Mancha **tourist office** (Pt. Bisagra, s/n, tel. 92/522-0843, 9 A.M.–6 P.M. Mon.–Fri., 9 A.M.–7 P.M. Sat., 9 A.M.–3 P.M. Sun.) is located just outside the Puerta de Bisagra. There are three **local tourist offices** throughout the old city: in the city hall building on Plaza Ayuntamiento across from the cathedral; in Zococentro (C/ Sillería 14) just off of Plaza Zocodóver; and at the base of the escalators. These offices keep irregular hours, normally closing for lunch (except for Zococentro, which sports a modern café). If you head to any of them during the morning hours, they are sure to be open.

Your essential guide to Toledo should be *T-Descubre,* a free magazine published by advertisers with the support of the Chamber of Commerce. It covers all sights (including opening hours and prices), gives basic tourist information, and features interesting articles on Toledo culture and events. It is available all over town. Its website (www.t-descubre.com) is excellent. Another good Internet resource is www.toledoweb.org. Free maps are available just about everywhere, some good, some not so. Really, you only need a basic guideline as all sights are clearly laid out and locals are more than willing to point you in the right direction.

GETTING THERE AND AROUND
Train

With the opening of the AV *alta velocidad* (high-speed) train line between Madrid and Toledo, the travel time between the two cities has been reduced to 35 minutes. The train leaves daily, about once per hour, from **Atocha** (Metro: Atocha Renfe, www.renfe.es). Be sure to go to the Puerta del Toledo (AVE) side of the station. The cost is €8.30 one-way and there is a discount if you buy round-trip. Do not arrive at the station without already having a ticket. The lines for tickets can be upwards of an hour and it is common to see your train sell out while you wait in line. You can purchase over the Internet, but the lines to print your tickets can also be quite long. Most *agencias de viajes* (travel agents) sell tickets. A good bet is **Halcon Viajes** (Gran Vía 39, tel. 91/532-5971, 10 A.M.–8 P.M. Mon.–Sat.), which has offices all over the city. There is a €3 charge for the service.

From the train station in Toledo (a sight in itself with lovely tile work and Mudejar mo-

tifs), it is a steep uphill climb. **Local buses** (€0.80) leave from the stop in front of the station, turn right out of the main doors. Look for a bus going to Zocodóver (nos. 5, 6, or 7). You can also catch a cab for less than €4.

Bus

Though the bus takes twice as long, it is a surer bet, especially if you didn't buy train tickets ahead of time. Head to Madrid's **Estación Sur de Autobuses** (Metro: Méndez Álvaro) and go to counters 43–46 of **Continental-Auto** (www.continental-auto.net). Buses leave about every 30 minutes 6:45 A.M.–10 P.M. Monday–Saturday. On Sundays and holidays, buses run 8 A.M.–10 P.M. Be sure and buy a *directo* (direct service) ticket, otherwise you'll be stopping at half a dozen towns on the way. The direct route should take just about one hour and the ticket costs €4.25 one-way. The bus drops you off at Toledo's drab bus station just outside the medieval walls. Again, the walk into town is uphill, so catch a cab or local bus 6 to Plaza Zocodóver. You can also catch bus 12 to the base of the *escaleras mecánicos,* a long set of escalators that go up to the old town, ending not far from the Judería.

Car

The only reason to take a car to Toledo is if you are heading elsewhere afterwards. From Madrid catch the A-42 Carretera de Toledo to TO-20 and take Exit 69 to Toledo Mocejón. If your hotel does not have a parking garage, park in the *aparcamiento* located near the Puerta de Bisagra and ride the escalators up into town. The drive is about 80 kilometers (50 miles) and should take a little over an hour depending on traffic. Do not attempt to drive in Toledo Monumental, the curves are tight, the cobblestone streets are narrow, and tourists walking blind behind maps are everywhere. Several hotels have guest-only parking lots, be sure to ask when reserving.

Cuenca

Cuenca is a tiny spit of land on top of a steep outcrop of rock hemmed in by the Rivers Huecár and Jucár. The *casco viejo* (old town) is a magnificent achievement of medieval architecture, with the houses and churches rising right from the craggy rock. Wandering through its tangled streets of centuries old churches and stone houses, you'll stumble time and time again on sweeping views over the river gorges. Founded by Muslims as Kunka in 711, the town became Cuenca after Alfonso VIII's forces conquered it in 1177. In the Middle Ages, it flourished as a textile center and home of the Christian order of Santiago. Today, it is the capital of the region of the same name and a UNESCO World Heritage Site. Though extremely popular with Spanish tourists, it is visited by few American tourists, which is too bad as it is really a magical town worth at least an overnight visit.

SIGHTS

Cuenca's most interesting sights are clustered together in the old town, high above the river gorges. They can easily be covered in a morning's time, but if you are not into uphill climbing, you might take it a little slower. Local buses 1 and 2 circle around the perimeter of the old town and go as high as the Castillo, a former military building at the top of the town. You could start there and then walk your way down. The important thing is to not rush your visit. Get lost in Cuenca's medieval jungle of tiny streets. Prowl through ancient covered alleyways. Linger at tiny parks with spectacular views over the river gorges. Along the way, be sure and tread Calles San Pedro, Julián Romero, and Alfonso VIII. A stroll through Barrio San Martín, just south of the cathedral is a nice walk off of the main tourist path and into a charming slice of Cuenca life. If you'd

Cuenca's Ayuntamiento

© CANDY LEE LABALLE

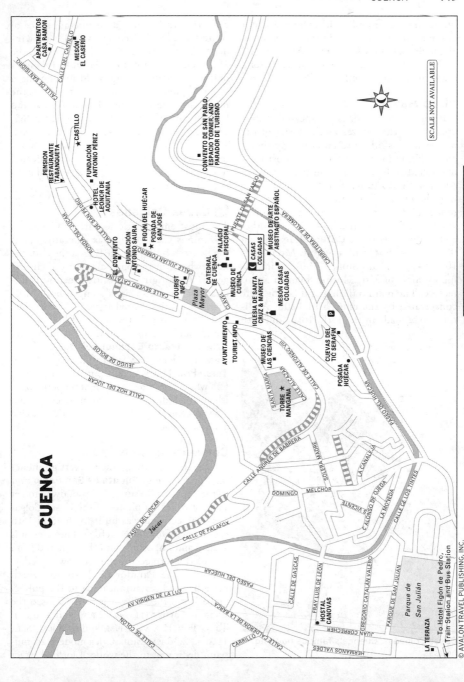

CUENCA

SCALE NOT AVAILABLE

APARTMENTOS CASA RAMON
MESÓN EL CASERÍO
CALLE DEL CASTILLO
CALLE DE SAN ISIDRO
★ CASTILLO
PENSION RESTAURANTE TABANQUETA
FUNDACIÓN ANTONIO PÉREZ
HOTEL LEONOR DE AQUITANIA
RONDA DEL JÚCAR
CALLE DE SAN PEDRO
CALLE JULIÁN ROMERO
FIGÓN DEL HUÉCAR
★ POSADA DE SAN JOSÉ
EL CONVENTO
FUNDACIÓN ANTONIO SAURA
CALLE SEVERO CATALINA
PALACIO EPISCOPAL
CONVENTO DE SAN PABLO, ESPACIO TORNER, AND PARADOR DE TURISMO
PUENTE DE SAN PABLO
CARRETERA DE PALOMERA
MUSEO DE ARTE ABSTRACTO ESPAÑOL
CASAS COLGADAS
TOURIST INFO
CATEDRAL DE CUENCA
MUSEO DE CUENCA
Plaza Mayor
MESÓN CASAS COLGADAS
IGLESIA DE SANTA CRUZ & MARKET
P
AYUNTAMIENTO
TOURIST INFO.
MUSEO DE LAS CIENCIAS
CUEVAS DEL TIO SERAFÍN
POSADA HUÉCAR
CALLE DE ALFONSO VIII
SANTA MARIA
★ TORRE MANGANA
CALLE LA CRUZ
JUEGO DE BOLOS
CALLE HOZ DEL JÚCAR
PASEO DEL HUÉCAR
CALLE ANDRÉS DE CABRERA
SOLERA MADRE
LA CANALEJA
LA MONEDA
DOMINGO
MELCHOR
S. VICENTE
C. ALONSO DE OJEDA
CALLE DE LOS TINTES
PASEO DEL JÚCAR
Júcar
CALLE DE PALAFOX
CALLE DE GASCAS
CALLE DE PEDRO
PASEO DEL HUÉCAR
PARQUE DE SAN JULIÁN
JUAN CORRECHER
GREGORIO CATALAN VALERO
Parque de San Julián
AV VIRGEN DE LA LUZ
FRAY LUIS DE LEÓN
HOSTAL CANOVAS
CALLE CALDERON DE LA BARCA
CARRILLO
HERMANOS VALDES
LA TERRAZA
CALLE DE COLÓN
To Hotel Figón de Pedro, Train Station and Bus Station

© AVALON TRAVEL PUBLISHING, INC.

like to hire a tour guide, either for a city tour or something more active in the surrounding areas, visit **Cuenca Activa** (C/ Alfonso VIII 43, tel. 96/924-1192, info@cuencactiva.com, www.cuencactiva.com).

Plaza Mayor

Cuenca's Plaza Mayor is a trapezoid-shaped open space that serves as the heart of the old town. It is full of restaurants and shops, and is home to two of Cuenca's most photographed sights. On its southern end, the **Ayuntamiento** (town hall) serves as a gate into the plaza. Completed in 1763, the baroque building sits atop three arches through which street level traffic flows. On the other end of the plaza is the **Catedral de Cuenca** (8:45 A.M.–2 P.M. and 4–6 P.M. Mon.–Fri., 10 A.M.–7 P.M. Sat.–Sun., €2.80), an imposing example of early Gothic Spanish architecture. The main building and facade were consecrated by the church in 1208. Additions were made in the 15th, 16th, and 17th

centuries. Inside, it is an exuberant space of stone arches and circular stained-glass windows. Around the back of the cathedral, the 13th-century **Palacio Episcopal** (bishop's palace) is an intriguing building housing a so-so religious museum. Across from it is the much more interesting **Museo de Cuenca** (C/ Obispo Valero, 12, tel. 96/921-3069, 11 A.M.–2 P.M. and 4–7 P.M. Tues.–Sat., 11 A.M.–2 P.M. Sun., extended hours in summer, €2.80), which has three floors dedicated to the archaeology, history, and cultural heritage of Cuenca.

Casas Colgadas

The most emblematic feature of Cuenca is its famous Casas Colgadas (literally, hanging houses). Built into the side of the cliff, the houses hang in the open air over the Huecár gorge. The origin of this architecture is unclear but local historians point to both Muslim and medieval predecessors. Today, they have been carefully restored and house a restaurant and a modern art museum, **Museo de Arte Abstracto Español** (tel. 96/921-2983, www.march.es, 11 A.M.–2 P.M. and 4–6 P.M. Tues.–Fri., 11 A.M.–2 P.M. and 4–8 P.M. Sat., €3), which boasts a spectrum of modern Spanish art, including a good sculpture collection. The gorgeous views from the galleries provide a dramatic backdrop.

Convento de San Pablo

Behind the cathedral, take the vertigo-inducing wooden bridge **Puente de San Pablo** over to the convent. Be sure to stop midway to get some of your best photos of the Casas Colgadas. The convent was built in the mid-16th century as a Dominican refuge. The exterior is austere and imposing and is best viewed from any of the terraces in the old town. Today, it houses the Parador de Turismo, which has a bar and restaurant open to the public. Since 2006, the convent has also housed the **Espacio Torner** (11 A.M.–2 P.M. and 4–6 P.M. Tues.–Fri., 11 A.M.–2 P.M. and 4–8 P.M. Sat., 11 A.M.–2:30 P.M. Sun., €3), a modern art museum dedicated to the work of local abstract

© CANDY LEE LABALLE

Casas Colgadas, Cuenca's famous hanging houses

sculptor Gustavo Torner. The intriguing interplay between the crisp, white gallery half-walls and the soaring Gothic ceilings is worth a visit alone.

Other Museums

Cuenca boasts several contemporary art museums. In addition to the Museo del Arte Abstracto Español and the Espacio Torner, there is the **Fundación Antonio Pérez** (C/ Julián Romero 20, tel. 96/923-0619, 10 A.M.–9 P.M. Mon.–Fri., 11 A.M.–9 P.M. Sat.–Sun., free), an extensive pop art collection which includes a few Warhols. It is housed in a spacious traditional building with wonderful views. More pop art can be found at the **Fundación Antonio Saura** (Pl. San Nicolás 4, tel. 96/923-6054, 11 A.M.–2 P.M. and 5–7 P.M. Thurs.–Tues., closed Wed., free) located in the restored Casa Zavala, an emblematic Cuenca house. Further down the hill, the **Museo de las Ciencias** (Pl. Merced 1, tel. 96/924-0320, 10 A.M.–2 P.M. and 4–8 P.M. Tues.–Sat., 10 A.M.–2 P.M. Sun., €1.20) is a delightful science museum with an attached planetarium. Check out the whimsical time machine near the front door.

ENTERTAINMENT AND EVENTS

Nightlife

Cuenca's nightlife scene is pretty low-key, though on the weekends it heats up. In the historic old town, try **Taberna/Discoteca Jovi** (C/ Colmillo 10, tel. 96/921-4284, 6:30 P.M.–2 A.M. Fri.–Sun.). Early evening, this is good spot for a coffee drink. Late night, it becomes a dance club with basic Spanish pop. **Vaya-Vaya** (C/ Bajada San Miguel, s/n, tel. 96/921-2175, 8 P.M.–4 A.M. Tues.–Sun.), just off the Plaza Mayor, is a good cocktail bar located in a cozy stone-walled house. Right next to the cathedral, **Los Elefantes** (C/ Severo Catalina 17) and **Las Tortugas** (C/ Severo Catalina 37) are two of the old town's oldest late-night bars. In the summer, outdoor bars pop up all around the Castillo, all the way at the top of the old town. Just

follow the music. If you are staying downhill in the new part of town, head to Plaza de la Hispanidad. There are bars all around the area, though the heaviest concentration is on **Calle San Francisco.** If you are getting tired of rustic-this and traditional-that, try **Sire** (C/ Sánchez Vera 9, tel. 96/923-2616), a super-slick upscale eatery that converts into a stylish drinking den at night.

Festivals and Events

Cuenca's Easter week **Semana Santa** processions are some of the best attended in Spain. (See sidebar *All About Semana Santa* in the *Andalucía* chapter.) They are held nightly from Palm Sunday to Easter Sunday. As with all Semana Santa processions, hooded participants march silently through the streets wielding candles and incense. Other participants loft heavy religious statues onto their shoulders and sway slowly from the cathedral through the steep, curving streets. Things get a little rowdy on Good Friday with the participation of *Las Turbas,* brotherhoods that accompany the march with drums, horns, and mournful wailing. They are also known as *los borrachos* (the drunks) because they swig from bottles of *resolí* throughout the procession. The tourist office provides an English-language booklet describing each procession and its route through the city.

At the end of August, Cuenca throws a boisterous bash called **San Julián.** Most of the action goes down at Parque de San Julián and includes musical performances and street parties. The festival also coincides with Cuenca's most important bullfighting event.

If you are in the region around September 21, you should make an effort to visit the **Fiesta San Mateo,** which lasts for a week around that date each year. Commemorating the 1177 capture of Cuenca from the Muslims, the fiesta has two parts: a solemn procession from the cathedral, and a wild free-for-all in the streets. The latter includes a bull run in Plaza Mayor, fireworks displays, live music, and late-night dancing in the streets.

SHOPPING

Cuenca is known for its ceramic work, which ranges from traditional to avant-garde. The best place to get a bit of both is at **Adrián** (Plaza Mayor, tel. 96/921-2828), named for master ceramicist Adrián Navarro. His son Rubén produces colorful, modern pieces for the shop. The **Iglesia de Santa Cruz** (C/ Santa Catalina, s/n, tel. 96/923-3184, 11 A.M.– 2 P.M. and 4–7 P.M. Tues.–Sat., 11 A.M.–2 P.M. Sun.) is a 16th-century church that houses the local arts and crafts center. Several artisans are on hand selling their wares. Cuenca's best traditional food shop is **El Convento** (C/ San Pedro 6, tel. 96/921-2959, 11 A.M.–2 P.M. and 4–8:30 P.M. Mon.–Sat.), which offers local pastries, saffron grown in the Cuenca region, artisan honey, and the most typical souvenir— the local liqueur *resolí* in a bottle shaped like the Casas Colgadas.

ACCOMMODATIONS
Under €50
The charming 【 **Posada Huécar** (Po. Huécar 3, tel. 96/921-4201, huecarposadahuecar .com, www.posadahuecar.com, €45) is located along the Huécar River, just downhill from the old town. The rooms have tiled floors and simple antiques. There is also a lovely garden. **Hostal Canovas** (C/ Fray Luis de León 38, tel. 96/921-3973, recepcion@ hostalcanovas.com, www.hostalcanovas.com, €45) is a family-owned hotel in the new town near the Plaza España. The rooms boast hardwood floors, burgundy curtains, and impressive views. Request a balcony for €10 more. If cheap and central is your thing, try the tiny **Pension Tabanqueta** (C/ Trabuco 13, tel.96/921-1290, €30), just south of the Castillo, on the Júcar river gorge. The six bare-bones rooms sport washbasins, but toilets and showers are shared. If you can get a room with a view over the gorge, it will more than make up for the austerity. It also has a homey, inexpensive restaurant with a terrace overlooking the river.

€50-100
【 **Posada de San José** (C/ Julián Romero 4, tel. 96/921-1300, info@posadasanjose.com, www.posadasanjose.com, €80) is a delightful inn tucked inside the former San José choir school behind a dramatic sculpted doorway. Canadian Jennifer and Spaniard Antonio have lovingly restored the building to its original beauty while incorporating all the modern perks. The airy rooms have a peaceful monastic feel with simple antiques and fresh flowers. Be sure to book one with a view over the Huécar river gorge. It will run about a dozen euros extra, but is worth it. Room 15 has its own terrace. There are also four double superiors, which have king-size beds and sitting rooms with a view. If you are on a budget, stay in one of the small street-side monk's rooms. You'll share a bath and won't have a view, but at €38 for a nicely decorated double, you really can't complain.

At the highest point in the old town, **Apartmentos Casa Ramon** (C/ La Paz, s/n, tel. 65/906-6204, www.casa-ramon.com, €70) has the best views of any accommodations in the city. This traditional Cuenca home features just two tourist apartments with nicely decorated living rooms, fully equipped kitchens, hydro-massage showers, and terraces. Apartments can hold up to five people and prices rise slightly as the number of people increase. If you are driving, there is a free public parking lot just behind the house. Just north of the train and bus stations, **Hotel Figón de Pedro** (C/ Cervantes 17, 96/922-4511, €60) is a basic mid-range hotel with no-nonsense, comfortable rooms, and a friendly staff. The biggest plus is the top-rated traditional dining room, which serves up true and tasty versions of Cuenca's specialties.

Over €100
The lovely **Leonor de Aquitania** (C/ San Pedro, 60, tel.96/923-1000, reservas@hotel leonordeaquitania.com, www.hotelleonorde aquitania.com, €106) is located in an elegantly restored 18th-century palace. The 49 cheery rooms have all the amenities. Views are either of the Huécar gorge or over the old city. The €9 breakfast is pricey, but the view from the cafe-

teria overlooking the river is priceless. Cuenca's **Parador de Turismo** (Convento de San Pablo, tel. 96/923-2320, cuenca@parador.es, www .parador.es, €135) is one of the most elegant in Spain. Set inside a 1523 monastery, it is a lovely example of late Gothic architecture with gorgeous carved stone walls and echoing hallways. The 63 rooms are superb and the best have views over the river and onto the Casas Colgadas. The food is not the best, as is common in paradors, but do be sure to enjoy breakfast from the outdoor terrace or the dining room, which is in the monastery's old chapel.

FOOD

As is typical in Castilla-La Mancha, Cuenca offers a game-based menu heavy on roasted meats, simply prepared vegetables, and hearty stews. Two local specialties draw from this background. *Morteruelo* is a liver pâté made with walnuts, cloves, and cinnamon. It tastes much better than it sounds when served warm on a piece of toast. *Zarajos* are goat intestines that are marinated in vinegar and spices, wrapped around a twig, and grilled over open coals. Again, the taste far exceeds the description. Around Cuenca are some of the largest garlic-growing farms and *ajo* appears in many dishes. The most popular is *ajoarriero*, a savory paste made from codfish, potatoes, and garlic. *Gazpacho pastor* is a large omelet made with game meat, usually rabbit, and served with unleavened bread and grapes. Grilled local *trucha* (trout) is also readily available. *Alajú*, Cuenca's most famous dessert, is a paste of almonds, honey, dried fruit, and cinnamon sandwiched between thin, crusty layers of cake. Finish your meal with a taste of *resolí*, a liqueur made from brandy, oranges, cinnamon, and coffee.

The number of restaurants in the old town are limited and spaces hard to come by on weekends at lunchtime. For some of the more popular locations, you can reserve a seat by dialing the **Cuenca reservation line** (tel. 90/110-0131). Unless otherwise noted

below, Cuenca restaurants follow standard Spanish opening hours (1:30–4:30 P.M. and 8:30–11 P.M.).

Local Cuisine

Specializing in local cuisine with a creative spin, **Figón del Huécar** (C/ Julián Romero 6, tel. 96/924-0062, closed Mon., €45) is one of Cuenca's top restaurants. The stone-floored dining room has a gorgeous view over the Huécar gorge. Another local legend is **Mesón Casas Colgadas** (C/ Canónigos, s/n, tel. 96/922-3509, closed Mon. P.M., €30, reservations recommended), where Spain's Prince Felipe and Princess Letizia dined on their honeymoon. Set right in one of the famous hanging houses of Cuenca, the atmosphere and the views are dazzling. The food keeps pace with a menu focused on high quality Castilian fare. For a completely different view, head underground to the **Cuevas del Tío Serafín** (Paseo del Huécar 2, tel. 96/922-9725, www.cuevadel tioserafin.com, closed Mon., €30). The "caves of Uncle Serafín" are built inside a cave that was originally used by Muslim occupants in the 8th century. The menu features Cuenca specialties as well as typical game dishes from Castilla-La Mancha. In the new town, at the top of the Hotel Alfonso VIII, **La Terraza** (Parque San Julián 3, tel. 96/921-4325, €20) offers value-priced meals along with a view over the lovely San Julián park.

Tapas

Though the dining room at **Posada San José** (C/ Julián Romero 4, tel. 96/921-1300, €20) seems perfect for long-lingering meals, this is one of the few hotel restaurants that features an all-tapas menu. *Raciones* run €6–14 and feature perfect renditions of local delicacies and Spanish standards. Share a few items and a bottle of wine while taking in the stunning view over the Huécar gorge. Further uphill, on the other side of the Castillo, **Mesón El Caserío** (C/ Larga 17, tel. 96/923-0021, €10) is famous both for its views and its generous tapas. An added bonus is that the kitchen is open all day. **Los Arcos** (C/ Severo Catalina 1, tel. 96/921-3806, 10 A.M.–midnight daily, €12) has a simple menu of tapas and sandwiches available all day. The bar looks out over the Júcar river gorge. There is also a more formal dining room downstairs.

INFORMATION

The **tourist office** (C/ Alfonso VIII 2, tel. 96/924-1051, 9:30 A.M.–2 P.M. and 4–7 P.M. daily, extended hours in summer) is very close to Plaza Mayor and can provide all the basic necessities. The best guide is *Cuenca Ciudad,* which is available at the tourist office for €1. If you are driving, stop at the **Centro de Recepción de Turistas** (Av. Cruz Roja 1, tel. 96/924-1050, www.turismocuenca.com). The English-speaking staff is very helpful. Be sure to pick up a copy of their free *La Agenda,* which gives a great overview of Cuenca, including several self-guided walks. The gift shop features all of Cuenca's local products at very good prices. There are no official tourism websites in English, though there is some basic information at the Spanish tourism website www.spain.info. In Spanish, two excellent websites are www .cuenca.es/turismo and www.todocuenca.es.

GETTING THERE AND AROUND

Four regional **trains** leave daily from Atocha (Metro: Atocha Renfe, www.renfe.es) start-ing at 8:50 A.M. and running about every three hours. The ride lasts 2.75 hours and costs €9.90 each way. The last train back to Madrid is at 6:45 P.M. These are hard-seated regional trains and they leave from the Cercanías side of the train station. **Bus** service to Cuenca is handled by **Auto-Res** (Estación de Autobuses Conde de Casal, Metro: Conde de Casal, www.auto-res.net) and is much more frequent with nine daily departures starting at 6:45 A.M. Normal fare is €9.75 one-way and takes 2.5 hours; express is €13.10 one-way and takes two hours. The last bus back from Cuenca is 8 P.M., 10 P.M. on Sundays. The train and bus stations in Cuenca are prac-tically next door to each other and both about 10 minutes walking uphill into the historic district. Catch local bus 1 or 2 to Plaza Mayor to save your legs.

If you are **driving** from Madrid, take M-30 out of the city heading in the direc-tion of Valencia. Then catch the E-901, again towards Valencia. Take Exit 79 onto N-400 and follow it towards Tarancón. Con-tinue until CU-11, which will take you into Cuenca. The drive is just over 160 kilome-ters (100 miles) and should take around two hours depending on traffic. Once in Cuenca, park at any *aparcamiento* and walk, cab, or bus into the historic zone, which is a steep labyrinth of streets that you do not want to drive in.

Southern Castilla-La Mancha

In the provinces of Toledo, Ciudad Real, and Albacete, the quintessential Quixote lands unfurl. Dry and vast, punctuated by olive groves and dusty villages, the region seems un-touched by modern times. Driving through, it is easy to imagine Don Quixote and San-cho Panza clopping along just over the next ridge. In 2005, on the 400th anniversary of the publication of the novel, the govern-ment of Castilla-La Mancha established 10 **Rutas de Don Quijote** (www.donquijotedela mancha2005.com) that weave through the southern areas of the region. Whether the routes cover the actual stomping grounds of the legendary Don is up for literary debate, but they make an excellent guide for discovering this little-known region of Spain. Each leg of the route is clearly marked and there are ample services including gas stations, restaurants, and hotels along the length of it. A modern-day errant knight couldn't ask for more.

The following list of towns can be followed

as a two- or three-day itinerary. If you prefer to not rent a car, most of the destinations are reachable by bus or train from Toledo or the drab industrial town of Ciudad Real. At any point, you can beeline back to Toledo, Madrid, or turn south to Andalucía.

◖ CONSUEGRA

Originally inhabited by the Romans, tiny Consuegra is a classic Manchego town of huddled buildings, medieval churches, and miles of dusty fields all around. It sits at the base of the Cerro Calderico hill, a low-lying, mottled patch of earth that would be forgettable were it not for the 12 **windmills** that line its crest like marching giants right from the warped mind of Don Quixote. Though hailing from the 15th century, the windmills have been carefully tended and four are still in working order. The aptly named "Sancho" mill rolls into action the second weekend of each month. The **tourist office** (92/547-5731, 10 A.M.–2 P.M. and 4:30–7 P.M. daily) is in the windmill named "Bolero," which is the closest to town. In the midst of the windmills lies the imposing **Castillo de Consuegra,** a 13th-century castle that looks like it is straight out of a fairy tale. If you are around in October, you may just be lucky enough to see the scorched earth turn purple as fields of saffron crocuses bloom. The flowers appear overnight and their bright red stigmas must be picked by hand immediately. Once dried, the resulting "red gold" can fetch up to $1,000 for a pound. In the last weekend of October, Consuegra celebrates the saffron harvest with the **Fiesta de la Rosa del Azafrán.**

Accommodations and Food

There is very little in way of accommodations in Consuegra. On the road leading to Toledo, **Las Provincias** (Ctra. Toledo-Alcázar, tel. 92/548-2000, €47) is the only hotel. It also has a decent restaurant. **Casa Caslida** (C/ Urda 26, tel. 67/739-4872) is a private home with rooms to let. For dining, there are several homey restaurants and bars serving basic Manchego cui-

sine. Two good bets are **Restaurante Castilla** (C/ Sertorío 18) and **Casa de la Tercia** (C/ Plus Ultra 5).

Getting There

The drive from Toledo to Consuegra is just over 70 kilometers (45 miles) and should take about an hour. From Toledo, take the N-401 south to Orgaz. There catch the CM-410 and head towards Mora. Switch to the CM-400 and finally to the TO-2011/Carretera de Turleque which will lead you into Consuegra.

◖ ALMAGRO

During the Middle Ages, Almagro was the capital of the Campo de Calatrava, the southern portion of Castilla-La Mancha, and the famed Knights of Calatrava had their headquarters here. In the 16th century, it became home to several royal bankers who refurbished the town to its present charm. They also introduced the art of lace making and you can find lovely pieces all around town. The regal, arcaded **Plaza Mayor** houses the city's famed **Corral de Comedias** (tel. 92/686-1539, www.corraldecomedias.com), Spain's best-preserved 17th-century theater. The stage is located in a 3,000-square-foot inner courtyard surrounded by wooden balconies for seating. Every July, it hosts the **Festival Internacional de Teatro Clásico,** one of the world's most prestigious classical theater festivals. The event was recently declared a Historic-Artistic Site by UNESCO. You can tour the theater when shows are not on, but the schedule and the pricing vary widely. Check with the **tourist office** (Plaza Mayor 1, tel. 92/686-0717) for details.

Accommodations and Food

◖ **La Casa del Rector** (C/ Pedro Oviedo, 8, tel. 92/626-1259, €120) is a beautiful inn tucked into a carefully restored 17th-century palace. The colorful rooms combine simple antiques with modern luxuries like orthopedic mattresses and whirlpool baths. Almagro's **Parador de Turismo** (Ronda San Francisco 31, tel. 92/686-0100, almagro@parador.es,

THE MAN BEHIND THE KNIGHT

Miguel de Cervantes y Saavedra led a life that surpasses anything you could ever read in a novel. He was born in 1547 in Alcalá de Henares but he lived in various Spanish cities during a lifetime of traveling, writing, and general mayhem. In 1569, he took on a position as the attendant to Cardinal Acquaviva in Italy. Two years later, Cervantes signed up to fight the Ottomans in the famed December 1571 Battle of Lepanto. During the battle, he lost the use of his left arm and earned the nickname *El Manco de Lepanto* (the one-armed man of Lepanto). Despite the injury, he continued on as a soldier. In 1575, on a sea voyage back to Spain, the ship was captured by Turkish pirates and Cervantes was taken to Algiers, where he was kept as a slave five years. Finally, Trinitarian monks intervened and helped Cervantes return to Spain.

Life took a mundane turn in Spain and the budding bard found himself in Valladolid working a series of sundry jobs that always left him penniless. In 1584, an affair with a barmaid resulted in the birth of his daughter Isabel. That same year, he married someone else – one Catalina de Salazar. Not surprisingly, the marriage was an unhappy one. Meanwhile, Cervantes became a public official and starting traveling through Andalucía to collect rents and taxes for the Spanish Armada. Being prone to trouble, along the way he ended up in jail in Sevilla for tax fraud. Literary legend holds it that most of *Don Quixote* was written here.

By 1608, Cervantes settled in Madrid and entered the most prolific part of his literary career. Madrid is where he came into his own as a playwright, poet and novelist. Cervantes' poetic works include the epic *Viaje al Parnaso* from 1614. His most well-known work as a playwright was published the following year as *Ocho Comedias y Ocho Entremeses Nuevos*. His novels include 1585's *La Galatea* and, of course, the world's most famous work of fiction: *El Ingenioso Hidalgo Don Quijote de la Mancha*, published in 1605. Don Quixote and

© CANDY LEE LABALLE

Taverns around here take their cue from Cervantes.

his faithful sidekick Sancho Panza have captured the imagination of readers worldwide ever since. On the 400th anniversary of the novel in 2005, Spain launched a full year of events celebrating the book and the writer. One of the most ambitious was the creation of ecotourism routes through southern Castilla-La Mancha, classic Quixote territory. Learn more about them at www.donquijotedela mancha2005.com.

The last years of Cervantes' illustrious life were especially prolific. He wrote the *Novelas Ejemplares*, published in 1613, and the second part of *Don Quixote*, published in 1615. He was a regular character at the cafés and bars around Calle Huertas in Madrid and contributed to the city's lively intellectual scene. He died in Madrid on April 23, 1616, which incidentally is the death date of record for Cervantes' contemporary, and possibly the only author more famous, Shakespeare.

www.parador.es, €135) is set in a gorgeous convent built in 1596. Rooms are in the former monks' cells and are immaculately serene. Many look out on one of the convent's 14 inner courtyards. For a cheap sleep, head to **Los Escudos** (C/ Bolaños 55, tel. 92/686-1574, €40). **El Corregidor** (C/ Jerónimo Ceballos 2, tel. 92/686-0648, €45) is one of the region's most celebrated restaurants. The food is a sophisticated blend of Manchego tradition and daring innovation. For a variety of tapas bars and cafés, head to the Plaza Mayor. A good bet is the popular **El Bar del Gordo** (Plaza Mayor 12).

Getting There

Almagro is 100 kilometers (62 miles) to the south of Consuegra. This route takes you through the back roads. Take the CM-400 to the E-5 in the direction of Córdoba. Take Exit 136 towards Ciudad Real. Near Puerto Lápice, catch the N-420 towards Ciudad Real/Damiel. Switch to the A-53 and as you approach Damiel, take Exit 15. Follow it until you get close to the town of Torralba de Calatrava. Take a left onto CR-P-5112. When you reach CM-412, take another left. This road will lead you straight into Almagro.

VALDEPEÑAS

It doesn't get more Quixotic than the purposeful little town of Valdepeñas. But for a charming blue- and white-fronted **Plaza España,** there is not much to see. Yet, tipplers all across Spain daily speak its name. As one of the largest wine regions, Valdepeñas has long been synonymous with cheap red table wine. Today, the Valdepeñas *denominación de origen* (D.O.) is starting to churn out finer wines designed to appease the current wine-crazy public. For an overview of local wine history, visit the **Museo del Vino** (C/ Princesa 39, tel. 92/632-1111, 10:30 A.M.–2 P.M. and 6 P.M.–8 P.M. Tues.–Sat., noon–2 P.M. Sun.), which is inside an old bodega. Better yet, visit one of the many bodegas in the region. The **tourist office** (Plaza España, s/n, tel. 92/631-2552) can give you informa-

tion and driving maps. The top-rated winemaker in the area is **Bodegas Real** located at the Finca Marisánchez Bodega (Ctra. Cózar, www.bodegas-real.com). Their Vega Ibor Crianza is a gorgeous wine at a very affordable price. Tours start in the vineyards and finish in the estate dining room with a wine tasting (lunch not included). Tours are conducted 10 A.M.–2 P.M. and 4–8 P.M. Mon.–Fri., 10 A.M.–3 P.M. Sat.–Sun., but reservations must be made ahead of time by calling their Madrid offices at 91/457-7588.

Accommodations and Food

There is little reason to stay overnight in Valdepeñas and practically nowhere to stay even if you wanted to. The closest decent hotel is the **Tryp el Hidalgo** (Ctra. Madrid-Cádiz, tel. 92/631-3088, €80), a four-star hotel on the edge of town. A much nicer option is to continue on to Villanueva de los Infantes. There are more choices for dining. **Mesón de la Viña** (C/ Guardia 13, tel. 92/632-3815) is the best tapas bar in town. Not surprisingly, the wine list is also excellent. On the road leading south to Andalucía, there are two excellent restaurants specializing in Castilian cuisine: **La Aguzadera** (tel. 92/632-3208, closed Mon.) and **Venta La Quintería** (tel. 92/633-8293, lunch only, closed Wed.).

Getting There

From Almagro, take the CM-412 towards Moral de Calatrava. This leads directly into Valdepeñas. The drive is just 35 kilometers (22 miles) and should take no longer than 40 minutes. As you approach Valdepeñas, you'll begin to see the vineyards and wine bodegas.

VILLANUEVA DE LOS INFANTES

Cervantes began *Don Quixote* with the line, "Somewhere in La Mancha, in a place whose name I do not care to remember." In doing so, he created a riddle that has intrigued readers for centuries. A recent theory, cooked up by team of professors from Madrid, is that the tiny village of Villanueva is the mystery town. Why? Well, it seems that the scholars calculated just how long an ancient horse and an overweight donkey can travel in one day and did the math from there. Their claim may be dubious, but Villanueva is still a charming place to visit. Start a walking tour in the lovely **Plaza Mayor,** where the tourist office is located. Be sure to visit the **Iglesia San Andrés,** an imposing medieval structure built in 1498.

Accommodations and Food

The best place to stay is the **Hospedería Real de Quevedo** (C/ Frailes 1, tel. 92/636-1788, www.hosteriasreales.com, info@hosteriasreales.com, €60), a 16th-century convent where the Spanish poet Quevedo lived and died. Conveniently, the town's best restaurant is also located here, the rustic **Santo Tomás Restaurante,** specializing in Manchego cuisine. There are also several cafés clustered around the Plaza Mayor.

Getting There

Villanueva de los Infantes is just 34 kilometers (21 miles) east of Valdepeñas. Catch the CM-412 towards Pozo de la Serna. Switch to the CM-3127, also called Carretera de Manzanares. This road will lead you directly into town. The entire trip should last about half an hour.

◖ EL TOBOSO

Of all the towns in Castilla-La Mancha that clamor for a bit of Don Quixote fame, only El Toboso has true bragging rights. It was one of the few towns actually named in the novel, and fans will recognize it as the home of the Don's love, Dulcinea. In the middle of town is a statue of the errant knight bowing before the startled lady. You can also visit the **Casa de Dulcinea** (C/ Don Quixote 1, tel. 92/519-7288, closed Mon.), a re-creation of a 14th-century home. **Museo Cervantino** (C/ Daoiz y Velarde 3, closed Mon.) holds a vast collection of foreign-language editions of the novel, many signed by dignitaries. The **tourist office** (tel. 92/556-8226) is right next door.

Accommodations and Food

The finest place to stay is the **Casa de la Torre** (C/ Antonio Machado 16, tel. 92/556-8006, €90), an elegantly restored palace in the heart of the old town. Another charmer is the rustic **Hostal El Quixote** (Av. Castilla-La Mancha 20, tel. 92/519-7398). There are restaurants and bars throughout town with names like Rocinante, Dulcinea, and Sancho Panza. They all offer La Mancha specialties and boast rustic atmospheres. Try **Mesón La Noria de Dulcinea** (C/ Don Quixote 3, tel. 92/556-8192).

Getting There

The drive north to El Toboso from Villanueva de los Infantes leads right through the heart of La Mancha. Olive trees punctuate the miles and miles of brown, khaki, and tan earth. Above, the sky rolls on infinitely in all directions. Midway through the journey, you'll pass the **Parque Natural Lagunas,** a rare bit of wet green relief in the midst of the drabness. Here you can pull off to see the **Lagunas de Ruidera,** a series of small lakes which Don Quixote mistook for maidens under a spell.

Catch CM-3129 north out of Villanueva, to N-430. In the town of Ruidera, switch to the CM-3115, which winds through the park. Continue towards Tomelloso, switching to the CM-3103, which will lead you right into El Toboso. The drive is around 110 miles (70 miles) long and should last close to two hours.

CAMPO DE CRIPTANA

A typical Manchego town of whitewashed houses and narrow streets, there is little of interest to the visitor in the city itself. The real draw is the surrounding landscape dotted with 15th-century **windmills,** several of which house tiny museums detailing the workings of windmills. Another excellent reason to visit Campo de Criptana is the vineyards of **El Vínculo** (Av. Juan Carlos 1, tel. 92/656-3709, www.el

vinculo.com), which produces some of the best wines in the country. Tours can be arranged by calling ahead.

Accommodations and Food

There are several places to stay in town, but the most charming is the **Casa de los Tres Cielos** (C/ Libertad 11, tel. 92/656-3790, www.casa los3cielos.com), a restored mansion. Along the same lines is the lovely **Casa de la Torrecilla** (C/ Cardenal Monescillo 15, tel. 92/658-9130, www.casadelatorrecilla.com, €55), which has a spectacular inner courtyard. For dining, head out to one of the surrounding bodegas for a classic local meal. In town, try **Restaurante Bahía de María** (C/ Tercia 11, tel. 92/556-3865) for a creative twist on Castilian fare.

CASTILLA Y LEÓN

It is in the hilly plateaus of Castilla y León that modern Spain was born—when Catholic monarchs Isabel and Fernando vowed to conquer the country, expel the Moors, and extend the Spanish empire into the New World. By the end of the 15th century, they had done just that. Their far-reaching power still echoes today in the hundreds of castles, cathedrals, and fortresses that dot the region. UNESCO has designated seven monuments in the region as World Heritage Sites: the Cathedral of Burgos, one of the largest Gothic structures in the world; the archaeological site of Atapuerca, where 800,000-year-old human remains give evidence of Europe's oldest civilization; the medieval walled city of Ávila; the monument-rich town of Salamanca, which boasts one of Europe's oldest universities; Segovia, which houses both a Roman aqueduct and a fairy-tale castle; Las Médulas, the rocky remains of a Roman mining field; and the Camino de Santiago, which cuts right across the northern edge of the region from Burgos to León.

Castilla y León is one of the largest of Spain's autonomous regions, comprising a huge chunk of the northwestern part of the country. Most of the land is a brown plateau crisscrossed by rivers and verdant valleys. It is surrounded by mountains on most sides—the Picos de Europa in the northwest, the Pyrenees in the northeast, and the Sierra de Gredos and Sierra de Guadarrama in the south.

The low valleys fed by the many rivers, particularly the Río Duero, are rife with vineyards that produce some of the country's best wines. The region boasts five D.O.s, or

© CANDY LEE LABALLE

HIGHLIGHTS

■ **Aqueduct:** This marvel of Roman engineering has loomed proudly over Segovia since the 2nd century. Its 204,000 stone blocks, forming 118 arches that reach over 27 meters at their highest, will leave you awestruck (page 164).

■ **La Granja Palace:** Like a mini-Versailles in the mottled hills of Segovia, this magnificent display of Spanish Bourbon extravagance pales only in comparison to its elegant gardens, which boast two dozen fantastical 19th-century fountains (page 170).

■ **La Muralla:** Ávila has the best preserved medieval wall in Spain, a Middle Age marvel of engineering that will leave you speechless with its enormity. Walking along it is to travel back 10 centuries through Spanish history (page 171).

■ **Plaza Mayor:** Surrounded by majestic, turret-topped buildings that shimmer with a distinctive golden hue, this broad plaza in Salamanca is arguably Spain's finest. Enjoying a glass of wine at one of its many sidewalk cafés as the sun goes down – painting the plaza in a rich tapestry of orange and pink – is an experience you won't soon forget (page 178).

■ **Catedral de León:** With nearly 1,858 square meters of vibrant stained-glass windows, León's cathedral is easily one of the most beautiful in the world. To witness the sun falling through its jewel-colored panes is to witness an ethereal beauty that has seduced visitors for centuries (page 183).

■ **Astorga:** Set in the lush green hills of rural León, this postcard-perfect town boasts the remains of its Roman founders, a magnificent medieval wall, a modernist fairy-tale palace, ancient religious significance, and even a mecca for chocaholics (page 190).

■ **Catedral de Burgos:** This Gothic masterpiece is a massive fantasy of gargoyles, frosting-like baroque touches, webs of flying buttresses, and fanciful filigreed spires that seem suspended from the sky. It looms over the city in a majestic glory that dates back to the 13th century (page 192).

■ **Santo Domingo de Silos:** The monolithic monastery of Santo Domingo de Silos provides a spectacular Romanesque background to the ethereal voices of its chart-topping chanting monks. Both the building and the music date back to the 10th century (page 201).

LOOK FOR ■ TO FIND RECOMMENDED SIGHTS, ACTIVITIES, DINING, AND LODGING.

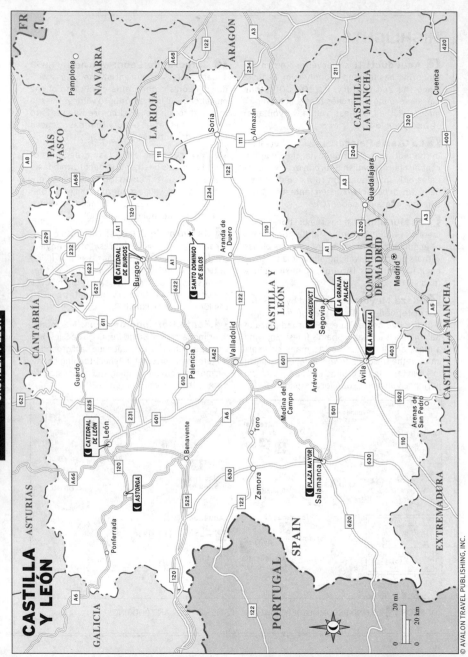

CASTILLA Y LEÓN

FR

PAMPLONA ○

NAVARRA

PAÍS VASCO

LA RIOJA

ARAGÓN

A8

A68

A68

122

A68

234

A3

Soria

Almazán

111

111

111

CASTILLA-LA MANCHA

211

Cuenca

420

320

629

232

234

122

204

320

400

623

120

122

110

A3

Guadalajara

627

CATEDRAL DE BURGOS

A1

Aranda de Duero

A3

A1

A5

SANTO DOMINGO DE SILOS ★

CANTABRIA

611

622

Burgos

A1

AQUEDUCT

LA GRANJA PALACE

320

COMUNIDAD DE MADRID

Madrid ✪

122

CASTILLA Y LEÓN

Valladolid

Segovia

LA MURALLA

403

CASTILLA-LA MANCHA

621

625

A62

Palencia

601

Ávila

502

Guardo

610

Arévalo

610

A66

231

A6

Medina del Campo

501

Arenas de San Pedro

CATEDRAL DE LEÓN

León

601

Benavente

630

Toro

110

120

ASTORGA

525

Zamora

630

630

EXTREMADURA

Ponferrada

122

PLAZA MAYOR
Salamanca

620

A6

120

PORTUGAL

SPAIN

122

CASTILLA Y LEÓN

GALICIA

ASTURIAS

20 mi

20 km

denominaciones de origen (appellations), including Rueda, Cigales, and Toro in the center of the region; Bierzo in the northwest; and the famed Ribera del Duero in the southeast. The hearty reds and crisp whites are paired with a rugged cuisine based on roasted meats. With Extremadura, Castilla y León shares the nickname *España del Asado* (Spain of the Roast). The single most popular dish is *cochinillo,* roasted suckling pig. The method is the same throughout the region—after 21 days of mother's milk, the piglet is roasted in a terra-cotta pot and sent sizzling to the table. *Cordero* and *lechazo,* lamb and suckling lamb, respectively, are also consumed with relish. As in most of Spain, cured meats and sausages are common. Incidentally, foodies swear that the *jamón* from Guijuelo in Salamanca is the best in the country.

PLANNING YOUR TIME

If you're based in Madrid and short on time, Segovia is the best day trip. Just over two hours away, this atmospheric city offers a touristic feast—Roman ruins, medieval walls, Romanesque churches, quaint squares, winding cobblestone lanes—in an area easily walked in a morning. With a day or two extra, consider an overnight trip to Salamanca or Ávila, both just a few hours from Madrid and each teeming with history, mystery, and great photo ops. Burgos is accessible from Madrid, País Vasco, and La Rioja, and if you're doing a wine tour in that region, it would be a shame to not make the two-hour detour to see the city's splendid cathedral. León is the least accessible from any other major tourist destination and requires at least an overnight stay.

To experience a truly off-the-beaten-path trip and see Spain at arguably its most Spanish, rent a car for a week. Starting in Madrid, drive clockwise through Ávila, Salamanca, up to León, over to Burgos, and down to Segovia. Take a night in each town and maybe an extra on the long leg up to León. You will find a Spain not yet trampled by tourism—crumbling hilltop castles, Roman ruins, century-old bodegas, sheep-dotted farmland, and ancient villages tucked in rolling green valleys or stuck on top of craggy mountain peaks. The best time to enjoy such a trip is spring or fall. The winters are viciously cold with piercing winds, while the summers are ungodly hot.

Segovia

Riding atop a ridge fringed green with trees, the city of Segovia emerges like a ship from the very core of Castile. From the aqueduct slicing across the Southern edge of the old town to the Alcázar anchoring the Northern end, Segovia is the history of Castile write large in the stones of ages—squat Roman blocks, fanciful Gothic spires, etched medieval facades. However, the real pleasure of Segovia is not found ticking sights off a monumental checklist. Instead, it is the simple delight of getting lost in the narrow alleys and almond-colored squares that spiderweb the old quarter. Even UNESCO had trouble choosing just one building and awarded Segovia World Heritage status for its "aqueduct and old town."

Segovia began life as the Roman military outpost of Segóbriga sometime around 80 B.C. Little is known about it, but the aqueduct's massive size indicates that it must have been quite large. After the fall of Rome, the Visigoths took over, only to be usurped by the Moors 200 years later. By the 11th century, fighting between the Moors and the Christians from Castile was a way of life. The Alcázar, a medieval Christian castle bearing a Moorish name, attests to this war-marred, intertwining history.

The Moors were firmly trounced out of Segovia in 1085, and the town soon became a favorite retreat of Castilian royalty. A dozen brooding Romanesque churches were built within the walls of the town and Catholicism and commerce began to grow. Before long,

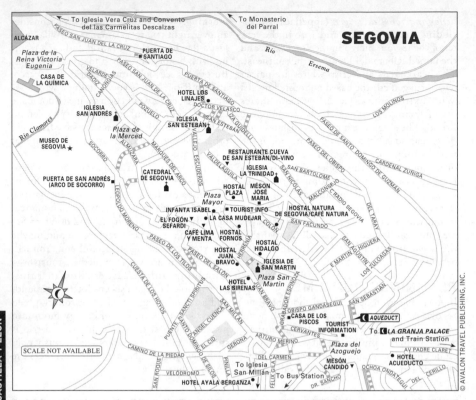

SEGOVIA

© AVALON TRAVEL PUBLISHING, INC.

Segovia was a medieval powerhouse fueled by a thriving textile industry. The high life didn't last, and as the Spanish kings lost control of the country's riches starting in the 1600s, Segovia, too, began a slow decline into centuries of neglect. The Civil War and Franco's subsequent rule also took their tolls and Segovia festered as just another dusty Castilian town with an illustrious past. Fortunately, tourism stepped in and since the 1980s, Segovia has received an infusion of visitors—and money. The new capital has been used to upkeep the town's treasures, including a much-needed restoration project for the aqueduct begun in 1997.

SIGHTS

Starting from the train or bus station, visiting Segovia means weaving through its charming streets up to the Alcázar and back down again. The most logical tour would start just outside of the old town near the bus station in the barrio of San Millán. You could spend a few hours winding your way up to the Alcázar, visit a traditional restaurant for a leisurely lunch, and then stroll down to the aqueduct before heading home. If you are really tight on time, take a cab directly to the Alcázar and start your tour from there. Be sure to buy a map beforehand as there is no tourist office in that part of town. Grab a snack or lunch in the Plaza Mayor and then finish up at the aqueduct where you can catch a cab back to the bus or train.

Aqueduct

Segovia's Roman *acueducto* is one of Spain's most astonishing sights. Rising 91 feet over

Plaza Azoguejo, the aqueduct was built in the 1st century A.D. to provide water to Segóbriga. The source of the water was the river Frío several kilometers to the east of the city. Originally, the aqueduct was over 15 kilometers (nine miles) long; the section that remains today is just under 0.8 kilometer (0.5 mile). An aqueduct is designed to transport water over long distances through a slightly descending shallow channel. To maintain the level of the water flow when the aqueduct crosses a valley, it must be propped up on arches. That is exactly what you see in Plaza Azoguejo. In its Roman heyday, the aqueduct once channeled water at eight gallons per second.

The most impressive aspect of the aqueduct is the fact that neither mortar nor cementing of any kind was used to hold the 20,000 granite blocks together—it is all the result of incredible Roman engineering. Of the 118 arches, 36 were seriously damaged during an 11th-century battle with the Moors. Four hundred years later, Queen Isabel had Catholic monks repair the damage. While they were at it, they replaced the Roman statue of Hercules that once stood in the central nook with a more Christian Virgin Mary. Each year in a pomp-filled ceremony, a Spanish soldier rappels to the top of the aqueduct to drape a fresh military banner across the virgin's torso. To get a close-up view of the aqueduct, climb the stairs to the right leading up out of the plaza. For a less touristy experience, go left and follow the aqueduct along its length to the edges of the city where it reaches ground level near a large roadway.

Barrio San Millán

Between the aqueduct and the bus station, the Barrio San Millán is home to Segovia's best preserved Romanesque church, **Iglesia San Millán** (Av. Fernández Ladreda, s/n). Built on the grounds of a Muslim temple, the massive church has distinctive Moorish flourishes. Typical of Segovian churches built in that time, San Millán features a covered porch, which served as a meeting place for the town's movers and shakers during the Middle Ages.

All along Avenida Fernández Ladreda there are sidewalk cafés and arty boutiques. Throughout the barrio, and in all of the old quarters of Segovia, you'll notice buildings with elaborately decorated exteriors. This local style, called *esgrafiado,* was created by covering the building in stucco and then chipping it off according to a stenciled design.

Barrio San Martín

Running from the aqueduct to the Plaza Mayor, the Barrio San Martín is full of charming plazas, gardens, palaces, and Romanesque churches. **Plaza San Martín** is one of Segovia's quaintest. At its center is a statue of Juan Bravo, the 15th-century local nobleman who led the War of the Comuneros, an ill-fated revolt against Carlos I. For his effort, Bravo lost his head but became a local hero. Also in the plaza is the 12th-century **Iglesia de San Martín.** Another Romanesque church not to be missed is the carefully restored 12th-century **Iglesia La Trinidad** (C/ Trinidad 2). Note that, aside from the cathedral, most of Segovia's churches are closed except during official masses. Check with the tourist office for schedules.

While wandering this neighborhood, look for the **Casa de los Picos** (C/ Juan Bravo 33), a 15th-century mansion covered in diamond-shaped stone points. Rumor has it that a treasure is hidden behind one of the points. Though not open to the public, it currently houses the Segovia Art School and students and teachers are not opposed to the odd tourist popping in to see the lovely tiled courtyard. To re-orientate yourself, follow the signs to the **Plaza Mayor,** the social and commercial hub of the old town. It was here in the plaza, just in front of the cathedral, where Isabel the Catholic was crowned Queen of Castile.

Catedral de Segovia

Nicknamed the "great lady of cathedrals" for its elegance and symmetry, the Catedral de Segovia (Pl. Mayor, s/n, 10 A.M.–5:30 P.M. daily Oct.–Mar., 10 A.M.–7 P.M. daily Apr.–Sept., €2, free Sun. A.M.) was one of the last Gothic cathedrals built in Spain. Segovia's original cathedral stood in the plaza in front of the Alcázar, but after it burned down in 1520, Carlos I ordered the new one built on its current spot. The exterior is a stunning example of Gothic flamboyance, with spiky turrets, flying buttresses, and leering gargoyles. Built in the same sand-colored stone as the rest of the old town, the cathedral blends nicely into the landscape. The interior is surprisingly serene, dominated by green marble choir stalls at its center. Look for the atmospheric cloister, which survived the original fire and was moved stone by stone to its current location.

Judería and Barrio San Esteban

Just behind the cathedral is Segovia's old Jewish quarter. Like the rest of the town, it is a web of tiny streets that open suddenly onto lovely plazas. Seek out the peaceful **Plaza de la Merced**. On its edges rests another example of Segovia's Romanesque heritage, the 12th-century **Iglesia San Andrés**. Take the picturesque route up to the Alcázar along Calle Socorro. Look for the **Puerta de San Andrés,** also called the Arco de Socorro, which was one of the seven stone arches that gave access to the Jewish quarter.

The **Museo de Segovia** (C/ Socorro 11, tel. 92/146-0615) is a hodge-podge of religious artifacts, anthropological finds, and art from the various cultures that once thrived in Segovia. The best part of the museum is its location right in one of the town's old walls. The views are spectacular, but the museum is scheduled to undergo restorations into 2007. Visit the tourist office for the latest on opening dates and hours. Another jewel in this area is **Iglesia San Esteban** situated in the plaza of the same name. The church was burned down and rebuilt in the 1800s, but the intriguing Byzantine tower dates to the 13th century and, at nearly 175 feet, is the highest Romanesque tower in Spain.

Alcázar

The third of Segovia's must-see sights is the magical **Alcázar** (Pl. Reina Victoria Eugenia, s/n, tel. 92/146-0759, www.alcazardesegovia.com,

10 A.M.–6 P.M. daily Oct.–Mar., 10 A.M.–7 P.M. daily Apr.–Sept., €3.50, buy tickets in the Casa de la Quimica to the left of the castle). The soaring cone-topped turrets of Segovia's famed castle are instantly familiar to fans of Disneyland. Rumor has it that Walt took inspiration for his fairyland castle from the Alcázar. The first evidence of a castle on this spot dates from 1122, shortly after the Moors were ousted. By the 13th century, it had become a favorite retreat for royalty, who enjoyed both the lovely views and excellent hunting in the surrounding regions. Due to its location at the top of a cliff carved out by the valleys of the converging Eresma and Clamores, it was also easily defended.

Throughout the Middle Ages the Alcázar was the sight of some of Old Castile's most important events. Isabel first met Fernando here. The pair later pledged their support of Christopher Columbus (Colón in Spanish) at the castle. Over a century later, King Felipe II married his fourth wife, Anna of Austria, here. Along with the rest of Spain in the 18th and 19th centuries, the Alcázar fell on hard times and entered a long period of disuse. It eventually became a prison and later a military academy. In 1862, a fire nearly destroyed it. The eventual rebuilding in the 1880s resulted in the castle's current fairy-tale form.

Check out the Chamber of the Kings with its elaborate gilded ceiling or the surprisingly small royal bedrooms. In the chapel, look for the painting of Spain's patron saint Santiago (Saint James). His nickname was Moor-slayer, and the painting grotesquely pays homage to that title. Climb the 156 slow-winding, stone stairs to the top of the **Torre Juan II** for amazing views of Segovia and the surrounding fields. The hike up is not for the weak of knees, wide of hips, or frail of heart. Steps are high and the spiraling staircase tiny. Only two people, one going up, another down can squeeze through at a time. The view compensates, with a breathtaking 360-degree panorama of the Castilian hillsides.

Valle de Eresma

The lush valley of the Eresma River, way below the outcrop on which the Alcázar sits, offers the best views of Segovia. Have your camera ready! There are a few sites worth visiting in the valley. It will take a few hours to see them all, so plan accordingly. If you are not driving, head for the **Puerta de Santiago** and walk down the steps to the main road below. From there, follow the signs for the *ruta turistica* and head for the **Iglesia Vera Cruz** (Crta. Zamarramala, s/n, 10:30 A.M.–1:30 P.M. and 3:30–7 P.M. Tues.–Sun., closed Mon. and Nov., €1.50). The church was built in 1208 by the Knights Templar, but it became a regular parish church when they were disbanded in 1312. Its 12-sided design is said to emulate the Church of the Holy Sepulchre in Jerusalem. Inside there is a two-story inner chamber where the knights held their secret rituals. It is surrounded by an outer room open to churchgoers. When the knights were around, the church housed a sliver of wood from the actual cross of Christ, hence the name Vera Cruz, or true cross.

Nearby is the **Convento de las Carmelitas Descalzas** (C/ Alameda de la Fuencisla, s/n, tel. 92/143-1349, 9:30 A.M.–1:30 P.M. and 4–7 P.M. Tues.–Sun.), founded by Saint John in 1558. The saint, known as San Juan de la Cruz, was so beloved by the people of Segovia that after he was buried in Andalucía, a crew of Segovians was dispatched to steal his body. The pope intervened and ordered that the saint be dismembered. His holy arms and legs were kept in Andalucía and the rest of his remains went to Segovia. Backtrack along the main road to get to the **Monasterio del Parral** (C/ Alameda del Eresma, s/n, 10 A.M.–12:30 P.M. and 4:15–6 P.M. daily, free), a 15th-century monastery built by Henry IV. The imposing complex houses a Gothic church and two serene cloisters.

ENTERTAINMENT AND EVENTS
Nightlife
Nightlife in Segovia is tame compared to the nearby party capitals of Madrid and Salamanca. Still, being Spanish, nocturnal revelry blows away almost any you might find stateside. The best area for bar-hopping is Plaza Mayor and there are a few late-night discos around the aqueduct. For a riotous cocktail experience, head to **Café Bar Menorá** (C/ San Frutos 21, tel. 92/146-3031) next to the cathedral. By day it's your basic bar serving coffees and beers. By night, it converts into a theme party from "country" to "funk." For a more laid-back night, go to **El Patio** (C/ Doctor Castelo 2) on the opposite side of the cathedral. The Irish pub **Canavan's** (Pl. Rubia 2, tel. 92/146-0252) is one of the liveliest bars in town. It is always full of English-speaking locals. They also offer a hefty free tapa with each beer.

Festivals and Events
If you are in Segovia the second week of May, don't be surprised to find the streets teeming with purple-headed giants, life-sized dolls, and colorful characters on stilts. It's just the tongue-twisting festival of **Titirimundo** (www.titirimundi .com), an international puppet festival that draws dozens of puppeteers and street theater groups from around the world. Free performances are held daily in Segovia's streets and plazas. Next up are the lively **Fiestas de San Juan y San Pedro** held the last weekend of June. Highlights include street fairs, nightly fireworks, and the town's most important bullfights.

ACCOMMODATIONS
Under €50
Hostal Fornos (C/ Infanta Isabel 13, tel. 92/146-0198, info@hostalfornos.com, www .hostalfornos.com, €45) is a step up from your basic cheap pension, with spacious rooms recently refurbished in green and terra-cotta. **Hostal Plaza** (C/ Cronista Lecea 11, tel. 92/146-0303, informacion@hotel-plaza.com, www.hostal-plaza.com, €42) offers a warren of drab but clean rooms in a great location. Cheap charmer **Hostal Juan Bravo** (C/ Juan Bravo 12, tel. 92/146-3413, €38) hides clean, updated rooms behind a run-down facade.

€50-100
One of the newest hostals in Segovia, **Natura de Segovia** (C/ Colón 5–7, tel. 92/146-6710,

info@naturadesegovia.com, www.naturade segovia.com, €70) is also one of the most charming. Stylishly blending rustic comfort with modern touches, this cozy family-run inn offers great value just steps from Plaza Mayor. **Hotel Acueducto** (C/ Padre Claret 10, tel. 90/225-0550, reservas@hotelacueducto.com, www.hotelacueducto.com, €88) claims the best views of the aqueduct from its rooftop terrace. The rooms are airy retreats done in white and blue, featuring all the modern amenities. If you're driving, check the hotel's website. They have conveniently photographed all the road signs from various cities leading into Segovia. **Las Sirenas** (C/ Juan Bravo 30, tel. 92/146-2663, www.hotelsirenas.com, €80) boasts a slightly battered elegance, comfortable rooms, and a spacious balcony to catch the sunset over Segovia. **Hostal Hidalgo** (C/ José Canalejas 3, tel. 92/146-3529, informacion@el-hidalgo.com, www.el-hidalgo.com, €55) offers basic rooms done up in rustic style. Ask for one with a view over the church of San Martín. The restaurant is popular with locals for its delicious take on classic Castilian dishes.

Over €100

Giving Segovia a much needed shot of boutique style is the gorgeous (C La Casa Mudejar (C/ Isabel la Católica 8, tel. 92/146-6250, info@lacasamudejar.com, www.lacasamudejar.com, €125). To stay here is to sleep among the history of Segovia—the basement houses Roman stairs, the building itself was a prominent residence in the Jewish quarter during the Middle Ages, and the dining room is set in a 15th-century converted patio. Each of its 40 rooms is named for towns in the province of Segovia and are meticulously decorated with Moorish touches, several with spectacular views. The charming **Hotel Ayala Berganza** (C/ Carretas 5, tel. 92/146-0448, ayalaberganza@partnerhotels.com, www.partner-hotels.com, €110) is built in a 15th-century palace that has been declared a historic monument. The 16 rooms are lavishly decorated and the service is top-notch. The only problem is that the hotel is tricky to find. It is located in Barrio San Millán, but just

two minutes walking to the aqueduct. Map it out before you go. **Los Linajes** (C/ Doctor Velasco 9, tel. 92/146-0479, €105) offers one of the prettiest locations of any hotel. Set in the northern walls of the city, overlooking the Eresma valley, the rustic hotel has lovely gardens and a terrace with a view. Request a room with a balcony if the weather is warm. The 19th-century **Infanta Isabel** (Pl. Mayor 12, tel. 92/146-1300, admin@hotelinfantaisabel.com, www.hotelinfantaisabel.com, €100), overlooking the Plaza Mayor, is a long-time favorite. The location is fantastic and if you score a room with a balcony on the plaza, your view will be magnificent. Though the rooms are a bit dated, they are still comfortable and feature all the top amenities. This is a favorite among older travelers.

FOOD

Though you can find *cochinillo* (roasted suckling pig) throughout Spain, gourmands worldwide claim that Segovia prepares the best. Whether it is the age-old roasting methods— a sprinkling of coarse salt, some fresh herbs, a well-worn terra-cotta roasting pan—or secret local roasting rites shared only by Segovian chefs, there is no denying that Segovia's suckling pig is melt-in-the-mouth good. One of the local tableside tricks is to cut the tender piglet with the side of a dinner plate. Two more hearty specialties to look out for are *judiones de la granja,* large white beans cooked with pork and spices, and *sopa castellana,* a simple broth soup seasoned with garlic, ham, and topped with an egg. The local dessert is *ponche segoviano,* a sponge cake soaked in orange liqueur, filled with custard, and topped with marzipan.

Cafés and Desserts

Your best bet for a great café experience is to try one of the many bars that line Plaza Mayor, especially in warmer months when tables are out in the plaza. Most serve breakfast, sandwiches, tapas, coffee, and drinks pretty much all day. The prices are slightly higher than what you'd pay elsewhere in town, but the view of the cathedral and the buzzing vibe of the plaza make the extra few euros worth it. Be on the look out for the art deco **La Concepción** (Pl. Mayor 15, tel. 92/146-0930, 9 A.M.–2 A.M. daily), a local favorite nicknamed "La Concha." In addition, the back-room restaurant is one of the best in the city, with a menu offering creative spins on local specialties plus an extensive wine list. Make reservations for dinner and expect to pay €40 per person. Escape the bustle of Plaza Mayor in the stylish **Natura Café** (C/ Colón 5–7, tel. 92/146-3079, 8 A.M.–11 P.M. daily, €5), which offers coffees and light fare all day long. For a sweet infusion, head to **Lima y Menta** (C/ Isabel la Católica 2, tel. 92/146-2141, 9:30 A.M.–9 P.M. daily, €5), a modern pastry shop with traditional offerings.

Gourmet
For something a little different, dine in a 600-year-old well at **Cueva de San Esteban** (C/ Valdeláguila 15, tel. 92/146-0982, 10 A.M.–midnight daily, €35). The elegant dining room is built inside of a medieval *aljibe* (stone water tank). The amusing menu dedicated to various saints includes Spanish favorites from *tortilla* to *jamón,* as well as upscale takes on grilled fish, meat, and vegetables. Owner Lucio won Spain's top sommelier award in 2002 and his intriguing wine list shows it. If you prefer lighter fare, visit their 16th-century patio or rustic bar for tapas. Kick the creativity up a notch at Lucio's newest restaurant, **Di-Vino** (C/ Valdeláguila 7, tel. 92/146-1650, 1–4 P.M. and 7:30 P.M.–midnight daily, €40), built specifically to house his 11,000-bottle collection of wine. In a dining room that is half rustic comfort, half modern swish, the award-winning chef offers creative interpretations of the local fare. Keep the bill under control by trying their *tosta* wine combos. A slab of toast topped with savory goodies is paired with wine for about €3 each. The latest trend in Spanish dining is Sephardic cooking—dishes based on medieval Jewish fare—and **El Fogón Sefardí** (C/ Judería Vieja 17, tel. 92/146-6250, 1:30–4:30 P.M. and 8:30–11:30 P.M. daily, €30) does it beautifully. Try the eggplant stuffed with pine nuts and almonds or the salad with dried fruits.

Local Cuisine
There are no shortages of restaurants in Segovia serving up carnivorous feasts based around *cochinillo.* You'll see the little piggies hanging in windows all over town and, quite disturbingly, a common souvenir is a stuffed animal *cochinillo* with a deliciously cute grin. The two most famous restaurants are Cándido and José María. The historic **Cándido** (Pl. Azoguejo 5, tel. 92/142-5911, www.mesondecandido.es, 1–4:30 P.M. and 8–11 P.M. daily, €40) commands the best location, with an upper-level dining room overlooking the aqueduct and a terrace tucked practically underneath it. Though foodies say the fare served here is not tops, the thousands of happy tourists that fill up at Cándido each year don't complain. ◖ **José María** (C/ Cronista Lecea 11, tel. 92/146-6017, 1–4 P.M. and 8–11:30 P.M. daily, €35), opened by a wine fanatic who trained at Cándido, offers what many locals swear is the best Castilian fare in Segovia. The restaurant also helped put the wines of Ribera del Duero on the map by exclusively offering them over the traditional rioja. In fact, the restaurant owns its own Ribera bodega, which produces the lovely Pago de Carraovejas wine. The rowdy bar upfront is usually packed with tapas-quaffing locals. Join them if you are not in the mood for a heavy meal.

Tapas
Good tapas can be found throughout the old town and you can't go wrong at any of the bars in the Plaza Mayor. A good one to try is **La Taurina** (Pl. Mayor 8, tel. 92/146-0902), a bull-crazy bar offering tapas all day. To tapa with the locals, head to popular—and cheap—**Bar San Martín** (Pl. San Martín 3, tel. 92/146-2466, €12). During the warmer months, opt for a fountain-side table in the plaza. **Vadiam** (C/ Padre Claret 29, tel. 92/143-5103, €8) is a cozy favorite with a large variety of tapas. The house specialty is the infamous *tortilla española.* **Correos** (Pl. San Facundo 4, tel. 92/146-3041, €15) offers homemade tapas on one side

of the bar, and hot chocolates and pastries on the other. It also houses a curious museum of old liqueur bottles.

INFORMATION

The local tourist office is housed in the **Centro de Recepción de Visitantes** (Pl. Azoguejo, s/n, 10 A.M.–8 P.M. daily) and is a great place to get oriented. This tourist office/shop/museum features a model of the city, tons of brochures, and helpful English-speaking attendants. They also offer occasional walking tours of the town. The **regional tourist office** (Pl. Mayor 10, 9 A.M.–2 P.M. and 5–8 P.M. daily, longer hours in summer) has local information plus maps and brochures on sights further afield in the province of Segovia. For Internet information in English, try the official Spanish tourism website www.spain.info. If you can manage Spanish, see www.infosegovia.com.

GETTING THERE AND AROUND
Bus

Bus is the best way to travel to Segovia from Madrid. Buses are run by **La Sepulvedana** (Po. Florída 11, Metro: Príncipe Pío, www.lasepulvedana.es, €6) and leave about every half-hour. The trip lasts a bit over one hour. The **bus station in Segovia** (Po. Ezequiel González 12) is about a 10-minute walk to the aqueduct. Turn right out of the station and then left on Avenida Fernández Ladreda. Follow it up to the aqueduct. You may want to stop on the way to see the Iglesia San Millán and the Iglesia San Clemente, both of which lie on this broad avenue. From Segovia, you can continue by bus to Ávila or beyond.

Train

There is little reason to take the local train to Segovia unless you absolutely can't stand buses, as it takes twice as long. There are nine trains that leave from Madrid's Atocha station daily. Go to the *cercanías* side of the station. The train station in Segovia is over 1.6 kilometers (one mile) from the old town. Catch local bus 3 or take a cab for around €4.

Car

From Madrid, catch the A-6 to Guadarrama and through the toll tunnel, then veer right onto the N-603. The drive is almost 100 kilometers (60 miles)and should take about 1.5 hours. Metered street parking only runs for a maximum of two hours, a major inconvenience if you are sightseeing. You'd be better off following the large blue "P" signs to a parking lot, though on Saturdays after 2 P.M. and on Sundays, street parking is free.

VICINITY OF SEGOVIA
◖ La Granja Palace

If you have time, make a detour from Segovia to the Bourbon palace of **La Granja de San Ildefonso** (Pl. España 17, Real Sitio de San Ildefonso, tel. 92/147-0019, www.patrimonio nacional.es, 10 A.M.–6 P.M. Tues.–Sun. Apr.–Sept., 10 A.M.–1:30 P.M. and 3–5 P.M. Tues.–Sat., 10 A.M.–2 P.M. Sun. Oct.–Mar., €5). Nestled at the foot of the Sierra Guadarrama mountains 11 kilometers (seven miles) east of Segovia, this Versailles-style palace was built in 1721 by Felipe V, who grew up in the real Versailles with his grandfather King Louis XIV. While the palace is impressive with its Bourbon opulence, Flemish tapestries, and regal crystal display, the real jewel of *La Granja* (the farm) is its sumptuous gardens. Felipe had Europe's best gardeners create a lush park-like garden with 26 sculptured fountains that pay homage to a pantheon of mythical gods. Several, such as the fountain "La Fama," once shot spouts of water as high as 100 feet into the air. The fountains, built in the early 18th century, are only turned on a few times per year (May 30, July 25, and August 25). Also, during spring, summer, and fall, if the water tables are not too low, four of the fountains rush into life at exactly 5:30 P.M. on Wednesday, Saturday, and Sunday. This grand 10-minute display costs €3.40. In the church next to the palace lie the bodies of Felipe and his Italian wife Isabel. Also on the grounds is the Royal Glass Factory of La Granja, an 18th-century structure with an ongoing collection devoted to the art of glassmaking. Note, though the palace is closed Mondays, the gardens remain open and are free.

Though your best bet for both dining and dreaming is to head back to Segovia or onto Madrid, if you must stay overnight, check in to **Las Fuentes** (C/ Padre Claret 6, tel. 92/147-1024, €100), an elegantly restored mansion with a tranquil flowered courtyard. The plain Jane **Hotel Roma** (C/ Guardas 2, tel. 92/147-0752, www.hotelroma.org, €52) offers neat rooms at reasonable rates. For bottom-of-the-barrel rates, the place to go is **Pozo de la Nieve** (C/ Baños 4, tel. 92/147-0598, €30), a clean pension with shared baths.

There are several cafés and tapas bars around the town's central square, Plaza de los Dolores. Look for **Casa Zaca** (C/ Embajadores 6, tel. 92/147-0087), a very popular lunch-only spot offering hearty fare at homey prices. Have a grander meal next door at **La Chata** (C/ Embajadores 3, tel. 92/147-1500, €20), a classic Castilian restaurant. Try their *torrijas* (a type of bread pudding) for dessert. At the **Bar Restaurante La Terraza** (C/ Puerta Segovia 2, tel. 92/147-0311) tuck into traditional tapas on their shady terrace.

There are 14 buses per day from Segovia to La Granja. They leave from the **La Sepulvedana station** (Po. Ezequiel González 12). The ride is about 20 minutes. There are also two daily direct buses from Madrid, also operated by La Sepulvedana (Po. Florida 11), but it's easier to go to Segovia and then travel to La Granja from there. If you are driving from Segovia, take CL-601 south out of town and straight there. From Madrid, take the A-6 to Collado Villalba, then the M-601 north.

Ávila

Nicknamed the "city of saints and stones," Ávila is a medieval wonderland, jam-packed with solemn gray Romanesque and Gothic architecture, above all, the magnificent solid granite wall surrounding the old city. Saints are honored with no less than 30 religious buildings, many dedicated to Ávila's homegrown Saint Teresa. Though it lacks the big sights of Segovia or Salamanca, Ávila offers a glimpse into Spain's medieval past not yet trampled by millions of modern-day tourists. Make the effort to at least spend a morning here.

Celtiberian tribes made the first settlement at present-day Ávila around 700 B.C. Later conquered by the Romans, Ávila was a fractious outpost for centuries. From the 9th to the 11th centuries, the city bounced back and forth between Muslim and Christian rule until the fall of nearby Toledo in 1085 put the area firmly under Christian rule. By the 13th century, Ávila had become a thriving commercial center with a powerful noble class. As you walk the streets, you'll see the remnants of their palatial mansions, many still bearing noble coats of arms. By the dawn of the 17th century, the glory days for Ávila were over. The Civil War and the years of Franco's dictatorship further dragged down the town's fortunes, turning it into just another backwater Spanish town. Not until the late 20th century did the town start to rebound. Today, Ávila's city walls—the best preserved in the country—are a UNESCO World Heritage Site and are the foundation upon which the town's tourism industry is based.

SIGHTS
◖ La Muralla

A great way to begin a day in Ávila is with a stroll along the sentry path that tops the medieval wall surrounding the city (tel. 92/025-5088, 11 A.M.–6 P.M. Tues.–Sun. Oct.–Apr., 11 A.M.–8 P.M. Tues.–Sun. May–Sept., €3.50). The views are magnificent! To call La Muralla imposing is to gravely underestimate its enormity. Looping around the city for 2.4 kilometers (1.5 miles), the granite wall is Europe's best-preserved example of medieval defense

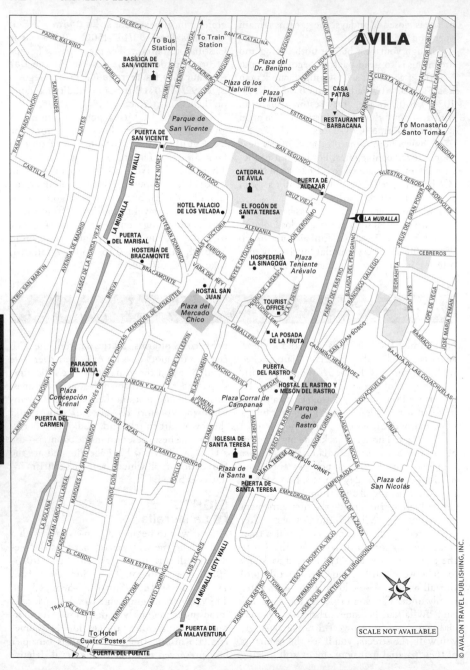

ÁVILA

To Bus Station
To Train Station

BASÍLICA DE SAN VICENTE

Plaza del Dr. Benigno

Plaza de los Nalvillos

Plaza de Italia

CASA PATAS

RESTAURANTE BARBACANA

To Monasterio Santo Tomás

PUERTA DE SAN VICENTE

Parque de San Vicente

LA MURALLA (CITY WALL)

CATEDRAL DE ÁVILA

PUERTA DE ALCÁZAR

CRUZ VIEJA

LA MURALLA

HOTEL PALACIO DE LOS VELADA

EL FOGÓN DE SANTA TERESA

PUERTA DEL MARISAL

HOSTERÍA DE BRACAMONTE

HOSPEDERÍA LA SINAGOGA

Plaza Teniente Arévalo

HOSTAL SAN JUAN

Plaza del Mercado Chico

TOURIST OFFICE

LA POSADA DE LA FRUTA

PARADOR DEL ÁVILA

Plaza Concepción Arénal

PUERTA DEL CARMEN

PUERTA DEL RASTRO

HOSTAL EL RASTRO Y MESÓN DEL RASTRO

Plaza Corral de Campanas

Parque del Rastro

IGLESIA DE SANTA TERESA

Plaza de la Santa

PUERTA DE SANTA TERESA

Plaza de San Nicolás

To Hotel Cuatro Postes

PUERTA DE LA MALAVENTURA

PUERTA DEL PUENTE

LA MURALLA (CITY WALL)

SCALE NOT AVAILABLE

Ávila's medieval wall has stood for more than 700 years.

planning. Begun in the 11th century and completed by the 14th, the crenellated wall is anchored with 90 towers, over 2,500 merlons (the spiky peaks that crown the length of the wall), and nine arched gateways into the city. The most remarkable gates are the **Puerta de San Vincente** and **Puerta del Alcázar,** both flanked by towers over 65 feet high. The latter gives access to the sentry path.

Catedral de Ávila

Originally planned as a Romanesque church, the Catedral de Ávila (Pl. de Catedral, s/n, tel. 92/021-1641, 9:30 A.M.–1:30 P.M. and 3:30–8 P.M. daily May–Sept., 10 A.M.–1:30 P.M.and 3:30–6 P.M. daily Oct.–Apr., €2.50) became the first Gothic church built in Spain. Built right into the city's walls, it served as both a house of worship and a part of the town's defense plan. Its massive granite apse forms the central buttress in the town's eastern wall. Inside, the red and white limestone columns and the inner sanctum are both impressive. There is also a museum with paintings by El Greco.

Basílica de San Vicente

Just outside the city walls, Basílica de San Vicente (Pl. San Vicente, tel. 92/025-5230 10 A.M.–2 P.M. and 4–6:30 P.M. daily, €1.20) is one of Ávila's most impressive buildings, dating back to the 11th century. Like many churches in the region, the basilica was begun in one architectural style (Romanesque) and completed in another (Gothic). It is named after San Vicente, who, along with his two sisters Cristeta and Sabina, was slaughtered by Roman soldiers on this site in the 4th century.

Monasterio Santo Tomás

Built towards the end of the 15th century, Monasterio Santo Tomás (Pl. Granada 1, tel. 92/035-2237, museum 11 A.M.–12:45 P.M. and 4–6 P.M. Tues.–Sun., cloisters 10 A.M.–1 P.M. and 4–8 P.M. daily, €1.50) houses three beautiful cloisters. The most notable is the Reyes (Kings Cloister), named for Isabel and Fernando, who attended mass here. It has a magnificent Mudejar ceiling.

Iglesia de Santa Teresa

Built on the birthplace of the saint herself, Iglesia de Santa Teresa (tel. 92/021-1030, 8:30 A.M.–1:30 P.M. and 3:30–8:30 P.M. daily, free) is the base for the worldwide Saint Teresa following. The room where she was born now serves as a chapel. In the next room over, you can get an up-close glimpse at the saint's holy index finger. Encased in airtight glass lies a decaying finger reputed to belong to the saint herself.

ACCOMMODATIONS
Under €50

The rooms at **Hostal San Juan** (C/ Communeros de Castilla 3, tel. 92/025-1475, €36) may lack character but the staff more than makes up for it. A favorite of bargain hunters is **El Rastro** (Pl. Rastro 1, tel. 92/021-1218, www.elrastroavila.com, €41), a rustic inn built right into the city's famous walls.

€50-100

For great views of Ávila's walls, stay at **Cuatro Postes** (Av. Salamanca 23, 92/022-0000, www.hotelcuartopostes.com, €55), which sits atop the town's best lookout point. For a bit of history, book a night at **Hospedería la Sinagoga** (C/ Reyes Católicos 22, tel. 92/453-0609, €82), a renovated old synagogue with distinctive Jewish architectural details still present alongside modern comforts.

Over €100

The most sought-after hotel in the region is the medieval ◖ **Palacio de los Velada** (Pl. Catedral 10, tel. 92/025-5100, www.velada hoteles.com, €125), where guests are treated like the royalty who slumbered here centuries ago, if not better, as even the Kings of Castile couldn't have imagined all the modern luxuries on offer here. Two blocks northwest of Plaza del Mercado Chico is the state-run **Parador del Ávila** (Marqués de Camales de Chozas 2, tel. 92/021-1340, www.parador.es, €127). This majestic parador sits on a ridge overlooking the Adaja River and boasts an elegant courtyard perfect for lounging and recently updated rooms.

FOOD

As throughout Castile, the local cuisine is based on roasted suckling pig and lamb. For variety, Ávila also specializes in *chuletón de ternera* (veal T-bone steak). Vegetarians will delight over the native haricot beans, which are so distinctive they've been awarded their own appellation from Spanish gastronomic authorities. Santa Teresa left her mark all over Ávila, but the sweetest relic she left behind is *yemas de Santa Teresa,* a sugary concoction made with egg yolks. You can find them in the windows of nearly every pastry and souvenir shop in town.

Local Cuisine

Ávila has a slightly limited restaurant scene but there are a few places worth checking out. Within the walls, take a walk from Plaza del Mercado Chico along Calle Vallespin and compare menus and prices at a number of decent establishments.

Those who judge **Casa Felipe** (Pl. Mercado Chico 12, tel. 92/021-3924, €22) by its very modest exterior will miss out on this cozy restaurant serving excellent local cuisine. In warm weather, head straight for at **La Posada de la Fruta** (Pl. Pedro Dávila 8, tel. 92/022-0984, €15), a great place to relax and have some drinks. When you get hungry, head inside to the dining room to sample traditional fare. For a more refined ambience, check out **El Fogón de Santa Teresa** (Pl. Catedral 9, tel. 92/021-1023). The dining room is bathed in a golden light that is the perfect backdrop for a romantic meal. For a more rustic feel, head to **Hostería de Bracamonte** (C/ Bracamonte 6, closed Tues.), located in a converted Renaissance mansion. The house specialty is *codero asado* (roasted lamb).

Tapas

For a pleasant bar with good tapas, try **Casa Patas** (C/ San Millán 4, closed Wed. and Sept.). It has a small dining room open in the evenings only. **Barbacana** (Pl. Santa Teresa 8, tel. 92/022-0011) has a menu that ranges from breakfast to dinner, but their excellent tapas are their claim to fame. Next to the *hostal* of the same name, **Mesón del Rastro** (Pl. Rastro 1) is an excellent tapas bar with a wide variety of offerings. For the best beer in town, make your way to **Gambrinus** (Av. de Portugal 15, tel. 92/025-7273). This chain bar always comes through with top-quality tapped beer and tapas.

INFORMATION

The local **tourist office** (Pl. Pedro Dávila 4 tel. 92/021-1387, www.avilaturismo.com) can provide you with a surplus of information about the city, but Ávila is so easily explored that you might want to skip it. You can get a decent map at any souvenir shop or just pop into the first hotel you see for a free one.

GETTING THERE AND AROUND
Train

More than 30 trains travel the 1.5-hour ride from Madrid (€5.60) to **Ávila's train station** (Po. Estación). Be sure to book the direct service; the local *cercanías* train is a long, hard-seated affair. If you want to continue on, it is a 1.5-hour ride to Salamanca (€5). You can also get direct service to Burgos, Léon, and Valladolid. La Muralla is 20 minutes walking west out of the station.

Bus

Buses depart from **Ávila's bus station** (Avenida de Madrid) for Madrid (€6.30), Salamanca (€4.65), and Segovia (€3.75).

Car

Traveling to Madrid by car, head northeast on N-110 and at Villacastín turn onto the N-6 or the parallel A-6 *autopista* (toll road). To get to Salamanca head north on the N-501, the N-110 heads east towards Segovia and west to Plasencia. Take N-403 north for Valladolid.

VICINITY OF ÁVILA
Sierra de Gredos

This rambling mountain range bristles with dark forests and pristine lakes. It is the perfect natural antidote to medieval church and Gothic facade overload. The Sierra offers ample outside activities including hiking, mountain biking, rock climbing, and canoeing. Even if you're not the outdoorsy type, a simple drive through the area can be a peaceful experience. It's best to go in spring or fall because the heat is unbearable in the summer, and the cold deathly in winter.

For guided walking tours in English call **Turactiv** (Navarredonda de Gredos, Ávila, tel. 67/865-4242, info@turactiv.com, www.turactiv.com), which offers day trips and overnight excursions with varying levels of difficulty. You can also try Madrid-based American expat Anne Pinder, who runs **www.puentespain.com** and offers custom-made hikes and walks.

You can take a bus through the range but they run infrequently and not on the weekends. Renting a car is the best way to enjoy these mountains at your own pace. There are three main routes through the Sierra. The C-502 runs north and south along an old Roman road. The C-500 has some of the best views from the road and takes you through many scenic villages. On the southern face of the range is the C-501, giving you a peasant ride from Arenas de San Pedro on your way to the cozy village of Candeleda.

CASTILLA Y LEÓN

Salamanca

Salamanca is an architectural stunner with a wealth of sand-colored, elaborate Plateresque buildings that date back to the town's medieval glory days as home to one of the world's most prestigious universities. The college spirit is alive and well so many centuries later and the town buzzes year-round with academic purpose and legendary nightlife. The two sides balance each other nicely. During the day, join the locals relaxing in the Plaza Mayor, the unrivaled heart of the city, or visit the dozen or so historic university buildings that line the town's elegant streets. Later, well after sundown, mix it with the college kids at any of the hundreds of bars that pump out music and drink until well into the next day. If you don't want to do an overnight, there is a 6 A.M. train from Salamanca to Madrid every morning.

Like much of Spain, Salamanca's distant past was defined by warfare and shifting political rule. Carthaginian leader Hannibal wrested control of the area from Celtiberian settlers in the 3rd century and the town was born. Later, as the Romans moved into power, they used the town as a stopping point on their trading route across Spain. Centuries later, the Moors took control of the city. Christian forces claimed the city in 1085, finally ushering in a period of relative calm. This paved the way for the largest event in the history of Salamanca—the founding of the university in 1218. Two centuries later, it had become one of the best—and wealthiest—in Europe. Literary and academic life were good for Salamanca and most of the exuberant buildings that line the town today were built during this golden era. However, Salamanca began to fall out of academic favor under the religiously conservative rule of Felipe II. From the 18th to the mid-20th century, the town followed the rest of Spain into economic downfall and oppressive dictatorship. Franco, who was notoriously anti-intellectual, allowed

Salamanca's Plaza Mayor draws young and old.

© ZIVILE VITEIKAITE

CASTILLA Y LEÓN

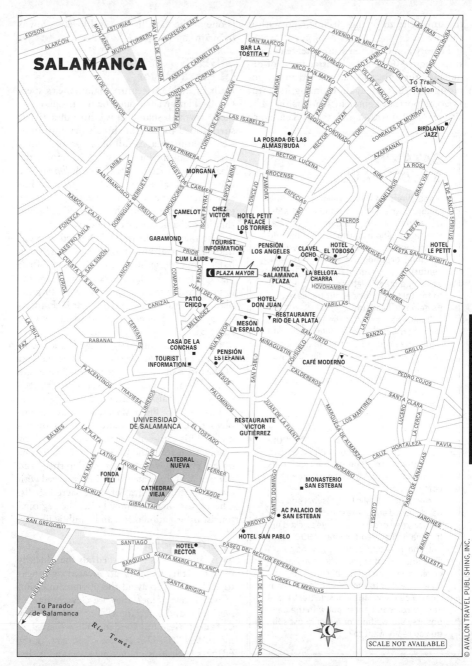

SALAMANCA

© AVALON TRAVEL PUBLISHING, INC.

SCALE NOT AVAILABLE

the university to further decline, and with it the city.

History and common sense intervened and since the 1980s and the reinstatement of democracy, the university has enjoyed an invigorating rebirth, once again claiming its status as an important center of scholarship. The city rebounded with it and, today, Salamanca is one of the most lively—and lovely—towns in Spain.

SIGHTS
Plaza Mayor

Built in the 18th century, Salamanca's spectacular Plaza Mayor puts the main squares of most towns to shame. It is a hive of activity, surrounded by elegant three-story buildings that sit atop arcades full of shops and cafés. Like most of the buildings in Salamanca, the plaza is constructed of *piedra de Villamayor,* a fine-grained sandstone native to the area. Pliable when extracted from the earth, the stone gradually hardens into the rich golden brown that is so characteristic of the city.

The plaza has historically served as Salamanca's central hub, hosting debates, town halls, and even bullfights. At the heart of the plaza is the clock, a landmark that serves as the town's favorite meeting spot. Surrounding the plaza are statues of famous Spaniards. Franco's is easy to spot: Students regularly deface it with spray paint.

Despite its historical significance and architectural beauty, the plaza is still an active part of the city's social life. The sidewalk cafés are full to the brim most warm evenings with residents nearly outnumbering tourists.

Just south of Plaza Mayor, seek out the emblematic **Casa de las Conchas** (C/ Compañía 2). This 15th-century mansion was built by a nobleman from the Order of Santiago. The order's symbol is the *concha* (scallop shell) and the facade of this stately building is carved with over 400 stone replicas of these sacred shells. The House of Shells now holds the regional tourist information office and a public library.

The Cathedrals

Salamanca boasts two cathedrals that, luckily for foot-weary travelers, are located right next to each other. To avoid the obvious question of which one's older, they are cleverly named *vieja* (old) and *nueva* (new). The 12th-century **Catedral Vieja** (C/ Cardenal Pla y Deniel, s/n, tel. 92/321-7476, 10 A.M.–7:30 P.M. daily, €3) was built in Romanesque style and is dis-

SATAN'S STUDY HALL

If you overdose on the religiosity of Salamanca's many *iglesias* and *catedrales,* try taking a walk on the dark side of Salamanca. Legend has it that the Cueva de Salamanca once served as Satan's private teaching ground. The story goes back centuries and even Cervantes, Spain's esteemed man of letters, gave credence to the tale in a story about the cave and its demonic academy.

Rumor has it that in the 14th century, local bad boy Enrique Villena tutored under the Lord of Darkness in the occult sciences. The price for the lessons was nothing less than the student's soul. Villena didn't like that idea and refused to comply. The devil was naturally incensed, yet before he could demand his payment Villena escaped the cave. The devil set out in pursuit, but Villena eluded him. His shadow, however, did not, and the devil devoured it. Poor Villena had to roam the earth alone for the rest of his life without even his shadow to keep him company.

When the Catholic Kings Isabel and Fernando heard about the evil doings in Salamanca, they ordered the cave bricked up. It remained sealed for nearly 500 years until the local tourist board saw the cave's potential tourist appeal. The cave was uncovered, restored, and opened to visitors. Take a peek into the den of darkness at Cuesta de Carvajal, alongside the Villena Tower. You can't enter, but with the devil possibly still waiting for his long-lost soul, do you really want to?

tinctive for its Torre del Gallo, a scaly, Byzantine dome topped with a rooster. Inside, the 1445 altarpiece is an impressive collection of 54 vividly painted tablets detailing the story of Christ. In the Capilla de Santa Bárbara see the well-worn feet of the tomb of Bishop Lucero. An old university tradition required students to spend the night before an important exam studying in the chapel with their feet propped up on those of the bishop.

Begun in the 16th century, the **Catedral Nueva** (tel. 92/321-7476, 9 A.M.–8 P.M. daily, €3) was added on to well into the 18th century, giving the mostly Gothic structure Renaissance and baroque flourishes. Before entering, marvel at the intricately carved **Puerta del Nacimiemieto.** Next, make your way to the flamboyant **Puerta de Ramos** and seek out the unusual sculptures of an astronaut and a lion eating an ice cream. Both were added by good-natured stonemasons during the last restoration.

The University

The **Edificio Histórico de la Universidad de Salamanca** (Patio de Escuelas, s/n, tel. 92/329-4400, 9:30 A.M.–1:30 P.M. and 4–7 P.M. Mon.–Fri., 9:30 A.M.–1 P.M. and 4–6:30 P.M. Sat., 10 A.M.–1 P.M. Sun., €4) is the university's main building. Founded in 1218, the school became a university in 1254. At the pinnacle of its educational and cultural reach in the 15th and 16th centuries, it enrolled over 10,000 students in 25 colleges and boasted the world's most important astronomy department. Columbus consulted with it before heading out to sea.

Queen Isabel was a benefactor of the school, and her bust, alongside that of her husband, King Fernando, dominate the Plateresque facade of the building. They are surrounded by lifelike depictions of heroes, biblical scenes, and noble coats of arms. However, these images are not what draw the rapt attention of the masses staring and pointing at the facade. There's a tiny frog hidden amongst the imagery, and legend has it that anyone who can spot the frog is granted good luck for a year. Dur-

COURTESY OF SOTUR

Edificio Histórico de la Universidad de Salamanca

ing exams, you can find students taking time away from studying in hopes that the friendly amphibian can make up for a semester of too much *discoteca* not enough *biblioteca* (library). Speaking of which, the university's library is one of the oldest in Europe and houses over 2,800 ancient manuscripts. Inside, seek out the whimsical Renaissance stairway featuring giant insects and bishops popping out of pots. The cloisters, around which the old lecture rooms were built, are also worth seeing.

Monasterio San Esteban

The monks of Monasterio San Esteban (Pl. Concilio de Trento, tel. 92/321-5000, 4–8 P.M. Mon. and Tues., 9:30 A.M.–1:30 P.M. and 4–8 P.M. Wed.–Sat., 9:30 A.M.–1:30 P.M. Sun.) were one of the first to take Christopher Columbus's ideas seriously. They helped him secure an audience with Queen Isabel and the rest is world history. The monastery is an interesting mix of Gothic and Renaissance styles, while the western facade is a Plateresque masterpiece depicting the martyrdom of St. Stephen.

CASTILLA Y LEÓN

Puente Romano

Dating back to the 1st century, the Puente Romano (Av. San Gregorio, tel. 92/326-8571), a well-preserved stone Roman bridge, stretches across the river Tormes. With its 26 arches, the 400-meter bridge was part of the Roman silver road. Now it offers some of the best views in all of Salamanca.

ENTERTAINMENT AND EVENTS
Nightlife

The only way to truly understand Salamanca's famed nightlife is to experience it. Students from all over the world come to Salamanca to study Spanish, or at least that's what they tell their parents. The real reason is to revel in the all-night madness that the locals call *la marcha*. For some all-night fun, remember that pubs stay open until 4 A.M., discos until 7 A.M., and there are always a smattering of "after hours" that start at 6 A.M. and go into midday. Look for flyers and cards on the street and in bars.

To ease into the night, try **Birdland Jazz** (C/ Azafranal 57). Like its name suggests, the background music is jazz and the vibe is relaxing. Another chilled-out spot is **Juanita** (Pl. San Boal), with soft lighting and an emphasis on good conversation with friends. For a more upbeat vibe, grab a stool at **Café Moderno** (Gran Vía 75), which is extremely popular thanks to unique theme nights. Hang out with the local avant-garde at **Clavel Ocho** (C/ Clavel 8). Try to snag a spot on the terrace. Kick it up a notch (or is that a shot?) at **Chupiteria** (Pl. Monterrey), which translates as the "shot bar." All they serve is *chupitos* (shots) of liqueur that come in dozens of different flavors. Everyone makes a stop here during a night out in Salamanca.

Although it's a university town, it is still Spain and going out to a night club means dressing nice. Leave your Gap T-shirt and shorts in your suitcase or you might be left out in the street by the bouncer. The fun doesn't start at **La Posada de las Almas** (Pl. San Boal 7) until around 3 A.M. but when it does, this dollhouse-inspired club is the place to be for the student crowd. For a more mixed crowd, try the massive **Morgana** (C/ Iscar Peira 30), famous for attracting both teens and middle-agers. The decor is medieval sorcerer meets King Arthur and the music varies from techno downstairs to Latino upstairs. Sporting a similar medieval vibe is sister bar **Camelot** (C/ Bordadores 3), where you feel like you just stepped into a scene from *The Sword and the Stone*. Push your way to the center of the very crowded dance floor or go upstairs for a quieter setting. If you enjoyed the Plaza Mayor, head to **Cum Laude** (C/ Prior 7), where the dance floor is a replica of the stately plaza. It is a great late-night spot, but it's also open during the day for a cup of coffee.

If you're still up at 5 A.M., go to **Garamond** (C/ Prior 24), where the best Spanish music keeps the 30-something crowd jumping all night long. **Buda** (Pl. San Boal 5) gets started in the wee hours, and its Far East decor draws a far-out, trendy crowd.

Festivals and Events

Lunes de Aguas is a family celebration with a seedy background. In the olden days, the city's prostitutes were banished to the other side of the river during Lent. On the second Monday after Easter, a priest would take a boat across the river and escort the ladies back to the city brothels. Today, this tradition is celebrated by families who spend the day picnicking on the river. Salamanca celebrates its patron saint San Juan for four days starting around June 12 with the **Fiesta de San Juan de Sahagun**. There is non-stop partying in the streets, food booths, concerts, and fireworks. Things get even wilder the first week of September for the town's female patron saint during the **Fiestas de la Virgen de la Vega,** which is accompanied by Salamanca's most important bullfights.

ACCOMMODATIONS

For help booking rooms throughout Salamanca city and province, visit www.hosteleriade salamanca.org.

Under €50

Right on Plaza Mayor, **Pension Los Angeles** (Pl. Mayor 10, tel. 92/321-8166 €43) offers outrageously cheap prices. Another budget option just off Rúa Mayor is **Pensión Estefania** (C/ Jesus 5, tel. 92/321-7372, €45). If you want your own bathroom, you'll have to spend a bit extra. Practically in the shadow of the cathedrals, **Fonda Feli** (C/ Libreros 58, tel. 92/321-6010, €40) offers simple rooms. If you want to get away from the noise of Salamanca's nightlife, **Hotel Le Petit** (Ronda Sancti-Spiritus 39, tel. 92/360-0773, www.lepetithotel.net, €49) offers rooms with lots of lace and embroidered wallpaper.

€50-100

The **Hotel San Polo** (C/ Arroyo de Santo Domingo 2, tel. 92/321-1177, hotelsanpolo@hotelsanpolo.com, www.hotelsanpolo.com, €96), run by the Best Western chain, is built within the ruins of the 11th-century Romanesque church of San Polo. The ruins have been incorporated into the modern building, making it truly unique. It will cost you a bit more, but do ask for a room with a view of the cathedrals. Thanks to its restored facade, **Hotel Salamanca Plaza** (Pl. Mercado 16, tel. 92/327-2250, www.salamancaplaza.com, €72) has a historical feel along with its comfortable and modern rooms. Close to Plaza Mayor, **El Toboso** (C/ Clavel 7, tel. 92/327-1462, €45) offers a rustic charm with its wood-paneled rooms. **Hotel Don Juan** (C/ Quintana 6, tel. 92/326-1473, info@hoteldonjuan-salamanca.com, www.hoteldonjuan-salamanca.com, €72) is located on a pedestrian street just minutes from the Plaza Mayor. Rooms have seen better days, but they are clean and the staff is friendly.

Over €100

Travelers agree that **Hotel Rector** (Po. Rector Esperabe 10, tel. 92/321-8482, hotelrector@telefonica.net, www.hotelrector.com, €130) is the best hotel in Salamanca. Located in one of the town's typical golden-hued Plateresque buildings, the family-run property features 13 rooms lovingly decorated with mahogany furnishings and marble bathrooms. There is a hotel bar and a salon with modern stained glass windows. The elegant, small **Hotel Petit Palace Las Torres** (C/ Concejo 4, tel. 92/321-2100, www.hotelpetitpalacelastorres.com, €130) is located on the backside of the Plaza Mayor, and if you upgrade to a suite your balcony will open right onto this gorgeous Salamanca jewel. For a shot of modernity amidst all the antiquity, head to the **AC Palacio de San Esteban** (C/ Arroyo de Santo Domingo 3, tel. 92/326-2296, www.ac-hotels.com, €138). Built in a 16th-century convent, this five-star hotel offers all the modern touches you could want, from sleek furnishings to mosaic-tiled baths.

Although it's located on a hill on the other side of the Rivers Tormes, the **Parador de Salamanca** (C/ Teso de la Feria 2, tel. 92/319-2082, www.parador.es, €119) makes up for the distance with its panoramic views of town. Not as spectacular as other paradors in the chain, here you must settle for the vista, the marble and wood interior, and the swimming pool.

FOOD

Salamancan fare is based on roasted meat. Two of the specialties are *cochinillo* (suckling pig) and *cabrito* (young goat). There are also some innovative restaurants featuring daring new chefs.

Gourmet

At his self-named restaurant, **Víctor Gutiérrez** (C/ San Pablo 66, tel. 92/326-2973, closed Sun., €50) whips up some of the most creative meals in Salamanca. His dishes take their cue from the seasons and he is equally adept at fish as he is at game. Another culinary Victor is Victoriano Salvador, who trained in France to perfect the stunning cuisine he serves at **Chez Victor** (C/ Espoz y Mina 26, tel. 92/321-3123, closed Mon. and Sun. P.M., €41), one of the most acclaimed restaurants in Castilla y León. Specialties include freshly prepared fish with nouveau French touches.

Local Cuisine

Despite boasting only four tables (or maybe because of it), **Mesón La Espada** (C/ Sánchez

Barbero 5, closed Wed., €15) is one of the most popular places in town. Specialties include herb-laced salads and delicious roasted meats *a la espada,* which are served in traditional clay pots. **Río de la Plata** (Pl. Peso 1, tel. 92/321-9005, closed Mon. P.M. and Tues., €40) is a top-rated traditional dining room with exquisite renditions of local favorites, particularly *lechazo,* roasted suckling lamb. Opened in 1902, **La Bellota Charra** (Pl. Mercado 8, tel. 92/321-9657) is right next to the city's fresh food market, which allows its chefs to get first dibs on the best produce of the day. *Jamón* is one of their specialties, and it hangs by the dozen above the bar, where you'd do well to sit if the popular dining room is too full.

Tapas

When locals want to tapas-hop, they head for **Calle Van Dyck.** It's lined with great little tapas bars, and you can't go wrong with any of them. This area is a bit out of the main tourist zone, but it's worth it for the quality of the food and the chance to mingle with someone other than college students. Just remember, Spaniards wouldn't think of visiting a tapas bar before 9 P.M.—don't go any earlier or you'll be all alone.

Back in the center, it is standing room only at **Bambú** (C/ Prior 4), which has been sating students' appetites for years. Tapas come in huge portions, and even if you only order a drink you'll get a freebie side of something yummy. Right on Plaza Mayor, **❰ Mesón Cervantes** (Pl. Mayor 15, tel. 92/321-7213) is as famous with locals as it is with tourists and students. Everything is excellent and the drink to wash it down with is the homemade sangria. Go early to snag a table on the plaza. **Patio Chico** (C/ Meléndez 13, 92/326-8616) has an extensive selection of tapas lined up on the bar. They also do excellent grilled meats. **Antonio Bar** (C/ Dimas Madariaga 30, tel. 92/322-5020) is famous city-wide for their *patatas bravas,* fried potatoes served with spicy tomato sauce. As traditional as they come, Antonio's is said to be frequented by bullfighters. *¡Ole!* **La Tostita** (Pl. San Marcos, s/n) packs in the crowds with their tasty tapas on toast. Try the *gambas* (shrimp with aioli).

INFORMATION

The **Municipal Tourist Office** (Pl. Mayor 12, tel. 92/321-8342, 9 A.M.–2 P.M. and 4:30–6:30 P.M. daily) offers information and maps on just the city while the **Regional Tourist Office** (C/ Rúa Mayor 10, tel. 92/326-8571, 9 A.M.–2 P.M. and 5–7 P.M. daily), located in the Casa de las Conchas, offers information on both the city and the surrounding Salamanca province.

GETTING THERE AND AROUND

Train

Renfe (tel. 90/224-0202, www.renfe.es) runs several daily trains to Salamanca from Madrid, Ávila, and Valladolid. The town is also easily accessed by train from Galicia and País Vasco.

Bus

Salamanca's bus station (Av. Filiberto Villalobos, tel. 92/323-6717) is in the northwest of the town. **Auto Res** (tel. 90/202-0999, www.auto-res.net) has over 20 daily buses to Madrid (€15), six to Valladolid (€6.55), and four to Ávila (€4.80).

Car

From Madrid, take the A-6 towards A Coruña. Take exit 81 to AP-51 towards Ávila. Switch to N-110 and then N-501, which leads into Salamanca. From town, the N-630 heads North to Zamora and beyond.

VICININTY OF SALAMANCA

Toro

Everyone in the know thinks the wines of the Castilla y León province of Toro are the next big thing. Toro sits on the western leg of the Duero River, famous for watering the valleys that produce the world-renowned Ribera del Duero wines. The wines of Toro, traditionally big, powerful, and dark—not unlike a *toro* (fighting bull)—are made from the dominant grape of the region, Tinta de Toro (which is pretty much the same as Spain's famed *tempranillo* grape). Packing a heavy alcoholic punch, this is what Spaniards used to drink to get drunk. In recent years, local winemakers decided to tame this wily wine, reducing the alcohol, and refining the taste. The results have been more than promising, and wines wearing the Toro D.O. have won international awards.

Wine tourism specialists such as **Cellar Tours** (www.cellartours.com) can help set up an exclusive tour to some of the wineries in the area. You can also plan your own tour by visiting www.dotoro.es, but it is a bit tricky as wine tourism in this region is still new (and English is not widely spoken). The **Toro tourist office** (Pl. Mayor 6, tel. 98/069-4747) can also help with winery visits. One winery that readily accepts visits by prior arrangement is **Bodegas Fariña** (Camino del Palo, s/n, tel. 98/057-7673, www.bodegasfarina.com), one of the best bodegas in the region.

The town of Toro is a historic treasure jammed with Romanesque and Mudejar buildings, reflecting its past as a frontier in the wars between the Moors and the Christians. A good place to stay is **Hotel Juan II** (Po. Espolón 1, tel. 98/069-0300, www.hoteljuanii.com, €78), located next to Toro's 13th-century cathedral.

Though connected by bus to cities throughout Castilla y León, this area is best explored by car as many of the region's bodegas lie well outside Toro's city limits. Toro is located on the CL-519 local road and is easily accessed from Salamanca, León, or Valladolid.

León

Once upon a time, León was the busy capital of medieval Spain's ever-growing Christian empire. That glory is still evident in the crowning jewel that is the city's cathedral. The Christian domination of the city began by the 10th century when King Ordoño II of Asturias set up royal shop here. By the 1200s, it had become the capital of the powerful kingdom of León. However, long before the Christian kings claimed the town for their own, the Romans had settled here as early as A.D. 70. They called it Legio Septima for the seventh Roman legion that was based here. They used the city as a base to control the extraction of gold from the mines in nearby Las Médulas. Their presence is also still evident, especially in the surreal moonscape of the mines themselves.

Like the rest of the Spanish empire, León began to lose its luster by the 17th century. It fell into backwater status and floundered for centuries. However, by the 19th century, the old Roman pursuit of mining was taken up in earnest and the city enjoyed a comeback that continues to this day. Well off the tourist track, stoic León is a wealthy provincial town that boasts one of the country's most respected universities. As a result, it bristles with trendy cafés, bustling streets, and a wild nightlife scene. It's also an important landmark on the Camino de Santiago. If you look down, you will see the golden scallops embedded in the roads of the old town, leading the way for the pilgrims.

SIGHTS
◖ Catedral de León

The ultimate in Castilian sanctuaries, León's 13th-century Catedral (Pl. Regla, tel. 98/723-6405, www.catedraldeleon.org, 10 A.M.–2 P.M. and 4–7 P.M. daily June–Sept., 10 A.M.–2 P.M. and 5–8 P.M. Tues.–Sun. Oct.–May, €1.70) is arguably the most magnificent example of Spanish Gothic architecture in the world. At least UNESCO thought so when it awarded the cathedral one of its exclusive Heritage of Humanity ratings. The exterior, with its imposing stone towers anchoring the building, are in stark contrast to the ephemeral stained glass windows that make up the bulk of the cathedral's upper reaches. There are over 125 jewel-colored windows covering a staggering 19,375 square feet. The star of this glorious

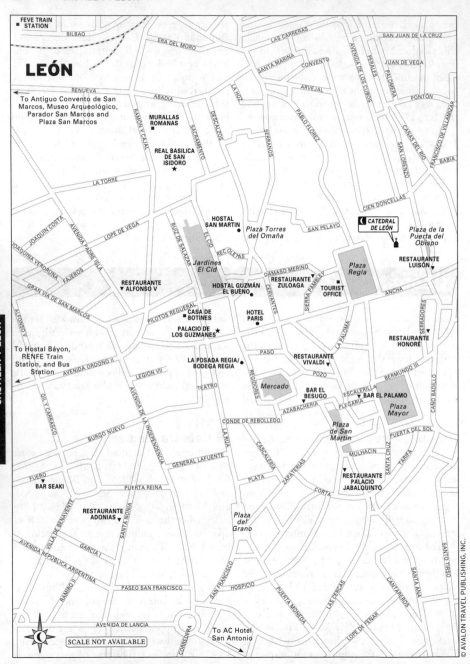

LEÓN

FEVE TRAIN STATION

BILBAO

ERA DEL MORO

LAS CARRERAS

SAN JUAN DE LA CRUZ

RENUEVA

To Antiguo Convento de San
Marcos, Museo Arqueológico,
Parador San Marcos and
Plaza San Marcos

ABADIA

SANTA MARINA

CONVENTO

AVENIDA DE LOS CUBOS

PERALES

JUAN DE VEGA

PALOMERA

PONTÓN

MURALLAS
ROMANAS

RAMÓN Y CAJAL

DESCALZOS

SACRAMENTO

ARVEJAL

PABLO FLÓREZ

CAÑAS DEL RÍO

SAN LORENZO

FRANCISCO DE VILLAMIZAR

BABIA

REAL BASILICA
DE SAN
ISIDORO
★

LA TORRE

LA HOZ

SERRANOS

CIEN DONCELLAS

HOSTAL
SAN MARTIN

Plaza Torres
del Omaña

SAN PELAYO

CATEDRAL
DE LEÓN

Plaza de la
Puerta del
Obispo

LOPE DE VEGA

JOAQUÍN COSTA

AVENIDA PADRE ISLA

EL CID

RUIZ DE SALAZAR

RECOLETAS

Jardines
El Cid

Plaza
Regla

RESTAURANTE
LUISÓN

JOAQUINA VERORUÑA

FAJEROS

RESTAURANTE
▼ ALFONSO V

DÁMASO MERINO

RESTAURANTE
ZULOAGA

CERVANTES

SIERRA PAMBLEY

ANCHA

GRAN VÍA DE SAN MARCOS

HOSTAL GUZMÁN
EL BUENO

TOURIST
OFFICE

SERRADORES

ALFONSO V

PILOTOS REGUERAL

CASA DE
BOTINES

HOTEL
PARIS

LA PALOMA

RESTAURANTE
HONORÉ

PALACIO DE
LOS GUZMANES ★

PASO

To Hostal Báyon,
RENFE Train
Station, and Bus
Station

AVENIDA ORDOÑO II

LEGIÓN VII

LA POSADA REGIA/
BODEGA REGIA

REGIDORES

RESTAURANTE
VIVALDI ▼

POZO

BERMUNDO III

GIL Y CARRASCO

AVENIDA DE LA INDEPENDENCIA

TEATRO

Mercado

BAR EL
BESUGO

ESCALERILLA

PLEGARIA

BAR EL PALAMO

CANO BADILLO

Plaza
Mayor

BURGO NUEVO

AZABACHERÍA

Plaza
de San
Martín

PUERTA DEL SOL

FUERO

CONDE DE REBOLLEDO

LA RÚA

CASCALERÍA

MULHACÍN

SANTA CRUZ

TARIFA

BAR SEAKI

GENERAL LAFUENTE

RESTAURANTE
PALACIO
JABALQUINTO

RESTAURANTE
ADONIAS ▼

PUERTA REINA

PLATA

ZAPATERÍAS

CORTA

VILLA DE BENAVENTE

SANTA NONIA

GARCÍA I

Plaza
del
Grano

SANTO TIRSO

AVENIDA REPÚBLICA ARGENTINA

BAMIRO II

PASEO SAN FRANCISCO

SAN FRANCISCO

HOSPICIO

PUERTA MONEDA

LAS CERCAS

CANTAREROS

SANTA ANA

AVENIDA DE LANCIA

CORREDERA

To AC Hotel
San Antonio

SCALE NOT AVAILABLE

© CANDY LEE LABALLE

León's cathedral has nearly 20,000 square feet of stained glass.

display of glass art is the giant rose window on the main facade. Installed from the 13th to 20th century, the glass windows shimmer with vibrant color. They are best appreciated from within, when the afternoon sun pours through them, filling the sandstone interior with a magical explosion of bejeweled shafts of light. One beam from the rose window is concentrated on the gilded altar, which sits along with the intricately carved choir stalls behind a glass wall. Be sure to stroll through the *claustro* (cloister) with its icing-like stone ceiling.

Real Basílica de San Isidoro

Built into the city walls in the 11th century, the regal sandstone Real Basílica de San Isidoro (Pl. San Isidoro 4, tel. 98/787-5088, 9 A.M.– 8 P.M. Mon.–Sat., 9 A.M.–2 P.M. Sun. July and Aug., 9 A.M.–1:30 P.M. and 4–7 P.M. Mon.– Sat., 9 A.M.–2 P.M. Sun. Sept.–June, free) was constructed on top of a 9th-century church to house the remains of San Isidoro and San Vicente. The saint's remains were laid to rest with those of a few dozen Castilian and Leonese roy-

als in the **Panteón de los Reyes** (€3.50), nicknamed the "Sistine Chapel of Romanesque art" for its brightly colored ceiling frescoes. However, the Panteón now lies empty—French troops destroyed the royal graves during the Napoleonic wars.

Convento de San Marcos

The opulent Antiguo Convento de San Marcos (Pl. San Marcos, s/n, tel. 98/723-7300, 10 A.M.–2 P.M. and 5–8 P.M. Tues.–Sat., 10 A.M.–2 P.M. Sun., closed Mon., €2.50) was originally a humble lodging for the weary knights of the Order of Saint James and for centuries, the building served as a resting point for pilgrims on the road to Santiago. In 1513, the very Catholic King Fernando decreed that the holy knights deserved better lodging and ordered the construction of the building standing today. Its most astonishing feature is its Plateresque facade, which looks more like a rich tapestry of sculpted knights and lords than a church front. The convent also houses the **Museo Arqueológico** (10 A.M.–2 P.M. and 5–8 P.M. daily), which has a fascinating collection of artifacts covering the city's past from Paleolithic, through Roman, to medieval epochs.

Palacio de los Guzmanes

Though construction work on the 16th-century Palacio de los Guzmanes (Pl. San Marcelo 6, tel. 98/729-2100, 10 A.M.–5 P.M. Mon.–Fri., closed Sat. and Sun.) was never completed, its intriguing facade is worth checking out. Its shape is trapezoidal and it has four towers, one at each corner. Today, it is the home of the León Regional Government. Guided visits are free of charge but in Spanish only and must be booked ahead by phone. Across the plaza, look for the **Casa de Botines** (Pl. San Marcelo, s/n). Barcelona's famed architectural genius Antoni Gaudí was commissioned to create the building in 1891. The result is decidedly modernist with distinctive medieval touches like whimsical pointed turrets. The building was declared a Historic Monument in 1969 and today is owned by a bank.

Roman Walls

Circling the old town of León, you can find impressive remains of the Murallas Romanas, Roman walls that stood at least as far back as the 1st century A.D. The walls were restored by Kings Alfonso V and Alfonso IX to delineate León and create new entranceways to the medieval city. The best remains are behind Plaza de San Isidoro, along Calle Ancha, and near Plaza Mayor. The tourist office can provide a *"ruta romana,"* a map of a Roman walking path to follow.

ENTERTAINMENT AND EVENTS
Nightlife

Barrio Húmedo, the nickname given to the oldest part of León, means "the wet district." It's a good reference to both the large number of bars packed into this small area and the copious amounts of drink consumed there. Barrio Húmedo is centered on the Plaza Mayor and spreads out in a web of streets that includes other plazas such as the Plaza del Grano, Plaza de San Martín, and the majestic Plaza Regla in front of the cathedral. The majority of the nightlife throbs as a result of León's large student population. To join in the fun, just wander the streets and stop when you find music you like and a crowd you want to be a part of. Most bars close at 4:30 A.M., while discos can stay open until dawn.

Start your night low-key at **La Galocha** (C/ Juan de Arfe), a local favorite for a quiet drink. Another good first drink bar is **Coolbar** (C/ Murias de Paredes), which true to its name is cool and laid-back with a very friendly staff. Kick things up a bit at **La Glam** (C/ Platerías), which bills itself as the place where the party never stops. Music is raucous and the crowd diverse—everyone makes a stop here during a night out in the barrio. The über-trendy **Danzatoria** (C/ Plegarias) is currently the place to be for León's young and beautiful. At **Pub El Toro** (C/ Mariano Domínguez Berrueta), the music is loud, danceable pop.

If you need a dose of disco, head to **Oh! León** (Av. Alcalde Miguel Castaño), which features a packed dance floor, multi-colored lasers

scanning the crowd, smoke machines, and DJs spinning the latest bass-pounding dance music. For a late night fix, try **La Tropi** (C/ Fuero 3), where dancing continues until 10 A.M.—just in time for breakfast.

Festivals and Events

León's party scene gets even wilder the last week of June when the town celebrates its patron saints with the **Fiestas de San Juan y San Pedro.** Much of the activity is concentrated in the Plaza Mayor, including concerts, performances, and a tasty *sopa de ajo* (traditional garlic soup) cook-off. If you like fish, head to León in May or June for the **Semana Internacional de la Trucha** (International Trout Week). The region of León is threaded with rivers teeming with tasty trout. There are fishing competitions, concerts, parties, and best of all, city-wide gastronomic competitions. In October, the **Fiestas de San Froilán y Las Cantaderas** pay homage to the long-ago time when León gave the Moorish king of Granada 100 maidens as a form of tribute. The *cantaderas* are locals dressed in the style of the Moors. The festivities include processions of decorated horse-drawn carriages, food booths (including several serving savory local sausages), and fireworks.

ACCOMMODATIONS
Under €50

Situated in a recently remodeled 18th-century building, **Hostal San Martín** (Pl. Torres de Omaña 1, tel. 98/787-5187, €36) offers well-lit rooms with balconies. In addition to rock-bottom prices, the owner is friendly and the bathrooms are spotless. The brightly painted **Hostal Báyon** (C/ Alcázar 7, tel. 98/725-4288, €23) is León's most relaxed *hostal.* Its amiable, young owner goes out of the way to make you feel at home after a long day of sightseeing.

€50-100

Guzmán El Bueno (C/ López Castrillón 6, tel. 98/723-6412, €63) is a no-frills hotel that has been popular with travelers on a budget for years. For a step up, book a night at **Hotel**

Paris (C/ Ancha 18, tel. 98/723-8600, www. hotelparisleon.com, €55), a very centrally located hotel with nicely decorated rooms and all the modern conveniences. **AC San Antonio** (C/ Velázquez 14, tel. 98/721-8444, www. ac-hotels.com, €79) offers everything expected of a four-star hotel with all the contemporary style expected of the AC chain.

Over €100
Spend a night or two surrounded by Plateresque and Renaissance masterpieces at **Parador San Marcos** (Pl. San Marcos 4, 98/723-7300, leon@parador.cs, www.parador.es, €175). The art history lesson begins with the facade of the 16th-century convent and continues throughout the lobby and into the rooms. The interior cloisters are spectacular and if you spring for a suite your room will open right onto them. Avoid the modern wing, however. **(La Posada Regia** (C/ Regidores 9, tel. 98/721-3173, www.regialeon.com, €100) is easily the most charming accommodation in town. Just steps from the cathedral, it is perfectly located in a building constructed in 1370. The family that owns it today has added many lovely touches like woven floor rugs, antique headboards, and comfy bathrobes.

FOOD
León takes gastronomic pride in its local fresh fish. The king of the table is *trucha* (trout) and you'll find it prepared in dozens of different ways. Of course, being entrenched firmly in Castile traditions, roasted meats, especially lamb and goat, take pride of place on many tables. One of León's most acclaimed specialties—and a taste sensation you should not miss—is *cecina,* beef cured in the same way as *jamón.* Served in transparent slivers, it is melt-in-the-mouth delicious.

Gourmet
(Palacio Jabalquinto (C/ Juan de Arfe 2, tel. 98/721-5322, closed Sun. and Mon. P.M., €30), set in a 17th-century palace, is a must for foodies. Dishes are so thoughtfully presented you'll feel almost guilty destroying the art of it just to satisfy your taste buds. However, from your first bite you'll discover that the visual can't compete with the exquisite flavors. Try the *rape* (monkfish) if it's available. For innovative fare with French/Basque touches, make a reservation at top-rated **Alfonso V** (Av. Padre Isla 1, tel. 98/722-0900, closed Sun. P.M., €40). Order anything with seafood or tuck into the tasting menu for a delicious review of what the talented chef is capable of.

If you are a true food-lover, head directly to **Vivaldi** (C/ Platerías 4, tel. 98/726-0760, closed Sun. and Mon., €50), a top-rated dining room offering impeccable local dishes with elegant touches. The roasted lamb with pine nuts, cheese shavings, and honey oil is divine. The wine cellar has over 200 different bottles to choice from, including fine wines from the León region.

Local Cuisine
The rustic **Bodega Regia** (C/ Regidores 9, tel. 98/721-3173, closed Sun., €37) incorporates one of León's old Roman walls into its dining room. Not to be outdone by history, the kitchen serves up award-winning local fare including fresh fish, roasted meats, and cured sausages. Local favorite, **Adonías** (C/ Santa Nonia 16, tel. 98/720-6768, closed Sun., €35) is famed for its *cochinillo* (roasted suckling pig), which is served on colorful ceramic plates. Impeccably fresh fish from the Cantabrian Sea are also specialties. **Restaurante Zuloaga** (C/ Sierra Pambley 3, tel. 98/723-7814, €25) offers creative takes on fish and meats in a stunning building lined with mosaics. There is also a very romantic interior garden. For local delicacies at rock-bottom prices, head to the neighborhood favorite **Restaurante Luisón** (Pl. Puerta Obispo 16, tel. 98/725-4029, €10). Try *botillo berciano,* a fall-off-the-bone pork dish. If you've really worked up an appetite, try the laid-back **Restaurante Honoré** (C/ Serradores 6, €15), famous among travelers for its massive portions.

Tapas
For hard-core tapas-hopping, head straight to Barrio Húmedo, popular for its excellent tapas

SPANISH WINE: BEYOND RIOJA!

Spanish wine today is in the middle of a revolution, undergoing a vast transformation and modernization. There are high-quality wines of every color being made in every corner of Spain using the latest viticulture and winemaking techniques. These wines are gaining recognition throughout the wine world for excellence. This newfound fame means that prices are rising, but Spain still represents the best value in the European wine scene and possibly in the world.

Spanish wines are classified by their *denominación de origen*, abbreviated D.O., an appellation rating that not only indicates where the grapes for a particular wine were grown, but also ensures that the wine is made to quality standards. For years, the reputation of Spanish wine was built upon the great wines of only one D.O., **Rioja.** Rioja's illustrious reputation dates back hundreds of years and until the mid-20th century it was only these wines that were consumed abroad. **Ribera del Duero** was the next region to gain fame, largely due to the efforts of two of Spain's best wineries, Vega Sicilia and Pesquera. Today Ribera del Duero is considered an equal to Rioja, producing some of Spain's best red wines.

Both of these famous regions still dominate the internal Spanish wine market, and are served in every bar and restaurant in Spain. Many wine lists in more traditional restaurants only have wines from these two regions, a fact that is hard to believe in a nation where there are 64 official D.O.s producing hundreds of great wines. Modern restaurants and the trendy wine bars popping up in Spain's larger cities are now offering extensive wine selections from all over Spain, and the public – in Spain and abroad – is getting savvy to the variety available.

Wines from regions other than Rioja and Ribera del Duero also tend to be much better values. While visiting Spain and eating out, look for wines from other regions; usually they are offered with a much lower mark-up on restaurant wine lists. Back home, ask your local wine merchant for bottles from some of these new regions; you'll almost certainly find some. Spanish fine wine exports are rising dramatically every year. The United Kingdom is Spain's first customer for exports, the United States is third, so these wines are becoming easier to find all the time.

Somontano, a wine region in rugged Aragón in the northeast of Spain, produces outstanding quality at great prices. It's hard to find a bad wine from here. Great red and white wines are made from both indigenous varieties such as Tempranillo and Garnacha, as well as French varieties, such as Cabernet Sauvignon and Chardonnay. Look for wineries such as Viñas del Vero and Enate. Other great wine regions in Aragón include Campo de Borja and Cariñena.

Toro is located down river from Ribera del Duero on the Duero River. Robust, hearty reds are made here from Tinta de Toro, a variety of the famous Spanish grape Tempranillo. The wines are tremendous and usually very cheap. Look for wines such as Elias Mora, Rejadorada,

and because many are served free with the purchase of a drink. The trick to getting the freebies is to order your drink alone. Most tapas bars are known for a particular dish. Mosey on up to any bar and ask for the specialty or just point to what everyone else is having. The practice in León, as in the rest of Spain, is to have one tapa and then move on to the next bar.

El Latino (Pl. San Martín 10) is famous for shrimp wrapped in bacon and doused in cheese. Across the street, the charming old inn **Llar** (Pl. San Martín 9) has been pleasing locals for 20 years with excellent *patatas ali-oli,* potatoes drenched in garlic mayonnaise. At **La Bicha** (Pl. Tiendas) try any of the sausages, though the house favorite is *morcilla* (blood sausage). **Celso II** (C/ Azabacheria 12) is where to head for delicious *pulpo* (octopus). Next door, **El Besugo** (C/ Azabacheria 10) has wonderful fresh grilled sardines. **El Palomo** (C/ Escalerilla 8) offers exquisite red peppers from Bierzo and clams cooked in wine. **Seaki** (C/ Fuero 11) serves scrumptious *gabardines* (fried shrimp).

Cyan, Vega Sauco, Quinta de Quietud, and many more. Some amazing wines from this region representing some of the top wines in Spain are Pintia, Numanthia, and San Roman.

Bierzo, the current darling of top wine critics, is located in the northwest of Spain. It is renowned for its red wines made from the little-known Mencia grape. Many winemakers from other regions are starting vineyards in this small area. Great wineries to look for include Domino de Tares, Tilenus, Petalos del Bierzo, and Pittacum.

Montsant is a small mountain region in Cataluña that has started producing some amazing red wines that rival the more famous, intense wines from neighboring **Priorat** – a world-class region producing wines with the reputation and prices to match. Montsant is a fairly new appellation producing similar wines at a much lower price. These are blended wines made from indigenous grapes such as Garnacha and Cariñena and French varieties such as Cabernet Sauvignon and Merlot. If you come across any of these wines, try them, but be on the lookout for bottles from Capcanes, Venus la Universal, Laurona, Perlat, and Etim.

La Mancha, long the origin of some of the worst table wines in Spain, is quickly reforming its image by producing some of the best-value red wines in Spain. A hot, arid area in the center of the country, the region produces robust wines made from multiple types of grapes, particularly Tempranillo (also called Cencibel

here). Wineries to look for include El Vinculo, Finca Antigua, Fontal, and Mano a Mano.

Vinos de la Tierra are "country wines" from around Spain. This is a hot new category for winemakers outside the legally delimited D.O. regions and for those who don't want to put up with the many constraints in the appellation system. In this category of wine, a wine-maker has much more freedom to create. Some of Spain's top wines are made in this category, and also some of the best-value wines. High-end wines include Abadia Retuerta, Dehesa del Carrizal, Mauro, Leda, Vallegarcia, and Pago del Ama. For value look for Finca la Estacada, Martue, Corpus del Muni, Duraron, and Torre de Barreda

There are many more up-and-coming regions in Cataluña, making both red and white wines. Good choices include Terra Alta, Conca de Barbera, and Penedès. Valencia is also starting to produce some fantastic red wines. Look for Jumilla, Alicante, Bullas, and Utiel Requena. Navarra is making some lovely wines of all colors. Also look for whites from Rueda and Rías Baixas in Galicia.

Spain's wine panorama is vast and complicated, but there are spectacular wines and incredible values everywhere you look. Spain's international reputation is on the rise, so learn and drink all you can while the values are still there. Be adventurous in your wine exploration and don't be afraid to go beyond rioja!

Contributed by Mary O'Connor, Wine Director of Madrid-based Planeta Vino, www.planeta vino.net.

INFORMATION

The main **tourist office** (Pl. Regla 3 tel. 98/723-7082) is right in front of the cathedral. This is a regional office, so they can also provide you with information about any town in Castilla y León.

GETTING THERE AND AROUND

Train

León is well-connected to major cities such as Madrid, Burgos, and Santiago by several daily trains that leave from the **Estación de Renfe** (C/ Astorga 11, tel. 90/224-0202, www .renfe.es) which is across the river from the city center. There are also smaller, narrow gauge tracks that head to País Vasco. They depart from **Estación de FEVE** (Av. Padre Isla 48, tel. 98/727-1210, www.feve.es).

Bus

León's **Estación de Autobuses** (Po. Sáenz de Miera, s/n, tel. 98/721-1000) connects León to almost every city in Spain. Bus is the easiest and cheapest way to travel in this region. Check with the bus station either in León or in your city of departure. The main operating company is **Alsa** (tel. 90/242-2242, www.alsa.es).

Car

To get to León from Madrid, take the A-6 towards A Coruña, then switch to the AP-6. Change back to the A-6 as you approach León. Change to the A-66, take exit 149, and finally CL-622. León sits on the N-630, which connects it to Oviedo in the north and Salamanca in the south. The N-120 goes west to Galicia via Astorga, where it merges with the A-6. The N-601 heads southeast towards Valladolid. If you want to drive from León to explore the region, **Avis** (www.avis.es) and **Europcar** (www.europcar.es) are both located at the Renfe station.

VICINITY OF LEÓN
◖ Astorga

The postcard perfect village of Astorga is jam packed with history from its medieval walls to its Roman ruins and Gaudí architecture. On the holy side, it's one of the most important stops on the Camino de Santiago, the thousand-year-old pilgrim's path through Spain to Santiago. In Astorga, the main trails from France and Portugal merge. Upon hitting town, road-weary pilgrims make their way directly to the **Catedral de Santa María** (Pl. Catedral, s/n, 10 A.M.–2 P.M. and 4–8 P.M. daily summer, 11 A.M.–2 P.M. and 3:30–6:30 P.M. daily winter, €2.50), an imposing Gothic structure begun in 1471 and finished three centuries later. Architectural buffs head instead for the **Palacio Episcopal,** just next door. Designed by Antoni Gaudí, this modernist wonderland was commissioned to be the bishop's palace in 1887. When the bishop died six years later, Gaudí was given full reign over the design and let loose his distinctive fantastical touches on the building. Pure fairy tale on the outside, playful extravagance on the inside, the palace is a must-see.

Founded in 19 B.C. as Asturica Augusta, a Roman military camp, Astorga is rife with

Roman ruins. Check out the **Museo Romano** (Pl. San Bartolomé 2, tel. 98/761-6937, 10 A.M.–1:30 P.M. and 4–6 P.M. Tues.–Sat., 10 A.M.–1:30 P.M. Sun., closed Mon. , €2.50), which houses artifacts and an interactive display. The **tourist office** (Pl. Eduardo de Castro, 5, tel. 98/761-8222) offers tours of the Roman ruins. The tour is in Spanish only but is a delightful time with a few scares along the way.

Add a sweet stop to the end of your sightseeing with a visit to Astorga's **Museo de Chocolate** (C/ José María Goy 5, 10:30 A.M.–2 P.M. and 4:30–7 P.M. Tues.–Sat., 10:30 A.M.–2 P.M. Sun.–Mon., €1). For centuries, Astorga was famous for its chocolate and this quirky museum honors that past with a display of old chocolate-making machinery and advertisements. At the end, you get a sweet sample.

With so much to do in this tiny town, you might want to stay the night. The **Casa de Tepa** (C/ Santiago 2, tel. 98/760-3299, www .casadetepa.com, €90) is one of the most charming hotels in all of León province. Set in an 18th-century pilgrims' hospital, the hotel features classically furnished rooms situated around an elegant glass-walled garden. **Hotel Gaudí** (C/ Eduardo de Castro 6, tel. 98/761-5654, €65) boasts gorgeous nighttime views of the cathedral and Gaudí's palace. **Hotel Asturplaza** (Pl. España 2 and 3, tel. 98/761-8900, asturplaza@asturplaza.com, www.astur plaza.com, €80) has clean, bright rooms, many with excellent views on the plaza. There is also a good restaurant, **Los Hornos,** and a glass-roofed bar, **Patio de Cristal.**

For top-rated local cuisine, head to **Casa Maragata** (C/ Húsar Tiburcio 2, tel. 98/761-8118, €18). Hours are erratic, so call ahead. ◖ **La Peseta** (Pl. San Bartolomé 3, tel. 98/761-7275) was a favorite of author James Michener in the 1960s. It is still going strong, offering Castilian fare amid walls laden with history. For cheap tapas and beer, try the café/bar **GPS** (C/ La Bañeza 9), a local favorite.

There are daily **buses** from León and Madrid into Astorga's bus station. The **train station,** serviced by Renfe (www.renfe.es), is several kilometers outside of town, and has a few connections per day with León. If you are driving, it's only 60 kilometers (37 miles) from León. Take the N-630, switch to the toll road AP-71, and finally to the N-6.

Las Médulas

During the Roman Empire, the Las Médulas mines were the prime contributor to Roman coffers. Estimates vary, but the extracted gold totaled somewhere around five million pounds—that is, 2,500 tons! The mining was done by over 60,000 slaves who dug underground tunnels of up to 40 kilometers (25 miles) in length and then flushed them with water to extract the gold. They called the process *ruina montium,* and true to its name, it destroyed the hills to get at the gold. This dangerous process went on for some 250 years, claiming the lives of thousands and constitut-ing the world's first environmental disaster. Nearly 2,000 years later, what remains is a lunar-like landscape of eroded red earth and jagged, rocky spikes—all that is left of the acres of hills that were once here. UNESCO has deemed this bizarrely beautiful place a World Heritage Site, due to the evidence the area shows of Roman ingenuity. The thousands that lost their lives digging the gold might not agree.

You need a car to explore this region. The village of Las Médulas lies about 160 kilometers (100 miles) east of León. Catch the toll road AP-71 out of town and switch to the A-6. Follow the signs towards Toral de los Vados, then towards Carucedo. Finally, enter the town of Orellan and follow that to the village. The mines are about 3.2 kilometers (two miles) beyond that.

Burgos

Running along the lush banks of the rushing River Arlanzón, Burgos is one of Spain's most delightful cities. It hums with an unassuming vibe that seems to take its wealth of elegant promenades, medieval squares, and gothic buildings in laid-back stride. Then again, bowing for centuries under the looming bulk of its astonishing cathedral would shush any town into modesty.

Burgos's quiet pride could also be due to its centuries-long military history. It was founded in 884 by the Castilian kings as a fortress to ward off both the advancing Moors and the fractious Kingdom of Navarra. A castle was built on a hill rising above the river and the town became secure enough to serve for centuries as the seat of the Kingdom of León. During the Christian Reconquest, Burgos blossomed into a thriving medieval trade center shuttling wool to the North and iron to the South of the peninsula. Meanwhile, the religious significance of the Camino de Santiago grew, and Burgos became an important stop for medieval pilgrims. The cathedral and a host of ornate churches and buildings were raised during this time.

In the 17th and 18th centuries, Burgos suffered along with the rest of the country as Spain began to tumble from its perch as the world's most far-reaching power. In 1808, Napoleon's forces occupied the city and vicious fighting—as well as a fair amount of pillaging—laid waste to many of the town's architectural treasures, including the castle. The cathedral escaped with only a few of its stained glass windows destroyed. The 19th century was a time of earnest rebuilding for Burgos fueled mainly by an industrial boom. It recovered enough to attract the attention of Franco, who made the town his headquarters during the Civil War. After the war, the Nationalist government encouraged industrial development in the region, resulting in a level of prosperity that is still evident in Burgos today.

Burgos shakes off its refined airs the week of June 29 and bursts into frivolity with the **Fiestas de San Pedro y San Pablo** in celebration of the town's patron saints. Events include bullfights, live music, fairs, fireworks, and all-night dancing in the streets. The tastiest aspect of the event is the city-wide tapas competition. Each tapas bar sets up a stand in the street and offers one cold tapa and one hot one. Locals then vote on their favorite. The best part is the price—just €2 for one savory snack—drink included! It is an excellent time to visit town, though book ahead as half of Spain will heading this way. The only time to avoid Burgos is during winter when the temperatures drop to a bone-chilling freeze.

SIGHTS
◖ Catedral de Burgos

No building is more emblematic in Burgos than its Catedral (Pl. Santa María, s/n, tel. 94/720-4712, www.catedralde burgos.es, 9:30 A.M.–7:15 P.M. daily in summer, 9:30 A.M.–1:15 P.M. and 4–7:15 P.M. daily in spring and fall, 10 A.M.–1:15 P.M. and 4–5:45 P.M. daily in winter, €4). Begun in 1221 on the orders of King Fernando, the bulk of the cathedral was completed in only 40 years.

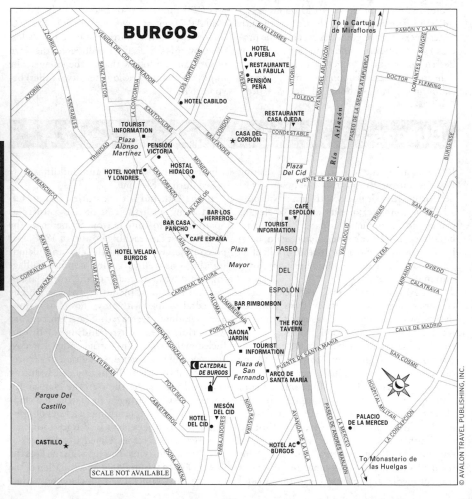

COURTESY OF BURGOS PATRONATO DE TURISMO

Catedral de Burgos

Take a walk around the outside to get the full effect of the sheer size of the building with its two 84-meter towers, intricate webs of flying buttresses, and dozens of latticed Gothic spires. You'll come across postcards that show the cathedral looking gloomy under a veneer gray. Thanks to a years-long cleaning process completed in 2006, it now shines in its original creamy-white stone finish.

At the Plaza Rey San Fernando, look for the door of **El Sarmental.** Finished in 1235, many historians consider it the best example of Gothic sculpture in existence. Enter the cathedral through the reception just to the left of the Sarmental. Here you can rent the highly recommended audio-guide (€3.50). As you tour, keep in mind that the cathedral is still an active house of worship and masses occur throughout the day.

The cathedral features three large naves and 13 ornate chapels. The central nave, called **Crucero y Cimborrio** is truly astonishing with a starburst ceiling and soaring windows. It is a fitting burial spot for El Cid who, along with his wife Jimena, lies beneath a simple stone slab in the nave's center. (See sidebar, *El Cid: Fact and Fiction*.) On the southern wall of the nave is the gorgeous **rosetón,** a six-meter wide stained glass rose window completed in 1240. Directly opposite is the elaborate **Escalera Dorada,** the Golden Stairway, which was completed in 1492 to allow worshipers to enter from the Puerta Alta. The cathedral is tucked into the side of the hill and this long-shuttered door is located at street height, about 7.6 meters above the cathedral floor. Beyond the main altar, look for the **Capilla de Condestables.** Commissioned by the wealthy Constable of Castile, Fernández de Velasco in 1482, the chapel, with its intricate stone work, sumptuous art, and dramatic nest of dual stars cut into the ceiling, is nearly a cathedral in itself.

The favorite sight of the cathedral's youngest visitors is **Papamoscas,** a 600-year-old mechanical puppet that heralds the hours. His name, which roughly translates as "flycatcher," refers to the way he opens his mouth wide with each toll of the hour. A smaller

CASTILLA Y LEÓN

EL CID: FACT AND FICTION

Throughout Castile you'll run across the name El Cid Campeador. Born Rodrigo Díaz de Vivar around 1043 in Vivar (Bivar), a few miles outside of Burgos, he was a medieval warrior famed for his brilliant tactics on the battlefield. He liked to fight, and didn't really care for whom he did battle. He fought for the Christians against the Moors, then switched to fighting for the Moors against the Christians. His legendary name reflects his conflicting loyalties. El Cid is from the Arabic word *al sayyid*, which means "lord." Campeador is Spanish for "champion."

El Cid's father was a minor nobleman and friend of King Fernando I of Castile. The King had El Cid educated in the court, where the

El Cid, Burgos's homegrown legend

boy proved particularly adept in military matters. Upon his death in 1065, Fernando divided Castile among his five royal heirs. This didn't sit well with the oldest son, Sancho II, who set out to take the lands away from his siblings. His long-time friend El Cid joined him in battle and soon earned respect across Castile for his daring military maneuvers. Several times when Sancho's forces faced imminent defeat, El Cid saved the day with then unheard of military strategies such as psychological warfare, decoys, and surprise attacks. El Cid was named commander of the Castilian troops. Soon Sancho had conquered the lands of his brothers Alfonso and Garcia, exiling them to Toledo. His sister Elvira fell next. In 1072, Sancho and El Cid laid siege to Zamora, the stronghold of his other sister, Urraca. The battle had barely begun when one of Urraca's soldiers killed Sancho in a plot widely contributed to Alfonso. As Sancho had no wife or children, all of his possessions fell to Alfonso, who soon took control of all of Castile.

Naturally, El Cid feared for his life, as he had waged war upon the new king. However, politics intervened. The king was from León and the Castilian people didn't like that. Legend has it that no one was brave enough to administer the oath of leadership – except El Cid. As a Castilian and a famed warrior, the people trusted him. The king didn't feel the same. To ensure loyalty, he made El Cid part of the royal family by marrying him to his niece Jimena in 1074. Then, just to be sure, he had El Cid removed from his position as military leader. For several years, El Cid led a relatively quiet

medieval puppet, Martinillo, announces the quarter- and half-hours. In contrast to the playful puppets, the **Cristo de Burgos** is downright eerie. Covered in buffalo hide, this life-size figure of Christ was made in the 14th century and features human hair and fingernails. Legend claims that both must be trimmed every eight days. The statue is kept in the **Capilla del Santísimo de Burgos,** a private worship temple open only for mass,

not tourism. Do not try to enter if you are not a believer. Creepy as it is, the statue is venerated throughout Burgos and indeed the world; it is extremely disrespectful to enter the chapel solely for the purpose of gawking.

Be sure to wander the medieval hallways of the claustros, the high and low cloisters, which are a close second to the Sarmental door for their Gothic brilliance. Other don't-miss sights include the **Sacristía Mayor,** built in 1765 and

life as a judge in Alfonso's court. But battle soon called.

During a trip to Andalucía to collect funds from the court of Sevilla on behalf of Alfonso, El Cid entered into an unauthorized battle with the Moors in Granada. Alfonso was incensed. Matters were made worse when court enemies of El Cid also accused him of dipping into the Sevillian tithe. When El Cid returned to Castile, Alfonso promptly exiled him from the kingdom. Thus began El Cid's life as a mercenary soldier, fighting indifferently on behalf of both the Christians and the Moors. Regardless of the enemy, El Cid always won the battle and his fame as a brilliant warrior began to reach epic proportions.

By 1080, El Cid was contracted as a military leader for the Moorish king of Zaragoza, Yusuf al-Mutamin. For years he served Yusuf and his son, fighting against Christian forces and other Moorish kingdoms. Meanwhile, Alfonso was furiously fighting his own battles, including a vicious defeat at the hands of Almoravid troops from Morocco. Following the loss, Alfonso called for El Cid to return from exile. He refused. During this time, Christian forces captured Toledo from the Moors, marking the beginning of the end of Muslim rule in Spain.

El Cid was done fighting for others. Educated in the Castilian court, employed in the Moorish court, he had enough knowledge and influence to pursue his own political ambitions. With an army built of both Christians and Moors, El Cid laid siege to Valencia in 1092. By 1094, the city was his. Though officially under the flag of Alfonso, in reality El Cid was an independent leader of the fiefdom of Valencia and ruled there until his death in 1099. The Moors almost immediately began to wage war to regain the city. Legend says that Jimena tied her dead husband to a horse and sent it into battle. At the sight of the famed warrior El Cid, the Moors retreated in fear. Jimena couldn't hold off the Moors for long however and Alfonso soon sent troops to help. When defeat loomed, Alfonso had Valencia burned to the ground and Jimena escaped with El Cid's body to Burgos.

In death, El Cid was converted from a talented gun-for-hire into a larger-than-life Christian soldier – loyal, brave, and dedicated to the Kings of Castile. This legend sprung into popular literature as early as the 1200s with the publication of what many consider the first great work of Spanish literature, *Cantar de Mio Cid*, by an unknown medieval poet. In 1636, a French playwright penned *Le Cid*. In 1885, the opera *Le Cid* debuted. It remains a favorite of Spanish opera star Placido Domingo. In 1961, Hollywood produced *El Cid*, starring Charlton Heston in the title role and Sophía Loren as Jimena. A lavish animated feature, *El Cid the Legend*, debuted in 2003.

Today, El Cid rests in a tomb alongside Jimena, beneath the central dome of the magnificent cathedral of Burgos. His sword is on display in Toledo's military museum at the Alcázar. Throughout Spain, stories about the great warrior abound and the line between fact and fiction has long been blurred. Whoever El Cid really was, one thing is certain – today he is a true legend and a powerful symbol of Spanish historical might.

rife with religious artistry, the **coro,** elaborately carved choir stalls made of inlaid walnut which date from 1550, and the **Girola,** a curved wall of Gothic stone carving.

Burgos is an important point on the **Camino de Santiago** and thousands of pilgrims visit the cathedral each year. The camino passes along Calle Fernán González, right behind the cathedral. You'll see the metal scallop shells tapped into the road. The scallop shell has been a symbol of the camino and of Saint James for centuries. Dozens of theories explain why. One of the most logical says that the camino ends at the sea and to prove you've been there, you must collect a scallop shell. Even if you are not a pilgrim, following the camino through Burgos makes for an enjoyable walk.

Paseo del Espolón

In front of the cathedral, the **Arco de Santa**

María was once an entrance through the city's medieval walls. Built in the 13th century, it was remodeled to look like a fortress with anchoring towers in the 16th century. Pass through the arch to get to the **Paseo del Espolón.** This tree-lined promenade follows the Arlanzón River with a lovely cascade of sidewalk cafés, manicured trees, flower gardens, and benches. On sunny days, it is the most popular spot in town. During the evening, frogs along the riverbank drown out the nearby traffic with their melodic croaking. The Paseo ends at the **Plaza del Cid** where the warrior himself is ensconced on his trusty steed Babieca. Sword drawn, beard flowing, El Cid seems poised to ward off any would-be attackers approaching from across the San Pueblo bridge. Turn left off the Paseo and follow Calle Santander to the **Casa del Cordón,** the 15th-century palace where the Catholic Kings greeted Christopher Columbus after his second voyage to the New World. Today, it houses a bank and if you decide to exchange your money here (9:30 A.M.–2 P.M. Mon.–Fri., closed Sat. and Sun.), you can get a glimpse inside the historical building. Directly north of the Paseo is the **Plaza Mayor,** a spacious plaza lined with shops, cafés, and restaurants.

Monasterio de las Huelgas

The second most important monument in Burgos is the Monasterio de las Huelgas (C/ Los Compases, s/n, tel. 94/720-1630, www.patrimonio nacional.es, 10 A.M.–1:15 P.M. and 3:45–5:45 P.M. Tues.–Sat., 10:30 A.M.–2:15 P.M. Sun., €5). Originally built as a royal retreat by Alfonso VIII and his wife Leonor of England in 1187, the building was donated to the Cistercian nuns soon after. It has been home to the cloistered sect ever since. For centuries, it was the most powerful monastery in Spain and its abbess was second only to the queen in power. The current abbess and the few remaining nuns live a quiet life of contemplation, while the monastery bustles around them as one of Burgos's busiest monuments.

The main chapel contains the remains of Alfonso, Leonor, and dozens of their closest relatives and former abbesses of the monastery.

© CANDY LEE LABALLE

This medieval statue has a moveable arm that once knighted brothers into the Order of Santiago.

During the 1800s, as Napoleon's troops were retreating from Spain, French soldiers desecrated the tombs, robbing them of whatever treasures lay within. The one tomb they missed revealed such a wealth of jewels and medieval clothing that it formed the basis of the **Museo de Ricas Telas,** a museum of medieval fabric housed within the monastery.

The echoing cloister, **Claustro de San Fernando,** surrounds an open courtyard above which the current nuns live. Though badly damaged, the ceiling of the cloister reveals distinctive Mudejar designs of Persian peacocks and geometric shapes. The loveliest part of the complex is **Las Claustrillas,** a small, contemplative cloister surrounding a manicured garden. This is where the kings would relax when they stayed in the monastery. In the nearby **Capilla de Santiago** (Chapel of Saint James), a medieval statue of Saint James hangs on the wall under a magnificently carved Mudejar ceiling. In the 13th century, it was a tradition for men to enter the Order of Santiago only after being knighted by this very statue, which features a moveable arm holding an outstretched sword specially built for knighting purposes.

The monastery is located on the West side of the city, a half-hour walk from the center. You can also catch local bus 7 from Plaza Primo de Rivera. It leaves every 20 minutes and costs €1.

La Cartuja de Miraflores

On the Eastern edge of the city lies La Cartuja de Miraflores (Ctra. de la Cartuja, s/n, www .cartuja.org, 10:15 A.M.–3 P.M. and 4–6 P.M. Mon.–Sat, 11 A.M.–3 P.M. and 4–6 P.M. Sun., free). Work began on this Gothic structure in 1441 and was finished under the command of Queen Isabel, who had the tombs of her parents, Juan II of Castile and Isabel of Portugal, installed here. The best architects of the age worked on the tombs, sepulchers, and altars; and together they are considered by art historians to be one of the best collections of the elaborate Isabelline Gothic style. Walking to Cartuja will take close to an hour; it's better to shell out for a 10-minute cab ride. However, if you are visiting Burgos in summer, consider the **Tren Cartuja de Miraflores,** a tourist train that goes to Cartuja daily at 5 P.M. in July, August, and September. The €3 ride leaves from Plaza del Rey San Fernando, in front of the tourist office.

Sightseeing by Train

Though Burgos is compact and walkable, there are a few sights you might want to take in via the **Tren Turístico** (Oficina de Turismo, Pl. Rey San Fernando 2, tel. 94/728-8874, €3). Though its faux train look is kitschy, it's actually a great way to see the city if you're not a walker or are short on time. Kids like it, too. The 45-minute route leaves from in front of the tourist office at the cathedral and travels past the sights of Burgos and up to the **Castillo,** a ruined medieval castle looking over the city. The train leaves every hour 11 A.M.–9 P.M., though departures are greatly reduced in winter months. Another excellent option is the

Ruta de la Luz (€3.50), the same train, only during a spectacular evening route that takes in the dramatically lit monuments of Burgos. Departure time varies with the season, but is always after sunset.

ACCOMMODATIONS
Under €50

For a cheap sleep, try **Pensión Victoria** (C/ San Juan 3, tel. 94/720-1542, €35). Bathrooms are shared, but it is immaculately clean and the family that runs it is very friendly. A bit more charming is the **Pensión Peña** (C/ La Puebla 18, tel. 94/720-6323, €30). Another good cheapie is **Hostal Hidalgo** (C/ Almirante Bonifaz 14, tel. 94/720-3481, €40).

€50–100

Hotel Cabildo (Av. Cid 2, tel. 94/725-7840, cabildo@hotelcabildo.com, www.hotelcabildo .com, €100) is a new three-star hotel done up in a modern palette of brown and cream with comfortable mattresses, flat-screen televisions, and well-appointed baths. It is an extremely good value for the price. With many rooms overlooking the cathedral, **Hotel del Cid** (Pl. Santa María 8, tel. 94/720-8715, €75) has the best location in town. Run by the Lopéz family, which owns the venerable Mesón del Cid restaurant, this cozy hotel offers old-world charm and friendly, personal attention. **Hotel Norte y Londres** (Pl. Alonso Martínez 10, tel. 94/726-4125, €70) was popular among diplomats during Franco's regime. Today it retains its exclusive airs, but at user-friendly prices. Its in-house restaurant, Colonial, is quite good. Another excellent mid-range choice is **Hotel La Puebla** (C/ La Puebla 20, tel. 94/720-0011, €70), a traditional hotel with ultra-modern touches.

Over €100

Palacio de la Merced (C/ Merced 13, tel. 94/747-9900, www.nh-hotels.com, €160) is easily the most luxurious hotel in the city center. Built within an austere 17th-century monastery that hides a breathtaking interior cloister and echoing arched hallways, the Merced offers all the top amenities characteristic of the posh NH chain. Beds are very comfy, rooms are contemporary lush (think thick-striped linens and modern Spanish art), service is impeccable, and the location—on the banks of the River Arlanzón across from the cathedral—can't be beat. Check the website before booking, there are often deals for as little as €89 per night. The **Velada Burgos** (C/ Fernán González 10, tel. 94/725-7680, www.veladahoteles.com, €130) is a lovely, small hotel tucked into a 16th-century house just behind the cathedral. Formerly the Hotel Palacio de los Blasones, the Velada does a nice job of combining the medieval ambience of the building (Gothic archways, stone walls)—with contemporary style (modern furniture, glass flooring). Another good choice right near the cathedral is the **AC Burgos** (Av. de la Isla 7, tel. 94/725-7966, www.ac-hotels.com, €124), a modern hotel with excellent service and comfortable beds. Try to get a room with a view over the river and the cathedral. **Landa Palace** (Ctra. N-1, km. 235, Villagonzalo Pedernales, www.landapalace.es, tel. 94/725-7777, €230) is the haunt of kings, politicians, and superstars when they are in Burgos. The hotel's medieval grandeur is evident from the lavishly decorated rooms (many with whirlpool baths) and sprawling stone terraces to the suits of armor and antiques in the reception area. In a nod to modernity, there is a spectacular swimming pool located in a vaulted room with soaring ironwork windows, and just in case you need it, a helicopter landing pad. Suites feature private terraces looking out on the unspoiled, rolling landscape of Burgos province. It's outside of town but if you can afford to stay here, you can afford a taxi ride into the center. The majestic Landa Restaurant is top-rated for its exquisite Castilian cuisine.

FOOD

Burgos is a meat and more meat kind of town. The local *carne* of choice is *lechazo,* roasted suckling lamb. Prepared simply in a terra-cotta pot, it literally melts in the mouth. Another Burgos favorite is *olla podrida.* Translated as "rotten pot," it is actually a savory meat and

sausage stew. *Setas* (wild mushrooms) flourish in the region and appear in many dishes or are served simply grilled. Burgos also provides two of Spain's most quintessential products to the rest of the country. *Queso de Burgos* is a soft, creamy sheeps' milk cheese that is often served as a dessert with walnuts and honey. *Morcilla de Burgos* is a savory blood sausage seasoned with onion, black pepper, and fluffed up with rice. It appears on menus alone or in dishes across Spain. Though the American palate is resistant to *morcilla* at first, those who do take the bite often become quite addicted. If you make it to Burgos, it would be a culinary sin not to try it.

Cafés and Desserts

There are several lovely cafés along the Paseo Espolón, the most popular of which is **Café Espolón** (Po. Espolón 1, tel. 94/727-9976). Located in the theater of the same name, this elegant café is a favorite meeting place for locals and tourists alike. In warmer months, its sidewalk seating is the best in town. **Café España** (C/ Laín Calvo 12, tel. 94/720-5337) is a popular belle epoque bar serving specialty coffees and pastries by day, cocktails and live piano music by night. In a narrow room connecting the plaza in front of the cathedral with Paseo Espolón, **The Fox Tavern** (Po. Espolón 4, tel. 94/727-3311) is a lively Irish bar with filling breakfasts and hearty lunch menus.

Local Cuisine

Try *lechazo* at 🄲 **Mesón del Cid** (Pl. Santa María 8, tel. 94/720-8715, www.mesondelcid.es, 1–4 P.M. and 8–11:30 P.M. daily, €30), a restaurant that has been run by the same family for three generations. Though you can find similar local specialties for lower prices elsewhere, nothing tops El Cid's spectacular setting in a rustic 16th-century building with dining rooms looking onto the cathedral. If you can have only one meal in Burgos, have it here. Another classic is **Casa Ojeda** (C/ Vitoria 5, tel. 94/720-9052, www.grupoojeda.com, 1:30–4:30 P.M. and 8–11 P.M. Mon.–Sat., 1:30–4:30 P.M. Sun., €40), which is hailed in gastronomic circles throughout Spain. The upstairs dining room oozes refined elegance while the boisterous downstairs bar packs in the locals. Ojeda also houses an impressive wine cellar and a small gourmet shop. For a creative take on traditional fare, head to **La Fábula** (C/ La Puebla 18, tel. 94/726-3092, 1:30–4:30 P.M. and 8–11 P.M. Tues.–Sat., 1:30–4:30 P.M. Sun., closed Mon., €40). They usually have a wide selection of fresh fish available, which can be a great break from the meat fest offered at other restaurants.

Tapas

Though there are good tapas bars all over the city, the greatest concentration is in the old town, near Plaza Mayor, particularly along **Calle Sombrería** and **Calle San Lorenzo.** Hours are 1:30–4:30 P.M. and 8 P.M.–midnight. The tradition in Burgos is to tapa-hop, spending no more than half an hour in any one bar. For this reason, most bars have one or two house specialties. Two of the most traditional—and most popular—tapas bars are **Casa Pancho** (C/ San Lorenzo 15, tel. 94/720-3405), famous for its *botones* (giant mushrooms stuffed with bacon), and **Los Herreros** (C/ San Lorenzo 20, tel. 94/720-2448), which specializes in a tapa called *cojonudo* (a quail's egg fried with chorizo). For something a bit more upscale, head around the corner to **La Favorita** (C/ Avellanos 8, tel. 94/720-5949), a boisterous blend of tradition and modernity. Try their *huevos rotos* (fried eggs with potatoes and ham). **Bar Rimbombin** (C/ Sombrerería 6, tel. 94/720-9396) is a gritty little place with a devoted local following addicted to their *alpargatas* (thick slabs of bread slathered with olive oil, tomato, and ham). One of the most charming bars is **Gaona Jardín** (C/ Sombrería 29, tel. 94/720-6191). Unlike most tapas bars in the area, this one has ample seating and a lovely garden right in the center of the bar. The specialty is grilled foie gras with a wild mushroom sauce.

INFORMATION

There are two main **city tourist offices.** One is near the Teatro Principal (Po. Espolón,

s/n, tel. 94/728-8874, 10:30 A.M.–2 P.M. and 4:30–7:30 P.M. Mon.–Sat., 10:30 A.M.–2 P.M. Sun., longer hours in summer). The other is in front of the cathedral (Pl. Rey San Fernando, tel. 94/728-8874, 10:30 A.M.–2 P.M. and 4:30–7:30 P.M. Mon.–Sat., 10:30 A.M.–2 P.M. Sun., longer hours in summer). The Burgos **regional tourist office** (C/ Asunción de Nuestra Señora 3, tel. 94/727-9432, info@patroturisbur.es, www.patroturisbur.com, 10 A.M.–2 P.M. and 5–8 P.M. daily) can provide information about sights throughout the Burgos region, including the archeological site at Atapuerca and the singing monks in Santo Domingo de Silos. Finally, there is a very capable **Castilla y León tourist office** (Pl. Alonso Martínez 7, tel. 94/720-3125) with extensive information and excellent maps on the entire region including Segovia, Ávila, León, and Salamanca.

GETTING THERE AND AROUND

Train

Renfe (www.renfe.es) runs daily trains to and from the **Burgos train station** (Pl. Estación, s/n), connecting to Barcelona, the País Vasco, Aragón, and Castilla y León. When traveling by train, take the intercity trains, which provide the most direct route. However, the trains are not as direct as the buses and normally cost more. The station began renovations late in 2006 and is expected to move out of the city in the future.

Bus

From Madrid, the best way to Burgos is by bus, which runs much more frequently than the train. **Continental Auto** (C/ Miranda 3, tel. 90/233-0400, www.continental-auto.es) has several daily buses to and from Madrid (€14, 2.25 hours). There are also direct routes to and from the País Vasco and other cities in Castilla y León.

Car

Burgos is easily reached by car from any major city. From Madrid, take the A-1 towards Burgos. Near the end of the journey, catch the

THE OLD, OLD BONES OF BURGOS

Spanish poet and philosopher Miguel de Unamuno (1864-1936) wrote "There is no landscape without history," and when it comes to Atapuerca, it could not be more true. In 1863, Spanish engineers were working on a railroad path through the Sierra de Atapuerca, about 10 miles east of Burgos city. After cutting a trench 0.8 kilometer long and 20 meters deep, workers found a paleontological puzzle – layers of a long-gone existence including hundreds of animal fossils and a few pottery fragments. The train tracks stopped and archaeologists stepped in.

Serious digging at Atapuerca began in earnest in 1976. Archaeologists spend lifetimes looking for just one fragment of bone, one sign of ancient life calling out to the present. What the Spanish archaeologists found at Atapuerca was much, much more. Each day revealed new findings. By 1989, over 300 human remains had been uncovered. Archaeologists also discovered why the area was so rich in human remains. In an excavation site called La Galería, evidence of a natural hole in the earth revealed thousands of animal remains.

Hundreds of thousands of years ago, animals including deer, horses, and even rhinoceroses regularly tripped to their deaths in this deep hole. At the bottom, ancient humans waited with crude stone tools. There they dismembered the animal for food. Fire had not yet been discovered so the meat was consumed raw.

Through the first half of the 1990s, Atapuerca delivered even more insights into the past. The *Sima de los Huesos* (pit of bones) proved especially rich, eventually revealing the remains of 32 individuals from the *Homo heidelbergensis* species, direct descendents of the Neanderthals. The cluster of so many individuals together has made archaeologists suspect that the site was a burial ground, which would make it the first evidence of burial in Europe. Meanwhile, digging continued, going deeper into the earth and further back in time. In 1992, human remains were dated to 300,000 years old. In 1994, the pit revealed a tooth dating back 800,000 years, thus confirming Atapuerca as the home of the oldest-known Europeans.

E-80 towards Burgos/Santander. Take *salida* (exit) 3 right into the city. From Barcelona, it is a very hilly six-hour drive along the toll highways AP-2 towards Zaragoza, switching to the AP-68 into Burgos.

VICINITY OF BURGOS
Covarrubias

Surrounded by pink-hued caves, thick stands of cherry and juniper trees, and the rolling green banks of the River Arlanza, Covarrubias sits about 40 kilometers (25 miles) south and a few centuries away from Burgos. Almost perfectly preserved, the village is made up of a tiny jumble of white medieval houses built of exposed timbers and stone-walled arcades. While wandering through, look for the **Colegiata de San Cosme y San Damián** (tel. 94/740-6311, 10:30 A.M.–2 P.M. and 4–7 P.M. Wed.–Mon., closed Tues.), a Gothic church founded in the 7th century and rebuilt in the 12th and 15th. The interior is both eerie and ornate, housing the tombs of long-dead Castile royals like Fernán González, the first count of Castile. There is also a spectacular, colored triptych, *Adoración de los Magos,* attributed to Spanish gothic sculptor Gil de Siloé. To get details on this and other sites of interest, as well as information on outdoor activities around Covarrubias, visit the **tourist office** (C/ Monseñor Vargas, s/n, tel. 94/740-6461, closed Mon.).

There are about half a dozen places to stay, the best of which is the **Hotel Rural Rey Chindasvinto** (Pl. Rey Chindasvinto 5, tel. 94/740-6560, www.hotelchindasvinto.com, €55). Though the building is old, the rooms are updated with modern, yet rustic, touches. Another good option is **Hotel Doña Sancha** (C/ Victor Barbadillo 25, tel. 94/740-6400, info@hoteldonasancha.com, www.hoteldona

On July 8, 1994, in an excavation called Gran Dolina, archaeologists found teeth, jaw bones, and skull fragments of six individuals. Research on the pieces revealed one of the most shocking discoveries in the field of archaeology. The individuals were different from all other discovered species of hominid. In 1997, Atapuerca presented to the world evidence of a new species, *Homo antecessor*. This finding put Atapuerca on the map as the most significant archaeological site in Europe and one of the most important in the world. Research and humanity awards were bestowed on the site and Atapuerca was named a World Heritage Site by UNESCO.

Digging has continued in earnest and Atapuerca has complied, revealing ever older evidence of human life. By 2001, a new excavation pit called Sima del Elefante was begun. It was named "elephant" after the remains of a hippopotamus were mistaken for an elephant. The crew was about to change the name when a researcher found the remains of an actual elephant. The site has so far been dated to over a million years ago.

Unfortunately, Atapuerca is difficult to visit. There is no public transportation so a car is required (or you could take a taxi from Burgos for about €20 each way). Currently, the site can be accessed from either the village of Atapuerca or Ibeas de Juarros, the latter being the easier of the two to access. From Burgos, take the N-120 straight to the town. Register for a tour at **Emiliano Aguirre Recepción** (tel. 94/742-1462, www .atapuerca.net, €4). The informative two-hour tour will be led by a very passionate archaeological doctoral student. However, they don't all speak English. In order to promote the site and archaeology in general, Atapuerca, the city of Burgos, and several prominent universities have teamed up to build the **Museo del la Evolución Humana,** an ambitious multimillion-euro project that will rival New York's American Museum of Natural History in scope. In addition to a cutting-edge interactive museum, the complex will house research facilities and educational departments. It is slated to open in 2010, and as the ongoing research at Atapuerca will comprise the foundation of the museum, it is expected that visits to the actual site will be easier to make.

sancha.com, €50). Standing just on the edge of town, its 14 quaint rooms offer gorgeous views of the village. The hotel also operates **Casa Rural Don Dimas,** a fully equipped apartment in the center of Covarrubias.

The best restaurant in town is **De Galo** (C/ Monseñor Vargas, 10, tel. 94/740-6393, €25), set in an antiquated home and featuring grilled game and fish. Call ahead as the hours are sporadic. For something more casual, but just as delicious, head to the local favorite, **Casa Galín** (Pl. Doña Urraca 4, tel. 94/740-6552).

There are two buses per day that leave from Burgos to Covarrubias operated by **Autocares Arceredillo** (C/ Miranda 3, tel. 94/748-5266, €2.50). The earliest ride out is at 1 P.M. If you are driving, take the A-1 towards Madrid and take exit 230 towards Sarracin. From there, switch to the N-234 and finally the BU-901, which leads into town.

◖ Santo Domingo de Silos

This tiny village is dominated by the spectacular **Monasterio de Santo Domingo de Silos** (C/ Santo Domingo 2, tel. 94/739-0049, 10 A.M.– 1 P.M. and 4:30–6 P.M. Mon.–Sat., 4:30–6 P.M. Sun., €3), an active Benedictine monastery that is one of the most celebrated Romanesque buildings in Spain. Located on the site of a Visigothic church, it was built in 929 by Saint Domingo, whose remains lie within the edifice. The most striking feature of the monastery is its cloister, built in the 11th and 12th centuries by Mudejar architects. It features lifelike carvings of Christ and various saints as well as impressive stonework at the top of its many columns. The monastery's 18th-century pharmacy is worth a peek for its large collection of antique medical instruments.

While most of Spain's religious monuments draw visitors solely on the basis of their architectural beauty, the Monasterio de Santo

FROM CHURCH CHANTING TO CHART TOPPING

Record companies are always looking for hits. In 1994, that search took EMI to the tiny medieval village of Santo Domingo de Silos, just south of Burgos, and to the Benedictine monks of the local abbey. Since the 1800s, the monks had performed their masses in Gregorian chants, a type of monophonic singing popular in the Catholic Church during the 9th century. By the 1950s, the Santo Domingo monks had formed a choir under the direction of a group of Benedictine monks, under the direction of their brother Ismael Fernández de la Cuesta, who later left the order to become director of Spain's musicology society. The monks put out several local recordings throughout the decades and, in 1993, a Spanish label compiled the recordings into a two-disc set called *Canto Gregoriano*. It became a surprise hit in Europe and EMI came calling. The American record giant cut the recording down to one disc, gave it some slick packaging, and whipped up a New Age marketing campaign. Under the name **Chant,** the album shot up the 1994 record charts, selling over six million copies. The music seemed to be the perfect cure for the stresses of modern life. The resultant media frenzy turned tiny Santo Domingo de Silos into a tourist destination and made the monks minor superstars. Gregorian chanting became a hot genre and sparked a flood of imitators, both authentic and not so. To the monks' shock, the music went more mainstream than they had ever anticipated, appearing in techno remixes and, reputedly, at least once in a porn movie soundtrack.

As with all media-fueled trends, the buzz died down pretty quickly and Santo Domingo de Silos went back to its sleepy self. Though the monks continue to record CDs and curious fans still people the audience during their Gregorian masses, life has gone back to normal for the singing monks. Their ancient music is still their own and still fuels their daily masses and permeates their monastic lives. Unfortunately, as is the case with many abbeys, the monks are growing old and there are very few younger converts willing to take on the life. What will happen to the order and the music is unclear. One thing is sure: Their recordings will carry on the tradition of their voices and the timeless beauty of Gregorian chanting for centuries to come. That is something to sing about.

To see the singing monks for yourself, you must attend mass. The monks do not give concerts or hold performances; the chanting is how they perform their religious services. There are several masses throughout the day and all are open to the public and free of charge. The only mass held entirely in chant is called Visperas; it occurs daily at 7 P.M. and lasts just over 2.5 hours. In summer, the Thursday service is held at 8 P.M. The daily 9 A.M. mass is partly held in chanting. Contact the **Monasterio de Santo Domingo de Silos** (tel. 94/739-0049) for more information.

Domingo de Silos also attracts attention because of its singing monks. In accordance with a Benedictine tradition, the monks hold most of their masses in Gregorian Chant. After topping the American music charts with their chanting, the monks—and the monastery—became international celebrities. (See sidebar, *From Church Chanting to Chart Topping.*)

If you are a single male looking for a contemplative retreat, you can stay at the monastery for a minimum of three days, maximum of eight. Contact **Padre Hospedería** (tel. 94/739-0049, silos@arrakis.es, €28). Lodging is austere but comfortable and includes three square meals per day. Though you are expected to eat with the monks, for the rest of the day you are left alone. If you prefer something a bit less monastic, try the competent **Hotel Santo Domingo de Silos** (C/ Santo Domingo, s/n, tel. 94/739-0053, www.hotelsantodomingodesilos.com, €50). The best hotel in town is **Tres Coronas** (Pl. Mayor 6, tel. 94/739-0047, reservas@hoteltrescoronasdesilos.com, www.hoteltrescoronasdesilos.com, €71), set in an 18th-century mansion that has been retrofitted to its past Castilian glory. **Arco de San Juan**

(C/ Pradera de San Juan 1, tel. 94/739-0074, €50) is right next to the cloister and offers comfortable rooms and a delightful garden. Each of these hotels features a good restaurant with local specialties, though the most acclaimed is **Casa Emerterio** at Tres Coronas.

The only way into Santo Domingo de Silos by public transportation is the bus from Burgos, **Autocares Arceredillo** (C/ Miranda 3, tel. 94/748-5266, €3). By car, take the A-1 towards Madrid and take exit 230 towards Sarracin. From there, switch to the N-234 and finally the BU-903, which leads into the center of town.

Ribera del Duero

At the southern tip of the Burgos province lies Ribera del Duero, Spain's most famous wine region after La Rioja. The vineyards roll north and south of the River Duero and extend into the provinces of Valladolid, Segovia, and Soria. The climate is harsh; Winter's heavy snows and volatile storms give way to a summer pierced by dry, coarse winds and long days of scorching sun. The result is hardy *tempranillo* grapes, which give Ribera del Duero wines their distinctive silkiness, intense flavor, and ruby color. There are dozens of bodegas including Spain's most prestigious winemaker, **Vega Sicilia** (www.vega-sicilia.com), producer of the country's most glorious (and expensive) wines. Two more renowned winemakers in the region are **Pesquera** and **Pago de Carraovejas**.

Wine tourism is still catching on in Ribera del Duero, and many bodegas are not open to the public. Still others, because of their exclusivity refuse to accept visitors unless they are VIPs or part of an elite tour. If you'd like a high-end tour to some of the more selective bodegas, contact **Cellar Tours** (tel. 91/521-3939, info@cellartours.com, www.cellartours.com), a luxury wine tourism operator based in Madrid and run by native Californian Genevieve McCarthy.

For a self-guided tour, **Peñafiel** in Valladolid makes an excellent base. The fortified town was built in 1307 and boasts one of the best-preserved castles in Castile. This massive structure once warded off advancing Moors and fractious Christian lords. Today, it houses the **Museo Provincial del Vino** (tel. 98/388-1199, www.museodelvinodevalladolid .es). There are several bodegas in town, but the most spectacular in the area is about 29 kilometers (18 miles) to the east. **Abadía Retuerta** (Abadía Santa María de Retuerta, Sárdon de Duero, Valladolid, tel. 98/368-0314, www .abadia-retuerta.com, €9) is headquartered in a 12th-century Romanesque abbey, which itself is worth seeing. Wine visits are normally held each morning and conclude with a tasting of three wines. Advance reservations are required. For complete information on bodegas and activities in the area, visit the **tourist office** (Pl. Coso 2, tel. 98/388-1526).

In Peñafiel, stay at the **Hotel Ribera del Duero** (Av. Escalona, 17, tel. 98/387-3111, www.hotelriberadelduero.com, €70), an elegant hotel built with wine tourism in mind. The friendly staff can help you arrange visits to various bodegas. For an unforgettable dining experience, head to **Molino de Palacios** (Av. Constitución 16, tel. 98/388-0505, closed Sun. P.M. and Mon., €35) where you can dine on succulent *lechazo* (roasted lamb) in a 16th-century water mill.

Another good base for Ribera del Duero wine tourism is **Aranda de Duero** in the province of Burgos. The **tourist office** (Pl. Mayor, s/n, tel. 94/751-0476) has information, maps, and suggested routes for the entire Ribera del Duero region. While in town, rest your wine-weary head at a bodega. **Hotel Torremilanos** (Finca Torremilanos, s/n, tel. 94/751-2852, hotel@torremilanos.com, www.torremilanos .com, €150) is a sprawling *finca* (country estate) that houses an excellent four-star hotel and a historic vineyard. Rooms are simple for the price, but service is impeccable and views of the surrounding vineyards are soul-soothing. The hotel's bodega, **Peñalba Lopez,** is a century-old estate worth a visit whether you stay here or not. The best *asador* (grill house) in town is the atmospheric **Mesón de la Villa** (Pl. Mayor, 3, tel. 94/750-1025, closed Mon., €35). In addition to sinfully delicious lamb, the restaurant specializes in *escabeches de caza,* savory house-pickled meats, and for the non-carnivore, there are platters of wild mushrooms and white asparagus.

Though both Peñafiel and Aranda de Duero are linked by bus and train to most major cities in Spain, the only feasible way to visit Ribera del Duero is by car. Aranda de Duero, the capital of the region lies on the N-1, just over 80 kilometers (50 miles) south of Burgos and about 160 kilometers (100 miles) north of Madrid. From there, it is a 40-kilometer (25-mile) ride on the N-122 to Peñafiel. Road N-122 actually cuts through the heart of this wine country and there are dozens of bodegas all along it. Contact the Castilla y León tourist office in either town for maps of the region. If your Spanish is up to par, check www.lariberadelduero.com for routes and itineraries and always be sure to contact the bodegas beforehand to confirm visiting hours and make reservations.

BARCELONA

When speaking of world-class cities, Barcelona falls off the tongue as easily as Paris, London, and Rome. Sure, Madrid, with at least a million more inhabitants, is Spain's capital city, but it is beautiful Barcelona that captures the imagination. Cosmopolitan and vibrant, fashion-forward and sophisticated, edgy and affluent, Barcelona oozes a European flair that transcends nationality. More than any other Spanish city, Barcelona is European—from its Roman roots to its internationally acclaimed architecture. Home to one of Spain's largest expat communities (brilliantly evoked in the 1994 film *Barcelona),* Barcelona's streets teem with globe-hopping jet-setters, dream-seeking immigrants, and hordes of people whose passports are stamped "citizen of the world."

They are drawn (as are five million tourists per year) to Barcelona's thousand and one charms. Take in the orderly opulence of Eixample, the bohemian grit of El Raval, and the dark medieval alleys of Barri Gòtic in one day. Lunch on simply grilled shrimp in a Barceloneta bar, then dine on cutting-edge New Catalan Cuisine at a haute spot. Lose yourself in a concert at the modernist masterpiece Palau de la Música Catalana or lose your head dancing to a world-famous DJ at an all-night party. Buy the fixings for a picnic at La Boqueria, one of the world's most atmospheric markets, then go spread your blanket at Parc Güell, one of the world's most whimsical parks. Tramp through history along the way. Visit Els Quatre Gats, where Picasso had his first art show. Walk through the tranquil Plaça de Sant Felip Neri, where shrapnel marks attest to the

HIGHLIGHTS

 Mercat de la Boqueria: This wrought-iron and stained-glass jewel is a feast for the senses. With dozens of artfully composed food stalls, rumor has it that if you can't find a food item in Boqueria, it just doesn't exist (page 215).

Barri Gòtic: This warren of tiny streets is where Barcelona got its start some 2,000 years ago. Get lost here amid the twisting alleys of medieval buildings, Gothic churches, and Roman ruins (page 221).

Museu Picasso: Located in a lovely cluster of medieval mansions, the world's largest collection of Picasso's early works reveals the development of his artistic genius (page 226).

Santa María del Mar: Soaring above the trendy barrio of El Born, this Catalan Gothic church, built in 1384, will lift your spirits with its spacious interior full of light and grace (page 227).

Barceloneta: Whether you elbow your way to a tapas bar in this old fishing barrio, stroll the beach at sunset, or dance till dawn in one of the mega-clubs on Port Olímpic, a visit to Barcelona's Mediterranean coast is a must (page 228).

Fundació Joan Miró: Created by Miró himself before his death in 1983, this magnificent museum offers an expansive overview of one of the most influential artists of the 20th century. Spanning surrealism, Dadaism, and modernism, the collection includes paintings, sculptures, ceramics, and tapestries (page 232).

La Pedrera: When it was completed in 1910, Casa Milà shocked the world and earned the disparaging nickname *pedrera* (stone quarry). Nearly a century later, La Pedrera is hailed as one of the most innovative and important structures in the history of architecture. It is also one of Barcelona's top sights. Not bad for a pile of rocks (page 238).

La Sagrada Família: The temple – begun in 1882 and unfinished to this day – has both mystified and mesmerized visitors for over a century. It is easily the most recognizable building in the world and a testament to the vision and genius of Antoni Gaudí (page 239).

Parc Güell: Forming the third point in the triangle of must-see Gaudí works, this park is a wonderland of color and architectural whimsy. It is also free, making it one of the best bargains in the world (page 244).

Montserrat: Just a half-hour train ride and a heart-stopping cable car away rises the jagged mount of Montserrat. Home of the internationally venerated Virgin of Montserrat, one very massive monastery, Europe's oldest boys' choir, dazzling views that take in both the Pyrenees and the Mediterranean Sea, and a dozen scenic hikes, Montserrat is the perfect vacation from your Barcelona vacation (page 291).

LOOK FOR  TO FIND RECOMMENDED SIGHTS, ACTIVITIES, NIGHTLIFE, DINING, AND LODGING.

violence of the Spanish Civil War. Stop in the Plaça del Rei, where the Catholic Kings Isabel and Fernando greeted Columbus after one of his New World journeys. Walk out onto the home field of the world's most famous soccer team, FC Barcelona. Have a cup of coffee in La Granja, where the back dining room boasts a 2,000-year-old Roman wall. Do all of this and still have the option of a morning hike in the green hills of Montjuïc or Tibidabo, a bike ride along the beach, a swim in the Mediterranean, or a half-hour escape to the mythical mountain of Montserrat.

Of course, all that history and nature is backdrop to Barcelona's artistic wonders. The city has long had a manic obsession with design—notice the whimsical street lamps on Passeig de Gràcia, the proliferation of public sculptures, the shop windows that resemble art galleries. In addition to Picasso, who spent his formative years here, Joan Miró lived, worked, and founded one of Spain's best museums in Barcelona. When he died in 1983, the city held what amounted to no less than a state funeral. Surrealistic master Salvador Dalí, born in nearby Figueres, held many of his earliest shows in the city. Writers from Jean Genet and Orson Welles to renowned art critic Robert Hughes have drawn inspiration from the city. Today, young artists by the galleryful call Barcelona home. They are joined by soon-to-be famous designers, semi-famous writers, and a host of other creative types. Yet, one artistic son in particular has left a mark so indelible on the city as to become synonymous with it—Antoni Gaudí. The most famous of a talented group of *modernisme* (Catalan art nouveau) architects that flourished in Barcelona in the early 20th century, Gaudí created groundbreaking buildings that over 100 years later still have admirers shaking their heads in wonder. If for no other reason, Barcelona is worth a trip just to see La Sagrada Família, the architect's final and yet-unfinished masterpiece.

Yet for all of Barcelona's style and sizzle, it is very much a traditional town, capital of the fiercely independent, supremely self-confident region of Cataluña. Back when Spain was battling the Moors in an effort to become Spain, Barcelona was already a world power with outposts throughout the Mediterranean, a powerful maritime industry, and a wealthy, educated citizenry. In 1238, Barcelona gave birth to Cataluña's first Generalitat, or self-ruling government. That early independence goes a long way towards explaining the city's deep-rooted pride. You'll hear the Catalan language spoken in shops, see it on street signs, buses, and menus. Every weekend, in front of the cathedral and the town hall, hundreds of Catalans of all ages join hands together to perform the *sardana,* an ancient Catalan dance. As any self-respecting local will tell you, Barcelona is not in Spain, it's in Cataluña.

It is true. Barcelona is not the land of stereotypical Spain. There is no bullfighting and the flamenco that happens does so strictly for tourists. If you want Spain, go to Madrid, Andalucía, or Castilla. If you want a dynamic, dazzling, dizzying city that offers all of the above plus a million things more, go to Barcelona. At the top of Las Ramblas you'll find a fountain where legend has it that if you drink from its gurgling water you'll forever return to the city. Even if you don't take a sip, a visit to Barcelona is guaranteed to stay with you forever. Like Gaudí's works, it is monumental, moving, magical, and immensely memorable.

PLANNING YOUR TIME

If you have just one day in Barcelona, do two things: Plan a return trip ASAP, then head straight to La Sagrada Família. There is no other building in the world like it and to see it rise, all molten stone and organic towers, from the tidy grid of Eixample is a sight you'll never forget. With a hefty morning available, you can also manage to see Gaudí's other masterpieces, Parc Güell and La Pedrera. Two days is a bit better, but you'll be running to take in the best of the sights. (See sidebar, *Two Days in Barcelona.*) Three days is more like it and to really see the city, it is the minimal amount of time you'll need. Follow the two-day itinerary, then add Montjuïc and Raval on day three. If

BARCELONA

BARCELONA

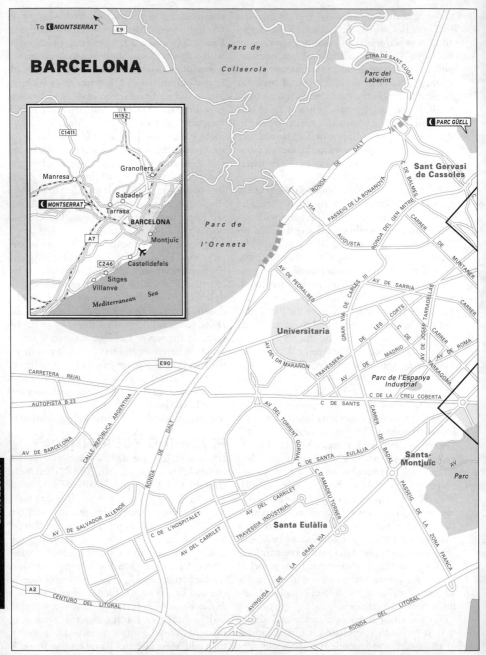

To **MONTSERRAT** E9

BARCELONA

Parc de
Collserola

CTRA DE SANT CUGAT

Parc del
Laberint

PARC GÜELL

Sant Gervasi
de Cassoles

N152
C1411

Granollers
Manresa
Sabadell
MONTSERRAT
Tarrasa
BARCELONA
A7
Montjuïc
C246
Castelldefels
Sitges
Villanve
Mediterranean Sea

Parc de
l'Oreneta

RONDA DE DALT
VIA
PASSEIG DE LA BONANOVA
RONDA DEL GEN MITRE
AUGUSTA
CARRER
DE
MUNTANER

AV DE PEDRALBES
GRAN VIA DE CARLES III
AV DE SARRIA
DE LES CORTS
C. DE MADRID
AV DE JOSEP TARRADELLAS
CARRER
AV DE ROMA
CARRER
DE TARRAGONA

Universitaria

AV DEL DR MARAÑON
TRAVESSERA
DE
AV
DE SANTS

Parc de l'Espanya
Industrial

C DE LA CREU COBERTA

E90

CARRETERA REIAL
AUTOPISTA B-23

C DE SANTS
CARRER
DE BADAL
Sants-
Montjuïc
AV
Parc

AV DE BARCELONA
CALLE REPÚBLICA ARGENTINA
RONDA DE DALT
AV DEL TORRENT GORNAL
C DE SANTA EULÀLIA
C D'AMADEU TORNER
PASSEIG DE LA ZONA FRANCA

AV DE SALVADOR ALLENDE
C DE L'HOSPITALET
AV DEL CARRILET
AV DEL CARRILET
TRAVESSIA INDÚSTRIAL
Santa Eulàlia

A2
CENTURO DEL LITORAL
AVINGUDA DE LA GRAN VIA
RONDA DEL LITORAL

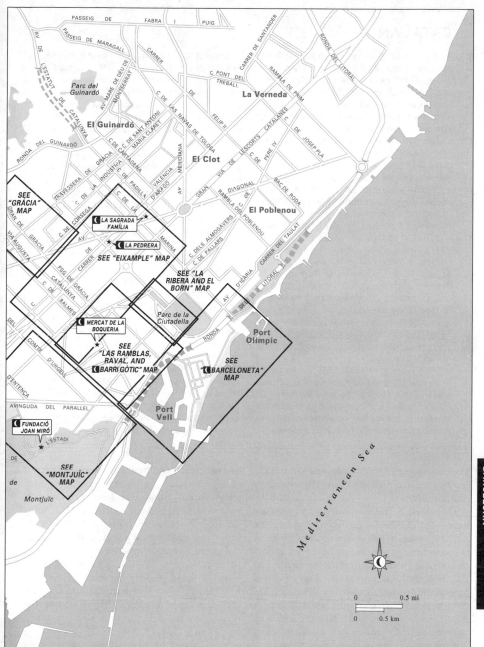

PASSEIG DE FABRA I PUIG
PASSEIG DE MARAGALL
CARRER
AV. DE L'ESTATUT
DE CATALUNYA
Parc del Guinardó
AV. MARE DE DEU DE MONTSERRAT
C. PONT DEL TREBALL
CARRER DE SANTANDER
RONDA DEL LITORAL
RAMBLA DE PRIM
El Guinardó
RONDA DEL GUINARDÓ
C. DE SANT ANTONI MARIA CLARET
C. DE LAS NAVAS DE TOLOSA
FELIP II
La Verneda
C. DE LESCORTS CATALANES
C. DE JOSEP PLA
TRAVESSERA DE GRACIA
C. DE LA INDÚSTRIA
C. DE CARTAGENA
VALENCIA
C. D'ARAGÓ
MERIDIANA
El Clot
C. DE PERE IV
GRAN VIA DE LES CORTS CATALANES
DIAGONAL
SAC DE RODA
C. DE CORSEGA
C. DE LA
RAMBLA DEL POBLENOU
El Poblenou

SEE "GRÀCIA" MAP
GRAN DE GRACIA
VIA AUGUSTA
C. DE CORSEGA
AV. DE
CARRER
★ ◖ LA SAGRADA FAMÍLIA ★
★ ◖ LA PEDRERA
SEE "EIXAMPLE" MAP
PSG DE GRACIA
C. DE BALMES
MARINA
C. DELS ALMOGAVERS
C. DE PALLARS
SEE "LA RIBERA AND EL BORN" MAP
CARRER DEL TAULAT
D'ICÀRIA
RONDA DEL LITORAL

DEL
COMTE D'URGELL
C.
◖ MERCAT DE LA BOQUERIA
★
SEE "LAS RAMBLAS, RAVAL, AND BARRI GÒTIC" MAP ◖
Pàrc de la Ciutadella
RONDA
Port Olímpic
SEE ◖ BARCELONETA MAP

D'ENTENÇA
AVINGUDA DEL PARALLEL
◖ FUNDACIÓ JOAN MIRÓ
L'ESTADI
★
DE
SEE "MONTJUÏC" MAP
de
Montjuïc
Port Vell

Mediterranean Sea

0   0.5 mi
0   0.5 km

BARCELONA

CATALAN

You've boned up on your high school Spanish, picked up a phrasebook, and memorized a few key things like where is the bathroom and how much are the clams; then you arrive in Barcelona and immediately notice the signs are posted with words you don't recognize and people are speaking in a tongue that sounds nothing like what you heard in the last Almodóvar film. No, you are not crazy. As locals will eagerly point out, you are no longer in Spain, you are in Cataluña.

Catalan (*català* in Catalan) is the official co-language of Cataluña, along with Spanish, which is more rightly called *Castellano* (Castilian Spanish). It is a Romance language that sounds and looks to the uninitiated like a blend between Spanish and French. However, it is its own language, at least as old as the other Romance languages, and is spoken by an estimated 10 million people. In addition to Cataluña, it is used in the Islas Baleares, Valencia, and Murcia. It is the main language of the small country of Andorra and is also spoken in parts of southern France and on the Italian island of Sardinia.

After years of linguistic oppression under Franco, when speaking a word of Catalan was reason for suspicion and possibly even jail, Catalan is back with a vengeance. It is taught in schools, used in official government communications, and is common in public signage.

A visitor to Cataluña should bear in mind a few things when navigating in this linguistic territory. First, almost everyone also speaks and understands Castilian Spanish, so if your Spanish is up to par, you should have no trouble communicating in this region. (Of course, in highly touristic areas such as Barcelona, English will also be quite common.) That said, you should remember to be culturally sensitive regarding the language. Never imply that Catalan is a dialect of Spanish – it is not. In fact, considering the complicated political history of Cataluña and Spain, the language of Catalan is a vital, integral part of Catalan identity and culture. If you really want to tickle the local fancy, learn a few simple phrases such as "good day" and "thank you."

From the most practical perspective, the main problems a tourist will have are with street signs, addresses, opening hours, and postings in train and bus stations. Part of the clash will happen if you buy maps or guides outside of Cataluña. They may very well use Spanish vocabulary, rather than Catalan. The following brief list should help. Though if you are unsure, ask a local, *Parles anglès?* (Do you speak English?) Just offering that little bit of Catalan is enough to warm a local's heart and get them to go out of their way to help you figure out what you need to know.

you can squeeze in half a day more, catch the train to the magnificent mountain monastery of Montserrat.

Dedicated Barcelona-philes—and they are legion—swear there is no bad time to visit the city. However, if you've been to Barcelona in the smothering mid-August heat with hordes of sunburned tourists jamming themselves into the shops and restaurants that haven't closed for vacation—you'd probably disagree. Another reason to avoid August is that it is peak public works season. With half the locals on vacation for the entire month, the city figures it is the perfect time to shut down metro lines,

detour streets, and basically make a whole lot of noise and dust. Summer in general is pretty tough in Barcelona. The heat is oppressive, prices inflated, and the tourists at their most teeming. If you do go, book your hotel in advance and make sure it has air-conditioning.

For the complete opposite experience, head there off-season. Wintertime is cold with wisps of wind peeling off the surrounding hills but still just enough sunshine to keep vacationers happy. However, Barcelona weather is notoriously fickle and rain, sleet, and even snow can suddenly descend. If you go during this time, pack sweaters, a waterproof

NUMBERS

one	*un/a*
two	*dos/dues*
three	*tres*
four	*quatre*
five	*cinc*
six	*sis*
seven	*set*
eight	*vuit*
nine	*nou*
ten	*deu*

DAYS OF THE WEEK

Monday	*dilluns*
Tuesday	*dimarts*
Wednesday	*dimecres*
Thursday	*dijous*
Friday	*divendres*
Saturday	*dissabte*
Sunday	*diumenge*

MONTHS

January	*gener*
February	*febrer*
March	*març*
April	*abril*
May	*maig*
June	*juny*
July	*juliol*
August	*agost*
September	*setembre*
October	*octubre*
November	*novembre*
December	*desembre*

DIRECTIONS

left	*esquerra*
right	*dreta*
Street	*Carrer*
Boulevard	*Passeig*
Avenue	*Avinguda*
Square	*Plaça*

TRAVEL

train station	*estació de tren*
airport	*aeroport*
bus station	*estació d'autobusos*
exit	*sortida*
north	*nord*
south	*sud*
west	*oest*
east	*est*

USEFUL PHRASES

hello	*hola*
goodbye	*adéu*
good day/night	*bon dia/bona nit*
please	*si us plau*
excuse me	*perdoni*
How much...	*Quant costa...*
open	*obert*
closed	*tancat*
thank you	*gràcies*

jacket, hats, scarves, and gloves. Optimists can pack sunscreen, too. Spring is as beautiful in Barcelona as it is just about anywhere. The trees on the Ramblas unfurl their shady leaves. Colorful tulips and flowers pop up in gardens and balconied pots. And the sun, feeling a bit bold, steps out to play spreading light and warmth all over the city. However, possibly the best time to visit Barcelona is fall, particularly the still-balmy month of October. Locals have returned from vacation and there is a palpable optimism in the air. The sea is still warm enough for swimming and the beachside bars still buzzing. Tourists have thinned out and prices are ratcheted down from summertime highs.

HISTORY

Around 15 B.C. the Romans built a military camp near Mons Taber, a hill that once stood where the Plaça de Sant Jaume is today. Despite the commanding name Colonia Julia Augusta Faventia Paterna Barcino, the outpost was not much more than a walled encampment with a population of 1,000—nearby Tarragona was the real Roman powerhouse in this region. In the 5th century, the Visigoths sacked the city. Two centuries later, the Moors arrived. In 801, the Franks who ruled

THE TWO-DAY BEST OF BARCELONA

Take your vitamins and slap on your comfiest shoes – this two-day itinerary of the best of Barcelona will keep you busy!

DAY 1

On day one, head straight to **El Born** and have a light breakfast at the café across the street from the **Museu Picasso.** Enter the museum at opening time (10 A.M.) to enjoy a couple of crowd-free hours wandering the museum's medieval halls and taking in Picasso's brilliance. Next, cross Vía Laietana to **Barri Gòtic** and take an amble through Barcelona's 2,000-year-old core. Be sure to pass the **Catedral de Barcelona** and the **Museu d'Història de la Ciutat.** If you are into Gothic grandeur, step into the first. If you prefer Roman history, choose the latter. Both will run you about an hour. Around 2 P.M., hop the metro at Jaume I and take it one stop to Barceloneta (or if you are up to it, walk– it is only 10 minutes away). There, have a sit-down seafood lunch at **El Rey de la Gamba** or try the boisterous tapas bar **Jai-Ca** for their famous fried seafood snacks. After lunch, head to the beach and rest your feet in the sand or have a refreshing, cold drink at one of the *chiringuitos* (beachside bars). Next, walk over to **Port Vell** and take the classic Barcelona stroll up **Las Ramblas,** stopping at the belle epoque **Café de L'Opera** for a refreshment and the **Mercat de la Boqueria** for some serious fruit and vegetable ogling. After arriving at Plaça de Catalunya, hop the metro back to your hotel for a siesta and a shower.

Come evening, you have two options. If you plan ahead and can score tickets to a performance at the *modernisme* masterpiece **Palau de la Música Catalana,** do it. If not, head to Plaça de Espanya and walk up to the **Magic Fountain** for the spectacular light and music show. In both cases, afterwards, head to **El Born** for an evening stroll in its Gothic streets and a dinner of Catalan tapas at classic **Cal Pep** or cutting-edge **Comerç.** Finish with drinks at one of the terrace bars on **Passeig del Born.**

DAY 2

On day two, think Gaudí. You can either buy a one-day pass for the **Barcelona Bus Turístic** and do the "red route" or head to the Passeig de Gràcia metro stop, and walk up to the **Manzana de la Discordia** and then to **La Pedrera.** Have breakfast at a café beneath either of these lovely buildings or – to get away from your fellow tourists – pop over to the parallel **Rambla de Catalunya,** where locals walk their dogs and chat on benches. Next, catch the metro to **La Sagrada Família** and spend an hour wandering through what is quite possibly the most famous building in the world. At a corner store, grab the fixings for an impromptu lunch and head to **Parc Güell** by metro (Lessops stop) or catch a cab if your feet are screaming. Enjoy the view and a picnic in this colorful wonderland. After lunch, metro to Plaça de Espanya and take a stroll through the **Museu Nacional d'Art de Catalunya** for an overview of Catalan art. When done, it is time for a siesta.

Come evening, head to Eixample for an elegant last night. If the terrace at **La Pedrera** is open, start there. Consider dinner at one of Barcelona's top-rated restaurants such as **Cinc Sentits** or **Gaig** (reservations required at both). If you want something more earthy, head back to the **Barri Gòtic** and have tapas along Carrer de Avinyo and drinks later on Carrer de En'Gignas.

the areas of France and Germany captured Barcelona. The city and its surroundings served as a buffer zone between the Frankish empire in the north and the Moors in the south. Christened the Marca Hispania, the area corresponded with Cataluña's current boundaries and many historians contribute the origins of Catalan culture and language to this era.

The first Count of Barcelona was the delightfully named Wilfred the Hairy. In 878, he established a dynasty that would rule Barcelona for five centuries. With its enviable port, Barcelona grew in power and wealth. As it did, it achieved greater independence from the Franks and by the 10th century it had its own nation-state. In 1137, the marriage of Ramon

Berneguer, Count of Barcelona, with Petronila of Aragón, joined Cataluña with Aragón to create the Crown of Aragón. Operating out of the Drassanes naval yards—located at the southern end of present-day Las Ramblas—it became one of the mightiest seafaring powers in the Middle Ages with territories as far flung as Italy and Greece. This was the Barcelona's golden Gothic age, as evidenced by the majestic buildings throughout Barri Gòtic.

In 1479, Fernando, King of Aragón, married Isabel, Queen of Castile, in a union that would change not only Spain, but the world. As the Catholic monarchs turned their focus on expelling the Moors from the peninsula, Barcelona was relegated to backseat status. Though Isabel and Fernando greeted Columbus in Barcelona in the Plaça del Rei after one of his maiden voyages to the New World, the royal pair later sought to limit Barcelona's power by authorizing only one port in the country to deal with the New World—Sevilla. Barcelona was prevented from doing the two things it did best—sailing and commerce. In 1561, when Madrid was named capital of Spain, Barcelona's fate as the second city of Spain was sealed.

Through the 16th and 17th centuries, unrest simmered in Cataluña. In 1641, an independent Catalan Republic was declared in Barcelona. It was quickly squashed by Madrid. After the 1700 death of Carlos II sparked the War of Spanish Succession (1705–1714), Barcelona and the Catalans supported the Austrian Hapsburg dynasty. When the Bourbon King Felipe V won, Barcelona was punished. The city was besieged on September 11, 1714 (now celebrated as Cataluña Day). The Generalitat was abolished, Catalan language and culture were curtailed, and half of the Ribera working-class district was demolished to build the Ciutadella, a massive fort where Felipe's troops could keep watch over Barcelona.

Over the 18th century, Spain toppled from its position as a great empire—due mainly to the loss of funds expended in constant warfare. After the 1808–1814 War of Independence (Peninsular War) with France, Spanish power, centralized in Madrid, basically left Barcelona

alone. Though there were occasional Catalan uprisings, Barcelona turned its energies to the Industrial Revolution. The city underwent a magnificent financial revival during the late 1800s. The Eixample was laid and Barcelona's famed *modernisme* architectural movement began. Emboldened by its renewed wealth and power, Catalan nationalism grew. Three more Catalan Republics were declared: in 1873, 1931, and 1934. The last was proclaimed just before the Spanish Civil War (1936–1939). In the war, Cataluña sided with the Republicans against Franco and his Nationalist army and Barcelona became a major stronghold of Republican resistance. After the war ended in 1939 with Franco's victory, Cataluña experienced the worst oppression of its history. The language was forbidden—books were burned, street names were changed—and expressions of Catalan culture were banned. Any allusion to autonomy was grounds for arrest. Thousands of Catalan activists—real or suspected—disappeared into the prison at Castell de Montjuïc. Yet, the language and culture were deeply rooted and throughout Franco's 36-year rule, the Catalans furtively guarded both.

The night of Franco's 1975 death, millions of Barcelonans poured into the streets and joyously danced away the dark, oppressive night. In the 1978, the Spanish Constitution granted Cataluña home rule and Barcelona's Generalitat was reinstated. The following year, the Estatut d'Autonomia (statute of autonomy) was enacted, declaring Cataluña a nationality with Barcelona as its governing seat. Catalan language and culture were revived. Children began learning Catalan in school and government and media began operating in the language. Today, nearly all Barcelonans understand and use Catalan.

The push for increased Catalan autonomy continued through the 1990s, though it was kept in check by the conservative ruling party, Partido Popular. When the socialist PSOE party took power in 2004, the Catalans found an ally and the pursuit for autonomy was invigorated. In 2006, the Catalans voted to extend their rights under the *estatut*. The new

BARCELONA

statute makes Cataluña's self-government one of the most advanced in Spain and—in a move that makes the prosperous, hard-working populace very happy—limits the export of Catalan wealth to Madrid's central government. Still, as an autonomous region within Spain, Cataluña has no official recognition at the international level. For this reason, the proud Catalans still raise their metaphorical fist, reminding its millions of yearly visitors—on posters, graffiti, and in word—"you are not in Spain, you are in Cataluña."

Sights

Barcelona can be roughly divided into three main areas for exploring. The Ciutat Vella is Barcelona's oldest area. It is where the Romans first settled, and later the Catalan rulers. It runs south from Plaça de Catalunya to the sea and is divided into the neighborhoods of El Raval and Barri Gòtic by Las Ramblas, plus El Born. You'll find here Gothic churches, medieval buildings, and Roman ruins. To the north, Eixample unfolds in a precise grid of broad blocks lined by magnificent mansions including several designed by modernist madman Antoni Gaudí. Along the Mediterranean Sea lie Barcelona's two ports, old (Vell) and new (Olímpic), separated by Barceloneta, a traditional fishermen's barrio. Man-made beaches run the length of the area. Other areas include Montjuïc, a seaside mountain on the west of the city, and Gràcia, a charming working-class barrio.

LAS RAMBLAS

Running for 1.2 kilometers (0.75 mile) through the historic heart of Barcelona, Las Ramblas is at once lazily ambling towards the sea and rushing full-steam-ahead with life—the good, the bad, and the oddly entertaining. If it seems more like a river of humanity than a street, there is some historical precedence for that. Las Ramblas follows the path of an old stream (*rambla* in Arabic) that ran alongside the medieval wall that once stood here. Today, Las Ramblas is synonymous with Barcelona for tourists and it is often their first destination. It is definitely something to see—historic buildings, traditional bird and flower stalls, and perhaps the biggest attraction of all, the living statues. Painted up as mythical figures, monsters, even political personas such as Che Guevara, they stand frozen on their podiums until someone drops a coin in the bucket at their feet. Then they do a little act or pose for a photo. Dozens of them line Las Ramblas drawing photo-wielding crowds. But beware—where there are crowds, there are pickpockets. Keep your hand on your purse, your camera strap around your waist, and your wallet tucked way down your front pants pocket. Behind tourists, petty thieves and con artists are Las Ramblas' most populous demographic. Don't even think about engaging in one of their gambling schemes—you will lose your money and whatever else they can fleece off you while you are distracted by their sucker's game.

Las Ramblas is also lined with bars, restaurants, and hotels. If you like people-watching, grab a seat on one of the benches and watch the world flow by. Well, the tourist world; about the only thing you won't find on Las Ramblas is locals. Most Barcelonans—and settled expats—steer clear of this street, sticking instead to hipper hoods like Raval to the west of the Ramblas or Born to the east. You'd do good to join them. Take the requisite walk down Las Ramblas, but when you are ready to dine, have some drinks, or do a little shopping, duck off and head in search of the real Barcelona.

Plaça de Catalunya

Las Ramblas is actually a series of five *ramblas* that start at the Plaça de Catalunya, Barcelona's busiest, broadest square. To its north lies Eixample. The plaza is a hive of activity with buses, both local and tourist, stopping here.

Underneath the plaza is a subway stop and a local *cercanías* train stop. There is also a massive, well-equipped tourist office and souvenir shop. Tucked in around the buzz are benches, trees, and patches of grass—most given over to kissing couples, half-dozing seniors, and picnicking backpackers. Beyond that are shopping meccas like the mammoth **El Corte Inglés** (Metro: Pl. Catalunya, 10 A.M.–10 P.M. Mon.–Sat., closed Sun.), Spain's favorite department store where you can get everything from guidebooks to walking shoes. Their 9th-floor cafeteria offers great views with coffee. Moving south out of the plaza **Rambla Canaletes,** the first leg of Las Ramblas, unfolds. It is named for the black-and-gold iron fountain at its start. Legend has it that if you drink from it, you'll never leave Barcelona. If you duck down Carrer Canuda to the left, you'll come to **Plaça Vila de Madrid,** a cozy neighborhood plaza that is home to Roman tombs from Barcino, the Roman town that stood here over 2,000 years ago.

La Mercat de la Boqueria

© CANDY LEE LABALLE

Rambla Estudis

The next section of Las Ramblas, Rambla Estudis is named for L'Estudi General, a university that once stood here, but it is locally known as the Rambla dels Ocells (*rambla* of the birds) for the stalls of twittering birds that line this part of the road. At the corner of Carrer del Carme on the right, the looming **Església de Betlem** is one of Barcelona's few baroque masterpieces. Built between 1681 and 1732, the former Jesuit church features a richly textured stone exterior. Across the street, the 1790 **Palau Moja** (C/ Portaferrissa 1) has a tapestry-like exterior. There are occasional exhibitions held here and if one is on, you should pop in for a glimpse at the sumptuous interior. Back on the other side of the Rambla, **Palau de la Virreina** (Rambla 99, tel. 93/316-1000, Tues.–Sat. 11 A.M.–8 P.M., 11 A.M.–2:30 P.M. Sun.) is a restored 18th-century palace that now serves as a cultural center with galleries mainly devoted to contemporary art. There is also a walk-in office for information on cultural events throughout the city.

⬛ Mercat de la Boqueria

In the center of the **Rambla Sant Josep,** the Mercat de la Boqueria (Rambla 91, Metro: Liceu, 8 A.M.–8 P.M. Mon.–Sat., closed Sun.), built between 1836 and 1840, stands as a glorious temple to all things edible. Beyond the soaring wrought-iron-and-stained-glass arch, food stalls stretch for nearly a block. Fruit and vegetables are piled in artistic displays, and fish is laid out in glistening rows. There are jars of spices, vats of fat, juicy olives, sacks of dried beans, bags of nuts, mounds of cheese, legs of *jamón,* and stacks of eggs. It is as much a visual feast as a mouthwatering one. The artful displays make you wonder if there is not a competition among the stalls for the best display. Look for the stall **Pons** for fruit and **Petras** for wild mushrooms. The fruit stalls near the front sell juices and fruit bowls ready to go, while way back, on the right, you can find dozens of different types of olives. Ask for *cien gramos* for a fistful. Try to hit the market in the early morning to see it at its most local—and liveliest.

BARCELONA

LAS RAMBLAS, EL RAVAL, AND █ BARRI GÒTIC

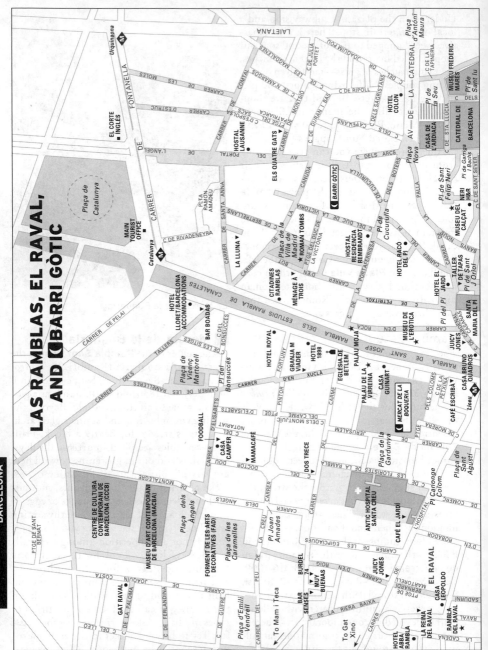

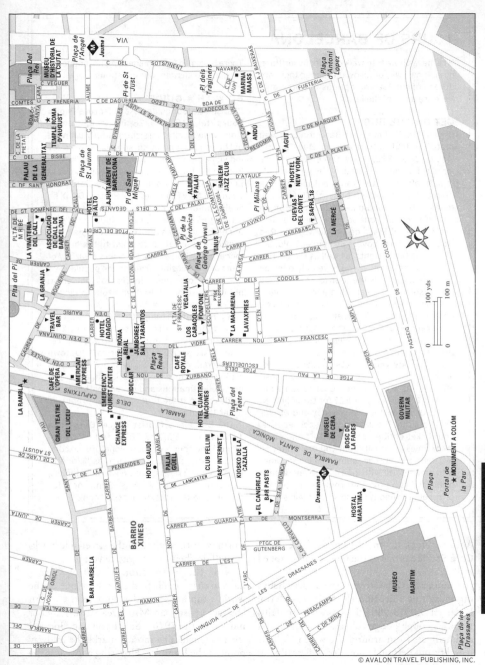

BARCELONA

TOURS OF BARCELONA

Whether you want to walk or ride, fly, or float, go your own way or follow the leader, there are dozens of sightseeing options in Barcelona. Here are a few of the best.

GET ON THE BUS

If your time is limited in Barcelona, or you prefer not to do lots of walking, **Bus Turístic** (tel.93/285-3832, www.barcelonaturisme .com) is for you. Operated jointly by the city's tourism office and the transit authority, these bright double-decker buses follow three touristic routes and make 42 stops. Hop on and off to create your perfect tour. The main bus depot is at Plaça de Catalunya. The **Red Route** (northern) covers Eixample, Tibidabo, and all the Gaudí sights, as well as the barrios of Gràcia and Raval. If you have only one day in Barcelona, this is the tour to do. The **Blue Route** (southern) covers Montjuïc and its various sights, including Poble Espanyol, Port Vell, Barceloneta, Port Olímpic, and the Barri Gòtic. The **Green Route** covers the coast from Port Olímpic to the Forum convention center. It is the least interesting of the three.

You can **buy your tickets** onboard the bus, at any tourist office, or online with the transit authority at www.tmb.net. Cost for an adult ticket is €18 for one day, €22 for two. Children 12 and under cost €11 for one day and €14 for two. Note that the days must be consecutive. Your ticket entitles you to get off and on as many times as you like, but you are limited to five transfers between routes. The ticket comes with a mini-guide with information about each of the sights on the tour route and a packet of discount coupons to use at the main sights.

There is also an English-speaking host onboard each bus to answer your questions.

GO WITH A GUIDE

Charismatic tour guide José Soler runs **Pepito Tours** (tel. 61/505-9326, info@pepitotours .com, www.pepitotours.com), a fully licensed outfit specializing in personalized tours for individuals and small groups. Having lived in Boston for three years, José speaks flawless English. As the author of the book *Barcelona Then and Now* (Thunder Bay Press, 2006), he is also an expert on his beloved hometown. During tours, he always has a binder handy full of photos of the way the city used to be. They provide a fascinating contrast to the buzz of modern-day Barcelona. He offers a variety of tours on his website, including the popular "Art and Wine" tours and side trips to Montserrat, but he is also happy to devise tours specially suited for your interests.

My Favorite Things (tel. 63/726-5405, www.myft.net) offers a series of walking tours, including jaunts called "Sweet Barcelona," "Art Nouveau Discoveries," "Uptown Barcelona," and "The Raval Tour," as well as walks that focus on food, design, and art. The unique destinations and cheery patter of the guides make these tours a fun, different way to see the city.

The Barcelona tourist office, **Barcelona Turisme** (tel. 93/285-3832, teltur@barcel onaturisme.com, www.barcelonaturisme.com) runs several classic tours such as "Modernisme" (4 P.M. Fri. and Sat., 6 P.M. in summer), "Picasso" (10:30 A.M. Tues.-Sun., includes entrance to the Museu Picasso), and "Gòtic"

About a block down, the colorful facade of **Café Escriba** is one of the most photographed in Barcelona.

Almost across the street is the underwhelming **Museu de l'Eròtica** (Rambla 96, Metro: Liceu, tel. 93/318-9865, 10 A.M.–10 P.M. daily, €7.50), a hodge-podge collection of sexual art and artifacts from around the world. A little naughty, but definitely not nice, it is really not

worth your time, though the street-side hawkers will do their best to entice you in.

Near the intersection of Carrer Cardenal Casañas, you'll find a work by one of the world's top artists under your feet. Catalan abstract artist Joan Miró created this anchor mosaic in the 1970s. See if you can find the tile he signed. The mosaic marks the midway point in the Ramblas. Hovering above it is the

(10 A.M. daily). Tours run about two hours and cost €9-11. Tickets can be bought at any tourism office, but tours leave from the Plaça de Catalunya main office.

BY AIR OR SEA

Lifestyle Barcelona (C/ Balmes 184, tel. 93/270-2048, info@lifestylebarcelona .com, www.lifestylebarcelona.com, 9 A.M.-7 P.M. Mon.-Fri.) arranges "experiences" in and around Barcelona. Wet and wild adventures include Jet Skiing in the Mediterranean, scuba diving along the Costa Brava, and sailing on a catamaran. High-flying experiences include a ride in an acrobatic plane, skydiving, or even a flight lesson. Other options include archery lessons, a night at the opera, a ride in a hot-air balloon, or a trip to see a Barça soccer game. The list goes on and on. Check their website for details.

For a tamer, but still thrilling, tour, contact **Cat Helicopters** (Heliport, Moll Adossat, tel. 93/224-0410, info@cathelicopters.com, www .cathelicopters.com), which offers 10-minute helicopter flights over Barcelona's main attractions – an amazing way to see La Sagrada Família – for €80. Longer flights to Montserrat run €240.

Strictly by sea, **Barcelona Turisme** offers "Barcelona Mar" (11:30 A.M. Wed. and Sun. Apr., May, June, and Oct., 5 P.M. Wed. and Sat. June–Sept., €28), small group tours by sailboat along the city's coast. During the tour, you'll receive an introduction to basic sailing techniques and have a chance to help pilot the boat. At the end of the cruise, you'll celebrate your maiden voyage with a glass of *cava*.

ON TWO WHEELS OR THREE

Zippy, easy, and fun, Segways – the two-wheeled, self-balancing, electric-powered "human transporters" – are fast becoming a popular way to do sightseeing. **Barcelona Glides** (tel. 93/268-9536, info@spainglides .com, www.spainglides.com, 11 A.M. and 5 P.M. daily Mar.-Nov., 11 A.M. daily Dec.-Feb., €60) offers two-hour rides past Barcelona's most intriguing sights. Tours start off at Plaça Sant Jaume. After a 30-minute training session, you're on your way. Things to know: You must weigh 100-250 pounds; 15 is the minimum age; and, if you must carry a bag, make it a backpack, as shoulder bags can knock novice gliders off-balance. Make reservations online well in advance, as the glides are very popular.

Turn heads as you tour the Barri Gòtic on the back of a pedal-powered Velotaxi – think an updated, modern rickshaw and you get the idea. **Trixi Tours** (tel. 93/310-1379, www .trixi.com) has a fleet of 10 Velotaxis moving all through the city, mainly on bicycle paths and narrow lanes where cars can't maneuver. They can be rented by the quarter-hour: 15 minutes for €6; 30 minutes for €10; and one hour for €18. Don't worry about the "poor driver." The driving team consists of a group of hunks from Cataluña and Europe. Aged 25-35, they are proud of their abilities to power the bikes. (Okay, the small electric motor that kicks in on upward climbs helps!) Drivers all speak English and will take you anywhere along the tourist routes, stopping to let you take photos whenever you want. Pick-up points are Plaça de la Catedral and the Columbus monument.

19th-century **Casa Bruno Quadros,** covered inexplicably in Asian imagery—unfurled fans, dainty umbrellas, and roaring dragons.

Rambla de Caputxins

Also called the Rambla del Centre, this stretch houses the **Gran Teatre de Liceu** (Rambla 51–59, Metro: Liceu, tel. 93/485-9913, tours 10 A.M.–1 P.M. daily, free), Barcelona's celebrated—and much maligned—opera house. Opened in 1847, it suffered a fire in 1861, was bombed in a terrorist attack by an anarchist in 1893, and was devastated by another fire in 1994. Completely remodeled and retrofitted, the opera house now hosts a vigorous season of operas, musicals, and plays to sell-out audiences. Moving south, take a left at Carrer Colom and you'll land in one of Barcelona's most picturesque squares, the 19th-century **Plaça Reial.** Laid out in a perfect rectangle, the arcaded plaza is dotted with palm trees, benches, and two whimsical iron lights designed by a young Antoni Gaudí. The plaza is lined with sidewalk cafés, trendy restaurants, nightclubs, and cheap hotels. It also draws a hefty bunch of drunks, though the city is trying to ward that off with constant police presence.

Rambla de Santa Mònica

This is the final stretch of Las Ramblas as it leads to the sea, and also the seediest stretch of the road, especially after nightfall. In addition to sex shops and transvestites, you'll find Internet cafés and Barcelona's wax museum, **Museu de Cera** (Rambla 4–6, Metro: Drassanes, tel. 93/317-2649, www.museo cerabcn.com, 10 A.M.–10 P.M. daily in summer, closes at lunchtime the rest of the year, €7.50) housed in a lovely building just off an alley. It is a pretty standard wax museum with all your regular stars as well as the requisite house of horrors. Kids will like it, while adults will enjoy the attached **Bosc de les Fades,** an enchanted forest posing as a café.

The **Museu Marítim** (Av. Drassanes, s/n, tel. 93/342-9920, Metro: Drassanes, www.museu maritimbarcelona.com, 10 A.M.–8 P.M. daily, €6) recounts Spain's rich seafaring history in the converted confines of Barcelona's original shipyards dating from the 13th century. Built to supply the Catalan royal fleet with the naval might needed to wrest control of the Mediterranean from the wily Venetians, the cavernous stone hallways of the shipyards were in continuous use until the 18th century.

Sitting across from the shipyards, at the center of Plaça Portal de la Pau, is the famed Columbus-topped tower, **Monument a Colom** (tel. 93/221-9226, Metro: Drassanes, 9 A.M.–8:30 P.M. summer, reduced hours rest of the year, €2). Built for the 1888 Universal Exhibition, the 170-foot tower can be ascended via an elevator. The views are great, even though the crowds, especially in summer, can be stifling.

EL RAVAL

Running along the west side of Las Ramblas, El Raval is one of Barcelona's most distinctive barrios. It is also its most notorious. Built mainly as a housing area for workers that emigrated here after the Civil War to seek work in the city's factories, it quickly became synonymous with petty crime, drugs, and prostitution. By the 1920s, it had earned the nickname Barri Xines, or Chinatown—not because of a profusion of Chinese immigrants, but rather because a local journalist compared it to the then-seedy Chinatown of San Francisco. French literary bad boy, Jean Genet, crawled these streets and described the barrio as a bohemian, cut-throat, poverty-stricken slum in his 1964 memoir *The Thief's Journal.* Parts of the barrio, especially around the plaza named for the author, are still very sordid. Carrer Sant Ramon is lined with prostitutes day and night despite the city's 2006 ordinance that levies hefty fines on both the working women and their clients. South towards the sea is a dirty warren of fleabag hotels, junkies, and petty thieves. However, up north, towards Ronda de Sant Antoni, gentrification is baring its shiny smile. In 2000, the city tore down several blocks of squalid apartment buildings to build the **Rambla del Raval,** a long, wide plaza lined with palm trees, benches, and one very fat black cat. Bohemian cafés and trendy restaurants soon began opening their doors along

ART TICKET

For €20, the Art Ticket (www.articket bcn.org) allows you to visit seven of the city's top museums, including heavy-hitters Museu Picasso, Fundació Joan Miró, Fundació Antoni Tàpies, and MACBA. But to get your money's worth, you'd have to visit at least these four. You can buy the ticket at any of the participating museums or in the tourist offices, and must use the ticket within a six-month period.

its length. Just north of that, the Museu d'Art Contemporani de Barcelona, a massive modern art complex that opened in 1995, has enlivened the surrounding blocks with art galleries, hip boutiques, and trendy restaurants and bars. Meanwhile, the barrio still serves as the number one destination for the city's immigrant population, particularly Pakistani, North African, and Filipino. The result is a vibrant, edgy cultural mix that has spawned its own verb—*ravalejar,* which has a decidedly bohemian meaning of wandering the streets, enjoying the artistic and diverse cultures, and fostering a healthy appreciation for the barrio's seedy edges.

Museu d'Art Contemporani de Barcelona

The main destination for visitors to Raval is the Museu d'Art Contemporani de Barcelona (Pl. dels Angels 1, Metro: Universitat, tel. 93/412-0810, www.macba.es, 11 A.M.–7:30 P.M. Mon.–Sat., 10 A.M.–3 P.M. Sun., closed Tues., €7.5, €4 for specific exhibitions), better known as MACBA. Designed by American architect Richard Meier, the massive white complex seems almost like a spaceship dropped in among its shabby apartment-block neighbors. Within, large skylights illuminate a permanent collection that includes works by international artists such as Paul Klee and Jean-Michel Basquiat, however the bulk is dedicated to Catalan artists. There are always at least three excellent exhibitions going on as well as a variety of performance events. Outside, the museum has become a mecca of sorts for the city's skateboarders.

Palau Güell

Just off the Rambla, the Palau Güell (C/ Nou de la Rambla 3–5, Metro: Drassanes, tel. 93/317-3974) was one of Gaudí's first house projects. Built in 1886, it features two elaborate wrought-iron doorways etched with the letters "E" and "G," for Eusebi Güell, the financier who commissioned the house. The main interior feature is the large domed hall that soars from the 1st floor straight up to the

Carrer Bisbe in the Barri Gòtic

© CANDY LEE LABALLE

roof. Gaudí's imagination and Güell's wealth are on display in the textiles and furnishings throughout. The roof features the humanoid chimney pots that Gaudí is so famed for. The building began undergoing an extensive restoration project in 2006 that is scheduled to be completed by August 2007. Locals in the know expect it will be much longer. Check at the tourist office for the latest.

◖ BARRI GÒTIC

The oldest quarter of Barcelona is also the most atmospheric. Wedged between Las Ramblas and Vía Laietana, Plaça de Catalunya to the north and the Port to the south, Barri Gòtic is Barcelona's past and future. It consists of dozens of tiny, cobbled alleyways snaking past 15th-century buildings draped with 20th-century laundry. Trendy cafés and bars place their sidewalk tables in the shadow of Roman walls. Modern art galleries are tucked into medieval homes. The stately seat of Cataluña's government vies for attention amidst rows of stylish shops. This is the Barcelona you want to spend

BARCELONA

time in, not with your checklist of must-see sights in hand, but rather with your eyes and mind wide open, ready to turn this way or that as the twisting alleys beckon. Wander, shop, eat, repeat. Along the way you'll take in some of Barcelona's most ancient sights.

Catedral de Barcelona

Sitting in the center of the city's Roman heart, the Catedral de Barcelona (Pl. Seu 3, Metro: Jaume I, tel. 93/342-8260, 8 A.M.–12:45 P.M. and 5:15–7:30 P.M. Mon.–Sat., 8 A.M.–1:45 P.M. and 5:15–7:45 P.M. Sun., €4) is a bulking display of Gothic somberness.

Begun in 1298, it took over 600 years to complete. Legend has it that the Native Americans that Columbus shipped to Spain were baptized here. Beneath the main altar rests the tomb of Saint Eulàlia, Barcelona's patron. She was just 13 when the Romans crucified her on an X-shaped cross for being a Christian. You'll see Xs carved throughout the chapel. Also look for the elaborately carved choir stalls from the 14th and 15th centuries. The faithful are not allowed to sit on sacred images, so the carvings are decidedly un-Christian. The most delightful part of the cathedral lies through the elaborate Romanesque door to the right

PUBLIC DISPLAYS OF CATALAN AFFECTION

The *sardana* is a pure, folkloric expression of Catalan culture, pride, and unity. The origins of this circle dance are murky. Some say it was adopted from the Greeks back when their outposts dotted the Catalan coast over 2,000 years ago. This belief probably arises from the fact that in both the Greek national dance and in the *sardana*, dancers form a circle, holding hands. Another theory points to the island of Sardinia where the powerful seafaring Catalans ruled in the 15th century. This would explain the dance's name, but is still quite unlikely. What is known for fact is that the dance became very popular in Cataluña during the Renaixença, the Catalan renaissance that took root in the 19th century. The dance came to be so synonymous with Catalan identity and culture that Franco banned it during his 36 years of dictatorial rule. After his death, and Cataluña's subsequent increased autonomy, the *sardana* came out of the closet and into the streets. Today, it is danced all over Cataluña at public festivals and private celebrations.

To begin a *sardana*, dancers clasp hands and with raised arms form a circle. It can be as small as two people, as large as several dozen. If it gets too big, new circles are formed. Anyone can join the circle at any time, but not between a man and his partner to his right. A circle may consist of young and old, wealthy and poor, lawyer and lout. The symbolism is

clear – no matter their station in life, the dancers are Catalans first and foremost. The spirit of unity created by the *sardana* is its most impressive accomplishment.

Except at festivals and folk performances, the dancers don't wear special costumes, but the traditional footwear is a type of espadrille with a flat, pliable bottom and long ribbons wrapping around the ankle. Though casual observers often comment that the dance is very simple, look closely at the feet of the dancers, as this is where all the action takes place. A concise series of steps, points, crossed feet, and heel lifts are performed in a measured manner in tune to the music. It is actually quite complicated. So how do so many ordinary citizens know this fancy footwork? Simple. The Catalan government has offered free lessons for the past 30 years. Every June, hundreds of kids take part in the classes, usually held in Plaça de Catalunya on Saturdays at 10:30 A.M.

The dance is accompanied by a *cobla* band of 11 musicians playing regional instruments such as the *flabiol* (a one-handed flute) and a *tambori* drum, plus conventional reed and brass instruments.

See this expression of Catalan pride for yourself in front of the Catedral de Barcelona in Barri Gòtic every Saturday at 6:30 P.M. and on Sundays at noon, or in Plaça Sant Jaume on Sundays at 6 P.M.

of Eulàlia's crypt. The cloisters are a magnificent display of Gothic whimsy. At the center is a courtyard full of palm trees and exactly 13 geese in honor of Eulàlia. In medieval times, the geese were used as an alarm system, honking at intruders.

In front of the cathedral is the broad plaza, **Plaça de la Seu,** lined with sidewalk cafés and hotels. On its southern edge is the **Museu Frederic Marès** (Pl. Sant Iu 5, Metro: Jaume I, tel. 93/310-5800, 10 A.M.–7 P.M. Tues.–Sat., 10 A.M.–3 P.M. Sun., closed Mon., €3), a Gothic palace that houses a very eccentric collection of Romanesque religious art and Victorian knickknacks. Just down the road, **Casa de L'Ardiaca** (C/ Santa Llúcia 1, Metro: Jaume I, tel. 93/318-1342, 10 A.M.–2 P.M. and 4–8 P.M. Mon.–Sat.,10 A.M.–2 P.M. Sun.) is a 12th-century Gothic building with distinctive modernist touches, such as the marble mailbox near the front door. Several of the interior walls are Roman. Be sure and visit the lovely courtyard which features a fountain that takes center stage with the annual *l'ou com balla,* or dancing egg. An egg is placed atop the fountain's waters each June to celebrate Corpus Christi.

Plaça de Sant Felip Neri is worth seeking out. This quiet, atmospheric space is completely enclosed by buildings, including the church that gives the plaza its name. On its facade you'll see shrapnel marks from a bomb that was dropped in the plaza during the Civil War—schoolchildren and priests were the victims. It was reformed in the mid-20th century. Shoe lovers get a kick out of the **Museu del Calçat** (Pl. Sant Felip Neri 5, Metro: Jaume I, tel. 93/301-4533, 11 A.M.–2 P.M. Tues.–Sat., €2.50), a shoe museum built in the original shoemakers' guild. There is just one café in the plaza—the posh **Neri,** which is part of the Hotel Neri.

Plaça del Rei

The Plaça del Rei is an atmospheric plaza hemmed in by four hulking, gray medieval buildings. It was once the seat of the Royal Palace, and later the site of Inquisition trials. Today,

it hosts concerts and open-air theater performances. The most impressive of the buildings houses the **Museu d'Història de la Ciutat** (C/ Beguer, s/n, Metro: Jaume I, tel. 93/315-1111, 10 A.M.–8 P.M. Tues.–Sat., 10 A.M.–3 P.M. Sun., closed at lunchtime in winter, €4). The museum takes you on a journey through 2,000 years of Barcelona's history. The most interesting bit is at the bottom of a long elevator ride where you'll step out into A.D. 600 and the ruins of Barcino, Roman Barcelona.

See more Roman history around the corner. The **Temple Roma d'August** (C/ Paradis 10, Metro: Jaume I, 10 A.M.–2 P.M. and 4–8 P.M. Mon.–Sat.,10 A.M.–2 P.M. Sun.) consists of three massive columns left over from the Roman temple that once stood guard over Barcino. They are tucked into the courtyard of an office building and free to visit. There is also a Roman tower and the remains of the Roman walls that surrounded Barcino on the road between Plaça E. Vilanova and Plaça Traginer. In the latter you can have lunch at a sidewalk café right under the tower. You'll also find the tiny slip of a street, Carrer Jupi. Its colorful murals and oversized flowers are the handiwork of Argentinean artist and true Barcelona bohemian **Marina Maass** (C/ Jupi 4, tel. 93/310-6803, www.marinamaass.com). You'll see her joyful graffiti all over town, but this is her stomping ground. She makes whimsical dolls, mobiles, paintings, and more. Hours are by appointment, but if you're lucky she'll be around. If not, just enjoy the colorful magic she's wrought on this dark, medieval alleyway.

Plaça de San Jaume

The broad Plaça de San Jaume is home to two of the most important political buildings in Cataluña—the **Ajuntament de Barcelona,** city hall, and **Palau de la Generalitat,** seat of the Catalan government. As a result, the square plays frequent host to political rallies and demonstrations. All the streets leading off of the plaza are full of shops and cafés. Make a U-turn behind the Generalitat onto **Carrer Bisbe.** Over the pedestrian street is a gorgeous Gothic bridge. Despite its authentic appearance, it was built in 1929—still it makes for a great photo and a lovely stroll.

El Call

To the east of Plaça San Jaume, Jewish Barcelona unravels in a web of dark, medieval alleyways. The word *call* is Hebrew for "community," and many of the streets here bear that name. El Call lies roughly between the plaza, Carrer Banys Nous, Carrer de Ferran, and the Església de Santa María. Archaeologists have determined that there was a Jewish presence in this area as far back as A.D. 212. During the Call's height in the 13th century, it was home to a thriving community that made up 15 percent of Barcelona's population and was the locus of the city's intellectual and financial center. However, the Catholic Kings pursued a vicious pogrom against Spain's Jews and the Call was brutally attacked in 1391. Over 1,000 Jews were killed and many more fled. Those who remained were forced to convert to Catholicism. By the early 1400s, the Call was no more and over the centuries, it was built over and the synagogues converted to other uses. In the mid-1990s, a team of investigators began to unearth the long-lost **Sinagoga Mayor,** the main synagogue of Barcelona's medieval Jewish population. Today, it houses the **Associacío de Call de Barcelona** (C/ Marlet 5, Metro: Jaume I, tel. 93/317-0790, www.calldebarcelona.org, 11 A.M.–6 P.M. Mon.–Fri. and 11 A.M.–3 P.M. Sat.–Sun., €2). You can see the building's 5th-century foundation through glass floors and visit the recreated congregational space. The organization can also arrange walking tours through the surrounding streets where they will point out evidence of the 13th-century Jewish community.

Plaça del Pi and Plaça de Sant Josep Oriol

These two adjoining plazas are among the most delightful in Barcelona. Plaça del Pi is shaded by a giant pine tree (*pi* in Catalan) and lined with cozy cafés. The adjoining Plaça de Sant Josep Oriol hosts an artist market on the weekends. The plazas are joined by the massive bulk of the **Parròquia Santa María del Pi** (Metro: Liceu, tel. 93/318-4743, 5–8 P.M. Tues.–Thurs., 10 A.M.–1 P.M. Sat.–Sun., free), a Gothic church built at the end of the 14th century.

LA RIBERA AND EL BORN

As is typical in so many of Spain's old cities, the name of this barrio—which is separated from the Barri Gòtic by Vía Laietana—is up for debate. City maps routinely label it La Ribera, Born, Sant Pere, and Santa Caterina, however the name that everyone on the street uses is El Born (Borne in Catalan). Though for clarification, we can consider Ribera to be everything north of Carrer de la Princesa and Born everything south. While there are a few key sights in Ribera, it is El Born where you will want to spend your time. While still maintaining the same mysterious medieval air as nearby Barri Gòtic, El Born bristles as the city's newfound haven of hip. It is loaded with the kind of boutiques, jewelry shops, and art galleries that require serious credit limits. In between are trendy eateries, classy cocktail

an ancient alleyway through El Born

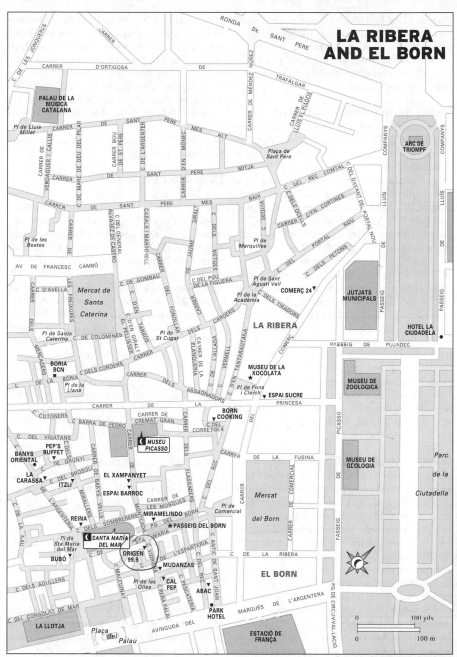

LA RIBERA AND EL BORN

RONDA DE SANT PERE

CARRER D'ORTIGOSA

CARRER DE MÉNDEZ NÚÑEZ

TRAFALGAR

CARRER DE LLUÍS EL PIADÓS

C DE LES JONQUERES

CARRER

PALAU DE LA MÚSICA CATALANA

Pl de Lluís Millet

CARRER DEL PILAR

DE SANT PERE MÉS ALT

C DE L'ARGENTER

CARRER DEN MONEC

Plaça de Sant Pere

CARRER DE VERDAGUER I CALLIS

C DE MARE DE DEU DEL PILAR

CARRER BOU DE ST PERE

CARRER

DE SANT PERE MITJA

C DEL REC COMTAL

C DE DAVANT DE

PORTAL NOU

ARC DE TRIOMPF

COMPANYS

COMPANYS

CARRER

Pl de les Beates

CARRER DEL GENERAL ÁLVAREZ DE CASTRO

CASALS I MARTORELL

C DE JAUME GIRALT

DE SANT PERE MÉS

BAIX SEQUIA

Pl de Marquilles

CARRER D'EN CORTINES

C DEL REC COMTAL

PORTAL NOU

LLUÍS

DE

LLUÍS

AV DE FRANCESC CAMBÓ

C DELS

FREIXURES

Mercat de Santa Caterina

C DE GOMBAU

C D'EN TARROS

DEL FONOLLAR

C DEL POU DE LA FIGUERA

Pl de Sant Agustí Vell

COMERÇ 24

JUTJATS MUNICIPALS

PASSEIG

PASSEIG

HOTEL LA CIUDADELA

C D'AVELLA

Pl de Santa Caterina

C DE COLOMINES

C D'EN GIRALT EL PELLISSER

Pl de St Cugat

CARRERS

Pl de la Acadèmia

C DELS TIRADORS

LA RIBERA

MERCADERS

BORIA BCN

C DELS CORDERS

DELS

CARRER DE LA FLANDUERIA

DELS

C DE L'ALLADA

VERMELL

C D'EN TANTARANTANA

COMERÇ

PASSEIG DE PUJADES

C DE LA BORIA

Pl de la Llana

DELS

ASSAONADORS

Pl de Pons i Clerch

MUSEU DE LA XOCOLATA

ESPAI SUCRE

MUSEU DE ZOOLOGICA

PICASSO

CARRER DE COTONERS

C BARRA DE FERRO

CARRER DE CREMAT GRAN

C DEL CORRETGER

BORN COOKING

PRINCESA

C DEL VIGATANS

PEP'S BUFFET

MUSEU PICASSO

DE LA FUSINA

MUSEU DE GEOLOGIA

Parc de la Ciutadella

BANYS ORIENTAL

LA CARASSA

ITZLI

DE GRUNYI

C DE BANYS VELLS

EL XAMPANYET

ESPAI BARROC

DELS

FLASSADERS

C DEL REC

CARRER

DE LA COMERCIAL

PASSEIG

REINA

MIRALLERS

C DE L'ARGENTERIA

DELS SOMBRERERS

MONTCADA

MIRAMELINDO

CARRER DE LES MOSQUES

PG

Pl de Comercial

BORN

Mercat del Born

Pl de Sta Maria del Mar

SANTA MARÍA DEL MAR

PASSEIG DEL BORN

SANTA MARIA

C DE L'ESPARTERIA

C ANTIC DE SANT JOAN

C DE LA RIBERA

BUBÓ

ORIGEN 99.9

MUDANZAS

C DEL REC

PG DE CIRCUVVALLACIÓ

C MALCUINAT

Pl de les Olles

CAL PEP

CREBA PALA

C PESCATERIA

ABAC

EL BORN

C DELS AGULLERS

PARK HOTEL

MARQUÉS DE L'ARGENTERA

C DEL CONSOLAT DE MAR

LA LLOTJA

Plaça del Palau

AVINGUDA DEL

ESTACIÓ DE FRANÇA

BARCELONA

0   100 yds

0   100 m

© AVALON TRAVEL PUBLISHING, INC.

bars, and laid-back sidewalk cafés. The barrio was once little more than a marketplace full of wholesale shops and creaky-tabled cafés. If you are intrepid and poke around a bit, you'll still find a bit of that old-time Born in traditional cafés and shops.

Palau de la Música Catalana

At the northwestern tip of Ribera, the Palau de la Música Catalana (C/ Sant Francesc de Paula 2, Metro: Urquinaona, tel. 93/295-7200, www.palaumusica.org, 10 A.M.–7 P.M. daily July and Aug., 10 A.M.–3:30 P.M. daily Sept.–June, €8) is one of Spain's leading concert halls. It also happens to be a modernist masterpiece. Designed and built by Lluís Domènech i Montaner between 1905 and 1908, this sumptuous building was declared a UNESCO World Heritage Site in 1997. The exterior is a marvel of colorful tiles depicting Catalan music as a playful female nymph surrounded by a chorus of singers. Inside, the star attraction is the dazzling stained-glass ceiling. More stained glass surrounds the audience, letting in a brilliant flow of colored light that seems in harmony with the music. In addition to a roster of local and Spanish performers and groups, international talents from Yo-Yo Ma to the Buena Vista Social Club have played here. Performances are usually held September–June, with regular concerts Sunday mornings at 11 A.M. Tickets run from a few euros to over €100.

Mercat de Santa Caterina

Spain has been undergoing an incredible flurry of architectural experimentation for the last dozen years, and Barcelona is right at the forefront. One building that has garnered international acclaim is the Mercat de Santa Caterina (Av. Francesc Cambo, s/n, Metro: Jaume I, tel. 93/319-2135, www.mercatsantacaterina.net). A faltering 19th-century neighborhood market, Santa Caterina underwent a major renovation in 1998. It took nearly eight years to finish due to the discovery of the remains of a medieval monastery and a Roman necropolis beneath the market. When it finally opened, it was deemed a visual masterpiece—at once

crisp and clean, whimsical and fun. The interior is a soaring space with a blond wood ceiling that resembles upturned boats. Beneath are food stalls, a supermarket, and a restaurant. Below, a glass floor reveals the uncovered archaeological remains. However, it's the birds and those living in the upper floors of the surrounding buildings that have the best view of the market. The undulating roof is covered in over 300,000 hexagonal tiles in 67 fruit-and-vegetable tinted hues.

◖ Museu Picasso

Five lovely medieval palaces have been linked together to house Museu Picasso (C/ Montcada 15–23, tel. 93/319-6310, www.museupicasso.bcn.es, 10 A.M.–8 P.M. Tues.–Sun., €6), an up-close look at Pablo Picasso's progress from child prodigy to 20th-century master through 3,500 of his works. The collection is chronologically divided into periods of Picasso's artistic life and as you work your way through, the effect is a dazzling insight into the artist's development. The works that demonstrate his Blue Period (1901–1904) comprise one of the world's most extensive collections of this era, which is dominated by the color blue and the symbolism of the figures in the paintings, many with sad, grief-stricken, or desperate expressions. Other important periods on display include Málaga, which stems from his childhood in that seaside town and includes portraits of his father and local fishermen. Picasso lived here from the age of 14 to 23, and the Barcelona collection documents the life-long love affair Picasso had with the city. The paintings reveal the artist's everyday life and surroundings from the seaside shacks of Barceloneta to the rooftops of the cluttered city.

One of the highlights of the museum is the room dedicated to *Las Meninas.* Picasso had admired the masterpiece by Velázquez since he was a child. He also thought of himself as a painter of paintings and took works by other artists as a motif just like any other subject. Here he exhausts *Las Meninas* in several paintings based on the form, rhythm, color, and movement of the original.

As one of Barcelona's top tourist destinations, the museum can get very crowded. Unless you want to jostle with school kids for a view of the works, go right at opening time, or during lunch (2–4 P.M.) when the kids (and most Spaniards) will be dining. Free guided tours in English are held on Thursdays at 6 P.M. and Saturdays at noon.

Santa María del Mar

Completed in 1384, the majestic Església de Santa Maria del Mar (Pl. Santa María 1, Metro: Jaume I, tel. 93/310-2390, 10 A.M.–1:30 P.M. and 4:30–8 P.M. daily, free) is considered one of the world's best examples of Catalan Gothic architecture. More austere than standard Gothic, this architectural style employed soaring pointed vaults, massive cliff-like walls, heavy stone columns, and little ornamentation except for large rose windows. The interior of the church is lofty and impossibly light and beautiful, especially with the sun streaming in through the windows. With

© CANDY LEE LABALLE

the back door of Santa María del Mar in El Born

excellent acoustics, the church often hosts concerts of classical and jazz music.

Passeig del Born

The church is surrounded on all sides by pedestrian streets lined with cafés, bars, and über cool shops. The main see-and-be-seen route is the Passeig del Born, a swathe of greenery and park benches. Back in the medieval day, horseback soldiers in metal mesh armor held jousting tournaments here. The pathway ends at the massive 19th-century iron-and-glass **Mercat del Born,** a glorious homage to the industrial age. Built in 1873, the building served as the city's wholesale market until 1973 when it was abandoned. Three decades later, the city has begun refurbishing the market to serve as a cultural center. In the process, the remains of 17th-century homes and streets were uncovered. A planned glass floor will allow visitors to view these remains.

Tempting the sweet-toothed, the **Museu de la Xocalata** (C/ Comerç 36, Metro: Jaume 1, tel. 93/268-7878, www.museudela xocolata.com, 10 A.M.–7 P.M. Mon.–Sat., 10 A.M.–3 P.M. Sun., free) is just a few blocks north of the market. Run by the chocolate-makers' guild, this scrumptious museum offers the history of everyone's favorite indulgence. However, it is the smell of the place that will make you swoon, as dozens of would-be pastry chefs whip up decadent creations. The local monuments—La Sagrada Família, the cathedral—rendered in chocolate will just plain wow you. There is a free little taste at the end of the tour and, of course, you are welcome to buy as much as you can devour. During the warmer months, the museum often sponsors "Jazz y Chocolate" concerts in their lovely garden.

Parc de la Ciutadella

On the edge of Born, Parc de la Ciutadella, Barcelona's most central park, is a great place to escape from the narrow sidewalks, noisy streets, and general mayhem of the city. After ascending to the Spanish throne, Felipe V had half of La Ribera/El Born torn down and built a large, star-shaped *ciutadella* (citadel) in 1714 in order to keep an eye on the wily, nationalist-minded locals. Naturally, the Catalans loathed it. In 1869, General Prim (immortalized in statue here) had the citadel destroyed and turned into a park. The only part of the citadel to survive the wrecking ball was the arsenal, which now houses the **Parlament de Catalunya** (tel. 93/304-6500, 9 A.M.–2 P.M. and 4–8 P.M., free). The park is also home to a sad, little **Parc Zoologic** (tel. 93/225-6780, www.zoobarcelona.com, 10 A.M.–7 P.M. daily June–Sept., 10 A.M.–6 P.M. daily Oct., 10 A.M.–5 P.M. daily Nov.–Feb., 10 A.M.–6 P.M. daily Mar.–May, €13, kids €8.30), where panthers and other majestic species pace anxiously back and forth in tiny, chain-linked cages. Plans are in the works to move the zoo to a more modern, animal-friendly facility but progress is slow. The most striking sight in the park is the **waterfall Cascada,** with its two grand stairways, towering arch, and classical statues surrounding a dramatic tumble of water that pours into a pond below. The baroque structure was designed by Josep Fontsère with his top student at the time—the soon-to-be-very-famous Antoni Gaudí—creating the rocks as his first work of public art.

◖ BARCELONETA

The working-class barrio of Barceloneta is a triangular wedge of tidy, tightly knit streets teeming with colorful apartment blocks, old-timey seafood restaurants, dive bars, and lots of lively street life. Built in the mid-1800s as an attempt at urban planning, the barrio quickly became the residence of choice for the city's sea-faring residents. Despite the gentrification that is encroaching it on all sides, this sea breeze–whipped barrio is on a very slow boat to change. Its main drag, the **Passeig de Joan de Borbó,** is lined with brightly lit, checked-tablecloth dining rooms serving up seafood of every species imaginable. The western tip of Barceloneta ends at the Port Vell, the city's old port just south of Las Ramblas. Along the Mediterranean, the

© CANDY LEE LABALLE

a street in the working-class barrio of Barceloneta

lively seaside promenade, **Passeig Marítim,** stretches east all the way to the Port Olímpic, the posh new port built for the 1992 Olympics. The promenade draws legions of walkers, joggers, bikers, skateboarders, and bladers. Between the two ports runs four kilometers (2.5 miles) of trucked-in sand and transplanted palm trees—part of the legacy of the city's Olympic beautification project. The beaches are wildly popular round the clock. By day, oiled-up sun worshippers cram every meter of sand. By night, college kids—complete with their carry-out bottles of booze—take over and the beach turns into a decadent bash where just about anything goes. The more discriminating hang out at one of the many *chiringuitos* (beachside bars) that dot the sand.

Port Vell

In Barcelona's medieval heyday as a seafaring power, Port Vell (Catalan for "old port") was a hive of activity with ships going in and out, including those of Christopher Columbus.

© CANDY LEE LABALLE

The Christopher Columbus monument soars above Port Vell.

By the Industrial Age, Barcelona's focus was squarely on industry and the lovely waterfront was hidden behind ugly warehouses, truck-clogged roads, and railroad tracks. Barcelona soon became known as a town that lived "with its back to the sea." The azure shimmer of the Mediterranean was a part of the city in the way a dusty field on the outskirts of town is—there, but incidental. By the 20th century, the waterfront had fallen into a very shameful state of seediness. It might have stayed that way were it not for the Olympics. With the whole world coming to watch, Barcelona kicked into high gear, polishing up the old port, laying kilometers of beaches, and connecting the Barceloneta promenade to the new Olympic port. Today, Port Vell is a top attraction, boasting one of Europe's best aquariums and an upscale mall. Its cruise ship–filled harbor is surrounded by a series of *molls* (wharves) teeming with restaurants and bars. Cruise ships from around the world dock here, giving it a bustling, festive feel.

From the Ciutat Vella, access Port Vell via the **Rambla del Mar.** Built in 1994, this suspended extension of Las Ramblas is seemingly adrift in wooden waves. At its end you'll find one of the city's most upscale malls, **Maremagnum.** At night the mall offers posh nightclubs for the young and way too rich. Just beyond the mall is Port Vell's most distinctive feature—the bright white monolith that is the **L'Aquàrium de Barcelona** (Moll d'Espanya, s/n, Metro: Drassanes, tel. 93/221-7474, www.aquarium bcn.com, 9:30 A.M.–9 P.M. daily, later hours in summer, €15, kids €10). With 10 tanks swarming with Mediterranean marine life, it is one of the world's largest collections of species from this ancient sea. There are also tanks dedicated to creatures from the Red Sea, the Caribbean, Australia's Great Barrier Reef, and Hawaii. However, what everyone remembers are the sharks. As visitors walk through an eerily lit, 262-foot glass tunnel, sharks of various species swim around—curiously or hungrily, it is hard to tell. Qualified divers can swim with the sharks in a specially designed four-hour course. The cost is €300, the experience priceless. Next to the aquarium, another kids' favorite is the **IMAX Port Vell** (tel. 93/225-1111, www.imaxintegral.com). Films are offered in IMAX super-sized screens, semispherical Omnimax screens, or in heart-racing 3-D.

Port Vell is also the launching pad for two great ways to see Barcelona—by air and by sea. From either the World Trade Center on the Moll de Barcelona or in front of the Platja de Santa Miquel beach closer to Barceloneta, catch the **Transbordador Aeri** (tel. 93/225-2718, 11 A.M.–8 P.M. daily summer, 10:45 A.M.–7 P.M. daily winter, €9). The gondola offers a bird's-eye view of the Ciutat Vella as it soars up to the Torre del Miramor on the top of Montjuïc. However, be aware that in summer at peak hours, the wait can be up to an hour for the two-minute ride. Your best bet is to go as early as you possibly can. If you prefer a view from the water, head to the foot of the Columbus monument and catch one of the quaint, double-decker wooden

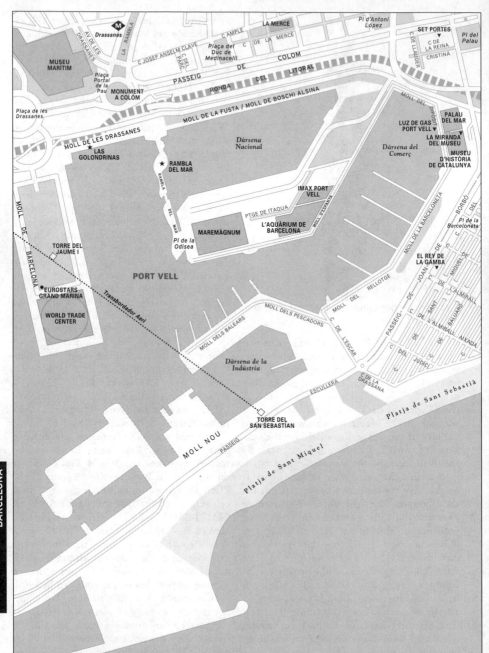

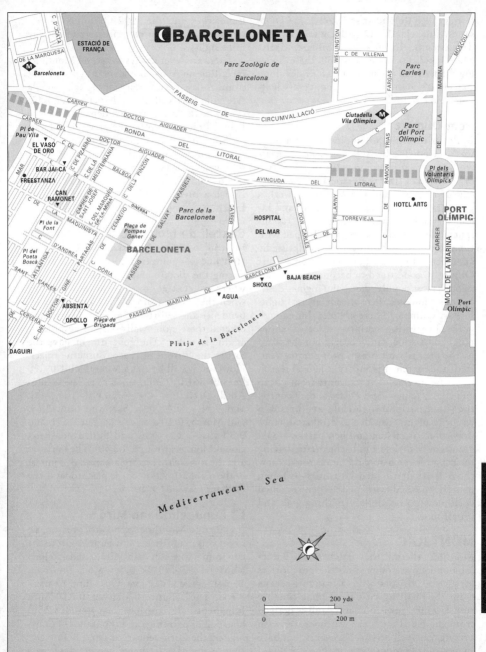

© AVALON TRAVEL PUBLISHING, INC.

ferries called **Golondrinas** (Moll de Les Drassanes, s/n, tel. 93/442-3106, www.lasgolondrinas.com, 11:30 A.M.–7:30 P.M. daily, €12.50, kids €6.30). Since 1888, these "swallows" have been taking visitors for rides along Barcelona's coast. Tours run about every half-hour and last 1.5 hours.

Port Olímpic

Built for the 1992 Olympics, Port Olímpic was developed to house athletes and officials with an eye on future uses for the city. Two of Barcelona's first skyscrapers were erected (the Hotel Arts and the Mapfre Tower), a yacht-friendly port was constructed, and kilometers of boardwalk with space for restaurants, bars, and shop were lain. Topped with the giant *Peix*, a whimsical fish sculpture by architectural wonder-boy Frank Gehry, Port Olímpic was destined to become one of Barcelona's most popular day—and night—destinations. However, there are not any real sights in Port Olímpic. There are pleasant enough parks, interesting sculptures, lots of shopping, and a wide, sandy beach, but the truth is, the area is a bit brash, over-commercialized, and extremely touristy. The real reason to go is the tide of restaurants from cheap and cheery to posh and pricey, and, of course, the seaside strip of nightclubs and bars. On weekend nights, this den of drink and dance draws dozens of stag and hen parties—wild groups of bachelors and bachelorettes having their last hurrah before the vows. You'll know them by their themed costumes—women usually adorned with plastic penises, men with blow-up sex dolls. Anything goes and usually does.

MONTJUÏC

Montjuïc, the hill that watches over Barcelona and slopes down into the port, offers locals and visitors alike a tranquil escape from the bustling city. The name roughly translates to "Jewish Mount" and is derived from the fact that there was once a Jewish cemetery here. The two big events that have shaped today's Montjuïc were the 1929 World

Exposition and the 1992 Olympic Games; remains from both constitute much of the hill's sights.

There are several ways to ascend Montjuïc, including on foot—not a good idea on a hot summer day. If you aren't taking the gondola ride from Port Vell, the easiest approach is via the funicular cable car that departs from the Paral.lel metro stop on the green line. Once on Montjuïc, you could walk to the various sights, but you'll spend more time doing so than you will at the sights. Instead, use public bus 50, 55, or 193. In the summer, there is also a Bus Parc Montjuïc from Plaça de Espanya.

Castell de Montjuïc

Built in 1640 as a defensive fort, **Castell de Montjuïc** was converted into a political prison during the dictatorship of Franco. This was where the central government took activists when they voiced support for Catalan independence and self-rule. Hundreds of prisoners entered these stone walls only to never leave again. In 2004, the government gave the fort to the European Peace Museum project. However, it still houses a **Museu Militar** (tel. 93/329-8613, 9:30 A.M.–8 P.M. Tues.–Sun. April–Oct., 9:30 A.M.–6:30 P.M. Tues.–Fri. and 9:30 A.M.–8 P.M. Sat. and Sun. Nov. and March, 9:30 A.M.–5 P.M. Tues.–Fri. and 9:30 A.M.–7 P.M. Sat. and Sun. Dec.–Feb., closed Mon. year-round, €2.50). The museum and the fort's dark history are in stark contrast to the main attraction of the place today—the brilliant views over the city.

🕊 Fundació Joan Miró

If you go to Montjuïc for no other reason, do so for this magnificent museum. A gift to the city from native son Joan Miró, Fundació Joan Miró (tel. 93/443-9470, www.bcn.fjmiro.es, 10 A.M.–7 P.M. Tues.–Sat. Oct.–Jun., 10 A.M.–8 P.M. Tues.–Sat., 10 A.M.–2:30 P.M. Sun. July–Sept., closed Mon. year-round, €7.50) houses 240 paintings and thousands of drawings by the 20th-century master. Before getting to the Miró-flavored center, you'll pass

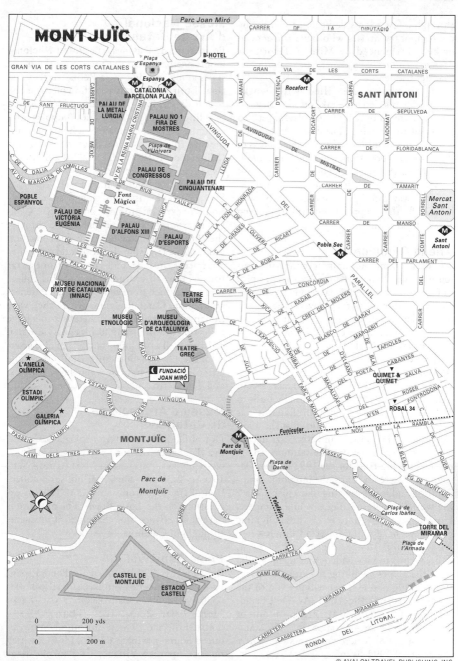

MONTJUÏC

Parc Joan Miró

GRAN VIA DE LES CORTS CATALANES

Plaça d'Espanya

B-HOTEL

Espanya

CATALONIA BARCELONA PLAZA

PALAU DE LA METAL·LÚRGIA

PALAU NO 1 FIRA DE MOSTRES

Plaça de l'Univers

PALAU DE CONGRESSOS

PALAU DEL CINQUANTENARI

POBLE ESPANYOL

Font Màgica

PALAU DE VICTÒRIA EUGÈNIA

PALAU D'ALFONS XIII

PALAU D'ESPORTS

MUSEU NACIONAL D'ART DE CATALUNYA (MNAC)

TEATRE LLIURE

MUSEU ETNOLÒGIC

MUSEU D'ARQUEOLOGIA DE CATALUNYA

TEATRE GREC

L'ANELLA OLÍMPICA

FUNDACIÓ JOAN MIRÓ

ESTADI OLÍMPIC

GALERIA OLÍMPICA

MONTJUÏC

Parc de Montjuïc

Parc de Montjuïc

Plaça de Dante

Funicular

CASTELL DE MONTJUÏC

ESTACIÓ CASTELL

GRAN VIA DE LES CORTS CATALANES

VILAMARÍ

D'ENTENÇA

Rocafort

CALABRIA

SANT ANTONI

CARRER DE SEPÚLVEDA

CARRER DE VILADOMAT

CARRER DE FLORIDABLANCA

MISTRAL

TAMARIT

Mercat Sant Antoni

MANSO

Sant Antoni

Poble Sec

CARRER DEL PARLAMENT

PARAL·LEL

LA CONCORDIA

DE LA CREU DELS MOLERS

DE GARAY

MARGARIT

TAPIOLES

POETA

CABANYES

SALVÀ

QUIMET & QUIMET

ROSER

FONTRODONA

ROSAL 34

RAMBLA

PASSEIG

MIRAMAR

Plaça de Carlos Ibáñez

MONTJUÏC

TORRE DEL MIRAMAR

Plaça de l'Armada

Teleféric

CARRETERA

CAMÍ DEL MAR

MIRAMAR

MIRAMAR

LITORAL

RONDA DEL

0   200 yds

0   200 m

through a few rooms dedicated to works by contemporary artists who have influenced or been influenced by Miró. A favorite is *Mercury Fountain* by American sculptor Alexander Calder.

Miró's rooms are filled with works showcasing his signature take on surrealism— art that seems at once light and playful yet also powerful and moving. The drama and uncertainty of the Spanish Civil War comes across in many of his works from the summer of 1934. He termed this period "wild paintings" and they are some of his best pieces. After making your way through the museum, step onto the roof for the sculptures and the surrounding views of Barcelona.

Anella Olímpica

It is just a few minutes walk from the Miró museum to the Olympic Ring (Anella Olímpica in Catalan) of the 1992 Barcelona Olympics. This collection of sports leftovers is at the top of Barcelona's touted sights-to-see. It is hard to know why. They are each dull in their own laborious ways, though if you are a major sports nut, you might be interested. The **Estadi Olímpic** (Av. De l'Estadi, tel. 93/426-2089, 10 A.M.–6 P.M. daily Oct.–Apr., 10 A.M.–8 P.M. daily May–Sept., free) was originally built in 1929 for the World Exposition. Later, it was hoped that the stadium would host the 1936 Olympics. Alas, Hitler and his Nazi nation got the games in Berlin. The stadium finally reached the big-time for the 1992 games. Despite ongoing renovations, the interior is disappointing and looks nothing like a place where the world's greatest athletes would compete. However, if you want to relive those Olympic glory days, head to the **Galería Olimpíca** (tel. 93/426-0660, 10 A.M.–1 P.M. and 4–6 P.M. daily, €2.50) to view videos and memorabilia from the games. Walking towards the spaceship-looking phone tower will get you to the **Piscines Bernat Picornell** (Av. De l'Estadi 30–40, tel. 93/423-4041, 7 A.M.–midnight Mon.–Fri., 7 A.M.–9 P.M. Sat., 7:30 A.M.– 4 P.M. Sun., €8), where you can swim where the greats of 1992 swam.

Museu Nacional d'Art de Catalunya

From Plaça de Espanya, the **Palau Nacional** looms on the horizon at the top of the many stairs along Avenida de la Reina María Cristina. Built in 1929 as the showpiece of the World Exposition, the Palau is a long-winged building bursting with domes, cupolas, and columns. Revamped in 1995, it houses the impressive Museu Nacional d'Art de Catalunya (Mirador del Palau 6, tel. 93/622-0360, Metro: Espanya, mnac@mnac.es, www.mnac.es, 10 A.M.–7 P.M. Tues.–Sat., 10 A.M.–2:30 P.M. Sun., €5). The mission of this massive collection is to explain, promote, and preserve Catalan art from the Romanesque period through the 20th century. The Romanesque collection is one of the largest in the world and comprises altarpieces, murals, and artwork from as far back as the 9th century. Most of this collection was rescued from churches in the Pyrenees and remote Catalan regions where they were in danger of destruction. There is also a large collection of work from 20th-century Catalan artists as well as an important group of masters from the Thyssen-Bornemisza collection. The latter includes works by Velázquez, Rubens, and Tintoretto.

Museu d'Arqueologia de Catalunya

Downhill, the Museu d'Arqueologia de Catalunya (Pg. Santa Madrona 39, tel. 93/424-6577, www.mac.es, 9:30 A.M.–7 P.M. Tues.–Sat., 10 A.M.–2:30 P.M. Sun., €3) houses a collection of findings from Greek and Roman excavations on the Costa Brava. The museum is part of a network of archaeological musuems throughout Cataluña.

Poble Espanyol

Built for the 1929 World's Fair, Poble Espanyol (Av. Marquès de Comillas, s/n, tel. 93/508-6330, www.poble-espanyol.com, 9 A.M.–8 P.M. Mon., 9 A.M.–2 A.M. Tues.–Thurs., 9 A.M.– 4 A.M. Fri.–Sat., 9 A.M.–midnight Sun., reduced hours in winter, €7.50, kids €4), which means "Spanish Village," is a mini-village showcasing the various architectural styles of Spain. You enter through the medieval walls of Ávila. Inside you can visit a typical white-washed Andalusian street, check out the Mudejar tower of Utebo in Aragón, or wander through a Basque barrio. There are dozens of booths selling crafts from around Spain as well as high-quality art.

It is about a 15-minute walk from Plaça Espanya or you can catch local bus 13 or 50. At night, the entrance fee is €4, but if you have a reservation at one of the many restaurants in the complex, the fee should be waived. A full list of the restaurants can be found on the website. There are also two massive discos.

Font Màgica

At the top of the Avenida de María Cristina, just before the escalators to the Palau Nacional, is the Font Màgica. During the day, it is not much more than a massive, foam-spraying fountain, surrounded by a few sidewalk cafés. Come sundown, classical music booms out of speakers, and the fountain turns into a glowing, dancing merry-go-round of water. Colored lights bathe the soaring and dipping sprays of water as the assembled crowd goes "ahh." May–September, the show starts at 9 P.M. The rest of the year, it is earlier. Go about an hour before sunset to get one of the few terrace tables.

EIXAMPLE

By the late 19th century, Barcelona was growing too big for its Gothic britches. It needed an expansion—a word that translates as *ensanche* in Spanish, *eixample* in Catalan. A then-novel grid of orderly blocks, their corners cut off to let in the sun (and give room to turning horse-drawn carriages), was laid out north of Plaça de Catalunya. Almost immediately, rich locals snapped up the land and spared no expense in building elaborate mansions. The result is a neighborhood of distinctive grace. Buildings sport brocaded facades, fanciful iron balconies, and stained glass windows. The most elaborate were built by the architects of *modernisme,* the Catalan art nouveau movement

that took root in the late 19th century. It is characterized by the choice of curves over straight lines, a penchant for asymmetry, and the use of exuberant shapes, elaborate decoration, bright colors, and organic motifs. Antoni Gaudí is the best-known architect from this movement. Along with his contemporaries Lluís Domènech i Montaner and Josep Puig i Cadafalch, he left his unique mark all over Eixample. His works—including the surrealistic La Sagrada Família church—are Barcelona's number one attraction.

Locals think of Eixample (eye-SHAMplah) in terms of right (Eixample Dreta) and left (Eixample Esquerra). Tourists think of it in terms of Gaudí and shopping. You can visit all of Gaudí's top works walking, but your feet will suffer for it. The sights are blocks apart. While these blocks are lovely to look at, dotted with boutiques and cafés here and there, the bulk of the area is residential. Get familiar with the easy-to-navigate metro or opt for the red route of the hop-on, hop-off tour bus run by **Bus Turistic** (Pl. Catalunya, www.tmb.net). (See sidebar, *Tours of Barcelona.*)

However, not all of Eixample's architecture is historic. The **Torre Agbar** (www.torreagbar .com), sitting on the less-than-glorious Plaça de les Glories Catalanes in the southeastern part of Eixample, is one of the world's most exciting new structures. Designed by French architect Jean Nouvel, the 31-story skyscraper—with a not very subtle phallic shape—is covered by thousands of LCD filaments. Pass by on weekend nights to see the building lit up in a rainbow of shimmering color.

Eixample is also home to Barcelona's gay and lesbian community. Known as "Gayxample," Eixample Esquerra around the streets of Casanova, Muntaner, Balmes, and Aribau is dotted with gay and lesbian bars, restaurants, boutiques, and hairdressers.

Passeig de Gràcia

Passeig de Gràcia is everything a good street should be—broad, efficient, lined with sidewalk cafés and good shopping. It is also blessed with some of the most magnificent buildings

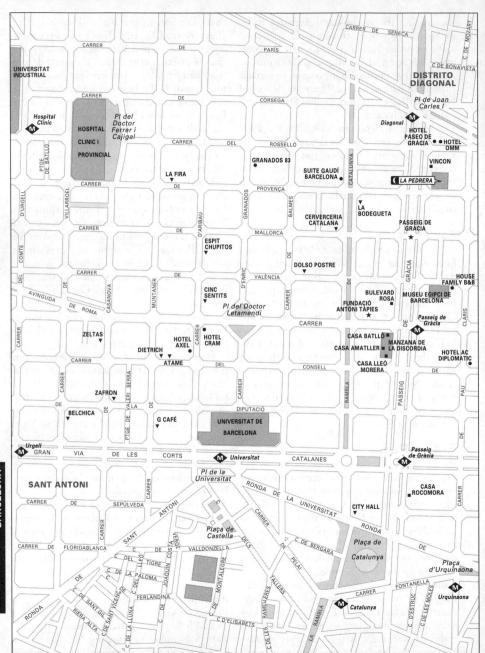

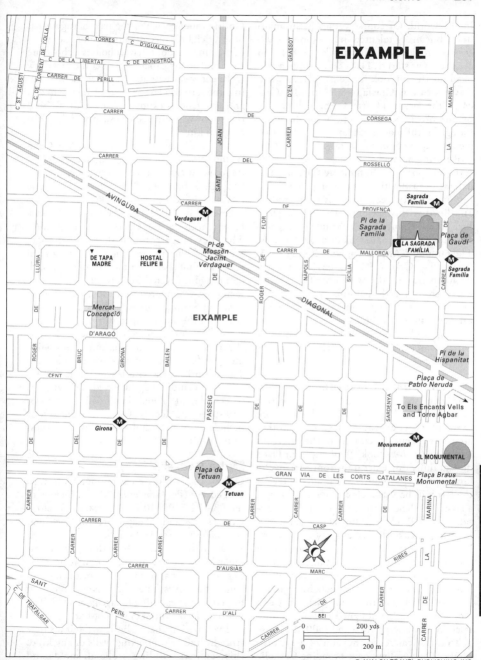

in the world. Of course Gaudí is the main draw, but many talented, lesser-known *modernisme* architects left their mark as well. If you are walking, start at Plaça de Catalunya and head north and look for gems such as **Casa Rocomora** (Pg. Gràcia 6–8, Metro: Pg. Gràcia) at the corner of Carrer Casp. Built in 1914 by the brothers Bonaventura and Joaquim Basegoda, this house has fanciful turrets that seem straight out of a fairy tale.

Running parallel to Passieg de Gràcia is its tranquil opposite—**Rambla de Catalunya,** a delightful road with a pedestrian path tunneling under leafy trees right down the middle and lined with sidewalk cafés and benches. Just off the Rambla, visit the intriguing museum of one of Spain's modern art legends. The **Fundació Antoni Tàpies** (C/ Aragó 255, Metro: Pg. Gràcia, 93/487-0315, www.fundaciotapies.org, 10 A.M.–8 P.M. Tues.–Sun., €4.50) showcases the paintings and sculptures of Catalan artist Tàpies in an airy, converted former publishing house. From the street, look up and you'll see his famed tangle of wire, *Cloud and Chair,* escaping from its rooftop confines.

Manzana de la Discordia

The English name of this intriguing trio of buildings is "block of discord." It's more than appropriate, as right next to each other are three excellent examples of the divergent styles *modernisme* took. Walking from Plaça de Catalunya or emerging from Metro: Pg. Gràcia, the first house you'll encounter on the left will be **Casa Lleó Morera** (No. 35), a lavish residence built by Domènech i Montaner from 1902 to 1906. Its exterior is full of wedding cake flourishes and floral motifs. Privately owned, the interior is not open to the public; however the recent installment of a Loewe VIP room has opened up part of the house to very wealthy shoppers by appointment only (tel. 93/216-0400). Next up, **Casa Amatller** (No. 41) designed by Puig i Cadafalch. Built between 1898 and 1900, the house is a fantastical representation of a Flemish house. The windows have brooding Catholic Gothic touches, while the pale orange walls have a rich brocaded quality. Visitors can wander the main floor freely. It houses a chocolate store and an art gallery, however the real draw is the entryway with its elaborately carved ceiling, the stained glass above the stone staircase, and the general exuberance of it all. Behind the shop, you can see the surprisingly plain original kitchen.

The undisputed star of the block is **Casa Batlló** (No. 43, Metro: Pg. Gràcia, tel. 93/216-0306, www.casabatllo.es, 9 A.M.–8 P.M. daily, €16). Built between 1904 and 1906, it is one of Gaudí's most famous works. The exterior is covered in colorful broken bits of tiles in a favorite technique of Gaudí's called *trencadís.* The tiles range through shades of orange, green, and blue and seem to reflect a tranquil sea. The roof soars and buckles like the back of a dragon, covered in scaly blue-green tiles. It has been compared to the mythical dragon slain by Saint George (Sant Jordi in Catalan) with the cross-topped turret as the saint's sword. The interpretation makes sense. Jordi is the patron saint of Cataluña and Gaudí—like most *modernisme* architects—was pro-Catalan. Though pricey, the visit is worth it just to escape into Gaudí's magical world of curvilinear spaces, playful colored glass, floating windows, and surprising details. The audio-guided tour includes visits to several rooms as well as access to the rooftop.

◖ La Pedrera

One of the world's most famous buildings, La Pedrera (Pg. Gràcia 92, Metro: Diagonal, tel. 93/484-5900, 10 A.M.–8 P.M. daily, €8) is Gaudí's most radical departure from the Catalan *modernisme* style. Built between 1906 and 1910 for the wealthy Milà family, the apartment block's exterior is an undulating mass of gray stone that seems to pulsate outward in concentric waves. The balconies are a tangle of forged iron resembling foliage gone wild. The flat roof hosts a forest of warrior-like chimneys and ventilation shafts. Built without a single straight line or supporting walls of any kind, this seminal building broke all molds and

the undulating facade of Gaudí's La Pedrera

earned World Heritage status in 1984. Today, it is an architectural icon drawing thousands of visitors each year. Yet, back when it was under construction, public opinion was decidedly less favorable. Locals and other architects found it ungainly and unattractive. Even the Milà family, who had commissioned it under the name Casa Milà, was not impressed. Because of its gray hulking exterior, critics labeled it La Pedrera (the stone quarry) and the name stuck.

Tours include a very informative audioguide that takes you through the house including a visit to the *Pis de la Pedrera,* a recreated modernist apartment on the 4th floor. The **Espai Gaudí** in the attic offers an informative multimedia look at Gaudí and his work. The roof offers spectacular views over Passeig de Gràcia, as well as an up-close glance at those emblematic chimney-monsters. Fridays and Saturdays in the summer, the rooftop terrace hosts **La Pedrera de Nit,** an open-air concert series that features intriguing musical acts. Tickets start at €12 and include your first drink. Call (tel. 90/210-1212) to reserve, as seats fill up quickly.

La Sagrada Família

The Temple Expiatori de la Sagrada Família (Pl. Sagrada Família, tel. 93/207-3031, www .sagradafamilia.org, 9 A.M.–8 P.M. daily Apr.–Sept., 9 A.M.–6 P.M. daily Oct.–Mar., €8), simply known as La Sagrada Família, is the most popular sight in Barcelona. It is also the most awesome—in the truest, jaw-dropping sense of the word. Looking like giant sand-colored dripping candles, La Sagrada Família will stop you in your tracks. It is not an understatement to say that this is the most famous—and most intriguing—building in the world. The final masterpiece of Antoni Gaudí, the church is expected to be finished in 2041.

The first stone of La Sagrada Família was laid in 1882 under the direction of an architect named Francisco de Paula del Villar. However, a year into the project, 31-year-old Gaudí took over as lead architect. He

ARCHITECTURAL MADMAN, MONUMENTAL GENIUS

Antoni Gaudí was born June 25, 1852, near Tarragona, Cataluña. As a child he suffered from rheumatic problems and was often confined to bed. More than one observer has wondered if Gaudí's hours alone in his sickbed gave flight to the imagination that would make him a genius architect. As he became older, his health improved and he took on a more active role in school. His artistic talents revealed themselves early on as he became the illustrator for his school newsletter and designed scenes for the school plays.

In 1868, Gaudí moved to Barcelona to study architecture. He wasn't the best of students, but he was the most intriguing. One of his professors famously claimed about Gaudí's schoolwork that it was either insane or genius. That summation still seems apt today. Gaudí did not limit himself to architecture classes. He also studied philosophy, history, and economics. His reasoning was that architecture did not depend solely on aesthetics, but also on the social and political environment surrounding the building project.

After earning the title of architect in 1878, Gaudí began to explore possibilities in his work. While his first projects were apprenticeships with established architects working on conventional projects such as the monastery in Montserrat, Gaudí sought inspiration in Gothic designs, Asian influences, and above all, in nature. He was enthralled with the organic shapes prevalent in the natural world. When art nouveau with its emphasis on fluid-

ity and curvature appeared at the beginning of the 19th century, Gaudí became an eager convert, shunning straight lines and rigidity in favor of bends and bows, curls and coils. This soon morphed into the eclectic, personal style that the world knows as Gaudí.

Barcelona in the early 1900s was booming. The textile industry in particular had led to the creation of a rich bourgeoisie very interested in two things: showing off their wealth and supporting the arts. It was a perfect time to be an architect! After one of his designs was presented at the World's Fair in Paris in 1878, Gaudí began to gain fame. This led to his meeting with **Eusebi Güell,** a rich industrialist who would later become Gaudí's most devout patron as well as a lifelong friend.

In 1882, work began on **La Sagrada Família** with one of Gaudí's former professors, Francisco de Paula del Villar, as lead architect. Work had barely begun when the builders clashed with del Villar and he quit. This led to the young Gaudí being assigned the job. He took over in 1883 and worked on the project until his death 43 years later. Meanwhile, his work became the rage among the wealthy – and bold – elite. He was commissioned to design **Casa Vicens, Casa Calvet,** and **Palau Güell** in Barcelona. On the Cantabrian coast, he built the **El Capricho** palace in Comillas. In Astorga, León, he designed the **Palacio de Astorga** for the local bishop. In León capital, he created the **Casa de los Botines.**

Despite the waves his undulating works

would eventually dedicate his life to building the church, which he took on as both an architectural challenge and a spiritual mission. Gaudí's first act was to change the design from neo-Gothic to his signature take on Catalan *modernisme,* replete with forms and imagery from nature.

Gaudí referred to La Sagrada Família as "the last great sanctuary for Christendom" and the architectural details of the building are a pictorial history of the Catholic church. The most striking feature are the spindle-

shaped towers, representing the apostles, the evangelists, the Virgin Mary, and Jesus Christ. The latter of these is the tallest, though not as tall as the nearby hill of Montjuïc, for Gaudí believed that his work should not surpass that of God.

Each of the church's three grand facades depicts major events in the life of Christ and of the church. Facing the rising sun in the east, the **Nativity Facade** is a celebration of the birth of Jesus Christ and the miracle of God's manifestation as a human. It is a riot of flora

were creating in artistic, architectural, and society circles, Gaudí was ignored by Barcelona officials. The city commissioned only two small projects – **the street lamps in Plaça Reial** and **Plaça de Palau.** Only once did he receive the city award for Building of the Year – in 1900 for Casa Calvet, his least extravagant building.

That same year, Gaudí began work on **Parc Güell,** which was to become a wealthy suburb. It was a monumental proposal and one of the first truly environmentally friendly development projects. Gaudí insisted that the land not be altered and not a single tree felled. In addition, he incorporated salvaged ceramics in the construction. Only two of the planned 60 homes were built and, in 1905, Gaudí moved into one of them with his father and niece.

In 1904, Gaudí received the commission for one of his most famous works – **Casa Batlló.** Built on the fashionable Passeig de Gràcia, the house surprised everyone with its heaving balconies, sea-colored tile exterior, wavy roof, and helmeted chimneys. Upon its completion, Gaudí was immediately contracted by politician Pere Milá to build his home, also on Passeig de Gràcia. **Casa Milá** became one of Gaudí's most complete expressions of the harmony of organic shape and form – there is not a single straight line in the entire building. The exterior is covered in natural gray stone from a local quarry. Locals and city officials alike were not happy with the building. The city tried repeatedly to stop the project on permit violations. Neighbors, aghast at what looked to them like a giant molten rock, nicknamed the building **La Pedrera,** the stone quarry. The name stuck and the building, finished in 1910, is one of Barcelona's top tourist attractions.

In 1911, Gaudí fell ill and, believing his death was near, made out his will. He survived the illness but became increasingly reclusive and religious, spurred on by a series of personal tragedies. His beloved niece died in 1912, leaving him alone in his home. In 1915, construction on La Sagrada Família nearly stopped due to financial problems. In 1918, his dear friend and patron Eusebi Güell died. As the years passed, Gaudí began to shun all outward signs of prosperity, took to dressing in old clothes, and turned his full attention to completing La Sagrada Família. On June 7, 1926, he was hit by a public tram as he crossed Gran Vía. Because of his ragged clothing, taxi drivers refused to transfer him to a hospital. When he finally was taken to a charity hospital, he was in grave condition and on June 12 he died. Thousands of Barcelonans turned out for his funeral. In homage to his work, Gaudí's body was buried in the crypt at La Sagrada Família.

Today, more than 75 years after his passing, Gaudí is lauded as Barcelona's most gifted son. His works are the number one tourist attraction in the city and the entire world knows his name. Seven of his works were collectively named a UNESCO World Heritage Site in 1984. For more information on the man and his work, visit www.gaudiclub.com.

and fauna stitched around scenes from Jesus's childhood. It can be mesmerizing and you might consider bringing binoculars in order to fully appreciate its detail. This was the only facade to be completed under the watchful eye of Gaudí.

The **Passion Facade,** on the southwestern side of the church, pays mournful homage to the passion and death of Jesus Christ. Created by sculptor Josep María Subirachs, chosen to complete the facade according to Gaudí's plans, the facade is an austere contrast to the Nativity Facade. Subirachs, an avowed atheist, later claimed his work had nothing to do with Gaudí. Nonetheless, he paid homage to Gaudí by sculpting the master architect above the left side of the main entry. Subirachs also drew his inspiration for the Roman soldiers from Gaudí's helmeted chimneys on the roof of La Pedrera. Upon its completion, the southern front, known as the **Glorification Facade,** will be the largest of all.

When Gaudí died in 1926, only the Nativity Facade, one tower, the apse, and the crypt

the Nativity Facade, La Sagrada Família

tivity and Passion Facades, the naves and the cloisters, the crypt where Gaudí is buried, and the ground-floor **Museu Gaudí,** featuring models of a completed Sagrada Família. You are also free to climb the towers of the Nativity Facade, but this is not a good idea if you are even slightly claustrophobic. For €2, you can take an elevator up the Passion Facade. For a detailed description of the temple, rent the audio-guide for €3.50.

Some visitors complain that the interior is not worth the price of the visit. If you might be one of those turned off by hammering, scaffolding, and dozens of camera-toting tourists and school kids, then grab a seat at one of the dozens of sidewalk cafés that circle the church. Prices are high for coffee (€2), but cheap compared to the entrance ticket—plus you can stay as long as you want.

GRÀCIA

Up until the 20th century, the working-class barrio of Gràcia was its own village. Home to factory workers and the poorly paid, it was a hotbed of Catalan nationalism. The famed Passeig de Gràcia is so named as it was the only road leading from Barcelona to Gràcia. In 1897, in the midst of its expansion north, Barcelona swallowed Gràcia whole. However, it couldn't ingest the barrio's distinctive personality. Sprawling north and east of the intersection of Avinguda Diagonal and Vía Augusta, Gràcia is still headstrong and proud—though many of the factory workers have been replaced by artists and fervent nationalist attitudes by a pervasive bohemian air. Gràcia is also extremely popular with expats, including Americans, Brits, Africans, and Middle Easterners. The result is a roiling cultural pot of Lebanese restaurants, English-language cinemas, traditional food markets, artist workshops, laid-back bars, jugglers on street corners, guitarists strumming in plazas, hip couples pushing expensive strollers, and lifelong residents soaking up the sun on benches. The barrio is also home to one of Barcelona's most colorful and most traditional festivals—Fiestas de Gràcia in August.

were finished. Because he was constantly improvising and changing the design as construction was going on, he left few complete designs and models behind. What was left was destroyed during the Civil War. Though many have continued to work with Gaudí's best interest at heart, we will never truly know just what the architectural genius envisioned upon the church's completion. Construction continues at a snail's pace due mainly to lack of funding (the building is supported by donors) and regular debate over each architectural move.

If you want to visit La Sagrada Família, know that it is wildly popular. Over a million people visit it annually, putting it up there with the Museo del Prado in Madrid and the Alhambra in Granada as the top sights in Spain. It is best to go first thing in the morning, not only to avoid the crowds, but because it is so overwhelming you'll want to arrive at your freshest, rather than weary after a day of sightseeing.

Your entry ticket gets you access to the Na-

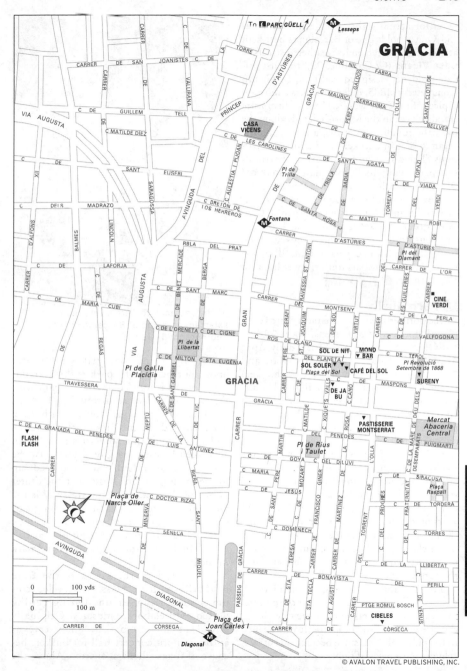

As for actual sights with a monumental "S," Gràcia holds one of Barcelona's best-kept architectural secrets in its weathered streets—**Casa Vicens** (C/ Carolines 22), the first private residence designed and built by Gaudí. Completed in 1883, it demonstrates a restraint typical of his early works. Hints of his future floridity exist in the Moorish details along the roof, the rough brick walls, and the colored ceramic tiles in checkerboard and floral patterns. The other sight to see is the barrio itself, particularly its lively squares. **Plaça del Diamont** was the setting for a famous Catalan novel named for the square, which documented life in Gràcia during the Spanish Civil War. **Plaça del Sol** is aptly named, for the sun pours into this open square by day. After nightfall, locals and expats rush in, filling the many surrounding bars until the wee hours of the morning.

◖ Parc Güell

At the northern reaches of Gràcia, Parc Güell (C/ d'Olot 7, Metro: Lesseps, 9 A.M.–9 P.M. daily June–Sept., 9 A.M.–8 P.M. daily Apr., May, Oct., 9 A.M.–7 P.M. daily Mar. and Nov., 10 A.M.–6 P.M. daily Dec.–Feb., free) is one of Barcelona's most delightful spots. Designed by Gaudí, the park is frisky and colorful, whimsical and magical—a perfect place to while away a few hours, perhaps with a picnic lunch.

In 1900, Gaudí was commissioned by the wealthy Catalan Eusebi Güell (one of the architect's greatest patrons) to create a model suburb on the hill of El Carmel at the edges of the then-limits of the city. Gaudí spent 14 years on the project until it became clear that the intended residents of the park—Barcelona's upper classes—had no interest in moving out of the city center. All that was completed was the park's entrance, two gatehouses, a pavilion and terrace, and two houses. Though it was a financial failure for Güell, the park soon became an architectural gem for the city. When the city acquired the property, it was opened to the public and has since become one of Barcelona's most beloved sights.

At the entrance to Parc Güell, the tiled salamander is one of Barcelona's most photographed sites.

The first thing that strikes the visitor upon approaching the park is the juxtaposition of the bright colors of the park with the parched landscape surrounding it. At its entrance, the stone gatehouses, with wavy multi-colored tile mosaics on the windows and roofs, look like something out of an acid-laced Hansel and Gretel tale. Past the entrance, a large double stairway leads up to the main pavilion. Resting at the center of one of the islands in the stairway is the most famous creature in the park—a giant, ceramic tile–covered salamander. You'll be hard-pressed to get a clear shot of it as this is the single most-photographed landmark in the park.

At the top of the stairs is the **Sala Hipòstila** with 86 classically styled columns supporting an undulating ceiling dotted with elaborate mosaics. Originally intended to house a market, it now serves as an impromptu concert hall for buskers because of its excellent acoustics. Above the *sala* rests the **Teatro Griego,** a large open-air plaza boasting views straight out to the Mediterranean Sea. Twisting like a snake on the plaza's edge is the park's second-most favorite sight—the bench **Banc de Trencadís.** *Trencadís* refers to the technique of creating mosaics with colorful bits of broken tile.

Only two of the park's proposed houses were built and sold, one to Gaudí himself—where he spent 20 years of his life. Today, it serves as the **Casa Museu Gaudí** (tel. 93/219-3811, 10 A.M.–8 P.M. daily Apr.–Sept., 10 A.M.–6 P.M. daily Oct.–Mar., €4).

To get to the park, take the metro to Lessops and then catch local bus 24 (€1.30) to the park's entrance. Be sure to pick up a sandwich at the shop next to the metro stop for an impromptu picnic in the park.

Nightlife

Barcelona nightlife is as eclectic as the city itself. Traditional Catalan *cava* bars, über-chic nightclubs, Irish pubs, live jazz spots, karaoke bars, open-air beachside party shacks, cozy wine bars, gay and lesbian discos, Latin dance clubs, and ancient neighborhood dives jostle for real estate all over town. Not a few visitors have joked that the "bar" in Barcelona comes from the sheer diversity and number of watering holes in town. For listings, try the Spanish-language *Guía de Ocío,* a weekly cultural magazine available at newsstands for €1. In English, consult any of the half-dozen free magazines that you will find in hotels, bars, and restaurants. Online, try www.bcn-nightlife.com and www.barcelonaconnect.com. For gay and lesbian nightlife, visit www.gaybarcelona.com.

A night out in Barcelona begins around 9 P.M. with wine and tapas (or a light meal). Next, hit a few easy-talking bars between 11 P.M. and 1 A.M. After that, dance clubs and live music venues reach their peak around 3 A.M.—closing time for many places. Later, the big clubs rock steady until sun-up. **Las Ramblas and Barri Gòtic** have the largest number of bars catering to tourists—particularly backpackers and bachelor/ette partygoers. **Raval** draws artists and expats to its gritty, avant-garde bars. **El Born** features stylish, urbane wine and cocktail bars. **Port Olímpic** boasts a string of big, brash, booming discos. **Eixample** bursts with upscale, very trendy drinking spots, as well as the best gay nightlife in town. **Gràcia** offers cheap, cheerful pubs and clubs catering to a mostly local, mostly young crowd.

One thing to keep in mind as you head out for the night is the distance between your hotel and your drinking hole. Taxis—especially Thursday through Sunday—are extremely scarce. If you are heading home between the peak hours of 2 and 3 A.M., you may find yourself walking. If you head home before 1 A.M. or after 5 A.M., you can catch the subway.

Drink prices in Barcelona are higher than elsewhere in Spain, yet still cheap compared to the United States or Great Britain. A *caña* (small draft beer) runs around €1.50 and a glass of wine will rarely exceed €2.50. *Copas* (mixed drinks) run €4–7. Of course, location amps up price, and the trendier the place the more you'll pay. Prices are also higher at *chiringuitos* (beachside bars)—but you are paying for the view. Remember that most dance clubs will charge an *entrada* (cover charge) of between €5–20. Often, you'll receive a slip of paper good for one *consumpción* (drink) in exchange for your cover. This is valid for your first drink, whether you choose a cheap beer or a pricey cocktail. (See sidebar, *A Nightlife Survival Guide,* in the *Essentials* chapter.)

LAS RAMBLAS
Bars

⟨ Bosc de les Fades (Pg. Banca 7, Metro: Drassanes, tel. 93/317-2649, 10:30 A.M.–1 A.M. Mon.–Thurs., 11 A.M.–2 A.M. Fri.–Sat., 11 A.M.–1 A.M. Sun.), run by the wax museum next door, translates to "Forest of the Fairies"—a very apt description of this magical bar. Lit only by candles, the bar hosts moss-draped trees, waterfalls, and fairies. Full of nooks and crannies, it is the perfect place to head for a romantic start to a date. **Bar Boadas** (C/ Tallers 1, tel. 93/318-9592, noon–2 A.M. Mon.–Sat., closed Sun.), established in 1933, oozes classic charm from an era way bygone. The original owner got his start in Havana and the decor has something of Colonial Cuban decadence to it. The cocktail to drink is a perfectly rendered Cuban-style *mojito*. The black-suited mixologists behind the bar also whip up classic (pricey) cocktails from whiskey sours to martinis. On the opposite end of the style meter (and the opposite end of Las Ramblas), join the locals at the walk-up window that is **Kiosko de la Cazalla** (C/ Arc del Teatre, s/n, 10 A.M.–10 P.M. Mon.–Sat., closed Sun.). Since 1912, this literal hole-in-the-wall has served up cold beers, olives, and the house specialty, *cazalla,* a raisin-flavored liquor with the kick of ouzo and none of the smoothness. Wash it down with a *café solo* (small cup of strong coffee). Owner Ángel is a former journalist and an affable encyclopedia of knowledge on traditional bars and restaurants in Barcelona. The raucous **Sidecar** (Pl. Reial 7, Metro: Liceu, tel. 93/302-1586, 6 P.M.–3 A.M. Mon.–Sat., closed Sun.) is a punk and funk kind of place commanding a large corner of the Plaça Reial. Their Monday anti-karaoke nights led by local expat comedian Rachel Arieff are wildly popular. Get there before 10 P.M. if you want any chance of singing your favorite Andy Gibb or Devo song.

Dance Clubs

Club Fellini (La Rambla 27, Metro: Drassanes, www.clubfellini.com, 12:30–5 A.M. Thurs.–Sat., Mon.–Sat. in summer, €15) has three dance rooms dedicated to house and techno with a little inspiration from punk, disco, and classic rock. It often hosts top international DJs. Check clothing shops in the area for discount entry coupons. **Café Royale** (C/ Nou de Zurbano 3, Metro: Liceu, tel. 93/412-1433, 5 P.M.–2:30 A.M. Fri. and Sat.) is a sexy, two-floored club with very deep sofas and deeper beats. The music is a modern blend of funk and soul with occasional forays into Latin jazz and bossa nova. Sophisticated touches like chandeliers and huge bouquets of fresh flowers keep local trendies coming back.

Jazz and Live Music

Opened in 1947, **Bar Pastis** (C/ Santa Mònica 4, Metro: Drassanes, tel. 93/318-7980, 8 P.M.–2 A.M. Tues.–Sun., closed Mon.) is a classic Barcelona watering hole with a turn-of-the-century French twist. When the stage is not given over to jazz performers, French crooners, tango orchestras, or local guitar players, Edith Piaf records wail on the sound system. If you go before 11 P.M., you'll likely be nursing your vermouth alone. **Jamboree** (Pl. Reial 17, Metro: Liceu, tel. 93/319-1789, 11 P.M.–5 A.M. daily, cover varies) is a long-time blues and jazz favorite that once hosted Chet Baker, Ella Fitzgerald, and Lionel Hampton. Today, you're more likely to catch a local combo enthusiastically performing anything from Chicago blues to Latin swing. When the musicians pack up their instruments, DJs take over, pumping out a vibey mix of hip-hop and world music to a very enthusiastic 20-something crowd. The club shares its nighttime party with the attached flamenco *tablao,* Sala Tarantos.

EL RAVAL
Bars

The most classic of Barcelona's rough-and-tumble dive bars, **Marsella** (C/ Sant Pau 65, Metro: Drassanes, 6 P.M.–2 A.M. Tues.–Sat., closed Sun. and Mon.) is a step back in grit-wizened time. The decor hasn't changed much since the place opened in 1820—and judging by the thickness of the dust on some of the bottles, there hasn't been much cleaning going on either. Still, this has been a mandatory stop during a night out in El Raval since Picasso and Dalí drank here. Nowadays, in one evening, everyone from yupsters to hipsters, dentally challenged old men to strawberry-cheeked working girls will make their way through. The specialty is absinthe and there are dozens of flavors on offer. Just be aware, Marsella is decidedly on the seedier side of Raval and the side street, Sant Ramon, is locally known as "hooker street." If you are jumpy, don't go here alone, and when you leave, don't go south. Head north to the Rambla de Raval and Carrer de Carme, where you'll find tons of trendy bars. **Bar Senses** (C/ Carme 74, Metro: Catalunya, 6 P.M.–2 A.M. Tues.–Sun., closed Mon.) is a laid-back bar that draws area hipsters with its mix of funk and house music; the kick-back comfy beanbag seating helps. **Muy Buenas** (C/ Carme 63, Metro: Catalunya, tel. 93/442-5053, noon–2:30 A.M. daily) has been serving up cold beer and homey tapas since 1928. The decor—all tobacco-stained walls, marble counters, and swirling wooden details—hasn't changed much over the last seven decades and that is just the way the devoted regulars like it.

Dance Clubs
La Paloma (C/ Tigre 57, tel. 93/317-7225, 6 P.M.–5 A.M. Thurs.–Sun.) opened as a dancehall in 1903 and is still going strong. In its heyday it drew the likes of Picasso and Hemingway; more recently it served as the venue for the premiere of Almodóvar's *All About My Mother*. A live orchestra plays big-band, mambo, and anything ballroom until 2:30 A.M. After that, DJs take over and techno finishes out the night. Friday and Saturday nights are particularly wild as the "So Rebel Club" party takes over the decks and the dance floor. It is worth a visit for the elaborate, gilded, red velvet interior replete with chandeliers, a VIP balcony, and a grand stage—all original. On the way out, you'll be greeted by a mime; his finger over his mouth reminds you to keep quiet, neighbors are sleeping.

Gay and Lesbian
Drawing a raucous gay, lesbian, and straight (but never narrow) crowd, **El Cangrejo** (C/ Montserrat 9, Metro: Drassanes, tel. 93/301-2978, 11 P.M.–4 A.M. Wed.–Sat.) is a kitschy classic that was a major venue during the *movida*, the raucous club-fueled culture that

exploded in the 1980s after Franco's death. Today, it is a bit shabby but still puts on a good show—not unlike the drag queens who perform here almost nightly. The music is pure old-school Spanish pop and the crowd—almost all local—sings along all night. At **Burdel 74** (C/ Carme 74, Metro: Liceu, tel. 93/442-6986, 7 P.M.–2:30 A.M. Tues.–Sat., cover varies) you can see wacky cabaret performances, drag queens, and avant-garde live music. The decor is brothel chic and the clients are a mix of gay and straight locals and expats.

BARRI GÒTIC
Bars
Sexy without being self-conscious, **Andú** (C/ Correu Vell 3, Metro: Jaume I, 7 P.M.–3 A.M. daily) has an underground claim on coolest bar in the Barri Gòtic—a tough call in a quarter busting at its medieval seams with cool bars. The wine list is impressive, the jazz on the stereo eclectic, and the mismatched antique furniture, old instruments, and dim lighting perfect for a romantic encounter. Owned by a pair of expats—Canadian Lee Courchesne and Australian Brenden Smith—this swank little hole is popular with expats, artists, musicians, and anyone else lucky enough to stumble upon it. There is also a tasty selection of simple tapas. Around the corner, **Milk Bar** (C/ Gignàs 21, Metro: Jaume I, tel. 93/268-0922, 6:30 P.M.–3 A.M. daily) has been voted "coolest new bar" in Barcelona. It is boudoir chic with brocaded walls, red-hued lighting, and fashionable furniture. Run by Irish expats, Milk doubles as a bistro, serving hipped-up hamburgers and a Sunday brunch to die for (noon–4 P.M. Sun.). It is a great place to start the night, even if the fame it has garnered has led staff to a very unfortunate state of un-cool disdain. Down the street, the **Cuevas del Conte** (C/ Gignàs 2, Metro: Drassanes, 7 P.M.–2:30 A.M. Wed.–Mon., closed Tues.) is a fantastic grotto-like warren of mosaic tiles, dripping candles, and rustic wood furniture. The staff are extremely friendly, the music is a blend of Latin and low-key techno, and the drinks are delicious. Happy hour, 7–10 P.M.,

BARCELONA

features €4 cocktails; after that, the "cocktail of the day" is just €4.50.

The English-speaking **Travel Bar** (C/ Boqueria 27, Metro: Liceu, tel. 93/342-5252, 10 A.M.–3 A.M. daily) is all things to all travelers, provided they are under 30—a lot under 30. This raucous café/bar/Internet spot/meeting point was built by travelers for travelers and serves as ground zero for most backpackers visiting the city. Their "Smashed Bar Crawl" (9:30 P.M. Tues., Thurs., and Sat., €15) takes travelers on a crawl to four bars and one club and features loads of drinking and the kind of stuff you might see on a *Girls Gone Wild* video.

Dance Clubs

Fonfone (C/ Escudellers 24, Metro: Liceu, 10 P.M.–2:30 A.M. daily, cover varies) is a jam-'em-in, play-it-loud kind of club with a musical bent toward funk, breaks, electronic, and hip-hop. Long and lean and glowing green, it is a perfect place to get your groove up and running at the start of the night. **La Macarena** (C/ Nou de Sant Francesc 5, Metro: Drassanes, 11:30 P.M.–4:30 A.M. daily, €5 cover) has nothing at all to do with the cheesy song of the same name. This small dance club built on the grounds of an old flamenco *tablao* is a mecca for electronic-music aficionados. It attracts the best DJs from around the world and prides itself at being at the forefront of this sound. Catch the beat at Macarena—but be ready, this place is not about posing, flirting, or flitting about—it is a venue for pure music worshipping. Hail the DJ.

Gay and Lesbian

At the northern reaches of Barri Gòtic is one of Barcelona's premier gay discos. **Salvation** (Ronda Sant Pere 19–21, Metro: Urquinaona, midnight–5 A.M. Fri. and Sat., cover varies) features happy hour from opening until 1:30 A.M. but things don't get hot here until after 3 A.M. After that a wall of sound—progressive techno, trance, house, and dance—electrifies thousands of happy, dancing boys (and a few girls) until the wee hours.

Jazz and Live Music

The miniscule **Harlem Jazz Club** (C/ Comtessa de Sobradiel 8, Metro: Jaume I, tel. 93/310-0755, 10 A.M.–3 A.M. Tues.–Sun., closed Mon., cover varies) is one of Barcelona's most-revered live jazz clubs. If you manage to snag one of their few tables, most nights you'll be treated to a very good, often classic, set of music. **El Monasterio** (Po. Isabel II 4, Metro: Jaume I, 8 P.M.–3 A.M. daily, cover varies) is a cavernous club/cafeteria/live music venue. Located at the end of Vía Laetana, near the seafront, the multiplex features a lively, popular outdoor terrace—get there early if you want a seat. Downstairs, there is a grand piano and a regular roster of live music acts from tango to rock to singer-songwriter.

LA RIBERA AND EL BORN

Bars

On the southern edge of Born, **Mudanzas** (C/ Vidriería 15, Metro: Jaume I, tel. 93/319-1137, 10 A.M.–2:30 A.M. daily) is delightfully misnamed. *Mudanza* means "a move," and that is the last thing you want to do once you settle in at this trendy bar. It has a sexy intellectual vibe fueled by a lively crowd full of creative types in black-framed glasses. During the day, it is a low-key place for a sandwich or a fresh juice. **Miramelindo** (Pg. del Born 15, Metro: Jaume I, tel. 93/310-3727, 8 P.M.–3 A.M. daily) is a cavernous space with a tropical feel. All that is missing is a guy in a Panama hat chomping on a Cuban. Instead, you'll find low-key Latin music and fruity cocktails. Try their *coctel de coco,* a delectable coconut milk and cognac concoction. **El Nus** (C/ Mirallers 5, Metro: Jaume I, tel. 93/319-5355, 7:30 P.M.–2 A.M. Thurs.–Tues., closed Wed.) has a battered elegance reminiscent of old New Orleans. The cocktails are straightforward and the music is an eclectic mix of whatever tickles owner Toni's fancy, though he leans towards classic jazz.

Founded in 1929, **(El Xampanyet** (C/ Montcada 22, Metro: Jaume I, tel. 93/319-7003, noon–4 P.M. and 6:30–11:30 P.M. Mon.–Sat., closed Sun.) is a local legend. This traditional bar jammed with wobbly marble tables, antique fixtures, and aging locals serves several *cavas* by the glass. The simple tapas include the house specialty, fresh anchovies. Whether you go for a light meal at lunch or as a first stop to start the evening, you will not regret your visit to this most traditional of Barcelona's bars. Just go early as it gets wildly packed.

Jazz and Live Music

Espai Barroc (C/ Montcada 20, Metro: Jaume I, tel. 93/310-0673, 8 P.M.–2 A.M. Tues.–Sat., 6 P.M.–10 P.M. Sun., cover varies) is a "baroque bar" located in Palau Dalmases, a 14th-century palace replete with ornate decor, heavy tapestries, dramatic frescoes, and lots of candles—all perfectly decadent and excessive. There is music every night, usually baroque, chamber music, or opera. At least one night a week is given over to flamenco (currently Tuesdays at 10 P.M.).

BARCELONETA

When considering nightlife in this swath of city by the sea, think: Barceloneta equals neighborhood dives and wine bars; the beachfront equals *chiringuitos* and impromptu parties on the sand; Port Olímpic equals late-night/early-morning mega-discos.

Bars

Absenta (C/ San Carlos 36, Metro: Barceloneta, tel. 93/221-5785, 11 A.M.–2 A.M. daily) is a good old dive with modern aspirations like Internet access and yummy tapas. It draws as many locals as it does tourists, all clamoring after a taste of their more than 20 types of absinthe. **Luz de Gas Port Vell** (Moll del Diposit, Metro: Barceloneta, tel. 93/209-7711, noon–3 A.M. daily), located on a boat docked across from the Palau del Mar, is a classy place for a beer by day and a glass of wine by candlelight at night. The music is terribly cheesy 1990s soft rock, but the atmosphere, surrounded by the bobbing yachts in the harbor, is romantic.

Chiringuitos

Summer nightlife in Barcelona means *chiringuitos*, beachside bars that offer snacks and ice cream by day, cocktails and cool beats by night. There are several running the length of Barcelona's beaches. Drinks tend to be pricey—€8 or higher—but you can't beat the ambience. Most are open all day and close around midnight or 1 A.M. The further you get from Barceloneta, the more adventurous the bars are in terms of music. Try **El Chiringuito** (Platja de Bogatell, Metro: Llacuna), which spins low-vibe techno and rents deck chairs to take on the sand, or **Chiringuito Nova Ola** (Platja Nueva Mar Bella, Metro: Selva del Mar), which features funky daytime parties with DJs pumping deep funk, soul, and lounge.

Dance Clubs

There are many dance clubs clustered on the boardwalks of Port Olímpic. Of those, the most hyped is **Baja Beach** (Po. Marítimo 34, Metro: Ciutadella Vila Olímpica, tel. 93/225-9100, www.bajabeach.es, noon–5 A.M. daily), a tropical playground for grown-ups. There are girls in bikinis selling beer, muscle-ripped go-go boys dancing on tables, palm trees, sand, volleyball tournaments, swimsuit competitions, and waitstaff dressed as lifeguards. During the day there is a menu of so-so salads, sandwiches, and seafood served on the boardwalk terrace. Early evening, live music from Latin to reggae to Brazilian accompanies diners. By nightfall, DJs kick in with full-volume techno and electronic dance music. Take note, this place is huge with British bachelor/bachelorette parties and if your visit corresponds with one you should expect total drunken mayhem. A few doors down and a world of hip away, **Shoko** (Pg. Marítim 36, Metro: Ciutadella Vila Olímpica, tel. 93/225-9200, midnight–3 A.M. Thurs.–Sun., cover varies) is a trendy Japanese restaurant by day, sophisticated dance club by night. Amid a forest of black bamboo, Barcelona's beautiful people dance to a mixture of house, hip-hop, and funk. There are often special guest DJs, including international stars.

MONTJUÏC
Dance Clubs

In the cavernous **Space** (C/ Tarragona 141,

Metro: Espanya or Tarragona, www.spacebar celona.com, midnight–6 A.M. Fri. and Sat., €15), top Spanish and international DJs spin hard house and new techno to enthusiastic crowds of thousands. There are go-go dancers everywhere, four massive bars, and a stellar sound system. Prices can go up if a top DJ is playing. Check trendy stores and bars for discount flyers. In Poble Espanyol, **Discotheque** (tel. 93/426-5237, www.clubdiscothequebcn .com, midnight–6 A.M. Fri. and Sat., cover varies) is flashy with just enough trashy to make it interesting. This big, bold, laser-lit club pumps out intense dance, house, and electronic music to a beautiful young crowd that is split about evenly between locals and tourists. It is a regular stop on the roster of top international DJs. In warmer months, Discotheque gives way to **La Terrrazza** (tel. 93/272-4980, www.la terrrazza.com, midnight–6 A.M. Fri. and Sat.), a massive open-air club that features the same hot music. Laser lights are replaced by Barcelona's glittering night sky.

EIXAMPLE
Bars
La Fira (C/ Provença 171, Metro: Hospital Clínic, tel. 93/978-1096, 11 P.M.–3 A.M. Mon.–Thurs., 11 P.M.–5 A.M. Fri.–Sat., closed Sun.) is a fun fair for grown-ups. The Ricky Martin look-alike owner got his hands on an out-of-business amusement park and filled his bar with crazy mirrors, carousel horses, giant masks, and swings at the bar—only in Barcelona! **Espit Chupitos** (C/ Aribau 77, Metro: Universitat, 10:30 P.M.–2:30 A.M. Mon.–Sat., closed Sun.) is a rowdy hole-in-the-wall dominated by a giant white sign on the wall listing the over 500 *chupito* (shot) flavors available (€1.50 each). **Belchica** (C/ Villaroel 60, Metro: Urgell, 6 P.M.–3 A.M. Mon.–Fri., 7 P.M.–3 A.M. Sat., 7 P.M.–1 A.M. Sun.) is Barcelona's only Belgian bar. With over 40 Belgian beers available, sophisticated decor, and Internet access, this has become a favorite haunt of the city's expats. So much so that Wednesday nights feature language-exchange parties between English-speakers and Spaniards.

Dance Clubs
The very hip resident DJs at **Distrito Diagonal** (Av. Diagonal 442,Metro: Diagonal, tel. 93/415-4635, www.distritodiagonal.com, 11 P.M.–4:30 A.M. Fri. and Sat. only) spin a meaty mix of deep house, garage, and beyond. The crowd is more than up for it, keeping the dance floor packed until closing. **City Hall** (Rambla de Catalunya 2, Metro: Catalunya, tel. 93/317-2177, www.cityhall-bcn .com, midnight–5:30 A.M. daily), located just off the northern edge of Plaça de Catalunya, is a pulsating maze of hip-hop, funk, house and backbeat. The DJs know how to keep the clamoring crowd of 20-somethings dizzy with anticipation over what they might spin next. Each night features a different party, so check the website for the latest.

Gay and Lesbian
The left side of Eixample is referred to as Gaixample due to heavy dose of gay and lesbian bars in the area. For a guide to gay and lesbian life in Barcelona, look for the free *Official Gay and Lesbian Tourist Guide* at a tourism office. Also run an Internet search—there are dozens of sites devoted to gay and lesbian life in Barcelona. **Zeltas** (C/ Casanova 75, Metro: Universitat, 11 P.M.–3 A.M. daily) is the place to start a night out on the gay/lesbian scene. This bustling three-room lounge features infectious house music, low lighting, gauzy curtained bars, and very beautiful boys and girls. **G Café** (C/ Muntaner 24, Metro: Universitat, tel. 7 P.M.–3 A.M. Tues.–Sun., closed Mon.) is a Gaudí-inspired club offering sophisticated cocktails to a discriminating crowd. **Dietrich** (C/ Consell de Cent 255, Metro: Pg. Gràcia, tel. 93/451-7707, 6 P.M.–3 A.M. daily) is a long-time favorite on the Barcelona gay and lesbian scene. Around 1 A.M., a drag queen takes the stage in an elaborately choreographed show. The rest of the time the crowd mingles on the dance floor. Next door, **Atame** (C/ Consell de Cent 257, Metro: Pg. Gràcia, tel. 93/454-9273, 6 P.M.–2:30 A.M. daily) heats up the dance floor with a crowd-pleasing blend of international and Spanish pop. **D-MER** (C/

Plató 13, Metro: Muntaner, tel. 93/201-6207, 11 P.M.–4 A.M. Thurs.–Sat.) looks more like a strip club than the city's premier women-only lesbian disco—but that is exactly what it is.

Jazz and Live Music

Luz de Gas (C/ Muntaner 246 Metro: Diagonal, tel. 93/209-7711, www.luzdegas.com, 11 P.M.–5 A.M. Thurs.–Sat., cover from €12) is an opulent music hall dripping in oversized chandeliers and red velvet curtains. Built at the turn of the 20th century, it is one of Barcelona's current "it" clubs for live music. The regular program features local jazz, blues, and Dixieland bands with a smattering of international acts.

GRÀCIA
Bars

Plaça del Sol is ground zero for partying in Gràcia. For the most part the crowds partake in *botellón,* an illegal practice of drinking in the streets. Cops tend to look the other way as long as things don't get too out of hand. If you prefer a less perilous piece of the action, pull up a stool at either **Café del Sol** (Pl. Sol 16, noon–3 A.M. daily) or **Sol de Nit** (Pl. Sol 9, tel. 93/237-3937, noon–3 A.M. daily). These sister bars feature old-timey decor, raucous crowds, and coveted outdoor seating in warmer

months. During the day, they are both very laid-back, serving up a few simple tapas and salads. **Mond Bar** (Pl. Sol 21, tel. 93/272-0910, Metro: Diagonal or FCG:Gràcia, 8:30 P.M.–2 A.M. daily) follows the philosophy of "pop will set you free." Maybe that is why the jukebox loaded down with indie pop is free. The interior is modern with a hint of kitsch and the crowd is laid-back and friendly. Another good place to get a groove on in Gràcia is **Carrer Francisco Giner,** where bars and clubs are lined up one after the other.

Dance Clubs

Cibeles (C/ Còrsega 363, Metro: Diagonal or FCG:Gràcia, tel. 93/457-3877, 11 P.M.–5 A.M., Thurs.–Sun., €10) is a swish ballroom on a grand scale. Music ranges from tango to techno and Friday nights are given over to the long-running **Mond Club** party, where an eclectic mix of pop and indie music attracts Gràcia's hippest 20-somethings. **Otto Zutz** (C/ Lincoln 15, Metro: Fontana or FCG:Gràcia, tel. 93/238-0722, 11 P.M.–5 A.M. Wed.–Sun., cover varies) offers three floors of New York–style clubbing fun. Music varies from house to funk to soul, while the people remain the same—beautiful, young, and quite often "someone." Come dressed to thrill with cash to spare.

Entertainment and Events

THE ARTS

Barcelona has long shimmered with creativity, from Gaudí and Picasso to the artistic shot in the arm that MACBA gave the city. For the most complete listing of venues and events, consult the Spanish-language *Guía del Ocio,* available from any newsstand, visit the tourist office or their website (www.barcelonaturisme.com), or look for the free guide *See Barcelona.* Any of the half-dozen free English publications that you will find around the city will also cover current events.

Cultural Centers

CaixaForum (Av. Marquès de Comillas, s/n, Metro: Espanya, tel. 93/476-8600, www.fundacio.lacaixa.es, 10 A.M.–8 P.M. Tues.–Sun., closed Mon.) is one of the city's most vibrant contemporary arts centers. Located in a gorgeously restored *modernisme* factory, the center—financed by the powerful Catalan savings bank La Caixa—possesses an impressive permanent collection of 20th-century art and sponsors intriguing exhibits in its three spacious foyers. It also hosts live events—mainly modern dance and world music. At the end of Las

Ramblas, **Centre d'Art Santa Mònica** (Rambla 7, Metro: Drassanes, tel. 93/316-2810, 11 A.M.–8 P.M. Tues.–Sat., 11 A.M.–3 P.M. Sun., closed Mon.) is a cool, inviting modern art space. Mounting shows in a variety of mediums, it has a reputation for exhibitions of complex, often perplexing works by major up-and-comers on the international art scene. The space also has a great café (tel. 93/342-5275, noon–1 A.M. Tues.–Sun., closed Mon., €18) with a modern tiki-style terrace. Another hotbed of modern artistic movement is the **Centre de Cultura Contemporánia de Barcelona** (C/ Montalegre 5, Metro: Universitat, tel. 93/306-4100, www.cccb.org, 11 A.M.–2 P.M. and 4–8 P.M. Tues., Thurs., and Fri., 11 A.M.–8 P.M. Wed. and Sat., 11 A.M.–7 P.M. Sun., extended hours in summer, €6), better known as the CCCB. Though often lumped in under the shadow of MACBA, this buzzing center hosts a vast array of events that would keep even a seasoned arthound panting. The annual program includes film retrospectives, dance programs, literary events, and—as a partner of Sonar (see *Festivals*)—electronic music concerts. The center's **C3 Bar** draws an expected arty, neo-hippie crowd.

Dance

Dance performances, from time-honored to ground-breaking, take place all over town bars, art galleries, and major venues. **Mercat de les Flors** (C/ Lleida 59, Metro: Espanya, tel. 93/426-1875, www.mercatflors.org) is one of the city's most traditional dance venues. Located in a spectacular, soaring space that was originally built as the Palace of Agriculture for the 1929 world exhibition, the theater hosts an impressive year-round roster of dance events, as well as big-name concerts and musical festivals. **Teatre Victòria** (Av. Paral.lel 65, Metro: Paral.lel, tel. 93/329-9189, www.teatrevictoria.com) has traditionally featured ballet and modern dance troupes, though recently it has hosted popular musicals such as *Grease,* as well as modern plays such as *Hysteria,* directed by American film actor John Malkovich.

Film

As in the rest of Spain, Barcelona's film houses were forbidden from showing films in any language other than Spanish during the Franco regime. As a result, the tradition of dubbing films is very strong and most Spaniards would not consider seeing a film that wasn't dubbed. Fortunately, Barcelona, being both a cosmopolitan town and home to a massive English-speaking expat community, has a good range of films shown in *V.O.* (original version). Check the latest issue of *Guía del Ocio* for listings. It is in Spanish, so just go to the back and look for "cine," then search for films with "V.O." next to them, and remember, Spain uses the military clock. **Casablanca** (Pg. Gràcia 115, Metro: Diagonal, tel. 93/218-4345) shows independent art-house films from around the world—all in V.O., with Spanish subtitles. **Filmoteca** (Av. Sarrià 33, Metro: Hospial Clínic, tel. 93/410-7590) shows oldies-but-goodies such as *West Side Story* and *Casablanca* for less than €3 a ticket. **Cine Verdi** (C/ Verdi 32, Metro: Fontana or FCG:Gràcia, tel. 93/238-7990) offers five screens of new releases in V.O. Around the corner, its sister venue, **Verdi Park Cine** (C/ Torrijos 49, Metro: Fontana or FCG:Gràcia, tel. 93/238-7990), has an additional four screens. **Icaria-Yelmo Cineplex** (C/ Salvador Espriú 61, Metro: Ciutadella Vila Olímpica, tel. 93/221-7585) is located in the El Centre de la Vila mall and has 15 screens showing the latest releases in V.O.

Every July, an open-air cinema is set up in Montjuïc, **Sala M** (tel. 93/302-3553, www.salamontjuic.com), using one of the walls of the castle for the screen. The program includes film classics from Billy Wilder to Woody Allen, as well as international indie films. All are shown in V.O. and cost just €2. Pack a picnic and make a night of it.

Flamenco

At **Tablao Flamenco Cordobes** (La Rambla 35, Metro: Drassanes, tel. 93/317-5711, tablao@tablaocordobes.com, www.tablaocordobes.com, 7 P.M.–midnight daily, €60 for dinner and show, €30 show only, discounts for kids), you know you are not in Barcelona anymore when you reach the glass doors—

complete with silhouetted flamenco dancer handles. These give way to a spectacularly tiled entry reminiscent of a very stylized Andalucía. In the upper dining rooms, the opulence continues with Moorish arches, gold detailing, and lots of tiles. Despite a reputation as a bit of tourist trap, top dancers from the world of flamenco have performed here. Be sure to reserve ahead, tour groups often book this place solid. Dinners start at 7 P.M., 8:30 P.M., and 10 P.M. with shows starting at 8:15 P.M., 10 P.M., and 11:30 P.M. **Sala Tarantos** (Pl. Reial 17, Metro: Liceu, tel. 93/319-1789, 9 P.M.–midnight daily, €12–18) is much more low-key (well, once you get past the gaudy Gaudí-inspired entryway). The simple *tablao* offers three half-hour shows per night featuring up-and-coming flamenco talent. Shows are at 8:30, 9:30, and 10:30 P.M. Keep an eye out for discount flyers in bars and shops around the neighborhood and also look for an employee passing out discount coupons in the street outside, especially on slow weekdays. In Poble Espanyol, **Tablao de Carmen** (C/ Arcos 9, Metro: Espanya, tel. 93/325-6895, www.tablaodecarmen.com, closed Mon., €31 show only) is named for the great flamenco dancer Carmen Amaya, who made her debut on the grounds of this *tablao* in 1929. In this simple Andalusian-style room, passionate dancers and musicians perform six nights per week. The first show is at 7:45 P.M. and the second at 10 P.M. If you choose to dine, the price goes up to €59–83, depending on the selected menu. Reservations are suggested.

Opera and Classical Music

In addition to performances at Palau de la Música Catalana (see *Sights*), great music can be heard at many venues around town. Opera fans are in luck, as Barcelona's **Gran Teatre de Liceu** (Rambla 51–59, tel. 93/485-9913, www .liceubarcelona.com) is one of Europe's grandest opera houses. Seating nearly 3,000, it runs a lively schedule of operas from classics such as *Madame Butterfly* to family-friendly shows such as *Puss in Boots*. It also hosts classical orchestras and international ballet companies. During intermission, be sure to visit the opulent Salon of Mirrors. You can get tickets via the theater's website or by visiting the box office (2–8:30 P.M. Mon.–Fri.). The day of the show, if tickets are not sold out, those under 26 and over 65 can get seats at a substantial discount. For classical music, **L'Auditori de Barcelona** (C/ Lepant 150, Metro: Glòries or Marina, www.auditori .org, tel. 93/247-9300) is the massive, modern home of Barcelona's Symphony Orchestra. Tickets can be purchased on the website or at the ticket office (noon–9 P.M. Mon.–Sat.).

Theater and Musicals

Barcelona is home base for a handful of internationally renowned theater groups. Foremost among them is **La Fura dels Baus** (www.la fura.com). This energetic troupe creates intentionally provocative works that explode on stage in a blur of image, sound, text, music, and physicality. Always controversial, often funny, a performance by this group is a must if you are fan of avant-garde theater and if your Spanish is up to par. Another troupe to look out for is **El Tricicle**, a trio of comedians who perform in mime—clearing up the pesky problem of language. Barcelona also hosts theater festivals and events, large and small, the most esteemed of which is **Festival del Grec** (see *Festivals*). Regarding venues, **Teatre Lliure** (Pl. Margarida Xirgu 1, Metro: Espanya or Poble Sec, tel. 93/289-2770) is one of the most important in Cataluña. Founded in 1976, the theater is famous for its productions of contemporary dramas as well as the re-working of classic texts. The ticket office is open Monday–Friday 11 A.M.–3 P.M. and 4:30– 8 P.M., as well as one hour before shows. **Teatre Grec** (Pg. Santa Madrona 36, Metro: Espanya, tel. 93/316-1000) is an ancient Greek amphitheater—built in 1929. It goes into high gear during the Festival del Grec. **Teatre Romea** (C/ Hospital 51, Metro: Liceu, tel. 93/301-5504, www.teatreromea.com) is notable for its artistic director, Catalan Calixto Bieito. He is world-renowned for the heightened sense of drama and violence he imbues in productions from Shakespeare to Tennessee Williams. However, all productions are in Spanish.

BARCELONA

FESTIVALS

Barcelona loves to throw a party and festivals take place year-round. The tourist office or any of the free English-language magazines, such as *Barcelona Connect,* will have complete details. Online, check the Agenda section of www.barcelonaturisme.com. Official holidays, on which all but the largest of sights and restaurants close, include: January 1 and 6; Easter Friday and Monday; May 1; June 24; August 15; September 11 and 24; November 1; December 6, 8, and 25.

Spring

April 23 is celebrated as **La Diada de Sant Jordi** (Saint George's Day). Jordi is the patron saint of Cataluña and this is a public holiday. It coincides with World Book Day and the tradition is to give gifts of books and roses. It is estimated that book sales in Barcelona triple on this day. Late May or early June, **Festa dels Cors Corals** occurs in Barceloneta. Held in honor of Passover, the event consists of dozens of neighborhood *corals* (singing groups) taking to the streets of the barrio in outrageous homemade costumes. They are famous for being horrible singers and have the politically incorrect nickname *coro mudo* (deaf choir). Regardless, the party is a wild affair marked by good cheer, lots of drink, and a deafening fireworks display.

Summer

The night of June 23 is celebrated throughout Cataluña and Valencia as **Nit de Foc** (night of fire) in honor of Sant Joan (Saint John). Barcelona lets loose a barrage of fireworks, street parties, and bonfires on the beach. While people eat the traditional pastry *coca de Sant Joan,* the city undergoes an aural assault as every kid (young and not so) sets off firecrackers. The explosions usually begin a few days before the festivities and continue until the supply is exhausted. Bring earplugs—you will need them. Mid-June brings the **Sonar Festival** (www.sonar.es), a three-day celebration of "advanced music and multimedia arts." For technophiles worldwide that translates into a massive techno and electronic music festival. In addition to the official (and expensive) events held at MACBA, world-famous DJs—underground, mainstream, and legendary—play at clubs, private gigs, and even beaches all over town. Book this one early—it is hot. From the end of June to mid-August, the **Festival del Grec** (www.barcelonafestival.com) brings theater, music, and dance troupes from around the world to the city. Though the top acts perform to paying audiences at the Teatre Grec located in Montjuïc, there are dozens of free (or very cheap) performances all over the city. August brings the most traditional party of the year, **Festa de Gràcia.** The barrio of Gràcia busts out in full party regalia the last half of the month. In addition to all night revelry, food stalls, and live bands in the squares, the most distinctive part of the fiesta is the street-decorating competition. Streets are transformed into fairy forests, space landscapes, and colorful, magical gardens. The quality of the decor and the total transformation that occurs makes this one of the more delightful parties in Spain.

Fall

Barcelona's patron saint is celebrated the week of September 24 with the **Festa de la Merce.** In addition to the usual roster of Spanish fun—food booths, dancing in the streets, parades, and fireworks—this festival is known for its *correfocs.* These fire-breathing dragons wind their way through the streets on the last Saturday or Sunday of the festival armed with firecrackers. They are not afraid to use them to get through the crowds so wear long sleeves and get out of their way. Recent years have brought *castellers* to the Merce. Normally seen only in small Catalan villages, *castellers* are human towers created by several layers of men standing on each others' shoulders. Once built, a boy—as young as five years old—clambers to the top. When he descends, the tower starts to dismantle. A recent Barcelona castle reached a record 10 layers high. Catalan competitiveness means you can expect to see similar attempts at future festivals.

Winter

The city celebrates **Carnival** with two weeks of festivities that culminate in the kitschily named **Barnaval** parade on the last Saturday of the festivities. It features floats, costumed revelers, and dancing in the street. For real carnival decadence a la New Orleans or Río, head to Sitges

(see *Vicinity of Barcelona*). On Ash Wednesday, the **Burial of the Sardine** takes place in Barceloneta. An event popular throughout Spain, its origins go back to Franco's ban on Carnival festivities. Because funeral processions were allowed, party-minded Spaniards concocted the death of a sardine as cover for a parade.

Shopping

SHOPPING DISTRICTS

If you have a little shopping problem, Barcelona is going to show you no sympathy. Barcelona's tourism office has created a consortium of shops under the label **Barcelona Shopping Line**. A free map, available at the tourist office, includes details on hundreds of shops. Better yet, hop their bright blue **Bus Shopping Line** (Pl. Catalunya, runs 7:30 A.M.–9:45 P.M. daily), also called by the unlikely name of **Tomb**. It travels a route past the city's top shops and malls. When shopping, remember to request tax-free forms whenever you spend over €90.15. (See *Money* in *Essentials* for more information about recouping your sales tax.) Also keep in mind that despite Barcelona's reputation as a worldly capital of culture, it still succumbs to old-world Spanish hours. Though there are more and more exceptions, particularly in touristy areas, shopping hours are 10 A.M.–2 P.M. and 5–8 P.M. and most stores close Saturday P.M. and all day Sunday.

Ciutat Vella

In Ciutat Vella, the oldest part of Barcelona comprising Las Ramblas, Barri Gòtic, El Born, and Raval, shopping runs from the kitsch to the cutting-edge. Shopping on Las Ramblas itself is pretty limited to souvenirs, newsstands, and those famous live-bird stalls. However, there are trendy designer shops selling clothes and household goods tucked all around the side streets, just keep your eyes peeled. A good mall in this area is **El Triangulo** (C/ Pelai 39, Metro: Catalunya, tel. 93/318-0108, www .triangle.es, 10 A.M.–10 P.M. Mon–Sat., closed

Sun.) on the southwestern edge of Plaça de Catalunya. It houses the music/books/electronics mega-store **FNAC,** a handful of trendy fashion chains, including everyone's favorite Spanish shoe store, Camper, and an absolutely magnificent Sephora perfumery, complete with its own fashion runway. On the other side of the plaza, **El Corte Inglés** (www.elcorte ingles.es, 9 A.M.–8 P.M. daily) looms large as both an orientating landmark and a one-stop shopping mecca. From designer duds to Barça jerseys, maps to stamps, imported cheese to Q-tips, El Corte Inglés has it all. At the opposite end of Las Ramblas, beyond Columbus and the wooden Rambla del Mar footbridge is **Maremagnum** (tel. 93/225-8100, www.mare magnum.es, 11 A.M.–11 P.M. daily). Looking for all the world like a shopping arcade in an airport, this mall has a handful of clothing shops aimed at the under-20 buns-of-steel set, a few upscale souvenir shops, and several restaurants and clubs that stay open until the wee hours with canned Euro-pop and overpriced drinks. Avoid it.

Barri Gòtic is home to the bustling shoppers alley of **Avinguda Portal de l'Ángel,** which runs from Plaça de Catalunya to the cathedral. It is jammed with mid-priced clothing and shoe stores, including the two Spanish chains that are slowly dressing the 30-somethings of the world—Zara and Mango. A bit less commercial is **Carrer de la Portaferrissa,** which is a hive of boutiques with a serious bohemian air.

Where shopping really gets interesting is El Born. Here artists and designers have set up dozens of shops that transcend trendy. Privately owned boutiques sell clothing, jewelry, shoes, housewares, candles, accessories, and art that appeal to all tastes but just one pocketbook—thick! Across Las Ramblas, in Raval there are more artist-run boutiques, though the edge here is harsher and the styles more urban.

Montjuïc

Montjuïc is home to one of the city's most lavish malls, **Gran Vía 2** (Gran Vía 75, Metro: Espanya, tel. 90/230-1444, 10 A.M.–10 P.M. Mon.–Sat., closed Sun.), with inlaid marble walkways, mammoth chandeliers, and hundreds of shops and cafés. There is also a very large Carrefour grocery store. **Las Arenas** (Plaça de Espanya, s/n) is a new leisure center and mall currently being built in Las Arenas, Barcelona's once-bustling bullring, built in 1900. The last fight at Las Arenas took place in 1977 and with Cataluña's subsequent ban on bullfighting, this once-proud red-brick structure was crumbling into decrepit disuse. As almost all travelers from Barcelona's airport to the center pass by this plaza, something had to be done. Cue Richard Rogers, the British architectural superstar. Along with a team of Catalan architects, his group has begun revamping the bullring. When it is complete (possibly by 2007) it will house dozen of shops and restaurants. At the center of the ring—where proud matadors once faced charging bulls—will be a tranquil garden. **Poble Espanyol** features a village of over 40 artisans producing everything from lifelike puppets to silver jewelry.

Eixample

The broad, busy **Passeig de Gràcia,** home to two of Gaudí's most-beloved buildings—the Casa Battló and La Pedrera—is also a bustling shopping spot. There are mainstream shops like Diesel and Tommy Hilfiger, haute haunts like Cartier and Loewe, and mass-market pleasers like Zara. There is also an upscale mall, **Bulevard Rosa** (Paseo de Gràcia 51, Metro: Pg. Gràcia, tel. 93/215-8331, 10:30 A.M.–9 P.M. Mon.–Sat., closed Sun.), with more than 100 shops. The other main shopping road in Eix-

ample is **Avinguda Diagonal,** particularly between the Passeig de Gràcia and Plaça María Cristina. This is where you will find your very exclusive, high-end shops—the kind that have top-hatted doormen and free parking lanes for chauffeured cars. An excellent mall in this area is the monolithic **L'illa Diagonal** (Av. Diagonal 545, Metro: María Cristina, tel. 93/444-0000, 10 A.M.–9:30 P.M. Mon.–Sat., closed Sun.) with hundreds of shops from tony to trendy.

TYPICALLY SPANISH SHOPS
Accessories

An embroidered shawl is required wear for weddings, funerals, and all the high-brow events in between. No self-respecting *señora* would have less than two in her closet. Pick one up at Barcelona's most famous purveyor, **Rafa Teja Atelier** (C/ Santa María 18, Metro: Jaume I, tel. 93/310-2785, 11 A.M.–9 P.M. Mon.–Sat., noon–3 P.M. Sun.). If you want to go all out in traditional Spanish wear, try **Flora Albaicín** (C/ Canuda 3, Metro: Catalunya, tel. 93/302-1035, 10:30 A.M.–1 P.M. and 5–8 P.M. Mon.–Sat., closed Sun.). This tiny shop dresses flamenco dancers in frills, ruffles, and lots of polka dots. Prices start around €200, but if you just want a little flamenco bling, go for a head comb or set of brightly colored bangles—*ole!*

Espadrilles

In recent years, espadrilles have landed on catwalks and among the footwear offerings of designers from Tommy Hilfiger to Ralph Lauren, but if you want the real deal, you'll have to visit an *alpargatera*—an espadrille shop. The name derives from *alpargata,* the rope-like material used for the soles of these comfy shoes. Slip into a pair or two (at €8, why not?) at **La Manual Alpargatera** (C/ Avinyó 7, Metro: Liceu, tel. 93/301-0172, 9:30 A.M.–1:30 P.M. and 4:30–8:30 P.M. Mon.–Fri.). Opened in 1941, this old-fashioned shop is lined with well-worn wooden benches and creaky ceiling-high shelves jammed with colorful espadrilles. The smell of fresh rope is intoxicating. In the workshop out back you can make out a staff of master espadrille-makers cutting and seaming made-to-order shoes. Choose from a variety of fun styles or just stick to the tried-and-classic slip-on.

Housewares

One of the most famous shops in Barcelona, **Vincon** (Pg. Gràcia 96, Metro: Diagonal, tel. 93/215-6050, www.vincon.com, 10 A.M.–8:30 P.M. Mon.–Sat.), founded in 1934, was one of the first shops to bring contemporary house ware designs to the general public. It evolved into a haven of hip over the decades and in the years just after Franco's death, before nightclub culture really took off, this was the place to go to pick up a date. Today, it is the place to see the latest in functional design, though you might have little need for an €8 egg holder or a gigantic glowing flowerpot. For something more traditional, think ceramics. A good place to stock up is **Art Escudellers** (C/ Escudellars 23, Metro: Liceu, tel. 93/412-6801, 11 A.M.–11 P.M. daily), a warehouse of ceramics from all over Spain. Upstairs, you'll find the usual suspects—plates, water pitchers, and tiles—downstairs there are more arty pieces, plus a small café and wine cellar.

Jewelry

Founded in 1839, **Bagués-Masriera** (La Rambla 105, Metro: Liceu, tel. 93/481-7050, 10:30 A.M.–2:30 P.M. and 4:30–8 P.M. Mon.–Fri., 11 A.M.–2 P.M. Sat.) creates exquisite *modernisme* jewelry using original designs from Lluís Masriera, a jewelry designer working at the turn of the 20th century. This elegant shop has developed a following among royalty and celebrities. You will not find designs like this anywhere else in the world, so if you have been thinking of splurging on a piece of jewelry, now is the time.

CIGARS, FOOD, AND WINE
Cigars

Gimeno (La Rambla 100, Metro: Liceu, tel. 93/318-4947, 9:30 A.M.–8 P.M. Mon.–Sat., closed Sun.) has been selling the world's best tobacco to discriminating Barcelonans since 1920. This is the place to stock up on your Cu-bans—just be sure and smoke them before you return to the United States, where the cigars are still banned. The shop recently inaugurated the El Rincón del Gourmet, a section of the store dedicated to not only the finest cigars, but also excellent wines and liqueurs.

Olive Oil

Olisoliva (Mercat de Sant Caterina, Av. Francesc Cambó, s/n, Metro: Jaume I, tel. 93/268-1472, 9 A.M.–2 P.M. Mon., 9 A.M.–3:30 P.M. Tues. and Wed., 9 A.M.–8:30 P.M. Thurs. and Fri.) specializes in extra-virgin olive oil from throughout Spain, with an emphasis on the delicate, almost floral oils of Cataluña. (See sidebar, *Liquid Gold,* in the *Andalucía* chapter.)

Savories

Opened in 1851, the friendly, family-run **Casa Gispert** (C/ Sombrerers 23, Metro: Jaume I, tel. 93/319-7547, www.casagispert.com, 9:30 A.M.–2 P.M. and 4–7:30 P.M. Tues.–Fri., 10 A.M.–2 P.M. and 5–8 P.M. Sat.) feels like an old country store with its long butcherblock counter, bushels of fresh-roasted nuts, and wooden shelves bowing under with herb-infused honey, dried peppers, jarred saffron, olive oils, aged vinegars, teas, coffees, and chocolates. If you are lucky, you'll arrive as they are roasting nuts in the antique, hand-turned oven out back.

Sweets

Chocolate (*xocolat* in Catalan) is a local addiction and you'll find specialty chocolate shops all over town. The lovely, old-fashioned **Fargas** (C/ Pi 16, Metro: Liceu, tel. 93/320-0342, 10 A.M.–2 P.M. and 5–8 P.M. Mon.–Sat., closed Sun.) has been selling exquisite chocolates and candies since 1827. It is a point of pilgrimage for locals during Easter when the lines can snake out of the door. **Xocoa** (C/ Carme 3, Metro: Liceu, tel. 93/304-2360, 10 A.M.–9 P.M. daily) is a very modern chocolate shop in a lovely art nouveau storefront built in 1890. Just off Las Ramblas, this is one very sweet detour you'll want to make. **Cacao Sampaka** (C/ Consell de Cent 292, tel. 93/272-0833, Metro: Pg. Gràcia, 10 A.M.–10 P.M. Mon.–Sat., closed

Sun.) is the Prada of chocolate—sleek, stylish, and sinfully expensive. Chocolate here might be paired with candied violets or dusted with exotic spices, or hail from Papua New Guinea, Venezuela, or Madagascar. Visit their tasting room in the back of the shop.

Looking more like a trendy jewelry store than a candy shop, **Pappabubble** (C/ Ample 28, tel. 93/268-8625, 11 A.M.–2 P.M. and 5–8:30 P.M. Mon.–Sat.) is actually a sleek laboratory of taste where a couple of Australian expats create their own brand of hard candies. Around 30 flavors are available at any time—from fiery cinnamon to tart lime to seasonal treats like coconut in summer or honey-anise in winter. Prices start at €5.50 for a 200-gram bag.

Wine

Located in the savory shadow of the Mercat de la Boqueria, the picturesque **El Celler de la Boqueria** (tel. 93/301-9427, Metro: Liceu, 8 A.M.–8 P.M. Mon.–Sat., closed Sun.) is filled—from its creaky wood floors to its dusky ceiling—with wines from all over Spain, including an impressive selection of Catalan vintages. With thousands of wines from Spain and beyond, the modern, spacious **Lavinia** (Av. Diagonal 605, Metro: María Cristina, tel. 93/363-4445, 10 A.M.–9 P.M. Mon.–Sat., closed Sun.) is Spain's premier wine shop and one of Europe's largest. With hundreds of bottles of Spanish sparkling wine in stock, the folks at **Xampany** (C/ Valencia 200, Metro: Hospital Clínic, tel. 93/453-9338, 10 A.M.–2 P.M. and 4:30–9 P.M. Mon.–Fri., 10 A.M.–2 P.M. Sat., closed Sun.) are Barcelona's *cava* experts.

ENGLISH-LANGUAGE BOOKS

Hibernian Book Shop (C/ Montseny 17, Metro: Fontana, tel. 93/217-4796, www.hibernianbooks.com, 4–8:30 P.M. Mon., 10:30 A.M.–8:30 P.M. Tues.–Sat., closed Sun.) is a cozy secondhand English bookstore. There are over 30,000 titles on hand and a few cozy chairs where you can slip back and peruse a few. **Elephant Bookshop** (C/ Creu de Molers 12, Metro: Paral.lel, tel. 93/443-0594, www.lfant.biz, 10 A.M.–8 P.M. daily) started out selling only new books, but has since expanded to have a very good secondhand selection.

FLEA MARKETS

Barcelona's largest flea market, **Els Encants Vells** (C/ Dos de Maig 186, Metro: Glories, 9 A.M.–6 P.M. Mon., Wed., Fri., and Sat.), is a riot of color and action. With over 500 stalls vying for your attention, you may actually get very little shopping done. Bargains are to be found, especially on silver jewelry and used leather jackets. The funky little **Mercat de la Barceloneta** (Pl. Font 12, Metro: Barceloneta, 10 A.M.–3 P.M. Mon.–Sat., closed Sun.) is a treasure trove of junk and jewels and a perfect place to get a feel for this quaint barrio. **Plaça de Sant Josep Oriol** converts into an artists' flea market every Saturday 10 A.M.–3 P.M. Some of the work is very good and the prices are surprisingly reasonable.

SPANISH FASHION
Chains

On the cheap-and-chic end of things, **Zara** (10 A.M.–9 P.M. Mon.–Sat., closed Sun.) with locations everywhere, is the place to stock up on Euro fashions on a budget. One of their largest stores sits at the mouth of the Passeig de Gràcia subway stop. The chain runs a discount shop called **Lefties** (Moll de Espanya, s/n, tel. 93/225-8572, 10 A.M.–8 P.M. Mon.–Sat., closed Sun.) where you can find major bargains. Just be careful, they are not opposed to putting items with permanent stains, ripped zippers, and irreparable holes onto the shelves. Both of these stores stock menswear as well as women's. The other outfitter of choice for Spain's fashion-conscious budget watchers—female only—is **Mango,** also with locations all over town. One of the biggest (Pg. Gràcia 65, Metro: Pg. Gràcia, tel. 93/215-7530, 10 A.M.–9 P.M. Mon.–Sat., closed Sun.) is a good place to kick off a shopping spree.

Designer Shops

Barcelona is right up there with Paris and Milan for its fashion-forward design. Most haute shops are located in Eixample, while the funkier up-and-comers hawk their wares in Raval and Gràcia. (See sidebar, *Spanish Style from A to Z*, in the *Madrid* chapter.)

The undisputed king of Catalan fashion design is Antonio Miró. His original shop, opened in 1967, **Groc** (Rambla Catalunya 100, Metro: Catalunya, tel. 93/215-7778, 10 A.M.–2 P.M. and 4:30–8:30 P.M. Mon.–Sat., closed Sun.) is where he made his name, creating avant-garde fashions for 1970s and 1980s trendsetters. Run by his family, Groc is still the place to go for Miró's fashion-forward designs as well as a sampling of pieces by other top designers. At his eponymous **Antonio Miró** (C/ Consell de Cent 349, Metro: Pg. Gràcia, tel. 93/487-0670, call for appointment), find impeccably tailored suits and immensely wearable casual wear for men and women. Another fashion legend, Catalan designer **Josep Font** (C/ Provença 30, Metro: Pg. Gràcia, tel. 93/487-2110, 10:30 A.M.–8 P.M. Mon.–Sat., closed Sun.) is famed for his exquisite fabrics and attention to detail. His women's fashions are classic with just a touch of modernity. For luscious women's wear, visit the shop of **Lydia Delgado** (C/ Minerva 21, Metro: Diagonal, tel. 93/415-9998, www.lydiadelgado.es, 10 A.M.–2 P.M. 4:30–8:30 P.M. Mon.–Sat., closed Sun.). Her pieces are feminine without being saccharine and her fabrics are simply luxurious. Darlings of the jet-set who prefer to look jetlagged head straight to **Custo Barcelona** (Pl. Olles 7, Metro: Barceloneta, tel. 93/268-7893, 10 A.M.–10 P.M.

Mon.–Sat., closed Sun.). The super-label got its start in Barcelona and runs operations out of its flagship store in El Born. **SO_DA** (C/ Avinyó 24, Metro: Jaume I, tel. 93/342-4529, 10 A.M.–8 P.M. Mon.–Sat., closed Sun.) sells the sleekest clothes in town—and quite possibly in all of Spain. Prices are dangerously high, but at least you won't catch anyone else wearing your purchase. Come evening, console your overspent budget with a drink at the bar that opens up after the boutique closes down. For leather goods, the only place to go is the world-famous Spanish purveyor of luxury, **Loewe** (Pg. Gràcia 35, Metro: Pg. Gràcia, tel. 93/216-0400, by appointment). Housed in a spectacular *modernisme* building designed by Lluís Domènech i Montaner, this is quite likely the only Loewe shop where the setting competes with the buttery soft handbags.

If your wallet is starting to protest, but your heart wants more, Barcelona has a couple of great discount designer shops. **Contribuciones y Moda** (C/ Riera Sant Miquel 30, Metro: Diagonal, tel. 93/218-7140, 11 A.M.–2 P.M. and 5–9 P.M., Mon.–Fri., 11 A.M.–2 P.M. Sat., closed Sun.), just inside the Gràcia district, offers deeply discounted clothes from labels like Cacharel and Comme des Garçons. **Stockland** (C/ Comtal 22, Metro: Urquinaona, tel. 93/318-0331, 10 A.M.–8:30 P.M. Mon.–Sat., closed Sun.) offers last-of-the-season pieces by top Spanish designers. For something fancy, head upstairs to the party-gown room.

Sports and Recreation

To many people around the world, Barcelona is synonymous with *fútbol* (soccer). The red-and-blue striped jerseys of FC Barcelona, the city's top-ranked team, are the most popular souvenir item in town. You'll see hordes of European and Latin American kids decked out in them all over Las Ramblas.

Barcelona also boasts many other recreational activities. In addition to the Gaudí wonderland of Parc Güell and the historical

park of Ciutadella (see *Sights*), Barcelona has several parks worth a detour. It also has over 3.2 kilometers (two miles) of sandy beaches. Granted, they are man-made, created as part of the 1992 Olympics makeover and each year they have to be re-filled as the sand washes away, but how many other major European cities can boast such lovely Mediterranean beaches just a quick subway ride away?

However, if you want to witness the spectacle

that so enamored Hemingway and that later became synonymous with Spain for so many tourists—bullfighting—you'll have to go elsewhere. In 2004, Barcelona became the first Spanish city to ban bullfighting. In 2006, Cataluña classified the sport under the category of animal cruelty—effectively banning it throughout the region. Though the government claims that the measure represents the opinion of the majority of Catalans, cynics point out that the move was yet another in a series to assert Catalan independence from Madrid, where bullfighting is revered. Barcelona's oldest ring, Las Arenas, has been transformed into a shopping and leisure center.

BEACHES

While Barcelona's beach waters are not the clearest, they are perfectly safe for swimming. Keep an eye out for the colored flags indicating water conditions. Green means calm seas. Yellow indicates rough waters and demands caution. Red means the sea is too dangerous and swimming is forbidden. Also listen for a call over the loudspeaker of *medusas* (jellyfish). They tend to arrive in shoals and it is advised that you get out of the water until they are gone. Their stings are very painful.

In addition to swimming and sunbathing, Barcelona's beaches are famous for their **chiringuitos,** beachside bars that may be no more than a shack in the sand or a full-on restaurant serving seafood and sandwiches. In all, you'll find drinks from coffee to wine and you can get most things to go to take with you onto the beach. Many, particularly around those along Bogatell and Mar Bella, sponsor all-day/all-night dance parties with DJs spinning the latest in techno music. Officially, they have to close at 1 A.M., though the four closest to the city on Barceloneta shut down at midnight. However, not everyone goes home. Many people bring their own drinks and hang out until the wee hours. Even more common, after the clubs shut down at 6 A.M., there are often impromptu after-parties that spring up and go strong until the sun is too hot to bear.

While catching your rays by day, keep an eye

TRY TRASH-CAN THERAPY: THROW YOUR TRASH IN THE CAN. YOU'LL FEEL BETTER.

Barcelona takes a light-hearted approach to keeping the beaches clean.

© CANDY LEE LABALLE

out for **Bambolino,** the donut man. He usually crawls the beaches barefoot, a tray of donuts balanced on his head.

Of course safety can not be overlooked. Do not leave any belongings unattended to go swimming. Use one of the locker facilities or better yet, bring nothing. Your towels, books, and shoes will more than likely be left alone, but any bags will be rifled through or outright stolen. And don't sleep on the beach. Many a drunken tourist has decided to sleep it off on the beach only to wake up and find their pockets emptied. Do not be one of the victims. Regarding medical safety, don't forget your sunscreen. The Mediterranean sun can be vicious, even on a hazy day. Don't ruin your vacation with a painful sunburn.

The closest beach to the city center is **Barceloneta** (Metro: Barceloneta). It is also the most crowded. The average age of beach-goers hovers around 20 and a haze of Spring Break–style debauchery hovers over the area. There is long boardwalk along the beach that goes as far as Port Olímpic. About midway down is the **Poliesportiu Maríti** (9 A.M.–7:30 P.M. daily), a facility with showers and lockers where you can also get your beach ball inflated. **Sant Sebastía** and **Sant Miguel** are the two smaller beaches to the right of Barceloneta. They border Port Vell and are decidedly calmer—and less attractive—than Barceloneta. This is a good place to watch the massive cruise ships pull into the port. **Nova Icària** (Metro: Ciutadella Vila Olímpica) is a popular slip of sand bordering the shops and restaurants of Port Olímpic. It has the usual beach amenities from lifeguards to ice-cream hawkers and is popular with families. The next beach down is **Bogatell** (Metro: Llacuna). It is a long stretch of sand with volleyball nets, deck chairs, and a *chiringuito* that can get quite thumping at night with DJs spinning the latest in techno music. The farthest beaches on the stretch of Barcelona's coast are **Mar Bella** and **Nova Mar Bella** (Metro: Poblenou or Selva de Mar). These are some of the most peaceful beaches in the city. They are also the unofficial nudist beaches, however most days the clothed bathers outnumber the unclothed.

BIKING

The cyclist can take advantage of over 97 kilometers (60 miles) of bike lanes in Barcelona. If you are a novice biker, stick to one of the established lanes. A map can be downloaded from www.bcn.es/bicicleta/pdf/mapabici.pdf. The main lane is along Avinguda Diagonal and it is very popular, especially on weekdays with local two-wheeled commuters. On the weekend, it can be a pleasant way to see the city—with the added bonus of dozens of sidewalk cafés, perfect for a mid-ride snack. The city allows bikes to be taken on the subway, just not during rush hours. The bike transport hours are 5–6:30 A.M., 9:30 A.M.–4:30 P.M., and 8:30 P.M. until closing Monday–Friday. On weekends and public holidays, as well as during all of July and August, you can travel on the subway with your bike all day. Remember to carry your bike to the end of the carriage and on Line 2 (the purple line), there are special areas for bikes. You can take a bike on the Montjuïc funicular anytime.

Cussons Hansmann (Av. Príncep d'Astúries 21, Metro: Fontana, tel. 93/217-2354 or 60/699-7659, jaume@cussons-hansmann .com, www.cussons-hansmann.com), run by the charming Jaume Cussons, offers biking (and walking and mini-van) tours of the city and surroundings. The emphasis is on culture and the guests tend to be well traveled and enthusiastic about discovering Barcelona. Bike tours (€35) depart at 9:30 A.M. and 3:30 P.M. Tuesday–Sunday and last about four hours, including a tapas stop—bikes, maps, insurance, and lots of laughs are included. Reservations are required. **Fat Tire Bike Tour** (C/ Escudellers 48, Metro: Drassanes, tel. 93/301-3612, www .fattirebiketoursbarcelona.com, 10 A.M.–7 P.M. daily) offers tours (€22) every day in the summer at 11:30 A.M., 4:30 P.M., and 7 P.M. The rest of the year, tours are at noon. Tours leave from Plaça Sant Jaume on the Carrer Ferran side. No need to reserve, just show up in the plaza and look for the guide in the Fat Tire T-shirt. These popular tours are led by young bilingual guides who are a whole lot of fun, but the tour can get crowded. If you would rather go on your own, you can rent bikes at the shop for €7 for three hours. A full day runs €15. **Barna Bikes** (C/ Pas de Sota La Muralla 3, Metro: Barceloneta, tel. 93/269-0204, www.barnabike.com, 10 A.M.–9:30 P.M. daily) is your one-stop rental shop for all things on wheels— bikes, electric bikes, tandems, go-karts, electric skateboards, even the Trikkn-6, an odd-looking triangular scooter (you'll see them cruising the boardwalk between the ports). They also offer bike tours, including a very cool nighttime ride. Reservations required.

PARKS

Tibidabo, located on the mount of the same name at the northern edge of Barcelona, offers the most breathtaking views of the city. The best way to access Tibidabo is via funicular. Take the commuter train L7 to FCG:Av. Tibidabo. Exit and catch the Tramvía Blau, a cable car that takes you to the base of the funicular. The tram/funicular combo runs 10 A.M.–6 P.M. daily and costs €3.50 roundtrip. Both the tram and the funicular were built in the late 19th century during Barcelona's golden age of public works. They also can get quite crowded. If you are hearty, you might take the funicular up and then walk down the mountain. At the top of the funicular is the **Tibidabo Parc d'Atracciones** (tel. 93/211-7942, www.tibidabo.es, €22, kids €11). This is Spain's oldest amusement park and it offers blend of nostalgia—antique plane rides, elaborate merry-go-rounds—as well as modern adrenaline rushes; see the brand new El Pèndol, which flings riders into a 125-foot drop. Hours vary wildly, though in summer it is usually open noon–11 P.M. Check the website to be sure. Also on Tibidabo is **Temple de Sagrat Cor,** a rather kitschy temple with a commanding view over the city. For an even more elevated view of the city, head up the **Torre de Collserola** (tel. 93/406-9354, 11 A.M.–2:30 P.M. and 3:30–7 P.M. Wed.–Sun., closed Mon. and Tues., €5.20, kids free). Built for the 1992 Olympics by British architect Norman Foster, the unique tower—secured by guy lines to the ground—serves mainly as a television and radio transmitter, but the 10th floor is open to visitors.

Located on Montjuïc, a few minutes walk from the Estadi Olímpic, **Jardí Botánic** (C/ Dr. Font i Quer 2, Metro: Espanya, tel. 93/426-4935, www.jardibotanic.bcn.es, 10 A.M.–8 P.M. daily summer, reduced winter hours, €3) is a park within a park. It houses a collection of over 2,000 species of plants from world regions climatically similar to Barcelona. A curious fact to think about as you walk through admiring the flora is that the gardens are built upon an old landfill, giving every dump around the world some hope.

SOCCER

The *fútbol* (soccer) season runs September– May and most Sundays there are games. If you can't get to a match while in town, pop into any corner bar with a television and join in the local fun. A good spot is **Jai-Ca** in Barceloneta (see *Food),* it's the home of an official Barcelona fan club.

FC Barcelona (www.fcbarcelona.com) got their start in 1899 and has since become a Catalan institution. Nicknamed Barça, the team has earned the motto *"més que un club"* ("more than a club"). There are nearly 150,000 fans signed up as *socios* (members) of Barça and around 1,800 fan clubs worldwide. Barça has been a member of the 1st division of La Liga (the Spanish soccer league) since its founding in 1928. The team scored league championships that first year and has repeated the victory 17 times, including the 2005–2006 season. They have also won the UEFA Champions league twice, most recently in 2006, and four European Winner Cups. Barça players are world superstars and during 2006 embarked on a sell-out tour of the United States.

If Barça is playing in town, try and get tickets by visiting the box office of their home base, the 100,000-seat **Camp Nou** (Av. Arístides Maillol, s/n, tel. 90/218-9900, 9 A.M.–1:30 P.M. and 3–6 P.M. Mon.–Thurs., 9 A.M.–2:30 Fri., 9 A.M.–1:30 P.M. Sat.). For more information on the team and getting tickets, visit the English-language fan site, www.fcbes.com. If you can't make a game, visit the **FC Barcelona Museum** (Camp Nou, tel. 93/496-3600, 10 A.M.–6:30 P.M. Mon.–Sat., 10 A.M.–2 P.M. Sun., €11) for a tour that includes the chance to sit in the players' box, visit the changing rooms, and walk out onto the field. Rumor has it that the museum is even more popular than La Sagrada Família, so expect crowds. Also, if you or your kids are really big fans, bring money to burn. The attached souvenir shop has everything from official jerseys to framed posters to bags of Barça chips.

Barcelona's second team, **RCD Espanyol** (www.rcdespanyol.com), plays at the 56,000-seat Estadi Lluís Companys—the former 1992 Olympic stadium. Despite disappearing in the shadow of their superstar brethren at Barça, they are the sixth-most successful soccer team in Spain.

Accommodations

LAS RAMBLAS
Staying on Las Ramblas evokes one of two reactions—love it or loathe it. Some people find the bustling mass of humanity that jams Las Ramblas day and night invigorating; others find it just plain tawdry. You'll have to decide for yourself.

Under €50
Hostal Maritima (La Rambla 4, tel. 93/302-3152, Metro: Drassanes, €40) is about as cheap as it gets around here—without being downright scary. Rooms are very basic, if shabby, and very noisy. But the location, right near the metro stop, is perfect and backpackers love the washing machine and luggage storage. **Hostal Residencia Rembrandt** (C/ Puertaferrisa, 23, Metro: Liceu, tel. 93/318-1011, info@hostalrembrandt.com, www.hostalrembrandt.com, €50) is a dirt-cheap place with amenities like maid service and a lovely tiled courtyard where the breakfasts are sometimes served. Bathrooms are shared and the staff is not the friendliest, but you can't complain at these prices. If you want an en-suite bath, the price rises to €65.

€50-100
Located at the top of Las Ramblas, the best thing **Hotel Lloret** (Rambla Canaletes 125, Metro: Catalunya, tel. 93/317-3366, info@hlloret.com, www.hlloret.com, €75) has going for it is location. Rooms are small and uninspired, but well maintained and clean. If you get one on Las Ramblas, the people-watching from the balcony is superb, but sleeping could be a problem—bring earplugs. There is Wi-Fi if you need it and a large salon where you can kick back on a sofa and plan your day. The owners also run **Barcelona Accommodations** (Rambla Canaletes 125, tel. 93/317-8356, info@bcn-accommodation.com, www.bcn-accommodation.com, €90), a group of fully equipped apartments for rent by the day. They are located on Las Ramblas on Carrer Tallers. There is no room service or cleaning during your visit (though you will be assessed a €30 fee for cleaning after your departure), however the freedom of your own apartment with kitchen is worth it. **Hotel Roma Reial** (Pl. Reial 11, tel. 93/302-0366, info@hotel-romareial.com, www.hotel-romareial.com, €70) is a cheap and cheerful spot right on the bustling Plaça Reial. If you get a room with a balcony overlooking the plaza, it will be noisy, but you'll be entertained day and night. Rooms are clean and the staff is friendly, but be aware that this hotel is popular with often-rowdy school groups. At the southern end of Las Ramblas, **Hotel Cuatro Naciones** (La Rambla 40, tel. 93/317-3624, www.h4n.com, €85) is a little past its prime, but rooms are clean and the black-and-white tiled lobby is a throwback to another era. Its walls are covered with illustrious patrons who stayed here, from Albert Einstein to Buffalo Bill. There is also free Wi-Fi.

BARCELONA

€100-200

If you are traveling with a family or in a small group, consider renting an apartment at **Citadines Ramblas** (La Rambla 122, tel. 90/220-0699, Metro: Liceu, info@citadines.com, www.citadines.com, €136–240). These fully furnished studio and one-bedroom apartments sleep up to four at a fraction of the cost of four-star hotel. They are decorated in pale, outdated shades of turquoise and orange, but they are very comfortable. There is a grocery store across the street where you can stock the fridge. **Hotel Royal** (La Rambla 117, tel. 93/301-9400, hotelroyal@hroyal.com, www.hroyal.com, €135) is an excellent hotel right in the heart of things. If you splurge for a designer suite, you'll have sound-proofed windows opening up over Las Ramblas and a chic modern room that is black, gray, and blonde wood all over. You'll also have access to a private salon with unlimited free soft drinks, *cava,* and chocolates. The attached La Poma restaurant serves excellent grilled meats and fresh pizzas, but skip the overpriced breakfast buffet. **Olivia Plaza** (Pl. Catalunya 19, Metro: Catalunya, tel. 93/316-8700, info@oliviaplazahotel.com, www.oliviaplazahotel.com, €129) is an absolutely gorgeous hotel for the money. The rooms are smart and contemporary with nice touches like Wi-Fi and double-head showers. The staff is extremely attentive and the public rooms are comfortable and chic. Request an upper floor for a view over bustling Plaza Catalunya.

Over €200

Hotel 1898 (La Rambla 109, tel. 93/552-9552, 1898@nnhotels.es, www.nnhotels.es, €250) is an oasis of tranquility and elegance right in the heart of Las Ramblas. Built in a tobacco factory from the 19th century, the hotel retains an upscale colonial air with a spectacular lobby full of leather sofas, thick-striped walls, and evocative black-and-white photography. The rooms are spacious and feature top amenities like plasma TVs, high-end toiletries, bathrobes, and slippers. There is even a menu of special pillows that you can order from reception. After a tiring day of sightseeing, relax in the basement sauna and whirlpool or head up to the rooftop pool for a cool dip under the stars.

EL RAVAL

If you want to be in the artiest, grittiest, most bohemian part of town, El Raval is where to head. Just be aware that this is still a neighborhood on the cusp. Gentrification has stretched out its tendrils, but has yet to take root. Alongside the trendy bars, innovative restaurants, and funky shops/art galleries, you'll still have to contend with prostitutes, pimps, and pushers. It is a good choice if you are young, hip, and streetwise, less so if you are not. Hotels run in the mid- to upper range here. The five-star places haven't moved in yet, and believe me, you don't want to stay at a cheapie in this barrio.

€50-100

◖ **Gat Xino** (C/ Hospital 149–155, Metro: Liceu, tel. 93/324-8833, hostalgatraval@gataccommodation.com, www.gataccommodation.com, €74) is a new boutique hotel dedicated to providing style and value. The sparkling white rooms are enhanced with apple-green walls and graffiti wall lamps. However, they are small and the free Wi-Fi is intermittent depending on your room location. The free breakfast is a standard European spread of pastries, cereal, coffee, and juice, but the dining room is too small to suit the hotel when full. Their sister location, **Gat Raval** (C/ Joaquín Costa 44, Metro: Universitat, tel. 93/481-6670, hostalgatraval@gataccommodation.com, €75), is nearly identical, but if you are willing to share a bath, you can drop the price by about €10 per night. Despite minor complaints, both properties are a happy stylish change from most of the dreary dorms in this price range.

€100-200

In the northern reaches of El Raval, **Hotel Mesón Castilla** (C/ Valdoncella 5, Metro: Universitat, hmesoncastilla@teleline.es, www.husa.es, €125) is a charming, old-fashioned hotel aptly run by the Husa chain. Decor is medieval Castilian and the rooms are surprisingly spacious. In warmer months, enjoy breakfast in the lovely gardened courtyard. **Hotel Abba Rambla** (Rambla del Raval 4, tel. 93/505-5400, rambla@abbahoteles.com, www.abba hoteles.com, €120) was the first major hotel to be built on the tree-lined Rambla del Raval and it is still the most stylish. Its 49 rooms feature comfortable modern decor, parquet floors, plasma televisions, and lovely toiletries. Request one that looks over the Rambla. Just a block off Las Ramblas into Raval, **Hotel Gaudí** (C/ Nou de la Rambla 12, Metro: Drassanes, tel. 93/317-9032, gaudi@hotelgaudi.es, www .hotelgaudi.es, €140) takes its design inspiration from the architectural maestro himself with a wavy, tiled pond in the lobby pond bursting with faux-Gaudí chimneys. The rooms don't have such whimsy and are quite plain, with a decor somewhere between bland and geriatric. Your best bet is to request a room on the street high up enough to look out over the real Gaudí work on the Palau Güell across the street.

Over €200
You've bought the shoes, now tuck them under the bed at the house that Camper built! Owned by the super Spanish shoe brand, **Casa Camper** (C/ Elisabets 11, Metro: Liceu, tel. 93/342-6280, www.camper.es, €225) has set style-setting tongues wagging since it opened. With a look somewhere between Polynesian and urban loft, luxury and asceticism, Camper has created an imminently comfortable and very cool hotel. Rooms are actually two-in-one. The sleeping area—with impossibly cushy bedding—and the luxe bath are located on the interior side of the building with a view on the hotel's unique vertical garden. The lounge area—with flat-screen television, sofa, and hammock for dozing—is directly across the hall with a balcony overlooking the street. Suites are similar, but the two areas are integrated and much more spacious. Nice touches include a café serving free breakfast and snacks 24 hours a day, including packed lunches to go (great for a picnic or to take up to the rooftop terrace), Camper-brand slippers and robes in the bath, a free hip guide to the city, Wi-Fi,

and a commitment to environmental friendliness (shower water is recycled to run the sewage system). There are also very strict policies against tipping and smoking.

BARRI GÓTIC
Under €50
Gothic Point Youth Hostel (C/ Vigatans 5, Metro: Jaume I, tel. 93/268-7808, info@gothic point.com, www.gothicpoint.com, €17–22 for a dorm bed, breakfast included) is a fun, boisterous youth hostel. The colorful main room is the perfect spot to meet fellow travelers. The hostel arranges walking, biking, and tapas tours, and provides free Internet and extensive tourist information including maps and magazines. It is very popular, so book early. Preferred booking is through www.gomio.com, which will also score you a 10 percent discount. **Hostel New York** (C/ Gignàs 6, Metro: Drassanes, tel. 93/315-0304, newyork@bcnalberg .com, www.bcnalberg.com, €20.50 for a dorm bed), is in the heart of the Barri Gòtic's major partying zone. Guests get free Internet, access to the kitchen, and use of the lovely rooftop terrace. Its sister property, **Alberg Palau** (C/ Palau 6, Metro: Jaume I, tel. 93/412-5080, palau@bcnalberg.com, www.bcnalberg.com, €20.50 for a dorm bed) is in a relatively calmer part of the Barri Gòtic and located in a lovely old palace full of old-fashioned furnishings, black-and-white tiled floors, and chandeliers.

About the only halfway decent place in this price category that is not a youth hostel is **Hostal Lausanne** (Av. Portal de l'Angel, 24, www.hostallausanne.com, tel. 93/302-1139, €48). The spectacular entry gives way to a seen-better-days warren of simple rooms. Baths are shared, but if you are willing to pay €60 you can get your own.

€50-100
El Jardí (Pl. Sant Josep Oriol 1, Metro: Liceu, tel. 93/301-5900, reservations@hoteljardi-barce lona.com, www.hoteljardi-barcelona.com, €70), located above one of the Barri Gòtic's prettiest plazas, is a decent bargain. If you can, splurge for the €96 exterior with private terrace, as the

regular rooms are very small. Plus the charm of this place is the view over the gothic Santa María del Pi church. The biggest drawback is the flight of stairs you have to go up to get to the rather antiseptic reception desk. The other floors have an elevator. **Hotel Adagio** (C/ Ferran 21, Metro: Catalunya, book@adagiohotel.com, www.adagiohotel.com, €85) is everything you could hope for in a budget hotel—the rooms and public areas are bright and clean, the staff is friendly and helpful, and the location is divine. On the downside, rooms are small and lack views, but that is to be expected at these prices in the heart of the Gothic district.

€100-200

Hotel Racó del Pi (C/ del Pi 7, Metro: Liceu, h10.raco.delpi@h10.es, www.h10hotels.com, €148) is a lovely mix of modern and rustic with parquet floors, exposed beam ceilings, and high-tech amenities. The glass of *cava* on arrival is a nice touch and the whirlpool baths are a welcome luxury. **Hotel Rialto** (C/ Ferran 42, Metro: Jaume I, reserve@gargallo-hotels .com, www.gargallo-hotels.com, €130) oozes old-world charm from the modernist-inspired furnishing to the soaring ceilings. Though the rooms could use a face-lift, the hotel—located in the house where artist Joan Miró was born—has charm, location, and a good restaurant. **Hotel Medinaceli** (Pl. Duc de Medinaceli 8, Metro: Drassanes, reserve@gargallo-hotels.com, www .gargallo-hotels.com, €155) is a sleek yet classy choice on a charming plaza in southern edge of the Barri Gòtic. The rooms are tight, but soothing in tones of orange and beige—though the odd satin duvets lend them a burlesque feel.

Over €200

Neri H&R (C/ Sant Sever 5, tel. 93/304-0655, info@hotelneri.com, www.hotelneri .com, €250) is easily Barcelona's sexiest boutique hotel. Built in an 18th-century palace off the tranquil Plaça de Sant Felip Neri, the rooms meld the opulence of their bygone glory with the sleekest in modern design. The effect is somewhere between *Dangerous Liaisons* and *The Fifth Element*. As they say in Spain, it

is *muy* fashion and *muy* exclusive. Book early and luxuriate. On the opposite end of the style meter, **Hotel Colon** (Av. Catedral 7, Metro: Jaume I, info@hotelcolon.es, www.hotelcolon .es, €250) is a grande dame of Barcelona's hotel scene. This is the kind of place for people who believe hotels should be refined, elegant, and very traditional. The plush rooms are colorful—if a bit out-of-date—with heavy curtains, marble baths, and very comfy beds. Be sure to book a room with a view over the cathedral—a dreamy sight as you tuck in for the night. Skip the so-so, overpriced buffet breakfast and head instead to any of the dozens of cafés that line the surrounding streets.

LA RIBERA AND EL BORN

This area has traditionally been short on accommodations, but since its revival as the city's haven of hip, stylish, smaller *hostales* and hotels are popping up in this area—if these recommendations don't suit you, do an Internet search for newer properties.

€50-100

Banys Oriental (C/ Argenteria 37, Metro: Jaume I, tel. 93/268-8460, www.hotelbanys orientals.com, €95) is a hip and sophisticated hotel right on one of El Born's most popular pedestrian streets. Rooms are crisp, clean, and contemporary and the wonderful walk-in showers are a welcome respite after a Barcelona day or night. At this price, it is amazing to note that the hotel made the *Condé Nast* list of 50 best hotels in 2004. The in-house restaurant, Senyor Parellades, is one of the area's best for creative Catalan food. **Hotel La Ciudadela** (Po. Luis Companys 2, Metro: Arc de Triomf, tel. 93/309-9597, reservas@ciudadelparc.com, www.ciudadelaparc.com, €78), located right in front of the Parc de la Ciutadella, is an excellent inexpensive choice. The simple rooms are airy and bright and the café features Spanish and Catalan comfort food served on three lovely terraces. **Hostal Fontanella** (Vía Laietana 71, tel. 93/317-5943, barcelona@hostal fontanella.com, www.hostalfontanella.com, €71) is a nice, inexpensive *hostal* on the edge of

Barri Gòtic with El Born. The decor is a little dated, but the rooms are comfortable and the staff is friendly. If price is a problem, forego the in-room bath for a substantial discount.

€100-200

The family-run **Park Hotel** (Av. Marqués de L'Argentera 11, Metro: Jaume I, tel. 93/319-6000, www.parkhotelbarcelona.com, €125) combines old-world luxury (an elegant, post–World War I building with a stunning spiral staircase and sleek, mosaic bar) with modern, minimalist design (gray and pale wood rooms with large light-streaming windows and Wi-Fi). Service is very attentive and the buffet breakfast—loaded with lovely pastries—is actually worth springing for (though check their website for all-inclusive deals). The hotel is across from the Parc de la Ciutadella on the edge of Born and just a 10-minute walk from the beach. **HCC Montblanc** (Vía Laietana 61, Metro: Catalunya, tel. 93/343-5555, www.montblanchotel barcelona.com, €150) is a classically styled new hotel with all the amenities you could want—Internet access, spacious bathrooms, helpful staff—plus one you will really appreciate—a swimming pool. It is small, but after a day of cement-pounding, you'll dive right in. On check-in, you'll also receive a coupon for a free glass of *cava* at the hotel's piano bar.

Over €200

Boria BCN (C/ Boria 24, Metro: Jaume I, tel. 93/295-5893, boriabcn@boriabcn.com, www .boriabcn.com, €239) is a gorgeous alternative to a hotel with a small collection of suites, junior suites, and lofts. The sleek spaces feature dark hardwood floors, fluffy down comforters, high-tech work centers, kitchens, washing machines, and bathrooms that look like they were set up for a home design shoot. The loft can hold up to four people, making it surprisingly affordable.

BARCELONETA

Working class Barceloneta, loaded with block apartments and seafood restaurants, has almost nil in the way of accommodations. Hard-working Port Vell to the west and the posh Port Olímpic to the east make up for it with accommodations running from mid-range to luxe. Though Port Olímpic offers some of the most exclusive lodgings in town, it is a bit out of the center. If you are planning on dining and drinking in the Ciutat Vella, you'll have to take taxis (about €10 one-way).

€50-100

Freestanza (C/ Sant Miguel 10, Metro: Barceloneta, tel. 68/749-4266, info@freestanza.com, www.freestanza.com, €65) rents funky little studio apartments in Barceloneta. Brightly decorated with full baths and kitchens, these cozy, fun properties make a great alternative to a hotel. You forego the safety net of a front desk, but the freedom of your own place by the sea more than makes up for it. There are also double rooms available at €50.

€100-200

Marina View B&B (Pg. Colom, s/n, Metro: Drassanes, tel. 60/920-6493, info@marina viewbcn.com, www.marinaviewbcn.com, €140) is a cozy inn right on the waterfront promenade between Las Ramblas and La Barceloneta. There are five classic rooms, each with their own bath. Affable owner José María goes out of his way to make your stay fantastic, even providing breakfast in bed if you want it. On the opposite end of the size scale, the 235-room **Eurostars Grand Marina** (Moll de Barcelona, s/n, Metro: Drassanes, tel. 93/603-9000, info@grandmarinahotel.com, www .grandmarinahotel.com, €180) offers five-star service in a contemporary hotel overlooking Port Vell. The spacious rooms have a Nordic look to them with blonde wood and minimalist cream furnishings. Baths are luxurious, with whirlpool tubs and separate walk-in showers. There is also a gym and a pool overlooking the cruise ships in the harbor. Be sure to request an upper floor for the best views.

Over in Port Olímpic, **Barcelona Marina** (Av. Bogatell 64, Metro: Ciutadella Vila Olímpica, tel. 93/309-7917, h10.marina.barcelona@ h10.es, €168) looks like a bland office building from the outside but gives way to a tranquil split-level lobby with trees, white stones, and flowing water. Rooms are equally relaxed yet stylish. There is an in-house wellness center with gym facilities and a nice indoor pool. The restaurant is a bit overpriced and you'd do much better hitting any of the seafood places along the waterfront.

Over €200

Looming over Port Olímpic in one of Barcelona's first skyscrapers, the **Hotel Arts** (C/ Marina 19–21, Metro: Ciutadella Vila Olímpica, tel. 93/221-1000, www.ritzcarlton.com, starting at €325) has been Barcelona's hotel of choice for international movers and shakers since it opened. Today, it is not alone in the posh-hotel biz in town, but it is still a leader for its sheer luxury—thanks mainly to the exacting standards of the Ritz Carlton chain. Rooms are spacious, modern retreats in neutral tones of cream and black. Most have spectacular views over the port and the Mediterranean. Staff is very attentive and accommodating. The in-house restaurants, **Enoteca** and **Arola** (named for chef Sergi Arola), are both excellent, though pricey.

MONTJUÏC

As home to Barcelona's busiest convention halls, Fira, Montjuïc hotels are very firmly business class, most in the mid-price range.

€100-200

B-Hotel (Gran Vía 389, Metro: Espanya, tel. 93/552-9500, b-hotel@nnhotels.com, www.nnhotels.com, €160) is a trendy hotel that still manages to retain a laid-back attitude. The rooms have a rustic-chic look with weathered wood, slate-colored blankets, and a very amusing mood lighting system (it make take you all of your stay to figure it out!). Request an upper floor for great views. The rooftop infinity pool is perfectly dreamy, especially at sunset. **Catalonia Barcelona Plaza** (Pl. Espanya 6–8, Metro: Espanya, tel. 93/426-2600, €140) sits in the heart of Plaça de Espanya with the mount of Montjuïc filling the view from most of the windows. Though the rooms are spa-

cious and well appointed, they lack charm. The rooftop pool and great views from the upper floors compensate, but the best thing about this hotel is ease of access. The Aero Bus from the airport drops off and picks up right in front and the metro is just below.

EIXAMPLE
€50-100

Hotel Paseo de Gràcia (Pg. Gràcia 102, tel. 93/215-5824, hotelpdg@terra.es, €78) offers classic, if shabby, rooms at a great price on one of the best stretches of real estate in Barcelona. You'll sleep within walking distance of La Pedrera and can use the money you save on this room at some of the shops along the Passeig de Gràcia. **House Family B&B** (C/ Valencia 286, Metro: Pg. Gràcia, tel. 93/215-7934, barcelona@housefamily.com, www.housefamily.com, €82), located in a tidy apartment, is like staying in a friend's home. There is a communal living area with satellite television, a small kitchen, and two bathrooms that are shared among the five rooms. You are given your own key to come and go as you please and the English-speaking owner Montserrat is extremely accommodating and full of suggestions on what to do and where to go. **Suite Gaudí Barcelona** (Rambla Catalunya 103, Metro: Diagonal, tel. 93/215-0658, www.suitegaudibarcelona.com, €70) is a colorful family-owned *hostal* with a very friendly staff and lovely rooms that include wonderfully tiled baths. If you share a bath, prices drop by about €15. **Hostal Felipe II** (C/ Mallorca 329, Metro: Verdaguer, tel. 93/458-7758, info@ hotelfelipe2.com, www.hotelfelipe2.com, €60) is a delightful charmer for the price and quality. Rooms are small but bright, with new furnishings and Internet. Prices go even lower if you book a single or forego a private bath.

€100-200

Hotel Axel (C/ Aribau 33, tel. 93/323-9393, www.axelhotels.com, €185) bills itself as a hetero-friendly hotel, but it is sizzles as a super-stylish gay and lesbian retreat located in the heart of "Gayxample." The rooms are oases of cool white with luxe touches like plush towels, high-thread-count linens, and Wi-Fi. The rooftop Sky Bar is one of the see-and-be-seen places in town, though it is open to the public only on Wednesday nights and Sundays. **Hotel AC Diplomatic** (C/ Pau Claris 122, Metro: Pg. Gràcia, tel. 93/272-3810, diplomatic@ac-hotels .com, www.ac-hotels.com, €200) combines sleek modern detailing with classic hotel ambience. The rooms are minimalist and loaded with perks like free beer and soft drinks in the mini-bar, upscale toiletries, plush robes, complimentary umbrellas, and comfy beds piled high with fine linens. As is true in all AC Hotels, the staff is extraordinarily helpful. There is also a small pool on the roof.

Over €200

Eixample's gridded streets have been sprouting up designer hotels like weeds. With cutting-edge architecture and quirky attention to detail, they provoke, pamper, and occasionally perplex—but never will they leave you bored. Just remember to always check the Internet before booking. Prices change constantly and if you are vigilant, you can snag any of the following rooms for well less than €200.

Opened in 2006, **Granados 83** (C/ Enric Granados 83, Metro: Diagonal, tel. 93/492-9670, granados83@derbyhotels.com, www .derbyhotels.com, €235) is all rusted steel and brushed glass. Rooms have a distinct Soho loft look with deep orange walls, leather sofas, dark wood floors, and black bed linens. There is a stylish rooftop terrace with a tiny slip of a pool and lovely views over Eixample. **Hotel Omm** (C/ Rosselló 265, Metro: Diagonal, tel. 93/445-4000, reservas@hotelomm.es, www .hotelomm.es, €290) shivers with understated coolness the moment you enter the lobby. Head upstairs and you'll be confronted with long dark hallways with black rubber floors and very spare filament lighting. From there, pass into your room—a light airy den of sophisticated modernism with luxury touches like oak flooring, cushy beds, plush towels, and spacious baths. The rooftop terrace and pool offer magnificent views over La Pedrera. The downstairs bar is wildly popular with Barcelona's hottest young things, but go only if you are willing to fight for a spot—despite claiming to reserve the "red sofa" for guests, the reality is it is all about who you know and how cool you go. The hotel's restaurant Moo is run by the famous Roca brothers, who own the Can Roca near Girona. Food is as inventive as the hotel and priced to match. **Hotel Cram** (C/ Aribau 54, Metro: Hospital Clínic, tel. 93/216-7700, www.hotelcram.com, €240) hides an ultra-modern hotel with a striking circular courtyard behind a very classic Eixample facade. The name is a misnomer, as the rooms are anything but cramped. Airy, spacious, and light, they are accented in autumnal colors and feature all the high-tech amenities such as Wi-Fi, interactive flat-screen televisions, and a variety of lighting choices with names like "fiesta," "romance," and "night light." The black-coated staff is both efficient and friendly. Cram also houses the Restaurante Gaig, a pool, a gym, and a trendy nightclub.

If you prefer more classic style, Eixample also delivers, most notably with the sumptuous **Casa Fuster** (Pg. Gràcia 132, Metro: Diagonal, tel. 93/255-3000, info@hotelcasa fuster.com, www.hotelcasafuster.com, €330). This 1908 modernist mansion designed by Lluís Domènech i Montaner underwent an €80 million renovation in 2004 to become one of Barcelona's most luxurious five-star hotels. Rooms are sublime with gilt-framed mirrors, heavy curtained windows, boutique toiletries, plush linens, and deliriously comfortable beds. The hotel's public rooms take advantage of the buildings modernist origins and add curvaceous antiques and oversized chandeliers. On the roof, a gorgeous, pillared terrace looks over Eixample while a lovely—though small—pool offers cool relief after a hard day of sightseeing. The Café Viennese is a luxurious retreat for a coffee. The only complaint is that there is no concierge, so come prepared with enough knowledge to get you around to what you want to see and do.

BARCELONA

Food

When the *New York Times* ran a cover story in their Sunday magazine hailing Cataluña as the new mecca of gastronomy and Barcelona's native son, Ferran Adrià (of El Bullí in Roses, Girona) as quite possibly the best chef in the world, foodies worldwide packed up their forks and headed for Barcelona's tables. Innovative tapas and delicious, homey Catalan traditional dishes are all yummy highlights of a Barcelona culinary tour. Typical Catalan dishes found in Barcelona and throughout the region include *pa amb tomàquet,* a thick slice of bread rubbed with tomato, garlic, olive oil, and salt; *butifarra blanc,* a mild, white sausage; *butifarra negre,* blood sausage; *escalivada,* a cold side dish of marinated vegetables; *fideuà,* a Catalan paella made with noodles instead of rice; *arròs negre,* a paella blackened by squid ink; *suquet,* fish and potato soup; and *calçots,* a mild green onion, often roasted over an open fire and eaten with *romesco,* a chunky sauce made of red pepper, garlic, hazelnuts, almonds, and olive oil. The classic dessert is *crema catalana,* the local version of crème brûlée.

For a little of that Adrià-inspired avant-garde, the sky is the limit to what creative Barcelonan chefs will whip up. Places like Abac, Espai Sucre, and Comerç 24 are famed across the world, but be aware that Barcelona's culinary scene is a living, evolving movement. For the latest in gastronomic advances, peruse the Spain forums of www.egullet.com, one of the top culinary websites in the world. Also check out the English version of www.lomejordelagastronomia.com, edited by Rafael García Santos, one of Spain's foremost culinary critics.

LAS RAMBLAS

If you are on the backpacker's bread-and-cheese diet, Las Ramblas offers enough cheapie fast-food places to meet your budget—

The goodies inside pastry shop Escribà are as deliciously beautiful as the exterior.

© CANDY LEE LABALLE

WHAT'S COOKING IN BARCELONA

After enjoying so many tasty Catalan dishes in Barcelona, you may wonder – can I try that at home? You betcha! Just pay a visit to one of these culinary gurus and you'll be Catalan in the kitchen in no time.

THE GOURMET BACKPACKER

The Barcelona backpacker's best friend, the rowdy, raucous **Travel Bar** (C/ Boqueria 27, Metro: Liceu, tel. 93/342-5252) offers €15 Spanish cooking courses aimed at travelers who usually stick to cheese and bread in an effort to do Europe on a budget. These fun classes are held right in the bar and include how-tos on paella, gazpacho, tapas, and sangria. Of course, afterwards you get to eat and drink it all. Classes are currently held Mondays at 5 P.M., but that is subject to change. Give them a call or pass by for the latest schedule.

COOKING ON LAS RAMBLAS

The cheerful little cooking school **Cook and Taste** (Rambla 58, Metro: Liceu, 93/302-1320, info@cookandtaste.net, www.cookandtaste .net) offers half-day seminars on the art of basic Spanish and Catalan fare. Classes take place in a bright, spacious kitchen right in the middle of Las Ramblas. The menu changes depending on the season, but it always includes the classic dessert crema catalana. The price is right at just €50 per person, which includes a lunch of what you just prepared plus sangria or wine. You can also opt to join the instructor in the Mercat de la Boqueria for a tour and a tapa as you pick out that day's ingredients (€10 extra). There are also specialized seminars for seasoned cooks (€110). All classes are held in English.

IN THE KITCHEN WITH A CATALAN CHEF

In the words of a famous American chef, kick it up a notch with a private culinary class with Catalan chef Jaume Brichs. **Cellar Tours** (tel. 91/521-3939, info@cellartours.com, www.cellar tours.com), a Madrid-based luxury wine and gastronomy tour company run by Californian Genevieve McCarthy, has paired with Chef Brichs to offer a half-day culinary extravaganza. The course starts with a tour of Mercat de la Boqueria, where you will learn how to choose truffles, olive oil, and the freshest of seafood. After shopping, you'll have an aperitif at one of the best bars in the market. Next, you will be whisked off to a private loft with a gourmet kitchen where the chef will reveal his secrets for some wonderful Catalan classics including fideuà, a type of paella made with noodles. Finally, you'll eat your creations from the loft's terrace overlooking a spectacular view of the city. Prices run €300, but keep in mind that the course is private, the attention to detail impeccable, the lessons intriguing, the food exquisite, and the experience priceless. Cellar Tours also offers a range of luxury food and wine tours in Cataluña and beyond.

TAPAS-HOPPING WITH THE EXPERTS

The gourmands at Barcelona-based **Food Wine Tours** (Ronda Universitat 12, tel. 93/317 1909, www.foodwinetours.com) offer a weekend tapas-crawl through Las Ramblas and Barri Gòtic. As you savor the local flavors, your bilingual guide will give you the background scoop on tapas and Spanish cuisine. The tour, which includes five tapas and two glasses of wine or beer, costs €60. The company also offers group cooking classes and specialized food tours.

WALKING GOURMET TOURS

The **Barcelona Tourism Office** (Pl. Catalunya 17, tel. 93/285-3832, www.barcelonaturisme .com) offers walking tours with an emphasis on Barcelona's culinary heritage. You'll pass through the Mercat de la Boqueria, as well as several classic tapas bars, cafés, and restaurants. As of this writing, the tour leaves every Friday at 11 A.M. from the tourist office beneath Plaça Catalunya (show up early to register, the office is usually a madhouse). The tours are held in English and cost just €11.

and, of course, it is home to the gorgeous Mercat de la Boqueria, where a healthy, hearty lunch can be put together for under €5. There are also several wonderful, atmospheric old cafés perfect for people-watching. Other than these, the bulk of the places on Las Ramblas are pure tourist traps with second-rate food at first-rate prices. Nonetheless, I have scoured Las Ramblas, looking for the best of the best, and found quite a few places worth a chair at the table.

Cafés and Desserts

Just off Las Ramblas, on the Raval side, **Granja M. Viader** (C/ Xuclà 4–6, Metro: Catalunya, tel. 93/318-3486, 9 A.M.–1:30 P.M. and 5–8:30 P.M. Tues.–Sat., 9 A.M.–1:30 P.M. Mon., closed Sun., €5) is an old-world café that was founded in 1870. The owner is reputed to have invented Cacaolat, the bottled chocolate drink that is served by the boatload here. There are also tasty pastries and a carry-out deli counter. A perfect café to while away the afternoon is the grand **Café de L'Opera** (La Rambla 74, tel. 93/317-7585, www.cafeoperabcn.com, 8 A.M.–2 A.M. daily). Founded in 1929, this perennial favorite is one of the few places on Las Ramblas where the locals almost outnumber the tourists. The drinks menu is long on coffees, teas, *batidos* (milkshakes), and juices. They also mix a mean cocktail and offer gin, whiskey, and vodka menus. Though there is a full menu, the best bet here is a simple breakfast pastry or a sandwich at lunch. For something heartier, go elsewhere. **Escribà** (La Rambla 83, tel. 93/301-6027, 8:30 A.M.–9 P.M. daily) is the city's most photographed pastry shop. Built in 1820, the corner shop sports a glittering green, violet, and gold mosaic facade topped by florally stained glass. There are dozens of sweet delicacies from pastries and cakes to homemade chocolates on offer.

Tapas

There are lots of bars in and around the Mercat de la Boqueria to grab a tapa and a cold beer. Three of the best follow. ◖ **Bar**

Pinotxo (Mercat de la Boqueria, stalls 66–67, 6 A.M.–4 P.M. Mon.–Sat., closed Sun.) is a boisterous walk-up bar right in the thick of things at the market. Presided over by septuagenarian Joan Bayan since forever, this tiny spot has made huge culinary waves round the world, appearing in such foodie tomes as *Saveur.* There is no menu and the waiter—often Bayan himself—will ask you *"pescado o carne?"* ("fish or meat?"). The former is your best bet and two of the house favorites are *revuelto de gambas* (scrambled eggs with shrimp) and *chipirónes con mongetes* (tiny squid sautéed with white beans and olive oil). Go early to have a coffee and croissant with the local food vendors. **Papitu** (Pl. Galdric, s/n, 9 A.M.–midnight Mon.–Sat., 11 A.M.–6 P.M. Sun., €12), just behind the market, draws a decidedly bohemian crowd to its sidewalk terrace. As the walk-up bar pumps out flamenco music, waiters serve a variety of tapas, sandwiches, and fresh-from-the-market treats. **Casa Guinart** (La Rambla 95, tel. 93/317-8887, 9 A.M.–9 P.M. Mon.–Sat., closed Sun., €12) is a tiny deli counter founded in 1899. The walls are laden with shelves jammed with local products, olive oils, wines, and sweets. The meat counter boasts locally cured sausages such as *butifarra,* chorizos, and artisan cheeses. Just beyond that is a tiny bar where you can snack on *flautas* (€1.40): thin, crusty baguettes stuffed with sausage or cheese. If you want something more substantial, there is a simple dining room upstairs that serves a creative *menú del día* for just €10.

Vegetarian

With its psychedelic graffiti paint job, dreadlocked staff, and long bar laden with fruits and vegetables, **Juicy Jones** (C/ Cardenal Casañas 7, Metro: Liceu, noon–11:30 P.M. daily, €9) could seduce even meat-eaters into going veg for a day. The bar serves a dozen different juices and the dark, cozy dining room out back features a menu bursting with creative dishes, many vegan. The tiny restaurant and bar **Ménage à Trois** (C/ Bot 4, tel. 93/301-5542, 1–4:15 P.M. and 9 P.M.–1 A.M. daily,

€15) features an eclectic little menu of crepes, pastas, salads, couscous, and vegetable pâtés. The emphasis is only really fresh, seasonal produce and many dishes have Asian touches. Even though it is just a block off Las Ramblas, next to the exposed Roman crypts, it is very much a locals' hang-out. The decor is pure kitsch, with birdcages jammed with superhero dolls, and the bar hops until well after the kitchen closes.

EL RAVAL

Who knows what style gods deemed it so, but gentrification always seems to bring with it good eating. El Raval, slowly undergoing hippification—MACBA, cool boutiques, expensive lofts—has been sprouting up edgy dining spots as fast as chefs can whip up their latest foamed whatever. Fortunately, still being rough around its art-galleried edges, this "bad" barrio also offers some of the city's most classic restaurants. Of course, by now you've heard all the warnings, but it bears repeating—if you are alone or squeamish about the junkies and hookers that are prevalent in the southern reaches of this 'hood, walk in by daylight and catch a cab out after dark.

Fusion Cuisine

It is hard to know how to classify **Dos Trece** (C/ Carme 40, tel. 93/301-7306, www.dostrece.net, 1:30 P.M.–3 A.M. Tues.–Sun., closed Mon., €18). By day, it serves up some of the freshest food with a Mediterranean/Mexican twist. Basmati rice salad (with almonds, oranges, and green olives), gazpacho with strawberry puree, shrimp tacos, and nachos are just a few of the regular offerings. However, what packs in the expat crowd every Sunday are the best brunches in Spain—eggs Benedict, pancakes, and Bloody Marys—oh my! By night, this haven of hip turns down the light and turns up the beats with DJs and live musical acts. The place is so cool, it even has its own radio station. There is also free Wi-Fi during the day if you just want to nurse a *café con leche* and surf the Web. **Mamacafè** (C/ Doctor Dou 10, Metro: Liceu, tel. 93/301-

2940, 1–4 P.M. and 9 P.M.–midnight Mon.–Sat., closed Sun., €20) resembles your mama's place only if she happens to be art-school hep. This place just shivers with coolness from the exposed air vents to the projected slides on the walls. The food is cool too, with the emphasis on fresh and fun. Tuna steak with sweet onion compote, monkfish cooked Indian-style, and crunchy ravioli with Brie and tomato marmalade are typical.

Local Cuisine

With its upscale Catalan cuisine, **La Reina del Raval** (Ramla del Raval 3, Metro: Liceu, tel. 93/443-3655, 1:30–3:30 P.M. and 8:30 P.M.–midnight Mon.–Sat., closed Sun., €30) is the newest player on Raval's hot dining scene. In a loft-like space of stone and steel, the chef gives traditional Catalan staples such as rabbit, duck, and cod classic treatments with an occasional creative touch. The emphasis is on the quality of the ingredients. The tiny bar serves over a 100 different cocktails to a very lively crowd on the sidewalk terrace. In the evening a DJ provides music. A more traditional local spot is the historic **Casa Leopoldo** (C/ Sant Rafael 24, Metro: Liceu, tel. 93/441-3014, 1:30–4 P.M. and 9–11 P.M. Tues.–Sat., 1:30–4 P.M. Sun. closed Mon., €25). Located on the seedier side of Raval, this classic dining room has been serving top-notch Catalan fare to grateful locals since the 1930s.

Tapas

El Jardí (C/ Hospital 56, Metro: Liceu, tel. 93/329-1550, 11 A.M.–11 P.M. Mon.–Sat., closed Sun., €8) is hidden in a Gothic garden surrounded by a medieval hospital and ancient library. Amidst trees and ancient statues, little old ladies gossip on benches while dreadlocked buskers juggle. A little food booth serves the tables that are scattered throughout the grounds. The tapas are local from *pa amb tomàquet,* the classic Catalan dish of bread with tomato and olive oil, to foie gras on toast, *jamón,* and *tortilla.* Go here early in your trip because you will want to return. The setting is absolutely divine and just far enough off the tourist path to give it a real local vibe. For a more traditional tapas bar, try ◖ **Mam i Teca** (C/ Lluna 4, tel. 93/441-3335, 1–4 P.M. and 8:30 P.M.–midnight Sun., Mon., and Wed.–Fri., 8:30 P.M.–midnight Sat., closed Tues., €20). The owners are food nuts and scour the country for the finest ingredients for their basic tapas. The charcuterie list is divine—from the white Catalan sausage *butifarra* to the best *jamón* money can buy to *mojama,* delicious dry-cured tuna from Cádiz. Their grilled shrimp are exquisite with a good salty sea taste and their sautéed mushrooms with garlic are made for sopping up with crusty bread. There is also a list of artisan cheeses from around the country offered by species—goat, sheep, and cow. The ambience is as simple and good as the menu—citrus-colored walls, chandelier lighting, and low-key jazz. The interesting wine list and welcoming English-speaking staff make this a cut way above your typical barrio bar. The only drawback is size—it's tiny, and the six tables go fast. Reservations are accepted.

© CANDY LEE LABALLE

Get a juice fix at hippy hangout Juicy Jones.

Vegetarian

Juicy Jones (C/ Hospital 74, Metro: Liceu, noon–11:30 P.M. daily, €9) is the twin sister to the restaurant of the same name off Las Ramblas. Healthy, hearty, and oh-so-hip—this colorful restaurant will give you a veggie fix without breaking your bank. **Foodball** (C/ Elisabets 9, Metro: Catalunya, tel. 93/270-1363, 11 A.M.–11 P.M. daily, €15) is foot-forward shoemaker Camper's foray into fast food. The airy space almost seems like it could be a minimalist shoe shop, but sure enough, walk up to the counter and you'll find balls of food (hence the name). The balls might be rice stuffed with tofu, seitan, red beans, mushrooms, or a few dozen other macrobiotic and vegan options. There are also soups-of-the-day, fresh juices, and hemp beer.

BARRI GÒTIC

Head to the Barri Gòtic for cozy cafés with actual Roman walls, traditional tapas, and cheap eats aimed squarely at a young, fun, and full of rum international crowd.

Cafés and Desserts

La Granja (C/ Banys Nous 4, Metro: Jaume I, tel. 93/302-6975, 9:30 A.M.–2 P.M. and 5–9 P.M. daily) is a ramshackle café with the look of an old country store. It opened in 1872, but the foundations of this room go back much further. The exposed stone wall in the back room is one of the original Roman walls of the city. Have a tea, coffee, or piece of chocolate cake sitting with your back leaning against history. For a bit of artistic history, head to **Els Quatre Gats** (C/ Montsió 3, Metro: Jaume I, tel. 93/302-4140, 8 A.M.–2 A.M. daily), one of Barcelona's most-storied cafés. Opened at the end of the 19th century, the café became a destination for the city's artists, thinkers, and bohemians. Picasso began hanging out here at 17 and had his first art exhibition on these walls. The tandem bicycle picture that adorns the restaurant and menus was designed by the artist himself. Today, the café maintains a stylish old-world feel boasting an interesting decor of rustic and modernist. It is a great place for a coffee in the afternoon.

Traditional Catalan food is also served but it tends to be pricey.

Fusion Cuisine

With a decidedly shabby-chic flair, the deli counter/cozy diner **Venus** (C/ Avinyó 25, Metro: Jaume I, tel. 93/301-1585, noon–midnight Mon.–Sat., closed Sun., €15) offers creative sandwiches and salads with Asian, Arabic, and Italian touches. There is a good selection of wine by the glass and a regular roster of art from local artists. **Margarita Blue** (C/ Josep Anselm Clavé 6, Metro: Drassanes, tel. 93/412-5489, 7 P.M.–3 A.M. daily) offers a Soho vibe with a side of Latin cool. The menu is Mexican-Spanish and makes good use of the ample fresh seafood available in Barcelona. The long bar, under oversized antique mirrors, draws a good-looking crowd of 30-somethings—both local and tourist—quaffing down the delectable house margaritas until closing. There are a roster of house DJs who spin an infectious mix of Latin-tinged house, and a couple of nights a week a local magician drops in to do his trick thing.

Local Cuisine

Since 1835, **Los Caracoles** (C/ Escudellers 14, Metro: Drassanes, tel. 93/302-3185, 1 P.M.–midnight daily, €20) has been serving Catalan comfort food: *arròs negre* (rice in squid ink), grilled seafood, roasted chicken, and their namesake *caracoles,* snails stewed in spicy tomato sauce. The interior looks like something out of an old Spanish film— jamón– dangling over the bar, vats of wine, colorful tiles, fat exposed beams, pots hanging from the ceiling. The dining rooms are scattered in a warren of rooms, but you can also just have tapas at the bar. **Agut** (C/ Gignàs 16, Metro: Jaume I, tel. 93/315-1709, 1:30–4 P.M. and 9 P.M.–midnight Tues.–Sat., 1:30–4 P.M. Sun., closed Mon., €18) serves some of the most traditional Catalan fare in the city. The restaurant, oozing a charming, faded glamour, has been run by the Agut family for decades and it is a well-loved favorite with upstanding locals decked out in pearls

and good shoes. The yellowed walls are covered in colorful contemporary art by local painters, the tables are linen-topped and a bit wobbly, the service is both attentive and assured. Everything is exquisite, particularly the seafood dishes, but if you are feeling really hedonistic, have the house specialty: *chuletón del buey,* a massive oxen chop, perfectly grilled and big enough for two. If you don't order it, the table next to you will—and boy will you be jealous.

Quick Bites

Fast food had never tasted so good! **Buenas Migas** (C/ Baixada de Santa Clara 2, Metro: Jaume I, tel. 93/319-1380, 10 A.M.–midnight daily, €10) elevates traditional focaccia (chewy olive oil–infused bread) to a very delicious art. There are dozens of type on offer from sweet to savory. Take out a sandwich for a picnic in front of the nearby cathedral or eat in at one of the tiny wooden tables—the aroma of baking focaccia is enough to lull you into staying long after you've licked up your last crumb. There are several locations throughout the city.

Romantic

Set in a early 20th-century modernist palace, **La Lluna** (C/ Sant Bonaventura 7, Metro: Catalunya, tel. 93/342-4479, 1:30–4 P.M. Mon.–Wed., 1:30–4 P.M. and 9–11:30 P.M. Thurs.–Sat., closed Sun., €28) is at once elegant, romantic, and old-worldly. The menu features the freshest Mediterranean ingredients with very creative touches, such as lentil salad with pickled tuna, grilled sea bream with sun-dried tomato oil, and pasta with squid ribbons and romesco mousse. Lunch is an unbelievable bargain at €12 including wine. **Safrá 18** (C/ Ample 18, Metro: Jaume I, tel. 93/268-7427, 9 A.M.–1 P.M. daily, €20) just feels European. Colored in a palette of spices with wooden tables and soft lighting, it is the perfect backdrop for the minimalist Mediterranean menu of carpaccio, risotto, and grilled steak perfectly sized for sharing.

Tapas

La Vinateria del Call (C/ San Domènec del Call 9, Metro: Liceu, tel. 93/302-6092, 8:30 P.M.–1 A.M. daily) is an atmospheric old wine bar. Under candlelight, it serves up an impressive list of Spanish wines plus simple tapas of cured cheeses and meats to a dedicated crowd of locals and the few happy tourists that stumble upon it. Try the *cecina* (cured beef)—it is decadently good. The very stylish **Taller de Tapas** (Pl. Sant Josep Oriol 9, tel. 93/301-8020, 9:30 A.M.–midnight Mon.–Sat., noon–midnight Sun., €15) serves up traditional tapas based on high-quality ingredients. Run by hip British expat Kate Preston, Taller draws a young, sophisticated local crowd. There is a second location in Born (C/ Argentaria 51, tel. 93/268-8559).

Vegetarian

Vegetalia (C/ Escudellers 54, tel. 93/317-3331, 11 A.M.–11 P.M. daily, €10) is an oasis of blonde wood, yellow walls, and lots of plants, right off of the down-and-dirty Plaça George Orwell. Food is ridiculously cheap for the excellent quality and there is quite a lot for the hardcore vegan. If you are really hungry, go for the "Full Monty;" at €18 it is the most expensive plate on the menu, but you'll get enough veg and healthiness to wipe out your carnivorous sins for a year.

LA RIBERA AND EL BORN

Sexy, stylish Ribera/Born is seething with upscale wine bars, designer bakeries, foodie temples, and—for those who like it laid-back and old school—a handful of traditional corner bars. Insiders consider Born the place to have a first date—especially if you want it to segue into a little more.

Cafés and Desserts

Looking more like a designer jewelry shop than a pastry shop, **Bubó** (C/ Caputxes 10, Metro: Jaume I, tel. 93/268-7224, www.bubo. ws, 4–10 P.M. Mon., 11 A.M.–10 P.M. Tues.– Thurs., 10 A.M.–1 A.M. Fri.–Sun., €10) offers gorgeous jewel-like individual cakes and pastries. The brainchild of master pastry chef Carles Mampel, Bubó does carry-out or sit-in service. **Born Cooking** (C/ Corretger 9, Metro: Jaume I, tel. 93/310-5999, noon–9 P.M. Mon., Thurs., and Fri., 11 A.M.– 9:30 P.M. Sat.–Sun., closed Tues. and Wed., €5) was the first American-style bakery in Barcelona. Run by a native New Yorker, this homey little shop churns out excellent cookies, cheesecakes, and brownies to a very dedicated expat and local crowd. Salads and sandwiches are also on offer.

Gourmet

Abac (C/ Rec 79–89, Metro: Jaume I, tel. 93/319-6600, 8:30–10:30 P.M. Mon., 1:30– 3:30 P.M. and 8:30–10:30 P.M. Tues.–Sat., closed Sun., €95, reservations required) is one of the world's best restaurants. Chef and owner Xavier Pellicer creates what he calls *cuisine d'auteur* and what tasters call highly inventive flights of fancy. In a spare dining room of blonde wood, gracious waiters in gray Nehru jackets deliver dishes such as a tarte tatin of eels with apples and artichokes, smoked sardine and apricot sorbet, and Iberian suckling pig with fried mango sticks. The best option is to submit to the chef's whim with his tasting menu. **Espai Sucre** (C/ Princesa 53, Metro: Arc de Triomf, tel. 93/268-1630, www.espaisucre.com, 9– 11:30 P.M. Tues.–Sat., closed Sun. and Mon., €50)—the Sweet Space—is the experimental sweet-food restaurant run by world-renowned pastry chef Jordi Butrón. Though you could easily call this a desserts-only restaurant, the philosophy behind the menu is more to move sweet flavors from the dessert tray and into the main courses. He has created a series of tasting menus that tantalize the sweet buds with sophisticated flavors and spices while binding the courses together with a few savory interludes. A typical menu might include a manchego cheese tart with pineapple and thyme; cold Ceylon tea soup with spices and fruits; or spicy milk with citrus and arugula. The flavors are deep, sublime, and addictive. Make reservations, as this sweet spot is hot.

And, take note that weekends feature only two seatings: 8:30 P.M. and 11 P.M. Expect to see more sweet menus popping up the world over, as the cooking school that Jordi runs in the space is very highly regarded and very well attended. The ant over the front door is not meant to scare; Jordi chose it as his symbol because it represents hard work.

Local Cuisine

Pep's Buffet (C/ Grunyi 5, Metro: Jaume I, tel. 93/310-0709, 8:30 P.M.–1 A.M. Tues.–Sat., closed Sun. and Mon., €20) offers a feast of Catalan home-cooking in a 17th-century fisherman's house. The choices can be overwhelming, so let Pep and his crew help you decide. Winners include the leek and garlic omelet and the rabbit braised in rosemary. For a modern, fun take on Catalan tradition, try **◖ Origen 99.9** (C/ Vidrieria 6, Metro: Jaume I, tel. 93/310-7531, www.origen99.com, €15), where 99.9 percent of the products used in the restaurant hail from Cataluña, from olive oil from Lérida to cheeses made in the Pyrenees to wines from Penedès and Priorat. The menu is presented in a give-away magazine that gives a bilingual history of all the dishes as well as interesting facts about Catalan food and recipes. There are also locations in Gràcia and Eixample.

Quick Bites

Itztli (C/ Mirallers 7, Metro: Arc de Triomf, tel. 93/319-6875, noon–11 P.M. Tues.–Sun., closed Mon., €8) is a tiny deli counter serving excellent Mexican carry-out such as tamales, tacos, and burritos. The ingredients are impeccably fresh and the service is too. If you want to eat in, there is a tiny counter in the window, perfect for people-watching.

Romantic

◖ La Carassa (C/ Brossolí 1, Metro: Jaume I, tel. 93/310-3306, 9–11 P.M. Mon.–Sat., closed Sun., €30) has been serving fondue to cozy couples since 1979. The 10-table restaurant looks like the attic of an old, rich aunt, jammed with antiques and mismatched fur-nishings, lacey tablecloths, dripping candelabras, and exposed beamed ceilings. The menu is strictly fondue and be aware that *fosa* with one "s" refers to melting cheese while *fossa*, with two, means raw meat or fish that is cooked at the table in a pot of hot broth or sputtering olive oil. This place is very popular and very small, so make reservations. **Reina** (C/ Sombrerers 3, Metro: Jaume I, tel. 93/319-5371, 8:30 P.M.–1 A.M. daily, €25) is the perfect place for a second date—it is way too sexy for a first date. Cozy tables are set beneath deep red walls and the lighting is very low. The French-Catalan menu is heavy on seafood with a few stellar meat dishes—try the *margret de pato* (duck breast with caramelized apples). After dinner, the house music is turned up and the place becomes a lounge.

Tapas

Cal Pep (Pl. Olles 8, tel. 93/310-7961, 1–4:30 P.M. Mon., 1–4:30 P.M. and 8:30–11:30 P.M. Tues.–Sat., closed Sun. and Aug., €18) is a Barcelona institution. Tucked on a tiny square near the Museu Picasso, this boisterous bar is presided over by chef and owner Pep and his team of white-coated waiters. The seafood tapas are some of the best in the city. For dessert, try their signature *crema catalana*. The innovative tapas bar **Comerç 24** (C/ Comerç 24, Metro: Arc de Triomf, tel. 93/319-2102, www.comerc24.com, 1:30–3:30 P.M. and 8:30 P.M.–midnight Tues.–Sat., closed Sun. and Mon., €45) glows brightly on the radar of foodies worldwide. Run by chef Carles Abellan, a nine-year apprentice to superstar chef Ferran Adrià at world-acclaimed El Bulli, this stylish dining room—exposed kitchen, charcoal-colored walls, lights made from drum cymbals—aims to make food fun with a menu of edgy, gourmet tapas drawn from various cooking styles. The menu is a work of art in continuous, delicious process, but look out for the *kinder egg,* named for a German chocolate egg. Here it is actually a boiled egg white, the interior scooped out, blended with black truffles, and stuffed back in. Other delights are tuna sashimi pizza with a dash of wasabi, crusty prawns with romesco sauce, and for the meat lover, foie gras and truffle hamburger. There are three seatings and reservations are highly suggested—you can easily make them on the restaurant's website. The one fly in the mousse is the service—it is painstakingly slow.

BARCELONETA

It is no surprise that Barceloneta—the city's original fishermen's quarter—offers traditional takes on impeccably fresh seafood. Hemmed in by two upscale ports, this area also serves some of the town's most creative food.

Cafés and Desserts

Daguiri (C/ Grau i Torras 59, Metro: Barceloneta, tel. 93/221-5109,10 A.M.–midnight daily, €10) is a laid-back café/bar/art gallery right on a plaza overlooking the beach. The name is a play on Spanish slang for foreigner, *guiri,* and the menu makes a play for Barcelona's large expat community with overstuffed sandwiches, cheesy garlic bread, chips and dips, and yummy carrot cake. By day, linger over a coffee and take advantage of their free Wi-Fi and large selection of foreign newspapers. By evening, have a snack on the terrace while watching the sunset over the beach. **La Miranda del Museu** (Pl. Pau Vila 3, Metro: Barceloneta, tel. 93/225-5007, 10 A.M.–7 P.M. Tues.–Sat., 10 A.M.–5 P.M. Sun., closed Mon.), located on top of the Museu d'Història de Catalunya, is a wonderful escape from the tourist crush. The sunny roof terrace has ample space, great views, and a very reasonable menu of Catalan specialties.

Gourmet

Set Portes (Pg. D'Isabel II 14, Metro: Barceloneta, tel. 93/319-3033, 1 P.M.–1 A.M. daily, €40), which means "seven doors," has a warren of as many dining rooms. Located in the monumental **Pòrtics d'en Xifré,** this legendary restaurant has served excellent Catalan seafood dishes to distinguished diners from King Juan Carlos to revolutionary Che Guevara since it opened its doors in 1836. Amid 19th-century belle epoque glory, have the long-coated waiters bring you either the *zarzuela,* a fish stew with lobster, or the paella of the day. Reservations are suggested.

Quick Bites

At Port Olímpic, **Delicamon** (C/ Marina, Metro: Ciutadella Vila Olímpica, tel. 93/225-3061, 9 A.M.–10 P.M. daily, €8) offers a healthy array of self-serve sandwiches, salads, and juices, as well as grilled panini and pizzas. Eat in the fast-food-ish interior or on the bright terrace. Facing the beach, **Opollo** (Pg. Marítim, s/n, Metro: Ciutadella Vila Olímpica. 93/224-0353, €8) is a hip, utilitarian space serving succulent roasted chickens to eat in at wood-block communal tables or carry out to the beach. It is close to the intersection of Carrer de L'Almirall Cervera.

Seafood

All along Passeig Joan de Borbó (separating Port Vell from Barceloneta) are neon-bright seafood joints packed with tourists coaxed in by the barkers out front. You can't go wrong at any of them for basic grilled, boiled, or fried seafood, but one favorite worth ducking into is **El Rey de la Gamba** (No. 53, Metro: Barceloneta, tel. 93/225-6401, 10 A.M.–1 A.M. Thurs.–Tues., closed Wed., €20), "the King of Shrimp," which offers excellent platters of its grilled namesake as well as aromatic pots of steamed mussels. For a little more atmosphere, head back into the barrio of Barceloneta and straight to **Can Ramonet** (C/ Maquinista 17, Metro: Barceloneta, tel. 93/319-3064, 1 P.M.–2 A.M. daily, €30), the barrio's oldest bar. The front room features wine barrel tables and a colorful bar display of fresh fish and vegetables. The exposed brick dining rooms out back are both rustic and elegant. Of course, the thing to have is fresh fish; ask for the *surgencia* (daily special). In warmer weather, there is a cozy little gardened dining area.

Along the beach, try **Agua** (Pg. Marítim 30, Metro: Ciutadella Vila Olímpica, tel. 93/225-1272, 1:30–4 P.M. and 8:30 P.M.–midnight daily, later on weekends, €30), which takes the tried-and-true nautical theme and infuses it with style. The excellent menu includes succulent monkfish, fresh pasta with prawns, lobster with rice, and, for meat-lovers, juicy, thick steaks. Dine on the terrace that borders the beach or inside with the beautiful people that clamor for seats here. Reservations are strongly suggested.

Tapas

Bar Jai-Ca (C/ Ginebra 13, Metro: Barceloneta, tel. 93/319-5002, 10 A.M.–1 A.M. daily, €12) is one of those fun corner bars that would be your favorite neighborhood spot if you lived here. With a cracked tile floor, creaky little tables, wine barrels behind the bar, and an always smiling staff, this barrio favorite serves up excellent fried seafood and cold beer to a very loyal local crowd. Try the *txokos* (fried squid), reputed to be the best in

town. During Barça soccer games, it gets wild here as this is home base for one of the team's most fervent fan clubs. **El Vaso de Oro** (C/ Balboa 6, Metro: Barceloneta, tel. 93/319-3098, 9 A.M.–midnight daily, closed Sept.) serves mounds of classic tapas (try the spicy tuna) to happy locals jammed elbow-to-elbow. If you are intimidated by crowded bars where you have to shout your order, go around 1 P.M. or 7 P.M.

MONTJUÏC
Tapas

In the barrio below Montjuïc—Poble Sec—you'll find the usual array of traditional restaurants, fast-food joints, and everything in between, including one very wonderful tapas bar, (**Quimet & Quimet** (C/ Poeta Cabanyes 25, Metro: Paral.lel, tel. 93/442-3142, noon–4 P.M. and 7–10:30 P.M. Mon.–Fri., noon–4 P.M. Sat., closed Sun., €20). Run by the Quimet family for five generations, this pint-sized bodega features just three tables but a world of amazing flavors. Rumor has it that

© CANDY LEE LABALLE

Barceloneta favorite Bar Jai-Ca draws locals and tourists to its friendly corner.

even the leader of the Catalan culinary revolution, Ferran Adrià, eats here. What's the kitchen's secret? A can opener. Spain has a long tradition of producing excellent canned and preserved seafood and vegetables. The Quimet family takes these lovely products and creates sublime treats such as salmon with Greek yogurt and truffled honey, caramelized tomato with anchovies, and cod with olive puree. The bar also has one of the best wine lists in Barcelona for a bar of its size. If you prefer beer, try the Quimet & Quimet house brew.

Rosal 34 (C/ Roser 34, tel. 93/324-9046, 1–4:30 P.M. Mon., 1–4:30 P.M. and 8:30–11:30 pm Tues.–Sat., closed Sun., €30) is one of the newest darlings on Barcelona's culinary scene. Founded by the grandfather of the current chef Josep and maitre d' Oscar in 1958, this classic tavern has received a seriously modern makeover complete with an industrial interior and semi-open kitchen. The menu, which focuses almost exclusively on tapas, is also a mix of tradition and daring. Dishes run the gamut from classically grilled anchovies to clams steamed with vanilla to deconstructed *patatas bravas* (fried potatoes with spicy tomato sauce). The wine list is also quite good, with bottles starting at just €11.

EIXAMPLE
Cafés and Desserts

Dolso Postre (C/ Valencia 227, Metro: Diagonal or Passeig de Gràcia, tel. 93/487-5964, 9 A.M.–1 A.M. Mon.–Fri., 11 A.M.–1 A.M. Sat., €15) is a sleek little haven of milk and honey. There are homemade ice creams, chocolates, and decadent desserts of all flavors. The menu changes constantly but ginger cream is a repeat winner. The floral dining room and black slate floor make it a stylish place for a light lunch or romantic dinner. The very short menu features sweet touches—hake with cherries, tuna salad with sweet corn puree. The daytime menu costs €12. At night, it's €25. **Café Viennese** (Pg. Gràcia 132, Metro: Diagonal), located in the posh Hotel Casa Fuster, is quite possibly the loveliest café/bar in Barcelona. Amid a refined den of marble columns, soaring iron-framed windows, velvet striped chairs, and a mile-long curvaceous red couch, hotel guests and discriminating locals sip coffee and cocktails.

Gourmet

Cinc Sentits (C/ Aribau 58, Metro: Pg. Gràcia, tel. 93/323-9490, www.cincsentits.com, €85)—run by self-taught chef Jordi Artal, his sister Amelia, and mother Roser—has been enchanting diners since opening in 2004. In a minimalist yet comfortable dining room, Jordi attempts to stimulate the five senses—hence the restaurant's name. One way he achieves this is by presenting a colorful, textured array of small plates in his tasting menus. The result is you never get bored—each bite is as seductive as the next. Treats might include an *ajoblanco* (traditional Spanish garlic and almond soup) topped with shrimp and an almond sorbet; monkfish with black olive compote, lemon caramel, and asparagus tips; or slow-roasted suckling pig with apples in two textures. His cuisine is winning raves among famously fickle foodies for being innovative, intriguing, and most importantly, delicious. Reservations are required; all staff speak English. Located in the stylish Hotel Cram, **Gaig** (C/ Aragó 214, Metro: Hospital Clínic, www.restaurantgaig .com, 1:30–3:30 P.M. and 9–11 P.M. Mon.– Sat., 9–11 P.M. Sun., €90), under the direction of esteemed Catalan chef Carlos Gaig, is one of Spain's top-rated restaurants. Chef Gaig follows the simple philosophy of using only the best, ripest, freshest products. The luxurious dining room, managed by Gaig's wife, the elegant Fina Navarro, only adds to the culinary experience. Because ingredients rule the menu, choose the chef's tasting menu of the day.

Tapas

Local favorite **De Tapa Madre** (C/ Mallorca 301, tel. 93/459-3134, www.detapamadre .com, 8 A.M.–midnight daily, €15) is the place to go in Eixample for classic Spanish tapas

Pastisseria Montserrat has been serving pastries to residents of Gràcia for over a century.

and home cooking. The menu is heavy on the cold meats from *jamón* to *morcilla* (blood sausage) but there are also wonderful homemade *croquetas,* stuffed red peppers, scrambled eggs with wild mushrooms, and fresh seafood—grilled or fried. The *menú del día* is a great value at €12. **La Bodegueta** (Rambla de Catalunya 100, Metro: Diagonal, tel. 93/215-4894, 7 A.M.–1:30 A.M. daily, €12), founded in 1940, appeals to a mostly neighborhood crowd with simple tapas of Catalan sausages, cheeses, and *tortillas.* Wine is drinkable and cheap, vermouth comes on tap, and the bartender really does seem to know everyone's name. In a barrio where almost every bar/café has jumped on the newer, trendier, shinier bandwagon, this old-world bodega, with its tarnished tiles and worn marble bar, remains tastefully the same. Another traditional favorite is **Cerverceria Catalana** (C/ Mallorca 236, Metro: Pg. Gràcia, tel. 93/216-0368, 8 A.M.–1:30 A.M. daily). It lives up to its name with a large selection of beers from around the world, but the real star of this cozy bar

is its tempting tapas, beautifully laid out on the bar—all you have to do is point at the savory Russian salad, the kebobs of shrimp, the *jamón* and tomato toast, the sautéed mushrooms, the deliciously fried artichokes, and so on and so on.

GRÀCIA
Quick Bites
For a carry-out from the past, visit **Pastisseria Montserrat** (Trav. Gràcia 172, tel. 93/218-4743, 9 A.M.–9 P.M. daily). Founded in 1870, the pastry shop with its crooked wooden floor, oversized glass cases, shelves lined with local goodies, and white-aproned staff looks like it must have back when Gaudí was stomping these streets. Take a sweet pastry to go, or if you crave something savory, try one of the stuffed croissants. For something a little more modern, **De Ja Bu** (Pl. Sol 1, 11 A.M.–11 P.M. Tues.–Sat., closed Mon., €8) delivers with a roster of fresh sandwiches, fun salads, fruit smoothies, and stuffed potatoes. There are quite a few vegetarian and vegan dishes

on offer, too. The enthusiastic young owner lived in England for several years and speaks the Queen's English perfectly. There are a few stools to eat inside, but a better option is to head out to the square in front.

Tapas

Sol Soler (Pl. Sol 21, tel. 93/277-4440, noon–2 A.M. daily, €8) is the kind of place that spawns poetry—cracked tile floor, rickety marble tables, dusky antique mirrors on the wall. It attracts a distinctive bohemian, arty crowd that tucks hungrily into the cheap, tasty tapas. Daily offerings might include couscous, chicken wings, and quiche and never cost more than €3. At **Flash Flash** (C/ Granada del Penedès, 25, Metro: Diagonal, tel. 93/237-0990, 1 P.M.–1:30 A.M. daily, €12) the ubiquitous Spanish omelet, *tortilla,* reigns supreme. There are over 70 types on the menu, plus burgers and salads. The black-and-white mod decor is original. This is the kind of place that was hip when it was founded in 1970 (by a top fashion photographer, hence the name) and continues to be hip today. **Sureny** (Pl. Revolució 17, tel. 93/213-7556, Metro: Fontana, 8:30 P.M.–12 A.M. Tues.–Thurs., 8:30 P.M.–1 A.M. Fri. and Sat., 1–3:30 P.M. and 8:30 P.M.–midnight Sun.) is an unassuming bar with surprising tapas. Ahead-of-the-mill fare might include venison with tangerine sauce and violet chips; foie gras with currant puree; or tempura-battered spring onions.

Information and Services

Tourist and Travel Information

The main **Barcelona Tourist Office** (Pl. Catalunya, s/n, tel. 80/711-7222, teltur@barcelona turisme.com, www.barcelonaturisme.com, 9 A.M.–9 P.M. daily) is located underneath Plaza Catalunya and is a hive of activity. In addition to a counter full of attendants (take a number, get in line), there is a hotel booking service, guided tour information, and a gift shop. There are also tourist offices at Sants train station and the airport (terminal 1 and 2). There are mini-tourist offices in front of the Columbus monument at the water and in front of Las Ramblas 115. They are bright red with a large lower-case "I" on top. In summer, tourist booths are set up in Plaça Espanya, La Sagrada Família, and on Passeig Joan de Borbó in La Barceloneta. For regional information, the **Cataluña Tourist Office** (Pg. Gràcia 107, tel. 93/238-4000, www .catalunyaturisme.com, 10 A.M.–7 P.M. Mon.–Sat., 10 A.M.–2 P.M. Sun.) offers support and services for travels throughout Cataluña, including Sitges and Montserrat.

The most comprehensive freebie guide aimed at tourists is **See Barcelona,** a half-sized magazine loaded with information from history and holidays to museums and bars. It features wonderful photography and excellent walking tours for all the barrios of Barcelona. Also look out for **Barcelona Connect** (www .barcelonaconnect.com), an expat magazine offering a lot of useful information for the visitor. Thanks to Barcelona's large expat community, there are several free English-language periodicals available, including the glossy **Metropolitan** (www.barcelona-metropolitan.com), the weekly paper **BCN Week** (www.bcnweek.com), and the pocket-sized **Miniguide** (www.barcelona-inside.com). In addition to these websites, visit www.softguide-barcelona.com, an accommodations, dining, and shopping guide, and the incredibly useful, very frank www.barcelona-tourist-guide.com.

Banks and Currency Exchange

Barcelona is teeming with **ATMs,** Of them, those from **La Caixa,** with its red-and-blue star logo designed by Miró, tend to work the best and allow for the largest withdrawals. In the airport, skip the non-bank machines near the baggage counter and instead use the bank-affiliated machines on the far left of the arrivals lounge.

With the ease of ATMs, debit cards, and

Look for the red-and-white cubes for all tourist information in Barcelona.

credit cards, it is almost archaic to **exchange U.S. dollars,** but if you feel more comfortable with bringing your stash of cash, you'll have to make a *cambio* (exchange). The best rates will be at big banks such as **La Caixa** and **BBVA,** both of which have branches in Terminal A and B of the airport. The BBVA closes at 3 P.M. while La Caixa stays open until 10 P.M. Both are shut on the weekends, but they have automatic currency-exchange machines running 24 hours. In the main tourist zones, just look for any office with either the word *banco* (bank) or *caixa* (cashier) in the title.

If you have brought **travelers checks** from Thomas Cook, Visa, or American Express, the same major banks as above will change them and department stores, top hotels, and chain restaurants should accept them—though don't count on it. A good alternative is the American Express travel card—just like a credit card, but not. There are two **American Express** offices in Barcelona: Passeig de Gràcia 101 (tel. 93/415-2371) and Rambla 74 (tel. 93/301-1166).

If you need to have money wired, **Western**

Union (www.westernunion.com, tel. 800/325-6000) has agreements with dozens of companies in Barcelona. You'll have to coordinate the exchange with someone stateside and if you do not have a passport to receive the money, you will have to create a question and answer pass code with your contact. The company that works with them the most is **Change Express** (Rambla 45, tel. 93/412-5478, 8 A.M.–midnight daily). There are several more branches all around Barcelona. The larger post offices in Barcelona also serve as Western Union sites.

As throughout Spain, most Barcelona businesses accept American Express, Visa, and Mastercard, whether credit or debit. Other cards are not accepted, so leave them at home. It is advisable to use your cards to pay for big-ticket items like your hotel bill, a splurge at a top restaurant, or a purchase in a major store. Do not use your credit card for smaller shops and stores. It is not practice in Spain to obscure credit card numbers from sales receipts and you are more likely to run into problems with a smaller business. Be sure and read *Money* in *Essentials* for complete coverage of currency and banking matters in Spain.

Communications

To buy stamps, head to any *estanco* (tobacco shop). They are throughout the city and easily identified by a brown and yellow sign that says "Tabacos." Bright yellow *correo* mailboxes are all over town. The **central post office** (Vía Laietana 1, tel. 93/486-8050, 8:30–10 P.M. Mon.–Sat., noon–10 P.M. Sun.) provides complete postal service.

Most hotels and many cafés now provide Internet or Wi-Fi as standard service. If yours doesn't, there are Internet cafés all over the town. The most central—and with dozens of terminals, the biggest—is **Easy Internet** (Rambla 31, Metro: Drassanes, 8 A.M.–11 P.M. daily). Bring coins and purchase a ticket to use the computers from the machine by the front door. There is a Subway sandwich shop in the lobby, but please don't ask the attendants for help with the Internet—they don't know and frankly don't care. **BBiGG** (C/ Comtal 9, Metro: Catalunya,

© CANDY LEE LABALLE

BARCELONA

DON'T BE A VICTIM

Though crime is discussed in the *Essentials* chapter under *Health and Safety*, the following crime-prevention tips bear repeating, as Barcelona seethes with petty thieves (though violent crime is rare). Unfortunately, if you are going to be robbed in Spain, odds are, it will happen here. Does that mean Barcelona is not safe or that you should cancel your trip? No way. Barcelona is an amazing, vibrant town that deserves to be explored at your leisure. However, being aware of the high level of pickpocketing and purse- and camera-snatching and practicing the following basic tips can help ensure that you are not a victim. The majority of thieves are both lazy and cautious; they look for easy victims that they can rob quickly, quietly, and easily. Do not be easy!

Finally, even though Barcelona is being singled out here, petty crime against tourists is a problem to be aware of in all the major touristic cities including Madrid, Granada, and Sevilla.

These tips have been adapted from an article written by Dr. John Bolton, editor of the excellent website www.barcelona-tourist-guide.com.

STAY CONNECTED

The simplest way to not be robbed is to stay connected to your belongings at all times. Purses should have straps long enough to fit over your shoulder and across the chest. Keep the bag part in front of you, zippered shut, with your hand on it at all times. Backpacks (not recommended) should be zippered at all times and worn around the front when you are in crowds. Any valuables should be kept deeply within the bag, far from the opening. However, be aware that thieves do not only stick their hands in bags and backpacks but have been known to slit them open, particularly in crowded places.

When you are in a restaurant, bar, or Internet café, do not let go of your bag. Do not hang it on the back of a chair. Do not put it on the floor at your feet. Instead, keep your bag on your lap, with your arm through the strap, or slip your leg through the strap if you will put it on the floor. If you go the floor route, you can also slip the leg of your chair through the strap. Again, none of this will ensure you won't get robbed (strap slitting is common), but again, it makes you a less easy target.

Be sure and stay connected to your goods at places like nightclubs and beaches as well. Do not leave your bag or valuables unattended while you dance or swim.

Finally, when taking photos or videos, always have the camera strap wrapped firmly around your wrist – several times if possible. When the camera or video recorder is not being used, keep it tucked in your bag. If you use a shoulder or neck strap, again, keep the item in front of you and your hand on it when moving through the crowds. Thieves who see a valuable item hanging from a string will sometimes make a run at it whether it is on your body or not, particularly if they think they can overpower you. Many a victim has ended up with a bruised neck, sprained ankle, or worse after falling as a thief pulled the item right off their body.

CHUCK THE BACKPACK

Unless there is a reason why you truly need a backpack, chuck it. One, it pegs you as a tourist and thus a potential victim. Two, in order to get at anything, you have to swing it off your back and go rooting. Three, you have to put it down at cafés and bars. A much better option is an across-the-shoulder bag, similar to the bags that bike couriers and postal workers use. One, you can access your goods even while walking. Two, you can keep your hand on your goods at all times. Three, if you stop in a bar or café, you don't have to remove the bag from your shoulders. Just remember, as you move about, keep the bag part in front of you, not swung to the side or back. If back problems are an issue, remember to switch the bag from shoulder to shoulder periodically.

BACK TO THE WALL

You will have to stop and check maps, subway guides, and this guidebook on occasion. When doing so, assume that a thief is checking you out, hoping to take advantage of your distraction to pickpocket or bag-snatch you. Make it that much harder by backing up to a wall before looking at your maps and guides. It is much more difficult for a thief to sneak up on you this way. Practice this technique in bus stations, train terminals, and airports. This trick is also useful when taking photos – though not always practical.

DIVIDE YOUR ASSETS

Keep small bills and loose change in one pocket in order to easily pay for subway tickets, coffees, and museum entrances. Keep your larger bills and credit cards elsewhere – perhaps in an inner pocket or a money belt. Never remove the larger bills in public. Step into a bathroom and shift the bills out as needed. Never, ever flaunt large bills or a wad of money in transport stations. These places teem with thieves.

Related to this, don't take more money with you than you will need for a day. You will need a picture ID if you want to use a credit card – a driver's license is usually fine. However, to be sure, have a copy of your passport with you. Leave your passport in your hotel for safekeeping.

CULTIVATE A CROWD MENTALITY

Whenever you are in a crowd – on the subway, watching a street performer, on a busy sidewalk – keep a crowd mentality. That is, be aware that thieves use the jostle and bustle of the crowd to pick pockets, often looking victims right in the face while they do it. When you are in a crowd, pull your bag to your chest, put your hand in your pocket over your money, and keep a close grip on your valuables. A thief will recognize this and go after a less-vigilant, easier victim instead.

BEWARE OF THE BIRD POOP

This is an oldie but still icky. You are walking along and suddenly something wet and mucky lands on your shoulders. Immediately some kind soul – speaking English, no less – ap-

pears, claiming a bird pooped on you. They have water and tissue and begin trying to clean you up. They are robbing you. Put your hand on your valuables and get away, even if you have to run. Do not talk or engage with the "helper." It takes less than 20 seconds to slip your wallet away – don't give them even a second.

Related to this, do not let anyone distract you for any reason. Another common scam is they come at you with an open map asking for directions. While you are poring over the map, their hands are beneath it entering your bag or their friend is behind you doing the same. Other distractions include trying to sell you a flower or a sprig of rosemary. Again, your first step always is to put your hand on your goods, say no, and walk away. Do not worry about seeming rude; someone who is not a thief will not take offense (actually, they won't be there in the first place), only a thief will feign indignity.

DON'T GET ANGRY, GET AWAY

If you catch a thief mid-action, you will naturally be angry. Don't let that feeling translate into action. Do not, under any circumstances, attempt to retaliate physically. Thieves often work in teams. You only see the one with his (or her) hand in your bag, but guaranteed there are four or five nearby and if you confront one physically, the others will descend upon you faster than you can think. It is not worth it. If you do catch a thief at work, look them in the eye, and they will slink away. If a police officer is nearby, you can try pointing the thief out, but the sad reality is they probably won't care and by the time you even get to the officer, the thief will be long gone.

BE ALERT IN UNLIKELY PLACES

Thieves have taken to committing their crimes in unlikely places. Shops are very popular – from cheap department stores to upscale boutiques. As you are checking out the goods, a thief may be checking out you. Again, keep your hand on your goods and keep an eye on your back. If someone is shopping too close

(continues on next page)

DON'T BE A VICTIM (CONTINUED)

to you, move away. If someone attempts to rob you, point it out to a shop employee, as they actually are much more responsive than the police. If you are trying on clothes, do not put your valuables on the floor of the dressing room where someone can stick their hand in and snatch your bag. Hang your valuables on the clothing hook.

Of course, you know to be vigilant in bus and train stations. That should extend to airports. Super-cheap flights throughout Europe means that a thief can pick up a €30 ticket to London then spend the day robbing unsuspecting travelers in the departures lounge. Again, stay connected to your goods and you should be fine.

DON'T GO IT ALONE

If you are traveling alone, exercise normal precautions when returning to your hotel late at night. If you are staying in a particularly desolate area, it is worthwhile to take a cab simply for safety's sake, even if you are on a budget. If you feel uncomfortable at any time

or accosted on an empty road, turn, run, and scream "Socorro!" (Help!).

WHAT IF THEY GET YOU?

If you are a victim, report the crime to the police. If you were insured, most insurance policies will require a police report. If your passport was stolen, you will have to visit your consulate to get a replacement. Both this chapter and the *Madrid* chapter have more information under *Emergency Services*. If you feel that a store, restaurant, or hotel in some way facilitated the robbery, demand the *hojas de reclamación*, an official complaint form that all businesses must report to the government. Businesses do not like to have these filled out and will often become quite helpful when you demand one.

HAVE FUN

Being aware and practicing these tips will help you ward off robberies and let you have a safe trip. Don't let thieves dampen your vacation. Your focus should be on fun, not fear.

tel. 93/301-4020, 9 A.M.–11 P.M. daily) is Easy's biggest rival. In Eixample, get your fix at **People Web** (C/ Provença 367, Metro: Verdaguer, tel. 93/207-0197, 11 A.M.–11 P.M. Mon.–Fri., 6 P.M.–11 P.M. Sat.–Sun.), a cheery little cybercafé with wicker chairs and a cold-drink-laden cooler. You can also make photocopies, buy phone cards, and top off your cell phone. For more office services, including software-loaded computers and printing, head to the 24-hour **Workcenter** (Av. Diagonal 439, Metro: Diagonal, tel. 93/390-1101). There are several more locations in town; see www.workcenter.es for the one nearest you. You'll have to buy a card and deposit money on it to use the computers, but if you are traveling in Spain after leaving Barcelona, Workcenter has locations in most major cities. Remember, Internet cafés are breeding grounds for thieves. Keep your bag on your lap or on the floor with the strap around you leg. Do not let your guard down for even a minute.

The most convenient—and safest—way to stay in touch with loved ones back home is to get a **cell phone.** If you will be in Spain for a week or two, consider renting a cell phone from **Onspanishtime** (www.onspanishtime.com). Run by an American expat, the company rents and delivers cell phones throughout Spain at rates much better than similar American-based companies. If you will bring your own phone but want a local SIM card, Onspanishtime can help there too. If you will be staying a month or more, you can buy a phone with a *tarjeta SIM de pre-pago* (a pay-as-you-go card). Any electronic shop will sell them, but to ensure quality of service and product, try El Corte Inglés, FNAC, or specialty shops like **The Phone House** (Rambla de Catalunya 31, Metro: Pg. Gràcia, tel. 90/288-7325, 10 A.M.–2 P.M. and 4:30–8:30 P.M.). Look also for the red **Vodafone** shops that are all over town. In any of these places you should be able to find a phone for as low as €40.

The **area code** for Barcelona is 93. (See *Communications and Media* in the *Essentials* chapter for more on calling to and from Spain.)

Emergency Services

For general emergencies, including crime, dialing 112 works in all of Spain. The **Guàrdia Urbana** is the local police force and they run a special **Tourist Center** (Rambla 43, tel. 93/290-3440, 7 A.M.–midnight Sun.–Thurs., 7 A.M.–2 A.M. Fri. and Sat.) to help visitors who have been the victim of a crime. There is always an English-speaking officer on duty. Staff can help you contact your local consulate as well as take the *denuncia* (police report) that will be necessary in order to get a replacement passport if it was stolen. The office can also help with medical needs. If you cannot get to the office, Spain has an **English-speaking crime hotline** at tel. 90/210-2112 (8 A.M.–midnight daily). You will be able to make your report on the phone and will be instructed to the nearest police station where you can sign it and get a copy. To replace the passport, go to the **U.S. Consulate** (Pg. Reina Elisenda 23, FCG. Reina Elisenda, tel. 93/280-2227, 9 A.M.–1 P.M. Mon.–Fri.), but call first to ensure you bring the correct documents and the right amount of money. To speak to an after-hours U.S. duty office, call 91/587-2200.

For **emergency medical services,** dial 061 for an ambulance or head to the *urgencias* (emergency) of any major hospital. **Hospital Clínic i Provincial** (C/ Villarroel 170, Metro: Hospital Clínic, tel. 93/227-5400), located in the southwest quadrant of Eixample, is accustomed to dealing with English-speakers. They can also handle non-emergency needs. Before leaving the United States, you should contact your health insurance provider to find out about reimbursement of medical expenses. The American embassy's website, www.embusa.es, also provides a wealth of medical and dental information—click on U.S. Citizen Services.

Most minor problems, from colds to traveler's diarrhea, can be treated with a visit to a *farmacia* (pharmacy). Pharmacies take turns performing as *farmacias de guardia* (24-hour pharmacies). Head to the closest pharmacy to your hotel and there will be a posting of where the nearest open pharmacy is. You can also head to the following 24-hour pharmacies: on La Rambla, **Farmacia Clapes Antoja** (La Rambla 98); in Eixample, **Farmacia Laguna Ventosa** (C/ Provença 459).

Laundry Services

Catch up on laundry at **LavaXpres** in Raval (C/ Ferlandina 34, Metro: Sant Antoni) or in Las Ramblas (C/ Nou de Sant Francesc 5, Metro: Liceu). Both fully automatic stations are open 8 A.M.–10 P.M. daily. A wash or a dry starts at €3.50. Prices increase with load size. Bring change. In Gràcia, get your load done at the cleverly named **Laundry** (Pl. Sol 11, Metro: Fontana or FCG:Gràcia, 7 A.M.–11 P.M. daily). Washing starts at €3.25. Grab a table at the terrace right in front of the laundry and sip as your clothes tumble. In Born, try **Lavomatic** (C/ Consolat del Mar 43, Metro: Barceloneta, 9 A.M.–9 P.M. Mon.–Sat., closed Sun.). A load

a modernist *farmacia* on Las Ramblas

of wash costs €4 and drying starts at €0.80 per five minutes.

Luggage Storage

At the airport, luggage storage is located in Terminal B. The Estació Sants train station offers luggage storage near the back of the station, by the golden arches of America's favorite hamburger. The Nord bus station has lockers in the outside bus depot. At all three places, rates start at about €4.50 for 24 hours; bring change or small bills for the machines. If you lose your key, you'll have to pay about €10 in replacement fines.

Getting There

Air

Barcelona Airport (tel. 90/240-4704, press 9 for English, www.aena.es), also called El Prat de Llobregat, is located about 13 kilometers (eight miles) southwest of the city center. It has three terminals (A, B, and C). Most U.S. carriers land at Terminal A, though check with your onboard crew to be sure. The airport's English website has extensive information about flights, terminals, and which airlines land where. You'll find the usual ATMs, money exchange, shops, restaurants, car rental agencies, and tourist booths in Terminals A and B.

Most flights from the United States connect in Madrid. If you are planning on seeing both cities, it makes financial and logistical sense to disembark in Madrid, spend a few days, then take an inexpensive national flight to Barcelona on one of the Spanish companies, such as Spanair (www.spanair.com), Air Eurpoa (www.aireuropa.com), or Iberia (www.iberia .com). You can book with them directly online or by visiting any travel agent in Madrid, or if your Spanish is up to speed, you can find the best deals at E-Dreams (www.edreams.es).

There are several ways to **transfer to the city center**, though the cheapest and easiest is by bus. **Aero Bus** (tel. 93/415-6020, €3.60) leaves every 12 minutes 6 A.M.–1 A.M. daily. The route stops at all three airport terminals and travels to Plaça de Catalunya via Plaça Espanya in a one-way direction. Both plazas are home to metro stations that can then take you almost anywhere in the city. To get to the airport, catch the Aerobus from Plaça de Catalunya, just in front of the El Corte Inglés. The ride, under optimal traffic conditions, lasts about 30 minutes, though count on 45 for traffic. Also, there is usually quite a long line at Plaça de Catalunya. Expect to take up to 15 minutes to board a bus.

A **taxi** from the airport to Plaça de Catalunya should run about €20, with a minimum fee of €11.70. There is an automatic airport surcharge of €2.90 and each piece of luggage costs €0.90. The taxis are black and yellow and will be lined up outside the arrivals terminals. You'll be directed to take the first taxi in line. Most taxi drivers have long ago given up ripping off tourists, but to be safe, insist that the meter be turned on (if it is not) and ask for *una factura* (a receipt).

Getting from the airport by **train** (every half-hour, 6 A.M.–10 P.M. daily, €2.30) is the least attractive option due mainly to the very long walk from the airport to the train station. Exit your terminal and proceed to the long bridge that takes you to the Prat train station. It takes about 15–20 minutes to walk—not fun with luggage. The train stops in Sants, Passeig de Gràcia, and França. This option is more feasible if you will be traveling directly out of Barcelona via the Sants or França stations.

Train

Barcelona has two train stations, França and Sants. Trains for both stations are run by the Spanish railroad, **Renfe** (tel. 90/224-0202, www.renfe.es), and also serve local FCG lines. **Estació de Sants** (Pl. dels Països Catalans, s/n, Metro: Estació Sants) is located in Eixample and is the main station for all national and some international journeys. It connects with the metro lines L3 (green) and L5 (blue). The other station, **Estació de França** (Av. Marquès de l'Argentera, s/n, Metro: Barceloneta) offers a few international destinations (Paris, Zurich, and Milan) through the Elipsos service (www .elipsos.com), as well as several trains with destinations throughout Cataluña. It is about two blocks away from the Barceloneta (L4, yellow) metro station. Both stations have all the usual amenities like cafés, luggage storage, ATMs, and tourist information. Taxis are also stationed in front of both and there is a €0.90 charge for each piece of luggage.

Bus

Barcelona's **Estació del Nord** (C/ Alí-bei 80, Metro: Arc de Triomf, tel. 90/226-0606, www .barcelonanord.com) is the city's main bus hub. It offers lockers, parcel service, restaurants, and tourist information. In Spain, which bus company you travel with will depend on where you are going. Because not all bus companies are based at Nord—in fact some depart from their own offices—be sure to check Nord's website before you head over there. If you cannot find your destination on the Nord site, go to any *agencia de viajes* (travel agent)—El Corte Inglés is a good choice and agents usually speak English—and purchase your ticket there. You may be charged a fee of a few euros for the issuance of the ticket, but it is worth it to save the time and hassle trying to figure it out for yourself.

Ferry

If you are traveling to or from the Islas Baleares (Mallorca, Menorca, Ibiza), you will pass through the **Estació Marítim** (Moll de Barcelona, s/n, tel. 93/412-7914), located south of the Columbus statue. **Trasmediterránea** (tel. 90/245-4645, www.trasmediterranea.com) runs half a dozen trips per day to/from the islands and Valencia.

Car

If you are arriving from France or other points north, Barcelona sits on the AP-7/C-33 highway. You can enter the city via the surrounding ring roads or by taking Avinguda Meridiana, which leads right to the center. From Andalucía and the south, you'll catch the AP-2 into the city and enter via Avinguda Diagonal. Traffic in Barcelona can be vicious, especially during rush hours, and it is not recommended that you use a car to get around town. Parking garages can be prohibitively expensive—up to €26 per day. If you will have a car during your visit, it is a good idea to pick a hotel that has its own parking facilities. Street parking is scarce and limited to zones painted blue (for visitors) and green (for residents). In the latter, visitors can park, but only for a short amount of time. In both cases, buy a parking ticket from either the blue or green machine that is located on the block where you are parking. This ticket must be displayed in your window.

Getting Around

Walking in the Ciutat Vella is easy, as it is compact and small; however, to get out to Eixample, Parc Güell, Port Olímpic, or Montjuïc you'll need to take public transport. With an extensive network of subways, trams, commuter trains, and buses, the visitor can get to just about any point in the city easily, quickly, and cheaply. If you are staying at least three days, it is worthwhile to buy the **T-10**, a 10-ride pass that is good for the subway, the buses, and

the commuter trains (FCG) within Zone 1 (the central area of town that few tourists will ever have the need to leave). It costs €6.65 and is valid for 10 trips. Individual tickets cost €1.20, so the T-10 provides savings of €5.35 (a little more than continental breakfast for two). If you are traveling in a couple or group, the same ticket can be used by each person. As you enter, each person must run the ticket through the machine. However, be sure to stick together;

if one of you transfers off onto another subway line and gets caught by authorities without a ticket, a fine will be issued. For all details about the T-10 and the Barcelona public transport system, visit www.tmb.es.

Metro

As in the rest of Spain, the subway system in Barcelona is called the metro. It has five lines covering 123 stations throughout the city. The lines are numbered and color-coded: L1 is red; L2 purple; L3 green; L4 yellow; and L5 blue. Almost all guidebooks have a metro map printed in them and you can get copies of the map at any tourist office. The trick to finding your way through the system is knowing the destination of the line you will take. Lines are named by their final point. So L2 purple is called Paral.lel-Pep Ventura, as those are its two end points. Determine where you are on the map and where you have to go, then look for the end point in the same direction. Ticket machines are located in the *boca* (mouth) of the metro stations and are easy to use, especially when you select the "English" function. Some stations also have a manned counter, but don't expect the attendant to speak English. Tickets cost €1.20, but the aforementioned T-10 is a much better bargain if you will use the system over a couple of days. The timetable for the metro is 5 A.M.–midnight, Sunday–Thursday and 5 A.M.–2 A.M. on weekends.

A word of caution: The metro stations—especially busy ones like Catalunya and Passeig de Gràcia—are natural congregating spots for thieves and pickpockets. Always have your money for the ticket in an easily accessible front pocket so you don't have to fish out your money belt or wallet in public. Also, be aware of your belongings at all times. The thieves don't just prey on everyone. They watch the crowd and go after the person that seems the most lost, confused, or distracted. Figure out where you are going before you arrive to the ticket counter and have your loose change ready; these two simple steps will decrease your odds of being a victim. Of course, practice common sense on the metro as well, meaning hands on your purses, wallets in front pockets, and backpacks turned around to the front.

Bus

Like the metro, Barcelona's city buses are efficient and inexpensive (€1.20). They also travel a much wider distance than the metros with over 80 routes. However, the bus is much more complicated to figure out. You have to know the city fairly well to find your line or your stop. You'll most likely use the bus to and from your hotel (ask the front desk for the specifics) or to Montjuïc or Parc Güell. Tickets cost €1.20 per ride or you can use the T-10 pass. Timetables vary on the line, but generally run 6 A.M.–11:30 P.M. After hours, there are 16 **Nit Bus** lines that provide service 10:30 P.M.–5 A.M. All but four of the lines pass through Plaça de Catalunya. Like the day buses, the night buses require a healthy knowledge of the city. Your best bet is to ask at your hotel for the nearest night bus line. You can also peruse www.tmb.es. Finally, note that the T-10 will not work on night buses; instead, purchase a €1.05 ticket when boarding the bus.

Commuter Train

Barcelona has a far-reaching network of commuter trains called Ferrocarrils de la Generalitat, known by the acronym **FCG** (tel. 93/205-1515, www.fgc.es). The main stations are in Plaça de Espanya and Plaça de Catalunya. You most likely will use the FCG if you go to the amusement park of Tibidabo or to the barrio of Gràcia, as the area is poorly served by metro. For trips to Sitges, the FCG is also the way to go.

Taxi

Barcelona has a fleet of over 11,000 taxis that buzz all over the city. They are very distinctive, painted black and yellow. To hail one, head to the closest big street and hold out your arm for any taxi you see sporting a lit green lamp on top. The light indicates the cab is free. Between 6 A.M.–10 P.M., *tarif 2* is in effect and the starting fare is €1.30 and increases by €0.74 each kilometer. *Tarif 1* is slightly higher and applies to night hours. There is a €3 supplement for entering or leaving the airport and €0.90 for each piece of luggage.

After the metro closes, the clamor for taxis can get severe. It is not uncommon to witness scuffles among people waiting for taxis along major thoroughfares and you may end up walking home. You have three options: familiarize yourself with the night bus system before going out, don't go stray too far from your hotel, or—our favorite—stay out until the metro starts up again at 5 A.M.

Car Rental

If you want to rent a car to take out of the city, along the coast, or into the Penedès wine region, Terminal B at the airport is your best bet for variety. **Hertz** (tel. 93/298-3637, www .hertz.es), **Avis** (tel. 93/298-3601, www.avis .es), **National Atesa** (tel. 93/298-3433, www .atesa.es), and **Europcar** (tel. 932 983 300, www.europcar.es) are all located right next to each other. You can find the best rates online by visiting a broker such as www.carbookers .com or www.easycar.com.

Vicinity of Barcelona

◖ MONTSERRAT

Just 40 kilometers (25 miles) northwest of Barcelona, the nearly mythical massif of Montserrat rises dramatically from the banks of the Llobregat River. Reaching over 1,219 meters (4,000 feet) at its highest peak, Montserrat is a natural wonder that began some 25 million years ago when this entire region was still below the sea. Some heavy geological twisting and turning, a few melted glaciers, the recession of the sea, and millions of years of sun, rain, wind, and sleet gave birth to Montserrat as we know it today. The faithful prefer the origin myth contained in a favorite hymn that sings of the mountain being sawed into shape by baby angels. Whichever theory you prefer, there is no denying it is a magical place. Massive sepia-colored columns seem to melt together in a soaring mass 9.7 kilometers (six miles) long and 4.8 kilometers (three miles) wide. Tucked all around its surface are plunging gorges, misshapen caves, and tufts of dark green vegetation. From a distance, the top of the mountain is outlined as jagged peaks across the sky. It is a truly dramatic sight that has not only given the mountain its name—*serrat* means "jagged" in Catalan—but has inspired countless legends. One claims that the Arthurian knight Parzival found the Holy Grail here. That story, in turn, inspired Wagner to pen his opera *Parsifal*.

However, the legend that most important to Montserrat is that of the Virgen de Montserrat. The story goes, Saint Peter traveled to the mountain not long after Jesus's death to hide a statue of the Virgin Mary carved by none other than Saint Luke. Centuries passed and the statue was lost. In 880, some shepherds (isn't it always the shepherds?) saw a bright light and were led to a grotto where they uncovered the long-lost statue. When a local bishop tried to move it to an appropriate chapel, the small statue was found to be too heavy. As a result the first shrine on the mountain was built. By the 9th century, there were four chapels in the mountain. Only that of St. Acisclo remains in the gardens of the present-day monastery. The mountain and the Virgin are among the most venerated holy sights in the world—the holiest in Cataluña—and thousands of pilgrims make their way here daily to pay their respects to the Virgin and ask for her blessings. It is particularly popular with newlyweds who seek the blessing of their union.

Sights

Monestir de Montserrat (tel. 93/877-7766, www.abadiamontserrat.net, 7 A.M.–8:30 P.M. daily May–Nov., 7 A.M.–7:30 P.M. daily Dec.–April, free) is a structure that would be impressive in its size were it anywhere else other than beneath the looming peaks of Montserrat. The original monastery was founded in 1025 and was firmly Romanesque in style. Home to an order of Benedictine monks, the monastery was expanded upon greatly over the centuries and became very rich thanks to faithful patrons. In 1811, Napoleon's troops looted and destroyed the sanctuary during the Peninsular War. The current monastery is a result of a decades-long rebuilding process in the mid-1800s. It is currently home to around four-dozen monks. During your visit, be sure to visit the gift shop where you can buy chocolates and liqueurs made by their blessed hands.

The main sight in the monastery is the statue of the **Virgen de Montserrat.** In the late 12th century, a new image of the Virgin was sculpted. Nicknamed La Moreneta (which translates variously from the cutesy "little brown one" to the regal "black Madonna"), the statue is a truly lovely example of Romanesque sculpture. Her skin is dark brown, her nose elongated out of proportion, her blank eyes transfixed on some holy thought. On her golden-clad knee is the baby Jesus as a toddler. In her hand is a globe, which is what pilgrims touch when they come to see her. Actually, it is all they can touch as the rest of her is behind protective glass. Incidentally, it is unclear where the original statue went. In 1881, the Virgin of Montserrat was declared the Patron Saint of Cataluña. Visit her 8–10:30 A.M. and noon–6:30 P.M. daily. But be aware, on weekends and on her two feast days, April 27 and September 8, lines can be up to an hour long. If you get a chance, step behind the statue where the faithful dip personal items in the font of baptismal water to soak up good blessings.

The monastery is also home to the **Escolania,** an internationally renowned boys' choir founded in the 14th century. The singers, aged 9–14, are educated and trained at the monastery. Hear their angelic voices at 1 P.M. Monday–Friday and noon and 6:45 P.M. on Sundays. They do not perform on Saturdays, or during the month of July. Get there early if you want to get a spot in the church. Also, be aware, if it is Sunday and you are relying on public transportation off of the mountain, the last cable-car down is at 6:45 P.M., so you'll have to be sure and attend the noon service.

The complex also houses the **Museu de Montserrat** (10 A.M.–7 P.M. daily, €6.50). where over 1,300 works of art—all gifts to the monastery—are displayed. There are quite a few masters, including El Greco, Michelangelo, Monet, Dalí, and Picasso.

The mountain also provides wonderful hikes and nature trails. Visit the **Montserrat Information Office** (9 A.M.–7:40 P.M. daily), located inside the complex after you exit the cable car, for maps and details on the various routes around the mountain. If you don't want to hike, there are two funiculars that go to the mountain's two most popular spots. **Santa Cova** (the holy grotto) is where the original statue was found. Today, there is a replica of the current statue in the grotto. The funicular (€2.50 round-trip) cuts 20 minutes off the 40-minute hike. **Sant Joan** is the highest peak on the mountain and affords stunning views out to the Pyrenees in the north and the Mediterranean Sea in the east. The funicular (€6.10 round-trip) drops you on the top. From there, there are six established hiking routes of varying difficulties and lengths.–Before setting out, be sure you have good walking shoes and a sweater or jacket; Montserrat is quite a bit cooler than Barcelona.

For complete information on Montserrat and all its sights and activities, visit the excellent www.montserratvisita.com.

Accommodations and Food

The majority of visitors to Montserrat just do a day trip, which makes spending the night a lovely option for getting away from it all. There are only two places to stay, both on the monastery complex. **Hotel Abat Cisneros** (tel. 93/877-7701, reserves@larsa-montserrat .com, €78) offers unpretentious rooms in a cozy annex of the monastery. The hotel also runs the **Abat Marcet Apartments,** which can house up to four people for long-term stays. For dining, the hotel offers a good, if pricey, restaurant. There is also **Restaurant Montserrat,** an elegant dining room with wonderful picture windows looking over the mountain. It is a surprisingly good value at around €16 per head. Also on the monastery complex is a self-service restaurant, a bar, and a cafeteria. However, most people bring their lunch from Barcelona and enjoy a picnic outdoors.

Getting There and Around

Montserrat is an easy trip to manage on your own, though there are no shortage of companies willing to haul you up. The most straightforward route is to head to Plaça de Espanya and catch the **FCG train** (every hour starting at 8:36 A.M., €12 round-trip). It will deposit you at the **Aeri Cable Car** (9:25 A.M.–1:45 P.M. and 2:20–6:45 P.M. Mar.–Oct., 10:10 A.M.–1:45 and 2:20–5:45 P.M. Nov.–Feb., €7 round-trip) which goes up 1,219 meters (4,000 feet) in five minutes. The views are awesome—but not for those with fear of heights. Alternately, you can take the FCG to the Monistrol stop, instead of the Aeri, and catch a train called **Cremellera** (8 A.M.–9 P.M., €8.70).

You can also buy the **Trans Montserrat** ticket (€19), which includes the train to Montserrat, the cable car or train ride up to the monastery, plus tickets for the funiculars that ascend to Santa Cova and Sant Joan. You can buy the ticket at any of the FCG stations or during shopping hours at the FCG booth in the El Triangle mall at the top of Las Ramblas in Plaça de Catalunya.

If you want to skip the hassle of juggling time schedules and buying tickets, a packaged tour might be for you. One of the better ones is from **Rabbie's Explore Catalunya** (tel. 93/211-9566, www.rabbies.eu.com, €39). The tour includes transport and an English-speaking tour guide, but it is structured so that you can also take off and do your own thing. On the way down, the tour stops at **Friexenet,** one of Cataluña's biggest *cava* producers. Lunch and extras are not included. Convenience and guidance are.

SITGES

South of Barcelona, 35 kilometers (22 miles) down the coast, sits Sitges. Boasting an excellent beach, a picturesque medieval quarter, and a sprinkling of modernist buildings, this once-sleepy fishing village stepped into the limelight as the resort of choice for wealthy Barcelonans in the early 20th century. More recently, it has gained fame as one of Europe's premier gay and lesbian resorts. However, the reality is that multi-faceted Sitges is a grab bag of fun in the sun for just about anyone. Larger hotels cater to families and all-night DJ parties keep Barcelona's club kids happy. There are also golf courses, lively tapas bars, and kilometers of lovely beach. Despite the heavy tourist development, Sitges has managed to retain quite a bit of charm and style. It is worth a day visit from Barcelona, if for nothing else but to enjoy its beaches. Alternatively, some people choose to base themselves in Sitges and take the half-hour train ride into Barcelona. Upon arriving in Sitges, visit the **tourist office** (C/ Sinia Morera, 1, tel. 93/894-5004, www.sitgestour.com).

Sights

The historic old district is dotted with lovely 18th- and 19th-century mansions, called Americanos because they were built by returning Spaniards who had found their fortunes in the New World. They run the gamut from Neoclassic to *modernisme*. The area also houses a trio of museums. **Museu Cau Ferrat** (C/ Fonollar, s/n, tel. 93/894-0364, hours vary, €3) is the former home of one of the leaders of the Catalan *modernisme* movement, Santiago Rusiñol. It contains works by the artist himself as well as a diverse collection from El Greco to Picasso. The museum also houses the world's largest collection of wrought-iron crosses. Nearby, **Museo Maricel** (C/ Fonallar, s/n, tel. 93/894-0364, hours vary, €3) houses an impressive collection of medieval paintings and artwork as well as modern works related to Sitges. The building is a gorgeous mansion from the early 21st century. **Museo Romántico** (C/ Sant Gaudenci, tel. 93/894-2969, hours vary, €3) is an 18th-century Catalan mansion that has been preserved as it was at the height of its glory. It houses a collection of 400 antique dolls. During your stroll, seek out **Calle Bosc,** the oldest street in Sitges and one of the most charming. The 17th-century **Sant Bartomeu i Santa Tecla** church sits on a hill rising from the city. Climb up to it to get a panoramic view of the city and the sea.

Beaches

There are nine beaches heading south from the city. The seaside promenade begins at the southern end of town and runs alongside the beaches for about three kilometers (nearly two miles). Along the way you'll find dozens of *chiringuitos* (beachside bars) serving tapas, beers, and fun in equal measure. You can also rent umbrellas and lounge chairs along the beaches. The further you get from the city, the less crowded it will be. The **Bossa Rodona** beach has traditionally been the "gay" beach, but in recent years, as the town has become more popular, the gay and lesbian crowds have dispersed and can be found on any of the beaches. **Balmins,** about a 20-minute walk down the promenade, is a nudist beach.

Festivals

The annual **Carnival** celebration in Sitges is a bacchanalian, booze-soaked, bare-chested (and other body parts!) fest that lasts for just about a week—and takes two to recover from. Called Carnestoltes in Catalan, this carnival,

---

A PENEDÈS SELF-DRIVE TOUR

The Penedès wine region is famed worldwide for its wonderful *cava,* Spanish sparkling wine, but the region also produces lovely, delicate whites and hearty reds. For the wine-loving tourist, a tour through Penedès is a real treat. The best way to see the wine country is by car, as many of the wineries are spread out and the best restaurants are not reachable by public transport. The following itinerary takes in the best cellars, some delightful pueblos, and some stunning cuisine.

DAY 1: BARCELONA-SUBIRATS-SANT PAU D'ORDAL-CAPELLADES

From Barcelona, head west to the wine hamlet of **Subirats.** First stop is **Sumarroca** (Crta. de Sant Sadurní a Gelida, km. 4, Barrio El Rebato, 08739 Subirats, tel. 93/891-1092, sumarroca@sumarroca.es, www.sumarroca .es), a historic and prestigious winery. Visit the vineyards and ancient caves and then enjoy a tasting of *cavas* and still wines. After this visit, head up to see the ruins of the ancient castle attached to the **Santuari de la Mare de Déu de la Font Santa.** Enjoy the fresh country air, take some photos, and move on to the next village of **Sant Pau d'Ordal.** Lunch is at the unforgettable **Cal Xim** (Pl. Subirats 5, Sant Pau d'Ordal, tel. 93/899-3092, www.calxim.com), located right in the village. Santi is the charming owner. Enjoy roast duck, artisan cheeses, and one of the best wine lists in Spain.

After lunch, visit the charming winery of **Albet i Noya** (Can Vendrell de la Codina, 08739 Sant Pau d'Ordal, tel. 93/899-4812, albetinoya@ albetinoya.com, www.albetinoya.com), Spain's leading organic producer. The very charming Josep Maria is the winemaker and for an extra fee, he will give you the tour himself. This estate makes exquisite wines, our favorite being *Reserva Martí* (with his son's baby handprints on the label). The on-site shop, **Can Vendrell,** is lovely and you can request to taste (and pay) for as many wines as you like. Your hotel tonight, located in **Capellades,** is rustic converted manor house **Tall de Conill** (Pl. Àngel Guimerà 11, 08785 Capellades, tel. 93/801-0130, talldeconill@talldeconill.com, www.tall deconill.com, €75).

DAY 2: CAPELLADES-SANT MARTÍ SARROCA-PACS DEL PENEDÈS-VILAFRANCA DEL PENEDÈS

After a rustic Catalan breakfast, drive to **Sant Martí Sarroca,** where you can visit the 11th-century **Castle** (by appointment only, tel. 93/899-1669) with its huge kitchens, Gothic hallways, and Romanesque wine cellar. Also interesting is the Romanesque church of **Santa María,** which dates back to the 12th century

like all carnivals around the world, has its roots in Catholicism. However, here those roots have been bleached blonde and dressed in a gold-lamé thong. Official acts include parades held on the Sunday and Tuesday of the event. Expect drag queens galore, elaborate costumes, intricate dance routines, and flower-bedecked floats boasting giant sound systems, dozens of dancing riders, and even bars. Following the parade on Tuesday, a wild all-night party envelopes the city. Forget about sleeping. Though technically this event is open to all—and families are in attendance at the parades—this is a gay and lesbian party. If you are even slightly homophobic, you'll be miserable. If you are open-minded, you'll have a great time. If you are gay or lesbian plus open-minded, you'll have the time of your life. Naturally, rooms are in short supply and hotels book out fast. Reserve well in advance if you plan on attending or find a place in Barcelona and take the train in for the fun.

While not officially a festival, the summer months of **July and August** transform Sitges into a massive party. It is very crowded, and again, the gay and lesbian vibe is strong. Expect lots of all-night beach parties, themed events, and general revelry all summer long. Book ahead.

---

and was restored in 1906 by the *modernista* architect Josep Puig i Cadafalch. Next stop is **Pacs del Penedès,** home of the superb **Bodegas Miguel Torres** (Finca El Maset, Pacs del Penedès, tel. 93/817-7568, www.torres.es), the founders of wine tourism in Spain. This is a very interesting, Napa-style visit, complete with a presentation video, a train ride through the winery, and a trip through a "sensory tunnel" – a unique experience that gives a vivid explanation of the varied aromas of wine.

After your visit and tasting, head to **Vilafranca del Penedès** for an aperitif at **Taverna Inzolia Wine Bar** (C/ Palma 21, Vilafranca del Penedès, tel. 93/818-1938, www.inzolia .com), followed by lunch at the adorable **El Gat Blau** (C/ Amàlia Soler 120, Vilafranca del Penedès, tel. 93/890-4126). After lunch, stroll around the old town of Vilafranca, before heading to **Museu de Vilafranca/Museu del Vi** (Pl. Jaume I I, 08720 Vilafranca del Penedès, tel. 93/890-0582, www.museudelvi.org), a fascinating museum detailing the region's ancient wine history. In the late afternoon, take in more sightseeing or head back to your little hotel in Capellades.

DAY 3: CAPELLADES-SANT SADURNI D'ANOIA-BARCELONA
Begin the day with a visit to the *modernista*

winery of **Codorníu** (Av. Codorníu, s/n, 08770 Sant Sadurní d'Anoia, tel. 93/891-3342, www .codorniu.com). One of the oldest wine-making families in Spain, Codorníu has been making wine commercially since 1551! Their *cavas* are world famous. The winery is often full of Spanish families with kids in tow, but is still a very enjoyable experience. The wine caves are spectacular, the shop is excellent, and who can resist a free glass of bubbly? After your visit here, head into the town of **Sant Sadurní d'Anoia,** where you can visit the baroque church of **San Sadurní.** Lunch is at **Cal Blay** (C/ Josep Rovira 9, Sant Sadurní d'Anoia, tel. 93/891-0022, www.calblay.com), a gourmet haven famed for its creative cuisine. After lunch, enjoy a walk around before heading back to Barcelona.

NOTES AND CONTACTS
Please keep in mind that all wineries must be contacted by email, fax, or phone beforehand in order to schedule appointments. Wineries do not accept visits without appointment. Additional information can be found at www.enoturismealtpenedes.net and www .dopenedes.es.

This tour was designed exclusively for *Moon Spain* by Genevieve McCarthy of www.cellar tours.com.

BARCELONA

Accommodations

Lodging in Sitges tends to be of the upscale, stylish hotel variety, with most rooms topping €100 per night. If you have a smaller budget, consider an apartment rental or accept being a bit out of the center or away from the beach. (Keep in mind, Sitges is tiny and you can get just about anywhere in under 10 minutes.) **Los Globos** (Av. Mare de Déu de Montserrat 43, tel. 93/894-9374, www.los-globos.com, €85) is a lovingly run inn on the beach in a residential zone of Sitges, about 15 minutes walking to the old town. Rooms are spacious and bright and six of the doubles have their own private garden. It is a perfect retreat from the madness of the town if you are staying for carnival or in the summer. **Hotel Suber** (Po. Ribera, s/n, tel. 93/894-0066, info@matasarnalot .com, www.hotelsubur.com, €85) is one of Sitges's oldest hotels. Situated in the spot where the beach meets the old town, the location is superb. Rooms are spacious and bright, if a bit outdated, and many have balconies with lovely views over the town and the sea.

In the over-€100 range, try **El Xalet** (C/ Illa de Cuba 21, tel. 93/811-0070, info@ elxalet.com, www.elxalet.com, €95). Located in the center of town, it is an absolutely gorgeous 19th-century chalet (*xalet* in Catalan) with wonderful *modernisme* details. Expect chandeliers, stained-glass windows, intricately tiled floors, and antiques. Service is apt and friendly plus there is a small pool and a rooftop terrace for relaxing. **Hotel La Niña** (Po. Ribera 65, tel. 93/811-3540, www.laninahotel.com, €140) opened in 2004 right on the town's main beach. Rooms are lovely oases of blue and gold, and seaside rooms boast balconies onto the Mediterranean. Service is impeccable and the hotel has a small rooftop pool and terrace where you can enjoy breakfast overlooking the old town and the sea. The property also runs the **Santa María** and **La Pinta** hotels, all accessed via their website. **San Sebastián Playa** (Port Alegre 53, tel. 93/894-8676, www.hotelsansebastian.com, €200) is one of the top-rated hotels in Sitges, offering a winning combination of Mediterranean tranquility and modern amenities. Right

on the beach in the old town, the hotel offers a lovely pool area and a lively disco. Be sure to book this one through an online agent as prices can come in at less than half.

Though the majority of hotels in Sitges attract a mix of straight and gay/lesbian clientele, there are a couple particularly popular among the latter. **Hotel El Cid** (C/ San José 39, tel. 93/894-1842, www.hotelsitges.com, closed Oct.–May, €85) is one of the better bargains in town. Close to the beach with its own pool, the rooms are fairly non-descript but comfortable (except there is no air-conditioning). Many boast balconies over the bustling street below. Staff is friendly and the in-house bar is nice, but skip the stale breakfast buffet and go to a café. **Hotel Romantic** (C/ Sant Isidre 33, tel. 93/894-8375, www.hotelromantic .com €115) is as romantic as its name suggests with antiques, lots of cherubs about, and old-fashioned furnishings. Some rooms are way past their prime and it'd behoove you to see the room before accepting the key.

Lately, an apartment rental boom has taken over Sitges, providing an alternative to hotels. If you are traveling with a few friends, renting an apartment is much cheaper than getting a hotel. However, in most cases you will need to stay for at least three days. An Internet search will turn up half-a-dozen bookers. Two good ones are www.fabsitges.com and www.sitges .bz. For gay and lesbian travelers, try specialist www.staygaybarcelona.net, which rents gay-friendly apartments in Sitges, Barcelona, and all over the region.

Food

Tapas bars and traditional Spanish restaurants abound in the old town. In addition, there are *chiringuitos* all along the beach offering basic Spanish fare and good seafood. Sitges also has a handful of top-rated restaurants. **El Vivero** (Playa San Sebastián, Po. Balmins, s/n, tel. 93/894-2149, €35) offers sublime seafood and paellas with a lovely view over the old town and the sea. **Maricel** (Po. Ribera 6, tel. 93/894-2054, closed Tues. P.M. and Wed., €50) offers creative cuisine utilizing the best of local seafood and produce. The dining room is elegant and traditional; leave your flip flops in the hotel.

Getting There and Around

Sitges is easily accessed from Barcelona via a 40-minute ride on the regional Cercanías trains run by **Renfe** (tel. 90/224-0202, www.renfe.es/cercanias). From the Sants train station, catch the C2 train. It runs about every 20 minutes 6 A.M.–midnight. The last train out of Sitges is 10:26 P.M. If you are **renting a car** in Barcelona to tour the coast and Cataluña, Sitges is a 45-minute drive on the C-32, which you can catch just outside of the city. If you are flying into Barcelona, take the **bus** from the airport right into Sitges. It is operated by **Monbus** (tel. 93/893-7060, www.monbus.es).

In town, there is a cheap and easy bus that goes up and down the beaches. You can also take taxis, but ask for a price and *una factura* (receipt) upon entering the cab, as Sitges's taxi drivers are notorious for padding the fares.

PENEDÈS

Barcelona lies less than half an hour from one of Spain's most exciting wine regions— Penedès. This is the home of the world-famous *cava*, Spain's bubbly version of sparkling wine. Americans will be most familiar with the distinctive black bottles of the region's top producer **Freixenet** (Av. Joan Sala 2, Sant Sadurni d'Anoia, tel. 93/891-7000, www.freixenet.es). It is one of the few Penedès wineries that can be visited via public transportation. The free tour lasts 1.5 hours and concludes with a tasting (11 A.M., noon, 1 P.M., 4, P.M., and 5 P.M. Mon.–Thurs., 10 A.M., 11 A.M., noon, and 1 P.M. Fri., 10 A.M. and 1 P.M. Sat. and Sun.).

Information

For a totally off-the-beaten path trip through this wine region, see the sidebar, *A Penedès Self-Drive Tour*, created exclusively for this book by **Cellar Tours** (www.cellartours.com), a luxury wine-tour operator.

Getting There

Access Sant Sadurni d'Anoia, home of Freixenet, via the Cercanías regional train run by **Renfe** (tel. 90/224-0202, www.renfe.es/cercanias). Catch the C4 from either Plaça de Catalunya or the Sants station. Freixenet is right across the highway upon exiting the train station.

CATALUÑA

Occupying a triangle of land that forms Spain's northeastern tip, Cataluña (Catalunya in the local language Catalan, Catalonia in English) possesses an almost embarrassing wealth of beauty—from the dramatic Costa Brava, where the lumbering Pyrenees meet the sea in a tumultuous and beautiful clash, to the lush valleys and soaring peaks rising inland, to the sugarfine beaches snaking out from Barcelona in both directions. History has left its beauty mark as well in the Roman ruins of Tarragona, the medieval Jewish quarter of Girona, and the Greek remains in Empúries. Art has had its say, too, thanks to the homegrown Catalan artist Salvador Dalí. His surrealistic imprint is palpable all over the tiny towns of Cadaqués and Figueres.

Cataluña is more than its land, however. It is also a deeply rooted culture with its own traditions and language, both of which are fiercely protected and passionately promoted. The Catalan language is taught in schools, used in print and press, and serves as the official language of the local government. Culturally, Cataluña is known for hard work, shrewd negotiations, and frugal habits. A popular saying "El Català de les padres fa pa," means "A Catalan can make bread from stones" and is an accurate metaphor. No other region in Spain is wealthier or more industrious. However, Cataluña's nose-to-the-grindstone attitude is matched by its throw-your-hands-in-the-air frivolity. Catalan popular customs are full of charming, even quirky, traditions, from human castle builders to fire-spewing dragons, solemn folk dances to barbecued onion festivals. There are festivals held throughout the region every

© FRANCESC TUR/PATRONAT DE TURISME COSTA BRAVA GIRONA

HIGHLIGHTS

《 Girona: Ancient, moody, beautiful Girona offers an atmospheric and historically important medieval Jewish quarter, 12th-century Arabic baths, and a colorful riverfront. It also makes a great base for serious biking – just ask Lance Armstrong, who owns a home here (page 302).

《 Empúries: On the edge of the fishing town/resort of L'Escala, the ancient site of Empúries offers excellent remains of the 6th-century B.C. Greek town that once stood here and the Roman settlement that usurped it (page 311).

《 Cadaqués: One of the most scenic fishing villages on the Costa Brava, Cadaqués is also home to the whimsy of man in the Casa-Museu de Salvador Dalí, Salvador Dalí's longtime home, and the whimsy of nature at the dramatic Cap de Creus peninsula, where the Pyrenees meet the deep blue sea (page 313).

《 Teatre-Museu Dalí: Created by the artist himself, this wacky, wonderful museum offers an amazing voyage into the mind of a true artistic genius (page 317).

《 Tarragona: The provincial capital of Tarragona was once one of ancient Rome's capital cities. That Roman legacy is seen in a dozen major ruins scattered about this Mediterranean city (page 320).

《 Valls: Pint-sized Valls may be way, way off the tourist map, but it's firmly on the culinary map thanks to its boisterous yearly onion barbecue, Gran Festa de la Calçotada. If you are in Spain near the end of January, don't miss it (page 327).

《 Besalú: With its unusual 12th-century fortified bridge, rare 11th-century Jewish baths,

and lovely panoramic views, this tiny medieval jewel is worth seeking out (page 331).

《 Vall D'Aran: The only Spanish section of the Pyrenees lying on the northern face of the mountains, this glorious valley is a natural paradise. Ski the peaks with royalty and celebrities during the winter or bike and hike in the butterfly-filled valley in the summer (page 336).

LOOK FOR **《** TO FIND RECOMMENDED SIGHTS, ACTIVITIES, DINING, AND LODGING.

single weekend. Check with a company such as culTOURa (www.cultourabcn.com) to see what is happening during your visit.

Cataluña is also famous for its cuisine. This is the stomping grounds for Ferran Adrià, arguably the most visionary chef the world has ever seen. His foams and gels and deconstructed food have inspired thousands of chefs and spawned a Catalan revolution in food. However,

even the great chef will confess that it all begins with ingredients, and few lands are as blessed with such an abundance of quality produce and products. Shrimp and snails, monkfish and cod, rabbit and duck, sweet green onions and fat asparagus, red peppers and tomatoes, eggplants and artichokes, figs and hazelnuts, rice and beans. All of these have been combined for centuries in dishes that are as old as the culture

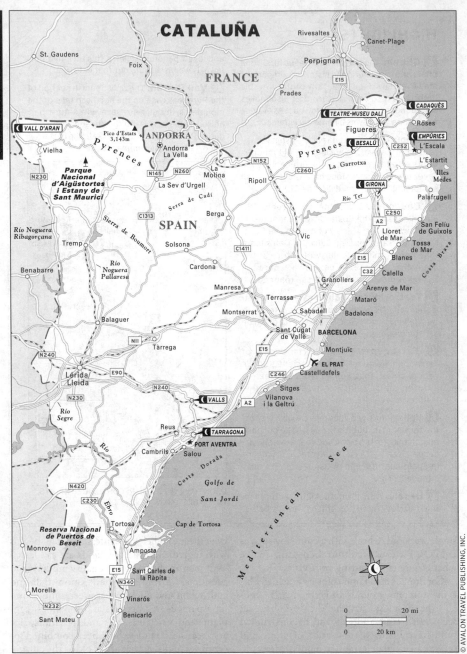

itself. *Arros negre* (rice with squid), *suquet* (fish and seafood stew), *anec amb figues* (duck with figs), *escudella* (a sausage and meat stew with peppers and cinnamon), *esqueixada* (salted cod salad), and *mandonguilles amb sepia* (meatballs with cuttlefish) barely scratch the surface of this varied, subtle, surprising cuisine. As you travel, always seek out the local specialty. And if you really want to know more, check out the wonderful book *Catalan Cuisine* by famed food writer Colman Andrews.

PLANNING YOUR TIME

If you are short on time and using Barcelona as your base, consider a day trip to either Figueres or Tarragona. The former offers the wonderful, wacky world of Dalí, the latter, a Roman wonderland. Both are reached via train from Barcelona in less than two hours and both offer just enough to keep you busy for a full morning. If you have a bit more time, head to the lovely city of Girona. Despite its medieval charms, natural beauty, and bustling cultural life, it remains off the radar for most tourists, meaning it is a good place to escape the crowds of Barcelona. It is also home to the most important Jewish quarter in Cataluña (it's reputed to be the birthplace of Kaballah) and Jewish culture and history are taken seriously here. If you have an interest in Judaism, you will not be disappointed. To properly see Girona (and recover from the steep up-and-down of its streets), you'll need to spend the night. The next day you can train to Figueres, and then return back to Barcelona in the evening.

If you have a week, you can't go wrong lazing your way up the Costa Brava from Barcelona. The coast is dotted with beautiful coves, bustling resorts, and fascinating ruins. Review the options, choose a few, and go. Public transport is a possibility, but if you really want to enjoy this wild area, rent a car. If you are a foodie, plan ahead, and get very lucky, you can combine the tour with dinner at the restaurant that has been voted the best in the world: El Bulli, located in Roses. (See sidebar, *El Bulli: The Most Sought-After Reservation in the World*.)

Cataluña is blessed with a mild climate year-round. It does get broiling hot in summer, particularly on the southern Costa Brava and Costa Dorada, but nothing compared with the scorching temperatures in Andalucía. In winter, it will be too cold to swim, but still nice enough for walks on the beach and coffee at an outside terrace. On the northern stretch of the Costa Brava, winter often brings with it a wind called *Tramontana* that blows wildly and that has over the millennia carved much of the wild landscape of the seaside cliffs.

July and August are peak Spanish vacation times and the coastal towns fill to brimming. Traffic jams clog the mountain roads and towels and umbrellas cover every bit of sand. Restaurants are packed, bars are thumping, and there is a general fiesta feeling in the air wherever you go. Some people find this exhilarating, others horrifying. If you are of the latter, try the shoulder months of May and June or September and October. If you are more interested in peaceful contemplation and local culture, consider traveling the coast in fall or early winter (keep in mind that many places in this region shut down in February). You'll mingle with locals and enjoy the grateful attention of restaurateurs and hotel keeps—at prices much lower than the summertime highs. You won't have to wait in line to see Dalí and you'll get great, people-free photos of the scenery. If you are traveling the last week of January, you have to detour to Valls to take part in their famed Calçotada, a village-wide barbecued onion festival. It is a delight—culinarily and culturally—and not to be missed.

Costa Brava

Snaking along the entire coast of the province of Girona (Gerona in Catalan), the Costa Brava offers 256 kilometers (159 miles) of Mediterranean-lapped beaches and cliff-backed inlets. The name Costa Brava means "rugged coast" and most of it is just that—rocky and tumultuous. After all, this is where the majestic Pyrenees tumble into the sea. The result is hundreds of beautiful coves tucked beneath pine tree–topped crests and hugging shimmering turquoise waters. In the 1950s, this area underwent a transformation from sleepy fishing villages to sangria-fueled playgrounds for Northern European package tourists. Lloret del Mar suffered the worst of it thanks to its once-stunning beach. Other villages—Tossa de Mar, L'Estartit, L'Escala, Roses—have fared better and offer resort amenities alongside unspoiled natural resources. Further north, Cadaqués is one of the quaintest villages on the coast and home to an intriguing museum dedicated to the works of Spanish surrealist Salvador Dalí. Inland, the town of Figueres is another stop on the Dalí route with its monumental Teatre-Museu Dalí, built by the artist himself.

The capital of this region is Girona, a delightful town with one of the most atmospheric *calls* (Jewish quarters) in Spain. It is a good base from which to explore the Costa Brava as it is well-connected via public roads and it boasts its own airport—a nice alternative to flying into Barcelona. Girona also makes a good jumping-off spot to explore the Catalan Pyrenees, which rise along the north of the province and stretch inland towards Aragón.

◖ GIRONA

Spread over a clutch of hills at the confluence of the Rivers Onyar and Ter, Girona (Gerona in Catalan) has 2,000 years of history. Founded by the Romans as Gerunda, it was a fortress point on the Vía Augusta, the ancient road from Rome to Cádiz. Visigoths later ruled it, then the Moors in quick succession. Charlemagne's Frankish troops captured the town in 785 and made it one of the courts of Cataluña. Despite another brief occupation by the Moors, Girona remained firmly under Christian control. In the 11th century, it was declared a city under the Crown of Aragón. From the 9th century onwards, Girona's Jewish population flourished, economically, socially, and intellectually. Many scholars believe that it was in Girona that the mystical branch of Judaism called Kaballah was born. By the 14th century, widespread anti-Semitism was spreading across Spain. In 1492, the Catholic Kings Isabel and Fernando gave expulsion orders forcing all Jews to either convert or leave the country. Girona's Jewish quarter, the **Call,** was built over and lost for six centuries. Historians, with the help of the Catalan, local, and even Israeli governments have located and recovered much of it and today the Call is one of Girona's top tourist attractions, as well as the center of much research into Cataluña's and Spain's medieval Jewish populations.

Sights

Pretty much everything you will want to see is located in the **Barri Vell,** the old quarter of Girona located on the east side of the Onyar. However, the best place to start a walking tour of Girona—and get a morning coffee while you're at it—is the buzzing **Plaça de l'Independència,** located on the western side of the river. Built in the 19th century on the site of a former Augustine monastery, the plaza is encircled by an elegant checkerboard floor arcade sheltering popular cafés, tapas bars, and shops. Walk south along the river (*riu* in Catalan) to get the most picturesque view of old Girona. Rising on the opposite bank are a jumble of centuries-old buildings painted in a sepia palette of orange, yellow, and ochre. The spire of the cathedral rises solemnly up from behind.

Crossing the river on the **Pont de San Agusti,** turn right onto Girona's favorite see-and-be-seen strolling spot—the lively **Rambla**

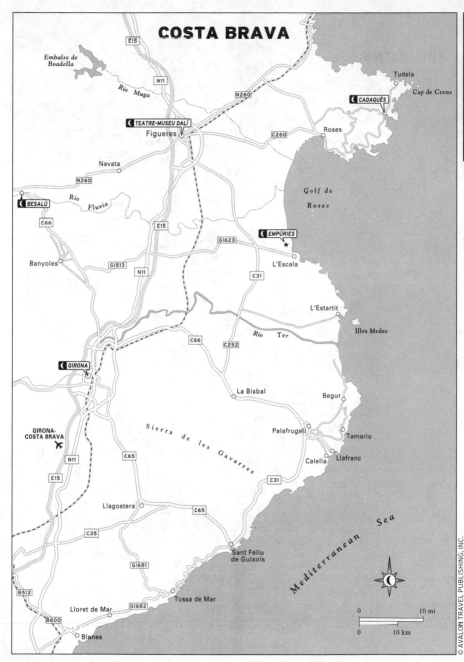

COSTA BRAVA

Embalse de Boadella

E15

Río Muga

N11

N260

Tudela

Cap de Creus

((CADAQUÉS

((TEATRE-MUSEU DALÍ

Figueres

C260

Roses

Navata

N260

Golf de Roses

((BESALÚ

Río Fluvià

C66

E15

GI623

((EMPÚRIES

Banyoles

GI513

N11

L'Escala

C31

L'Estartit

Illes Medes

C66

C252

Río Ter

((GIRONA

La Bisbal

Begur

GIRONA-COSTA BRAVA ✈

Sierra de les Gavarres

Palafrugell

Tamariu

N11

C65

Calella

Llafranc

E15

C31

Llagostera

C65

C35

Mediterranean Sea

B512

Sant Feliu de Guíxois

GI681

B600

GI682

Tossa de Mar

Lloret de Mar

Blanes

0   10 mi

0   10 km

CATALUÑA

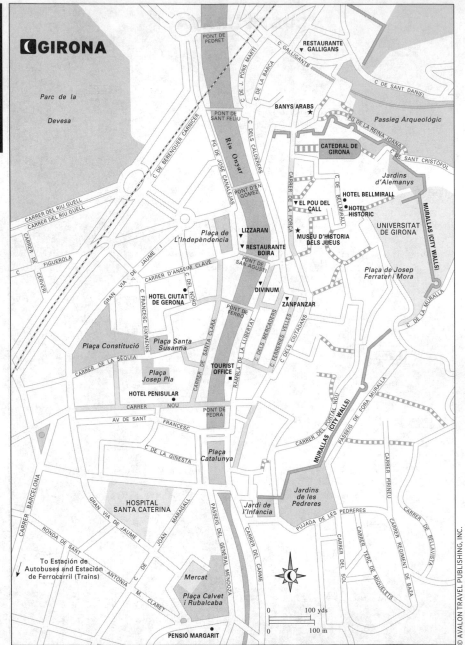

GIRONA

Parc de la
Devesa

RESTAURANTE
GALLIGANS

PONT DE
PEDRET

C. GALLIGANTS

C. DE J. PONS MARTI

C. DE LA BARCA

C. DE SANT DANIEL

BANYS ARABS ★

Passieg Arqueológic

PONT DE
SANT FELIU

PG DE LA REINA JOANA

CATEDRAL DE
GIRONA

C. DE SANT CRISTÒFOL

PG DE JOSE CANALEJAS

Ríu Onyar

C. DELS CALDERENS

CARRER DE BERENGUER CARNICER

CARRER DEL RIU GUELL
CARRER DEL RIU GUELL

CARRER DE JAUME I

C. DE FIGUEROLA

C. CERVERI

GRAN VIA DE JAUME I

C. FRANCESC EIXIMENIS

C. DEL NORD

CARRER D'ANSELM CLAVE

PONT D'EN
GOMEZ

Plaça de
L'Independencia

Jardins
d'Alemanys

HOTEL BELLMIRALL

C. DE BELLMIRALL

▼ EL POU DEL
CALL

● HOTEL
HISTÒRIC

UNIVERSITAT
DE GIRONA

CARRER DE LA FORÇA

MURALLAS (CITY WALLS)

LIZZARAN ▼

★ MUSEU D'HISTORIA
DELS JUEUS

▼ RESTAURANTE
BOIRA

PONT DE
SAN AGUSTÍ

Plaça de Josep
Ferrater i Mora

HOTEL CIUTAT
DE GERONA

▼ DIVINUM

C. DE LA MURALLA

PONT DE
FERRO

CARRER DE SANTA CLARA

ZANPANZAR

C. DELS MERCADERS

C. FERRERIES VELLES

C. DELS CIUTADANS

Plaça Constitució

Plaça Santa
Susanna

RAMBLA DE LA LIBERTAT

CARRER DE LA SEQUIA

Plaça
Josep Pla

TOURIST
OFFICE

MURALLAS (CITY WALLS)

PASSEIG DE FORA MURALLA

HOTEL PENISULAR ●

CARRER   NOU

PONT DE
PEDRA

CARRER DEL PORTAL NOU

AV DE SANT

FRANCESC

CARRER PIRINEU

C. DE LA GINESTA

Plaça
Catalunya

CARRER DE BELLAVISTA

CARRER BARCELONA

GRAN VIA DE JAUME I

JOAN MARAGALL

PASSEIG DEL GENERAL MENDOZA

CARRER DEL CARME

Jardi de
L'Infancia

Jardins
de les
Pedreres

PUJADA DE LES PEDRERES

CARRER DEL SOL

CARRER REGIMENT DE BAZA

CARRER TERÇ DE MIQUELETS

HOSPITAL
SANTA CATERINA

RONDA DE SANT

ANTONIA

M. CLARET

C. DE

To Estación de
Autobuses and Estación
de Ferrocarril (Trains)

Mercat

Plaça Calvet
i Rubalcaba

PENSIÓ MARGARIT ●

0   100 yds
0   100 m

© AVALON TRAVEL PUBLISHING, INC.

© CULTOURA/WWW.CULT3URABCN.COM

The River Onyar runs through the old heart of Girona.

de la Llibertat, a riverfront walkway lined with cafés and home to the main branch of the tourist office. Make a U-turn and head back north along the river to the **Banys Arabs** (C/ Rei Ferran el Catòlic, s/n, tel. 97/221-3262, €1.60), 12th-century Arab baths that were built by Moorish architects under the auspices of the Christians. The baths are a blend of Romanesque and Muslim design.

The baths sit at the base of a dramatic neoclassical set of 90 steps that lead up to the imposing **Catedral de Girona** (Pl. Catedral, s/n, tel. 97/221-5814, 10 A.M.–8 P.M. daily, €3). Built during the 11th, 12th, and 14th centuries, the cathedral is a mix of styles. The facade is baroque while its single bell tower is Romanesque. Inside, the Gothic nave is famed for its vast size. Some 23 meters (75 feet) across, it was the widest nave in the world when it was built and today is barely three meters (10 feet) shorter than that of the Vatican. The elegant 14th-century cloister has an unusual trapezoid shape dictated by the land upon which the cathedral stands. The cathedral's museum,

Museu-Tresor de la Catedral, houses a wealth of sacred and religious art including the famed *Tapis de la Creacío,* an 11th-century Romanesque tapestry detailing the creation story. This brilliant work of medieval art is a must-see.

Moving up and beyond the cathedral, the recently refurbished 14th-century **Murallas** (city walls) wrap around the Barri Vell, offering spectacular views over the slate-roofed houses, the river, and the rolling countryside in the distance. Access them via the **Passieg Arqueológic** and through the gate in the **Jardins de la Francesa.**

Just south of the cathedral is the **Call,** Girona's old Jewish quarter. Based on and around **Carrer de la Força,** this atmospheric warren of ashen granite buildings and pearl grey cobblestones is a truly delightful labyrinth. It is also an evocative reminder of the lively Jewish population that once lived here and was forcibly dispersed more than 600 years ago. For more about the neighborhood and Girona's Jewish history, visit the **Museu d'Història dels Jueus** (C/ Força 8, tel. 97/221-6761, 10 A.M.–6 P.M. Mon.–Sat. Nov.–Apr., 10 A.M.–8 P.M. Mon.–Sat. May–Oct., 10 A.M.–3 P.M. Sun. year-round, €2), which recreates Jewish life in medieval Cataluña through artifacts and interactive displays. The museum's collection of medieval Jewish tombstones is one of the most important in the world. The museum can also arrange walking tours of the Call and special Sephardic dinners at local restaurants.

Festivals and Events

One of the loveliest festivals in Spain happens here in May. **Girona, Temps de Flors** is a citywide exhibit of flowers and floral displays. Streets, parks, alleyways, even window boxes, are turned into florid displays of creativity that is not limited to real flowers. Paper flowers, flowered T-shirts growing from oversized pots, statues sculpted of flowers, giant photographs of flowers, and more have all made their appearance in Girona during this colorful fiesta. Many houses and buildings normally closed to the public open for the event, which usually occurs sometime around May 14–21.

At the end of October, the town lets loose in a wild celebration called **Festa y Fira de Sant Narcís,** the Festa Major (main festival) of the city. There are street parties, live bands, fireworks, and the peculiar Catalan tradition of *castellers,* groups of people that form trembling human towers up to nine layers high. (See the sidebar *Catalan Festivals.*)

Biking

For over a decade, Girona has served as a second home and training base for top American cyclists. Seven-time Tour de France winner Lance Armstrong owns a home here, and before retiring from cycling in 2005 he spent more than half the year living and training here. Many members of the elite Discovery Channel Pro Cycling Team (formerly the U.S. Postal team) also train here. American Olympians including Dede Demet Barry live here part-time. They are drawn to the surrounding terrain, which is perfect for training. Just a few minutes from the city center, cyclists find themselves on tranquil roads that lead up into the foothills of the Pyrenees or ramble along the coast.

Many tour operators have begun offering biking trips to Girona. They tend to be aimed at serious riders and involve intense training runs. However, they also offer Catalan fun—daytrips to Barcelona, meals in rustic mountain restaurants, sightseeing in Cataluña. Two top operators are **Bike Cat** (www.bikecat.com), which often pairs with celebrity cyclists to develop intense trips, and **Marty Jemison Cycling Tours** (www.martyjemison.com), run by former Discovery Channel team member Marty Jemison. These trips are not cheap (starting around €1,800 not including airfare) but the bikers who attend think the price is worth it. There are also several bike shops and tour guides in town. **Ciclo Turisme** (C/ Impressors Oliva 4, tel. 97/222-1047, www.cicloturisme.com) offers beginning biking tours that last from one day to one week. They also rent bikes (€20 per day) if you want to head out on your own. **Vies Verdes de Girona** (Pg. Sant Marti 4, tel. 97/218-5199, www.viesverdes.org) is an organization that

Girona is a favorite training spot for world-class bikers.

manages the "Vies Verdes" (greenways), rural biking trails throughout Cataluña. Their website is informative but difficult to get around. At the very bottom in the right, click "EN" for the English version.

Accommodations

At the low scale of lodgings, consider **Pensió Margarit** (C/ Ultonia 1, tel. 97/220-1066, www.hotelmargarit.com, €40), located on the western side of the Riu Onyar, just a few blocks from the train/bus station. This family-run property offers simply decorated, clean rooms at a rock-bottom price that includes breakfast. **Hotel Penisular** (C/ Nou 3, tel. 97/220-3800, www.novarahotels.com, €70) faces a lively pedestrian shopping street. Rooms are classically furnished and feature surprisingly large baths. The public areas are modern and elegant.

Bellmirall (C/ Bellmirall 3, tel. 97/220-4009, www.grn.es/bellmirall, €70) is easily the most charming lodging in Girona. Located in a historic stone mansion deep in the Barri Vell, not far from the cathedral, this small inn boasts stone walls, an atmospheric inner courtyard, and original artwork throughout (one of the owners is a painter). The downside is that it can be tough to find and is way uphill—take a cab. The other problem is the cathedral. The massive bells chime around the clock. Bring earplugs. ◖ **Hotel Històric** (C/ Bellmirall 4, tel. 97/222-3583, www.historic.go.to, €115) shares the same pluses (charming location, medieval atmosphere) and minuses (hard to find, ringing bells) as the Bellmirall, but adds a lot of contemporary style alongside inimitable details like actual Roman walls. Starting at €90, the hotel also offers full-service apartments. This is the home-away-from-home for many U.S. cycling champions.

Hotel Ciutat de Gerona (C/ Nord 2, tel. 97/248-3038, www.hotel-ciutatdegirona.com, €120) is the place to go for upscale, big-hotel luxuries. Rooms are very modern in shades of white, gray, and red. Service is impeccable. The hotel is located on a pedestrian street and if you are driving, you'll need to have the hotel open the road for you. Detailed directions are on their website.

Food

At the heart of Cataluña's culinary revolution, Girona offers several options for gastronomic tourism—from the haute to the hearty. Starting with tapas, try **Divinum** (C/ Argenteria 12, tel. 97/222-2153), famed for its excellent artisan cheeses and wine list. **Zanpanzar** (C/ Corte Reial 10, tel. 97/221-2843, 1–4 P.M. and 9–11:30 P.M. Tues.–Sun., closed Mon.) offers a wide array of Basque-style tapas. **Lizarran** (Pl. l'Independència 14, tel. 97/221-8150, 11 A.M.– midnight daily) is a Spain-wide chain offering inexpensive tapas and, at this location, a wonderful view. Ask for a plate and then choose what you want from the bar. Hot tapas will be offered to you as they come out of the dining room. Conserve your toothpicks, as this is how your bill is calculated at the end. Each tapa runs €1–2.

For hearty Catalan fare, try **El Pou del Call** (C/ Força 14, tel. 97/222-3774, 2:30 – 5 P.M. and 8 –11 P.M. Tues.–Sun., 2:30–5 P.M. Mon., €30). Located in the heart of the Call, this local favorite offers traditional dishes like *fideuà*, Catalan noodle paella made with clams. **Boira** (Pl. l'Independència 17, tel. 97/221-9605, 1–4 P.M. and 8–11 P.M. Tues.– Sun., closed Mon., €35) is located in a corner of the lively plaza and offers a rowdy tapas bar downstairs. Upstairs, an elegant white tablecloth dining room offers excellent Catalan fare and lovely views over the river. **Galligans** (Pl. Santa Llucia 4, tel. 97/220-9654, 1–3:30 P.M. and 8:30–11 P.M. Mon.–Sat., closed Sun., €40) offers creative Catalan cuisine based on market produce and products. For dessert don't miss their white chocolate and pistachio soup.

Just outside of Girona is ◖ **El Celler de Can Roca** (Ctra. Taialá 40, tel. 97/222-2157, www.elcellerdecanroca.com, 1–3:30 P.M. and 9–11:30 P.M. Tues.–Sat., closed Sun. and Mon., €75), a culinary reference when speaking of new Catalan cuisine and one of the top restaurants in Spain; it's earned a host of awards and acclaim. The chefs and staff at world-famous El Bulli are said to be fans. Run by the three Roca brothers, the elegant dining room offers both creative and classic takes on Catalan tradition, with menu themes such as Cuisine of Tradition, Cuisine of Contrasts, Cuisine of Memory, and Cuisine of the Seasons. Their wine list is one of the best in the region. Reservations are required.

Information

The main **tourist office** (Rambla de la Llibertat 1, tel. 97/222-6575, 8 A.M.–8 P.M. Mon.–Fri., 8 A.M.–2 P.M. and 4 P.M.–8 P.M. Sat., 9 A.M.–2 P.M. Sun.) offers extensive city information as well as maps and guides to the Costa Brava and Cataluña in general. The local tourist website www.ajuntament.gi is lovely to look at, but very confusing. You will do better with www.costabrava.org and www.catalunya turisme.com. An unofficial site, run by a very dedicated expat living in Barcelona, is www .girona-tourist-guide.com. It is practical, informative, and easy to use.

Getting There and Around

Girona's **Aeroport** (tel. 97/218-6600, www .aena.es) is less than 13 kilometers (eight miles) from the city and receives flights from around Spain via **Iberia** (www.iberia.es) and **Air Europa** (www.aireuropa.com). It also serves many discount airlines originating in the United Kingdom, including **Ryanair** (www.ryanair.com).

There are several **airport shuttles** that leave the airport heading to downtown Girona (€1.70) and Barcelona (€11). The shuttle stop is right outside the arrivals terminal; stop first at the tourist office for schedules. There are also buses from the airport that travel up and down the Costa Brava. A taxi from the airport into Girona should be less than €20.

The **Estación de Ferrocarril** (Pl. Espanya, s/n) is run by **Renfe** (tel. 90/224-0202, www .renfe.es) and offers daily trains to Figueres, Barcelona, and beyond.

The **Estación de Autobuses** (tel. 97/221-2319, Pl. Espanya, s/n) is serviced by several companies offering transport throughout Cataluña and beyond. **Sagales/Barcelona Bus** (tel. 90/213-0014, www.sagales.com) runs buses from Barcelona throughout the Costa Brava, including Girona and Figueres. **SARFA** (tel. 90/230-2025, www.sarfa.com) offers buses along the coast including Tossa de Mar, L'Escala, Cadaqués, and Roses. **Autocars Roca** (tel. 97/223-6059) also offers service up and down the Costa Brava.

By car, Girona lies on the AP-7/E-15, also known as the Autopista del Mediterráneo, which travels along the coast from Murcia in the south to France in the north, passing Barcelona on the way. From Madrid, take the A-2 to Barcelona, and then swing north on the AP-7.

There are car rental agencies, including **Hertz** (www.hertz.es), **Avis** (www.avis.es), and **Europcar** (www.europcar.es), located at the airport. There are several parking lots throughout Girona indicated by a large blue "P." Along the Riu Onyar, beneath the train trestle, is a free, public lot. Don't attempt to drive into the Barri Vell, as it is a warren of dead-end streets, many no wider than 2.4 meters (eight feet), and all steeply uphill.

TOSSA DE MAR

Marc Chagall fell in love with tiny Tossa de Mar when he visited in the 1930s. He christened it "Blue Paradise" and if you squint past the buzzing holiday resorts, you can see what he meant. Shimmering in the sun high above the town are the walls and turrets that make Tossa one of Cataluña's best preserved medieval cities. The walls were built between the 12th and 14th centuries and boast three perfectly preserved watchtowers. The area tucked into the arc made by the walls is the **Vila Vella** (old town), a moody labyrinth of tiny cobbled streets ripe for wandering. The **Museu Municipal** (Pl. Roig i Soler 1, tel. 97/234-0709, €3), opened in 1935, was Spain's first contemporary art museum and is still the only one to house works by the modernist master Chagall. There are also pieces by local Catalan bad boy Salvador Dalí.

Beaches

There are four beaches right in town and a dozen more stretching to the north and south of the city. The main beach, **Platja Gran**, is a wide swathe of golden sand offering every amenity you could need. Alongside it runs the **Passeig del Mar,** which is lined with bars and cafés.

Accommodations

Lodging in Tossa is plentiful, but rooms book up very quickly in July and August; advance reservations are necessary. The cheap and cheerful **Fonda Lluna** (C/ Roqueta 20, tel. 97/234-0365, www.fondalluna.com, €35) offers very simple rooms and shared baths in the Vila Vella. **Cap D'Or** (Pg. Vila Vella 1, tel. 97/234-0081, €65) sits at the junction between the beach and the old town. Rooms are very simple and a bit noisy, but the view over the sea is lovely. **Hotel Mar Menuda** (Platja Mar Menuda, s/n, tel. 97/234-1000, €120) is located on the quiet Mar Menuda beach just minutes north from the Vila Vella. Rooms are simply furnished but very well maintained and the staff (trained by owner Best Western) is accommodating. Be sure and request a sea-facing room as it makes all the difference in the world. The hotel also arranges a wide variety of water sports and activities.

Food

The waterfront and the Vila Vella are jammed with restaurants serving everything from pizza to paella. For delicious Catalan cuisine, seek out the tiny Carrer Portal, which is jammed with excellent restaurants. **Can Pini** (C/ Portal 14, tel. 97/234-0297, www.canpini.com, 1–4 P.M. Sun.–Fri., 1–4 P.M. and 8–11 P.M. Sat., €20) boasts a quaint patio brimming with flowers and a stone-walled dining room lined with antique prints. Food is homey, classic Catalan with an emphasis on exquisite seafood dishes. **La Cuina de Can Simón** (C/ Portal 24, tel. 97/234-1269, 1–4 P.M. and 8–11 P.M. Mon.–Sat., 1 –4 P.M. Sun., closed Mon. and Tues. in winter, €50) is one of the top-rated restaurants in Cataluña. The antique-filled dining room is the sight for extremely creative and seductive cuisine. Typical dishes might include shrimp ravioli with beluga caviar or squid-ink paella with artichoke; however, the best bet is the chef's tasting menu.

Getting There

By bus, Tossa is reached via **SARFA** (tel. 90/230-2025, www.sarfa.com) from Barcelona or Girona. The **Estación de Autobuses** (Av. Pelegrí 25) is also the locale of the main tourist office. By car, Tossa is accessed via the GI-682, which can easily be reached from Girona to the northwest or Barcelona to the south.

PALAFRUGELL

The inland town of Palafrugell is about as sleepy as can be considering its location in the heart of the Costa Brava. The town itself offers a few sights—the 16th-century Gothic church of **Sant Martí** and the lively **Plaça Nova,** which is home to bars, cafés, and boutiques—however, the real draw of this town is its trio of tiny, pine tree–shaded coves located on the craggy coast just 3.2 kilometers (two miles) away: Calella, Llafranc, and Tamariu.

Calella is the largest of the three and has a wide, rocky bay dotted with fishing boats. The shore is rimmed by whitewashed houses that rise up into a maze of tranquil, cobbled streets. About a 45-minute walk south along the beach brings you to the **Castell i Jardins de Cap Roig,** a lush botanical garden laid out on top of a rocky headland. From here you can see the green and gray humps of **Illas Formigues,** a tiny archipelago of uninhabited islands.

Llafranc lies at the end of a lovely 20-minute walk north. The path takes you above a stretch of dramatic coast. The cove features a shimmering stretch of sand backed by a pine tree–shaded promenade beyond which a stretch of whitewashed buildings leading into a warren of streets dotted with lovely plazas and even lovelier villas.

Tamariu is the prettiest, and the smallest, of the coves. Protected by a rocky outcroppings topped with pine trees, the beach is a perfect little crescent of golden sand. Its shady beachside walkway gives way to tiny streets that snake uphill into the shady little town.

Accommodations and Food

Lodging is plentiful in Palafrugell proper and in the three coves, though in the former rooms tend to be cheaper. Remember to book ahead in July and August and expect prices to drop the rest of the year. In Palafrugell, try **Hostal Plaja** (C/ Sant Sebastià 34, tel. 97/261-0828, www.hostalplaja.com, €70), a charming little *hostal* with simple rooms and adequate service. In Calella, **Hotel Alga** (Av. Costa Blanca 55, tel. 97/261-7080, www.novarahotels.com, €100) offers contemporary, spacious rooms—many with a view—and all the upscale amenities including a lovely pool. In Llafranc, **Hotel Terramar** (Pg. Cypsela 1, tel. 97/230-0200, www.hterramar.com, €103) offers minimal, spacious rooms with excellent views. In Tamariu, **Hotel Tamariu** (Pg. Mar 2, tel. 97/262-0031, www.tamariu.com, €120) is located right on the beach and features cozy rooms with pinstriped linens. Many have views and balconies. The hotel also has a set of apartments available for longer-term rental. The in-house restaurant serves excellent Catalan fare with an emphasis on seafood.

The most luxurious and romantic lodging in this area is 《 **El Far de Sant Sebastià** (Platja de Llafranc, s/n, tel. 97/230-1639, www.elfar.net, €300). Located in a lovingly restored stone inn attached to a 17th-century shrine and 15th-century watchtower, the hotel offers sensual old-world elegance. At the top of a cliff overlooking the sea, you will have the sensation that you are sleeping right above the Mediterranean's waves—and you are. Rooms are spacious, comfortable, and sophisticated, each with balconies or terraces (more expensive). Even if you do not stay here, consider a meal on their gorgeous terrace perched high above the sea.

In addition to the hotel restaurants mentioned above, seafood and Catalan fare is plentiful in this area. In Palafrugell, try **La Casona** (Paraje la Sauleda 4, tel. 97/230-3661, 2–4 P.M. and 8–11 P.M. Tues.–Sat., 2–4 P.M. Sun., closed Mon., €24), where the house specialty is *arròs negre* (paella made with squid ink and calamari). In Tamariu, **Royal** (Pg. Mar 9, tel. 97/262-0041, €20) has a bright little terrace where excellent seafood is served, particularly the *suquet,* a savory Catalan fish stew.

Find a variety of places in Llafranc along the seafront boardwalk.

Getting There

Palafrugell's **bus station** (C/ Torres Jonama 73) is serviced by **SARFA** (tel. 90/230-2025, www.sarfa.com), which runs daily routes to Barcelona and locations throughout Costa Brava. Public buses make the route from the Palafrugell bus station to the coves. By car, reach Palafrugell via the C-31, which winds along the Costa Brava and is accessed from Girona and Barcelona via the AP-7/E-15.

L'ESTARTIT AND ILLES MEDES

L'Estartit (also known as Torroella de Montgri-L'Estartit) is another sun-n-fun resort blessed with an expansive beach wrapped around a sapphire blue bay. Just inland from the beach is a long, uninspiring row of blocky hotels and apartment buildings. The town itself offers little beyond packaged-tour bliss, however, it makes the perfect staging post for exploring the underwater wonderland around the Illes Medes, a protected collection of rocky islands that rise up dramatically a few kilometers off the L'Estartit coast. Beneath the waters, this archipelago is home to some 1,000 species of marine life and a glorious kaleidoscopic world of sea flora. Millenia of turbulent sea action against the soft limestone of the islands have also resulted in a cathedral of underwater caves, some passing right through the base of the islands.

Diving

Excellent information about Illes Medes in English, including a list of dive operators, can be found at www.visitestartit.com. One to try is **Calypso Diving International** (tel. 97/275-1488, www.grn.es/calypso), run by an Englishman who has lived in Spain for 35 years and is a retired professional diver. His multicultural staff speak a half-dozen languages.

Accommodations and Food

As a resort, L'Estartit has a wealth of accommodations, but none quite as atmospheric as

Hotel Moli Del Mig (Cami Moli del Mig, s/n, tel. 97/275-5396, www.molidelmig.com, €150). Located in the town of Torroella de Montgri, just inland from the L'Estartit beach, this sexy little inn is built within a 15th-century flour mill and boasts sleek styling, luxury linens, and every perk you could want from plasma televisions to internet to high-end toiletries. The restaurant is one of the best in the region and for just €30 you can add half-board to your stay—a gourmet six-course meal complemented by excellent regional wines. The hotel is owned by the friendly folks from Ciclo Turisme in Girona and therefore bikers are catered for with bike rental, maps, and optional guided biking tours.

Back on the beach, **Hotel Bell Aire** (C/ Església 39, tel. 97/275-1302, closed Oct.–Mar., €80) offers spacious, if dowdy, rooms with balconies. They arrange diving packages as well. **Hotel Santa Anna** (C/ Port 46, tel. 97/275-1326, www.hotelsantaanna.com, €65) has a big-resort feel complete with classically styled rooms and a beachside pool.

Excellent seafood can be found anywhere on the Passeig Marítim, but one place worth seeking out is the rambunctious **La Gaviota** (Pg. Marítim 92, tel. 97/277-0728, 1–4 P.M. and 8–11 P.M. Tues.–Sun., closed Mon., €25), which serves wonderful seaside views along with traditional Catalan recipes.

Getting There

By bus, L'Estartit is serviced by **AMPSA** (tel. 97/275-8233, www.ampsa.org), which runs a regular line between Girona, Torroella de Montgri, and L'Estartit. **SARFA** (tel. 90/230-2025, www.sarfa.com) has buses from Barcelona. By car, Torroella de Montgri-L'Estartit is located a few kilometers off the AP-7/E-15, which runs from Barcelona through Girona and into Figueres.

L'ESCALA

L'Escala is another fairly built-up (and bland) resort with a wide stretch of high-rise-lined sand stretching to the south along the Passeig del Mar. Up in town, things are bit more interesting with an atmospheric old city center of winding cobbled streets lined with whitewashed buildings. These tiny roads tumble down to more isolated, rockier coves tucked along the northern part of the city. Many are dotted with fishing boats, as this town still very much makes a livelihood off of the sea. *Anxoves de L'Escala* (anchovies from L'Escala) are a culinary delight sought after throughout Spain.

As quaint as it all is, there is really only one reason to choose L'Escala as your Costa Brava village *du jour*—the nearby archaeological site of Empúries.

Empúries

The ancient town of Empúries was founded by the Greeks in the 6th century B.C. as a lively port and market town; they named it Emporion, which quite simply means "market." Some 400 years later, the Romans arrived and set up a military encampment here. In the 1st century B.C., they added their own town, Municipium Emporiae, which grew until it overtook that of the original Greek settlement. In the 3rd century A.D., the Romans abandoned the town. After nearly 1,000 years of continuous settlement, the town fell into disuse and disrepair. In 1908, archaeological excavations to recover Empúries were begun. They continue to this day. Wandering through the vast site—full of rooms, forums, and mosaic floorings—is a magical passage to the past and a truly delightful alternative to the sun and sand sameness of the Costa Brava.

Entrance to the ruins is at the **Museu d'Arqueologia de Catalunya** (tel. 97/277-0208, www.mac.es, 10 A.M.–6 P.M. daily Oct.–May, 10 A.M.–8 P.M. daily June–Sept., €2.40). Reach it by walking along the L'Escala promenade and then following the coast past a breathtaking view of cobalt seas and tiny coves bathed in the white lace of waves. In inclement weather, make the 0.8-kilometer (0.5-mile) drive to the museum's parking lot.

Accommodations and Food

Hostal El Roser (C/ Església 7, tel. 97/277-0219, www.elroserhostal.com, €50) is a quaint family-run *hostal* in the center of the old town. Rooms are old-fashioned and comfy and the in-house restaurant is excellent. **Hotel Can Miquel** (Platja Montgo, s/n, tel. 97/277-1452, www.can-miquel.com, €75) offers a big-resort feel with small-hotel charm. Rooms are simply decorated but you will spend little time in them as the hotel boasts a pool, tennis courts, a mini-golf course, and, just steps away, the big, blue Mediterranean Sea. The hotels above also feature restaurants and more can be found along Passeig del Mar as well as in the old town. **Sotavent** (C/ Camí Ample 13, tel. 97/277-3053, 10 A.M.–midnight daily, closed Nov.–Mar., €15) offers traditional Mediterranean fare at excellent prices. **Els Pescadors** (Port d'en Perris 3, tel. 97/277-0728, closed in Nov., €35) is located right on the fishing port and oozes maritime charm. Of course, fresh fish is the only thing to order. In Sant Martí, the village just north of Empúries, ◖ **Mesón del Conde** (Pl. Major 4, tel. 97/277-0306, closed Mon. P.M. and Tues., €30) is worth seeking out. In a rose-hued rustic dining room centered around a massive fireplace, hearty Catalan fare is served. If available, try their excellent *calçots* (mild green onions) grilled over an open fire and served with *romesco*, a chunky sauce made of red pepper, garlic, nuts, and olive oil.

Getting There

L'Escala's **bus station** (Pl. Escoles 1) is also home to the tourist office. Bus companies serving the town include **SARFA** (tel. 90/230-2025, www.sarfa.com), with daily routes to Barcelona, Figueres, and Girona. By car, L'Escala lies on the tiny GI-623, which can be reached via the C-31. Consult a good map as the roads are quite small and route names change frequently.

ROSES

Sitting at the northern tip of the impossibly blue Gulf of Roses, the resort town of Roses offers breathtaking views of what can really be described as a *costa brava* (rugged coast)—deeply green with wild tufts of rock rising from the sandy coves far below. Flowing into the bay beneath the town is a turquoise swatch of clear, calm waters, dotted most days with fishing and pleasure boats. This perch was sought after as far back as 776 B.C., when the Greeks set up the town of Rhode here. Nearly eight centuries later, the Romans moved in and still later, the Christians. The remains of their 11th-century Romanesque **Ciudadela** (fortress) still loom over the town. Down below, some four kilometers (2.5 miles) of fine, sandy beach and dozens of crystal clear coves entice swimmers, divers, and sailors and have led to the development of a buzzing little resort. However, the town's greatest claim to fame is the world's most acclaimed restaurant, El Bulli.

Accommodations

Though many people with dinner reservations choose to drive or taxi in from Barcelona or Girona, each method has its drawback. The drive winds along a sheer cliff high over the sea. If you've had a bottle of wine, you might not want to attempt this at night—and of course, there is the recent toughening of Spain's drunk driving laws to consider. Taxis from either city could cost nearly as much as the dinner itself. Instead, consider staying in Roses. As a resort community, there is no lack of lodging from cheap and cheerful to pricey and posh.

If you are saving all your euros to pay for the meal, consider sleeping super cheap right next door at the campground, **Cala Montjoi Ciudad de Vacaciones** (Ctra. Roca, s/n, tel. 97/225-6212, www.montjoi.com, closed Oct.–Mar.). Very simple, sparse bungalows run €50 and include a creaky bed and private bath. The big plus is you can walk to El Bulli in under a minute. **Hotel Coral Platja** (Av. Rhode 28, tel. 97/225-2110, www.prestige hotels.com, €75) offers resort services that are just downscale enough to keep the prices low. Rooms are adequate and many have balconies overlooking the beach. Prestige operates four more similarly priced hotels in Roses. **Hotel Vistabella** (Av. Díaz Pacheco 26, tel. 97/225-6200, www.vistabellahotel.com, €260) is where to go if luxury is the objective and price no object. Rooms have a kooky, old-world charm, similar to what you might expect if you stayed with a wealthy, eccentric artist.

The suite (€850) is decorated with golden eggs that would make Dalí happy. Views, service, and amenities are five-star. Rates drop considerably off-season and a four-day package with breakfast for two people runs just €460, making this luxury property surprisingly affordable. If you have three days to spare, consider staying at the charming 🄲 **Castello Circle Aparthotel** (C/ Juan Alcover 28, tel. 97/225-7195, www.castellocircle.com, €66), a rustic, whitewashed house draped in bougainvillea in the hills above the Gulf of Roses. These cozy studio apartments feature mini-kitchens; however, the real jewel of the place is its spectacular terrace overlooking the sea. The German owner, Wolf, is delightfully gruff and he runs a lively bar and restaurant as well. There is a three-day minimum stay and prices drop if you stay for longer than a week.

Food
The real buzz of Roses comes from the tree-dappled ridge above town. This is the home of 🄲 **El Bulli** (Cala Montjoi, s/n, tel. 97/215-0457, www.elbulli.com, 7:30–9:30 P.M. Wed.–Sun. April–June, 7:30–9:30 P.M. daily July–Sept., closed Oct.–Mar.), the restaurant that has changed the way the world thinks about food. Led by the innovative Ferran Adrià, El Bulli has earned the number-one spot in esteemed food tome *Restaurant* magazine's world rankings of 2006 and an encyclopedia's worth of praise, analysis, and even research. The restaurant is only open six months out of the year; the other six Adrià and crew retreat to a Barcelona laboratory to create new taste experiments. Often cited as a master of "molecular gastronomy," this is the man who created "culinary foam" by adding the essence of a food to a gelatin and then pumping it through a whipped-cream canister. He has also explored new concepts like hot jellies and food "cooked" in liquid nitrogen. For full details on the El Bulli experience, read the sidebar *El Bulli: The Most Sought-After Reservation in the World* by food writer Megan Cytron. She was lucky to get in. Only 8,000 dinners are served per year and upwards of 500,000

people clamor for those seats. The reservation list is opened mid October and is usually full before the month is out. The set menu of 30–40 tasting plates runs around €200 per person (not including beverages) and lasts about five hours.

Getting There
All **trains** between Barcelona and France stop at nearby Figueres—17.7 kilometers (11 miles) inland—where you can catch a taxi for around €40. See train schedules at **Renfe** (tel. 90/224-0202, www.renfe.es). By bus, Roses is serviced by **SARFA** (tel. 90/230-2025, www.sarfa.com), which connects it to Figueres and Cadaqués.

By car, reach Roses via the AP-7/E-15 highway. Coming from Barcelona or points south, take *Salida* (exit) 4 towards Figueres/Roses. Follow the N-2 towards Roses and exit C-260 into town.

🄲 CADAQUÉS
Many swear that Cadaqués is the loveliest town on the Costa Brava. A cluster of brilliant white buildings topped by sloping terra-cotta roofs hug a rocky bay burbling with fishing boats. Above, a carpet of green treetops creeps up a rugged hill. All around grayish-blue mountains loom in the distance while the Mediterranean laps the shores with deep cobalt blue possessiveness. The stretch of coast from Roses to Cadaqués is one of the most rugged on the Costa Brava. The terrain is more jagged, the fauna sparser and wilder. The beaches are smaller and rockier, the coves more secluded and tranquil. The turbulent landscape has prevented the type of resort development seen further south, though this is still a popular destination for Spanish and French vacationers in July and August. They are drawn not only to the natural beauty of the place, but also to the charming village itself. Presided over by the white Gothic hulk of the 17th-century **Santa María** church, the town crawls up the hill in a tangle of narrow alleyways lined with wrought iron window grilles draped in colorful flowers. In the warmer months, these tiny streets buzz with art galleries, artists'

CATALUÑA

EL BULLI: THE MOST SOUGHT-AFTER RESERVATION IN THE WORLD

Cooking is a language through which all the following properties may be expressed: harmony, creativity, happiness, beauty, poetry, complexity, magic, humor, provocation, and culture.

A Synthesis of elBulli Cuisine, a 23-point manifesto presented by Ferran Adrià in 2006

The adventure begins with a jaw-dropping drive from the town of Roses on the Costa Brava. The road to El Bulli winds up into the wild rocky capes of the Cap Creus National Park, with no guardrails between the trickle of cars headed to the restaurant and the waves pounding on the rocks below. The setting is spectacular – the exceedingly rare sort of unspoiled coastline that time has forgotten. As you descend into a piney cove, a modest sign points the way to the Michelin three-star Restaurante El Bulli, a stone house nestled into a Zen-garden nook of Cala Montjoi. Given the cinematic quality of the approach, you cannot help but feel spirited away to a storybook alternate reality. After all, Cala Montjoi is just a few miles down the rugged coast from Cadaqués, Salvador Dalí's dreamy fishing village retreat. Here, Chef Ferran Adrià, yet another Spanish genius with a knack for the surreal and theatrical, has captured the attention of people worldwide, drawing his inspiration from the very same azure sea (and the delicious creatures that live beneath it).

Perhaps best known as the man who pondered the flavor and texture of the sea foam on the beach below and brought it right into his kitchen, Adrià has stood the culinary world on its head by adopting a scientific methodology to examine the essence of flavor, while – in a very Spanish and Catalan fashion – infusing theater, art, and play into the dining experience.

As you sit on the terrace perched above a deserted Mediterranean beach, a waiter

© FRANCESC GUILLAMET

The world's most inventive chef, Ferran Adrià, at work.

swoops in with a flourish: "Take this and eat it right away in two bites. It's humid today and it won't hold up even a moment longer." It is a *ninfa de algodón,* literally, a cotton nymph, gastronomically, a re-conceptualized Vietnamese garden roll – a gossamer layer of cotton candy wrapped around finely chopped peanuts, tender shoots of cilantro, impossibly tiny shrimp, and perhaps fairy dust. As promised, it self-destructs the moment you bite into it: a burst of sweet and savory flavor, soft and crunchy texture, cold and warm – the essence of a traditional Vietnamese garden roll – but to the second power. It is as if the idea of the original had been distilled into something more pure and intense. All of the courses are a bit like this – fragile and ephemeral, plucked from their natural habitat at the most succulent moment possible, and prepared for this precise moment in time.

What makes this restaurant so special is not only the wild inventiveness of the mastermind Adrià (and his equally brilliant brother Albert), but also the flawless and playful execution of the staff. If there are 50 people dining each night, there is, at the very least, an equal number of waiters and cooks swarming silently behind the scenes to ensure that each course is prepared and delivered with impeccable timing. *Stagiaires* (chefs in training) come from all over the world to work for free at the restaurant.

El Bulli is only open April–October. The rest of the year, Adrià and crew research new ideas and techniques at a workshop in Barcelona (El Bulli taller), which are then put into practice at the restaurant during the dining season. Adrià is clearly not interested in cutting any corners or even in making a profit at the restaurant. There are loftier goals bandied about: revolution, manifesto, research, philosophy, and even social change.

Despite the serious-sounding philosophical underpinnings and scientific methodology, El Bulli is not a stuffy, intimidating three-star restaurant. The food, presentation, setting, and service are all infused with a profound sense of lightness and humor. Diners at El Bulli do not see the menu until the end of the night, documenting exactly what each person ate and drank. Although there is no ordering à la carte, the 30-plus-course tasting menu is different every day – always making use of the very freshest seasonal ingredients and focusing particularly on seafood and vegetables. Courses from my recent dinner included parmeggiano marshmallows, black olive Oreos with bitter cream, and spherical olives (the intense flavor of an olive liquefied and contained by a trompe l'oeil gelatin exterior). For one course, there was a specially designed fork with a hollow space for an herb sprig. As you take a bite, the herb is held just under your nose so that your sense of smell communicates the flavor of mint while you taste buds transmit passionfruit, ensuring that every sense is engaged in the experience.

The end result is, of course, more than just a meal. At El Bulli, diners put five hours of their lives into Adrià's hands and he controls every bite, taste, smell, vision, and sound – creating a complete experience. Adrià has said, "Cuisine is not something to be had, but a state to be in." At times Adrià sounds more like a Buddhist monk than a chef, and perhaps this explains why many consider El Bulli to be a gastronomic temple worthy of a such a long pilgrimage.

The logistics: Those in the know email their requests to bulli@elbulli.com the day that the restaurant closes (usually around October 15) to request a slot for the following year. Many wait years to get a reservation – planning their trips around any available date and not the other way around. The 2006 tasting menu cost about €200 – the upper echelon by Spanish standards, but considered a great bargain for a three-star meal in nearly any other country. The wine list is very reasonably priced.

No reservation? Adrià is involved in two two-star restaurants in Spain – **Restaurante La Terraza** (El Casino de Madrid, C/ Alcalá 15, Madrid, tel. 91/532-1275) and **Hacienda Benazuza** (also known as El Bulli hotel, San Lúcar la Mayo, tel. 95/570-3344, www.elbullihotel.com), located 24 kilometers (15 miles) outside of Sevilla. He has also launched a chain of fast-food cafés called **Fast Good** (locations in Madrid, with Barcelona, Valencia, and Las Palmas de Gran Canaria to follow) and has developed products for the home kitchen – olive oils, espresso, wine, chocolate, and even a brand of delicious herb-infused potato chips. He has also very generously documented every recipe and technique involved in creating the dishes from the past 12 years at El Bulli in a series of beautiful cookbooks. Curiously, very few, if any, have managed to replicate them successfully.

(Contributed by Madrid-based foodie and journalist Megan Cytron, who writes frequently on Spanish food and gastronomy.)

workshops, boutiques, and bars that manage to be both rustic and arty.

The bohemian air is a holdover from Cadaqués' time in the very trendy sun when Salvador Dalí lived and worked here. Born in nearby Figueres, Dalí often spent summers as a child here. He returned in the 1920s and 1930s bringing with him an entourage of art world figures. He bought a clutch of fisherman cottages in the adjacent bay of **Port Lligat** (also spelled Portlligat) and built an extravagant home and workshop where he began to live full-time after the Spanish Civil War. By then, he was a major international art star and tiny Cadaqués became a haunt of the rich, bohemian, and famous—Brigitte Bardot, Man Ray, Walt Disney, Mick Jagger—all drawn to the outrageous, creative lifestyle led by Dalí and his wife Gala. He lived the final decades of his life here before moving to Gala's Púbol Castle in 1982, then finally to Figueres, where he died in 1989. Though the jet set is long gone, Dalí's fantastical home still draws crowds. (See sidebar, *The Surrealistic Life of Salvador Dalí.*)

the lovely fishing village of Cadaqués

© FRANCESC TUR/PATRONAT DE TURISME COSTA BRAVA GIRONA

Casa-Museu de Salvador Dalí

The Casa-Museu de Salvador Dalí (C/ Port Lligat, s/n, tel. 97/225-1015, pllgrups@dali-estate .org, www.salvador-dali.org, 10:30 A.M.–6 P.M. Tues.–Sun. Mar. 15–June 14 and Sept. 16–Jan. 7, 10:30 A.M.–9 P.M. daily June 15–Sept. 15, closed Jan. 8–Mar. 14, €8, reservations are mandatory) is a fantastical voyage into the inner life of this controversial 20th-century genius. Highlights include the stuffed and bejeweled polar bear presiding over the entrance hall, Dali and Gala's theatrical colorful canopied beds, and the provocative penis-shaped swimming pool around which sits a plastic pink sofa shaped like a pair of lips, Pirelli tire posters, and an Ali Baba sitting area shaded by a snake-adorned awning.

Tours are conducted every 10 minutes and to join one you must reserve in advance via the website, email, or phone. You must arrive 30 minutes early to pick up and pay for your ticket. Non-flash photography is allowed, but no equipment such as tripods may be used. Additional details can be found at www .salvador-dali.org.

Cap de Creus

Cadaqués sits on the Cap de Creus peninsula where the very last bit of the Pyrenees rumbles down into the sea. It is a stony, bald land mottled with tufts of wild foliage and bizarre formations of slate-colored rock. The ragged shores are chewed away by deep blue spurs of the Mediterranean Sea. Dalí described the landscape as "a grandiose delirium of geography," a statement that stands as probably the best description of the area. Since 1988 the area has been deemed a protected park, **Parc Natural del Cap de Creus.** Information, maps, and walking routes can be found at the Cadaqués **tourist office** (C/ Cotxe 2, tel. 97/225-8315).

Accommodations

Hostal Marina (C/ La Riera 3, tel. 97/215-9091, €55) is cheap and cheerful and just steps from the harbor. **Hotel Misty** (Ctra. Port Lligat, s/n, tel. 97/225-8962, www.hotel-misty

.com, €55), located on the road between Cadaqués and Port Lligat, is a comfortable family run inn with a peaceful garden and pool area. **(Hotel La Residencia** (Av. Caritat Sarinyana 1, tel. 97/225-8312, www.laresidencia.net, €100) oozes Dalí-esque charm with a jumble of antiques, paintings, sculptures, tapestries, collectibles (see the amazing walking sticks), and a big, white bulldog named Dama. Rooms are a bit of a letdown after the dramatic public areas, but they boast stunning views over the town and sea. Vintage champagne and beluga caviar is available round the clock and you can buy original Dalí-signed prints from the front desk. **Hotel Port Lligat** (Platja Port Lligat, s/n, tel. 97/225-8162, www.port-lligat.nct, €77) is located steps from Dalí's house and has quaint little rooms decorated with Dalí memorabilia. Many rooms have views and a couple have terraces (costs extra). The outdoor pool with whirlpool is a nice touch.

Food
(Casa Anita (C/ Miquel Roset 16, tel. 97/225-8471, 1:30–3 p.m. and 8:30–10:30 p.m. Tues.–Sun., closed Mon., €18) has been serving homey Catalan fare for over 40 years. The narrow arched dining room is lined with photos of happy guests including celebrities like Kirk Douglas and King Juan Carlos of Spain. Tables are heavy wood, draped in checkered tablecloths, and meant for sharing. The house specialties are simply grilled sardines and shrimp and the savory fish stew *suquet*. Meals are finished with a *porrón* being passed around. It is a glass jug filled with sweet muscatel wine from which guests pour a long swig right into their mouths while holding the jug far above their head. Yes, it can get messy. Next door is the lively **Anita Nit,** a bar that buzzes until the wee hours. **Can Rafa** (C/ Passeig 7, tel. 97/215-9401, closed Sun. p.m. and Wed., €35) is another local favorite. In the simple dining room, the kitchen turns out some of the highest-rated Catalan food in the region. Try the savory *arroz de cabra* (rice with goat). A tiny street-side terrace faces the sea. If you make it up to the lighthouse in Cap de Creus, be

sure and drop into the **Restaurant Cap de Creus** (tel. 97/219-9005, www.cbrava.com/ restcap.uk.htm, noon–9:30 p.m. Sun.–Thurs., 11 a.m.–midnight Fri. and Sat., closed Nov.) run by British expat Chris Little. Along with simple, hearty Spanish fare, the restaurant offers spectacular views over the protected park and the dramatic shoreline.

Getting There
Cadaqués is served by bus via **SARFA** (tel. 90/230-2025, www.sarfa.com), which has daily connections to Figueres, Roses, Girona, and Barcelona. By car, Cadaqués is most easily accessed via the AP-7/E-15 highway that runs from the French border through Girona and down past Barcelona. Take the exit for Roses and follow the signs to Cadaqués.

FIGUERES
Just 32 kilometers (20 miles) inland from Dalí's artistic home lies his natal one; the artist was born in the town of Figueres in 1904. Today, it is a buzzing little town that lives off the tourist trade generated by its most famous son.

(Teatre-Museu Dalí
The Teatre-Museu Dalí (Pl. Gala-Salvador Dalí 5, tel. 97/267-7500, www.salvador-dali .org, 10:30 a.m.–5:45 p.m. daily Oct.–June, 9 a.m.–7:45 p.m. daily July–Sept., €10) averages more than a million visitors per year, making it the fourth-most-visited attraction in Spain behind the Prado in Madrid, the Picasso museum in Barcelona, and Barcelona's Camp Nou soccer stadium. The museum is located in Figueres' old opera house, which was badly damaged during the Spanish Civil War. Dalí began designing the museum in the early 1960s, planning it as the greatest collection of his work in the world. The artist was involved in all aspects of the museum's design and was on hand when it was inaugurated in 1974.

Approaching the museum from the street, the first thing that strikes you is the deep red walls topped by giant eggs—not unlike a fairytale castle you might find in a Humpty Dumpty tale. The tower, **Torre Galatea,** is where the

THE SURREALISTIC LIFE OF SALVADOR DALÍ

He is one of the visionary few that managed to transcend self to embrace the status of an adjective. The word Dalí evokes a kooky wildness, an expectation of the unexpected – melting clocks, elephants on stick-thin legs, Mae West's lips as a sofa, a lobster as a phone. As one of the pioneers of the surrealist art movement – he once proclaimed, "surrealism is me" – Salvador Dalí was one of the most important artists of the 20th century. Viewers, critics, and even history have loved or loathed him, but have never, ever been indifferent.

Born with the unwieldy name of Salvador Felipe Jacinto Dalí Domènech in the Catalan town of Figueres in 1904, Dalí had his first art exhibit in the local municipal theater when he was just 15 years old. That theater later became home to the Teatre-Museu Dalí, one of Spain's most-visited museums. As a child his family spent summers in nearby Cadaqués on the Mediterranean coast, an almost lunar land of crumbling rock, bald trees, and vast, wild beaches. This landscape became a motif in many of his works.

In 1922, he moved to Madrid to study art and immediately fell in with some of Spain's most visionary artists, including poet Federico García Lorca and filmmaker Luis Buñuel. After thrilling classmates with his avant-garde approaches to art, he was kicked out of the academy just before his final exams for claiming that no one on the staff was good enough

to grade him. Unruffled, he headed to Paris where he met one of his artistic idols, Pablo Picasso. Though he was influenced by the cubist master, he soon fell into the burgeoning surrealist movement and in 1927 produced his first important painting in this genre, *Honey is Sweeter than Blood*.

During the summer of 1929, surrealist poet Paul Eluard visited Dalí in Cadaqués. He had his Russian wife, Gala, with him. Though Gala was 11 years older than Dalí (and married), the pair fell hard for each other. She became his muse, model, and constant companion. He was so enamored of her that he even began to sign his name, Gala-Dalí. They moved in together immediately and were married in 1934.

In the 1930s, Dalí began to receive critical acclaim and fame. His 1931 painting, *The Persistence of Memory*, also known as the "melting clocks" painting, became one of the most famous works in surrealism. Dalí drew his inspiration for this painting from exploring his subconscious and his dreams in a method he called "paranoiac-critical," or the ability to draw connections between items that had no rational connections.

After spending World War I living in the United States, in 1942, Dalí and Gala returned to live in Port Lligat, a fishing hamlet on the edge of Cadaqués. At this point Franco was in power and Dalí's choice to live in Spain angered many of his contemporaries. He was

artist lived the last five years of his life. After dying here, he was buried in a crypt beneath the stage area of the museum. Within, the surrealism is palpable. Note the *Rainy Cadillac*, a large black Cadillac which, when fed a Euro coin, gets a car wash—on the inside. (Be sure and have change on hand as many of the items in the museum spring to life with the insertion of a coin.) In the colossal painting *Gala Nude Watching the Sea Which, at a Distance of 20 Meters, Turns Into the Portrait of Abraham Lincoln (Homage to Rothko)* a nude Gala does indeed morph into a portrait of Abraham Lincoln. The furnished living room, *Sala de Mae West*, melts

into a portrait of the sultry American actress complete with red sofa lips, fireplace nostrils, and the world's largest wig. Amidst the illusions and absurdities are thousands of works spanning the career and styles of this monumental artist, including many technically brilliant realist paintings that remind the viewer that Dalí was a gifted painter long before he became a provocative master of surrealism. Masterpieces to seek out include *Soft Self-Portrait with Grilled Bacon, The Spectre of Sex Appeal, Napoleon's Nose Transformed into a Pregnant Woman Strolling Her Shadow with Melancholic amongst Original Ruins*, and *Galatea of the Spheres*. Adjacent to

expelled from the French surrealist group and earned the sobriquet "avida dollars," an anagram of his name that translates into "eager for dollars." Over the next few decades, Dalí's behavior was as outrageous as his paintings. He sent Franco congratulatory letters for killing political prisoners. Once, after a bad olive harvest, the government was prepared to offer financial compensation to the farmers. Dalí wrote to Franco that the trees of Cadaqués were fine, thus denying the local farmers of the government money. Because of his total association of himself as part and parcel of surrealism, it is hard to judge whether his acts were truly political in nature or just extensions of his art into his life.

His private life was also quite surreal. Gala went to live in the town of Pubol in an elaborate castle that Dalí decorated in his whimsical way for her. He signed an agreement saying he would never visit her unless she requested it – she rarely did so. By all accounts, physical contact between the pair was non-existent. She is known to have had many young lovers throughout their marriage, often lavishing them with gifts bought with Dalí's money. Meanwhile, she shrewdly managed Dalí's career, hurting many people in the process and earning a reputation as a domineering manipulator. For his part, Dalí claimed that Gala saved him from madness and early death and he worshiped her unabashedly.

For the next several decades, Dalí continued to live at Port Lligat creating art and provoking critical discussion. He explored mediums such as holography, photography, fashion, and film and acquired cult status for his eccentricities. His distinctive handlebar mustache soon became an icon. Tiny Cadaqués became the hub of a curious mix of international bohemianism and the jet-set lifestyle. Walt Disney was a regular and Dalí collaborated with him on an animated short, *Destino*, which was released posthumously in 2003.

In the 1960s, Dalí began working on the Teatre-Museu Dalí in Figueres. He was involved in all aspects of building the museum, which opened in 1974. He once dramatically claimed that he and Gala would pour gold down on Figueres and the entire region. The museum has done just that – it pulls in millions of euros in revenue each year and has turned the otherwise forgettable town of Figueres into a major destination.

After Gala died in 1982, Dalí became despondent. He moved into the Pubol castle, but after a suspicious fire in the room beneath his bedroom, friends intervened and brought him back to Cadaqués. Eventually, he was moved into the tower of the museum in Figueres where he died in 1989 at the age of 84. He was buried in the crypt beneath the stage of the museum.

the museum is the **Dalí-Joies,** a collection of jewelry designed by Dalí. Entrance is included with general admission to the museum.

In August, the museum holds **Dalí de Nit** (10 P.M.–1 A.M. daily, €12), a nighttime visit to the museum. It includes a glass of *cava* (Catalan sparkling wine) and a video presentation. It is a wonderful way to explore the museum as the crowds are much smaller and the atmosphere much more jovial. Tickets can only be purchased online.

Accommodations and Food

La Barretina (C/ Lausaca 13, tel. 97/267-

3425, www.hostallabarretina.com, €45) is just off the buzzing La Rambla and offers very simple rooms with newish baths. The cozy hotel restaurant offers decent Catalan fare at decent prices. **Hotel Plaza Dalia** (C/ Pujada del Castell 14, tel. 97/251-4540, www.hotelplazadalia .com, €85) is a kitschy little hotel just around the corner from the museum that takes heavy design inspiration from its illustrious neighbor—with spidery-armed clocks, overstuffed furnishings, a disco ball column in the lobby, blinking lights around the balconies, and lots of Dalí-esque paintings everywhere. Rooms are comfy and spacious, but pretty basic. There is a lively restaurant attached with a festive terrace. **Hotel Durán** (C/ Lausaca 5, tel. 97/250-1250, www.hotelduran.com, €110) is one of Figueres' classic old hotels. Rooms are minimalist and modern with light-colored wood and colorful accents, however the real treat of this hotel is its atmospheric restaurant **Durán** (€30), which has been serving hungry travelers since 1855, including Dalí who had a private table here. The restaurant is famed throughout the region for exquisite Catalan fare such as fish stew, stuffed rabbit in wine, and meatballs with cuttlefish.

Inexpensive cafés and tapas bars can be found around Plaça del Sol and along La Rambla. For a café with bohemian pedigree, seek out **Casino Menestral Figuerenc** (C/ Ample 17), located in an early 20th-century cultural center. In addition to the café, it houses an exhibition center and a nightclub. For inexpensive Catalan fare, try **El Gallo Rojo** (Baixada de la Mercè 4, tel. 97/250-5536, €18), which offers a very good lunchtime menu. Foodies should hop directly in their cars and head for **Restaurante Ampurdan** (Ctra. N-2, Av. Salvador Dalí 170, tel. 97/250-0562, www.hotel emporda.com, €60), located in what on first glance seems to be a dull concrete hotel block on the highway. Indeed, the rooms, though nice enough, are nothing compared to the food, which has garnered three decades' worth of praise from loyal customers. Cuisine is best described as nouvelle Catalan, taking impeccably fresh local produce, seafood, and game and preparing it with subtle, artistic takes on traditional techniques. The hotel, managed by Sercotel (www.sercotelhoteles.com), has doubles starting at €80.

Information

The **Tourist Information Center** (Pl. Sol, s/n, tel. 97/250-3155, www.figueresciutat.com) has all the information you could want, including complete hotel listings should you decide suddenly to stay the night and the above selections are booked. During the summer, information points are also open in Plaça de l'Estació and Plaça Gala-Salvador Dalí (hours vary by season).

Getting There

Figueres' **Estació de Renfe** receives trains from Barcelona (two hours) and elsewhere. All trains are operated by **Renfe** (tel. 90/224-0202, www.renfe.es). **Bus** service is provided by **SARFA** (tel. 90/230-2025, www.sarfa.com) with connections to Barcelona, Girona, and other points in Cataluña. By car, Figueres is easily accessed as it lies on the AP-7/E-15 that runs north to France and south to Girona, Barcelona, and beyond.

Costa Dorada

Stretching south from Barcelona is the Costa Dorada (Daurada in Catalan), the "golden coast." Despite its name, the beaches here are less than inviting—dull, narrow, and lined by soulless little resorts of concrete and glass. The one glorious exception is Sitges (covered in the *Barcelona* chapter). Nonetheless, this coast does have one main draw worthy of a one- or two-day detour: the magical city of Tarragona and its wealth of 2,000 year-old Roman ruins. Those traveling with kids may want to linger a bit longer at the coast's PortAventura, Spain's largest amusement park. Foodies traveling in January should grab a bib and make a beeline for Valls and the world's most famous barbecued onion festival.

TARRAGONA

Less than 90 kilometers (60 miles) down the coast from Barcelona, the provincial capital of Tarragona often gets overlooked by holiday-makers heading to Cataluña. That was anything but the case some 2,000 years ago when Roman Barcino paled in comparison to the mighty city of Tarraco, capital of Hispania and the second-most important city in the Roman

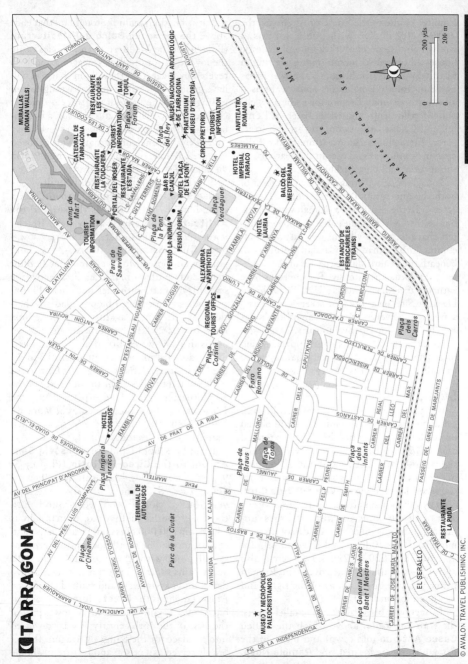

TARRAGONA

MURALLAS
(ROMAN WALLS)

PSG TORROJA

PSG DE SANT ANTONI

RESTAURANTE
LES COQUES

BAR
TOFUL

Plaça de
Forum

MUSEU NACIONAL ARQUEOLÒGIC
DE TARRAGONA

Plaça
del Rey

VIA AUGUSTA

PRAETORIUM/
MUSEU D'HISTORIA

TOURIST
INFORMATION

ANFITEATRO
ROMANO

CATEDRAL DE
TARRAGONA

C. DE LES COQUES

TOURIST
INFORMATION

CIRCO-PRETORIO

RESTAURANTE
LA CUCAFERA

RESTAURANTE
L'ESTADA

CARRER MAJOR

C. DELS FERRERS

C. DE CAVALLERS

TOURIST
INFORMATION

PORTAL DEL ROSER

HOTEL
IMPERIAL
TARRACO

PALMERES

BAR EL
CANJIL

BALCO DEL
MEDITERRANI

Camp de
Mart

Plaça de
la Font

HOTEL PLAÇA
DE LA FONT

RAMBLA VELLA

AV R MARIA CRISTINA

AV R MARIA CRISTINA

TOURIST
INFORMATION

C. DE SANT DOMENEC

PENSIÓ LA NORIA

PENSIÓ FORUM

RAMBLA

Plaça
Verdaguer

PEIXATERIA

VIA DE WILLIAM J BRYANT

PLATJA

PASSEIG MARITIM RAFAEL DE CASANOVA

Parc de
Saavedra

VIA DE L'IMPERI ROMÀ

RAMBLA NOVA

BAIXADA DE

HOTEL
LAURIA

ALEXANDRA
APARTHOTEL

CARRER D'AUGUST

AV DE CATALUNYA

CARRER ANTONI ROVIRA

CARRER DE PIN I SOLER

AVINGUDA D'ESTANISLAU FIGUERES

REGIONAL
TOURIST OFFICE

GOV. GONZALEZ

CARRER D'ARMANYA

CARRER DE PONS D'ICART

ESTANCIÓ DE
FERROCARRILES
(TRAINS)

AV DE PAU CASALS

C. DEL

NOVA

Plaça
Corsini

CARRER

DE

CARDENAL CERVANTES

REDING

Foro
Romano

C DOROSI

C DE BARCELONA

CARRER D'APODACA

CARRER DE TRUJILLO

Plaça
dels
Carros

C MARQUES DE QUAD EL-JELU

HOTEL
COSMOS

RAMBLA

AV DE PRAT DE LA RIBA

DELS

C. DE MISERICORDIA

CARRER DE

CASTAÑOS

CAPUTXINS

CARRER DEL MAR

Plaça
Imperial
Tarraco

MARTELL

PERE

MALLORCA

Plaça de
Braus

Plaça de
Toros

JAUMEL

CARRER DE PEDRELL

CARRER DELS

CARRER REIAL

CARRER DEL LLEO

PASSEIG DEL GREMI DE MAREJANTS

AV DEL PRINCIPAT D'ANDORRA

TERMINAL DE
AUTOBUSOS

Parc de la Ciutat

AVINGUDA DE RAMON Y CAJAL

CARRER DE

DE

FELP

CARRER DE SMITH

AV DEL PPES LLUIS COMPANYS

Plaça
d'Orleans

AVINGUDA DE ROMA

CARRER D'ENRIC D'OSSO

AV DEL CARDENAL VIDAL I BARRAQUER

CARRER DE MANUEL DE FALLA

CARRER DE F BASTOS

CARRER DE TORRES JORDI

CARRER DE JOSE MARIA MALATO

CARRER DE TRAFALGAR

EL SERRALLO

RESTAURANTE
LA PUDA

MUSEO Y NECRÓPOLIS
PALEOCRISTIANOS

Plaça General Domènec
Batet I Mestres

PG DE LA INDEPENDENCIA

N

Mediterranean Sea

platja de miracle

0   200 yds
0   200 m

Empire. Home to the Emperor Augustus, the ancient city buzzed with public forums, a Roman circus, an amphitheater, and majestic houses all bound within an impressive ring of fortified walls. At the height of its power it was home to 30,000 inhabitants and was praised all over the Roman Empire for its beauty, climate, fertile fields, and wine. Later, as Rome fell and Christianity swooped through in its place, Tarragona became a stronghold for the faith in Spain. It is said that in the year A.D. 58 the apostle Paul preached here.

Today, modern Tarragona offers the best of both the ancient and modern world. Trendy cafés sit in the shadow of a Roman wall, traffic buzzes through the same gates that once admitted chariots, and a vibrant festival scene celebrates both Roman and Catalan culture—all beneath the beautiful blue specter of the Mediterranean Sea. The extensive Roman ruins have earned Tarragona status as a UNESCO World Heritage Site, meaning tourist services are well supported; however, this is still an off-the-radar stop for most non-Spanish tourists. Those who do come, often do so as day-trippers, which means if you stay the night, you'll have a chance to really enjoy this seaside city's charms.

Sights

When planning a trip to Tarragona, keep in mind that all public monuments are closed on Monday. In summer, hours are extended and uninterrupted, while in winter most sights close for lunch 1:30–4 P.M. If you plan on being very ambitious and getting an early start, consider buying the **Tarra-GO-na Card.** Sold by the tourism office, it offers free admission to all museums and historical sites, unlimited transport on city buses, discounts, and more. Cost is €10 for a 24-hour card, €15 for 48 hours, and €20 for 72 hours. There is also an €8 pass available that covers the Roman ruins; you can buy it at any of the sights and it is good for one year.

Tarragona is bisected by two parallel streets: the **Rambla Vella,** above which the walled **Casco Antiguo** (old town) and many of the Roman ruins are located, and **Rambla Nova,** the city's bustling main thoroughfare that ends above the sea at the **Balcó del Mediterràni** (Balcony of the Mediterranean). This is easily the loveliest spot in all of Tarragona and is so revered by locals that they claim that you will have good luck if you touch the wrought-iron railing here. The lookout sits some 40 meters (130 feet) above the sea and takes in a breathtaking wash of sparkling blue—a view surely shared by the ancient Romans who so loved this area. Below, the fine sand beach of **Platja de Miracle** stretches invitingly.

To the left of the Balcony, follow the **Passeig de les Palmeres** and then make a scramble downhill towards the sea and the **Anfiteatro Romano** (Parque del Miracle, 9 A.M.–9 P.M. Tues.–Sat. summer, 9 A.M.–5 P.M. Tues.–Sat. winter, 10 A.M.–3 P.M. Sun. year-round, closed Mon. year-round, €2). Built in the 2nd century A.D. into a hillside above the sea, this oval amphitheater once held 14,000 spectators who enjoyed bloody gladiator battles that pitted man against beast or against man. In A.D. 259, Bishop Fructousus and two of his deacons were burned alive here. Their martyrdom led to their eventual sainthood. In the 6th century, defiant Visigothic Christians built a small basilica right in the center of the amphitheater. It was later expanded into the 12th-century Romanesque church, **Mare de Deu del Miracle,** Mary of the Miracle, which stands in shambles today.

Head back uphill and cross **Passeig Sant Antoni** to the **Circo-Pretorio** (Pl. Rey 5, 9 A.M.–9 P.M. Tues.–Sat. summer, 9 A.M.–7 P.M. Tues.–Sat. winter, 10 A.M.–3 P.M. Sun. year-round, closed Mon. year-round, €2), the site of the 1st century B.C. Roman Circus where some 30,000 fans could watch horse and chariot races. The small portion that remains standing today is within the old Roman walls and retains some unique features such as underground passageways and vaulted chambers. At the far end is the **Praetorium,** a tower that once housed stairs leading to the lower part of the city. In the 16th century, it was converted into a palace for the Kings of Aragón. It later briefly served as a prison and is currently home

© CULTOURA/WWW.CULTOURABCN.COM

The Anfiteatro Romano is among the ruins from the ancient Roman city of Tarraco.

to the **Museu d'Història,** Tarragona's history museum. Climb to the top of the tower for an ancient view of old Tarraco with the Circus, the Amphitheater, and the sea laid out below as they have been for millennia.

Next door, the **Museu Nacional Arqueológic de Tarragona** (Pl. Rey 5, tel. 97/723-6209, www.mnat.es, 10 A.M.–8 P.M. Tues.–Sat. summer, 9:30 A.M.–1:30 P.M. and 3:30–7 P.M. Tues.–Sat. winter, 10 A.M.–2 P.M. Sun. year-round, closed Mon. year-round, €2.40) helps give context to the various ruins with an impressive collection of artifacts from art and coins to everyday items like kitchen utensils, hair pins, jewelry, baby rattles, and dolls.

The narrow warren of streets north of the Plaça del Rey is Tarragona's atmospheric **Call,** or Jewish Quarter, particularly along **Carrer Talavera** and **Plaça dels Angels.** This area thrived until the 14th and 15th centuries when Christian intolerance forced Jews to flee the country or convert. Further north among the tangled streets, stands the **Catedral de Tarragona** (Pl. Seu, tel. 97/723-8685, €2.40).

Begun in the 12th century on the grounds of a Moorish mosque, the white and yellow building features Romanesque and Gothic details and a massive rose window.

Exit the old town at the **Portal del Roser** and turn right onto the **Passeig Arqueológic** footpath. It follows the remains of Tarraco's Roman walls, some of the best conserved outside of Italy. They were originally built around 218 B.C. and added onto extensively between the 16th and 18th centuries.

In the newer part of town, south of Rambla Nova, there are a few more sights worth seeking out, including the **Foro Romano** (C/ Lleida, s/n, 9 A.M.–9 P.M. Tues.–Sat. summer, 9 A.M.–5 P.M. Tues.–Sat. winter, 10 A.M.–3 P.M. Sun. year-round, closed Mon. year-round, €2). Built in the 2nd or 3rd century B.C., this forum was the center of political and administrative life for Tarraco. The remains include part of the basilica, which once held the halls of justice. Closer to the river, the **Museo y Necrópolis Paleocristianos** (Av. Ramón y Cajal 80, tel. 97/721-1175) is the site of over 2,000 burials

CATALAN FESTIVALS

Play hard, work hard is ingrained in the Catalan lifestyle. The rigorous working day is compensated for with the relentless urge to celebrate – be it a national holiday, a Saturday night on the town, or a local festival. The latter, called *festes,* are vibrant celebrations that happen throughout the whole year. Barely a weekend goes by without at least one Catalan town holding a party. Cataluña has always had a strong agricultural economy and its *festes* are based on important moments in the agricultural calendar, such as the beginning and ending of seasons, purification and fertility ceremonies, seed sowing, and the harvest. With the advent of Christianity, many of these festivals that were associated with nature came to be replaced by Christian celebrations known as feast days, held in commemoration of specific saints.

While each town holds several *festes* throughout the year, the biggest celebration is known as a *Festa Major* and can last 2–7 days. Most towns have two of these major festivals throughout the course of the year, one in winter, the other in summer. August and January are the two most popular months for the *Festa Major.* In Barcelona, the Gràcia neighborhood celebrates its *Festa Major* during the third week of August while Barcelona's *Festa Major,* the "Mercé," takes place on September 24.

The elements that define a *Festa Major* are similar in every town across Cataluña. In addition to a religious event, such as a mass or procession, there is usually a communal meal eaten outdoors and accompanied by shared wine from a *porró,* a glass container with a spout to pour the wine through the air and straight into the mouth, an all-night performance by famous musicians, and a huge fireworks display. Catalan festivals also include the following traditional elements.

Giants and Dragons: These vibrant folkloric processions, or *cercavila,* include fantastical dragons, 12-foot giants, enormous-headed dwarfs, magical fire dancers, and lively musicians that wind their way through the festival streets.

Devils and Fire Throwing: The *Correfoc* (Fire Run) and *Ball de Diables* (Devil's Dance) are the most stunning elements of Catalan festivals. Devil figures, stemming from pagan legends, run through dusk-darkened streets brandishing sparking forks, live fireworks, and shooting flames.

Human Castles: The infamous human towers known as *castellers* originated in the region of Valls in Tarragona. Hundreds of people balance on each other's shoulders to create great trembling towers up to nine stories high, accompanied by the traditional Catalan musicians called *grallers.* Ecstatic applause adds to the tense excitement and electric atmosphere as a small child clambers to the top to "crown" the tower.

Traditional Catalan Dancing: Town squares burst into life with displays of vibrant Catalan dancing, or *balles,* including: *Ball dels Gegants* (the Dance of the Giants) featuring gigantic figures, *Ball de Gitanes* (Gypsy Dance), *Ball de Bastons* (Stick Dance), and the classic Catalan Sardana (circle dance).

Up until recently, the *Festa Major* had not been well known in the English-speaking world. This is partly due to the personal nature of the *festa* as an event passed down over the generations by the people of a town and maintained strictly for their own pleasure – as part of their cultural inheritance. As travel to and interest in Cataluña has extended well beyond the bounds of Barcelona, more and more tourists are discovering the hard-earned, vibrantly lived, traditional fun of the Catalan *festes.*

Contributed by Genevieve Shaw, co-founder and operator of culTOURa (tel. 93/473-1731, www.cultourabcn.com), which leads day trips to Catalan festivals year-round.

dating from the Roman era through to the 7th century. The site is currently closed for additional archaeological research but there is an ongoing exhibit about the necropolis at the archaeological museum.

Festivals and Events

The Tarragona calendar is chock full of fun and festivals. Their **Carnival,** held around the end of February, is one of the most delirious in Cataluña, with elaborate floats, costuming, and all-night dancing in the streets the last weekend of the event. New Orleans sends its own carnival sounds to Tarragona the first week of April when the **Festival de Dixieland** (www.dixielandtarragona.com) comes marching in with hundreds of performances in dozens of venues. **Tarraco Viva** is a celebration of the town's Roman past held the last two weeks of May. In addition to mock gladiator battles, parades of costumed Roman soldiers, theater, and music, the festival has an academic side with conferences and workshops.

Tarragona's blow-out bash, **Santa Tecla,** is held the third week of September with 10 days of revelry culminating on the 24th. Catalan traditions dating back centuries are a major component of the festivities—traditional dances, ancient spoken-word performances, *correfocs* (fire-spewing devils that run through the crowded streets), and *castellers* (human castles). The event is rounded off with non-stop partying accompanied by dozens of live music performances and massive fireworks displays.

During the first weekend of October of even years (2008, 2010, etc.) Tarragona's bullring hosts the **Concurso de Castells,** a human castles competition. (For more on *castellers,* see the *Valls* section later in this chapter.)

Beaches

Tarragona's beaches are made of fine golden sand and are lapped by waters warm enough for swimming from June through September. The main city beach, **Platja de Miracle,** stretches for nearly 0.8 kilometers (0.5 mile) along the Passeig Rafael de Casanovas. It has a long boardwalk and every amenity you could

want from *chiringuitos* (beachside bars) to lifeguards, showers, and shops. Stretching north are dozens of coves and sparkling beaches. **Arrabassada** and **Savinosa** also offer long stretches of golden sand, promenades, and amenities, but they are less crowded and less urban than Miracle. At the latter, nudism is practiced on the far end near the dunes. The best beach is **Platja Llarga,** which unfurls for nearly 3.2 kilometers (two miles) in a stunning arc of golden sand backed by verdant hills. Public buses 1 and 9 go to all of these beaches. Beyond them, the **Punta de la Mora** nature preserve has two lovely coves, **Cala Fonda** and **Cala de la Roca Plana,** both wild and beautiful and backed by rocky hills. Nudism is practiced at both. Public bus 9 accesses this area.

Accommodations

In the **under €50** category, you can't go wrong with the cheap and cheerful **Pensió La Noria** (Pl. Font 53, tel. 97/723-8717, €45). Rooms (which are accessed via the ground floor restaurant) are nothing special but the price is right and the location—just steps from the old town—is priceless. At **Pensió Forum** (Pl. Font 37, tel. 97/721-1333, €40) you save even more, as bathrooms are shared. Rooms are a bit dumpy, but the backpackers who fill this place don't seem to mind. **Hotel Cosmos** (C/ Estanislao Figueras 57, tel. 97/724-3987, www .hotelcosmostarragona.com, €50) is a new, airy property not far from the buzzy traffic circle of Plaça Imperial Tarraco. Rooms are clean and updated and service is attentive and friendly.

In the **€50-100** price range, the best is **Hotel Lauria** (Rambla Nova 20, tel. 97/723-6712, www.hlauria.es, €68), an old-fashioned hotel right in the heart of the commercial district, steps away from the Balcony. Rooms are comfortable and spacious, if a tad dated. The hotel also boasts a serene garden/pool area. **Alexandra Aparthotel** (Rambla Nova 71, tel. 97/724-8701, www.ah-alexandra.com €70) offers elegant, modern mini-apartments complete with kitchenettes and complemented by hotel amenities such as room and maid service, a 24-hour lobby, and a tiny, but refreshing swimming pool. The apartments are comfortable retreats done in airy, Mediterranean colors and feature nice touches like fresh flowers and Internet service. 🄲 **Hotel Plaça de la Font** (Pl. Font 26, tel. 97/724-0882, www.hotelpdela font.com, €60) is a charming little hotel on the busiest plaza in town. Rooms are simple and warm with stylish little touches of bright color. A room overlooking the plaza costs a bit more, but is worth it if you like people-watching, not so much if you prefer silence. **Hotel La Nuria** (Vía Augusta 145, tel. 97/723-5011, www.hotel nuria.com, €80) is a very stylish little hotel located on the edge of town—perfect for those driving in. Public transport easily sweeps you into downtown Tarragona in minutes. The minimalist rooms feature balconies and Wi-Fi.

Over €100, the **Imperial Tarraco** (Pg. Palmeres, s/n, tel. 97/723-3040, hotelimp erialtarraco@husa.es, www.husa.es, €110) is a big brash sweep of a hotel offering resort-like amenities and spacious rooms with views over either the sea or the Roman ruins of old Tarraco. Request a room with a balcony. The decor, both public and private, is an early-1990s attempt at style—black leather, dark colors—that could use a re-do. Nonetheless, everything is comfortable, the staff is attentive, the large pool is inviting, and the outdoor dining areas are romantic. Prices drop on the weekend as this hotel mainly caters to the business traveler. **Royal Tarraco** (C/ Sant Auguri 5, tel. 97/722-8880, www.royaltarraco .net, €110) offers spacious, functional rooms in a hotel full of amenities such as a large fitness center, swimming pools, a sauna and beauty spa, and much more. The gardened terrace is a lovely place for coffee or breakfast. Rates drop on the weekends.

If you want the laid-back buzz of a **campground** combined with excellent facilities, head to **Las Palmeras** (Ctra. N-340, km. 1168, Platja Llarga, tel. 97/720-7817, www.laspalmeras.com, closed Nov.–Mar.). It costs €20 to pitch a tent and €80 for a charming cabin that sleeps up to six (discounts in off-season). The grounds are gorgeous, laid out along a stunning stretch of pristine coast

boasting a sugar-fine beach. There is a store, bar, and restaurant on the grounds and Tarragona city is barely 6.5 kilometers (four miles) away, easily accessible via public bus (line 1 or 9) or taxi.

Food

For a plethora of tapas bars from traditional to trendy, head to the Casco Antiguo. Seek out the retro-hip vibe at **Bar Toful** (Arc de Sant Bernat 4, tel. 97/721-4216, 8 A.M.–midnight daily), which serves as a sort of ground zero during the Santa Tecla fiestas. The house specialty is *espineta amb cargolins* (tuna with snails), which is much tastier than it sounds. Laid-back sidewalk cafés that segue into late-night drinking spots crowd the bustling Plaça de la Font. Buzzing local favorite **El Candil** (Pl. Font 13, 9 A.M.–3 P.M. and 5 P.M.–1:30 A.M. Sun.–Thurs., 9 A.M.–3 P.M. and 5 P.M.–3 A.M. Sat. and Sun.) attracts tapas-quaffing locals and tourists by day and an up-for-it, thirsty college crowd by night. More upscale bars and cafés (plus the best shopping in town) can be found on Rambla Nova.

Local Tarragona fare is Catalan in origin and has a decidedly surf-and-turf flavor. A local favorite is *romesco de peix,* a fish stew with a sauce made from almonds and hazelnuts. For inexpensive fare, try **La Cucafera** (C/ Santiago Rusiñol 5, tel. 97/724-2007, €15), located near the cathedral with a great terrace in warmer months. **L'Estada** (C/ Major 4, tel. 97/723-2298, €15) is located in a medieval house in the Casco Antiguo and has a lively tapas bar in addition to a cozy stone-walled dining room.

For gourmet fare, head where the savvy foodies do: **Les Coques** (C/ Sant Llorenç 15, tel. 97/722-8300, closed Sun., €50). Located in a centuries-old house in the heart of the Casco Antiguo, this atmospheric restaurant offers succulent fare from the sea—*pulpitos y gambas de Tarragona* (a grilled plate of local shrimp and calamari)—and the land—*cabrito al horno* (oven-roasted suckling goat). The atmosphere couldn't be more romantic, set off with candles, chandeliers, and arched stone walls. The wine list and the service are also superb. If you want the best seafood in town, hop a cab to **El Serallo,** the fishing port. The streets here teem with everything from seafood shanties to linen-tableclothed haute temples. A good in-between is **La Puda** (Muelle Pescadores 25, tel. 97/721-1511, 1–4 P.M. and 8–11 P.M. daily, €35), which offers everything from simply grilled fish and fried seafood to elegant stews and Catalan recipes.

Information

The main **tourist office** (C/ Major 39, tel. 97/725-0795) is open year-round with seasonal information points in the Plaça Imperial Tarraco, the Portal del Rosa, and the Rambla Vella near Vía Augusta. The **regional Cataluña tourism office** (C/ Fortuny 4, tel. 97/723-3415, www.catalunyaturisme.com) offers excellent regional information including accommodations listings.

The tourist office's website, www.tarragonaturisme.es, is one of the best online resources available in English. The Costa Daurada site, www.costadaurada.org, offers more limited information, while the commercial www.eurotarragona.com is a grab bag of information. The best website for Tarragona's Roman ruins is that of the archaeology museum, www.mnat.es.

Getting There

Tarragona can be reached via plane at the regional **Aeropuerto de Reus** (tel. 97/777-9832, www.aena.es), 13 kilometers (eight miles) inland from the city. It is served by the Spanish airline **Iberia** (www.iberia.es), which offers daily flights from major cities in Spain, as well as the cut-rate U.K. airline **Ryanair** (www.ryanair.com), which offers flights to/from London, Dublin, and Frankfurt. From the airport, there is a shuttle bus run by **Hispano Igualadina** (tel. 97/777-0698).

Tarragona's **Estació de Ferrocarriles** (Pl. Pedrera) is located just above the beach in the new part of town, about 10 minutes walking (uphill) to Rambla Nova. It is operated by **Renfe** (tel. 90/224-0202, www.renfe.es). There are several trains daily to/from Barce-

lona. The Euromed is the fastest at under an hour, but also the most expensive at €17 each way. The Catalunya Express and the Regional take around an hour and 15 minutes but cost under €6.

The **Terminal de Autobusos** (Pl. Imprerial Tarraco, tel. 97/722-9126) is serviced by **ALSA** (tel. 90/242-2242, www.alsa.es) with buses to Barcelona, Valencia, Málaga, Madrid, and most major cities in Spain, as well as local buses to towns throughout the Costa Dorada and Tarragona province. This is the least attractive way to travel to Tarragona.

By car, Tarragona is located on the AP-7/ E-15 that runs north past Barcelona to Girona, Figueres, and France. The road goes south along the Mediterranean to Valencia and into Murcia and Andalucía.

◖ VALLS

The little inland town of Valls, just 19 kilometers (12 miles) due north of Tarragona city, seems as sleepy a Catalan village as can be; outside of its two main festivals, there is not much going on. However, tiny Valls is considered the home base of two of Cataluña's quirkier traditions—*calçotadas,* communal green spring onions barbecues, and *castellers,* the building of human towers.

Valls' historic center has a few key places worth wandering through. The main square **El Pati** was once part of a defensive castle. The only remaining evidence of the fortress is the stone arch leading into the plaza. Stretching from the plaza, the pedestrian **Carrer de la Cort** is the town's main commercial hub and home to the **tourist office** (C/ Cort 61, tel. 97/761-2530). Nearby stands the **Capilla de Roser,** a chapel boasting walls covered in 2,600 17th-century glazed tiles that colorfully and graphically depict the Battle of Lepanto. The church also houses a collection of 12th-century clocks. At the end of Carrer de la Cort is the Plaça del Blat, home to the **Ayuntamiento** (town hall). Beyond that is the 16th-century **Sant Joan Baptista** church with its 74-meter high Gothic tower as spindly as a spring onion itself. It often serves as the backdrop for the *castellers.*

Festivals and Events

Valls holds its renowned **Gran Festa de la Calçotada** on the last Sunday in January. The festival celebrates the harvest of the *calçots,* a type of long green onion that is specifically grown in the region. In fact, Valls claims to have invented the onion when a local farmer pulled up and then replanted a crop of white onions. He then protected the resultant green shoot as it grew. The result was an elongated, white, sweet-tasting onion protected by a sheath of green external layers—not unlike an overgrown green onion. The *calçots* are harvested and sent directly to the barbecue pit—washing off the dirt is frowned upon. They are grilled until the outer leaves turn black and then wrapped in newspaper to allow the sweet inner onion to steam. To eat them, you strip off the burnt layers, dip the white center into a savory *salvitxada* sauce made of tomatoes, spicy red peppers, garlic, almonds, hazelnuts, olive oil, and red wine vinegar, hold it over your head, and let it slide into your mouth. It is messy and wherever *calçots* are served, so are plastic bibs.

The festival kicks off early Sunday morning in the Plaça del Blat with a *salvitxada* contest. Behind a long, rickety table, sweat-browed, yet smiling, señoras armed with mortars and pestles grind out their best recipes. At another table, piles of muddied *calçots* fresh from the ground await judgment. Over in El Pati, hearty eaters from around Cataluña participate in a *calçot*-eating contest. The winner can down nearly 200 *calçots* in 45 minutes. Meanwhile, over in Plaça del Oli, bonfires of vine shoots are being tended. Great iron grids are dropped upon them creating massive barbecue pits. Men dressed in the traditional costume of floppy red hats and hip sashes pile the *calçots* onto the fire as a line of eager locals grow. For around €5 you get a plastic bag with 10 steaming, wrapped *calçots,* a plastic tub of *salvitxada,* a hunk of bread, some wine, and a plastic bib. For the rest of the day, people peel, dip, slurp, and repeat. This is a food fest you don't want to miss. If you do go, expect to be with a lot of locals. Despite the fame the event has received

castellers in Tarragona

© CULTOURA/WWW.CULTOURABCN.COM

in foodie press worldwide, this party is still way off the beaten path.

Valls is also considered one of the birthplaces of the **castellers,** or human castle builders. This uniquely Catalan tradition involves group of competing *colles* that create castles that normally reach up to six layers. On the ground, a large group of very strong, broad men forms a solid base. The next layer of between two and four men climbs up, and so on. Once built, a young child of five or six, scampers up to "crown" the tower. When he (or she) raises his little arms to the surrounding crowd, cheers erupt and the *colle* begins to dismount. The most important *casteller* event in Cataluña happens in Valls during the **Feste Santa Úrsula** held the closest Sunday to October 21.

Castellers are also an important part of festivals throughout Cataluña and recent attempts in Barcelona to reach unheard-of heights of 10 layers have become part of that city's **La Mercè** festivals in September. If you are in Barcelona and want to experience a Catalan festival such as these, contact **culTOURa** (tel. 93/473-1731, www

.cultourabcn.com) run by an English expat and Catalan festival researcher and writer, Genevieve Shaw. She leads tours to festivals every weekend. (For more on Catalan festivals in general, see sidebar, *Catalan Festivals*.)

Accommodations and Food

There is not a whole lot going on in Valls' lodging scene. Again, it is just not set up for tourists. You may consider staying in Tarragona and catching the bus or a cab into town for the festivals. **Hostal Torreblanca** (Ctra. Pla de Santa María 86, tel. 97/760-1022, €40) is as simple as can be. Located on a bustling road, it can be loud, however the lovely view out the windows makes up for it. **Casa Felix** (Ctra. N-240, km. 17, tel. 97/760-9090, www.felix hotel.net, €80) is a rambling, 56-room hotel on the highway towards Tarragona. Rooms are bland but adequate. There is also a large restaurant that serves *calçots* along with other Catalan classics. **Hotel Class Valls** (Pg. President Tarradellas, s/n, tel. 97/760-8090, www.hotel classvalls.com, €88) is the nicest hotel in town. Opened in July 2005, this modern property features stylish, spacious rooms and excellent service. Amenities include a pool and Wi-Fi.

Even if you can't make the festival, *calçots* are in season from November to April and can be enjoyed throughout the region at rambling farmhouse restaurants. The longtime local favorite is **Masia Bou** (Crta. N-240, km. 21, tel. 97/760-0427, 1–4 P.M. and 9–11 P.M. Tues.–Sun., 1–4 P.M. Mon., €40), owned by the Gatell family. In addition to *calçots,* they serve exquisite Catalan fare like *escudella* stew and *buñuelos de avellanas* (hazelnut fritters) for dessert. Just north of Valls, **Cal Ganxo** (C/ Església 13, tel. 97/760-5960, 1–3:30 P.M. daily, closed evenings) in the town of Masmolets is one of the region's top-rated Catalan restaurants serving fare similar to Masia Bou, in an equally charming farmhouse.

Getting There

Autocars Plana (www.autocarsplana.com) offers several buses per day to Valls from Tar-ragona, including a night bus. By car, take the N-240 from Tarragona straight to Valls.

PORTAVENTURA

On the opposite end of the culture scale, PortAventura (Av. Pere Molas, km. 7, tel. 90/220-2220, www.portaventura.es) is one of Europe's most popular amusement parks. Roller coasters, thrill rides, water slides, magic shows, food booths, exhibitions, games, and more are spread over five thematic "worlds," including the Far West, China, Mediterranean, Polynesia, and Mexico. The top attraction is the **Dragan Khan** roller coaster, one of the world's biggest with eight upside-down loops. Other thrilling rides include the **Tutuki Splash** water chute and the **Hurakan Condor** vertical drop.

Prices vary, but generally start at €37 for ages 11 and up. Under 11 costs €24. You can buy single-day passes at the gate only. The confusing Internet booking engine is set up for 7- and 14-day passes only. Most hotels and travel agencies can also book your tickets.

Hours vary wildly according to the month, but in the summer the park is generally open 10 A.M.–midnight. Check the website for specific hours during your visit.

Accommodations

There are three massive resort hotels located right on the sight of the park: **Hotel PortAventura, Hotel El Paso,** and **Hotel Caribe.** Prices average around €100 per night and rooms can be booked right at www.port aventura.es. They offer every resort amenity you could want, from themed restaurants to pools to tennis courts.

Getting There

If you are flying in to either Barcelona's El Prat airport or Reus, there are **PortAventura shuttle buses** (tel. 97/777-9090). If traveling by **train,** PortAventura has its own stop. Service is run by **Renfe** (tel. 90/224-0202, www.renfe .es). By bus, **Autocars Plana** (www.autocars plana.com) provides service from Tarragona and Barcelona. By car, take the AP-7/E-15 highway to exit 35 which leads straight to the park.

CATALUÑA

Catalan Pyrenees

Though paling in comparison to the higher, wilder, more mountain-y peaks that dominate Aragón's central chunk of the range, the Catalan Pyrenees do offer some spectacularly beautiful scenery—such as the green valleys and crystal lakes of the Parc Nacional d'Aigüestortes i Estany de Sant Maurici and the rambling hills of La Garrotxa. And unlike the Aragonese section, the Catalan Pyrenees are a whole lot more hospitable. Man and nature have lived here in harmony for centuries and the whole region is dotted with medieval villages, Romanesque churches, and rambling fieldstone farmhouses. Some of the loveliest areas—including the storybook village of Besalú—are located in the foothills of the Pyrenees that bubble up in the northern area of the province of Girona. Further north, the Vall d'Aran is home to the upscale ski resort Baqueira-Beret, which counts among its regular clients the Spanish Royal Family.

Do your homework before embarking into this area. The information here is intended as an introduction, not as a guide to mountaineering or hiking in the Pyrenees. Look for books such as *Walks and Climbs in the Pyrenees* by Kev Reynolds or *Through the Spanish Pyrenees: GR11* by Paul Lucia. A general book on Spanish natural parks with solid information on the Pyrenees is *Wild Spain* by Frederic V. Grunfeld. For more detailed information, turn to Editorial Alpina (www.editorialalpina.com) and its cartographic maps and books. In each of the tourist offices listed below, you'll find more information and most of these towns will have at least one dedicated mountaineering store. If you will be in Barcelona, pay a visit to **Federació d'Entitats Excursionistes de Catalunya** (La Rambla 41, tel. 93/412-0777, www.feec.org), a group that manages excursions, routes, and *refugios* (mountain huts) in the Catalan Pyrenees. Their website is only partially in English,

The ancient volcanic landscape of La Garrotxa is a hiker's paradise.

but the Spanish section is excellent. More information can be found at www.cataloniapyrenees.com and www.parcsdecatalunya.net.

LA GARROTXA

La Garrotxa is an ancient swath of land that stretches north and east of Girona city. A protected natural zone, it is the greatest example of volcanic landscape on the Iberian Peninsula. With over 30 inactive volcanoes and lava basalt valleys teeming with verdant forests of cork, oak, and beech trees, it makes for some of the most pleasant low-level hiking and biking in Cataluña. Trails range from half-hour strolls to strenuous hikes. You can plan walks on your own or contact an operator such as **Puente Spain** (www.puentespain.com), owned by Anne Pinder, an American expat who confesses that La Garrotxa is her favorite region of Spain.

◖ Besalú

On the main road leading towards Olot, Besalú is one of the most magical medieval towns in Spain. You know you are in for something special as you cross the 12th-century Gothic stone bridge high above the Fluvià. Tiny, twisting lanes lead to a medieval core based around the lovely **Plaça de la Llibertat,** also known as Plaça Major. It shelters a clutch of cafés, shops, and the **tourist office** (tel. 97/259-1240). The town is also home to an atmospheric **Call** (medieval Jewish quarter) that houses some of the best-preserved *mikvehs* (Jewish baths) in Europe. They date from the 11th century.

Castellfollit de la Roca

After passing Besalú, drivers get a spectacular glimpse of Castellfollit de la Roca, roughly translated as "Mad Castle of the Rock." This rambling old village is laid out like a train track along the top of a sheer vertical cliff. It offers delightful strolling opportunities punctuated by breathtaking lookout points. Seek out the **Museu de l'Embotit** (Crta. de Girona 10, tel. 97/229-4463, www.museudelembotit.com), a sausage museum that is equal parts kitsch and quaint, and—if you like sausage—very delicious, too. Despite its tiny size, this village has one of the more impressive municipal websites (www.castellfollitdelaroca.org) in Spain, chock-full of English information about the town and La Garrotxa.

Olot

The bustling little town of Olot is the main staging zone for exploring La Garrotxa. Though rather dreary along its edges, it gives way to an elegant center of 18th- and 19th-century buildings, including a smattering of intriguing early 20th-century *modernisme* (Catalan art nouveau) buildings. Earthquakes destroyed the earlier medieval town in the 15th century. The **Museu de la Garrotxa** (C/ Hospici 8, €2) is located in an 18th-century hospice and holds a nice collection of modernist paintings including works by Santiago Rusiñol, one of the leaders of *modernisme* (of which Antoni Gaudí was the most famous member). The hospice also houses the **tourist office** (tel. 97/226-0141).

Accommodations and Food

You could easily stay in either Girona or Figueres, visiting La Garrotxa in day trips. If you do plan to stay overnight, in Olot consider the excellent **La Perla** (Ctra. La Deu 9, tel. 97/226-2326, www.laperlahotels.com, €75), which offers modern, cozy rooms and a decent restaurant. The hotel's reception also serves as an official tourist point for La Garrotxa with maps, trail information, and more. Guides and bike rentals are available. On the cheap and cheerful side, **La Vila** (C/ Sant Roc 1, tel. 97/226-9807, €40) has basic but functional rooms overlooking a lively square. For dining in town, try **Can Guix** (C/ Mulleras 3, tel. 97/226-1040, closed Sun., €18), which offers inexpensive Catalan fare in a rowdy dining room full of Spanish families. Just outside of town, **Les Cols** (Ctra. Canya, tel. 97/226-9209, €45) is a rambling, old farmhouse and is very stylishly refurbished. Food is a modern, elegant take on Catalan classics, with dishes like lamb cooked in sheep milk and thyme or creamy wild mushroom paella. The grounds feature a beautiful garden and terrace.

In Besalú, **Els Jardines de la Martana** (C/ Pont 2, tel. 97/259-0009, www.lamartana.com, €105) is a dreamy little inn located steps from the medieval bridge. It features simple, cozy rooms, most with spectacular views over the mountains or the bridge. Public spaces include a salon with a fireplace, a quaint tiled breakfast room, and a very romantic terrace. **Hostal Siqués** (Av. Lluís Companys 6, tel. 97/259-0110, www.grupcalparent.com, €60) offers style-less little rooms that are deeply compensated for when they come with a view—request one! The hotel also has a pool and one of the most charming restaurants in town: **Fonda Siqués** (€20), featuring a rustic stone-walled dining room. More atmospheric eats can by found at **Pont Vell** (C/ Pont Vell 24, tel. 97/259-1027, €35), which offers lovely views of the medieval bridge alongside hearty, market-fresh Catalan fare.

Information

Get maps, walking routes, and more at the La Garrotxa museum/information center, **Casal dels Volcans** (Av. Santa Coloma 43, tel. 97/226-6202, closed Mon., €2) located in Olot. On the Internet, www.parcsdecatalunya.net offers detailed information on the park. Cataluña's www.catalunyaturismo.com also offers good information.

Getting There and Around

The best way to explore this area is via car, though there are local daily buses into Besalú and Olot from both Girona and Figueres. Check with the bus stations in those cities. By car, La Garrotxa is easily accessible from either Girona or Figueres. From Girona, follow the C-66 northwest to Besalú, from there the N-260 (also known as the Carretera de Olot) leads into Olot. From Figueres, you can take the N-260 directly.

PARC NACIONAL D'AIGÜESTORTES I ESTANY DE SANT MAURICI

The only national park located in Cataluña, Parc Nacional d'Aigüestortes i Estany de Sant Maurici is also one of the loveliest in Spain, brimming with lush meadows, dramatic mountains, and over 200 cool, clear glacial lakes (*estany* in Catalan). It stays a sensual deep green thanks to the heavy rain and snowfall that is common to this area—upwards of 50 days of rain per year, 100 of snow. The park is located in the northwest of Cataluña right in the heart of the Pyrenees and just kilometers from the Aragón border. It is bordered to the north by a crest of high mountains reaching nearly 3,050 meters (10,000 feet). The name Aigüestortes means "twisted waters" in Catalan and indeed the park is riddled with innumerable streams and rivers. This zone lies in the western edge of the park along the **Vall de Boí.** The second part of its name, Sant Maurici, refers to the gorgeous lake of Sant Maurici located in the eastern part of the park and accessed via the village of Espot. The two areas can be considered separately from a tourist's point of view.

The park has some very strict rules that serve to preserve its beauty: no cars, no motorized vehicles of any sort, no camping, no fires, no pets. Access, however is free, and there are *refugios* (mountain huts) where you can stay for less than €15 per night. A meal costs about the same.

Barruera

The western entrance to the park is through Barruera, a tiny stone village boasting an impressive Romanesque church, **Sant Feliu.** Along with other Romanesque churches in the Vall de Boí, Sant Feliu was awarded UNESCO World Heritage designation. The **tourist office** (Crta. Caldes de Boí, s/n, tel. 97/369-4000, www.vallboi.com) offers maps and routes to visit the churches as well as information on the park itself.

Espot

The eastern entrance of the park is located in the quaint little town of Espot located at the heart of the Escrita river valley. At its entrance is a picturesque stone bridge, **Pont de la Capella.** Small, but lively, you can find anything you need in Espot to prepare for your

© CULTOURA/WWW.CULTOURABCN.COM

a centuries-old Romanesque church in the Vall de Boí

excursion into the park. Nearby, **Espot Esqui** (Crta. Berradé, s/n, tel. 97/362-4058, www .espotesqui.net) offers nearly 32 kilometers (20 miles) of trails and a host of ski and snow activities, most aimed at casual and family skiers.

Accommodations and Food

The two most popular *refugios* in the park are the 66-bed **Refugi d'Amitges** (tel. 97/325-0109, www.amitges.com), near the Amitges lakes at 2,414 meters (7,920 feet), and the 26-bed **Refugi Ernest Mallafré** (tel. 97/325-0105), also known as the Refugi de Sant Maurici, located near the lake of the same name at the base of Mount Els Encantats. Both require advance booking in July and August. See www .feec.org for complete details on all the *refugios* in the park and surrounding areas.

In Barruera, **Hotel Alta Muntanya** (Ctra. Durro 4, tel. 97/369-4075, www .alta-muntanya.com, €80) is tucked into a lovely stone building and features very cozy two- and four-bed apartments with a garden, a barbecue pit, and an inviting pool. They also

arrange all sorts of activities in the park. In the Boí Valley, **Hotel Boí Taüll Resort** (tel. 97/369-6000 or 90/240-6660, www.boitaull resort.es, €80) is a charming mountain hotel and ski resort that offers cozy rooms and a wealth of activities from skiing and hiking to guided tours of the area's Romanesque churches. The resort also has a restaurant and bar.

In Espot, **Hotel Roca Blanca** (C/ Esglé-sia, s/n, tel. 97/362-4156, www.rocablanca .net, €100) offers cozy mountain lodging with modern, upscale style and spectacular views. Staff can arrange tours and activities.

Information

There are two Centres del Parc where you can get complete information, register for hikes, reserve a spot in a *refugio*, and much more: **Casa del Parc de Boí** (C/ Graieres 2, tel. 97/369-6189) and **Casa del Parc de Espot** (C/ Prat del Guarda 4, tel. 97/362-4036). As in any mountainous region such as the Catalan Pyrenees, do not try to exceed your own abilities. Do not head off marked trails unless you are

WALKING IN SPAIN

Spain offers some of the best terrain for walkers. A large part of the country is some kind of wilderness, from mountains to wild coasts to sparsely populated plains. Along the way, the scenery is amazingly varied with many kilometers of paths meandering between tiny villages. Local people are friendly, and though they may not understand why anyone would want to *walk* to the next village, they will happily explain the route, often offering a story about the friendly rivalry between the two villages. Add good weather and an excellent public transportation system, and Spain comes out with high marks as a destination for both long-distance hikes and day walks. This is still a fairly well-kept secret, because with the exception of a few classic routes, Spain's trails are pleasantly free of crowds.

However, as good as Spain's walking may be, maps are not always accurate. This is improving as the official topographical maps are updated, but it is a good idea to carry two different maps when walking in remote areas. Also, getting pre-trip trail information can be difficult even in Spanish. This is starting to improve as more walking books are published and enthusiasts are posting information on the Internet, but getting information in English is time-consuming and, at times, impossible. In addition, there is very little trail maintenance in Spain, so some trails may be overgrown or eroded. Main trails are usually fine, but minor trails or remote areas may be uncomfortable for inexperienced walkers.

WALKING TRAILS IN SPAIN

Spain's walking trails follow European trail standards and are divided into **GR trails** (*gran recorrido* or long distance, marked with horizontal red-and-white stripes) and **PR trails** (*pequeño recorrido*, shorter distance, marked yellow-and-white). Generally speaking, these trails are fantastic, offering a wonderful way to see Spain on foot, with about 28,165 kilometers (17,500 miles) of marked routes all over the country. There are a couple of bumps, however. Some of the trails are not marked sufficiently

and there are occasional tricky spots that are really too difficult for these kinds of routes.

Unfortunately, it is difficult to find general information on Spain's GR and PR trails in English. An Internet search will reveal the basics and www.wikipedia.com has a list of all the trails in the European system (search for "GR Footpath").The website www.traildatabase.org is also a good source of information. The Spanish trails are managed by the Federación española de deportes de montaña y escalada (www.fedme.es). If you click the "senderismo" ("hiking") link on the home page, you'll receive a map of Spain with links to different regions and their trails. It's best to decide the route you will hike and then buy a guide and maps specifically for that route.

RAIL-TRAILS

Many of Spain's old rail lines have been converted into walking and biking trails. These Vías Verdes (Green Ways) are great for walking. On www.viaverdes.com (in Spanish and English), the best-equipped trails are highlighted in green while the less-developed trails are in brown. As well as having fewer bikers, the less-developed rail-trails often have more interesting walking, peppered with adventures like enormous mud puddles, rocky footing, dark tunnels, or missing bridges. Currently there are about 1,515 kilometers (940 miles) of fully equipped rail-trails and many more kilometers under development.

ROUTES THROUGH SPAIN

Most people have heard of the Camino de Santiago (Saint James' Way), the classic pilgrimage road across northern Spain to Santiago de Compostela. As a well-marked, well-traveled, and world-famous route, it is extremely popular, drawing thousands of pilgrims/hikers per year. For walkers in search of a less-trod path, Spain offers several routes that attract far fewer travelers. One of the most enjoyable is the Vía de la Plata (Silver Road), an old Roman road that runs from Gijón in the north of Spain straight down south to Andalucía. Information can be found in specialized hiking stores or on www.spain.info, the official Spanish tourism site. Click "what to do," then "great routes."

NATURAL PARKS

There are lots of parks in Spain at the national, regional, and local level. Many parks have trails but again, getting information isn't always easy. For national parks the best source of information is the Spanish Environmental Ministry website, www.mma.es (partly in English). It has a list of national parks on the home page, all linked to additional information. For regional parks, a web search with the name of a region plus the words "parques" "medioambiente" or "espacios naturales" should lead to the regional environmental organization and links to the region's parks.

MAPS AND BOOKS

Topographical maps for the entire country are published by the SGE (Army Geographic Service) and the IGN (National Geographical Institute). The maps are identified by a numbered grid system and are available in various metric scales suitable for walking. In addition to the official topographical maps, the following publishers are good for walking maps: **Tienda Verde** (www.tiendaverde.org) and **Editorial Alpina** (www.editorialalpina.com) provide general maps covering all of Spain. **Pirineo** (www.editorialpirineo.com) is especially good for Aragón, **Adrados** (www.infopicos.com) for the Picos de Europa, and **Penibética** (www.penibetica.com) for Andalucía.

Books are available from all of these publishers and can be found at specialty hiking and mountaineering stores in the United States as well as in Spain. In Madrid, one of the best stores to visit is **Desnivel** (Pl. Matute 6, tel. 90/224-8848, www.desnivel.com). In Barcelona try, **Quera** (C/ Petritxol 2, tel. 93/318-0743, www.llibreriaquera.com).

SUGGESTED WALKING AREAS

Pyrenees: Between Spain and France, this mountain range has something for everyone, from challenging technical climbing to easy valley routes between villages. Specific places to consider include: the Salazar and Roncal valleys in the western Pyrenees (Navarra); Ordesa–Monte Perdido National Park and Benasque in the central Pyrenees (Aragón); and Vall d'Aran and Aigüestortes-Estany Sant Maurici in the eastern Pyrenees (Cataluña). For a multi-day, challenging through-hike, the GR11 Trans-Pyrenees trail connects the Mediterranean and the Bay of Biscay. There are many books that cover this route and there is ample information available online. It is one of the most popular in Europe.

Picos de Europa: Just inland from Spain's northern coast, the upper reaches of these beautiful limestone mountains offer challenging hiking for strong, experienced walkers; casual hikers should stick to the easier valley routes. All walkers choosing the Picos should do thorough research and take suitable precautions as there is very little infrastructure, weather changes can be dramatic and sudden, and most trails are steep and rocky. Suggestions for easier routes include Garganta de Cares and the lakes near Covadonga.

Guadarrama: This range of mountains is only about an hour north of Madrid and offers a surprising number of lovely, relatively unused trails. It's easy to get to the mountains by train and bus, so day hikes are a real option to satisfy travelers on museum overload. Specific places with easy access: Cercedilla valley; La Pedriza (a UNESCO Biosphere Reserve); the Cotos and Navacerrada passes; and around the cultural sites of La Granja Palace and San Lorenzo del Escorial Monastery. For through-hiking, try the long-distance GR10 walking trail.

(*Contributed by Anne Pinder, owner of www.puentespain.com and an avid Spanish hiker.*)

completely prepared, skilled in mountaineering, well equipped, and fit. A good book to look for is *Guía Parque Nacional d'Aigüestortes i Estany de Sant Maurici* from Editorial Alpina. The website for Refugi d'Amitges, www.amitges .com, is an excellent resource. Another more basic resource is www.parcsdecatalunya.net.

Getting There and Around

If you are traveling by public transport to Espot, **Alsina Graells** (www.alsinagraells.es) will get you from Barcelona or Lérida only as far as the La Torrassa dam between the villages of Escaló and La Guingueta. From there you have an eight-kilometer (five-mile) walk (though hitching is not unknown in these parts) to Espot. There is no public transport to the park's entrance. There is very limited public transport into Vall d'Boí.

By car, the easiest access into the park is from Lérida, which lies on the A-2 that runs from Madrid to Barcelona. For Barruera and Boí, take the N-230 north to the L-500. For Espot, get the C-13 a few kilometers outside of Lérida and follow it to the N-260 at Puimanyons, catching the C-13 again at Sort. Finally, take the LV-5004 into Espot. Always get proper maps and up-to-date directions before leaving your city of origin.

◖ VALL D'ARAN

There are many who will swear that the Vall d'Aran is the valley to end all valleys. Indeed, the word *aran* means "valley" in the local dialect. In Vall d'Aran you will find an impossibly green valley teeming with meadows and forests and surrounded on all sides by soaring snow-capped Pyrenees peaks. In spring, the valley explodes into color as dozens of native flowers bloom, attracting an equal colorful rush of butterflies. The valley is located in the northeastern corner of Cataluña and is the only part of the Catalan Pyrenees that sits on the northern side of the range facing France, rather than Spain. Its main river, the Garonne, rumbles down through France before spilling into the Atlantic Ocean near Bordeaux. This unique geographic position helps keep the val-

ley wet and cold. It also has allowed inhabitants to maintain linguistic ties with their French neighbors. The local language is called Aranés and is related to the French Gascon dialect, Basque, and Catalan. Of course, heavily reliant on tourism, locals also speak Spanish and quite often English and French—but that has not stopped activists from spray-painting local names on street signs.

Find good information about the region at the Vall d'Aran tourism website, www.torisme aran.org. Editorial Alpina (www.editorial alpina.com) prints *Guía Vall d'Aran,* which is a very complete resource.

Vielha

The capital of the Vall d'Aran, Vielha (Viella in Spanish) was a sleepy medieval town until a 1948 tunnel made it, and the snowy peaks nearby, accessible year-round. Since then, the ski trade has grown expansively and Vielha looks like pretty much like any other sprawling ski resort. There are a few sights worth seeking out, including the Romanesque **Església de Sant Miquèu** with its imposing 14th-century bell tower. It sits on the lively **Place dera Glèsia,** which serves as the old town's social hub. Within the church is the *Cristo de Mig Aran,* a 12th-century polychrome wood carving that is an exceptional example of medieval sculpture. There are various villages and medieval ruins to be explored north of the town. Visit the **tourist office** (C/ Sarriulera 10, tel. 97/364-0110) for maps and information.

Salardú

Just 9.6 kilometers (six miles) east of Vielha, Salardú also makes a good base for exploring the valley. Its sharply rising stone streets house the 13th-century **Església de Sant Andreu,** an eloquent example of Pyrenees Romanesque architecture. The church shelters the 12th-century wooden carving, *Cristo de Salardú,* said to have arrived to the village by miraculously floating up the Garonne river from the Atlantic. The **tourist office** (Trauèssa de Balmes 2, tel. 97/364-5197) offers extensive information on the valley.

Biking

Though this area is known for its ski resorts, in spring and summer it makes a delightful "off-season" place for biking, a fact that the enthusiastic group **Pedals de Foc** (C/ Arnals 8, tel. 97/364-3662, www.pedalsdefoc.com) wants to promote. They have set up a 225-kilometer (140-mile) loop that starts in Vielha, goes into Aigüestortes, and returns to the Vall d'Aran. They arrange lodging in rustic hotels and tiny *cases de pages* (rural houses), including one that is 1,000 years old! You can also choose to include meals—a wise idea, as many of the lodgings are renowned for their country cooking. Throughout the route you have the support of a local biking guide. When you complete the trip you are awarded a special Pedals de Foc T-shirt. While the rides are not super-challenging, you will need to be in shape. It is recommended that you bring your own mountain bike, but the group is currently working with a local provider to offer rentals. This organization is fairly new, so check their website for the latest. Depending on the number of days, the number of riders in your group, and your meal options, prices run €50–200 per day.

Skiing

The ski resort of **Baqueira Beret** (tel. 97/364-3068, www.baqueira.es) is the poshest resort in Spain. The Spanish Royal Family have a chalet here and King Juan Carlos I is a regular on the slopes. As to be expected, it is expensive, starting at €40.50 for a one-day pass (though seasoned European skiers will point out that those prices are cheap compared to France, Switzerland, or even Italy). Located 1,500 meters (4,920 feet) above sea level, the resort features nearly 105 kilometers (65 miles) of pistes including three beginner, 38 easy, 25 advanced, and 6 expert runs. There are also seven kilometers of cross-country trails. The resort is known for its giant slalom run and a few local outfitters provide helicopter outings to even higher peaks. Jumbled around the resort are four ski schools (with some 300 instructors), dozens of bars and restaurants, several very upscale hotels, and attendant boutiques and ski shops. But keep in mind, this is a Spanish resort through and through. Almost all signs and menus are in Spanish (or Aranés, or Catalan) and Spanish cultural quirks are practiced—long lunches, dinner at 11 P.M., a very lively bar scene. Of course, you can manipulate this to your skiing advantage. Head to the slopes at 9 A.M. and you'll be rewarded with no lines; have lunch at noon and you can be back on the slopes by 2 P.M. when all the Spaniards have piled into the restaurants.

Accommodations and Food

In Viehla, **Casa Vicenta** (C/ Camin Reiau 3, tel. 97/364-0819, €45) is about as cheap as it gets. The friendly staff compensate for the sparse rooms. **Hotel Pirene** (Crta. Túnel, s/n, tel. 97/364-0075, www.hotelpirene.com, €95) offers bright, modern rooms with spectacular views. A few kilometers south of town, the spectacular **Parador de Artiés** (Crta. Baqueira Beret, s/n, tel. 97/364-0801, arties@parador.es, www.parador.es, €130) is a romantic mountain chalet. Rooms are a bit fussy with a pastel, country style, but the views over the Pyrenees are jaw-dropping and the pool is inviting in summer. Dine at **Basteret** (C/ Major 6, tel. 97/364-0714, €15), a simple little dining room offering classic Aranese fare—a hearty mix of mountain cooking with elegant French and Catalan touches. Typical dishes include *olla aranesa,* a thick stew with several kinds of meat, beans, and vegetables and *pitxana,* lamb seasoned with saffron and stuffed with mushrooms. **Era Mola** (C/ Marrec 14, tel. 97/364-2419, €40, reservations required) is one of the most acclaimed dining rooms in the Pyrenees. Set in an atmospheric old stable, the restaurant (also called Gustavo-María José) serves succulent Aranese fare brimming with goodies like duck breast, truffles, foie gras, and wild mushrooms.

If you prefer to be minutes from the pistes, **Hotel Tuc Blanc** (tel. 97/364-4350, www.hoteltucblanc.com, €130) is one of the more affordable options in Baqueira Beret. Rooms are spacious and cozily decorated, if a bit bland. **Meliá Royal Tanau Boutique Hotel**

(tel. 97/364-4446, www.solmelia.com, €500 and up) is the choice of the jet-set (or those with the credit to fake it), with lushly modern rooms and all the luxury amenities money can buy—from Thai massages to haute cuisine. It is open only December–April and there is a five-night minimum stay. Dining options in Baqueira Beret are plentiful and run the gamut from tapas bars to temples of fine cuisine. For a memorable experience head to the Dracula's Castle of **Cap del Port** (tel. 97/325-0082, €25) for goat chops, venison steaks, and sautéed mountain mushrooms. It is located at the crest of the Port dera Bonaigua pass. Back in town, **Tamarro** (tel. 97/364-4322) is a very popular tapas and wine bar with giant picture windows perfect for people-watching.

Getting There and Around

By bus, **Alsina Graells** (www.alsinagraells.es) offers routes to Vielha from Lérida and Barcelona. Within the Vall d'Aran, you'll have to rely on taxis (tel. 97/364-0195) or seasonal public bus service.

By car, the easiest access to the Vall d'Aran is from Lérida which lies on the A-2 Madrid-Barcelona highway. From Lérida, take the N-230 straight north for about 160 kilometers (100 miles). Enter the Túnel de Vielha and you are there. The C-28 road runs east from Vielha to Salardú, Artíes, and Baqueira.

ARAGÓN

Geographically defined by the Pyrenees in the north, the Ebro river valley in the center, and the Iberian mountains in the south, Aragón is a swath of northern Spain that is famed both for its beautiful landscapes and its role in the history of Spain. Northern Aragón, which comprises the province of Huesca, is home to several lovely national parks, dozens of rushing rivers, and the highest peaks of the majestic Pyrenees, all offering a thrilling roster of outdoor adventures. Southern Aragón, also known as the province of Teruel, is a rough-and-tumble land of red earth, disorderly mountains, and vast tracts of empty land lying between tiny, sparsely populated villages. Central Aragón, which includes the province of Zaragoza, is home to the bustling capital city of the same name. The fifth-largest city in Spain, Zaragoza is a delightful detour off the Madrid-Barcelona-Andalucía tourist track. Scattered throughout all three provinces are legacies of Aragón's tumultuous history—perfectly preserved medieval villages, imposing monasteries, Romanesque churches, earth-colored fortresses, and Mudejar masterpieces.

As throughout Spain, cuisine plays an important role in the cultural heritage of Aragón. It is hearty and meat-based. Taking pride of place on most menus is *ternasco,* lamb that is raised and slaughtered according to very strict regulations imposed by the Aragón government. It is considered the most tender and succulent lamb in the country. Stews and roasted game are also popular, but thanks to the many rivers crisscrossing the province of Huesca,

© ZARAGOZA TURISMO

HIGHLIGHTS

◖ Basílica del Pilar: Dominating the Zaragoza skyline with its colorful domes and spiraling towers, this holy shrine is an exuberant display of baroque architecture and home to the venerated Virgin of the Pillar. The festival in her honor every October is one of Spain's best (page 346).

◖ Tarazona: Way, way off the beaten path, the atmospheric town of Tarazona features medieval houses carved into a hillside high above a meandering river and surrounded by dramatic mountains (page 355).

◖ Teruel Capital: This bustling provincial capital features four World Heritage Mudejar towers dating from the 14th century and a pair of ill-fated 13th-century lovers resting together for eternity in a set of elaborately carved hand-holding tombs (page 356).

◖ Albarracín: A fairy tale wrought in centuries-old stone and wood, Albarracín is more a museum of time gone by than a town. Its medieval streets, lined with stone mansions boasting massive coats of arms, give a clue to the wealth that once flourished here (page 358).

◖ Barbastro: As capital of the Somontano wine-producing region, this town makes the perfect base to explore this area. Somontano is very up-and-coming and the bodegas, tucked in a landscape of green hills, wildflowers, and medieval ruins, are very open to guests (page 364).

◖ Aínsa: Perfectly preserved within its ring of 12th-century stone walls, this magical little village offers a majestic Plaza Mayor, spectacular views of the Pyrenees, and an excellent jumping-off point for mountain adventures (page 365).

◖ Parque Nacional de Ordesa y Monte Perdido: A protected park within the Spanish Pyrenees, this gorgeous natural wonderland offers not only some of the mountain range's highest peaks, but also trails in the lush valleys that are accessible even to casual walkers (page 368).

LOOK FOR ◖ TO FIND RECOMMENDED SIGHTS, ACTIVITIES, DINING, AND LODGING.

ARAGÓN

ARAGÓN

Pamplona

Estella

Embalse de Yesa

Jaca

SPAIN

FRANCE

Parc National des Pyrénées

Vielha

Benasque

PARQUE NACIONAL DE ORDESA Y MONTE PERDIDO

NAVARRA

Olite

★ SAN JUAN DE PEÑA

Loarre

Ayerbe

AÍNSA

Parque Natural de la Sierra y Cañones de Guara

LA RIOJA

Huesca

Benabarre

Tudela

Borja

TARAZONA

Zuera

ARAGÓN

BARBASTRO

Monzón

N230

Lérida/Lleida

CASTILLA Y LEÓN

Zaragoza

BASÍLICA DEL PILAR

CATALUÑA

Calatayud

Fuentedetodos

Belchite

Caspe

Daroca

Híjar

Alcañiz

Móra

Molina de Aragón

Monreal del Campo

Montalbán

Monroyo

Reserva Nacional de Puertos de Beseit

Tortosa

E15

CASTILLA- LA MANCHA

Amposta

ALBARRACÍN

Morella

TERUEL CAPITAL

Vinarós

0   20 mi

0   20 km

Castelló

Landete

Mediterranean Sea

VALENCIA

Sagunto

© AVALON TRAVEL PUBLISHING, INC.

THE WORLD'S FIRST POWER COUPLE

The marriage of Isabel of Castile and Fernando II of Aragón was one of the most powerful unions in the history of the world. Their combined kingdoms led to the creation of modern Spain as it is known today. Along they way, the very devout pair installed Roman Catholicism as the state religion and created the Inquisition to enforce it. They mercilessly expelled the Jewish population from the country and, in 1492, did the same with the Moors. The pair also financed the four voyages of Columbus.

Isabel (1451–1504) spent much of her childhood in Segovia. Even at a young age, she proved adept at manipulating those around her. She managed to convince the king, her half-brother Henry IV, that she, rather than the king's own daughter, Juana of Portugal, should inherit his crown. (Her manipulations were aided by rumors that the king was impotent and that Juana was not his legitimate child.) As Isabel was consolidating her place in the Castilian court, Fernando II (1452–1516) was in line to inherit the crown of Aragón from his father, King Juan II. The pair married in 1469. When Henry IV died in 1474, Isabel had herself crowned Queen of Castile and Fernando

became king. Their ascension was challenged on behalf of Juana of Portugal and a war of succession broke out. Fernando beat the challengers back in 1476, sparking a long line of near invincibility.

In 1479, Fernando's father died and the pair became King and Queen of Aragón, uniting their powerful kingdoms and laying the foundation for what would become Spain. In 1480, they oversaw the creation of a codex of laws to govern their nascent nation. It vested all power with the royal house. Roman Catholicism was declared the official religion of their reign, partly out of their own devotion to the faith, but mostly as a way to control the fractious nation and solidify their power.

Pope Sixtus IV issued a papal bull giving Isabel and Fernando the power to implement the Inquisition and appoint three grand inquisitors to investigate heretics and other threats (real or politically motivated) to the church. Converted Jews were seen as the greatest threat. In the 1390s, a series of bloody pogroms had forced Jews to abandon Spain or convert to Catholicism. Though many had accepted baptism as Catholics, these *conversos*

---

local Aragonese cuisine is also know for its *trucha* (trout). Of course, no region in Spain would be complete without *jamón* (cured ham), and *jamón* with the Tereul *denominación de origen* (appellation or D.O.) is revered throughout the country. Look for *chilindrón,* a dish that combines chicken with Teruel *jamón,* garlic, and sherry. Thanks to the rich *huertas* (farmland) in Aragón, produce and fruit are abundant. The *melocotones* (peaches) from Calanda are famed and often appear on dessert menus stewed in red wine.

Aragón is home to four wine-producing areas—Cariñera, Campo de Borja, Calatayud, and Somontano. The latter is making major press in the wine world with its rich, savory reds. Based around the city of Barbastro, the Somantano region makes a perfect tour well off the beaten path in Aragón.

PLANNING YOUR TIME

If you have a minimum of time and want a bit of Spanish culture relatively free of tourists, hop the AVE high-speed train to Zaragoza. This regional capital offers everything you could want from a historic Spanish town—an awe-inspiring cathedral, Mudejar architecture, Roman ruins, a medieval core meant for wandering, and a very lively tapas/bar scene. Located on the wide banks of the Río Ebro, it is also a very lovely town. Best of all, outside of its grand fiesta the week of October 12, it is little visited, meaning no lines at sights, no hassles with petty pickpockets, and no feeling of being one of the touristic herd. If you have two days, add the city of Aínsa or Tarazona—both medieval wonderlands. Which you choose will depend on your tastes and your flexibility—renting a car is always the best option. With three days, spend the first in Zaragoza,

were highly suspect. On the one hand, many believed that they continued to practice Judaism in secret, but the real reason lay on the uglier hand. Many *conversos* were wealthier Jews who later used their money and education to rise through the political ranks, posing a potential threat to Isabel and Fernando's burgeoning Catholic kingdom. The Inquisition not only rooted out suspect *conversos* but anyone else who was suspected of undermining either Catholicism or the reign of the Catholic Kings, as Isabel and Fernando soon became known. Trials were barely veiled condemnations of death.

As the Inquisition rooted out heretics within their kingdom, Isabel and Fernando took up the cause of the Christian Reconquest of Spain to root out the last Moorish strongholds on the peninsula. They advanced continually into the south of Spain, eventually conquering all Muslim territories except Granada. In 1492, after nearly a decade of warfare, Granada fell to Isabel and Fernando. The powerful pair had succeeded in capturing the entire peninsula (with the exception of Portugal) for Spain. One of their first acts following this victory was to expel all remaining Jews and Muslims from the country – further solidifying their power of a united Catholic kingdom.

The year 1492 was also important for the pair, as Christopher Columbus (Colón in Spanish) set sail under the Spanish flag to discover a new route to India. As history knows, Columbus and his men found the Americas instead. In later years, these new lands would become Spanish territories and supply the Spanish crown with gold, cocoa, and vast wealth. In return, Spanish conquistadors decimated native civilizations, enslaved native citizens, and forced the spread of Catholicism throughout Latin America.

The Catholic Kings succeeded in their goals on an unprecedented international level. By the time of their deaths, there was one united Spain, devoutly Catholic, and rapidly growing very rich. By the time their grandson Carlos ascended to the throne, the Kingdom of Spain was the world's largest empire – with vast wealth, immense power, and lands stretching halfway around the world. Rather than simply rule as king over such a dominion, Carlos became the Holy Roman Emperor.

travel via car to Barbastro and spend a day exploring the wine bodegas of Somontano, finish up with a trip to Aínsa and, if you are really ambitious, a half-day excursion into the Parque Nacional de Ordesa y Monte Perdido. Of course, if you are a seasoned climber and camper, you could easily spend two weeks in the Aragonese Pyrenees alone. Just be sure to be well prepared and equipped with the knowledge and experience that these peaks demand.

Weatherwise, the only time you want to avoid this region is the depths of winter. Southern Aragón is home to Spain's coldest winter temperatures (conversely their summers are savagely hot). The northern region and the Pyrenees are draped in snow and many roads will be impassable in winter. Another time to consider avoiding Aragón is from mid-July through August. This is peak Spanish travel time and the only time you may have trouble getting reservations at hotels—booking ahead will be essential. For hiking and walking in the national parks, spring couldn't be better. The rivers rumble to life, wildflowers burst into color, and the temperatures are comfortable.

Keep in mind as you plan a visit to this region that Aragón is made up of three provinces, Zaragoza, Huesca, and Teruel, each with capital cities of the same name.

HISTORY

The history of Aragón is in many ways the history of modern Spain. Iberians and other tribes originally called this territory home. With the rise of the Roman Empire and the founding of Hispania (Roman lands on the Iberian Peninsula), Aragón was populated by Roman towns—including Cesaraugusta, which later became Zaragoza. At its Roman height, it was home to 30,000 inhabitants. The modern city offers testament to this Roman heyday with a wealth of Roman ruins. When the Moorish conquests began in the 8th century, Cesaraugusta was captured, renamed Saraqusta, and made the capital city of a powerful *taifa* (Moorish state). During this time the spectacular **La Aljafería** palace was built. In 1081, El Cid, the great Spanish warrior, began working as soldier-for-hire for the Moorish leader of Saraqusta, Yusuf al-Mutamin.

The region was conquered by Christian forces in 1118 and christened the Kingdom of Aragón. The Christian royals moved into the Aljafería palace and subsequent kings were crowned in Zaragoza's La Seo cathedral—a must-see sight in the city. The 1150 marriage of Queen Petronila of Aragón and Count Ramón Berenguer of Barcelona led to the creation of the Crown of Aragón. Despite the name, this entity had its powerful roots firmly in Barcelona and Cataluña. The Catalans, through commercial and naval expertise, soon conquered lands as far off as Sardinia for the Crown of Aragón. Power shifted dramatically in 1469 when Fernando, King of Aragón, married Isabel, Queen of Castile. They turned their considerable powers to conquering Spain, expelling the Moors, and spreading Catholicism. Aragón and Cataluña both took a back seat as this process—nothing less than the founding of modern-day Spain—unfolded.

The 19th and 20th centuries brought tragedy to Zaragoza and the region. First the Napoleonic invasions laid siege to the city. Locals fought back bravely, earning Zaragoza the logo, *siempre heróica e inmortal* (always heroic and immortal). The site of some of the heaviest fighting was the Plaza de los Sitios. During the Spanish Civil War, Zaragoza was a stronghold of Franco's Nationalist troops and therefore a target of great interest to the Republicans as control of Zaragoza meant control of the north. As a result, some of the most violent and destructive battles were waged in the towns and fields in southern Aragón, as the Republicans attempted to advance towards

Zaragoza. One of the worst was the Battle of the Ebro, which lasted from July to November of 1938. Though the Republicans began strong, they were no match for the Nationalists' air support. When it was over, nearly 37,000 men were dead. It is considered one of the decisive battles in the war and the start of the downfall of the Republican forces. Another vicious battle in the region occurred in 1937 in the town of Belchite. Though it was also a Nationalist victory, its place in the history books belongs less to the battle than to the aftermath. City leaders, rather than rebuild, left the devastated city of Belchite standing in its post-war rubble. It is a moving reminder of the devastation of warfare.

The post-Franco democratization of Spain has brought economic advancement to the region, particularly Zaragoza. The AVE high-speed train has put the city firmly on the map, increasing both tourism and business. The scheduled 2008 World's Expo is expected to do for Zaragoza what the 1992 Olympics did for Barcelona—introduce the city to the world. Northern Aragón thrives mainly on the tourism trade generated by the natural wealth of the Pyrenees. Skiing, hiking, climbing, canyoning, white-water rafting, and more are all serious activities here and have given rise to a vast tourism industry that runs the gamut from lodgings and restaurants to sports shops and adventure tour operators. Southern Aragón (Teruel) has had a rougher go of it. Roads are poor and train transport is extremely limited. Activists have started Teruel Existe to draw attention to their plight and to lobby for support. Others have looked to the heart and organized Caravanas de Mujeres, caravans of eligible women who are brought to small Teruel villages to meet the mostly male, mostly single population. Such events are celebrated in many towns on May 28. Teruel is still the most difficult place for tourists to access, but for those intrepid few who do the rewards are unspoiled Spanish countryside and a real glance to the past. The city of Albarracín is particularly worth the effort.

Zaragoza

Straddling the Río Ebro, Zaragoza (tha-ra-GO-tha) is Spain's fifth-largest city and the capital of Aragón. Though it rarely makes the the Spanish tourist's must-see list, it is a charming provincial capital that boasts 2,000 years of illustrious history and a handful of truly inspiring sights—the massive Basílica del Pilar, the lovely Mudejar La Seo cathedral, and the imposing Moorish fortress of La Aljafería among them. Zaragoza is also a thoroughly modern city with a healthy economic base fueled by industry and a long reputation for hard work. It is home to the Universidad de Zaragoza, one of Spain's most prestigious public universities and host to a yearly influx of foreign students who do their semester abroad here. As such, the cultural scene and nightlife are positively buzzing. Despite all of this, Zaragoza has a refreshing lack of tourists. The city hopes to change that with their hosting of the 2008 World Expo. If you are in Spain then, make the effort to attend the fair, which will focus on water. (See sidebar, *World's Water Fair.*)

Zaragoza is mid-way between Madrid and Barcelona and lies on the AVE (high-speed) railway between the two. The Madrid–Zaragoza route is already up and running, connecting the two cities in less than two hours. (The AVE tracks to Barcelona are projected to be completed by 2008, though geological problems in western Aragón and Cataluña are affecting construction.) If you are driving the Madrid–Barcelona route, Zaragoza definitely deserves a one-day detour. It is also a good place to start a tour north into the Aragonese Pyrenees, the most spectacular section of the majestic mountain range.

SIGHTS

The bulk of Zaragoza's sights lie within the cluster of streets that make up the **Casco Histórico,** the city's old historical center. It is bound by the Río Ebro to the north, the **Murallas Romanas** (Roman Walls) to the west, and the sweeping arc of **Calle Coso,** which runs from the Roman walls around the Casco Histórico and back up to the river.

Plaza del Pilar

The elegant Plaza del Pilar rolls out like an expansive granite welcome mat to the city. Stretching along the Río Ebro from the **Plaza Cesár Augusto** in the west to the **Plaza La Seo** in the east, it is lined with Zaragoza's most important buildings, including its two cathedrals (Pilar and La Seo) as well as dozens of lively cafés. If you are short on time, this is the place to head.

Along its eastern end, the remains of the Murallas Romanas give testament to Zaragoza's Roman ancestry. The walls were built soon after the Romans founded the city as Caesaraugusta in 14 B.C. and measured much longer than the 100-meter (330-foot) piece that stands today. At the north end of the walls looms the **Torreón de la Zuda** (Glorieta de Pío XII, s/n), a 10th-century tower that was once part of a Moorish castle. Today, it houses the municipal tourist office. On the upper levels, you can get wonderful views over the river and the roof of the Basílica del Pilar.

Next to the tower stands the **Iglesia de San Juan de los Panetes** (C/ Salduba 3), an 18th-century baroque church famous for its curious eight-sided leaning brick tower. It is built atop the remains of the Moorish castle that the Torreón de la Zuda once belonged to.

On the western end, the **Plaza La Seo** is home to the elegant **La Lonja** (tel. 97/639-7239, 10 A.M.–2 P.M. and 5–9 P.M. Tues.–Sat., 10 A.M.–2 P.M. Sun., closed Mon., free). Built in the 16th century as a public market and trading place for local merchants, it is a stunning example of the Aragonese Renaissance style.

The plaza is also home to the **Museo del Foro de Caesaraugusta** (Pl. Seo 3, tel. 97/639-9752, 10 A.M.–2 P.M. and 5–8 P.M. Tues.–Sat., 10 A.M.–2 P.M. Sun., closed Mon., €2), which houses the remains of a Roman market and forum excavated in the plaza as well as many Roman artifacts. While here, you can purchase an *entrada conjunta* (combined entry pass) for €6 that allows you access to all of the city's Roman ruins.

Directly behind La Lonja is the **Puente de Piedra.** This 15th-century bridge has been repaired many times due to damage from flooding. Walk out about mid-way to get the best photographs of Basílica del Pilar.

☾ Basílica del Pilar

Soaring up from the southern banks of the Río Ebro are the four spires of the Basílica de Nuestra Señora del Pilar (tel. 97/639-7497, 5:45 A.M.–8:30 P.M. daily winter, 5:45 A.M.–9:30 P.M. daily summer, free). Simply called "El Pilar," the cathedral takes pride of place on the Plaza del Pilar. Legend has it that around A.D. 40, the Virgin Mary traveled to this spot to visit Santiago (Saint James), who was doing missionary work among the heathens of Iberia. She carried with her a wooden post (*pilar* in Spanish), planted it in the ground, climbed atop, and exhorted Santiago to build a shrine on this spot so that believers would have a place to ask for her intervention. Thus the Virgen del Pilar and the first cult of Mary was born. As the patron of all of Hispanidad (the entire Hispanic world), she is one of the most venerated of all the Catholic icons. She is also the patron of the Guardia Civil (Spain's Civil Guard). During the Civil War, she

© ZARAGOZA TURISMO

aerial view of the Basílica del Pilar

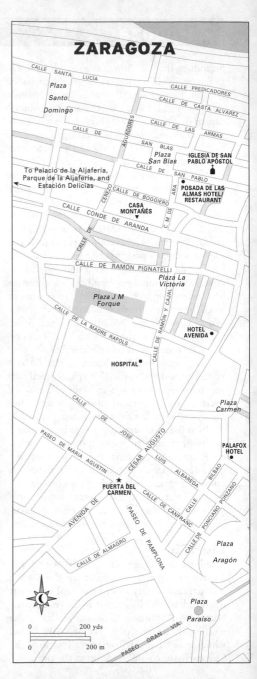

ZARAGOZA

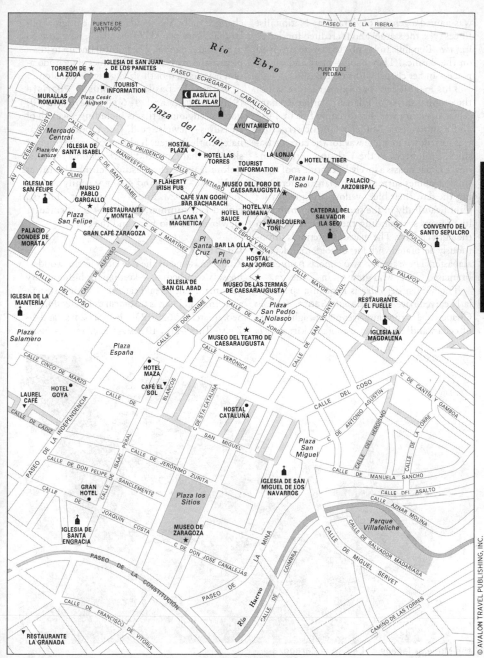

was named a general of Zaragoza's Nationalist forces (yes, the statue) and is credited for defusing two Republican bombs that were dropped on the Basílica. They hang—inert and out of place—in her chapel within the Basílica.

This magnificent baroque structure is not the original shrine of Pilar. An earlier Romanesque structure was destroyed by fire in 1443 and a subsequent Mudejar-Gothic structure was torn down to make way for the current Basílica. Built between the 17th and 18th centuries, El Pilar boasts a lovely Byzantine roof of 10 smaller domes surrounding a larger one. During the day, their blue, yellow, and green tiles glint beautifully in the sun. The four minaret-like towers surrounding them were erected in the 20th century. The spacious interior is sumptuously decorated with lots of gold, marble, and alabaster. There are also two cupolas painted by Francisco Goya, who grew up in Zaragoza.

The Virgen del Pilar is kept in a spectacularly carved nave in the **Capilla Santa,** or Holy Chapel. She is tiny, just over a foot high, carved of cedar, and clad in an elaborate skirt that is changed daily. She stands upon the original pillar that Mary planted for Santiago, now covered in silver and marble. The faithful line up to kiss a piece of the marble pillar. Centuries of such adoration have left a mouth-sized gouge in the stone.

Within the Basílica, the **Museo Pilarista** (9 A.M.–2 P.M. and 4–6 P.M. daily, €1.50) houses religious artifacts including a wealth of treasures—jewels, gold, fine tapestries—donated to the Virgen. It also displays the original sketches that Goya did for the cupola frescoes. Before leaving the Basílica, climb the tower (9:30 A.M.–2 P.M. and 4–6 P.M. daily winter, 9:30 A.M.–2 P.M. and 4–7 P.M. Sat.–Thurs., closed Fri. summer, €1.50) for a spectacular view over the Río Ebro and the city.

La Seo

Zaragoza is one of the few cities in the world to boast two cathedrals—keeping the bishop a very busy man. The second cathedral, lying just steps away from El Pilar, is **Catedral del Salvador** (Pl. Seo, s/n, tel. 97/629-1238, 10 A.M.–2 P.M. and 4–7 P.M. Tues.–Fri., 10 A.M.–1 P.M. and 4–7 P.M.

the Mudejar facade of La Seo in Zaragoza

© ZARAGOZA TURISMO

WORLD'S WATER FAIR

The 1992 World Expo put the Andalusian city of Sevilla brightly in the international spotlight. In 2008, the Expo Zaragoza is expected to do the same for this oft-overlooked Spanish city. Zaragoza beat out contending cities in Greece and Italy by proposing a world's fair based on "Water and Sustainable Development." June 14–September 14, 2008, Zaragoza will host upwards of 70 countries. Guests will be based in large pavilions according to eco-geographical areas such as "Islands and Coasts," "Tropical Jungles," and "High Plains and Mountains." Each country will present its own approaches to water preservation and sustainability. Spain, which has recently suffered some of the worst droughts in its history, is presenting a pavilion that will provoke serious discussion of water shortage problems with the hopes of finding solutions on a global level. There will also be a "Water Pavilion" that will host exhibitions on global water issues and serve as a place to share and promote solutions to the world's water woes. The Expo site will encompass nearly a 1.3-square-kilometer (0.5-square-mile) area in a crook of the Ebro River.

The Expo is expected to bring 7.5 million visitors to Zaragoza, create nearly 10,000 jobs, and rake in over a billion dollars in income. It is also expected to provide a major long-term boost to the city and region. Hotels, public buildings, and infrastructure have already been put in place to handle the influx of visitors and exhibitors.

Zaragoza is currently one of Spain's best-kept secrets – a bustling provincial capital boasting a dynamic cultural, historic, and architectural heritage – and city leaders hope that after the event, Zaragoza will take its place as one of Spain's premier cities. Located almost directly between Madrid and Barcelona and serving as a major hub of Spain's high-speed train system AVE, Zaragoza just might do it.

If you will be traveling in Spain during the summer of 2008, you should make an attempt to visit Expo Zaragoza. Remember, you will have to reserve ahead for accommodations or take the AVE train in from Madrid for just a day. Find more information about the event at www.zaragozaexpo2008.es.

ARAGÓN

Sat., 10 A.M.–12 P.M. and 4–7 P.M. Sun., closes one hour earlier in winter, closed Mon., €2), better known as La Seo. Sitting on the site of a former Visigothic church, later a Moorish mosque, La Seo was built in the 12th century and added onto through the 18th. Its best feature is its northern wall (facing the river), a stunning display of Mudejar style, comprised of an intricate mosaic of red bricks and colored tiles. Inside, the 15th-century alabaster altar is quite lovely. The cathedral is home to the **Museo de Tapices** (€1.50), an extraordinary collection of medieval tapestries. Your ticket allows access to the **Capitular,** a cathedral museum housing the skull of Saint Dominguito del Val who was martyred in Zaragoza.

Casco Histórico

The Casco Histórico is dotted with several worthy sights that illustrate the tangled history of Zaragoza. Seek out the 14th-century Mude-

jar churches of **La Magdalena** (Pl. Magdalena, tel. 97/639-9745), with its gorgeous brickwork tower, and **San Gil Abad** (C/ Don Jaime I, 15), with a slightly less impressive tower.

Roman history can be found in the **Museo de las Termas de Caesaraugusta** (C/ San Juan y San Pedro 3, tel. 97/629-7279, 10 A.M.–2 P.M. and 5–8 P.M. Tues.–Sat., 10 A.M.–2 P.M. Sun., closed Mon., €2, or €6 for access to all Zaragoza's Roman ruins). These public baths date from the 1st century and were uncovered during roadwork in the 1980s. Nearby, the **Museo del Teatro de Caesaraugusta** (C/ San Jorge 12, tel. 97/620-5088, 10 A.M.–9 P.M. Tues.–Sat., 10 A.M.–2 P.M. Sun., €3) houses a Roman theater that also dates back to the 1st century. You can get a good glimpse from the street if you don't feel like entering the museum.

Twentieth-century art can be found at **Museo Pablo Gargallo** (Pl. San Felipe 3, tel. 97/639-2058, 9 A.M.–2 P.M. and 5–9 P.M. Tues.–Sat., 9 A.M.–2 P.M. Sun., closed Mon., free), a lovely 17th-century palace housing the work of Pablo Gargallo (1881–1934), a Zaragoza native and prolific sculptor.

On the eastern edge of the Casco Histórico is the impressive glass and iron **Mercado Central** (Av. César Augusto, s/n, 8 A.M.–2 P.M. Mon.–Sat., closed Sun.). This modernist masterpiece dates from 1903 and still serves as the city's central market. Get there early to see it at its liveliest.

Plaza de España

On the southern edge of the Casco Histórico lies the bustling Plaza de España, brimming with sidewalk cafés, tapas bars, and restaurants. Leading south off of the plaza is **Paseo de la Independencía,** a broad, tree-lined avenue lined with boutiques and department stores. Just off the Paseo, **Iglesia de Santa Engracia** (Pl. Santa Engracia, s/n, tel. 97/622-5879, 9:30 A.M.–1:15 P.M. and 5:30–8:30 P.M. Sun., 7:30–8:30 P.M. Sat., free) is a 16th-century church housing 9th-century tombs behind its Plateresque facade. The stone sarcophagi are said to contain the bones of dozens of Christian martyrs, including Saint Engracia.

A few blocks west is the **Museo de Zaragoza** (Pl. Sitios 6, tel. 97/622-2181, 10 A.M.–2 P.M. and 5–8 P.M. Tues.–Sat., 10 A.M.–2 P.M. Sun., closed Mon., free). The museum has two distinct parts: archaeology and fine arts. The former has pieces dating back to prehistoric times, while the latter has an excellent collection of paintings by native son Francisco Goya.

La Aljafería

West of the Casco Histórico, the Palacio de la Aljafería (C/ Diputados, s/n, tel. 97/628-9683, 10 A.M.–2 P.M. and 4:30–8 P.M. Sat.–Wed. 4:30–8 P.M. Fri. April–Oct., 10 A.M.–2 P.M. and 4–6:30 P.M. Mon.–Wed. and Sat. 4–6:30 P.M. Fri. 10 A.M.–2 P.M. Sun. Nov.–Mar., €3) rises as a sand-colored reminder of Moorish history from the verdant park surrounding it. Built in the 11th century as both a pleasure palace and a defensive fort, this building is one of Spain's finest Moorish structures. The mosque is a particularly lush example of Moorish design. The oldest part of the structure, the **Torre del Trovadar** served as the setting for Verdi's 1853 opera *Il Trovatore.* Within the walls are two lovely patios. The gothic pieces were added by the Catholic Kings Isabel and Fernando who resided here briefly. In the 15th century, the palace became the local head of the Inquisition. Today, it houses the Aragonese parliament.

ENTERTAINMENT AND EVENTS
Nightlife

Zaragoza is famed throughout Spain for the ferocity of its *la marcha* (nightlife), which is fueled in large part by the city's universities, but also by the local obsession with being out and about. Bars, cafés, and tapas bars can be found all over town. For the thickest concentration, head to the Casco Histórico between Calle Don Jaime I and the Central Mercado.

Start the night at the low-key **Café Van Gogh** (C/ Espoz y Mina 12), a cozy favorite with brick walls laden with local art. Sharing the same address, **Bar Bacharach** (as in crooner Burt) is a hipster homage to the 1970s. Complete with checkered couches and stencils of Bacharach himself on the wall, you'll feel like you've walked into your really mod friend's apartment for a drink. The music ranges from Johnny Cash to Lou Reed and, of course, Burt Bacharach. Across the street, **La Casa Magnetica** (C/ Espoz y Mina 19) has the feel of a funhouse that's been converted into a neighborhood nightclub—complete with disco balls, black lights, and loud colors. The music—from Jamiroquai to Prince—is equally loud. **P. Flaherty** (C/ Alfonso I 39, tel. 97/629-8094) is a boisterous Irish pub with a multicultural, English-speaking staff and very good pints. **El Marqués de Carabás** (C/ Contamina 2) is off-the-hook Spanish fun. The place is nothing special to look at, but the crowd, amped on cheap drinks and seriously loud Spanish pop, go wild until the wee hours. Just south of Calle Coso, and out of the Casco Histórico, seek out **El Sol** (C/ Blancas 4, tel. 97/621-1055), a café/bar jammed with old neon advertising signs hanging on the tiled walls. For late-night dance action, try **La**

Casa del Loco (C/ Mayor 10), a longtime favorite on the Zaragoza night scene. It's big, brash, and bold and filled with good-looking, party-loving locals. There is usually a line by 2 A.M. on the weekends and you can expect to pay €8 for a cocktail. Music is a mix of pop, house, and a smattering of Euro-trash. For the latest on late-night parties, keep an eye out during the day for flyers in shops and restaurants and posters in the Casco Histórico announcing upcoming DJ shows.

Festivals and Events

Mid-October, Zaragoza goes wild in celebration of their patroness with the **Fiestas de Nuestra Señora de Pilar.** The nine day celebration kicks off on October 12, the official day of the Virgin, with an Ofrenda de Flores, an offering of flowers woven into a massive cape flowing from the statue, which is placed in Plaza del Pilar for the occasion. There are several other religious events and even more purely festive ones. By day there are folk dances, sports competitions, and parades of *cabezudos*, costumed figures with enormous heads that chase the local children around town. At night there are street parties, food booths, live music, fireworks, and up-'til-dawn carousing. Book ahead if you plan on attending.

There are several more traditional festivals around the calendar. The **Fiestas de San Jorge,** held on April 23 to celebrate the patron saint of Aragón, features live bands in the streets and free guided tours of the local government offices. **Semana Santa** (Easter Week) is celebrated with processions accompanied by deafening drums. There is also one decidedly non-traditional party that is gaining in fame each year: the **Zaragoza Ciudad Hip Hop Festival.** Held the last weekend in June, it brings hip-hop artists from around the globe as well as huge crowds drawn to the both the music and the array of attendant activities—from breakdancing to skateboarding to graffiti demonstrations.

ACCOMMODATIONS

When considering accommodations in Zaragoza, keep in mind that prices can double (or more) during the Fiestas del Pilar in October. Rooms in the Casco Histórico or on Plaza del Pilar can be noisy due to both constant foot traffic and the hourly cacophony of chiming church bells.

Under €50

◖ Hostal Plaza (Pl. Pilar 14, tel. 97/629-4830, €48) is located in an antique-filled building facing the Basílica. Rooms are surprisingly cheerful for the price. Request one with a view for a memorable stay. **Posada de las Almas** (C/ San Pablo 22, tel. 97/643-9700, €45) offers 20 basic rooms in a family-run *hostal* just 10 minutes walking to Plaza del Pilar. The attached restaurant is famed for its hearty Spanish fare. **Hostal Cataluña** (C/ Coso 94, tel. 97/621-6938, www.zaragoza-ciudad.com/hostalcataluna, €48) is a *hostal* with hotel illusions. Located less than a block from Plaza de España, this old-fashioned property has comfortable—if tired—rooms and a friendly staff. Request an upper floor for a view and skip the overpriced, under-stocked breakfast buffet. **San Jorge** (C/ Mayor 4, tel. 97/639-7462, €39) offers basic, clean rooms at rock-bottom prices in the heart of the Casco Histórico.

€50-100

Hotel Las Torres (Pl. Pilar 11, tel. 97/639-4250, www.hotel-lastorres.com, €55) is located in an absolutely charming building right on the Plaza del Pilar. Many of the (somewhat small) rooms feature floor-to-ceiling windows, allowing you to doze off with the lit-up Basílica as your nightlight. **Hotel Avenida** (Av. César Augusto 55, tel. 97/643-9300, www.hotelavenida-zaragoza.com, €55), close to the Mercado Central, offers updated, basic rooms with large baths for a very economical price. **El Tibur** (Pl. Seo 2, tel. 97/620-2000, www.hoteltibur.com, €70) offers comfortable, if bland, rooms in one of the best locations in town. **Vía Romana** (C/ Don Jaime I 54, tel. 97/639-8215, viaromana@husa.es, www.husa.es, €80) offers an ideal location, right in the center of the Casco Histórico, just moments walking to all of the city's sights. Rooms are modern and updated and run with usual Husa efficiency, however avoid the 4th floor, which is accessed via a stairwell (not an elevator) and features small, dark rooms. **Hotel Maza** (Pl. España 7, tel. 97/622-9355, www.hotelmaza.com, €60) offers 54 decent-sized rooms in an antique-filled hotel right on the buzzing Plaza de España. **Hotel Sauce** (C/ Espoz y Min, 33, tel. 97/620-5050, www.hotelsauce.com, €60) offers sherbet-colored rooms in a tidy little hotel in the Casco Histórico.

Over €100

Gran Hotel (C/ Joaquín Costa 5, tel. 97/622-1901, nhgranhotel@nh-hotels.com, www.nh-hotels .com, €120) is a classic of Zaragoza society, having been inaugurated by King Alfonso XIII himself in 1929. Rooms are traditionally appointed, service is impeccable, and there is a noble air permeating the place. If you are going at Easter time, the processions pass right in front of the hotel. It is a thrilling sight, but be prepared for the loud banging of drums. **Hotel Goya** (C/ Cinco de Marzo 5, tel. 97/622-9331, hotelgoya@palafoxhoteles.com, www.palafoxhoteles.com, €140) is one of Zaragoza's classic hotels. Rooms are spacious compared to many in the city center and a styled in a very traditional chain hotel palette of burgundy and green. Prices are cut nearly in half on weekends. **Palafox Hotel** (C/ Casa Jiménez, s/n, tel. 97/623-7700, hotelpalafox@palafoxhoteles.com, www.palafoxhoteles.com, €178) is one of the few five-star hotels in town—and the most centrally located. Rooms are spacious and stylishly decorated in warm colors. Despite the location (five minutes from the Casco Histórico, 10 from El Pilar), the rooms are very quiet. Service is discreet yet attentive. Prices drop to €110 on weekends.

FOOD
Cafés and Desserts

The cafés with the best views are those lining Plaza del Pilar. Just be aware that you'll pay extra for the privilege. Another good bet is along the Roman walls, just north of the Mercado Central, where there are several cafés specializing in everything from hot chocolate to cold milkshakes. ◖ **Gran Café Zaragoza** (C/ Alfonso I 25, 9 A.M.–midnight daily) is a lovely belle epoque café located in an old jewelry store that boasts heavy marble counters and red vel-

vet curtains. It is an excellent place for coffee any time of day. **Laurel Café** (C/ San Diego 3, tel. 97/623-9829, 8 A.M.–11 P.M. Sun.–Thurs., 8 A.M.–3 A.M. Fri.–Sat.), a modern spot a few blocks off Paseo de la Independencía, offers an extensive menu of teas, coffees, and *batidos* (milkshakes). There is also a short list of sandwiches and salads. **Tetería Al-Harin** (C/ Don Teobaldo 16, tel. 97/639-4163) takes the Mudejar styling from nearby Iglesia de la Magdalena and brings it inside. This Moroccan tea house is the perfect retreat for mint-infused green tea, cardamom-flavored coffees, and sticky sweet pastries served atop low-lying brass tables.

Gourmet

◖ **Montal** (C/ Torrenueva 29, tel. 97/629-8998, 1–3 P.M. and 8:30–10 P.M. Mon.–Fri., 1–3 P.M. Sat., closed Sun., €35) offers excellent Spanish and international fare in one of the loveliest dining rooms in Spain—an old Aragonese palace boasting a 16th-century cloister with delicate arches and intricate stonework. The Montal family has run a charcuterie and wine shop at this location since 1919 (currently the city's best gourmet shop), insuring the restaurant the most exquisite cured hams and wines. **La Granada** (C/ San Ignacio de Loyola 14, tel. 97/622-3903, 1:30–4 P.M. and 9–11 P.M. Mon.–Sat., closed Sun., €45) is one of Zaragoza's most exciting restaurants. Drawing from the best of Aragonese products and produce, the kitchen adds distinctive postmodern touches. **Los Borrachos** (Po. Sagasta 64, tel. 97/627-5036, 1–4 P.M. and 9–midnight Tues.–Sun., closed Mon., €36) is a serious, dignified, and extremely elegant dining room accustomed to serving royalty, both blue-blooded and celebrity. Food leans towards solid, delicious interpretations of classic Aragonese dishes. Game is a specialty.

Local Cuisine

La Posada de las Almas (C/ San Pablo 33, tel. 97/643-9700, 1–3:30 P.M. and 9–11:30 P.M. daily, €20) has been serving rustic Spanish fare to happy locals for decades. The dining area is a warren of antiquated rooms with stained glass, tiled walls, and heavy wood furnishings. **El**

Fuelle (C/ Mayor 59, tel. 97/639-8033, 1:30–4 P.M. and 8:30–11 P.M. Mon.–Sat., 1–5 P.M. Sun., €20) oozes rustic charm with a decor of farm implements and flea market finds. The food is suitably pastoral with dishes like *migas* (savory fried bread crumbs) taking pride of place on the menu. It also has a lively tapas bar. **La Bodega de Chema** (C/ Latassa 34, tel. 97/655-5014, 1–4 P.M. and 9–10:30P.M. Mon.–Sat., 1–4 P.M. Sun., €18) is famed for its hearty meat dishes, particularly *cabrito asado* (roasted goat). **Casa Montañés** (C/ Conde Aranda 22, tel. 97/644-1018, 1–4 P.M. and 9 P.M.–midnight daily, €25) offers a variety of seafood dishes alongside meatier Aragonese fare.

Tapas

For more tapas bars than you can jab a toothpick at, head to the famed **El Tubo** in the Casco Histórico, a jumble of streets between Calle Alfonso and Calle Don Jaime I and south of Calle Espoz y Mina. Most bars have their own specialty and a safe bet is to order whatever everyone else is having; however, you might want to think twice before going for the *tortilla de sesos* (pig's brain omelet). Another excellent tapas zone is around the Plaza Santa Marta, behind La Seo. Tapas bars in Zaragoza are generally open from 1–4 P.M. and 8 P.M.–midnight, with many places closing either Sunday or Monday. If you find one of the places listed below closed, don't fret, it's guaranteed there is another one open nearby.

Cervecería Marpy (Pl. Santa Marta 8, tel. 97/639-2613) offers classic tapas in a festive bar decorated with bullfighting memorabilia (including one very large bull's head) and bright red and blue furnishings. The owner Antonio is a hoot, just be careful—he may try to talk you into his house specialty—*criadillas* (bull testicles). **La Olla** (C/ Mayor, 1, tel. 97/639-8257) offers a gleaming counter top full of tapas in a cheery yellow and blue tiled bar. Have the *gambas al ajillo* (garlic shrimp) with a glass of *vermut* (red vermouth) right from the barrel. **Marisquería Toñi** (C/ Don Jaime I 40, tel. 97/639 0414) is a shellfish haven with raw oysters shucked behind the bar, boiled shrimp piled under glass,

and succulent fresh anchovies simmering in olive oil baths studded with garlic. **El Gastrónomo** (C/ Mártires 6, tel. 97/629-6433) has a medieval dining room complete with hulking stone pillars. They serve an excellent variety of tapas.

INFORMATION

The **municipal tourist offices** (Pl. Pilar, s/n, tel. 97/639-3537, 10 A.M.–8 P.M. daily and Torreón de la Zuda, Glorieta de Pío XII, s/n, tel. 97/620-1200, 10 A.M.–2 P.M. and 4:30–8 P.M. Mon.–Sat.,10 A.M.–2 P.M. Sun.) are extremely well stocked with ample information in English and extremely friendly staff. There are also information points at the train station and the airport. Their website (www.zaragozaturismo.es) is good, but much of it is still in Spanish only. That is being changed in anticipation of the 2008 Expo.

If you plan on touring other areas of Aragón, including the Pyrenees, visit the **regional tourist office** (Av. César Augusto 25, tel. 97/628-2181).

GETTING THERE AND AROUND
Air

Aeropuerto de Zaragoza (Crta. Aeropuerto, s/n, tel. 97/671-2300, www.aena.es) is about 10 kilometers (six miles) outside of the city and receives daily flights from cities throughout Spain via **Air Europa** (www.aireuropa.com) and **Iberia** (www.iberia.es). (However, if you are traveling from Madrid, the AVE high-speed train is your best bet.) The airport also receives direct flights via **Ryanair** (www.ryanair.com) from London's Stansted Airport. By the time the 2008 Expo kicks off, the airport should have increased international services.

To get into the city from the airport, catch a taxi for €15–20 or hop on the bus. It leaves from in front of the terminal every half-hour and takes about 25 minutes to get into town. Get a schedule of stops at the tourist booth in the airport.

Train

Zaragoza's train station, **Estación Delicias** (Av. Rioja 33) is gleaming, modern structure run by **Renfe** (tel. 90/224-0202, www.renfe.es).

There are 13 daily high-speed AVE trains to Madrid (€43) as well as regular service to cities throughout Aragón (five to Huesca, three to Teruel) and the rest of Spain (15 to Barcelona). The station is near the La Aljafería palace, about 15 minutes walking to the center. Local bus 51 will get you as close as Paseo de la Constitución. A cab will run less than €10.

Bus

Taking a bus out of Zaragoza can be a complicated affair as there is no single bus station. Each of the dozen bus companies operates from its own depot. If you are traveling into Zaragoza by bus, it is a good idea to do research at your bus station of origin to determine where you will catch your bus in Zaragoza. **Alsa/Agredasa** (Po. María Agustin 7, tel. 97/622-9343, www.agredasa.com or www.alsa.es) serves most major cities, including Barcelona, Bilbao, Madrid, and Santiago de Compostela. **Alosa** (Po. María Agustin 7, tel. 90/221-0700, www.alosa.es) serves Huesca and Jaca. **Autobuses Jiménez** (C/ Juan Pablo Bone, 13, tel. 97/627-6179, www.grupo-jimenez.com) serves the Costa Blanca, including Alicante and Valencia, as well as La Rioja and Burgos. It is also the connection to Teruel. **Autobuses Conda** (Av. Navarra 81, tel. 97/633-3372, www.conda.es) serves Pamplona and San Sebastián.

Car

Zaragoza lies on the A-2/N-2 that runs Madrid–Zaragoza–Barcelona. It also sits on the A-68 highway that connects to Bilbao. The N-330 goes south towards Teruel and north to France. The N-232 runs northwest to Logroño and Santander.

If you want to rent a car to explore Aragón, **Avis** (www.avis.es), **Hertz** (www.hertz.es), and **Europcar** (www.europcar.es) each have offices in the airport.

VICINITY OF ZARAGOZA
Fuendetodos

If you are driving to the south and are a fan of Spanish artist Francisco de Goya y Lucientes, consider detouring to tiny Fuendetodos (population 170). The artist was born in 1746 in this dusty little hamlet some 48 kilometers (30 miles) southeast of Zaragoza. The **Casa Natal de Goya** (tel. 97/614-3830, 11 A.M.–2 P.M. and 4–7 P.M. Wed.–Mon., closed Tues., €1.80) is the humble stone house where Goya spent the early years of his life. It has been decorated to evoke a 17th-century feel down to the simple rough-hewn furnishings and utensils. There are also several of his works as well as informative displays (in Spanish) about his life. Down the street, the **Museo del Grabado** (same hours, phone, price) houses an extensive collection of etchings and prints by Goya, including a delightful series called *Caprichos* (whims) and *Disparates* (absurdities), which some claim are among Goya's most profound works.

Outside of the Goya goodies, there is little to see other than a nice respite of slow-moving, back-country Aragonese life. You can enjoy an excellent local meal at **Mesón de la Maja** (Pl. Goya, s/n). "Maja" is slang for "kind woman," and it is true—the women running this rustic inn are extremely accommodating. Their roasted meats are equally delicious.

Get there by car following the N-330 south from Zaragoza. At Botorrita, switch to the A-2101, which leads into town. There are a couple of buses a day from Zaragoza, but in order to avoid an overnight, take the **Samur Buil** bus (C/ Borao 13, tel. 97/643-4304) at 10 A.M. It returns from Fuendetodos at 3 P.M.

Belchite

Aragón's countryside saw some of the fiercest fighting during the Spanish Civil War (1936–1939). Zaragoza was a Nationalist stronghold under the control of Franco's forces. In attempt to make inroads into Aragón, the Republican forces started an offensive in the area, entering Belchite on August 24. They were met with strong resistance from local Nationalists and a fierce battled ensued. The fighting was particularly brutal, going from house to house, citizen to citizen. When it was over—15 days later—over 6,000 people were dead. Houses, churches, schools, shops, restaurants, and plazas had been reduced to smoldering rubble. When the war was finally over, the surviving citizens of Belchite turned to rebuilding. However, rather than repair the damage, they built a new town next to the remains of the old, choosing to leave the remains of old Belchite as a testament to the horrors of war. It is an eerily moving place. Walking around the skeleton houses, the gaping wounds of the old church, it is impossible not to make comparisons that continue to wage today and wonder, if all Belchite suffered, if the seven decades of testament that this ravaged old town has offered, were just in vain.

The best access to Belchite is **via car.** From Zaragoza, take the N-232 towards Alcañiz and switch to the A-222, then follow the signs. From Fuendetodos, follow the A-220 east about 21 kilometers (13 miles).

◖ Tarazona

Sitting in a verdant valley just 80 kilometers (50 miles) northwest of Zaragoza is one of Aragón's medieval jewels. Beneath the looming hulk of Mount Moncaya (2,286 meters/7,500 feet) and straddling the meandering Río Queiles, lovely little Tarazona boasts one of the country's most atmospheric old quarters. Called the **Barrios Altos** (Upper Town), it is a tangle of ancient alleyways winding precariously around a hilltop. Many of the oldest houses are carved right into the hillside. The heart of town is the **Plaza de España** flanked by the 16th-century **Ayuntamiento** (town hall) with its sumptuous facade that includes a magnificent frieze detailing key events in Spanish history. Looming above the Barrios Altos is the **Iglesia de Santa María Magdalena** with its elegant 12th-century Mudejar tower. From the church you can get a magnificent view over the city, including a glimpse of Spain's most unusual **Plaza de Toros.** Built in 1792, this bull ring is actually composed of 32 apartments whose flat, windowed backsides join together in a circle to form the ring. The apartments are still occupied though it has been a long time since bulls were fought here.

Recently, historians have discovered important documents relating to Tarazona's long-lost Jewish population (expelled from the country in 1492 by Fernando and Isabel, the Catholic Kings). The **Judería** (Jewish quarter), situated on Rúas (Calles) Altas and Bajas, is notable for its *casas colgadas,* or hanging houses, called such because they cling to the side of the hill. Get your best view of them from Calle Judería.

In the lower, newer town, on the banks of the river is the monumental **Catedral de Nuestra Señora de la Huerta.** A stone and brick testament to the myriad of styles popular in this region, the cathedral boasts a unique brick dome similar to La Seo in Zaragoza and a Mudejar tower, as well as Gothic, Romanesque, and Renaissance details. The interior is said to be magnificent, however it has been closed to the public since 1985 due to structural damage and a very long-term reconstruction project.

If you end up in town on August 27, you'll witness one of Spain's more bizarre festivals. At noon, the Cipotegato, a giant figure on stilts dressed in a colorful harlequin outfit emerges and takes a walk around town—or attempts to. Townspeople halt his progress by pelting him with tomatoes.

It is recommended that you stay overnight to really enjoy the medieval vibe of this little town which is particularly atmospheric after dark—though you might want to make it a weekend, during the week it's a ghost town. **Hostal Santa Águeda** (C/ Visconti 26, tel. 97/664-0054, www.santaagueda.com, €60) is a lovely medieval house that has been converted into an inn. Rooms are individually decorated and feature homey antiques and country styling. **Condes de Visconti** (C/ Visconti 15, tel. 97/664-4908, www.condesdevisconti.com, €77) is a charming inn located in a 16th-century palace. Rooms have a rustic chic look with lovely linens, antiques, and artwork. Service is friendly and the in-house restaurant is excellent. The best restaurant in the town is **Brujas de Bécquer** (Ctra. Zaragoza, s/n, tel. 97/664-0400), which offers exquisite Aragonese fare.

By car, Tarazona lies on the N-121, about 19 kilometers (12 miles) south of the AP-68, which connects Zaragoza to Logroño in La Rioja. By bus from Zaragoza, take **Autobuses Therpasa** (C/ General Sueiro 22, tel. 97/622-5723, www.therpasa.es).

Southern Aragón

Comprising the province of Teruel, southern Aragón offers a geographic variety that rambles through a military roster of colors—flaxen plains, khaki brown plateaus, olive green scrubland. Then, when you least expect it, turning a curve on one of the nearly impassible old roads that spiderweb this vast land, a jade green mountain rises suddenly from a verdant valley threaded with ambling blue rivers. The variety is thanks to the Sistema Ibérico mountain range that riddles the region and protects it from both cool Atlantic air and moist warm Mediterranean winds. The result is a harsh, almost violent climate—searing hot in summer, bone-cracking cold in winter. This region has a history that is equally severe, marred by military conquest and carnage. The Romans vanquished the Iberians. The Christians and Moors clashed viciously for centuries here. During the Spanish Civil War, some of the most brutal, soul-crushing battles were waged in these desert-colored lands.

Today, the land is still as forlorn and frozen in time as the dinosaur tracks that cross it. Poverty is high, birth rates low, emigration constant. In 1999, fed up and frustrated, regional activists formed the social movement Teruel Existe (Teruel Exists) to draw attention to their plight and demand government aid and support to develop infrastructures, highways, education, and opportunities. One initiative has focused on tourism. Within the centuries of torment in these troubled lands, there were pockets of cultural advancement, particularly during Muslim rule, and southern Aragón is home to some of the most spectacular Moorish structures in the country as well as several impressive medieval cathedrals and castles. The combination of the remoteness of the land, the lack of access (Teruel was the last province in the country to receive public highways), and the historic poverty has kept tourists away—still keeps tourists away. Which is exactly what makes this region such an enchanting place to visit—it's a truly remote slice of traditional Spanish life—just a few hours away from Zaragoza, Madrid, Barcelona, or Valencia. If you like to take the paths way, way beyond beaten and don't mind your culture undiluted by marketing, free from sidewalk barkers, and blissfully silent—Southern Aragón is for you. Just be ready to rent a car, be flexible, and get familiar with your phrasebook—English is not spoken.

◖ TERUEL CAPITAL

On a plateau some 914 meters (3,000 feet) above sea level, the provincial capital of Teruel rises like an oasis of urbanity in the sparse countryside. Modern and lively, the town of 33,000 boasts a medieval center of charming plazas, winding streets, and a glorious clutch of Mudejar towers that figure among the UNESCO World Heritage Sites. An architectural movement that emerged around the 12th century as master Moorish builders began to carry out public works on behalf of the Christian rulers, Mudejar employed Muslim design motifs with Western structural styles. Brick became the main building block, in part because it was cheap. To beautify this humble material, the Moorish builders experimented with elaborate tiling and layering techniques. Nowhere in Spain did this style reach such sophistication as it did in Teruel.

Sights

If you are entering the city via train, the first evidence that you are entering Teruel Ciudad Mudejar is **La Escalinata,** an impressive set of stairs leading from the train platform into the **Casco Histórico** (historic quarter). Built in 1920, the stairs are decorated in neo-Mudejar style replete with brickwork and colorful tiles. At the top of the stairs is a mural of Teruel's famous, ill-fated lovers, Isabel and Diego. Once you enter the old quarter, the first of Teruel's spectacular towers comes into view. The 131-foot **Torre del Salvador** (C/ Salvador, s/n, 11–2 P.M. and 4:30–7:30 P.M. Tues.–Sat. in winter,

Teruel's Mudejar towers loom over the old city center.

ARAGÓN

what—or whom—lies beneath. Within the church of San Pedro is the **Mausoleo de los Amantes** (9:30 A.M.–8:30 P.M. daily summer and 10 A.M.–2 P.M. and 4–8 P.M. daily winter, €3)—the Mausoleum of the Lovers. Legend has it that sometime in the 13th century, Isabel de Segura and Diego de Marcilla fell madly in love. She was rich, he was not. Her father refused to consent to marriage until Diego had amassed a fortune. He went forth into the world and over five long years finally gained the wealth he needed to wed Isabel. However, he was too late. Isabel's impatient father had betrothed her to a wealthy man from Albarracín and Diego arrived on the eve of the wedding. He implored Isabel for just one last kiss. When she refused, Diego, heartsick and longing, died right at her feet. The next day, dressed in her wedding gown, Isabel approached Diego's body as it lay in wake in the church of San Pedro. She leaned over and finally gave him the kiss he had died for. As her lips touched his, she too was consumed by a grief too harsh to bear and fell dead herself. The ill-fated lovers lie today in matching tombs, carved with their likenesses, their alabaster hands reaching out to touch between the sarcophagi. The mausoleum is a popular pilgrimage for young newlyweds hoping also to spend eternity together.

A visit to the lively **Plaza del Torico** finishes a tour of Teruel. At its center is a soaring white column on top of which sits a sculpture of a *toro*, a fighting bull with a star between its horns. It is the symbol of the city. The *toro* figures prominently in the annual fiestas of the city. Around the plaza are several attractive buildings, particularly the **Casa Art Noveau** as well as cafés and shops.

Festivals

For several days around February 14, the citizens of Teruel don their medieval finery to celebrate **Las Bodas de Isabel de Segura,** the Weddings of Isabel de Segura. The entire town takes on a festive medieval air as the tragedy of the Lovers of Teruel is honored in a series of activities and events. The second week of July, Teruel throws its main bash, **La Vaquilla del**

daily in summer, €2.50) was built in 1677 but dates back to the 14th century. The most sumptuous of the town's towers, Salvador features an elaborate red brick facade decorated with green and white tiles. It seems almost brocaded. Like all the towers in Teruel, it is separate from its church—just as Muslim minarets are separate from their mosques. This is the only tower which visitors are allowed to ascend. A few blocks away, **Torre de San Martín** (Pl. Pérez Prado, s/n) was built in 1315 and is very similar to Salvador, though a bit less spectacular.

The **Catedral de Santa María de Mediavilla** (Pl. Catedral, s/n, 11 A.M.–2 P.M. and 4–7 P.M. Mon.–Sat., 4–7 P.M. Sun., €3) boasts not only a magnificent tower, but a brick-covered Mudejar dome. Inside the cathedral, don't miss the exquisitely carved wooden ceiling.

The fourth of Teruel's towers is **Torre de San Pedro** (C/ Matías Abad, s/n), built in the 14th century. It is the least grand of the group, but that is like saying that a pink rose is less beautiful than a red one. However, the tower definitely pales in popularity to

© CANDY LEE LABALLE

Ángel. As in nearby Pamplona, the event involves bull runs through the town's streets, but about the only guests are locals—Hemingway never wrote about this place. The festivities include street parties, live music, and fireworks.

Accommodations

Hostal Alcazaba (C/ Joaquín Costa 34, tel. 97/861-0761, €42) offers lovely, very clean rooms for an excellent price. **Hotel Oriente** (Av. Sagunto 7, tel. 97/860-1550, €70) is located just outside the Casco Histórico and offers comfortable rooms brimming with rustic style. **Torico Plaza** (C/ Yagüe Salas 5, tel. 97/860-8655, toricoplaza@sercotel.es, www .bacohoteles.com, €84) has the best location, right on the Plaza del Torico. It also boasts spacious, comfortable rooms. On the outskirts of town lies the **Parador de Teruel** (Ctra. Sagunto-Burgos, N-234, tel. 97/860-1800, teruel@parador.es, www.parador.es, €110). Unlike most properties in the Parador chain, this is not a historic building. It is a modern "palace" that incorporates Mudejar styling throughout. It does have lovely views over the city and its towers and a pool—a nice touch in the dog heat of summer.

Food

Like all Aragonese food, Teruel's cuisine is hearty and heavy on the roasts and stews. Teruel also produces some of the best *jamón* in Spain, and you'll find it on offer all over town. **Los Juncos** (C/ Ramón y Cajal 16, tel. 97/860-2423, 9 A.M.–midnight Mon.–Sat., closed Sun.) offers Basque-style tapas, but for a more substantial meal, try **Torre del Salvador** (C/ Salvador, s/n, tel. 97/860-5263, 1:30–3:30 P.M. and 9–11 P.M. Tues.–Sat., 1:30–3:30 P.M. Sun., closed Mon., €15) at the foot of the tower of the same name. Their specialty is *berenjenas gratinadas* (baked eggplant). **Mesón Óvalo** (Po. Óvalo 6, tel. 97/860-9862, closed Mon., €25) is a rustic house with rustic fare such as *setas silvestres* (sautéed wild mushrooms) and *cordero* (lamb). **La Menta** (C/ Bartlomé Esteban 10, tel. 97/860-7532, closed Sun., €30) is the most acclaimed restaurant in town. The Barcelona-trained chef takes local fare and adds sophisticated touches. A delicious case in point is the *entrecot al cava* (steak in sparkling wine).

Information

The **tourist office** (C/ Tomás Nogués 1, tel. 97/860-2279) offers city as well as regional office. The best website is http://turismo.teruel .net, but it is only in Spanish.

Getting There

You begin to understand why the citizens of this region started the Teruel Existe campaign when you learn that Teruel's **Estación de Ferrocarril** only receives trains from Zaragoza, making it the only provincial capital not connected via rail to Madrid. From Zaragoza, **Renfe** (tel. 90/224-0202, www.renfe.es) offers three trains per day.

The **Terminal de Autobuses** (Ronda de Ambeles, s/n) has daily buses to Madrid and Valencia via **Samar** (tel. 97/860-3450); to Zaragoza via **Tezasa** (tel. 97/860-1014); and to Barcelona via **La Rapida** (tel. 97/860-2004).

By car, Teruel is not connected via major highways. It lies on the national road N-234, which goes from Sagunto in Valencia to Burgos in Castilla-La Mancha. From Zaragoza, take the N-330 south, then switch to the N-234. From Valencia city, take the A-7 to the N-234.

🄲 ALBARRACÍN

Located within the Montes Universales mountain range, the tiny village of Albarracín sits 1,171 meters (3,841 feet) above sea level. The first hint it is a place straight out of a fairy tale appears as you approach the town. Rising in a pink sandstone swath along a hill above the town are the ancient Moorish walls—an imposing sight that once stopped medieval armies in their tracks and that today cause modern hearts to leap. The town itself is much smaller than the massive walls portend, but more atmospheric than even the Brothers Grimm could have conjured. Clinging to the top of a ridge, surrounded on three sides by the Río Guadalaviar, Albarracín is a frozen moment of medieval time. You could spend hours wander-

© CANDY-LEE LABALLE

The tiny medieval village of Albarracín is one of the most charming in Spain.

ing its narrow streets. Half-timbered houses with iron-framed doors heave over cobbled lanes. Ancient aristocratic mansions crumble romantically. Their massive crests attesting to the immense wealth once present here—from 1170 to 1285, Albarracín was an independent Christian kingdom, rich from livestock and trade. Prior to that, in the 11th century, this tiny outpost was an independent *taifa* (Moorish state) called Ibn Razín (from which the current name is derived). The walls and remains of the **Castillo de El Andador** (castle) date from this period. The southernmost tower, the **Torre de Doña Blanca,** was built in the 13th century and still stands guard over the city. Legend has it that on full moons, a ghostly woman dressed in white emerges from the tower to bath in the river below. Some say she was an Aragonese princess imprisoned by the queen; others believe she was a Christian in love with a Jewish man and when the Jews were expelled from Spain she retreated to the tower in despair.

Other sights of interest within the town include the 16th-century cathedral and the rambling 11th-century Plaza Mayor surrounded by impressive stone buildings. A few kilometers outside of town, tucked into a natural park, are several well-preserved *pinturas rupestres* (prehistoric paintings) dating to 6000 B.C. Check with the **Centro de Estudios Rupestres** (C/ Catedral 5, tel. 97/871-0251) for maps and access information. The **tourist office** (C/ Diputación 4, tel. 97/871-0251) can also offer information as well as details on dining and sleeping in and around town.

Accommodations

(Posada del Adarve (C/ Portal de Molina 23, tel. 97/870-0304, www.posada-adarve .com, €57), located in a historic building erected right in the old city walls in 1731, is the most precious of Albarracín's handful of lodgings. With only five rooms to attend to, the staff is very accommodating. **Hostal Los Palacios** (C/ Los Palacios 24, tel. 97/870-0327, www.montepalacios.com, €40) offers 14 rustic rooms (stone walls, beamed ceilings) very close to the Plaza Mayor. Many of the rooms boast spectacular views over the mountain. **La Casona del Ajímez** (C/ San Juan 2, tel. 97/871-0321, www.casonadelajimez.com, €75) sits above town, tucked beneath the ruins of the 10th-century castle in a 200-year-old home that once housed local priests. The six rooms evoke that spirituality with rooms reflecting Christian, Jewish, and Muslim cultures. The views are spectacular. **Hotel Albarracín** (C/ Azagra, s/n, tel. 97/871-0011, www.gargallo-hotels.com, €120) is the best-rated accommodation in town. Owned by a prestigious Catalan chain, this small hotel is located in a Renaissance stone palace and comes with all the amenities including a swimming pool.

Food

For tapas, head to **Aben Razín** (Pl. Mayor, s/n), a stone-walled tavern that looks like it has been serving drinks since the Middle Ages. It offers good tapas and coffees by day, beer and cocktails by night. **La Covacha** (C/ Chorro 31, tel. 97/871-0030, 11 A.M.–10 P.M. Mon.–Sat., closed Sun.) is known for its excellent *embutidos* (cured meats) and wines. It also houses a small shop specializing in regional crafts and artisan food products.

In addition to the hotels, which each house their own rustic restaurants, try **Mesón del Gallo** (C/ Los Puentes 1, tel. 97/871-0386, 2–4 P.M. and 8:30–10:30 P.M. daily, €10), which offers classic dishes beneath a rough-hewn beam ceiling. Specialties include *salmon al hojaldre* (salmon in puff pastry) and *chuletas de cordero* (lamb chops). **El Bodegón** (C/ Azagra 2, tel. 97/870-0355, 1:30–4 P.M. and 8:30–11 P.M. Tues.–Sat., 1:30–4 P.M. Sun., closed Mon., €18) offers Aragonese fare such as *migas con uvas* (sweet and savory bread stuff with sausage and grapes). **El Rincón del Chorro** (C/ Chorro 15, tel. 97/871-0112, 2–4 P.M. and 9 P.M.–midnight daily June–Oct., 2–4 P.M. and 9–midnight Fri. and Sat. Nov.–May, €30) is Albarracín's most acclaimed restaurant. In a dining room that is more sophisticated than rustic, the classic fare includes *solomillo* (filet with an anchovy sauce) and excellent *asados* (roasted meats).

Getting There

There is one bus per day to Albarracín. It leaves Teruel's **Terminal de Autobuses** (tel. 97/860-2680) at 3:30 P.M. and returns the following morning at 8:55 A.M. The bus runs Monday through Saturday only, not on Sundays nor holidays.

By car, Albarracín is located off of the N-234, which runs from Sagunto in Valencia to Burgos in Castilla-La Mancha. From Teruel follow the winding A-1512 east. It should take under an hour. If driving in winter, exercise extreme caution on the winding, hilly roads.

Northern Aragón

The northern part of Aragón encompasses the province of Huesca. From Zaragoza, there is a slow rise up from the Río Ebro to the buzzing capital of the region, Huesca city, just north of which sits the Parque Natural de la Sierra y Cañones de Guara, a natural park of spectacular canyons carved by a series of rushing rivers. To the east spreads the mottled fields of Somontano, one of Spain's most exciting wine-producing areas. Continuing north, the land swoops and soars upward, rapidly becoming the hallowed peaks of the Pyrenees.

HUESCA

The city of Huesca is a not very attractive town surrounded by extremely attractive scenery. As the provincial capital of the region, however, it is well connected to transport and offers just about anything a traveler could need. It is also a great base for exploring the gorgeous park, Sierra y Cañones de Guara, which rises just kilometers outside of the city.

The city was first founded by Iberian tribes as Bolskan. When the Romans moved in, they renamed it Osca and founded a

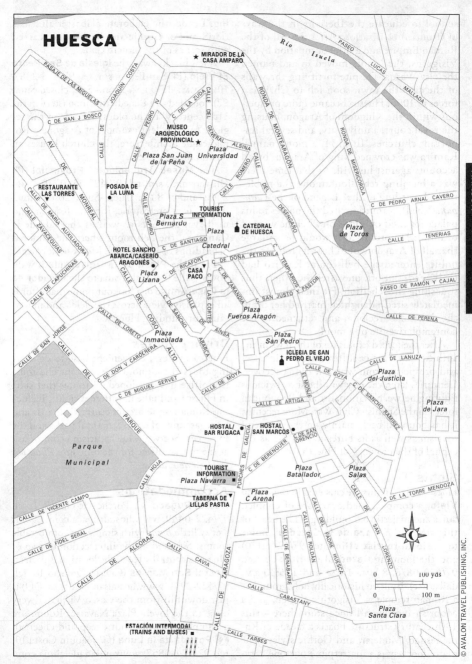

HUESCA

Río Isuela

PASEO DE LUCAS

MALLADA

RONDA DE MONTEARAGÓN

PASAJE DE LAS MIGUELAS

JOAQUÍN COSTA

CALLE DE PEDRO IV

C DE SAN J BOSCO

CALLE DE LA ZUDA

CALLE DEL GENERAL ALSINA

★ MIRADOR DE LA CASA AMPARO

AV DE MONREAL

MUSEO ARQUEOLÓGICO PROVINCIAL ★

Plaza San Juan de la Peña

Plaza Universidad

CALLE DEL ROMERO

RONDA DE MISERICORDIA

▼ RESTAURANTE LAS TORRES

CALLE DE MARÍA AUXILIADORA

● POSADA DE LA LUNA

CALLE SUSPIRO

Plaza S Bernardo

TOURIST INFORMATION ■

Plaza Catedral

✝ CATEDRAL DE HUESCA

C DE PEDRO ARNAL CAVERO

Plaza de Toros

CALLE TENERIAS

CALLE ZAYACEQUIAS

CALLE DE CAPUCHINAS

C DE SANTIAGO

C DE RICAFORT

CASA PACO ▼

C DE DOÑA PETRONILA

C DE ZARANDIA

C DEL

CALLE DE TEMPLARIOS

HOTEL SANCHO ABARCA/CASERÍO ARAGONÉS ●

Plaza Lizana

CALLE DE SANCHO

CALLE DE LAS CORTES

C SAN JUSTO Y PASTOR

PASEO DE RAMÓN Y CAJAL

CALLE DEL COSO ALTO

CALLE DE LORETO

CALLE DE SAN JORGE

CALLE DEL

Plaza Fueros Aragón

CALLE DE PERENA

Plaza Inmaculada

CALLE DE AINSA

CALLE DE ABARCA

Plaza San Pedro

C DE DON V CARDERERA

✝ IGLESIA DE SAN PEDRO EL VIEJO

CALLE DE GOYA

EL MONTE

CALLE DE LANUZA

Plaza del Justicia

C DE MIGUEL SERVET

CALLE DE MOYA

C DE SANCHO RAMÍREZ

Plaza de Jara

Parque Municipal

CALLE DE ARTIGA

CALLE HOJA

PARQUE

HOSTAL/ BAR RUGACA ■

HOSTAL SAN MARCOS ■

CALLE DE BERENGUER

PORCHES DE GALICIA

● C DE SAN ORENCIO

Plaza Batallador

Plaza Salas

C DE LA TORRE MENDOZA

TOURIST INFORMATION ■

Plaza Navarra

Plaza C Arenal

CALLE DEL PADRE HUESCA

CALLE DE

CALLE DEL ROLDÁN

CALLE DE VICENTE CAMPO

TABERNA DE ▼ LILLAS PASTIA

CALLE DE BENABARRE

CALLE DE SAN LORENZO

CALLE DE FIDEL SERAL

CALLE DE ALCORAZ

CALLE

CAVIA

CALLE DE ZARAGOZA

CALLE CABASTANY

0   100 yds

0   100 m

Plaza Santa Clara

ESTACIÓN INTERMODAL (TRAINS AND BUSES) ■

CALLE TARBES

ARAGÓN

school to educate the Iberians in the ways of (Roman) civilization. After the fall of the Roman Empire and a brief occupation by the Visigoths, the Moors moved in and named the city Wasqa. Despite fortifying the walls of the city, the town soon fell to Christian forces in 1096. Huesca became quite prosperous within the Kingdom of Aragón, housing the royal court, a university, and several important churches. In 1134, a monk named Ramiro was crowned king of Aragón, by all accounts against his will. At that time there was a burbling rebellion among the noblemen. According to the "Legend of the *Campana*" (bell), Ramiro invited the nobles to his palace for their opinions on a bell he wanted to build. He promised it would be so large that all of Aragón would hear its toll. As the nobles entered the bell room, Ramiro had their heads cut off, one after the other, thus squashing the rebellion. He then almost immediately sired a daughter, married her off to the duke of Barcelona, and returned to the contemplative life of a monk.

After the forced expulsion of the Jews in the 14th century, Huesca suffered a loss of intellect and prosperity from which it didn't recover. Centuries later, the city was the site of vicious fighting between Nationalist and Republican forces in the Spanish Civil War. More recently, it has bounced back mainly on the thrust of tourism as well as its bureaucratic role as the capital of the province of Huesca.

Sights

Huesca's main sights are clustered in the **Casco Viejo,** a compact medieval core of cobbled lanes and majestic old buildings. The heart of this area is the **Plaza de la Catedral,** home to the **local tourist office** (tel. 97/429-2170) and the looming **Catedral de Huesca** (tel. 97/422-0676, 8 A.M.–1 P.M. and 4–6:30 P.M. daily, free). Built on historically holy ground—a Roman temple, a Visigothic church, and a Moorish mosque all once stood here—this 13th-century structure boasts a facade of Romanesque, Mudejar, and Gothic styles. The main doorway is a masterpiece of stone carv-

ing. Inside, the elaborate alabaster altar is a florid mix of Gothic and Renaissance carved with scenes of the Crucifixion.

A few blocks away, the **Iglesia de San Pedro El Viejo** (Pl. San Pedro, s/n, tel. 97/422-2387, 10:30 A.M.–1:30 P.M. Mon.–Sat., closed Sun., €2), founded as a Benedictine monastery in the 11th century, is the oldest church in the region. An excellent example of Aragonese Romanesque architecture, the church houses an outstanding cloister.

The **Museo Arqueológico Provincial** (Pl. Universidad, s/n, tel. 97/422-1540, 10 A.M.– 2 P.M. and 5–8 P.M. Tues.–Sun., closed Mon., free) houses prehistoric, Iberian, Roman, and medieval artifacts as well as the Sala de la Campana, the bell room where the rumored beheadings of Ramiro the Monk took place.

From the **Plaza de la Universidad,** walk down Calle General Alsina to the **Mirador de la Casa Amparo,** a lookout point that affords an expansive view across the fields and mountains surrounding Huesca.

Driving Routes

Huesca makes a convenient base to do driving tours throughout the region. The tourism office has developed 13 routes that start in Huesca and take in different sights, including Romanesque architecture, vineyards and bodegas, and, of course, natural parks and the Pyrenees. See www.huecaturismo.com or ask at the tourist office for the brochure *Rutas por la Hoya de Huesca.*

Accommodations

Hostal Rugaca (C/ Porches de Galicia 1, tel. 97/422-6449, www.hostalrugaca.com, €50) is a cozy little *hostal* with simple yet comfortable rooms. Situated at the intersection of two of Huesca's central streets, the location is perfect. **Hostal San Marcos** (C/ San Orencio 10, tel. 97/422-2931, www.hostalsanmarcos.es, €49) is just downhill from the Casco Viejo and very close to the lovely Plaza Navarra. Rooms are as simple as can be, but cheap and cheerful. **◖ Posada de la Luna** (C/ Joaquín Costa 10, tel. 97/424-0857, www.posadadelaluna.com,

€120), opened in 2004, has finally brought some style to Huesca's very staid lodging scene. Built right into the medieval walls of the city, La Luna combines modern furniture, bright colors, and rustic touches with details like whirlpool baths, heated towel racks, and Wi-Fi. It is fast becoming the hotel of choice for discriminating visitors. Book ahead. **Hotel Sancho Abarca** (Pl. Lizana 13, tel. 97/422-0650, www.hotelsanchoabarca.com, €110) offers more classic style in a palatial stone building on one of Huesca's nicest plazas.

Food

In the Casco Viejo, find bar after tasty tapas bar on Calles Padre Huesca, San Orencio, and Berenguer. **Bar Rugaca** (C/ Porches de Galicia 1, tel. 97/422-003, 9 A.M.–midnight daily), located on the ground floor of the *hostal* of the same name, is famed for their delicious seafood tapas—especially *langostinos con guindilla* (shrimp sautéed with spicy red peppers). **Caserío Aragonés** (Pl. Lizana 13, tel. 97/422-0650, 1–3:30 P.M. and 8:30–10:30 P.M. daily, €25), located on the ground floor of the Hotel Sancho Abarca, has been serving exquisite local fare since 1943. Try the **migas** (savory breadcrumbs) or *ternasco* (succulent Aragonese lamb).

Lately, Huesca has become an unlikely spot for gourmet dining. The very elegant ◖ **Taberna de Lillas Pastia** (Pl. Navarra 4, tel. 97/421-1691, 1:30–3:30 P.M. and 8:30–10:30 P.M. Tues.–Sat., closed Sun. and Mon., €46), located in the modernist Casino building, is known for its innovative cuisne that incorporates local ingredients. Consider *bacalao con miel* (cod encrusted in honey), *arroz de olivas negras* (rice with black olives and basil), or *pollo Manchego* (chicken with apples and Manchego cheese). **Las Torres** (C/ María Auxiliadora 3, tel. 97/422-8213, 1–3 P.M. and 8:30–10:30 P.M. Mon.–Sat., closed Sun., €42) has some of the most sought-after tables in Aragón. The cuisine is delightfully innovative and changes seasonally. Make reservations and go with the chef's *surgencia* (suggestion).

Getting There

Huesca lies on the AVE high-speed railway from Madrid with two trains leaving the capital city daily (4 P.M. and 9 P.M., €47.90) and arriving in Huesca in just over two hours. The train makes a stop in Zaragoza. By bus, **Alosa** (tel. 90/221-0700, www.alosa.es) runs from/to Zaragoza, Pamplona, Barcelona, and Lérida, as well as to cities in Huesca province, including Jaca and Barbastro. Both trains and buses arrive at the modern **Estación Intermodal** (C/ José Gil Cavez, s/n), about 10 minutes walking uphill to Plaza Navarra.

By car, Huesca lies on the N-330 that goes south to Zaragoza and north to France. It is also on the N-240, which leads to Lérida where you can catch the A-2 to Barcelona. The A-132 goes to Pamplona.

LOARRE

An easy day-trip from Huesca (or a detour on your way North to the Pyrenees) is the tiny village of Loarre (pop. 44), home to **Castillo de Loarre** (www.castillodeloarre.org, 10 A.M.–2 P.M. and 4–8 P.M. daily June 16–Sept. 15, 11 A.M.–1:30 P.M. and 3–5:30 P.M. daily Nov. 1–Feb. 28, 10 A.M.–2 P.M. and 4–7 P.M. daily Mar. 1–June 15 and Sept. 16–Oct. 31, €2). Built in the 11th and 12th centuries, this massive fortress is so cleverly tucked into a rock outcropping that despite its size, it is almost easy to miss. It is a joy to explore with its exquisitely preserved towers, dungeon, and even a medieval bathroom. Parts of the 2005 Ridley Scott film *Kingdom of Heaven* starring Orlando Bloom were filmed here.

Loarre lies 35 kilometers (22 miles) west of Huesca. Take A-132 west and then catch A-1206 into Loarre.

PARQUE NATURAL DE LA SIERRA Y CAÑONES DE GUARA

Lying between the city of Huesca and Barbastro is the Parque Natural de la Sierra y Cañones de Guara, a 474-square-kilometer (183-square-mile) park that is comprised of a dramatic landscape of canyons and cold rushing rivers—a very popular day escape from Huesca city. The **Huesca tourism office** (Pl. Catedral 1, tel. 97/429-2170) and the **Barbastro tourism office** (Av. La Merced, 64, tel. 97/430-8350) can provide maps and access information plus a list of activities outfitters, unfortunately most will speak only Spanish. In Barbastro, **Guara Tours** (C/ San Ramón 19, tel. 97/430-8318, www.guaratours.com) arranges multi-adventure tours from white-water rafting to climbing. They also offer vineyard and wine-tasting tours in Somontano.

The park is particularly popular for canyoning. The most popular canyon in the park is **Cañon del Vero.** To visit it, you'll have to head for the tiny village of **Alquézar** (tourist office, tel. 97/431-8940, www.alquezar.org). Find more information in English at www.cai aragon.com (click on "What to Do" and follow the links to "Canyoning") and www.guara.org (click "Routes," then "Canyoning").

◖ BARBASTRO

Barbastro is the main city of the Somontano wine-making region. It is also a key city in Spanish history. The Crown of Aragón was ordained here when Petronila, Queen of Aragón was married to Ramon Berenguer, Count of Barcelona, thus uniting Cataluña and Aragón. Barbastro also has religious pedigree as the birthplace of Josemaría Escrivá de Balaguer, the Catholic priest who founded the powerful and secretive lay movement, Opus Dei. Escrivá was canonized as a saint in 2002.

Barbastro's **Casco Viejo** (old quarter) is dominated by the 16th-century **Catedral de Santa María,** which possesses a lovely alabaster altar beneath a lofty nave held up by gorgeous pillars. The **Plaza Mayor** with its majestic 16th-century **Ayuntamiento** (town hall) is also worthy of a visit. However, the best reason to visit Barbastro is to plan a tour of the surrounding wineries. It is also a good access point into the Cañones de Guara park.

Bodegas and Wine Tourism

Though there are four wine-growing regions in Aragón that have the distinction of a *denomi-*

nación de origen (appellation), better known as a D.O., it is **Somontano** that has wine lovers worldwide giddy. Using popular grapes such as cabernet sauvignon, merlot, chardonnay, gerwurtztraminer, and the Spanish stand-by, tempranillo, Somontano wineries are producing hearty, flavorful reds and fruity, rich whites. Wine tourism has been very slow in coming to Spain. La Rioja's Alavesa region has led the way (see *Rioja Alavesa* in the *País Vasco, La Rioja, and Navarra* chapter), with the rest of La Rioja and Ribera del Duero in Burgos starting to catch up. Somontano's top wineries have not hesitated to jump on the wine-wagon and three of the top producers—Enate, Viñas del Vero, and Bodegas Pirineos—have rolled out the barrel and welcome visitors with open bottles. The first step in planning a tour should be a visit to www.somontano.org. In Barbastro, stop in the **Complejo de San Julián y Santa Lucía** (Av. La Merced 64, tel. 97/430-6006), which houses the Somontano regulation and tourism agencies as well as the local tourist offices and a

the wine cellar at Enate, one of Somontano's best bodegas

wine museum. Note that this tour can be done only by car. And remember, despite the publicized opening hours, reservations are required. You can make them via phone, Internet, or in the San Julián complex.

Alternatively, if money is no object and you want a truly luxurious approach to this region, contact **Cellar Tours** (www.cellartours.org). Run by an American expat from California, it is one of the best fully licensed wine-tour operators in Spain.

Bodega Pirineos (Crta. Barbastro-Naval, km. 3.5, tel. 97/431-1289, bpvisitas@bodega pirineos.com, www.bodegapirineos.com), located on the outskirts of Barbastro, offers visits 10 A.M.–2 P.M. and 4–7 P.M. Monday–Friday, and on Saturdays by special arrangement only. The bodega is closed on Sundays. The €3 entrance includes a guided tour and tasting.

One of Somontano's most prestigious bodegas, **Viñas del Vero** (Crta. Barbastro-Naval, km. 3.7, tel. 97/430-2216, marketing@vinas delvero.es, www.vinasdelvero.es) is located in the Finca de San Marcos and offers tours 10 A.M.–2 P.M. and 4–7 P.M. Monday–Friday and 10 A.M.–2 P.M. on Saturday. Saturday evening and Sunday appointments are only by special arrangement.

Enate (Crta. Barbastro-Naval, km. 9, tel. 97/430-2580, bodega@enate.es, www.enate.es) is located in the village of Salas Bajas and offers tours at 10:30 A.M., 11:30 A.M., and 5 P.M. Monday–Thursday; 10:30 A.M. and 11:30 A.M. on Friday; and 10 A.M. and 12 P.M. on Saturday. It is closed Sunday.

Accommodations and Food

Gran Hotel Ciudad de Barbastro (Pl. Mercado 4, tel. 97/430-8900, www.ghbarbastro .com, €80) is the city's best hotel, offering classic yet sleek rooms and excellent service. Upgrading to a €130 suite gets you a whirlpool bath and a balcony overlooking the mountains. **Hostal Clemente** (C/ Corona de Aragón 5, tel. 97/431-0186, €65) offers clean, simple rooms and one of the city's most beloved restaurants, **Pablo's,** which offers traditional Aragonese fare. Gourmands should head to **Flor** (C/ Goya

3, tel. 97/431-1056, closed Sun. P.M., €35), Barbastro's top-rated dining room for modern cuisine based on Aragonese tradition.

In the wine region, consider the lovely *casa rural* **[El Puntillo** (C/ Iglesia 4, tel. 97/431-8168, www.elpuntillo.com, €65–75), which offers cozy, country-style rooms lovingly attended to by owners Oscar and Mireya. The pair also has a wonderful little restaurant serving Aragonese fare with distinctive modern touches. Of course, the wine list offers nothing but the best Somontano wines. For additional accommodations throughout the wine region, www.somontano .org offers an exhaustive list of options.

Getting There

There is limited bus service from Huesca via **Alosa** (tel. 90/221-0700, www.alosa.es), but you will need a car to explore the wine regions. From Huesca, take N-240 to Barbastro. From Barcelona, take A-2 to Lérida, then the N-240 into Barbastro.

[AÍNSA

The tiny village of Aínsa has been declared a national Spanish treasure for good reason—it is quite simply one of the loveliest villages in the Pyrenees and one of the best-preserved medieval villages in Europe. Once the capital of the ancient kingdom of Sobrarbe, Aínsa has perfectly preserved medieval walls encircling a spider's web of cobbled lanes and tidy stone houses. At the top of the town, the broad, arcaded **Plaza Mayor** dates to the 12th century. It is home to the equally ancient **Colegiata de Santa María,** a brooding Romanesque church that hides a surprisingly lovely cloister. On the northeastern side of town lies the rambling remains of the **Castillo** (fortified castle). The pentagonal tower dates back to the 11th century but the rest of the structure was built in the 16th as a defense against the invasion-prone French.

Sports and Recreation

Sitting at the confluence of the Río Ara and Río Cinca, Aínsa also boasts some of the region's best white-water rafting. The new town, which sprawls beneath the medieval center,

ARAGÓN

is home to several outfitters including the friendly **Aguablancas** (Av. Sobrarbe 11, tel. 97/451-0008, www.aguasblancas.com). The **tourist office** (Av. Pirenaica 1, tel. 97/450-0767) has a complete listing as well as routes for self-guided activities.

Accommodations

Casa El Hospital (C/ Santa Cruz 3, tel. 97/450-0750, www.caselhospital.com, €45) is located in a stone house right in the Casco Viejo, adjacent to an ancient pilgrims' hospital. Rooms are very simple, but atmospheric. **Posada Real** (Pl. Mayor 6, tel. 97/450-0977, www.posadareal.com, €85) has six rustic rooms in a refurbished inn replete with exposed woodwork, stone-flooring, and country antiques. Each room looks out onto the magnificent Plaza Mayor. **Los Arcos** (Pl. Mayor 23, tel. 97/450-0016, www.hotellosarcosainsa.com, €100) is also located right in the plaza but offers more style as well as nice touches like hydro-massage showers and Internet. Two rooms look out over the Plaza Mayor, while the rest have views onto the Pyrenees.

Food

L'Alfil (C/ Travesera, s/n, tel. 97/450-0299, 1–11 P.M. Mon.–Sat., closed Sun.) offers tapas and sandwiches accompanied by house-made red vermouth and excellent Somontano wines. **❰ Bodegas de Sobrarbe** (Pl. Mayor 2, tel. 97/450-0237, 12:30–4 P.M. and 8:30–11 P.M. daily, closed Jan. and Feb., €25) is located inside an 11th-century stone wine cellar and is famed for its succulent **codero asado** (roasted lamb) and *lomo de jabalí* (wild boar with apple puree). **Bodegón del Mallacán** (Pl. Mayor 6, tel. 97/450-0977, 12:30–3:30 P.M. and 8:30–11 P.M. daily, closed Jan., €25), located on the ground floor of the Posada Real, is gourmet gone earthy, with wild mushroom salads topped with slivers of foie gras, roasted game, and ice cream made from wild strawberries. Tables are set beneath the ancient porticos of the Plaza Mayor in warmer months.

Getting There

By car, the easiest route into Aínsa is via Barbastro, which lies on the N-240 that runs from Tarragona to San Sebastián. From Barbastro, take the N-123 towards Benabarre, and switch to the N-138 towards Aínsa and France. By bus, from Barbastro **Autocares Cortes** (tel. 97/647-0614) offers limited service. **Alosa** (tel. 90/221-0700, www.alosa.es) offer one daily route from Zaragoza.

Aragonese Pyrenees

Aragón is home to the steepest, wildest section of the Pyrenees. The range's highest peaks—Aneto (3,404 meters/11,168 feet), Posets (3,375 meters/11,072 feet), and Monte Perdido (3,355 meters/11,007 feet)—lie between the Aragonese towns of Jaca in the west and Benasque in the east. At the center of this section is the Parque Nacional de Ordesa y Monte Perdido, 155 square kilometers (60 square miles) of protected land that includes some of the Pyrenees' most beautiful peaks and valleys.

Hiking ranges from easy to extremely challenging. If you plan on bagging the highest mountains, you should be experienced and do your homework. Books to get you started include *Walks and Climbs in the Pyrenees* by Kev Reynolds or *Through the Spanish Pyrenees: GR11* by Paul Lucia. A general book on Spanish geography with basic information on the Pyrenees is *Wild Spain* by Frederic V. Grunfeld.

An Internet search will bring up many more resources, though unfortunately most of the official websites are in Spanish only. **Puente Spain** (www.puentespain.com) can offer generalized info on hiking in Spain. (See sidebar, *Walking in Spain,* in the *Essentials* chapter.) You should be able to purchase all your maps and guides in the United States; however, if you are flying into Madrid, the specialized book and map store **Desnivel** (Pl. Matute 6,

Metro: Sol, tel. 90/224-8848) is dedicated to all things adventure, particularly mountaineering. For detailed maps, look for the publisher Editorial Alpina (www.editorial alpina.com).

JACA

The largest town in the Aragonese Pyrenees, Jaca is the most popular base for walkers, hikers, and skiers. A major Christian stronghold during the Reconquista, Jaca was briefly the capital of Aragón in the 8th century. Today, it has a few worthwhile sights, including the Romanesque **Catedral de San Pedro** (Pl. San Pedro, s/n), built in the 11th century. Above the city is the imposing **Ciudadela**, a five-sided citadel built in the 16th century. The city also boasts typical medieval architecture, a lively restaurant and bar scene, and several shops and outfitters that make their living off providing tourists with information, excursions, and equipment for Pyrenees adventures. The **tourist office** (C/ Regimiento de Galicia 2, tel. 97/436-0098) is the logical place to start. It also sells guidebooks and maps. Next door, **Mountain Travel** (tel. 97/449-5615, www .mountaintravel.net) arranges all types of outdoor activities from rafting to hiking. They also run mountaineering classes.

Skiing

Just north of Jaca are two excellent ski stations. **Candanchú** (www.candanchu.com) has 60 kilometers (37 miles) of pistes with runs from beginners to expert. Of the 12 black expert runs, several are known for their steep drops. Nearby, **Astún** (www.astun.com) has 40 kilometers (25 miles) of pistes; the majority are intermediate, though there are also a few green beginner runs as well as black expert runs. Both ski stations offer restaurants, schools, and children's activities. Skiers can purchase joint passes good at both stations. To reach the stations from Jaca, take N-330 north.

Accommodations

Hostal Paris (Pl. San Pedro 5, www.jaca.com/ hostalparis, €35) offers the cheapest (nice) accommodation in town. Located right in front of the cathedral, this historic property offers warm, woody rooms and shared baths. **Hotel Jaqués** (C/ Unión Jaquesa 4, tel. 97/435-6424, www.hoteljaques.com, €70), opened in 2003, offers simple yet stylish rooms. There is also a good restaurant and a lively tapas bar. **Gran Hotel** (Po. Constitución 1, tel. 97/436-0900, www.inturmark.es, closed Nov., €90) offers a clubby, ski-lodge feel and spacious functional rooms—plus a swimming pool and garden for the summer months. **Hotel Conde Aznar** (Po. Constitución 3, tel. 97/436-1050, www.condeaznar.com, €90) is the most stylish hotel in town. The individually decorated rooms are sophisticated retreats of antiques and luxury details like whirlpool baths and pillow menus. The hotel's restaurant, **La Cocina Aragonesa,** is the highest-rated (and most expensive) in Jaca.

Food

In addition to the hotel restaurants, try **Casa Fau** (Pl. Catedral, s/n, tel. 97/436-1719, 1–10 P.M. Tues.–Sat., closed Mon., €15). Since 1957, this cozy bar/restaurant in the Romanesque shadows of the cathedral has been serving tapas and Aragonian mountain fare to ravenous, rambunctious crowds. **La Tasca de Ana** (Pl. Ramiro I 3, tel. 97/436-4726, €20) is another local favorite. In a rustic setting with wine barrel tables and exposed beam ceilings, Ana and crew serve a wealth of traditional Spanish tapas plus excellent cured Aragonese *jamón* and artisan cheeses. **El Rincón de la Catedral** (Pl. Catedral 4, tel. 97/435-5920) offers something different with French-inspired savory tortes, pastries, and salads.

Getting There

By bus, **Alosa** (tel. 90/221-0700, www.alosa.es) has daily runs from Zaragoza, passing through Huesca. By car, access Jaca by following the N-330 north from Huesca or Zaragoza.

SAN JUAN DE LA PEÑA

If you are driving into Jaca, consider a detour to the spectacular **Monasterio de San Juan**

ARAGÓN

de la Peña (tel. 97/435-5119, www.monasterio sanjuan.com, €4.50). In 724, the nobles of the Kingdom of Sobrarbe gathered here to declare holy war on the Moorish invaders. Since that moment, this monastery has been considered the seat of the Aragonese Reconquest. Built into a cliffside, the monastery is so cleverly concealed that the Moors did not ever stumble across it. Legend has it that the Holy Grail was safely hidden here for centuries.

Composed of two layers, the monastery features a 10th-century Mozarabic chapel underground, and above that a 12th-century cloister built beneath a massive rock overhang. The columns and capitals of the cloister are some of the most delightful examples of Romanesque religious sculpture in the region. Within are the tombs of several Aragonese kings.

Hours vary wildly month to month but in general, the monastery is open 10 A.M.–2 P.M. and 4–7 P.M. daily. In winter, the hours are greatly reduced and it is closed on Mondays.

Getting There

The monastery is located 24 kilometers (15 miles) west of Jaca. Take the N-240 in the direction of Pamplona, then switch to the A-1603 into town. Follow the signs for the *viejo* (old) monastery; the *nuevo* (new) monastery is modern and bland. In summer, you have to park next to the new monastery and take a shuttle bus the 13 kilometers (eight miles) to *el viejo*.

◖ PARQUE NACIONAL DE ORDESA Y MONTE PERDIDO

The Parque Nacional de Ordesa y Monte Perdido, tucked on the Spanish side of the Pyrenees in Northern Aragón, is one of the most beautiful of Spain's national parks. The park is known for its contrasts—cold and dry among the snow-mottled peaks and verdant and wet in the valleys in meadows. In late spring, hundreds of waterfalls burble to life as the mountain snow melts and the green valleys explode in color with fields of wildflowers. It is home to some of the mountain range's tallest peaks including the Tres Sorores (Three Sisters), a trio

of mountains that top 3,048 meters (10,000 feet) and create the lush valleys the park is known for—Ordesa, Pineta, Añisclo, and Escuaín. These deep valleys have prompted many to nickname the park "Spain's Grand Canyon." The highest of the three peaks is Monte Perdido at 3,355 meters (11,007 feet).

The Ordesa park is crisscrossed by mountain trails called *gran recorrido* (long trails), or GR, and *pequeño recorrido* (short trails), or PR. The GR11 is a 414-kilometer (257-mile) path that crosses the Spanish portion of the Pyrenees from Cataluña to the Cantabrian Sea. It passes right through the Ordesa park. Within the park there are dozens of trails that go from beginner to seasoned alpinist. They are well marked and maintained. One of the most popular is the **Circo de Soaso,** a 5-hour hike that is excellent for inexperienced hikers and those wanting a somewhat easy walk (though there are a few challenging stretches). It takes in beautiful waterfalls and stunning vistas along the way.

The park is open May–mid-November, however snow can still be a problem in May, October, and November. August is peak Spanish tourism season and the park reaches maximum capacity during this time. For these reasons, June, early July, and early September are your best bets for good weather and fewer people.

Information and Services

The park is accessed via the town of **Torla,** located about mid-way between Jaca and Aínsa. Stock up on supplies here, as there are limited goods in the park itself. You can also pick up maps and information. The **Torla Oficina de Turismo** (C/ Fatas 7, tel. 97/448-6378 or 97/450-2043) is only open July–September. The **Centro de Visitantes** (tel. 97/448-6421, 10 A.M.–1 P.M. and 4:30–8 P.M. daily, July–Oct.) is located on the road between Torla and the Pradera de Ordesa (the entrance and car park). At both spots, you can get loads of information and buy maps and guides.

Look for the English-language book *Ordesa and Monte Perdido* by Editorial Alpina (www .editorialalpina.com). The best website about

ARAGÓN

© SUNNY SEVILLA

The Aragonese Pyrenees are at their loveliest in the Parque Nacional de Ordesa y Monte Perdido.

the park is www.ordesa.com, but it is in Spanish only. Some English information can be found at http://reddeparquesnacionales.mma.es, the official website for Spain's national parks.

Accommodations and Food

As a protected Spanish parkland and a UNESCO biosphere reserve, access to the park is limited to 1,500 people per day. Camping with or without a tent is restricted to spots above 1,795 meters (6,890 feet) and only on the condition that the campsite is dismantled and abandoned at sunrise. The park houses many *refugios* (mountain *hostales*) that offer very simple beds, cooking facilities, baths, and cold showers for less than €5 per person. They fill up fast, so get on the trail early. In peak season, if the *refugio* is full, you'll be allowed to camp next to it. A limited list of *refugios* is available on www.ordesa.com, and the Centro de Visitantes can provide more information.

On the road to the Pradera de Ordesa, **Hotel Edelweiss** (Av. Ordesa, s/n, tel. 97/448-6173,

€55) is a charming mountain hotel with simple rooms offering spectacular views. In town, **Albergue Lucien Briet** (Av. Francia, s/n, tel. 97/448-6221, €12 per bunk) is a youth hostel with a vast room that sleeps up to 30. **Hotel Villa de Torla** (Pl. Aragón, 1, tel. 97/448-6156, www.hotelvilladetorla.com, €67) is one of Torla's favorite mountain hotels with charming rooms, rustic details, and a very friendly staff. Sharing a bath knocks the price down €10; going outside the month of August, drops it another €10.

There are restaurants and tapas bars throughout Torla, however their hours are seasonal. From Easter until the end of September, most restaurants are open every day from 1 P.M.–10 P.M. The rest of the year, hours are limited. **El Rebeco** (C/ Fatas, s/n, tel. 97/448-6068, €15), located in a cozy stone house, boasts a large open fireplace and a kitchen famous for its hearty mountain fare such as grilled meats and stews. **Bar La Brecha** (Av. Francia, s/n, tel. 97/448-6221), next door to the Lucien Briet youth hostel, is much more laid-back with tapas and beers served in equal proportions to a rowdy crowd of locals and tourists.

Getting There and Around

By bus to Torla, **Alosa** (tel. 90/221-0700, www.alosa.es) provides daily service from Huesca and Jaca. From Aínsa and many of the tiny mountain towns, **Hudebus** (tel. 97/421-3277) offers daily service.

By car, Torla is located on the winding A-135 that snakes north off of the N-260. From Aínsa, follow the N-260 northwest to the A-135. The trip is about 45 kilometers (28 miles). From Jaca, take the N-330/E-7 east to the N-260 and finally the A-135. The total length of the trip is 56 kilometers (35 miles).

To get to the Pradera de Ordesa from Torla, just follow the 6.4-kilometer (four-mile) road, Avenida Ordesa, to its end. The parking lot costs €0.60 per hour. After 24 hours, there is a 20 percent discount. Road access is limited July–October and you may be obligated to park in Torla and take the shuttle bus. It leaves every 20 minutes from Torla to Ordesa and runs 7 A.M.–7 P.M. to the Pradera de Ordesa with one stop at the Centro de Visitantes (be sure to exit here for maps and info) and returns to Torla up until 9 P.M. The cost is €3.30.

BENASQUE

The tiny mountain village of Benasque boasts a 13th-century Romanesque church, the **Iglesia Parroquial de Santa María,** several romantically tattered stone mansions, and a charming medieval center. However, the real draw of Benasque is its location. It is the perfect jumping-off point for serious mountaineers and hikers wanting to explore the picturesque **Valle de Benasque,** home to some of the Pyrenees most forbidding mountains—including the highest in the range, **Aneto.** At 3,404 meters (11,168 feet) above sea level, the mountain supports Spain's largest glacier at 163 hectares (403 acres)—though it is melting fast and environmentalists predict it will be gone by the late 21st century. **Posets** at 3,375 meters (11,072 feet) is the second-highest mountain in the range and is also located here.

Hiking and Climbing

Aneto and Posets provide decent challenges for serious, experienced climbers. Do your homework and consult websites such as the detailed www.summitpost.org or www.peakbagger.com for information. Proper equipment, including crampons and ice axes, are required. The best maps are from Editorial Alpina (www.editorialalpina.com).

Before embarking on any activities in the area, pay a visit to the **tourist office** (C/ San Sebastián 5, tel. 97/455-1289). They offer maps, guides, and information of rental equipment and tour operators in town. Several hiking stores in town rent equipment and sell maps. **Viajes Benasque** (Av. Francia, tel. 97/455-2127, www.viajesbenasque.com) is a local outfitter that arranges all sorts of hiking and climbing excursions in the region, as well as skiing and rafting. Another reputable provider is **Sin Fronteras Adventure** (Crta. Benasque, s/n, tel. 97/455-0177, www.sinfronterasadventure.com).

Skiing

Just 6.4 kilometers (four miles) outside of Benasque is the tiny town of Cerler and its world-class ski station, **Aramón Cerler** (www.cerler.com). One of the highest ski stations in the Pyrenees, Cerler boasts 60 kilometers (37 miles) of pistes, including nine beginner, 17 intermediate, and nine expert black runs. There are also restaurants, a children's play area, and a ski school.

Accommodations and Food

If you will be camping in the mountains, there are several campsites and *refugios*; your best bet is to get a complete listing from the tourist office or by visiting www.benasque.com. In town, the **Hotel Solana** (Pl. Mayor 5, tel. 97/455-1019, www.hotelsolanabenas.com, €50) offers cozy rooms with lots of wood detailing in a charming stone house right at the center of town. For €40, you can stay in their first-floor *"hostal"* rooms which are a bit less quaint than the upper "hotel" lodgings. The hotel has a lively plaza-level bar/restaurant. **Hotel San Marsial** (Av. Francia 75, tel. 97/455-1616, www.hotelsanmarsial.com, €100) offers homey rooms full of antiques and quilted blankets—many with wonderful views—on the edge of town. The hotel also rents apartments beginning at €300 per week in the low season, €750 in the high (July and August).

Rabasón (C/ Mayor 27, 11 A.M.–10 P.M. daily) is a typical tapas bar located in a rustic stone building. At night, it becomes the town's liveliest bar. **El Pesebre** (C/ Mayor 45, tel. 97/455-1507, 1–3:30 P.M. and 8–10:30 P.M. daily, €30) offers excellent roasted meats and game as well as delicious homemade desserts.

Getting There

By bus, Benasque is located on the A-139, which intersects with the N-260 to the south. **Alosa** (tel. 90/221-0700, www.alosa.es) runs daily buses from Huesca, Barbastro, Zaragoza, Lérida, and Barcelona into Benasque.

PAÍS VASCO, LA RIOJA, AND NAVARRA

Clustered together in the north of Spain in a luxuriant green corner formed by the Cantabrian Sea and the French border, the autonomous regions of País Vasco, La Rioja, and Navarra share a land that is wildly diverse. País Vasco boasts a gorgeous coast of wild seas, untamed beaches, and dramatic cliffs. Inland, the deep green hills roll across the north of the region and into Navarra, slowly climbing to meet the majestic Pyrenees in the east. Along the way, ancient forests grow in even more ancient valleys. In southern País Vasco, the Ebro River courses through La Rioja and into Navarra, carving out wide undulating valleys. Protected from the Cantabrian winds by a wall of mountains, the area receives warm breezes from the Mediterranean and lots of sun. The result is the world-famous Rioja wine vineyards, which spill over into all three regions. Southern La Rioja and southern Navarra are drier, flatter, and hotter than the rest of the region, sharing more in common with the brown lands of Castile to the south.

Culturally, the region is both Basque and Spanish. According to the Spanish autonomy agreements of 1981, the País Vasco (Basque Country in English, Euskadi in Basque) consists of three provinces, Vizcaya, Guipúzcoa, and Álava. However, Basque heritage deems that the Basque country include northern Navarra and parts of southern France. People of Pamplona and northern Navarra identify as both Navarrese and Basque. Southern Navarra and all of La Rioja are firmly Castilian. (See sidebar, *A Basic Basque Primer.*)

Politics and geography aside, this tiny corner

HIGHLIGHTS

◖ **Parte Vieja:** San Sebastián is a delight for the senses and nowhere is that more evident than in the city's Parte Vieja. Its centuries-old cobbled lanes teem with medieval buildings and award-winning tapas bars (page 377).

◖ **Hondarribia:** Tucked above a colorful fishing port is this charming medieval town, where you can sleep in a 10th-century palace that once hosted the Catholic Kings Isabel and Fernando (page 392).

◖ **Museo Guggenheim:** Pictures hardly do justice to the whimsical grandeur of Frank Gehry's masterpiece, the Museo Guggenheim. Inside and out, it hypnotizes with its soaring spaces and unexpected curves. The museum revitalized the once-grungy town of Bilbao, which now offers the visitor elegant riverside walks, moody medieval quarter, and world-class Basque food (page 400).

◖ **Casco Antiguo:** The capital of La Rioja, Logroño is the perfect place to set off on a winery tour, but not before spending a night grazing on the delicious tapas on offer in Casco Antiguo, especially the famous Calle Laurel (page 416).

◖ **Haro:** Home to over a dozen wineries, the cozy town of Haro merits its nickname of "the wine capital of Rioja." It makes a great base for a wine tour through the bodegas of La Rioja (page 423).

◖ **San Millán de la Cogolla:** In this sleepy little town tucked on the side of a verdant mountain in southern La Rioja, the Suso Monastery, begun in the 6th century, features Visigothic, Arabic, and Romanesque architectural details. Sleep next door at the 11th-century Yuso Monastery (page 426).

◖ **Laguardia:** One of the most enchanting towns in all of Spain, medieval Laguardia boasts intact 13th-century walls, atmospheric plazas, gourmet restaurants, cozy inns, and several underground wineries. It is perfect on its own or as a base for exploring the Basque region of Rioja – Rioja Alavesa (page 429).

◖ **San Fermín:** Immortalized by Ernest Hemingway, mythologized by thousands of hard-partying college students, and venerated by Pamplona's red-kerchief-wearing locals, the raucous frivolity of San Fermín is something that must be experienced once in your lifetime (page 438).

◖ **Olite:** Just south of Pamplona, a fairy-tale castle full of soaring pointy-topped stone towers rises from the brown fields. Once the 15th-century home of the Kings of Navarra, this Gothic wonderland is yours for exploring or, better yet, stay the night in one of its wings (page 442).

◖ **Ochagavía:** A picture postcard come to life, the medieval stone village of Ochagavía is tucked deep within a valley of the Pyrenees. Way off the beaten path, this is the perfect place to check into a *casa rural* (country inn) and check out of 21st-century life for a while (page 444).

LOOK FOR ◖ TO FIND RECOMMENDED SIGHTS, ACTIVITIES, DINING, AND LODGING.

PAÍS VASCO

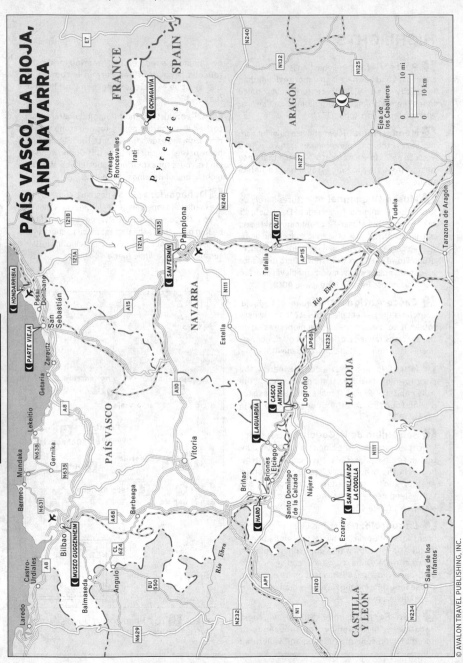

PAÍS VASCO, LA RIOJA, AND NAVARRA

of Spain offers visitors a world of culture, food, and wine. Consider the astonishing Guggenheim Museum in Bilbao, the running of the bulls at San Fermín in Pamplona, the sophisticated wineries of La Rioja, the gourmet food served at hundreds of bars in San Sebastián, the frozen-in-time fishing villages along the Basque coast, the sand-colored medieval churches that seem to rise right from the earth of La Rioja and southern Navarra.

Foodies and regular people who just love to eat will be thrilled in this region. País Vasco, with San Sebastián leading the way, has elevated local dishes to culinary heights with a New Basque Cuisine that has the gastronomic press around the world dizzy with praise, scrambling for adjectives other than the most accurate—astonishing, unbelievable, delicious. However, traditional Basque cuisine is equally wonderful. Based on impeccably fresh seafood, seasonal produce, local game, and subtly flavored sauces, it is both homey and sophisticated, nourishing and delicious. Moving south into La Rioja, the food becomes decidedly more earthy—thick bean stews, cod in wine, lamb chops grilled over vine shoots. It is paired with world-class rioja from the local bodegas—refreshingly affordable compared to their American and French counterparts. Navarra too offers its own wonderful wines, similar to rioja but under a different *denominación de origen,* or D.O. (appellation).

Outside of the main cities and festivals, the region is delightfully undeveloped by tourism. Sure, you will find five-star hotels, world-class restaurants, and a good smattering of sophisticated travelers, but nothing compared to the crowds in Andalucía, Barcelona, Madrid, or the Mediterranean coasts. Part of the reason is that it is a bit harder to travel here. You will need a car if you really want to explore the area. Another reason is the lack of English spoken. Even in sophisticated cities like San Sebastián, few service people (outside of top hotel staff) can manage beyond the most basic "Hello, three euros please" English. What this means is that you will have to be a little more daring

if you want to explore this area. Get a good phrasebook, bone up on a little Spanish, buy a Spanish road atlas (and maybe a wine guide), rent a car, and go. País Vasco, La Rioja, and Navarra will provoke your taste buds, douse your dreams with fine wine, stimulate your mind with avant architecture and medieval history, and most importantly, sate your desire for an astonishing, unbelievable, different kind of Spanish vacation.

PLANNING YOUR TIME

For the truly time-crunched, consider flying into Bilbao for a one-day immersion in Basque art and gastronomy. There are several low-cost flights daily from most cities in Spain, especially Madrid and Barcelona. Check with a local *agencia de viajes* (travel agent), Iberia (www.iberia.com), or Spanair (www.spanair.com). Bilbao not only offers the Guggenheim—one of the world's most impressive buildings—but a charming old quarter, a beautiful riverside promenade, and lots of good eating. To fit in San Sebastián too, you will need at least three days. An excellent tour of the entire region by car can by done in under a week, taking in these two Basque cities, plus the La Rioja wine region, and, if you are ambitious, Pamplona.

Year-round, this region has a milder climate than much of Spain. Summer brings the warmest weather, with averages around 24°C (75°F), warmer in La Rioja and southern Navarra. One thing to keep in mind is that the nights here can be cool, even in summer—bring a light sweater when going out at night. Winter hovers around 4°C (40°F), lower in the south and fluctuating quite a bit with cold winds from the Atlantic. Winter in the Western Pyrenees in Navarra is cold and snowy and much of the region will be impassable in the depth of winter. Fall and winter bring quite a bit of rain to the entire area.

From a fiesta viewpoint, if you are looking to run with the bulls (or at least watch), you need to be in Pamplona July 6–14. Summer brings large-scale music festivals and raucous village parties to the area. One of the funnest (and messiest) is the Batalla del Vino in Haro—it is basically a town-wide wine fight. October in La Rioja means *la vendimia,* the wine harvest. Though the date is never known until a few weeks before—it depends on Mother Nature—if you travel to Spain during that time, it is worth checking with a La Rioja tourism office to find out the dates.

San Sebastián

San Sebastián is a bit of unexpected grace in the middle of one of Spain's most rugged coasts. Hugging the Bay of La Concha, the town is protected from the full force of the Cantabrian Sea by the bay and its looming Isle of Santa Clara. Its eastern edge is guarded by the thickly wooded Mount Igeldo, while the twin peak of Mount Urgull stands over the west. Between the two runs the most beautiful urban beach in Spain, La Concha. The name means "seashell" and refers to the beach's scallop shell shape. Lined by a broad promenade, the golden beach is one of the most sought-after destinations for Spanish travelers. It is also making its name internationally, not only for star-studded events such as its Cannes-rivaling film festival or its acclaimed jazz festival, but for something much more fundamental—its food. Ask any Spaniard about San Sebastián and the first thing they'll tell you about are the *pintxos* (spelled *pinchos* in the rest of Spain). The "tx" is classic Basque spelling and a *pintxo* itself is a culinary Basque art. The bars of San Sebastián's pedestrian medieval quarter, the Parte Vieja, bow under the weight of platter after platter of *pintxos* from items as simple as grilled wild mushrooms to elaborate mini-dishes involving half a dozen ingredients and a presentation that requires an engineering degree to comprehend. However, San Sebastián's food extends well beyond the miniature and straight into the stars—Michelin stars that is. This tiny town boasts more stars per square foot than any other. (See sidebar, *Dining with the Stars.*)

In between devouring as much as you possibly can (after all, *pintxos* are so small, three more couldn't hurt), you can take in San Sebastián's gritty port; its lopsided cube of post-modernism called the Kursaal; its belle epoque mansions lining the Urumea River; or quite simply grab a bench on the Concha promenade and bask in San Sebastián's natural beauty—the deep green of its mountains, the sapphire sparkle of its sea, the inviting white embrace of its beach.

To fully enjoy this delightful city, you need at least two days. Spend one relaxing on the beach, followed by a leisurely stroll to Monte Urgull for the funicular car ride to the top. Hit the *pintxo* bars in the Parte Vieja for dinner. The next day, either rent a bike to explore the city further or take an early bus to the nearby port town of Hondarribia, where you can have lunch on the fishing port. More *pintxos* for dinner or splurge for a table at one of the Michelin-rated restaurants. The ideal time to visit San Sebastián is June–October, when the sea is at its warmest and the city bristles with activity. (Check *Festivals and Events* because if you head down during an event such as the film festival, you'll be looking at triple costs for hotel rooms.) Also, note that San Sebastián is extremely popular in summer, so book ahead by contacting the hotel directly or using a reputable online booker. If you can hold off your trip until October, and don't mind the water and wind a bit chilly, you'll have the city mostly to yourself and the locals.

The city's **tourist office** rents an audio guide for €10 that is okay, but overloaded with facts that only a history buff could appreciate. There is also a tourist bus, **Donosti Tour Fuenterrabía** (tel. 69/642-9847, €12, children €6), which operates from a booth across the street from the tourist office, right in front of Teatro Victoria Eugenia. Though the town is small enough to walk and lacks the major sights that would keep you busy, this hop-on, hop-off bus is perfect for folks who can't handle heavy walking or for those with kids. It is also a quick way to get an overview of the city. During the summer, the route includes a visit to the Museo Chillida Leku in Hernani.

If you are 20-something—or just wish you were—check out **Enjoy SS** (Kursaal Center, tel. 94/300-5060). They arrange fun events squarely aimed at the international backpacker clientele. Excursions include *pintxos* tours, a party boat cruise in the bay, bike tours, and trips to nearby towns. Enjoy is run by a team of locals and expats who know and love San Sebastián.

SIGHTS

The best sight of San Sebastián is the lovely crescent-shaped city itself with its elegant streets, tidy historic quarter, broad boardwalks, and shimmering beaches. Seeing the actual "sights" should take no longer than an afternoon; drinking in the charm of this picture-perfect town could take a few delicious days longer.

◖ Parte Vieja

The compact Parte Vieja (old quarter) is tucked in a nook formed by the sheer climb of Monte Urgull, the portside of the Bay of La Concha, and the River Urumea. Though the local tourist maps are great, this is a wonderful place to get lost and it is so small that you'll never really get off track. Just be aware that street names in the Parte Vieja use the Basque word *kalea*, rather than *calle*.

Over 1,000 years ago, this neighborhood comprised the whole of San Sebastián and though the narrow streets still bear a medieval air (especially at night under the orange glow of the street lamps), the Parte Vieja burned to the ground several times over the centuries, most recently on August 31, 1813. The only street to survive that fire was renamed **31 de Agosto.** Today, a candlelight vigil is held every year on this date.

During your rambling, look for the elegant **Plaza de la Constitución** with its yellow painted shutters. It used to serve as the city's bullring. The numbers above the windows were private seats held by wealthy patrons. You could own your apartment, but not your balcony. Be sure to have a coffee at one of the many cafés lining the plaza. Nestled against the side of Monte Urgull, you'll find San Sebastián's most interesting museum, **Museo San Telmo** (Pl. Zuloaga 1, tel. 94/348-1580, 10:30 A.M.–1:30 P.M. and 4–7:30 P.M. Tues.–Sat., 10:30 A.M.–2 P.M., free). Set in a lovely Dominican convent with an exquisite cloister, it houses minor works by major artists, including El Greco, Rubens, and Goya, as well as displays on Basque culture and art. The opposite end of the Parte Vieja is bounded by the bustling **Alameda del Boulevard** (locally called "el Bulevar"). It boasts dozens of cafés, ice-cream shops, and bars as well as the lively market **Bretxa.** Upstairs, it is a standard mall. In the basement, it is a fish, meat, and produce market. In the early mornings, the city's top chefs trek here to find that day's special. You might just want to stock up on picnic fixings for the beach.

Paseo del Muelle

Starting from the Parte Vieja, the colorful Paseo del Muelle runs alongside San Sebastián's port. It is lined with seafood shacks, souvenir shops, and laundry hanging from balconies overhead. The tiny port is jammed with a rainbow of boats of all sizes. Hop one called **Barco Ciudad San Sebastián** (Po. Muelle, s/n, 94/328-1488, €7, children €4) for a cruise around the bay and to the island of Santa Clara. Boat trips leave hourly 1–8 P.M. (closed during lunch). San Sebastian's rinky-dink **Aquarium** (Pl. Carlos Blasco de Imaz 1, tel. 94/344-0099, www.aquariumss.com, 10 A.M.–8 P.M. daily Apr.–June, 10 A.M.–9 P.M. daily July–Aug., 10 A.M.–7 P.M. Mon.–Fri. and 10 A.M.–8 P.M. Sat.–Sun Sept.–Mar., €9, children €5) offers a walk beneath a shark-filled tank and the chance to touch tamer fish in a petting tank. The **Museo Naval** (Po. Muelle 24, tel. 94/343-0051, €1.50) reveals the intertwined history of Basque culture and the sea. Even if you don't understand the Spanish translations, the model ships are cool to look at.

PAÍS VASCO

PAÍS VASCO

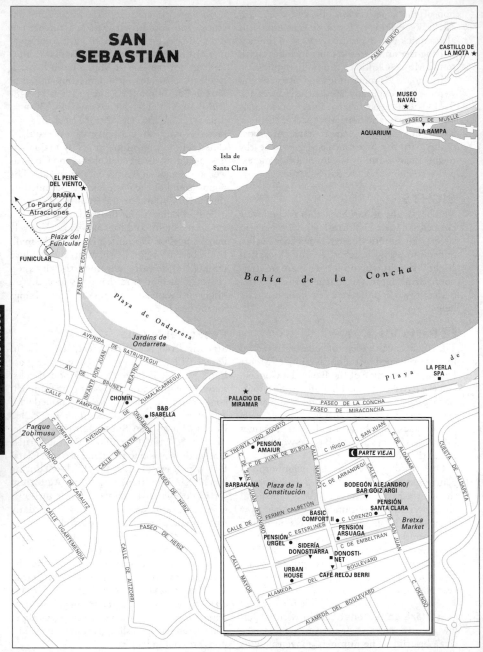

SAN SEBASTIÁN

CASTILLO DE LA MOTA ★

PASEO NUEVO

MUSEO NAVAL ★

PASEO DE MUELLE

AQUARIUM ★ LA RAMPA ▼

Isla de Santa Clara

EL PEINE DEL VIENTO ★

BRANKA ▼

To Parque de Atracciones

Plaza del Funicular

FUNICULAR

PASEO DE EDUARDO CHILLIDA

Bahía de la Concha

Playa de Ondarreta

Jardíns de Ondarreta

AVENIDA DE SATRUSTEGUI

AV DE PAMPLONA

INFANTE DON JUAN

C DE BRUNET

BEATRIZ

ZUMALACARREGUI

CHOMIN ●

DE ONDARBIDE

B&B ISABELLA ●

CALLE DE MATIA

Playa de la Concha

LA PERLA SPA ★

PALACIO DE MIRAMAR ★

PASEO DE LA CONCHA

PASEO DE MIRACONCHA

Parque Zubimusu

C TORENTO

C LOGROÑO

AVENIDA

C DE ZARAUTZ

PASEO DE HERIZ

CALLE UGARTEMENDIA

PASEO DE HERIZ

CALLE DE AITZORRI

CALLE MAYOR

C TREINTA UNO AGOSTO

PENSIÓN AMAIUR ●

C DE JUAN DE BILBOA

C SAN JUAN JERONIMO

BARBAKANA ▼

Plaza de la Constitución

CALLE DE FERMIN CALBETÓN

PENSIÓN URGEL ●

C ESTERLINES

SIDERÍA DONOSTIARRA ▼

URBAN HOUSE ●

ALAMEDA

C NARRICA

C IÑIGO

C SAN JUAN

C DE ARRANDEGI

BASIC COMFORT II ●

C LORENZO

PENSIÓN ARSUAGA ●

C DE EMBELTRAN

DONOSTI- NET ■

CAFÉ RELOJ BERRI ●

ALAMEDA DEL BOULEVARD

☾ PARTE VIEJA

C DE ALDAMAR

BODEGÓN ALEJANDRO/ BAR GOIZ ARGI ▼

PENSIÓN SANTA CLARA ●

Bretxa Market

C DE SAN JUAN

BOULEVARD

CUESTA DE ALDAPETA

C OKENDO

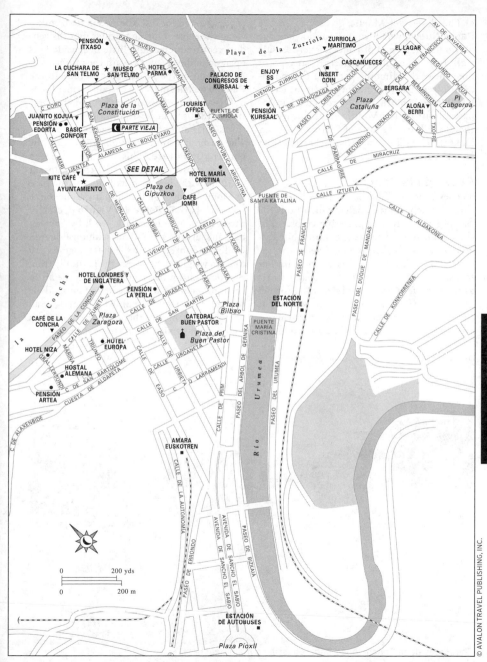

PENSIÓN ITXASO

PASEO NUEVO DE SALAMANCA

CALLE DE SALAMANCA

Playa de la Zurriola

ZURRIOLA MARÍTIMO

EL LAGAR

AV DE NAVARRA

LA CUCHARA DE SAN TELMO

MUSEO SAN TELMO

HOTEL PARMA

CASCANUECES

CALLE DE SAN FRANCISCO

SEGUNDO IZPIZUA

CALLE DE BERMINGHAM

PALACIO DE CONGRESOS DE KURSAAL

ENJOY SS

INSERT COIN

AVENIDA ZURRIOLA

BERGARA

Pl Zubgeroa

C CORO

ALDAMAR

TOURIST OFFICE

C DE SAN JERÓNIMO

Plaza de la Constitución

PUENTE DE ZURRIOLA

PENSIÓN KURSAAL

C DE USANDIZAGA

PASEO DE CRISTOBAL COLON

CALLE DE ZABALETA

Plaza Cataluña

ALOÑA BERRI

ESNAOLA

GRAN VIA

C TXOFRE

JUANITO KOJUA

PENSIÓN EDORTA

BASIC CONFORT

PARTE VIEJA

CALLE MAYOR

ALAMEDA DEL BOULEVARD

C DE IRABAGIRE

SECUNDINO

CALLE

DE MIRACRUZ

CALLE MARI

IJENTEA

SEE DETAIL

C DE OKENDO

PASEO REPÚBLICA ARGENTINA

KITE CAFÉ

AYUNTAMIENTO

C DE HERNANI

HOTEL MARÍA CRISTINA

Plaza de Gipuzkoa

CAFÉ IOMBI

PUENTE DE SANTA KATALINA

CALLE IZTUETA

CALLE DE ALDAKONEA

C ANDIA

CALLE GARIBAI

C TXURRUCA

AVENIDA DE LA LIBERTAD

C ETXAIDE

PASEO DE FRANCIA

PASEO DEL DUQUE DE MANDAS

CALLE DE KONKORRENEA

HOTEL LONDRES Y DE INGLATERA

PENSIÓN LA PERLA

CALLE DE SAN MARCIAL

C BERGARA

C GETARIA

Concha

PASEO DE LA CONCHA

CALLE DE ZUBIETA

CALLE DE ARRASATE

CALLE DE SAN MARTIN

Plaza Bilbao

ESTACIÓN DEL NORTE

CALLE DEL DUQUE DE MANDAS

CAFÉ DE LA CONCHA

Plaza Zaragoza

CALLE DE SAN MARTIN

CATEDRAL BUEN PASTOR

Plaza del Buen Pastor

PUENTE MARÍA CRISTINA

la

HOTEL NIZA

GRAL LERSUNDI

MARINA

TRIUNFO

HOTEL EUROPA

CALLE DE URDANETA

PASEO DEL ARBOL DE GERNIKA

Río Urumea

PASEO DEL URUMEA

HOSTAL ALEMANA

C DE SAN BARTOLOMÉ

CALLE DE URBIETA

D LARRAMENDI

PENSIÓN ARTEA

CUESTA DE ALDAPETA

CALLE DE EASO

C DE ALAXENBIDE

AMARA EUSKOTREN

CALLE DE PRIM

AVENIDA DE SANCHO EL SABIO

CALLE DE LA AUTONOMÍA

0 200 yds

0 200 m

PASEO DE ERRONDO

PASEO DE BIZKAIA

AVENIDA DE SANCHO EL SABIO

ESTACIÓN DE AUTOBUSES

Plaza PíoXII

© AVALON TRAVEL PUBLISHING, INC.

PAÍS VASCO

The Paseo del Muelle gives way to the **Paseo Nuevo,** which wraps around the edge of Monte Urgull and provides a lovely seaside walk (jog, bike, inline skate). At any point take one of the climbing paths up the mountain to see the ruins of the medieval castle **Castillo de la Mota,** which protected San Sebastián during the Middle Ages. Nearby is the rather kitschy statue of Christ that overlooks the city. The view of San Sebastián from Monte Urgull is classic.

Paseo de la Concha

The jewel of San Sebastián is the white shell-shaped beach of La Concha, which hugs the Bay of La Concha in a glittering embrace. In the middle of the bay sits the uninhabited island of Santa Clara. Its presence keeps the waters calm. Hearty swimmers often swim out to the island in summer. The beach starts at the majestic **Casa Consistorial,** a former grand casino built in 1882 that now serves as the Ayuntamiento (town hall). From there a series of seaside parks and white-stoned prom-enades stretch for 3.2 kilometers (two miles) along the shore. During warmer months vendors rent umbrellas and little beachside bars open up in the arcade beneath the promenade. At the end of the beach, you'll come to the **Palacio de Miramar,** the elegant former home of Queen María Cristina who summered here in the 1800s. The surrounding gardens are spectacular and offer lovely views of the bay. The beach continues though now under the name of **Ondarreta.** This is where the queen and her consorts used to take royal dips. If you follow the beach to its finish at the base of Monte Igeldo, you'll eventually come to the sculpture park **El Peine del Viento** (Comb of the Winds), an emblematic work by San Sebastián's favorite artistic son, sculptor Eduardo Chillida. Giant steel claws, 9,000 kilograms (10 tons) in weight, seem to emerge naturally from the rocky cliff walls, trying to catch the air in their grip. **Monte Ugeldo** can be mounted via funicular (hours vary, €2). At the top is a sad little amusement park that pales in comparison to the thrilling view over San Sebastián.

The Paseo de la Concha hugs San Sebastián's main beach.

Centro and Gros

Along the banks of the River Urumea, the newer part of San Sebastián unfolds. Well, if you consider the 19th century new. The houses along the river are majestic testaments to a lovely era long gone. The bridges and riverside paths make for an excellent stroll. In this area, also called **Centro Romántico,** you'll find excellent pedestrian shopping zones, restaurants and bars where the locals go, and upscale hotels. The city's cathedral **Buen Pastor** (Pl. Buen Pastor, s/n) sends its 250-foot Gothic spire up here as well. During your wanderings, look for the landscaped **Plaza de Gipuzkoa,** a lush oasis of green in the middle of the commotion. Cross either the Puente de Zurriola or the Puente Santa Catalina to get to the cozy little neighborhood of **Gros,** home to some of the most-acclaimed *pintxo* bars in town. Though just 10 minutes walking from the Parte Vieja, this area is mostly devoid of tourists. Its slip of a beach, **Playa de la Zurriola,** is a favorite of surfers with its constant rolling waves. It is also home to the glowing cubes of glass called the **Palacio de Congresos de Kursaal,** a multi-function space hosting concerts, conventions, and the famous San Sebastián Film Festival. Designed by architect Rafael Moneo, the building is breathtaking when lit at night.

Museo Chillida Leku

Eduardo Chillida was born in San Sebastián in 1924 and went on to become one of the most important contemporary sculptors in the world. He won numerous prestigious prizes during his lifetime and his work was collected by galleries and famous museums, including the Metropolitan in New York and the Art Institute in Chicago. When he died in 2002, Spain lost a great artist but gained a legend. The 16th-century farmhouse that he converted into his studio has now been refitted as the Museo Chillida Leku (C/ Jauregui 66, Hernani, tel. 94/333-6006, www.eduardochillida.com, 10:30 A.M.–3 P.M. Wed.–Sun., closed Tues. Sept.–June, 10:30 A.M.–8 P.M. Mon.–Sat., 10:30 A.M.–3 P.M. Sun. July–Aug., €8). It houses over 100 of his works and the

PAÍS VASCO

The glass cubes of the Palacio de Congresos de Kursaal soar above the Zurriola bridge.

pastoral gardens are dotted with over 40 more. The sculptures are made mainly of iron and granite and despite their heaviness seem perfectly suited for this sedate landscape of beech, oak, and magnolia trees. Get there by taking a 25-minute ride on bus G2 from Calle Okendo. It costs €1 and leaves every half-hour 7 A.M.–10 P.M.

ENTERTAINMENT AND EVENTS
Nightlife

A night out in San Sebastián usually begins in the Parte Vieja. As the *pintxo* bars shutter down, the tiny bars tucked between fill up. Things don't get started until around midnight and will go strong until 2 A.M., a bit later on weekends. Head out during the early week and you'll find breathing room and crowds above 25. On the weekends, both the age level and the personal space level drop. Your best bet is to wander around until you hear music you like and a crowd you'd like to join. Barring that, here are a few places to get started. **Bar Zibbibo** (Pl. Sarriegi 8) serves up fine sangria and funky house. **Argia** (C/ Pescadería 3) keeps heads bopping to pop rock. **Mendaur** (C/ Fermín Calbetón 8) cranks it up with hard house. Down the street, **Loretxu** (C/ Fermín Calbetón 26) features pop rock. **Tik Tak** (C/ Embeltran 11) offers easy dancing music.

In Gros, facing Zurriola beach, you'll find one of the most popular clubs in town **Ondarra 16 Bis** (Av. Zurriola 16). It draws an arty crowd to its laid-back ground-level bar while the smoky basement pulls in the young hipster set for live indie music. Monday features a popular open-mic night. For a classier night out, head to the **Museo del Whisky** (Boulevard 5), which features a piano player and classic cocktails. Ask for a piece of their gin-and-tonic-flavored candy. Another sophisticated choice is the bar/terrace of the swanky **Branka** (Po. Eduardo Chillida 13), located close to the El Peine del Viento sculpture. Listen to jazz as you watch the stars dance on the waves of the bay below. Branka also houses a gourmet restaurant and a decent café.

Most of the late-night dance clubs are located on the La Concha promenade. Everyone's favorite mega-disco is **Bataplán** (Po. Concha, s/n, €12 cover). Popular with exchange students and San Sebastián's moneyed under-30 crowd, Bataplán pumps out standard house and techno with an occasional bit of hip-hop. Practically next door **La Rotunda** (Po. Concha, s/n, €18 cover) is a bit swisher, attracting a 25-and-up crowd. The view is spectacular with circular windows overlooking the beach and the island of Santa Clara lit up at night. **La Kabutzia** (Po. Concha, s/n), located on the edge of the Parte Vieja in front of the town hall, draws a 40-something crowd with Spanish pop and classic disco. It is located in the upper half of a private club that resembles a boat and features great views over the bay. A late-night spot in Gros fronting the Zurriola beach is **ZM** (Po. Zurriola 41, tel. 94/329-7853, €10 cover), the abbreviated name the restaurant Zurriola Marítimo takes on at night. The music is Spanish pop, the drinks are classic mixes, and the crowd 30-something. It doesn't get madly crowded, which is a plus for claustrophobic types.

Festivals and Events

If you'll be in San Sebastián the third weekend of January, bring earplugs for the celebration of **Tamborrada**. At midnight on January 19, thousands of uniformed drummers take to the streets of the Parte Vieja and begin beating their drums as they parade around. They keep it up for 24 hours, with only a short break around dawn for a brandy breakfast. It is said the tradition started centuries ago when a chef went to draw water from the town's well. He began to sing and soon, others in line to draw water began to accompany him by beating their pots. Today, the different drumming groups are made up from various gastronomic societies, which accounts for the various chefs you'll see in the processions.

Thudding drums are traded for silkier beats the third week of July when the **Festival de Jazz** comes to town. For over four decades, top names in jazz have descended upon San

Sebastián for a week's worth of concerts. Recently the repertoire has expanded to include artists like Bob Dylan, Dr. John, Erykah Badu, and Van Morrison. The event is open to all with a mixture of free and ticketed events. Get all the details at the official website, www.jazzaldia.com.

August is when San Sebastián shakes off its elegant persona and gets down and funky with **Semana Grande.** The week-long event (usually around August 15) is a joyous celebration jam-packed with nightly concerts, dancing in the streets, food stands, fireworks, a fun fair, and San Sebastián's most important bullfighting events. A month later, locals take to the water for the annual **Regatas de Traineras,** regatta races from La Concha, out past Santa Clara Island.

The third week in September, Hollywood directors, film stars, and the movers and shakers of cinema arrive for the **Festival Internacional de Cine,** Spain's version of Cannes. For over 50 years, the event has grown in prestige, rivaling the French festival. It is an exciting time to be in the city, but if you want to go, book way in advance and expect to pay triple for your room.

SPORTS AND RECREATION
Biking
San Sebastián is a bike-friendly town threaded with dedicated bike paths. You are also allowed to bring bikes on the local trains. At the tourist office or one of the bike rental companies, pick up the handy map, **Pedal Round the City,** which lays out several routes and also covers all the legalities of biking in English and Spanish. Rent a bike at **Bici Rent Donosti** (Av. Zurriola 22, tel. 65/572-4458), across from Zurriola beach. Prices start from around €5 per hour depending on the season, the length of rental, and the type of bike rented. An antiquated two-seater is among the offerings. Down the street, **Aritz Rental Bike Center** (Av. Zurriola 30, tel. 94/332-2640) rents bikes and also offers guided bike tours of the city and surroundings. In the Centro, try **Comet** (Av. Libertad 6, tel. 94/342-2351).

Surfing
Though the waves are not as big as elsewhere on Spain's northern coast, San Sebastián offers consistent, long swells at the pristine Zurriola beach. If you are a beginner, intermediate, or even advanced, **Puka Surf** (Av. Zurriola 24, tel. 94/332-0068, www.pukasurf.com) should be your first stop. In addition to selling and renting boards and wetsuits, they give classes to all levels. In conjunction with Urban House (see *Accommodations*), they have created **Urbansurf San Sebastian** (94/342-8154, www.urbansurfsansebastian.com), an ideal program for young people who want to learn surfing cheaply. Their packages include accommodation in one of the Urban Houses, breakfast, daily lessons with a qualified instructor (in English), board and wetsuit rental, and insurance. Urbansurf also arranges "surfaris" to famous surfing spots nearby, including Mundaka and Zarautz. Weekend packages start at €131 and two weeks are just €602. There is a discount if you sign up with friends.

Spa
After her royal doctor recommended she bathe in waters off of La Concha to cure her skin ailments, Queen Isabel became a regular visitor to San Sebastián. Queen María Cristina of Spain also chose San Sebastián's sea for its restive properties and built royal bath houses along the beach, one of which has been converted into the luxurious day spa **La Perla** (Po. Concha, s/n, tel. 94/345-8856, www.la-perla.net). In a 15,000-foot beachfront complex, the spa offers massages, facials, pedicures, manicures, peelings, and several different body wraps designed to relax and rejuvenate mind, body, and skin tone. Many of the treatments rely on the curative powers of the local sea water, including their exclusive Circuito Talaso, a circuit of treatments that include a hydro-massage pool, a heated pool, a whirlpool with a view of the bay, saunas, cold-water pools, and saltwater steam rooms. A three-hour session costs €25 and is guaranteed to relax even the weariest of travelers. Reservations are required. There is also a creative restaurant set inside a spaceship-shaped

room overlooking the beach. Combination spa and meal packages run €60. Finally, the complex includes a very trendy bar. Unfortunately, the bar is run by a snippy staff—the only sour note in an otherwise wonderful place.

ACCOMMODATIONS

If you need help securing accommodations, try the one-stop online reservation system run by the San Sebastián tourism board, www.san sebastianreservas.com. Their toll number is 90/244-3442.

Under €50

As a mecca for both surfers and European backpackers, San Sebastián has a good smattering of youth hostels and very low-end rooms with shared baths. They tend to book early and stay full throughout the summer months. Most are clustered in the Parte Vieja; just look up for signs that say *pension*. Backpackers can't go wrong with **Urban House** (Boulevard 26, tel. 94/342-8154, www.enjoyss.com), a new concept in hostelling run by lifelong San Sebastián resident Pablo Portero. Pablo and partners run three "houses" in the center of San Sebastián. Just don't call them hostels! The idea is to provide a space that is as comfortable as home. Guests are given their own keys and treated like family members. Dormitory rooms for up to eight run around €16 per person. Doubles are just €34. Bathrooms are shared and there is a fully stocked kitchen. Staff go out of their way to introduce guests and often lead *pintxos* and bar tours.

For something more private, try the lovely **(Pensión Amaiur** (C/ 31 de Agosto 44, tel. 94/342-9654, www.pensionamaiur.com, €48). Yes, bathrooms are shared, but the rooms are cozily decorated with lovely details like lace curtains, wicker furniture, and flowers on the balconies. You'll feel like you are staying in someone's home. **San Lorenzo** (C/ San Lorenzo 2, tel. 94/342-5516, www.pensionsan lorenzo.com, €48) offers five very basic rooms with en-suite baths. A few doors down, **Santa Clara** (C/ San Lorenzo 6, tel. 94/343-1203, €50) offers just a bit more color in the rooms

for just a few euros more. At **Loinaz** (C/ San Lorenzo 17, tel. 94/342-6714, www.pension loinaz.com, €50) you get a lot more charm for the price, but the bathrooms are shared. Another cheap charmer is **Arsuaga** (C/ Narrika 3, tel. 94/342-0681, €38), which offers rustic rooms with shared baths for rock-bottom prices. Out of the Parte Vieja, try **La Perla** (C/ Loiola 10, tel. 94/342-8123, www.pension laperla.com, €50), which has quaint rooms with hardwood floors in a quiet part of town. Request a room with a view of the cathedral.

€50-100

In addition to its great location on the edge of the Parte Vieja, the major selling point of **(Pensión Itxasoa** (C/ San Juan 14, tel. 94/342-0132, itxasoa@pensionesconencanto .com, www.pensionesconencanto.com, €60) is its extremely friendly staff. The views of the sea don't hurt. There are only five rooms so book early. If you opt for the €3 breakfast, it will be brought to your room. Itxasoa also organizes trips to nearby towns including a dinner in a authentic cider house located in the hills surrounding San Sebastián. **Edorta** (C/ Puerto 15, tel. 94/342-3773, www.pension edorta.com, €70) is a rustic haven of stone walls and wood floors. Street rooms can be noisy, which explains the higher price for interior rooms. If you opt to share a bath, the price goes down to €50. **Pensión Urgel** (C/ Esterlines 10, tel. 94/343-0047, €56) is another charming value, with wrought-iron headboards and soothing yellow walls. Another good value is the stylish **Basic Confort** (C/ Puerto 17, tel. 94/342-2581, www.basicconfort.com, €80) and its sister property **Basic Confort II** (C/ San Lorenzo 12), both of which feature brightly colored rooms named for cities around the world. **Pensión Alameda** (Boulevard 16, tel. 94/342-6449, www.pensionalameda.com, €80) has a great location on the Boulevard and features good sized rooms with hardwood floors and contemporary decor.

Outside of the Parte Vieja, head across the river to the trendy Gros district and **Pensión Kursaal** (C/ Peña y Goñi 2, tel. 94/329-2666, kursaal@pensionesconencanto.com, www.pensionesconencanto.com, €60), just steps from the surfers' beach of Zurriola. It offers personalized service and breakfast in bed. Another lovely bargain is **Hostal Alemana** (C/ San Martín 53, tel. 94/346-2544, www.hostal alemana.com, €90), located just blocks behind La Concha. On the top floor of a stately building, the *hostal* features large cream-colored rooms with comfy beds and all the usual amenities. **Pensión Artea** (C/ San Bartolomé 33, tel. 04/345-5100, www.pension artea.com, €63) offers stylish, if small, rooms just a few blocks from the beach.

For more bargain hotels, head to the residential zone of Ondarreta, just behind the Ondarreta beach, the former playground of royalty. **Chomin** (Av. Infanta Beatriz 16, tel. 94/331-7312, www.restaurantechomin.com, €80) offers a dose of grandmotherly charm in this small inn located in a converted summer house. The downstairs restaurant of the same name is excellent, if a bit stuffy. **B&B Isabella** (C/ Ondarbide 1, tel. 94/321-8324, www.roomsisabella.com, €60) rents four comfortable rooms and two small apartments. The house features a great terrace with views over the bay and Island Santa Clara.

Over €100

Run by the family of artist Eduardo Chillida, the ◖ **Hotel Niza** (C/ Zubieta 56, tel. 94/342-6663, niza@hotelniza.com, www.hotelniza.com, €120) is a longtime local favorite. Nearly half of the rooms face the bay and you should definitely request one early. The service is personable and the location, smack in the middle of the Concha boardwalk, is perfect. There is an okay pizzeria and a wonderful bar/cafeteria facing the bay. A few blocks away, another good option is the **Hotel Europa** (C/ San Martín 52, tel. 94/347-0880, europa@hotel-europa.com, www.hotel-europa.com, €165), an antique-laden hotel featuring all the amenities including bathrobes. Beach towels are provided in the summer. You can't go wrong at the modern **Tryp Orly** (Pl. Zaragoza 4, tel. 94/346-3200, tryp.orly@solmelia.com, www.solmelia.com,

€160), a member of the venerable Meliá chain of hotels. Check the Internet before booking as rooms are often discounted. **Parma** (C/ General Jáuregui 11, tel. 94/342-8893, www.hotel parma.com, €124) is a smart hotel offering personal attention. Book ahead to get a room with a view of the bay.

With its history as a retreat for royalty, both blue-blooded and Hollywood, San Sebastián has a couple of top-end accommodations. One of the best is the elegant, if somewhat stuffy, **Londres y de Inglatera** (C/ Zubieta 2, tel. 94/344-0770, rcservas@hlondres.com, www.hlondres.com, €144–222), with its prime location on La Concha. Rooms with a view cost more but are worth it. Expect old-world elegance, impeccable service, and very comfortable beds. The other top spot in town is the prestigious five-star **María Cristina** (C/ Okendo 1, tel. 94/343-7600, hmc@westin.com, www.westin.com/mariacristina, €300) inaugurated by Queen María Cristina herself in 1912. It is a favorite of the A-list celebrities that descend upon San Sebastián during the September film festival. Out of season, prices dip below €200.

FOOD

San Sebastián, along with Bilbao and Cataluña, is at the forefront of Spanish cuisine. Making waves worldwide, the refined flavors of local dishes—impeccable seafood, fresh vegetables, carefully rendered sauces—are as easy to come by in a corner dive as they are in a fine dining room. The suggestions below have been carefully—and deliciously—researched, but don't be afraid to explore. Go where the locals are, follow your nose to a sumptuous smell. If you are disappointed (which is highly unlikely), don't fret, it is only a *pintxo* after all—pay up and move to the next *pintxo* bar.

Food and Wine Tours

If you'd rather let someone else take the reigns on a tour through San Sebastián's food, there are several gastronomic tour operators to meet all budgets. At the rock-bottom end of the spectrum are the friendly folk at **Enjoy SS** (Kursaal

ART OF FOOD: A *PINTXO* PRIMER

Throughout País Vasco, you'll find bar tops laden with tiny, bite-sized snacks. Though they resemble tapas, they are actually *pintxos*, with the requisite Basque "tx" in the spelling. In other parts of Spain they are spelled *pincho*, a word that roughly translates as a "bite" or "pinch." In País Vasco, they mean one thing – gastronomic heaven. Imagine the scene. It's 9 P.M. in San Sebastián, you duck into a bar in the Parte Vieja. It is a typical Spanish watering hole – legs of ham hanging from the walls, a few rustic wooden tables crowded with plates and glasses, lots of laughing people standing around the bar – until you get closer to the bar and lean in for a drink order. The entire length is covered in platter after platter of *pintxos* – *jamón* and tomato on toast, crab tartlets, cod-stuffed red peppers, fresh marinated anchovies, wild mushroom omelet, shrimp with aioli, monkfish with leek, duck breast with pear, and on and on and on. As one platter is finished, the waiters lay out another. Behind the bar are more dishes waiting to be heated, cheeses waiting to be cut, cured hams and sausages waiting to be sliced. It is a sight that is at once enticing and forbidding. After all, just how do you join the *pintxos* party? A little bit of background information will help.

WHAT?

A Basque *pintxo* can be as simple as green olives marinated with garlic, however in recent years the País Vasco has emerged as one of the most culinary relevant regions of the world. Since the 19th century, *txokos*, men-only Basque gastronomic societies, have created a legacy of fine cooking. Today's top Basque chefs, known for their innovation and commit-

ment to fresh, local ingredients, have garnered worldwide cult status and their restaurants have become gastronomic meccas. The humble little *pintxo* was not immune and has evolved into *alta cocina en miniatura* (haute cuisine in miniature). *Pintxos* now include many ingredients and careful elaboration. You might find baby squid stuffed with onion and eggplant, zucchini layered with creamed crab, poached quail eggs with foie and caramel sauce, cod with smoked peppers and peach puree. In some bars, such as **Aloña Berri** in San Sebastián or **Sagartoki** in Vitoria, you will encounter ornate works of art posing as *pintxos*. Some are so complex that you'll need the bartender's advice on how to eat them.

WHERE?

A *pintxo* bar is any place *pintxos* are served. It may be a full-fledged restaurant with a small bar up front, a trendy wine bar, a rowdy dive, or a basic bar as described above. Almost anywhere you go in País Vasco will offer a few *pintxo* bars, though no town in the world has embraced *pintxos* like San Sebastián. In the Parte Vieja, there are dozens of *pintxo* bars on every street.

Most *pintxo* bars are standing-room only. While there may be a few tables, they fill up by 10 P.M. and are situated far from the delicious bar-top action. Though several items such as *txangurro* (spider crab, served baked in a tartlet or as stuffing) and *gilda* (a skewer of green olives, fresh anchovies, and spicy green peppers) are common across the board, most *pintxo* bars specialize in one particular item. Always ask what is *la especialidad de la casa* to know what the specialty is – or just point to

Center, tel. 94/300-5060). They offer *pintxos* tours (€25) as well as a series of themed dinners, including a trek to a nearby cider house (during season). Closely involved with the hostel/backpacker/surfer scene, Enjoy draws a 20-something international crowd looking for fun to go with all the good food. Madrid-based **Planeta Vino** (tel. 91/310-2855, 68/030-1024,

info@planetavino.net, www.planetavino.net), run by American expat Mary O'Connor and her Basque husband Miguel de Moral, offers a well-priced *pintxos* tour by prior arrangement, in addition to their usual roster of wine events. At the luxe end of the scale, try **Cellar Tours** (tel. 91/521-3939, info@cellartours.com, www.cellartours.com), run by Madrid-based Cali-

what everyone else is having. Another old but still good piece of advice is to look at the floor to gauge the quality of the food. In Spain, it is customary to toss napkins, toothpicks, and even olive pits on the floor. Spaniards say that the more trash on the floor, the better the food must be. It is a philosophy that pretty much holds true.

HOW?

Going out for an evening of *pintxos* in País Vasco is so much a part of the culture that it has its own word, *txikiteo*. The rules are deliciously simple – move, move, move. The idea is to hit three or four or more *pintxo* bars in a night, enjoying one or two snacks in each. By the end of the evening, you've had the equivalent of a good meal with the fun of a pub crawl. In the bars, you can either take what you want directly from the platters or point a few things out to the bartender who will then pile the *pintxos* on a plate for you. Some *pintxos* will have to be heated before serving, so before you bite into an unbaked tartlet, consult the bartender first.

Pintxo bars generally operate 8:30 P.M.– midnight. Tourists like to hit the bars early to avoid crowds, which is not a bad idea as the bars do get incredibly crowded, particularly between 10 P.M. and 11 P.M. However, this is also the most exciting time to be in a *pintxo* bar. To join the boisterous fun, just wiggle your way to the bar (local etiquette means folks will shift to accommodate you), look over what you want, catch the bartender's eye, and point.

The accompanying drink of choice is *txakoli* (cha-KO-lee), a fizzy, light white wine produced in País Vasco. It is poured from a height to cre-ate bubbles and served in a short, squat glass. You can, of course, drink whatever you want, but you might want to forego beer as it tends to fill you up, leaving less room for *pintxos*.

HOW MUCH?

Pintxos generally run €1.50–3, though complicated haute cuisine dishes may go up to €5. A glass of wine or *txakoli* is less than €2. For a good night of eating and drinking, expect to pay about €30 per person. You will have to pay cash, as *pintxo* bars do not accept credit cards.

Unlike in the United States, you are not expected to pay as you go. Rather, when you are ready to leave, ask the bartender for *la cuenta* (the bill). He will more than likely recite what you ate and drank to confirm. Sometimes, he'll ask you what you had. Do not think of lying to save money. The *pintxos* culture is a lovely tradition where the bars and chefs truly want to please you, sharing their culinary heritage freely. Respect their kindness and culture by being honest. Besides, the bartenders have a very accurate memory. If you fudge it, they usually know – leading to a very awkward and embarrassing moment for you.

MORE INFORMATION

The Internet is loaded with information detailing *pintxos* and the *txikiteo*. Most American foodie magazines and websites have covered the topic extensively. A perusal of the Spain forums at www.egullet.com will reveal lots of insider tips, while the San Sebastián-based site www.todopintxos.com offers a round-up (with photos) of the city's best *pintxos*, news and information on chefs and dishes, and suggested *pintxo* routes.

fornian Genevieve McCarthy, a fully licensed wine tour specialist who also arranges San Sebastián tours. Another top-end provider is **Tenedor Tours** (tel. 94/331-3929, info@tenedor tours.com, www.tenedortours.com), run by ex–New Yorker Gabriella Ranelli de Aguirre, who has been based in San Sebastián more than a dozen years. She offers a variety of tours throughout the Basque country, most with a gastronomic twist. She can also arrange one-day private guided tours of San Sebastián's dining scene—from *pintxos* to Michelin stars.

Cafés and Desserts

Pastry-making is an art in San Sebastián and you'll find charming bakeries scattered

DINING WITH THE STARS

San Sebastián is a culinary mecca. The city holds 14 Michelin stars (and counting), more per capita than any other city in the world. The current exalted state owes a debt to the New Basque Cuisine Movement started by local chefs Juan Mari Arzak and Pedro Subijana in the mid-1970s. After stints in the great kitchens of France, the two young chefs returned to their native San Sebastián to apply new techniques and concepts to local cuisine. Basque cooking was already established as the best in Spain with a reputation for excellent raw ingredients and delicate preparations. Arzak and Subijana began the task of lightening up the traditional dishes and emphasizing the remarkable local products. A new generation – most of whom have worked in the kitchens of the two masters – continues to innovate, while Arzak and Subijana continue at the top of their game.

The key ingredients in the food of the Basque Country are freshly caught fish, locally raised meats, and fresh-from-the-farm produce. For example, when the first fava beans of the season are rushed to market, it's a culinary event. Classic dishes include slowly braised beef cheeks and oxtail that falls from the bone at the merest prod of a fork. Grilled fish is often served whole, with olive oil, garlic, and a bit of cider vinegar. While prime product still plays a great part in Basque cuisine, the chefs at the forefront heighten the flavors with complex yet subtle treatments. Everything is seasonal. Sauces are kept to a minimum, often substituted for rich broths and vegetable infusions. In the new cuisine, chefs use myriad spices – ginger, saffron – and seamlessly integrate them into magical combinations. Varied textures will surprise and entertain you.

The stars come out every night in San Sebastián (except on Monday) and the following list includes the best of the best. However, the vibrancy of the restaurant scene in San Sebastián means that there are always new stars on the rise. If you are truly a foodie, keep an eye on the Spanish forum of www.egullet .com. Note that all of the following require advance reservations, which can be handled online. Finally, be sure to check the exact arrival directions ahead of time. Several of the following are well outside the city center and require a car or a taxi ride.

Akelarre (Paseo Padre Orcolaga 56, tel. 94/331-1209, restaurante@akelarre.net, www .akelarre.net, closed Sun. P.M., Mon. and Tues. in winter, Feb., and the first fortnight in Oct.). Chef Pedro Subijana serves impeccable meals in an elegant setting with glorious views over the Cantabrian Sea. Specialties include cuttlefish with Venere rice and sea bass with gooseneck barnacles, olive oil pearls, and arugula. The highly recommended tasting menu is €100 without wine.

---

throughout the city. One of the best products is a decadent almond- and raisin-studded brioche that you will find widely available for breakfast. With a *café con leche* you have a yummy way to start the day. Beneath the arcade of the bustling Alameda del Boulevard are several cafés/bars that serve continental breakfasts by day, cocktails by night. They also all feature sidewalk seating in warmer months. Try **Reloj Berri** (Boulevard 20, tel. 94/342-9709, 8 A.M.– 3 A.M. daily), a modern bar with a capable staff. **Kite Café** (C/ Ingentea 4, tel. 94/342-5593, 7:30 A.M.–11 P.M. daily), right across from the town hall, offers free Wi-Fi with your break-

fast. For strictly coffee and drinks, head to **Ostertz** (Po. Muelle 11, tel. 94/342-5387, 12–11 P.M. daily), a gritty portside bar popular with both fishermen and bohemians.

If you want something more substantial than *pintxos* but don't have the trust fund needed for San Sebastián's Michelin-starred haute spots, here are a few café alternatives. Right on the Concha boardwalk, the nautically themed **Café de la Concha** (Po. Concha, 12, tel. 94/347-3600, noon–2 A.M. daily, €18) boasts a large terrace overlooking the bay and a menu of tasty basics such as sandwiches, hamburgers, and pastas. In the Centro,

Arzak (Alto de Miracruz 21, tel. 94/327-8465, restaurante@arzak.es, www.arzak.es, closed Sun. P.M., Mon. and Tues. in winter, and the last fortnight in June and Nov.). Juan Mari Arzak and his daughter Elena share their Michelin three-starred kitchen and oversee a research laboratory where their food is constantly evolving. Deep knowledge of their land and clientele allow them to use cutting-edge techniques to create a surprising, delightful, and refined cuisine. You will never be disappointed. Lamb in a veil of *café con leche* is a specialty. Average price is €120 without wine.

Martín Berasategui (Loidi Kalea 4 in Lasarte, tel. 94/336-6471, info@restaurantemartinberasategui.com, closed Sun. P.M., Mon. and Tues., and Dec. 15–Jan. 15). Martín Berasategui's flagship restaurant in Lasarte is a grand affair with a lovely terrace for summer nights. The extensive tasting menu (€130 without wine) is, in effect, the chef's greatest hits. From 2001, there's his classic roast Dover sole with clam oil, citrus fruit, black mint, dried tangerine, and walnut powder. One of the best from 2006 was octopus in four textures with king crab juice, an octopus broth bonbon, paprika foam, and ice herbs.

Mugaritz (Aldura Aldea 20, Caserio Otzazulueta in Renteria, tel. 94/351-8343, info@mugaritz.com, www.mugaritz.com, closed Sun. P.M., Mon. and Tues. A.M. in winter, Easter, and Dec. 15–Jan. 15). Andoni Luis Aduritz is a cerebral chef. His attention to detail is far-reaching and from the moment you arrive at his beautiful remote farmhouse, all of your senses will be on high alert. Flavors are sublime and textures unexpected – nothing is what it seems. He is a master of foie gras and a wizard with oysters and sea urchin. Treat yourself to a tasting menu. There are two – one at €85 and the other at €110, not including wine. The wine cellar is contemporary and Ruth, the wine steward, is a wealth of information.

Zuberoa Jatetxea (Iturriotz Auzoa 8 in Oyarzun, tel. 94/349-1228, zuberoa@zuberoa.com, www.zuberoa.com, closed Sun. and Wed., the first fortnight of Jan., and the second fortnights of Apr. and Oct.). Chef Hilario Arbelaitz serves elaborate, soul-satisfying food in his family's 600-year-old farmhouse. The covered terrace is ideal in warmer months, and menus change seasonally. Try the grilled scallop with wild mushroom and celery vinaigrette in spring or roasted squab with rosemary and truffled cabbage in fall. The tasting menu is €105 without wine.

Contributed by Gabriella Ranelli de Aguirre, founder of Tenedor Tours (www.tenedortours.com) and a food and wine specialist who has been based in San Sebastián since 1989.

PAÍS VASCO

Iombi (Pl. Guipúzcoa 15, tel. 94/342-8423, 9 A.M.–9 P.M. Tues.–Sun., closed Mon., €15) offers modern dishes—including lots of large-enough-to-share salads—at reasonable prices. The hearty *menú del día* is a bargain at €11. Another bonus is that the kitchen stays open all day. In the Parte Vieja, tuck into tasty salads and chunky sandwiches at the young and funky **Barbakana** (C/ San Jerónimo 20, tel. 94/342-1127, 11:30 A.M.–4:30 P.M. and 7:30–11 P.M. daily, €15). Across the bridge in Gros, **Zurriola Marítimo** (Po. Zurriola 41, tel. 94/329-7853, 10 A.M.–2 A.M. daily, €20) offers upscale basics from *pintxos* to sandwiches in a soaring glass and steel loft. The best feature of the building is the glass wall overlooking the rolling waves of the Cantabrian Sea. If you are out late at night and realize the *pintxos* you devoured hours early have now left you hungry, head to **Va Bene** (Boulevard 14, tel. 94/342-2416, 11 A.M.–1A.M. daily) for decent burgers served late.

Gourmet

San Sebastián is home to some of the most revered restaurants in the world and boasts more Michelin stars than any other city of its size in the world. In case you don't know Michelin, it rates the world's top restaurants with stars for quality. Tiny San Sebastián boasts 14 stars among a handful of places that serve as culinary meccas for the world's most discriminating palates. Reservations and a wad of cash are recommended. (See sidebar, *Dining with the Stars*.)

Local Cuisine

Traditional Basque food relies heavily on bounties from the sea and San Sebastián has several great places to try a Basque take on seafood. San Sebastián's restaurants generally follow standard Spanish dining hours from 1:30–4 P.M. and 8:30–11 P.M. Most establishments also close either one or two days per week as noted in the listings below.

Since 1947, the simple dining room of **Juanito Kojua** (C/ Puerto 14, tel. 94/342-0180, closed Sun. P.M. and Mon., €35) has been serving fish and shellfish according to traditional Basque recipes. Try their *bacalao al pilpil,* a classic cod dish. For more seafood options, head to Paseo del Muelle. The most highly rated restaurant along this stretch is **La Rampa** (Po. Muelle 26, tel. 94/342-1652, closed Tues. and Wed., €35), next to the aquarium. It offers a sophisticated dining room with rustic touches. If the weather is nice, sit on the terrace overlooking the port. The other restaurants on the port are just a smidgen cheaper, but also offer impeccably fresh fish and seafood.

For insight into how one of the world's top chefs, Martín Berasategui, got his start, try ◖ **Bodegón Alejandro** (C/ Fermín Cabeltón 4, tel. 94/342-7158, closed Sun. P.M. and Mon., €40, reservations required), the traditional Basque restaurant owned by his family. The menu is always set for the day and includes a starter, entrée, and dessert. Dishes might include a local favorite of scrambled eggs with cod and raisins, grilled turbot with a spicy garlic sauce, or roasted pork in wine. For a more affordable taste of tradition, head over to Gros and the charming little **Cascanueces** (Po. Colón 46, tel. 94/327-8839, €25) for classics like hake stuffed with crab and mushrooms and warm seafood salad. The weekday menu is just €11.

Another Basque product is *sidra,* naturally fermented cider. (See sidebar, Sidra, Sidrerías, y Chigres, *Oh My!,* in the *Cantabria and Asturias* chapter.) Though most of the cider houses lie a good 20 minutes by cab out of the center (ask your hotel if they can arrange a visit), there are a couple rowdy *sidrerías (sagardotegia* in Basque) right in town. They all feature rustic decor, long wooden tables, and a set menu that includes scrambled eggs with cod, a green salad, a T-bone steak, and cheese and quince jelly for dessert. Of course, all the cider you can drink is included. In the Parte Vieja, try **Sidrería Donostiarra** (C/ Embeltran 5, 94/342-0421, www.sidreriadonostiarra.net, closed Sun. P.M. and Mon., €27). In the center, try **El Aurrera** (C/ Urbieta 12, tel. 94/342-3182, closed Sun. P.M., €19–24).

Pintxos

San Sebastián elevates the *pintxo* (see sidebar, *Art of Food: A* Pintxo *Primer)* to nearly sacred status. There are several annual *pintxo* competitions and a year-round rivalry between bars trying to outdo each other with their creativity. The best places to *txiquiteo* (eat *pintxos* in Basque) are Parte Vieja and Gros. Always ask for the specialty of the house, and of course, do like the locals and keep moving—one pinxto, one drink, one bar. Hours are usually 11 A.M.–3 P.M. and 8–11 P.M., and remember that the good stuff will be gone by 10 P.M., so go early.

In the Parte Vieja, try award-winning **Bar Txeptxa** (C/ Pescadería 5, closed Mon.) for *anchoas* (anchovies). Nothing like the salty slivers tossed onto American pizzas, these are plump, white, impeccably fresh fish bursting with the crisp taste of the sea. Txeptxa prepares them 14 ways, but the best is *jardinera* in a tangy salsa of tomato, peppers, onions, and vinegar. Note the worldwide press coverage on the walls. Keep up the seafood theme at **Bar Goiz Argi** (C/ Fermín Calbetón 4, tel. 94/342-5204, closed Mon.) for amazing *brocheta de gambas* (shrimp kebobs). For the freshest in produce, head to **Ganbara** (C/ San Jerónimo 21, tel. 94/342-2575). Choose any of the *pintxos* on the bar, but for the house specialty, *setas silvestres* (wild mushrooms), you'll have to order a *ración* (€14–22). The tiny 【 **La Cuchara de San Telmo** (C/ 31 de Agosto 28, tel. 94/342-0840, closed Mon.) has been making waves among locals and foodies since it opened a few years back. Unlike other bars, nothing is on the counters—everything is prepared to order by two young chefs who trained under culinary legend Ferran Adrià. The house specialty is melt-in-the-mouth foie gras served with apple compote. Their small dab of risotto with blue cheese is heavenly. Cuchara can be tricky to find as it is actually on an alley behind 31 de Agosto. Look for the tables next to the church. Another haute spot is **Gandaria** (C/ 31 de Agosto 23), which specializes in meat treats such as *solomillo con pimientos* (filet with green peppers).

Across the river in Gros is perhaps the most famous gourmet *pintxo* bar in San Sebastián. 【 **Aloña Berri** (C/ Bermingham 24, tel. 94/329-0818, closed Mon.) has won numerous awards and—even more important in food-obsessed San Sebastián—the admiration of the region's top chefs. The self-taught owner José Ramón Elizonda (Joserra to his friends) grew up in his parents' *pintxo* bar and dedicated himself to the art of *alta cocina en miniatura* (miniature haute cuisine) from a young age. His award-winning *equilibrio de mar* is a work of art which must be eaten as follows: savor the one-inch square of sea-flavored rice, let the sugar crystal snowflake studded with pink peppercorns melt on your tongue, eat the squid stuffed with seafood, drink the seafood stock with martini. It is a surreal experience. Though the rule is to always keep moving during your *pintxo* tour, this is one place you may want to linger. In fact there is a *menú degustación* (tasting menu) of nine of these lovely creations, plus dessert, for just €29. A few blocks away, **El Lagar** (C/ Zabaleta 55, tel. 94/332-0329) is a sleek contrast to the traditional bars that flood the Parte Vieja. It is also one of the few to specialize in wines by the glass. Their top *pintxo* is *huevos estrellados*, a perfectly fried egg served atop a tiny stew of potatoes and wild mushrooms. Also in this part of town, don't miss the local favorite **Bergara**

(C/ General Artetxe 8), a rustic bar with wood bench seating. They recently won an award for "best *pintxo* bar" in Guipúzcoa. Try *rape con puerros* (monkfish with a leek sauce) or *delicias de pato con calvados* (duck with pear liqueur).

INFORMATION AND SERVICES

The best place to stock up on information about San Sebastián and surrounding villages is the **regional tourist office** (C/ Reina Regente 3, tel. 94/348-1166, 9 A.M.–1:30 P.M. and 3:30–7 P.M. Mon.–Sat., 10 A.M.–2 P.M. Sun.). Located at the end of the Boulevard, about a block off the river, the office has friendly English-speaking staff, loads of maps and magazines, and bus schedules for all the surrounding villages. Their comprehensive English website (www.sansebastianturismo.com) is also a great resource. Another excellent source of local information is **Enjoy SS** (Kursaal Center, tel. 94/300-5060), a tourist initiative with the philosophy of promoting independent travel. Though their focus tends to be on younger travelers, their green tourist map is a comprehensive and it is also the only one in town to feature the Parte Vieja blown up so you can actually see the streets.

If you need to check email, in the Parte Vieja head to **Donosti-NET** (C/ Narrika 3, tel. 94/342-9497, 9 A.M.–11 P.M. daily), a friendly cybercafé with coffee. At **Cibernet World** (C/ Aldamar, 3, tel. 94/342-0651) you can also store your luggage for a reasonable fee. In Gros, fronting the Zurriola beach, **Insert Coin** (C/ Ramón y Cajal 1, tel. 94/327-4571, 10 A.M.–10 P.M. daily) has several computers as well as a convenience store.

GETTING THERE
Air

There are daily flights into San Sebastián from most major Spanish cities. The airport is in Hondarribia (Fuenterrabía in Spanish), about 20 kilometers (13 miles) outside of the city. Get into town via the green Interbus buses. They drop off in Plaza de Gipuzkoa. The ride takes about 40 minutes and costs €1.50.

PAÍS VASCO

Bring change. If you prefer a taxi, it will run about €24. International flights land in Biarritz, just over the border in France. There are buses and trains into San Sebastián, but you'll have to take a taxi to the stations (the train station is closer and thus cheaper). The **Pesa bus company** (tel. 90/210-1210) departs every half-hour for San Sebastián and leaves you in Plaza Pío XII. The train is called Topo and run by Euskotren (www.euskotren.es).

Train

If traveling by train, you'll arrive at the Renfe **Estación del Norte** (Po. Francia, tel. 90/224-0202). You'll exit at the river near the Puente María Cristina. There is a taxi stand and you can get most anyplace in town for under €8. Local buses run nearby as well, but check with your hotel to which you should catch. Trains from France and towns near the French border land at the **Amara Euskotren stop** (Pl. Easo 9, tel. 90/254-3210), about a 15-minute walk to the center of town. If you have luggage, do your back a favor and grab a taxi, rides should be less than €10.

Bus

The main bus stop in San Sebastián is at Plaza Pío XII. Bus companies including **Pesa** (serving Bilbao, Lekeitio, Vitoria, Biarritz) and **Continental** (serving Madrid and Burgos) have their offices around the corner at Avenida Sancho El Sabio. Other companies leave from smaller stops around the city. Check with the tourist office for details.

Car

San Sebastián lies on the coastal highway A-8/ E-70, a major road that is easily accessed via other highways from regions throughout Spain. Upon approaching the town, take the exit toward Amara and follow the *centro ciudad* signs into town. If your hotel doesn't provide parking, look for a "P" indicating public parking nearby.

GETTING AROUND

San Sebastián is compact and easily walkable, however if your feet need a rest, the town is ser-

viced by an excellent public bus system. The main stop is along the Boulevard. Taxis are also cheap and plentiful, though in San Sebastián the trend is to call **Radio Taxi Donosti** (tel. 94/346-4646) or head to a taxi stand, marked with a large T on tourist maps. The main taxi stand is on the Boulevard, close to the Ayuntamiento.

The city makes an excellent base for exploring the dramatic Basque coast by car. There are several reputable rental car agencies in town including **Hertz** (Av. Zubieta 5, tel. 94/346-1084) and **Avis** (C/ Triunfo 2, tel. 94/346-1556. **Europcar** (tel. 94/332-2304) has offices at the main train station.

VICINITY OF SAN SEBASTIÁN
🄲 Hondarribia

Founded in 1203, Hondarribia (Fuenterrabía in Spanish, though the Basque name is the one most commonly used) is a speck of a town surrounded by wild coasts, sheep-dotted farm land, and medieval remnants of history long gone. Words like charming, enchanting, and rustic don't even begin to capture the delights of this tiny fishing village. It deserves at least a day detour from San Sebastián. Though it is on the border with France, Hondarribia is less a border town than it is the very essence of País Vasco. The town itself is divided into two parts, with the modern new city below, and the walled, medieval village above. Head straight there, stopping at the **tourist office** (C/ Javier Ugarte 6, tel. 94/364-5458, 9 A.M.–1:30 P.M. and 4–6:30 P.M. Mon.–Fri., 10 A.M.–2 P.M. Sat., closed Sun.) on the way. Their self-guided tour in English is excellent. You enter the walled town through the 15th-century **Puerta de Santa María.** All along Calle Mayor to the Plaza de Armas you'll pass by traditional homes with their ancient coats of arms still intact. The plaza is dominated by the **Palacio de Carlos V**, first built in the 10th century and extended to its current size in the 16th. It currently houses one of Spain's most romantic paradors (state-run luxury hotels built in historic buildings). You can have a drink at the bar, but the terrace is reserved for guests only.

La Marina is Hondarribia's quaint port full of brightly colored boats. Look for **Calle San**

Pedro, lined with wood-beamed Basque houses with flower-laden iron balconies and red, blue, and green shutters.

If you decide to stay the night and want to do it in style, head directly to the Palacio Carlos V **Parador de Turismo** (Pl. Armas 14, tel. 94/364-5500, hondarribia@parador.es, www.parador.es, €190). The infamous Catholic Kings Fernando and Isabel stayed within the castle's eight-foot-thick walls a few centuries back. With all the suits of armor, tapestries, and antiques about, it is easy to imagine the royal couple wandering the halls. For more modern luxury at a lower price, try the **Hotel Obispo** (Pl. Obispo 1, tel.94/364-5400, www.hotelobispo.com, €125, breakfast included) set in a sumptuously restored 15th-century bishop's mansion. Another sweet option is the charming **Hotel Palacete** (Pl. Guipuzcoa 5, tel. 94/364-0813, www.hotelpalacete.net, €75), a smartly renovated mansion in the old town. Prices don't go much lower than €60 in the high season, and the best of the lot at this price is **Pensión Txoko Goxua** (C/ Murrua 22, tel. 94/364-4658, www.txoko goxoa.com, €60), on the edge of the walled town; it features simply decorated rooms in an inn run by an extraordinarily friendly family.

As in all of País Vasco, there are excellent dining opportunities throughout Hondarribia. Any of the bars along Calle San Pedro make excellent *pintxos* stops and many offer good value *menú del día*. Try **Gran Sol** (C/ San Pedro 65, tel. 94/364-2701) run by two up-and-coming chefs who regularly score awards for their innovative *pintxos*. A local favorite is **Hermandad de Pescadores** (C/ Zuloaga 12, 94/364-2738), where mounds of impeccably fresh seafood are served to boisterous families squeezed in at wooden communal tables. Reservations on weekends are recommended. If you are craving gourmet, head to **Alameda** (C/ Alameda 1, tel. 94/364-2789, www.rest alameda.com, closed Sun. P.M. and Mon., €75), which has one of the most exciting young chefs working in new Basque cuisine, Gorka Txapartegi. The menu is varied according to seasonal specialties and the chef's whim. Your best bet is one of the tasting menus that range €39–62.

Get to Hondarribia by **Interbus** (tel. 94/364-1302), which leaves every 20–30 minutes from Plaza Gipuzkoa, takes 40 minutes, and costs €1.50. If driving, take the A-8 or the N-1 in the direction of Irun. Exit when you see signs for Hondarribia/Fuenterrabía.

Pasai Donibane

An excellent morning trip from San Sebastián is the tiny port town of Pasai Donibane (Pasajes San Juan in Spanish). Though less charming than Hondarribia, it is a whole lot less touristed and makes for a great escape off the beaten path. A good idea would be to arrive around 1 P.M., see the city, and settle in for a luscious seafood lunch before heading back to San Sebastián. The old medieval town consists of one cobblestone, narrow street snaking along the River Oiartzun and a busy harbor lined with colorful boats. Larger ships pass through regularly on their way out to the Gulf of Biscay. The street, **Calle San Juan,** goes under ancient houses built into the cliff walls above and over bayside houses that seem to rise right from the water. In 1846, Victor Hugo lived at number 63. The building now holds the **tourist office** and a pokey costume museum. Look for the picturesque plaza about midway down the street, lined with colorful buildings draped in laundry. Here you can catch the green boat across the river to Pasajes San Pedro.

There are several restaurants, all offering seafood and local Basque dishes. The best is **Casa Cámara** (tel. 94/352-3699, closed Sun. P.M. and Mon., €35) an elegant dining room surrounded by windows overlooking the bay. Also try the charming **Mirones** (tel. 94/351-9271, closed Wed., €25), a rustic, florally decorated room with a great enclosed porch. For a cheap eat, **Ongi Etorri** (tel. 94/352-4588, closed Thurs., €12) can't be beat for their shrimp and calamari.

To get there by from San Sebastián catch the green H1 **bus** from Plaza Gipuzkoa. It takes about 15 minutes and costs €1. Be sure and ask the bus driver to advise you of the stop. At the bus stop, make a U-turn and walk downhill towards the water. Continue straight until you reach the old town. The town is basically

PAÍS VASCO

© CANDY LEE LABALLE

waterfront houses in the tiny fishing village of Pasai Donibane

a suburb of San Sebastián. Unless you are continuing on to Hondarribia by car, you should stick to public transport.

Zarautz

The long beach of Zarautz, lapped by a constant roll of frothy waves, has made this sleeping fishing town an international surfing destination. Each year it hosts world-class surfing contests. One of Spain's top board makers, **Pukas Surf** (C/ Nafarroa 4, tel. 94/383-5821), is based here and offers rentals and lessons as well as a full line of surf gear and supplies. Even if you don't surf, the 2.4-kilometer-long (1.5-mile-long) beach lined with a lovely modern promenade is worth a day trip. But beware, it packs out on weekends with hordes of local families. There is not much to see in the old town other than a few churches and lovely plazas. For complete details, as well as up-to-date surf information, contact the ultra-friendly folks at the **tourist office** (C/ Nafarroa Kale, 3 tel. 94/383-0990, www.turismozarautz.com).

If you are a foodie, you can't miss the namesake restaurant of Spain's first celebrity chef, **Karlos Arguiñano** (C/ Mendilauta 13, tel. 94/313-0000, www.hotelka.com, €60). You can enjoy cutting-edge Basque cuisine in the elegant inner dining room or more traditional (and less expensive) fare in the dining room that looks out on the sea. The complex also houses a cozy four-star hotel with spectacular views. Doubles run about €160 but check the website for cut-rate dining/sleeping deals. For cheaper sleeps, try the charming **Txiki Polit Guest House** (Plaza Musika, s/n, tel. 94/383-5357, www.txikipolit.com, €55). It also boasts a lively bar with a terrace.

Get to Zarautz via the **Euskotren** from the Amara station in San Sebastián. If you are driving, take A-8 or N-634 heading towards Bilbao.

Getaria

The medieval fishing village of Getaria oozes provincial Basque charm. Surrounding by lush fertile hillsides, it is also a major producer of *txakoli* (pronounced chak-o-LEE), the fizzy white wine ubiquitous in País Vasco. It is celebrated here with a raucous festival the first week in August. Getaria is a picturesque blanket of medieval homes hugging the steep slope down to the bay. Look for the 15th-century **Iglesia San Salvador,** which houses a model ship and the grave of native son Sebastián de Elkano, the first sailor to go around the world. The huge monument to him in the middle of town is a lively meeting point. Getaria was also the birthplace of the world famous fashion designer Cristóbal Balenciaga and the intriguing **Museo Balenciaga** (Parque Aldamar 3, tel. 94/300-4777) is dedicated to his designs. Be sure to walk along the wharf to the *ratón,* a mouse-shaped peninsula that ends at the mount of San Antón. The views from the top are stunning. And if you are in need of a bit of sand and surf,

the town also boasts two decent beaches. The **tourist office** (Parque Aldamar 2, tel 94/314-0957) is small and only open in the summer.

Getaria has less than a dozen places to stay and nothing very high-end. Try the basic **San Prudencio** (Barrio San Prudencio 4, tel. 94/314-0411, €36). The **Getariano** (C/ Herrerieta 3, tel. 94/314-0567, €54) is a bit more upscale. For some of the best grilled fish you'll eat in your life, head to **Elkano** (C/ Herrerieta 2, tel. 94/314-0614, €60). They also offer innovative takes on traditional Basque cuisine. For cheaper eats, try the laidback bar/restaurant **San Anton** (C/ Puerto 9, tel. 94/314-0324, €20).

Getting to Getaria is most convenient from San Sebastián by **Euskotren** leaving from the Amara station. The ride is just under an hour. If driving, follow N-634 along the coast.

Bilbao

Nestled in the deep folds of the coastal hills of the País Vasco and hugging the undulating banks of the River Nervión as it spills out into the coast's deepest estuary, Bilbao (Bilbo in Basque) has long benefited from this location. Founded in 1300 by the Lord of Vizcaya, Diego López de Haro, the town quickly became an important trading port, shipping iron and wool to Northern Europe. By the 1800s the city was one of Spain's wealthiest, fueled by a network of iron mines and its excellent port. The industrialization continued through the Franco regime with many car-manufacturing plants settling in the region. The prosperity was great, but so was the damage to the city. Bilbao soon became known as the ugly stepsister to San Sebastián's fairy-tale beauty. The surrounding mountains captured the vile exhaust from the hundreds of factories and plants, and the industrious city went about its business under a gloomy cloud of pollution and indifference.

All that changed with the opening of the Guggenheim Museum in 1997. The Frank Gehry–designed building became an instant

cultural landmark and drew over 1.5 million visitors its first year. Inspired by a gust of creativity, commerce, and bold confidence, the city turned its hardworking attitude towards cleaning up Bilbao and presenting a glowing face to the world. The gritty ports along the river were converted into parks, housing, restaurants, and cultural centers. International architects were invited to join Gehry in creating public works. Top British architect Norman Foster designed the city's subway system. Innovative Spanish architect Santiago Calatrava built a new airport and a footbridge across the river. The city polished up its charming Casco Viejo (old city center) and connected it to the Guggenheim with a sleek new tram system. Meanwhile, hoteliers decided to build showcase designer hotels here, including the Miró, designed by fashion maverick Antonio Miró, and the Gran Domine, which consistently rates as one of the top hotels in the world. At the same time, Basque cuisine was ascending to the top of gastronomy ratings and foodies worldwide were aiming their forks at local tables.

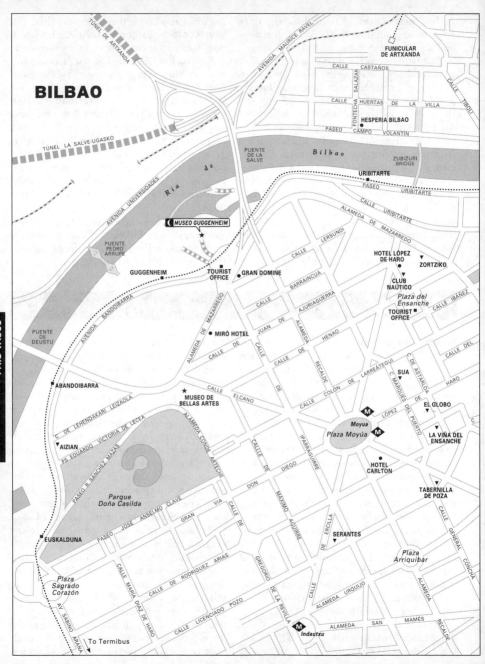

PAÍS VASCO

BILBAO

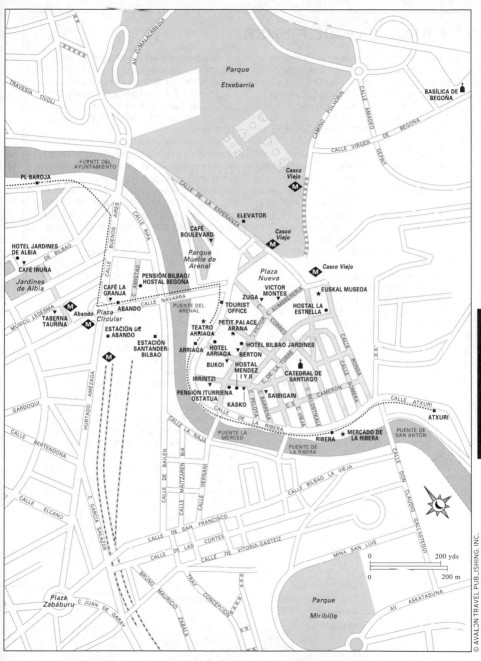

PAÍS VASCO

A BASIC BASQUE PRIMER

Though the País Vasco is an autonomous region within Spain, culturally, historically, and linguistically, it is called *Euskadi* (collection of Basques) and includes the Spanish provinces of País Vasco (Vizcaya, Guipúzcoa, and Álava) plus northern Navarra. These Spanish Basque lands are part of a greater territory called *Euskal Herria*, which includes three regions in France: Zuberoa (Soule in French), Behe Nafarroa (Basse-Navarre), and Lapurdi (Labourd). Euskal Herria is located in the Western Pyrenees and bordered by the Cantabrian Sea. The lush valleys and wildly indented coastlines of this region comprise some of the most spectacular landscapes in Europe. They are also some of the most rugged, a fact that has kept the Basques geographically isolated for millennia.

Archaeology suggests the Basque lands have been inhabited since the late Paleolithic era – 10,000–40,000 years ago. Research into morphology further suggests that current Basques are descended from the peoples who lived during that time and some have proposed that modern Basques descend directly from Cro-Magnon man. How the ancient Basques got into this region is unknown, but their presence as distinctive tribal cultures was documented by the Romans. Though the Romans set up the city of Pompaelo in the Basque settlement of Iruña (present-day Pamplona), they were not able to subjugate the Basque tribes. The Basques later fought off the Visigoths and the Moors, keeping their heritage relatively free from the influence of invading cultures. Part of their isolationist success came about simply because their lands were not the easiest to negotiate. Only in the 20th century did routes through the Basque regions of the Pyrenees become passable.

One influence that did infiltrate the Basque culture was Christianity, arriving with the Visigoths in the 3rd or 4th century. By the Middle Ages, the Basques were devoutly Christian and one of Christianity's most venerated figures, Iñigo de Loyola, the founder of the Jesuits, was Basque.

During the Spanish Reconquista, the Basques were less a political entity than a confederacy of aligned tribes, often under control of other groups including the Franks in the 8th and 9th centuries and the Kingdom of Navarra from the 10th century onwards. As the various kingdoms were consolidated into one nation, the Basque lands fell under the command of the Kingdom of Castile and, eventually, Spain. During this time, the Basques were granted *fueros*, or laws that allowed for a strong measure of autonomy. The origins of this sovereignty date to a 1513 statute enacted by Fernando I of Aragón (one half of the power couple Isabel and Fernando, the Catholic Kings). Subsequent kings reinforced and ratified this statute that today is the basis for Basque claims to autonomy. The system of self-rule under the Spanish king was respected throughout Hapsburg rule often as a means of keeping the fractious Basques in line and ensuring their loyalty to the Spanish nation overall. In the Middle Ages, the Basques proved themselves to be talented and fearless sailors. Much of the crew for Columbus's voyage to the New World was composed of Basque sailors. Centuries later, the País Vasco was one of the first to embrace the industrial revolution particularly in the prosperous town of Bilbao.

By the 19th century, many of the *fuero* rights were being chipped away by the central government and a desire for Basque autonomy was simmering. This boiled over into full-fledged nationalist sentiment in the late 19th century thanks in great part to Basque scholar Sabino de Arana y Goiri. Born in Bilbao, he was a vehement defender of Basque culture and wrote several influential books and articles claiming that the Basques were a unique race and had sole rights to the original Basque lands. In 1894, he founded the first Basque nationalist political party, called Eusko Alderdi Jeltzalea (EAJ) in Basque and Partido Nacionalista Vasco (PNV) in Castilian Spanish.

In 1936, the Spanish republic officially granted autonomy to a Basque region that included the provinces of Vizcaya and Guipúzcoa (Álava and Navarra declined participation). The new Basque government adopted their own flag and installed an army. Of course, by this time, the Civil War had begun. The Basques supported the Republican forces because the Republicans supported regional autonomy. Franco's Nationalist forces retaliated with vicious attacks on Basque lands including the infamous attack on the town of Guernica in April of 1937, captured poignantly by Picasso in his painting of the same name. Following Franco's victory, Basque culture and language – along with other regional languages – were oppressed. Legitimate political entities such as the PNV continued to operate, however within the terms of Franco's regime.

ETA

In 1959, Euskadi Ta Askatasuna (ETA, Basque Homeland and Freedom) was formed by radicals who felt the PNV was too moderate in its opposition to Franco. Their goal was to create an independent Basque country including both Spanish and French Basque lands. Their means of achieving this goal have included kidnappings, murders, and bombings. Since ETA's founding, over 900 people have been killed by the group – including dozens of innocent civilians. Both the European Union and the United States have labeled ETA a terrorist group – a feeling also held by many Spaniards. In the Basque country itself, there are deep divisions over ETA and its political wing Batasuna. It is a division that has torn apart communities and instilled a deep sense of distrust and fear in the region.

In 2006, ETA declared a ceasefire for the first time in its history. The socialist-led government (PSOE) responded cautiously with an attempt at creating a dialogue. Nonetheless, in December 2006, ETA bombed a parking lot at an airport in Madrid. Two people were killed.

TOURISTS IN PAÍS VASCO

ETA and Basque separatism have not affected tourists. On the contrary, the Basque people are warmly receptive and open to visitors. A tourist will have no problems enjoying the wonderful landscape, food, and cities of País Vasco. Though you will hear Basque spoken and see it written, most locals will speak Castilian Spanish, particularly in big cities and in popular tourist areas such as the wine region of Rioja Alavesa and the coastal resort towns. However, you may have more difficulty off the beaten path in remote, interior towns.

Do keep in mind that ETA and Basque nationalism are very volatile subjects. Families, neighbors, and friends have been sharply divided on this difficult matter for over five decades. It is unwise for anyone, including a tourist, to speak about it casually. Respect the Basque people and enjoy your vacation in the País Vasco by practicing a don't-ask-don't-tell policy.

PAÍS VASCO

Bilbao was ready, serving up a delicious roster of internationally renowned chefs and world-class restaurants.

Though it is still the Guggenheim that draws the masses, the savvy visitor will find a lot more to see. The sixth-largest city in Spain and capital of the Vizcaya (Bizkaia in Basque) region of País Vasco, bustling Bilbao is a cosmopolitan retreat well on its way to becoming one of Europe's greatest comeback cities. Go and be a part of it. Just not on Mondays when the Guggenheim is closed. In July and August, the museum opens up on Monday, but most other sights, as well as many restaurants, remain closed. Also, come prepared for rain with an umbrella and waterproof shoes. Bilbao gets as much rain as Seattle.

SIGHTS
◖ Museo Guggenheim

Called *el Goog* by the locals, the Museo Guggenheim (Av. Abandoibarra Et 2, tel. 94/435-9080, informacion@guggenheim-bilbao.es, www.guggenheim-bilbao.es, 10 A.M.–8 P.M. Tues.–Sun., closed Mon. except in July and Aug., €10–13, under 12 free) has single-handedly changed the face—and fate—of Bilbao. Designed by famed North American architect Frank Gehry, the curvaceous titanium exterior has been compared to a ship, a fish, even a cauliflower. Whatever it is, it has won accolades in both the realms of architecture and art and has become one of the world's most important structures. Be sure to view it from opposite the River Nervión to get the best view and lovely photos of the building reflected in the river. Near the entrance of the museum you'll find *Puppy,* a 12-foot-high dog sculpted of greenery and flowers by the pop artist Jeff Koons. Out back, facing the river, is French artist Yves Klein's *Fire Fountain,* a series of fountains that shoot flames from a bed of water. Inside, the piece not to miss is *A Matter of Time* by American sculptor Richard Serra. A commentary on the physicality of space, the work consists of eight massive rusted steel pieces that form towering walkways, spirals, and mazes. As the viewer walks inside the pieces, perspective shifts and the result is a dizzying, unforgettable sensation of space in motion.

The bulk of the museum is given over to temporary exhibits, shows dedicated to specific artists, and retrospectives of movements. Prices to enter the museum vary depending on the current exhibits and include a very comprehensive (almost too comprehensive) audio-guide that includes interviews with the artists. **Free guided tours** are conducted daily at 11 A.M., 12:30 P.M., 4:30 P.M., and 6:30 P.M. You must sign up 30 minutes beforehand and the tour is offered in English or Spanish depending on demand. On weekends, get to the museum early or expect to wait in line up to an hour.

Getting to the museum is easy from almost anywhere in town thanks to the Euskotran tram system; just get off at the Guggenheim stop. If you are staying across the river, cross over on the **Zubizuri** footbridge, an architectural masterpiece in itself. Designed by Santiago Calatrava, it features a transparent walkway reminiscent of a fish's backbone and soaring fin-like supports. Also within walking distance is the **Funicular de Artxanda** (7:15 A.M.–10 P.M. daily, €0.80), a climbing tram on the riverbank opposite the Guggenheim. Built in 1915, it ascends 226 meters (740 feet) to provide spectacular views over Bilbao and the Guggenheim. At the top is a picnic area where locals go to sip *txakoli,* the fizzy Basque wine, at open-air bars. Reach the funicular by taking Calle Múgica y Butrón uphill.

Museo de Bellas Artes

Bilbao's fine arts museum, the Museo de Bellas Artes (Pl. Museo, 2, tel. 94/439-6060, www.museobilbao.com, 10 A.M.–8 P.M. Tues.–Sat., 10 A.M.–2 P.M. Sun., €5, Wed. free) offers a classical contrast to the Guggenheim's contemporary collection. It houses works by El Greco, Goya, and Gauguin and regularly hosts excellent temporary exhibits. It is a pleasant five-minute walk from the Guggenheim. The museum sits on the edge of the gorgeous **Doña Casilda** park, a perfect respite from a heavy day of art-seeing.

Abando

Forming the modern heart of Bilbao, the Abando district (also called Ensanche) is an elegant grid of streets built in the 19th century and criss-crossed by several diagonal boulevards. They are lined with cafés, restaurants, and shops and deserve at least a morning's worth of exploration. Orientate yourself by heading for either a plaza or a bridge. **Plaza Moyúa** sits at the center of this area and is home to the **Palacio de Chavarri,** an 1894 mansion that features several ornate balconies and windows, each different. **Plaza del Ensanche** is nothing to rave about, but it does house the main tourist office. It is also very close to a tiny jewel of a park, **Jardines Albia,** bursting with flowers and lined with benches. The busy **Plaza Circular** (called Plaza España during Franco's regime) marks the beginning of Bilbao's grandest avenue, the Gran Vía Don Diego López de Haro, **Gran Vía** for short. It is also home to the **Estación de Abando,** the main train station. Check out its lovely glass and iron gate featuring a mural of Bilbao's industrial background.

Several bridges cross the River Nervión and make lovely sights in themselves. The one you'll use most will be the **Puente del Arenal** which connects Abando with the Casco Viejo, Bilbao's oldest quarter. Just to the west of the bridge, look for the **Estación Santander-Bilbao,** built in 1898 and boasting a lovely green and blue tiled exterior and soaring ceilings. If you are coming or going to Santander, you'll depart or arrive here.

Casco Viejo

The Casco Viejo consists of a warren of narrow, cobblestone streets that form the historic heart of Bilbao. When the city was founded in 1300, it consisted of the **Siete Calles,** seven parallel streets that run down to the river and still serve as the lifeblood of this lively zone. They are teeming with boutiques, bars, and bakeries. Above, wrought-iron balconies support pots of colorful flowers. Entering the Casco Viejo by the Arenal bridge, you'll pass in front of one of Spain's best opera houses,

the narrow medieval streets of Bilbao's Casco Viejo

Teatro Arriaga, a copy of the Opera Garnier in Paris. Across from the theater is the **Muelle de Arenal,** a small riverside park that features a glorious Art Noveau pavilion in glass and steel. It hosts free classical music concerts on Sundays in warmer months. Follow Calle Correo and look for the **Plaza Nueva,** an elegant square enclosed by 19th-century buildings sitting above a lovely arcaded walkway. It boasts several of Bilbao's favorite *pintxo* bars and a colorful Sunday flea market.

A few blocks away get an crash course in Basque culture at **Euskal Museoa** (Pl. Miguel Unamuno 4, tel. 94/415-5423, 11 A.M.–5 P.M. Tues.–Sat., 11 A.M.–2 P.M. Sun., €3). Built in an old Jesuit cloister, the museum offers prehistoric and historic reflections on Basque culture. Around the back of the museum, the **Catedral de Santiago** bursts from the tiny maze of the Casco Viejo with a lovely Gothic spire. Completed in the 14th and 15th centuries, the church was the center of town for centuries. Walking around the imposing gray facade, it is curious to note that the ground level of the

© CANDY LEE LABALLE

PAÍS VASCO

church houses decidedly non-denominational shops including a tobacconist and a jeweler. On the edge of the Casco Viejo, along the river, pay a morning visit to the bustling **Mercado de la Ribera.** This glass and steel market building, built in 1929, is the largest covered market in Europe. Go early to see all the action between local chefs, grandmothers with carts, and vendors.

On the opposite end of the neighborhood, just north of the Plaza Nueva, behind the Iglesia de San Nicolas, take the 24-hour, city-run elevator (€0.30) to get a lovely bird's-eye view over old Bilbao. From there, it is a five-minute walk to **Basílica de Begoña,** an imposing 16th-century church that serves as the cathedral of Bilbao and a pilgrimage point for followers of Saint Begoña, the town's patron saint.

Beaches

On a sunny summer day, do like the locals and head to the beach. You can take the metro to the Neguri stop and visit **Getxo.** Exit the metro and walk past the lovely 19th-century mansions to get to the Paseo. Follow that to the Puerto Deportivo boardwalk, which offers casual restaurants and *pintxo* bars, along a lovely stretch of sand. Other metro-accessible beaches are **Las Arenas** at the Algorta metro stop, and **Sopelana** at the Plentzia stop.

ENTERTAINMENT AND EVENTS
Nightlife

Nightlife in Bilbao can be divided into under-25 and over-25. The younger set concentrates in the Casco Viejo, especially in the dozens of bars that line Calle Barrencalle Barrena. It stays rowdy until around 3 A.M. Join the fun at either **El Surtidor** (No. 12) or **El Último Tranvía** (No. 10), two of the most typical bars of this area, featuring cheap cocktails and really loud Spanish electronic music called *bakalao*. For something more sophisticated head out of the old town. Along Alameda de Mazarredo there is a cluster of trendy bars offering a mix of cool cocktails and hip beats. Try **Miró Bar** (No. 77) in the hotel of the same name for low-key acid jazz.

Class (No. 20) is a den of, well, class that goes from breakfast to nightcaps in a single leap. For a big disco experience, head to **Loft** (C/ Alameda Urquijo 34), a three-story mega-club with theme nights. For hard house and techno, try **Titanio Club** (C/ Alameda Rekalde 18).

Festivals and Events

Bilbao shakes off its reserved airs and gets downright crazy during **Semana Grande** (Aste Nagusia in Basque), a two-week-long celebration around August 15. There are daily concerts from traditional Basque tunes to classical to techno. The Abando's major plazas and the Casco Viejo turn into massive outdoor parties complete with food booths, games, dancing, and fireworks displays. The fun starts up around 10 P.M. and continues until 6 A.M. Meanwhile, **Herri Kilorak** takes place. These traditional rural sports competitions include events like chopping wood, tossing bales of hay, and arm wrestling. However, the most popular of the competitors are the stone lifters. Dressed in leather padding, Amazon-sized strongmen lift stones weighing 90–275 kilograms (200–600 pounds). In some cases they just lift them to their shoulders, in others they actually roll the stone over the back of their neck. Ouch!

In November, things take a lighter turn when puppets take over during the **International Puppet Festival.** Later that month, indie film buffs descend on the city for the **International Documentary and Film Festival.**

ACCOMMODATIONS
Under €50

Your cheapest housing in Bilbao will be found scattered throughout the Casco Viejo. **Hostal La Estrella** (C/ María Muñoz 6, tel. 94/416-4066, www.hostallaestrella.com, €48) features very basic rooms at rock-bottom prices. The bar downstairs can get lively and offers a cheap continental breakfast. **Mendez I y II** (C/ Santa María 13, tel. 94/416-0364, www.pension mendez.com, €38–50) is another basic cheap sleep in the Casco Viejo. Mendez I has shared baths and lower prices. The quirky **Hostal Begoña** (C/ Amistad-Adiskidetasun 2, tel.

94/423-0134, www.hostalbegona.com, €49), Just across the river from the Teatro Arriaga, features colorful rooms and an accommodating staff. Just upstairs is **Pensión Bilbao** (C/ Amistad-Adiskidetasun 2, tel. 94/424-6943, www.pensionbilbao.com, €50), which is spotless but a little lacking in the charm department.

€50-100

Iturriena Ostatua (C/ Santa María 14, tel. 94/416-1500, €70) offers the most charm for your dollar in Bilbao. Full of rustic touches like exposed beam ceilings, lace curtains, flower-laden balconies, antique-filled hallways, and deeply colored walls, this cheap charmer feels like an exclusive inn. The staff contribute to that impression with non-flagging smiles and helpful advice. For something a bit slicker, try **Bilbao Jardines** (C/ Jardines 9, tel. 94.479-4210, www.hotelbilbaojardines.com, €70), a new hotel with modernist aspirations at two-star prices. Rooms are light, airy, and very spacious, if a bit drably decorated. Wi-Fi is free, but sketchy on the 2nd and 4th floors. Staff is ultra-friendly and the location just a block from the Arriaga Euskotran stop, is ideal. Also in the Casco Viejo is the cheap and cheerful **Hotel Arriaga** (C/ Ribera 3, tel. 94/479-0001, info@hotelarriaga.org, www.hotelarriaga.org, €60), a plant- and antique-filled hotel across from the Teatro Arriaga. It has an elevator, a parking garage (for a fee), and Wi-Fi. A few doors down, the **Petit Palace Arana** (C/ Bidebarrieta 2, tel. 94/415-6411, arana@hthoteles.com, www.hthoteles.com, €95) offers all the modern amenities expected from the High Tech chain, including contemporary furnishings, hydro-jet showers, and Wi-Fi.

Over €100

Most of the top-end hotels are clustered across the river from the Guggenheim or in the Abando. The best of the lot is **Miró Hotel** (Alameda Mazarredo 77, tel. 94/661-1880, info@mirohotelbilbao.com, www.mirohotelbilbao.com, €135) designed by Spanish fashion legend Antonio Miró. This is the kind of place that puts the "ooh" in boutique—all sleek and modern but with personal touches like fresh flowers, gourmet cookies left bedside, and a decadent basement whirlpool and steam room. Most rooms have amazing views over the Guggenheim. Competing for the title of coolest hotel is the extravagant **Gran Domine** (C/ Alameda Mazarredo 61, tel. 94/425-3300, www.granhoteldominebilbao.com, €180). From the 75-foot stone and glass sculpture towering in the atrium to the spacious stone bathrooms to the spectacular views from the rooftop terrace where breakfast is served, you know you are somewhere special every moment you spend in this hotel. The in-house bar, Splash and Crash, makes some of the best (and most expensive) cocktails in town. Another den of modernity is **Hesperia Bilbao** (C/ Campo Volatín 28, tel. 94/405-1100, hotel@hesperia-bilbao.com, www.hesperia-bilbao.com, €100), which is unmissable with its rainbow of colored glass balconies overlooking the river. A €15 upgrade gets you a Guggenheim view. Service is very attentive and the glass-fronted bar, a chic respite after all-day street-stomping.

For a little less flash, head to the **Jardines de Albia** (C/ San Vicente 6, tel. 94/435-4140, jardinesalbia@husa.es, www.husa.es, €110) a very hotel-esque accommodation with comfortable, quiet rooms and a very gracious staff. Located in the Abando district, midway between the Guggenheim and the Casco Viejo, the location couldn't be better. There is also a gorgeous park across the street and the wonderful Café Iruña is on the same square. A few blocks away is the classic **Hotel Carlton** (Pl. Moyúa 2, tel. 94/416-2200, carlton@aranzazu-hotels.com, www.aranzazu-hotels.com, €150). In its heyday it was a favorite haunt of Ernest Hemingway and Ava Gardner. Today, its glamour is a bit faded and its rooms just a shade shabby. Still, the service is stellar and the old-world charm intact. The current hotel of choice for the literati and glitterati is the **Lopez de Haro** (C/ Obispo Orueta 2, tel. 94/423-5500, lh@hotellopezdeharo.com, www.hotellopezdeharo.com, €180), a luxurious five-star classically decorated in a posh country-club style.

FOOD

The Basque take their dining seriously and Bilbao is no exception. From gourmet haunts to gritty *pintxo* bars, there is more eating to be done in this small city than in many cities twice the size. For a complete overview, ask for the *Best Gastronomy Map* (www.bilbao estimula.com) at the tourist office or your hotel. It's in Spanish, but all the award-winning restaurants and *pintxo* bars are listed along with their contact information, best dish, and closing time. If you are not sure where to go, pull up at a bar somewhere, whip out the map, and then ask the nearest local to point out their favorites. Note that most restaurants in Bilbao stick closely to standard Spanish dining hours (1:30–4 P.M. and 8–11 P.M. daily) and close one day a week, usually on Monday.

Cafés and Desserts

Bilbao is home to a trio of gorgeous turn-of-the-20th-century cafés that multitask as breakfast stops, lunch rooms, and *pintxo* bars. Since 1903, **Café Iruña** (Jardines de Albia, s/n, tel. 94/423-7021) has drawn a dedicated local crowd as well as lots of very happy tourists. The front area is a monument of Andalusian tiles and great *pintxos.* Try the *pincho moruno,* a kebob of pork marinated in Moroccan spices. The back dining room looks like an extension of the Alhambra in Granada, full of Moorish architectural touches, gorgeous tile work, and an intricately carved ceiling. The delicious *menú del día* is a great bargain at €13. During warmer months, the café sets out tables in the lovely tree-lined plaza, Jardines de Albia, just in front. Opened in 1926, **La Granja** (Pl. Circular 3, tel. 94/423-0813) is a favorite meeting spot for locals. It offers continental breakfasts, sandwiches, and decent *pintxos* throughout the day. Across from the Teatro Arriaga, **Café Boulevard** (C/ Arenal, 3, tel. 94/415-3128), which opened its doors in 1871, has a lovely copper-colored carved ceiling. It is a great place to breakfast if you are staying in the Casco Viejo. For more information on all three cafés, see www.cafesdebilbao.net.

Gourmet

Bilbao is right up there with San Sebastián in terms of gastronomic excellence and one of the best restaurants can be found right at the city's most popular sight. Under the direction of Spanish super chef, Martín Berasategui, the **Restaurant Guggenheim Bilbao** (tel. 94/423-9333, www.martinberasategui.com, 1:30–3:30 P.M. and 9–10:30 P.M. Wed.–Sun., 1:30–3:30 P.M. Tues., closed Mon., €60, reservations required). The food is as exciting as the building itself, and with tasting menus starting at just €18, it is much more affordable than Berastegui's namesake restaurant outside of San Sebastián. The menu changes seasonally and might include dishes like roasted vine tomatoes stuffed with black risotto, fresh oysters with crunchy cherries, or vacuum-cooked lamb in a sherry broth laced with candied lemon. The most famous of Bilbao's gourmet temples is **Zortziko** (Alameda de Mazarredo 17, tel. 94/423-9743, www.zortziko.es, €80, reservations required), led by chef Daniel Garcia, a major player in the world of New Basque Cuisine. Service is impeccable, the French Empire–style dining room is serene, and the cutting-edge food is simply stunning. The menu changes seasonally, but recent dishes included cod with a gelatin of peppers, rabbit stuffed with dates, and scallops on a bed of tomato carpaccio. The best bet is the chef's tasting menu.

The hottest young chef in town is José Miguel Olazabalaga and his restaurant **Aizian** (Av. Lehendakari Leizaola 29, 94/428-0039, www.restaurante-aizian.com, closed Sun., €65) draws foodies from around the world to its striking wood-striped dining room. You might start with fresh anchovy lasagna with black olives and yogurt ice cream, segue into monkfish wrapped in bacon with tomato jam or veal with candied black olives and chestnuts, and then finish up with a dessert of strawberry soup with a wine brioche.

If you want gourmet at backpacker prices, head to Abando and the darling of young movers and shakers, **Sua** (C/ Marqués del Puerto 4, tel. 94/423-2292, 1:30–4 P.M. and 9–11 P.M. Tues.–Sat., 1:30–4 P.M. Mon., closed Sun.).

The brainchild of one of Spain's foremost chefs, Aitor Elizegui, this red-and-black bistro serves creative menus based on cooking temperatures. The different dishes feature Asian, North American, and French touches. The best value are the daily menus for €10 and €14.

Local Cuisine

The Casco Viejo is full of traditional Basque restaurants. The most fun of the lot are the cider bars, called *sagardotegia* in Basque. (See sidebar, Sidra, Sidrerías, y Chigres, *Oh My!*, in the *Cantabria and Asturias* chapter.) Try the rustic **Arriaga Asador** (C/ Santa María 13, tel. 94/416-5670, closed Mon.), where their set cider menu is €25. For a little more variety, head to the equally rustic **Saibigain** (C/ Barrencalle Barrena 16, tel. 94/415-0123), a cozy dining room with classic Basque menus starting at €18 per person.

Berton (C/ Jardines 11, tel. 94/416-7035) specializes in smoked fishes and cured meats, especially *jamón,* and is very popular with the young and hip of Bilbao. Around the corner, **Bukoi** (C/ Nueva, s/n, tel. 94/479-0093) boasts a turn-of-the-20th-century hand-cranked contraption that slices *jamón* to transparently thin, melt-in-your-mouth slices. Their *pintxos* are also wonderful, especially the deep-fried stuffed squid, *txipience*. For quirky takes on traditional ingredients, don't miss **Kasko** (C/ Santa María 16, tel. 94/410-6231, 11 A.M.– 5 P.M. Mon.–Thurs., 11 A.M.–11 P.M. Fri.– Sat., closed Sun.). It gets packed with locals at lunchtime tucking into the massive *menú del día* for just €9.50.

For high-end Basque tradition with elegance and prices to match, try **Club Náutico** (C/ Obispo Orueta 2, tel. 94/423-5500, €50), one of the top restaurants in town. During the week there is an excellent lunch menu available for €29.50 that draws a lot of serious suits. On Saturday and Sundays, there is a truly decadent lunch buffet for €35.

Pintxos

As in the rest of the País Vasco, tapas in Bilbao are called pintxos and consist of elaborate bite-sized snacks. (See sidebar, *Art of Food: A* Pintxo *Primer.*) Locals head out for *pintxos* around 9 P.M. and make the round of several bars before calling it a night. The highest concentration of *pintxo* bars is in the Casco Viejo. Hours generally run 8 P.M.–midnight, with many bars closing either Sunday or Monday.

One of the best *pintxo* bars is also the newest, **¶ Zuga** (Pl. Nueva 4, tel. 94/415-2344). In this tiny cove of modernity, right on the traditional Plaza Nueva, sample the specialty of the day—sure to be a work of art posing as food. They do a lovely foie gras served with pear puree. Also on the plaza is the world-famous **Victor Montes** (Pl. Nueva 2, tel. 94/415-1678, www.victormontesbilbao.com), a small black-and-gold, belle epoque bar/restaurant. Bartenders and waiters wear suits and the few tables fill up early with tourists. It is charming enough and worth a visit for a quick *pintxo,* but the food is wildly overpriced and not as good as what you'll find elsewhere in town. Next door, a better option is **Café Bar Bilbao** (Pl. Nueva 6, tel. 94/415-1671). Opened in 1911, this blue- and white-tiled local favorite often wins local *pintxos* competitions. Try the *bacalao al pil-pil,* a classic cod dish. For a bit of hard-core local tradition, head to **Bizkaia Bi** (Jardines 2, tel. 94/415-2308), a no-nonsense Basque bar serving basic *pintxos* like toast topped with scrambled eggs and mushrooms. A bit more upscale is the pop-art bar **Irrintzi** (C/ Santa María 8, tel. 94/4156-7616), dominated by a long bar laden with creative *pintxos.* Try *anchoas,* fresh anchovies topped with caramelized onions, or *croquetas de txipiron,* croquettes stuffed with squid.

More great *pintxos* can be found in Abando, the newer part of town. Especially along Calle Licenciado Poza, locally called "Pozas." The street is lined with *pintxo* bars, all filled with locals. Only 10 minutes walking from either the Casco Viejo or the Guggenheim, this is a very delicious detour. At **Tabernilla de Poza** (C/ Licenciado Poza 3, tel. 94/443-5009), a very traditional bar where carafes of wine are served in earthenware jugs, try anything with *bonito,* a type of tuna. **Serantes** (Licenciado Poza 16,

TRAVELER'S BASQUE

Since Franco's death and the 1981 installation of democracy, Basque culture has enjoyed a resurgence. Basque traditions have been revived including folklore, regional dances, music, and the popular sport, *pelota*, played with a ball and wooden racquet-like object. The Herri Kilorak, a series of Paul Bunyan-type events, including competitions for chopping wood, tossing bales of hay, and stone lifting, have become a regular feature of Basque society.

However, perhaps the strongest resurgence of Basque culture has been its language. The Basque tongue (called Euskara in País Vasco) is a linguistic puzzle that has challenged researchers for decades. What is known is that the language predates Indo-European tongues and has some links with ancient languages of Central Asia and pre-Arabic languages of Northern Africa. Because of the millennia-long isolation of the Basques in their remote valleys, the language has retained its own structure and phonology – unique in all the world. Outlawed under Franco, it has come back with a vengeance. It is the official co-language (with Castilian Spanish) of the País Vasco and there are an estimated million people who currently speak it.

The traveler will mainly encounter Basque on street signs, maps, and menus. Again, unless you are really off the beaten path, locals will usually speak Spanish, English, and/or French, so you should have no linguistic barriers to your pursuit of a Basque good time. The following brief glossary covers the words you'll most likely encounter. There is no need to memorize words or phrases; the Basque people are generous and kind enough to not expect a tourist to speak their native tongue. However, taking the time to learn and use simple phrases such as *Kaixo!* (hello, pronounced KAI-sho), *Agur!* (goodbye, ah-GOOR), and *Eskerrik Asko* (thank you, es-kay-REEK as-KOH) is a much-appreciated gesture of respect and friendliness.

CITY PLACE NAMES (SPANISH LISTED FIRST)

Álava	Araba
Bilbao	Bilbo
Guernica	Gernika
Guipúzcoa	Gipuzkoa
Fuenterrabía	Hondarribia
Nafarroa	Navarra
Pamplona	Iruña
San Sebastián	Donostia
Vitoria	Gaxteiz
Vizcaya	Bizkaia

COMMON WORDS

Airport	Aireportua
Bathroom	Komunak
Beach	Hondartza
Caution	Kontuzi
City Center	Erdialdea
Hotel	Hotela
Main Street	Kale Nagusia
Parking	Aparkalekua
Restaurant	Jatetxea
Street	Kalea
Tourist Office	Turismo Bulegoa
Welcome	Ongi etorri

tel. 94/421-2129) has excellent seafood tapas as well as a variety of *tortillas*. There is also a very highly regarded restaurant attached. By Plaza Circular, head to **Taberna Taurina** (C/ Ledesma 5, tel. 94/424-1381), a bullfighting bar with delicious chorizo *pintxos*. Also be on the look out for Calle Diputación, a pedestrian street bisecting the Gran Vía. It is filled with sidewalk tables in warmer months and the tapas bars tend to be filled with locals. The tiny, upscale **El Globo** (C/ Diputación 8, tel. 94/415-4221) is wildly popular with the after-work set and its *pintxos* regularly win awards from local gastronomic societies. The specialty is *gratinado de txangurro*, a baked crab spread. If it is too crowded, as it often is, head to the more spacious—and more rustic—**La Viña del Ensanche** (C/ Diputación 10, tel. 94/415-5615, closed Sun.), a boisterous bar featuring top wines by the glass as well as *jamón jabugo*, the best *jamón* made in Spain.

INFORMATION

Tourist offices are conveniently located near the top sights in Bilbao and also at the airport. There is a mini-office next to the Guggenheim (11 A.M.–6 P.M. Tues.–Sat., 11 A.M.–2 P.M. Sun.) and another at Teatro Arriaga (11 A.M.–2 P.M. and 5–7:30 P.M. Mon.–Fri., 9:30 A.M.–2 P.M. and 5–7:30 P.M. Sat., 9:30 A.M.–2 P.M. Sun.). The **main office** (Pl. Ensanche 11, 9 A.M.–2 P.M. and 5–7 P.M. Mon.–Fri.) is a bit out of the way, but offers more information.

The best free map you can get is the blue-and-white Bilbao Plano, available at tourist offices and most hotels. Also look for the very informative Bilbao Guide, a free monthly publication of the city that provides details on museums, restaurants, bars, and hotels. Online, the best website for all your tourist needs is www.bilbao.net/bilbaoturismo. It is in English and easy to navigate.

GETTING THERE
Air

It is often cheaper to fly to Bilbao from Barcelona or Madrid then to take either the train or the bus. Check with an *agencia de viajes* in either city for tickets that can run as low as €35 one-way. Bilbao's **airport** (tel. 94/471-0301) is located in Loiu, about 30 minutes outside of the city. A **Bizkai Bus** (€1.20) runs every half-hour from the Termibus station at Metro: San Mamés to the airport. The same bus stops in Plaza Moyúa, just next to the Carlton Hotel.

Train

If you are coming from Santander, Bilbao is serviced at the gorgeous, tiled **FEVE train station** (www.feve.es). All other destinations are served by the **Estación de Abando** (www.vente.es). Unfortunately, train service is long-winded in País Vasco, and often your best bet is bus.

Bus

Alsa, Auto-Continental, and the Basque company **Pesa** make regular stops at the **Termibus Station** (tel. 94/439-5205), an open-air bus

the 19th-century tiled facade of the old Santander-Bilbao train station

© CANDY LEE LABALLE

stop a few kilometers west of the Guggenheim. Termibus is connected to the Metro: San Mamés, as well as the local tram, Euskotran.

GETTING AROUND

Bilbao is one of the easiest Spanish cities to get around in. The main tourist drag—from the Guggenheim in the west, through the central area of Abando, and into the Casco Viejo—can be walked in under 45 minutes. Of course, if you want to do like the locals and visit cafés and *pintxo* bars along the way, it will take you longer. The Guggenheim is connected to the Casco Viejo by the spanking-clean **Euskotren** (6:30 A.M.–11:30 P.M., €1), a tram system running along the River Nervión. Bring coins and buy your ticket before boarding the tram, using the automated ticket dispenser. Also take note that the Casco Viejo stop is called Arriaga and located next to the theater of the same name. The **Metro Bilbao** (6:30 A.M.–11 P.M., €1) subway system is extremely convenient and clean, not to mention sleek, as the stations were designed by Norman Foster, one of the world's greatest living architects. Use the automated ticket dispensers located in each metro station to purchase your ticket. Most of your travels will take place in Zone A, but if not, be sure and buy the correct ticket.

VICINITY OF BILBAO
Guernica

Throughout Spanish history, the small town of Guernica (Gernika in Basque) served as a potent symbol of Basque nationalism. Under an ancient oak tree, Spanish kings would swear to uphold Basque liberties in exchange for Basque support of their own quests for power. During the Spanish Civil War, this symbolism got under Franco's skin and he asked his friend Hitler for some help in quashing the pesky Basques. In April of 1937, the German dictator complied, using the opportunity to test out some of his bombers. On a market day, when the streets were full of women, children, and the elderly going about their daily activities, the German bombers flew overhead and

saturated the town with bombs. Almost 2,000 people died. It was the first time in the world that such a horrific attack had been taken against civilians and the world was outraged. In reaction, Picasso captured the nightmare in his haunting work, *Guernica* (see Museo Reina Sofía under *Sights* in the *Madrid* chapter). In 1997, the German government made an effort at reparation by sponsoring a sports complex in the city. Miraculously, the famed Basque oak tree survived the attack and today stands as a potent symbol of freedom and hope. You can see it at **Casa de Juntas** in the city center. The only other sight worth seeing in town is the **Parque de los Pueblos de Europa,** which sports two sculptures by famed Basque sculptor Eduardo Chillida. There are a few hotels but the town, despite its chilling history, warrants little more than a day visit, easily accomplished in a 45-minute Renfe train ride from Bilbao. The train leaves from the Estación de Abando. If you are driving, take the A-8 East towards Donostia/San Sebastián. Exit 18 will lead you right to Gernika/Guernica.

waiting for a wave in Mundaka

© CANDY LEE LABALLE

Mundaka

If you are a surfer, you have heard about Mundaka and its famous wave. The coast boasts an amazing left-turning swell that has made this tiny fishing village one of the top surfing spots in the world. Each year, the unassuming town of 2,000 would welcome up to 10,000 surfers and hangers-on each September and October when the wave was it its most powerful. Unfortunately, in 2004 the wave all but disappeared. Research has pointed to a local shipyard that dredged the nearby sea bed in order to facilitate the movement of ships in and out of the estuary. Controversy ensued, pitting the surfers and the locals who depend on their business against the shippers and the government agency that approved the dredging. After the 2005 World Championship Tour (one of Europe's most important surfing events) was cancelled, action to repair the damage was undertaken. By 2006, the wave had almost completely recovered and the surfers have returned in droves. Even if you are not a surfer, Mundaka is still worth a visit for its lovely beach and charming fishing port.

There are mid-priced accommodations throughout town. Try **Hotel Mundaka** (C/ Florentino Larrínaga 9, tel. 94/687-6158, www.hotelmundaka.com, €60), a basic hotel that also organizes outdoors activities. **Hotel El Puerto** (C/ Portu Kalea 1, tel. www.hotelelpuerto.com, 94/687-6725, €75) is a former fisherman's house that has been converted into a charming inn with gorgeous views over the port.

From Bilbao, Mundaka is a one-hour ride on the Renfe, leaving from Estación de Abando. By car, head to Guernica on the A-8 then use the N-634 to transfer to the BI-635 and then the BI-2235 into Mundaka.

Lekeitio

About midway between Bilbao and San Sebastián, smack center in one of the loveliest stretches of the Basque coast, Lekeitio is a sleepy fishing village with gorgeous views of the seas and the inland Cantabrian hills. Despite its beauty, it still lures more fish than tourists and makes for a great off-the-beaten path escape. It has two fine beaches (the better of the two is east of the river) and a bustling harbor. The town itself is a maze of colorful fishermen's cottages crawling up a steep hill overlooking the bay with its tiny central island.

The best lodging in town is the very hotelesque **Emperatriz Zita** (Santa Elena s/n, tel. 94/684-2655, €80). A more charming option is the **Zubieta** (Portal de Atea s/n, tel. 94/684-3030, €80), a 17th-century palace with lovely gardens. There are dozens of seafood shacks and tapas bars tucked behind the harbor, just wander around until you find one full of locals. For a fine dining experience, head to **Oxangoiti** (C/ Gamarra 2, tel. 94/684-3151, closed Mon., €45), one of the region's best seafood restaurants set in a lovely 17th-century home. For good food at good prices, try **Txalupa** (C/ Txatxo Kaia s/n, tel. 94/684-1386, €20).

From Bilbao, Lekeitio is about an hour away by bus. There is no train service. Catch a Vizcay bus from the Termibus station. If you are driving, take the A-8 east towards Donostia/San Sebastián. Catch exit 18 towards Gernika/Guernica and then switch to N-634 and them almost immediately switch to BI-635. After 14 kilometers (8.7 miles), change to the BI-2238 which leads right into Lekeitio.

Vitoria

Self-sufficient and hard-working, Vitoria has a thoroughly urban style that befits the capital city of País Vasco. Despite an industrious legacy that allowed the city to flourish throughout the centuries, Vitoria retains an elegant air, defined by broad avenues, palatial buildings, and well-tended parks. It also has one of the highest standards of living in Spain based on such things as work, schools, green spaces, and cultural centers. Though off the radar for most tourists, Vitoria offers a pleasant respite for visitors. It is also a good place to start a La Rioja wine tour, though it is not the most convenient place to base yourself.

Founded as a fortress town by Sancho el Sabio of Navarra in 1181, Vitoria (Gasteiz in Basque) lay on the disputed frontier between Navarra and Castile and suffered nearly a century of warfare before finally falling into the hands of Alfonso VIII in 1200. Over the centuries, the same strategic location that made the town such a hot spot, also allowed it to become a vibrant trading center for wool and iron. As a result, Vitoria grew very rich. By the 1800s, the town had spread well beyond its Casco Medieval (medieval center) and gave rise to elegant avenues lined with Renaissance palaces and churches. In 1981, after the death of Franco and the launch of democracy, Vitoria was named capital of País Vasco. Far from the heated factions demanding Basque autonomy that are common to coastal and mountain villages, level-headed Vitoria has proven to be an excellent capital.

Vitoria serves up two of Spain's most famed festivals. In July, the streets vibrate with jazzy beats as world-class musicians such as Wynton Marsalis and Sonny Rollins descend upon the town for the **Festival de Jazz de Vitoria-Gasteiz** (www.jazzvitoria.com). In August, events turn local with the raucous **Fiesta del la Virgen Blanca,** six days of wild partying in celebration of the Virgin Blanca, patron saint of Vitoria. The fests kicks off on the 4th when Celedón, a beret-wearing puppet in worker's clothes, descends like Mary Poppins under an umbrella from the top of the cathedral to start the festivities. On the 10th, he glides back up and away into the tower to signal the end of the fun. The days in between feature the usual Spanish pastimes of late-night street parties, fireworks, food booths, and concerts.

SIGHTS
Casco Medieval
The site of the original medieval town of Vitoria, the Casco Medieval lies almost at the geographic center of the city. It consists of a series of concentric streets that slowly expanded as the pebble of time sent the city further out from the old center. At the far south is the **Plaza de España** (also called Plaza Nueva), a rather austere sand-colored square built in the 19th century. Its arcaded walkways shade several traditional cafés and shops. Just next door is the **Plaza de la Virgen Blanca,** an open triangle of green ringed by noble houses sporting distinctive glass bay windows trimmed in white. In the center is a monument to Wellington, who defeated Napoleon's forces here in 1813. Dominating the northern tip of the plaza is the **Iglesia de San Miguel,** a 14th-century Gothic structure that houses a statue of the Virgen Blanca in a niche between two gaping archways.

Behind the church, follow Calle Frey Zacarías up past several lovely Renaissance palaces including the colossal **Palacio de Montehermoso** (corner of Cantón de la Soledad), built in 1524. Further up is the immaculately preserved **Palacio de Escoriaza-Esquibel.** Built in 1540 by a royal doctor, it has a stunning Plateresque facade and an impressive inner courtyard.

Just east, follow Calle Gasteiz to one of Spain's most unusual attractions, the **Museo Fournier de Naipes** (C/ Cuchillería 54, tel. 94/518-1920, 10 A.M.–2 P.M. and 4–6:30 P.M. Tues.–Fri., 10 A.M.–2 P.M. Sat., 11 A.M.–2 P.M. Sun., free), otherwise known as the card museum. In 1868, Heraclio Fournier founded

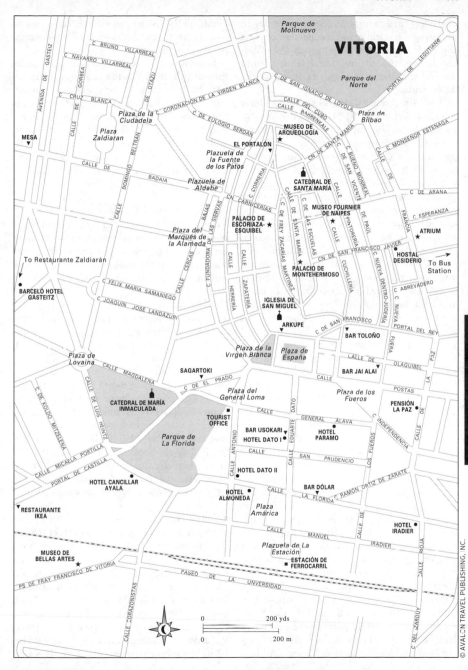

VITORIA

Parque de Molinuevo

Parque del Norte

C BRUNO VILLARREAL
C NAVARRO VILLARREAL
AVENIDA DE GASTEIZ
C DE GORBEA
C CRUZ BLANCA
DE OTAZU
CORONACION DE LA VIRGEN BLANCA
C DE EULOGIO SERDAN
Plaza de la Ciudadela
Plaza Zaldiaran
MESA
CALLE DE
C DE SAN IGNACIO DE LOYOLA
CALLE DEL CUBO
CALLE BARRENKALE
Plaza de Bílbao
CN DE SANTA MARIA
C DE SAN VICENTE
C BUENO MONREAL
PORTAL DE LEGUTIANO
C MONSEÑOR ESTENAGA
MUSEO DE ARQUEOLOGÍA ★
EL PORTALÓN ▼
Plazuela de la Fuente de los Patos
C CORRERIA
BADAIA
DOMINGO BELTRAN
CALLE DE
Plazuela de Aldabe
CN CARNICERIAS
BAJAS
CN CORRERIA
CATEDRAL DE SANTA MARÍA ♦
C DE ARANA
MUSEO FOURNIER DE NAIPES ★
C DE LAS ESCUELAS
PINTORERIA
C DE SANTA MARIA
C DE FREY ZACARIAS MARTINEZ
PALACIO DE ESCORIAZA-ESQUIBEL ★
Plaza del Marqués de la Alameda
C DE LAS SIERVAS
CALLE CERCAS
CALLE FUNDADORA
CALLE
CALLE ZAPATERIA
HERRERIA
C FELIX MARIA SAMANIEGO
C JOAQUIN JOSÉ LANDÁZURI
To Restaurante Zaldiarán
BARCELÓ HOTEL GASTEIZ ▼
PALACIO DE MONTEHERMOSO ★
CN DE SAN FRANCISCO JAVIER
CUCHILLERIA
C NUEVA DENTRO-JUDERIA
FRANCIA
C ESPERANZA
ATRIUM ●
HOSTAL DESIDERIO ●
To Bus Station →
IGLESIA DE SAN MIGUEL ♦
ARKUPE ▼
C DE SAN FRANCISCO
C NUEVA
C ABREVADERO
PORTAL DEL REY
BAR TOLOÑO ●
Plaza de Lovaina
CALLE MAGDALENA
Plaza de la Virgen Blanca
Plaza de España
LALLE DE
OLAGUIBEL
PAZ
FUERA
LA
SAGARTOKI ▼
C DE EL PRADO
BAR JAI ALAI ●
CATEDRAL DE MARÍA INMACULADA ♦
C DE LUIS HEINTZ
CALLE DE KOLDO MITXELENA
Parque de La Florida
Plaza del General Loma
Plaza de los Fueros
DATO
CALLE
POSTAS
PENSIÓN LA PAZ ●
TOURIST OFFICE ■
BAR USOKARI ●
HOTEL DATO I ●
EDUARTE
GENERAL ALAVA
HOTEL PARAMO ●
C INDEPENDENCIA
LOS FUEROS
CALLE DE
CALLE MICAELA PORTILLA
PORTAL DE CASTILLA
HOTEL CANCILLAR AYALA
CALLE ANTONIO
HOTEL DATO II ●
SAN PRUDENCIO
RESTAURANTE IKEA ▼
HOTEL ALMONEDA ●
CALLE
Plaza Amárica
BAR DÓLAR ●
C LA FLORIDA
C RAMON ORTIZ DE ZARATE
CALLE DE
ROJA
HOTEL IRADIER ●
MUSEO DE BELLAS ARTES ★
PS DE FRAY FRANCISCO DE VITORIA
CALLE CORAZONISTAS
PASEO DE LA UNIVERSIDAD
MANUEL IRADIER
Plazuela de La Estación
ESTACIÓN DE FERROCARRIL ■
CALLE DEL IZARDUY

0   200 yds
0   200 m

PAÍS VASCO

a playing-card factory and soon after began amassing the world's largest collection of playing cards. Housed in the gorgeous 1525 Palacio de Bendaña, the museum has cards from around the world dating as far back as the 12th century.

The 14th-century **Catedral de Santa María** (C/ Cuchillería 95, tel. 94/512-2160, fundacion@catedralvitoria.com, www.catedralvitoria.com, €3) is a must-see. Currently undergoing an expansive decade-long restoration project, the cathedral is open to the public, providing a rare glimpse into the delicate restoration process. The tourist office can help you make reservations or you can do so yourself on the cathedral's website. If you can't (or don't want to) go inside, be sure to at least have a look at the cathedral's exquisite Gothic doorway.

At the northern tip of the Casco Medieval, you can get a good glimpse of what Middle Ages Vitoria looked like among a row of wood and brick buildings that date to the 15th century. The best preserved of these structures is **El Portalón** (C/ Correría 151), built over 500 years ago to lodge traveling merchants. Today, it houses one of the city's finest restaurants. Just across the street, the **Museo de Arqueología** (C/ Correría 16, tel. 94/518-1922, 10 A.M.–2 P.M. and 4–6:30 P.M. Tues.–Fri., 10 A.M.–2 P.M. Sat., 11 A.M.–2 P.M. Sun., free) is housed in a similar 16th-century structure. The collection includes Roman and neolithic remains as well as a collection of unique Basque funerary items.

Ensanche

As in the rest of Spain, Ensanche, from the Spanish word for "enlargement," refers to the part of the city that expanded beyond the original old quarter. Vitoria's Ensanche pours east and south of the Casco Medieval in an elegant grid of majestic buildings and well-groomed parks. Its eastern border with the Casco Medieval also houses **ATRIUM** (C/ Francia 24, tel. 94/520-9000, www.atrium.org, 11 A.M.–8 P.M. Tues.–Fri., 10:30 A.M.–8 P.M. Sat. and Sun., €4.50). Built as a third point in the triangle of Basque modern art that includes Bilbao's Guggenheim and San Sebastián's Museo Chillida-Leku, ATRIUM has an eclectic collection of modern art that includes work by top contemporary Basque artists.

Southwest of the Casco Medieval, the graceful **Parque de la Florida** is a large botanical park built in the style of a romantic French 19th-century garden. A few blocks south is the **Museo de Bellas Artes** (Paseo de Fray Francisco 8, tel. 94/518-1918, 10 A.M.–2 P.M. and 4–6:30 P.M. Tues.–Fri., 10 A.M–2 P.M. Sat., 11 A.M.–2 P.M. Sun., free), which features a collection of Spanish classics including appearances by Picasso and Ribera.

ACCOMMODATIONS

Vitoria's hotel market is squarely aimed at the business traveler. As a result, there are few budget options. The upside is that prices drop substantially come the weekend. If you can, check the Internet for the best deals.

Under €50

The two best places in town for a cheap sleep are **Dato** (C/ Eduardo Dato 28, tel. 94/514-7230, www.hoteldato.com, €47) and **Dato II** (C/ San Antonio 17, tel. 94/513-0400, €41). Located around the corner from each other, the two Datos offer cozy rooms full of art and antiques with a few kitschy boudoir pieces thrown in for fun. The owners couldn't be nicer and the location, about halfway between the train station and the Casco Medieval, couldn't be better. If they are booked, just walk around this area. There are dozens of *pensiones* clustered here. A decent choice is **La Paz** (C/ La Paz 3, tel. 94/513-9666, €45) with very basic rooms.

€50-100

For a good mid-range place, try **Hotel Iradier** (C/ Florida 49, tel. 94/527-9066, www.hoteliradier.com, €53). Rooms are a bit heavy on the brass fittings, but clean and comfortable. On the edge of the Casco Medieval, **Hostal Desiderio** (C/ Colegio San Prudencio 2, tel. 94/525-1700, €55) has very basic but spacious rooms. Also close to the center is **Hotel Paramo** (C/ General Alava 11, tel. 94/514-0240, www.hotelparamo.com, €75). It is a little dark inside and done up in worn out 1980s decor, but it is professionally run and the bathrooms are spacious.

Over €100

Barely edging into this category is the homey **Hotel Almoneda** (C/ Florida 7, tel. 94/515-4084, www.hotelalmoneda.com, €105). Built in an old Basque townhouse, the family-run hotel offers rustic decor and friendly service. A nice, unexpected touch is that the hotel donates a portion of each room price to Amnesty International. One of the nicest hotels in town is the ultra-modern **Canciller Ayala** (C/ Ramón y Cajal 5, tel. 94/513 0000, nhcanciller ayala@nh-hotels.com, www.nh-hotels.com, €120). Service and amenities are top-notch as is standard for this chain. The location next to Parque de la Florida is also very lovely. **Barceló Hotel Gasteiz** (Av. Gasteiz 45, tel. 94/522-8100, www.bchoteles.com, €120), a ways out of town, offers the sleek style the Barceló chain is known for at much cheaper prices than their other city locations. It is very convenient to access from the airport and has ample parking if you will be driving on to La Rioja.

If you are driving and want a bit of medieval luxury, head to the **Parador de Argómaniz** (Ctra. N-1, km. 362, Argómaniz, tel. 94/529-3200, argomaniz@parador.es, www.parador .es, €120), a majestic 17th-century stone palace just 15 minutes east of the city. It is set in a lovely garden with soaring views across the plains of Álava. Rooms feature hardwood floors, antiques, and luxurious baths. The regal dining room turns out excellent Basque fare and the large selection of Rioja Alavesa wines is surprisingly good value.

FOOD

Vitoria sits at a delicious crossroads of cuisine. The sophisticated flavors of the Basque country blend with the rustic fare of La Rioja to create truly unique local dishes. A specialty you shouldn't miss is *perrotxikos,* wild mushrooms typical to the region. They come whipped in a *revuelto* of scrambled eggs, served as a side sauce for grilled meats, or deliciously grilled alone.

Like the rest of the Basque country, Vitoria has award-winning *pintxo* bars and cutting-edge Basque temples of gastronomy.

Gourmet

If you want a taste of the world-acclaimed New Basque Cuisine, Vitoria can comply. The ultra-modern **Zaldiarán** (Av. Gasteiz, 21, tel. 94/513-4822, www.restaurantezaldiaran.com, 1–3:30 P.M. and 9–11 P.M. Mon.–Sat., closed Sun., €60) has earned legions of fans worldwide with the creations of Patxi Eceiza, such as carpaccio of prawn with celery ice cream, sole with a citronella foam and dried fruit, and icy spiced jelly with citrus sorbet and pepper crystals. Try the tasting menu for the best experience. **Ikea** (Av. Portal de Castilla 27, tel. 94/514-4747, 1–3:30 P.M. and 8–11 P.M. daily, €60) has long been the height of culinary acclaim in the city serving exquisite renditions of Basque dishes with modern touches that enhance rather than change local flavors. (It has nothing to do with the furnishing giant of the same name.)

Local Cuisine

The atmospheric **El Portalón** (C/ Correría 151, tel. 94/514-4201, www.restauranteelportalon .com, 1–3:30 P.M. and 9–11:30 P.M. Mon.–Sat., closed Sun., €40) is spread over three floors of a historic 15th-century building in Vitoria's Casco Viejo. You'll feel like you are dining in the Middle Ages among the wrought-iron chandeliers, heavy beamed ceilings, ancient brick walls, and eerie paintings of long-gone noblemen. The food is also a throwback to more rustic times, heavy on grilled meats and traditional Basque dishes such as *merluza* (hake). If you eat at only one place in town, make this it. For acclaimed classic Basque cuisine, head to the family-run **Arkupe** (C/ Mateo Moraza 13, tel. 94/523-0080, 1:30–3:30 P.M. and 9–11:30 P.M. daily, €30). For inexpensive local fare, try **Mesa** (C/ Chile 1, tel. 94/522-8494, €18), which prides itself on the freshness of its ingredients.

Pintxos

Vitoria's *pintxo* bars often open in the morning for coffee around 9 A.M. and stay open until the last *pintxo* is gone, usually around midnight and a bit later on weekends. To understand the level of art that a *pintxo* can achieve you have to visit ❰❰ **Sagartoki** (C/ Prado 18, tel. 94/528-8676, closed Sun.). At the prestigious 2005 San Sebastián food competition, its young chef Senen González beat out several world-renowned chefs to score the top prize for the best *pintxos* bar in Spain. His winning mini-dishes included a puff pastry layered with potato and smoked fish with a foam of white garlic and a lasagna of wild mushrooms with spore ice cream. He is always creating new taste experiments and a visit to his tapas bar will be an unforgettable culinary adventure. If you want something more traditional, try the attached *asador* (grill house), famed for its top-quality meats and excellent grilling techniques.

Another gourmet favorite is **Bar Dólar** (C/ Florida 26, tel. 94/523-0071), known for creative takes on Spanish standards such as *solomillo*, a bit of grilled filet served with pears and foie gras. At **Bar Usokari** (C/ Eduardo Dato 25, tel. 94/523-4152), try excellent cold *pintxos* like marinated *pochas* (broad white beans). At **Jai Alai** (C/ Fueros 7, tel. 94/525-9878) is a local favorite that prepares huge portions of rustic *pintxos*. **Bar Toloño** (C/ Cuesta de San Francisco 3, tel. 94/523-3336, closed Tues.) serves both creative and traditional *pintxos*.

INFORMATION

The **main tourist office** (Plaza General Loma 1, tel. 94/516-1598, 10 A.M.–7 P.M. Mon.–Sat. and 11 A.M.–2 P.M. Sun.) can provide local city information as well as regional information for Álava and the Rioja Alavesa wine region. Their English-language website (www.vitoria-gasteiz .org) is excellent.

GETTING THERE AND AROUND
Air
If you are flying from within Spain, you will land at the **Vitoria-Gasteiz Airport (VIT)** (tel. 94/516-3591), located just eight kilometers (five miles) out of the city. Iberia is the main airline serving the airport. Taxis in Vitoria go by the length of time spent in the cab as opposed to distance, therefore they are more expensive than in similar-sized cities. If there is a taxi waiting out front of the airport, the ride should cost €15–20. If you must call a **Radio Taxi** (tel. 94/527-3500), it will cost more as the meter is turned on as soon as the taxi accepts the call. There is a public bus that departs from the airport, usually timed to leave according to the arrival flights. It takes 15 minutes and costs €3.

Train
Vitoria's Renfe **train station** (C/ Eduardo Dato, 46, tel. 90/224-0202, www.renfe.es) is a sight in itself, decorated in a Moorish style that evokes Bollywood brashness with its wildly colored tiles. Train service is your best bet for national trips throughout Spain.

Bus
Vitoria's **bus station** (C/ Los Herrán 50, tel. 94/525-8400) is a 10-minute walk to the east of the Casco Medieval. It is served by Spain's biggest bus companies including **Continental** and **Alsa,** as well as País Vasco's largest company, **Pesa.** For most travel within País Vasco, bus is both faster and cheaper than train.

Car
With broad avenues and less traffic, Vitoria is one of the easier cities to get around in car; however, if your hotel is in the city center, you'd be better off by foot. If you decide to use Vitoria as your starting point for exploring the La Rioja wine region, you can rent a car at **Avis** (tel. 94/527-6539) or **Europcar** (tel. 94/516-3644), both of which are located in the airport.

Logroño

Thanks mainly to the booming wine industry, modern, hard-working Logroño is an important agricultural and industrial city. It modestly flaunts its wealth in a series of elegant streets punctuated by broad squares, medieval churches, modern shops, and dozens of *pincho* bars. Though there is very little to see sight-wise, it is a pleasant town with a lovely location on the Río Ebro. As the capital of La Rioja, it makes an excellent base to start a tour of the region's wineries, but for charm, you'd be better off in Laguardia. If you are traveling by bus, you'll find it easiest to use Logroño as your main base, as it is connected by several daily buses to all the nearby wine villages.

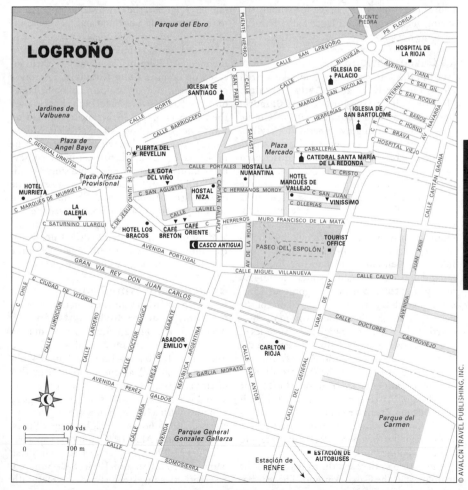

PAÍS VASCO

SIGHTS

A logical place to start a walking tour of Logroño is **Paseo del Espolón.** This broad, graceful plaza, dotted with trees and lined with sidewalk cafés, marks the barrier between the old historic part of town, the Casco Antiguo, and the new commercial zone. At its center is a sculpture of General Espartero, a local 18th-century military leader who helped repel the advances of Napoleon in Spain. The sculpture is famous in La Rioja for the gargantuan size of the testicles on the general's horse. When a local does something brave (or stupid) the saying goes, "you have bigger balls than Espartero's horse."

Casco Antiguo

Head to the Casco Antiguo and take a stroll along the lovely arcaded **Calle Portales.** Here you will find the 16th-century **Catedral Santa María de la Redonda** with its Gothic twin towers looming over the town's skyline. At the very top of the towers a flock of storks has taken up residence. Around sunset each evening, they retire to their giant nests in an impressive flurry of flight. The portico of the church is a feast of baroque religious sculpture. The church faces the cozy **Plaza del Mercado,** which is lined with sidewalk cafés in warmer months. For more impressive religious architecture, seek out the 12th-century Romanesque **Iglesia de Palacio** with its outstanding cloister and unusual eight-sided spire. The **Iglesia de San Bartolomé** features a gorgeous 13th-century Gothic portico, considered one of the best in La Rioja. The Casco Antiguo is bordered by the Río Ebro, which boasts a series of peaceful, green parks including the **Parque del Ebro** and the **Parque de la Ribera.** You can cross the river by either the **Puente Piedra,** the stone bridge, or the **Puente Hierro,** the iron bridge. At the end of the iron bridge is the **Bodegas Franco Españolas** (tel. 94/125-1300), the only winery located inside the city. Unfortunately, they don't offer tours except to large pre-booked groups.

Interesting as they are, the sights are not the main draw in the Casco Antiguo. The real rea-son to go is the *pinchos.* Around 9 P.M., the pedestrian street of **Calle Laurel** comes alive with hundreds of hungry locals and tourists. It is lined with dozens of *pincho* bars and just about every night of the week, the atmosphere is that of a ravenous, roving street party. Be sure to plan your visit to Logroño for just before sunset. When you finish with the visual sights, you can tuck into the tasty ones.

Camino de Santiago

For six centuries before Rioja wine brought fame to Logroño, the city owed its importance to the **Camino de Santiago** and the thousands of pilgrims who walked it each year. As such, many of Logroño's monuments are related to the medieval Pilgrims' Way, most of them located on or near **Calle Ruavieja,** Logroño's oldest street. A giant sculpture of Saint James on horseback, sword held high, hovers over the doorway of the 16th-century **Iglesia de Santiago.** At his horse's feet are slain Moors. Saint James is also known as Matamoros (the Moor slayer) for appearing on his horse several centuries after his death and single-hand-edly killing 10,000 Moors during a key battle of Christian Reconquest. The backside of the church boasts a lovely view over the Río Ebro. The last interesting spot on the Camino leading out of the old city is the **Puerta del Revellín,** the only remaining gate from the mostly gone medieval walls of the city.

Bodegas and Wine Tourism

A good place to get an introduction to wine is at the **Bodega-Museo Ontañón** (Av. Aragón 3, tel. 94/123-4200, www.ontanon.es, 10:30 A.M.–1:30 P.M. and 4–6:30 P.M. Tues.–Sat., 10:30 A.M.–1:30 P.M. Sun., €4, reservations required), a winery and museum that offers visits and tastings in a rustic bodega decorated with local art. Most of the other good wineries with visiting hours are on the outskirts of Logroño or in neighboring villages. **Bodegas Juan Alcorta** (Camino de Lapuebla, tel. 94/127-9900, 11 A.M., 1 P.M., and 4 P.M. Mon.–Fri., 11 A.M. and 1 P.M. Sat.–Sun., €3, reservations suggested) is an architecturally

La Rioja's vineyards have spurred the wine industry in Logroño.

striking winery on the road to Fuenmayor. The tour includes an overview of the winemaking process and a tasting of one wine.

In Fuenmayor, a suburb just a few kilometers from Logroño, you'll find one of the newest bodegas to visit. Unlike the current trend of building ultra-modern bodegas by world-famous architects, **Marques de Arviza** (C/ Bodegas San Cristóbal 34, Fuenmayor, tel. 94/145-1245, €5, reservations required) has looked to the past and built a lovely, rustic bodega and visitors center in an old wine factory from 1874. Below the complex are 400 meters (1,312 feet) of wine caves dating to the 16th century. A tour begins in the bodega, which artfully combines the old with the new thanks to sculptor Faustino Aizcorbe, who designed the space. Visitors continue through the stone- and earth-lined caves, ending with a wine tasting 11 meters (36 feet) below ground. The woman currently in charge of the bodega is Elsa Ubis, an enthusiastic young winemaker with an incredible passion for the vine. Look out for her new wines—unnamed as of the date

of this publication—in coming years. She is a name to watch.

If you'd like to set up an exclusive visit to some of the smaller vineyards in the area, contact Gonzalo Gonzalo, another exciting young winemaker. He is currently producing lovely handcrafted wines for his boutique bodega **The Wine Love** (tel. 63/563-7336, www.the winelove.com) and for the exciting new **Lazurus Wines** (www.lazaruswine.com). He is passionate about La Rioja and happy to help visitors meet other winemakers like himself.

If you would like to do a more intensive wine-tasting (*cata* in Spanish), visit the friendly folk at **Vinissimo** (C/ San Juan 23, tel. 94/125-8828, closed Mon. P.M. and Tues.), a wine shop and bar that offers an introduction to rioja with a tasting of six wines for €15. The tasting can be conducted in English with advance notice. A more straight forward tasting school is **Cofradía del Vino de Rioja** (C/ Horno 1, tel. 94/125-0852), offering *catas* every Monday–Saturday at 7 P.M. Reservations are required and prices start around €18.

ENTERTAINMENT AND EVENTS

Nightlife

Logroño's nightlife is very low-key compared to many Spanish cities. Most of the action happens in the Casco Antiguo, particularly along Calle Marqués de San Nicólas and Calle Mayor. In warmer weather, the terraces in front of the **Plaza del Parlamento** stay open very late. Bringing the newest in music to the oldest of quarters is **Bossanova** (C/ San Nicolás 69). **La Luna** (C/ Bretón de los Herreros 56) serves up indie rock and poetry readings to Logroño's hip young things. For a 1970s rock feel with a riotous mix of music from London punk to California surf, try **Stereo** (C/ Sagasta 19). **El Sueño de la Musa** (Plaza del Mercado 8) offers modern music and cocktails until the wee hours.

Festivals and Events

The week of June 11, Logroño celebrates the **Fiestas de San Bernabé,** commemorating the town's resistance against a siege by the French in 1521. The attacking forces could not get past Logroño's thick city walls, so they surrounded the town in the hopes of starving the residents out. The wily locals snuck over the walls under the cover of night to fish in the River Ebro. This allowed them to outlast the French occupation and maintain hold of their city. Today, local groups fish in the river and distribute their catch free to the citizens during the fiestas. There are also parades, street parties, and concerts. The third week of September, Logroño really lets loose at the **Fiestas de San Mateo.** There are daily bull runs through the streets, though by local custom, cows are substituted for bulls. The real bulls appear in the local *plaza del toros* for La Rioja's most prestigious bullfighting events. There are also all-night street parties with live bands, food booths serving local specialties like lamb chops grilled on grapevine shoots, and nightly firework displays. The drink of the party is *zurracapote,* a blend of red wine, cinnamon, and sugar. San Mateo corresponds with **La**

Vendimia, the Rioja wine harvest, which is celebrated throughout the region with street parties and activities. On the 21st, there is a traditional crushing of the grapes by barefooted locals in traditional costume. The first jug of juice extracted is devoted to the Virgin of Valvanera.

ACCOMMODATIONS

Under €50

Located near the Paseo del Espolón, **Hostal Niza** (C/ Capitán Gallarza 13, tel. 94/120-6044, €50) is the nicest accommodation you'll find in this price range. In the Casco Antiguo, try **Hostal La Numantina** (C/ Sagasta 4, tel. 94/125-1411, €46) for decent but noisy rooms. **Pensión Cinco Villas** (C/ Labradores 21, tel. 65/597-8575, €36) is about 10 minutes from the Casco Antiguo, but you won't find rooms cheaper.

€50-100

The stylish ❰❰ **Hotel Marqués de Vallejo** (C/ Marqués de Vallejo 8, tel. 94/124-8333, info@hotelmarquesdevallejo.com, www.hotelmarquesdevallejo.com, €100) features rooms that manage to be ultra-modern and super-cozy all at once with bold colors, blocky furnishings, warm wood paneling, and plump, cushy linens. Another good choice is the more traditional **Herencia Rioja** (C/ Marqués de Murrieta 14, tel. 94/121-0222, €85), run by the upscale NH chain. A few blocks away, the **Hotel Murrieta** (C/ Marqués de Murrieta 1, tel. 94/122-4150, €80) is another aptly run, modern hotel.

Over €100

On one of the city center's liveliest streets, **Los Bracos** (C/ Bretón de los Herreros 29, tel. 94/122-6608, €115) offers top-notch service in a lovely hotel. Rooms are cozily decorated and have lovely touches like fresh flowers. The grande dame of Logroño hotels is the **Carlton Rioja** (Gran Vía 5, tel. 94/124-2100, www.pretur.com, €140) a sleek, new four-star hotel located in the newer part of town, but still close enough to walk to the Casco Antiguo in 10 minutes.

FOOD

Cafés and Desserts

Your best bet for a good café for breakfast, coffees, sandwiches, and ice cream is Calle Bretón, an elegant avenue graced by the theater of the same name. There are several open-all-day cafés lining the street and most put out sidewalk tables in warmer months. For old-world elegance, head to **Café Bretón** (C/ Bretón 32, tel. 94/128-6038, 8 A.M.–midnight daily). If you prefer something a bit more modern with a low-key techno soundtrack, try **Café Oriente** (C/ Bretón 38).

Local Cuisine

The same rich land and sheltered climate that has allowed La Rioja's grapes to dominate the wine world also fuels La Rioja's rich gastronomic history. It is a cuisine based on vegetables freshly pulled from the earth at their peak of ripeness. Peppers, asparagus, and artichokes take starring roles in some of the region's most delicious dishes, including *menestra,* a savory vegetable medley. Beans are also integral to the diet, particularly *caparrones,* fat red beans, and *pochas,* broad white beans; both are served stewed with chorizo. Chorizo also plays the key role in *patatas a la Riojana,* a thick potato stew seasoned with the distinctive red sausage. For centuries, Rioja has also been prime pastureland for livestock and there is a long tradition of excellent roasted meats. By far, the most popular dish is *chuletas al sarmiento,* tender lamb chops grilled over a fire of grapevine twigs. As the capital of La Rioja, Logroño has hundreds of restaurants proffering these local treats. Here are a few of the best.

Run by the same family for four generations, **Cachetero** (C/ Laurel 3, tel. 94/122-8463, 1:30–3:30 P.M. and 9–11 P.M. Mon.–Sat., 1:30–3:30 P.M. Wed. only, closed Sun., €40) is one of La Rioja's best restaurants for truly classic Riojan dishes. It also boasts a rotating list of over 100 different Rioja wines. **Asador Emilio** (Av. República Argentina, 8, tel. 94/125-8844, 1–3:30 P.M. and 9–11:30 P.M. Mon.–Sat., 1 3:30 P.M. Wed. only, closed Sun., €35), tucked into a rustic house with an intricately carved ceiling, serves to-die-for grilled lamb and the freshest of vegetables. For a modern twist on Riojan tradition, try **La Galería** (C/ Saturnino Ulargui 5, tel. 94/120-7366, 2–3:45 P.M. and 9–11 P.M., closed Sun., €40).

Pinchos

Logroño is famous for its *pinchos*—small, bite-sized snacks that cost just over a euro each. In the heart of the old town, look for **Calle Laurel** and the tiny streets that branch off of it. You'll find dozens of tiny bars lined up, each specializing in a different tasty treat. The local tradition is to *pincho*-hop—one glass of wine, one *pincho,* move on. Continue until full. The pincho bars are normally open from noon to 3 P.M. and in the evening from 8 P.M. to midnight. On the weekends hours are extended to 1 A.M.

Some winners include **Blanco y Negro** (Travesía Laurel 1), a gritty little place with wonderful *bacalao con pimientos* (cod with olive oil and green peppers). At **Bar Ángel** (C/ Laurel 12) go for *champiñones* (sautéed mushrooms with garlic). The rustically charming—down to its checkered tablecloths—**Bar Muro** (C/ Laurel 36) features *setas con jamón* (wild mushrooms with *jamón* on toast). At **Casa Pali** (C/ Laurel 11) try *berenjenas con queso* (eggplant with cheese). For seafood tapas, especially shrimp and calamari, head to **La Casita** (C/ Laurel 13). Around the corner from Calle Laurel, find some of the most-renowned *pinchos* in Logroño at 【 **La Gota del Vino** (C/ San Agustin 14). Their *espinacas con jamón* (sautéed spinach with *jamón*) is so tasty it even made the foodie press in the United States. As the name suggests, there are also amazing wines—rioja only, thank you—by the glass, many starting at just one euro.

INFORMATION

La Rioja has one of the most helpful and well equipped tourist agencies in all of Spain. The **regional tourist office** (Paseo del Espolón, s/n, tel. 94/129-1260, 10 A.M.–2 P.M. and 5–8 P.M. daily, extended hours in summer) offers countless maps, driving routes, and wine information as well as guides to bodegas, hotels, and restaurants. The best wine tourism guide they offer is the bilingual (Spanish and English) *Datos Enoturismo,* a 150-page booklet offering complete information on all bodegas open to the public in the region. Their website (www.lariojaturismo.com) is also excellent. Logroño's **local tourist office** (C/ Portales 39, tel. 94/127-3353) has information only about the city, and frankly, you'll need a lot more than that to tour La Rioja properly.

GETTING THERE
Air
Air Nostrum (tel. 90/240-0500, www.airnostrum.es), a regional wing of Iberia, makes daily flights to Logroño from Madrid and Barcelona. If you are tight on time, this could be a good option. The **Logroño-Agoncillo (RJL) Airport** (tel. 94/127-7400) is 12.8 kilometers (eight miles) outside of the city, less than a €10 cab ride.

Train
Renfe (tel. 90/224-3402, www.renfe.es, €49) runs one train per day to Logroño from Madrid at 6:10 P.M. and takes just under four hours. However, there are several speedy AVE trains from Madrid to Zaragoza and you can easily transfer from there. The ride is just under four hours. It leaves Logroño at 8 A.M. only. Logroño's train station is located in Plaza Europa, about 10 minutes walking from the Casco Antiguo.

Bus
Logroño's **bus station** (Av. de España 1, tel. 94/123-5983) services both national and regional buses. The best way to arrive in town from Madrid is by **Continental** (tel. 90/233-0400, www.continental-auto.es), which leaves from Avenida de America hourly. The ride is about four hours and costs €18, however splurging for the *gran clase,* at €28, is worth it for the large seats, free snacks, and helpful attendant. There are also daily buses to and from Pamplona, Burgos, Vitoria, and San Sebastián.

Car
Logroño is well connected to all major roads by the A-12 as well as several national roads: N-232, N-120, and N-111. If you are going to use Logroño as your base for traveling La Rioja by car, **Avis** (tel. 90/218-0854, www.avis.es) is located at the train station and **Hertz** (tel. 90/240-2405, www.hertz.es) is at the airport.

Rioja Alta

West from Logroño, Rioja Alta unfurls in a pastoral wave of white-tipped hills, deep green valleys, and acres upon acres of vineyards. Bound to the north by País Vasco, to the west by Burgos, and to the south by the low-lying mountains that give way to Castilla y León, this is classic Spanish wine country, home to dozens of medieval villages and hundreds of bodegas. Even though it is the River Oja that gives this region its name, it is the River Ebro that feeds the valleys and nourishes the grapes. You'll cross it time and again as you traipse through the region. The northern banks of the river give way to Rioja Alavesa, the part of La Rioja that falls within the País Vasco. Though the geographical line has both political and historical significance to locals, a visitor won't notice much of a difference.

The best way to explore this area is by car. Rent one in Logroño or Vitoria, then hit the tourist office for maps and bodega information. Some of the towns below are accessible by bus, but you will need to be very flexible in your travels and limited in your scope. A third option is to check into one of the finer hotels in the region. They will often handle your wine tourism needs, including transport to and from the bodegas.

BRIONES
From Logroño, Briones is one of the first stops you should make on any wine tour through La

Rioja. The village, set on a hill jutting high above the vineyards below, has the same charm you'll find throughout La Rioja—winding medieval streets, ancient plazas, and a smattering of hulking gothic churches. The most important is the 16th-century **Santa María de la Asunción** (tel. 94/132-2216) with its incredible golden altar soaring to the church's roof. The main plaza is surrounded by a warren of narrow streets dotted with restaurants and bars and makes for a pleasant morning stroll. Along **Calle San Juan,** the views over the vineyards and the looping flow of the River Ebro are lovely.

Bodegas and Wine Tourism

The prestigious family bodega **Dinastía Vivanco** put sleepy little Briones on the wine tourism map in 2004 when it opened **Museo de la Cultura del Vino** (tel. 90/232-0001, www.dinastiavivanco.es, 10 A.M.–6 P.M. Tues.–Sun., extended hours in summer, €6).

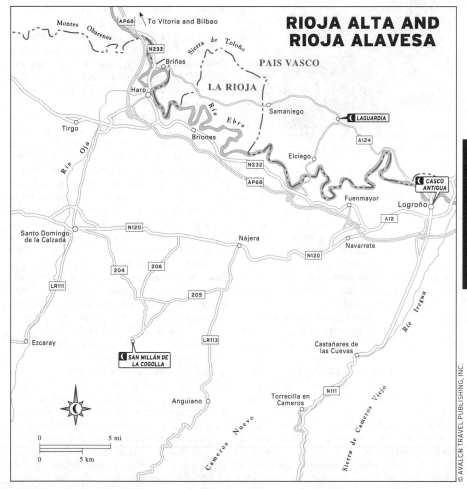

RIOJA ALTA AND RIOJA ALAVESA

PAÍS VASCO

Bodegas Muga in Haro is one of the friendliest bodegas in La Rioja.

This spectacular multimillion-euro complex houses an interactive museum detailing the entire wine-making process from soil cultivation to wine barrel construction to bottling techniques. In the Bacchus garden you can see different varieties of grapes growing. There is also a massive collection of *sacacorchos* (wine openers), and a fine art collection with pieces ranging from Roman artifacts to Picasso. It will take about two hours to work your way through. Unfortunately, all the videos and displays are only in Spanish—a very poor move considering the popularity of wine tourism worldwide. However, there are audio-guides in English for €2 more. At the end of the tour, you are served one of the bodega's wines, but the bartender seems to know little about it. Despite these missteps, it is still a fascinating visit.

Visit one of the smallest—and most highly regarded—winemakers in La Rioja at **Bodega Miguel Merino** (Crta. de Logroño 16, tel. 94/132-2263, info@miguelmerino.com, www.miguelmerino.com, reservations required).

Miguel is extremely friendly and very proud of his lovely bodega and delicious wines. Also, because his winery is small, you'll receive the most personalized attention you'll encounter throughout your wine travels in La Rioja.

Accommodations and Food

There is very little by way of accommodations in Briones, but what there is oozes charm. The quaint **Casa Rural Mesón del Briones** (Trav. de la Estación 3, tel. 94/132-2178, www.brioneslarioja.com/elmeson, €45) is run by lifelong resident Mari Cruz Díaz Matute and offers rustic furnishings, stone walls, and very friendly service. The elegant **Los Calaos** (C/San Juan 13, tel. 94/132-2131, www.loscalaos debriones.com, €58) features gorgeously appointed rooms full of antiques, several with lovely views over the valley. The hotel sits atop its own wine cellar.

For dining, **Los Calaos** (1–3:30 P.M. and 8–10:30 P.M. Mon.–Sat., 1–3:30 P.M. Sun., €25) also offers excellent Riojan cuisine in a lovely country-style dining room full of antique wine-making equipment. Their *chuletillas al sarmiento* (baby lamb chops grilled over vine twigs) are sumptuous. The **Museo de la Cultura del Vino** (tel. 94/132-2340, 1:30–3:30 P.M. and 8:30–10:30 P.M. Tues.–Sat., 1:30–3:30 P.M. Sun., closed Mon.) boasts a sleek, round dining room jutting over the vineyards below with spectacular wrap-around windows. Set menus run €24–58 and focus firmly on local specialties with a few modern touches. Reservations are imperative as the entire dining room is often booked out to large groups in advance. If you'd like a bit of the local cuisine with actual locals, drive across the highway from the museum to the gas station. Yes, the gas station! **Restaurante Briones** (tel. 94/132-2080, 1:30–4 P.M. and 8:30–11:30 Mon.–Fri., 1:30–4 P.M. Sat., closed Sun.) is connected to a 24-hour gas station and features excellent rustic fare in huge portions. A *menú del día* runs just €9 and may start with a plate of potatoes with chorizo (be sure and tell the server to stop serving or your bowl will be overflowing) and finish with a grilled steak. Of course, excellent rioja is available at the kind of prices you'd expect in a gas station. The large dining room is very popular with wine workers and you may be just about the only tourist in the place.

Getting There and Around
From Logroño's **bus station** (Av. de España 1, tel. 94/123-5983), catch the bus that is heading to Haro. If driving, follow the AP-68 out of town in the direction of Burgos/Vitoria/Bilbao. Take exit 10 towards the town of Cenicero and then switch to the N-232 (also called the Carretera de Logroño) into Briones.

❰ HARO
Perched at the junction of the River Ebro and the River Tirón, the hard-working town of Haro is often dubbed the wine capital of La Rioja. The old town is a horseshoe-shaped collection of cobbled streets and crumbling 16th-century noblemen's houses surrounding a central square, **Plaza de la Paz**. The main sight of interest is the 16th-century **Iglesia de Santo Tomás**, which boasts a spectacular Plateresque portico. If you are driving through La Rioja, Haro merits a few hours' stop, with a visit to a bodega or two. If you are traveling by bus, your best bet is to stay overnight and take advantage of the many bodegas that are located within town.

Bodegas and Wine Tourism
On the edge of Haro, just across the River Tirón from the old town, is the **Barrio de la Estación** where several wineries are located, most open to visitors. The neighborhood takes its name from the adjacent train station. Before long-distance trucking, bodegas relied on rail service to move their wine cross-country; for that reason the oldest bodegas in the country are located next to train stations. If you are driving, the barrio is located on the A-3023 road and there is a free parking lot on the roundabout as you approach town.

The most charming of the bodegas—and the most accommodating for English-speakers—is **Bodegas Muga** (tel. 94/131-1825, info@bodegasmuga.com, www.bodegasmuga.com, tour at 11 A.M. Mon.–Sat. Sept.–May, 10 A.M.

Mon.–Sat. Jun.–Aug., €5). One of Spain's oldest wineries, Muga offers a comprehensive tour in its charming facilities, ending with a tasting of two wines. Unlike most bodegas in the region, Muga does not require advance notice to join a tour. Just show up. Another venerable winemaker, **Bodegas Bilbainas** (tel. 94/131-0147, www.bodegasbilbainas.com, tour at 10 A.M., 11 A.M., and noon Tues.–Sat., 11 A.M. Sun., closed Mon.) offers tours in its majestic 150-year-old cellars. Reservations are suggested every day but Friday and English-language tours must be requested ahead of time. **Bodegas CVNE** (tel. 94/130-4800, www.cvne.com, 11 A.M.–2 P.M. and 6–9 P.M. daily) is another charming century-old bodega. The rest of the wineries are by appointment only—though that is changing fast as locals catch on to the wine-tourism craze. You can get the latest information by picking up the free *Bodegas of Haro* guide at the **tourist office** (Pl. Monseñor Florentino Rodríguez, s/n, tel. 94/130-3366, 10 A.M.–2 P.M. Mon.–Sat.). For a comprehensive introduction to local winemaking, visit the **Estación Enológica y Museo del Vino** (C/ Bretón de los Herreros, s/n, tel. 94/131-0547, 10 A.M.–2 P.M. and 4–8 P.M. Mon.–Sat., 10 A.M.–2 P.M. Sun., free), an interesting little wine museum—though all the displays are in Spanish.

Shopping
If you are not going to travel through the bodegas in La Rioja, Haro is a great place to stock up on wines at bodega prices. Try the **La Catedral de los Vinos** (C/ Santo Tomás 4, tel. 94/131-2144) with its impressive selection and accommodating English-speaking staff. A few doors down is the much more rustic **Mi Bodega** (C/ Santo Tomás 13, tel. 94/130-4003), whose dark cellars are lined with thousands of choice riojas to suit all budgets. At **Bar Oñate** (Pl. de la Paz 11, tel. 94/131-0010) you can try before you buy.

Festivals and Events
Haro is at its liveliest the last week of June for festivals in honor of **San Juan, San Pedro,**

and **San Felices.** June 24–28, the town hosts nightly parties, fireworks, and outdoor concerts. There are also daily *encierros* (bull runs) through the streets. However, Haro uses cows instead of bulls. Though less dangerous, at nearly 450 kilograms (0.5 ton) each, they still pack a powerful wallop. Of course, all the festivities are accompanied with rivers of Rioja wine. On June 29, things get wet and wild for the annual **Batalla del Vino** (wine battle). Hundreds of locals dressed in white climb the local mountain, Bilibio, all the while spraying each other with wine. They descend a few hours later, completely drunk and soaking wet, their white clothes dyed a deep pink. If you decide to join them, wear something you don't mind throwing away. Also be sure to bring along a *bota,* a traditional Spanish wine skin made of leather. It straps around your neck and can hold up to two bottles of wine for drinking or spraying.

Accommodations

The most luxurious housing in town is **Hotel Los Agustinos** (C/ San Agustín 2, tel. 94/131-1308, www.aranzazu-hotels.com, €103), tucked into a 1373 convent that later did time as a medieval prison. The interior cloister—lined with graffiti from the Middle Ages—has been turned into a modern salon with sleek furnishings and oversized lamps and mirrors. About three kilometers (two miles) outside of Haro, the nicest place to stay is the famed **Hospedería Señorío de Casalarreina** (Pl. Santo Domingo de Guzmán 6, Casalarreina, tel. 94/132-4730, www.hotelesconencanto.org, €150), a lavishly updated bishop's palace from 1509. Staff can arrange any wine-related activity from a private winery tour to dinner in a wine cellar to a spa treatment based on the anti-oxidant properties of grapes.

For cheaper sleeps, try **Pensión la Peña** (Pl. de la Paz 17, tel. 94/131-0022, €36), which features decent rooms, many with balconies overlooking the plaza. **Pensión Vega** (Pl. de Juan García Gato 1, tel. 94/130-3280, €30) offers very basic rooms with the cheapest prices in town.

Food

For *pinchos,* head to Calle Santo Tomás, which is lined with wonderful bars featuring mouthwatering snacks and delicious wines. **Mesón de Berones** (C/ Santo Tomás 26, tel. 94/131-0707, 1–3 P.M. and 8–11 P.M. daily), a local favorite, serves up giant-sized tapas. Another good bet is **Beethoven** (C/ Santo Tomás 10, tel. 94/131-0018, 1–3 P.M. and 8–11 P.M. daily), which has a charming tapas bar as well as a rustic dining room featuring traditional Riojan fare. For cutting-edge cuisine, head to the ultra-modern **Las Duelas** (Pl. Monseñor F. Rodríguez, tel. 94/130-4463, 1:30–3:30 P.M. and 8:30 –11 P.M. Tues.–Sat., 1:30–3:30 P.M. Mon., closed Sun., €45) located in Hotel Los Agustinos. Their risotto with wild mushrooms and parmesan foam is at once homey and haute. Get back to basics at the world-famous **Casa Terete** (C/ Lucrecia Arana 17, tel. 94/131-0023, 1:15–4 P.M. and 8:30 –11 P.M. Tues.–Sat., 1:15–4 P.M. Mon., closed Sun., €30), serving wood-roasted lamb since 1877. You'll sit at long, wooden tables with hordes of locals tucking into the house specialty, *menestra de verduras* (sautéed mixed vegetables).

Getting There and Around

If you don't have a car, the best way into Haro from Logroño is by bus. Daily buses leave from the **bus station** (Av. de España 1, tel. 94/123-5983) starting at 7:30 A.M. and running every two hours or less. The ride takes 50 minutes and costs €3. The last bus from Haro is 8:30 P.M. From **Haro's bus station** (Av. Santo Domingo) you can catch daily buses to towns throughout the region. Buses also run daily to and from Vitoria and Burgos. Trains run very infrequently and cost more than double. If you are driving, take the AP-68 out of Logroño in the direction of Burgos/Vitoria/Bilbao, then follow exit 9 for Haro.

BRIÑAS

About three kilometers (two miles) north of Haro, the tiny medieval village of Briñas is as sleepy as it is charming. Its steep cobbled streets are lined with crumbling stately homes, many for sale. The town is dominated by the colossal 16th-century church, **Nuestra Señora de la Asunción** (Pl. Constitución, s/n, open during mass only). Briñas lies along a thick stretch of the River Ebro and there is a very romantic riverside walk that will make you feel as if you were stepping back in time. Across the river is nothing but vineyards as far as the horizon— no industry, no housing, no electric lighting.

Heredad Baños Bezares (C/ Solana 20, tel. 94/131-2423, €5) is a lovely riverside bodega that accepts visits by appointment during the week and anytime 10 A.M.–6 P.M. on weekends. If you want the visit in English, you must call ahead.

Accommodations

One of the loveliest accommodations in the region is located here. **Hospedería Señorío de Briñas** (Travesía Calle Real 3, tel. 94/130-4224, €110), a splendidly appointed 18th-century palace, offers antique-filled rooms, divine food, and impeccable personal service including a wide range of wine-related activities.

Getting There and Around

This is a destination for drivers only. Catch the N-124 from Haro. It is less than a 10-minute drive away.

NÁJERA

Tucked against a cliff of pink-tinged rocks and tangled green trees, the old town of Nájera straddles a wide bend in the River Najerilla. Like all towns in La Rioja, wine is both symbolically and financially important to this medieval town, but it is the Camino de Santiago that gives Nájera its fame. It is the first town of note on the Camino after pilgrims leave Logroño and their destination is the colossal 15th-century **Monasterio de Santa María la Real** (Plaza de Santa María 1, tel. 94/136-3650, €2). Legend says that back in 1085, King García III was hunting in the woods that then covered the town when he stumbled upon a cave containing a statue of the Virgin Mary. Being a religious sort, he built a church right on the spot. Five hundred years later, the cur-

the cloister of the 15th-century Monasterio de Santa María la Real in Nájera

© CANDY LEE LABALLE

rent monastery was added on. You can still see the miraculous statue today. It is tucked in an appropriately cave-like space behind a row of sarcophagi containing the remains of 10th- and 11th-century kings of Navarra. Be sure to visit the Gothic cloister with its two-dozen arches, each intricately carved in different patterns. You'll notice most of the heads cut off from the statues. Locals say French troops did the beheading during the Napoleonic invasions in the early 1800s.

Accommodations and Food

The nicest hotel in town is the romantic **Hotel Duques de Nájera** (C/ Carmen 7, tel. 94/141-0421, info@hotelduquesdenajera.com, www .hotelduquesdenajera.com, €75). For an inexpensive yet charming stay, try **Hostal Ciudad de Nájera** (Cuarta Calleja San Miguel 14, tel. 94/136-0660, www.ciudaddenajera.com, €50), which features brightly painted rooms and its own bodega with rustic local fare.

Dine where the locals do at the cozy **La Amistad** (C/ La Cruz 6, tel. 94/136-0877,

1:30–3:30 P.M. and 8–10:30 P.M. Wed.–Mon., €25). Their specialty is *cordero asado* (roasted lamb). At **El Mono** (C/ Mayor 43, tel. 94/136-3028, 1:30–4 P.M. and 8:30–11 P.M. Thurs.–Tues., €20), fish takes center plate with the *rape* (monkfish) stuffed with lobster being the star. For a quick snack or coffee, you can't beat one of the riverside terraces for their wonderful views.

Getting There and Around
Buses leave for Nájera about every half-hour from Logroño's **bus station** (Av. de España 1, tel. 94/123-5983). It's a 30-minute ride. If you are in Vitoria or Burgos, check their bus schedules as there are occasional trips to Nájera. By car, take the A-12 out of Logroño towards Navarrete. Switch to the N-120, which leads right into town.

SANTO DOMINGO DE LA CALZADA
The bustling little town of Santo Domingo de la Calzada was built by an 11th-century saint who dedicated his life to assisting pilgrims on the road to Santiago. Domingo was his name, and building *calzadas* (causeways) was his game. One thousand years later, the town is still a stopping point for pilgrims from around the world. Visit Santo Domingo's sacred bones in the **Catedral** (Plaza del Santo, s/n, 10 A.M.–1 P.M. and 4–6:30 P.M. Mon.–Sat., reserved for worship only on Sun., €3), a converted Romanic church first built in the early 12th century. Its 230-foot baroque tower was built on the opposite side of the plaza in 1762. Though the cathedral's ornate gilt altar, marble tombs, and impressive choir are intriguing, the real draw is the iron Gothic henhouse that is built into the cathedral's walls. Since 1460, the church's faithful have kept a pair of live chickens here in honor of a local legend. In the 1400s, a German pilgrim refused the advances of an innkeeper's daughter. Her pride bruised, she sought revenge by planting a silver goblet in his backpack and then claiming robbery. The hapless pilgrim was summarily hung. A few days later, his parents, on their own return from Santiago, found their son alive. When a local judge heard this during his dinner, he pointed at his plate and claimed indignantly, "he is as dead as this chicken." The roasted bird promptly sprouted feathers, stood up from the plate, and began to sing.

Accommodations and Food
There is really not much to keep you in Santo Domingo, but if you do decide to stay you can enjoy one of the most historic paradors in Spain. **Parador de Santo Domingo de la Calzada** (Pl. del Santo 3, tel. 94/134-0300, sto.domingo@parador.es, www.parador.es, €140) is built in a 12th-century pilgrim's hospital and features Gothic arches, wooden coffered ceilings, and classically appointed rooms. For a cheaper sleep, go see the Cistercian nuns who run the cozy two-star **Hospedería Cisterciense** (C/ Pinar 2, tel. 94/134-0700, €50). For dining, the **Parador** (1:30 –4 P.M. and 8:30 –11 P.M. daily, €30) offers classic Riojan dishes in a regal dining room. Equally delicious, yet a bit cheaper, is **El Rincón de Emilio** (Pl. Bonifacio Gil 7, tel. 94/134-0990, 1:30–4 P.M. and 8–11 P.M. daily, €25), a rustic dining room that is very popular with locals. For similar fare with the option of tapas, try **Restaurante Casa Madariaga** (Pl. Ayuntamiento 7, tel. 94/134-0130, 1–4 P.M. and 8:30–11 P.M. Tues.–Sat., closed Mon., €15), which also has a bustling terrace in the summer.

Getting There and Around
There are several daily buses to and from Logroño's **bus station** (Av. de España 1, tel. 94/123-5983) starting at 7:15 A.M. with the last at 8 P.M. If traveling by car, Santo Domingo is located on the N-120, which connects it to Logroño.

◀ SAN MILLÁN DE LA COGOLLA
The medieval village of San Millán de la Cogolla is nestled in a deep valley thick with trees and lush hills on the edge of the Montes de Suso. A quiet, monastic enclave, it houses two of the most historic religious buildings in all of Spain, both World Heritage Sites. The vil-

lage is named for Saint Millán, a 5th-century monk who lived in the caves here for most of his 101 years. In 550, the Visigoths built a church into the side of one of the higher hills and the saint began to do his Lenten penance in its dark rooms. He was eventually buried here. Over the centuries, the church was added onto by both Arabs and Christians and eventually the imposing structure came to be known as the **Monasterio de Suso** (tel. 94/137-3082, 9:30 A.M.–1:30 P.M. and 3:30–6:30 P.M. Tues.–Sat., €3). Today, its fame comes not only from its architectural beauty, but also from its role as the birthplace of the Spanish language. In the 10th century, a studious monk made a few notes in the margins of a book on Saint Augustine using the local vernacular Spanish, rather than Latin. Those 43 words are the first written evidence of the language.

In the 11th century, the pious and possessive King García III decided to move San Millán's bones to his base in nearby Nájera. Legend has it that once the oxen bearing the carriage with the saint's remains reached the bottom of the hill, they stopped, refusing to budge another inch. The king took it as a sign and ordered the building of the colossal **Monasterio de Yuso** (tel. 94/137-3049, 10 A.M.–1:30 P.M. and 4–6:30 P.M. Tues.–Sat., €3.50). Rebuilt in the 16th century, the building earned the nickname "El Escorial of La Rioja" for its vastness. Today, it is most famous for its library, which houses the oldest documents written in Spanish—including the first compilation of Spanish grammar. The monk-led tour is extremely detailed and exhausting. If you are not turned on by grammatical history, you might just take a quick walk around.

Accommodations and Food
The landscape around San Millán de la Cogolla is a pastoral dream of verdant green hills, thick stands of trees, and rolling acres of vineyards. It is barely touched by traffic, and there are few electric lights and no pollution. It is a lovely place to visit if you just want to do nothing but sip good wine and slip back in time. There is no better place to do that than

the Yuso monastery, which houses the atmospheric **Hospedería Monasterio San Millán** (tel. 94/137-3277, hospederia@sanmillan.com, www.sanmillan.com, closed Jan., €112). A feeling of old-world luxury permeates the rooms, which are done up in rich colors and antique furnishings. Views are either of the monastery itself or of the lovely countryside. The dining room (8:30–11 P.M. Mon.–Fri., 1:30–3:30 P.M. and 8:30–11 P.M. Sat. and Sun., €40) is elegant and warm with a menu of Riojan and Spanish specialties that are surprisingly reasonable. Be sure to order the house-made wine. For more low-key lodging, try **La Calera** (Crta. Lugar del Río, s/n, tel. 94/137-3268, €70), a beautiful family-run inn featuring romantic rooms complete with canopied beds. There is also a very good restaurant.

Getting There and Around
You'll need a car to get to San Millán de la Cogolla. From Santo Domingo de la Calzada take the LR-204. From Nájera, catch the LR-206.

EZCARAY
Sitting in the foothills of the Sierra de la Demanda, the mountain range that divides La Rioja from Burgos, Ezcaray is a cozy little town that offers the best of mountaineering activities along with world-class dining and accommodations, plus the oh-so-priceless trait of being quiet, peaceful, and very lovely. Straddling the River Oja, the town is a tidy web of quaint plazas, cobbled streets, and wooden arcaded walkways. The main architectural gem is the 12th-century **Iglesia de Santa María la Mayor,** which looks like a medieval fortress with its towers anchoring the corners of the building. Though the medieval town center is small, hosting just over 1,000 full-time residents, it is surrounded by blocks of new housing that serve as second homes for many families from the País Vasco. On weekends, when the tourists are in town, Ezcaray has a buzzy, fun feel. In warmer months, there are free classical music concerts in the main square and restaurants and bars put tables out. During the week and off-season, the town is downright

CANDY LEE LABALLE

Centuries-old wood beams are typical in Ezcaray.

PAÍS VASCO

sleepy. In winter months, Ezcaray comes to life with skiers, again, mostly on the weekends. To get complete information on activities including skiing and hiking, visit the friendly **tourist office** (C/ Sagastía 1, tel. 94/125-4679).

Sports and Recreation

The main draw to Ezcaray is its ski station **Valdezcaray** (Av. de Navarra 11, tel. 90/235-0235, oficinas@valdezcaray.es, www.valdez caray.es), located at the peak of the highest mountain in the Sierra de Demanda. Extremely popular with Spanish families, Valdezcaray features more than a dozen pistes, including two black expert runs, ten red intermediate runs, and two yellow off-piste slopes. Skiing for one day runs €25 in the high season, €18 for kids 10 and under. Full equipment rental is €18.50, €15.50 for kids. You can also rent skis and equipment slightly cheaper at **El Fuerte** (C/ Museo Etnográfico 2) in Ezcaray. Get to Valdezcaray via the **Bus Blanco** (tel. 94/124-1733 or 94/130-5614) that leaves Ezcaray several times per day.

If you are already a seasoned skier and want to try something different, contact **Torocuervo** (tel. 66/152-4628 or 69/603-3334), which promotes and teaches telemark, a skiing technique that dates back to the invention of the sport. Classes run from €20 for two hours.

The gentle mountains around Ezcaray are crisscrossed by streams and relatively untouched by human encroachment. Ten minutes walking from the town center and you'll find yourself alone in a pristine paradise. It is the perfect place for hiking and mountain biking. The tourist office will be able to provide you with maps and information to create a self-guided tour. If you prefer some professional intervention, contact **Red Rioja** (Ronda de los Cuarteles, Logroño, tel. 94/150-9010, www .redrioja.com). Run by Ezcaray native Octavio Cidre, Red Rioja can arrange anything from a brief hike to a one-week biking trek through the vineyards of La Rioja.

Accommodations and Food

The cheapest housing in town is also the most historic. The Real Fábrica de Tejidos was a royal fabric factory established in 1752. Today, it's been restored to house the **Albergue de la Real Fábrica** (C/ Santo Domingo, s/n, tel. 94/135-4477, €34 for doubles, €18 for a bunk). Baths are shared, but for the price, you can't complain. In winter, it is very popular so book ahead. The stylish **Casa Masip** (Av. Academia Militar 6, tel. 94/135-4327, www .casamasip.com, €90) combines boutique hotel touches with a homey feel. The bright, airy rooms surround a lovely stone-floored garden. The hotel also boasts an elegant dining room and a rowdy *pincho* bar, both packed on weekends. The most elegant hotel in town is the **Palacio Azcarate** (C/ Héroes del Alcázar 8, tel. 94/142-7282, info@palacio azcarate.com, www.palacioazcarate.com, €95). The hardwood-floored rooms boast rich fabrics, antique furnishings, and large, luxurious baths. The hotel also has a white-linen-tablecloth dining room and an English pub.

Tiny Ezcaray is home to one of Spain's most celebrated restaurants. **El Portal** (C/ Héroes del

Alcázar 2, tel. 94/135-4047, www.echaurren .com, 1:30–3:30 P.M. and 9.15–11 P.M. Tues.– Sun., closed Mon., €65) opened in 2004 and received one Michelin star soon after. Chef Francis Paniego offers avant-garde dishes like translucent gazpacho, *jamón* ice cream, and sweet-and-sour foie gras. For something more traditional, try his mother Marisa Sánchez's restaurant, **Echaurren** (1:30–3:30 P.M. and 9:15–11 P.M. daily, €40), located in the same building. It has won several top Spanish awards over the years with homey Riojan dishes. Both restaurants are situated in the lovely three-star Echaurren hotel (€80).

Getting There and Around

By car from most major cities in the region, take the N-120 to Santo Domingo de la Calzada and switch to the LR-111, which leads right into Ezcaray. There are three daily buses from Logroño's **bus station** (Av. de España 1, tel. 94/123-5983). The ride is just over an hour.

Rioja Alavesa

The Rioja wine-making region extends into the southern part of Álava, one of the three provinces of the País Vasco. A visit to the Rioja bodegas would not be complete without a de-tour through this region called Rioja Alavesa. Geographically, the region is indistinguishable from Rioja Alta. Touristically, it's years ahead, boasting cutting-edge architecture, perfectly restored medieval wine cellars, and dozens of enchanting inns. The difference is not in the wine, but in the money. The Basque gov-ernment has taken a proactive stance towards tourism and supports businesses and individ-uals involved in the field. La Rioja is slowly catching up. The result is a little something for everyone. For unabashed charm, head to Rioja Alavesa. For a grittier, off-the-beaten-path allure, visit Rioja Alta. Of course, with increased worldwide interest in wine tourism, expect those generalizations to blur over the next decade.

◪ LAGUARDIA

The medieval town of Laguardia is one of the most beautiful in all of Spain. Sitting on a lofty perch high above the River Ebro, it is completely enclosed by six-foot thick medi-eval walls dating from the 13th century. De-spite several episodes of war and bombardment through the centuries, they are intact and still boast working doors. In medieval times these doors would shut at sunset and late arrivals to the city would have to summon the key holder for access. A walk around the walls is a must, including a stroll along the **Paseo del Collado,** a lovely, tree-lined walk wrapping around the outside of Laguardia and boasting spectacular views of the valleys below and the dramatically carved cliffs of the Sierra de Cantabria moun-tain range in the distance.

Back inside the walls, let yourself get lost in the town's delightful grid of pedestrian streets lined with taverns, bodegas, wine shops, and palaces emblazoned with coats of arms of long-gone nobility. Balconies are often draped with bunches of red peppers drying in the sun. Called *pimientos de piquillo,* they are a staple of both Basque and Riojan cuisines. The lively heart of Laguardia is the **Plaza Mayor,** over which a whimsical 19th-century clock heralds the time at noon and 8 P.M. with a mechanical show of dancing puppets.

Laguardia's most beloved sight is hidden within the walls of the **Iglesia de Santa María de los Reyes,** built between the 12th and 14th centuries. Like most of the church porticos built during that epoch, the doorway was ren-dered in a joyous polychrome of bright colors. Unlike most—in fact, almost all—the portico of Laguardia's church was closed behind an ex-terior wall. The result is the best-preserved me-dieval portico in Spain, looking pretty much the same as it did 600 years ago. Unfortunately, the church is closed except to tours run by the

tourist office (Pl. San Juan, s/n, tel.94/560-0845, www.laguardia-alava.com, 10 A.M.–2 P.M. and 4–7 P.M. Mon.–Sat.,10 A.M.–2 P.M. Sun.). They are usually held twice a day and cost €2. The tourist office can also provide you with all the information you need to tour the bodegas both of Laguardia and the surrounding Rioja lands.

Bodegas and Wine Tourism

One of Laguardia's most fascinating aspects is its *cuevas* (caves). The town rests upon a honeycomb of over 300 caves reaching some 15 meters (50 feet) into the earth. Locals say that underground Laguardia is twice as large as the aboveground town. Built in the Middle Ages, the cellars are mostly privately owned and closed to the public. One glorious exception is **Bodega El Fabulista** (Pl. San Juan, s/n, tel. 94/562-1192, info@bodegaelfabulista.com, www.bodegaelfabulista.com, 11:30 A.M., 1 P.M., 5:30 P.M., and 7 P.M. Mon.–Sat., €5), located next to the tourist office. Housing the town's largest system of caves, the bodega has been producing wine since the Middle Ages. Tours are normally offered in Spanish, though English can be arranged by calling ahead. Owned and operated by the passionate winemaker Eusebio Santamaria, Fabulista produces thousands of bottles of wine each year. If you arrive on the *vendimia* (harvest day), which usually falls in late October, you can see the grapes being unloaded into the fermentation tanks. A lucky few are invited to hop in and give the grapes a good stomping. The tour continues through the underground den of caves where the wine is stored and aged. At the end, you'll taste a red and a white. Back upstairs, in the shop, if Eusebio still has some bottles of his velvety 2001 vintage available, buy as many as you can carry. Another bodega within the city walls is **Carlos San Pedro Pérez de Viñaspre** (C/ Páganos 44, tel. 94/560-0146, www.bodegas carlossampedro.com, by appointment only) located near the Puerta de Páganos town gate. The San Pedro family has made wine for over 500 years and is in the process of expanding their business through the construction of a new bodega outside of the town.

Pimientos de piquillo drying on balconies are a common sight in medieval Laguardia.

While walking around Laguardia's walls, you'll notice a sweep of silver undulating atop a low-lying rust-red building in the valley below. This is the showcase winery of **Ysois Bodegas** (Camino de la Hoya, s/n, tel. 94/560-0640, 11 A.M., 1 P.M., and 4 P.M. Mon.–Fri., 11 A.M. and 1 P.M. Sat. and Sun., €3, reservations suggested). The titanium-topped building was designed by famed Spanish architect Santiago Calatrava and houses a state-of-the-art winery owned by the conglomerate Bodegas y Bebidas. The bodega produces the so-so Ysois Reserva wine, which you'll taste on tour.

Along this same road are a series of bodegas, most welcoming guests by appointment. For a complete listing, ask the tourist office for the *Ruta del Vino Rioja Alavesa* booklet or visit www.rutadelvinoderiojaalavesa.com. One of the few that doesn't require advance booking is the **Bodegas Palacio** (C/ San Lázaro 1, tel. 94/560-0057, www.habarcelo.es, 1 P.M. Tues.–Fri., 12:30 P.M. and 1:30 P.M. Sat. and Sun., €3), located on the road below Laguardia.

Accommodations

About the cheapest lodging you'll find in Laguardia is **Agroturismo Larretxori** (Portal de Páganos, s/n, tel. 94/560-0763, larretxori@euskalnet.net, €40), a family-run three-room *casa rural* with plain-Jane decor that is easily trumped by the drop-dead gorgeous valley views. For a few euros more, you can stay at the cozy **Hotel Pachico** (C/ Sancho Abarca 20, tel. 94/560-0009, hotel@pachico.com, €55), a tiny hotel just outside the old city walls. Be sure and ask for a room overlooking the valley. The hotel has a decent restaurant serving local specialties at very reasonable prices. **Hotel Marixa** (C/ Sancho Abarca 8, tel. 94/560-0165, €65) is a nice-enough mid-priced lodging with a highly acclaimed restaurant featuring classic Riojan dishes like roasted lamb and white beans. A meal with wine will run about €40.

The most luxurious option in town is the **Castillo El Collado** (Po. El Collado 1, tel. 94/562-1200, www.hotelcollado.com, €110), a restored noblemen's house. The eight rooms are sumptuously decorated with antiques, Andalusian tiles, and fine linens. For €45 more, the "Amor y locura" (love and madness) suite is located in the turret with sweeping views and a whirlpool bath. Another lovely choice within the city walls is the antique-filled **Posada Mayor de Migueloa** (C/ Mayor 20, tel. 94/562-1175, www.mayordemigueloa.com, €105) located in a 17th-century mansion on Laguardia's main pedestrian street. Owned by a noted winemaker, the inn features a wonderful restaurant and an underground bodega.

In the valley below the city walls, there are several more sleeping options, including at the **Antigua Bodega de Don Cosme Palacio** (Ctra. Elciego, s/n, tel. 94/562-1195, €85). Each room is named for a grape variety and is beautifully decorated. "Tempranillo" boasts the best views of the surrounding vineyards. There is also a wine bar where you can sample Palacio's wine, as well as an excellent restaurant. Your booking also gets you a free tour of the bodega right next door. If you are getting a bit tired of charming, rustic, and cozy, head to the shiny, new four-star **Hotel Villa de Laguardia** (Po. San Raimundo 15, tel. 94/560-0560, info@hotelvilladelaguardia.com, www.hotelvilladelaguardia.com, €135), which features classically decorated rooms with nice touches like big, cushy bathrobes and complimentary wine.

Food

In addition to the fine hotel restaurants, **Biazteri** (C/ Berberana 2, tel. 94/560-0026, 1–4 P.M. and 9–11 P.M. daily, €15) offers homey local cuisine in a wood-beamed dining room decorated with antique wine-making implements. Check out their glass-roofed wine cellar. The *menú del día* is a bargain at €9 and includes the house-made rioja. The restaurant also has a small *hostal* with seven very basic double rooms (€50) and two quadruples (€85). For more innovative tastes, **Amelibia** (C/ Barbacana 14, tel. 94/562-1207, 1–3:30 P.M. Sun.–Wed., 1–3:30 P.M. and 9–11 P.M. Thurs.–Sat., €45) offers a seasonal tasting menu with items such as swiss chard in pumpkin sauce, local piquillo peppers stuffed with squid, and monkfish with pistachio. The modern dining room takes advantage of the splendid views with big picture windows.

For a serious infusion of Basque culture, head to **Batxoki** (C/ Mayor 22, tel. 94/560-0192, 10 A.M.–midnight daily), a traditional *pintxo* bar run by the Basque Nationalist Party. **Arbulu** (C/ Mayor 41, tel. 94/560-0791, 7 A.M.–3 P.M. and 6–11 P.M. daily) is a local favorite that starts with coffee and croissants in the morning and switches to sandwiches and *pintxos* by the afternoon. If you are in town on a Sunday, head to **La Muralla** (C/ Páganos 42, tel. 94/560-0198) for the best homemade *croquetas* in town. The rest of the week they serve up basic fare at basic prices.

Getting There and Around

Laguardia is accessed by daily buses from Vitoria (C/ Los Herrán 50, tel. 94/525-8400) and Logroño (Av. de España 1, tel. 94/123-5983). If you are driving, Laguardia is located on the A-124. Connect to it from Vitoria via the A-2124, from Logroño via the LR-132.

ELCIEGO

The tiny village of Elciego has long been an insider's stop off for good wine as home to the esteemed winery Marqués de Riscal. Today, it is on the map of culture vultures worldwide thanks to that company's new winery complex designed by architect Frank Gehry. Gehry's Guggenheim in Bilbao is credited with single-handedly saving Bilbao from the tourism wastelands. It is hoped he'll do the same for Rioja Alavesa. The **Marqués de Riscal Ciudad del Vino** (C/ Torrea 1, tel. 94/428-0000, www.marquederiscal.com), opened in July 2006, is a multimillion-euro wine complex that includes a luxury boutique hotel, a decadent "vinotherapy" spa, a world-class restaurant, a wine museum, boutiques, and bodega offices. The **Hotel Marqués de Riscal** (94/428-0000, www.starwoodhotels, €350 and up) is run by the prestigious Starwood group and includes 43 suites lavished with details like fine furnishings, sumptuous bathrobes, Wi-Fi, state-of-the-art audio and television equipment, marble baths, and soaring views over medieval Elciego and the surrounding vineyards. The museum details the entire wine-making process from land cultivation to wine tasting through interactive and traditional displays. The restaurant, under the guidance of Francis Paniego, owner of El Portal/Echaurren in Ezcaray, is expected to become an international dining destination. Finally, the Caudalie Vinothérapie Spa offers the latest in luxury spa treatments—all based on the antioxidant powers of grapes.

Like the Guggenheim, the building itself is expected to be a major draw. Composed of layered rivers of titanium tinted in shades of gold and pink, the ambitious edifice reflects the changing colors of Rioja from the piercing blue sky to the green, gold, and red leaves of the vineyards. As with all of Gehry's work, the building has drawn the ire of tradition-minded critics who disparage the building as nothing more than a giant crushed can. Fortunately for Marqués de Riscal, they are outweighed by fans who hail it as a singular creation of architectural genius. Either way, it is expected to draw hordes of tourists. To deal with the influx, roads, gas stations, hotels, and restaurants are furiously being built.

Accommodations and Food

If you can't score (or can't afford) reservations at Marqués de Riscal, **Hotel Villa de Elciego** (C/ Norte 1, tel. 94/560-6597, €60) has long been the village's hotel of choice, with 18 cozy rooms and a rustic wood-paneled attic bar with lovely views out to the Cantabrian mountains. With the Gehry-spurred increase in tourism that is expected, prices may soon be rising. It also has a very good restaurant offering succulent renditions of local specialties paired with excellent riojas.

Getting There and Around

There is very infrequent bus service from Logoño and Vitoria, but that is expected to change by mid-2007. Driving from Vitoria, take the A-2124 for about 32 kilometers (20 miles) then switch to the A-3212. From Logroño, take the N-232 towards Santander/ Vitoria and then switch to the A-3210, which will take you right into town.

Navarra

Tucked into a diamond-shaped piece of land separated from France by the Pyrenees, bordered by País Vasco to the west, Aragón to the east, and La Rioja to the south, Navarra has long enjoyed an independence unique in Spain. Its origins are in the 9th century when the local rulers ran the Frankish troops from the region and the nascent Kingdom of Pamplona was created. By the 11th century, the region had expanded and become the independent Kingdom of Navarra. Its stature grew due to the Camino de Santiago (Saint James' Way), which crossed right through the center of the region. In 1512, Navarra was taken over by the Castilian Kings, however the region was allowed to maintain its autonomy and self-rule as and independent kingdom under the flag of Castilian Spain—mainly because any attempt to limit their self-governing privileges resulted in massive revolts. It was just easier to let the Navarrese be. During the Spanish Civil War, Navarra sided with Franco, as much to protect their own self-interests as to advance the cause of Spanish nationalism and Catholicism (much of Navarra is deeply Catholic to this day). As a result, post-war Navarra was allowed to remain independent—the only autonomous region in all of Spain during Franco's reign.

The region today is comprised of three very distinctive zones: the green and misty north, which includes the western stretch of the Pyrenees; Pamplona, one of the world's most famous towns thanks to its San Fermín festival; and the arid south, watered by the River Ebro and home to sun-baked plains, vineyards, wheat fields, and castles. The northern region, along with Pamplona, is considered Basque in culture and heritage and you will hear Basque spoken and see it on street signs and publications. In many tiny mountain villages, Basque may be the principal language. Southern Navarra identifies more with Castilian Spain and is very similar in landscape to much of Castile.

Navarra is famed throughout Spain for its gastronomy, particularly its extraordinary produce. White asparagus grows here up to an inch thick in diameter. Nicknamed *cojonudo,* which translates roughly as "damn good," they are usually preserved in cans or jars and served with a light mayonnaise sauce. *Pimientos de Piquillo* (small sweet red peppers) are another famed local product. They are usually roasted and sold bottled or canned. Chefs then stuff them with anything from tuna to ground beef. The rivers teem with *trucha* (trout) that is often served *a la Navarra* (sautéed with cured ham). Cheeses to look out for include *roncal,* made from sheep's milk and possessing a distinctive spicy flavor and very buttery texture. *Idiazábal* is typical from the Basque region and is a very intense sheeps' milk cheese. Navarra also has its own D.O. (wine appellation); expect almost everywhere you eat in Navarra to serve only Navarrese wines.

PAMPLONA

Called *Iruña,* which simply means "the city" in Basque, Pamplona is infamous the world over thanks to Ernest Hemingway's 1926 novel *The Sun Also Rises,* which describes the city's San Fermín festivals (also known as the "running of the bulls") in vivid terms.

However, long before Papa and his pals visited the city, Pamplona was a legendary Spanish capital. The Romans founded it as Pompaelo or Pompelo and used it as the capital city of their Vascones region. By the time the Visigoths took control in 409, very little of Pamplona's Roman culture remained. On the brink between Northern Europe and the Moors coming up from the south, the city was the locus of much fighting between the 6th and 10th centuries. In the 11th century, as the capital of the Kingdom of Navarra, Pamplona flourished, particularly thanks to the Camino de Santiago (Saint James' Way), which spurred the city's growth as a trade center. During the Napoleonic Wars, French troops occupied the city from 1808 to 1813, leaving quite a bit of destruction in their wake. Later, during the

PAÍS VASCO

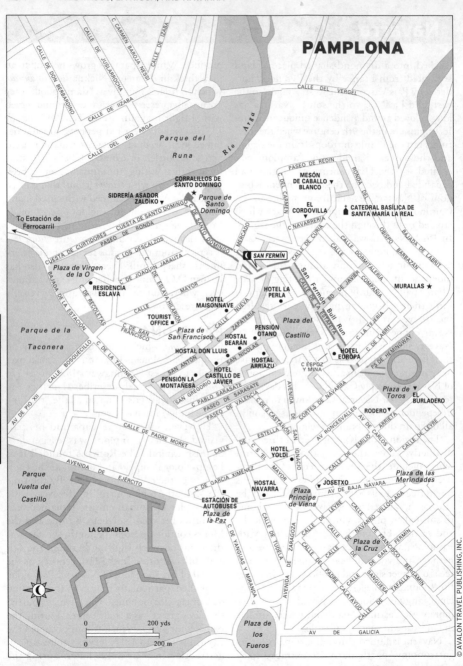

PAMPLONA

CALLE DE DON BERBARDINO
C. CARMEN BAROJA NESSI
CALLE DE IZABA
CALLE DE JUSLARROCHA

CALLE DE IZABA
CALLE DEL VERGEL
CALLE DEL RÍO ARGA
CALLE DEL RÍO ARGA

Parque del
Runa

Río Arga

PASEO DE REDIN

CORRALILLOS DE
SANTO DOMINGO

MESÓN
DE CABALLO ▼
BLANCO

SIDRERÍA ASADOR
ZALDIKO ▼

Parque de
Santo
Domingo

EL
CORDOVILLA ▼

✝ CATEDRAL BASÍLICA DE
SANTA MARÍA LA REAL

To Estación de
Ferrocarril

C. DE SANTO DOMINGO
CUESTA DE SANTO DOMINGO
CUESTA DE CURTIDORES
PASEO DE RONDA
C. DE MERCADO
C. NAVARRERÍA
C. DEL CARMEN

RONDA DEL
OBISPO · BARBAZÁN
BAJADA DE LABRIT

☾ SAN FERMÍN

CALLE DE CURIA

CALLE DORMITALERÍA

Plaza de Virgen
de la O

C. LOS DESCALZOS

BAJADA DE LA ESTACIÓN

RESIDENCIA
ESLAVA

C. DE JOAQUÍN JARAUTA
C. DE ESLAVA
MAYOR
HILARIÓN

San Fermín Bull Run
CALLE DE LA ESTAFETA
BD DE JAVIER COMPAÑÍA
C. LA TEJERÍA

MURALLAS ★

HOTEL LA
PERLA

C. DE RECOLETAS
C. DE SAN
FRANCISCO

HOTEL
MAISONNAVE

CALLE NUEVA
ZAPATERÍA

Plaza del
Castillo

C. DE LABRIT

TOURIST
OFFICE ■

PS. DE HEMINGWAY

Parque de la
Taconera

C. BOSQUECILLO
C. DE LA TACONERA

Plaza de
San Francisco

HOSTAL
BEARÁN

PENSIÓN
OTANO ▼

HOTEL
EUROPA

HOSTAL DON LLUIS
SAN ANTÓN
SAN GREGORIO
C. DE PABLO SARASATE
PASEO DE SARASATE
PASEO DE VALENCIA

SAN NICOLÁS

HOSTAL
ARRIAZU

C ESPOZ
Y MINA

Plaza de
Toros

EL
BURLADERO

AV DE PÍO XII

PENSIÓN LA
MONTAÑESA

HOTEL
CASTILLO DE
JAVIER

AVENIDA DE CARLOS III
AV DE RONCESVALLES
AV DE ARRIETA

RODERO ▼

AVENIDA DE CORTES DE NAVARRA
AVENIDA DE SAN IGNACIO

CALLE DE PADRE MORET

CALLE DE
C. ESTELLA
C. S. E.

CALLE DE EMILIO
AV DE CARLOS III

CALLE DE LEYRE

AVENIDA DE EJÉRCITO

HOTEL
YOLDI

MAYOR

Plaza de las
Merindades

Parque
Vuelta del
Castillo

C. DE GARCÍA XIMÉNEZ

HOSTAL
NAVARRA

JOSETXO ▼

AV DE BAJA NAVARA

CALLE DE LEYRE
CALLE DE NAVARRO VILLOSLADA

LA CUIDADELA

ESTACIÓN DE
AUTOBUSES

Plaza de
la Paz

Plaza
Príncipe
de Viana

CALLE DE SAN FRANCISCO

Plaza de
la Cruz

C. DE YANGUAS Y MIRANDA
CALLE DE TUDELA
AVENIDA DE ZARAGOZA
C. DE GASTAÑÓN
CALLE DE FRANCISCO
CALLE DEL PADRE CALATAYUD
C. SANGUESA
CALLE DE SAN FERMÍN
BERGAMÍN
CALLE DE TAFALLA

0   200 yds
0   200 m

Plaza de
los
Fueros

AV DE GALICIA

© AVALON TRAVEL PUBLISHING, INC.

Civil War, Pamplona was an early stronghold of Franco's Republican troops and was granted autonomous privileges after the war (as the capital of the Kingdom of Navarra). The city has since proved to be hard-working, hearty, and self-sufficient. It is home to one of Europe's top universities, Universidad de Navarra, and boasts a lively industrial base including a large Volkswagen factory just outside of town.

Wrapped by the River Arga, Pamplona has as much greenery as it does cement, with half a dozen gorgeous parks scattered throughout the city. Along with its lively economy, vibrant cultural life, and excellent infrastructure, for several years the city has been rated as having the highest quality of life in Spain. That said, the casual tourist might find it a bit dull. The town is lovely enough and the nightlife is lively thanks to the university students, but that is about it. It makes a good base to explore the nearby Navarrese Pyrenees, and of course, if you want to experience the fiesta to end all fiestas—San Fermín—Pamplona is your place; just book your hotel way ahead of time.

Plaza del Castillo is lined with sidewalk cafés. During Sanfermines, this is party ground zero.

Sights

The main sights are within easy walking distance of each other in the **Casco Antiguo,** Pamplona's oldest quarter located on the southern banks of the River Arga. The heart of this area is the broad **Plaza del Castillo,** which also serves as ground zero for all the San Fermín mayhem. When not in fiesta mode, it is a bustling plaza surrounded by arcaded cafés and filled with locals. Off the eastern edge of the plaza is the medieval **Judería** (Jewish quarter). Today it is a buzzy area full of shops, tapas bars, and restaurants. Not far away is the lovely 14th-century **Catedral Basílica de Santa María la Real** (C/ Curia, tel. 94/821-0827, 10 A.M.–1:30 P.M. and 4 P.M.–7 P.M. Mon.–Fri. and 10:30 A.M.–1:30 P.M. Sat., Sun. for worship only, €3.60), built atop a Romanesque church. When completed, it was the second-largest cathedral in Spain behind that of León and its facade was said to be a marvel of Gothic architecture. Unfortunately, it was covered up by a rather plain neoclassical facade in the 18th century. Within, the Gothic naves are still quite spectacular. They give shelter to the tombs of the 15th-century Navarrese royals, King Carlos III and Queen Leonor. The cloisters are also magnificent, especially the Puerta Preciosa "Precious Door," a very good description. The cathedral also houses the **Museo Diocesano,** a collection of religious ornaments dating from the 11th century. Behind the cathedral is a well-preserved segment of the city's 16th-century **Murallas,** the fortified walls that held off advancing armies for centuries. The view from up top is expansive. Head through one of the gates and down to the river, then look up to see just how impressive these walls once were.

Back in the center, head south along the walls to the **Plaza del Toros,** one of the largest bullrings in Spain. It is the serves as the finishing point for the San Fermín *encierros* (running of the bulls). In front is **Paseo Ernest Hemingway,** a tree-lined walkway with a bust of the writer. The starting point of the *encierro* is at the opposite end

RUNNING WITH THE BULLS: WHAT YOU NEED TO KNOW

© SEVE PONCE DE LEON

the infamous running of the bulls at Sanfermines

Many people believe visitors should not run with the bulls. It is extremely dangerous and often deadly. There have been 13 deaths since 1924, including Chicago native Matthew Tasio, a 22-year-old who was gored to death in 1995. General consensus is that he lacked the basic knowledge of how to run. However, even skill does not guarantee survival. In 2003, Pamplona native Fermín Etxeberria Irañeta, who had run for decades, was killed. The bottom line is that no matter how much you know, the 450-kilogram (1,000-pound) bulls are wild and very dangerous. That said, thousands choose to run with the bulls each year. If you are among them, please become as informed about the event as possible. Knowledge can make the difference between the experience of a lifetime or the end of your life.

BEFORE RUNNING

The most important first step to take before running is to decide definitively whether you will or will not run. Do not make the mistake of deciding that you won't run, partying all night, and then changing your mind in the morning. Your lack of knowledge about what will happen is not only dangerous for yourself, but for other runners. If you think you are even slightly likely to run, get prepared.

First, read all you can about the event. The Internet is loaded with information, including www.pamplona.net, www.sanfermin.com, and the blog www.bullrunning.info.

Once in town, look for the official flyers detailing the dos and don'ts of running with the bulls. Be sure and read the entire pamphlet. It is also a good idea to talk with an experienced runner for first-hand, practical information. On the morning of the run, officials will announce the rules in various languages. Ask someone if you are not sure of anything.

The day before, walk the length of the run and decide which section you will run. It is not advised to run the entire course. Learn more about the various sections of the run — which are safer,

easier, harder – through your research. Also, do not attempt to run if you are out of shape.

Do not party all night. Quit drinking early enough so you will be sober by 8 A.M. (and preferably hangover-free). You will need your wits about you. If you are visibly drunk, you will be tossed from the run – more for the safety of the other runners, than for yourself.

BASIC RULES

The basic rules of the run are posted on various websites and printed by the tourist office. They are intended to make this extremely dangerous event somewhat less dangerous. For that reason, the rules are not just enforced by police and run officials, but by locals as well. If the locals catch you breaking the rules – and potentially putting their lives at risk – they will not take it lightly and you may end up on the receiving end of a few serious blows. The rules are as follows:

1. You must be at least 18 years old and male.

2. You must be on the running course by 7:30 A.M. and can only enter through official gates; do not jump over the barricades as you will be arrested or, as stated above, beaten up by irate locals.

3. Do not block any part of the run or place yourself in any restricted areas of the run.

4. Do not hide in corners, entryways to buildings, or any other place on the route without the intention of running. Actual runners may need to dive into these spaces to save their lives.

5. Do not run under influence of alcohol or drugs.

6. Do not carry any object that could put any runner in danger, including yourself. Cameras, backpacks, and other items are strictly forbidden, as they will slow you down. Do not even think of stopping to take a photo during the run.

7. You must wear appropriate clothing and footwear, and nothing that will cause you to slip, fall, or otherwise be hindered.

8. Do not attempt to attract the bull's attention or touch the bull in anyway. Pulling its tail is strictly forbidden, and again, you may be attacked by other runners if you try to do so. The most dangerous thing that can happen is if the bull gets separated from the pack. He will become wild, unpredictable and extremely dangerous. Most deaths occur in this situation.

9. Do not hit the bull with a rolled-up newspaper. You have seen people running with rolled-up papers. Contrary to popular misconception, they are not for hitting the bull. Rather, a loose bull will go after a moving object. The idea is that if a bull is bearing down on you, throwing the paper will distract his attention from you to the newspaper.

10. Do not stop or slow down in the run. This can cause the runners behind you to trip, creating a very dangerous situation.

11. Once the bulls pass you, stop running. If you continue, there is a chance one of the bulls may notice the movement behind him and turn around, creating a dangerous situation.

12. Once you are in the bullring, head immediately for protection behind one of the walls. There are other runners behind you, so you must get out of the way. Do not try to attract the bulls. Let the bull handlers corral them into the ring.

13. Finally, the **most important thing to know:** If you fall down, stay down. Wrap your hands around your head and stay still. A bull is only attracted to moving objects. If you look like a lump on the ground, it will pass you. You may get stepped on or kicked and end up with serious bruises, but you'll live. Matthew Tasio died because he didn't know this. He fell and stood up. The crowd went wild, screaming at him to get down but it was too late. A 450-kilogram (1,000-pound) bull was attracted to his movement and within seconds had run his horns right through Matthew's body.

Once the danger is over, someone will tap you to let you know you can get up. If you've been injured, medics waiting all along the route will attend to you immediately. Pamplona has a well-trained medical force experienced in bull-running injuries.

BOTTOM LINE

My advice is to NOT run. If you will anyway, for the safety of yourself and the other runners, be prepared and follow the rules.

of the Casco Antiguo at the **Corralillos de Santo Domingo,** a city gate. Nearby is the **Museo de Navarra** (C/ Santo Domingo 47, 10 A.M.–2 P.M. and 5 P.M.–7 P.M. Mon.–Sat. and 11 A.M.–2 P.M. Sun., €2). Originally a 16th-century hospital, the museum now houses a collection of Roman artifacts and paintings from the Gothic and Renaissance periods.

West of the Casco Antiguo, the massive Parque de la Ciudadela is home to **La Ciudadela,** a 16th-century citadel constructed under order of Fernando the Catholic King of Castile to fortify the city and protect it from invasion. Just north is **Parque de la Taconera.** Both parks are wonderful expanses of green in the midst of the bustling city. But come Pamplona, the parks—especially Ciudadela—is party central as thousands of college kids from around the world bed down in the park in lieu of springing for a room.

Nightlife

During San Fermín, the party flows like alcohol onto the streets of the old quarter. You will have no problem finding a place to drink and dance. In fact many impromptu bars emerge from grocers and clothing stores. Most places set up counters right on the street, in effect turning the entire street into a bar. Many add dance floors and live music, all day long. The rest of the year, the highest concentration of bars in the city is on Calles San Nicolas, San Gregorio, and Comedias. Plaza del Castillo is also a great place to meet locals and tourists while enjoying drinks in the open air. Try **Casino Eslava** (Pl. Castillo 16, tel. 94/821-2937). Open all day with coffees and snacks, by evening it becomes a popular place to start the night. Around the corner is **La Granja** (C/ Estafeta 71), essential to any bar-crawl route. **Fitero** (C/ Estafeta 58), just down the street, attracts an up-for-anything university crowd.

Pamplona has a lively nightclub scene on the weekends. **Friday** (Pl. Castillo 8, weekends only) is one of the few places to dance late night in Plaza del Castillo. The music is house and the crowd local and under 30. A couple blocks South of the Plaza de Toros, **By By** (C/ Abejeras 11, Thurs.–Sat.), an old favorite on the Pamplona nightclub scene, draws a boisterous crowd with a mix of Spanish pop and dance favorites. Just southwest of the Ciudadela, **Singular** (Av. Pío XII 1, 11 P.M.–4 A.M., weekends only) is shiny disco playing fun pop music from The Beatles to U2 via The Cure, REM, and Depeche Mode. In the same building, **Plural** (Av. Pío XII 1) is the place to go for drag queens, go-go boys (and a few girls), and all-out liberal-minded bacchanalia against a background of peppy house music.

◖ San Fermín

Every July 6–14, the world converges upon Pamplona for the festival of San Fermín (often spelled Sanfermines), swelling the population from just under 200,000 to well over a million. Although similar events take place all over Spain throughout the year, thanks to Ernest Hemingway, the festival has been immortalized and "running with the bulls in Pamplona" has become a rite of passage for young men the world over (women are not allowed to run).

The fiesta honors the devout saint San Fermín, an early bishop of Pamplona who was beheaded in France around the 3rd century for preaching Christianity. (What would he think of the current bacchanalia held in his honor?) His official feast day is July 7, and there is a solemn procession held in the streets at 10 A.M., during which a wooden statue of the saint is paraded. During the bull runs, those who narrowly escape injury are said to be protected by the cape of San Fermín.

The most distinctive feature of San Fermín is the daily bull run held on July 7–14. Called *encierro,* a word that means "the enclosing," it refers to the practical origins of the bull run— to get the bulls from their pens into the enclosure of the bull ring. The run starts at 8 A.M. each morning of the festival. The route begins at Cuesta de Santo Domingo and travels down Calle Santo Domingo past the Ayuntamiento (Town Hall), takes a dangerous turn onto Calle Mercaderes, then another onto Calle Estafeta. This leads to the Plaza de Toros. At the start of the bull run, a flare is shot to signal that the

bulls have been released. A few moments later, a second shot signals all the bulls are in the street and running. A third shot means they have all entered the ring, and a fourth signals that all the bulls are safely in their pens. The length of the route is just over 0.8 kilometer (0.5 mile) and should take under two minutes if all goes well. The longest run occurred in 1980, when bulls got separated form the pack. The run took over 10 minutes and left two runners dead. In the bullring, after the bulls have been herded into the pens, several heifers are released. The crowds run with them, taunt them, and basically play at being a matador. However, even though the heifers are small compared to the bulls, they still weigh several hundred kilograms and pack a serious wallop if they hit you. (See sidebar, *Running With the Bulls: What You Need to Know*)

Watching the bull run requires some pluck and luck. Failing that, money helps. First, take note that there are two layers of fencing separating the crowd from the runners. The space in between is reserved for medics, police, and a few press photographers. Don't take up a spot where there is only one fence; at some point before the run, the authorities will move you so that they can erect a second fence. For the most part the fences are pretty high and it is difficult to see over them. A good spot to head is Calle Santo Domingo near the start of the run. The sidewalk is elevated some six meters (20 feet) off the street so there is no need for fencing. There is a railing and benches. If you want to sit here, get there by 5:30 A.M. and don't move. Bring food, drinks, and a friend to hold your spot should you need to use the bathroom. You can also watch the run from a balcony by booking a "Balcony VIP" with **Erreka** (C/ Curia 18, tel. 94/822-1506 or 65/909-9547, info@erreka.net, www.erreka .net). For around €70, you can watch the bull run from a 2nd-floor balcony with a bilingual guide who will explain the history of the event. A buffet breakfast is included. Lots of locals also rent out space on their balconies, just look around for flyers or wave up to the folks in their balcony. Another place to watch the run is

at its finale in the bullring. Tickets costs under €6. The daily bull run is also shown on a giant screen hung in the Plaza del Castillo. Finally, be aware that the first weekend of the festival is the most crowded, so going later in the week might improve your viewing chances.

The bull runs are hardly the only event in San Fermín. The festival kicks off with the **Txupinazo,** held on July 6. In the morning, thousands of locals dressed in the official San Fermín uniform of white pants and shirts with a red neckerchief, cram the Plaza Consistorial for the mayor's declaration of the start of San Fermín. A rocket is set off precisely at noon and simultaneously the crowd uncorks thousands of bottles of sparkling wine—very little is drunk, a lot gets sprayed and spilled. This act sets off the wild revelry that will engulf the town for the next week. The fiesta closes at midnight on July 14 with the **Pobre de Mí,** a candlelit procession that translates as "Poor Me."

Throughout the fiesta, **corridas** (bullfights) are held each evening at 6:30 P.M. Tickets are sold out far in advance, however, by law the bull ring must reserve 10 percent of the tickets for sale the morning of the fight. You'd have to line up early to get them—missing the bull run in the process. There is a continued problem with scalpers taking over the line and purchasing all the tickets only to re-sell them at a very large mark-up. If you really want to attend, just stand around the front of the plaza, a scalper will approach you—though it is a good idea to have a Spanish-speaker on hand to do the negotiations. Expect to pay €20–50.

Inside the bullring, the upper levels are taken over by *peñas,* private social clubs that set much of the raucous tone of the fiestas. They have their own brass bands, flags, and colors. Their clubs are concentrated on Calle Jarauta and are open to the public around the clock throughout the fiesta. Their boisterous bars are definitely the most fun place to be. Every night, their brass bands lead spirited musical processions through the streets.

Around 11 P.M. a fireworks display is held near the Ciudadela. There is also a fun fair, food booths, mobile bars, and music, dancing, and drinking non-stop. The whole city becomes quite a mess with the ground covered in an inch of broken glass and muck that you don't even want to know about. Do not wear sandals—the biggest injury recorded by local medics is cut feet.

Foreigners have introduced their own events to San Fermín as well. On July 5, People for the Ethical Treatment of Animals (PETA) stages a **Running of the Nudes** along the route of the bull run. As the name suggests, the runners are naked. Of course, PETA's goal is to protest the bull runs and bull fights of the festival, but most curious locals just go to watch the naked *guiris* (foreigners). With constant press coverage, the run gains more participants each year and has become a fun alternative for tourists who agree with PETA's views. See www.running ofthenudes.com for more.

Another foreign addition is the **Navarrería Fountain Jump,** begun by Australians several years ago. Tourists, often extremely drunk, climb to the top of the fountain and jump into the arms of the waiting crowd. Technically, it is illegal, but the police seem to not intervene and the locals just look the other way. However, as injuries have increased (including several quite serious), crackdowns by police may increase as well.

A word about **accommodations.** If you can't live without a cozy bed and warm shower, be sure to reserve your hotel room at least by January—and expect to pay triple prices. If you can't get a reservation—or can't afford one—do like the thousands of other tourists and sleep in the parks or plazas. Follow your city map to a patch of green and bed down, though consider doing so by day—after the bull run and before the night's festivities have reached full boil. The further you go from the center, the quieter it will be. Be aware that July nights in Pamplona are quite cold. You'll need a sweater or a sleeping bag to sleep at night. Also, sleeping tourists are prime targets for thieves. Sleep with friends and keep all of your valuables on your body—preferably inside your clothing. Thieves have been known to slit open sleeping bags with travelers dozing inside. You can also

lock up valuables at the *consigna* (left luggage) that sets up in the **Escuelas de San Francisco** in Plaza San Francisco. The lines are usually quite long and you may be asked to show ID. Public bathrooms are set up in the Parque de la Ciudadela and around town and there are **public showers** (C/ Eslava, tel. 94/822-1738) where you can bath and wash your clothes for a small fee.

Finally, another option, especially if you are in a city like Madrid or Barcelona, is to check with a local youth hostel or *agencia de viaje* (travel agent) for overnight trips to the event. They will usually arrive in the city around nightfall and leave the next morning soon after the bull run—you sleep on the bus.

For more on the event, any Internet search will bring up tons of information, but the most complete—and objective—is www.sanfermin. com, run by the Pamplona-based design company Kukuxumusu. Their colorful t-shirts (on sale throughout Pamplona and in their shops all over Spain) are the most stylish souvenirs you could ask for.

Accommodations

The prices listed here are for all seasons except San Fermín. During the fiesta, expect rates to at least triple. Remember to book way in advance for San Fermín. Some recommend booking a year in advance, however, the hotels often don't set their prices for the year until after Christmas and subsequently won't accept reservations until after that. You can also try to rent a private apartment or room by visiting the notice boards of www.sanfermin.com.

In the **Under €50** category, **Pensión Otano** (C/ San Nicolás 5, tel. 94/822-5095, www .casaotano.com, €45) is a simple, comfortable pension with a very good traditional Navarrese restaurant right downstairs. It is in the heart of the tapas/bar-hopping zone. **Pensión La Montañesa** (C/ San Gregorio 2, tel. 94/822-4380, €35) is barely better than dumpy. Rooms are small, baths are shared, and beds are lumpy, but the price was made for budget travelers and the location in the old town is perfect. **Hostal Don Lluis** (C/ San Nicolás 24, tel. 94/821-0499, €45) also has a good location, but the rooms are nicer than the Montañesa. **Hostal Bearán** (C/ San Nicolás 25, 94/822-3428, €42) is another good, cheap sleep. There are also several low-rent places near the bus station.

At **€50-100**, try the Victorian-styled **Hostal Arriazu** (C/ Comedias 14, tel. 94/821-0202, www.hostalarriazu.com, €65). Though the rooms are tiny, the location more than makes up for it—just steps from lively Plaza del Castillo. **Residencia Eslava** (Pl. Virgen de la O 7, tel. 94/822-2270, www.hotel-eslava.com, €55) is a charming, inexpensive option located on a hill on the edge of the historic center. The friendly family that runs it and the wonderful views of the city's old walls compensate for the rather dull rooms. There is also a wonderful rustic bar on the 1st floor. **Hostal Navarra** (C/ Tudela 9, tel. 94/822-3426, info@hostal navarra.com, www.hostalnavarra.com, €60), very close to the bus station, feels more like a hotel than a *hostal* with light, airy rooms and efficient service. **Hotel Castillo de Javier** (C/ San Nicolás 50, tel. 94/820-3040, www.hotel castillodejavier.com, €65) is well located on a main tapas/bar street and features clean, updated rooms and a friendly 1st-floor bar.

Many of the hotels in the **over-€100** price range drop rates on the weekends (excluding San Fermín, of course). Situated south of the Ciudadela, **AC Ciudad de Pamplona** (C/ Iturrama 21, tel. 94/8260-6011, www.ac-hotels .com, €112) is a modern hotel with comfortable, spacious rooms and good amenities. Located 15 minutes walking from the old town, it is a good choice if you need a break from the pandemonium of San Fermín. However, being close to the University of Navarra means there are plenty of bars and restaurants nearby—skip the hotel's overpriced breakfast buffet. **Yoldi** (Av. San Ignacio 11, tel. 94/822-4800, www.hotel yoldi.com, €130) is a well-maintained modern hotel popular with bullfighting fans. It is just south of the old center and a few blocks from the bullring. **◖ Hotel Maisonnave** (C/ Nueva 20, tel. 94/822-2600, www.hotelmaisonnave .es, €102), located between Plaza San Francisco

and Plaza del Castillo, is the perfect option for the seasoned, sophisticated traveler. Rooms are modern and comfortable and there are luxury touches, including a sauna.

The famous **Hotel La Perla** (Pl. Castillo, tel. 94/822-7706), where Ernest Hemingway is rumored to have watched his first bull run, is one of only two hotels with balconies overlooking the run. It is undergoing a long-overdue face-lift and is expected to re-open sometime in 2007 as a boutique hotel. The other hotel with a view is the **Europa** (C/ Espoz y Mina 11, tel. 94/822-1800, europa@hreuropa.com, www.hreuropa.com, €120), a classy property with an acclaimed restaurant. However rooms here are often reserved strictly for VIPs during the festival.

Food

The Plaza del Castillo is a local favorite for open-all-day, people-watching **cafés.** One of the best is the belle epoque **Café Iruña** (Pl. Castillo 44, tel. 94/822-2064, 9 A.M.–10 P.M. daily), which has been serving breakfasts, light lunches, and lots of coffee on its marble tables since 1888. **Bar Café Niza** (C/ Duque de Ahumada 2, tel. 94/822-5958, 7:30 A.M.–2:30 A.M. daily) is an old-fashioned café that is wildly popular during the bull runs when those who'd rather not be crushed up against the barriers— or trampled by bulls—watch the event on a large-screen television with a cup of hot chocolate and *txurros* (fried dough sticks).

It is easy to find *pintxos* in the Casco Antiguo, just walk in any direction and follow the locals. The basic rule, which applies throughout Spain, is that if it is crowded, it's good. Most are open from noon–3 P.M. and again from 8 P.M.–midnight. **◖ Baserri** (C/ San Nicolás 32, tel. 94/822-2021) has won numerous pintxo competitions over the years for its innovative mini works of culinary art, such as venison with wild mushrooms, rosemary salsa, and almond vinaigrette. Vegetarians will be delighted with Baserri's attached vegetarian restaurant **Sarasate. El Gaucho** (C/ Espoz y Mina 7, tel. 94/822-5073) is a classy bodega serving creative and traditional *pintxos*

PAÍS VASCO

and wines from Navarra. **Mesón de Caballo Blanco** (C/ Redín, s/n, tel. 94/821-1504) serves traditional *pintxos* and meals on a lovely terrace overlooking the old city walls. **El Cordovilla** (C/ Navarrería 8, tel. 94/822-2034) arguably serves the largest *pintxos* in the world (try their fried calamari with peppers). The place gets packed early, wait your turn and you will not be disappointed!

For delicious local cuisine you are spoiled for choice in Pamplona. **Casa Paco** (C/ Lindachiquia 20, tel. 94/822-5105, 1:30–3:30 P.M. and 9–11 P.M. daily, €15) is a top-rated traditional restaurant serving exquisite Navarrese fare. Just be aware, their house specialty, *callos,* is tripe. **Sidrería Asador Zaldiko** (Cuesta de Santo Domingo 39, tel. 94/822-2277, €35), located near the start of the bull run, is a traditional Basque cider house with hearty grilled meats and lots of hard cider. **El Burladero** (C/ Emilio Arrieta 9, tel. 94/822-8034, 1:30–3:30 P.M. and 8:30–11 P.M. daily) is an elegant dining room close to the bullring. Decorated with stylish bullfighting posters and memorabilia, it is popular with locals after bullfights.

Pamplona has several gourmet spots, including the acclaimed **Rodero** (C/ Emilio Arrieta 3, tel. 94/822-8035, 1:30–3:30 P.M. and 9–11 P.M. Mon.–Sat., closed Sun., €65). The restaurant has been in the Rodero family for 40 years, but young gun Koldo Rodero has thoroughly modernized the once traditional menu with surprisingly good dishes like sweet tomato with pepper ice cream, duck liver with quince jelly and truffle butter, and seared mullet with fruit tea infusion. The best bet is the gastronomic menu of the chef's choices. Book ahead as this sleek dining room is very popular. **Josetxo** (Pl. del Príncipe de Viana 1, tel. 94/822-2097, 1:30–3:30 P.M. and 9–11 P.M. Mon.–Sat., closed Sun., €50) is another family-run dining institution in Pamplona. Located in a lovingly restored 19th-century mansion, the restaurant turns out impeccable Basque dishes with modern touches such as shrimp salad with pickled tomatoes, shellfish pastry, or grilled monkfish brochette with chive cream. They also boast a stellar wine cellar.

Information

The **tourist office** (C/ Eslava 1, tel. 84/842-0420, www.turismo.navarra.es, 10 A.M.–2 P.M. and 4 P.M.–7 P.M. Mon.–Sat., and 10 A.M.–2 P.M. Sun.) is near Plaza San Francisco in the old quarter. For additional information, visit www.pamplona.es and click on "Tourism."

Getting There and Around

Pamplona's **Noáin Airport** (Crta. Zaragoza, tel. 94/816-8700, www.aena.es), about 6.5 kilometers (four miles) out of the city, offers domestic service to cities throughout Spain via **Iberia** (www.iberia.es). If you are coming from outside of Spain, your best bet is to fly into Bilbao and then transfer to Pamplona via train, bus, or rental car. (Bus is your best bet, cheap and under two hours). From the airport in Pamplona, taxi is the only option (about €15).

Pamplona's **train station** (Av. San Jorge, s/n) is northwest of the Casco Viejo and operated by **Renfe** (tel. 90/224-0202, www.renfe.es), with trains going all over the country.

A number of bus companies operate out of the centrally located **Estación de Autobuses** (C/ Conde Oliveto, s/n, tel. 94/822-3854). Transport services are offered between cities throughout Spain and you should not have a problem reaching Pamplona by bus, regardless of your origin point. Schedules and fares vary by company.

If **driving,** the A-15 links Pamplona to San Sebastian in the north and Madrid in the south. To get to France, use NA-135 and the Belate Tunnel. Parking during San Fermín can be both scarce and expensive; try to rent your car after leaving the festival.

VICINITY OF PAMPLONA
Olite

If you are driving to or from Pamplona, it is worth your time to make a 44-kilometer (27-mile) detour south to the town of Olite. As you approach, the medieval stone towers and slate cone tops of the **Palacio Real** (tel. 94/874-0035, €3) rises up magically from the plains to greet you. Built in the 15th century, this fairy-tale castle is the best example of civil Gothic structure in the world and provides a fascinating glimpse into life in the Middle Ages—well, at least the lives of the Kings of Navarra. The town also has a number of 12th- and 13th-century Romanesque churches. It is a delightful visit, but for a night worth remembering, consider staying in the wing of the castle that has been turned into **Parador de Olite** (Pl. Teobaldos 2, tel. 98/474-0000, olite@parador .es, www.parador.es, €120).

Getting there from Pamplona, follow A-15 south and switch to N-121 to Olite.

WESTERN PYRENEES

The majestic Pyrenees begin their rapid ascent in the northeastern region of Navarra. Separating Navarra from France, this western section of the mountains is the gentlest area of the range. For centuries these relatively low mountains and valleys have served as a passageway into and out of Spain for conquerors, soldiers, and pilgrims. Today, the area attracts Spanish and European nature-lovers with its dramatic carpet of green, rising summits, deep valleys, and pristine forests. Dotted with tiny mountain villages of white houses edged in gray brick and topped with steep rust-colored roofs, sprinkled with Romanesque ruins, riddled with rivers and waterfalls, and blessed with ancient beech forests, the Western Pyrenees offer a picturesque escape to travelers in the region—and provide the perfect post–San Fermín antidote.

You'll need a car and at least two days to visit here (though you could easily spend a month). You'll also need some vacationing pluck. This is not roll-out-the-welcome-mat Spain. Don't expect people to speak English and, in many cases, even Spanish takes second seat to Basque. You'll find very few big hotels, if any. In their place are dozens of *casas rurales* (rural houses), which are often converted centuries-old farmhouses. In English, find them at www.top rural.com. A more extensive list is in Spanish at www.hotelesruralesnavarra.es. Any Navarra tourist office should also be able to provide you with a list and some may even do the booking for you. Other services like shops and gas stations are limited as well. When you see a village, stock up on what you need. And always be on the lookout for local food products, especially cheeses and jarred vegetables—both prized gastronomic items outside of Navarra. Finally, don't be afraid to go exploring beyond the limited information covered below. The Navarra tourism office in Pamplona, and online at www.turismo.navarra.es, has wonderful information. Be bold and create your own fantasy trip in these age-old mountains. One last tip, when sussing out food, go wherever the other cars are going—never judge a place by the way it look. The dumpiest hovel may have exquisite food—the locals will know, so follow them.

If you'd like to explore this area but prefer to do so with a guide, contact **Puente Turismo Activo** (info@puentespain.com, www.puente spain.com). Run by native Iowan Anne Pinder, who has lived in Spain 20 years, the company specializes in hikes and walks in the foothills of the Pyrenees and elsewhere in Spain. (See sidebar, *Walking in Spain,* in the *Essentials* chapter.)

Orreaga-Roncesvalles

The historical village of Orreaga-Roncesvalles is the starting point for the majority of the pilgrims walking the Camino de Santiago. The first name is Basque and the second is Spanish, and depending on the map, you'll find one or both of these names. Surrounded by ancient green forests of beech, fir, and oak, and sheltered by the broad rise of the Ibañeta pass, Orreaga-Roncesvalles is a truly lovely Pyrenean village. The main sight is the **Real Colegiata de Santa María,** a 13th-century church that was once a hospice for pilgrims. The Gothic altar is still the sight of daily masses for pilgrims (8 P.M. Mon.–Fri., 7 P.M. Sat. and Sun.). The adjacent **Sala Capitular** holds the tomb of legendary Spanish King Sancho VII El Fuerte (the strong). The chains and clubs displayed at the head of his tomb are said to be spoils of the famed battle of Navas de Tolosa in 1212, in which Sancho's troops dealt the Moors a crushing blow. This battle is considered the defining moment in the Christian Reconquest. The town also has a clutch of other religious buildings dating from the 13th–18th centuries.

If you want to talk a walk in the woods surrounding the village, visit the **tourist office** (C/ Antiguo Molino, s/n, tel. 94/876-0301), which can provide maps and tips.

Among **accommodations,** the **Albergue Orreaga** (tel. 94/876-0015) is a youth hostel, located in an former pilgrims' hospital adjacent to the Colegiata. **Casa de los Beneficiados** (tel. 94/876-0105, www.casadebeneficiados .com, €60) offers two-, four-, and six-person apartments in a reformed 18th-century building. Apartments feature hewn stone floors and clean modern furnishings. A few kilometers outside of town in the village of Burguete, **Hotel Loizu** (C/ San Nicolás 13, tel. 94/879-0453, www.hotelloizu.com, €80) is a charming mountain mansion that has been converted into a lovely rural hotel.

Getting there, from Pamplona, follow the N-135 about 48 kilometers (30 miles) to the northeast. From San Sebastián, the easiest route is to head into Pamplona first by taking the A-15 there.

Selva de Irati

Just south of the French border, tucked between two valleys is the Selva de Irati. It is Europe's second-largest birch forest and the best preserved with over 168 square kilometers (65 square miles) of nearly untouched land. Watering it is the rambling River Irati, which falls into a shimmering turquoise lake called **Embalse de Irabia.** A protected reserve, it provides habitat for countless birds and mammals including wild boar and deer. There are several walking paths and the information booth at the entrance to the forest can provide maps. Also visit www.turismo.navarra.es for information in English; www.irati.org has more complete information, but in Spanish only. The most visually stunning time to visit the forest is in fall when the leaves are changing color. Summer is good too, as a respite from the heat in the rest of the country. Remember to pack your lunch and water, as there is very limited service in the park. Fortunately, the region all

around is famous for its wonderful cheeses and cured meats—perfect fare for a picnic in an ancient forest.

To get to Selva de Irata, leave Pamplona in the direction of France on N-135. After passing Aurizberri-Espinal, catch NA-140 to Aribe, then follow the sights to Orbaitzeta. From there you can enter the forest. Be sure and consult the tourist offices in Pamplona (or wherever you set off from) and get the latest maps and directions, as these small roads sometimes close due to work or weather.

◖ Ochagavía

On the other side of the Irati forest, in the picturesque Valle del Salazar (Salazar Valley), lies the enchanting village of Ochagavía. You'll feel like you fell right into a picture book when you enter this tiny town of 650. Steep-roofed white houses rise proudly against a soaring background of dense green mountains. A trickling river flows under a medieval arched bridge. Cobbled streets lead to a Romanesque stone church with an elegant tower. Sitting about one kilometer (nearly 0.5 mile) above sea level and well protected by the mountains, Ochagavía is a fresh breath of air, a clean, crisp magical place. However, this peaceful charm hides a sad background. In the 18th century during a war with the French, troops laid siege to the town and burned it nearly to the ground. The current layout of *caserios* (large houses) stems from a 19th-century rebuilding. A persistent rumor says the town is named Ochagavía from the fact that only eight (*ocho*) houses were left standing after the fire, yet historical documents refer to the town's existence as the capital of the Valle del Salazar as far back as the 11th century.

The town has given Navarra a folk custom known as the *dazantes de Ochagavía,* roughly the "dancers." Each September 8, a *romería* (pilgrimage) is held and the townsfolk perform these ancient dances in costume. Eight dancers in bright green and red costumes perform dances with sticks under the direction of *El Bobo,* literally "the idiot," a figure dressed as a harlequin.

There are a handful of wonderful *casas rurales* in Ochagavia. If the following aren't available, check with the **tourist office** (C/ Labaría, s/n) for assistance, or just ask a villager. Though many of these places prefer to rent by the weekend or week only, you can always inquire about a single night. **Casa Mantxoalorra II** (C/ Mantxoalorra 1, tel. 94/889-0513, gabrielintxusta@wanadoo.es, €190 for the weekend) is pure rustic charm with stone walls, a big fireplace, and a garden with views to the mountains. **Casa Burret** (C/ Labaría, s/n, tel. 94/889-0335, €300 for the weekend) offers similar accommodations. **Hotel Rural Besaro** (tel. 94/889-0350, www.besaro.org, €65) is an enchanting mountain hotel about three kilometers (two miles) outside of Ochagavía. The charming staff also arrange all sorts of activities in the surrounding countryside. For dining, wander around to any of the little restaurants that are in the town. The local specialty is *migas,* a type of bread stuffing made with savory sausage.

To reach Ochagavía from Pamplona, follow the Autovía del Pirineo A-21 to Venta de Judas where it merges with NA-150. Continue on to Lumbier (amazing views out the window!) and then switch to the N-178 and then the NA-178. Follow the signs to Ochagavía.

PAÍS VASCO

CANTABRIA AND ASTURIAS

Few foreign tourists venture far enough from the beaten path to make it to beautiful Asturias and Cantabria in the very heart of La Costa Verde, the green coast. This is not the Spain of flamenco and bullfighting, nor the dusty plains of the Meseta. Think more of the green rumpled hills of Ireland, the rocky coast of Maine, the sheer cliffs of Galway, and the moors of Scotland. Add a backdrop of snow-capped mountain peaks riddled with crystal-clear mountain streams coursing down through dramatic gorges out to the Cantabrian Sea and you start to get an idea of just how unexpectedly breathtaking this region is. In place of the big hotels, golf courses, and other tourist amenities so rife on the Mediterranean coast, Asturias and Cantabria offer tranquil, unspoiled, rural hideaways popular with Spanish travelers

and ecotourists. The region is a walker's paradise, with tiny roads and trails cutting through the mountains and farmland. Yet, thanks to the pilgrim routes to Santiago and a thriving network of rural houses and bed-and-breakfasts, this region is remarkably well equipped to receive tourists looking for a truly different Spanish experience.

If there is one catch, it would be the climate. All of that green thrives thanks to very damp and cool weather year-round. The conditions can turn on a dime from bright and sunny to damp and chilly, even at the height of summer. It can stay misty and foggy for days on one beach and be perfectly sunny on the next one. For those traveling in July and August, this region can provide a well-needed respite from the oppressive heat and relentless tourism

© MEGAN CYTRON

HIGHLIGHTS

◖ **Santillana del Mar:** One of the best-preserved medieval villages in Spain, pint-sized Santillana del Mar captivates the imagination with its cobblestone streets, majestic stone mansions, and imposing 12th-century Romanesque church (page 462).

◖ **Cuevas de Altamira:** Though you can't enter the actual caves, the Museo de Altamira offers a fascinating reproduction of these caves and their colorful 20,000-year-old paintings (page 462).

◖ **Playa de las Cuevas del Mar:** Sea Caves Beach is appropriately named. Wedged between beaches pockmarked with caves, this beautiful beach is one of the few that offers a straight line of sight to the soaring Picos de Europa mountains just a few miles inland (page 469).

◖ **Cudillero:** Climbing up from its horsshoe-shaped port in a jumble of colorful buildings, the fishing village of Cudillero is arguably the most picturesque on the Asturian coast (page 473).

◖ **Pre-Romanesque Architecture:** The bustling capital city of Asturias, Oviedo is also the capital of pre-Romanesque architecture in Spain with a clutch of UNESCO World Heritage buildings dating back to the 9th century. The city also offers a lively university vibe and a street lined with boisterous cider houses (page 479).

◖ **Fuente Dé:** Sitting well above sea level at the base of a soaring rocky cliff in the Picos de Europa, Fuente Dé is famous for its cable car that climbs up the 0.8-kilometer (0.5-mile) cliff in under four minutes. Up top, the views are stunning. Have a picnic or try one of the easy hiking trails (page 485).

◖ **Covadonga:** This most venerated of Spanish pilgrimage sites also boasts some of the loveliest scenery in Asturias – particularly the shimmering glacier lakes of Enol and Ercina sitting some 1,100 meters (3,600 feet) above sea level (page 488).

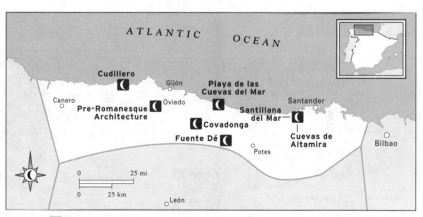

LOOK FOR ◖ TO FIND RECOMMENDED SIGHTS, ACTIVITIES, DINING, AND LODGING.

SIDRA, SIDRERÍAS, Y CHIGRES, OH MY!

Ah! – to be in a *chigre* (cider bar, also known as *sidrería*, or *sagardotegia* in Basque) with sawdust-strewn floors, monstrous crustaceans on display at the bar, and the acrobatic prowess of the *sidra* (cider) pourer on display. In northern Spain, one of the best ways to get a taste of the local flavor – in more ways than one – is to visit a *sidrería*. These are earthy neighborhood spots where you can get a good bite to eat and, of course, enjoy *sidra*.

Sidra is made from apples grown mainly in the areas around Gijón, Villaviciosa, Nava, and Sariego. It is brewed in a *llagar* (cider brewery), some of which are available for visits. The production of cider in this region dates back to 781 in the Monasterio de San Vicente. There is a carbonated variety available on tap, which is sweet, but the real treat is the drier, bottled variety, which is naturally carbonated due to the fermentation process and the unique method of pouring.

Drinking a beverage does not generally involve elaborate instructions, but in this case visitors may be baffled when they see how *sidra* is served. First, the *escanciador* (the person whose job it is to pour cider) will bring a tall green bottle and a squat wide-mouthed glass to the table. Looking anywhere but at the glass or the bottle, he (in rare cases, she) will raise the bottle high overhead with one hand and hold the glass as low as possible with the other hand. He will then pour a thin stream of cider and allow it to splash around the edges and into (and out of) the glass, making it as fizzy and aromatic as possible. Here, style is key. The best pourers make it into a sort of performance art to prove their superior technique. After pouring, he will present the glass to be drunk in one shot (called a *culete* or *culín* – which means "little butt"). No sipping or savoring allowed – freshly poured cider should go right down the hatch! Well-seasoned *sidra* drinkers leave a tiny amount in the glass to swirl around (ostensibly to clean the rather plentiful dregs out of the glass) and then chuck it with a flourish on the floor (hence, the sawdust). When you are ready for another round, flag the cider pourer down and he will repeat the process as many times as you can handle.

Aside from the cider and jovial atmosphere, the next best thing about *sidrerías* is the food. At the bar, expect to find fresh seafood on display: *centollo* (spider crabs), *buey de mar* (giant crabs that look like they have been fed steroids), *nécora* (a very delicate and flavorful crab – the best of the lot), *cigalas* (large hard-shelled shrimp), and anything else plucked fresh from the sea that day. Another perfect foil for *sidra* are the wonderful blue cheeses from the Picos de Europa mountains: *gamonedo*, *cabrales*, *picón-treviso*, and *valdeón*.

For more information about Asturian *sidra*, visit the **Museo de la Sidra de Asturias** (Pl. Príncipe de Asturias, in Nava, 35 kilometers/22 miles east of Oviedo, tel. 98/571-7422, www.museodelasidra.com). To see a cider factory in action, visit **Llagar Trabanco** (La Vandera, near Gijón, tel. 98/513-6462), where you see the traditional production techniques that are still in practice today.

(Contributed by Madrid-based journalist Megan Cytron, who writes frequently on Asturias.)

in other parts of Spain. Just be sure to pack a rain jacket and some warm layers—just in case. In the winter and off-season, the coastal areas tend to have milder—albeit wetter—weather than the bone-chilling high plains in the center of Spain.

While you can find moderate hustle and bustle in some of the bigger cities, urban life is pretty much incidental to the rural. The capital cities of Santander and Oviedo make for good points of departure, rather than dazzling destinations, and the other big cities are mostly unattractive industrial ports best skipped. It is not that there is nothing to see. Oviedo and its surroundings have been declared a UNESCO World Heritage Site for its impressive 1,100-year-old pre-Romanesque churches. Santander has a distinctive, upper-crust charm and a dream location right on a stunning bay. But there is no denying that the real allure here lies in the countryside.

The 800-kilometer-long (500-mile-long) Cantabrian mountain range dominates the interior of these two regions and divides it from the rest of Spain. In Asturias, the coastline borders on the melodramatic—sheer cliffs dotted by a series of sandy coves and sprinkled with quaint little fishing villages. Just a few kilometers beyond the coast, the mountains rise straight from sea level up to 2,652 meters (8,700 feet) in the Picos de Europa. Many of its peaks are snow-capped year-round. The coastline in Cantabria is a bit less rugged, with longer, wider beaches—some famed for excellent surfing—and more developed vacation villages, especially at the east end.

Another draw is the gastronomy that the region has to offer. *Mar y montaña*—Spanish for "surf and turf"—sums it up. On the sea side, fresh seafood caught on the coast and in the *rías* (estuaries) is abundant and delicious. Look for fresh *dorada* (sea bass), *merluza* (hake), *sepia* (cuttlefish), and more. There is also a dizzying array of shellfish. From the earth, you'll find a variety of farm products. These regions are known for their wonderful dairy products, particularly the artisan blue cheeses, such as the world-famous Cabrales. Cows, goats, and sheep easily outnumber the people, and what a life they lead, grazing free-range on fresh hay and grass. Their milk is reputed to have more vitamins because of their happy lifestyles and healthy diets. The beef and pork products are also excellent, particularly homemade smoked sausages such as chorizo and cured *lomo* (pork loin). The national dish of Asturias is *fabada asturiana* and in Cantabria *cocido montañés*, both stick-to-your-ribs white-bean stews with an ever-changing combination of pork products added. *Fabes con almejas,* fat white beans with clams and saffron, is a dish that should not be missed. In the late fall, *pote de castañas* (chestnut soup) is worth seeking out.

Sidra (hard cider) is the drink of choice. (See sidebar, Sidra, Sidrerías, y Chigres, *Oh My!*) The fruity pour is also an ingredient in many of the region's dishes, such as *merluza a la sidra*

and *chorizo a la sidra*. Most meals end with a complimentary shot of *orujo* or *hierba* (strong liqueurs often flavored with herbs). The best places to sample seafood at a reasonable price are the *sidrerías/chigres* (cider bars) and seaside *marisquerías* (simple seafood restaurants)—even the smallest towns will have one or two.

PLANNING YOUR TIME

It is nearly impossible to make a day trip into this region unless you are passing through on your way to somewhere else. Plan at least two or three days (longer if you are a nature-lover, hiker or just looking to get away from it all). And though you will be able to take some limited buses and trains, outside of the main cities you'll need to travel by car. With two days, spend the night in Santander and head to the Altamira cave in the morning. (See sidebar, *Prehistoric Cave Paintings.*) After, take a quick look at the touristy but well-preserved medieval town of Santillana del Mar. Take the coastal road to Comillas and have a peek at the outside of Gaudí's art nouveau house, El Capricho (The Whim). Then head just over the border to Asturias and the beach town of Llanes to spend the night. Pack a picnic lunch of local cheese, sausage, and cider and spend the next day relaxing and exploring the wild beaches near Llanes. If you have a third day, either head to Oviedo to see the pre-Romanesque architecture, or head up into the Picos de Europa mountains hugging the River Deva through Panes, the narrow gorge of la Hermida, crossing back into Cantabria, passing the cheese-making town of Potes, and finally turning off to head up, up, up to Fuente Dé. Do not be deceived by the short distances: These 65 kilometers (40 miles) are an all-day journey. Once you reach the end of the road, you can take a gondola up the remaining 914 meters (3,000 feet)—those with fear of heights need not attempt this—to get a bird's-eye view of the pristine beauty of this region. If time permits there are hiking trails that depart from the summit and, if you are in the mood for a splurge and want a break from the mountain roads, there is a modern parador (state-run luxury hotel), just at the end of the gondola ride.

HISTORY

Cut off from the rest of Spain by the Cantabrian mountains, Asturias and Cantabria have followed their own historic trajectories for millennia. The prehistoric cultures of the fertile coastal plains left behind cave paintings, tools, and other artifacts. The Celts built their *castros* (fortified towns), mined gold, and left behind a musical and cultural legacy that persists to this day. It took the Romans two centuries to colonize and "romanize" the Celts (who, like those who would follow, used their superior knowledge of the landscape to wage relentless guerilla warfare). The Romans extended their mining operations in this area and some of those ruins still dot the area. When the Roman Empire crumbled, the Visigoths soon found their way to Spain around 412. Almost exactly 300 years later, the Moors conquered the peninsula. Though Asturias and Cantabria were under Muslim control, the mountainous interior of the Picos never fell completely into the hands of the Muslim empire. As such, it became a hotbed of Christian upstarts. (See sidebar, *The Cradle of the Reconquista*.)

Asturias and Cantabria are two of only a handful of Spanish regions that experienced the Industrial Revolution prior to the mid-20th century—primarily through the foreign-owned mining industry, which extracted coal and iron. For a time, this brought some economic vitality to the primarily agricultural region. Meanwhile, *hidalgos* (those with some modest measure of nobility usually bought at a price) headed for the Americas to seek their fortunes. When the Latin American countries won their independence from Spain in the 19th century, many of these *indianos* returned to their tiny pueblos in Asturias and Cantabria bringing along fabulous wealth. They built colorful mansions, Casas de los Indianos, in ostentatious contrast to the humble local cottages and farmhouses. Some of the best examples are whimsical art nouveau or *modernista* masterpieces such as the Gaudí house at Comillas and the Hotel Palacete Peñalba in Figueras.

As all of this happened, the century turned, mining profits sagged, and the working and living conditions of the miners worsened. In the first third of the 20th century the tension mounted. In the traditionally conservative region of Asturias, workers began to organize and formed a movement to fight the policies of the newly elected right-wing government. Armed with ammunition seized from government forces and factories, and even primitive catapults and dynamite and rocks from the mines, the workers revolted on October 4, 1934, proclaiming a general strike. The revolt fanned out from the town of Mieres and the strikers quickly gained control of most of Asturias. National troops were sent to crush the rebellion—mainly mercenaries from North Africa who were under the command of none other than General Francisco Franco. After two weeks of ferocious fighting, the uprising failed and the rebels fled into the mountains. With a crushing brutality, under Franco the national forces hunted down and captured the organizers and strikers. In the end, over 2,000 miners were killed and as many as 30,000 imprisoned. This event is viewed by many historians as a training ground and catalyst for the Spanish Civil War, which broke out two years later on July 18, 1936, when Franco, once again, moved his troops from Morocco into the Peninsula. In retaliation, after the Civil War, the Kingdom of Asturias was symbolically slighted when it was renamed the Province of Oviedo.

After the uprising, another wave of Asturians and Cantabrians took the well-beaten path to neighboring Galicia and set sail for the Americas. The mining industry declined and the region, once again, came to depend on agriculture, primarily dairy farming and corn, another contribution from the New World *indianos*. In the last half of the 20th century, as in nearly all of Spain, the population of the small villages in the region decreased substantially, with young people heading to the big cities in search of jobs and education. The past decades have seen an increase in tourism and investment and many small towns are recovering their traditions and economy through rural tourism and modest development.

Santander

Hugging the tranquil waters of the Bay of Santander—the jagged, white-capped mountains of the Cordillera Cantábrica hazing slate gray and blue in the distance—is Santander, the capital of Cantabria. After nearly burning to the ground in 1941, it was rebuilt in an orderly—almost too much so—fashion. The result is a forced elegance that is rather modern and dull. However, this slowly gives way to an attractive seaside that has drawn upper crust Spaniards to its shores for centuries. The town reaches full-on, postcard-perfect beauty at the resort of El Sardinero with its turn-of-the-20th-century mansions and wide, sandy beaches.

Santander was put on the physical map in 21 B.C. when the Romans established a outpost here and named it Portus Victoriae. The town landed on Spanish maps in 1187 and throughout the centuries waxed and waned as an important port. Santander made the social map in the 1900s when King Alfonso XIII deigned to spend his summers here. Hundreds of court hangers-on followed and Santander's reputation as an excusive summer retreat was cemented. Plazas were built, promenades laid, and elegant palaces erected—particularly in the El Sardinero area. Combined with the rebuilt center, they give Santander an air of old-world refinement that more than matches its royal reputation.

The town is particularly buzzy during summer when Spanish tourists and international students descend in droves. Come August, the **Festival Internacional de Santander,** a world-class music and dance festival, draws artists and fans from around the world. Book early. Santander also makes the perfect base from which to explore the lovely Cantabrian coast.

SIGHTS
City Center
There are a handful of worthwhile sights in the center of town, the best being the **Iglesia Catedral de Nuestra Señora de la Asunción** (Pl. Obispo José E. Eguino, s/n, tel. 94/222-

6024, 10 A.M.–1 P.M. and 4:30–7:30 P.M. Mon.–Sat., 8 A.M.–2 P.M. and 5–8 P.M. Sun., free). It sits on the location of the long-gone abbey of San Emerterio, built in the 8th century on the very ground where the skulls of Christian martyrs Saint Emeterio and Saint Celedonio were found. The pair now serve as Santander's patron saints. The current cathedral actually consists of two 13th-century churches, built one above the other. After the 1941 fire, the upper church underwent major work to recapture its original Gothic grandeur, including a spectacular interior cloister. The lower church, **Iglesia del Santísimo** (C/ Somorrostro, 8 A.M.–1 P.M. and 5–8 P.M.), sits above exposed Roman ruins, and houses the original Romanesque crypt where you can visit the aforementioned skulls, thankfully hidden within silver vessels.

The **Museo Municipal de Bellas Artes** (C/ Rubio 6, tel. 94/220-3120, 10:30 A.M.–1 P.M. and 4–7 P.M. Mon.–Fri., 10:30 A.M.–1 P.M. Sat., closed Sun., free) holds a small collection of mostly Cantabrian landscape paintings plus a few minor Goyas. The **Museo de Prehistoria y Arqueología de Cantabria** (C/ Casimiro Sainz 4, tel. 94/220-7105, 10 A.M.–1 P.M. and 4–7 P.M. Mon.–Sat., 11 A.M.–2 P.M. Sun.) houses over 1,200 objects, many dating from the Paleolithic and Iron Ages.

If you'd like to just wander around the city center, good places to start are **Plaza Porticada** and the streets around the town hall, or **Ayuntamiento. Plaza Cañadio** is where to head for lively tapas bars and watering holes. As the night progresses, the area around this square fills up with college students out on the party prowl.

Paseo de Pereda
The lovely Paseo de Pereda goes along the **Bahía del Santander** and is lined with majestic buildings that house banks and businesses, upscale shops, and dozens of quaint cafés. On warm nights, many set out sidewalk

terraces that draw well-heeled locals out in droves. Join them. One of the most impressive buildings along this route is the headquarters of the **Banco de Santander** (Po. Pereda 9–12). With its massive arch over Calle Martillo, this was one of the few edifices that survived the 1941 fire. The Paseo continues past the beautiful **Jardines de Pereda,** an oasis of flowering trees, trickling fountains, and inviting benches. At about the midway point of the Paseo is the **Palacete del Embarcadero** (tel. 94/231-4060, 11 a.m.–1:30 p.m. and 6–9 p.m. Tues.–Sat., closed Mon. and Sun., free), a lovely modernist palace on the sea that has sea-themed art shows. You can also catch small boats—called *reginas*—across the bay or to the gorgeous beach of **Puntal** and the villages of **Somo** and **Pedreña.** The boats take off every

half-hour, weather permitting and a round-trip ticket costs €3.50. Contact **Los Reginas** (tel. 94/221-6753, www.losreginas.com) for more information or just show up at the Palacete. If you do nothing else in Santander, take this ferry ride—the views are spectacular. You can also enjoy wonderful seafood at a handful of seaside shacks in Somo and Pedreña.

El Sardinero

The **Avenida Reina Victoria** runs along a stunning stretch of the bay. Here the water shimmers blue and green, reflecting the clouds above as clearly as a mirror. The Avenue ends at **El Sardinero,** the former royal playground of King Alfonso and crew. This majestic barrio is lined with regal mansions that have since been converted into hotels, restaurants, and residences.

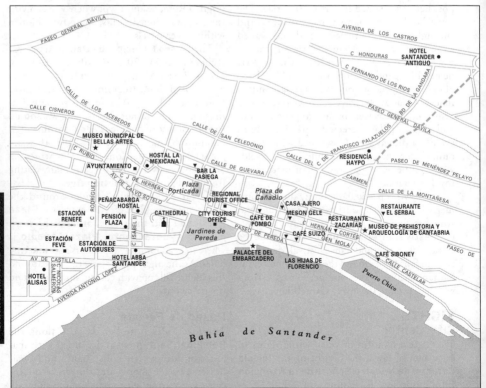

The King's palace-away-from-palace sits on the **Peninsula de la Magdalena,** which separates the bay from the Cantabrian Sea. **Palacio de la Magdalena** (8 A.M.–8:30 P.M. daily Oct.–May, 8 A.M.–10 P.M. daily June–Sept.) built between 1909 and 1911, was a gift to the king and his English queen Eugenia and resembles an English estate. Since 1932, the palace has hosted the summer school of the Universidad Internacional de Menéndez Pelayo, which draws hundreds of foreign students each year. The views from the cliff where the palace sits are spectacular—the water a searing blue dotted with bobbing boats. The entire 24 hectares (59 acres) of the peninsula have been converted into a park where seniors play cards under shady trees, young people rent bikes, and families bask in the view.

Whether or not you are a gambler, **Gran** **Casino de Sardinero** (Pl. Italia, s/n) is worth a look. The elegant belle epoque building hails from the early 20th century and houses an upscale gaming center—blackjack, roulette, poker, and slots—as well as a formal restaurant.

From the city center, you can get to El Sardinero and Magdalena via local bus 1, 2, or 3.

Beaches

The most popular beach in Santander is the long, wide golden sand of **Playa de Sardinero,** divided midway through by a lovely park. It proudly boasts its ranking as one of the top 10 cleanest beaches in the world. South of it, the smaller **Playa del Camello** features a bustling, elegant boardwalk with several cafés. The lovely **Playa de la Magdalena** swoops along the base of the peninsula of the same name.

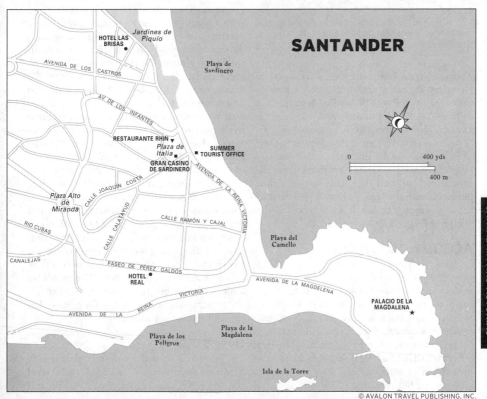

©C. BOLTON

Santander's popular beach, Playa de Sardinero

Anchored in the waters are several rafts, perfect for swimming out to and sunbathing. Closer to town, the small **Playa de los Peligros** is home to several sailing, kayaking, and windsurfing schools. There is also a lively beachside bar. To escape the crowds, hop the *regina* (ferry-taxi) from the Palacete del Embarcadero to the 3.2-kilometer (two-mile) **Playa del Puntal,** a stunning stretch of sand that curls out on a thin peninsula into the sea. Nudism is practiced in the dune areas. The beach is connected to the village of Pedreña by a long bridge.

ACCOMMODATIONS

Lodging in Santander is surprisingly cheap nine months out of the year. Come summer, prices can triple and bookings go fast. If you are planning on visiting in August—prime tourist time—book well ahead. Also be sure to take into consideration if you will be staying in the city center or in El Sardinero. The two are separated by the long boardwalk-lined Avenida Reina Victoria, about a 20-minute walk, a 10-minute bus ride, or a €5 cab.

Under €50

On a tight budget or just want to reconnect with your inner child? Book a stay at **Haypo** (C/ Francisco Palazueles 21, tel. 94/221-7753, €16 for a dorm bed), which shares space with a preschool and offers basic youth hostel accommodations. **Peñacabarga Hostal** (C/ Emilio Pino 4, tel. 94/203-7742, €45) offers very simple rooms right next to Iglesia de Santísimo. The beds at **Santander Antiguo** (Av. Castros 65, tel. 94/231-8565, servicios@santander antiguo.com, www.santanderantiguo.com, €43) are draped in colorful quilts and each room has Internet access. There is also a good café with excellent local seafood.

€50-100

The lovely **Abba Santander** (C/ Calderón de la Barca 3, tel. 94/221-2450, www.abba santanderhotel.com, €80) is a classic hotel with Queen Anne–style furnishings, lovely marble baths, and an efficient, accommodating staff. Wi-Fi is available throughout the hotel. **Hostal La Mexicana** (C/ Juan de Herrera 3, tel. 94/222-2354, www.hostalla mexicana.com, €59) boasts friendly staff who will make you feel at home from the time you walk through the door. Rooms are decorated in simple wooden antiques and there is a comfortable lounge where guests mingle. **Pension Plaza** (C/ Cadiz 13, tel. 94/221-2967, www .pension-plaza.com, €58) has simple rooms and an inattentive staff, but the location close to the train and bus stations makes it ideal for a quick visit to town. **Hotel Alisas** (C/ Nicolás Salmerón 3, tel. 94/222-2750, hotel. alisas@celuisma.com, www.celuisma.com, €75) is a nicely kept modern hotel close to the fisherman's port and the sea, yet only a five-minute walk to the bus station. The rooms are a bit outdated, but the service is excellent. If the breakfast is not included in the price—skip it, and head for a nearby café.

Over €100

The best accommodations in Santander are in El Sardinero and the top of the crop is **Hotel Real** (Po. Pérez Galdós 28, tel. 94/227-2550, real santander@husa.es, www.hotelreal.es, €284), located in a regal 19th-century building originally erected to house King Alfonso's courtiers. Run by the excellent Husa chain, the hotel features all the expected five-star amenities, an impeccably trained staff, and richly decorated rooms, many with lovely views over the sea. If you can, upgrade to a room with a balcony. For a more laid-back—but just as lovely—experience, try the family-run **(** **Hotel Las Brisas** (C/ La Braña 14, tel. 94/227-5011, info@hotel esensantander.com, www.hotelesensantander .com, €100), located in a charming, early 20th-century mansion a stone's throw from the beach. The country floral decorated rooms are quirky, cozy, and very comfortable, while the staff are friendly and accommodating. If you'll be staying for a week or more, inquire about the vacation apartments Las Brisas manages.

FOOD
Cafés and Desserts
Café Suizo (Po. Pereda 28, tel. 94/221-5864) is a bright, split-level café where you can enjoy a light breakfast or snack at the long, winding pink bar or on the sidewalk terrace where a bow-tied waiter will serve you. **Café de Pombo** (C/ Hernan Cortes 21, tel. 94/222-3224) has the feel of a 1920s parlor with a polished wooden bar and comfy benches lining the wall. If the weather is nice, sit outside on the shady Plaza Pombo. **Siboney** (C/ Castelar 7, tel. 94/231-3062) offers great views of the port and is a popular place to start the evening.

Gourmet
Located in Puerto Chico, **El Serbal** (C/ Andres del Río 7, tel. 94/222-2515, 1:30–4 P.M. and 9–11:30 P.M. Tues.–Sat., 1:30–4 P.M. Sun., closed Mon., closed Feb., €55) is one of a handful of top gourmet spots in Santander. Set in a sea of traditional seafood houses, it defiantly offers something daring in the casual, modern confines of its checkerboard-floored dining room. Sublime offerings include cherry gazpacho with pickled tuna, baked ray with wild mushrooms and olive pasta, or quail stuffed with rose petals and foie. The wine list is quite extensive

with offerings from all over the world. Nearby, **Zacarías** (C/ Hernán Cortes 38, tel. 94/221 2333, noon–4 P.M. and 8 P.M.–midnight daily, closed Sun. in winter, €40) is owned by chef and Cantabrian gastronomic expert Zacarías Puente-Herboso, and offers exquisite takes on regional specialties in a charming marina setting.

Local Cuisine
In Santander, local food means seafood and there is no better place to tuck into straight-from-the-boat goodies than the **Barrio Pesquero,** a rough-and-tumble fishermen's neighborhood located at the Puerto Pesquero (catch local bus number 4 to get there). Forget stylish decor, these places are about good eating and boisterous fun. Most of the cooking happens on the sidewalk, with fish grilling and paella cooking all along Calle Marqués de la Ensenada. One of the local favorites to seek out is **La Gaviota** (Marqués de la Ensenada 32, tel. 94/222-1132, 1–4 P.M. and 9 P.M.–midnight daily, €8), where a barker works to get people into the cozy, white-table-clothed dining room. It's not a tough sell and he's having the time of his life. On the other end of the refinement scale, over in El Sardinero, try **Restaurante Rhin** (Pl. Italia, s/n, tel. 94/227-0868, 1:45–3:45 P.M. and 9–11:45 P.M. daily, €50) in the hotel of the same name. With a gorgeous terrace overlooking the beach, it is perfect for a leisurely lunch or a romantic dinner. Grilled seafood and fish are an excellent bet here. In the center of town, head to **Mesón Gele** (C/ Eduardo Benot 4, tel. 94/222-1021, noon–4 P.M. and 7 P.M.–1 A.M. Tues.– Sat., closed Mon. and Sun., €20); exposed beams and wine cellar decor make for an atmospheric dining experience. Start with the regional specialty *sopa de marisco,* a simmering pot of fresh seafood stew.

Tapas
Santander's city center teems with lively tapas bars. As in the rest of Spain, they are generally open from 1–4 P.M. and from 8 P.M.–midnight. The exposed brick walls and pastoral murals give **Casa Ajero** (C/ Daoiz y Velarde 18, tel. 94/221-8386) a quiet, rustic feel. Pull up to the red-and-white checkered bar and

order a tapa of sardines caught that morning. **Las Hijas de Florencio** (Po. Pereda 23, tel. 94/231-0475) is a traditional Spanish tapas house with legs of cured ham and wine glasses hanging above the bar. The seafood tapas can be had inside or at the terrace on the sidewalk. **La Pasiega** (C/ Rualasal 15, tel. 94/222-7434) is a cozy, neighborhood bar that keeps a steady stream of locals happily stuffed with simple, traditional tapas.

INFORMATION

The main **tourist office** (Jardines de Pereda s/n, tel. 94/220-3000, 8:30 A.M.–7 P.M. Mon.–Fri. 10 A.M.–2 P.M. Sat. and Sun. Sept.–April, 8:30 A.M.–7 P.M. Mon.–Fri. 10 A.M.–7 P.M. Sat. and Sun. May–June, 9 A.M.–9 P.M. daily July–Aug.), located in the gardens along Paseo Pereda, offers extensive information on the city and surrounding beaches. In the summer, there is an information stand in Plaza Italia at El Sardinero. The **regional tourist office** (C/ Hernán Cortés 4, tel. 90/111-1112, 9:30 A.M.–1:30 P.M. and 4–7 P.M. daily, phone service from 9 A.M.–9 P.M. daily) is located in the Mercado del Este and has information all about Cantabria.

GETTING THERE AND AROUND
Air

The **Aeropuerto de Santander** is close to town and receives direct flights from throughout Europe, while Iberia connects it to most major cities in Spain. The eight-minute taxi ride into town should run about €8. Just to the right of the taxi stand is the **airport bus** (every half-hour, €1.50) that delivers tourists right to the bus station in the center of town. If you will be exploring the Cantabrian and Asturian coast by car after arriving, the airport has offices for **Avis** (www.avis.es), **Europcar** (www.europcar.es), and **Hertz** (www.hertz.es).

Bus

Santander's bus station (C/ Navas de Tolosa, s/n, tel. 94/221-1995, www.santandereabus.com) has connections via **Alsa** (www.alsa.es) to points along the coast, including País Vasco and on into France. **Continental** (www.continental-auto.es) offers six trips daily to Burgos and Madrid. It also serves Salamanca, Zaragoza, Barcelona, and Valladolid.

Train

The Santander train station (Pl. de las Estaciones, s/n) serves two rail lines. **FEVE** (tel. 94/220-9522, www.feve.es) travels the northern coast of Spain with three trains to and from Bilbao and two trains heading west to San Vicente de la Barquera, Llanes, and Oviedo. **Renfe** (tel. 94/228-0202, www.renfe.es) has several daily trains to and from Madrid, as well as connections throughout Spain.

Local Transportation

Though Santander is small enough to be walkable, if you want to easily move between the city center, the ports, and El Sardinero, you'll need to take the local buses. The nine bus lines running throughout the city are easy to figure out. Cost is €1 but if you are traveling in a group or will be in town for a few days, buy a 10-trip *bono* for €5.20.

East of Santander

A top tourist trail for Spanish tourists, the eastern coast of Cantabria stretches from the Bahía de Santander to the fishing village of Castro-Urdiales on the border with the País Vasco. Nicknamed the Costa Esmeralda (Emerald Coast), it is an undulating stretch of deep green earth, icy blue waters, golden white sands, and slate-colored cliffs pockmarked with lovely coves. If you had two days to travel, you could start off from Santander and spend the morning stopping off in the small seaside towns of Isla and Noja. Have lunch in Santoña, then continue into Laredo for the evening. The next day, head to Castro-Urdiales where you can have lunch before returning to Santander or continuing on towards Bilbao. Of course, half the joy of a trip such as this is stopping off at any village that catches your fancy. What they all hold in common is spectacular scenery, impeccable seafood, friendly locals, and a glimpse into a slow-paced, rustic Spain that is a delightful departure from the stereotyped sun-and-sand resorts of the southern coasts. If traveling by public transport, head by bus to Laredo, then take the ferry to Santoña and back. Depending on your timeframe, continue east on another bus or return to Santander.

SANTOÑA

The lovely fishing village of Santoña sits at the base of a slip of land that juts out into the sea. It is surrounded by salt marshes and excellent beaches. The village was guarded by the remnants of its defensive past, including the forts of **San Martín, San Carlos,** and **Napolean,** the last of which boasts 760 very high stone steps. The local industry is canning and the tuna and anchovies that are canned here are sought after throughout Spain for their high quality. Naturally, the town's patron saint is Santa María del Puerto, guardian of *pescadores* (fishermen).

Sights

In the evenings, locals gather in **Plaza San Antonio,** where kids run about and older citizens tell animated stories. During the evening, be sure to visit the port where you can enjoy the sunset followed by the lights of the town of Laredo twinkling across the bay. To the north of town, **Playa Berria** is one of the most stunning beaches on the open waters of the Cantabrian Sea. Inland, the pristine *marismas* (salt marshes) play host to dozens of species of migratory birds, so many in fact that the area has been designated a protected bird habitat by the RAMSAR international conservation committee. For more information on the habitat, the beaches, or charming Santoña, visit the very friendly staff at the **tourist office** (Palacio Manzanedo, tel. 94/266-0066).

Accommodations

If you want to stay on the beach **Hotel Miramar** (Av. Berria, s/n, tel. 94/266-0006, €60) is the place to be. The name Miramar says it all: You can look at the sea from your room. **Hotel El Parque** (C/ General Sagardia 15, tel. 94/266-2198, €42) is a simple hotel located close to the tourist office, Plaza San Antonio, and a very lovely park.

Food

Pretty much everything you'll eat in Santoña will come from the sea. In Plaza Manuel Andujar look for the sign with the shrimp holding a green beer bottle, when you see it you've arrived at **La Casa de las Gambas** (Pl. Manuel Andujar, s/n, tel. 94/267-1939). The House of Shrimp (also known as Bar Oasis) offers high-quality seafood at fast-food prices. *Gambillas* only cost €1, so order a few. **Restaurante Brisa** (El Pasaje, s/n, tel. 94/266-1293, 1–3:30 P.M and 8 P.M.–midnight daily, €20) offers waterfront dining just steps from the ferry to Laredo. To experience the bustle of local Santoña, have a meal at **Casa Tino** (Pl. San Antonio, s/n, tel. 94/266-1645, 9:30 A.M.–11 P.M. Mon.–Sat., closed Sun.) where the delectable house specialty is *paella de mariscos* (seafood paella, Cantabrian-style)!

Getting There

By car from Santander, you have two options to get to Santoña. If pressed for time, take the highway A-8 to Laredo, park, then catch the **Santa Clara de Asís ferry** (tel. 94/260-5903) across the bay. If you have time and fancy a winding, country road within sight of the sea, take A-8 out of Santander and then switch to the CA-141 at the town of El Astillero. If traveling by public transport, **Alsa** (www.alsa.es) runs buses from the Santander bus station.

LAREDO

Situated between the river Treto and the Bay of Santoña, Laredo is a cozy seaside town with a spectacular beach. Founded in 1200, by King Alfonso VIII, Laredo was once the royal port of Northern Spain. However, after centuries of naval attacks and a handful of epidemics, it lost that honor to Santander. The town suffered through several centuries of decline until it resurfaced as a major center for canning sardines and other seafood. The boom continued when the town became a major Spanish tourist destination in the 1960s and '70s. The tradition of summering in Laredo continues today and one of the main reasons is the gorgeous **Playa Salvé**—about five kilometers (three miles) of glistening fine golden sand hugging the turquoise waters in a perfect half-moon arc. Running the length of the beach is the **Paseo Marítimo,** a broad, elegant boardwalk lined with cafés, bars, and benches perfect for watching the sunset. Just don't look back—the 1970s housing boom left behind kilometers of squat, ugly apartment blocks that is a marring, jarring contrast to the sea and sand.

At the southern end of the beach is **Puebla Vieja,** a well-conserved medieval grid of streets called *ruas* crammed with noble houses dating to the 16th century. The Gothic church, **Iglesia de Santa María de la Asunción,** sits at the top of Rua Santa María and houses a magnificent Flemish altarpiece as well as a pair of eagle-shaped brass choir desks—a gift from the Holy Roman Emperor Carlos V during his 16th-century visit to Laredo.

When the day is coming to an end, head to the **Puerto de Laredo** and catch a *barco* (boat) for a sunset cruise around the bay. Operated by **Santa Clara de Asís** (tel. 94/260-5903), the boat takes you across to Santoña where you can disembark or you can stay onboard for the return to Laredo. The ride is about an hour each way.

The **tourist office** (Alameda de Miramar, s/n, tel. 94/261-1096), located between the Puebla Vieja and the beach, can help you set up activities such as horseback riding, boat tours, camping, and more.

Festivals

The last Friday in August, Laredo blooms into festivity with the **Batalla de Flores.** This Battle of Flowers commences with a spectacular parade of flower-covered floats. The rest of the day is given over to street parties, live music, fireworks, and boisterous revelry until late in the night. If you want to be part of the fun, book your room early or drive in from Santander.

Accommodations

About a block from the beach, **Hotel Montecristo** (C/ Calvo Sotelo 2, tel. 94/260-5700, €83) is a lovely Cantabrian retreat with a Mediterranean feel. Rooms are spare but rustic and the white-walled courtyard houses a cozy little café. The staff is very accommodating. **Hotel Ancla** (C/ González Gallego 10, tel. 94/260-5500, €89) boasts a maritime theme with anchors and tide charts located all over the property. There are even golden anchors on the blue rugs in the rooms.

Food

Just steps from the beach, **El Pescador** (Av. Victoria 2, tel. 94/260-6638, €12) serves delectable seafood on their ocean breeze–kissed terrace. It's a hang out for many locals who while away hours playing cards at the bar. **Camarote** (Av. Victoria, s/n, tel. 94/260-6707, 1–3:30 P.M. and 9–11 P.M. daily, closed

9–11 P.M. Sun. in winter, €33) is a top-rated gourmet spot that does delicious wonders with the simplest of fresh seafood and fish.

Getting There
By car from Santander, the A-8 highway reaches Laredo in about 40 minutes. If traveling by public transport, **Alsa** (www.alsa.es) runs buses from the Santander bus station. You can get off in Santoña and take the ferry to Laredo, or just go straight to the city.

CASTRO-URDIALES
Just over the border from the País Vasco, Castro-Urdiales is a quaint fishing village with spectacular beaches stretching out along the sea in both directions. Founded in 1136, the town is lorded over by the dramatically Gothic **Iglesia de Santa María de la Asunción** (10 A.M.–1:30 P.M. and 4–7 P.M. daily, free). Built between the 13th and 15th centuries, this massive church is the largest of its kind in Cantabria. Climb the stairs leading up the church. When you reach the top you'll be amazed at how the cliffs drop off into the sea where schools of fish swim purposefully in the clear waters. You'll also get a great view of the so-called **Puente Romano** (Roman bridge). It is actually medieval. Next to the church, the **Castillo Faro** is a medieval castle that now houses the town's lighthouse.

The lifeblood of the city is its busy little port bursting day and night with colorful fishing boats. In the 13th and 14th centuries, it served as the country's most important whaling port. Surrounded by houses sporting white-framed glass galleries, it is a picturesque spot where you can watch the fishermen lug in their catch, then mosey up to one of the surrounding restaurants to eat it. In the tangle of streets behind the port, seek out **Rua de Ardigales.** Once an old Roman road, it is now a lively pedestrian street with medieval houses, many now housing excellent tapas bars.

On the northern side of the port is **Playa de Ostende,** an idyllic swimming cove dotted with dramatic boulders. To the south, **Playa Brazomar** offers the same natural beauty com-

© C. BOLTON

The port of Castro-Urdiales sits below the medieval Iglesia de Santa María de la Asunción.

plemented with man-made slides and floating docks. The beaches are within a 10-minute walk from each other. For information on the beaches, the sights, and more, visit the friendly **tourism office** (Av. de la Constitution, tel. 94/287-1512) at the port.

Accommodations
At the comfortable **Hotel Miramar** (Av. La Playa 1, tel. 94/286-0204, €105) you can step right out of your hotel onto the beach. The rooms come with peaceful ocean views and there is a good café/bar. **Pensión La Mar** (C/ La Mar 27, tel. 94/287-1188, €55), at almost half the price, is still comfy, though you'll have to hoof it to the beach.

Food
On a lovely summer day in Castro-Urdiales, there's no better place to be than the buzzing **€ Asador Perla** (€8), a giant white tent set up right on the fishing wharf. It houses a massive grill run by a grillmaster who has been keeping

CANTABRIA AND ASTURIAS

the tentfuls happy with the freshest grilled sardines in town for years. For a more traditional dining experience head to the acclaimed **Mesón Marinero** (C/ Correría 23, tel. 94/286-0005, www.mesonmarinero.com, 1–4 P.M. and 8–11 P.M. daily, €20), where locals and fishermen clamor at the bar for delicious, massive seafood tapas. For a full meal, head upstairs to the dining room overlooking the port—very charming!

Getting There
From Santander, follow the A-8 highway to Castro-Urdiales. Buses depart to and from Santander daily, run by **Alsa** (www.alsa.es).

West of Santander

The western coast of Cantabria offers a perfect vacation—from monument-rich towns to beyond-quaint fishing villages, fine-sanded beaches to pre-historic caves, simple seafood shacks to avant-garde dining—all on a stretch of glorious green coast bathed by rolling sea blue waves.

⚔ SANTILLANA DEL MAR
Back in 1575, Santillana del Mar set its destiny to become a major tourist town. It wasn't a conscious choice but by enforcing strict building codes, Middle Ages locals ensured their cobbled stone streets and medieval village would endure for centuries to come. Today, Santillana del Mar is one of the best-preserved medieval villages in Spain and a national monument. If you can overlook the profusion of tacky souvenir shops and the packs of school children, you can almost imagine raggedy-robed shepherds scuttling along the cobblestones while velvet-caped nobles stroll through accompanied by their entourage toting torches for light. Better yet, after the hordes of tourists have bussed out, stay the night and experience the centuries-old silence of these ancient streets. Famously called "the prettiest village in Spain" by Jean Paul Sartre, Santillana del Mar—which despite its name is not on the sea—can capture the imagination for hours, even though there are only three streets and one major sight, the **Colegiata de Santa Juliana** (Pl. Abad Francisco Navarro, s/n, tel. 94/284-0317, 10 A.M.–1:30 P.M. and 4–6:30 P.M. Tues.–Sun. Nov.–Mar., 10 A.M.–1:30 P.M. and 4–7:30 P.M. Wed.–Mon. April–Oct., €3). Built in the 12th century, it is Cantabria's finest example of Romanesque architecture and the final resting place of the town's and church's namesake, Santa Juliana, a 3rd-century martyr whose remains somehow made the journey to Santillana del Mar after her death. Be sure to see the atmospheric cloister with its skillfully sculpted capitals. A visit to the Colegiata also grants you entry into the **Museo Diocesano** (tel. 94/ 284-0317, 10 A.M.–2 P.M. and 4–7 P.M. Tues.–Sun., closed Mon.). Located in a 16th-century convent just outside the town walls, the museum houses a large collection of religious art and artifacts dating back several centuries.

⚔ Cuevas de Altamira
About three kilometers (two miles) outside of Santillana sit the 20,000-year-old Altamira Caves, often called the "Sistine Chapel of prehistoric art" for the extensive, colorful art that lines the caves. The caves are closed to the public due to their fragility, but you can learn all about them and see replicas at the **Museo de Altamira** (Av. Sanz de Sautuola, s/n, tel. 94/281-8815, http://museodealtamira.mcu .es, 9:30 A.M.–7:30 P.M. Tues.–Sat., 9:30 P.M.–3 P.M. Sun., reduced hours in winter, €2.40). Advance tickets are available (and recommended) from any branch of Banco Santander Central Hispano. (For more on the caves, see sidebar, *Prehistoric Cave Paintings*.)

Accommodations
For modern luxury with medieval flare, check into the ⚔ **Parador de Santillana Gil Blas** (Pl. Ramón Pelayo, s/n, tel. 94/202-8028, santillanagb@parador.es, www.parador.es,

PREHISTORIC CAVE PAINTINGS

Cantabria and Asturias are home to some of the oldest and most interesting prehistoric cave drawings and paintings in Europe. The caves of **Altamira**, located near Santillana del Mar in Cantabria, offer the best example from an artistic standpoint. In 1879, Marcelino Sanz de Sautuola, a lawyer and amateur archaeologist, was exploring a hilltop cave located on land that he owned. He had explored it several times before, finding minor drawings in the anterooms. On this particular day, he brought along María, his five-year-old daughter. Striking off on her own, she spotted some peculiar drawings on the ceiling of the cave and said: *¡Mira, Papa, bueyes!* (Look, Papa, oxen!) – coining the name of the cave, Altamira (High Look).

The oxen turned out to be bison, horses, deer, and a series of handprints and negative images of hands. Sautuola deduced that the paintings were from the prehistoric period, but his findings were ridiculed at the time – the condition and style of the drawings was so unusual that few believed they could be prehistoric. It was not until many years after his death that the true significance of his findings was finally recognized.

What makes Altamira so special is the artistic merit of the drawings and their spectacular conservation. The cave is thought to have been hermetically sealed by a rockslide for at least 13,000 years, which protected the drawings from the elements. More remarkable still, the artist, or artists, who produced the works were extraordinarily gifted and were many millennia ahead of their time. Picasso, upon seeing the cave paintings, declared them to be entirely "modern," saying famously, "after Altamira everything is decadence." He and other artists such as Joan Miró incorporated Altamira forms into their art. The bull in Picasso's masterpiece *Guernica* (in Madrid's Museo Reina Sofía) is thought to be a direct descendent of an Altamira bison.

Unfortunately, due to the delicate nature of the cave, it is no longer open to the general public for visits. To meet public demand, the government constructed the **NeoCueva** (new cave) right next door at the Museo de Altamira – a perfect replica of the cave with the drawings reproduced using the same technique as the originals. There is another older and smaller replica of the cave in the Museo Arqueológico in Madrid.

OTHER CAVES

There are many other caves in the area that are also worth a visit. Some are rather rustic, others more accessible. Call ahead to reserve and get specific details.

Cuevas El Castillo y Las Monedas (Puente Viesgo, Cantabria, tel. 94/259-8425) offers two adjoining caves with modest prehistoric art and interesting rock formations.

Cueva El Pendo (El Churi, Escobedo de Camargo Cantabria, tel. 94/225-9214) is a large cave featuring important Paleolithic findings, including a 20,000-year-old "Frieze of Paintings." Because of an ongoing archaeological excavation, only 150 visitors are allowed in per day.

Cueva Ardines y Cueva Tito Bustillo (Ribadesella, Asturias, tel. 98/586-1118) are ancient caves with 20,000-year-old prehistoric paintings. The site has a museum as well.

(Contributed by Madrid-based journalist Megan Cytron, who writes frequently on Asturias.)

€130) located in a 17th-century mansion dripping with regal touches like ornate antiques, chandeliers, rich drapes, and dark hardwood floors. Just next door is **Parador de Santillana** (Pl. Ramón Pelayo, s/n, tel. 94/281-8000, santillana@parador.es, www.parador.es, €130), set in a newly constructed building in the style of a traditional Cantabrian stone house. Outside of the old village, **Hotel Cuevas I y II** (Av. Antonio Sandi 4, tel. 94/281-8384, €50) is a lovely stone manor converted into a small rustic hotel comprised of two buildings with a lovely outdoor sitting area between them.

Food

If you visit in summer, don't miss dining in a

a medieval stone wall in Santillana del Mar

stone-walled garden. **Mesón de los Villa** (C/ Santo Domingo 5, tel. 94/281-8015, 11 A.M.–10 P.M. summer only, €13) offers inexpensive Cantabrian fare in a lovely medieval courtyard full of flowering trees and chirping birds. The servers, decked in French maid outfits, add a kitschy touch. Nearby, **Terraza El Jardín** (C/ El Cantón, 13, tel. 94/281-8388, 11 A.M.–10 P.M. daily summer only, €10) is also set in an atmospheric medieval garden. Both restaurants offer light fare from sandwiches to sweets, including the local specialty *bizcocho con leche,* a sponge cake moistened with milk. For a tasty Cantabrian meal year-round, visit the warren of rustic rooms that make up the restaurant of the **Hotel Altamira** (C/ Cantón, 1, tel. 94/281-8025, 1:15–4 P.M. and 8–11 P.M. daily, €25). The fare is fish and seafood served simply steamed or grilled.

Getting There

If driving, head west out of Santander along the A-67. Take exit 16 and at Polanco, turn left

onto CA-300. Switch to CA-131 and follow it into town. By public transport, **La Cantabrica** (tel. 94/272-0822) runs seven buses a day during the week from Santander, five on the weekends. The buses continue on to Comillas and San Vicente. The bus will drop you off right next to the tourist office, where you can inquire about transport to Altamira.

COMILLAS

Embraced by a glittering beach, nestled among verdant hills, Comillas seems as far removed from the cosmopolitan sheen of Barcelona as possible. Yet, the two seaside towns are linked by none other than the world's most famous architect—Antoni Gaudí. After King Alfonso XII spent the summers of 1881 and 1882 here, the town became über-fashionable among Spain's wealthy nobles—and would-be nobles. One of them, the Marqués de Comillas—a Catalan named Antonio López y López who bought his title after making a fortune in slave-trading and tobacco—had familial ties to Eusebi Güell, a friend and patron of Gaudí. That connection led to a commission that Gaudí accepted to build **El Capricho** (Parque del Sobrellano, s/n), a playful green-and yellow-tiled house covered in flowers and leaves. Over the main door stands the highest tower with sunflowers spiraling towards the roof.

The **tourist office** (tel. 94/272-2591, 9 A.M.–9 P.M. daily summer, 9 A.M.–2 P.M. and 4–6 P.M. Mon.–Sat. 10 A.M.–2 P.M. Sun. winter) is located underneath the city hall, right off Plaza El Corro.

Sights

The hilly, town houses the church **Capilla Panteón de los Marqueses de Comillas** (10 A.M.–9 P.M., €3) and the **Palacio de Sobrellano** with its minor collection of Gaudí-designed furnishings. Both neo-Gothic structures are only viewable through guided tours, normally starting every half hour. The large brick structure looming on the far hillside is the **Universidad Pontifica,** a rambling neo-Gothic building with Mudejar and modernist

the fanciful El Capricho house that Gaudí
built in Comillas

touches. Though closed to the public, you can
explore the grounds if you so desire.

In the summer, just about everyone you see
walking around Comillas has a beach towel
or umbrella under their arm. **Playa Comillas,**
the town's most central beach, wraps around
the cove beneath the historical center. About
five kilometers (three miles) to the west, the
Oyambre Nature Reserve features gorgeous
beaches backed by dramatic cliffs and dotted with unspoiled dunes. The beaches stay
full until nearly 8:30 P.M. Afterwards, everyone heads to **Plaza El Corro** and **Plaza de la
Constitución** for tapas and drinks.

Accommodations

Sleeping in Comillas could be one of the
highlights of your trip, no matter your price
range. Each of the handful of hotels has its
own personal quirk. If you're on a budget
yet still want to sleep close to El Capricho,
Hostal Fuente Real (Pl. Fuente Real 19,
tel. 94/272-0155, €35) is the place for you.
It is run by a charming mother/daughter duo

who welcome you as family to their simple
but comfortable rooms. A more cozy option
is **Posada La Solana Montañesa** (C/ La
Campa 22, tel. 94/272-1026, www.lasolana
montanesa.com, €65), a wonderful mountain home, just steps from the town's lively
medieval center. ⟨ **Marina de Campíos** (C/
General Piélagos 14, tel. 94/272-2754, www
.marinadecampios.com, €95) offers whimsical
rooms doused in bold colors. Named for fictional femme fatales, the rooms are so seductive that you may end up extending your stay.

Food

Restaurante Fuente Real (Pl. Fuente Real
4, tel. 94/272-2159, 1–4 P.M. and 8–11 P.M.
daily summer only, hours vary in winter, €19),
in the hotel of the same name, has been serving up rustic local grub since 1855. The *sopa
de mariscos* (seafood soup) is slurp-to-the-last-
sip good. For tasty fresh seafood tapas drop by
La Compuerta (C/ Cervantes 3, tel. 94/272-
0000, €10). It's empty before 10 P.M., after
that, the line snakes out the door.

The finest dining to be had in town is in
the house that Gaudí built. ⟨ **El Capricho
de Gaudí** (tel. 94/272-0365, 1–3:30 P.M. and
9–11 P.M. Mon.– Sat., 1–3:30 P.M. Sun., €35)
serves classic Cantabrian fare amidst Gaudí's
creative architecture.

Getting There

By car from Santander, take the A-67 west out of
town, then catch the A-8 towards Oviedo. Take
exit number 249 towards Comillas. Exit CA-135
and follow it into town. By bus, **La Cantabrica**
(tel. 94/272-0822) makes seven daily runs from
Santander, five on the weekends. The buses continue on to San Vicente. The main bus stop in
town is Plaza Fuente Real next to El Capricho.

SAN VICENTE DE LA BARQUERA

Once an important Roman port, San Vicente de
la Barquera received Spanish civil status in 1210.
Today, it is one of the most atmospheric fishing villages on the Cantbrian coast—all writh-
ing sea, medieval buildings, and heaving snow

© C. BOLTON

CANTABRIA AND ASTURIAS

capped Picos de Europa in the background, what Spanish poet Pérez Galdós once referred to as the "delirious geography" of the town.

Sights

Your first view of the town comes as you cross the **Puente de la Maza,** a 15th-century bridge boasting 28 ancient arches. Above the town looms the rambling **Castillo del Rey.** The castle once provided the old town with defensive protection; now it offers expansive views over the tumbling blue sea and surrounding green fields. Further up the hill, the 13th-century **Iglesia de Santa María de los Ángeles** looks more like a defensive structure than a religious building—quite fitting as it commands the highest point in town. It offers a few notable sights, including impressive Romanesque doors and a life-sized statue of Antonio del Corro, a 16th-century Inquisitor.

When descending the hill, detour through **Puerta de la Barrera,** a quiet staircase that leads to Plaza José Antonio. Be sure to look out for the arcaded porticoes of the **Plaza Mayor.** Back on the seafront, a centuries-old fishing port serves as base for a fleet of colorful fishing boats. It shivers with activity—boats unloading their catch of tuna and sardines, fishermen stringing nets, dinghies bobbing in the waves. The area is heavily scented with the smell of fresh fish, palpable even as you enter the gardens of the nearby **Parque Municipal.**

Accommodations

Hotel Luxón (Av. Miramar 1, tel. 94/271-0050, €67), a delightful stone mansion sitting on Plaza José Antonio, is constantly bathed with sea breezes. The hotel's grand parlor and front porch lend an aristocratic air and are perfect for lounging. **Hotel Boga Boga** (Pl. José Antonio 9, tel. 94/271-0135, €58) has a jaunty nautical theme and restaurant where the fresh seafood is accompanied by live music. Barely a block off the water's edge, **Hotel Canton** (C/ Padre Angel 8, tel. 94/271-1560, €64) has small but quaint rooms.

Food

When dining in San Vicente, think seafood, seafood, and more seafood. Restaurants stick

a stunning view from the Castillo del Rey in San Vicente de la Barquera

© C. BOLTON

with a tried-and-true nautical theme, but the one place that practically outdoes the port itself is **El Marinero** (Av. Generalísimo 23, tel. 94/271-0279, 1:30–4 P.M. and 8:30–11 P.M. daily, €17), with nets, buoys, and anchors dripping from the walls and ceilings. Fish straight off the boat are kept on ice on the terrace and orders come out of the kitchen piled high for the table to share. **Dulcinea** (Av. Miramar 16, tel. 94/271-0133, 1–3:30P.M. and 9–10:30 P.M. Fri.–Tues., 1–3:30 P.M. Wed., closed Thurs., €24) also serves heaping platters of seafood, though the house specialty is *arroz con bogavante* (rice with lobster). If you don't want a sit-down meal, take a spot at the bar where seafaring locals lean in over their wine glasses telling tall tales about the one that got away.

Getting There

Driving from Santander, take the A-67 west out of town, then switch to the A-8 towards Oviedo. Take exit 264 towards San Vicente de la Barquera and finally catch CA-843 into town. The **La Cantabrica** (tel. 94/272-0822) bus company provides several daily runs from Santander. Coming from Bilbao or Oviedo, the city is served by **Alsa** (www.alsa.es). By train, the narrow-gauge rail, **FEVE** (www.feve.es) stops here daily on its route between Santander and Oviedo.

Eastern Asturian Coast

The eastern coast of Asturias is marked by a rugged coastline with mountains just a few kilometers inland and a tiny strip of fertile farmland reaching right to the edge of the sea. The slow-chugging FEVE (www.feve.es) narrow-gauge railroad runs along the northern coast from Bilbao to Santander to Oviedo and on to Ferrol in Galicia. It is a beautiful route for those with the time, but perhaps the best practical use of the FEVE is to take it one or two stops and then lazily walk back to your home base through the beautiful countryside. There is also decent bus service throughout the coast provided by the ALSA company (www.alsa.es). However, to really enjoy this area, you'll have to rent a car. The coast is pockmarked with secluded coves, scenic overlooks, and the ruins of ancient villages—all accessible only by car. You can rent one in any of the larger cities including Gijón, Oviedo, and Santander.

LLANES

The delightful port town of Llanes and its surrounding beaches are the biggest tourist destination on the Asturian coast. It is easy to see why. Situated on a stunningly dramatic stretch of coast and nestled between the Cantabrian Sea and the foothills of the Picos de Europa, Llanes is brimming in natural beauty. There are several beaches and coves on both sides of the city.

The Llanes **tourist office** (C/ Alfonso IX, s/n, tel. 98/540-0164, 10 A.M.–2 P.M. and 5–9 P.M. daily summer, 10 A.M.–2 P.M. and 4–6:30 P.M. Mon.–Sat. 10 A.M.–2 P.M. Sun. winter) is housed in a medieval tower and can provide information on the town itself, the beaches, and excursions into the Picos de Europa.

Sights

The most spectacular beaches here are **Playa de Ballota** and **Playa del Andrín**, about 2.4 kilometers (1.5 miles) to the east. These twin crescents of white sand sit in front of a monolithic column of rock rising from the sea. Both are extremely secluded and nudism is not uncommon. From nearly all of these beaches, there are paths leading up onto the bluffs to a *mirador* (scenic view).

There are several cliffs along this stretch to the east of Llanes from Puerta to Buelna that also have *bufones* (blowholes) where, under the right conditions (best in fall and winter), the water pounds against holes in the cliff and a column of water shoots up. The best ones—**Santiuste, Vidiago, Arenillas, Punta**

Ballota, and Buelna—are off the N-634, accessible by paths through the fields. Further to the west, near the town of Naves (also accessible via footpath off N-634), is the truly bizarre geological phenomena of **Playa de Gulpiyuri.** This "beach" is in the middle of a pasture. There you will find a huge pit in the ground with a sandy beach at the bottom and a sort of tide pushing through subterranean passages.

Back in town, the old town is centered around **Plaza Cristo Rey,** a tranquil plaza partly surrounded by the remains of the town's nearly 305 meters (1,000 feet) of pre-Romanesque walls built around the 13th century. A scenic cliff top walk, **Paseo de San Pedro** leads to the **Playa del Sablón,** one of three beaches in the town. Many of the beaches have snack bars serving fresh seafood *a la plancha* (grilled). Do not hesitate to give it a try; beach food in Spain actually comes straight from the sea and rivals anything you'd find in a multi-starred restaurant. To see before you try, head to the port around 1 P.M., when the local fishermen sell their morning catch in a daily fish market. Walking along the port, you'll notice the brightly painted cubes along the seashore. This work of art, called *Los Cubos de la Memoria,* is actually part of the town's breakwater. The mayor commissioned a local artist to transform the dull grey cement cubes into this cheery work of public art. It now serves as a landmark to those out at sea.

Those with an interest in ancient history and time on their hands for an eight-kilometer (five-mile) hike inland will want to visit the Bronze Age dolmen, **Peña Tú** (tel. 98/541-1166, 9:30 A.M.–1:30 P.M. and 3:30–6 P.M. Wed.–Sun., closed Mon. and Tues., free) near Puertas de Vidiago. This huge block of stone in the shape of a head has paintings and carvings that date from neolithic times.

Accommodations

There is ample accommodation in Llanes, mainly of the rustic and charming type; however, if you show up in July or August without a reservation, you'll end up a little too rustic—without a place to stay. For historic charm, try **La Posada del Rey** (C/ Mayor, s/n, tel. 98/540-1332, €80), built on the location where medieval kings once slept. About three kilometers (two miles) outside of town, **(El Habana** (La Pereda, tel. 98/540-2526, www.elhabana.net, €90) is a gorgeous *casa rural* (country house) surrounding by lush greenery in the foothills of the Picos.

Food

Seafood is king in this seafaring town, and if you are a fan of *mariscos,* you'll be in heaven. Any place along the waterfront is bound to be delish, but one of the local favorites is **Barlovento** (C/ Genaro Riesstra, s/n, tel. 98/540-2562, closed Wed., €25), which does amazing things with oven-baked fish. For local Asturian fare with a creative kick, try **El Cuera** (Pl. Parrés Sobrino, 9, tel. 98/540-0054, 2–4 P.M. and 9–11 P.M. Wed.–Mon., €35). Just outside of town close to Puertes de Vidiago, there is a wonderful *sidreria,* **Sidrería Casa Poli** (tel. 98/541-1261), with a lovely outdoor patio.

Getting There

Entering Asturias from Cantabria on A-8, the main coastal road, Llanes is the first major town. The **FEVE train station** (C/ Estación, s/n, tel. 98/540-0182, www.feve.es) has limited daily trains to Oviedo and Santander. Bus service is handled by **Autobuses Easa** (Estación de Autobuses, tel. 98/540-2485, www.alsa.es), with daily buses to destinations throughout the region.

Vicinity of Llanes

There are beaches all along the stretch between Llanes and Ribadesella, any one of which would make for a lovely afternoon of exploring. Worth noting are the seashell-shaped **Playa de Torimbia** near Niembro—accessible only by a footpath down the cliff—and the much longer and wilder surf destination, **Playa de San Antolín,** visible going west just after the town Bedón from both coastal roads, but accessible only from the smaller AS-263.

◖ PLAYA DE LAS CUEVAS DEL MAR

Further along, just past the town of Nueva de Llanes off the smaller AS-263 is a gorgeous beach unlike any other. Playa de las Cuevas del Mar (Sea Caves Beach) is one of the few beaches where you can see straight back into the snow-capped Picos, and the backdrop will take your breath away. The beach is flanked with dark craggy rocks and shallow caves with a small mountain stream running into the sea. As picturesque cows graze nearby, you can cozy up to a tiny seafood shack for snacks. Watch out for the sneaky and sudden tide and be sure to place your belongings well back on the beach. You could explore here all day, following the paths leading up onto the cliffs. Do not worry about the fences: They are for keeping the cows in, not for keeping the people out. The path to the right leads to those tinkling cowbells that you can hear on the beach. There is a tiny chapel on top of the cape and a path leading down the other side to another deserted beach, **Playa de San Antonio.** The next beach over to the left and west of Cuevas del Mar is **Playa del Canal,** a lovely freak of nature. This extremely narrow beach is wedged in between two perfectly parallel cliffs that jut improbably far out into the sea creating a "canal." Because of this, the tide comes in here with a furious rush.

RIBADESELLA

Moving west along the Asturian coast, the next notable town is Ribadesella, a seaside port that is among the most developed and frequented by tourists. Here the Río Sella—one of the biggest rivers in the region—meanders into the Cantabrian Sea, dividing the town in two. The river hosts the town's main claim to fame, **Fiesta de las Piraguas y Descenso Internacional del Sella** (the Kayaking Festival and International Descent of the River Sella). Held the first Saturday in August, the party starts in the morning in the mountain town of Arriondas, where over 1,000 kayakers race (or, in many cases, less-aggressively float) down the steep 2.4-kilometer (1.5-mile) descent to the sea. By the time the racers make it to Ribadesella, the party is in full swing waiting for them. After the trophies are awarded, the whole town adjourns to the Campos de Ova park for an afternoon picnic with free-flowing cider and plenty of food and music. By late afternoon, in typical Spanish fashion, the crowd slides into a collective siesta under the shade of the trees, only to regroup a bit later back in town to party more seriously into the wee hours of the morning.

Ribadesella's **tourist office** is located on the Carretera Piconera (tel. 98/586-0038).

Sights

The western part of town is the older area, full of charm and good seafood in equal measure. The eastern part has the town beach, **Playa de Santa Marina. Cueva Tito Bustillo** (tel. 98/586-1118, 10 A.M.–4:15 Wed.–Sun., €2) is an ancient cave with 20,000-year-old prehistoric paintings of horses and bison galloping on its walls. Call for reservations in July and August. Just west of Ribadesella, about 1.5 kilometers (a mile or so) off the N-632 (and through an unexpected gorge), is the spectacular **Playa de la Vega,** a long, sandy surfer beach backed by cliffs. At the west end of the beach are paths leading up onto the cliffs where there are fossils and dinosaur footprints in the rocks.

Accommodations

The bulk of the town's lodging is located on the beach, including the oddly elegant **Ribadesella-Playa** (C/ Ricardo Cangas 3, tel. 98/586-0715, www.hotelribadesellaplaya.com, €100), a family-run hotel with recently renovated sea-colored rooms. Another family affair is **Hotel Boston** (C/ El Pico 7, tel. 98/586-0966, www.ovio-boston.com, €50), located in the city center. One of the cheapest places in town, it has colorful rooms and a decent bar/café.

Food

All along the beach are wonderful seafood restaurants and you can't go wrong popping into any of them. For excellent Asturian specialties

© MEGAN CYTRON

the remote Playa de la Vega just west of Ribadesella

with serious Asturian charm, head to the city center and **El Rompeolas** (C/ Manual Fdez. Juncos 11, tel. 98/586-0287, 10:30 A.M.–1 A.M. daily, €15). If you are not up for a full meal, have a cider and a few tapas at the lively bar. One of the best *sidrerías* in town is **Casa Gaspar** (C/ López Muñiz 6, tel. 98/586-0676, 1–4 P.M. and 7:30–midnight daily, €20), which sets up a hopping terrace in the warmer months.

Getting There

Ribadesella is located on the N-632 coastal road, also called the La Coruña-Santander road. The coastal **FEVE train** (tel. 98/586-0518, www.feve.es) stops here a few times per day at the station on the western edge of the old town. Buses come from Oviedo and other towns via **Autobuses Easa** (tel. 98/586-1303, www.alsa.es).

Vicinity of Ribadesella

Beyond Ribadesella, the **Sueve Mountains** rise up next to the sea. Off the N-632, above the town of Gobiendes. Follow the road signs to the **Mirador de Fito,** a hilltop lookout which provides a spectacular view of both the mountains and the sea. If you are lucky, you'll catch a glimpse of the wild ponies that live freely in the area. In 2004, the next town to the west, Colunga, opened the **Jurassic Museum of Asturias** (tel. 90/230-6600, www.museo jurasico.com, 10:30 A.M.–2:30 P.M. and 4–7 P.M. Wed.–Sun., 10:30 A.M.–2:30 P.M. Mon., closed Tues., €5.30, kids €3.18) to house the many dinosaur fossils found in the region. The building itself is built in the shape of a dinosaur footprint and overlooks what is locally called the Costa de la Jurásica, which includes **Playa de la Griega** and the quaint fishing villages of **Lastres** and **Tazones,** where many tracks have been discovered and preserved. The museum organizes tours to the nearby beaches to tour the fossils and footprints in the rocks. After a trip to the museum, if the weather is warm enough, children will enjoy the little beach, **Playa de la Isla,** with its shallow, calm lagoon and little island to swim out to.

If you decide to do an overnight in the area,

© KATIE PETRILLO

a cider house in Asturias

opt for the precious port town of Lastres and **Casa Eutimio** (C/ San Antonio, tel. 98/585-0012, €65), an 11-room hotel and restaurant in a restored mansion overlooking the harbor.

VILLAVICIOSA

Despite the vicious tinge to its name, Villaviciosa means "fertile land" and as Spain's apple capital, it lives up to it. Tucked in a beautiful green valley just off the coast, the town is surrounded by apple orchards, which means two things in Asturias—*sidra* and *sidrerías*. The town boasts several of the latter. Always lively, they really get going in the first half of September when the **Fiesta de la Manzana** (Apple Festival) takes place. The first apples are harvested and pressed, with the first *mosto* (juice) offered to the Virgin. Cider pouring competitions, tastings, and a whole lot of *sidra*-drinking goes on.

Sights

In addition to apples, this area teams with Romanesque buildings. In the town proper is the 13th-century Romanesque church **Iglesia de Santa María.** The nearby village of Valdediós is home to a working Cistercian monastery from the 13th century, but the tiny town's real jewel is the small, 9th-century pre-Romanesque church of **San Salvador de Valdediós,** known locally as the Conventín (tiny convent). Well-proportioned and intimate, it is everything that a country church should be.

If you prefer sandy beaches to stone churches, Villaviciosa delivers with several lovely coastal beaches located at the mouth of the Ría de Villaviciosa. The best is the 0.8-kilometer (0.5-mile) **Playa de Rodiles,** which boasts golden sand backed up against a lovely park full of shady trees and wooden picnic tables.

Accommodations and Food

Located on a flowered plaza, **El Manquin** (Pl. Santa Clara 2, tel. 98/589-00024, www.hotel manquin.com, €60) is a decent two-star hotel with large, bright rooms. For a more luxe setting, head to the inland village of Santa Eulalia, about 16 kilometers (10 miles) to the south, and **☾ Hotel Casona de Bustiello**

(Crta. Infiesto-Villaviciosa (AS-255), km. 16, tel. 98/571-0760, www.hotelcasonadebustiellos.com, closed Jan. and Feb., €75). This country estate has been converted into gorgeous 10-room hotel. The lovely grounds boast their own stable and horseback rides can be arranged. Both hotels have good dining rooms, but visiting Villaviciosa and not eating in a *sidería* would be criminal. One of the best in town is **El Congreso** (Pl. Ayuntamiento 25, tel. 98/589-1180), which has excellent seafood.

Getting There

Villaviciosa is located on the N-632, which connects to the A-8 and therefore the rest of Asturias. By bus, **ALSA** (C/ García Caveda 22, tel. 98/589-0118, www.alsa.es) runs several daily buses to and from Gijón and Oviedo. **Autocares Cabranes** (C/ Norberto de la Ballina, s/n, tel. 98/589-0761) does the same. There is no train service to Villaviciosa, but the **FEVE train** does stop in Infiesto, about 24 kilometers (15 miles) away. From there you'll have to hail a cab or befriend a local. Hitchhiking is not well accepted in Spain.

GIJÓN

The industrial seaside town of Gijón resembles a sprawling, bland suburb on the sea. It would be eminently skippable were it not for its size and location. Gijón is well connected by train, bus, and highway. It also a good place to stock up before an adventure in the Picos de Europa.

Even though it was destroyed during the Civil War and had to be completely rebuilt, the town itself does have a few historical sights including some that date back millennia to its Roman founding. There is also a lively cultural scene thanks to the presence of a large university. One thing that will strike the tourist, especially those already familiar with busy touristic hot spots such as the Costa del Sol, is that Gijón is a very Spanish town. Because of its lack of charm, it is not a tourist destination for foreigners; however, as most Spanish people like to vacation in the town from which their family came, during the summer, Gijón fills up with Spaniards visiting from all over the country.

Sights

If you do stop over in Xixón (as it's spelled in the Asturian dialect), you'll want to visit the historic quarter of town, which sits on the hillside of Santa Catalina and includes the fishing barrio of Cimadevilla. At the top of the hill is *Elogio del Horizonte* (Eulogy of the Horizon), a monumental work by famed Basque sculptor Eduardo Chillida. From the sculpture, you'll get some amazing views of the coast and sea. The streets between the port and the beach are worth a wander, dotted with lovely fishermen's houses, plazas, and Roman ruins. Seek out the **Plaza Mayor,** an elegant, arcaded promenade lined with cafés. Behind that, visit the **Termas Romanas** (C/ Campo Valdés, s/n, tel. 98/534-5147, 10 A.M.–1 P.M. and 5–8 P.M. Tues.–Sat., 10 A.M.–1 P.M. Sun., closed Mon., €3), Roman baths that date back to the epoch of Augustus.

Gijón's best beach, **Playa de San Lorenzo,** stretches west from the hilltop and a walk along its beachside promenade is a popular early-evening pastime. The town's busy harbor is to the east of the hill and you can find some good seafood shacks here, as well as another city beach, **Playa de Poniente.** Facing the port is the town's main **tourist office** (Dársena de Fomento 1, tel. 98/534-1771, 9 A.M.–10 P.M. daily summer, 9 A.M.–8 P.M. daily winter) where you can get local information as well as routes and excursions to surrounding sights and beaches.

Accommodations

Gijón has tons of housing options from the basic to the luxurious. Keep in mind that prices fluctuate wildly. During the busy summer months, prices are almost double what they are they rest of the year. The prices below reflect this busy high season.

At the top end, **Hernán Cortés** (C/ Fernández Vallín 5, tel. 98/534-6000, www.hotelhernancortes.es, €120) is an elegant hotel that just oozes old-world charm. Rooms are five-star with all the attendant amenities. Another luxe option is the **Parador de Gijón** (Parque de Isabel la Católica, s/n, tel. 98/537-0511, gijon@ parador.es, www.parador.es, €120), surrounded by a tranquil park. Though not a medieval castle or convent like many of the paradors, this 100-year-old bright red former mill is a delightful place to stay. The in-house restaurant serves excellent renditions of traditional Asturian fare. In the historic quarter, **Casona de Jovellanos** (Pl. Jovellanos 1, tel. 98/535-6151, €75) is a lovingly restored *casona* (mansion) with 13 hardwood-floor rooms and a boisterous in-house *sidrería*. For a truly tranquil experience, head east out of town a few kilometers to the village of Cabrueñes and **Hotel Quinta Duro** (Camino de las Quintas, 384 Cabrueñes, tel. 98/533-0443, www.hotelquintaduro.com, €106), an elegant rural hotel located on eight hectares (20 acres) of private parkland.

Food

Whether you're looking for a full meal or filling tapas, the family-friendly **Casa Tino** (C/ Alfredo Truán 9, tel. 98/534-1387, closed Thu., €25) delivers. **El Planeta** (Tránsito de las Ballenas 4, tel. 98/535-0056, closed Mon., €30), located in an elegantly reformed 19th-century mansion, serves freshly grilled fish and bubbly cider with views of the port. **Torremar** (C/ Ezcurida 120, tel. 98/533-0173, closed Tues., €20) does magical things with their grill, from fish to seafood to steaks. One of the best *sidrerías* is **Principado** (C/ Matemático Predrayer 3, tel. 98/534-8655, closed Mon. P.M. and Tues., €40), famed for its exquisite grilled seafood and meats.

Getting There

Gijón's train station (Av. Juan Carlos I, s/n. tel. 98/517-0202) is serviced by **Renfe** (tel. 90/224-0202, www.renfe.es), which connects Gijón with the rest of Spain including several daily trains to Santiago, Madrid, and Barcelona. The narrow-gauge coastal train **FEVE** (Pl. Humedal, s/n, tel. 98/534-2415, www.feve.es) goes to Ferrol, Santander, and Bilbao. Bus service to Gijón is provided by **ALSA** (C/ Magnus Blikstad 2, www.alsa.es) with daily connections to dozens of cities in Spain and even internationally. If you are **driving,** Gijón is located on the A-66, which connects it to central and Southern Spain. The N-632 connects it to the northern regions and the coast.

Western Asturian Coast

The western coast of Asturias is even more wild and desolate than that of the east. The landscape consists of low-slung green mountains threaded with beautiful valleys and clear rivers that pour out into to the sea. Pristine beaches and secluded coves are tucked into seaside cliffs. It is a truly breathtaking place, yet only at the height of summer will you have to share the beach with more than a handful of locals. Until very recently, this entire area was very difficult to reach by car and, as such, has remained relatively untouched by development and tourism (though the new superhighway A-8 is beginning to change this along the coast). One of the most interesting options for tourists looking to get away from it all is to rent a small *casa rural* (country cottage) or to stay in a *casa de aldea/casona* (bed-and-breakfast) and explore the area on foot, by bicycle, FEVE coastal train, and/or car. Heading west from Gijón, the most interesting coastal fishing towns are Cudillero, Luarca, and Castropol.

◖ CUDILLERO

A small dream town by the sea, Cudillero is often cited among the most charming towns in all of Spain—and for good reason. Nicknamed *anfiteatro* (amphitheater), the town is perfectly nestled into the cliffs surrounding the old harbor. A steep road of switchbacks descends into town (though there is a newer and more gentle approach from the west). Once at sea level, the

© MEGAN CYTRON

the harbor of the tiny Asturian fishing village of Cudillero

town's colorful houses rise up, appearing to be stacked, one on top of the other. A lighthouse guards the old harbor and there is a nice path to take you to the scenic view. Quaint as it is, Cudillero is still a fishing town and there is a newer, very active harbor just beyond the old one. Go at dusk to watch the fishing boats come in with the day's catch. After working up an appetite, you can head back into town to sample the fresh seafood at one of the many *sidrerías* around the harbor. In July and August, you can arrange boat excursions and sailing lessons. There are several lovely beaches around the town including **Playa de Aguilar** to the east, where several good hotels are located. The **tourist office** (C/ Puerto del Oeste, s/n, tel. 98/559-1377, 10 A.M.–2 P.M. and 4–7 P.M. Mon.–Fri., 11 A.M.–2 P.M. and 4–7 P.M. Sat., 11 A.M.–2 P.M. Sun., 10 A.M.–9 P.M. daily summer only) can help you plan out your visit. There is also free Internet access in the town's cultural center, **Casa de Cultura** (C/ García de la Concha, tel. 98/559-0168, 4–9 P.M. Mon.–Fri.).

Accommodations and Food

The loveliest lodging around is **Casona de la Paca** (El Pito, tel. 98/559-1303, www.casonadellapaca.com, €83), a lavishly converted 19th-century *indiano* mansion. The brightly painted building is tucked in a lovely garden with hundred-year-old trees. **La Casona de Pío** (C/ Riofrío 3, tel. 98/559-1512, €78) is a stone-walled rustic haven built in an old fish-salting factory near the port. It has an excellent restaurant, specializing in—surprise—fish. **Sidrería el Timón** (C/ Suárez Inclán 9, tel. 98/559-0755), next to the old port, is where you can rub elbows with the local fishermen after they return from sea at sundown. The *almejas* (clams) are a house specialty.

Getting There

Cudillero is located on the N-632, which runs along the coast. It connects to Oviedo in about 35 minutes. Both the **FEVE** (www.feve.es) rail and the **ALSA** bus company (www.alsa.es) make daily stops here.

Vicinity of Cudillero

Moving west from Cudillero on the main road (N-632) you will find the long beach of **Concha de Artedo,** a nice place to have lunch. The excellent **Restaurante Mariño** (tel. 98/559-1188, 1:30–4 P.M. and 9–11:30 P.M. Tues.–Sat., 1:30–4 P.M. Sun., closed Mon., €33) is located right on the beach.

On this stretch of road, the signage to the beaches is not always the best. Look for long white signs with black borders and, if need be, do not hesitate to flag someone down to ask *¿Dónde está la playa?* (DOHN-day est-TAH la PLY-ya, Where is the beach?) Many beaches are only accessible through foot or cart paths. Do not be deterred by fences; as long as you are respectful, it is perfectly acceptable to walk through the pastures—just watch out for livestock.

Next, turn off at **Oviñana** and follow the signs to the *faro* (lighthouse) at **Cabo Vidio.** Take the road until you have reached the end (the last bit is a doozy with the cliffs plunging down hundreds of meters on either side of the road). On a clear day, the view is spectacular and you can see all the way to Galicia. At sundown the sunset is incomparable and you can watch the lighthouses on the nearby capes turn on, one by one. On the west side of the lighthouse (left as you are facing it), there are paths that thread down the cliffs, through wild flowers, to the deserted beaches below. Pack snacks and water if you plan to make it down and back in one day.

PLAYA DEL SILENCIO

Back on the road going to the west, is the Playa del Silencio (Beach of Silence, also called Gavieiru). True to its name, this sliver of sand between the plunging cliffs is blissfully peaceful and remote. Turn off the coastal road at Castañera and follow the signs through the fields to the cliff. You can drive about halfway; pull off to the side and park when the road makes a sharp turn to the right (it will soon cease to be driveable!). Walk the rest of the way down the gravel road past the free roaming goats, sheep, and

horses. At the literal "end of the road," there will be stairs that take you down the rest of the way to the beach. Pack a picnic, contemplate the unusual rock formations, and enjoy the solitude.

LUARCA

The bustling fishing village of Luarca would make a good home base in the area. Tucked into an S-shaped cove against a backdrop of cliffs, it boasts a charming historical quarter and a bustling port teeming with brightly colored fishing boats. Its nickname is La Villa Blanca de la Costa Verde (the white village of the green coast), and its white houses do make a lovely contrast to the green and blue of the surrounding mountains and sea. Take a walk up to the **Faro de Punta Altaya** lighthouse for a breathtaking panoramic view. The town's popular beaches are unimaginatively named 1, 2, and 3, and are mostly gray sand. For a more rugged beach, head a few kilometers west to **Playa del Barayo,** accessible on foot from the town of Sabugo. This wide beach has dunes, a stream, and nearby wetlands to explore. There is good bird-watching in this area.

Luarca's **tourist office** (C/ Los Caleros 11, tel. 98/564-0083, 10 A.M.–2 P.M. and 4:30–6:30 P.M. Tues.–Fri., 10:30A.M.–2 P.M. and 5–7 P.M. Sat., noon–2 P.M. Sun., 10 A.M.–2 P.M. and 4–8 P.M. daily summer) can give you more details on the local flora and fauna-spotting opportunities.

Accommodations

Villa la Argentina (C/ Villar de Luarca, tel. 98/564-0102, www.villalaargentina.com, €84), an opulent *casa del indiano* built in 1899, is now a converted 12-room hotel. It sits atop a hill overlooking the town and boasts a good a restaurant, a pool, refined gardens, and even a small antiques museum. Closer to the beach, another majestic *casa del indiano* has been turned into **Villa de Luarca** (C/ Alvaro de Albornoz 6, tel. 98/547-0703, www.hotelvilladeluarca.com, €90) with 14 country-chic rooms. Get up close to harbor action at the **Hotel Báltico** (Paseo

© CELLAR TOURS/WWW.CELLARTOURS.COM

colorful fishing boats in the tiny port of Luarca

del Muelle 1, tel. 98/564-0991, €60), a decent two-star lodging right on the port.

Food

There are several great seafood places around the port. One of the local favorites is **El Sport** (C/ Rivero 9, tel. 98/564-1078), known for their delectable *empanada de merluza* (hake turnover). Another good choice is **El Barómetro** (Paseo del Muelle 5, tel. 98/547-0662, €20), which has a very good value *menú del día*.

A famous Spanish dining institution is just a few kilometers west in the town of Otur. Family-run **Casa Consuelo** (N-634, km. 317, tel. 98/564-1696, www.casaconsuelo.com, closed Mon. and Nov., €30, reservations suggested) has been serving up exquisite local Asturian fare for over 70 years. Their *fabada* (bean stew) is sublime, but the dish that keeps folks coming back is the *merluza* (hake) served with *angulas* (baby eels) and locally made blue cheese. It is divine. The wine cellar boasts over 20,000 bottles. If you eat so much that you can't possibly move, Casa

Consuelo also houses a large, comfortable hotel (tel. 98/547-0767, €65).

Getting There

Luarca is easily accessed via the N-634, also called the Santander-La Coruña road. Because it is the capital city of the Asturian region of Valdés, it also has better bus service than many of the seaside towns on the Costa Verde. **ALSA** (C/ García Prieto, s/n, tel. 98/589-0118, www .alsa.es) operates several daily buses to Oviedo, Gijón, and points beyond. The **FEVE** (Av. Estación, s/n, tel. 98/564-0552, www.feve.es) also stops here.

WEST TO GALICIA

Navia, with its paper mill and industry, may be one of the least-appealing towns in the region, but the Río Navia, which ends here, goes deep into the Asturian interior along a truly breath-taking valley. This is a good entryway into the interior if you are looking for an off-the-beaten-path escape. A few kilometers inland, tucked in the rolling green hills, are the Iron Age ruins of

Castros de Coaña (tel. 98/563-0801) dating from the 7th to the 2nd century B.C. It is one of the most extensive Celtic villages found in the Iberian Peninsula. The Celtiberians who lived in this area thrived primarily on hunting, gathering, and raising livestock, not agriculture. The ancient Greek historian Estrabon (1st century B.C.) wrote of the people from this area: "All of the inhabitants in the mountains are completely sober. They do not drink anything that is not water, they sleep on the floor, and [the men] wear their hair as long as the women do, though they tie it back with a band around their foreheads in battle... they sleep on straw beds and use wooden cups, like the Celts, and the women wear dresses with floral decoration." There is a small interpretive center that displays artifacts found at the site and also has good tourist information about the rest of the region. The ruins are a short walk away, set into the side of a hill and surrounded by farmhouses built from the very same slate rocks. There are remnants of the citadel, baths, basins, grain grinding stones,

and circular dwellings—all surrounded by a strong defensive wall. There are more *castros* dotting the Navia valley, but none as extensive as that found at Coaña.

Continuing to the west, back along the coast, is the tiny fishing village of **Viavélez,** which wraps around a little harbor. And just past the cliff-top town of **Valdepares** is the lovely **Playa de Porcía,** with its impressive salmon run March–July. Salmon was once so plentiful in the area that it was not valued at all. During a local miners' strike in 1934 one of the complaints was that the workers were fed too much salmon. The next stretch of beaches around the town of **Tapía de Casariego** is popular with surfers, **Playa de los Campos** in particular.

Castropol

The last Asturian coastal town before crossing the border into Galicia is the charming medieval village of Castropol, surrounded on three sides by water from a river, Río Eo, and an estuary, Ría de Ribadeo (named for the larger

© MEGAN CYTRON

CANTABRIA AND ASTURIAS

The Castros de Coaña are Celtic ruins dating back to the Iron Age.

Galician town on the other side of the river). Across the *ría* and still on the Asturias side is the small town of **Figueras** (not to be confused with the town of the same name in Cataluña) with its spectacular art nouveau hotel, ◖ **Palacete de Peñalba** (C/ Grande, s/n, tel. 98/563-6125, www.hotelpalacetepenalba.com, €99), a frosting yellow, curvaceous palace of a hotel built in 1912 by Angel Arbéx, a disciple of Gaudí. The *modernista* master's influence is visible throughout this sumptuous building. The in-house restaurant presents very simple, very good seafood. From Figueras it is possible to take a **boat excursion** up the Río Eo (tel. 98/563-6248), weather permitting (check with the **tourist office** on the main road). The easily accessible **Playa de Peñarronda** is popular with locals and even allows camping.

Oviedo

Moving inland from the coast, you come to the capital of Asturias. A pleasing blend of medieval and modern, Oviedo is a good place to spend a day or two and stock up on provisions before heading off to the Picos, the coast, or the remote interior. Like many small cities in Spain, Oviedo is compact and easily walkable—with a particularly lovely pedestrian historic quarter—while still having a surprisingly bustling restaurant scene and nightlife. However, the real treat in Oviedo is its collection of pre-Romanesque buildings and a tour of these 1,000-plus-year-old structures is a must. Just don't go counting on a vision of sunny Spain; Oviedo has fog an average of 100 days per year.

SIGHTS
El Catedral
El Catedral de San Salvador (Pl. Alfonso II, s/n, tel. 98/522-1033, 10 A.M.–1 P.M. and 4–7 P.M. Mon.–Sat., longer hours in summer, free, Cámara Santa €3) is quite a pastiche of styles—Visigoth, pre-Romanesque, Romanesque, Renaissance, and baroque elements are all incorporated into a Gothic structure that features a lacy 15th-century tower. You'll notice it is a bit lopsided. Two towers were planned, but a lack of funds curtailed the construction of the second so the tower stands alone. The pre-Romanesque chapel of San Miguel, **La Cámara Santa,** is a UNESCO World Heritage Site and an important stop for pilgrims on the Camino de Santiago. It houses two important and symbolic gold crosses from the 7th and 8th centuries (the Cross of the Angels and the Cross of Victory), the silver-plated Visigoth Arca Santa (Holy Chest) that was brought from Toledo when that town fell to the Moors, an agate-encrusted pre-Romanesque chest, and a 6th-century Byzantine diptych. The *torre vieja* (old tower), the carved El Salvador icon of Christ, and the six sculpted columns in the Cámara Santa date from the Romanesque period (1175–1578). Also of note are the baroque frescos on the sacristy vault.

Aside from the antiquities and architecture, part of the mystique of the Cámara Santa that has drawn pilgrims off the Camino for centuries can be attributed to the very curious (and, with all due respect, improbable) collection of relics collected there. Among them can be found five thorns from Christ's crown, a fragment of the actual cross he was crucified on, a cloth said to be his shroud, a sandal worn by St. Peter the Apostle, a piece of bread from the Last Supper, and a vial of Mary's breast milk.

Behind the cathedral, you'll find the **Museo Arqueológico de Asturias** (C/ San Vicente 5, tel. 98/521-5405, 10 A.M.–1:30 P.M. and 4–6 P.M. Tues.–Sat., 11 A.M.–1 P.M. Sun., closed Mon., free). This archaeology museum, located in the Monasterio de San Vicente, houses a trove of pre-Romanesque art and sculpture "rescued" from the tiny churches in the surrounding region. Be sure to walk through the lovely cloisters during your visit.

Plazas of Oviedo

From here, you can take a stroll through a series of adjoining plazas. **Plaza de Trascorrales** often has cultural exhibits in its old fish market. **Plaza Fontan,** with its colorful buildings and jewel-box market of iron and glass, was a public works project of the 18th-century Enlightenment—a marsh was drained and Oviedo gained one its most charming and well-loved public spaces. A lively little flea market sets up outside on Thursdays, Saturdays, Sundays, and public holidays. **Plaza de Daoíz y Velarde** is a good place to have a rest and a round of *sidra,* preferably at one of its lazy *terrazas* (outdoor cafes) if the weather permits.

La Universidad

Universidad de Oviedo (C/ San Francisco, s/n, tel. 98/510-3993, free) has a wonderfully three-dimensional, sculpted 16th-century Plateresque facade. Only the exterior of the monument and the cloistered interior courtyard are open for visits. The nearby and enormous **Campo de San Francisco** park—Oviedo's largest green space—is the gateway to the newer parts of the city. Its esplanades and winding wooded paths are a favorite local spot for a late-afternoon stroll and a great source of shade in the summer and people-watching year-round.

◖ Pre-Romanesque Architecture

The pre-Romanesque architectural style, which foreshadowed both Romanesque and Gothic, is typical throughout Asturias. Oviedo itself provides the opportunity to take in some of the most significant buildings. In addition to the Cámara Santa there is also **Iglesia de San Tirso, Santa María del Naranco, San Miguel de Lillo,** and **San Julián de los Prados,** all of them National Monuments. Together, these structures have earned World Heritage status from UNESCO. Touring these sights is a hypnotizing trip way back into the past, but you'll

have to get a good map from the tourist office and put on your walking shoes as they lie on the edges of the city. (For more on this architectural heritage, see sidebar, *Asturian Pre-Romanesque Art and Architecture.*)

ACCOMMODATIONS
€50-100

Hotel Carreño (C/ Monte Gamonal 4, tel. 98/511-8622, www.hotelcarreno.com, €60) is a well-appointed two-star hotel close to the train and bus stations. **El Ovetense** (C/ San Juan 6, tel. 98/522-0840, www.hotelovetense.com, €50) is a pretty standard cheap hotel with a boisterous *sidrería* (cider bar) in-house—perfect for stumbling back to your room!

Over €100

If you are a fan of very traditional, very upscale hotels, head to the five-star **Hotel de la Reconquista** (C/ Gil de Jaz 16, tel. 98/524-1100, www.hoteldelareconquista.com, €215), one of Spain's most prestigious hotels. Built in a 16th-century hospital, the hotel wraps around an austere interior patio. Inside, the decor is heavy on antiques (real and faux), religious painting, brocaded fabrics, while the exterior is a baroque fantasy of carved stone. At the opposite end of the style meter, the very modern **El Magistral** (C/ Jovellanos 3, tel. 98/520-4242, www.magistralhoteles.com, €105) is black, white, and shiny all over. A plus is that it is located right in the center of the city's sights. Another stylish good choice is ◖ **Libretto Hotel** (C/ Marqués de Santa Cruz 12, tel. 98/520-2004, www.librettohotel.com, €120). Located in a historic building overlooking the San Francisco park, this lovely hotel has taken opera as its decorating theme and musical notes and oversized black-and-white photos of opera stars distinguish the rooms.

FOOD
Local Cuisine

For fun with your food, head straight to a *sidrería.* There are several on Calle Gascona, known locally as the "boulevard of cider." Start at **Tierra Astur** (C/ Gascona 1, tel. 98/520-3411,

ASTURIAN PRE-ROMANESQUE ART AND ARCHITECTURE (A.D. 737–910)

During the first 250 years of Muslim rule in Spain, Christian artistic production was anything but prolific. As the only stable Christian realm during this time, Asturias is a notable exception and is home to much of Spain's best pre-Romanesque architecture from this period. These small churches and religious objects may seem modest when compared to the splendors of Al-Andalus, but what the sites lack in grandiose scale, they make up for in simple harmonious proportion and the introduction of light and height into what were previously dark, low-slung Christian temples. The significance of these structures extends beyond Spain because they laid the groundwork for the great movement of Romanesque art that swept through Europe at the beginning of the second millennium – culminating in the magnificent cathedral of Santiago.

The Asturian pre-Romanesque style is a synthesis of Roman, Visigoth, Mozarabic, Byzantine, and even Celtic motifs. The distinguishing characteristics of the architectural style are the impressive height of the buildings, barrel-vaulted ceilings, the numerical motif of three (for the trinity) in windows and decorations, and the organic and geometric motifs and carvings on interior columns and capitals. The structure also represented a technological advance – a new type of support (a precursor to the buttress) was devised on the outside to support the additional weight and verticality.

© MEGAN CYTRON

The pre-Romanesque San Miguel de Lillo is part of Oviedo's thousand-year-old heritage.

The best examples of this style are found in and around Oviedo, particularly on the outskirts of town. **San Julián de los Prados,** built in A.D. 812–842, is located within walking distance of the historic quarter beside a large highway in the neighborhood of Pumarín. It is the largest pre-Romanesque church in Spain

---

1 P.M.–midnight daily, €20) with its adjoining store, and work your way along from there. The city also boasts several nationally renowned culinary destinations including **Casa Fermín** (C/ San Francisco 8, tel. 98/521-6452, 1–4 P.M. and 8–11 P.M., closed Sun., €45). This elegant dining room has been serving classic Asturian fare since 1924, when it was opened by Luis Gil, a champion of the cuisine. Today, the current chef adds some creative touches to the dishes while remaining fully committed to a base of excellent local products.

Tapas

Throughout the historic center, especially around the cathedral, there are loads of tapas bars. A local favorite for fried shrimp and vermouth on tap is **La Paloma** (C/ Independencia 3, tel. 98/523-5397). For classic tapas in a classic space, head to **Casa Ramón** (Pl. Daoiz y Velarde 1, tel. 98/520-1415).

INFORMATION AND SERVICES

Maps and tourist information for all of Asturias are available from the **main tourist office** (C/

and one of the best preserved, particularly its medieval frescos and ornate window carvings (*celosias*). If it is locked, you can request the key (*llave*, YA-bay) at the priest's residence to the left of the main door.

On Mount Naranco – with a beautiful view of the mountains and Oviedo spread out below – **Santa María del Naranco** was built during the first half of the 9th century as a summer palace for the Asturian king Ramiro I. It was converted into a church between 900 and 1100 and is the only palace from the Visigoth period that has been preserved. It is notable for its Byzantine-influenced decorative carvings, unique two-level configuration (the temple is on the second level and is accessed via exterior stairs), porch, and tall trinity of windows and columns.

A short walk away is **San Miguel de Lillo,** the original church of Santa María, built in 848. Unfortunately, this church has suffered damages over the centuries and its interior configuration is not very well preserved. However, the Germanic style of decoration, ornate window carvings, and unusual sculpted jambs depicting circus scenes – complete with acrobats, a lion, and his tamer – are certainly worth a look.

The **Fuente de Foncalada,** a fountain built in the form of a tiny temple during the latter half of the 9th century, sits just outside Oviedo's original city walls and is the only public-works project conserved from this period.

In the old quarter of Oviedo, the **Cámara Santa** (now part of the Cathedral) was erected by King Alfonso II between 791 and 842. On display are several important pre-Romanesque relics, the most emblematic being two gold crosses – *Cruz de Los Ángeles* (Cross of the Angels) and *La Victoria* (the Cross of Victory). According to legend, this second cross is said to be the one that Don Pelayo brandished at the battle of Covadonga.

Other examples of architecture from the Asturian pre-Romanesque period worth a visit are **Santa María de Bendones** (in Bendones, about five kilometers/three miles from Oviedo), **San Pedro de Nora** (in San Pedro de Nora, about 11 kilometers/seven miles from Oviedo), **San Salvador de Valdediós** (in Valdediós near Villaviciosa, 40 kilometers/25 miles east of Oviedo), and the well-preserved **Santa Cristina de Lena** (in Pola de Lena, 48 kilometers/30 miles south of Oviedo), which is recognized along with the Cámara Santa, Santa María del Naranco, San Miguel de Lillo, and San Julián de los Prados as part of the Asturian UNESCO World Heritage Site. In many cases, visitors will arrive to find the doors of these churches locked. Provided that it is not lunchtime (2-4 P.M.) or late evening, ask around in the village to find the person who has the key – usually the town priest. Or, better yet, have a tourist office call ahead to arrange a visit.

Contributed by Madrid-based journalist Megan Cytron, who writes frequently on Asturias.

Marqués de Santa Cruz 1, tel. 98/522-7586, 10:30 A.M.–12:30 P.M. and 4:30–7:30 P.M. daily) in front of the cathedral. A smaller second branch is located at the east corner of the Parque San Francisco. **La Lila** (C/ la Lila 17, tel: 98/508-3400, 9 A.M.–9 P.M. Mon.–Fri.) offers free Internet access. If you are walking this way, do not miss the unexpected **Woody Allen statue** on Calle de las Milicias Nacionales. He spoke very favorably of Oviedo when he was in town to receive the Prince of Asturias Award, so the town could not help but erect a statue in his honor.

GETTING THERE AND AROUND

Air
The **Aeropuerto de Asturias** (tel. 98/512-7500) is located near Avilés on the coast, about 44 kilometers (27 miles) from Oviedo. It takes domestic flights from all over Spain and the low-cost carrier Easyjet flies in from London Stansted. There are public buses that connect regularly to Oviedo or you can catch a taxi for about €20.

Train
The **Estación del Norte** (C/ Uría, tel.

98/525-0202) handles both **Renfe** (tel. 90/224-0202, www.renfe.es) and **FEVE** (tel. 98/598-1700, www.feve.es) trains. Renfe connects Oviedo to all of Spain including Madrid, Barcelona, and as far away as Alicante. FEVE runs across the coast from País Vasco to Galicia.

Bus

The **Estación de Autobuses** (C/ Empresario Pepe Cosmen, s/n) has several bus companies, though the one with the widest network is **ALSA** (www.alsa.es,) which connects Oviedo to cities nationwide.

Car

If driving, Oviedo is accessed from the A-8 and N-632 from Cantabria and País Vasco, the N-634 from Galicia, and the N-630 and A-66 from the south.

Picos de Europa

Comprising most of the western interior of Asturias, part of Cantabria, and a bit of Castilla y León, the Picos de Europa is popular destination for Spanish tourists, but overlooked by nearly everyone else. It is a shame because this compact mountain range has much to offer: spectacular gorges, steeple-like peaks, verdant green valleys, ancient stone villages, great food, and friendly people. It is the largest national park in Spain (some say in Europe) and is well loved, not only for its natural beauty, but also because of its historic importance in the formation of the country. (See sidebar, *The Cradle of the Reconquista.*)

The Cantabrian mountains spread across Northern Spain, from east to west, partitioning the peninsula—green and misty mountains and coastal pastures to the north; semi-arid high Meseta (plateau) to the south. Right in the middle sit the Picos de Europa. Lying very close to the coast, the Picos span Asturias, Cantabria, and León. They soar suddenly up to 2,438 meters (8,000 feet) in under 21 kilometers (13 miles). The effect is almost surreal, with the snow-covered peaks towering above the beaches and surrounding pastureland.

Three river gorges divide the range into three tremendous *macizos* (massifs): Andara in the east, Urrieles in the center, and Cornión in the west. Across the range, there are 200 limestone peaks rising more than 1,981 meters (6,500 feet) above sea level with drops of up to 2,301 meters (7,550 feet). The highest summits are in the central section, with three rising above 2,438 meters (8,000 feet). There are three towns at the foot of the mountains that are popular base camps: Cangas de Onís, Arenas de Cabrales, and Potes (over the border in Cantabria). The mountains were formed by glacial action and the combination of millennia of glacial movement combined with slightly acidic rain on the limestone peaks resulted in erosion that led to the development of an immense underground drainage system full of caves. The deepest yet explored goes down over 1,372 meters (4,500 feet).

Opportunities for outdoor activities abound: rock climbing, spelunking, backcountry skiing, horseback riding, mountain biking, four-wheel-drive treks, fishing, bird-watching, canoeing, kayaking, and so on. Each of the main towns (Arriondas, Cangas de Onís, Arenas de Cabrales, and Potes) has tour operators and mountaineering stores where travelers can get maps or set off on guided treks. Most hotels in the area can also arrange activities or package tours for their guests. For those who prefer to ponder, rather than engage, nature, there are countless quaint historic inns, cottage rentals, and bed-and-breakfasts sprinkled throughout the Picos. Most have views of the mountains and outdoor patios where visitors can breathe it all in. There are relatively flat paths for easy walks in the river valleys and through the farmland. The area also has excellent gastronomic offerings.

When to Go

The weather in the Picos is notoriously fickle. You may step out in short sleeves and warm temperatures only to find yourself shivering under a damp, cold fog a few hours later. Even the summer months feature a few chilly, cloudy days, though there is usually enough sun to keep vacationers happy. Just be aware that July and August are the traditional vacation months for Spain and thousands of Spaniards flock to the Picos during these months. While crowds are barely a blip of what you'd find on the Mediterranean coasts, they are large enough to snap up hotel rooms and campgrounds. If you'll go during this time, book ahead. Better yet, try to arrange your trip in June or September. Both months boast some sunshine and thinning crowds. If you do travel off-season or in winter, expect desolation and snow. Many of the smaller towns all but shut down. Rural houses and campground often do close up. Plan ahead with bookings and you should be fine.

Safety

Driving at the higher altitudes can get dicey between October and May. It is best to avoid traveling to the Picos in the dead of winter, and if the weather is even a little chilly, take chains just to be safe (rental car companies all provide them). Even those used to higher altitudes may miscalculate how challenging the Picos can be, mainly due to the precipitous slopes and unpredictable weather and visibility. On a clear day, an impenetrable fog bank can suddenly roll in from the sea. It is important to notify someone of your whereabouts before you head out on a backcountry hike. Do not expect guardrails on the roads or trails, or even at most overlooks. Paths and stairs may get slippery when wet. It helps to remember that the Spanish have an "at your own risk" mentality about personal safety. Each year, a few adventurers underestimate the dangers and end up coming out in a body bag. It is a sure way to ruin a trip. When in doubt, play it safe or ask a local for advice. Your best bet is to sign up with an outfitter experienced in leading treks in the Picos. **Mountain Travel Sobek** (tel. 888/687-6235, www.mt

sobek.com), based in California, offers a solid trip into the Picos that has some easy days and some challenging ones. Their usual guide, Eric Perez, is one of the best in the region. Other decent companies are **Iberian Wildlife Tours** (tel. 94/273-5154, www.iberianwildlife.com), **Pico Verde** (www.picoverde.com), and **Pura Aventura** (www.pura-aventura.com). The latter two are based in the United Kingdom. If you are an experienced mountaineer and keen on going it alone, be sure and do your research at your local mountaineering shop, on the Internet, and in the library.

Getting There and Around

The only good way to visit this area is via car. If you had a few weeks to kill and were very experienced in mountaineering and hiking, you could hike around to many of the best spots— but if that is the case, you should be reading a specialized book on hiking in the Picos such as *Walks and Climbs in the Picos de Europa* or *Trekking and Climbing in Northern Spain*, not this brief introduction.

Public bus service is provided year-round by **EASA** (www.alsa.es) from Oviedo into Cangas de Onís, Arriondas, Infiesto, Ribadesella, Llanes, Onís, and Cabrales. From there, you'll have to hike around a bit or join an organized tour. From Cangas de Onís, there are daily busses to Covadonga, but the bus to the lakes only runs in summer. EASA also runs trips from Llanes and Ribadesella into the Cares gorge.

By car, where you enter the Picos depends on where you are coming from. Most likely that will be the coast—it is mighty hard to resist the pull of the mountains once you've seen theme towering, all jagged and white-capped, over the sea. If you are coming from Oviedo, you'll head east along N-634. From Ribadesella, go south on N-625. From the Cantabrian coast, access the Picos via N-621 south which you can catch near the town of Unquera on the Cantabria-Asturias border.

MASSIF ANDARA

The Andara Massif is the easternmost part of the range. In Spanish, it is often called the

THE CRADLE OF THE RECONQUISTA

Like all good nationalist stories, the story of the Christian Reconquista (reconquest) of Spain is a hodgepodge of history and mythology. However, one generally accepted fact is that the Reconquista was launched from the tiny kingdom of Asturias by a character named Don Pelayo. Born in Asturias, he was reputedly a descendent of Visigoth royalty. For many years, Pelayo attempted to establish a Christian kingdom in the isolated and mountainous north. Despite the lack of territorial unity, in A.D. 718 Pelayo was appointed King of Asturias by an assembly of tribal elders, according to the Visigoth political system. The capital was placed in the mountainous interior town of Cangas de Ónis, on the western fringe of the Picos de Europa.

The Battle of Covadonga is considered the watershed moment in Spanish history. In reality, it was but one battle in the midst of many skirmishes. The Moors were more interested in expanding into what is now France and the rest of Europe than in fully conquering Asturias. That is, until they lost the Battle of Toulouse in 721 and were driven back across the Pyrenees into Iberia. In an effort to solidify their political control of the Iberian Peninsula, a small delegation headed up by the general Alqama was sent to the north to negotiate with Don Pelayo. The details get fuzzy here, but what is known is that Don Pelayo refused to negotiate and retreated from Cangas de Ónis into the valley of Covadonga with his army and holed up in a cave (currently a shrine to the Virgin of Covadonga). Pelayo and his men laid in wait for the Moors – whose numbers vary widely depending on who is doing the counting. As the story goes, Pelayo and his men received a signal from the Virgin Mary telling them precisely when and how to attack. They took her holy advice and prevailed, forcing the Moors to retreat.

According to some accounts, the people of Asturias were so inspired by the defeat that they rose up and slaughtered the defeated Moors as they retreated to the other side of the Picos. According to a Muslim account of the same event, the Moorish delegation simply left because they could not negotiate with *asnos salvajes* (wild donkeys, referring to Pelayo and his soldiers). In retreat, it is believed that many Moors may have perished in a rockslide on the other side of the mountains.

In any case, the Battle of Covadonga has great symbolic importance as the first Christian victory against the Moors. Today, even though the present royal family is in no way descended from Pelayo, the heir to the Spanish throne, Prince Felipe, has the title of "Prince of Asturias," and Asturias is not merely an autonomous community, but rather the loftily titled Principado de Asturias due to its status as the first Christian kingdom established after the Moorish invasion.

(Contributed by Madrid-based journalist Megan Cytron, who writes frequently on Asturias.)

Macizo Oriental. This area is the most accessible, and therefore the most visited of the massifs in the Picos. Though purists lament the onslaught of summertime tourists, their presence means this area, especially the towns of Potes, is fully equipped to meet the needs of visitors from hard-core climbers seeking a thrill to car-trippers looking for good views and good food.

Desfiladero de la Hermida

Heading south on N-621 from the coast, the first town you hit is **Panes,** a fairly forgettable place that is good for gassing up and maybe grabbing a coffee. Continuing south, follow the River Deva up into the mountains and through a series of shifting microclimates and tiny towns. In the process you'll traverse a gorgeous, almost impossibly narrow gorge, Desfiladero de la Hermida. At its deepest point, the walls close in claustrophobically on either side, barely allowing any direct sunlight to penetrate. Having crossed over into Cantabria, you may want to make a quick stop in the nearly deserted town of **Liébana,** just a few kilometers to the east; it is home to one of the region's finest pre-Romanesque churches, the 10th-century **Iglesia de Santa María.** Ask the *cura* (priest) for the key. After a quick look, have an excellent *café* at the tiny shack next door. The church's only other companions are an olive tree and a yew tree, both planted when the church was built—over 1,000 years ago.

Potes

The largest town in Liébana, Potes is a popular base for exploring the central and eastern massifs. Bustling and cute, it also makes a good place to visit in itself. The old part of town is a web of narrow medieval streets lined with stately buildings that attest to Potes former splendor. Hulking over its center is the 15th-century **Torre Infantado**, a squat defensive building. If you are in Potes on a Monday, be sure to visit the traditional market.

The **tourist office** (Pl. Serna, s/n, tel. 94/273-0787, 10 A.M.–2 P.M. and 4–6 P.M. Thurs.–Mon., 10 A.M.–2 P.M. Tues.–Wed.) can provide tons of information on hikes and activities into Potes. You will also see tour outfitters and excursions offered all over town. If you stay in town, check with your hotel as most organize trips.

For accommodations, try **Casa Cayo** (C/ Cántabra 6, tel. 94/273-0150, www.casacayo .com, €60), a rustic lodge that has the added bonus of one of the town's best restaurants and its liveliest bar. Another decent option is **Hotel Dolnar** (C/ Amapola, s/n, tel. 94/273-1054, www.hoteldolnar.com, €55).

For complete packages, your best bet in the area is **Casa Gustavo** (Aliezo, tel. 94/273-2010, stuartsinpicos@terra.es, www.picos-accommodation.co.uk, €50), a few kilometers before Potes on the N-621. This rustic guesthouse is set in a 500-year-old converted farmhouse and run by British expats Mike and Lisa Stuart. Enthusiastic about their adopted homeland, the pair organize hikes, skiing, mountain biking, and other activities in the mountains. Homemade meals, when weather permits, are served in a courtyard with views of the mountains. There is an in-house library with guides on the Picos.

There are three buses daily from Santander to Potes run by **Palomera** (tel. 94/288-0611).

Fuente Dé

From Potes, there will be a great stream of cars heading up the highway to Fuente Dé. They are day-trippers headed to the **teleférico** (tel. 94/273-6610, 9 A.M.–8 P.M. daily summer, 10 A.M.–6 P.M. daily winter, €12.50, kids €4), a cable car that climbs alarmingly up the cliff nearly 0.8 kilometers (0.5 mile) in under four minutes. If you go on a summer weekend, there could be quite a wait. Buy a ticket as soon as you arrive and wait to hear your number called at the bar next door. Be sure to bring a jacket or sweater. even in summer, as it can get chilly up top.

At the top, you'll find an immensely beautiful area with stunning vistas and easy trails for walking. You can hike all day if you like, but remember to make it to the last cable car down. If you miss it—on purpose or not—you can spend the night at the simple hostel, **Refugio de Aliva** (tel. 94/256-3736, closed Oct.–May, €75), about a four-kilometer (2.5-mile) hike from the cable car; in summer you'll need to make reservations ahead of time. The hostel also has a restaurant serving hearty mountain fare. If you do not want to wait in line to go down, there is a long trail back down the mountain to the tiny village of **Espinama,** where you can stay at one of a handful of hostels. It may also be possible to arrange a four-wheel-drive trek back down, depending on the season—ask around in Espinama.

If you want to stay overnight in Fuente Dé, you have several choices including **Parador del Río Deva** (tel. 94/273-6651, fuentede@parador .es, www.parador.es, €110), a modern parador built in the style of a rustic ski lodge. The charming **Hotel Rebeco** (tel. 94/273-6601, www.liebanaypicosdeeuropa.com/guia/rebeco .htm, €75) is a more low-key option. The hotel runs activities and treks into the mountains.

If you are traveling by **public transportation,** the **Palomera** (tel. 94/288-0611) bus from Santander, travels from Potes to Fuente Dé three times a day, but only in summer.

MASSIF URRIELES

Located in the center of the Picos, the Urrieles is the most dramatic of the three massifs. It is home to the three of the highest peaks in the

Picos: Naranjo de Bulnes (2,519 meters/8,264 feet), Picotesorero (2,570 meters/8,432 feet), and, the highest in the range, Torre de Cerredo (2,648 meters/8,687 feet).

Arenas de Cabrales

The small town of Arenas de Cabrales, located on the AS-114, is a good base for exploring the Urrieles. Like Cangas, it is well equipped with mountaineering stores and tour operators. Despite the name, this is not the town responsible for making the famously potent artisan Cabrales blue cheese (which is made from a blend of sheep's, goat's, and cow's milk, then wrapped in leaves, and finally aged for months in caves). The main cheese towns are Panes, Potes, Sotres, Bejes, and Treviso. You can, however, buy lots of this love-it-or-hate-it cheese in town (and all through the region). Just be sure to pack the smelly stuff in an airtight container unless you want to make enemies wherever you travel. If you are in town the last Sunday in August, you can attend the **Feria de Cabrales,** a lively celebration of the cheese. In summer and on long weekends, the **tourist office** (tel. 98/584-6484) opens up in a kiosk on the town's main road.

A great place to stay on the edge of town is the **Hotel Torrecerredo** (Vega de Barrio, s/n, tel. 98/584-6640 info@picosadventure .com, www.hoteltorrecerredo.com, info@picos adventure.com, €60), an absolutely charming mountain inn run by an accommodating English/Spanish couple. The location of the hotel is so picturesque that it has been nicknamed, "the one-star hotel with the five-star view." Even if you don't stay here, check out their roster of activities from hiking to biking, open to all and reasonably priced. The restaurant also offers hearty Asturian fare with a good-value *menú del día.*

Desfiladero de las Cares

From Arenas, you can drive south on the AS-264 through the spectacular Desfiladero de las Cares, also called Garganta del Cares (Cares Gorge). This 1.6-kilometer-deep (one-mile) rift of nature separates the Cornión from the Urrieles massifs and is one of the most pop-ular walking spots in the Picos—some would say too popular, especially in July and August when the vacationing hordes descend. The river that once roared through the gorge has mostly been diverted into an enclosed canal as part of a hydroelectric project. The access path runs along the northern wall of the canal.

Bulnes

At the end of the Cares Gorge in the town of **Poncebos,** there is a new funicular that travels seven minutes through a two-kilometer (1.2-mile) tunnel to the mountaintop town of Bulnes. Until 2000, the only way to get to Bulnes was on foot. There are still no roads to the town. Those who want to get a taste of just how isolated life in this town was before the funicular can walk down the original burro path (1–1.5 hours) back to Poncebos.

Bulnes lies at the foot of the solid-rock peak of **Naranjo de Bulnes,** also known as Picu Urriellu in the local tongue. While not the highest in the Picos, it is arguably the most striking, with its sheer walls of limestone rising to over 2,438 meters (8,000 feet) full of fissures and crags, many laden with snow until well into spring. "Naranjo" (*naranco* in the local tongue) refers to the orange-hue the mountain takes on in the evening light. This is a rock-climber's paradise and a major destination for serious climbers in Spain and worldwide. It is also the Spanish mountain that has claimed the most lives. The first climber to conquer the mountain was Pedro Pidal, a Spanish aristocrat who ascended the peak with rudimentary equipment and a local guide in 1904. Pidal later went on to lead conservation in Spain and established the Western Massif as Spain's first national park. That park later expanded to include the current Picos. At the bottom of the peak, in tiny **Vega Urriellu,** there is a 90-bed *refugio* (mountain hut), **Delgado Ubeda** (tel. 98/592-5200), where you can book a no-frills bunk for less than €20 per person.

Cabrales Route

For those who want an invigorating (at times knuckle-whitening) drive (or those driven by a love of stinky cheese), the 11-kilometer (seven-mile) CA-1 road winds up and up from Poncebos through primitive tunnels to the small mountain farm town of **Sotres,** the summer home of the sheep, goats, and cows who produce the milk for the famed Cabrales cheese. The spring and summer mountain grass is highly prized for producing the best milk and cheese. From Sotres, there are hikes into the peaks. One of the most interesting leads to the small alpine lake, **Lago de las Moñetas,** and the nearly lunar landscape of the **Valle de las Moñetas.** The road continues on, crossing over into Cantabria to two other cheesemaking towns, **Treviso** and **Bejes.** The caves where these cheeses are aged are also on these slopes.

MASSIVE CORNIÓN

In Spanish, this zone is often called the Macizo Occidental (Western Massif). With its Peña Santa de Castilla summit rising to 2,596 meters (8,517 feet), it is the largest and most varied of the three massifs. Lying completely within Asturias, it is most easily accessed via Oviedo. Heading east on the N-634 from Oviedo, you will pass through the cider town of **Nava** with its green rolling hills, sheep, and **Museo de la Sidra** (Cider Museum). Next is **Infiesto,** a pretty town on the banks of the Río Piloña.

Cangas de Onís

When you get to Arriondas, take the turn off to Cangas de Onís. The biggest town in the interior, Cangas is a charming town along the Río Sella. It has a few sites, like the centuries-old **Monasterio de San Pedro de Villanueva** (which now serves as a parador overlooking town), a picturesque medieval bridge, and the tiny **Capilla de Santa Cruz,** which is erected over a Celtic dolmen. There is a tranquil, shaded central plaza lined with cafés and *sidrerías*. Cangas is the best place to stock up on provisions before heading up into the mountains. There is also a big Sunday market here with artisan and gastronomic products from the surrounding area. It is pretty much the only place to shop on Sundays, since most stores will be closed elsewhere in the region. Here you can arrange guided treks, canoe

and kayak trips, and other outdoorsy activities. Check with the **visitors center** (Casa Dago, tel. 98/584-8614, open year-round) and the mountaineering stores off the main plaza for details. Those less ambitious can do as the Spanish do and stop and have lunch, have a quick dip in the nearby Sella River (if the weather is warm enough), and then head on to nearby Covadonga or to the beautiful Desfiladero de los Beyos (Beyos Gorge) to the south on the N-625.

If you decide to stay overnight, Canga de Onís offers a variety of accommodations. The **Parador de Canga de Onís** (C/ Villanueva, s/n, tel. 98/584-9402, www.parador.es, €135) is the most luxurious splurge. Rumored to have been built by King Alfonso I in 746, this sprawling former monastery was a work in progress at least into the 18th century. Rooms are spacious and simply decorated and the restaurant offers hearty Asturian fare in a majestic setting. The parador can arrange outdoor activities. Another luxurious choice is **Hotel Aultre Naray** (in Peruyes, eight kilometers/ five miles outside of town, tel. 98/584-0808, www.aultrenaray.com, €95), a 10-room hotel in a renovated mansion with beautiful views of the mountains. An amazing mid-priced option is the lovely **Hotel Posada del Valle** (in Collia, near Arriondas, tel. 98/584-1157, www .posadadelvalle.com, closed Oct. 15–Mar. 31, €68). A converted 19th-century farmhouse, the hotel is surrounded by roaming sheep and a working organic farm. Guided walking and hiking tours (in English) into the surrounding Picos can be arranged. Even if you don't decide to visit the hotel, visit their website, which is a gold mine of information on the Asturian Picos. Back in town, there are several cheap and cheerful pensions, including the homey **Hospedaje Torreón** (C/ San Pelayo 32, tel. 98/584-8211, www.pensiontorreon.icspana .es, €45).

Food options run towards home-cooked Asturian meals with lots of white-bean stews, locally made cheeses and sausages, and fresh salmon and trout from the rivers. Fill up on these goodies and more at **Casa Juan** (Av. Covadonga

20, tel. 98/584-3012). **El Molín de la Pedrera** (C/ Río Güeña 2, tel. 98/584-9109, €27) is a *sidrería* in a rustic setting on the river.

◖ Covadonga

Covadonga (which means "lady of the cave") is a small town with lots of history in a beautiful natural setting that has been nearly completely overrun by tourists. This is one of the few sites in Asturias that is visited by the tour-bus set, due to its unequaled claim to fame as the site of the first battle in the (re)conquest of Spain. (See sidebar, *The Cradle of the Reconquista*.) This is where it all started. Here King Pelayo defeated the Moors in 722, starting the eight-century Reconquista to claim Spain for the Christian monarchs. Legend says that the Virgin Mary appeared to Pelayo's troops in a cave just before the battle. Suddenly, all the stones and arrows that the Moors had been throwing at them from the other side of the valley boomeranged back at them! Then, part of the mountain fell on top of them. According to the chroniclers, the Moorish army was left with only "thirty asses and ten women." Over a millennium later, the **Santuario de Covadonga** (tel. 98/584-6035, 9 A.M.–8 P.M. daily April–Sept., 9 A.M.–7 P.M. daily Oct.–Mar., free) was built next to the cave. The 19th-century shrine seems a bit out of place, but it is a major pilgrimage for Spaniards.

Pack a picnic lunch and head up the twisting road towards the mountain lakes of Enol and Ercina. For 12 kilometers (7.5 miles), the road twists through a rolling carpet of intense green, while all around, the jagged, white tips of the mountains reveal themselves. Halfway up the road, stop at the **Mirador de la Reina** lookout point for a truly breathtaking view. **Lago de Enol** is the first of these two glacier lakes. It sits 1,070 meters (3,510 feet) above sea level. Cows, sheep, and horses graze lazily around the edge of this crystal clear body of water, seeming to take no notice of the camera-crazy visitors all around. Continue on up to **Lago de Ercina.** Sitting at 1,108 meters (3,635 feet) above sea level, this stunning body of water dramatically changes color from blue to light green to dark green, with occasional swatches of red and yellow. This is due to the various plant species living in the lake and the changes in the light. The hordes of tourists tend to laze around for a siesta in the grass by the lakes. Join them or escape to solitude on one of the many marked hiking trails—and please, stay on the trails! In case you forget your provisions, there is also a small terrace bar near Lago de Enol, **Restaurante el Casín** (closed Jan. and Feb., €10). The traditional fare is almost as wonderful as the view. Be sure to bring a sweater or rain jacket, even in the summer temperatures can drop suddenly. During summer, there is a **EASA bus** (10 A.M.–6:30 P.M., €6) that leaves for the lakes several times a day from Covadonga. In August, the bus is mandatory. Cars are not allowed in due to the crush of visitors. You can drive up after 7 P.M., but before that time you'll have to get on the bus.

Desfiladero de los Beyos

The N-625 follows the Río Sella up into the stunning gorge of **Desfiladero de los Beyos.** The road itself is an amazing bit of engineering, but you'll be too blown away by the jaw-dropping natural sights to focus on the man-made. There are dozens of *miradores* (lookout points) along the way. If you continue on this road, you'll eventually land in the province of León in the region of Castilla y León.

Sports and Recreation

In Cangas de Onís, you can get all the information you need to plan your own mini-tours and walks through this region, however if you'd like something more organized or want to do an activity such as kayaking or four-wheeling (called "quad" in Spain), visit one of the many adventure outfitters in the region. Near Arriondas, halfway between Canga de Onís and Covadonga, **Frontera Verde** (El Portazgo, s/n, tel. 98/584-1457, info@frontera verde.com, www.fronteraverde.com) organizes trekking, canoeing, and other adventures in and around the Sella river basin. In the same town, **Aquassport** (C/ Juan Carlos I, s/n, tel. 98/584-0364, aquassport@canoasdelsella.com, www.aquassport.com) also offers a variety of activities, though canoeing is their specialty.

GALICIA

Comprising the northwest corner of the country, Galicia is Spain's most surprising landscape. Forget all your notions about the russet plains of Castilla-La Mancha, the golden brilliance of the Costa Blanca, and the whitewashed villages of Andalucía, Galicia is deep green Spain where the hills roll out in a thick blanket of velvet and everything is alive. It is also wet Spain, where rain falls 320 days per year and locals say, "Rain is Art." Looking upon Galicia's impressionist landscape of muted shades—slate-blue sky, gray-tinged clouds, moldering granite buildings, and still a thousand shades of green—it is hard to argue. This is also coastal Spain, where the land ends in a tumble of dramatic cliffs carved by millennia of waves from the Atlantic Ocean to the west and the Cantabrian Sea to the north. An eternity of tumult between land and sea has resulted in Galicia's most distinctive feature—its estuaries (*rías* in Spanish). These narrow fingers of ocean seep into the coast bringing calm waters, natural fishing ports, and beautiful beaches. In inland Galicia, the land is mountainous, thick with ancient forests and untamed valleys. It is colder in the winter, hotter in the summer, and more desolate year-round than the coasts. Anyone looking for a truly off-the-beaten path vacation will be thrilled with Galicia's rugged, rustic interior.

Culturally, Galicia has Celtic roots. The same peoples that millennia ago populated Ireland also lived here. The remains of their *castros* (dwellings) dot the region and their music echoes in the use of the *gaita,* or Spanish bagpipe, so common in this region. Galicia

HIGHLIGHTS

◖ **Catedral del Apóstol:** Though not the largest nor most dramatic of Spain's many cathedrals, Santiago's cathedral is surely the most mythical. The third-most important shrine in the Christian world and the raison d'être for millions of faithful pilgrims for nearly 1,000 years, this glorious display of faith writ large in gray Gothic stone is a delight for pilgrims and non-pilgrims alike (page 494).

◖ **La Coruña:** Surrounded by the battering Atlantic Ocean, this provincial capital boasts the world's only functioning Roman lighthouse, a bustling port lined with charming glass-balconied buildings, and an old medieval core that teems with tapas bars serving amazing seafood (page 506).

◖ **Cabo Ortegal:** Feel Zen-fully insignificant in the face of the monumental beauty of nature. Beneath a tiny lighthouse at the tip of this tiny Galician peninsula, dramatic cliffs plummet into the churning waters where the Cantabrian Sea and the Atlantic Ocean meet (page 511).

◖ **Finisterre:** Thought for centuries to be the end of the world, Finisterre still serves as a pilgrimage point for walkers on the Camino de Santiago. It also makes the perfect starting point for exploring the fabled Costa da Morte (Coast of Death), which runs north to La Coruña and is characterized by rugged cliffs, tumultuous waters, and secluded beaches (page 516).

◖ **Ría de Muros e Noia:** Offering the million and one joys of Galicia on a drivable-in-a-day *ría* (estuary), this area teems with colorful fishing ports, Gothic churches, golden beaches, and pint-sized waterfront plazas where the restaurants serve shellfish pulled fresh from the waters just hours before (page 517).

◖ **Pontevedra:** Often overshadowed by nearby Santiago, this provincial capital is a delightful surprise. Lording over its own *ría*, Pontevedra has an atmospheric medieval core

made up of a series of cobbled squares perfect for lingering over a bottle of Galician wine (page 523).

◖ **Baiona:** Facing the Atlantic, beautiful little Baiona offers a bustling fishing port lined with fresh-from-the-boat-seafood restaurants, a perfect crescent beach, and an 11th-century castle where you can spend the night (page 526).

◖ **Las Islas Cíes:** With its restricted access, this tiny archipelago offers intrepid campers a virtually deserted paradise of sugary white beaches, clear turquoise waters, and expansive views over the surrounding ocean (page 526).

LOOK FOR ◖ TO FIND RECOMMENDED SIGHTS, ACTIVITIES, DINING, AND LODGING.

GALICIA

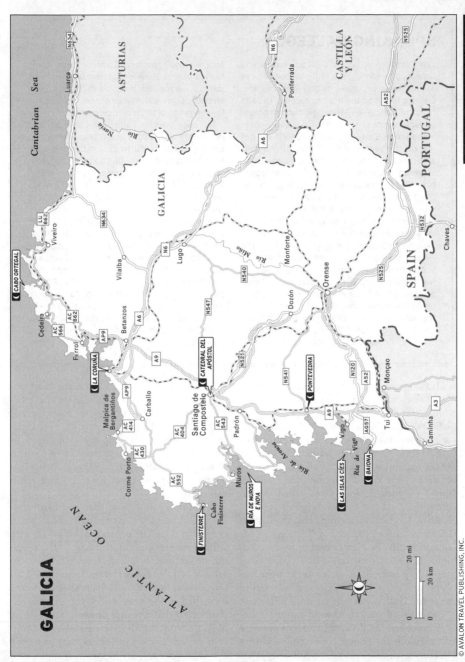

Cantabrian Sea

ASTURIAS

ATLANTIC OCEAN

GALICIA

CASTILLA Y LEÓN

PORTUGAL

SPAIN

N634
Luarca
Río Navia
N6
Ponterrada
N525
A52
N532
Chaves
LU 862
Viveiro
N634
Vilalba
Lugo
N6
Río Miño
Monforte
Orense
N525
Monção
N120
A52
A3
Caminha
Tui
[CABO ORTEGAL]
Cedeira
AC 862
AC 566
Ferrol
[LA CORUÑA]
AP9
Betanzos
A6
A9
N547
[CATEDRAL DEL APÓSTOL]
N540
Dozón
N541
[PONTEVEDRA]
N525
Malpica de Bergantiños
Carballo
AP9
AC 414
AC 404
Santiago de Compostela
AC 543
Padrón
A9
Vigo
AG57
[LAS ISLAS CÍES]
Ría de Vigo
[BAIONA]
Corme Porto
AC 430
AC 552
Muros
Cabo Finisterre
[FINISTERRE]
[RÍA DE MUROS E NOIA]
Ría de Arousa

20 mi
20 km

© AVALON TRAVEL PUBLISHING, INC.

SPEAKING GALLEGO

Like Catalan and Basque, Gallego (also spelled Galego, guy-YAY-go) is a regional language of Spain. However, unlike its linguistic cousins, Gallego is not so politically charged. Though it is the official co-language of the region, Gallego is not used as much in day-to-day conversation as Castilian Spanish. Only if you get way off the beaten path will you notice a shift with more rural dwellers speaking Gallego.

Gallego sounds like a mix between Spanish and Portuguese and both Portuguese and Gallego derive from the same ancient language. There are an estimated three million speakers of Gallego, mainly in Galicia, though great numbers of Galician immigrants in Argentina also speak the language. In fact, the Argentinean word for a Spaniard is "Gallego."

As with the other regional languages, Gallego was banned from governmental use and suppressed under Franco's regime – it didn't matter to the dictator one bit that he was born in the Galician town of Ferrol. Following his death and the subsequent democratization of the country, including increased regional autonomy, Gallego experienced a resurgence. It was named one of Spain's four *lenguas españolas* (official languages), installed in schools, used on public signs and in place names, and became the language of the local government.

Because Galicians all speak Castilian (and in tourist havens such as Santiago many also speak English), a tourist should have no trouble traveling in the region. The main confusion may arise with place names. On signs within Galicia, Gallego names are used, while maps are often printed with Spanish names, others with Gallego, some with both.

If you know Spanish, the main changes you'll notice are the articles. The Spanish "la" becomes a Gallego "A" as in A Coruña. The "el" becomes "O" as in O Grove. The language is also liberally peppered with the letter "x," which is pronounced "sh" as in Rías Baixas and generally replaces the "j" or "g" in Spanish, so Juan becomes Xuan. Learning to say *Bos días* (Good Day) and *Graciñas* (Thank You, grah-THEEN-yahs) is a sure way to impress the locals.

is also very much a seafaring culture, particularly along the coasts. The Phoenicians, the Romans, and the Visigoths all set up ports on Galicia's coasts. Since the dawn of Spanish history, sailors and fishermen made the coasts of Galicia their home. They made their fortunes off the sea and when they couldn't, they took off to the New World. For centuries, Gallegos (guy-YAY-goes, as locals are called) sailed across the Atlantic to seek brighter futures. So many landed in Argentina that the Argentinean word for Spaniard is "Gallego." This connection to the New World only served to highlight Galicia's separation from Spain. Geographically isolated by water to the west and north, mountains to the east, and Portugal to the south, Galicia was long regarded by the rest of Spain as a distant, backward cousin. It was only in the last few decades that highways were laid through the region connecting Galicia's big cities with Madrid and the rest of Spain.

One result of this isolation is the local language, Gallego, which falls somewhere between Spanish and Portuguese. Not nearly as in-your-face as Euskara in País Vasco or Catalan in Barcelona, the language crops up quite a bit on maps and street signs. Some words to keep in mind: *praza* is plaza, *praia* is playa (beach), *igrexa* is iglesia (church), and *rúa* is calle (street).

A local saying boasts that you can travel Galicia through its gastronomy. The coasts, entwined with the ocean, pockmarked with fishing villages and colorful ports, offer up exquisite seafood including *vieiras* (scallops), the symbol of Saint James and the Camino de Santiago; *ostras* (oysters), which are shucked by the bushelful in the streets of Vigo; and *percebes* (barnacles) that resemble dinosaur toes and are both gastronomically prized and astronomically priced. The sea also offers *pulpo* (octopus); the Galician specialty of boiled octopus with potatoes and paprika served on a wooden plate is widely famous. You'll find *pulperias* (octopus restaurants) all over the country. The land has also long given its bounty to the Galician table—often after a spell in storage in one of the traditional *hórreos* that cover the countryside. These tomb-shaped granaries, raised off the ground and topped with a cross, are built of stone and wood and help keep produce both dry and safe from rodents. *Cachelos* (Galician potatoes) are often paired with *grelos* (similar to turnip greens) and *lacón* (cured pork shoulder) to create hearty stews such as *caldo Gallego*. Empanadas are also famous throughout Spain. In their classic form, they are large pastry turnovers stuffed with tomatoes and meat, though anything might end up between the layers, from *pulpo* to *atun* (tuna). Galicia's land also offers several cheeses including *tetilla,* a cows' milk cheese formed in the shape of a woman's breast—hence the name. The inland rivers also nurse vast vineyards that have given rise to wonderful white wines that go perfectly with seafood. (See sidebar, *Wines from Galicia.*) For dessert, there is nothing better than *tarta de Santiago,* a rich, moist almond cake dusted in powdered sugar.

Outside of Spain, Galicia's claim to fame is the **Camino de Santiago.** Since its founding, nearly 1,000 years ago, the Camino (often called "The Way of Saint James" in English) has drawn millions of pilgrims to Santiago de Compostela, the burial place of Santiago (Saint James), apostle and patron saint of Spain. Today, Santiago remains one of Spain's most visited places. However, the tourist seeking a vacation worthy of being called a pilgrimage need look no further than Galicia's wild northern coasts—Costa da Morte and the Rías Altas—or the green, tangled interior to find a once-in-a-lifetime trip to a little-known world smack in the middle of the vacation paradise that is Spain.

PLANNING YOUR TIME

If your time is limited, head at least to Santiago de Compostela. Compact, evocative, and thick with history, this town is as good as any to get a feel for Galicia's underrated charms, as well as take in one of the world's most emotive cathedrals. You'll need at least a day and a night to really enjoy the city. With five days, you can drive from La Coruña along the dramatic Costa da Morte, and then cut inland to Santiago. Longer and the land and sea are the limit. If you are based in Madrid, Barcelona, or Andalucía, consider flying to Santiago or La Coruña. Spanish airlines often offer cut-rate prices on domestic flights. The train to Santiago is over eight hours. A plane is under two.

Weather-wise, try to avoid the region in winter unless you are attracted to gray skies, cold rain, and even snow and sleet in the interior. Summer is the best time for the coasts, with the most sun and warm weather, however avoid August when the Spanish populace takes vacation en masse, filling the coastal towns to the brim, particularly the Rías Baixas. Summer in the interior, especially in Ourense, can be brutal. Spring or fall is a better option. Festivals occur year-round, though many seafood festivals happen in late summer and fall. Attendance at a local festival is a wonderful way to experience the exuberant joy of the Galician lifestyle. Visit www.turgalicia.es and click on What to Do to plan your visit around a festival.

Santiago de Compostela

At the end of the millennia-old pilgrimage known as the Camino de Santiago lies the granite medieval city of Santiago de Compostela. Dominated by the monumental **Catedral del Apóstol**—Saint James' Cathedral—Santiago resonates with religious mystery. Its monuments rise proudly under a sheen of ancient green moss and a thousand shades of gray—the result of the rain that bathes this city more days than not. Its air is sweetened by the soft wail of bagpipes, an homage to its Celtic past. Its streets are lively, not only with the stream of pilgrims who arrive weary yet joyous to the city at the end of their pilgrimage, but also with the thousands of students who attend Santiago's university—one of the oldest in Spain.

Though the Celts, Romans, and Visigoths inhabited the area first, the story of Santiago really begins with Christianity. The city takes its name from Santiago Apóstol (St. James the Apostle), whose corpse is said to have been transported by his faithful servants from the Holy Land in A.D. 44. After maneuvering their stone boat across the treacherous seas, they buried the saint 16 kilometers (10 miles) from their landing site in the town of Padrón. The grave was forgotten until 813, when a star led a religious hermit to it. It was perfect timing. The Reconquista was just beginning and the Christian forces needed a rallying point—or a saint. After the local bishop confirmed the authenticity of the saint's remains, Santiago was proclaimed the patron saint of Christian Spain, and a church was built on the spot. Soon, the *campus stellae* (field of the star)—from which the name "Compostela" is derived—became a bustling town as Christians from across Europe made their way over the Pyrenees and through the Peninsula to pay homage to Saint James. Their footsteps wore the path of the Camino de Santiago that generations of pilgrims (and over 100,000 tourists per year) still follow today. (To make your own pilgrimage, see sidebars, *Show Me the Way* and *Tips for the Camino de Santiago*.)

As throughout much of northern Galicia, Santiago is a gray, rainy city. In winter, it can be quite cold—though never freezing. Summer brings more sunshine, but overcast days are not uncommon. If you can possibly arrange it—and you book in advance—head to Santiago the third week in July. This is when the city celebrates **Festividad de Apóstol**—the festival of Saint James the Apostle. At 11:30 P.M. the evening of the 24th, the spectacular Fuego del Apóstal (Apostle's fire) is held. The cathedral's main facade on Praza do Obradoiro is covered in fireworks, sparklers, and all manner of fizzy, fiery pyrotechnics. It is an awesome sight. The towers—which already look as if they could take off like baroque rockets into the heavens—are given a fire and light treatment that only adds to the effect. Get to the plaza early to secure a place—families with picnic baskets start showing up around 8:30 P.M. The 25th, a very solemn, moving mass, Ofrenda Nacional de Catedral, is held in the cathedral. A giant incense burner called Butafumeiro is swung through the church for the occasion. The rest of the days, the town erupts in a blowout bash full of food booths, live music, dancing in the streets, and parades full of *gigantes* and *cabezudos* (larger-than-life puppets and costumed figures). The 31st brings the event to a close with a dazzling fireworks show over the city.

SIGHTS

Although modern-day Santiago is a sizeable city of 93,000, most of what is worth seeing lies within the Casco Viejo (old town) and can be seen in just a day or two.

(Catedral del Apóstol

Spain is filled with churches, but none quite equal the grandeur of the Catedral del Apóstol (Pr. Obradoiro, s/n, tel. 98/156-0527, 7 A.M.–9 P.M. daily, free). Though not the biggest, nor the most elaborate, Santiago's cathedral is the most venerated. In fact, in the world it is the third-most important shrine

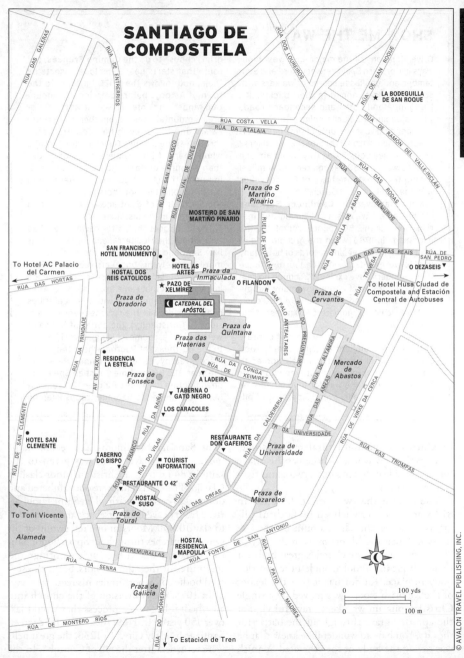

SANTIAGO DE COMPOSTELA

RÚA DAS GALERAS

RÚA DE ENTRERRIOS

RÚA DOS LOUREIROS

RÚA DE SAN ROQUE

★ LA BODEGUILLA DE SAN ROQUE

RÚA DE RAMÓN DEL VALLE-INCLÁN

RÚA COSTA VELLA
RÚA DA ATALAIA

RÚA DE SAN FRANCISCO

RÚA DO VAL DE DEUS

Praza de S Martiño Pinario

MOSTEIRO DE SAN MARTIÑO PINARIO

RUELA DE XERUSALÉN

RÚA DAS RODAS

RÚA DE ENTREMUROS

RÚA DE AIGALLA DE ABAIXO

RÚA DA DAS CASAS REAIS

RÚA TRAMESA

RÚA DE SAN PEDRO

SAN FRANCISCO HOTEL MONUMENTO

To Hotel AC Palacio del Carmen

RÚA DAS HORTAS

HOSTAL DOS REIS CATOLICOS

HOTEL AS ARTES

Praza da Inmaculada

O FILANDON ▼

O DEZASEIS ▼

★ PAZO DE XELMIREZ

Praza de Obradorio

☾ CATEDRAL DEL APÓSTOL

R SAN PALO

Praza de Cervantes

To Hotel Husa Ciudad de Compostela and Estación Central de Autobuses →

RÚA DO PREGUNTEIRO

RÚA DA TRINDADE

RESIDENCIA LA ESTELA

Praza da Quintana

Praza das Platerias

AV. DE RAXOI

Praza de Fonseca

RÚA DA RAIÑA

RÚA DA CONGA

RÚA DE XEIMIREZ

▼ A LADEIRA

▼ TABERNA O GATO NEGRO

RÚA DE ALTAMIRA

Mercado de Abastos

RÚA DAS ANEAS

RÚA DE VIRXE DA CERCA

HOTEL SAN CLEMENTE

RÚA DE SAN CLEMENTE

LOS CARACOLES

TR DA UNIVERSIDADE

RÚA DAS TROMPAS

RÚA DO FRANCO

RÚA DO VILAR

RESTAURANTE DON GAFEIROS

Praza de Universidade

CALDEIRERIA

TABERNO DO BISPO ▼

■ TOURIST INFORMATION

RÚA NOVA

RÚA DA

▼ RESTAURANTE O 42'

HOSTAL SUSO

RÚA DAS ORFAS

Praza de Mazarelos

To Toñi Vicente

Praza do Toural

R ENTREMURALLAS

HOSTAL RESIDENCIA MAPOULA

RÚA DE SAN ANTONIO

Alameda

RÚA DA SENRA

RÚA FONTE

RÚA DO PATIO DE MADRES

0   100 yds

0   100 m

Praza de Galicia

RÚA DO HORREO

RÚA DE MONTERO RÍOS

↓ To Estación de Tren

© AVALON TRAVEL PUBLISHING, INC.

SHOW ME THE WAY

Drive along any of the major east-west highways in Northern Spain between April and September and you'll see scores of walkers with scallop shells strapped to their backpacks, trudging along paths and secondary roads while slugging water, chomping granola bars, and spending vast amounts of time gazing off towards the horizon. Who are these walkers? What are they doing? And why would anyone want to walk the 805 kilometers (500 miles) linking the Navarrese town of Roncesvalles with the capital city of Galicia?

More than ever, the **Camino de Santiago** (Saint James' Way) is a hot hiking destination. Fewer than 2,500 people completed the pilgrimage in 1985, when the Archdiocese of Santiago started keeping records of how many people were undertaking the journey. Since then, numbers have exploded. Though no reliable statistics exist about how many people attempt the Camino, more than 194,000 completed at least 96 kilometers (60 miles) of the Way in 2004.

To speak of one Camino alone isn't entirely correct, since ancient pilgrims simply took the most direct routes from their homes to Santiago, stopping by whatever churches they could along the way for lodging and assistance. These days, over 90 percent of pilgrims choose to do the **Camino Francés,** the route that starts near Pamplona, bisects La Rioja, and follows the N-120 highway to the town of Astorga before crossing two mountain ranges and entering Galicia at the O Cebreiro mountain pass. From there, the route twists and turns along backcountry paths through some smaller Galician cities (and a whole ream of tiny hamlets, most no larger than a couple of dozen houses) before ending up at the Monte do Gozo – where (until recently) pilgrims got their first glimpse of the Cathedral of Santiago de Compostela shimmering in the distance.

The story goes that, after having preached throughout the Mediterranean for most of his life, Santiago (Saint James the Apostle, or, more precisely, his body) arrived in the Galician town of Padrón after a seven-day voyage in a stone boat that came from Palestine. After some heated negotiating with the local tribes (which resulted in their subsequent conversions to Christianity), the bones of the saint were laid to rest some 24 kilometers (15 miles) to the northeast of Padrón, where they were discovered by a shepherd named Pelayo in the year 813. By this time Christian Spain had been fighting the Moors for over 100 years. A hero was needed to help the troops keep up

for Christians, behind Jerusalem and Rome. Perhaps this is why it was chosen as the image for the flipside of Spain's one-, two-, and five-cent euro coins.

The church that was originally built in 813 was soon overwhelmed by faithful pilgrims. A larger church was built on the site in 896. When the Moors overran the city in 997, they snagged the church's great bells for their mosque in Córdoba, but left the apostle's body in place. Rumor has it that the leader of the Moorish troops was moved by a single Christian pilgrim who kept prayerful vigil at the apostle's grave throughout the battle for the city. You have to wonder if he knew that he was saving the body of the venerated Spanish

saint, Santiago Matamoros. The second name means "Moor-slayer" and was given to the saint in 844 during a Christian/Moor clash at Clavijo. The Christians were outnumbered and doomed to certain death when Saint James arrived from heaven on horseback and proceeded to slay 10,000 Moors in one fell swoop of his sword. Churches throughout Spain honor Santiago Matamoros with graphic paintings and sculptures of the saint on horseback, the severed bodies of Moors under his feet.

In 1075, the conversion of the church into a cathedral began—a process that would last over 150 years. In 1189, Alexander III decreed Santiago a "Holy City." In 1236, the great bells were returned after the fall of Córdoba. In the

the good fight and reports of Santiago Matamoros (Saint James the Moor-slayer) appearing at Reconquest battles throughout Castile soon started to spread. Once the Moors had been pushed out of Northern Spain, pilgrims started arriving from all over Europe, convinced that the powers of Santiago Matamoros could work wonders for them.

Early Christians believed completing any pilgrimage would earn the pilgrim some kind of reprieve after death. Those who reached Santiago could expect their time in purgatory to be reduced by half. Traveling to Santiago was considered a "safer" pilgrimage, compared to the risk of contracting illnesses from the swamps of Rome or getting your head lopped off on the treacherous path to Jerusalem. Modern reasons for undertaking the Camino are as varied as the pilgrims themselves. Some do it to gain peaceful time for reflection, others do it for the physical challenge, and many use it as an excuse to see some of the lesser-visited areas of Northern Spain. The vast majority of would-be pilgrims walk, but an increasing number are doing it by bicycle, on horseback, and (in the case of some very determined pilgrims) in wheelchairs.

Though the modern-day revival of the Camino hasn't totally turned around the econ-omies of many of the small towns along the route, the influx of walkers, bikers, and horse riders has helped several small-town entrepreneurs rethink the economic possibilities of the route. Therefore, along the way, you'll see bike shops, cobblers, and small hotels designed to cater to the needs of pilgrims. While the Camino has its sharks willing to make a fast euro off tired, hungry walkers, the vast majority of business owners along the Camino are shiningly honest and genuinely glad to see that people are visiting their communities (though they might not appear that way on a hot August afternoon with 15 thirsty pilgrims clamoring for Cokes and the bathroom).

Even if you don't choose to do the Camino, it's worth taking the time to stop in at some of the towns along the route to visit the churches and sights – such as the many paradors, which started out as hospitals and refuges for pilgrims. If you need a little extra inspiration, remember that the Camino crosses some of Spain's best wine regions: La Rioja, Navarra, and the Miño Valley, home to Galicia's crisp white ribeiro wine.

(Contributed by Patricia Dawn Severenuk, a Madrid-based writer and cycling tour guide who has done the Camino several times. Contact her at severenukdawn@yahoo.es.)

18th century, the local bishop decided that the most holy of Spain's cathedrals just wasn't holy-looking enough. He ordered the facelift that resulted in the baroque facade that we see today—though he left much of the medieval interior, including the original doors, intact. Today, the cathedral is a singular work boasting Romanesque, Plateresque, baroque, and neoclassical elements.

Since the cathedral grew in size as Santiago grew in importance, much of the structure is built right into the city and its four sides lead onto four major *prazas* (Gallego for "plaza"), making the cathedral appropriately omnipresent in the Casco Viejo.

The main entrance of the cathedral is from the broad Praza do Obradoiro. Here, the cathedral presents its exuberant 18th-century baroque facade. The two towers soar to the heavens while on the steeple between them Saint James looks out, standing just above his tomb—symbolized by a star (you'll see this star throughout the city). When you enter the cathedral, you'll come face-to-face with the most elaborate example of Romanesque structure in existence in Spain today—the cathedral's original medieval doorway, **Pórtico de la Gloria.** Sculpted in granite by Maestro Mateo from 1168–1188, the doorway is the cathedral's crowning glory. Its three doors depict the Apocalypse and the joy etched on the faces of the faithful is palpable. Saint James sits at the top of the middle pillar.

TIPS FOR THE CAMINO DE SANTIAGO

The image that most people have of walkers on the Camino de Santiago is of apple-cheeked pilgrims from all over the world, bouncing merrily down the path towards Santiago Cathedral. The reality is a lot uglier: blisters, sunburns, arguments at hostels, and, for some, the need to pack it in after only a few days' walking. As easy as it seems to do the Camino de Santiago – how tough can it be to walk 781 kilometers (485 miles)? – completing the Camino, and making sure you don't die in the process, is a lot easier with preparation, patience, and pluck. Here is a highly arbitrary list of tried and true tips to help you get through.

CONTACT A LOCAL CLUB

Your first step in planning your pilgrimage to Santiago is contacting your local or national Camino association to get advice and documentation that will allow you to shape your Camino trip. The most important document is the *credential*, a fold-out "passport" you get stamped at bars, restaurants, and refuges along the way that serves as proof that you've completed the requisite mileage to get the Compostela certificate at the end of the journey. In the United States, potential pilgrims can get information from **American Pilgrims on the Camino** (www.americanpilgrims.com). Canadians should get in touch with **The Little Company of Pilgrims** (www.santiago.ca), based in Toronto but with chapters nationwide.

DO YOUR HOMEWORK

The increasing popularity of the Camino has led to a similar increase of books being published about the route. They tend to fall into three categories: maps and guides (one upbeat and informative guide is *Walking the Camino de Santiago* by Vancouver's Pili Pala

Press); books detailing the spiritual experience (such as Shirley MacLaine's *The Camino: A Journey of the Spirit*); and the "how-did-I-survive-that" school of travel writing. The hands-down winner in this category has got to be Tim Moore's *Spanish Steps: One Man and His Ass on the Way to Santiago*, which describes Moore's trip on the back of a highly uncooperative donkey.

SET REASONABLE LIMITS

Determine ahead of time how much of the Camino you realistically can do. Be honest about what kind of shape you are in and how far you can walk or bike every day. Someone who is in shape can probably walk 19-26 kilometers (12-16 miles) per day or bike 65 kilometers (40 miles) per day. But to accomplish that much (and to do it consistently) it pays to...

GET IN SHAPE

The entire Camino is paved with the good intentions of would-be pilgrims who decided that they would get in shape on the way to Santiago, not the other way around. Keep in mind that Spain is one of the most mountainous countries in Europe, and that you'll need to take gear with you. All that exertion takes a toll even on the most buff bodies. Your feet, back, and legs will thank you for whatever preparation you do beforehand.

SAY NO TO NEW BOOTS

As a matter of fact, don't bring boots at all – unless you will be walking the Camino in the depths of winter. Camino veterans advise wearing walking shoes if you're going to be walking any other time of year. With the exception of a few stretches, the vast majority of the Camino runs along well-worn paths that don't require technical footwear. Just make sure that whatever you wear is broken-in, breathable, and comfortable.

PACK LIGHT

Do not pack too much. Are you really going to need that terry-cloth housecoat or your hardback copy of *The Complete Works of Stephen King?* Remember that unless you join a luxury Camino tour that hauls your luggage around for you, you will have to carry everything that you bring. It is wise to invest in backpacking gear such as an ultra-light sleeping bag, a travel towel, and fast-drying socks and clothing.

SEEK REFUGE ALTERNATIVES

If you're traveling by bicycle, be aware that not every refuge will agree to house your mode of transport. At some refuges, cyclists can't get a bed until after 8 P.M., the thinking being that if you've got another mode of transport, it's less bother for you to mosey down to the next refuge if this one is full. Also, be prepared for a nasty phenomenon called "the refuge rush," where pilgrims bolt to the closest refuge just before lunchtime and pack out all the beds. There are two ways to prevent this: either incorporate camping into your accommodation plans or alternate between hotels and refuges. Staying in hotels will increase a pilgrim's costs, but it is also a better bet for a quiet, restful night.

SHOW RESPECT

Be respectful of the reasons why others are doing the Camino, even if you do not agree with them. Some pilgrims do see the Camino as a type of walking therapy, some have purely religious reasons, and some just want a cheap walking holiday. There is no right way, no wrong way, and definitely no "holier than thou" way. Everybody who walks the Camino, whether hoofing it alone or cruising along with a luxury tour group, is contributing to keeping the Camino — and the businesses along the way — alive and vibrant.

KEEP A SENSE OF HUMOR

Sometimes keeping your sense of humor on the Camino is easier said than done, especially when you've got blisters on your blisters and the guy in the bunk next to you is snoring like a hyena in heat. When you start to lose it, find a quiet spot and focus on why you are doing the Camino. Keep a journal. Vent to a tree. Check in to a hotel for a cushy bed and a long soak in a tub. Whatever you do, don't let the anger or frustration get to you. It will defeat the purpose of your journey. Also remember: What doesn't kill you makes a great story to tell your family and friends when you get home.

BE FRIENDLY

Keep a friendly attitude and don't be afraid to greet fellow pilgrims with a hearty *Buen Camino!* Pilgrims consistently cite the fascinating people they've met while walking to Santiago as one of the best aspects of their long journey. Lifelong friendships are made every week on the Camino.

KNOW WHEN ENOUGH IS ENOUGH

No one gives out prizes for the pilgrim with the most blisters or the worst shin splints. There are no medals for surviving a third-degree sunburn or herniating a disc because your backpack is too heavy. The Camino will always be there, so there's no sense in punishing yourself to "beat" the Camino. There is a clear line between pilgrimage and martyrdom. You can always return and complete the journey at a later date.

(Contributed by Patricia Dawn Severenuk, a Madrid-based writer and cycling tour guide who has done the Camino several times. Contact her at severenukdawn@yahoo.es.)

The Catedral del Apóstol has drawn the faithful to Santiago for nearly a thousand years.

At its base is a golden *vieira* (scallop shell). The scallop shell is the symbol of the Camino. In the Middle Ages, pilgrims collected the shell straight from the sea on the Galician coast as proof of their journey. Modern-day pilgrims carry the shell symbol with them the length of their journey. You'll see shells throughout Santiago and embedded in the ground along the entire length of the Camino. Over the centuries, tens of thousands of pilgrims have bent at this pillar to kiss the shell. In doing so, they put their hand on the pillar and the indentation of their millions of fingers is clearly outlined. On the other side of the pillar, Maestro Mateo carved himself humbling offering the cathedral to God. His nickname, *O Santo dos Croques* (meaning "Saint Bump-on-the-Head"), comes from the age-old practice of the faithful bowing their head to his in the hopes that some of his genius would rub off on them.

Beyond the portico, the Romanesque nave of the church unfurls. Its well-preserved, barrel-vaulted interior is very much the same one that pilgrims saw over 800 years ago. The sides of the nave are lined with chapels. The first on the right, *Capilla del Relicario* (Chapel of the Reliquary), is the most important. It holds a gold crucifix dating to 874. Many believe this cross to contain a piece of the original *vera cruz* (true cross) that Jesus was crucified on.

At the end of the nave, the *altar mayor* (main altar) is baroque at its most gaudy—gilded and overwrought. Above it looms the original 12th-century sculpture of Santiago by Maestro Mateo. To the side of the altar, the extensive ropes and pulleys are for attaching the **Butafumeiro,** the world's largest censor (incense burner). Weighing 120 pounds, the Butafumeiro is hauled out on Feast Days and special celebrations. Eight priests, called *tiraboleiros,* operate the pulley system (designed in the Middle Ages) that allows the massive brass censor to swing forcefully and quickly across the length of the transept spewing smoke and incense over the congregation. This happens about two dozen times per year. Check with the tourist office to see if it will happen during your visit.

Beneath the ambulatory to the left is the crypt where Saint James' remains lie. His tomb is a simple silver box adorned with a star. This is where pilgrims have traditionally offered their prayers to the saint.

Before you leave the cathedral, check with the information office for a tour of the roof. Tours are offered regularly. When you exit the Praza del Obradoiro, visit the adjacent **Museo de Catedral** (10 A.M.–2 P.M. and 4–8 P.M. Mon.–Sat., 10 A.M.–2 P.M. Sun. summer; 10 A.M.–1:30 P.M. and 4–6:30 P.M. Mon.–Sat., 10 A.M.–1:30 P.M. Sun. winter, €5). The museum contains various relics from the cathedral, including the original stone choir which used to sit in front of the altar; the cloisters which house a fountain where pilgrims once bathed and the original cathedral bells that once adorned the mosque in Córdoba; and the crypt, also called the *catedral vieja* (old cathedral) due to its spectacular design. Created by Mateo, it features majestic stone columns with ornate capitals. Your museum ticket also provides access to the **Pazo de Xelmírez** (Gelmírez Palace). Built between the 12th and 13th centuries, it is a fine example of Romanesque civil architecture. Though the upper floors still serve as residence for the archbishop of Santiago, the lower are open to the public and provide a fascinating look into a medieval home, including the kitchen.

Praza do Obradoiro

Dating from the 12th century, when the workers building the cathedral lived and worked here, Praza do Obradoiro (workmen's square) is by far the most beautiful in Santiago—with each of its four sides composed of a historic building. Of course, the main focal point is the cathedral. To the left is the Plateresque **Hostal dos Reis Católicos,** a hospital founded in 1501 by the Catholic monarchs Isabel and Fernando as a place of rest for weary pilgrims. In 1953, it was converted into a luxury parador (state-run hotel). The hospital's former morgue is now the popular bar. Opposite the cathedral is the neoclassical **Ayuntamiento** (town hall) building, originally built in the 18th cen-

tury as the Pazo de Rajoy, a palatial seminary. If you take a glance upwards, you will find the statue of Santiago Matamoros, St. James the Moor-Slayer, perched atop a horse. The next building to the left is the main library of the **Universidad de Santiago,** Spain's third-oldest university, enrolling over 30,000 students each year.

Praza das Platerías

The Praza das Platerías (Silversmiths' Square) is named for the silversmith shops that once filled the arcades. The cathedral door opening onto this square is the **Puerta de las Platería** and is the only one of the doors that is originally Romanesque. The tower arising over the door is the **Torre de Berenguel,** first built in the 14th century. Over the centuries it was used as a watchtower to warn of advancing enemies. Now it houses the church's clock and bells. At the very top is a powerful beam light that shines out to pilgrims kilometers away on the Camino.

Praza da Quintana

The cathedral door facing this plaza is the **Puerta Santa,** the "Holy Door." It is only opened for services during an Año Xacobeo (Holy Year), which occurs when the Feast of Saint James (July 25) falls on a Sunday. The next Holy Year will be in 2010. The 1611 door is decorated with Saint James and the apostles. Across from the door is the austere facade of the **Convento de San Paio de Antelares.** Around back, the convent houses the **Museo de Arte Sacra** (10:30 A.M.–1:30 P.M. and 4–7 P.M. Mon.–Fri., 11 A.M.–2 P.M. and 4–7 P.M. Sat., closed Sun., €2), which has an interesting collection of religious artifacts related to the Camino and Saint James. Be sure to seek out the monastery's statue of a pregnant Virgin Mary—an image typical in Galicia.

Praza da Inmaculada

Medieval pilgrims following the French route of the Camino, entered the cathedral through the Praza da Inmaculada. Here the pilgrims bathed in the long-gone "Fountain of Paradise" before passing through the cathedral door. The door is the least interesting of the cathedral. Having suffered the worst of the 18th-century facelift, it is uninspired and dull. Opposite the cathedral stands the **Mosteiro de San Martiño Pinario** (tel. 98/158-3008, 10 A.M.–2 P.M. and 4–6 P.M. Tues.–Sun., closed Mon., free). Originally built in the 12th century, and massively reconstructed in the 17th, this Plateresque monastery was founded to assist medieval pilgrims. Road-weary pilgrims could throw off their ragged clothes here and receive new ones. Today, the monastery houses an ecclesiastical museum and the interactive world of **Galicia Digital** (10:30 A.M.–2 P.M. and 4–8:30 P.M. daily, free). This museum takes visitors on virtual 3-D tours of the cathedral—including a bumpy flight over its roof, a submarine ride through Galicia's waters, and a virtual tour of Santiago.

Mercado de Abastos

For an authentic old-world shopping experience, take a stroll through the long corridors of the **Mercado de Abastos** (Rúa das Ameas, s/n, 7:30 A.M.–2:30 P.M. Mon.–Sat., closed Sun.). The fertile lands and waters of Galicia yield super-size produce, soft and creamy cheeses, and the freshest of fish, all of which—and more—can be found here at this centuries-old market. Though it is open six days a week, the best and busiest times to visit are Tuesday, Thursday, and Saturday, the market days when locals do most of their shopping and all the stalls are open.

ACCOMMODATIONS

The best place to stay is in the old city, which offers a wide variety of accommodations. Whether you are looking for a deluxe hotel, a medieval parador, or a cheap hostel, Santiago's lifelong business has been catering to visitors. Just remember that tourism peaks in July and August so it's best to book your bed ahead of time.

Under €50

If you are traveling on a tight budget, check into **Hostal Residencia Mapoula** (Rúa das Orfas 38, tel. 98/158-0124, www.mapoula

.com, €39). Although a bit off the main drag, this *hostal* offers comfortable rooms with en suite baths, TVs, and telephones. The 10 rooms at **Hostal Suso** (Rúa do Villar 65, tel. 98/158-6611, €39) are spacious for the price and are equipped with clean bathrooms—always a plus at low-cost accommodations. **Residencia La Estela** (Av. Raxoi 1, tel. 98/158-2796, hostalestela@yahoo.es, €40) is basic and historic—the hotel's granite building dates back to 1666—and the location right next to the cathedral is perfect.

€50–100

Just off Praza do Obradoiro, **Hotel San Clemente** (Rúa de San Clemente 28, tel. 90/240-5858, www.pousadasdecompostla .com, €80) offers simple but pretty rooms. If you don't mind walking up a few flights of stairs with your luggage, ask to stay in the attic room, which has a skylight view of the cathedral. Conveniently located in the center of the Casco Viejo, **Hotel As Artes** (Travesa das Duas Portas 2, tel. 98/157-2590, www .asartes.com, €75) offers clean, cozy rooms with close up-views of the cathedral. Though not included in the room price, the very friendly owners serve a delicious and complete breakfast each morning—often hard to find in Spain. Another dependable mid-range hotel is **Husa Ciudad de Compostela** (Av. de Lugo 213, tel. 98/156-9323, ciudadcompostela@ husa.es, www.husa.es, €65). This chain hotel offers modern rooms and amenities in a convenient location only 10 minutes from the center of the old city.

Over €100

For a once-in-a-lifetime experience, check into five-star parador **Hostal dos Reis Catolicos** (Pr. Obradoiro 1, tel. 98/158-2200, santiago@ parador.es, www.parador.es, €200). Originally constructed to house the thousands of pilgrims making their way through the city, this 15th-century stone building of long corridors and sunny courtyards continues to house Santiago's journey-weary visitors. Wander its hallways and you'll stumble upon four spectacular inner courtyards. This is one of the more popular paradors, so be sure to book well in advance. **(San Francisco Hotel Monumento** (Campillo de San Francisco 3, tel. 98/158-1634, reservas@sanfranciscohm.com, www.sanfranciscohm.com, €125), housed in the lovely 13th-century Convento de San Francisco, is the perfect alternative if you can't get reservations at the parador (or your pocketbook balks). Though it has been thoroughly modernized—cushy beds, satellite TV, Internet—it retains medieval charm with exposed brick walls and a lovely enclosed courtyard. **AC Palacio del Carmen** (Rúa Oblatas, s/n, tel. 98/155-2444, pcarmen@ac-hotels.com, www.ac-hotels.com, €130) is housed in the former Convento de las Oblatas and offers modern luxuries alongside history. Just moments from the Praza de Obradoiro, it is located in a serene park setting.

FOOD
Local Cuisine
Many of the restaurants in the old city serve more or less the same food at the same price—seafood, Galician empanada, Spanish fare. However, a few places shine above the rest. **Restaurante O 42** (Rúa do Franco 42, tel. 98/157-0665, noon–4 P.M. and 8 P.M.–midnight Tues.–Sat., noon–4 P.M. Sun., closed Mon., €40) offers a wide variety of delectable Galician seafood tapas and full meals in an enchanting stone-walled dining room. Despite their hurried appearance—dashing constantly from kitchen to dining room—the staff are incredibly friendly. **Don Gafeiros** (Rúa Nova 23, tel. 98/158-3894, 1–3 P.M. and 8–10:30 P.M. Tues.–Sat., 1–3:30 P.M. Sun., closed Mon., €45) is commonly accepted as one of Santiago's best restaurants. The classic stone interior evokes a medieval feel, while the Galician dishes take you right to the sea. Try the house specialty *merluza en salsa verde con mariscos* (hake in green sauce with shellfish). Complement it with a bottle of wine from the restaurant's own bodega (winery). If you want to keep an eye on the tab, head to **Taberna O Gato Negro** (Rúa da Raiña, s/n, tel. 98/158-3105, noon–3 P.M. and 7:30–11 P.M. Mon.–Sat., noon–3 P.M. Sun., €15). Down a hefty platter of home-style seafood dishes with a ceramic pitcher of their crisp, white wine pulled directly from the barrel. There is no street sign, just keep an eye open for the black metal cat.

Just as pilgrims trek to Santiago's cathedral, foodies trek to **Toñi Vicente** (Rúa Rosalía do Castro 24, tel. 98/159-4100, 1:30–4 P.M. and 9 P.M.–midnight Mon.–Sat., closed Sun., €50), named for its highly acclaimed chef. Toñi imparts an original touch on local seafood including favorites such as *marinada de vieiras con caviar de salmón* (marinated scallops with salmon roe) or *rape envuelto en aceituna negra* (monkfish coated in black olives). Another foodie favorite, a few steps down the price scale, is **O dezaseis** (Rúa de San Pedro 16, tel. 98/157-7633, 1–4 P.M. and 8 P.M.–midnight Mon.–Sat., closed Sun., €25), which serves excellent local fare in an absolutely charming stone-walled dining room with a glass roof and lots of local folk art.

Tapas
Santiago's best tapas bars are concentrated in the old city, particularly on Rúa do Franco and Rúa da Raiña. Opening hours for tapas bars are flexible with some opening for breakfast, however most tapas bars are open from noon–4 P.M. and 7 P.M.–midnight. For an imaginative take on local seafood specialties, head to the upbeat **A Taberna do Bispo** (Rúa do Franco, 37, tel. 98/158-6045). Always packed with locals and tourists alike, this bar is not to be missed. Another bar putting a creative spin on tapas is **A Ladeira** (Rúa do Vilar 11). Try their *tortilla de pulpo* (octopus omelet) and *empanada de lomo y manzana* (pork and apple turnover). **Los Caracoles** (Rúa da Raiña 14, tel. 98/156-1498) is the place to go for *caracoles al albariño* (snails in wine sauce). If you're out for tapas in the dead of winter, **O filandon** (Rúa da Acibechería 6, tel. 98/157-2738) will warm you up with their tasty tapas served by a fireplace. **La Bodeguilla de San Roque** (Rúa San Roque 13) offers massive *raciones* (tapas sized for two). If you manage to snag a table

next to the kitchen, you will get to watch the waiters slice your ham and cheese. They also serve a variety of pâtés and *revueltos* (scrambled egg dishes).

INFORMATION

The main tourist office in Santiago, **Oficina Central de Información Turística Municipal** (Rúa do Vilar 63, tel. 98/155-4748, www.santiago turismo.com, 9 A.M.–9 P.M. daily summer, 9 A.M.–2 P.M. and 4–7 P.M. daily winter) can provide you with information on things to do in and around the city. They offer organized excursions to other Galician points of interest as well as activities and events in the city itself. Additional tourist information stations are scattered throughout the city. On the Internet, try www.santiagodecompostela.org for information on the city and www.turgalicia.es for more on Galicia.

GETTING THERE
Air

Santiago's **aeropuerto** (tel. 98/154-7500, www.aena.es) is 13 kilometers (eight miles) outside of town and accepts both domestic and international flights. Traveling from within Spain, you might find your cheapest way into Santiago is by plane. Check with the three top Spanish airlines, **Iberia** (tel. 90/240-0500, www.iberia.com), **Spanair** (tel. 90/213-1415, www.spanair.com), and **Air Europa** (tel. 90/240-1501, www.aireuropa.com) or any *agencia de viajes* (travel agent). To get into the city from the airport, catch the airport bus just outside the terminal. There is also a bus running to La Coruña. Taxis are pricey in Santiago and the ride to your hotel could cost up to €20.

Train

The **Estación de Tren** (Rúa do Hórreo, s/n, tel. 98/159-6050) lies on the outskirts of the city and is operated by **Renfe** (tel. 90/224-0202, www.renfe.es), which shuttles passengers between Santiago de Compostela and the major Galician cities of La Coruña (14 daily) Vigo (11 daily), and Ourense (8 daily). **TALGO** trains (www.renfe.es) connect Santiago to Madrid (two daily, eight hours), as well as other cities in Castilla y León. If you are going to train from Madrid to Galicia, consider upgrading to a sleeper car and endure the eight-hour journey asleep.

Bus

Santiago's **Estación Central de Autobuses** (C/ San Cayetano, s/n, tel. 98/154-2416) provides both urban and interurban service. Various bus lines travel to Galician destinations while **Alsa** (www.alsa.es) and **Eurolines** connect Santiago de Compostela with other Spanish cities such as Madrid, Bilbao, and beyond.

Car

There are several national highways into Santiago. Toll-road AP-9 runs along the Atlantic Ocean to La Coruña, Ferrol, Pontevedra, Vigo, and into Portugal. The northwest road, A-6, runs to the rest of Spain via Lugo and ends in Madrid. The N-634 runs across the northern coast, through Asturias, Cantabria, and into France.

Rías Altas

The craggy fissures of the Rías Altas course their way inland through the northwest corner of Galicia. Different maps give differing, often very exacting, opinions but generally the region called Rías Altas begins at the city of La Coruña and arcs northward along the Atlantic coast, turning east at the Cantabrian Sea and continuing until the Asturian border. The cluster of wide estuaries that separate the city of La Coruña from the city of Ferrol is also called the **Golfo Ártabro** (Gulf of Artabro). The bulk of the region lies in the province of La Coruña, while the coastal stretch towards Asturias lies in the province of Lugo. The waters of the Rías Altas are cold, the coasts are pockmarked with caves and coves, and beaches are wild and windswept. The whole region is steeped in a palette of deep blue seas, velvet green hillsides, and chalky gray skies. The most urban space in the Rías Altas is the city of La Coruña, the second-most populated town in Galicia behind Vigo. The most atmospheric place is Cabo Ortegal where the Atlantic Ocean and the Cantabrian Sea meet in a tumult of sea foam and soaring rock. As in all of Galicia, the weather is wet, windy, and cool. In summer, sun melts the foggy mists for days at a time and its possible to get a tan—but don't count on it. Pack a rain hat and slicker alongside your swimsuit.

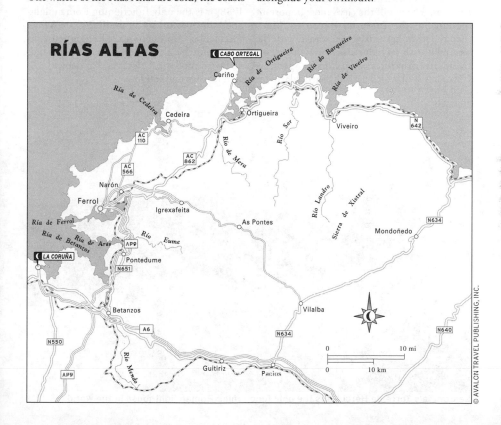

By far the best way to get around the Rías Altas is by renting a car in Santiago or La Coruña. There are regional buses that connect most of the towns below, but schedules are limited. Check **Alsa** (www.alsa.es) for the larger towns. **Rías Altas/Rialsa** (www.rialsa .com) runs from La Coruña to Cedeira while **Arriva** (tel. 90/227-7482, www.arriva.es) runs throughout the provinces of La Coruña and Lugo and is constantly expanding its circuit.

◖ LA CORUÑA

The bustling port city of La Coruña (A Coruña in Gallego) sits on a tree-shaped peninsula jutting out into a thick swath of Atlantic Ocean that forms the Ría de Coruña. Celts and other early peoples lived here as far back as 3000 B.C., but the town first took shape under the Romans. They built the city's most important monument, the **Torre de Hércules.** Since then the town has waxed and waned with the sea and its fishing industries. Though well off the tourist map for most visitors to Spain, La Coruña is well worth a visit—particularly for

those looking to escape the tourist hordes in nearby Santiago. Its dramatic situation, surrounded by the roiling waves of the Atlantic is a tempestuous counterpart to the locals who are unflaggingly helpful and friendly. Throw in excellent seafood, a lovely old town, a lively port, long sandy beaches, and you have a perfect Galician escape.

La Coruña can suffer the brunt of northern winds and even a sunny day may be windy and cool. Don't come here expecting long days on the beach.

Sights

La Coruña's most impressive sight is the **Torre de Hércules** (Av. Navarra, s/n, tel. 98/122-3730, 10 A.M.–6:45 P.M. daily, later in summer, €2), built in the 2nd century B.C. Reformed in 1788, it is the only functioning Roman lighthouse in the world. Climb the 242 steps for a spectacular view out to sea. The lighthouse sits on the northern tip of the city in a park studded with modern sculptures that depict Galician history and folklore.

© C. BOLTON

La Coruña's Torre de Hércules is the only functioning Roman lighthouse in the world.

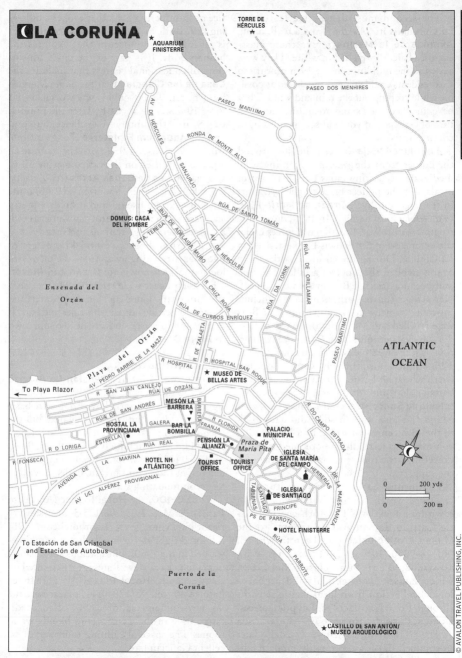

LA CORUÑA

★ AQUARIUM FINISTERRE

★ TORRE DE HÉRCULES

PASEO DOS MENHIRES

PASEO MARITIMO

AV. DE HÉRCULES

RONDA DE MONTE ALTO

R SANJURJO

RÚA DE SANTO TOMÁS

★ DOMUS: CASA DEL HOMBRE

RÚA DE ADELAIDA MURO

R STA. TERESA

AV. DE HÉRCULES

R CRUZ ROJA

RÚA DA TORRE

RÚA DE ORILLAMAR

Ensenada del Orzán

RÚA DE CURROS ENRÍQUEZ

R DE ZALAETA

R HOSPITAL

R HOSPITAL SAN ROQUE

PASEO MARITIMO

ATLANTIC OCEAN

Playa del Orzán

AV. PEDRO BARRIE DE LA MAZA

★ MUSEO DE BELLAS ARTES

To Playa Riazor →

R SAN JUAN CANLEJO

RÚA DE ORZÁN

RÚA DE SAN ANDRÉS

MESÓN LA BARRERA ▼

BARRERA

R FLORIDA

FRANJA

R DO CAMPO ESTRADA

HOSTAL LA PROVINCIANA ●

GALERA

BAR LA BOMBILLA ▼

ESTRELLA

PENSIÓN LA ALIANZA ■

Praza de María Pita

PALACIO ■ MUNICIPAL

R D LORIGA

RÚA REAL

HOTEL NH ● ATLÁNTICO

TOURIST OFFICE ■

TOURIST OFFICE ■

IGLESIA DE SANTA MARÍA DEL CAMPO

HERRERÍAS

R DE LA MAESTRANZA

R FONSECA

AVENIDA DE LA MARINA

AV DEL ALFÉREZ PROVISIONAL

TABERNAS

SANTIAGO

★ IGLESIA DE SANTIAGO

PRINCIPE

0   200 yds

0   200 m

PS DE PARROTE

● HOTEL FINISTERRE

RÚA DE PARROTE

↙ To Estación de San Cristobal and Estación de Autobus

Puerto de la Coruña

★ CASTILLO DE SAN ANTÓN/ MUSEO ARQUEOLÓGICO

The second most distinctive feature of La Coruña is its *galerías*. Take a walk along **Avenida de la Marina** to see these glass-enclosed balconies etched in white. They were added to the buildings in the 19th century so that residents could enjoy as much sun as possible while keeping out the rain and wind. They have since become a standard architectural feature of Galicia and you will see them in most coastal towns.

The **Ciudad Vieja** (old city) lies just around the corner from the *galerías*. Teeming with medieval streets, tiny tapas bars, and lots of locals, it is the perfect place to get lost. Start in the large and lively **Praza de María Pita,** named for a local heroine. In 1598, during the Anglo-Spanish War, British naval forces under the command of Sir Francis Drake arrived in La Coruña. During the ensuing battle, feisty María grabbed the lance of a fallen comrade and began attacking British soldiers herself. Her actions spurred other civilians—including more women—to take up arms. The Brits were repelled and María became a legend.

Also seek out **Iglesia de Santiago** (C/ Parrote 1), the city's oldest church. Built in the 12th century, it is primarily Romanesque but over the years it has received Gothic arches, a baroque altar, and 18th-century rose windows. **Iglesia de Santa María del Campo** (Pl. Santa María 1) is also Romanesque and dates back to the 13th century. Inside, notice its leaning columns, a rare result of poor medieval engineering—the roof is actually too heavy for the supports.

La Coruña has a few fine cultural attractions worth seeking out if you are in town for a few days. The 16th-century castle Castillo de San Antón is home to the **Museo Arqueológico** (Po. Parrote, s/n, tel. 98/118-9850, 10 A.M.–7:30 P.M. Tues.–Sat., 10 A.M.–2:30 P.M. Sun., closed Mon., €2), which houses a rather scattered archaeological collection from local Celtic remains through Roman artifacts via Egyptian pieces. **Domus: Casa del Hombre** (C/ Santa Teresa 1, tel. 98/118-9840, 10 A.M.–7 P.M. daily, later in summer, €2) is a thoroughly modern edifice of shimmering glass that evokes a billowing sail. Built in 1997, this "House of Man" is an interactive museum that explores the human body. It is part of the city's consortium of educational centers that includes the **Casa de las Ciencias** (Parque Santa Margarita, s/n, tel. 98/118-9844, www.casaciencias.org, 10 A.M.–7 P.M. daily, later in summer, €2), Spain's first interactive science museum, and the **Aquarium Finisterre** (Po. Marítimo, s/n, tel. 98/118-9842), a not-very-interesting aquarium focused on the varied marine life of Galicia. **Museo de Bellas Artes** (Av. Zalaeta, s/n, tel. 98/122-3723, hours vary, €2.40) is the city's fine arts museum and it holds a pretty standard collection of European works as well as some interesting etchings by Goya.

La Coruña boasts several kilometers of **beaches** stretching away from the city. Two located right in town are **Orzán** and **Riazor.** They each boast wide stretches of fine sand, the European "blue flag" for clean water, and a long promenade dotted with cafés and bars. If you want to practice nudism, head out of town to **Playa Barrañán.**

Accommodations

For **less than €50,** try **Pensión La Alianza** (C/ Riego de Agua 8, tel. 98/122-8114, €34), right off Praza de María Pita. Rooms are basic and a little dark and baths are shared, but the friendly staff make up for a lack of ambience. **Hostal La Provinciana** (C/ Rúa Nueva 9, tel. 98/122-0400, www.laprovinciana.net, €47) offers bright rooms and private baths, as well as an accommodating staff.

At **€50–100,** the **Hotel Riazor** (Av. Pedro Barrié de la Maza 29, tel. 98/125-3400, reservas@riazorhotel.com, www.riazorhotel.com, €90) is located right on the beach. Rooms are time-warped in the 1980s, but spacious and clean—upgrade to a sea view. Rates are discounted on the weekends. **Hotel Plaza** (Av. Fernández Latorre 45, tel. 98/129-0111, plaza@sercotel.es, www.hotelplaza.info, €90) offers meditative style in their cream and blonde-wood rooms. The space-age dining room serves excellent Galician fare.

Over €100, the **NH Atlántico** (Jardines Méndez Núñez, tel. 98/122-6500, nhatlantico@nh-hotels.com, www.nh-hotels.com, €105), located in a lovely central park, offers sophisticated, yet comfortable design in the hotel of choice for Spain's soccer teams when they play in town. **Hotel Finisterre** (Po. Parrote 2, tel. 98/120-5400, www.hesperia.com, €150) has long been La Coruña's top hotel and a 2003 makeover infused it with a much-needed shot of style. Today, it offers chic luxury in a perfect location on the water, steps from the old city. Run by the upscale Hespería chain, amenities and service are excellent.

Food

If you want to do some Galician-style tapas-hopping, go no further than the Ciudad Vieja where street after street is crammed with bars serving wonderful seafood tapas. If you want to do a little people-watching while you snack, the Praza de María Pita and the Paseo Marítimo are for you. (**La Bombilla** (C/ Torreiro 6, tel. 98/122-4691, 10 A.M.–midnight Thurs.–Tues.) is wildly famous among the locals whom are often overhead declaring, "the tapas here are better than my grandmother's." Tapas start at around €1 a piece and the place gets so crowded that you might end up scarfing your tapas on the sidewalk—you won't be alone. **Mesón La Barrera** (C/ La Barrera 22, tel. 98/122-7484, 9 A.M.–11 P.M. daily) is another local favorite with a bit more breathing room. Try the *tigres* (spicy tiger mussels).

To have what in-the-know locals swear is the best *pulpo* (octopus) in town, head to **A Lanchiña** (C/ Pérez Porto 1, tel. 98/192-2333, 11 A.M.–3:30 P.M. and 7 P.M.–midnight, Mon. and Wed.–Sat., 11 A.M.–3:30 P.M. Sun., closed Tues., €20), an atmospheric old restaurant near the train station. **El "10"** (Pr. España 8, tel. 98/120-7153, €25) is another noted *pulpería* famed for the freshness of its seafood and its simple, delicious preparations. **Artabria** (C/ Fernando Macías, 28, tel. 98/126-9646, 1:30–4 P.M. and 9–11 P.M. daily, €30) offers creative twists on Galician fare in a modern dining room decorated with the work of local artists. Their wine list is excellent. **Casa Pardo** (C/ Novoa Santos 15, tel. 98/128-0021, 1:30–4 P.M. and 9 P.M.–midnight Mon.–Sat., closed Sun., closed in March, €50) is one of La Coruña's most acclaimed restaurants. In a sophisticated dining room, the creative kitchen offers the freshest seafood as well as seasonal vegetables, mushrooms, and game.

Information

The **tourist office** (Pl. Ourense, s/n, tel. 98/118-4340, 10 A.M.–2 P.M. and 4–8 P.M. Mon.–Fri., closed Sat. and Sun.) is located on the Paseo Marítimo and there is an information kiosk in Praza de María Pita. Both can offer extensive information and maps for the city, as well as regional information.

Getting There

By air, La Coruña is served by the **Aeropuerto de Alvedro** (tel. 98/118-7200, www.aena.es), located about eight kilometers (five miles) outside of the city center. Flying is an attractive option from within Spain as **Iberia** (www.iberia.com) and **Spanair** (www.spanair.com) often offer cut-rate prices on domestic flights. There is an airport bus that runs into the city center hourly during the week.

By train, the **Estación de San Cristobal** (C/ Joaquín Planells, s/n) is serviced by **Renfe** (tel. 90/224-0202, www.renfe.es), with direct routes to Santiago and Vigo and long-distance routes to Bilbao, Barcelona, and Madrid. The **bus station** (C/ Caballeros 21, tel. 98/118-4335) is quite close to the train station and has connections to cities small and large throughout Galicia—remember, the easiest way to travel outside of the main cities is via bus. There are long-distance connections as well to Madrid, Barcelona, and beyond.

If you are traveling by car, La Coruña is located on the AP-9 toll road, which connects to Ferrol in the north and Santiago in the south. The A-6 connects the city to Madrid, via Lugo and Castilla y León. The N-634 runs from La Coruña across the north of the country and on into France.

BETANZOS

Once inhabited by Celts, Visigoths, and Romans, the romantically tattered town of Betanzos sits on a hill at the confluence of the rivers Mandeo and Mendo. Long ago, the rivers ran freely into the large Ría de Betanzos estuary, making this tiny town an important medieval port. The port brought riches into the city until the 18th century, when the rivers silted up and nearby La Coruña stole the seafaring show as the region's most important port. Soon little Betanzos became a living museum. Decidedly off the beaten path, the town is delightful simply for itself—ancient cobbled alleyways, medieval gates, mansions with their distinctive white *galerías* and balconies, and old stone bridges.

Sights

The town's lively center is the broad **Praza dos Irmáns García Naveira** with its elegant Versailles-style fountain. From there set out in search of a trio of Gothic churches. **Iglesia de Santiago** (Pr. Constitución, s/n) has a dramatic door based on the cathedral in Santiago. The 14th-century **Iglesia de Santa María do Azogue** (Pr. Fernán Pérez de Andrade, s/n) sits across from the 13th-century **Iglesia de San Francisco**. Within the latter is an intriguing 14th-century tomb lying upon the backs of a stone bear and boar. The tiny **Museo de Mariñas** (Rúa de Emilio Romay, tel: 98/177-3693, 10 A.M.–1 P.M. and 4–8 P.M. Mon.–Fri., 10:30 A.M.–1 P.M. Sat., closed Sun., €1.50) includes more stone tombs as well as medieval artifacts. The building also houses the **tourist office** (tel. 98/177-6666).

On August 16, Betanzos holds the lovely **Fiesta de San Roque,** where small flower-laden boats are sent down the river and giant paper hot-air balloons are released at midnight.

Accommodations and Food

Of the limited lodging in Betanzos, **Complejo San Roque** (Crta. Castilla 38, tel. 98/177-5555, www.complejosanroque.com, €85) is the most elegant, offering you a chance to sleep in a room lined by lovely Galician *galerías*. **Hotel Garelos Betanzos** (C/ Alfonso IX 8, tel. 98/177-5922, www.hotelgarelos.com, €80) offers classy, comfy rooms in a standard hotel. **Hotel Los Ángeles** (Rúa Los Ángeles 11, tel. 98/177-1511, €57) is basic and bland, but the rooms are spacious and cheap.

For cheap eats, check out the cafés on Praza dos Irmáns García Naveira or the tapas bars lining Venla de Campo. For excellent Galician fare, try **Mesón Pulpería Pirri** (C/ Valdoncel 3, tel. 98/177-2703, €20), which specializes in Galician-style octopus. **La Penela** (C/ Los Ferradores 21, tel. 98/177-3127, €25) offers succulent grilled meats in addition to the usual seafood and shellfish.

Getting There

By car, Betanzos is a half-hour drive from La Coruña. Take the AP-9 and then switch to the A-6. Several regional buses stop in Praza dos Irmáns García Naveira coming from La Coruña and Ferrol.

FERROL

Sitting across the wide, salty expanse of the Ría de Betanzos from La Coruña lies Ferrol, the other important port in the Rías Altas. Though it has a nice enough medieval core and a tidy 18th-century grid of elegant old mansions with picturesque *galerías,* there really is not much to see—nor much reason to stay. The town's biggest claim to fame is that Francisco Franco was born here in 1892. He later went on to become Dictator Franco and up until 2002 his statue stood proudly in the Praza de España. If you do end up here—transferring on a bus most likely—take a walk around **Barrio de la Magdalena** (the old town). The pedestrian streets **Rúa Real** and **Rúa Magdalena** are lined with cafés and shops, perfect for whiling away the hours until you leave.

Accommodations and Food

If you must spend the night, **El Suizo Hotel** (C/ Dolores 67, tel. 98/130-0400, €75) offers comfortable rooms with wood floors and marble bathrooms. **Hotel Real** (C/ Dolores 11, tel. 98/136-9255, €45) is a cheaper sleep with simple, modern rooms.

High ceilings give **Bla Bla Café** (C/ Real 193, tel. 98/135-0006, €7) an old-world feel—the large silver harp adds to that atmosphere. **A Gabeira** (C/ Lugar de Balón, tel. 98/131-6881, closed Mon. and Sun. evening, €40) is one of the best restaurants in the Rías Altas. Chef Miguel Ángel Campos is obsessed with technique and quality of ingredients and the result is a modern, delicious take on Galician fare. **Pataquiña** (C/ Dolores 35, tel. 98/135-2311, closed Sun. evenings in winter, €25) is a rustic Galician restaurant famed for its grilled seafood platters and savory *cazuelas* (seafood stews).

Getting There

By car, Ferrol is just a few kilometers off of the AP-9, which runs south to La Coruña and on to Santiago. From the AP-9, you can connect to the A-6 towards Madrid. Several buses per day run into Ferrol from La Coruña, Santiago, and other Galician towns. **Renfe** (tel. 90/224-0202, www.renfe.es) provides service between the city and La Coruña, while the narrow-gauge **FEVE** (tel. 94/220-9522, www.feve.es) runs from Ferrol across the northern coasts of Galicia, Asturias, Cantabria, and into País Vasco.

CEDEIRA

The tiny port town of Cedeira sits on the Ría of the same name. Its old center is charming with traditional *galerías* and excellent local seafood. From here, you can also explore some of the area's best *praias* (beaches). The in-town beach, **Praia Magdalena,** is fine enough, bordering a cove protected from the roiling rush of the Atlantic—perfect if you are traveling with small children. From the old town, if you head around the tip of the peninsula you can visit the protected wetlands of **Praia de Vilarrube,** which boasts a truly stunning beach tucked into a cove surrounded by dramatic cliffs—legend has it that a couple walking its shores will soon fall in love. To the south, near the town of Valdoviño, **Praia Frouexira** safeguards a lagoon that is one of the most important in Galicia for birdwatching. The nearby **Praia Pantín** hosts the international surfing competition Ferrolterra Pantín Classic (www.pantinclassic.com) and

though it is fairly remote, it has all the amenities a surfer (or swimmer) could need. In Cedeira's old town, the **tourist office** (C/ Ezequiel López 17, tel. 98/148-2187, 10:30 A.M.–1:30 P.M. and 5–8 P.M. Mon.–Fri., 10:30 A.M.–2 P.M. Sat., closed Sun.) can give you maps and access information for the beaches.

The mountains in this region are full of wild horses, which gives rise to one of Spain's most peculiar festivals, **Rapa das Bestas** (the "taming of the beasts"). (See sidebar, *Taming of the Beasts.*)

Accommodations and Food

If you decide to stay the night, try the lovely **Villa de Cedeira** (Campo do Hospital, s/n, tel. 98/141-1244, €46), located in the picturesque mountains surrounding Cedeira. You'll find excellent seafood throughout the old town and on the port facing the Ría. A great café to get a pulse on the town is **Café Bar a Marina** (Rúa do Marineiro 5, tel. 98/148-0137), which has good coffee and tea and often shows the work of Texas-born artist Jane Danko, who has a home in Cedeira. **A Revolta** (Po. Marítimo 37, tel. 98/148-0764) is a good choice for excellent fish and seafood right from the Ría. The restaurant also rents a couple of port-front vacation apartments. On the edge of town, **Casa Alonso** (Crta. Cedeira 88, tel. 98/138-3594, €20) offers a rustic Galician dining experience.

Getting There

Cedeira is about 32 kilometers (20 miles) north of Ferrol. By car, take the winding coastal road AC-566 north. There are regular buses via **Rialsa** (www.rialsa.com) from Ferrol.

◖ CABO ORTEGAL

Everything is in motion at Cabo Ortegal. The clouds crawl across a landscape of verdant mountains that suddenly, almost violently, plummet into an explosion of waves below. With the wind releasing its ancient howl, it is easy to feel insignificant. Standing high above the point where the Atlantic Ocean meets the Cantabrian Sea in an infinite stretch of undulating water, your sense of scale is truly tested.

What you thought were just dots on the ocean turn out to be seagulls and the small ripples hitting the rock islands are actually monumental waves. Standing watch over it all is a small red-and-white lighthouse.

Cabo Ortegal is about three kilometers (two miles) north of the tiny port of **Cariño,** tucked tightly into the valley between the mountains and the sea. There is a pleasant beach in town next to the port, **La Concha,** and several more east of town, lining the estuary.

Accommodations and Food

One of the very few places to stay in Cariño is **Hostal a Pedra** (Av. Fraga Iribarne, tel. 98/142-0300, €50), with simple accommodations and a very helpful staff. **Meson o Barometro** (Av. Fraga Iribarne s/n, tel. 98/142-0295) is an old-fashioned Galician eatery popular among locals who while away long afternoons playing cards here. On the road from Cariño to Cabo Ortegal is **Chiringuito San Xiao** (Ctra. Do Cabo Ortegal, tel. 63/098-3984, www.sanxiao.org, closed Mon.), a rustic bar/café on the edge of the mountain that offers amazing views along with good tapas.

Getting There and Around

From Ferrol, take the AC-862 to Mera, then switch to the AC-1051, a narrow, winding road with amazing vistas over the sea. It passes through Cariño and onto Cabo Ortegal. By bus, **Arriva** (www.arriva.es) offers transport only as far as Mera, about five kilometers (three miles) to the south.

VIVEIRO

Moving north and west along the coast, brings you to Viveiro. Surrounded by fragrant groves of eucalyptus, this bustling port town sits at the head of the Ría de Viveiro, one of the largest on the Cantabrian coast. The town's **Casco Viejo** (old quarter) boasts the remains of impressive medieval city walls including three original gates, the 13th-century **Porta de Vila,** the Romanesque **Porta do Velado,** and the 16th-century **Porta do Castelo,** also known as the gate of Carlos V. The latter leads into the

Praza de Pastor Díaz, Viveiro's lively main square. About a block away is the 12th-century **Iglesia Santa María del Campo,** a wonderfully preserved Romanesque church.

Viveiro's **beaches** are both lovely and popular—particularly with Spanish holidaymakers. The closest to the city is **Praia de Covas,** a wide beach facing the estuary that stretches about 1.5 kilometers (one mile). It is lined with a promenade that runs from the **Ponte Maior,** a 15th-century bridge that leads to the Porta de Castelo and into the old city. At the opposite end of the beach is **Os Castelos** (The Castles), a series of dramatic rock outcroppings. About three kilometers (two miles) north of Viveiro on the eastern side of the estuary, the beaches of Area-Faro run for 0.8 kilometers (0.5 mile) bordered by dunes and green hills. The **tourist office** (Av. Ramón Canosa, s/n, tel. 98/256-0879, 10:45 A.M.–2 P.M. and 5–8 P.M. Mon.–Sat. noon–2 P.M. Sun. July and Aug., 11 A.M.–2 P.M. and 5–8 P.M. Mon.–Sat. noon–2 P.M. Sun. Sept.–June) offers information and maps for the local beaches.

Accommodations and Food

As the most popular seaside resort in the province of Lugo, Viveiro offers a wide range of accommodations. If you are on a budget, stay in town at **Hotel Vila** (C/ Nicolás Montenegro 57, tel. 98/256-1331, €43), which offers decent rooms, though nothing special. On the beach in Covas, **Hotel Las Sirenas** (C/Sacido, s/n, tel. 98/256-0200, www.hotel-apartamentoslas sirenas.com, €145) offers spacious rooms with balconies. If you are driving and want a treat, try **Pazo da Trave** (A Trave, s/n, tel. 98/259-8163, www.pazodatrave.net, €91), a 16th-century noblemen's home that has been converted into a charming rural retreat.

Nito (Playa de Area, tel. 98/256-0987, 1:30–4 P.M. and 8:30–midnight daily, €45), one of the best restaurants in the region, is famed for the impeccable freshness of its seafood and fish. The dining room overlooking the beach is wonderful. In town, seek out the friendly **O Asador** (C/ Melitón Cortiñas 15, tel. 98/256-0688, www.oasador.com, €20), a long-time local favorite that churns out excellent Galician fare as well as succulent grilled meats. If you are really hungry, go for the *chuletón del buey,* a massive oxen steak.

Getting There

Viveiro sits on the N-642, which runs east to the Asturian coast where it meets up with N-634. By bus, **Arriva** (www.arriva.es) offers service from La Coruña and the Galician border town of Ribadeo. The narrow-gauge **FEVE** (tel. 94/220-9522, www.feve.es) runs from Ferrol across the northern coast of Spain as far as Bilbao, making a stop in Viveiro.

Costa da Morte

Running along a piece of coast mercilessly ravished by the Atlantic Ocean, the Costa da Morte earned its macabre name eons ago when ship after medieval wooden ship sunk in the impetuous waters off this coast. Ancient Celtic legends say that even whole villages have been captured and sunk by these waters. The scenery is as mysterious and mystical as the myths, full of theatrical cliffs, mist-soaked skies, churning seas, wild gray beaches, and some of the loveliest tangerine sunsets you'll see in your life. Just about the only thing not seductive about the region is the water-it's freezing, even in summer.

To really enjoy the landscape of Costa da Morte, you'll need a car. An excellent itinerary is to rent one in La Coruña, drive south along the coast and then cut inland to Santiago. Of course, you can also set off from Santiago or Pontevedra. If you are traveling by public transport, the main bus company servicing this region is **Arriva** (tel. 90/227-7482, www.arriva.es) and almost all buses to the Costa da Morte will pass through the town of Carballo. If you are planning on traveling this way, study the routes carefully and prepare to be flexible. Buses often do double duty as school buses.

MALPICA DE BERGANTIÑOS

Malpica de Bergantiños—known locally as Malpica—sits on a tiny slip of land jutting out into the Atlantic. The main road runs right down the middle. On the left, narrow alleys lead to the **Praia de Area Maior,** a crescent-shaped cove bookended by rolling green hills and rocky cliffs. Running the length of it is a lively boardwalk with a handful of cafés and bars. On the eastern side of the road you'll find the less-than-attractive port, heavily involved in the sardine trade. There is not much to do here, which makes Malpica the perfect place to do nothing but relax with the view and a good plate of shellfish.

Accommodations and Food

Kick back on the beach at one of a pair of inexpensive lodgings that are so close to the ocean, you'll feel like you are sleeping above the waves: **Pensión Barnovo** (C/ Emilio González 28, tel. 98/172-0017, €40) or **Hostal JB** (C/ Rueiro da Praia 3, tel. 98/172-1906, €42). **Café del Mar** (Po. Playa 1) is the place to grab cheap, fresh seafood tapas. For a bit of rustic pampering, check into **Refugio As Grozas** (Porto Barizo 40, tel. 98/172-1765, www.asgarzas.com, €54). This converted seaside house offers five cozy rooms brimming with understated elegance and stunning views (definitely upgrade to a room with a balcony). However, keep in mind that there only five rooms so you should book well in advance. The hotel also houses one of the best restaurants (closed Mon., €30) in the region. It is well-known for its *arroces,* rice dishes with seafood. For quality seafood, head across the street to **O Burato** (C/ Villar Amigo, s/n, tel. 98/172-0057). In the summer, the restaurant crams the side alley with tables full of locals.

Getting There

Malpica lies at the end of the AC-414, which connects it to the A-55 road that runs between La Coruña and Carballo.

COSTA DA MORTE

ATLANTIC OCEAN

Islas Sisargas

Malpica de
Bergantiños

LA CORUÑA

Corme
Porto

Corme
Aldea

Ría de Corme E Laxe

Laxe

Ponteceso

AC
414

AG59

Carballo

AC
430

Cabo Vilán

Ría de Camariñas

AC
432

AC
552

Camariñas

AC
400

N550

Muxia

Vimianzo

AC
440

Santa
Comba

AP9

Embalse de
Fervenza

Ría de Lires

Río Xallas

AC
546

Corcubión

FINISTERRE

A54

AC
400

Cabo
Finisterre

Ría de Corcubión

AC
550

Outes

Río Tambre

Santiago de
Compostela

CATEDRAL DEL
APÓSTOL

Muros

AC
543

Noia

AP9

Porto Do Son

Ría de Muros E Noia

RÍA DE MUROS
E NOIA

0   5 mi

0   5 km

Padrón

N550

AP53   N525

© AVALON TRAVEL PUBLISHING, INC.

CORME

The small fishing village of Corme Porto lies so far off the beaten tourist path that it doesn't even have a hotel—so make this a day trip. The town is a nearly vertical sweep of pastel buildings crawling up a hillside beyond which unfurls a vast swath of farmland known as Corme Aldea. At the top of the crest, modern windmills pump furiously against the azure sky. Park your car at the port and take the 30-minute walk out to the *faro* (lighthouse) along a narrow road that winds high above the crashing waves and a few scattered micro-beaches. The white crosses next to the lighthouse pay homage to the countless fishermen who lost their lives along these waters. Time your walk to be at the lighthouse for sunset when the clouds, ocean, and horizon meld together in a shimmering pallette of pink, red, and gold. You can enjoy it and still have time to make it back to town before it's completely dark. The town sits on **Ría de Corme e Laxe,** a lovely estuary lined with cozy beaches and clusters of brightly-colored fishing boats. Try the catch of the day at **O Biscoiteiro** (C/ Remedios 14, tel. 98/173-8376), which also offers a lively local atmosphere.

Getting There
Corme is on the AC-424, which connects it to the town of Ponteceso, where you can turn south toward Laxe or head to Carballo and on to La Coruña.

MUXÍA
Sitting on a finger of land on the southern side of the Ría de Camariñas, Muxía is yet another charming Costa da Morte fishing village. Its medieval center is picturesque with weathered buildings boasting white-framed *galerias* and crooked cobbled roads lined with tiny bars and shops. Long the locus of a busy fishing industry, the port has bustled back to life after intensive recovery efforts following the oil spill that marred the region in 2002. (See sidebar, Prestige *Oil Spill,* in the *Background* chapter.) Along the port, you'll see Lincoln Log–looking structures strung with thick, yellowing "nets." These are actually eels being dried out in a process that has been used since the 17th century.

Sights
The town has a small curve of a beach boasting clean, shallow waters. Nearby is the long, lovely beach of **Lago** backed by verdant hills and protected by rocky outcroppings. Take the walk out to the **Punta da Barca** lighthouse. On the way, you'll pass the early 18th-century **Nuestra Señora de la Barca,** one of the most venerated religious shrines in Galicia. Legends abound about the church and various miracles carried out by Santiago (Saint James) in this region. The very ground upon which you traverse to get to the church and lighthouse is composed of massive rocks, themselves considered holy. The second Sunday of September, the church is the locus of a very large pilgrimage. Of course, being Spain, that means the Saturday night before, this tiny town throws a party to rival the biggest in the country.

HÓRREOS
It does not take long for a visitor to Galicia or Asturias to notice that alongside nearly every small cottage or farm is a primitive and mysterious-looking one-story structure on four stone or wood posts. One could easily speculate that they are shrines, the homes of tiny spirits, or amazingly elaborate dog houses. Of course, this would be wrong. The structure is an *hórreo* and it is nothing more than a raised granary. The Spanish philosopher Ortega y Gasset called the *hórreo* "a temple of a very old religion" and, of course, he was right. The survival of the *hórreo* is a testament to the persistence of the small-scale micro-farming agrarian culture of this region.

According to an *hórreo* census (yes, there is such a thing) Asturias has the most *hórreos* with Galicia not far behind. Many of the *hórreos* date back centuries and at one time, they were so highly prized that a woman might bring one to her new home as a dowry when she married.

The *hórreo* is a very clever, functional design and is still used to store fruit, vegetables, grains, and other perishable items. There are often beautiful sheaves of corn hanging under the eaves on the outside. Being raised off the ground keeps out rodents and other pests and gives smaller livestock a place to stay dry underneath. In Galicia, *hórreos* are rectangular and are usually made of stone or brick and often topped with a cross. In Asturias, *hórreos* are made of slatted wood and nearly always perfectly square. In both places, they make wonderful photographic subjects. Check with the tourist office of the town you are visiting to find out the location of the nearest *hórreo*.

Accommodations and Food
To stay the night, go no further than the lovely **Hotel Rústico Muxía** (tel. 98/174-2441, www .hotelrusticomuxia.com, €70), a lovely stone inn that serves as a bit of a cultural center for the town. It also houses a lively wine bar and

restaurant. On the beach, try fisherman's-house-turned-hotel **Playa de Lago** (Praia de Lago, s/n, tel. 98/175-0793, www.hostalplaya delago.com, €40).

Getting There

Muxía lies on the AC-440, which runs into the AC-552 that goes between Finisterre and Carballo, then on to La Coruña.

🎵 FINISTERRE

Nearly 1,000 years ago, when the Camino de Santiago was first etched across the Iberian Peninsula, Finisterre (Fisterra in Gallego) was considered the end of the world (the name comes from the Latin *finis terrae,* or "land's end.") Pilgrims, upon reaching Santiago, still had to make it another 88 kilometers (55 miles) to the tip of the finger of land jutting into the ocean about three kilometers (two miles) beyond Finisterre. Here, they could gather a scallop shell from the beach to prove they had made it to Santiago—at least, according to one legend that explains why the scallop shell is the symbol of the Camino. Pilgrims

still flock here to stand on the rocky promontory overlooking the Cape of Finisterre. A lighthouse stands guard over the cape and most days, a lone bagpipe player provides a mournful wail—an appropriately dramatic soundtrack to the dropping cliffs and roaring waves below. However, the best views are to be had a little higher up by following the signs to **Vista Monte do Facho.** Notice the bed-shaped rocks along the coast on the way; an ancient Celtic legend says that childless couples who bed down on the rocks—preferably under a full moon—will get pregnant.

Back in town, there is little to stick around for. It is a cute-enough fishing village of granite houses clustered around the port, but nothing special. One sight worth seeking out is the **Castillo de San Carlos,** a small fort located behind the port. If you continue past it along **Paseo de Corveiro** you'll arrive at the tucked-away swimming hole of **Praia da Corveiro.**

Accommodations and Food

For a cheap place to sleep in town, **Hotel Finisterre** (C/ Bajada al Puerto 8, tel. 98/174-

Before Columbus, many thought Finisterre was the end of the world.

0000, €30) offers basic rooms, a friendly staff, and a location right next to the bus stop. For something more rustic, head just out of town to **Insula Finisterrae** (Lugar da Insua 76, tel. 98/171-2211, www.insulafinisterrae.com, €72), a gorgeously renovated farmhouse with huge wooden beams and stone walls. Out your window you get a stunning view of the town and ocean below.

O Centolo (Po. Puerto, s/n, tel. 98/174-0452), located on the port, is a modern restaurant serving simply prepared fish and seafood. **O Tearrón** (C/ Calafigueira 1, tel. 98/174-0112) is a bit more rough-and-rumble and a favorite with older locals who while away the afternoons here. Grab a table on the deck and order the catch of the day.

Getting There
The "end of the world" sits at the end of AC-445, which runs into the AC-552 that goes up to La Coruña (you can also detour off to Santiago). If you are traveling by bus, **Arriva** (tel. 90/227-7482, www.arriva.es) runs six buses daily to/from La Coruña and seven to/from Santiago de Compostela, with the last one leaving at 4:30 P.M. Check the route carefully, as some require bus changes.

Rías Baixas

The lower estuaries of the Galician coast— Rías Baixas (buy-SHUSS) in Gallego, Rías Bajas in Spanish—are markedly greener, tamer, and warmer than those of the Rías Altas. The region can generally be delineated as the coast and estuaries running south from Finisterre to the border of Portugal. Two of the estuaries—Ría de Pontevedra and Ría de Vigo—are home to the cities of Pontevedra and Vigo respectively. Temperatures are bit warmer in the Rías Baixas and the sun peeks out more often—but this is still Green Galicia—and an umbrella and rain jacket are required packing, even in summer. Also, in general, the further south you go, the more touristy it gets.

The estuaries of the Rías Baixas are big—so big in fact that local legend claims they are the result of God's handprint on the coast. Thanks to their proximity to big cities, including Santiago, many can be visited via public transportation. **Monbus** (tel. 90/215-8778 or 90/229-2900, www.monbus.es) travels the length of the coast from Muros down to Baiona. Schedules change daily and transfers will need to be made, but if you have the freedom and flexibility, it is possible to reach all of the places below via public bus.

◖ RÍA DE MUROS E NOIA
Just 40 kilometesr (25 miles) west of Santiago, the Ría de Muros e Noia is one of the easiest areas to visit if you are short on time. The estuary has the town of Muros at its northern edge, the town of Noia at its most inland point, and the fishing villages known as Porto do Son at its southern edge.

Muros
Muros is one of the more charming fishing villages you'll come across. Its medieval core is made up of lovely granite buildings boasting white-framed Galician *galerías,* narrow arcaded streets, and a majestic old public market. Throw in a bustling little fishing wharf, a hulking Gothic church, and miles of beach stretching in both directions from the town, and you have a lovely little vacation spot.

Noia
Noia (Noya in Spanish) is a cute little town with a very big ego—it advertises itself as the Florence of Galicia. Hmm. It is true that there are a handful of lovely churches—**Santa María la Nueva** with its extensive collection of gravestones from the Middle Ages and **San Martino** with its elaborate facade and rose windows— both built in a distinctive "Maritime Gothic"

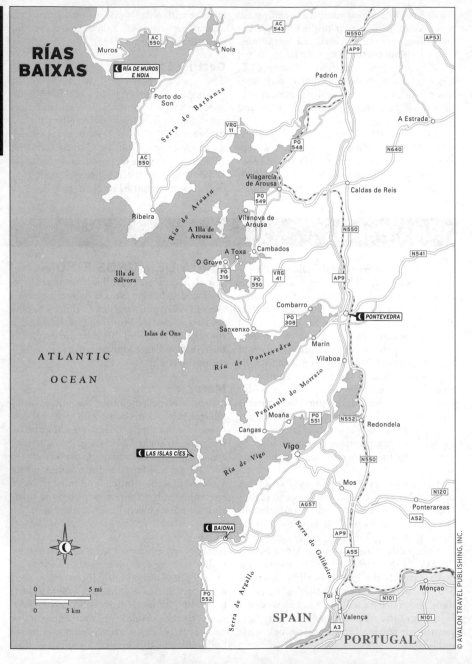

RÍAS
BAIXAS

RÍA DE MUROS
E NOIA

Muros

Noia

Padrón

A Estrada

Porto do
Son

Serra do Barbanza

AC
550

AC
543

N550

AP9

AP53

VRG
11

PO
548

N640

AC
550

Vilagarcía
de Arousa

Caldas de Reis

PO
549

Ribeira

Ría de Arousa

Vilanova de
Arousa

N550

A Illa de
Arousa

A Toxa   Cambados

N541

O Grove

Illa de
Sálvora

PO
316

PO
550

VRG
41

AP9

Combarro

PONTEVEDRA

PO
308

Islas de Ons

Sanxenxo

Marín

ATLANTIC

OCEAN

Ría de Pontevedra

Vilaboa

Península do Morrazo

Moaña

PO
551

N552

Redondela

Cangas

Vigo

LAS ISLAS CÍES

Ría de Vigo

N550

Mos

AG57

N120

Ponterareas

A52

BAIONA

Serra do Galiñeiro

AP9

A55

0   5 mi

0   5 km

PO
552

Serra de Argallo

Monçao

Tui

N101

SPAIN

Valença

A3

N101

PORTUGAL

style. However, what really makes Noia stand out is its ability to be all things Galician in such a small space—weathered granite buildings well over 500 years old, white-framed *galerías,* Galician culture and food, and a bustling fishing port. But, there is one big drawback to the town. Because it sits on the end of the estuary, where two rivers come to meet it, the water bordering the town is dirty and silt-filled. To get to the lovely beaches nearby, you'll have to hike out of town. **Praia de Testal** is the closest—about a 20-minute walk or 5-minute drive.

Porto do Son

Porto do Son is actually a collection of several speck-sized fishing villages, including **Porto Sin,** which has undergone a recent transformation as a port for leisure boats and aquatic activities. The village of **Xuño** boasts an original Roman bridge while **Baroña** houses the remains of an ancient Celtic dwelling *(castro)*—below which lies a nudist beach. However, the best "sight" in this area is nature, as the golden beaches running in both directions along the Atlantic are backed by earth-toned cliffs and beyond that the green peaks of the Serra do Barbanza mountain range.

Accommodations and Food

All around the perimeter of the Ría are accommodations and restaurants, mainly of the rustic, seaside type. In Muros, the **Pensión Ría de Muros** (Av. Castelao 53, tel. 98/182-6056, €60) is a good choice with spacious rooms and beach views. It's on a seaside road lined with decent seafood shacks, and you'll find lots of tapas bars in the old town. In Noia, try **Hotel Park** (C/ Barro, tel. 98/182-3729, www.hotelpark.es, €80), a small hotel with big-hotel aspirations. Located about 0.8 kilometers (0.5 mile) out of the city center on its own little beach, the rooms are a bit dreary, but the sea view compensates nicely. About 15 miles out of the city on the road towards Santiago, **Pesquería del Tambre** (Central del Tambre, Santa María de Roo, tel. 98/105-1620, www.pesqueriadeltambre.com, €85) is a gorgeous inn on the banks of the Tambre River.

Five stone houses have been lovingly restored to create this rustic retreat. It also houses an excellent restaurant. Prices are slashed by half during the off-season.

There are dozens of eating options—from gritty dives to upscale dining rooms—all along the coasts of the ría. The one thing they all share in common is impeccably fresh, perfectly prepared, simply delicious seafood. A local favorite, located in Noia, is **Ceboleiro** (C/ Galicia 14, tel. 98/182-4497). This traditional Galician house located right on the port is both elegant and rustic with a friendly staff and an impressive list of Galician wines.

Getting There

By car, follow the AC-543 straight west from Santiago. It meets the AC-550 in Noia, which wraps around the *ría* in both directions.

RÍA DE AROUSA

The broad Ría de Arousa is the largest of Galicia's estuaries. It is jammed with beaches, Celtic and Roman ruins, colorful fishing boats, *bateas* (mussel-farming rafts) anchored in the estuaries, and dozens of seaside villages. The northern bank runs along the mountains of Serra do Barbanza and is less populated than the southern coast. It has a few towns of note, including **Ribeira,** right on the Atlantic, but nothing really worth a detour.

The southern shore of the Ría is rimmed by a winding coastal road that offers lovely views across the estuary and out to the ocean. However, hidden beneath the natural beauty is a very ugly reality. The Ría de Arousa is one of the most active ports for drug smuggling in Europe. Galicia has long been known as the entrance to Europe for heroin and cocaine into the continent—its secluded coves and rural landscape gives the drug-runners natural cover. The towns of **Vilagarcía** and **Vilanova,** and the island **A Illa de Arousa,** have longstanding reputations for being particularly active in the illegal drug-running market. If that is not reason enough to avoid them, consider that most of the towns along this southern shore, including these three, are

GALICIA

WINES FROM GALICIA

The heavy rainfall and thick humidity that color Galicia's rolling hills in an infinite palette of green also water acre upon acre of vineyards. Though wine has been produced in this region for millennia, only in the last 20 years have Galicia's wines begun to garner critical acclaim. Though there is not enough sunlight to nourish grapes for rich, red wines, there is just enough for the production of the region's luminous, fruity, aromatic whites.

Five regions have been awarded with their own *denominación de origen*, or appellation, known as a D.O. (day-OH) in Spain. Many of the best producers are small boutique bodegas called *adegas*. If you travel in Galicia, you'll be hard-pressed to find anything other than Galician wines on offer; if you are elsewhere in Spain, get in a Gallego frame of mind by asking for one of the following wines by name.

RÍAS BAIXAS

The Rías Baixas vineyards give rise to the wonderful wines of the same name. Though 11 varieties of grapes are used, *albariño* accounts for 90 percent of the vineyard area and produces the region's best wines. Albariño wines are intensely fruity with intoxicating citrus bouquets. Bodegas to seek out include: **Pazo de Barrantes,** run by the same family (including a bona fide count) that owns the excellent Rioja bodega Marqués de Murrieta; **Bodegas Martin Codax,** which has garnered a following in the United States for its exquisite wines produced under the labels Martina Codax, Burgans, and Organistrum; **Bodegas Terras Gauda;** and **Bodega Palacio de Fefiñanes,** located in a stunning 17th-century palace in the town of Cambados, considered the capital of albariño.

RIBEIRO

The name means "riverbank" in Gallego and these light, crisp white wines (and a few reds) come from vineyards laid out along the Río Miño (Minho in Gallego) in the province of Ourense. For centuries, Ribeiro was known for its cloyingly sweet, high-alcohol wines called *tostados*. Today, thanks to innovative, independent bodegas who have insisted on using native grapes

---

pretty nondescript—cinder-block apartments crowded around scruffy ports. Yes, the scenery is still lovely and there are wonderful beaches and a smattering of Celtic and Roman ruins, but not much more.

Padrón

Unless you are driving in from the Ría de Muros e Noia in the north or up from Pontevedra, you'll enter this area through the city of Padrón, situated just inland from the estuary on the Río Ulla. The town is pretty nondescript and there is really no good reason to stick around—lunch maybe, or to fill up your gas tank—but Padrón holds a prominent place in both the sacred and the gastronomical realms of Spain. The holy fame stretches back almost 2,000 years when the stone boat carrying the body of Santiago (Saint James) landed in Padrón around A.D. 44. They hitched up here (*padrón* means memorial pillar) and then buried the body in the spot that is now Santiago de Compestela.

The tasty fame comes from the tiny green peppers that appear on tapas menus throughout the country under the name of *pimientos del Padrón*. About 2.5 centimeters (an inch) long and bright green, the peppers are served deep fried in olive oil and sprinkled with coarse salt. They have an almost sweet flavor and are wildly addictive. But be careful, for in every batch of mild peppers are a few that are searingly hot. Have a glass of wine handy just in case.

Cambados

The charming seaside village of Cambados has a majestic medieval core of stately stone buildings. The highlight is the elegant main square of **Praza de Fefiñanes,** lined with local crafts shops, wine bars, and one very palatial 17th-century palace. It houses **Bodega Palacio de Fefiñanes** (tel. 98/654-2204), one of the re-

and producing high-quality wines, Ribeiro is becoming famed for its "boutique" wines. **Viña Mein** is one of the best known of these bodegas, with wine sales throughout Spain, Europe, and in the United States. Their wines are complex, deeply aromatic, and honeyed. Look also for wines from **Rojo Bangueses Emilio.**

RIBEIRA SACRA

The Ribeira Sacra D.O. is located in the spectacularly dramatic region where the Rivers Miño and Sil converge, deep inside Galicia. The name translates to "sacred riverbank" because many of the bodegas in this area were (or still are) owned by monasteries built in the Middle Ages. The riverbanks in question are lofty slopes so steep that ladders have been fixed into the ground in many vineyards, giving the winemaker access to the vines. This region is known for its reds made from the *mencía* grape, which produces very intense, aromatic, full-bodied wines. Because of the near-inaccessibility of the vineyards, wine production uses traditional, mostly organic growing methods and producers tend to be small, individually owned farmhouses. Of the Galician wines, Ribeira Sacra are the hardest to find outside of the region.

MONTERREI

Meaning "king's mountain" in Gallego, Monterrei takes its name from the ancient hilltop fortress that overlooks the vineyards of this newer D.O. region. Located in the southern portion of Ourense, near the Portuguese border, Monterrei produces both fresh, fruity whites and *mencía* reds. These wines are still little known beyond Galicia.

VALDEORRAS

Located in eastern Galicia, along the River Sil, the Valdeorras D.O. region was known for its wine as far back as the Romans. Today, it is rebuilding a reputation by using new production techniques and ancient native grapes such as *godello*. This grape produces a richly scented, straw-colored white, while the *mencía* grape is used for reds. One of the best bodegas in the region is **Finca La Tapada.**

gion's top producers of the fragrant white wine *albariño*. Cambados is considered the capital of *albariño* country, which spreads for acres around the town; the first week of August there is a very lively wine festival, the **Festa do Viño Albariño.**

O Grove

A popular destination on the Ría de Arousa, O Grove has a long tradition of catering to tourists. It sits on the Atlantic end of the Ría on the tip of a cauliflower-shaped isthmus that was once a separate island. The town boasts a lively port, a pleasant seaside walk, inexpensive hotels and eateries, and dozens of spectacular beaches—particularly around the southern end of the isthmus leading to the Rías de Pontevedra. If you are in town the last week in September, O Grove throws a lively seafood festival, **Festa do Marisco,** with lots of traditional music, general revelry, and tons of delicious seafood—all accompanied by the delicious Galician white wine, albariño.

From O Grove, it is just a short walk over a pedestrian bridge to reach the quaint **A Toxa** (Toja in Spanish). A resort destination for well-heeled Galicians since the 19th century, the lush little islet boasts high-end resorts, bustling hotels, a lively casino, and a surprisingly modest, absolutely charming **Ermita de San Sebastián** church, which is covered in sea shells. Look closer and you'll see that most of the shells have been signed (some call it graffiti) by locals over the years. The island has been famous for centuries for the healing properties of its waters and Toja brand soaps are sought-after—though none are actually made on the island.

Accommodations and Food

As this area has long relied on tourism, there are many more upscale places to stay. In Cambados, the sumptuous **Parador de Cambados**

(Po. Calzada, s/n, tel. 98/654-2250, cambados@parador.es, www.parador.es, €140) is a gorgeous seafront manor with lovely gardens and an excellent wine cellar.

In O Grove, you are spoiled for choice, though in August—peak Spanish travel time—you will have to book ahead. **Hostal Monte Sol** (Rúa Castelao 160, tel. 98/673-0916, www.hostalmontesol.net, €50) is a charming property with basic rooms overlooking the water. **Villa Juanita** (Rúa Castelao 110, tel. 98/673-2309, www.villajuanita.com, €55) also offers rooms with a view plus a good restaurant. To really splash out, head to A Toxa and **Gran Hotel La Toja** (tel. 98/673-0025, www.hesperia.com, €160), a classic spa hotel that has definitely seen better days but is still stunning in its grandeur. Facilities include a day spa, a nine-hole golf course, indoor and outdoor pools, and an upscale restaurant.

Throughout the Ría de Arousa, you'll find delicious seafood almost anywhere—this region was built on the ocean's bounties. In O Grove, try **Restaurante Solaina** (Av. Beira-mar, s/n, tel. 98/673-2969). For a gourmet seafood fix, head to **El Crisol** (C/ Hospital 12, tel. 98/673-0029, closed Mon., €40), a top-rated O Grove restaurant with excellent rice dishes and—for the non-shellfish eater—exquisite grilled meats.

Getting There

Getting to and around Ría de Arousa by car is straightforward. From Santiago, follow the N-550 to Padrón. From there, follow the coastal roads of VRG-11 for the northern shore of the Ría de Arousa, or the PO-548 along the southern shore. If you are heading straight to O Grove, take the AP-9 (out of either Padrón or Santiago) and then switch to the VRG-41. Follow the signs to O Grove.

RÍA DE PONTEVEDRA

The Ría de Pontevedra is another large estuary fingering its way into the coast. It shares its name with both the province of Pontevedra as well as its bustling capital city. On the northern shore, near the Atlantic, is the popular resort

Traditional *hórreos* (stone granaries) are common all along the Galician coast.

© C. BOLTON

of **Sanxenxo**. Along with nearby **Portonovo,** this is the closest you'll get in Galicia to the built-up resort life so popular on Spain's southern coasts. In addition to Celtic ruins, Romaneseque churches, a thumping nightlife, and more wonderful seafood, the main draws here are the gorgeous beaches that snake west of Sanxenxo towards O Grove and the Ría de Arousa. One of the best is **Praia de Lanzada,** an enormous beach of fine, white sand.

Islas de Ons

Lanzada beach faces out to the Islas de Ons, one of a series of tiny archipelagos off the coast that make up the **Parque Nacional de las Islas Atlánticas de Galicia.** Theses islands (including Cíes) are uninhabited, emerald green oases rising from the ocean floor and provide home to a vast array of marine and birdlife. The beaches are wild, windswept, and mostly deserted. There are several companies running boats out to Ons, including **Cruceros Rías Baixas** (tel. 98/673-1343, €11), which offers eight daily trips to/from the islands in July, August, and September only. The trip lasts about 45 minutes and departs from both Sanxenxo and Portonovo. The embarkation points and ticket offices are clearly marked in the respective ports of each town. Up to 200 people are allowed to camp on Ons per night, with each party staying no more than five days. A *tarjeta de acampada* (camping permit) must be requested at the port where you buy the boat ticket. Reservations are not possible and in summer, the place fills quickly. If you do get a spot, be aware, the showers are cold and there is no potable water, you'll have to bring your own.

Combarro

The tiny fishing port of Combarro, located between Sanxenxo and the city of Pontevedra, is another spot worth visiting. Along its waterfront (Rúa do Mar) is a string of traditional *hórreos* (ancient stone granaries) that make for a lovely photograph.

Accommodations and Food

Accommodations on the Ría de Pontevedra,

especially around Sanxenxo and Portonovo, are of the bold, brash variety. Off-season, prices can drop to less than half. In-season, it is imperative to make reservations. In Sanxenxo, try **Hotel Carlos I** (C/ Vigo, s/n, tel. 98/672-7036, www.carlosprimero.com, €120), a new luxury property with cool, cream-colored rooms, an in-house spa, swimming pools, and lovely gardens. Request an ocean-facing room. Just 0.8 kilometer (0.5 mile) out of the resort, **Hotel Duna** (Playa de Canelas, tel. 98/669-1411, www.hotelduna.com, €70) is a charming smaller property right on a less-populated stretch of beach. Both hotels offer restaurants and there are loads of tapas bars and seafood shacks throughout the region. If you are a gourmand, you'll love **La Taberna de Rotilio** (Av. del Puerto 7, tel. 98/672-0200, closed Sun. in the evening and Mon. in winter, €40), located in the Sanxenxo hotel of the same name. This beachside dining room offers acclaimed traditional and regional takes on local seafood and produce.

Getting There

To travel around Ría de Pontevedra, follow the PO-308 from the city of Pontevedra and it will lead you straight to Sanxenxo via Combarro.

◖ PONTEVEDRA

As capital of the province of Pontevedra (one of the four provinces of Galicia), the small city of Pontevedra, surrounded by apartment blocks and commercial buildings, will do nothing to charm you on first approach. However, once you reach its **Casco Viejo,** you'll fall under its spell. It is hard to walk more than a block in the historical old town (locally called Zona Monumental) without stumbling upon a lovely old plaza full of lively cafés.

First founded by the Romans as Ad Duos Pontes, Pontevedra has been shaped by millennia of seafaring citizens. Rumors abound that Christopher Columbus was born here and that the *Santa María* was built in Pontevedra's shipyards. Until the river silted up in the 17th century, Pontevedra was a dynamic port thanks to the Río Lérez, which allowed ships from the

TAMING OF THE BEASTS

All along the Atlantic coast of Galicia are low-rolling hills and thick green pastures that are home to herds of wild horses. Local legends claim that the horses have been "fathered by the wind." Another story holds that during a 16th-century plague, two sisters begged San Lorenzo to intervene, promising the Saint two of their finest horses. The plague ended and the sisters kept their promise, releasing a pair of breeding horses into the wild each year on the saint's feast day. Over the centuries, the horses – protected from ranchers as holy property – formed large wild packs.

Just as the origins of the horses are steeped in mystery, the origin of the festival **Rapa das Bestas,** or "Taming of the Beasts," is murky. The Romans wrote about the natives of Galicia rounding up wild horses. Other legends say that the event began in medieval times because the horses were be-lieved to hold sacred powers. Whatever the origins, the "taming of the beasts" is held throughout Galicia June-August.

The Rapa das Bestas begins with an early-morning round-up of horses by livestock workers and others involved in the horse trade. The animals are then herded into a *curro*, a specially constructed corral surrounded by bleachers for the public. In the corral, expert handlers, called *agarradores* (which means "someone who seizes") wrestle with the wild animals until they can subdue them long enough to brand them and shear their manes. Once the animals have all been sheared, a typically wild Spanish fiesta commences.

Most Rapa das Bestas events take place in Pontevedra. Check with the Galician tourism website (www.turgalicia.es) to see if one will occur during your visit to the region. The most popular event happens in the town of Sabucedo (A Estrada in Gallego) on July 6.

Atlantic to dock in its wharves. Today, Pontevedra is the quintessential Galician town—surrounded by water and mountains, weathered by centuries of rain, tempered in mist, perfumed by the verdant hills of pine and eucalyptus surrounding it—it is a truly lovely place. And though not unknown touristically, it receives barely a fraction of the tourists as does nearby Santiago—allowing the intrepid visitor to discover a bit of authentic Galician life.

Sights

Pontevedra is bisected by the Río Lerez and nearly all the sights you'll want to visit are on its southern banks, including the Casco Viejo. Whether arriving by train, bus, or car, a natural starting point is the **Alameda,** a swath of 19th-century gardening elegance full of bright blooming trees, stone benches, and monuments and tiles in honor of a local victory over Napoleon's troops in 1808. Close to its end are the ruins of the 13th-century **Convento de Santo Domingo** (Po. Montero Ríos, s/n).

From there, if you are not following the tourist office's walking route, the best bet is to just wander the streets (*rúas* in Gallego) and plaza hop (*praza* in Gallego)—there is no "must-see" sight, but also no sight not worth seeing.

Praza de España is lorded over by the eclectic 19th-century **Ayuntamiento** (city hall). The **Praza da Peregrina** is home to the 18th-century **Santuario da Virxe Peregrina,** built with a scallop-shaped base in honor of pilgrims on their way to Santiago (Pontevedra is on the Portuguese leg of the Camino de Santiago). Just steps away is **Praza da Ferraría,** a broad, tree-lined plaza home to sidewalk cafés and concerts in the summer. Looming over the plaza is the 14th-century **church of San Francisco,** which, according to legend, was built by St. Francis of Assisi on his pilgrimage to Santiago. **Praza de Churros Enríquez** boasts both medieval charm and trendy eateries. **Praza Teucro** is a majestic old plaza surrounded the homes of long-dead noblemen. The facades of the houses still bear their family crests. At sunset, the place to be is

Praza das Cinco Rúas, where five bar-lined streets converge and the atmosphere is electric. **Praza de Leña** is one of the most beautiful in town with its flower-covered balconies and thriving cafés. It also houses the **Museo Provincial** (C/ Pasentería,10, tel. 98/685-1455, €2), home to a fascinating collection of Celtic jewelry and a perfectly preserved 18th-century Galician kitchen.

Accommodations

Under €50, Pension Casa Maruja (Av. Santa María 12, tel. 98/685-4901, €37), overlooking the lovely Praza Santa María, is a good cheap sleep despite the hideous fluorescent lighting. **Hotel Madrid** (C/ Andrés Mellado 5, tel. 98/686-5180, €45) offers very basic rooms. In the €50-100 range, try **Hotel México** (C/ Andrés Muruáis 10, tel. 98/685-9006, €52). Just off Praza Galicia, it features a helpful staff and comfy beds. **Hotel Rúas** (C/ Sarmiento 20, tel. 98/684-6416, €60) features low-rent rooms, but its location next door to Praza da Leña is perfect. **Over €100,** the best choice in town (and one of the best in the region) is **Parador de Pontevedra** (C/ Barón 19, tel. 91/516-6666, pontevedra@parador.es, www.parador .es, €140), a 16th-century stone mansion built upon Roman ruins.

Food

The Casco Viejo is flooded with tapas bars, from traditional Galician to cutting-edge trendy. For the former, try **Os Carballos** (Pr. Verdura 9, tel. 98/685-2078, 7 A.M.–1 A.M. Wed.–Sun.), a mom-and-daughter operation offering simple, savory Galician treats. **La Chata** (Pr. Curros Enríquez, s/n, noon–4 P.M. and 7 P.M.–midnight Mon.–Sat., closed Sun.) is a bit more modern with a focus on good wines to go with the tapas. The restaurant also runs the attached award-winning tapas bar, **A Casa do Lado** (Pr. Leña 1, tel. 98/686-0225), if you prefer a lighter meal.

Figueroa (Rúa Figueroa 14, tel. 98/684-6909, 12:30–4 P.M. and 8 –11:30 P.M. Tues.–Sat., 12:30–4 P.M. Sun., closed Mon., €15) is a simple yet elegant room offering exquisite sea-food against a background of old jazz. **Eirado da Leña** (Pr. Leña 1, tel. 98/686-0225, 1:30 4 P.M. and 9–11:30 P.M. Wed.–Sat., 1:30– 4 P.M. Mon.–Tues., closed Sun., €28) offers a sleek dining room with fresh flowers on every table and windows overlooking the plaza— it is one of the few places in town to offer a menu in English. **Alameda 10** (Alameda 10, tel. 98/685-7412, 1:30–3:30 P.M. and 9–11 P.M. Mon.–Sat., closed Sun., €40), one of Pontevedra's top restaurants, offers local dishes with creative touches. Try the *arroz de marisco* (rice with shellfish).

Information

The **city tourist office** (C/ General Gutiérrez Mellado 1, tel. 98/685-0814, 9:30 A.M.–2 P.M. and 4:30–7:30 P.M. Mon.–Fri., 10 A.M.–2 P.M. and 4:30–7:30 P.M. Sat., 10 A.M.–2 P.M. Sun. summer; 9:30 A.M.–2 P.M. and 4–6P.M. Mon.–Fri., 10A.M.–noon Sat., closed Sun. winter) offers a wide variety of information in English. Look for their walking route, which will give you the best overview of the city. The office of **Turismo Rías Baixas** (Pr. Santa María, s/n, tel. 98/684-2690, 9 A.M.–8 P.M. Mon.–Fri., 10 A.M.–2 P.M. Sat. and Sun) is the best source for free, English-language information about all of the Rías Baixas.

Getting There and Around

Pontevedra lies about 65 kilometers (40 miles) south of Santiago. Pontevedra's **Estación de Ferrocarril** (Av. Eduardo Pondal, s/n, tel. 98/685-1313) is run by **Renfe** (tel. 90/224-0202, www.renfe.es), which offers direct trains to Madrid; trips to other Spanish cities will more than likely stop in Vigo first. By bus, Pontevedra is serviced by the **Estacíon de Autobuses** (Rúa Calvo Sotelo, s/n, tel. 98/685-2408). The main service provider for routes out of Galicia is **Alsa** (www.alsa.cs). Note that the bus and train stations are located within a block of each other on the south side of town, about a €5 taxi into the center.

By car, reach Pontevedra via the rambling N-550 road or the faster AP-9 toll road. Tolls should not top €7. Follow the street signs into the center of town and to the Alameda, a main square with a large underground parking lot.

RÍA DE VIGO

The Ría de Vigo is the last of Galicia's great estuaries before the Portuguese border. Long and narrow, it boasts lovely beaches and rustic fishing villages—as well as Vigo, the largest city in Galicia. The Ría is also the locus of much fishing and industry traffic. At its deepest point in the coast it forms the inlet of San Simón, site of one of Europe's largest commercial oyster beds.

Cangas

On the northern shore, Cangas is a lively resort with a ramshackle medieval center and a handful of weather-beaten Romanesque churches. Its main beach, **Praia de Rodeira** is long and narrow with a beachside promenade. Heading west, towards the Atlantic, there are more pristine beaches including **Liméns** and **Nerga,** the latter of which is for nudists. For more seclusion, head inland on PO-305, which leads to Áldan, on the ría of the same name. It boasts many tiny coves and wild beaches. It is also accessed via boat from Vigo.

【 Baiona

Way down on the southern shore where the Ría de Vigo meets the Atlantic sits the fishing town of Baiona. Its biggest claim to fame came in 1493 when Columbus' ship *Pinta* landed here to tell of the discovery of the New World. Up until the 19th century, it was the busiest port until upstart Vigo usurped it. Today, it is popular vacation destination as well as a lively fishing town. The old town has an elegant medieval core and the in-town beach, **Santa Marta O Burgo** is a lovely crescent bathed by relatively calm waters. From the beach, the town's most prominent monument is visible: the **Castillo de Conde de Gondomar,** an 11th-century walled fortress. It is almost obligatory to make the climb up here to walk on the 2.5 kilometers (1.5 miles) of walls and watch the sunset.

Accommodations and Food

If you are not staying in Vigo, your most luxurious accommodations can be found in Baiona within the walls of the Gondomar fortress. The 【 **Parador de Baiona** (tel. 98/635-5000, baiona@parador.es, www.parador.es, €175) is a very cloak-and-dagger Galician palace with sumptuous rooms, stunning views, and an excellent traditional restaurant. This is a popular parador, so make reservations. In town, try cozy **Tres Carabelas** (C/ Ventura Misa 61, tel. 98/635-5133, www.hoteltrescarabelas.com, €60). The rooms are a bit outdated, but the location on a stone lane is very atmospheric. There are dozens of decent seafood restaurants and tapas bars in Baoina and along the port where you can eat for less than €20. If you want to splurge, the top-rated **O Moscón** (C/ Alférez Barreiro 2, tel. 98/635-5008, 1–4 P.M. and 8 P.M.–midnight daily, €30) is famed for its seafood, particularly *bogavante* (lobster); check the price before you order, as it can go sky high depending on the season.

【 LAS ISLAS CÍES

The shimmering jade islands of Cíes sit in the Atlantic Ocean just off the Ría de Vigo. A part of the **Parque Nacional de las Islas Atlánticas de Galicia,** the islands are protected parkland and only 2,200 people are allowed to visit per day. Oh, but what beauty those lucky few find—sugar-white secluded beaches, magical coves, turquoise-hued waters, unspoiled hills rolling with long grass flowing in the wind, astonishing views.

The archipelago is made up of three islands, Illa de San Martiño, Illa do Faro, and Illa do Monteagudo. The latter two are linked by a long neck of sand that forms a beach on the Atlantic side and the tranquil lagoon, Lago dos Nenos, on the other side. The beach is the locus of most tourist action, boasting campsites and a bar/restaurant/shop. Head away from it and you can find kilometers of beautiful solitude. The highest peak, at 198 meters (650 feet), affords expansive views over the islands and ocean.

© J. ALBERTOS/WWW.VIGOENFOTOS.COM

The protected islands of Cíes offer an unspoiled natural retreat.

Accommodations

If you want to camp on the island, you have to request a *tarjeta de acampada* (camping permit) from **Camping Illas Cíes** (tel. 98/643-8358, €5 per person plus €5 per tent) before you head to the isles. The office is located at the Naviera Mar de Ons booth in the boat terminal in Vigo.

Getting There

Naviera Mar de Ons (Estación Marítimo, C/ Canóvas del Castillo, Vigo, s/n, tel. 98/622-5272, www.mardeons.com, €15.50 round-trip) runs nine boats a day from Vigo to the islands during the summer season.

VIGO

Depending on your tastcs, vivacious Vigo is a welcome shot of urbanity in the green mists of tranquil Galicia—or a screeching, dirty intrusion of big city blight. As Galicia's largest city and a thriving hub of industry—fishing and automobiles—there is quite a bit of urban unpleasantness around the edges of town. However, despite what so many guidebooks say, it is not all that bad. There is a charming historical center, a bustling fishing port, lovely verdant parks, elegant promenades along the water, a few nice beaches, and a very lively social scene—locals are boisterous and friendly with an infectious love of life, and the nightlife in Vigo is one of the most intense in all of Spain. Of course, the local seafood is impeccable, and if you are an oyster fan, you're in luck—Vigo's waters produce most of Europe's oysters.

The prime location right on one of the region's most expansive bays has enticed seafaring settlers to Vigo from the Phoenicians to the Vikings. The Romans called the town Vicus Spacorum. In the 16th century, Sir Francis Drake—known locally as a pirate—raided Spanish ships as they entered the Ría de Vigo; to this day, rumors abound of sunken treasures of silver beneath the waters of Vigo.

Sights

Climbing up to the hilltop park of **Castelo do Castro** affords spectacular views of the city, the

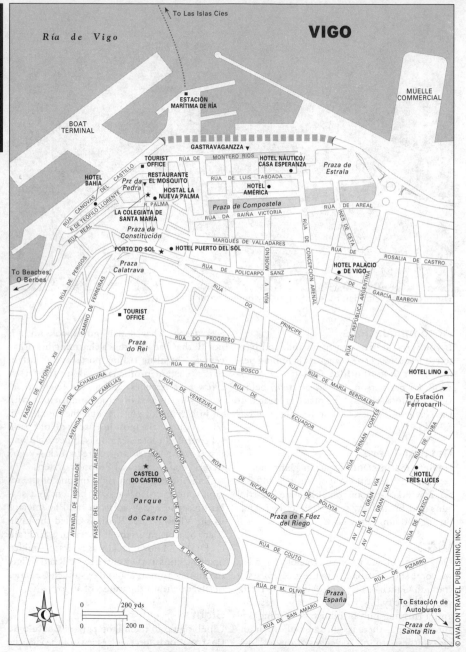

VIGO

To Las Islas Cies

Ría de Vigo

MUELLE
COMMERCIAL

ESTACIÓN
MARÍTIMA DE RÍA

BOAT
TERMINAL

GASTRAVAGANZZA

TOURIST OFFICE

RÚA DE MONTERO RIOS

HOTEL NÁUTICO/
CASA ESPERANZA

Praza de Estrala

HOTEL BAHÍA

Prz da Pedra

RESTAURANTE EL MOSQUITO

HOSTAL LA NUEVA PALMA

RÚA DE LUIS TABOADA

HOTEL AMÉRICA

R. PALMA

LA COLEGIATA DE SANTA MARÍA

Praza de Compostela

RÚA DE AREAL

RÚA DA RAIÑA VICTORIA

Praza da Constitución

MARQUÉS DE VALLADARES

PORTO DO SOL

HOTEL PUERTO DEL SOL

Praza Calatrava

RÚA DE POLICARPO SANZ

RÚA DE

HOTEL PALACIO DE VIGO

ROSALIA DE CASTRO

To Beaches,
O Berbes

RÚA
DO

RÚA V

CONCEPCIÓN ARENAL

AV. DE GARCÍA BARBON

TOURIST OFFICE

PRINCIPE

Praza do Rei

RÚA DO PROGRESO

RÚA DE RONDA DON BOSCO

RÚA DE MARIA BERDIALES

HOTEL LINO

RÚA DE

RÚA DE VENEZUELA

ECUADOR

To Estación
Ferrocarril

PASEO DOS CEDROS

RÚA

RÚA DE CUBA

CASTELO DO CASTRO

RÚA DE NICARAGUA

RÚA DE BOLIVIA

AV. DE LA GRAN VIA

HOTEL TRES LUCES

Parque do Castro

Praza de F Fdez del Riego

AV. DE LA GRAN VIA

RÚA DE MÉXICO

R. DE MANUEL

RÚA DE COUTO

RÚA DE PIZARRO

RÚA DE M. OLIVIE

Praza España

To Estación de Autobuses

RÚA DE SAN AMARO

Praza de Santa Rita

PASEO DE ALFONSO XII

RÚA DE CACHAMUIÑA

CAMINO DE FERREIRAS

RÚA DE PERIGOS

RÚA CANOVAS DEL CASTILLO

R DE TEOFILO LLORENTE

RÚA REAL

AVENIDA DE HISPANIDADE

PASEO DEL CRONISTA ALAREZ

AVENIDA DE LAS CAMELIAS

PASEO DE ROSALIA DE CASTRO

MORENO

RÚA DE INÉS DE CETA

RÚA HERNAN CORTES

RÚA DE REPÚBLICA ARGENTINA

0   200 yds

0   200 m

© AVALON TRAVEL PUBLISHING, INC.

Ría, and the Atlantic Ocean beyond. The park is named for the remains of a castle built by Felipe IV. Scattered around the hill are funerary artifacts attributed to Celtic tribes from the Iron Age.

Just below the hill, the **Casco Vello** (old town) unfurls in a web of medieval streets. The buzzing heart of the area is **Porto do Sol,** a good jumping-off point for exploring this area. Around the corner, **Praza da Constitución** is a broad, cobblestone plaza lined with cafés and bars—particularly hopping on weekend nights. Nearby, **La Colegiata de Santa María** (Pl. Iglesia, s/n) is Vigo's most popular house of worship. The church was built in the early 1800s to replace the original church that stood here before Drake torched it in 1589.

Follow **Rúa Real** into one of the most atmospheric parts of the Casco Vello. Up the stairs to **Rúa Teófil Llorente,** middle-aged women in white smocks and hair nets stand at granite tables shucking oysters. These women are Vigo's *ostereras* and they can shuck a dozen faster than you can dig out the €6 to pay for them. You can take a plate into any of the surrounding bars and suck them down along with a glass of *albariño.* The barrio of **O Berbés** is a traditional fishing quarter along Rúa Ribeira. It is one of the more picturesque areas of town with the ramshackle old homes propped up on stone arcades and the cobbled street laid out in a checkered pattern.

Beaches

Running west along the city, facing the Ría de Vigo and out towards the Atlantic, are a dozen or so beaches. The most popular—and closest to the city—is **Samil,** which boasts over 1.5 kilometers (over one mile) of fine sand, tranquil waters, and a view out to the islands of Cíes. It is lined with every amenity you could need—showers, bars, restaurants, ice-cream shops. Get there via public bus number C3, which you can catch in Porto do Sol. It runs every 15 minutes and costs €1.

Accommodations

Under €50, the Casco Vello is your best bet. **La Nueva Palma** (C/ Palma 7, tel. 98/643-

0678, €24), located just steps from Praza Constitución, is clean and homey despite its cheap price tag. Near the port, **Hotel Náutico** (C/ Luis Taboada 28, tel. 98/612-2440, €44) takes the maritime theme to the extreme with sailboats printed on the sheets.

Between **€50 and 100,** 🄲 **Puerta del Sol** (Porta do Sol 14, tel. 98/622-2364, www.vigonet.com/puertadelsol, €67) is a retreat of rustic sophistication set in a 19th-century palace on the border between the old town and the new commercial zone. **Hotel Lino** (C/ Lepanto 26, tel. 98/643-9311, www.hotel-lino.com, €65) is a large, remodeled hotel very close to the train station and some of the city's busier nightlife. If your room is on the street and it's a weekend, you'll need earplugs. **Hotel Tres Luces** (C/ Cuba 19, tel. 98/648-0250, www.hotel3luces.com, €85) offers refined elegance at surprisingly affordable prices in the upscale shopping area of town. **Hotel América** (C/ Pablo Morillo 6, tel. 98/643-8922, www.hotelamerica-vigo.com, €75) offers colorful, contemporary rooms near the water. Request one with a view.

Over €100, Vigo's first classic big hotel is still its favorite. Now run by the modern Husa chain, **Hotel Bahía** (C/ Canovas del Castillo 24, tel. 98/644-9656, www.hotelbahiade vigo.es, €145) features clean, spacious rooms (request an upper room overlooking the estuary) and an excellent location between the boat terminal and the old town. **Palacio de Vigo** (Av. García Barbón 17, tel. 98/643-3643, nh palaciodevigo@nh-hoteles.com, www.nh-hotels .com, €180) occupies an elegant turn-of-the-20th-century building about midway between the port and the Castro park. Rooms are classy and stylish and service is good. **Pazo de los Escudos** (Av. Atlantida 106, tel. 98/682-0820, www.pazolosescudos.com, €270) is located in a 19th-century stone palace right on the beach. Rooms are sumptuous, with modern touches like Bang & Olufsen stereos. The hotel's beachside restaurant is very good.

Food

Throughout the Casco Vello and O Berbés, there are countless tapas bars serving up fresh

GALICIA

© J. ALBERTOS/WWW.VIGOENFOTOS.COM

Enjoy freshly shucked oysters right on the streets of Vigo's Casco Vello.

seafood. **Rías Gallegas** (in front of Puerto Pesquero, tel. 98/622-2152, €20) serves outsized seafood platters of crab, lobster, shrimp, and pretty much anything else you can catch. One platter can easily feed two or three people. **Bar Cocedero La Piedra** (Rúa Pescadería 3, tel. 98/622-3765, €16) also dishes out quality seafood, including local oysters by the dozens. **Casa Esperanza** (C/ Luis Taboada 28, tel. 98/622-8615, 1–4 P.M. and 8–11 P.M. Mon.–Sat., closed Sun., €36) is one of Vigo's top-rated restaurants and specializes in classic Galician fare and, of course, seafood. **El Mosquito** (Pr. Pedra 4, tel. 98/622-4441, closed Sun., €50) has a quaint fishing wharf atmosphere and exquisite seafood—it is one of the best restaurants in town. For a modern change of pace, **Gastravaganzza** (C/ Montero Ríos 16, tel. 98/611-3313, 1–4 P.M. and 9–11:30 P.M. Tues.–Sat., 1–4 P.M. Sun., closed Mon., €25) isn't extravagant in name alone. Complete with couches and giant orbs of Christmas lights, it offers a creative take on local Galician fare with an exciting menu of pastas, salads, and meat dishes.

Information

There are several tourism offices around town. **Turismo de Vigo** (Rúa Teófilo Llorente 5, tel. 98/622-4757, www.turismodevigo .com, 10 A.M.–2 P.M. and 4–7:30 P.M. Tues.–Sun., 10 A.M.–2 P.M. Mon.) is the city office, but also offers a lot of information about the towns in the Ría de Vigo. Galicia has a **regional tourist office** (C/ Cánovas del Castillo 22, tel. 98/643-0577, www.turgalicia.es, 9:30 A.M.–2 P.M. and 4:30–7:30 P.M. Mon.–Fri., 10A.M.–2 P.M. and 4:30–7:30 P.M. Sat., closed Sun.) near the boat terminal. The latter has extensive information and maps on the Rías Baixas, the Rías Altas, and beyond. If your Spanish is up to par, peruse www .vigoenfotos.com, run by local photographer Javier Albertos Benayas. He publishes amazing photos of the Ría de Vigo and surroundings, as well as good tourist information.

Getting There and Around

By air, **Aeroporto Peinador** (tel. 98/626-8200), located about 11 kilometers (seven miles) outside of town, is perfect if you are traveling domestically within Spain as there are several daily (cheap) flights to Barcelona, Bilbao, Madrid, Vallodolid, and more. They are operated by **Spanair** (www.spanair.com) and **Iberia** (www.iberia.com). **Air France** also runs flights to Paris. Flights from elsewhere land in Santiago first.

By train, Vigo's **Estación Ferrocarril** (C/ Urzaiz, s/n) is run by **Renfe** (tel. 90/224-0202, www.renfe.es) and there are hourly trains to Pontevedra, Santiago de Compostela, and La Coruña. There are also daily trains to Madrid, Barcelona, and San Sebastián.

By bus, Vigo's **Estación de Autobuses** (Av. Madrid, s/n) offers routes throughout Galicia—mainly run by **Monbus** (www.monbus .es)—and to major destinations throughout Spain through **Alsa** (www.alsa.es).

By boat, the **Estación Marítima de Ría** (C/ Canóvas del Castillo, s/n) is the docking point for pleasure trips to villages on the Ría de Vigo, including charming Cangas, and the Islas de Cíes.

Interior Galicia

Of the four provinces that make up Galicia (La Coruña, Pontevedra, Lugo, and Ourense), only Ourense is completely inland, though the bulk of Interior Galicia is made up of Lugo province. Separation from the sea does not at all mean this area is dry. On the contrary, it is riddled with misty mountains, rushing rivers, and lazy lakes. The mountains separating interior Galicia from its coast and delineating its borders from Asturias and León are called the "backbone" of Galicia. They are mostly low and rolling, but Mount Peña Trevinca reaches approximately 2,070 meters (6,800 feet). The largest river running through interior Galicia is Río Miño (Minho), which waters the land and gives rise to several Spanish D.O.s (appellations) including the up-and-coming Ribeira Sacra. (See sidebar, *Wines from Galicia.*) Weather is more extreme, getting very cold in winter and hot in summer. Ourense has often topped the charts as Spain's hottest city in the summer months.

The region is one of Spain's most remote, with roads and access either limited or poor. Those who do venture in may think they fell into the past as farmers tend their postage-stamp-sized fields with donkey-drawn carts. Yet this region is also home to three vibrant cities—Santiago de Compostela, one of Spain's most visited cities, and the capital cities of Lugo and Ourense. The latter two are full of regional charms and far enough off the beaten path to present visitors with an authentic slice of Galician life.

Inland Galicia is also famed for the **Camino de Santiago,** the 800-year-old pilgrimage route that leads to the cathedral of Santiago, final resting place of Saint James (Santiago in Spanish). The last hump of the 805-kilometer (500-mile) journey cuts across the interior of Galicia and all but the coldest months bring pilgrims by the thousands shuffling through the rural landscape. You'll know them by their backpacks, staffs, scallop shells, and contemplative gazes. (See sidebars, *Show Me the Way* and *Tips for the Camino de Santiago.*)

If you want to learn more about this remote region, consider staying with those who know. British expats Ian and Irene Holliday fell in love with interior Galicia and bought a centuries-old stone farmhouse deep in the Ribiera Sacra wine-growing region. They have since converted it into the **Casa Santo Estevo** (www.ribeirasacra.com), a charming country inn surrounded by vineyards, valleys, and very old churches and ruins. The Hollidays are gracious hosts and passionate about the beauties of their adopted home. Their website is also a font of information on interior Galicia. As members of a local tourist consortium, they have dozens of contacts for everything from hiking to bodegas. Contact them to book a room and enjoy a way, way off-the-beaten-path vacation.

GALICIA

a rustic scene in interior Galicia

OURENSE

Sprawling along the banks of the Río Miño, Ourense (also called Orense) doesn't look like much on first approach. As with so many Spanish cities, it is rimmed by ugly urban sprawl, squat apartment blocks, and soulless commercial buildings. However, once inside the **Casco Vello** (the old town), Ourense reveals her charms in a warren of medieval squares, bustling café-lined streets, Romanesque churches, and Roman ruins. Off the tourist path, this lovely, accommodating town makes a good base for exploring villages in the surrounding countryside.

Sights

Ourense's sights are on the southern side of the Río Miño, which is crossed by a dramatic stone bridge called both **Ponte Maior** and **Ponte Romana.** The latter name refers to the base of the bridge, which is Roman and dates back to the reign of Emperor Augustus. The bulk of it was rebuilt as both a bridge and a fortress in the 13th century. More Roman ruins

can be found at **Las Burgas** (Pr. Burgas, s/n), the site of a Roman spa and bath built above a natural hot spring. The baths were expanded upon in the 17th and 19th centuries. Though long closed to public bathing, the waters still spout into a steaming pool. Think twice before sticking your hand in—the water has a median temperature of 66°C (150°F)!

In the heart of the Casco Vello stands the **Catedral do San Martiño** (Pr. Trigo 1), a hulking Romanesque treasure built in the 12th and 13th centuries on a former house of worship that dated to the 6th century. Of note is the western door, **Pórtico del Paraíso,** a 13th-century reproduction of the Pórtico de la Gloría on Santiago's cathedral. A small, attached museum holds various Romanesque pieces, including a rare 10th-century chess set carved of crystal. All around the cathedral are charming plazas perfect for getting lost in. Look for the arcaded **Praza Maior,** the Casco Vello's social hub. It is home to the **Museo Arqueológico** (Pr. Maior, s/n, tel. 98/822-3884), a regional archaeological museum housed in a 12th-century bishop's palace. Artifacts span history from Paleolithic times to the Renaissance. Of particular interest are the Celtic displays.

Accommodations

If on a tight budget, try **Hostal San Miguel II** (C/ San Miguel 14, tel. 98/823-9203, €25). Baths are shared, but the price is right and just downstairs is one of the best restaurants in the city, Restaurante Sanmiguel. **Río Miño** (C/ Juan XXIII, tel. 98/821-7594, €36) offers standard rooms with bath. Those on higher budgets should try **Hotel Francisco II** (C/ Bedoya 17, tel. 98/824-2095, www.ga-hoteles.es, € 90), a newish hotel in the city center with classic rooms and good views from the upper floors. **Gran Hotel San Martín** (C/ Curros Enríquez 1, tel. 98/837-1811, www.gh-hotels.com, €120) is a grand lodging with all the big-hotel trappings, spacious airy rooms, and attentive service. It also houses the highly rated San Martín restaurant.

Food

The Río Miño feeds the vineyards that give rise to wonderful Ribeiro wines and any meal in Ourense is bound to be complimented by these vinos and finished with a shot of *aguardiente,* the powerful liqueur made with the fermented remains of the wine-making process. Locals say it takes three people to have a glass—one to drink it and two to help him stagger home.

For tapas, head no further than the plazas and streets surrounding the cathedral. Locally called "Los Vinos," this area is jam-packed with traditional tapas joints and upscale wine bars. Try **A Porta da Aira** (C/ Hornos 2, tel. 98/825-0749, 1–3:30 P.M. and 8–11 P.M. Tues.–Sun., closed Mon.), famed for their *solomillo* (marinated steak) and *huevos rotos* (eggs with cured ham and potatoes). **Restaurante Sanmiguel** (C/ San Miguel 12, tel. 98/822-0795, 10:30 A.M.–1 A.M. daily, €30) has prided itself on Galician tradition since opening its doors in 1951. They have won numerous awards for quality, presentation, and taste; however, the best thing they have earned is a devoted local following. **A Taberna** (C/ Julio Prieto Nespereira, 32, tel. 98/824-3332,

1–4 P.M. and 9 P.M.–midnight Tues.–Sat., 1–4 P.M. Sun., closed Mon. €30) is a tiny dining room famous for its sublime renditions of classic Galician fare. Try their fish of the day *al horno* (oven-roasted with salt).

Information

The **city tourism office** (C/ Burgas 12, tel. 98/836-6064, www.turismourense.com, 9 A.M.–2 P.M. and 3–8 P.M. Mon.–Fri., 11 A.M.–2 P.M. Sat. and Sun.) offers city maps and discount packages for local hotels. The **Xunta de Galicia** (Ponte Maior/Ponte Romana, s/n, tel. 98/837-2020, 9 A.M.–2 P.M. and 4–8 P.M. Mon.–Fri., 10 A.M.–2 P.M. and 4–8 P.M. Sat., 10 A.M.–2 P.M. and 5–7 P.M. Sun. summer; 9 A.M.–2 P.M. and 4:30–6:30 P.M. Mon.–Fri., closed Sat. and Sun. winter) offers information and maps on all of Galicia.

Getting There

Ourense's train station is run by **Renfe** (tel. 90/224-0202, www.renfe.es) and is located about a half-hour walk on the other side of the river. There are daily long-distance trains to Madrid and beyond, as well as regional trains to Santiago and other points in Galicia. The **bus station** (Crta. Vigo 1, tel. 98/821-6027) is quite a ways out of the center of town and is serviced by several companies including **Alsa** (www.alsa.es) for connections outside of Galicia and **Monbus** (www.monbus.es) for connections within. By car, the A-52 connects to Madrid and Vigo. The N-540 goes north to Lugo. The N-525/AP-53 goes to Santiago.

LUGO

As the capital city of the region of the same name, Lugo is a thriving hub in what is mostly a rural, slow-moving region of Galicia. Originally a Celtic settlement (*Lugus* is often translated as Celtic for "sun god"), the town fell under Romans control in the 2nd century B.C. They re-christened it Lucus Augusti, made it capital of their Gallaecia province, and built the walls that still stand around the old city center—and which have been named a UNESCO World Heritage Site.

Sights

The main reason to visit Lugo is for its spectacular **Murallas Romanas** (Roman Walls). The best-preserved Roman fortification walls in Spain (some say in the world), the walls run for 2.5 kilometers (1.5 miles) around the city center, rise nearly 15 meters (50 feet) in places, and boast 71 round towers. They are in impeccable shape and as a UNESCO site are protected and well maintained. Access the walls via a rampart next to the cathedral in Praza Pío XII. They are free to visit and open 24 hours per day. Though the views have long been marred by urban sprawl, it is a thrill to walk the walls at night, taking the same steps that Roman sentries did over 2,000 years ago. Ten gateways provide access into the old city.

In addition to the walls, Lugo is full of Roman ruins. The tourist office can provide a complete listing with maps. Within the walls, seek out the **Casa de los Mosaicos** (C/ Doctor Castro, s/n), the remains of a Roman building lavishly decorated with mosaic tile work. Outside the walls, the **Termas Romanas** (Camino del Balneario, s/n, tel. 98/222-1228) are well-preserved Roman baths. The springs that fed the baths are still in use as a modern-day *balenario* (spa) and hotel erected on the same spot. The Roman ruins are contained within the ground floor. Close to the baths is a **Puente Romano** (Roman bridge) crossing the Miño.

Lugo's **Catedral** (Pr. Santa María, s/n, tel. 98/223-1038, free) is a lumbering baroque cathedral built in the 12th and 13th centuries and added onto in the 14th. Nearby, the **Museo Provincial** (Pr. Soledad 7, tel. 98/224-2112) has an extensive collection of old sundials and clocks as well as Roman artifacts and pre-Romanesque jewelry.

Outside of these few sights, there is little of interest to the camera-toting tourist. Lugo's charms rest instead within the plazas and old taverns of the walled town. Though don't expect picture perfect-charm—much of the town is neglected and bits are downright unattractive. However, the city is working to promote itself as a tourist destination, so you can expect improvement. Also, as Lugo is still way off the path for English-speaking tourists, the citizens and tourist offices tend to be very friendly and proud to point you towards their favorite sight, restaurant, or bar—they may even join you!

Accommodations

Sleeping with history comes cheap in Lugo. Very comfortable double rooms at the **(Balneario y Termas de Lugo** (Barrio del Puente, s/n, tel. 98/222-1228, www.balneario delugo.com, €58) come complete with one circuit in the hotel's spa—and, of course, you can visit the Roman baths on the ground floor. Spa treatments range from baths to massages to facials and start at €8. Even lower on the price scale is the cozy **Hostel Paramés** (C/ Progreso 28, tel. 98/222-6251, €28), which has a good Galician restaurant. The simple rooms at **Mar de Plata** (Ronda Muralla 5, tel. 98/222-8910, €30) come with views of the walls. If you want big hotel luxury, head to **Gran Hotel Lugo** (Av. Ramón Ferreiro 21, tel. 98/222-4152, www.gh-hoteles.com, €100), Lugo's most esteemed hotel. It offers spacious contemporary rooms in a large building located in a lovely garden just outside of the walls. It is mainly a business hotel, so prices go up during the week.

Food

For tapas, head to Praza del Campo and its surrounding streets: Rúa Nova, Rúa da Cruz, and Rúa Bispo Basulto. For dining, **Mesón de Alberto** (C/ Cruz 4, tel. 98/222-8310, 10:30 A.M.–4 P.M. and 8 P.M.–12:30 A.M. Mon.–Sat., closed Sun., €36) is a top-rated local favorite in a charming stone house. Food is pure Galician with just a hint of modernity. **Verruga** (C/ Cruz 12, tel. 98/222-9572, closed Sun. P.M. and Mon., €30) has offered classic Galician fare—particularly local fish—for over half a century. **Campos** (C/ Nova, 4, tel. 98/222-9743, closed Mon., €40) is Lugo's most acclaimed restaurant. Again, the fare is local Galician and the quality is impeccable.

Information

The **city tourism office** (Pr. Constitución, tel. 98/229-7347, www.lugoturismo.com,

10 A.M.–2 P.M. and 4:30–7 P.M. Mon –Fri,, 10 A.M.–2 P.M. Sat., closed Sun.) offers city maps and thematic walking tours such as "Lugo Romano." The **Xunta de Galicia** (Pr. Maior 27, tel. 98/223-1361, www.turgalicia .es, 10 A.M.–2 P.M. and 4–8 P.M. Mon.–Sun. summer; 10 A.M.–2 P.M. and 4–7 P.M. Mon.–Sat., closed Sun. winter) offers information and maps on all of Galicia.

Getting There
Lugo's **Estación de Tren** (Pr. Conde Fontao,

s/n) is operated by **Renfe** (tel. 90/224-0202, www.renfe.es) and located about 10 minutes from the city by foot. The **Estación de Autobuses** (Pr. Constitución, s/n, tel. 98/222-3985) is serviced by **Alsa** (www.alsa.es) and **Monbus** (www.monbus.es). By car, Lugo lies on the A-6/N-6 that runs from Madrid to La Coruña. Ourense is to the south, just over an hour, via the N-540. To Santiago, take the N-6 north, then swing south onto the N-634 (though there are also many small winding back roads between Lugo and Santiago).

EXTREMADURA

Lying on the border of Portugal, hemmed in by mountains and rivers all around, Extremadura is a nearly unspoiled tract of Spanish countryside. With just over one million people throughout the entire autonomous region, Extremadura is the least populated area in Spain. Once you get off the main roads, life slows to history's laborious pace. Ancient agricultural traditions of herding sheep, curing ham, making cheese, and pressing olives still dominate the countryside and small towns. Much of the land is worked by landless laborers and owned by absent landlords. Poverty has long been associated with this land and one of the most important films in Spanish social consciousness, Luis Buñuel's 1933 masterpiece *Tierra sin Pan (Land Without Bread)*, was filmed in Extremadura. It depicts the heart-wrenching poverty that gripped this area pre–Civil War. Though things are much improved, the image of Extremadura as a poor, backward land persists. For centuries, locals left the region by the boat, carriage, and trainload, seeking a brighter future in Sevilla, Madrid, Barcelona, and beyond. In the 15th century, some of the most famous conquistadors in the world hailed from Extremadura—Cortés, Pizarro, Nuñez de Balboa. The exodus continues today as young people look for more excitement and opportunities than sleepy Extremadura can offer.

This image of Extremadura is slowly being replaced with the recognition that this mostly unexploited land is a national treasure brimming with gorgeous valleys and rivers, pristine natural parks, forests of oak, cork, and olive trees, and kilometers of virgin land-

HIGHLIGHTS

■ Ciudad Monumental: One of the most atmospheric places in Spain, the aptly named "monumental city" of Cáceres is a perfectly preserved walled wonderland of stone mansions and palaces dating from the 15th and 16th centuries (page 543).

■ La Villa: Built of golden-hued stone by conquistadors who found their fortunes in the New World, the medieval core of Trujillo rises from the southern plains of Extremadura like an invitation back in time (page 550).

■ Guadalupe: Dominating its pint-sized medieval city, the massive monastery of Guadalupe, built between the 14th and 15th centuries, is one of the Hispanic world's most venerated shrines. It is also an expansive retrospective of Spanish architecture with Gothic, Mudejar, Renaissance, and baroque details (page 553).

■ Teatro y Anfiteatro Romano: When Mérida was one of the ancient Rome's most important cities, this theater and amphitheater were the star attractions – hosting both classic theater and gladiator battles. Modern Mérida's summer theater festival is held right in the nearly 2,000-year-old theater (page 558).

■ Casas Romanas: Roman Mérida was a wealthy retirement community for Roman soldiers and politicians. Insight into their ancient daily lives is displayed in the well-preserved ruins of their homes – from mosaic walls to interior plumbing (page 558).

■ Zafra: Between Mérida and Sevilla, charming Zafra is just far enough off the tourist trail to retain its true Spanish flavor. In addition to a lovely Plaza Mayor and a few centuries-old stone mansions, the joy of this town is spending the night in a 15th-century Mudejar palace (page 562).

LOOK FOR **■** TO FIND RECOMMENDED SIGHTS, ACTIVITIES, DINING, AND LODGING.

scape. Weekenders—mostly Spanish—have begun to arrive and *casas rurales* (country inns) are popping up in even the most desolate of towns. They are drawn also to a handful of cities boasting spectacular architecture. Cáceres and Trujillo shimmer with honeycombed centers lined with 16th-century stone mansions paid for by New World gold. Mérida boasts a wealth of Roman ruins—the most in Spain and some of the best preserved in

the world. Tiny Guadalupe is home to one of Spain's most impressive medieval monasteries and one of the Catholic world's most venerated images—the Virgen de Guadalupe. These four cities are Extremadura's jewels and will reward handsomely the intrepid traveler.

Extremadura's long agricultural tradition has given rise to foods and dishes that are prized throughout Spain and beyond and a trip in this land is a delicious gastronomic adventure. *Extremeño* cuisine, not surprisingly, is hearty and simple. Some of the best *jamón* in the country comes from Extremadura's famed dark-coated, black-hoofed Iberian pigs. *Jamón ibérico* is highly sought after throughout Spain and appears on all the finest menus. (See sidebar, Jamón, Jamón.) There are also dozens of other cured meat products, including chorizos and sausages. For the adventurous, try *morcilla patatera,* a blood sausage made with potatoes, paprika, and garlic. It is exquisite.

Extremadura also has a wonderful reputation for its *quesos* (cheeses). The star is *torta del Casar,* a creamy, almost liquid sheep's milk cheese that has a very strong, piquant flavor and a sumptuous buttery texture. Many restaurants in Extremadura will offer a *surtido* (selection) of *quesos, ibéricos* (cured Iberian pork products), or *embutidos* (cured meats in general). This is the best way to sample these delicious products. Remember, you can bring the cheese home—sealed, of course—but United

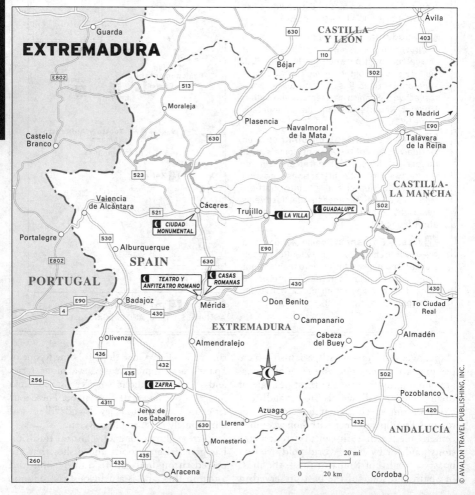

© AVALON TRAVEL PUBLISHING, INC.

States Customs does not allow the import of any meat products.

Other *extremeño* dishes you'll find on the menu are *calderetas* (stews, often of lamb or goat), *cordero asado* (roasted lamb), *migas* (a savory bread stuffing with chorizo), and *zarangollo* (a potato dish with roasted red peppers). While these dishes are all hearty, peasant fare, the region also has a tradition of sophisticated dishes, hailing mostly from monasteries that once served kings. The most famous is *perdiz a la Alcántara,* pheasant stuffed with truffles and pâté and marinated in port.

PLANNING YOUR TIME

Extremadura is divided into two provinces, Cáceres to the north and Badajoz in the south. Cáceres city is the capital of the former and an excellent place to begin touring Extremadura. Basing yourself there will allow you to either take buses or a rental car to the region's best sights—Trujillo, Guadalupe, and Mérida. At an absolute minimum, in a day and a half you can see the jeweled cities of Cáceres and Trujillo. Visiting the other two towns will re-

quire two more days. An itinerary would be to spend the first day and night one in Cáceres. Day two, travel to Guadalupe, see the monastery, then backtrack to Trujillo and spend the night. Day three, head down to Mérida and spend the day and night among the city's amazing Roman ruins. Day four, head back to your city of origin. If you have more time and are willing to rent a car, hop on a bike, or slap on hiking shoes and a backpack, consider getting off the beaten path and onto the Roman one. The Vía de la Plata is a 2,000-year-old Roman road that stretches from Gijón on the Sea of Cantabria to Sevilla in Andalucía and cuts right through the center of Extremadura, north to south. (See sidebar, *On the Roman Road Again.*)

Weather-wise, you want to avoid Extremadura in July and August when the daily temperatures can reach up to 38°C (100°F). Winter, on the other extreme, can be very cold. The best time to visit is fall or spring. Though book ahead if traveling to Cáceres or Trujillo in May—the WOMAD festival takes over the region and hotels go very fast.

Cáceres

The medieval city of Cáceres is located on the undulating khaki-colored countryside almost in the center of Extremadura. It is famed for its excess of monumental buildings from the 15th and 16th centuries that rise from the city's historic heart as golden-hued testament to Cáceres' ancient wealth and prestige. Although human settlements have been present in Cáceres since prehistoric times, it wasn't until 34 B.C. that the Romans founded the town they called Norba Caesarina. They built a defensive wall—parts of which can still be seen today—and designed the first urban center on the site. After a decline during the Visigothic domination of Iberia, the town reclaimed its importance under the Moors when it was turned into a strategic military point, with a new defensive wall, a mosque, and an *alcazar* (citadel).

King Alfonso IX conquered the town in 1229 and added Cáceres to his growing Castilian Kingdom. From this point, rather than fighting external enemies, the local nobility fought viciously to gain power over the city's government. The noble families attacked each other from high towers built on top of their palaces—all located within the town walls. It wasn't until 1477, when Queen Isabel the Catholic ordered the towers destroyed, that the fighting stopped.

Cáceres is also well-known for its conquistadors and explorers. Many of the town's residents left their homes in the early days of the conquests in America, returning home with fortunes to build palaces and other monumental structures. Most of the city's important historic and impressive

EXTREMADURA

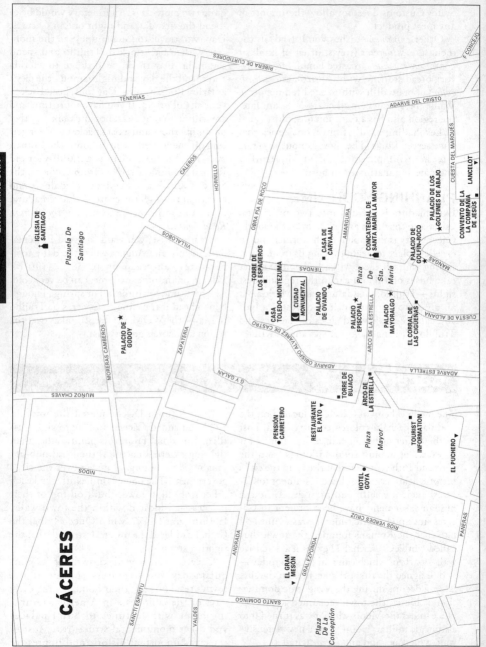

CÁCERES

IGLESIA DE SANTIAGO

Plazuela De Santiago

RIBERA DE CURTIDORES

TENERÍAS

ADARVE DEL CRISTO

CUESTA DEL MARQUÉS

CALEROS

HORNILLO

OBRA PÍA DE ROCO

PALACIO DE LOS GOLFINES DE ABAJO

LANCELOT

CONVENTO DE LA COMPAÑÍA DE JESÚS

VILLALOBOS

SOBOLOBOS

AMARGURA

CASA DE CARVAJAL

CONCATEDRAL DE SANTA MARÍA LA MAYOR

PALACIO DE GOLFÍN-ROCO

TORRE DE LOS ESPADEROS

TIENDAS

MANOS

MORERAS CAMBEROS

PALACIO DE GODOY

ZAPATERÍA

ADARVE OBISPO ÁLVAREZ DE CASTRO

CASA TOLEDO-MONTEZUMA

CIUDAD MONUMENTAL

PALACIO DE OVANDO

Plaza De Sta. María

PALACIO EPISCOPAL

ARCO DE LA ESTRELLA

PALACIO MAYORALGO

EL CORRAL DE LAS CIGÜEÑAS

CUESTA DE ALDANA

MUÑOZ CHAVES

G Y GALÁN

TORRE DE BUJACO

ARCO DE LA ESTRELLA

ADARVE ESTRELLA

NIDOS

PENSIÓN CARRETERO

RESTAURANTE EL PATO

Plaza Mayor

TOURIST INFORMATION

EL PUCHERO

ANDRADA

SANTO DOMINGO

GRAL ESPONDA

RÍOS VERDES CRUZ

HOTEL GOYA

PANERAS

SANCTI ESPÍRITU

VALDÉS

EL GRAN MESÓN

Plaza De La Concepción

F CONCEJO

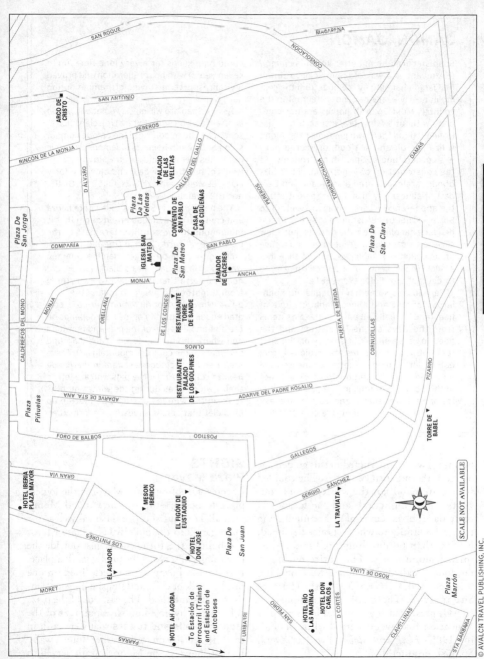

EXTREMADURA

SAN ROQUE

MAGDALENA

CONSOLACIÓN

■ ARCO DE CRISTO

SAN ANTONIO

PEREROS

RINCÓN DE LA MONJA

D. ÁLVARO

★ PALACIO DE LAS VELETAS

CALLEJÓN DEL GALLO

Plaza De Las Veletas

DAMAS

TORNEMOCHADA

PEREROS

Plaza De San Jorge

COMPANÍA

IGLESIA SAN MATEO †

■ CONVENTO DE SAN PABLO

■ CASA DE LAS CIGÜEÑAS

Plaza De Sta. Clara

SAN PABLO

Plaza De San Mateo

PARADOR DE CÁCERES

ANCHA

MONJA

CALDEREROS DEL MONO

MONJA

ORELLANA

DE LOS CONDES

RESTAURANTE TORRE DE SANDE

OLMOS

PUERTA DE MÉRIDA

CORNUDILLAS

RESTAURANTE PALACIO DE LOS GOLFINES

ADARVE DE STA. ANA

ADARVE DEL PADRE ROSALIO

PIZARRO

Plaza Piñuelas

▼ TORRE DE BABEL

FORO DE BALBOS

POSTIGO

GALLEGOS

HOTEL IBERIA PLAZA MAYOR ●

GRAN VÍA

▼ MESÓN IBÉRICO

EL FIGÓN DE EUSTAQUIO ▼

Plaza De San Juan

SERGIO SÁNCHEZ

LA TRAVIATA ▼

LOS PINTORES

HOTEL DON JOSÉ ●

EL ASADOR ▼

ROSO DE LUNA

Plaza Marrón

MORET

● HOTEL AH AGORA

To Estación de Ferrocarril (Trains) and Estación de Autobuses

F. URIBARRI

SAN PEDRO

HOTEL RÍO ● LAS MARINAS

HOTEL DON ● CARLOS

D. CORTÉS

CLAVELLINAS

STA. BÁRBARA

PARRAS

SCALE NOT AVAILABLE

JAMÓN, JAMÓN

Spanish cured ham, better known as *jamón* (HA-moan), is a way of life in Spain. You will find *jamón* hanging by the hoof from the ceiling in nearly every bar and restaurant in the country. Most Spanish homes are not complete without a *jamonera*, a special rack designed to hold their own personal ham. Along with olive oil and seafood, dry-cured pork is a cornerstone of Spanish gastronomy. To the consternation of vegetarians, little bits of ham are considered a spice and can be a part of almost any dish. Do not be put off by the appearance – certainly many visitors to Spain will not be accustomed to seeing an appendage dangling from the rafters – but a few slices on a sandwich, wrapped around a slice of melon in the summer, or, best of all, eaten straight in thin hand-cut slices could make you forget that prosciutto even exists.

Perhaps, as some have suggested, Spaniards' fervent and almost fanatical love of ham (and virtually all parts of the pig) stems from the days of the Inquisition and the need to prove one's Christianity on the spot (both Jews and Muslims are forbidden from eating pork). In any case, cured meats were an ancient and ingenious part of the diet in the poorest regions in Spain, such as Extremadura, Andalucía, and Castile. In these semi-arid and less-than-fertile climates, dry-cured ham keeps for a very long time (up to seven years) with no refrigeration and proved a vital resource in staving off famine during hard times.

As any Spaniard will quickly point out, *jamón* is also good for you. Extensive scientific research has been done into the unique composition and health benefits of *jamón*. Like olive oil, it has been found to contain very high levels of healthy omega-3 and omega-6 fatty acids, as well as antioxidants, folic acid, B1, B6, and B12 vitamins.

The best *jamón* in Spain is called **pata negra** and comes from a unique breed of pig that is indigenous to the southwestern part of the peninsula: *el cerdo ibérico* (the Iberian pig). This pig tends to be darker than the common white pig and usually has a black hoof – *pata negra*, a term that is applied to everything from tomatoes to music to mean "the very best." However, not all *jamón ibérico* is created equal. The quality of the ham depends on the diet and lifestyle of the pigs and how long and where the ham is cured (usually around two years in the cool, dry mountain air). There are three basic categories. **Jamón ibérico de bellota** comes from lucky pigs who are left to their own devices during the winter months to roam the wooded pastures and fatten up on a diet that consists mostly of acorns (*bel-*

---

buildings were constructed in this golden age of the 15th and 16th centuries. The cobbled streets are winding, the churches and convents are monumental, and the facades of the palaces boast coats of arms announcing the grand family to whom it once belonged. No less than 60 buildings are listed as historical monuments. The entire old quarter, locally called the Ciudad Monumental, was declared a UNESCO World Heritage Site in 1986. The medieval atmosphere is so well preserved that Cáceres has served as a location for several period films, including 1985's *Flesh and Blood* as well as several Spanish productions.

SIGHTS
Plaza Mayor

Cáceres' rambling Plaza Mayor is the logical place to begin a tour of the Ciudad Monumental. The tourist office is here as well as the main gate into the old city. The Plaza Mayor was built in the 16th century just outside the town walls to serve as the public market place. It still has a buzzy market feel, lined on one side by outdoor cafés and shops selling local artisan crafts and food. The east side of the plaza is bordered by an impressive remnant of the **Moorish walls and towers** that were built in the 12th century on top of earlier Roman walls. In their heyday, the Moorish walls served to

Iotas) from holm oaks and cork trees. **Jamón ibérico de recebo** comes from pigs that are allowed to feed free-range on acorns and are then fattened up at the end of the season with a high-quality grain. **Jamón ibérico de pienso** is the least prized and comes from pigs that are generally kept in stables and are fed a diet of feed and grass.

Jamón serrano (literally "mountain ham"), also known as **jamón curado** (cured ham), is made from common white pigs. While it is delicious – particularly that from Teruel – it cannot compete with the sweet flavor, marbled composition, and nutty richness of *jamón ibérico*. Due to USDA regulations, *pata negra* and the best *jamón serrano* are not available in the United States.

In case you still are not convinced that the Spanish take their ham very, very seriously – as with wine, cheese, and other delicacies – there is a governing body that regulates the entire *jamón*-making process to ensure that the quality of the product is tightly controlled. Those regions that have been proven to produce an outstanding product can receive a *denominación de origen* or D.O., an appellation. The following regions have D.O. status for *jamón ibérico*: Dehesa de Extremadura, Guijuelo, Los Pedroches, and Jamón de Huelva, also known as Jabugo, for the main ham-producing town in this region. Two specific brands are often cited as the best: 5J (Cinco Jotas) from Sánchez Romero Carvajal (D.O. Huelva) and Joselito Reserva (D.O. Guijuelo). There are two D.O. designations for regular, non-*ibérico jamón serrano*: Jamón de Teruel and Jamón de Trévelez.

At a price of up to €120 per kilo (about €55 per pound), a love of *jamón* could turn into a costly addiction. Luckily, a few divine slices with the accompaniment of a fine sherry are really all one needs to appreciate the rich and complex flavor. You can sample *jamón* in tapas bars and restaurants. If it is not on the menu, you can nearly always ask for it. An even better and more affordable option is to have a picnic – buy 100 grams of the very best ham you can afford at a market *charcutería* or *fiambrería* (stores that sell cold cuts). To find a sublime ham, look for meat that is marbled with golden-colored fat (remember, it is good for you and the fat has a wonderful nutty flavor). Ask to have it hand cut (*cortado a mano*); the meat is so delicate and buttery that a machine slicer can damage it.

(*Contributed by Megan Cytron, who lives in Madrid and has been studying and writing about Spanish language, literature, and culture for over 15 years. She eats* jamón *almost every day.*)

---

defend the city from Christian attacks. Today, the towers are home to boat-sized storks' nests. The most impressive tower is **Torre de Bujaco** (10 A.M.–2 P.M. and 5:30–8:30 P.M. Mon.–Sat., closed Sun., free), a square tower in excellent condition. The steps next to it lead to the **Arco de la Estrella** also known as the Puerta Nueva, the impressive official entrance to the old city. Though the gate was built in the 15th century, its lovely baroque facade was added in the 18th century. Just to the north of here is **Casa Toledo-Montezuma,** where it is said that one of Cortés's men brought back one of the most treasured prizes from America—the Aztec emperor's daughter as his bride.

◖ Ciudad Monumental

Continue through the gate and into the walled enclosure to the Plaza de Santa María, a charming little square that is home to the **Concatedral de Santa María la Mayor** (9:30 A.M.–2 P.M. and 5–7:30 P.M. Mon.–Sat., 8:30 A.M.–2 P.M. and 4–7:30 P.M. Sun., free), the most important church in the city. The church was finished in the 16th century, after several hundred years of construction. This explains the combination of architectural styles that include two Gothic facades and a Renaissance tower. Within are the Renaissance and Gothic tombs of many of Cáceres' wealthy families. Don't miss the 16th-century Plateresque altar. An engraving of the Black Christ, the organ, and the alabaster baptismal fonts are also worth a look. If you are single and would rather not be, be sure to kiss the feet of the shiny-toed San Pedro of Alcántara on the outside corner as you exit. Legend says that if you do so, you will soon find a spouse! The plaza is also home to the **Palacio Episcopal,** begun in the 13th century; the **Palacio Mayoralgo,** a 16th-century palace with an impressive coat of arms from the noble Blazquez family; and the beautiful **Palacio de Ovando,** a 16th-century palace reformed in the 18th century with a half-moon-shaped door.

Turn left onto Calle Tiendas to admire the 16th-century **Casa de Carvajal** with its lovely corner balcony, courtyard, and cylindrical Muslim tower dating from the 12th century. A little further down the street brings you to the **Torre de los Espaderos,** a 14th-century Mudejar tower.

Round a few more corners toward the sloping Calle Aldana and along the way you will pass the Renaissance-era **Palacio de la Diputación**

© CELLAR TOURS/WWW.CELLARTOURS.COM

an alley lined with 16th-century stone mansions in Cáceres

and the 16th-century **Palacio de Golfin-Roco** before you are struck by the magnificent view of the **Convento de la La Compañía de Jesús** (Pl. San Jorge, s/n, 11 A.M.–2 P.M. and 5:30–8 P.M. daily, free) rising at the end of Calle Caldereros del Mono. The baroque convent dates from the 18th century and is a pleasing contrast to the medieval and Renaissance buildings around it. It is especially impressive at night when lit up. Plaza de San Jorge is also home to the massive 15th-century **Palacio de los Golfines de Abajo,** one of the most representative buildings of the city. This Gothic palace/fortress is where the Catholic monarchs Fernando and Isabel stayed when in town and what stands out most are the uneven towers and the elaborate coats of arms decorating the facade.

Walk up the slight slope of the Cuesta de la Companía, and you will come onto the **Plaza San Mateo,** surrounded by yet another cluster of fascinating historic buildings—including the 15th-century **Casa de Las Cigueñas,** one of the few buildings that was allowed to keep its battlement tower by special privilege of Queen Isabel. The plaza is also home to **Convento de San Pablo,** a 15th-century Gothic convent and church and **Iglesia San Mateo,** a 14th-century church, erected on the grounds of an Arab mosque. The church was added on to in the 16th, 18th, and 20th centuries.

Just east of San Mateo is the magnificent 16th-century **Palacio de las Veletas** (Pl. Veletas, s/n, 9:30 A.M.–2:30 P.M. and 5–8:30 P.M. Tues.–Sat., 10 A.M.–2 P.M. Sun., closed Mon., €1.50). Remodeled with a Renaissance facade in the 18th century, the building looks pretty much in line with all the other magnificent monuments in the old quarter, but it was built on the site of a 12th-century Moorish citadel building. The original interior *aljibe* (cistern) is the second largest that is still intact in the world (the largest is in Istanbul). The building's interior boasts row upon row of arches and columns. Though built in the Renaissance period and of Tuscan style, they evoke images of the great mosque in Córdoba.

Continue east into the **Barrio San Antonio,** which was once the Barrio Judio, or old Jewish

The buildings of Cáceres's Ciudad Monumental boast mammoth stone crests.

Quarter. Here the **Arco de Cristo** is the only city gate that survives from the original Roman wall. In this barrio, the best thing to do is just get lost in its twisting streets full of medieval houses and modern cafés and bar.

Outside the Ciudad Monumental
There are a few notable sights outside of the old quarter, in particular, the **Iglesia de Santiago** (Pl. Santiago, s/n), a 14th-century Gothic church with a gloomy, looming facade and fanciful 16th-century interior naves and vaulted ceilings. Closer to the Plaza Mayer, just outside the old town is the 16th-century **Palacio de Godoy** (C/ Camberos) with its fascinating corner balcony.

ENTERTAINMENT AND EVENTS
Nightlife
The Plaza Mayor is the party focal point for the city's large university crowd. It has several bars with terraces plus clubs like **Berlin Rock Bar** (Pl. Mayor 21) and the very popular pub **Belle**

Epoque (C/ General Ezponda) just off the plaza. Many of the kids just skip the bars altogether and have a *botellón* (a BYOB street party) right in the middle of the plaza. Older (or at least more discriminating) partiers head just south of the Ciudad Monumental to **Calle Pizarro** and surrounding streets which teems with bar after lively bar filled to bursting until the wee hours. Try the **Torre de Babel** (C/ Pizarro 8) or the trendy **La Traviata** (C/ Sergio Sánchez 7), which has DJs and art expositions. If you want something a little quieter, head to **El Corral de las Cigüeñas** (C/ Cuesta de Aldana 6), a converted medieval house and garden where you can relax in the peaceful sunshine over a coffee by day and listen to live music (jazz, blues, and flamenco) over a glass of wine by night. Not far from here you'll find the English pub **Lancelot** (C/ Rincón de la Monja 2), a buzzing bar with a decidedly medieval feel. Located in a centuries old palace, the bar is popular all day and night. The owner Georges is Spanish though his family is British and he loves to practice his English while talking about Cáceres.

Festivals and Events
Aside from the many traditional holidays celebrated throughout Spain, including a magnificent Semana Santa celebration, Cáceres has its own local parties, the best of which is **Fiesta de San Jorge** (Saint George's Day). Every April 23, the city congregates in Plaza Mayor to watch a battle between the *moros y cristianos* (Moors and Christians). Townspeople, dressed in elaborate medieval costumes as factions of Christian and Moorish soldiers, relive the battles of King Alfonso's men as they won the region back from the Moors. Then there is a reenactment of St. George, the patron saint of the town, killing a mythical dragon. The event concludes with a bang of all-night partying beneath a massive fireworks show.

In May, thousands of spectators from throughout Europe flock to the outskirts of Cáceres for the **WOMAD** (World of Music, Art, and Dance) festival. Founded in 1982 by musician Peter Gabriel, the event (www.womad.org) is one of the planet's premier world music festivals, drawing top artists from around the globe.

EXTREMADURA

ACCOMMODATIONS
Under €50

It isn't hard to find cheap sleeps in the center of Cáceres. **Hotel Goya** (Pl. Mayor 31, tel. 92/724-9950, www.hotelgoya.net, €45) is located right on the city's liveliest plaza. Exterior rooms cost a bit more (€54), but remember that this is party central; the people-watching will be fun, but bring earplugs if you expect to sleep. **Pensión Carretero** (Pl. Mayor 23, tel. 92/724-7482, €25) is about as low as you can go. Rooms are very basic, but the location rocks. **Hostal Alqazeres** (C/ Camino Llano 34, tel. 92/722-7000, €37) is also very simple, yet clean, and the staff is absolutely accommodating. In the new part of the city, closer to both the train and bus stations, you'll find **Hostal Neptuno** (Av. Alemania 19, tel. 92/723-6423), a two-star lodging in a new building.

€50-100

Hotel Iberia Plaza Mayor (C/ Pintores 2 tel. 92/724-7634, www.iberiahotel.com, €55) is located in an 18th-century palace right off the Plaza Mayor. Each room is individually decorated and features antique headboards. The antiques continue throughout the house, including in the brothel-meets–Queen Anne salon. **Don José** (C/ Pintores 28, tel. 92/721-2192, www.hoteldonjose.net, €50) has a lovely stone entrance that leads to a new, very clean place to sleep. **Hotel Iberia Plaza de América** (C/ Hermandad 12, tel. 92/721-0906, www.iberiahotel.com, €62) has the same antique styling as its Plaza Mayor sister, but in a new building with a bit more space to the rooms. It is a 10-minute walk from the Ciudad Monumental. **Hotel Don Carlos** (C/ Donoso Cortés 15 tel. 92/722-5356, www.hoteldoncarlos caceres.net, €70) is a wonderfully renovated old house with rustic details. Some rooms can be on the small side, so don't hesitate to request a change if needed. It is located very close to the nightlife zone of Calle Pizarro.

Over €100

◖ Parador de Cáceres (C/ Ancha 6, tel. 92/721-1759, caceres@parador.es, www.parador.es, €135) is one of the most atmospheric paradors (luxury state-run hotels) in Spain. Housed in a 14th-century conquistador mansion in the Ciudad Monumental, the parador features spacious rooms and bathrooms and majestic public spaces. The in-house restaurant, Torreorgaz, serves exquisite local fare. **Río Las Marinas** (C/ San Pedro 16 tel. 92/721-4578, www.gruporio dehoteles.com, €125) is a very central, very comfortable four-star hotel. The sophisticated, yet rustic, rooms feature whirlpool baths and comfortable mattresses. **Hotel AH Agora** (C/ Parras 25, tel. 92/762-6360, www.ahhotels.com, €135) is a modern, sleek hotel with airy, spacious rooms done up in contemporary, pale shades with red accents. It is located less than 10 minutes from Plaza Mayor. A little further out from the center is the **Hotel Extremadura** (Av. Virgen de Guadalupe 28, tel. 92/762-9639, www.extremadurahotel.com, €120), with sleek, modern rooms, large bathrooms, and a refreshing pool. It's a good choice for those driving into town, as it's located on the main road to Salamanca and has an underground parking lot (€10).

FOOD
Gourmet

Atrio (Av. España 30, Bloque 4, tel. 92/724-2928, 2–4 P.M. and 9–11 P.M. Mon.–Sat., 2–4 P.M. Sun., €100) was voted by *Wine Spectator* as having one of the best wine lists in the world. With a cellar of over 25,000 bottles and no less than 2,000 on the list at any given time, the wine list is indeed spectacular. Packaged as an art book, you can take a copy home for around €80. Wine bottle prices run from €30 to over €3,000. The wine is paired with adventurous Spanish and *extremeño* fare prepared with an emphasis on impeccable ingredients and creative touches. Game is always a good bet here. The restaurant is warm and elegant and the service friendly. Make reservations. **Torre de Sande** (C/ Condes 3, tel. 92/721-1147, 2–4 P.M. and 9:30–11:30 P.M. Tues.–Sat., 2–4 P.M. Mon., closed Sun., €40) offers creative local cuisine in a restored 15th-century palace. Sit in the lovely gardened terrace in warm weather. **Palacio de los Golfines** (C/ Adarve del Padre Rosalío 2, tel. 92/724-2414) is located in an atmospheric 15th-century palace. The cuisine relies on local produce and the chef's creative touch. Try any of their exquisite seafood dishes.

Local Cuisine

(**El Figón de Eustaquio** (Pl. San Juan14, tel. 92/724-4362, €25) serves the heartiest of *extremeño* fare such as partridge stew and roasted venison in a cozy warren of dining rooms. **El Galeón** (C/ Motril, 3, tel. 92/721-3609, 1:30–4 P.M. and 8:30 P.M.–midnight daily, €18) is famed for its meat dishes, especially *solomillo ibérico al Jerez* (Iberian pork loin in sherry). **Mesón Ibérico** (Pl. San Juan 10, tel. 92/722-2959) has wonderful cured hams and excellent game, particularly *conejo al ajillo* (rabbit in garlic). **El Gran Mesón** (C/ General Ezponda 7, tel. tel. 92/724-7726, €20) is decorated with bullfighting memorabilia and serves regional cuisine with just a hint of modernity.

Tapas

The Plaza Mayor is lined with boisterous bars where the tapas are hearty and the wine is *pitarra* (home brew). **Restaurante El Pato** (Pl. Mayor 12, tel. 92/724-8736, noon–4 P.M. and 8 P.M.–midnight daily) is a classic, serving local specialties including the house favorite *ancas de rana* (frog legs). They also offer a wonderful variety of local goat cheeses. **El Puchero** (Pl. Mayor 9, tel. 92/724-5497, 1–4:30 P.M. and 9:30 P.M.–midnight daily) is another favorite with cheap tapas and a very lively terrace. **La Fusa** (C/ San Pedro 4, tel. 92/721-3351, 2–4 P.M. and 8–11 P.M. daily) draws design inspiration from the Ciudad Monumental with a very cloak-and-dagger interior. It would be kitschy if it weren't actually medieval. **El Asador** (C/ Moret 34, tel. 92/722-3837, 1:30–4 P.M. and 8:30 P.M.–1:30 A.M. daily) is known for its simple yet sophisticated tapas, such as a wide variety of artisan cheeses. They also have an excellent wine list by the glass. Note that each of these tapas bars also has an attached restaurant serving traditional fare.

INFORMATION

The **regional tourist office** (Pl. Mayor 3, tel. 92/701-0834, www.turisimoextremadura.com, 9:30 A.M.–2 P.M. and 4–6:30 P.M. Mon.–Fri., 9:45 A.M.–2 P.M. Sat.–Sun.) is your best bet for information on both Cáceres and Extremadura in general. The local tourist office is right next door, but they have very little information in English. At both, you can sign up for **guided walking tours** (€4) that take you around the network of tiny streets and squares and explain the overlapping stories of each of the dozens of historic sites.

GETTING THERE
Train

The **Estación de Ferrocarril** (Av. Alemania, tel. 92/722-5061) is run by **Renfe** (tel. 90/224-0202, www.renfe.es), which has daily trains to Badajoz, Madrid, Sevilla, and Barcelona.

Bus

Cáceres' **Estación de Autobuses** (C/ Tunez, s/n, tel. 92/723-2550, www.estacionautobuses .com) is serviced by **Auto-Res** (tel. 90/202-0999, www.auto-res.net), which goes pretty much anywhere in Spain. **Mirat** (tel. 92/723-4863, www.mirat.net) handles many of the local connections through Extremadura including to Guadalupe (1 and 5 P.M. Mon.–Fri., 1 P.M. Sat.) and Trujillo (1, 3, and 5 P.M. Mon.–Fri., 1 P.M. Sat.).

Car

Cáceres sits on the N-630, which runs north–south right through Extremadura. Going east–west, Cáceres is on the N-521 running to Trujillo, where you can catch the A-5/E-90 north towards Madrid.

VICINITY OF CÁCERES
Alcántara

Just over an hour northeast of Cáceres lies the sun-baked village of Alcántara. Separated from Portugal by a border locally called La Raya, it makes a good stop if you are driving into Portugal—if for no other reason than to see its outstanding **Puente Romano** (Roman

Bridge). Built around A.D. 2, the bridge sits on the western edge of town, a living testament to the engineering skills of the Romans. Spanning the Río Tajo, the stone structure measures over 193 meters (636 feet), rises some 65 meters (213 feet), and consists of six half-moon arches. At the center is an arch believed to have been built in honor of Roman Emperor Trajan, but it bears plaques honoring Fernando and Isabel, the Catholic Kings. In a niche, at the entrance to the bridge, is a plaque bearing the name of its long-dead Roman builder: Cayo Julio Lacer. Very close to the bridge is the **Embalse de Alcántara,** a huge reservoir created by a massive dam—the second largest in Europe.

In town, the most enjoyable sight is the dusky little town itself. During the Reconquista, Alcántara was the seat of the powerful *Orden de Alcántara,* a group of knights who controlled a great deal of land. They built the **Convento de San Benito** (C/ Regimiento de Argel 43, tel. 93/739-0080, closed Sun. P.M., free) in the 1600s. A pleasing blend of Gothic, Renaissance, and Plateresque architecture styles, the building has a stunning double-layered cloister and lovely inner chapels. During the Napoleonic invasion of Spain in the 1800s, French troops took a recipe book from the convent that dated back to the time of the Order of Alcántara. It was sent back to France and the dishes were incorporated into French cuisine. The dish *perdices a la moda de Alcántara* (pheasant cooked with truffles and port) continues to be very popular. The convent has been impeccably restored and is a cultural center today.

If you decide to stay the night, consider a *casa rural* (a rural B&B). **Casa Candi** (C/ Cuartro Calles 8, tel. 92/739-0028, €55) is located right in the historic center of the village and has four rustic-chic rooms with magnificent stone floors. **Casa San Antonio** (C/ San Antón 40, tel. 92/739-0822, €45) boasts a charming interior patio and three very cozy rooms. There is a kitchen available as well. The few restaurants in town all offer local classics. Try the famous Alcántara pheasant at **Gundín** (Pl. Portugal 4, tel. 92/739-0143, 1–3:30 P.M. and 8 P.M.–midnight daily).

Get to Alcántara by car. Take the N-521 west, catch the EX-207 north, and follow the signs to Alcántara.

Trujillo

Like Laguardia in País Vasco, Toledo in Castilla-La Mancha, and Ávila in Castilla y León, Trujillo has the ability to transport the visitor to a time long-gone—particularly at sunset, when the falling light paints the entire town in shimmering shades of dusty pink and copper. With a clutch of finely preserved 15th- and 16th-century russet-colored stone mansions, a fine Plaza Mayor, Arabic defense walls, and a rambling Roman/Moorish/Castilian castle, Trujillo is Spanish history writ in stone. Nicknamed the "Cradle of the Conquistadors," Trujillo was the birthplace of Francisco Pizarro (1476–1541), who, along with his four stepbrothers, sought adventure and fortune in the New World. His name has become synonymous with the founding of Peru (and the decimation of Incan civilization). Francisco de Orellana (1500–1549) founded parts of Ecuador and was the first European to sail down the Amazon. He gave the river its name when he wrote of fierce women warriors attacking his ships. It is more likely that the attackers were long-haired natives, but the name Amazon—from the ancient Roman word for a female gladiator—stuck.

Founded by the Romans and later inhabited by the Visigoths, Trujillo fell under Moorish control in the 8th century. As had their predecessors, they settled on top of a hill and built the walls that still protect the upper portion of the city. They also expanded the Roman castle. This area of Trujillo is called La Villa today. After centuries of struggle, Trujillo was captured by the Christians in the 13th century.

ON THE ROMAN ROAD AGAIN

Evidence of Roman rule on the Iberian Peninsula is scattered across the country – the aqueduct in Segovia, Roman walls in Barcelona, baths in Zaragoza. One Roman legacy actually runs across the country. Originally built to connect the Roman cities of Augusta Emerita (Mérida, Extremadura) and Asturica Augusta (Astorga, León), the Vía de la Plata (Silver Route) crosses through the heart of Extremadura on its journey. A branch in the south stems off to Sevilla, while in the north it continues into Castilla y León and Asturias. The route is an increasingly popular alternative path to Santiago and is often called the Camino Mozárabe. Despite its modern translation, the name Vía de la Plata comes from the Arabic word *balat*, meaning "paved path."

After leaving Sevilla and heading north, the Vía de la Plata hits Extremadura, where it passes Zafra, Mérida, Trujillo, and Cáceres. In Castilla y León, it goes through Salamanca, Zamora, and Astorga, where it meets up with the Camino Francés, the popular northern pilgrim route from France to Santiago. The Vía de la Plata continues from Astorga north to Gijón on the Asturian coast. The total length from Sevilla to Gijón is about 1,000 kilometers (600 miles).

During its 2,000-year-plus existence, the road served every epoch of Spanish history. Citizens and soldiers under the rule of the Roman emperors Trajan and Hadrian walked this path, spreading Roman culture throughout Iberia. Later the Moors used it to make inroads into the peninsula. Christians in the Middle Ages traveled the path as pilgrims on the way to Santiago. Later, it became a popular path for shepherds moving their flocks between towns and pastures. With such a diverse past, the Vía de la Plata is not surprisingly full of historical treasure. The most intriguing aspect for many who walk the path is that miles of it are still paved with the original Roman roads complete with ancient mile makers called *miliarios*.

If you'd like to plan a walking route of the Vía de la Plata, start by doing some web research. If you are going to use the route as a basis for your pilgrimage to Santiago, you can't go wrong with a visit to the comprehensive www .santiago-compostela.net (and clicking on "Vía de la Plata") or www.theviadelaplata.com. For non-Camino related options, including suggestions on *casa rurals* (rural B&Bs), visit www .ruralplan.com and click on "Tourist Routes" and then "Vía de la Plata" in the drop-down window. The tourist site specifically for the route is www.rutadelaplata.com.

When Trujillo's conquistadors returned from their voyages in the New World, they brought with them vast riches and built many of the city's most atmospheric stone palaces, both within the walls of the upper town and in the lower portion of town around Plaza Mayor. This part of the city is called the Cuidad Extramuro (City Outside of the Walls).

SIGHTS

A walking tour of Trujillo most logically begins in the Plaza Mayor, Trujillo's bustling nerve center. The tourist office is located there and can help arrange walking tours of the city, as well as provide maps and information. But be ready: Most of the city rambles upward on crooked, cobbled streets. If you're not feeling fit or are pressed for time, take a cab to the Castillo (castle) and wind your way down. While you are exploring, be sure to turn your camera skywards. Trujillo's towers and roofs play host to large colonies of *cigueñas* (storks). Their massive nests, hanging precariously on ancient stone towers, are impressive.

Plaza Mayor

Trujillo's broad Plaza Mayor is as perfect a town plaza as it can be. Begun in the 16th century, it is lined with majestic Italian Renaissance buildings and modern, bustling cafés. Throughout the year, it hosts cultural events, concerts, and markets. At the center of the Plaza Mayor is a statue honoring Trujillo's most famous son, Francisco Pizarro. Built by an American sculptor in the 1920s, the equestrian statue has a twin in Lima, Peru.

Soaring behind the statue on the northeast corner of the plaza is the **Iglesia de San Martín,** a 16th-century Gothic church with a beautifully carved ceiling and a baroque organ. If you are lucky, the choir will be rehearsing on the night of your visit. Moving clockwise, the **Palacio de los Duques de San Carlos** (9:30 A.M.–2 P.M. and 4:30–6:30 P.M. Mon.–Sat., 10 A.M.–noon Sun., €1.30) was built in the 16th and 17th centuries and boasts a dramatic facade, a beautiful inner courtyard, and an impressive stone staircase. Today, it is home to an order of nuns who sell homemade sweets. The next building is the **Palacio de los Marqueses de Piedras Albas,** a Renaissance palace from the 16th century inspired by the Italian style, particularly of Florence. It has a wonderful interior courtyard with a double cloister, but it is not always open to the public.

A 10th-century Moorish castle still watches over Trujillo.

Palacio del Marqués de la Conquista, built in the 16th century, has the most dramatic facade of Plaza Mayor's buildings. Built for Hernando Pizarro (brother of Francisco) and his wife Francisca Pizarro Yupanqui (daughter of Pizarro and his Incan consort Inés, sister of the Incan emperor Atahualpa)—and yes, that means the happy couple were not only man and wife but uncle and niece, the Plateresque exterior of the building depicts the brothers' exploits in the New World. The two couples appear on the corner of the building in an elaborately carved balcony. Other carvings show the King of Spain, the Incan emperor, and lots of gold. The building is not open to the public. Behind this building, at the end of tiny Calle Cañón de la Carcel, stands **Palacio de los Orellana-Pizarro** (10 A.M.–1 P.M. and 4–6 P.M. Mon.–Fri., 11 A.M.–2 P.M. and 4:30–7 P.M. Sat. and Sun., free). Originally a minifortress, in the 16th century it was converted into a palace with a magnificent Renaissance courtyard. Miguel de Cervantes spent some time here after being released from prison in Sevilla. Today it houses a school.

◖ La Villa

The old walled part of the city is the perfect place to get lost. Enter through one of the four gates still standing (originally there were seven). **Puerta de Santiago** is just above the Plaza Mayor. Next to it is the **Iglesia de Santiago,** a 16th-century church built upon a base of a 13th-century Romanesque church. Continue uphill to the **Iglesia Santa María de Mayor** (tel. 92/732-3005, 10 A.M.–2 P.M. and 4–7 P.M. daily, longer hours in summer, €1.25). Originally built on the site of an Arabic mosque in the 13th century, the church underwent major restoration in the 16th century and today boasts Romanesque, Gothic, and Renaissance elements. It has a fine rose window and an outstanding Plateresque choir.

There is a trio of interesting museums to seek out in La Villa. **Museo de Traje** (10 A.M.–2 P.M. and 4:30–8:30 P.M. daily, €1.50) is a collection of clothing and costumes dating back to the 18th century, including several reproduction pieces of older outfits. It is housed in a former convent and offers a visual insight into how the residents who built this city dressed as they walked its cobbled alleyways. **Museo Casa Pizarro** (10 A.M.–2 P.M. and 4–7 P.M. daily, €1.30) is located in Francisco Pizarro's ancestral home and houses a collection of art and artifacts illustrating the connections between Spain and the New World, particularly those forged by Pizarro. Incidentally, it is unlikely the conqueror ever lived here; before he made his fortune in the New World, he was the poor, illegitimate son of a philandering local man. **Museo de la Coria** (tel. 92/732-1898, 11:30–2 P.M. weekends only, free) is housed in a former convent on the city's northwest walls. For this reason, it has a fortress-like appearance. Inside are lovely plant-filled courtyards and an extensive display of art and artifacts illustrating Spain's conquests and campaigns in the New World.

At the highest point in La Villa—a hill called Cabezo de Zorro (Fox's Head)—sits the **Castillo** (10 A.M.–2 P.M. and 4–7 P.M. daily, later in summer, €1.30), the 10th-century Moorish castle. The grounds house a 16th-century church, two Moorish *aljibes* (cisterns), and an image of Trujillo's patron saint, Virgen de la Victoria, who is credited with helping the Christians capture the city from the Moors. The views from the castle are the main reason to visit—the panoramic vistas over the city and the surrounding countryside are spectacular.

ACCOMMODATIONS
Under €50
Hostal Nuria (Pl. Mayor 17, tel. 92/732-0907, €40) offers five cozy rooms with the basic amenities (air-conditioning, en-suite baths) and a couple of the rooms open up onto the Plaza Mayor. It is noisy, but the view is worth it. **Hostal Restaurante Trujillo** (C/ Francisco Pizarro 4, tel. 92/732-2274, www.hostal trujillo.com, €38) is located in the 15th-century Hospital del Espíritu Santo, about a 10-minute walk south of Plaza Mayor. The walls are stone, the halls feature suits of armor, and the rooms are adequate, though nothing spe-

cial compared to the rest of the building. The restaurant is particularly good and very atmospheric set under medieval stone arches. Parking is available. **Hostal Mesón Hueso** (C/ Arquillo 4, tel. 92/7322-2820, www.hostal hueso.com, €45) offers basic, yet spacious, rooms in a rustic stone palace just around the corner from the Plaza Mayor. The owners arrange many outdoor activities.

€50-100
Posada Dos Orillas (C/ Cambrones 6, tel. 92/765-9079, www.dosorillas.com, €100) is an enchanting family-run inn located within the walls of La Villa. The 13 rooms are named for Latin American countries and feature low-key antiques, stone walls, rustic wood ceilings, and comfortable linens. The staff is accommodating and the in-house restaurant offers excellent Spanish and Mediterranean fare. **Hotel Victoria** (C/ Campillo 22, tel. 92/732-1819, €72), about a 10-minute walk southeast of Plaza Mayor, is a new hotel located in a lovely 19th-century building. Rooms are decorated in a mix of modern and traditional and the staff is very friendly. There is also a pool, parking, and a good in-house restaurant. **Las Cigüeñas** (Av. Madrid, s/n, tel. 92/732-1250, www.hotel asciguenas.com, €85) is located on the east side of town and is perfect for those who are driving in from Madrid. Rooms are spacious and decorated in a pleasing blend of antiques and old-fashioned charm. The in-house restaurant, La Bodega, is excellent, but often booked out for weddings; check before showing up.

Over €100
The **Parador de Trujillo** (C/ Santa Beatriz de Silva 1, tel. 92/732-1350, trujillo@parador.es, www.parador.es, €120) is located in the 16th-century Convento de Santa Clara, a five-minute walk east of the Plaza Mayor. It boasts two peaceful Renaissance cloisters, a magical stone palace, and echoing ancient hallways. The rooms are spacious, feature terra-cotta floors, and were recently redecorated in a rustic-modern style that manages to retain the 16th-century spirit of the building. Baths

EXTREMADURA

feature whirlpool tubs, a wonderful modern addition that you'll appreciate after a day of climbing Trujillo's cobbled streets. **Isla del Gallo** (Pl. Aragón 2, tel. 92/732-0243, www.isladelgallo.com, €120) is an absolutely charming hotel located in a traditional Trujillo house painted the color of the sunset. Rooms are individually decorated with antiques and local art and each is named for a Trujillo conquistador. **Palacio de Santa Marta** (C/ Ballesteros 6, tel. 92/732-3165, nhpalaciodesantamarta@nh-hotels.com, www.nh-hotels.com, €125) is located in the majestic Santa Marta palace built in the 16th century. The stylish Spanish hotel chain NH converted it in 2004 into a very sleek, very comfortable four-star hotel. The location, just in front of the Plaza Mayor, is perfect. **Meliá Trujillo** (Pl.Campillo 1, tel. 92/745-8900, melia.trujillo@solmelia.com, www.solmelia .com, €130) is located in the converted 16th-century Convento de San Antonio. Rooms are decorated in a classic style with lots of heavy striped fabrics and antiques. The inner courtyard has been converted into a divine retreat with comfortable, shady seating areas and a lovely pool.

FOOD
Gourmet
Located in the Hotel Isla del Gallo, **Huaylas Nusta** (Pl. Aragón 2, tel. 92/732-0243, 1:30–4 P.M. and 8:30–11 P.M. Tues.–Sun., closed Mon., €36) is under the direction of chef Ignacio Uraín, who trained with the god of New Basque Cuisine, Juan Mari Arzak. He offers a very subtle, harmonious menu of local ingredients with creative Basque touches. The dining room is sophisticated yet warm and inviting. Reservations are suggested.

Local Cuisine
El Bizcocho Plaza (Pl. Mayor 8, tel. 92/732-2017, 1–4:30 P.M. and 8–11:30 P.M. daily, €30) is one of the most popular restaurants in town. In a rustic stone-walled dining room, the kitchen serves classic *extremeño* fare with just a hint of creativity. Start with a plate of *quesos y embutidos* (artisan cheeses and cured meats). **Asador Corral del Rey** (Pl. Corral del Rey 2, tel. 92/732-1780, 1–4 P.M. and 8–11 P.M. Mon.–Sat., closed 8–11 P.M. Sun., €35) comprises three traditional Trujillo dining rooms and is famed for working with the seasons to serve only the most exquisite local dishes. Both meat and fish dishes are excellent, but the best bet is to choose the chef's *surgencia* (suggestion). **Pizarro** (Pl. Mayor 13, tel. 92/732-0255, 1–5 P.M. Wed.–Mon., closed Tues., €25) serves homey, hearty local fare in a very popular upstairs dining room. The house specialty is *gallina trufada* (young chicken cooked with truffles). For an inexpensive local meal, try **El Bizcocho** (Pl. Molinillo 1, tel. 92/732-0518, 1:30–4:30 P.M. daily, €15), which offers an extensive menu of *extremeño* classics at very economical prices. The *cordero asado* (roasted lamb) is a favorite. This restaurant is owned by the same family that owns the pricier El Bizcocho Plaza.

Tapas
Plaza Mayor is lined with cafés and restaurants, most of which feature lively tapas bars. Also take a walk down Calle Garcia, which teems with tapas bars and wine bars. **Mesón La Troya** (Pl. Mayor 10, tel. 92/732-1364, 1–4:30 P.M. and 8:30–11:30 P.M. daily) is a boisterous favorite drawing as many locals as tourists. Beneath walls covered in photos of celebrities posing with owner Concha, the bar serves heaping *raciones* (tapas sized for sharing) of *extremeño* treats such as *migas* (savory breadcrumbs fried with sausage). The dining room out back offers a fixed menu (around €20) that features massive portions. Go only if you are starving and be sure and have *caldereta de cordero,* a local stew made with lamb.

INFORMATION AND SERVICES
Trujillo's **tourist office** (Pl. Mayor, s/n, tel. 92/732-2677, www.ayto-trujillo.com, 9:30 A.M.–2 P.M. and 4–6:30 P.M. Mon.–Fri., 9:45 A.M.–2 P.M. Sat.–Sun.) offers maps and

information about the city and its sights. They sell an *abono*, a €6.75 pass that covers entry into various sights. It is a good deal if you speak Spanish because it includes a guided tour (11 A.M. and 5 P.M. daily). There are currently no plans to offer an English-language tour. **Gárgola Trujillo** (Pl. Mayor 17, tel. 92/732-3225) is a tourism company offering alternative activities in and around Trujillo including biking, hiking, and hot-air balloon rides.

GETTING THERE
Bus
Trujillo's **Estación de Autobuses** (Av. Miajadas, s/n, tel. 92/732-1202) is on the outskirts of town near the A-5 highway. There are no local buses to get you into town, but it is only a five-minute taxi ride. The main bus company is **Auto-Res** (tel. 90/202-0999, www.auto-res.net), which goes pretty much anywhere in Spain. **Mirat** (tel. 92/723-4863, www.mirat.net) handles much of the local connections through Extremadura, including routes to Guadalupe and Cáceres.

Car
Trujillo lies on the A-5/E-90, also called the Madrid–Badajoz highway. The N-521 runs west to Cáceres and east into Toledo. There is no driving in La Villa, so if you are driving into town, try to book a hotel with parking or take advantage of one of the public lots marked by a large blue "P."

VICINITY OF TRUJILLO
◖ Guadalupe
The dusty little village of Guadalupe is home to one of the most impressive monasteries in Spain and is the locus of one of the most venerated holy figures in the Catholic world—the Virgin of Guadalupe. The dark-faced statue distinctively clad in a long A-shaped gown is said to have been carved by Saint Luke. It was eventually given to the Bishop of Sevilla, but during the Moorish invasions of the 8th century, the statue was sent out of Sevilla for safekeeping. A group of priests buried the statue in the green valley along the Río Guadalupe and there it was lost until a 13th-century shepherd

EXTREMADURA

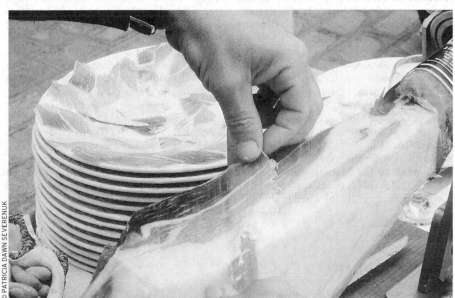

© PATRICIA DAWN SEVERENUK

Extremadura is famed throughout Spain for its succulent *jamón ibérico*.

had a vision that led him to the statue. A small shrine to the Virgin was built and it soon attracted many faithful Christian soldiers—including King Alfonso XI, who invoked the Virgin's name before entering into the Battle of Río Salado in 1340. When the Christian forces defeated the Moors, Alfonso XI gave thanks by ordering the construction of the **Real Monasterio de Guadalupe** (tel. 92/736-7000, 9:30 A.M.–1 P.M. and 3:30–6:30 P.M. daily, €3). The monumental structure, built in the 14th and 15th centuries, soon became a pilgrimage sight that rivaled Santiago de Compostela. The Virgen de Guadalupe was named the patron of all the territories founded in the New World—hence the Caribbean island of Guadalupe and the large Mexican city.

The monastery has Gothic, Mudejar, Renaissance, and baroque details and the exterior boasts eight large quadrangular towers. The **Basílica** has a lusciously carved exterior. Inside are three naves, a walnut choir, and the **Camarín de la Virgen,** a baroque marble chamber that houses the Virgen de Guadalupe. The **Claustro Mudejar** is a gorgeously carved interior cloister in the Mudejar style with an elaborate Gothic temple at its center. The **Claustro Gótico** was built in the 16th century and consists of three arched galleries. The monastery also houses an embroidery museum and an art museum. The latter holds several important works by court painter Francisco Zurbarán and one by Goya. The monastery was declared a UNESCO World Heritage Site in 1993.

True to its historic origins as a pilgrimage center, Guadalupe offers quite a bit of accommodationsfor the traveler. The **Parador de Guadalupe** (C/ Marqués de la Romana 12, tel. 92/736-7075, guadalupe@parador.es, www.parador.es, €120) is located in the 15th-century Hospital de San Juan de Bautista, a hospital and hostel for pilgrims. It has simple Mudejar detailing with soothing white arches, a lush garden, and a lovely pool. Request a room overlooking the monastery. Or, better yet, stay at the monastery. The **Hospedería del Real Monasterio** (Pl. Juan Carlos I, s/n, tel. 92/736-7000, hospedería@monasterio guadalupe.com, www.monasterioguadalupe .com, closed Jan. 15–Feb. 15, €65) is a group of monks' rooms surrounding the Gothic cloister that now provide guests with a historic night's stay. Rooms are simple but lovely with antiques and an inimitable peaceful atmosphere. **Posada del Rincón** (Pl. Santa María de Guadalupe, tel. 92/736-7114, www.posadadelrincon .com, €72) is an old stone and wood house that has been converted into a charming family-run inn with a lively bar, peaceful garden, and excellent local restaurant.

For local food, try **Mesón El Cordero** (C/ Alfonso Onceno 27, tel. 92/736-7131, closed Mon., €20), a rustic dining room with wonderful views of the mountains surrounding Guadalupe. Try the house specialties: *cordero asado* (roasted lamb) and *perdices escabechadas* (preserved pheasant). The **Hospedería del Real Monasterio** (Pl. Juan Carlos I, s/n, tel. 92/736-7000, 1:30–3:30 P.M. and 9–10:30 P.M. daily, €30) runs an excellent *extremeño* restaurant in the Gothic cloister of the monastery. You can have a full meal or just a coffee in the cloister.

Car is the best way to get to Guadalupe. From the A-5/E-90 Madrid–Badajoz highway, take EX-118 near Navalmoral de la Mata and follow it south. From Cáceres, **Mirat** (tel. 92/723-4863, www.mirat.net) runs buses at 1 and 5 P.M. Monday–Friday, and at 1 P.M. on Saturday. In either case, you'll have to spend the night to take the bus out the next day.

Mérida

The city of Mérida was founded in 25 B.C. as Augusta Emerita, a settlement for veterans of the fifth and 10th Roman legions. At that point Roman Hispania consisted of three regions—Bética, Tarraconense, and Lusitania. Emerita became the capital of the latter. It rose in power and prominence to become one of the ancient world's 10 most important cities. Located on the Vía de la Plata, Mérida grew very rich, as evidenced by the wealth of monuments still standing today—theaters, temples, houses, and public works. After Rome fell, the Visigoths moved in and made the town their capital. The Moors arrived in the 8th century, built a fortress, and dismantled many of the Roman ruins to use the stone to help build the Moorish cities of Granada and Córdoba in Andalucía. Mérida fell to the Christians in 1230 and over the following centuries continued to decline in importance. It seemed no one wanted this Roman treasure. Today, it is the capital of Extremadura and a bustling town of nearly 60,000 that enjoys a hearty tourism trade thanks to its Roman heritage and a world-class theater festival held each July.

SIGHTS

Spread throughout the **Casco Viejo** (old town) of Mérida, the main sights can be taken in during a morning's stroll. Opening hours (9:30 A.M.–1:45 P.M. and 5–7:15 daily summer, 9:30 A.M.–1:45 P.M. and 4–6:15 P.M. daily winter) are the same for all monuments, except as noted below. You can purchase an **entrada conjunta** (€9), which allows access to the Roman theater, Amphitheater, Alcazaba fortress, Casa del Mitreo, and the Roman Circus, among other sites. You can purchase the ticket at any of these monuments. You save over €8 if you visit just the above sites alone.

Puente Romano

Spanning the Río Guadiana, Mérida's magnificent Roman bridge is the longest in Spain. With 64 granite arches, it stretches a kilome-ter (about 0.5 mile). Up until 1993, it served as the main entrance into the city. Now the modern Puente Luisitania bridge designed by Spanish architect Santiago Calatrava handles the traffic, though pedestrians can still walk across the Roman bridge. At the end of the bridge is the **Alcazaba** (Pl. Rastro, s/n, tel. 92/400-3438, €3.50) a Moorish fortification built in A.D. 835. The interior is a cross-section of Mérida's culture. Along the outside are Roman walls and in the basement is a massive Roman cistern capable of filtering river water for consumption. Stone pillars carved by the Visigoths frame the doorway leading down to the cistern. The fort also contains the remains of a building belonging to the Knights of Santiago and a number of Roman houses with intriguing mosaic floors. Just north of the Alcazaba is the **Plaza de España,** the heart of modern Mérida. Running just south of the plaza is **Calle John Lennon,** which is appropriately the main nightlife strip in town.

Templo de Diana

Standing nearly at the center of town, this majestic colonnaded structure (C/ Romero Leal) served as a temple to the goddess Diana in Augusta Emerita. In the 16th century, a local count incorporated the temple into his palace. More recently, excavations have been conducted to recuperate the temple and now it stands as a hybrid structure—Roman in front, Renaissance in back. Access is not allowed and the surrounding ground is an ongoing archaeological site and home to a colony of cats. In fact, there are as many tourists cooing at the felines as awing at the building.

Museo Nacional de Arte Romano

Just before arriving to the Roman theater and amphitheater complex, you come to the Museo Nacional de Arte Romano (C/ José Ramón Mélida, s/n, tel. 92/431-1690, 10 A.M.–2 P.M. and 4–9 P.M. daily Mar.–Nov., 10 A.M.–2 P.M. and

EXTREMADURA

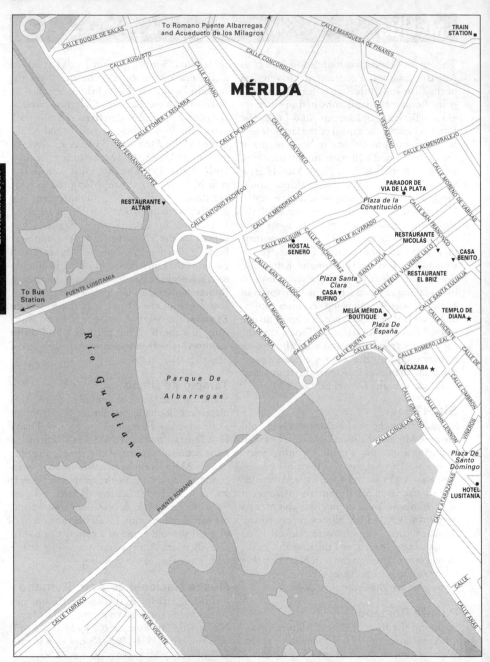

MÉRIDA

To Romano Puente Albarregas
and Acueducto de los Milagros

TRAIN
STATION

CALLE DUQUE DE SALAS

CALLE MARQUESA DE PINARES

CALLE AUGUSTO

CALLE CONCORDIA

CALLE ADRIANO

CALLE FOMER Y SEGARRA

AV JOSE FERNANDEZ LOPEZ

CALLE DE MUZA

CALLE DEL CALVARIO

CALLE VESPASIANO

CALLE ALMENDRALEJO

CALLE MORENO DE VARGAS

CALLE ANTONIO PACHECO

PARADOR DE
VIA DE LA PLATA

Plaza de la
Constitución

RESTAURANTE
ALTAIR

CALLE ALMENDRALEJO

CALLE SAN FRANCISCO

CALLE ALVARADO

RESTAURANTE
NICOLÁS

CALLE HOLGUIN
CALLE SANCHO PEREZ

HOSTAL
SENERO

SANTA JULIA

CASA
BENITO

CALLE FELIX VALVERDE LILLO

RESTAURANTE
EL BRIZ

CALLE SAN SALVADOR

Plaza Santa
Clara

CASA
RUFINO

CALLE SANTA EULALIA

CALLE MORERIA

To Bus
Station

PUENTE LUSITANIA

PASEO DE ROMA

MELÍA MÉRIDA
BOUTIQUE

TEMPLO DE
DIANA

Plaza De
España

CALLE VICENTE

CALLE ARQUITAS

Río Guadiana

CALLE PUENTE

CALLE CAVA

CALLE ROMERO LEAL

CALLE DE

ALCAZABA

Parque De
Albarregas

CALLE CIMBRON

CALLE GRACIANO

CALLE JOHN LENNON

VINEROS

CALLE CINUELAS

Plaza De
Santo
Domingo

PUENTE ROMANO

CALLE ATARAZANAS

HOTEL
LUSITANIA

CALLE TABRACO

AV DE VICENTE

CALLE

CALLE AXAS

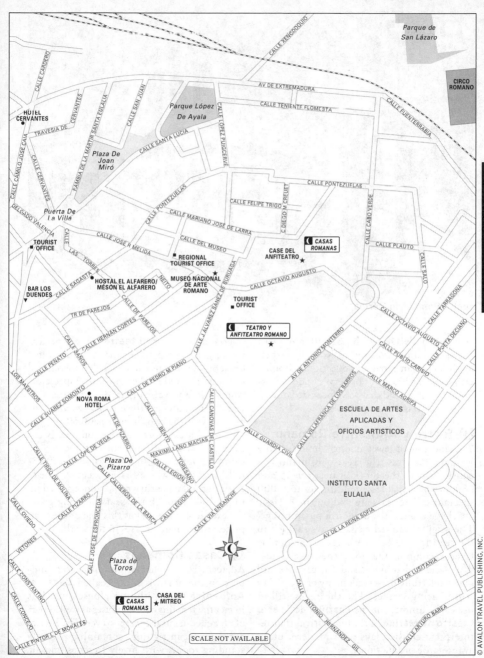

EXTREMADURA

EXTREMADURA

© BRANDON LANE FERGUSON

Teatro Romano in Mérida

4–6 P.M. daily Dec.–Feb., €2.40), a modern structure built according to Roman aesthetics. It houses an extensive collection of Roman artifacts. The basement preserves under a glass floor a Roman road that was uncovered during construction of the museum.

🎦 Teatro y Anfiteatro Romano

The undisputed jewel among Mérida's many Roman treasures, the Teatro Romano is a classic Roman theater built between 15 and 16 B.C. and capable of holding up to 6,000 spectators. The seats are laid out in a classic arc shape around the orchestra pit and stage. The original vaulted passageways that led to the seating area are still intact. The double layer of columns that form the stage's backdrop were added in the 2nd century A.D. and are wonderfully preserved, many of the niches still housing statues. The theater is still in use each summer for the **Festival de Teatro Clásico de Mérida,** a theater festival that reinterprets classic plays with modern, often avant-garde productions.

Next door is the **Anfiteatro** (Amphitheater), where gladiator battles pitting man against beast or man against man were held. Founded in 8 A.D., it could hold up to 14,000 spectators who sat in an oval ring around the arena. If you did not purchase the *entrada conjunta,* the price to visit the two theaters is €6.50.

A few blocks north of the complex is the third pinnacle of Roman entertainment—the **Circo Romano** (€3.50), a 0.4-kilometer (0.25-mile) oval track where chariot races were held. Built in the 1st century A.D., it once seated up to 30,000. Though the seats are long gone, the excellent track makes this one of the best-preserved Roman circuses in the world.

🎦 Casas Romanas

Adjacent to the theater-amphitheater complex on the north is the so-called **Casa del Anfiteatro** (Amphitheater House), which is in fact the remains of two houses as well as part of an aqueduct and a water tower. The houses are the most intriguing, containing partially standing rooms with lovely frescoes, mosaic tile floors, and the original piping that brought water into the bathing areas of the house. They offer a fascinating glimpse into upper-class life in Augusta Emerita. An even better example of a Roman home is just south, behind the bull ring. Dating from the 2nd century, **Casa del Mitreo** (Cerro de San Albín, s/n, €4) is a truly beautiful Roman house that belonged to a prominent family. The colorful mosaics throughout are stunning, especially the *Mosaico Cosmogónico,* which depicts the cosmos of heaven, earth, and the seas.

Los Acueductos

Over eight kilometers (five miles) of Roman aqucducts still stand around the city. They were built to transport water from the man-made lagoons on the outskirts of Augusta Emerita. The best remains are those of the **Acueducto de los Milagros** on the north end of town, near the train station. The aqueduct once ran for nearly a kilometer (over 0.5 mile) and rose over 24 meters (80 feet) at its highest point. Just west of the aqueduct is another bridge, the **Romano Puente Albarregas,** which crosses the Río Albarregas. It consists of five arches and spans some 122 meters (400 feet).

ACCOMMODATIONS
Under €50

(**Hostal El Alfarero** (C/ Sagasta 40, tel. 92/430-3183, info@hostalelalfarero.com, www.hostalelalfarero.com, €45) is located just steps from the theater-amphitheater complex on one of Mérida's most popular tapas-hopping streets. Rooms have very simple yet stylish furnishings, and lovely details like ceramic painted sinks and hydro-jet showers. There is work by local artists hanging throughout the building as well as two charming plant-festooned patios. **Hostal Senero** (C/ Holguín 12, tel. 92/431-7207, www.hostalsenero.com, €38) offers very basic rooms in a converted yellow and white house just steps from the lively Plaza de España. The public rooms and hallways boast charming Andalusian tiling. Not all have air-conditioning—in summer, check before booking. **Hotel Lusitania** (C/ Oviedo 12,

tel. 92/431-6112, €50) offers 20 decent rooms with large baths in a very central location close to the theater.

€50-100

Hotel Cervantes (C/ Camilo José Cela 10, tel. 92/431-4961, infomacion@hotelcervantes .com, www.hotelcervantes.com, €70) is an old-fashioned hotel with spacious, classically decorated rooms. There is a lively bar downstairs and a parking garage (costs extra). Skip the restaurant; it's okay, but nothing special considering the many other charming options in town. **Nova Roma Hotel** (C/ Suárez Somonte 42, tel. 92/431-1261, www.novaroma.com, €86) is a fairly new property with decent-sized rooms and all the basic amenities you'll need. Decor is surprisingly dated and the staff is hit-and-miss on the friendliness front.

Over €100

Hotel Velada Mérida (Av. Princesa Sofía, s/n, tel. 92/431-5110, www.veladahotels.com, €109) has very comfortable rooms offering sophisticated style in a recently refurbished hotel. There is a lovely garden and a small—but refreshing—pool. Prices go down to around €70 on weekends. The in-house restaurant, La Alcazaba, is highly rated. It is about a 10-minute walk to the Roman theater from here. **Parador de Vía de la Plata** (Pl. Constitución 3, tel. 92/431-3800, merida@parador.es, www .parador.es, €135) is located in a whitewashed Andalusian-style 18th-century convent. It was built atop a Roman temple and in the interior some Roman columns are still visible. Rooms are airy and light with wonderful architectural details like vaulted ceilings and exposed beams. There is also a lovely garden, a pool, and a good restaurant. **Meliá Mérida Boutique** (Pl. España 19, tel. 92/438-3800, melia.merida@ solmelia.com, www.solmelia.com, €135) has the best location in town, right on the lively Plaza de España. It is also the only five-star in town. Built in what were once two former palaces, the rooms are spacious and designed with colorful Moroccan touches. There is a wonderful interior patio, with bright blue walls and

EXTREMADURA

lots of tiles, that help bring natural light into the hotel. Amenities include a pool and a parking garage—but for less than half the cost of parking at the hotel, you can park in a nearby public lot.

FOOD
Gourmet
Altair (Av. José Fernández López, s/n, tel. 92/430-4512, 2–4 P.M. and 9–11 P.M. Mon.–Sat., closed Sun., €50) is one of Extremadura's top-rated restaurants, with award-winning dishes that combine exquisite local products with restrained creative touches. Located on the Río Guadiana, the dining room looks onto the Roman bridge—simply stunning when lit up at night. Try the *patito* (duck with honey and figs) or the *bacalao* (cod baked with garlic). Better yet, opt for the chef's tasting menu, a bargain at €30.

Local Cuisine
In warmer months, head to Calle José Ramón Mélida. The entire street leading up to the Roman theater is lined with boisterous restaurants serving hearty local fare. The outside tables are the place to see and be seen. Nearby Calle Sagasta is another good foodie street.

Owned by the *hostal* of the same name, **Mesón El Alfarero** (C/ Sagasta 29, tel. 92/430-2959, 1:30–3:45 P.M. and 8:30–11 P.M. daily, €20) is a rustic dining room set in an old ceramic workshop where Spain's Queen Sofía once took classes. The menu is classic *extremeño* fare. Try *tortilla de espárragos* (asparagus omelet), *quesos surtidos* (mixed artisan cheeses), or any of their meat dishes. The menu is extensive so ask the waiter for recommendations or just point to what the table next to you is having. The locals always know the best dishes to have. **Nicolás** (C/ Félix Valverde Lillo, 13, tel. 92/431-9610, closed Sun., €35) is a rustic dining room with wooden walls and a cozy garden. The kitchen is acclaimed for its exquisite local fare. Two house specialties to lick your fingers for are *cordero a la ciruela* (lamb with plums) and *solomillo ibérico a la pimienta* (Iberian pork loin in peppercorn sauce). **El Briz**

(C/ Félix Valverde Lillo 5, tel. 92/431-9307, 2–4 P.M. and 9–11 P.M. daily, €15) is a no-nonsense dining room tucked behind a lively tapas bar. Tables are covered in paper, walls are layered with cork, and the food is straightforward and homey—with an emphasis on stews and grilled meats.

Tapas
Plaza España is lined with cafés and tapas bars, as are the streets between Templo de Diana and the Roman theater. **Casa Benito** (C/ San Francisco 3, tel. 92/433-0769, 1:30–4 P.M. and 8:30–11 P.M. daily) is a rambling tapas bar/restaurant that offers classic Spanish and *extremeño* dishes to a very dedicated clientele. The interior is warm and cozy with brick walls lined with bullfighting memorabilia and old black-and-white photographs of Mérida. Outside, a large terrace is set up under the glass and iron awing of the old central marketplace. **Casa Rufino** (Pl. Santa Clara 2, tel. 92/431-2001, 1–4 P.M. and 9 P.M.–midnight daily) is a rowdy tapas bar offering a wide range of *raciones* (tapas sized for sharing). Try their wonderful cheeses and cured meats. **Los Duendes** (C/ Berzocana 1, tel. 92/437-4400, 1:30–4:30 P.M. and 9–11:30 P.M. daily) offers a spectacular view in warmer months—tables are set right next to the Templo de Diana. But don't bother if the weather is cold, as the tapas are standard at best.

INFORMATION
The **regional tourist office** (C/ José Ramón Mélida, s/n, tel. 92/431-5353, www.turismo extremadura.com, 9:30 A.M.–1:45 P.M. and 5–7:45 P.M. Mon.–Fri., 10 A.M.–2 P.M. Sat., closed Sun.) is located next to the Roman theater. It has complete information on Mérida as well as Extremadura. The **Mérida tourism office** (C/ Santa Eulalia 66, tel. 92/438-0104, 9:30 A.M.–1:45 P.M. and 5–7:45 P.M. Mon.–Fri., 10 A.M.–2 P.M. Sat., closed Sun.) offers city-only information, as well as good guides to tapas and restaurants. Ask for their *Plano a Tapear,* which includes several coupons for inexpensive tapas at 18 tapas bars.

GETTING THERE
Train
The **Estación de Tren** (C/ Cardero, s/n) is operated by **Renfe** (tel. 90/224-0202, www.renfe.es) and has several daily direct trains to Badajoz, Sevilla, Cáceres, and Madrid. Other destinations may require a transfer. The station is located on the northern edge of the city, about a 15-minute walk to the Roman theater.

Bus
Mérida's **Estación de Autobuses** (Av. Libertad, s/n, tel. 92/437-1403) is located on the other side of the Río Guadiana, near the end of the Puente Luisitania.

Car
Mérida is located on the A-5/E-90 highway that runs from Madrid to Badajoz. There are parking lots throughout the town.

VICINITY OF MÉRIDA
Badajoz
Lying some 65 kilometesr (40 miles) to the west of Mérida, Badajoz rises up from the mottled plains of southern Extremadura like an oasis of urbanity—all glass, steel, and lots of people (with a population of 150,000 it is the largest of Extremadura's cities). However, only if you are truly starving for civilization is a detour here merited. There is little of interest to the tourist other than maybe a place to get a fill-up before heading into Portugal, just about seven kilometers (about four miles) away. The A-5/E-90, which runs from Madrid to Badajoz, is a convenient way to access Lisbon to the west or the Portuguese resort towns to the south on the coast.

So why is it so populous? Badajoz is both the regional capital of the province of Badajoz and it has a popular, highly regarded university. The students insure an ongoing cultural vivacity and booming nightlife year-round. By day, take a walk along the Río Guadiana to see the **Puente de Palmas,** a 16th-century stone bridge with 32 lovely arches. It ends in the **Puerta de Palmas,** the castle-like 16th-century entrance into the city. North along the river is the **Parque de la Alcazaba,** home to the **Alcazaba** (€1.30), the remains of a Moorish fortification with an impressive eight-sided tower, **Torre de Espantaperros.** Within the walls is a 16th-century palace that now serves as the regional **Museo Arqueológico.** It houses over 15,000 finds from throughout Badajoz, representing Roman, Visigoth, and Moorish cultures. In the center of town, the 13th-century **Catedral de San Juan Bautista** (Pl. España, s/n) soars over the buzzing Plaza de España looking more like a fort than a cathedral. The look was necessary as it was built during an era when the town was under regular siege and this spiritual sanctuary served many times as an actual sanctuary for the city's residents.

If you must stay the night, try the **Hotel Cervantes** (C/ Trinidad 2, tel. 92/422-3710, €40), a low-frills hotel overlooking the lovely Plaza Cervantes. **Badajoz Center** (Av. Damián Téllez Lafuente, s/n, tel. 92/421-2001, www.hotelescenter.es, €135) is a modern property in Badajoz's main commercial zone. Rooms are stylish and full amenities are standard. There is a parking garage in the hotel (costs extra). If you are a foodie, you are in luck as one of the best restaurants in Extremadura is located here. **Aldebarán** (Av. de Elvas, s/n, tel. 92/427-6837, closed Sun., €45) is an elegant dining room under the direction of a head chef who once ran the kitchen of Arzak in San Sebastián—one of the world's greatest restaurants. Food is a sophisticated blend of tradition and modernity with an emphasis on fresh, local ingredients. It is located in a suburb outside of town so you'll need to drive or take a cab. For a cheaper meal in town, try **La Toja** (C/ Sánchez de la Rocha 8, tel. 92/427-3477, 1–4:30 P.M. and 8:30 P.M.–midnight daily, €25), which offers hearty, heaping helpings of *extremeño* fare.

Badajoz is located at the end of the A-5/E-90 Madrid–Badajoz highway, which cuts through Trujillo and Mérida. From Cáceres, take the N-630 to Mérida, then the A-5/E-90 to Badajoz.

Badajoz is the only city in Extremadura to have an **airport** (tel. 92/421-0400, www.aena.es), located about 13 kilometers (eight miles)

EXTREMADURA

outside of the city. Exclusively served by the Spanish airline **Iberia** (tel. 90/240-0500, www.iberia.es), it is convenient if you are flying from within Spain into Extremadura. The **Estación de Ferrocarriles** (C/ Carolina Coronado, s/n) is served by **Renfe** (tel. 90/224-0202, www.renfe.es) with several trains per day to Mérida, Madrid, Barcelona, and beyond. The **Estación de Autobuses** (C/ José Rebollo López, s/n, tel. 92/422-8515) is served by several bus companies, the most popular being **Auto-Res** (tel. 90/202-0999, www.auto-res.net).

⟨ Zafra

About 65 kilometers (40 miles) due south of Mérida lies the pretty little village of Zafra. About halfway between Mérida and Sevilla, it makes a convenient stopping-off point. Though located on the Roman Vía de la Plata, the great Roman transit route from Gijón to Andalucía, there is very little left of the Roman presence. Evidence of Moorish rule is seen a bit more, particularly in the Mudejar influence in the town's most important sight—the **Alcázar de Zafra**, a 15th-century fortress-palace built by the Dukes of Feria. Today it houses one of the loveliest properties in the entire Parador chain. Even if you are not a guest, you can still pop in to see the elaborate marble courtyard. Be sure to stroll around Zafra's arcaded **Plaza Mayor,** which is actually two plazas in one: the 18th-century Plaza Grande, with a clutch of majestic buildings, and the 16th-century Plaza Chica, which once served as the town market. They are connected by an archway, and leading off in all directions are Zafra's finest streets.

It you decide to stay the night, you can't do better than the **Parador de Zafra** (Pl. Corazón de María 7, tel. 92/455-4540, zafra@parador.es, www.parador.es, €120), also called the Parador Hernán Cortés because the legendary explorer once stayed here before heading off on a voyage to the New World. Rooms are spacious and some boast astonishing coffered ceilings. ⟨ **Hotel Huerta Honda** (C/ López Asme 30, tel. 92/455-4100, info@hotelhuertahonda.com, www.hotelhuertahonda.com, €74) is an exquisite inn tucked into lovely stone mansion. Rooms seduce with a stylish blend of sophistication, fun, and a touch of ethnic flair—the Al Andalus suite (€150) is a fantasy world of canopies and fabrics that evoke a hedonistic Berber retreat. The in-house **Restaurante Barbacana** (closed Sun. P.M., €35) is the best-rated restaurant in town, serving excellent renditions of local *extremeño* fare in a very romantic dining room. The hotel also has a more moderately priced cafeteria and a lively bar. For tapas, head to the Plaza Mayor and **Monreal** (Pl. Chica 2, tel. 92/455-3023, noon–3 P.M. and 8 P.M.–midnight daily), a classic tavern that is a local favorite for its generous, hearty tapas.

Zafra's **Estación de Ferrocarril** (Av. Estación, s/n) is about 20 minutes by foot south of the city. It is served by **Renfe** (tel. 90/224-0202, www.renfe.es). The **Estación de Autobuses** (Crta. Badajoz-Granada, tel. 92/455-3907) is served by several companies, including **Alsa** (www.alsa.es).

ANDALUCÍA

Perhaps no region better evokes the sheer exuberance of Spain than does Andalucía. Ruled by the Moors for over 800 years, Al-Andalus, as they named it, was a vibrant, cultured, prosperous land while the rest of Europe shivered in the Dark Ages. Remnants of this great culture are everywhere, not only in monumental World Heritage Sites such as Granada's Alhambra, Córdoba's Mezquita, and Sevilla's Alcázar, but also in the tiny maze-like villages that dot the countryside. Thick-plastered white buildings clustered around winding alleyways—walls so close they almost kiss—honeycombed with plant-festooned inner patios are all architectural tricks to ward off the vicious heat of the sun. Travel to North Africa, and you'll see identically styled medinas. But Andalucía is more than its spectacular Moorish past. In the 15th

century, the Catholic Kings ushered in their own legacy of architecture and their Gothic, baroque, and Renaissance churches lend even the dustiest hillside pueblos an air of elegance.

Andalucía is Spanish culture at its most emblematic. Bullfighting, with its origins in Ronda, began as a way to train the cavalry officers of the Spanish military. It eventually became a proving ground for young aristocratic men eager to show their courageous mettle. Flamenco, like so many of the world's most moving indigenous art forms, began in poverty. The origins are murky, but clearly tied to the ramshackle communities where *gitanos* (Andalusian gypsies) poured out their souls in songs of love, yearning, pain, and improbable hope. Today, flamenco stars such as guitarist Paco de Lucía and dancer Sara Baras

ANDALUCÍA

HIGHLIGHTS

Barrio Santa Cruz: This centuries-old barrio is for feeding the senses. Postage-sized patios brim with greenery, 17th-century wrought-iron crosses rise from cobbled plazas rimmed with orange trees, and flamenco pours out of tiny bars where sherry is served from wooden vats (page 575).

Pueblos Blancos: Draped like a string of pearls in the mountains between Sevilla and Málaga are the picturesque "White Villages" of Andalucía. Clustered on hilltops around ancient churches and crumbling castles, these towns are a beautiful escape way off the beaten path (page 606).

Zahara de los Atunes: Still very much a tuna-fishing town, this little resort is blessed with a fine sweep of sand and is perfectly situated for exploring the lovely, still-wild beaches of the Costa de la Luz, the least-developed of Spain's *costas* (page 620).

La Mezquita: With a forest of columns, orange tree-filled patios, rainbow-colored mosaics, and exquisite marble carvings, this 9th-century former mosque is a marvel of Islamic architecture (page 631).

Écjia: This unassuming town lays way off the beaten path and offers an impressive wealth of Roman artifacts, Renaissance build-

ings, and a heavy dose of Andalusian charm undiluted by tourism (page 639).

La Ciudad: The old town of Ronda is one of the most charming of Andalucía's white pueblos and there is no better way to enjoy it than by getting lost in the crooked lanes of its hilltop La Ciudad barrio, the old Moorish quarter (page 653).

Alhambra: Quite simply one of the grandest buildings in the world, this fortress-palace dating from the 13th century offers a glimpse into the splendor of Moorish Al-Andalus (page 666).

El Albaicín: The old Moorish neighborhood of Granada is a magical place to wander past whitewashed buildings, bustling plazas, and Spain's most picturesque lookout, where you can watch the Alhambra melt into a shimmering wash of red and gold as the sun sets (page 671).

Cabo de Gata: This protected natural park offers some of the wildest, most untouched beaches on the Mediterranean coast (page 688).

Mojácar: Glistening white and blue under the Mediterranean sun, this tiny town wraps itself around a hilltop high above the sea, offering a labyrinth of flower-filled streets, tiny tapas bars, and art galleries (page 692).

LOOK FOR (TO FIND RECOMMENDED SIGHTS, ACTIVITIES, DINING, AND LODGING.

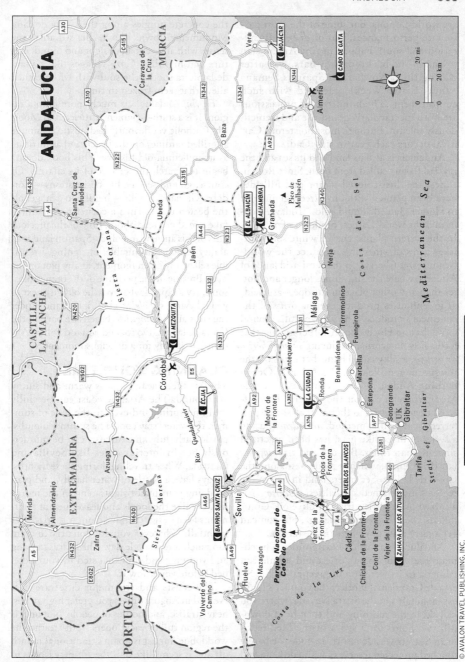

are world-famous, but some of the most passionate performances, full of *duende* (inspiration and soul), happen in tiny Andalusian towns in the backrooms of bars, way after closing time. Nowhere in Spain is Semana Santa (Easter Week) practiced with such commitment. The hundreds of processions are both spectacularly grandiose and tremendously solemn. Europe's most boisterous Carnival occurs each year in tiny Cádiz.

Andalucía is also its land and its sea and the myriad flavors culled from both. Since Roman times, the dust-colored plains and hillsides have been planted with olive trees, giving rise to Homer's fabled "liquid gold." Today, Andalucía is the world's largest producer of olive oil. In the eastern plains, chalky white soil nourishes acres of vines that produce the world-famous *jerez* (sherry). In the semi-arid lands of Almería, where the sun shines longer and hotter than any other place in Europe, vast fields of greenhouses produce the majority of the continent's produce. The verdant hills around Córdoba and Huelva nourish Iberian pigs that feed solely on acorns, producing *jamón ibérico de bellota,* a silky cured ham that melts on the tongue. For millennia, the Atlantic Ocean bathing Andalucía's western coast and the Mediterranean Sea on the eastern, have offered their bounties to Iberia's tables. The preferred local fishing method, *almadraba,* using a series of maze-like nets, has been practiced since Roman times. Be sure and try *mojama* (air-dried tuna), which is made best along the Costa de la Luz. Sea meets land in one of the region's most famed specialties, *pescaito frito,* a mixed plate of fish fried in olive oil. Gourmands swear it's best in Málaga, but you can get a tasty plate anywhere in the region.

Andalucía is a world of extremities. The climate goes from Spain's driest and sunniest in Almería to its wettest and greenest in the Sierra de Grazalema. It offers the country's highest mountains in the Sierra Nevada, where you can ski in the morning and then head downhill two hours for a swim in the Mediterranean Sea. Its seaside resorts include the barely touched protected reserve of Cabo de Gata and the concrete jungles along the Costa del Sol. Monumental towns like Sevilla stimulate the senses with an overload of sight and sound, culture and nightlife. Cozy villages like Zahara de la Sierra soothe the soul with whitewashed alleys that seem frozen in time.

En fin, Andalucía is much more than a region. It is a spirit—flamenco-fueled and Moorish, Catholic yet devoutly hedonistic, as simple as grilled sardines on the beach and as intricate as its millennia-old history. This book doesn't begin to scratch the surface of its charms. Of course, go and see the big destinations—Córdoba, Granada, Sevilla—but if you can, get off the beaten track. Turn a corner not planned, take a road not read about. One of the precious gifts of this ancient and oh-so-Spanish land is its ability to be its inimitable, intriguing, irresistible self at any given moment, at any plot on the map. Breathe in the perfume of the orange blossoms, try a tapa of whatever the old guy next to you is having, say *ole!* at a bullfight, dance under the stars at a *chiringuito* (beachside bar) on the Costa de la Luz. Do so, and you too will be Andalusian, if only for a delicious moment.

PLANNING YOUR TIME

The Mediterranean coast is warm and sunny year-round. The Atlantic coast can be chilly well into spring and even in the heat of summer, the waters stay cool. The summer months, particularly July and August, can be murderously hot in interior cities like Sevilla and Granada. When traveling during these months, always have a bottle of water handy, and plan on doing your major sightseeing in the morning. Do like the locals and leave the hot afternoons for a siesta, then head out for tapas after nightfall. Whatever you do, don't try to cram too much into a single day. The heat is sapping and you may end up exhausted in your hotel bed before you know it.

The coasts and the major cities are best avoided in August unless you prefer high prices, heavy traffic, and hordes of people. Not only is the region full of vacationers from around the world, but August is Spain's traditional month off and it seems like half the country flocks to

ANDALUCÍA AGAINST THE CLOCK

Assuming you'll be based out of Madrid, with **one day,** head straight to Sevilla on the 7 A.M. high-speed AVE train. Visit the Alcázar and the Cathedral in the morning, have a lingering lunch, maybe a boat ride on the river afterwards. Wander the Barrio Santa Cruz as the sun sets, have some tapas and a glass of *jerez,* then catch the 10 P.M. train back to Madrid.

With **two days,** follow the same itinerary as day one, but spend the night in Sevilla. The next morning catch the 9 A.M. AVE to Córdoba and spend the morning visiting the Mezquita. Have lunch in the Jewish quarter and then take one of the early-evening AVE trains back to Madrid.

With **three days,** you can work in Granada and its amazing Alhambra, but you'll have to take at least one bus and you must purchase your tickets to the monument in advance, requesting to enter the Alhambra in the afternoon. Start as before with the AVE to Sevilla, spend the day and night. The next morning, catch the 7 A.M. train to Granada. It is a three-hour ride. Check into your hotel and then make your way to your Alhambra visit. Spend the late afternoon exploring the Albaicín and enjoying tapas. If you are feeling energetic, take in a flamenco show in Sacromonte. The next morning, catch the 7:30 A.M. bus to Córdoba. It is another three-hour trip. Once there, head straight to the train station, where you can buy your evening AVE ticket to Madrid and lock up your luggage. After seeing La Mezquita and having lunch, head back to Madrid.

One **note of warning:** The AVE is extremely popular and books up quickly, especially on weekends. Try buying all of your tickets online at www.renfe.es before beginning your trip, or visit an *agencia de viajes* (travel agent) immediately upon landing in Madrid.

One option for the truly time-crunched is hiring a personal guide. Chicago native **Kelly O'Donnell** (tel. 60/718-4008, odkelly2002@yahoo.com, www.tourguideinspain.com) has been living in Spain since 1987 and offers custom-made itineraries for individuals and small groups throughout Spain, though the bulk of her work takes her to Andalucía. In addition to the big sights she takes visitors to back-road places such as a family-run olive oil factory in the Pueblos Blancos or a tiny ceramics studio in Jaén. For a set per-day price (based on your needs), she'll be your planner, driver, translator, and tour guide.

Andalucía. If you must travel in summer, plan ahead. Reservations will be necessary.

Spring is one of the best times to travel. The orange blossoms and jasmine are in bloom, the weather is warm and sunny, and the summer price increases haven't yet occurred. Go around Easter and you'll see some of the magnificent Semana Santa processions. Winter can be a treat, too. Though you'll be less likely to take advantage of the beaches, and you'll need a sweater or two, you will enjoy Andalucía's major sights with a lot fewer tourists than usual. Prices will be reduced, plus you won't have to worry so much about advance reservations. If you like parties, Cádiz offers the country's wildest Carnival in February.

To really see the best of Andalucía you need at least a week. Unfortunately, time and money constraints often mean the average American tourist has between one and three days for Andalucía. (If that is your case, see sidebar, *Andalucía Against the Clock.*)

A last bit of explanation as you plan your trip: Andalucía is made up of eight provinces, each named after its capital city. So, there is a Sevilla province, as well as a Sevilla city. In this chapter, the difference will be made clear, but you'll need to keep this in mind as you book hotels and travel. This book covers only the most accessible and enjoyable regions of Andalucía and is not an exhaustive guide. The larger cities are covered in detail, while smaller towns are grouped together under provincial or thematic headings. If you plan on spending intense time in any one area, check the Internet for the most up-to-date information and details, and bone up on your Spanish, since the best information will be in the native language.

Sevilla

"Seville doesn't have an ambience. It is ambience," James A. Michener once wrote. No statement could be more apt. More than any other city, sloe-eyed Sevilla (say-VEE-ya) evokes the sensuality of Andalucía—orange blossoms and Moorish arches; the clattering of castanets and the whish of a flouncy polka-dotted skirt; the crescendo of *ole!* rising from the bullring and the grandeur of medieval towers rising over a jumble of whitewashed buildings. Sevilla gave birth to some of the sultriest, bawdiest, most unforgettable lovers of literature—*Carmen, Don Juan,* and *The Barber of Seville.* Spain's beloved painter, Diego Velázquez (of *Las Meninas* fame), was born in Sevilla and Miguel de Cervantes did time in prison here, where, rumor has it, he began *Don Quixote.*

Today, as the bustling capital of Andalucía, the city of close to one million still inspires artists, musicians, and visitors alike. However, perhaps no one is quite as roused by Sevilla and its rich history and colorful culture as the Sevillanos (as locals are known) themselves. Each spring, locals throw two of the most vibrant celebrations in the country—Semana Santa and La Feria de Sevilla. The rest of the year, they go about their business as one of Andalucía's most prosperous city. Spaniards not from Sevilla label the city and its people, *pijo,* a word which translates loosely as "haughty." Maybe it is the stunning architectural legacy of the Moors, the medieval Christians, and the Renaissance. Maybe it is the heady scent of jasmine drenching the 600-year-old barrio of Santa Cruz. Maybe it is the cathedral of Sevilla—the largest Gothic church in the world. Maybe it is the Río Guadalquivir that runs through the city and for centuries served as the gateway to the New World. With all of these things and more, Sevillanos, quite rightly, have a lot to be proud of.

HISTORY

Legend holds that Hercules founded Sevilla. History points to the Romans who founded the city as Hispalis in 205 B.C. In 711, the Moors arrived from North Africa and a year later conquered Sevilla. They changed its name to Isbiliya and, during their 500-year reign over the city, turned it into a trading port and a vibrant city. When the Moorish kingdom of Al-Andalus broke apart, independent *taifas* (principalities) arose. Sevilla was one of them. From 1023 to 1091, it rose in prominence, reaching eventually as far west as Algarve and as far east as Murcia, even coming to dominate powerful Córdoba. In 1091, it fell to the Almoravids, Berber troops from North Africa. They fortified the city (the walls are still visible in the barrio of La Macarena) before being usurped by the Almohads, another North African group. It is they who built Sevilla's most emblematic structure, the La Giralda minaret that towers over the cathedral. They also built the Torre del Oro. However, neither fortifications, nor towers could prevent the advance of the Christian Reconquista troops.

In 1248, King Fernando III (the Saint), captured Isbiliya and re-christened it Sevilla. Under his rule, the newly Christian town flourished. In the 13th and 14th centuries, Jews migrated to the city and built a thriving *judería* (Jewish community) in present-day Barrio Santa Cruz. However, in 1391, fueled by a wave of anti-Semitism sweeping across Christian Spain, Sevilla unleashed a deadly pogrom on its Jewish population. The gates of the barrio were shut off and the Christian mobs went through massacring entire families. An estimated 4,000 people were killed, the rest were forced to flee. The synagogues were converted into churches and the barrio was christened Santa Cruz (Holy Cross).

After Granada fell in 1492 and Spain emerged as a unified nation, the Catholic Kings Fernando and Isabel looked to expand their country, their religion, and their fortunes. When their chosen explorer, Cristóbal Colón (Christopher Columbus), returned successfully from the New World, the kings established Sevilla as the sole port of trade with the Americas, ushering in the city's golden age. In the 16th and 17th centuries, Sevilla was the largest and wealthiest in Spain. However, in 1649, a plague decimated the population and the city rapidly declined in the following centuries—as did the rest of Spain. In the Spanish Civil War, it was one of the first to fall to Franco's troops.

Sevilla began to rebound after the death of Franco and the rise of democracy. The 1992 World's Fair did wonders for the city, bestowing it with a new airport, more hotels, and improved infrastructure. It also rekindled the city's tourism industry and today Sevilla is one of Spain's most popular destinations.

SIGHTS
Real Alcázar

Hidden behind unassuming brick walls is the Real Alcázar (tel. 95/450-2324, www.patronato-alcazarsevilla.es, 9:30 A.M.–7 P.M. Tues.–Sat., 9:30 A.M.–5 P.M. Sun. Apr.–Sept., 9:30 A.M.–5 P.M. Tues.–Sat., 9:30 A.M.–1:30 P.M. Sun. Oct.–Mar., €7), a UNESCO World Heritage Site. Designed by Moors yet commissioned by Christians, this collection of royal buildings is arguably Spain's best example of the eclectic architecture known as Mudejar.

The history of the Alcázar is one of continually shifting occupation, with each ruling sect tweaking and expanding the complex to suit their needs. Although a Christian basilica stood here as early as the 5th century, the Alcázar first began to take shape in the 10th century, when the construction of a fortress was ordered by Abd Al-Raman III. The Alcázar grew to include its first palaces, most notably the Al-Muwarak, as the site passed through the hands of the ruling Almoravids and then the Almohads in the following centuries. In 1248, Fernando III conquered Sevilla, bringing an end to the Moorish control of the city and taking over the Alcázar complex and the Moorish palaces within.

These earlier structures gave way to Alfonso X's Gothic palace, built in the 13th century, and finally, to the construction of the Palacio de Don Pedro I in the 14th. This is not to say,

however, that the Moorish palaces were lost, for although the subsequent additions enveloped the previous sites, the new palaces drew inspiration—and in some cases, materials— from the Moorish palaces. By the 17th century, the Alcázar's evolution slowed to a trickle. Except for the construction of a royal entrance hall and numerous restoration efforts, it stands today much the way it did back then.

The entrance to the complex, the **Puerta del León**—a grand red gate flanked by two towers and lorded over by a portrait of a heraldic lion— leads to the **Patio del León,** which curiously was once used as a theatre. Directly ahead stands an original 10th-century triple-arched wall that separates the patio from the larger courtyard to the south. Take the first left into the **Sala de la Justicia** (Hall of Justice) built under Alfonso XI in the 14th century. Most notably, this is where Pedro I, known variously as the Cruel or the Just, is rumored to have murdered his half-brother, Don Fadrique. Adjacent to the hall is the lovely **Patio del Yeso,** one of the best examples of the original Moorish palace.

Head back to the Patio del León and cross it to enter the **Casa de la Contratación** (House of Trade), created in 1503 to regulate commerce and trade between the Crown and the Spanish colonies. This was also the center for colonial judicial matters, overseas communication, and naval training. Housed in the adjacent **Sala de Audencias** (also known as the Cuarto del Almirante—Admiral's Quarters) is a 1535 painting by Alejo Fernández that is regarded as the earliest known work following Spain's discovery of the New World. The painting is dominated by the image of the Virgin Mary with open arms sheltering a group of Native Americans below. Fernando, Isabel, and their grandson Carlos I are to the right, Christopher Columbus and crew to the left, and a sea full of typical Spanish vessels at the bottom. Note the lovely, gilded coffered ceilings.

From here, you will spill out into the **Patio de la Montería,** a broad red- and white-tiled patio. The vast facade of the **Palacio de Don Pedro I** lines the patio. It is carved with both Arabic and Gothic inscriptions. Pass through

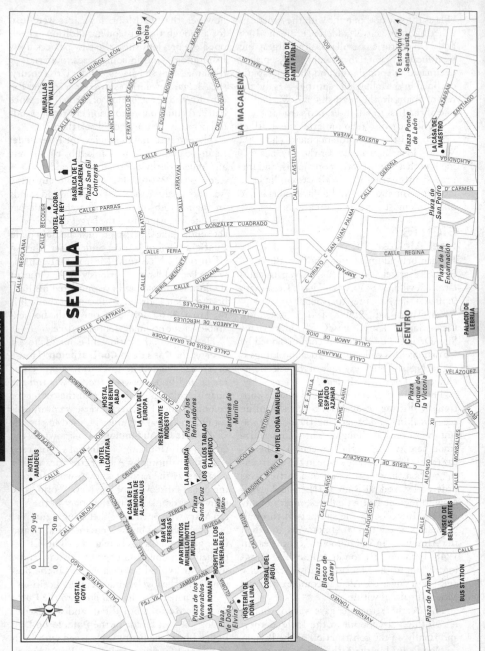

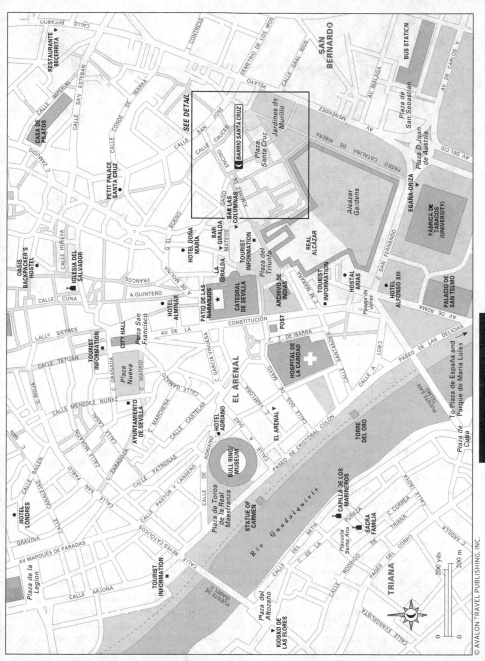

ANDALUCÍA

© SEVE PONCE DE LEON

the beautifully decorated Patio de las Doncellas in Sevilla's Real Alcázar

and into the beautiful **Patio de las Doncellas** (Patio of the Maidens). The walls are so deeply textured and colored that they appear to be tapestry rather than plaster work. It is simply breathtaking. The lower level of the patio is made up of intricately carved arches that are purely Moorish. Looking above them, notice how the more conventional second-story railings and arches differ. The upper section of the palace, begun under Carlos I in the 16th century by the Spanish architect Luis de Vega, blends with the bottom in a way that shouldn't work, but does. You are witnessing the marriage of lavish Moorish decoration with structured Renaissance configurations. Created by both Moor and Christian craftsmen from Toledo, Granada, and Sevilla, this is the essence of Mudejar architecture. Although the central pool is flanked by sunken gardens, this original detail of Moorish design was only recently restored. During the post-Reconquista remodeling, they were covered in marble. Interestingly, the 16th-century marble surface was recreated for scenes from Ridley Scott's 2005 film, *King-*

dom of Heaven. The bedrooms of the Moorish Kings were off this patio.

Adjacent to the patio is the 15th-century **Salón de Embajadores,** undoubtedly the most beautifully decorated room in the palace. It boasts an intricately carved wooden dome decorated with geometric star patterns representing the heavens. It also contains remnants from the earlier Moorish palace that stood here, including walls that date to the 11th century. This was the public room of the palace, used for functions such as the 1526 wedding of Carlos V and Isabel of Portugal. The lions and castles you see inlaid throughout signify Castilla y León.

If the Patio de las Doncellas was considered public space, the intimate **Patio de las Muñecas** (Patio of the Dolls) that lies adjacent was for private affairs. This was where the royal family hung out. The galleries surrounding it were their private rooms. The patio, which underwent 19th-century additions and decorations, gets its name from the four tiny faces carved on some of its arches. See if you can spot them. (Hint: Look on the arch leading into the patio.)

Leaving Pedro I's palace leads you into the **Salones de Carlos V,** built between 1576 and 1588 over Alfonso X's 13th-century Gothic palace. Within, you will find a roomful of tapestries as well as ancient Arabic texts and writings from Islamic Caliphates. The walls are a colorful excess of mosaics and tiles.

This final palace will release you to the **Jardines** (gardens) where you can soak up the aromas of fresh foliage as the breeze whisks by them. The large walkable **Galería de Grutescos,** which divides the newer 20th-century gardens to the east from the older original gardens to the west, offers the best views of both. The latter gardens hold a passageway that leads underground to the **Baños de Doña María de Padilla,** tucked cozily beneath Alfonso X's palace and the neighboring **Patio del Crucero.** Be sure not to miss them for they make for a delightful cave-like photo. Legend has it that María poured boiling oil over her face to repel King Pedro I's pursuit after he killed her husband. She became a nun and has since become a symbol of purity in Sevilla. Continue on to the **Apeadero,** the entrance hall which today welcomes the present King and Queen of Spain when they come to stay in their royal residence—located within the complex. Finally, the last section of the tour is ironically the oldest: the **Patio de las Banderas.** In the 10th century, this patio was where the soldiers were positioned to guard the original fortress.

The Real Alcázar sits on the south side of the Plaza del Triunfo, across from the cathedral, and west of the Barrio de Santa Cruz. Though the audio-guide can be long-winded, it is a delightful companion when touring the palaces and patios. It costs €3 and includes a free map.

Catedral y La Giralda

Traveling through Spain it is tempting to get cathedral-weary. Burgos, Salamanca, Barcelona, Toledo, you may think you've seen the best and the biggest. You are wrong. The

Catedral de Sevilla (Av. Constitución, s/n, tel. 95 421 4971, www.catedralsevilla.org, 11:30 A.M.–6 P.M. Mon.–Sat., 2:30 P.M.–7 P.M. Sun. Sept.–June, 9:30 A.M.–4:30 P.M. Mon.–Sat., 2:30 P.M.–7 P.M. Sun. July and Aug., €7) is the world's largest Gothic temple and the world's third-largest cathedral behind Saint Peter's in Rome and Saint Paul's in London. Add an impressive 800-year-old Moorish tower, and you have a cathedral that will renew your faith in sightseeing.

In the 12th century, a massive Muslim mosque stood on this site. Following Fernando III's conquest of Sevilla in the 13th century, the mosque was refitted and used as a Christian church. But at the start of the 14th century, the building was deemed inadequate, and rumor has it was decided to "make a church so huge that those who see it shall take us for mad." The exterior gives little clues to this decision. At first, its tangle of flying buttresses and jagged spikes poking into the sky make it appear unapproachable, thorny, a bit, well, mad. But

Catedral de Sevilla's columns tower over its visitors.

once you enter, apprehension melts into awe as the interior unveils some 40 massive columns, illuminated by stained-glass windows, curving into incredibly smooth domes.

The cathedral contains five naves—with the central one rising 40 meters (130 feet)—each a balance between lavish decorations and architectural simplicity. In the center, the **Capilla Mayor** (Main Chapel) is dominated by the *retablo* (altarpiece), a masterpiece that took 82 years to complete. Arguably the greatest of its kind, the altar includes hundreds of finely carved figures and ridiculous amounts of gold to depict 45 scenes from the life of Christ.

The southern, eastern, and northern walls of the cathedral are lined with treasures, but the most notable ones are as follows. On the southern side is the **Monumento a Colón** (Columbus Monument), thought to contain the remains of the Spanish explorer. The Dominican Republic, however, also claims to have his remains in its possession. In 2003, a Spanish research team began DNA analysis on the remains in the cathedral of Sevilla with the plan of comparing them to the DNA samples of his brother Diego and illegitimate son Hernando. Unfortunately, the Dominican Republic initially refused to allow access to their remains, only deepening suspicions that the tourism the site draws may be more important than the truth. Tests were ultimately inconclusive. Although Columbus requested in his will that he be buried in his newly discovered Hispaniola, he was first buried in Valladolid (where he died) before being moved to the Dominican Republic by his son Diego. After Cuba won its independence, however, his remains were brought to the cathedral in Sevilla. But in their haste to move the bones, the Spanish may have grabbed the wrong ones. Until further research, the true whereabouts of the famous explorer are up for debate.

Moving east, the **Sacristía de los Cálices** (Sacristy of the Chalices) houses many of the cathedral's treasures, including art by Goya and Zurbarán, among others. East of this is the Plateresque **Sacristía Mayor** (Main Sacristy), which contains the keys to the city given to Fer-

nando III by the Muslim and Jewish communities upon their surrender of Sevilla. Carved into them in Arabic are the words "May Allah render eternal the dominion of Islam in the city." Finally, at the southeastern corner of the cathedral is the magnificently domed ceiling of the **Sala Capitular** (Chapter House) and its *La Inmaculada (Immaculate Conception)*, Murillo's masterpiece from 1668.

Moving north, inside the **Capilla Real** (Royal Chapel) are the tombs of Fernando III the Saint (and a gold-plated glass urn with his remains), his descendant Pedro I (creator of the Alcázar), and Alfonso X, among others. If you wish to enter, do so only after you've visited the rest of the cathedral. The room must be entered through the **Puerta de los Palos** off the Plaza Virgen de los Reyes. It is reserved for prayer, so its exploration necessitates a level of silence and respect.

Just north of the Capilla Real is the only surviving structure of the original Islamic mosque, **La Giralda.** In medieval times, it was thought to be the tallest tower in the world. With the baroque belfry that was added by the Christians after the conquest of Sevilla, the tower now stands 97 meters (318 feet). Originally built in 1184, the base of the tower incorporated stones recovered from various Roman structures. It functioned both as a minaret to call the Muslims to prayer as well as a lookout tower. Along with their loss of the city, the Muslims purportedly wanted to take their prized tower down with them. But following the threat that "if they removed a single stone, they would all be put to sword," the tower was left intact. Interestingly, the design technically includes two towers, one inside the other. Between the two, 35 consecutive ramps lead to the upper terrace. Instead of steps, these ramps made it possible to ride to the top on horseback. The ascent affords great views of the city and the neighboring cathedral. In the 16th century, a set of bells was installed, as well as a bronze statue of Faith that acted as a weather vane. Named the *giraldillo* (that which turns), it is where the tower gets its name.

After descending the tower, exit into the

Patio de los Naranjos (Patio of the Oranges), where Muslim worshippers once ritually washed their hands before entering the mosque. It is planted with over 60 orange trees. From the central fountain, look back and compare the soft pink brick of the Giralda to the heavy grey stone of the Gothic cathedral. The exit, through the **Puerta del Perdón** (Gate of Pardon), lies on the northern side of this patio. This wonderfully arched original mosque entrance contains Arabic inscriptions on its doors.

Archivo de Indias

Between the cathedral and the Reales Alcázares, the Archivo General de Indias (Av. Constitución 3, tel. 95/421-1234, 10 A.M.–4 P.M. Mon.–Sat., 10 A.M.–2 P.M. Sun., free) is a collection of archives documenting the relationship of Spain with its New World colonies. It is a must for history buffs. The imposing building it is housed in was built by Spanish architect Juan de Herrera, who also built El Escorial outside of Madrid. It originally served as the merchants' exchange until King Carlos III chose it to serve as the repository of all documents related to Spain's explorations in the Americas. In 1503, Sevilla was appointed principal port for all dealings with the New World; hence there was a massive influx of such papers, maps, reports, expense accounts, and other information into the city. See it all—including documents bearing the signature of Christopher Columbus—here.

◀ Barrio Santa Cruz

Once the thriving medieval *judería* (Jewish quarter) of Sevilla, Barrio Santa Cruz is now the most atmospheric quarter of modern Sevilla. Read this, then put away the guidebook and the map and get lost. Bounded by Calle Mateos Gago, Calles Santa María la Blanca/San José, the Jardines de Murillo, and the Reales Alcázares, Barrio Santa Cruz is a tiny space offering a world of sensory overload. Immerse yourself.

Enter through the covered passageway in the Plaza del Triunfo next to the Alcázar. You'll emerge in **Patio de Banderas,** which is part of the Alcázar. The patio offers a postcard-perfect view of the Cathedral and La Giralda. At the far corner of the patio, pass through the **Arco de Judería** to enter the barrio. Within moments you'll be in Santa Cruz and its tangle of quaint streets with names like Vida (Life) and Muerte (Death). It is a magical maze of whitewashed walls draped in colorful bougainvillea, wrought-iron street lamps, colorful doors with intricately carved knockers, twisting cobbled streets, surprisingly lush patios, and ancient, cozy plazas. Though there are dozens of bars and cafés, this area is mostly residential and quiet. Unless you are there in the dog-heat of August, you may notice a slight drop in temperature. The streets were originally built close to maximize the shade from the hot Sevilla sun. Throughout the barrio you'll notice intricate iron latticework. It was a typical motif in 17th-century Sevilla. Also typical are the inner patios lined with tiles and filled with a jungle of plants and flowers. Again, they originally served as refuge from the heat in pre-air-conditioning days.

As you wander, look out for **Callejón del Agua.** Bordering the Alcázar, this lovely lane is crowded with white homes trimmed in ocher, several with large patios. Don't be afraid to stick your head in. It ends at **Plaza Alfaro,** where Rossini's Barber of Seville, Figaro, serenaded Rosina on her balcony. Beyond that is the delightful **Plaza Santa Cruz.** Bristling with orange trees and sweet-smelling flowers, it is the barrio's very heart. At its center, the ornate wrought-iron cross, *La Cerrajería,* dates from the 17th century. Follow Calle Mezquita to its end and you'll enter the **Plaza de los Refinadores,** which boasts a statue of the fictional bachelor-gone-bad, Don Juan, whose tale was first recounted by Spanish playwright Tirso de Molina around 1625, and was famously recreated in Mozart's 1787 opera *Don Giovanni.*

A few cobblestone alleys away, the **Casa de Murillo** (C/ Santa Teresa 8) houses several works by the Spanish painter Bartolomé Esteban Murillo. Born in the barrio in 1617, Murillo was a contemporary of Velázquez (also born in Sevilla) and his baroque paintings were the height of fashion in the 17th century. A more intriguing stop off is the nearby **Hospital de los Venerables** (Pl. Venerables 8, tel. 95/456-2696, 10 A.M.–2 P.M. and 4–8 P.M. daily, €4.75), an imposing 17th-century baroque hospital. Its inner red and white tiled patio and sunken gardens are spacious respite from the close quarters of the barrio. The gardens were designed to take advantage of the low water pressure once common in the area. Today, the hospital houses the Focus Abengoa cultural foundation, which hosts art exhibits. The plaza on which it sits drips with ambience and the tiny streets around it are some of the most enchanting in Santa Cruz, particularly **Calle Reinoso.** At the end of lovely Calle Gloria sits **Plaza de Doña Elvira,** named for Don Juan's love—whom he unceremoniously dumped to pursue another. It is one of the barrio's most beautiful, with a fringe of orange trees, tiled benches, and a twittering fountain. Another lovely pocket-sized square to visit is **Plaza Alianza,** with its white walls draped in colorful bougainvillea.

Marking the far end of the barrio are the **Jardines de Murillo,** an elegant strip of greenery that once served as the vegetable garden of the Alcázan. At the far end of the gardens is Sevilla's University, better known to fans of the opera *Carmen* as the **Fábrica de Tabacos** (tobacco factory) where Carmen rolled cigars on her thighs. When it was built in the mid-18th century, it was the largest industrial building in Europe, eventually employing some 3,000 *cigarreras* (female cigar-makers). It had stables for 400 mules, 21 fountains, 24 patios, 10 wells, and a nursery where its female staff could leave their babies. On school days up to 9 P.M., you are free to wander the ground floors if you don't mind bumping into thousands of students. It is closed to the public on Saturdays and Sundays.

El Centro

The center part of old Sevilla is is a bustling commercial zone of shops, restaurants, tapas bars, and hotel. At its heart is the elegant **Plaza Nueva,** presided over by the town hall, **Ayuntamiento de Sevilla** (tel. 95/459-0108, tours at 5:30 P.M. Tues.–Thurs., free), one of the most elaborate examples of Plateresque architecture in Andalucía. Built between 1527 to 1564, the building boasts an elaborate facade of historical and mythical figures. Get the best views from the **Plaza de San Francisco,** around the back. This broad plaza is the main square of Sevilla. It was originally the site of a Muslim market and later the locus for public auto-da-fés held under the Inquisition. Today, it is the sight of the city's main civic and social events.

Leading north away from the Ayuntamiento is **Calle Sierpes,** Sevilla's version of Rodeo Drive. Beyond that, the **Palacio de Lebrija** (C/ Cuna 8, tel. 95/422-7802, 10:30 A.M.–1:30 P.M. and 4:30–7:30 P.M. Mon.–Sat., 10 A.M.–1 P.M. Sat., closed Sun., €4) offers a gracious step into the distant past. Originally built in the 16th century and refurbished in 1914 by the Countess of Lebrija, the palace offers several ample hallways filled with archaeological finds of Roman, Greek, and Etruscan origin. The real jewel, however, is the spectacular inner courtyard featuring a Roman mosaic, Moorish arches, and exuberant tile work.

Nearby, the **Iglesia del Salvador** (Pl. Salvador, s/n, tel. 95/459-5405, 10 A.M.–1:30 P.M. and 4–7:30 P.M. Sat. and Sun., €2) looms in a colonial sheath of red break and minarets. Built between 1671 and 1712, it sits on the sight of a long succession of houses of worship—Roman, Visigoth, and Mozarabic. In the 11th century, the great mosque of Sevilla, Idn-Addabas, was built here. When the current church was built, one of the mosque's minarets was converted into a bell tower and the Patio de los Naranjos, a lovely courtyard filled with orange trees, was preserved. The church is undergoing restorations to reclaim its history and visitors traverse wooden planks under which the archaeological excavations are taking place. **Plaza Salvador** was the sight of the original Roman forum of Híspalis. Now, it is a lively square full of cafés and bars.

On the eastern edges of El Centro, **Casa de Pilatos** (Pl. Pilatos 1, tel. 95/422-5298, 9 A.M.–

6 P.M. daily, €8, €5 ground floor only) offers a glimpse into centuries of Spanish architecture. Built in the late 1500s, the house was modeled on that of Pontius Pilate in Jerusalem, hence the name. Its origins are Moorish, yet there are Gothic and Plateresque motifs throughout. The main facade is Renaissance with Gothic flourishes near the top. The spacious courtyard is a blend of Mudejar and Plateresque styles. With a full tour ticket, you can also visit the sumptuous upstairs living quarters replete with frescoes, oil paintings, and antiques.

On the opposite side of the barrio close to the river, find the **Museo de Bellas Artes** (Pl. Museo 9, tel. 95/422-0790, 2:30–8:30 P.M. Tues., 9 A.M.–8:30 P.M. Wed.–Sat., 9 A.M.– 2:30 P.M. Sun., €1.50). Built on the grounds of the Convento de la Merced (1612) in the mid-1800s, this collection of fine art is one of Spain's best—right up there with Madrid's Prado. It is particularly strong on lesser-known Spanish masters, including baroque painters Francisco de Zurbarán and Bartolome Estéban Murillo, both of whom lived in Sevilla. Pleasing the visitors looking to recognize a name, El Greco's *Retrato de Jorge Manuel*, a portrait of the artist's son is also here. Be sure to wander through the entrance hall and cloisters, which house a rich and varied collection of tiles from Sevilla. The plaza on which the museum sits hosts an artists market every Sunday morning.

Arenal

Between the cathedral area and the Río Guadalquivir is the barrio of Arenal, home to **Plaza de Toros de la Real Maestranza** (Po. Colón 12, tel. 95/422-4577, 9:30 A.M.–7 P.M. daily, closes at 3 P.M. the day of bullfights, €4), one of Spain's oldest and loveliest bullrings. Made famous in Bizet's *Carmen*, the ring, built between 1761 and 1881, features an understated baroque facade painted white with yellow trim. The main entrance, Puerta del Príncipe, has ornate 16th-century iron gates originally from a convent. When a matador has an exceptionally good fight, fans will carry him out of this gate on their shoulders. Along with the bullrings in Madrid and Ronda, La Maestranza is

considered one of the most prestigious rings in the world and matadors long to prove their bravery in front of its 14,000 seats, particularly during the Feria de Abril festivities. The tour of the bullring gives you access to the ring, the chapel where the matadors pray before a fight, the infirmary where they get stitched up if their prayers weren't heard, the Museo Taurino (a small but interesting collection of bullfighting memorabilia), and a fantastic gift shop. (If you would rather attend a bullfight, see *Bullfighting* under *Sports and Recreation*.)

Beyond the bullring is the **Hospital de la Caridad** (C/ Temprado 3, tel. 95/422-3232, 9 A.M.–1:30 P.M. and 3:30–7:30 P.M. Mon.–Sat., 9 A.M.–1:30 P.M. Sun., €4), a magnificent display of Christian piety etched in baroque grandeur. It was built in 1674 by Don Miguel de Mañara, a wealthy nobleman who fell into licentious ways after his young wife died. (A persistent legend says that he was the inspiration for Molina's *Don Juan*, but the play was written before Don Miguel was born.) Coming home after a wild night of debauchery, the dirty Don had a vision of his own decomposing body in a funeral procession and decided then and there to devote his life to charity—specifically the Brotherhood of Charity who lived in service of the poor and buried the unclaimed dead with their own hands. The hospital he built served as a refuge for the city's poor and destitute.

Within its elegant white and elegant facade are lovely arcaded courtyards, but the real jewel is the ornate church. On its walls hang canvasses that translate as the *Hieroglyphics of the End*, very gruesome depictions of the triumph of death over life. There are also several somber paintings by Murillo. The mood doesn't lighten up when you decipher the inscription over Don Manuel's crypt—"Here lies the dust and bones of the worst man to have lived on God's earth. Please pray for his soul."

Standing south of the Plaza de Toros and overlooking the banks of the Río Guadalquivir is the **Torre del Oro** (tel. 95/422-2419, 10 A.M.–2 P.M. Tues.–Fri., 11 A.M.–2 P.M. Sat.–Sun., €1), a 12-sided Moorish watchtower that

ANDALUCÍA

dates from 1220. It was constructed as part of the defensive rampart that ran up to the fortress Alcázar. The Moors would stretch a chain from the base of the tower across the river to another tower (since disappeared). This served as a barrier forcing boats that wished to enter the port of Sevilla to stop. It was this barrier that was broken by the Castilian naval commander Ramon de Bónifaz in 1248 and leading to Fernando III's capture of Sevilla. Used as a prison in the Middle Ages, this tower has narrowly escaped demolition and undergone many additions and restorations. It now houses a small naval museum and serves as an emblematic symbol of Sevilla. The origins of its name is lost but speculations say it may come from either the golden tiles that once adorned its facade or from the gold that was unloaded nearby during Sevilla's 15th-century heyday as the port to the Americas.

Plaza de España

This colorful, half-moon-shaped plaza and the nearby Parque de María Luisa are remnants of the 1929 Fair of the Americas held in Sevilla. The plaza is dominated by the Spanish Pavilion, which is decorated in motifs from Spain's grand cities. Starting with Álava and ending with Zaragoza, each city is honored with an elaborately tiled scene. You'll see Spanish visitors lining up for photos in front of their hometown's alcove. Grab a seat on one of the tiled benches around 8 P.M. and watch the locals stroll by on their evening paseo (stroll). You can also rent a rowboat on the moats that surround the plaza. On some evenings, the central fountain is lit with colored lights, adding to the festive atmosphere.

Stretching south from the plaza, **Parque de María Luisa** is one of the most elegant city parks in Spain. In an area about 130 hectares (0.5 mile square), a forest of over 3,500 orange, elm, palm, and pine trees provide shade for a tidy maze of bench-lined pathways, graceful fountains, and ornate pavilions. At the far end of the park, two of the pavilions have been turned into interesting museums. The Mudejar Pavilion houses the

Museo Artes y Costumbres Populares (Pl. América 3, tel. 95/423-2576, 2:30–8:30 P.M. Tues., 9 A.M.–8:30 P.M. Wed.–Sat., 9 A.M.–2:30 P.M. Sun., €1.50). (The building appeared in *Lawrence of Arabia* as an Arabic palace.) The museum is devoted to the folk arts and traditions of Andalucía and there are displays about bullfighting, flamenco, Semana Santa, and the Feria de Abril, bringing to vivid life the cultures and traditions that make Sevilla so unique. The Neo-Renaissance Pavilion is home to the **Museo Arqueológico de Sevilla** (Pl. América, s/n, tel. 95/423-2401, 2:30–8:30 P.M. Tues., 9 A.M.–8:30 P.M. Wed.–Sat., 9 A.M.–2:30 P.M. Sun., €1.50), one of the best archaeological museums in the country. The focus is on Roman remains, but there are also artifacts from the prehistoric eras, the Phoenicians, the Greeks, and the Carthaginians—all of whom once lived in the area of Sevilla. In the Phoenician section, don't miss the Carambolo Treasure, a collection of gold jewelry that dates to the 6th century and shows elements of Far East designs. Even though is the display features replicas, it is still fascinating to gaze upon such ancient expressions of vanity.

Triana

Across the Río Guadalquivir from the bullring sits the ancient barrio of Triana, a lively warren of narrow cobbled streets and winding alleys. Though not as picturesque as Santa Cruz, this barrio makes up for it with fewer tourists and more of a local village-within-a-city feel. Enter the barrio via **Puente de Triana** (officially named Puente Isabel II). At the end of the bridge is the **Plaza del Altonzano,** lined with houses bearing distinctive *miradores* (glass balconies). On the right you'll find a traditional market bustling with grocery-toting locals. The market sits on the sight of the long-gone Castilla San Jorge, a prison where those waiting Inquisition trials were held in misery. On the left, **Calle Betis** is home to dozens of lovely 18th-century mansions. As it follows the river, this street affords postcard-perfect views of the Torre del Oro, the bullring, and La Giralda rising in the distance. Lined with early evening bars and late-night clubs, Betis is also ground zero for Triana's lively *la marcha* (nightlife).

Named for the Roman emperor Trajan who was born outside of Sevilla, Triana has a long history as working-class. It has been home to *azulejo* tile factories since Roman times and almost all the tile work you'll see in Sevilla's churches, homes, and streets originated here. Of course, the barrio also took advantage of the local industry and many houses in Triana are covered in spectacular tiles. Located on **Calle Pelay** and **Calle Correa** are some of the best examples. To plan a little home decorating of your own, head to **Calles Callao, Antillano Campos,** and **Alfareria,** where several ceramics workshops are located.

For decades, Triana was home to Sevilla's *gitano* (Andalusian gypsy) community and the barrio is nicknamed the "Cradle of Flamenco." As you are wandering, look out for typical *gitano* homes called *corrales de vecinos.* These structures feature many apartments around a communal courtyard used by day for washing and cooking, by night for singing and dancing. The lovely **Casa de las Flores,** at Calle Castilla 16 is a perfect example.

Of course, as a good Catholic barrio in Sevilla—one of the most deeply religious of the Andalusian cities—religious events are paramount, including the spectacular solemnity of **Semana Santa.** Thousands line the streets of the barrio as no less than six fraternities of hooded penitents take to the streets, statues of their respective virgins mounted on their back. Some of these brotherhoods date back as far as the 1400s and of all the processions in Sevilla, those in Triana are among the most moving. The rest of the year, the faithful flock to **Capilla de los Marineros** (C/ Pureza 53) to see the venerated virgin, Esperanza de Triana. Other churches worth visiting are **Parroquia de Señora Santa Ana** (C/ Vázquez de Leca 1) near the Puente de San Telmo. Built in the 13th century, this Mudejar/Gothic church is the oldest in the city. The baptismal font called *pila de los gitanos* is said to impart flamenco talent on those baptized there.

Isla de la Cartuja

Just north of Triana, the Isla de Cartuja is not really an island at all, but rather a slip of land between two branches of the Río Guadalquivir. This was the location of the 1992 World's Fair. Four of the fair's pavilions have been converted into the **Isla Mágica** (tel. 90/216-1716, www.islamagica.es, 11 A.M.–10 P.M. daily, later in summer, €23.50, kids €16.50). The pairing of this 20th-century, tacky, overpriced amusement zone with the ancient historic center of Sevilla is a strange one at best. Adults should avoid it at all costs—there is enough wonder to be found in Sevilla's barrios. However, if you are traveling with antsy kids you might make a detour. The park is themed on Sevilla's past as a gateway to the New World—with pavilions named Quetzal, Gate to the Indies, Amazon, and El Dorado—each with its own rides and life-size cartoon characters. There are adrenaline-pumping roller coasters and wet and wild water rides as well as a Dimension 4 screen where you can watch films in 4-D. The park is small and can be "done" in a few hours. Consider making those evening hours when the prices drop to nearly half.

The isla is also home to the **Monasterio de Santa María de las Cuevas,** a 14th-century monastery complex that hosted Christopher Columbus during his layovers in Sevilla. Romantic legend holds that the great explorer planned out his early voyages within these walls. During the 1810–1812 occupation of the city by France, Napoleon's troops encamped at the monastery and destroyed much of its artwork. A few decades later, an Englishmen converted the monastery into a ceramics factory. Today, amid the restored confines of the monastery/factory, the **Centro Andaluz de Arte Contemporáneo** (tel. 95/503-7070, www.caac.es, 10 A.M.–9 P.M. Tues.–Fri., 11 A.M.–9 P.M. Sat., 10 A.M.–3 P.M. Sun., closed Mon., €1.80) is a focal point for modern art in Andalucía.

La Macarena

To the north of El Centro, the barrio of La Macarena is a jumble of working-class streets winding around a clutch of baroque churches.

ANDALUCÍA

This is local, inner-city Sevilla—old men in berets, grannies pulling shopping cars, beautiful young gay couples, neo-hippies, and dreadlocked artists—yet, despite being just a 10-minute walk from the cathedral, few tourists make it here.

The barrio lends its name to the **Basílica de la Macarena** (C/ Bécquer 1, tel. 95/490-1800, 9 A.M.–2 P.M. and 5–9 P.M. daily), home to Sevilla's most revered virgin, Nuestra Señora de la Esperanza. Her haunting image—sad dark eyes, crystal tears marring her rosy cheeks—appears all over Sevilla and during Semana Santa when the Brotherhood of Macarena carries her through the streets on Holy Thursday, the city reaches a religious frenzy. It is the highlight of the week's processions. La Macarena is the patron saint of gypsies and bullfighters and rumor has it that Joselito, the world-renowned matador from Sevilla, spent a fortune buying her four emeralds. When he was killed in the ring in 1920, the faithful dressed the virgin in mourning clothes for a month. See her jewels and costumes in the adjacent museum (€3).

The barrio's other religious monument worthy of a pilgrimage is **Convento de Santa Paula** (C/ Santa Paula 11, tel. 95/453-6330, 10:30 A.M.–1 P.M. Tues.–Sun., closed Mon., €2), a 15th-century convent with a fine Gothic facade and a glorious Mudejar cloister. It is still home to an order of nuns who whip up candies and cakes according to centuries-old recipes.

Along the northern edge of the barrio runs 400 meters (1,312 feet) of the city's original 12th-century walls. Lined with orange trees and double-parked cars, they seem almost forlorn in the midst of the bustling city. However, in their day they were part of one of the most fortified cities in Europe. Built by the Almoravids, Moors who ruled Andalusian in the 11th and 12th centuries, the walls once boasted 166 watchtowers and nine gates. Only three of the latter remain: the **Puerta de Córdoba,** the **Puerta Macarena,** and the **Postigo del Aceite.** Of the remaining watchtowers, the **Torre del Oro,** along the riverfront, is the most famous. The Puerta Macarena standing in front of the church of the same name ac-

the Torre del Oro

tually dates from the 2nd century A.D. when the Romans ruled the area. It is named after a Roman noble named Macarius.

ENTERTAINMENT AND EVENTS
Nightlife
If Sevilla by day is a visual feast of architectural styles and historical epochs, Sevilla by night is a dessert tray of variety, with hundreds of bars meeting every whim imaginable. In one night, you could hit a traditional tapas bar, a minimalist cocktail lounge, a flamenco *tablao*, and a thumping disco, all within a five-minute walk of each other. A generalized breakdown of nightlife zones are: Centro, particularly Plaza del Salvador and Plaza Alfalfa; Barrio Santa Cruz; around the cathedral, especially rocking Calle Mateos Gago; Calle Betis in Triana; and the edgy Alameda de Hércules, home to the city's largest concentration of gay and lesbian clubs, but also one of the least savory areas of the city. For a detailed list of gay and lesbian nightlife, go to www.turismo.sevilla.org and download their guide, *Guia Sevilla Para Gays y Lesbianas*. The local take on sangria is a boozy affair innocently named *Agua de Sevilla*. A potent potion of four liquors, pineapple juice, and sparkling wine, it is usually served by the pitcher and not recommended for drinking alone. Cheers!

In Sevilla, local fashion is to start at a tapas bar around 10 P.M. and then move onto a bar. When the bars close at 3 A.M., those who want more head to a *discoteca* or one of the handful of bars that stay open late.

Start the night with any of these choices. The rooftop terrace bar at **Hotel Doña María** (C/ Don Remondo 19, tel. 95/422-4990) is the most sophisticated place to begin an evening. The open-air bar overlooks the illuminated La Giralda, providing an unforgettable backdrop for a glass of wine or cold cocktail. Prices are hotel high, but the view is worth it. The bar is only open in warm weather, so call first if you are there during winter. Down on the ground, **El Perejil** (C/ Mateos Gago 20, tel. 95/421-8966) is a tiny slip of a place that has been a long-

time favorite of locals. Ask for a *vino de naranja*, a house specialty wine infused with oranges. Around the corner, **Bar Tenderete** (C/ Rodrigo Caro 3, tel. 95/422-0295) is a narrow bar jammed with antique clocks and radios. It is one of the few places in this part of town that stays open past 2 A.M. It is also a good place to catch live music from blues to flamenco. The red-hued **Zapata** (C/ Rodríguez Zapata 1, Thurs.–Sun. only) is a tiny haunt with Mexican aspirations. Their margaritas and tequila sunrises are sublime. **Antigüedades** (C/ Argote de Molina, 40, weekends only) is a warren of stuffed body parts and life-size dolls posed in all sorts of perplexing positions. This "work of art" is courtesy of the owner, who also serves up well-priced cocktails to a mix of locals and tourists.

Between El Centro and La Macarena in Plaza de los Terceros is the oldest bar in Sevilla, **El Rincóncillo** (C/ Gerona 40, tel. 95/422-3183). Founded in 1670, this atmospheric watering hole has been run by the same family for eight generations. Its rough wooden ceiling is hung with wrought-iron chandeliers and the bar is lined with centuries-old liquor bottles. Near Plaza Alfalfa, **Garlochi** (C/ Boteros 26) takes the spectacle of Spanish Catholicism and adds alcohol. Virgin Mary greets visitors just inside the door, walls are plastered with pictures of saints and more virgins, and flowers and candles jam every bit of free counter space. Naturally, the house cocktail is the Sangre de Cristo (Blood of Christ). Amen! Over on hopping Calle Pérez Galdos, you'll find tons of bars buzzing even on Monday nights. For *chupitos* (shots), try the tiny **Le Rebotica** (No. 11, tel. 95/422-1625), which serves over 50 different shooters (€1.50). It gets packed with the college crowds on weekends.

If you are ready to go late, know that the bigger dance clubs are usually open only on weekends and don't get going until 3 A.M. They'll finish up around dawn, depending on the bar's particular license. Most will charge a cover of €5–12. In exchange you'll receive a ticket good for your first drink. Near Plaza Alfalfa, **Berlin** (C/ Boteros, s/n, tel. 95/422-1697) is an eclectic bar that keeps disco hours. It is a

ANDALUCÍA

good place to chat up a local while listening to a mix of pop rock. **Catedral** (Cuesta del Rosario 12) takes its decor cue from Catholicism and its music from the post-modern international DJs. It is smaller than other discos, but also attracts a smaller, hipper crowd. The house DJ at **Elefunk** (C/ Adriano, 10) serves up an infectious mix of funk blended with a bit of jungle and hip-hop.

In Triana, the most famous mega-club has long been **Boss** (C/ Betis, 67, midnight–6 A.M. Wed.–Sun., often goes much later on weekends). With a stadium-sized dance floor, four bars, and a group of resident DJs pumping out the latest music, this place stays popular. The doormen are known to suffer from that peculiar "I am a doorman/god" disease, so go dressed well and with good manners—at least until you are inside where you can let loose with a crowd of hundreds. **Río Latino** (C/ Betis 40) serves up Spanish pop to a mostly Sevillano crowd.

West of Alameda de Hércules, **Weekend House Club** (Av. Torneo 43, 10:30 P.M.–7 A.M. Fri.–Sat.) takes its name from the music it pumps out—hard and heavy house. There are go-go dancers in cages, a towering drag queen named Barbie the Destroyer, and a roster of top international guest DJs. The crowd is a pretty mix of gay and straight all with one thing in common—a love of electronic music and all-night dancing. **Fun Club** (Alameda de Hércules, 84, 11 P.M.–8 A.M.) adds a little rock and roll to its musical line up of techno, drum-and-bass, and house. There are often concerts held early in the evening.

Flamenco

Many aficionados claim that flamenco was born in the barrio of Triana and that Sevilla is one of the finest places in the world to witness this exuberant, emotional, evocative art form. You'll see flyers and posters all over town. You'll also be constantly warned to stay away from "tourist traps" pumping out taped music and unskilled dancers. Honestly, there are not too many of those; this town—indeed the region of Andalucía—is crawling with seasoned,

talented, professional flamenco dancers, singers, and performers. Some shows are better—and aficionados claim, more authentic—than others, but if you are a novice, you are bound to have a good time no matter where you go.

The options are two: a big, splashy *tablao* (caberet), where there are several choreographed shows per night, often accompanied by dinner; or a flamenco bar, where the costumes might not be as fancy, the decor not as polished, but the improvised performance is guaranteed to be inspired. Take note, most of the *tablaos* offer an option for dinner. Skip it. Though decent enough, the meals are overpriced.

Boasting a solid reputation even among flamenco snobs, **El Arenal** (C/ Rodo 7, tel. 95/421-6492, www.tablaoelarenal.com, 8:30 P.M. and 10:30 P.M. daily, €34 show and one drink, €66 show with dinner) has been delighting visitors with authentic performances for over 25 years. The *tablao*, situated in a renovated 17th-century building, oozes Andalusian charm with bright tiles, deep yellow walls, and rustic wooden furniture. The show might include two guitarists, a percussionist tapping a *cajón* (a wooden box that the musician sits on top), and half-a-dozen dancers. The quality of the performance is high and the music impassioned—both tourists and performers seem to really enjoy themselves. **Los Gallos Tablao Flamenco** (Pl. Santa Cruz 11, tel. 95/421-6981, www.tablaolosgallos.com, 9 P.M. and 11 P.M. daily, €27 show and one drink) is a perennial favorite with excellent shows featuring passionate performers. Make reservations, and show up about 40 minutes early to snag a good seat. The one drawback of this charming spot is that it has become very, very popular with the tour group set. Though it doesn't affect the performance, it does make you feel like you are seeing a show back home in Duluth. **Casa de la Memoria de Al-Andalus** (C/ Ximénez de Enciso 28, 95/456-0670, 9 P.M. daily, €12), deep in the Barrio Santa Cruz, is a house of memories dedicated to the Jewish population who were massacred in the barrio in 1391. By day, it offers tours of its Sala Sefarad, a restored space showing elements of the Jewish homes typical to this barrio. By night, it becomes one of the most atmospheric *tablaos* in town. The show only—no drink, no food—is held in the Moorish-arched courtyard of the house. It may consist of two guitarists, a few singers, and a clutch of serious, impassioned dancers. Reservations are mandatory.

Triana is full of neighborhood bars where flamenco performances spontaneously occur. **Casa Anselma** (C/ Pagés del Corro 49, 11 P.M.–3 A.M. Mon.–Sat., closed Sun., though opening hours change often) is the most famous. There is no sign on the door, but you'll feel the flamenco spirit pouring out of the glowing blue, arched entryway (unless you arrive before 11 P.M. when the doors will still be closed). Inside is riot of Andalusian excess—colorful tiles, bullfighting posters, black-and-white photos of famous flamenco performers, deep orange walls, a bull's head over the bar, and above the stage a small shrine to the Virgin Mary, surrounded by electric candles. Presided over by the tough-as-long-red-nails Anselma—who often sings and dances herself—there are only two rules here: Enjoy the music and buy a drink. Anselma prowls the crowd to ensure everyone has something in their hands—Coke, whisky, beer—and will not let the show begin until she is satisfied. The reason is simple, there is no cover charge, therefore the drinks cover the expenses—and the musician's salaries. The shows—completely improvised—generally begin with a guitar player or two. Singers and dancers are not costumed and may very well be the person sitting next to you. One night, the crowd may be brought to tears by a particular song; on others, the entire room—mostly consisting of locals—may join in the singing and clapping. However, one song is always performed. Near the end of the night, Anselma calls for silence. The lights are lowered and the electric candles surrounding the virgin are lit up. All eyes face the virgin—La Paloma Blanca—while one of the performers sings a mournful song/prayer in her honor. Many audience members join in. It is a touching, unexpected, very Andalusian finish to a raucous night of fun.

Back near the cathedral, **La Carbonería**

(C/ Levies 18, tel. 95/421-4460, 8 P.M.–3 A.M. daily) is one of Sevilla's most famous bars and for good reason. Its cavernous rooms drip with atmosphere, from the wood-beamed ceiling to the fireplace in the bar to the large gardened terrace open in summer. It sponsors all sorts of free music shows—jazz, Arabic, blues—but it is famed for its flamenco shows. The stage is intimate and the music inspired. After the live show, flamenco is pumped through the stereo system while a mix of tourists and hip, young locals while away the night.

FESTIVALS AND EVENTS
Semana Santa

The celebration of Semana Santa reaches its zenith in Sevilla with more processions, more venerated virgins, and more crucified Christs than in any other town. With origins back to the 14th century, Sevilla's Semana Santa has 57 *cofradías* (brotherhoods) representing the city's churches with over 100 floats. Beginning on Palm Sunday, various brotherhoods begin their processions, carrying the statues of their Virgin Mary and Christ on flower-covered floats to the cathedral. The most anticipated day of Semana Santa is Good Thursday, when the city's most adored processions make their way through the crowded streets: El Silencio, El Gran Poder, La Macarena, El Calvario, La Esperanza de Triana, and Los Gitanos. If you make it to no other processions, try to make one of these for an intimate glimpse at the deep spirituality of the Sevillano people. (See sidebar, *All About Semana Santa*.)

La Feria de Abril

No festival better captures the proud exuberance of the city than the springtime Feria de Abril. The week-long event begins about two weeks after the end of Semana Santa, and therefore the date is dependent on Easter. The party is held at a mock village set up in a field on the far bank of the river and runs non-stop for a full seven days. Expect prancing horses, *señoritas* in flouncy dresses, dancing until daybreak, and free-flowing sherry. (See sidebar, *Seven Days in Sevilla*.)

SEVEN DAYS IN SEVILLA

During the **Feria de Abril** (also called the Feria de Sevilla), Sevilla throws a party that rivals New Orleans' Mardi Gras, Río's Carnival, and Munich's Oktoberfest. In stark contrast to the solemn grandeur of Semana Santa, which precedes it by mere weeks, *la feria* is an all-out city-wide bash dedicated to dancing and drinking, singing and socializing. For six days and nights Sevillanos attack this purpose with a passionate fervor, dancing from sundown to sun-up every night.

The atmosphere is pure magic. It all takes place just outside the old city center in a colorful pre-fabricated village, Real de la Feria, set up just for the event. The celebration kicks off the first Monday of the festival with the lighting of the massive arch that graces the entrance to the village. The crowd stretching down Calle Asunción vibrates with anticipation as the clock ticks down. At precisely the stroke of midnight, the thousands of lights that cover the arch explode into illumination and a river of merrymakers stream into the mock village. *La feria* has begun.

Inside, hundreds of *casetas* (replicas of whitewashed Andalusan houses) cram flower-lined pedestrian streets. Locals dress the part. For women, that means thick-ruffled, floor-length dresses in rainbow hues, long-fringed shawls, and an oversized flower tucked low behind one ear. Men jazz up in short-waisted coats and broad-brimmed flat-topped hats. Arm-in-arm they strut through the village beneath thousands of bright paper lanterns, seeing and being seen.

However, the real action takes place inside the *casetas*, which can hold anywhere from a few dozen to a thousand people. They crank out *sevillanas* (a popular variant of flamenco) and *jerez* (sherry) in equal portions. Heavy dancing starts up around 11 P.M. and the dance of the fair is *sevillanas*. Nothing like the focused intensity of flamenco, this popular dance follows a strict set of steps and is practiced in pairs. It is an extremely graceful dance full of twirling skirts, expressive arms, beckoning hands, and seductive smiles. Everyone from the tots to grannies dance it nonstop during the festivities.

Despite its grand scale, the *feria* is very much a local affair. Generation-spanning families come out in full force. Don't be surprised if you see an eight-year-old girl dancing with her grandfather at 4 A.M. Reflecting this cozy family nature are the *casetas* themselves. Most are sponsored by groups composed of friends and families known generically as *hermanos* (brotherhoods). Supported by member dues, these *casetas* are strictly private – you know someone or you don't go in. However, the festive nature of the fair means it's not too hard to meet a kind Sevillano and wrangle yourself an invite. If not, the public *casetas* are just as lively. Sponsored by corporations and public organizations, these *casetas* are usually massive and jam-packed with locals seeking a change of scenery, visitors from around Spain, American college students, and Japanese girls decked out in full-festival regalia dancing like pros. The *caseta municipal*, run by town hall, is the largest and liveliest.

The dancing goes until daybreak when everyone heads out for *churros y chocolate* (fried donut sticks and hot chocolate) at one of the dozens of stalls lining the fairgrounds. Later in the day, you can stop by the massive fun fair that accompanies the *feria*. Or if you prefer to just kick around the city center, you'll find the festive atmosphere permeating every corner bar. The *feria* coincides with Sevilla's bullfighting season and the Maestranza bullring attracts some of the best bullfighters in Spain.

From midday until about 8 P.M., men parade on horseback up and down the sandy streets of the village, while the ladies ride side-saddle behind them. As night falls, the horses make room for thousands of revelers dressed and ready for dancing. Around 10 P.M., the *casetas* fill anew. More dancing, more hand-clapping, more singing, more skirt-twirling, more sherry, more friends, more fun. Just more. This goes on every night until Sunday night when the *feria* culminates in a spectacular fireworks show.

Anyone can join in the fun, but you need to plan ahead. Most obviously, book your hotel early—up to six months—and expect to pay triple the normal rates. Getting to the fairground can be hectic, as nearly all of Andalucía is doing the same. The road leading to the fair can be claustrophobically jammed, so taxis will cost you a mint and buses will take forever. It is not that long a hike, so pop your dancing shoes into your bag and follow these directions: Cross the San Telmo bridge near the Torre del Oro. At Plaza de Cuba, turn left on Calle Asunción. Go straight until you run into the fair.

The drink of the fair is *jerez,* Andalusian sherry, often mixed into a spritzer with sweet soda and ice. Food is typically Andalusian, with fried fish, grilled seafood, and cured hams dominating the menus at the food stalls on the fairgrounds. The food is grossly overpriced—though the drinks are not—so if you are on a budget, eat before you arrive at the fair or bring a sandwich.

If you are in Madrid during the week of the fair and didn't know to reserve a room in time, reserve a spot on the Renfe AVE high-speed train to Sevilla. You can leave in the afternoon. Enjoy the fiesta until sun up, and then catch the morning train out. Sleep it off later.

Flamenco

Sevilla has a healthy roster of events related to flamenco. Every two years, the **Bienal de Flamenco** (www.bienal-flamenco.org) is held in September and October. Begun in 1980, it is one of the world's premier flamenco festivals and draws top acts to the city's top venues. Serious aficionados worldwide pour into town for the series of high-brow events. Tickets are expensive and should be bought in advance through the website or by calling 95/459-0867. In off years, the city sponsors a smaller, more local **Festivales de Flamenco de Sevilla.** The city also sponsors **Feria Mundial del Flamenco** (www.feriamundialdelflamenco.es), a trade fair that brings together artists, producers, and purveyors of flamenco goods from instruments to records. It is held in October yearly.

© SEVE PONCE DE LEON

Catch a local performance of the inherently Andalusian dance: flamenco.

SPORTS AND RECREATION
Arabic Baths

As in the rest of Andalucía's cities, Sevilla harkens back to its Moorish roots in food, architecture, and most pleasurably, in its *hammams,* or Arabic baths. The most sensuous is **Aire de Sevilla** (C/ Aire 15, tel. 95/501-0024, www .airedesevilla.com, 10 A.M.–2 A.M. daily, €20). Built on the grounds of an actual Arabic bath over 1,000 years old, this luxurious modern temple to relaxation is an experience you should not miss. Moroccan candelabras throw latticed shadows onto the deep orange walls, incense fuses with clouds of steam, and the sound of soft Arabic music mingles with the constant trickle of water. There are three large baths—hot, warm, and cold. As you move from one to the other, your body reacts to the temperature change. You can feel each vein coursing with life beneath your skin, your spine softens, your breathing deepens, your mind quiets. The baths are held every two hours, with the most popular times being after 8 P.M. and on the weekends. An optional 15-minute massage is an extra €8. After your bath, relax further with a specialty infusion in the attached Arabic tea room.

Bullfighting

Though there are a couple of bullfights held the two Sundays right after Semana Santa, the **Feria de Abril** kicks off Sevilla's bullfighting season. The series of bullfights held in conjunction with the festival is among the most prestigious in the world, right behind the San Isidro festival of Madrid. The Feria de Abril usually kicks off mid-April and lasts two weeks, with a bullfight every day. You can attempt to buy tickets at the bullring, but these bullfights are extremely popular and tickets are usually sold to season holders well in advance. After the Feria, there are usually fights every Sunday until October. May–September, most of the *corridas* (bullfights) are *novilladas,* meaning that the bullfighter is a novice—often in his teens. For a diehard fan, this makes an artistic difference; to the tourist, it just means tickets are about half what they'd cost for a big-name professional matador. Also, the *novilladas* can be exciting as the young guns are almost idiotically brave, doing things a more experienced matador never would. You can purchase tickets at the bullring or at **Empresa Pages** (C/ Adriano 37, tel. 95/450-1382), located right behind the ring. There are also various ticket stands set up around the city. They are convenient, but expect a 20 percent mark-up. Don't buy scalped tickets near the ring. Unless you know what you are looking for, you are apt to be ripped off. (For details on this most Spanish of sports, see sidebar, *Bullfighting,* in the *Background* chapter.)

ACCOMMODATIONS

Barrio Santa Cruz is surely the most atmospheric place to stay in Sevilla, but most of it is inaccessible by car so you will have to haul your luggage in from Plaza Santa Cruz. Consult with your hotel for the best options for arriving. If you stay anywhere else in the barrios discussed in this book, you'll be fine. The city is compact and walkable—with visual delights hidden around every corner. If you have trouble

booking a place on your own, try www.sol.com, an online booker specializing in Andalucía.

Under €50

As the capital and the largest city in Andalucía, Sevilla tends to be more expensive than other Andalusian cities. However you can find some decent, family-run *hostales* in this price range, as well as most of the city's youth hostels (*albergue* in Spanish). The best youth hostel is **Oasis Backpacker's Hostel** (C/ Don Alonso el Sabio 1, tel. 95/429-3777, info@oasissevilla.com, www.oasissevilla.com, €18 for a dorm bed), located in a renovated building with terra-cotta floors. The bright rooms and social areas are modern and cozy, and the rooftop terrace boasts an expansive view over the cityscape. The terrace also features a glass floor that lets sun shine into the hostel's inner courtyard. Guests appreciate backpacker standards like free Internet, continental breakfast, communal kitchen, and hostel-sponsored parties and bar crawls.

A step up from a youth hostel, **Hostal San Benito Abad** (C/ Canarios 4, tel. 95/441-5255, www.hostalsanbenito.com, €36) is as basic as you get. Located on a dead-end alley off the Plaza Santa María, this family-run place has eight small, darkish rooms overlooking an inner courtyard. **Hotel Londres** (C/ San Pedro Martir 1, tel. 95/450-2745, recepcion@londreshotel.com, www.londreshotel.com, €50), located near the Museo de Bellas Artes, is a cheap and cheerful hotel with charming Andalusian details and clean, if plain, rooms. Air-conditioning is standard, though it gets turned off when you leave the room. Remind them to turn it back on when you return. **Hostal Arias** (C/ Mariana de Pineda 9, tel. 95/422-6840, reservas@hostalarias.com, www.hostalarias.com, €50) features clean, airy rooms with odd, outdated decor. Heat and air-conditioning are standard.

Practically in the shadow of the Real Alcázar, **Pensión Alcázar** (C/ Dean Miranda 12, tel. 95/422-8457, info@pensionalcazar.com, www.pensionalcazar.com, €40) has gorgeously tiled hallways and a rooftop terrace with spectacular views. Opt for an upper-floor room that includes small terraces and air-conditioning. **Hostal Goya** (C/ Mateos Gago 31, tel. 95/421-1170, €45) features a lovely interior courtyard and smallish, clean, nicely decorated rooms. The staff is particularly friendly, even though English is not their strong suit. Make sure you see your room before you accept it, as there are a few duds. Also, remember that Mateos Gago is party central at night; if you have an exterior room, you'll need to be a heavy sleeper or use earplugs. Also, the cheapest rooms feature sinks and showers, but the toilets are down the hall. Prices go up for in-room toilets.

€50-100

Hostería de Doña Lina (C/ Gloria 7, tel. 95/421-0956, hlina@hlina.com, www.hlina.com, €60) is located right in Barrio Santa Cruz next to the Alcázar, fronting a lovely tiny square jammed with orange trees. The small hotel oozes charm—colorful tiles, blooming plants, Andalusian art—and the simple rooms feature all the creature comforts, including air-conditioning. Try to get the front room with a balcony for a breathtaking view of La Giralda. The hotel houses an excellent restaurant serving traditional fare, but be warned, the bill might very well exceed that of your hotel room. For a cheaper option, head to their tapas bar, Tapas Doña Lina. Also in Santa Cruz, **(C Hotel Amadeus** (C/ Farnesio 6, tel. 95/450-1443, hotelamadeussevilla@hotelamadeussevilla.com, www.hotelamadeussevilla.com, €92) is a gem of a small hotel. Taking classical music as a design cue, the hotel's 14 rooms, spread over two adjacent buildings, are lovingly styled with antiques, soothing walls, and refreshing linens. The common room feature Andalusian tiles, plants, artwork, more antiques, a grand piano, and a harp. On the roof, a modern gardened terrace offers lovely views over the barrio. **Hotel Doña Manuela** (Po. Catalina Ribera 2, tel. 95/454-6400, dmanuela@andalunet.com, www.grupo modesto.com, €95) is a gleaming new boutique hotel with an elegant old-world style. The cream-colored rooms boast updated antiques and colorful linens. Some have terraces opening onto the lovely Murillo parks. The rooftop sundeck gives an amazing view over the old town. The hotel owners also run the highly recommended restaurant Modesto. **Hotel Alcántara** (C/ Ximénez de Enciso 28, tel. 95/450-0595, info@hotelalcantara.net, www.hotelalcantara.net, €90) is a breath of modernity in the sometimes queasy quaintness of Santa Cruz. With the usual features like a central courtyard and an 18th-century carriage entryway, the hotel surprises with a clean, minimal interior. The rooms are calming shades of dusky green with blonde wood floors and marble baths. Staff are known for their friendliness and are happy to to help guests book flamenco shows and other activities. **Apartmentos Murillo** (C/ Reinoso 6, tel. 95/421-6095, www.hotelmurillo.com, €95) offers attractive apartments with kitchenettes (fridge, stove, and microwave) and sitting areas. The decor is sophisticated country with lots of bright colors, hardwood, and iron-framed furnishings. They have apartments that can sleep up to five comfortably. Around the corner, they run the equally stylish **Hotel Murillo** (€90). **Espacio Azahar** (C/ Jesús del Gran Pode, 28, tel. 95/438-4109, info@espacioazahar.com, www.espacioazahar.com, €98) is a new hotel in El Centro with just 14 rooms. Done in a Mediterranean palette of blue, yellow, and white, the rooms have thoughtful touches like latex mattresses, Tiffany-style lamps, plasma televisions, and Wi-Fi. The complex also includes a creative, upscale restaurant, Azahar, a coffee shop with homemade cakes, and the intriguing Terraza Universal Etnia, a rooftop lounge with Arabic and African design, a short menu with Asian and Spanish tapas, and a unique acclimatization system that allows the terrace to be used even in the cold clutch of winter.

€100-200

(C La Casa del Maestro (C/ Almudena 5, tel. 95/450-0007, reservas@lacasadelmaestro.com, www.lacasadelmaestro.com, €131) is located in the home of legendary flamenco guitarist and teacher, Manuel Serrapi Sánchez, better known as Niño Ricardo—the Maestro. The flamenco/Andalusian theme is throughout the hotel—lots of blue and yellow tiles, guitar motifs, and the placement of two *trajes de luces* (bullfighting suits) in niches along the stairs. The rooms, each individually named and decorated, soothe with muted colors and quaint sophistication, and details like wrought-iron headboards, wall tapestries, and plush linens. The rooftop garden is a nice refuge after a day of sightseeing. **Hotel Alminar** (C/ Álvarez Quintero 52, tel. 95/429-3913, reservas@hotelalminar.com, www.hotelalminar.com, €125) is the sister to Alcántara and has the same modern style, only more so. Bedrooms feature muted golden walls with chocolate trim and creamy flowing curtains. The bathrooms, with big tiled tubs, are a delight. The staff is very accommodating and ready to divulge a wealth of information about tapas bars, nightclubs, and flamenco. **Hotel Adriano** (C/ Adriano 12, tel. 95/429-3800, www.adrianohotel.com, €130) is located on a quiet street in Arenal, about a five-minute walk to the river, less than 10 to the cathedral. Its 34 clean, well-maintained rooms are classical with thick, striped burgundy furnishings and marble floors.

Hotel Doña María (C/ Don Remondo 19, tel. 95/422-4990, www.hdmaria.com, €135) is located in a 14th-century mansion that once belonged to the advisor to King Pedro I the Cruel. Far from cruel, this is one of the city's most charming hotels. Billed as a "hotel-museum" by its aristocratic owner, the property is crammed with antiques and artifacts attesting to Andalucía's glorious heritage. The rooftop deck boasts a bar and a pool where you can do laps in full view of La Giralda. **Petit Palace Santa Cruz** (C/ Muñoz y Pavón 18, 95/422-1032, sac@hthoteles.com, www.petit palace.com, €150), opened in April 2006, is located in a majestic 17th-century building near the cathedral. That is where the old-world charm stops. As a member of the sleek High Tech chain, decor and amenities are modern. The result is a futuristic palace of muted tones and inviting rooms. There aren't tubs, but the showers feature high-pressure hydro-massage functions. Wi-Fi is freely available. Located

in the barrio La Macarena, **◖ Alcoba del Rey** (C/ Becquer 9, tel. 95/491-5800, info@ alcobadelrey.com, www.alcobadelrey.com, €180) revels in Sevilla's Moorish heritage. On the grounds of a former Moorish palace, the owners have built a modern Moorish retreat. Guests enter a world of explosive color, trickling fountains, and tiled patios lush with sweet-smelling plants. Each room has been carefully decorated in its own individual style, though they share details such as brightly patterned ceilings, horseshoe-arched doorways, colorful silk throws, luxurious baths, and decadent bath products from Hermés. Avid collectors and importers, the owners have also placed every item in the hotel for sale. The only drawback is its location, some 25 minutes walking to the cathedral. Put on your comfiest shoes or hail a cab, since this hotel is worth the effort.

Over €200

Hotel Alfonso XIII (C/ San Fernando 2, tel. 95/491-7000, www.hotel-alfonsoxiii.com, €535) is not only the city's premier five-star hotel, but a sight in itself. Located next to the university (formerly *Carmen*'s tobacco factory), this Mudejar palace was built to house King Alfonso XIII and his royal guests during the 1929 exposition. Its huge inner courtyard is surrounded ornate archways, broad hallways boast acres of marble, walls are covered in gold and red silks, and the rooms are nothing short of sumptuous. Under the management of the Westin/Starwood luxury hotel chain, service and attention are outstanding. There is also a lovely pool and garden complex providing a perfect refuge after a day of sightseeing in Sevilla's hot sun. Note that the listed price is the rack rate for a double. You can slash that by more than a third if you use an online booker.

FOOD

As in the rest of Andalucía, Sevilla's local cuisine is based on cured hams and meat, game, seafood, and fresh produce. Local specialties to look out for are *pescaito frito* (a platter of fried fish and seafood), *coquinas* (small clams stewed in white wine), *puntillas* (fried baby squid), *pincho moruno* (a pork kebob seasoned with Moroccan spices), *solomillo al wisky* (steak marinated in a whisky sauce), *jamón jabugo* (very high-quality cured ham from nearby Huelva), *pringá* (a savory spread made of several blended meats and sausages), and for dessert, particularly during Semana Santa, *torrijas* (a version of French toast, often flavored with orange).

Your options for trying these tasty treats are limitless, with dozens of tapas bars and restaurants on every street. If it looks full of locals, it is probably a good bet. The following are tried and true suggestions, but don't be afraid to venture out on your own. Calle Mateos Gago is hard to beat for sheer variety, the Barrio Santa Cruz for charm, Triana and Macarena for local character.

Keep in mind that Sevilla's restaurants more or less follow Spanish opening hours of 1–4 P.M. and 8 P.M.–midnight. In the hottest months of summer, some places close down during the day altogether and in August they may shut down for the whole month. If you head out around 6 P.M. looking for food, you are bound to be disappointed. If you know you can't wait until 9 P.M. to eat, buy a few snacks at a grocery and have them in your room to tide you over until it is time for tapas-hopping or dinner.

Local Cuisine

The following are all in the Barrio Santa Cruz. **Modesto** (C/ Cano y Cueto 5, tel. 95/441-6811, noon–5 P.M. and 8 P.M.–2 A.M. daily, €32) has nothing to be modest about. Located near the Jardines de Murillo in Santa Cruz, this classic Andalusian restaurant has been pleasing locals since 1900. Specialties include *fritura el modesto* (shrimp fried with onions and green peppers) and *solomillo al wisky*. During warm weather, the terrace in the plaza opens up, though the restaurant's antique dining rooms are quite charming. **La Albahaca** (Pl. Santa Cruz 12, tel. 95/422-0714, 1–4:30 P.M. and 8 P.M.–midnight daily, €42) is set in a romantic 1920s Andalusian mansion. The equally divine food is Andalusian with Basque touches. **C Corral del Agua** (Callejón

del Agua 6, tel. 95/442-0714, noon–4 P.M. and 8 P.M.–midnight Mon.–Sat., closed Sun., €30) is one of the city's most romantic spots. In an ancient building amid flickering candles, lush flowering plants, and trickling fountains, the kitchen serves classic Andalusian fare like *ajoblanco* (a cold almond and grape soup) and *dorada al Tío Pepe* (sea bass in sherry). **La Cueva** (C/ Rodrigo Caro 18, tel. 95/421-3143, noon–4 P.M. and 8 P.M.–midnight daily, €25) with a terrace opening onto the charming Plaza Doña Elvira, is another lovely old Andalusian mansion. There are two rustic dining rooms complete with bulls' heads, but the flowering patios are the true delight and the perfect place to try one of the restaurant's signature rice dishes. At the end of the Murillo gardens, **Egaña-Oriza** (C/ San Fernando 41, tel. 95/422-7211, info@restauranteoriza.com, www.restauranteoriza.com, €50) is Sevilla's most gastronomically acclaimed restaurant. It is also quite arguably its most beautiful. The dining room, set in the glass and wrought-iron greenhouse of a 1926 mansion, shimmers with elegance and refinement. That feeling extends to the plate as well. The chef hails from País Vasco and creates a wonderful cuisine combining Basque delicacy with Andalusian heartiness. The result is dishes like warm partridge salad with sherry vinaigrette, roasted fish with capers and anchovies, and lobster salad with citrus. Half the fun of dining here is watching the crowd—this is *the* place for Sevilla's socialites and business leaders.

Between El Centro and La Macarena, **Becerrita** (C/ Recadero 9, tel. 95/441-2057, www.becerrita.com, 1–4:30 P.M. and 8–11:30 P.M. Mon.–Sat., 1–4:30 P.M. Sun., €40) is located in an elegant turn-of-the-20th-century mansion with fanciful murals, colorful ceramic walls, and rich wood trim. The food is pure Andalusian with a refined touch. Seafood dishes are particularly sublime—fresh tuna with aioli, monkfish with apples, and codfish gratin. It may be way off the beaten path on the outskirts of Triana, but **Poncio** (C/ Victoria 15, tel. 95/434-0010, www.poncio restaurantes.com, 1:30–4 P.M. and 9:30 P.M.–midnight Tues.–Sat., 1:30–4 P.M. Mon., closed

Sun., €36) has landed on the maps of foodies in Spain and beyond. In a lovely red dining room, chef Willy Moya, who studied at the Cordon Bleu in Paris, serves sophisticated Andalusian fare with dreamy desserts. Reservations are suggested.

Tapas

In Sevilla, tapa-hopping approaches religion. It is called the *tapeo* and on Saturdays and Sundays, it is the most popular way for locals to lunch. The bulk of your tapas-hopping will happen around the Cathedral and in Barrio Santa Cruz, where there are hundreds of great tapas bars, including the following. ❨ **Bar Giralda** (C/ Mateos Gago 1) is on the grounds of an ancient 10th-century *hammam*—you can see elements of the bathhouse in the solid columns and domed ceilings. The walls are elaborately tiled and the marble bar glistens with fresh fish ready to made into delicious *frituras* (fried fish platter) or delicious *pâté de cabracho* (mild fish spread). **Bar Belmonte** (C/ Mateos Gago 24) is named for the famed bullfighter Juan Belmonte, who was born in Triana. The bar is full of bullfighting memorabilia and the tapa to have is *albóndigas* (meatballs). **Las Columnas** (C/ Rodrigo Caro 1) is officially called Bodega Santa Cruz, but even locals don't know that. It is jam-packed day and night. Be brave, make your way through the crowd, and give your order. The bartender will write it on the wood-topped bar with the stub of chalk he carries behind his ear. The best tapas are *pringa* (a savory blend of sausages and other meats) and *flamenquin* (pork stuffed with cheese, wrapped in ham, and deep fried). **Las Teresas** (C/ Santa Teresa 2) is an atmospheric hole-in-the-wall with cured *jamón* legs hanging from the ceiling, tiled walls hung with bullfighting photos, and a bar lined with sherry bottles. Have a glass and splash out for a plate of *jamón jabugo*. **Casa Román** (Pl. Venerables 1) is famous for its *pan tumaca*, thick bread rubbed with tomato, garlic, and olive oil and topped with transparent slices of *jamón*. **La Cava del Europa** (C/ Santa María la Blanca 40) is a sleek little wine bar that shines like a beacon of modernity in Santa Cruz's sea of old tiles and Andalusian charm. The bar won Sevilla's award for best tapas in 2003 and the menu is peppered with delights like wonton of *sanfaina* (an eggplant and onion relish) or pungent Torta de la Serena cheese with tomato and ginger jelly. The menu changes with the seasons.

Moving out of Santa Cruz, you'll find many good tapas joints in El Centro, especially around Plaza Nueva and Plaza Salvador. Make an effort to track down ❨ **Entrecárceles** (C/ Faisanes 1). It was once the guard's quarters of the former royal prison where Cervantes once did time. Since 1894 it has been serving tapas and cold sherry. Today, the decor—an excessive riot of tiles and woodwork—remains the same though the tapas have taken a modern turn— foie gras with grapefruit puree or eggplant layered with cured salmon and shrimp.

In Triana, you again are spoiled for choice, especially along Calle San Jacinto. Try **Bar Oliva** (C/ San Jacinto 62), a 100 percent locals' place, for excellent fried seafood and grilled *solomillo*. One of the most famous tapas bars in the barrio is **Kiosko de las Flores** (Pl. Altozano, s/n), located right at the end of the Triana/Isabel II bridge. It is hard to say what is better—their *pescaito frito* or their view of the Torre del Oro, La Giralda, and cathedral on the other side of the river. Enjoy an inner view at the classic **Sol y Sombra** (C/ Castilla 151), named for the seating area of the bullring that is partly sunny, partly shady. The excessive bullfighting decor has an antiquated look that is both comfortable and timeless. Try the *revuelto de trigueros* (eggs scrambled with asparagus) and a glass of sherry.

In Macarena, **Bar Yebra** (C/ Medalla Milagosa 3) is legendary for their hearty, homey tapas. They claim to have invented the *revuelto de chorizo* (fried eggs with chorizo). It is delicious, but so are their more creative dishes like *rape con cava* (monkfish in sparkling wine), *bacalao con almendras* (cod with an almond sauce), and *jabalí con frambuesa* (wild boar with raspberries). Near the Macarena gate, **Bar Plata** (C/ Resolana 2) is an atmospheric tapas bar with a gorgeous coffered ceiling above the bar. The tapas are classic Andalucía and the bar is open all day from breakfast through dinner.

INFORMATION AND SERVICES
Tourist and Travel Information
In front of the Alcazares Reales is the **provincial tourist office** (Pl. Triunfo 1, tel. 95/421-0005). It offers complete city information, as well as details on the Sevilla province. The region of Andalucía has a **regional tourism office** (Av. Constitución 21, tel. 95/422-1404, , 9 A.M.–7:30 P.M. Mon.–Fri., 10 A.M.–2 P.M. and 3–7 P.M. Sat., 10A.M.–2 P.M. Sun.) behind the cathedral. It is an excellent place to stock up on information for all of Andalucía. Their city maps are particularly handy. There are also regional offices at the airport and the train station.

The tourism office operates www.turismo.sevilla.org, a fairly comprehensive site. Other good tourism sites include www.andalucia.org and www.andalucia.com. American expat Jeff Spielvogel runs the informative and fun www.exploreseville.com. If your Spanish is up to speed, www.elgiraldillo.es is the online version of Sevilla's entertainment guide.

The **local tourist office** (Pl. San Francisco 19, tel. 95/459-5288, 10 A.M.–2 P.M. and 5–8 P.M. Mon.–Sat., 11–2 P.M. Sun.) also offers free Internet service.

Internet Access
If your hotel doesn't provide Internet service, you'll have to find a *ciber* (pronounced THEE-ber). The main post office **Correos** (Av. Constitución 2, 8:30 A.M.–8:30 P.M.) has an Internet and calling center with very reasonable rates. **WorkCenter** (C/ San Fernando 1, tel. 95/422-0487, 7 A.M.–11 P.M. Mon.–Fri., 10 A.M.–2 P.M. and 4–9 P.M. Sat. and Sun.) has a bank of computers and offers full office and copying services. There are also small Internet and cybercafés all over the center.

GETTING THERE
Air
If you are flying into Sevilla, you'll land at **Aeropuerto de San Pablo,** about 13 kilometers (eight miles) outside of the city. To get into the city center, you can shell out €18 for a cab. This is fixed rate for day-time trips. On Sundays, holidays, and after 10 P.M. the rate rises to €20. You can also catch the EA (Especial Aeropuerto) bus located outside the terminal. It makes a stop at the train station before terminating in Puerta de Jerez, about a block from the cathedral. It costs €2.30 and runs every half-hour 6:15 A.M.–11:30 P.M. If you will be renting a car at the airport to take off on a tour in Andalucía, do yourself a favor and rent the car after your visit to Sevilla. The winding roads are constantly jammed with traffic, ongoing public works means main roads are chaotic, and parking lots (when you find one with space available), are expensive. You'll save money and hassle by bussing into town, enjoying your visit, then bussing back to the airport for your car.

Train
The main station in Sevilla is **Estación de Santa Justa** (Av. Kansas City, s/n, tel. 90/224-0202, www.renfe.es). It is located about a 20-minute walk northeast from the cathedral. A cab ride from the station to the center will run about €6 or you can catch local bus C2 or 32. The station offers daily trains to just about every town in Andalucía. The high-speed AVE train has more than 20 daily trips to Madrid. The AVE also goes to Córdoba in just 40 minutes, making a day trip there very doable. Keep in mind that the AVE trains are very popular and are often booked solid on the weekends. Do not think you will just mosey to the station and get a ticket. Purchase online several days in advance or if you prefer assistance, any *agencia de viajes* (travel agent) can book the train. They usually charge a few euros for the service, but the price is worth not having to stand in line at the train station.

Bus
Sevilla has two bus stations. Which you use depends on where you are going and where

ANDALUCÍA

you've been. **Prado de San Sebastián** (tel. 95/441-7111) serves most towns in Andalucía, except for Huelva. It is located very close to the University, across from the Murillo gardens. **Plaza de Armas** (Av. Cristo de la Expiración, s/n, tel. 95/490-8040), located near the Puente del Cachorro bridge, serves just about everywhere else, including Madrid, Barcelona, and Valencia.

Car

If you are driving into or out of Sevilla, you'll find it easily accessed from most any point in Spain. A-4 connects to Córdoba and Madrid. It is also the highway where Sevilla's airport is located. A-66 connects to Extremadura. A-92 running parallel with N-334 connects to Málaga. A-4 and the toll-road AP-4 go to Cádiz. It is recommended that you take the toll road. The total fees come to less than €7, but it is worth it as the A-4 is very crowded, especially on weekends. A-49 leads to Huelva.

GETTING AROUND
Bus

If you'll be spending the bulk of your time in Sevilla near the cathedral or Barrio Santa Cruz, you probably won't need to get on the bus. A pair of comfy shoes and a good map is all you'll need. However, if you want to venture further afield (La Macarena, Triana, El Centro) and don't want to walk, the local bus system is convenient and inexpensive. There are four circular lines (C1–4) that circle the city and several more that traverse it north–south and east–west. Almost all buses stop in Puerta de Jerez, near the cathedral, and Prado de San Sebastián, next to the university. Bus stations are all over the city and most have city maps indicating the routes. You can also get a bus map from the tourist office. Online, routes and information can be found on the official transit website (www.tussam.es), but it is in Spanish only. For English explanations, visit www.exploreseville.com.

Single tickets, called *univiaje,* cost €1 and can be bought right on the bus—exact change is preferred and required after 9 P.M. A 10-trip *bonobús* is €4.20 without transfer privileges and €5.15 with. You can buy this pass at any newsstand or in an *estanco* (tobacco shop), usually identified by the word *tabacos* on the door.

Taxis

White with a yellow sash across the rear door, Sevilla's fleet of taxis are inexpensive and efficient. The easiest means of hailing one is to just head to the closest big street or plaza. Luggage is surcharged. As in the rest of Spain, taxi drivers do not expect a tip, however it is normal to round off to the nearest euro. Also, remember to have small bills available, as many drivers will not accept a €50 bill. If you would like to schedule a taxi for an early-morning airport run or a late-night return from a restaurant, dial one of these numbers: 95/467-5555, 95/458-0000, or 95/462-2222. They won't speak English, so ask your hotel staff for assistance if you are unsure about your Spanish.

Car Rental

At the airport, there are five rental car companies: **Atesa** (www.atesa.es), **Avis** (www.avis.es), **Crown Car Hire** (www.crowncarhire.com), **Europcar** (www.europcar.es), and **Hertz** (www.hertz.es).

Cádiz Capital

Entering Cádiz (KA-deeth), you'll go through a depressing row of industrial hangers, shipping works, and uninspired 1970s housing. Then you pass through the city's 16th-century gates and quite suddenly you are transported into a magical maze of old cobbled lanes bursting at their cracked edges with palm trees and sweet-scented jasmine. Cádiz has the dilapidated charm of old Havana, with regal 18th-century buildings crumbling here and there, their soft limestone facades wind worn by centuries. Wooden doors open halfway to reveal an inner world of bright blue, white, and yellow tiles surrounding lush gardens of sunset-colored flowers. At any turn, you may end up under a medieval archway or standing atop a Roman ruin, and then quite suddenly, the narrow crook of the street gives way to a sea view. Surrounded on two sides by the Atlantic Ocean and on the third by the Bay of Cádiz, the 3,000-year-old-city of Cádiz is a captivating oasis of history and charm amidst the great, blue sea. Few tourists give it a thought, and that is a shame because it is also an oasis from the over-tourism that plagues other more sight-heavy cities in Andalucía. It is a bit of Andalucía where you can enjoy it as it is best enjoyed—slowly, savoring its quiet charms, the way you would a fine glass of sherry.

Set at the tip of a long peninsula that juts out into the Atlantic Ocean like a beckoning finger, Cádiz has an ancient seafaring history. Founded by the Phoenicians in 1100 B.C., and inhabited every since, it is the oldest continually occupied city in Western Europe. The Phoenicians called it Gadir and took advantage of the city's location to create an important shipping port. When the Romans took over nearly a 1,000 years later, they renamed it Gades. The city flourished as a naval base under the Romans and even served as the proving grounds for a young Julius Caesar—the future emperor held his first public office here.

After the fall of Rome, Visigoths and Moors both occupied the town, but it wasn't until the arrival of the Christians in the 13th century that Cádiz itself enjoyed the benefits of its great port. Christopher Columbus set forth on two of his trans-Atlantic journeys from Cádiz's port. In the 18th century, the River Guadalquivir silted up, preventing ships from traveling inland to Sevilla, and the Spanish Court moved the headquarters for all trade with the New World to Cádiz. As silver, gold, sugar, and cocoa began to flow through Cádiz's port, the town underwent a renaissance and soon became one of the most important commercial centers in Europe. The elegant mansions and squares that blanket the city hail from this era.

In 1812, in the midst of warfare with France, Spanish leaders gathered in Cádiz and signed the first Spanish constitution establishing a parliament and setting the standards that all future leaders would have to follow, more or less willingly. Cádiz itself served as the capital of Spain from 1810–1813. During the Civil War, Cádiz was one of the first cities to fall to Franco's forces. The Nationalist forces took advantage of Cádiz's port to move troops and shipments into the country. After the war, along with the rest of the country, Cádiz entered a downward spiral. In the late 20th century, because of its port and nearby military bases, Cádiz bounced back. Unlike so many other Andalusian towns, the city has not had to turn to tourism for economic recovery; as a result the tourist that does make it here will find it a refreshingly laid-back, even quiet—despite the bustling port. Except, of course, in February, when Cádiz throws Europe's most raucous Carnival party. If you want to attend, book far, far in advance.

SIGHTS

Cádiz is made up of two parts—the Centro Histórico, the old town that sits on the peninsula beyond the city gates, and the new town, which stretches along a skinny neck

ANDALUCÍA

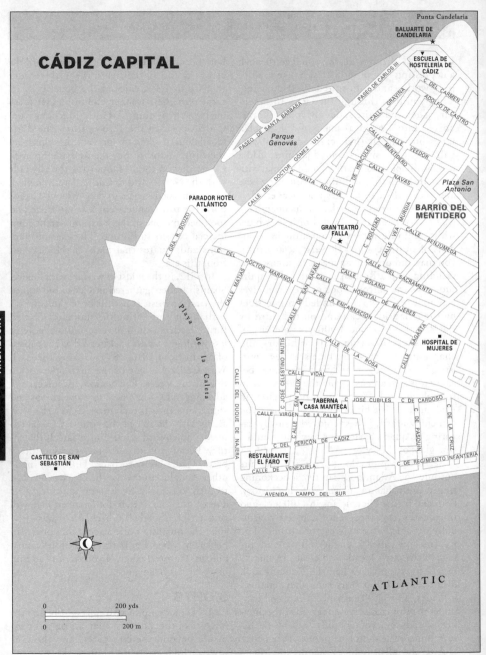

CÁDIZ CAPITAL

Punta Candelaria

BALUARTE DE
CANDELARIA

ESCUELA DE
HOSTELERÍA DE
CÁDIZ

C. DEL CARMEN

ADOLFO DE CASTRO

PASEO DE CARLOS III

CALLE GRAVINA

CALLE MENTIDERO

CALLE

VEEDOR

CALLE

C. DE HÉRCULES

NAVAS

Plaza San
Antonio

BARRIO DEL
MENTIDERO

PASEO DE SANTA BÁRBARA

Parque
Genovés

PASEO DE DOCTOR GÓMEZ ULLA

C. SANTA ROSALIA

C. DEL DOCTOR GÓMEZ ULLA

PARADOR HOTEL
ATLÁNTICO

C. GRA. R. BOUZO

C. SOLEDAD

CALLE VEA

MURGIA

CALLE BENJUMEDA

GRAN TEATRO
FALLA

CALLE DEL SACRAMENTO

CALLE SOLANO

C. DEL DOCTOR MARAÑON

CALLE MATÍAS

CALLE DE SAN RAFAEL

DEL HOSPITAL DE MUJERES

C. DE LA ENCARNACIÓN

CALLE

Playa de la Caleta

CALLE DE LA ROSA

SAGASTA

CALLE

HOSPITAL DE
MUJERES

CALLE DEL DUQUE DE NAJERA

C. JOSÉ CELESTINO MUTIS

CALLE VIDAL

CALLE SAN FELIX

TABERNA
CASA MANTECA

C. JOSÉ CUBILES

C. DE CARDOSO

C. DE PASQUIN

C. DE LA CRUZ

CALLE VIRGEN DE LA PALMA

C. DEL PERICÓN DE CÁDIZ

CASTILLO DE SAN
SEBASTIÁN

RESTAURANTE
EL FARO

CALLE DE VENEZUELA

C. DE REGIMIENTO INFANTERÍA

AVENIDA CAMPO DEL SUR

ATLANTIC

0   200 yds

0   200 m

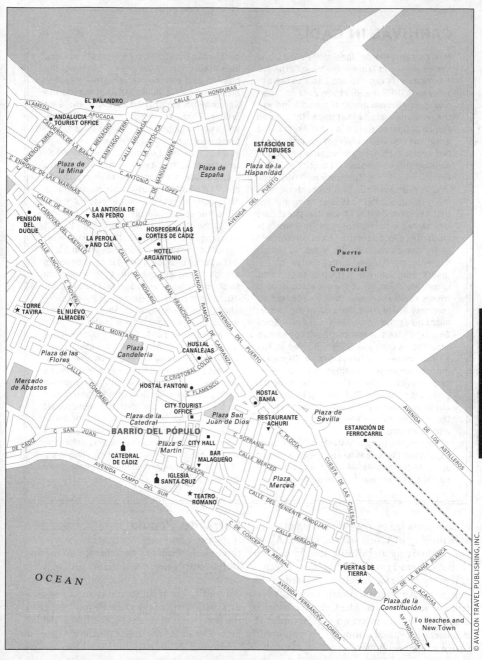

ANDALUCÍA

CARNIVAL IN CÁDIZ

New Orleans, Río de Janeiro, Trinidad, and Venice are world famous for their Carnivals. True hedonists know to add Cádiz to the list. This tiny 3,000-year-old town puts on a carnival party to rival any in the world and was the only Spanish city that blatantly ignored Franco's ban on Carnival. As in the rest of the world, the official Carnival season lasts about two weeks, culminating in a frenzy of bacchanalia on Shrove Tuesday (February 5, 2008; February 24, 2009; February 16, 2010). The streets teem with celebration each night of the festival, but the best time to visit is the first weekend. On that Friday, the streets are jam-packed with locals, American university students, and Spaniards from all corners of the peninsula. It is one massive, liquor-soaked, hand-clapping street party. The following night, Saturday, is the time to costume. Originality drives the costumes and groups of friends usually choose a theme and dress accordingly. There are no limits. A group of guys might go as the Space Girls, kind of a Spice Girls meets Martian meets drag queen get-up. Others really push boundaries, dressed as, say, a bedroom set – mattress and all. Of course mainstream nurses, cavemen, and clowns are very popular. If you really want to enjoy the party, get a costume. This will require planning ahead as costume shops will be down to nil by the time you arrive – and what is left will cost a small fortune.

Most nights, the party starts off in Plaza de España and Plaza de Mina and the crowds then spill into the streets. All the bars and *peñas* (social clubs) are open to the public and ven-

dors hawk sandwiches, rum, liters of soda, and beer at surprisingly low prices. This is not the place to go if you are even slightly agoraphobic. The crowd is thicker than at Macy's the Saturday before Christmas and a whole lot drunker. Forget trying to get into a bathroom, you'll wait all night; just join the folks squatting between cars. And don't even dare try to yawn or look tired because some nice Gaditano (as locals are called) will come right up to you, lock you in a bear hug screaming *"Que te pasa?"* ("What's wrong?") while motioning for his buddies to get you another drink. Ah, that is the true spirit of Carnival.

Like the other great Carnivals, Cádiz has it's own unique local flavor that is separate from the wild party that most tourists see. In Cádiz, it is a series of singing competitions between groups of amateur choruses that range from large *corros* (semi-professional choirs of 30-40) to small *cuartetos* (groups of 2-4 singers). The groups are made of locals and everyone in Cádiz has a singer or two in the family. In the weeks leading up to Carnival, competitions are held to determine the best groups in town. Originality is the key. The groups sing funny, sarcastic songs about the government, famous personalities, and key events that happened during the year. The final competition is held on the first day of Carnival and is broadcast live on national television. During the ensuing festivities, especially early evenings, you'll see bands of the costumed singers performing throughout the squares or participating in parades on floats. Get a schedule of events from the tourist office.

of land bounded by the Atlantic on one side and the Bay of Cádiz on the other. All of your sightseeing and dining should happen in the Centro Histórico. The best beaches and many of the top hotels are located in the new town. An efficient, inexpensive bus system connects the two. The Centro Histórico is small enough to bisect on foot in under 15 minutes, yet varied enough that you could easily wander for hours.

Barrio del Pópulo

If you enter the town by car or bus, you'll pass through the **Puertas de Tierra,** two massive 16th-century gates. The entrance arcs were cut out in the 20th century to accommodate modern traffic. The train station is just a few minutes' walk north of the gates. Beyond the gates, the first barrio of interest is the Barrio del Pópulo. The site of the oldest medieval village in Cádiz, it is delineated by three 13th-century arches that once served as entryways into this old barrio: **Arco del Pópulo, Arco de la Rosa,** and **Arco del Blanco.** The barrio is also home to Cádiz's busiest square, **Plaza San Juan de Dios,** a lovely wedge-shaped plaza that serves as the city's favorite meeting spot. Dozens of bars and cafés rim the plaza, all with tables out in warmer weather. On the hour, the clock on the neoclassical **Ayuntamiento** (town hall) rings out a snippet from the opera *El Sombrero de Tres Picos,* composed by Cádiz's native son, famed composer Manual de Falla. There is also a tourist office in the plaza. South of the town hall, fronting the ocean, are the recently uncovered remains of a **Teatro Romano** (Av. Campo Sur, s/n, 10 A.M.–2 P.M. daily, free), a Roman theater dating back to 70 or 60 B.C.

Just west of the theater is the looming white and taupe mass of the **Catedral de Cádiz** (Pl. Catedral, s/n, tel. 95/628-6154, 10 A.M.–1 P.M. and 4:30–7 P.M. Tues.–Fri., 10 A.M.–1 P.M. Sat., Sun. for worship only, €4). Begun in 1776, as Cádiz was enjoying its heyday as the port to the New World, the cathedral took 116 years to complete. As a result it is a mix of styles, from its lofty baroque facade to its neoclassical towers. It is capped by a massive golden cupola that glints in the sun and can be seen from kilometers out to sea. Within are a few choice paintings by Zurbarán and Murillo. What it lacks in ooh-and-ahh sights, it makes up for with its lack of tourists underfoot. This is a place were you can enjoy a cathedral the way it should be enjoyed—in silence. The western bell tower, **Torre Poniente** (10 A.M.–8 P.M. summer, 10 A.M.–6 P.M. winter, €3.50), rises 74 meters (243 feet) and offers visitors strong of leg and heart astonishing vistas over the rambling white maze of Cádiz and out to sea. Around the corner, through Arco de la Rosa, lies the old cathedral, **Iglesia Santa Cruz** (Pl. Santa Cruz, s/n). Built on a former mosque, the inner patio of the church retains Cádiz's only recovered examples of original Moorish architecture in the city.

Mercado de Abastos

West of the Barrio Pópulo, the winding pedestrian streets lead to the **Mercado de Abastos** (Pl. Libertad). This rambling market may have seen better days, but there is no better people-watching to be had in Cádiz than here on any given morning. Nearly everyone in town seems to congregate here for shopping and gossiping in equal measure. Take a walk around and maybe pick up lunch—the *pollo asado* stand out front offers amazing roasted chickens for less than €5. The streets around the plaza are usually lined with flea market booths selling everything from silver jewelry to used beach umbrellas. Just east of the market is the bustling little **Plaza de las Flores.** In addition to flower booths, the plaza has a handful of sidewalk cafés and the best fried fish shop in town—**Freiduría Las Flores.**

Weave your way northwest until you come to **Torre Tavira** (C/ Marqués del Real Tesoro 10, tel. 95/621-2910, www.torretavira.com, 10 A.M.–8 P.M. daily summer, 10 A.M.–6 P.M. daily winter, €3.50). Built in the 18th century, it was one of 160 watchtowers that rose up from the city to allow its citizens to keep an eye out to sea. Today, the Torre Tavira is the highest remaining tower at 45 meters (148 feet). From its roof, you'll get fantastic bird's-eye views. To get an even better look at the streets of Cádiz, the tower also operates a **Camera Obscura** that projects live images of the bustling city onto its screen. Views of the camera are given every half-hour. English is offered. Nearby, the **Hospital de Mujeres** (C/ Hospital de Mujeres 2, 10 A.M.–1 P.M. daily, free) is a stern 18th-century hospital that hides a delightfully over-the-top baroque chapel. It is home to the El Greco painting *Éxtasis de San Francisco.*

Barrio del Mentidero

The northwest quadrant of Cádiz is home to the Barrio del Mentidero and a clutch of delightful squares, the most famous of which is **Plaza de la Mina,** a cozy rectangle full of unkempt flowers and wildly leafed trees providing shelter from both wind and sun. The city's best museum, **Museo de Cádiz** (Pl. Mina, s/n, tel. 95/621-2281, 2:30–8 P.M. Tues., 9 A.M.–8:30 P.M. Wed.–Sat., 9:30 A.M.–2:30 P.M. Sun., €1.50) houses both

ANDALUCÍA

a fine arts and an archaeological collection. Of the former, expect a few works by Rubens, Zurbarán, Murillo, and Miró. In the latter—by far the more interesting part of the museum—there are quite a few Phoenician remains, including a stunning pair of white-stone sarcophagi carved in human likeness.

A block away, the broad **Plaza San Antonio,** dominated by the 17th-century baroque church of the same name, is a local meeting place. Lined with cafés and bars, this plaza hosts large concerts during Carnival, as well as the rest of the year. Check with the tourist office to see what's on. Another key spot for Carnival is the nearby **Gran Teatro Falla** (Pl. Fragela, s/n). This massive 19th-century redbrick theater is Cádiz's best example of Mudejar design. It hosts performances year-round, but during Carnival it is ground zero for choral competitions between local singing groups.

Barrio del Mentidero is bounded by two of Andalucía's most beautiful parks. To the north, running along the Bay of Cádiz, is the **Alameda Apodaca,** a long, narrow walk jammed with flowering bushes, giant ficus trees, colorfully tiled benches, and magnificent views over the bay. It is a favorite for strolling lovers and hopeful fishermen. On the Atlantic coast, separated from the Apodaca by the star-shaped **Baluarte de Candelaria,** a former bastion that now serves as a cultural center, lies the oceanfront **Parque Genovés.** This large swath of green is home to dozens of exotic trees and a lovely outdoor café.

BEACHES

Playa de la Caleta is the only beach in the historic town. A small, little crescent of golden sand, it is protected from the full force of the Atlantic by twin forts that sit on either edge of the beach—Santa Catalina and San Sebastián. It is a nice place to catch the sunset, but it can get very crowded during the day. In the new area of town (catch any local bus heading towards Avenida de Andalucía), long sandy beaches stretch for kilometers. The first is **Playa Santa María del Mar,** then **Playa de la Victoria, Playa de la Cortadura,** and fi-

Boats and sunbathers line the Playa de la Caleta.

© GLORIA MORÁN MORENO

nally **Playa del Chato.** All have promenades, cafés, and services such as changing rooms, showers, and toilets. However, the further you get away from the city, the fewer services you'll have. The upside is fewer people. And if you want to practice nudism, Chato is the place for you. It is also the most popular beach for Cádiz's substantial gay community.

ACCOMMODATIONS
Under €50
Unfortunately, in this price range, the historic center of Cádiz has a bad reputation for small, dank rooms, noise, and rude service. Partly this is due to the lack of space, partly it is due to a history of not quite being prepared for tourism. Prices also go way up during summer and Carnival. One decent exception is **Hostal Canalejas** (C/ Cristóbal Colón 5, tel. 95/626-4113, €50), which has small but updated rooms. They open onto a central shaft, so while there is no view, there is also no noise. Family-run **Hostal Fantoni** (C/ Flamenco 5, tel. 95/628-2704, www.hostalfantoni.net, €50) is located in a house that could use some remodeling. Cheaper rooms feature shared baths, but the rooftop terrace is a nice touch. **Hostal Bahía** (C/ Plocia 5, tel. 95/625-9061, €50) has nice, clean rooms with small balconies. They are planning renovations in 2007, so the quality—and the prices—may go up. **Hostal San Francisco** (C/ San Francisco 12, tel. 95/622-1842, €49) is very basic but friendly, as is the tiny **Pensión Del Duque** (C/ Ancha 13, tel. 95/622-2777, €40).

€50-100
▌ **Hospedería Las Cortes de Cádiz** (C/ San Francisco 9, tel. 95/622-0489, contacto@hotel lascortes.com, www.hotellascortes.com, €95) is set in a reformed 18th-century home and takes its design inspiration from the Spanish Constitution of 1812. It is a lot more charming than it sounds, with bright rooms decked in antiques. There is a lovely inner courtyard and the in-house gym has a sauna and whirlpool. **Hotel Argantonio** (C/ Argantonio 3, tel. 95/621-1640, www.hotelargantonio.com,

€90), opened May 2006, has brought some much needed style into Cádiz's hotel scene. The rooms are individually decorated in an eclectic blend of colonial and Arabic style and the in-house restaurant takes its cuisine seriously with a savory spread of Mediterranean and vegetarian dishes. **Hotel Regio** (Av. Ana de Viya 11, tel. 95/627-9331, hotregio@hotel regiocadiz.com, www.hotelregiocadiz.com, €80) is a modern facility in the new part of Cádiz just two minutes walking to Playa de la Victoria. Rooms are small but clean and updated, many with covered balconies, and the staff is very friendly.

Over €100
The **Parador Hotel Atlántico** (Av. Duque de Nájera 9, tel. 95/622-6905, cádiz@parador.es, www.parador.es, €120) is not the best in the Parador chain. It is blocky and modern and sorely in need of an update. However the views over the Atlantic are lovely, as is the hotel's large swimming pool and location in the Genovés park. The bar offers a decent—and surprisingly affordable—selection of tapas and wine and the morning breakfast buffet is actually quite good. **Hotel Playa Victoria** (Pl. Ingeniero La Cierva 4, tel. 95/620-5100, hotelplayavictoria@ palafoxhoteles.com, www.palafoxhoteles.com, €150) offers a big-hotel feel in cozy Cádiz. Situated a few minutes outside of the old city gates and right on a broad stretch of the Playa de la Victoria, this hotel offers good service, good rooms, and great views. The nearby **Tryp La Caleta** (Av. Almicar 47, tel. 95/627-9411, tryp.la.caleta@solmelia.com, www.solmelia .com, €130) is another apt choice offering lovely ocean views, a pool, and top-notch service.

FOOD
As in the rest of Andalucía, *pescaito frito* (fried fish) is king here. Local specialties that will have you licking your fingers are *cazón adobo* (marinated, fried shark) and *tortilla de camarones* (a fried patty of tiny shrimp). The best places to get a taste are the *freidurías* (fry shops) that are located all over town. These are carry-out places, so grab a paper cone and go make a

ANDALUCÍA

© PATRICIA DAWN SEVERENUK

Grilled and fried seafood is the specialty throughout Cádiz.

picnic on the beach. The hands-down favorite for locals and tourists alike is the **Freiduría Las Flores** in the plaza of the same name.

Local Cuisine

El Faro (C/ San Felix 15, tel. 95/621-1068, www.elfarodecadiz.com, daily, €40) has long been considered Cádiz's top-rated restaurant. It is surely one of the most romantic. Intricate ceramic tiles cover the walls from the floor up midway. Above that are brightly colored walls covered in oil paintings and old photos of Cádiz. The tables are covered in linen and the furniture is antique. Service is impeccable and the menu—consisting of classic Cádiz fish dishes—is award-winning. There are a couple of meat and vegetable dishes, but this a place to go for fish. ◖ **El Balandro** (Alameda Apodaca 22, tel. 95/622-0992, closed Sun. P.M. and Mon. in winter, €22) manages to combine elegance and fun in a bright, boisterous dining room where enthusiastic locals down excellent takes on local fare. Try the *choco* (grilled cuttlefish) or the *salmorejo* (a thick, savory

take on gazpacho). You can also dine at the bar. For a gastronomic experience that will surprise you, head to **Escuela de Hostelería de Cádiz** (Alameda Marqués de Comillas 2, tel. 96/580-8002, lunch Mon.–Fri. only, €25), the restaurant of the local cooking school. Dishes tend to be creative takes on local ingredients, such as a carpaccio of shrimp with caramelized mushrooms or medallions of monkfish baked with squid ink. Reservations are required. At **Achuri** (C/ Plocia 15, tel. 95/625-3613, closed Sun. P.M. and Wed., €30) the decor is nothing to get exciting about, but the very boisterous crowd doesn't mind as the chef's Andalusian-Basque dishes are downright sublime.

Tapas

One of the best zones to tapas-hop is Barrio la Viña, particularly Calle de la Palma and Plaza de la Tiza. This is where the locals go to gorge on fried fish, cured hams, and flowing *barbadillo,* a favorite local white wine. Of course, as any good tapas-hunter knows, you'll find the best places by following the paper napkin trail of the locals. **Taberna Casa Manteca** (C/ Corralón 66, tel. 95/621-3603, closed Sun.) is everything you imagine a good Andalusian bar to be—walls covered in bullfighting memorabilia, bar covered in blue-and-white tiles, and a ham slicer right next to the cash machine. Try a slice or two of *queso curado* (cured Manchego cheese) with a glass of *manzanilla* (dry sherry) pulled right from the barrel. The rustic **El Nuevo Almacen** (C/ Barrie 17, tel. 95/622-1033, closed Sun.) is dominated by a deli counter packed with local hams, sausages, and cheeses. The thing to have is *surtido de embutidos* (a cold-cut tray) and a glass of wine. **Malagueño** (C/ Mesón 5, tel. 95/626-2423, closed Sun.) is a cute hole-in-the-wall in the Barrio Pópulo with a massive tapas list. Try their *boquerones en vinagre* (marinated fresh anchovies). **La Antigua de San Pedro** (C/ San Pedro, s/n, tel. 95/622-0491, closed Mon.) is a spacious tapas bar offering a wide array of goodies. *Chapatas* (mini-sandwiches made with rustic bread and your choice of fillings) are the house favorite. **La Perola and Cía** (C/ Canovas del Castillo 34, tel. 95/607-6675) is a tapas innovator, combining Spanish standards with Moroccan influences. Try the *pastela* (a flaky pastry stuffed with chicken and raisins) or *pâté de cañaillas* (sea snail pâté).

INFORMATION

The **city tourist office** (Pl. San Juan de Dios 11, tel. 95/624-1001, 9 A.M.–2 P.M. and 4–7 P.M. Mon.–Fri., 10 A.M.–2 P.M. Sat., closed Sun.) offers complete information on the city as well as good information about Carnival. On the weekends, the office is closed, but a kiosk in the middle of the plaza is open. The **regional tourist office** (C/ Calderon de la Barca 1, tel. 95/621-1313) has great regional advice and the best maps for all the cities of Andalucía.

On the Internet, find good Cádiz information at www.guiadecadiz.com, though not all their English links work. Also visit the regional sites, www.andalucia.com and www.andalucia.org. The city's tourist website is buried deep within the all-Spanish www.aytocadiz.es/turismo.

GETTING THERE AND AROUND

Train

Cádiz's **Estación de Ferrocarril** (Pl. Sevilla, s/n) is serviced by **Renfe** (tel. 90/224-0202, www.renfe.es). You can take trains to most points from here, but if you are heading to Madrid, it is best to go first to Sevilla and then catch the AVE. Of course, remember, you should always book your train tickets early, especially on weekends. A good practice is to buy your return tickets as soon as you arrive at your destination.

Bus

The main **Estación de Autobuses** (Pl. Hispanidad 1, tel. 95/680-7059) services the bus companies **Transportes Comes** (tel. 90/219-0208, www.tgcomes.es) and **Los Amarillos** (tel. 95/628-5852, www.losamarillos.es), which provide connections throughout Andalucía.

Car

Cádiz is located at the end of the national highway A-4, which originates in Madrid and passes through Sevilla. The N-340/E-5 connects it to the Costa de la Luz.

Boat

Cádiz is connected to the nearby port (and sherry) town of El Puerto de Santa María via **El Vapor,** a ferry run by **Motonave** (Estación Marítimo, tel. 62/946-8014, €4), with departures about every two hours 10:15 A.M.–6:45 P.M. **Trasmediterranea** (tel. 90/245-4645, www.trasmediterranea.es) operates weekly service to the Canary Islands Tuesdays at 6 P.M.

Public Transport

If you are staying in the historic center and will be doing all your sightseeing there, you can travel easily by foot. If you are in the new part of town or want to head out to the beaches, you can take taxis or catch the local public buses, which are both convenient and inexpensive. The main stop is at Plaza de España. Number 1 runs along Avenida de Andalucía and Number 7 circles the old town and then takes the Atlantic road into the new town.

ANDALUCÍA

Provincia de Cádiz

The Province of Cádiz, one of eight that make up Andalucía, comprises the furthest reaches of Western Europe. At its southernmost tip, the continent of Africa is just over 11 kilometers (seven miles) away. Stretching east from the mouth of the Río Guadalquivir to Tarifa, north from the windswept coast to the rainy mountains of the Sierra de Grazalema, the province of Cádiz takes in wild, nearly undeveloped beaches, sleepy whitewashed villages, pastures where *toros* (fighting bulls) graze, acres of grapes destined to become *jerez* (sherry), and even another country—the British outpost of Gibraltar. This is not the Andalucía of jaw-dropping Moorish monuments or all-inclusive resorts. The charms are subtler here, hidden within the weave of everyday life—the smell of fish frying, the rattling clap of flamenco pouring out of a tinny radio in no-name bar, the swoosh of a salty wave pulling away from shore, incense smoke curling in the cupola of a medieval church, the low roar of horse hooves on the sand, the smile of a child kicking a soccer ball against a whitewashed wall. And then there is the light. The coast of Cádiz is called Costa de la Luz (Coast of Light). The sun falls here in bright, vivid hues, giving everything a shimmering glow—the golden sand dunes, the white-grained *albariza* soil that lends sherry its distinctive taste, and of course, the white buildings tucked in the hills. The latter has led to a whole new tourism initiative—Ruta de los Pueblos Blancos ("Route of the White Houses").

The seasons are mild. With 300 days of sun, the average temperature is 14°C (57°F). In summer, it moves up to the 30s (90s in °F). Winters can be bone-chilling. The most distinctive feature of the weather in Cádiz, especially along the coast, is the Levante. This strong easterly wind blows most days, some much stronger than others. It thrills the wind- and kite-surfers down near Tarifa, but legend has it that it can make locals go crazy. When someone has a bad day or acts out of character it's always blamed on the Levante.

The areas to explore can be divided into Jerez and the sherry region, the Pueblos Blancos, Costa de la Luz, and the capital city of Cádiz (covered separately). As you do, you will notice a very welcome thing about this part of Spain—the lack of development. Along the coast there is a law preventing buildings going up more than three stories, ensuring a perfect sea view for all and warding off the cement scars that have been forged on so many other Iberian coasts. And of course, the Levante wind has also dissuaded major resorts from setting up shop. As a result, there is less active tourism here. Don't expect the man at the gas station or the receptionist at your hotel to speak English. In fact, even if you speak Spanish, you might not understand a thing. Gaditanos (as locals are called) speak their own form of Spanish, dropping the final "s" off of words and cramming the rest of the letters together in a singsong patter that they call *andalu*. It is all just part of the charm. Cádiz is what it is. When you come to Cádiz, you need to fit in with its unhurried, age-old rhythm, wind and all. If you do, you'll have the time of your life.

JEREZ DE LA FRONTERA

No matter where you go in Jerez de la Frontera—usually just called Jerez (HER-reth)—it's hard to get away from the influence of the distinctive straw-colored wine named for the city. The name "sherry," which first entered the English language in the 1600s, was the British take on the city's name. Sherry, the drink (in Spanish, *jerez,* like the city) has been produced at least since Roman times and historians speculate that it was under the Moors that the production expanded—even though Muslim law forbid them from drinking it. The bottled gold entered the wine cabinets of the British upper class in the 16th century. Shakespeare lauded the drink in *Henry VI*. Wealthy British merchants eventually settled in Jerez—Harvey, Osborne, Sandeman—and helped build a sherry dynasty. The success of the wine helped tiny Jerez become a wealthy, upper-crust Spanish city—It was one of the first to get electric street lamps. Even today, Jerez, along with the towns of Puerto de Santa María and San Lucar de Barrameda, produces almost all of the world's sherry.

Though most visitors come to tour the many bodegas (wineries), Jerez offers a few other enticements. A legacy of its British aristocratic roots, Jerez's equestrian school and famous dancing Andalusian horses are not to be missed. Jerez also has deep flamenco roots and is considered one of the cradles of this Spanish indigenous art form; there are ample opportunities to see authentic performances in town. Jerez's old town offers a typically Andalusian warren of cobbled streets, lively tapas bars, and historic buildings. However, one of the best reasons to visit Jerez is that very few people do. It is just far enough off the beaten path to still be refreshingly authentic, charming, and very Spanish.

Sights

Most of Jerez's sights lie in the **Centro Histórico** within a 10-minute walk of the **Plaza del Arenal,** the bustling heart of town. The 12th-century **Alcázar de Jerez** (C/ Alameda Vieja, s/n, tel. 95/631-9798, 10 A.M.– 8 P.M. Mon.–Sat., 10 A.M.–3 P.M. Sun., €3.35) was built by the Moorish Caliphs of Sevilla as a last-ditch effort to ward of the advancing Christians. In 1264, Alfonso X captured the city and turned the fortress into a Castilian stronghold. Heavily restored over the last 50 years, the Alcazar is Jerez's oldest preserved building. Within are beautiful Moorish gardens that are tended to using the same plants and techniques that were used 1,000 years ago. The grounds also contain the remains of an Arabic bathhouse, an ancient olive oil mill, and the 18th-century **Palacio de Villavicencio,** which houses a **Camera Obscura** that provides great live views beyond the city limits out onto the sherry vineyards.

The **Catedral de Jerez** (P. Encarnación, s/n, free) isn't necessarily one of the prettiest in Spain. Due to lack of funds, it took over 150 years to build and a succession of architects gave it an unwieldy style, though it is predominantly baroque. The warehouse-like interior is worth visiting only to seek out the lovely painting, *Virgen Niña,* by Zurbarán. If you're in town during Semana Santa, the steps of the cathedral are a good place to catch the processions since almost all of them pass by here.

The northwest quadrant of the historic center is called **Barrio de Santiago,** a scenic neighborhood that also happens to be one of the hotbeds of flamenco. Don't be surprised if you hear some of the neighbors breaking into song or rhythmic clapping: many of flamenco's most notable names came from this barrio, and those two scruffy guys having coffee might just be working on the next blockbuster flamenco CD. The **Centro Andaluz de Flamenco** (Pl. San Juan 1, tel. 95/634-9265, 9 A.M.–2:30 P.M. Mon.–Fri., free) has one of Spain's most comprehensive holdings of flamenco music, videos, recordings, and publications, and anyone can access the archives (though the bulk are in Spanish). A small cinema on the second floor shows a new flamenco video every day, and the staff can provide information on flamenco schools, teachers, clubs, and classes. Nearby is the colossal **Iglesia de Santiago,** built under Alfonso X and showing a mix of baroque, Gothic, and Renaissance influences. Around the edges of this barrio on the streets of Ancha, Muro, and Porvera are remains of the city's original Moorish walls. Follow Calle Porvera south until it runs into Calle Larga, a lively pedestrian shopping zone full of bars, cafés, and boutiques.

Bodegas

A visit to the sherry bodegas of the city has been de rigueur for decades, but gone are the days when you could get staggeringly drunk on the free stuff; these days, visits proceed like clockwork, leading you directly into the souvenir shop once you've had a couple of tipples to loosen your purse strings. Most of the bodegas have a regular program of visits (some with tapas, all done in either English or Spanish). Just be aware, bodega tourism in Jerez

ANDALUCÍA

© CELLAR TOURS/WWW.CELLARTOURS.COM

sherry barrels in Jerez

is ever-evolving. Hours and offerings change quite a bit. Visit the tourist office for the latest information on who does what when.

González Byass (C/ Manuel María González 12, tel. 95/635-7000, www.bodegas tiopepe.com), which produces the famous Tío Pepe brand, is located very close to the Alcázar and offers one of the most enjoyable presentations in the city. Entering the grounds of the winery, one of the first things you see is La Concha (The Shell), a storage area designed by Gustave Eiffel— yes, of the Parisian tower. Your tour takes you past several other atmospheric storage spaces where wine casks are signed by famous people. Look out for the *ratoncitos felices* (happy mice). The bodega also offers a series of themed nights—wine harvest, flamenco, horses—that combine a bodega tour with a bit of local culture. At the end, you get to taste a few varieties of Tío Pepe. English tours (11:30 A.M.–6:30 P.M. Mon.–Sat., 11:30 A.M.–2 P.M. Sun., €8) are hourly and do not have to be reserved, but to be safe, visit their website or call the bodega.

Domecq (C/ San Ildefonso 3, tel. 95/615-1500, www.domecq.es), close to the cathedral, also offers well-organized, enjoyable tours. Founded in 1730, it is the oldest sherry producer in town and the bodega is absolutely gorgeous, with wonderful old Moorish details and patios. English tours (10 A.M.–2 P.M. Mon.–Fri., noon and 2 P.M. Sun., €10) are hourly and reservations are suggested.

Sandeman (C/ Pizarro 10, tel. 95/615-1711 or 95/631-2995, www.sandeman.com) is another good choice, especially if you are coming to town for the noon horse show at the Royal Andalusian School of Equestrian Art. The show ends at 1:30 P.M. and the bodega, right behind the school, begins an English tour at 2 or 2:30 P.M., depending on the day. The grounds are historic and lovely and the tour ends with a tasting. Sandeman is known in the United States for its port, but this facility is dedicated solely to its sherries. English tours (11 A.M.–2:30 P.M. Mon., Wed., and Fri., 10:30 A.M.–3 P.M. Tues. and Thurs., 11 A.M., 1 P.M., and 2 P.M. Sat., €6) do not need to be reserved, but again, it is suggested.

Entertainment

The **Real Escuela Andaluza de Arte Equestre** (Av. Abrantes, s/n, tel. 95/631-1111, www.realescuela.org), one of the world's most prestigious equestrian centers, is where regal Cartujana horses are trained in the art of dressage—the execution of precision movements in response to barely perceptible signals from a rider. Even if you're not much for horses, the elegance with which the horses move and almost dance to the music is astounding. Every week the school presents *Cómo Bailan los Caballos Andaluces (My, How the Andalusian Horses Dance!)*, an equestrian ballet accompanied by Spanish music and 18th-century costumes. Seats for the shows (noon Tues. and Thurs. Sept.–July, noon Fri. Aug., €17–23) should be reserved online.

Jerez has one of the strongest **flamenco** traditions in Andalucía. The **Barrio de Santiago,** the *gitano* quarter, has long been recognized as one of *the* places to learn about and hear authentic flamenco, including the local specialty, *bulerías de Jerez,* a more playful version of the original style that focuses on flamenco singing.

Visitors can enjoy good performances at the *tablaos* (flamenco cabarets), the best-known of which is **El Lagá del Tío Parrilla** (Pl. Mercado, s/n, tel. 95/633-8334) in the Barrio de San Mateo. **Tablao de Bereber** (C/ Cabezas 10, tel. 95/632-7327) is a relatively new establishment based out of the 800-year-old Palacio de Torres de Gaitán. **La Taberna** (C/ Angostillo de Santiago 3, tel. 95/633-8334, www.la tabernaflamenca.com) is another fine option. For more "authentic" experiences, try a *peña* (social club). Technically closed to the public, they often have open performances on Fridays and Saturdays. Try **La Buena Gente** (Pl. San Lucas 9), **Don Antonio Chacón** (C/ Salas 2), or **Tío José de Paula** (C/ Merced 11).

Festivals and Events

Hardly a month goes by that Jerez doesn't have some kind of fiesta taking place, and the three best celebrate the city's three favorite pastimes: sherry, horses, and flamenco. They are each very popular, so be sure to book ahead. For two weeks near the end of February, the **Festival Flamenco de Jerez** (www.festivaldejerez.es) takes over the city. Every night, the Teatro Villamarta (www.teatrovillamarta.com) hosts a different performance and many nationally famous flamenco dancers choose to use the festival as the place to debut their newest shows. It is possible to purchase tickets over the Internet (www.telentrada.com), eliminating the need to scrounge for tickets when you arrive.

The first week of May, the **Feria del Caballo** (Horse Fair) brings thousands of gorgeous, talented four-legged creatures to town along with the tens of thousands of two-legged creatures who train, ride, and simply love them. The week-long event features a packed roster of equestrian events and performances. Meanwhile, half of Jerez's high society don their best Andalusian wear—short jackets and broad-brimmed hats for the men, flouncy dresses for the women—and parade about town on their own steeds.

The second half of September brings the exuberant **Fiestas de Otoño,** when the locals celebrate the harvest of the sherry grapes with lively street fairs, more horse riding, lots of flamenco, and even more sherry.

Just when the calendar starts to look just a little too traditional, the bikers arrive. The **Circuito de Jerez** (www.circuitodejerez.com) hosts the **Campeonato de España de Motociclismo** (the Spanish motorcycle championships). This event draws a staggeringly huge number of motorcycle enthusiasts from all over Europe every year (the month varies). They take over the city popping wheelies, burning rubber, and whooping it up biker-style all weekend long.

Accommodations

In the **under €50** category, consider the homey **Ⓒ Riad** (tel. 95/634-6996, info@houseinjerez.com, www.houseinjerez.com, €60), a private apartment in the heart of the San Miguel flamenco district of Jerez. The one-bedroom oozes Andalusian charm and is perfect for two (but can accommodate four tightly). It has a kitchen, full bath, and a stereo system chock-full of flamenco CDs. The friendly Spanish-American owners live downstairs and guests are always invited to join them on their patio for a glass of sherry and lively talk of flamenco, Jerez, and Spain. Their website is a font of information on the city. **Hotel Nuevo** (C/ Caballeros 23, tel. 95/633-1600, nuevohotel1927@teleline.es, €40) is just steps from Plaza del Arenal, the heart of the city. Located in a 19th-century mansion, the rooms are straightforward and simple, but surprisingly comfortable and well kept for the price.

For **€50-100,** a good choice is **Hotel Serit** (C/ Higueras 7, tel. 95/634-0700, info@hotelserit.com, www.hotelserit.com, €66). It doesn't look like much from the outside and the rooms are pretty standard mid-range hotel fare, but what makes this little hotel so sweet is the wonderful family running it. They are extremely helpful and genuinely want all of their guests to enjoy Jerez. **La Casa Grande** (Pl. Angustias 3, tel. 95/634-5070, hotel@casagrande.com.es, www.casagrande.com.es, €90) is located in a splendid old mansion and features rooms laden with stylish antiques and a charming rooftop terrace.

In the **over €100** category, try the very popular **Hotel Royal Sherry Park** (Av. Álvaro Domecq 11, tel. 95/631-7614, sherrypark@ hipotels.com, www.hipotels.com, €110). About 15 minutes from the historic center and very close to the horse school, this full-service property has ample—if bland—rooms, a pool, and a decent breakfast spread. The choice of Jerez's movers and shakers has always been the **Hotel Villa Jerez** (Av. Álvaro Domecq 35, tel. 95/630-0600, reservas@villajerez.com, www .villajerez.com, €200). Located in a luxurious old villa, the rooms are spacious, the staff is accommodating, and the sophisticated Andalusian charm is palpable.

Food

Tapas abound throughout Jerez and some of the best are found at **Bar Juanito** (C/ Pescadería Vieja 8, tel. 95/633-4838, closed Mon.), which once won the award for "Best Tapas Bar in Spain." *Alcachofas* (artichokes) are the house specialty. **La Moderna** (C/ Larga, s/n, tel. 95/633-9956) is a Jerez institution where women in pearls tuck into tasty tapas alongside dreadlocked hippies. Flamenco is on the sound system and in the middle of the bar is a medieval well uncovered during renovations. **Taberna Marinera** (Pl. Rafael Rivero 2, tel. 95/633-4427) is another popular local choice with lots of seafood tapas. **Gallo Azul** (C/ Larga 2, tel. 95/632-6148) is located in a landmark building. Tapas are a tasty mix of modernity and tradition.

For a full meal, try the longtime local favorite, **La Mesa Redonda** (C/ Manuel de la Quintana 3, tel. 95/634-0069, closed Sun., €35), located near the bullring. The cozy dining room lined with culinary books is the perfect setting for classic local dishes culled from the kitchens of the bodega owners, as well as ancient Moorish dishes. Consider the seasonal menu, which is always sublime. **La Carbona**

(C/ San Francisco de Paula 2, tel. 95/634-7475, closed Tues.) offers succulent grilled meats in what was once a sherry warehouse.

Information

There are several **tourist offices** in town: The ones at Alameda Cristina, s/n (tel. 95/632-4747) and Calle Larga 39 (tel. 95/633-1162) are the most central. A third is in the airport.

Getting There

Jerez has its own airport, **Aeropuerto de la Parra** (tel. 95/615-0000), about 6.5 kilometers (four miles) outside of town. An **airport bus** (€1) will take you into Plaza de las Angustias, where local buses converge. From there it is an easy five-minute walk into the historic center, or you can catch a cab to your hotel. Some of the airport busses also travel to El Puerto Santa María and Cádiz.

Jerez's **Estación de Ferrocaril** (Pl. Estación, s/n) is operated by **Renfe** (tel. 90/224-0202, www.renfe.es), with direct train connections south to Cádiz and north to Sevilla. **Estación de Autobuses** (Pl. Estación, s/n, tel. 95/633-9666) is next to the train station and is serviced by several bus companies; the most far-reaching are **Transportes Comes** (tel. 90/219-0208, www.tgcomes.es) and **Los Amarillos** (tel. 95/628-5852, www.losamarillos.es), which provide connections throughout Andalucía.

◖ PUEBLOS BLANCOS

Small in size and dramatically situated on the tops of hills and the edges of gorges, the Pueblos Blancos of Andalucía were originally built as fortresses along what would have been the frontier between Christian and Moorish Spain—hence the "de la Frontera" tag used in many of their names. The whiteness comes from layers of whitewash used to reflect the hot sun. Over the centuries, the white coatings have built up so much that many of the buildings boast softened corners as round and smooth as the inner domes of the town's tiny medieval churches. Southern Spain is dotted by scores of such towns and the Ruta de los Pueblos Blancos (Route of the White Houses) will take you past the most emblematic and prettiest villages in a path lying between Sevilla and Málaga. You could also detour up from Cádiz to start the route. Once you reach Setenil de las Bodegas, it is less than a 30-minute drive to Ronda. From there you can easily slip down to Málaga city. This route can be done in a day and a half, but you may find yourself lingering longer in these magical white villages way off the beaten path. To design your own path or simply learn more about the Pueblos Blancos, visit the Cádiz provincial tourist website (www.cadizturismo.net) or the Andalucía websites (www.andalucia.com or www.andalucia.org). Also, if you don't have time to work a tour of these villages into your schedule, consider a day trip to Ronda. In Málaga province, Ronda is without compare the most atmospheric of all of Andalucía's Pueblo Blancos.

Though traveling by car is the best option to really enjoy this region, it is possible to take public transportation— namely the bus. Check with the stations in Ronda, Cádiz, or Sevilla for routes and hours or with **Transportes Comes** (tel. 90/219-0208, www.tgcomes.es) and **Los Amarillos** (tel. 95/628-5852, www.losamarillos.es). When driving, keep in mind that these towns were not meant for cars. Most of them are divided into the charming hilltop old town and the newer town down below. Park in the first lot you come across in the new town. Just look for the big blue letter "P." Local residents get a kick out of watching frustrated tourists trying to extricate their vehicles from dead-end streets up in the old towns.

Arcos de la Frontera

Sitting on a spur of rock more than 90 meters (300 feet) above the fertile valley of the Río Guadalete, Arcos de la Frontera is the gateway to the Pueblos Blancos. Founded by the Romans as Arco Briga, the village was in Moorish hands for centuries before becoming a Christian border town in the 13th century. Today, Arco's population of close to 30,000 is divided between the new town, down on the lower slopes of the ridge, and the **Casco Viejo** (old town) on the ridge. The Casco Viejo, with

its tangled labyrinth of streets, is where you'll spend your time. The winding Cuesta Belén street leads into the heart of the old town and the cobbled **Plaza de Cabildo,** the social center of the town. The parador occupies one side of the plaza. Next to it is the church of **Santa María de la Asunción,** whose original facade was destroyed during the same earthquake that leveled most of Lisbon in 1755. The interior still reveals its Gothic/Mudejar origins. Next is the **Ayuntamiento** (town hall). In the 15th century, the Catholic Kings Fernando and Isabel met to plan their attacks on the Moorish territories. Today, it houses the tourist information office. The plaza would be heartachingly picturesque were it not for the parking lot smack in the middle. Ignore it and head to the railing for a spectacular—if vertigo-inducing—view over the valley.

Turn on **Calle de los Escribanos** and start wandering, enjoying the quaint streets and peeking into the flowered courtyards where locals have traditionally passed the evenings with friends. Your goal is Iglesia San Pedro, but on the way seek out **Calle Cuna** and **Calle Maldonaldo,** two alley-like lanes lined with wrought-iron window grates and bright red geraniums. **Iglesia de San Pedro** is the most emblematic building of Arcos's skyline. This is where the bodies of Saint Victor and Saint Fructoso lie, semi-decomposed, in a glass case. It is possible to climb up to the top of the square-headed steeple, but be warned that it has high, narrow stairs and no handrail. The other distinctive monument rising from the white mass of Arcos is the **castle.** Originally built by the Moors, it was reconstructed to its present appearance in the 15th century by the Duke of Arcos. Today, it is privately owned.

If you decide to stay the night, Arcos offers a variety of accommodations, the best being **La Casa Grande** (C/ Maldonado 10, tel. 95/670-3930, info@lacasagrande.net, www.lacasagrande.net, €80). Located in a 1729 mansion, it is a gorgeous inn decorated in a sophisticated blend of Andalusian and Moroccan styles. Many rooms boast lovely views, but the rooms with private terraces have the best views.

The **Parador de Arcos de la Frontera** (Pl. Cabildo s/n, tel. 95/670-0500, arcos@parador .es, www.parador.es, €135), located in an old palace, offers stunning views over the river valley. **Hotel El Convento** (C/ Maldonado 2, tel. 95/670-2333, www.webdearcos.com/ elconvento, €85) is located in an old convent on one of Arco's most charming streets. Rooms ooze old-world class with antiques and stone floors and excellent views over the valley. Breakfast is served on a cliff-top terrace. **Callejón de las Monjas** (Callejón de las Monjas 4, tel. 95/670-2302, www.mesonelpatio .com, €35) offers simple, but cozy rooms.

For excellent local food, head to **El Patio** (Callejón de las Monjas 4, tel. 95/670-2302, €15), a cave-like bar lined with sherry barrels that offers wonderful tapas and rustic Andalusian fare. **El Convento** (C/ Maldonado 2, tel. 95/670-2333, €30), in the hotel of the same name, is one of the town's top-rated restaurants. Try their *abajao* (asparagus soup) or any of their game dishes. If you'd like to have tapas, head to Calle Dean Espinosa and around—or just follow the locals.

Arcos de la Frontera's **tourist office** (Pl. Cabildo 2, tel. 95/670-2264) is located in the town hall on the Plaza del Cabildo.

By car, Arcos is accessed via A-382, which connects it to Jerez, just 40 kilometers (25 miles) to the east. From Jerez, you can catch the A-4 south to Cádiz or north to Sevilla and eventually Madrid.

Of all the pueblos, Arcos has the best bus service. The **bus station** (C/ Corregidores, s/n, tel. 95/670-4977) is located in the new part of town. You can catch the Centro shuttle bus (every half-hour 8:15 A.M.–9:15 P.M. Mon.–Sat., €1), take a cab (less than €5), or walk 15 minutes uphill. Check the map posted in the bus station for directions.

Grazalema

Following the A-372 highway directly east out of Arcos, you head deep into the **Parque Natural de Sierra de Grazalema.** This UNESCO Biosphere Reserve houses the Sierra de Grazalema mountain range, a dramati-

cally rugged limestone massif. It brings a very unique microclimate to Andalucía (and Spain) with the highest rainfall of any other region in the country! The mountains rise 610–1,615 meters (2,000–5,300 feet) and are woven with spectacular gorges, pristine lakes, underground caves, and forests that are home to stands of ancient Spanish fir trees. It is a favorite of hikers and a wonderful cool escape from the summer heat in Andalucía, but visits are restricted due to the fragility of the ecosystem.

After heading over the Puerto del Boyar mountain pass, you enter the town of **Grazalema,** nestled in a gorge just below the peak of San Cristobal. Its name comes from its long-ago Arabic founders, Gran Zulema. The Duke of Arcos captured the town for the Catholic Kings in 1485. Over the next centuries, it prospered due mainly to its textile industry. The blankets woven in Grazalema are still a sought after piece of folkloric art. You'll see them on sale throughout the town. Outside of its inherent charm and dramatic setting, there is not much to see in Graza-

© PATRICIA DAWN SEVERENUK

Sierra de Grazalema

lema. Yet, most visitors are content to just wander the narrow alleys of white houses with their hanging pots of flowers and tiny courtyards. There is also a smattering of 17th- and 18th-century churches and a few Roman and Moorish remains. The remains of the 10th-century **Moorish castle** are particularly impressive.

Grazalema also has one of the wildest bull-centered festivals in the area—the Fiesta del Toro, held during the first week of July. The police cordon off the center of town and the town's population (minus the alcoholically impaired) spends four hours running away from the bull set loose in the town's center.

Of course, most visitors use the village as a base for exploring the Sierra de Grazalema and there are dozens of outfitters offering everything from guided hikes to mountain climbing. **Horizon** (C/ Dr. Mateos Gago 12, tel. 95/613-2363) is one of the most popular.

The best accommodations option is the **Hotel Fuerte Grazalema** (Baldio de los Alamillos, A-372, km. 53, tel. 95/613-3001, grazalema@fuertehoteles.com, www.hotel fuertegrazalema.com, €101), a sprawling new complex just seven minutes from Grazalema town. It offers all the amenities, including a pool with a view of the mountains. The hotel also offers a wide range of activity packages and has information on local hiking trails. In town, the cozy **Casa de las Piedras** (C/ Las Piedras 32, tel. 95/613-2014, info@casadelaspiedras.net, www .casadelaspiedras, €50) is located in one of the whitewashed houses on one of Grazalema's oldest streets. Rooms are colorful, the staff is accommodating, and there are a host of outdoor activities available. **Hotel Peñon Grande** (Pl. Pequeña 7, tel. 95/613-2434, www.hotel grazalema.com, €55) offers rustic rooms and modern baths, also in a traditional white-washed building.

For food, each of the hotels mentioned here

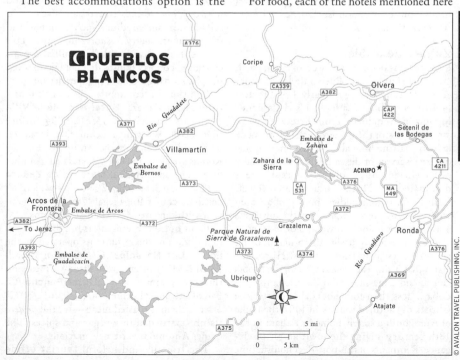

feature a traditional, local restaurant. Or you can walk around the Plaza España and check out the tapas bars and cafés. Two good bets for solid local fare are **Cádiz El Chico** (Pl. España 8, tel. 95/613-2027) and **Antonio Mangana Lamela** (C/ Real 23, tel. 95/671-6282).

For more information on visiting the Sierra de Grazalema or attending the local festivals, visit the town's small but friendly **tourist office** (Pl. España 11, tel. 95/613-2225). A British couple runs www.walkeurope.com from their gorgeous mountain home right outside of Grazalema. They are experts in the region and plan dozens of different hiking/lodging packages.

To get there from Arcos, take the A-372 into Grazalema. From Sevilla, follow the A-376 towards Costa del Sol, switch to the A-382 towards Antequera, Ronda, and Algodonales. Finally, switch to the CA-351 towards Zahara de la Sierra and follow it into Grazalema. Remember, this is mountain driving. When a heavy rain, or even a mist, falls, exercise extreme caution.

Zahara de la Sierra

Leaving Grazalema up and west of town, you'll cross the sierra at the Puerto de las Palomas (Pass of the Doves)—at nearly 1,350 meters (4,400 feet) above sea level, it's the second-highest in Andalucía. From here you get an amazing view of the white village of Zahara de la Sierra, sitting high above a shimmering turquoise reservoir of the same name. Like many of the villages in this area, Zahara's skyline is dominated by a 16th-century watch tower. Built by Christian soldiers on top of an even older Moorish tower, or *atalaya*, the tower sits at the highest point in town and once allowed soldiers to send light signals to neighboring communities to warn of attacks. Historians claim that, using the *atalaya* system, the Moors could send a message from Barcelona to Córdoba in less than four hours. Long after the Christians captured the city in 1407, the Duke of Arcos built a stately home in Zahara in the 18th century, giving the town an air of elegance. Remnants of this post-Reconquista time

are evident in the churches of **San Juan** and **Santa María de la Mesa,** both constructed in the 17th century. The main drag is the cobbled Calle San Juan and this is where you'll find the life of the pueblo. It also leads up to the watchtower, offering some spectacular views along the way.

Should you find yourself in Zahara during the summer months and suffering in the heat, don't despair. No self-respecting Andalusian town survives July and August without a pool and Zahara's very cool **municipal pool** (C/ Camino de la Fuente, tel. 95/612-3110) merits special mention, not only for its amazing views of the mountains, but also because you can use the complex (including a restaurant and snack bar) for a mere €3 and stay as long as you want.

Just outside of town, **El Vínculo** (Crta. Zahara-Grazalema, s/n, tel. 95/612-3002, www.molinoelvinculo.com) is a 17th-century olive oil *molino* (mill) that has been refurbished and now creates cold-pressed artesian olive oil and sells handmade products such as honey and sweet farmers' sherry. Visitors can see the whole process from olive to oil. The mill also rents charming country houses that hold up to seven people. starting at about €30 per person.

Additional accommodations can be found throughout Zahara. **Hotel Arco de la Villa** (Camino Nazarí, tel. 95/612-3254, info@tugasa.com, www.tugasa.com, €65) is tucked on the side of a cliff, on the way up to the castle. Rooms are clean and cozy, if outdated. Another lovely option is **Hostal Marqués de Zahara** (C/ San Juan 3, tel. 95/612-3061, www.marquesdezahara.com, €40), a regal 17th-century mansion with ten cozy, Castilian-style rooms.

Food options are many throughout town, in addition to the restaurants operated by the hotels. **Los Naranjos** (C/ San Juan 15, tel. 95/612-3314) offers great sit-down meals on their lively summer terrace. **Bar Pancho** (C/ Felix Rodríguez Fuente, s/n, tel. 95/612-3032) offers delicious roasted meats—try the *cordero* (lamb) marinated in vinegar and spices. The owner Antonio is extremely gracious.

The friendly and helpful **tourist office**

(Pl. Rey, tel. 95/612-3114) is located in the center of town, just under the castle peak. It also offers a myriad of activities from hiking to paragliding.

Getting there means driving as bus service is sporadic at best. Zahara de la Sierra lies on the CA-531, a winding mountain road that runs south to Grazalema. Just north of the CA-531, the A-382 runs from Jerez to Antequera, and connects to the A-376, which runs between Sevilla, Ronda, and the Costa del Sol.

Olvera

The northernmost Pueblo Blanco in the Cádiz province, Olvera has an ancient history. It was settled by the Phoenicians, then the Romans, but archaeology has revealed that it was a Paleolithic settlement as far back as 12,000 years ago. As in the rest of the Iberian Peninsula, the Visigoths took over after the Romans and then the Moors arrived in the 8th century. It was they who gave Olvera its current shape, building up the town as a defensive garrison that

© PATRICIA DAWN SEVERENUK

The ruins of a Moorish castle loom over the white houses of Olvera.

successfully held off the advancing Christians until 1327. Since then, its experienced similar ups and downs as in the rest of Spain, while continually eking out a living with olive-oil production. Some say the town's name comes from the Spanish word for olive, *oliva.*

Today, the intrepid visitor (for it's a long way off the beaten path) will find a perfect little white town spreading out like a wedding-gown train beneath its twin monuments of castle and church. The 12th-century **Castillo** was originally a Moorish castle/watchtower that served as part of the defensive system of the Granada Nasrid kingdom. The **Barrio de la Villa,** immediately below, is what remains of the old walled town, where Visigothic antiquities are still being found. Directly across the square sits the **Iglesia de la Encarnación,** rebuilt in the 17th century to replace a pre-Moorish Visigothic temple. About 1.5 kilometers (about a mile) out of town, on the road to Setenil, the **Ermita de Nuestra Señora de los Remedios** chapel contains the holy image of the town's patron saint, Our Lady of the Remedies.

Olvera is gradually becoming known as a good place to base yourself if you're into hiking, mountain biking, or horseback riding. The town's economy, dependent for so many years on the olive industry, has gotten a boost from local initiatives to bring more people to the area. One of the most ambitious is the **Vía Verde de la Sierra,** an old rail trail that is being converted into a biking and hiking path. Once done, it will reach all the way to Arcos de la Frontera. Right now it offers 37 kilometers (23 miles) of fairly level walking through tunnels and across gorgeous countryside. The Spanish-language website www.viasverdes.com offers extensive information.

The biggest hotel in town is the **Hotel Mesón Fuente del Pino** (Av. Julian Besteiro, s/n, tel. 95/613-0232, www.hotelfuente delpino.com, €60), which offers 20 simply decorated rooms in a rambling white house located on the A-382 Jerez-Antequera road. The restaurant offers excellent local food. If you are planning on hiking the Vía Verde, consider the **Antitgua Estación Vía Verde** (Camino de la

ANDALUCÍA

LIQUID GOLD

Called "liquid gold" by Homer and hailed as both a food and a medicine by Hippocrates, olive oil is anything but humble. For millennia it's been used to anoint kings and religious leaders. Greek mythology holds that the olive tree was a gift from Athena, goddess of wisdom. In Egypt the mighty Tutankhamen was entombed with olive branches. Biblical history says that Noah received the olive branch as a sign of peace following the floods. Despite this illustrious history, olive oil is still barely used outside of the Mediterranean region. Oh sure, in both the United States and the United Kingdom, top chefs and budding gourmets enthuse over *extra virgens* like religious converts, but when it comes to feeding the family, the masses stick to their tried and trusty butter and vegetable oils.

Too bad, since not only is olive oil delicious, it is also good for you. Unlike other oils, olive oil is rich in monounsaturated fat. What that means is that it lowers cholesterol, leading to a reduced risk of heart disease. It is also a great source of Vitamin E, an antioxidant linked with cancer prevention. If that doesn't make you want to trade in your old artery-cloggers, then the taste surely will. Nothing can stand up to the rich impact of a truly fine olive oil. And Spain, as the world's largest producer, has over 500 delicious brands on offer. The only problem is how to choose.

The term *virgen* means the oil has been obtained from the olive by solely mechanical means – no chemicals or heat. Of the virgin oils *extra virgen* is the finest and most flavorful. It is cold-pressed from the choicest fresh-picked olives and cannot exceed a maximum of one percent acidity. In general, the lower the acidic percentage, the more "perfect" the oil. However, this doesn't imply that oils above the one percent mark are inferior. Each *extra virgen* oil has its own distinct flavor and in general, the higher the number, the more robust the oil. Your taste buds are really the only way you can decide which level is for you.

Just a step down is *virgen fino*. Made from lesser-quality olives or subsequent pressings, these oils lack the intense richness of *extra virgens* yet are perfect for everyday use. *Aceite de oliva* is the stuff you see in big plastic jugs at supermarkets. It is basically refined oil obtained from inferior virgin oils by chemical means. For flavor, a measure of *extra virgen* is blended in. It is perfect for cooking.

As with wine, olive oil varies widely in taste and color depending on the type of olives used, the climate and soil where they are grown, and the producer's methods. Oils can be fruity or flowery, nutty or spicy, delicate or mild, and can range in color from pale champagne to deep green. With six *denominaciones de origen* from 22 growing regions, over 60 types of olives used in production, and countless blends, Spain's variety is astounding.

Estación, s/n, tel. 66/146-3207, €38), located in the old train station and recently remodeled. Good local food can be found all over the old town, but the aforementioned Mesón Fuente del Pino offers the best.

Olvera's **tourist office** (Pl. Iglesia, tel. 95/612-0816), located at the very top of the town between the church and the Moorish castle, can give you more information about the ever-increasing number of outdoors companies offering different activities, as well as maps and information on the Vía Verde.

To get there, take the A-382 from just north of Zahara. It runs just past Olvera and connects the town to Jerez in the west and Antequera in the east. It also bisects A-376, which goes north to Sevilla and south to Málaga and Costa del Sol.

Setenil de las Bodegas

Set in a deep cleavage of tufa rock and limestone 16 kilometers (10 miles) north of Ronda, Setenil de las Bodegas is the most dramatically situated of the Pueblos Blancas. Large sections of the old town have been built into the sides of two cliffs that were formed by the flow of the

Since Andalucía accounts for 80 percent of production, it gets the most fame – and Andalusian oils, primarily from Jaén and Córdoba, are fantastic. The most popular olive in the region is *picual*, which produces a slightly spicy oil that stands up well to robust foods. These oils are perfect for cooking and sautéing, but of course, for intense flavor you can also use them straight from the bottle drizzled over a salad or a thick slice of toasted bread.

The most delicate olive oils in Spain are produced in Cataluña from the *arbequina* olive. These olive oils are light and smooth with pleasant fruity undertones. They are impeccable as is, drizzled over delicate foods, or whisked into salad dressings, cold sauces, and mayonnaise.

TASTING NOTES

An olive oil's flavor depends on the year, the time the olive is picked, the production methods, and countless other factors. When you are shopping, it may help to keep in mind these very general tasting notes regarding some of the most common olive types.

Olive Type	Olive Oil Characteristics
Arbequina	Very fruity, smooth, and light
Cornicabra	Very aromatic, fresh, almost sweet
Empeltre	Very sweet and delicate
Hojiblanca	Very smooth and sweet
Lechín	Fragrant, fresh, a little spicy
Picual	Strong, piquant, almost spicy
Verdial	Very smooth, light, fresh

STORAGE NOTES

Though your bottle of olive oil may look gorgeous in the kitchen windowsill with the sun streaming golden-green through it, this is a sure way to destroy your precious oil. Always store olive oils away from heat and light. Tightly capped in a nice dark cupboard (not next to the stove) is the best way to preserve the oil's flavor and extend its shelf life (depending on the oil, up to two years, though most extra virgins are best if used in the first six months). Though some manufacturers suggest you refrigerate your oil, it is not a good idea. In order to use it you will have to let it warm to room temperature. Repeated cooling and warming traps moisture in the oil and leads to premature rancidity.

BUYING OLIVE OIL

A beautifully bottled Spanish *extra virgen* olive oil makes a very tasty souvenir. There are specialty olive oil shops in most major Spanish towns and you can also find an extensive selection at any El Corte Inglés department store.

Trejo River thousands of years ago. The soft tufa rock (formed by deposits on limestone) was pliable enough for residents to carve out dwellings and wine cellars, explaining the "de la Bodegas" part of the town's name. Until a phylloxera plague in the 1870s ruined the wine industry in all of Málaga province (and a good part of western Cádiz province, too), Setenil was one of the most important wine-producing towns in the region. The wine-making tradition is starting to come back again as smaller winemakers have reclaimed abandoned estates.

The town was originally inhabited by the Romans, and then the Moors centuries later. The name comes from the Latin Septern-Nihil, which means "seven times nothing" and refers to the number of times the Christians tried unsuccessfully to push the Moors out. They finally succeeded in 1484.

The real charm of tiny Setenil is found in wandering its narrow, steep streets with the cliffs above seeming to billow right over the rooftops. There are a few sights, including the remains of the 12th-century Moorish castle and the **Iglesia de la Encarnación,** an impressive

Gothic church that dates back to the 16th century. It was spared the worst violence exacted on many churches throughout the area during the Civil War. It houses an interesting 12-paneled Flemish painting that dates back to the 12th century. The church doesn't have set opening hours, but the tourist office can give you information about visits.

The **tourist office** (C/ Villa 2, tel. 95/613-4261) is housed in a medieval building with a notable wooden ceiling. You'll have to visit them if you want to arrange accommodations. Remarkably, there are no lodgings within the city itself. **Hotel Villa de Setenil** (C/ Callejón 10) is scheduled to open in 2007. However, there are many *casas rurales* (rural inns) around the region and the tourist office serves as their broker. You'll have more luck with food, as there are cafés and bars tucked throughout the streets. Try the **Restaurante Terraza El Mirador** (Pl. Andalucía, s/n, tel. 95/613-4261, closed Mon.), which offers amazing views over the valley accompanied by excellent grilled meats. If you are really hungry, go for their *parrillada surtida,* a mixed grill plate that stuffs two for €22.

Getting there by car, take the A-382 out of Olvera and then swing south on the tiny, windy CAP-4222. To get to Ronda, just 25 kilometers (16 miles) south, follow the signs out of town to the MA-486 and then switch to then the MA-449. It hooks up with the A-376 into Ronda.

COSTA DE LA LUZ

Cádiz's Costa de la Luz runs along the Atlantic ocean from just north of Cádiz city down to Tarifa at the southernmost tip of Spain. The beaches here are fine and gold and wide enough to land a jumbo jet. Backed by pine groves, windswept dunes, rugged cliffs, and saltwater marshes, these beaches are less developed and less crowded than those on the nearby Costa del Sol. Part of the reason is the climate. The waters of the Atlantic are colder and choppier than those of the warm, placid Mediterranean. The entire coast is also subject to the near constant blowing of the Levante, an

sunset on the Costa de la Luz

easterly wind. Access is difficult without a car, though infrequent busses do serve the main beaches. Travelers who take the time to get to see and know Costa de la Luz invariably fall in love with its unkempt charm and its famous coppery sunsets.

One thing to keep in mind when traveling here. This is one of the top destinations for vacationing Spaniards in July and August. While it doesn't get as unbearably crowded as the Costa del Sol or Costa Blanca, the fact that it has fewer lodgings means beds book fast. Unless you fancy sleeping in your car, plan ahead.

The best way to explore and enjoy this area is via car. Rent one in Cádiz and go. If you are reliant on public transportation, you'll have to be more flexible and travel light, but it is doable. **Transportes Comes** (tel. 90/219-0208, www.tgcomes.es) and **Los Amarillos** (tel. 95/628-5852, www.losamarillos.es), both based out of Cádiz, cover most of this area. Check at the bus station in Cádiz (Pl. Hispanidad, 1, tel. 95/680-7059) for schedules and rates.

Chiclana de la Frontera

Bordering the southern edge of the Bay of Cádiz nature reserve, charming Chiclana combines the sleepy feel of whitewashed Andalusian village with two fantastic beaches. It is a late bloomer by Spanish standards, not having been founded until 1303. Outside of its own cute self, the sights in Chiclana are few and mainly religious. On Calle de la Plaza, the 18th-century **Iglesia San Telmo** has an unusual angular bell tower. This street is also home to a lively weekly market held every Saturday morning. The 17th-century **Iglesia de Jesús Nazareno** boasts Cádiz's most impressive baroque doorway. Carved entirely in white Carrera marble, it blends in beautifully. The church has an attached convent where the nuns prepare the most delicious almond pastries. The 18th-century **Ermita de Santa Ana** is the Chiclana's most emblematic church as its massive dome towers over the town. Just off the coast, on a tiny islet named Sancti-Petri, the Phoenicians built the famous Towers of Hercules. Later, the Christians built a lighthouse

and defensive castle on the ruins of the towers. Those too now lay in ruins.

Chiclana's beaches are about five kilometers (three miles) outside of the town and are easily accessed via public bus. **La Barrosa** is a 6.5-kilometer (four-mile) swath of fine sand backed by dunes and stands of pine trees. Next to that is **Playa Sancti-Petri**, a gorgeous beach that fronts the Novo Sancti-Petri development, home to several resorts and a golf course.

Chiclana offers very limited accommodations within the old city and a resort's worth of options in Novo Sancti-Petri. There is really very little distinguishing Sancti-Petri's hotels one from the other. They are all big, brash, rambling resorts with massive pools, massive buffets, and easy access to unlimited sun and sand. In each, inquire about a sea-facing room. Also, there are no set addresses, they are all located on the road leading into Novo Sancti-Petri. Good choices include: **Iberostar Royal Andalus** (tel. 95/694-9109, www.iberostar.com, €110), which costs less than the others but the rooms boast circa-1980s decor; and **Meliá Sancti Petri Hotel and Golf** (tel. 95/649-1200, melia.sancti.petri@solmelia.com, www.solmelia.com, €250), which offers an amazing free-form pool and an 18-hole golf course right on the beach.

Like all the towns along the coast, Chiclana offers wonderful food based on the sea's bounty. The town has no shortage of tapas bars. One of the best is **Bodega San Sebastián** (C/ Mendaro 15, tel. 95/653-3232), which has an old sherry bar feel. For succulent grilled meats and fish, try **El Santuario de las Carnes** (C/ San Antonio 7, tel. 905/640-4264, closed Mon., €30).

Chiclana has two **tourist information offices:** In the town (C/ Vega 6, tel. 95/653-5969) and in Novo Sancti-Petri (Playa de la Barrosa, tel. 95/649-7234).

Getting there by car, leave Cádiz via the CA-33 towards San Fernando, then switch to the E-5/A-48 until Chiclana. It is about 24 kilometers (15 miles) and half an hour. If you are coming from Tarifa, take the same road, which is still called N-340 in parts.

Conil de la Frontera

Bigger than Chiclana, the bustling town of Conil is one of the most popular vacation spots for Spaniards. Archaeology suggests that the town was first inhabited by Phoenicians, who developed a fishing community here. Later, subsequent populations of Romans, Visigoths, and Moors each set up their own fishing industry here, each using the ancient technique of *almadraba*. The tuna fishing industry and the use of *almadrabas* continued through the Christian conquest and on until the present day.

From the sea, Conil looks like a maze of tiny white houses clamoring around a few rising structures—the town's churches. These are Conil's only real sights (though the charming cobbled town is something to see in its own right). In your wanderings, seek out the 14th-century **Torre de Guzmán,** built for the Reconquista hero Guzman el Bueno who famously allowed his son to be murdered at the gates of Tarifa, rather than give up the city.

Of course, Conil's real draw is its beaches which stretch out for kilometers in a long ribbon of fine sand and golden dunes. **Playa de la Fontinilla** is closest to the city and runs along **Paseo Marítimo** (boardwalk). **Playa Fuente del Gallo** is backed up against cliffs to the north of the town. Still further north are the **Calas de Roche,** secluded beaches and coves that are difficult to access, but worth the trouble. To the south, across the river, the beaches of **Castilnovo** and **Bateles** unfurl. These long beaches are very peaceful, backed up against salt marshes and grazing land.

One of Conil's other attractions is its **nightlife.** This is the busiest party capital on Costa de la Luz and locals pile in from the pueblos each weekend to partake. Of course, the most thumping season is summer and around Semana Santa (Easter Week). Bars heat up around 10 P.M. with mostly Spanish music and cheap cocktails. Nightclubs go nearly until sunset with loud techno and more cheap cocktails. Calle/Plaza de Goya is a good place to start as it is loaded wall to whitewashed wall with bars.

Because Conil is so popular with Spanish holiday-makers, there can be a crunch on accommodations in July and August. Book ahead. Here are a few recommendations, but you may need to check out a website, such as the Spanish-language www.hoteles-conil.com, which has hundreds of listings of everything from campsites to four-star resorts. **Pension la Villa** (Pl. España 6, tel. 95/644-1053, €45) offers simple, clean rooms in the center. **Hostal Renato** (C/ Hernan Cortes 12, tel. 95/644-2083, www.hostalrenato.com, €51) offers bright little rooms in the center of town. The beach is a five-minute walk away. For the resort experience, head to the beach and **Hotel Fuerte Conil** (Playa de la Fontanilla, s/n, tel. 95/644-3344, conil@fuertehoteles.com, www.fuertehoteles.com, €145). It offers spacious seafront rooms (worth the €20 extra), indoor and outdoor pools, an in-house spa, and a PADI-certified dive school. It is about 10 minutes walking to the center of Conil.

For good local food just wander around the old town. There are hundreds of cafés, bars, and restaurants serving everything from tapas to pizza to gourmet. Along the beaches, you'll find some of the best seafood. One to seek out is **La Fontanilla** (Camino de la Fontanilla, s/n, tel. 95/644-1130, closed Wed., Dec., and Jan., €30). Their seafood is impeccable and if you are feeling brave, have the *ortiguillas* (fried sea anemone), a local specialty.

Conil's **tourist office** (C/ Carretera 1, tel. 95/644-0501) runs a summer information kiosk in Plaza Santa Catalina.

Getting there is easy as Conil lies on the E-5/N-340/A-48, which runs from Cádiz to Tarifa. And yes, you may see all three names at different points in the road. It is the same highway, though the A-48 portion is much newer and wider.

Vejer de la Frontera

The lovely whitewashed village of Vejer is located about 10 kilometers (six miles) inland and 190 meters (625 feet) straight up from the coast, midway between Conil and Barbate. If you are making a tour of Costa de la Luz, it would be a shame to miss this beauty. Settled by the Phoenicians, the Romans, and the Moors, Vejer became part of Christian Spain in 1264. The Moorish legacy is the one most felt in the city and the labyrinth of white walls and crooked cobbled alleys feel at times like a medina. In fact, Vejer is considered one of the best examples of Andalusian-Arabic architecture along the coast—and indeed among the other more famous white villages.

Start a tour of the city in **Plaza de España,** a palm-tree-lined square famous for its frog-fonted fountain. When you pass through the 11th-century **Arco de la Villa,** you'll enter the past and Vejer's whitewashed wonder world of ancient alleys, postage-stamp-sized patios lined with bright flowers, and iron-grilled windows. Hidden among the streets are a handful of intriguing churches and at the very top, the fortified walls and remains of the 11th-century Moorish castle are worth exploring. As you turn corners and go up alleys, you'll quite suddenly come upon Vejer's other important sight—its view. On one side, it looks out over the coast and the blue expanse of the Atlantic. On the other, it looks towards the mottled green and brown lands of Andalucía and the Sierra de Grazalema beyond.

Just keep in mind before setting off that most of Vejer is uphill. If you are not feeling up to the climb, hire a cab to take you to the castle at the top and then wind your way down, stopping often to take in the view—or just a glass of wine with the locals at one of the dozens of tiny bars that line the tiny streets.

Vejer offers some of the most charming accommodations on Costa de la Luz. **[** **La Casa del Califa** (Pl. España 15, tel. 95/644-7730, www.lacasadelcalifa.com, €80) has been lovingly hobbled together from four houses that date back to the Moorish occupation of Vejer. The decor draws heavily from this past in a heavily spiced palette of colors and Moroccan furnishings. If you upgrade to "Emir" service you'll have fresh flowers, sparkling wine, and chocolates in your room upon arrival. **Convento San Francisco** (C/ Plazuela, s/n, tel. 95/645-1001, www.tugasa.com, €70),

located in a 17th-century convent, offers atmospheric rooms heavy on the Castilian decor—lots of dark wood and exposed brick.

You don't have to look hard for good food in Vejer. For tapas or light fare, try any of the half-dozen cafés rimming the Plaza de España. For something more substantial, try **La Refectorio** (C/ Plazuela, s/n). Attached to the Hotel Convento San Francisco, it offers creative takes on Andalusian fare. **Trafalgar** (Pl. España 10, tel. 95/644-7638, closed Mon. and Jan., €25) is located in a traditional Vejer house complete with flowering patio. The specialty is *secreto ibérico,* a tender cut of pork grilled over open flames.

The **tourist office** (C/ Marqués de Tamarón 10, tel. 95/645-0191) is a five-minute walk from Plaza de España. Be sure to pick up their map, but don't forget to put it down and just enjoy walking about as well—it's a hilltop, you can't get lost.

Get to Vejer from any town lying on the coastal E-5/N-340/A-48 road. Look for the exit to Vejer and then take it up the long, winding road until you reach Plaza de España. Park. Any further driving and you'll end up in a mire of ancient, unforgiving alleyways. If you are taking the bus, the bus stop is at the bottom of the hill in the new part of town. It is about a 20-minute walk up or you can just catch a cab.

Caños de Meca

Caños de Meca is so small that it is not even a town, but rather an extension of nearby Barbate (quite possibly the least picturesque place on the coast). Located in the natural park of La Breña, Caños de Meca is a stunning 11-kilometer (seven-mile) stretch of golden beach lined with jagged cliffs and pine tree groves. Up above the cliff runs the one road that constitutes the "village" of Caños de Meca, Avenida de Trafalgar. It is has a few small hotels, campsites, a grocery store, a handful of restaurants and bars, and a pharmacy. Despite its small size, Caños de Meca has a huge reputation as one of the most beautiful and most bohemian beaches in Spain. Neo-hippies, dreadlocked hipsters, and self-styled artists and musicians from across Spain and Europe

Palm trees line the beach at Caños de Meca.

flock here each summer to participate in drum circles on the beach, paint their bodies in the soft clay that oozes from the cliffs, dance until dawn in the *chiringuitos* (beachside bars), and sunbathe nude among the furthest rocky reaches of the beach. It is also a favorite destination for just about anyone looking for a laid-back, very unpretentious beach vacation. However, despite what the hotels and campgrounds say, it is not really a place for kids. Nor would anyone but the most young-spirited of those over 40 appreciate its particular charms.

As along the rest of the Costa de la Luz, the Atlantic here is chilly—even in the midst of summer—and the waves can be rough. However, the waters are crystal clear and the vistas breath-catching. The far, southeastern end of the beach, called **Las Cartinas,** is a stretch of sand that mingles with giant boulders, forming mini-coves; this is also the nudist part of Caños, perfect for getting rid of pesky tan lines. But be careful here come late day—the tide can rush in suddenly trapping you among the rocks.

Just above this point, on the other side of the cliff, stretches the **La Breña** natural reserve and park. Along its edge are marked trails leading the 13 kilometers (eight miles) to Barbate. It is a haven for nature lovers, full of rich fauna, fascinating birdlife—look out for the wide wingspan of the peregrine falcon—and amazing views over the Atlantic.

At the opposite end of the beach, moving west, is the famous **Faro de Trafalgar.** This lighthouse serves as a beacon over Trafalgar Bay, the sight where the invincible Spanish Armada was duly trounced by Lord Nelson in 1805. Napoleon had been throwing his weight around Europe since naming himself Emperor and the English were worried. They sent Nelson, a war-wizened and victorious admiral, out to sea in an attempt to stop Napoleon's navy. Spain, who was busy trying to maintain control over its unraveling empire in the Americas, did not want to get involved. Napoleon, veiling some serious threats, convinced them otherwise. So the Spanish Armada and the French Navy joined forces and went out to sea to meet Nelson and his sailors ship-to-ship. In

October of 1805, the two crews met within sight of the lighthouse and a vicious battle ensued. Despite being outnumbered, the British proved their naval mettle. The combined Spanish/French ships lost 7,000 sailors, while the Brits lost 450—among them Lord Nelson. He was wounded by a sniper near the end of the battle and lived just long enough to learn of his victory. The battle marked the end of Spain's centuries-long domination of the seas and launched Nelson into infamy. It didn't stop Napoleon however. He proceeded to stomp all over Europe, until another British leader, Lord Wellington, put a stop to him at Waterloo in 1815. Looking out at the tranquil sea from this point, it is hard to imagine the scene of smoking wooden warships, jettisoned bodies, and gunpowder smoke—but it happened, just 200 years ago.

By night, Caños de Meca thumps with music from half-a-dozen bars and *chiringuitos* (beachside bars), particularly in summer. The music stops when the last person leaves or just passes out on the beach. **Las Dunas** (Av. Trafalgar, s/n) is a favorite. Also, if the Jaima Moroccan tent is open, go, it is a spectacular hookah den complete with floor pillows and spice-colored canopies billowing out over the sea. However, it closes from year to year, plagued by ownership and/or legal problems.

Caños de Meca offers some interesting accommodations. **Casa Atrapasueños** (Las Acacias 186, tel. 60/903-2570, info@casas atrapa.com, www.casasatrapa.com, €100) is a collection of typical white Andalusian *casitas* (little houses) that can accommodate up to four people. They are simply decorated and feature baths with hydro-jet showers, orthopedic mattresses, and equipped kitchens. **Casas Karen** (Fuente del Madroño 6, tel. 95/643-7067, www.casaskaren.com, €100) offers a similar set of cozy little houses and cottages. The decor is a bit more interesting with an Andalucía meets "Gilligan's Island" feel, complete with hammocks in each house. There are also two *chozas* (bamboo and straw huts) that have been kitted-out with all the modern amenities, except for television and

air-conditioning. If you want to book a room by telephone, be sure to call between 9 A.M.– noon Monday–Friday. This is the only time when the company accepts phone calls. For a more traditional hotel, head to the newly built **Hotel La Breña** (Av. Trafalgar 4, tel. 95/643-7368, info@hotelbrena.com, www .hotelbrena.com, €65). It offers clean, modern rooms and one of the nicer restaurants in the area.

Many people who come to Caños de Meca do so to camp. There are a handful of campsites along the length of the beach. Each offer showers, laundry rooms, small shops, cafés, and bars. The latter are some of the hottest night spots in Caños, offering music and dancing until the wee hours. If you want to sleep at all, choose a plot as far away from the bar as possible—and bring earplugs as a back up. Particularly in summer, these "family friendly" campsites turn into wild party scenes reminiscent of Spring Break—only with flamenco instead of techno. **Camping Caños de Meca** (Crta. Vejer, s/n, tel. 95/643-7120, www .camping-canos-de-meca.com), with over 100 tree-shaded plots (€40 for a site with an electric hook-up for one car or caravan) plus bungalows (€65), is one of the quieter campgrounds. **Camping Camaleón** (Av. Trafalgar, s/n, tel. 95/643-7154) is party central come summertime as it packs out with groups of 20-somethings (and those who wish they were). The campsite's bar is one of the liveliest in town. There are full amenities—showers, laundry, food—but they can get downright filthy on August weekends—oddly, the guests don't seem to mind.

There are not a lot of food options in Caños de Meca. In addition to a few no-name bars and food booths, **La Pequeña Lulu** (Av. Trafalgar 2, tel. 95/643-7355) offers a wide variety of salads and vegetarian dishes. Though being deep Andalucía, meat and fish are always available. This is also one of the few places that stays open late (until 4 A.M.) year-round. **El Pirata** (Av. Trafalgar, s/n, tel. 95/643-7396) juts out over the beach and offers excellent seafood along with its spectacular views. Come back for a cocktail and the sunset. **El Jazmin** (Av. Trafalgar, s/n, tel. 95/643-7088, closed Nov.) offers award-winning tapas (really), Arabic-inspired fare, and great barbecued meats.

Getting to Caños de Meca by car is not difficult. From the E-5/N-340/A-48, take the Vejer-Caños de Meca exit and it will run you right into Avenida de Trafalgar. If you are bussing in from Cádiz or elsewhere, the stop is at the entrance to Caños de Meca at the start of Avenida de Trafalgar, close to El Pirata.

Barbate

Lying midway between Conil and Tarifa, Barbate is one of the bigger towns on the Costa de la Luz. It is also one of the least attractive. An ancient fishing town, it lost its charm a long time ago. (Maybe during the many aummers when dictator Francisco Franco vacationed here?) Now it is busy, bustling, and bland. However, it is packed with cheap sleeps so if you can't get a place in Caños, Zahara, or even Vejer, Barbate may have to do. Additionally, the only tourist information resource for Caños de Meca and Zahara de los Atunes is Barbate's **tourist office** (C/ Vázquez Mella, s/n, tel. 95/643-3962).

◖ Zahara de los Atunes

With a wide variety of accommodations, excellent dining, and a gorgeous beach, the perfect little beach village of Zahara de los Atunes makes an excellent base for exploring the Costa de la Luz. Located on the eastern edge of Barbate (of which it is a part), tiny Zahara gets its second name from its long history as a tuna-fishing community. The **Castillo de la Almadraba**, which now lie in ruins, was built in the 15th century by the Dukes of Medina Sidonia in order to protect their tuna fishing industry from pirates. Rumor has it that Miguel de Cervantes himself once worked in the tuna-processing plant here.

Though tuna fishing is still practiced, it has been supplanted by tourism as the town's main industry. Zahara is a popular resort with both Spaniards and Northern Europeans drawn to its gorgeous beaches—some 19 kilometers (12 miles) of them—and laid-back Andalusian lifestyle. There are two parts of the town. Closer to the main road is the older town, jammed with inexpensive lodgings, old-fashioned hotels, tapas bars, and seafood restaurants. At the end of a long road heading along the beach is the newer part, Atlanterra, home to many upscale private homes, expensive resorts, and a large German-speaking community.

Summer nights in Zahara can be quite lively—though without the hippy air that permeates Caños de Meca. Bars are all over the old town and usually go until about 2 A.M. On the beach, *chiringuitos* keep the party going until much later.

Zahara offers a wide-variety of accommodations considering its small size. Unless you arrive in July or August, you'll have no problem finding a place to stay. If you are looking for something cheaper than these recommendations, just look for *pensión* or *hostal*. And remember, all the prices listed in this book are for the high-season. Off-season, prices drop down to half. The town's classic hotel is **Doña Lola** (Pl. Thompson 1, tel. 95/643-9009, www.donalolazahara.com, €75), an authentic Andalusian hotel complete with whitewashed walls and lovely inner courtyards, with all the modern amenities—air-conditioning, a swimming pool, an outdoor garden with bar. **Gran Sol Hotel** (Av. Playa, s/n, tel. 95/643-9301) is just as its name implies, a grand old hotel—Cádiz style. The rooms have seen better days, but are clean and well maintained, and if you upgrade to a sea view, your own private balcony will open right over the Atlantic. Staff is friendly, but skip the restaurant, which is so-so and overpriced. **Casa Grande** (Av. Pradillo 57, tel. 95/643-9001, info@casagrandezahara.com, www.casagrandezahara.com, €95) is a lovely old Andalusian home offering rustic comfort just two minutes walking to the beach or three to the center of Zahara.

Zahara offers dozens of choices for food. Wander about the area between the town center and the beach to find where the locals go for tapas. Many agree the best are found at **Casa Juanito** (C/ Sagasta 7, tel. 95/643-9211), which offers nine different tapas takes on tuna. For a sit-down meal, try **Casa José María** (Pl. Marqués de Tamarón 3, tel. 95/643-9338) for genuine Andalusian dishes. Their *salmorejo* (a very thick gazpacho) is sublime, as is their *arroz negro* (paella cooked with squid and its ink). **La Botica** (C/ Real 13, tel. 95/643-9183) is a stone-walled bodega with excellent wines and, for a change from seafood, excellent roasted meats.

To get to Zahara, duck off the E-5/N-340/ A-48 at the sign for the Bar Venta de Retin. The road is A-5204, but it is poorly marked and Zahara de los Atunes may or may not appear.

Bolonia and Baelo Claudia

Sixteen kilometers (10 miles) northwest of Tarifa, along Bolonia Cove and near the town of El Lentiscal, the Roman ruins of Baelo Claudia are among the best-preserved in Andalusia. Though the town was established relatively late in the Roman era (it wasn't built until the 2nd century B.C.), it quickly became famous for the quality of its *garum,* a fermented fish sauce made from tuna or mackerel. Anthropologists suggest it'd turn stomachs today, but during the Roman days it was quite the delicacy. Within 300 years, the settlement went from being a mere trading post to a full *municipium* (self-governing town), complete with voting rights, under the rule of Emperor Claudius.

The ruins of **Baelo Claudia** (Ensenada de Bolonia s/n, tel. 95/668-8530, 10 A.M.–6 P.M. Tues.–Sat., later in summer, 10 A.M.–2 P.M. Sun., free) were discovered in 1917. As you enter, you encounter the three temples dedicated to Jupiter, Juno, and Minerva—the three great gods of imperial Rome. There is also a temple to the Egyptian goddess Isis, which faces onto the former law courts. Move closer to the beach, however, and you see the stone pits where the fish sauce was produced in four-foot-deep wells: fish heads, entrails, roe, and blood would be left to ferment in the sun's heat before being transferred to clay *amphorae* (containers) and sold throughout the empire. (The factory was located beside the water to facilitate garbage disposal and to allow brisk breezes to eliminate the smell.)

However, many people come to Bolonia for its lovely **beach** (www.playasdebolonia.com). Though it is windy, the peak of nearby mount San Bartolomé helps to somewhat minimize the effect of the winds whipping up from Tarifa. The breezes have traditionally kept the beach somewhat isolated, which for many visitors is the true charm of the place. It is not unusual to see a cow from a nearby farm come trotting along.

To the northwest of the village, the pristine sand dunes of **Punta Camarinal,** once a radar outpost for the Spanish Navy, are extremely popular with nudists.

Bolonia is also famous for its *chiringuitos* (beachside bars), with no less than six in a stretch of a few kilometers. These café/shacks serve coffees and light fare by day, cocktails and hot beats by night. The *chiringuito* closest to the ruins is renowned for its Brazilian rhythms. Grab a mojito, walk out the sand, and do a little rumba under the stars.

Accommodations in summer, especially August, can be scarce and often require a minimum two-night stay. Book ahead. **La Posada de Lola** (C/ El Lentiscal 26, tel. 95/668-8536, hostallola@cherrytel.com, www.hostallola .com, €55) has brightly colored rooms around a lovely garden. Many look out onto the Atlantic. Some have shared baths. **Hostal Los Jerezanos** (C/ El Lentiscal 5, tel. 95/668-8592, €89) is a great favorite of windsurfers and the owners are fonts of information on windsurfing and other activities in the area.

Bolonia is best accessed by car. It is located near the E-5/N-340/A-48, which runs from Cádiz to Tarifa. The turn-off is regional road CA-2216. From Tarifa, it is possible to get to the area by walking north along the beach, towards Punta Paloma. From Zahara de los Atunes, walk south through the Atlanterra subdivision, towards the lighthouse at Punta Camarinal; when you reach the lighthouse, you'll see a dirt track that goes up towards the Sierra de la Plata. After 20–30 minutes walking, turn right on the first paved road (going downhill). You can also catch an inexpensive taxi from either Tarifa or Zahara de los Atunes.

TARIFA

It is in Tarifa, the southernmost point in mainland Europe, just 11 kilometers (seven miles) from the coast of Africa, that the turbulent Atlantic and tranquil Mediterranean meet. This clash of two of the world's proudest bodies of water has given rise to rolling waves and swooping winds and led to Tarifa being nicknamed "City of Wind." Though it long kept holidaymakers at bay, the wind proved irresistible to extreme sports fans and the beaches north of town have become Europe's biggest wind- and kite-surfing destination. Tarifa also happens to be a perfect little Spanish village. Whitewashed buildings, a winding maze of old streets, medieval ruins, sandy beaches, a harbor lined with seafood restaurants, hopping tapas bars, and relatively few tourists compared with nearby Costa del Sol. It also offers easy boat access to Morocco. (See sidebar, *Tangier*.)

However, Tarifa is much more than wind, water, and wandering. This tiny town has played a pivotal role throughout Spanish history. Archeological evidence that indicates Tarifa was settled way before the Romans ever arrived. There is also proof that the Romans put roots nearby in Bolonia and that the Visigoths were afoot as well. However, the town takes its name from the Berber general Tarif ibn Malik. He led the first Moorish push into the peninsula, landing at Tarifa in 710. By 1085, the Christians were pounding at the door and for the next 300 years, battles at Tarifa were frequent. By 1295, Tarifa was in the hands of the Christian soldier Guzmán El Bueno. A faction of 5,000 Moorish troops arrived at the gates, with El Bueno's son as their prisoner. They threatened to kill the boy if Tarifa was not surrendered immediately. El Bueno famously replied, "I did not beget a son to be made use of against my country, but that he should serve her against her foes." With that he threw down his dagger. His son was killed, Tarifa remained in Christian hands, and El Bueno became a legend.

Today, evidence of the Moors is felt in the twisting, medina-like streets of the old town. Local fishermen still use an ancient Roman

Tarifa, Spain's southernmost town

© ARIELLE WEISMAN

technique of catching fish, called *almadraba,* that uses a circle of boats and large nets. The Christian legacy is seen in the castle named for El Bueno and in the solemn Semana Santa celebrations that take place each Easter.

Sights

Tarifa is relatively small and the main monuments can be seen in a morning, leaving you the rest of your time here to take advantage of the white sand beaches or pop over to Morocco or Gibraltar for the day. Begin your walking tour of Tarifa on the **Paseo de la Alameda,** a pedestrian way lined with palm trees and cafés. Enter the old walled city via Calle Guzmán el Bueno, which passes by the ruins of **Castillo de Guzmán El Bueno.** The castle was built in 960 by the Moors. Its irregular oblong shape is typical of Roman fortresses and has led to speculation that it sits on the site of an ancient Roman fort. On its east are two high towers. The castle is currently under long-term renovation and will remain closed to the public for several years. From the castle, continue on through the historic center to the charming, flower-festooned, blue-tiled **Plaza del Ayuntamiento** (Town Hall Plaza). Don't forget to visit the much-photographed frogs at the fountain in the center of the plaza! From the Ayuntamiento building, wind your way through the cobblestone streets to the **Iglesia San Mateo** (C/ Sancho IV El Bravo, 9 A.M.–1 P.M. and 5:30–9 P.M. daily, free), which was built in the 15th century in Mudejar style. However, a small tombstone inside is dedicated to an ancient Visigoth Christian, indicating that the church's history is much older. As you leave the old city, pass through the 8th-century **Puerta de Jerez,** one of the original three entrances to Tarifa.

For a breath of modernity amidst so much medieval history, take a stroll down **Calle Batalla del Salado.** This street is famous for its expensive surf shops. If you can't afford the prices, a good time can still be had window shopping—or wondering just how much money a dreadlocked surfer makes.

The cheapest way, of course, to enjoy the waters of Tarifa is to simply head to the **beaches.** On the Atlantic side, **Playa de los Lances** is Tarifa's most famous beach. Located just north of town, it offers nearly 10 kilometers (six miles) of white sand and lots of wind. Not so much fun for the bathers, but surfers love it. You'll see hundreds of them trying out their tricks at various levels of grace. Beyond that is **Playa de Valdevaqueros,** another kitesurfing paradise. On the Mediterranean, the aptly named **Playa Chica,** or small beach, is located on a narrow strip of sand on the isthmus leading out to **Isla de las Palomas.** Though equally as chilly as the Atlantic, the Mediterranean side makes for safer swimming, as it is sheltered and has less undertow. To get to the beaches, you'll need a car, or in the summer, you can catch a beach bus runs from the station (C/ Batalla del Salado 10, €2) every two hours.

Nightlife
Start the night slow at **Bamboo** (Po. Alameda 2, tel. 95/662-7304), a Moroccan hippy den with striped canopies, cushy pillows, tropi-cal cocktails, tasty tapas, and a chilled-out soundtrack. It's open all day serving a very late breakfast to the same folks who closed down the joint the night before. **Misiana** (C/ Sancho IV el Bravo 18, tel. 95/662-7083), located in the hotel of the same name, is a glamorous little café/bar that is so sleek it wouldn't be out of place in Soho. Get a Guinness fix at **Bean House** (C/ Sancho IV el Bravo 26, tel. 95/668-5253), a hopping Irish pub where everyone speaks English, the beer flows all night, and the music is often live. For a relaxed evening sipping good sangria (not boxed wine and fruit juice) and listening to live flamenco music, head to **Almedina** (C/ Almedina 3, www.almedinacafe.net). It doubles as a lively café by day.

Kick it up a few decibels at one of Tarifa's *discotecas*. **La Ruina** (C/ Santísima Trinidad 9) is one of the most popular places in town with a thumping mix of electronica, jungle, and world beats. The dance floor is hot. **Tanakas** (Pl. San Hiscio, s/n, tel. 95/668-0327) is famous for its late, late nights, and loud, loud techno-Spanish pop mix.

Sports and Recreation
Tarifa's infamous Levante (easterly) and Poniente (westerly) winds blow year-round, making Tarifa the place to go for aquatic sports like **windsurfing and kitesurfing.** If you already have your own gear, just head on down to the beach, but if you need a rental, visit **Art of Surfing** (C/ Batalla del Salado 47, tel. 95/668-5204, www.artofsurfing.com) for either wind- or kitesurfing gear. Though it will not by any means be a cheap ordeal, trained professionals can set you up with everything from equipment (€70 for one day) to lessons (€95–190, depending on the type of course). Playa los Lances hosts the annual **Red Bull Skyride Tarifa,** an international kitesurfing competition that draws the world's best kitesurfers every May. There are over 20 official kitesurfing schools in town and many more unofficial ones. Look out for flyers or head straight to **Max Sports** (Playa de Valdevaqueros, tel. 95/668-5277), near Hotel Hurricane, which

TANGIER

Just a 35-minute boat ride from Tarifa and 11 kilometers (seven miles) across the narrow Strait of Gibraltar, Tangier is the gateway to an exotic world. According to Berber legend, the city was founded upon the return of the dove to Noah's ark with soil in its claws, indicating the birth of a new world, or *tanja* in Berber. The ancient Greeks described the city as the most beautiful known to both man and the gods, and according to their mythology, the grotto that lies just outside Tangier is where Hercules once rested before attempting one of his 12 labors.

Because of its strategic location at the mouth of the Mediterranean, this historic North African city has served as a prime port for trade since the days of the Phoenicians and Romans. Its increasing importance has given rise to a history of invasion and foreign rule, to such an extent that in 1923, it was declared a tax-free international zone. Throughout the ages, Tangier has attracted all sorts of people, from Jews seeking refuge from the Spanish Inquisition and secret agents dealing in dirty business during World War II to famous artists and writers such as Henri Matisse and Tennessee Wil-

liams. Tangier even served as the site for the filming of one of the most famous movies of all time, *Casablanca*. Though Tangier now belongs to the Kingdom of Morocco, the centuries of European influence have left their mark on the city and its nearly 700,000 inhabitants. Today it is a popular destination for day-tripping tourists from Spain and wealthy African families.

Tangier is a bustling, cosmopolitan city with an old-world feel. Moroccans dressed in long, loose kaftans weave their way through the narrow streets and alleyways alongside their modern suit-wearing companions. Professions too are diverse. Some locals are snake charmers and spice vendors; others are businesspeople and tour guides. Nearly all have something they want to sell you, be it cheap jewelry or elegant rugs, and most are willing – actually expecting – to bargain with you. With starting prices so low, you'll feel almost guilty haggling, but it is part of the culture. Tangier's street vendors are notoriously persistent, so if you are not interested in making a deal with them, it's best not to get caught up in conversation in the first place. Don't bother changing your euros into Moroccan dirhams, which are non-

---

offers lessons starting at €100 for a one-day beginner course. In town, lessons at **Hotstick** (C/ Batalla del Salado 41, tel. 95/668-0419, kite@hotsticktarifa.com, www.hotsticktarifa.com) also begin at €100 per day.

The rough-and-tumble waters around Tarifa and the narrow Strait of Gibraltar are also prime ground for **dolphin- and whale-watching.** Dozens of outfits offer English-language journeys and about 90 percent of the time you'll see the massive mammals. The dolphins are so used to the boats that they will swim right up. The waters are home to dolphins and pilot whales year-round. Sperm whales are present May–July and orcas show up in July and August. **FIRMM** (C/ Pedro Cortés 4, tel. 95/662-7008, www.firmm.org) is the Foundation for Information and Research on Marine Mammals, a Swiss-run nonprofit

dedicating to studying and protecting marine mammals and their habitats. It offers educational whale-watching cruises up to five times per day April–October. Cost is €30, €20 up to age 14, €10 under age 6. There are also longer courses and activities as well. Three-day advance reservation by phone is required and payment is in cash only.

Accommodations

For **under €50,** you have a few decent choices. **Hostal Facundo** (C/ Batalla del Salado 47, tel. 95/668-4298, www.hostalfacundo.com, €30) is more cheap than cheerful, but the gnome-lined flowered courtyard is a treat. If you are really on a budget, you can get a bunk in a three- or six-bed dorm for just €15. **Hostal Villanueva** (Av. Andalucía 11, tel. 95/668-4149, €45) is a friendly, cozy option on the

convertible outside of the country; most merchants are more than willing to accept your more valuable European bills and coins over the local currency.

Tangier has as much to offer its visitors as they have to offer this gleaming, whitewashed city. The official incorporation of Tangier into Morocco in 1956 devastated the economy of this once-prosperous port, but thanks to the burgeoning tourist industry, the city has since made its comeback. Browse the stalls of the pungent **Grand Socco** market or take a stroll along the palm-lined boulevards that stretch endlessly along 21 kilometers (13 miles) of sandy beach. Grab a coffee at one of the many cafés on the French-inspired Boulevard Pasteur or make your way through the old city, dominated by the **Kasbah** (citadel) with its **Dar al Makhsen** (Sultan's palace), now the home to an important Moroccan art museum. Visit the imposing 17th-century **Grand Mesquite** built by Moulay Ismail, the leader who pacified the warring tribes of Morocco and expelled the intrusive Europeans from the region, or ponder the simple beauty of the tiny sugar cube houses sprinkled across the hillside, which give Tangier its nickname of the "White City." Climb to the highest point in the medina (old Arab town) in the cool of the evening to watch a brilliant sunset over the Atlantic and perhaps catch a glimpse of Spain in the distance. All things old and new, great and small, make Tangier a city worth detouring to on any trip to the far south of Spain.

The easiest – and most economical – way to visit Tangier from Spain is to sign up for a one-day excursion with **FRS** (tel. 956/681-830, www.frs.es). For just €56, you get a round-trip ferry ticket from Tarifa to Tangier, a guided tour of the city by bus and on foot (offered in both English and Spanish), visits to several bazaars, and a three-course traditional Moroccan meal serenaded by live music. However, if you choose to go to the city on your own, the round-trip ticket alone will cost you a whopping €52. Never will you more feel that you have gotten your money's worth than when you visit Tangier with the organized group! Purchase your ticket online or visit one of their various offices scattered around the port of Tarifa. And don't forget your passport – after all, you are traveling to another world.

edge of the old town. The terrace overlooking the city is a nice touch. The street out front can get loud, so request a room in the back or bring earplugs. **Hostal Africa** (C/ María Antonia Toledo 12, tel. 95/668-0220, €45) is another sweet little place to sleep with cheery rooms, a rooftop garden, and lots of North African flavor. Cash only.

In the **€50-100** range your options broaden. The pleasant ◖ **La Estrella de Tarifa** (C/ San Rosendo 2, tel. 95/668-1985, www.laestrelladetarifa.com, €86) offers Moroccan furnishings and fresh flowers. Their comfortable rooms painted in a soothing palette of white and cobalt blue add to the charm. **La Casa Amarilla** (C/ Sancho IV El Bravo 9, tel. 95/668-1993, www.lacasaamarilla.net, €66), or "The Yellow House," is in a beautifully restored 19th-century building on the city's most bustling street. Its lovely apartment-style rooms have marble floors, tiled walls, and lots of evocative Moroccan touches. It also houses top-rated restaurant **Bodega Casa Amarilla.**

For **over €100,** try the sleek new **Hotel Misiana** (C/ Sancho IV El Bravo 18, tel. 95/662-7083, reservas@misiana.com, www.misiana.com, €120). The entire complex—hotel, restaurant, and lounge—is a hip explosion of color and style. Rooms come in crayon-bright hues and feature fun details like floral lampshades, cowhide chair coverings, and glass-bead curtains. The top-floor suite is a dream with a massive terrace, a whirlpool tub, and a private elevator. The bar also happens to be the hottest spot in town for a night out. For more subdued elegance, head to **La Sacristía** (C/ San Donato 8, tel. 95/668-1759, tarifa@lasacristia.net, www.lasacristia.net, €145). Set in an 18th-century typical whitewashed Andalusian house, it doesn't look like much from the outside. However, step inside and you enter a world of rustic sophistication and charm. The 10 rooms surround a Moorish brick-arched courtyard and are individually decorated with antiques, fine linens, and artwork. The courtyard hosts live music most nights.

Two of the best hotels in Tarifa actually lie along the coast just outside the city. If you are willing to travel a bit to get to the center of town, these hotels will provide you with a true beach escape. **100 Percent Fun Hotel** (Crta. N-340, km. 76, tel. 95/668-0330, www.100x100fun.com, €92) is situated right on the beach in the midst of lush tropical gardens. Don't be deceived by the cheesy name; this hotel is a hidden gem with flower-filled gardens, Polynesian decor, a Tex-Mex restaurant, a swimming pool, and even a kitesurfing school. **Hotel Hurricane** (Crta. N-340, km. 78, tel. 95/668-4919, www.hotelhurricane .com, €155), also right on the coast, has the feel of a deep South plantation complete with shady verandas. Rooms face either the beach or the mountains.

Food

For café fare just wander around the old town, there are hundreds of options. **La Tribu** (C/ Luz, s/n) is where the kitesurfers go for fresh-from-the-oven pizzas and fruity cocktails. **Café Central** (C/ Sancho IV El Bravo 10, tel. 95/668-0590) is easily the most popular place in town, with its big, open-all-day terrace right on the Tarifa's most bustling street. It stays packed with a lively crowd of locals and tourists. The folks get younger—and livelier—as the night wears on. The quirky **Café Azul** (C/ Batalla del Salado 2, 9 A.M.–midnight daily) offers crepes, fresh fruit, smoothies, and other breakfast-y type foods until 3 P.M. daily. They also have a nice mix of intriguing hot sandwiches. The greenhouse decor is relaxing even if the planters sprouting balding dolls makes you think too much. **Mezcla** (C/ San Francisco 12, tel. 95/662-7465, 10 A.M.–1 A.M. daily), which means "mix" is Spanish, is just what its name implies. Part tapas bar, part sports bar, part bar bar, this comfortable place offers it all—including Wi-Fi.

Locals swear that the best tapas in town are on Calle Guzmán El Bueno. **Los Mellis** (No. 16) is a rowdy place where the tapas are plentiful, traditional, and very in demand. **Pasillo** (No. 14) is equally popular.

Tarifa's local cuisine is based on seafood and North African spices. For the former, **Bodega La Olla** (C/ Alcalde Juan Nuñez 7, tel. 95/668-4085, www.bodegalaolla.com, €10) offers an ocean's worth of fresh seafood and paellas on a terrace overlooking the port and Africa. **Morilla** (C/ Sancho IV El Bravo 2, tel. 95/668-1757, 8:30 A.M.–11:30 P.M. daily, €12) offers similar fare, with a view over the see-and-be-seen main thoroughfare of Tarifa. For a Moroccan/Asian twist, **Souk** (C/ Mar Tirreno 46, tel. 95/662-7065, www.souk-tarifa.com, 8–11:30 P.M. Wed.–Mon., €12) is the place to go. Food is served all day in their tranquil dining room adorned with candles and scented with a hint of exotic spices. Visit their mini-market tea room adjoined to the restaurant to sample and purchase some of their infusions.

Information

Check with Tarifa's **tourist office** (Po. Alameda, tel. 956/680-993, www.tarifaweb .com, 9 A.M.–3 P.M. daily) for the latest info on events and attractions. There are also several good websites about the city: www.windtarifa .com, www.gotarifa.com, and www.tarifa.net should get you started.

Getting There and Around

Via public transportation, there is only one way into Tarifa—bus. You will have to change buses in a larger Andalusian town in order to get just about anywhere else. Tarifa's bus station, located across from the gas station at the northern end of Calle Batalla del Salado, is serviced by **Transportes Comes** (tel. 90/219-0208, www.tgcomes.es), which runs daily buses to the neighboring town of Algeciras and also to the larger cities of Cádiz, Sevilla, and

Málaga, from where connections can be made to the rest of Spain.

The nearest train station is in Algeciras, which is lies about 30 minutes northeast of Tarifa. The **Estación de Renfe** (C/ San Bernardo, s/n, tel. 95/663-0202, www.renfe.es) links Algeciras with other Andalusian cities and beyond.

From the port of Tarifa, **FRS** (Av. Andalucía, tel. 95/668-1830, www.frs.es) runs several fast ferries a day to Tangier, Morocco (35 minutes, €29 one-way). (See sidebar, *Tangier.*)

By car, Tarifa is located on the N-340/E-5, which connects it to the costal cities of Cádiz in the northeast and Málaga in the northwest.

Córdoba

Until you've spent some time in the city and have had the opportunity to wander its atmospheric streets, it's hard to believe that the sleepy provincial capital of Córdoba was once one of the most important Islamic cities in the world, second only to Baghdad. Originally founded by the Romans, Córdoba rose in power and prestige under its Moorish rulers. Within its bustling walls Muslims, Jews, and Christians lived peacefully together in pursuit of common goals of education and art. The city soon became one of ancient Europe's most important seats of learning, giving rise to philosophers, scientists, poets, and artists. The legacy of that shimmering time resonates in the winding lanes around Córdoba's Mezquita. But Córdoba is also a very Spanish, very Andalusian town, with a rich tradition of flamenco and bullfighting. The two heritages blend sensuously to create a magical place—though you'll have to look for it. Today's city, bounded by the muddy riverbanks and modern, blocky apartment buildings, doesn't look like much on first glance. Dig deeper and you'll find it—Arabic Córdoba, Roman Córdoba, Andalusian Córdoba—coexisting with a modern, bustling population that holds a deep respect for its past.

© SEVE PONCE DE LEON

The morning sun pours through the narrow streets of Córdoba.

HISTORY

Though ancient peoples had always valued the fertility of the Guadalquivir Valley, it wasn't developed as an urban center until the arrival of the Romans, who could navigate their boats up the river. They founded the city of Corduba in 152 B.C. at the highest navigable point on the river. It soon became one of the empire's most important shipping ports in Hispania, transporting not only olive oil, but also wine and wheat back to ancient Rome. The most notable legacy of their rule is the Puente Romano crossing the river.

Not long after invading the Iberian Peninsula in 711, the Moors, under Abd ar-Rahman the First, made Córdoba their first capital city.

ANDALUCÍA

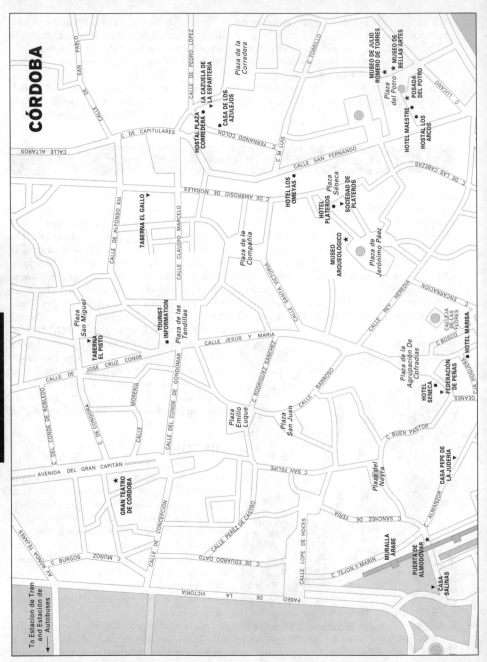

CÓRDOBA

ANDALUCÍA

To Estación de Tren
and Estación de
← Autobuses

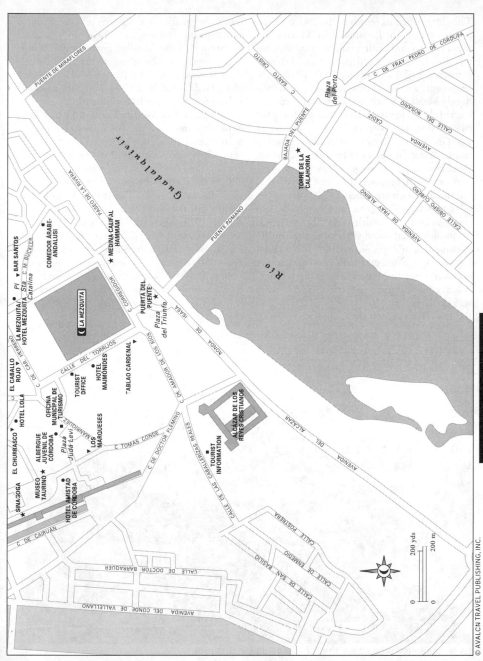

ANDALUCÍA

The city reached its zenith in the 10th century. It was not only the largest city in Western Europe, with roughly half a million residents, but was also the most sophisticated and learned. It attracted educated people from all over the continent, and its culture, though predominantly Muslim, welcomed Christian and Jewish thinkers. Jewish writer and philosopher Maimónides was born in Córdoba and wrote *The Guide of the Perplexed* in Arabic in part to reconcile the theologies of Judaism and Islam. Read it in full at www.sacred-texts.com.

As the seat of power of the Caliphate of Córdoba, which stretched as far west as Sevilla, north to Zaragoza, and east to Valencia, Córdoba was wealthy and vibrant. It was a Moorish wonderland with more than 1,000 mosques and 600 public baths. It had a thriving economy based on textiles and agriculture and was as bustling then as any modern capital is today. Some suggest that from 935 to 1013 it was the largest city in the world. However, in the mid-11th century, the Caliphate broke up into *taifas* (smaller, autonomous regions). Prone to infighting and warfare, the *taifas* brought instability to the Muslim government. The Christians took advantage of this to advance their Reconquest. King Fernando III's troops conquered Córdoba in 1236, and then used it as base for their attacks on Granada.

After the fall of Muslim Spain in 1492, Córdoba went into decline, and although a prosperous textile industry emerged in the 16th century, it never recovered its former glory. During the Napoleonic invasions of the early 1800s, the surrounding area saw some of the most dramatic battles. The region stayed dormant until the end of the Franco's dictatorship in 1975, when the Cordobeses (as locals are called) went left with a vengeance, electing one of the first communist city councils in Spain. Since then, Córdoba has employed the twin pillars of education and tourism to help its economy recover, marketing its history as the meeting point between the most prevalent cultures in the West.

La Mezquita looming above the Río Guadalquivir at sunset

SIGHTS
◖ La Mezquita

No matter where you go in the center of the city, the imposing bell tower and minaret of La Mezquita (C/ Cardenal Herrero 1, tel. 95/747-0512, 10 A.M.–5 P.M. Tues.–Sat. Jan. and Dec., 10 A.M.–5:30 P.M. Tues.–Sat. Feb. and Nov., 10 A.M.–6:30 P.M. Tues.–Sat. Mar. and July–Oct., 10 A.M.–7 P.M. Tues.–Sat. Apr.–June, 9:30 A.M.–2:30 P.M. Sun. and holidays year-round, €6.50) makes its presence felt. The third largest mosque in the world, the building is a layering of architectural styles, displaying the increasing grandeur of each successive leader, resulting in a striking, if jarring, end result.

The structure you see today was first built as a joint house of worship for the Visigoth Christian and Muslim communities. After the Muslim conquest of Spain in the early 8th century, Caliph Abd ar-Rahman I bought the church portion of the structure from the local Christian community, tore it down, and began working on the construction of the mosque in 785. It was completed 200 years later by the military leader Al-Mansur.

The mosque's formal entrance is the 14th century **Puerta del Perdón** (Door of Forgiveness), just right of the ticket office. The name refers to a medieval practice of forgiving debtors at this door on religious holidays. It opens into the **Patio de los Naranjos,** a broad garden studded with orange, palm, and olive trees. When the orange blossoms are in bloom, the fragrance is intoxicating. During the Moorish rule, this courtyard was used for ablutions, where worshippers would cleanse themselves in the fountains before entering the mosque. It was also the sight of intellectual lectures and teachings.

Entering the mosque is a breath-catching experience. A forest of jasper, onyx, marble, and granite columns seems to stretch out forever. Originally numbering 1,300, the 850 remaining columns have a double-arch design with red-and-white striped sandstone at the top. The open shape was meant to mimic the fronds of palm trees as well as to allow light to disperse more easily through the mosque.

The palm forest effect is greatly overwhelmed by the imposition of the main altar of the **Catedral,** which squats in the very center of the Mezquita. Though the Catedral, with its Gothic and baroque elements—is beautiful in its own way, the brusque imposition of one style onto another takes away from the artistry of the Christian temple. It's not unusual to see Mezquita visitors use the info pamphlets to block out the sight of one style in order to fully appreciate the other. The cathedral has an impressive red marble altar and two mahogany vestibules that feature life-sized marble replicas of a bull, a lion, and an eagle.

The cathedral is open to public worship and free to worshippers. In keeping with the incongruity of the building, locals often comment that they attend "mass at the mosque."

The east and west walls of the building contain several other minor chapels, but it's the south wall that draws the most attention. The *maksura,* the area where the caliph and his entourage once prayed, is decorated with an astounding collection of stucco carvings and a red, gold, blue, purple, and green mosaic incorporating quotes from the Koran. The focal point is the *mihrab.* A common feature in all mosques, the *mihrab* is the prayer niche. It always faces southeast in the direction of Mecca. Except here. Because the mosque was built on the grounds of the former Visigoth church and the surrounding sandy banks of the Guadalquivir were not stable, Córdoba's *mihrab* faces south. Elaborated in 822 to its current glory, the *mihrab* is a marvel of Islamic architecture. The shell-shaped ceiling is carved from a single block of marble designed to amplify sound throughout the entire Mezquita. However, entry is forbidden.

The **Torre de Alminar** is a Christian bell-tower built on top of the mosque's original minaret, which called the faithful to worship several times per day. You can ascend it for a bird's-eye view over old Córdoba. As you go up, notice the sealed-up arches and windows from the minaret.

If you are day-tripping into town solely to see La Mezquita, you can arrive at the Mezquita by

ANDALUCÍA

© SEVE PONCE DE LEON

a forest of Arabic arches in La Mezquita

taking public bus 3 from the bus/train station complex and exit at the riverside by the Hostal Maestre. The Mezquita is a few minutes walk from there. The bus costs €0.95 or you can take a cab for about €5.

Puente Romano

Just north of the Mezquita sits the **Calleja de las Flores,** probably the most photographed street in the entire city, especially when the geraniums are in bloom. However, there is more to see if you head south. Follow Calle Torrijos as you come out of the Mezquita to arrive at the **Puerta del Puente** (Bridge Gate), which takes you out onto the Puente Romano (Roman Bridge).

Until the end of the 16th century, it was possible to sail up the Guadalquivir River as far east as Córdoba, meaning that locally produced olive oil could be sold throughout the Roman empire. Looking downstream, you can see the old Islamic water wheel and millhouses. The city council is currently working with the engineering departments of several Spanish

universities to restore the mill complex to its former working state. The column that stands beside the Puerta del Puente, the **Triunfo de San Rafael,** bears a statue of San Rafael, patron saint of the city.

Alcázar de los Reyes Cristianos

The imposing hulk of the Alcazar de los Reyes Cristianos (Campo Santo de los Mártires, s/n, tel. 957/420-151, 10 a.m.–2 p.m. and 4:30–6:30 p.m. Tues.–Sat. Oct.–Apr., 10 a.m.–2 p.m. and 5:30–7:30 p.m. Tues.–Sat. May–June and Sept., 8:30 a.m.–2:30 p.m. Tues.–Sat. July–Aug., 9:30 a.m.–2:30 p.m. Sun. and holidays year-round, €2, free Fri.) stands guard over the river. Built in the 13th century as a palace for King Alfonso X the Wise, it's more infamously known as the headquarters of the Spanish Inquisition. Although it's nowhere near as spectacular as the Alcázar in Sevilla, it's still a noble structure in its own right, and the gardens provide a welcome respite from the heat of summer. The building houses the **Baños Califales,** an old royal bathhouse and several important mosaics, many of which were taken from Roman settlements in and around the city.

La Judería

Four sections of the **Muralla Árabe** (Moorish wall) remain, spread around Córdoba. The most-photographed section is the one that sits across from the Alcázar, running parallel to Calle Cairuán. At its end stands the **Puerta de Almodóvar**, the only remaining Moorish gate in the city. Next to it is a statue of Seneca, the Córdoba native who became a powerful philosopher in Rome. He was forced to commit suicide on the command of Emperor Nero. Pass through the gate to enter the Judería (Jewish quarter) of old Córdoba. Once upon a time, its narrow, winding streets of whitewashed houses were home to the city's prosperous Jewish community. Thanks to the religiously intolerant Catholic Monarchs, little remains today of their former glory. The one surviving **Sinagoga** (C/ Judíos 20, 10 A.M.–1:30 P.M. and 3:30–5:30 P.M. Tues.–Sat., 10 A.M.–1:30 P.M. Sun. and holidays, €0.30) offers a glimpse into Córdoba's rich Jewish heritage. Built in 1316, the interior of the synagogue is remarkably well conserved, especially the Mudejar stucco work lining the tops of the walls. Note the women's gallery at the top, which permitted females to worship without distracting the men at prayer.

The Judería no longer exclusively commemorates Jewish heritage. The **Museo Taurino** (Pl. Maimónides, s/n, tel. 95/720-1056, 10 A.M.–2 P.M. Tues.–Sat., 9:30 A.M.–3 P.M. Sun., €2.95), or Bullfighting Museum, celebrates local *toreros* (bullfighters). The museum houses the remains of Islero, the bull that killed the legendary bullfighter Manolete in 1947.

Plaza del Potro

Though most visitors to Córdoba focus on the area in and around the Judería and the Alcázar, wandering through the streets to the north and east reveals just as much of Córdoba's charm. Following the river upstream just past the Puente de Miraflores takes you to the Plaza del Potro, which gets its name from the small statue of a colt in the middle. To the left is the **Posada del Potro**, a 16th-century inn that has been converted into an exposition gallery. It's said that Miguel de Cervantes stayed here during his brief spell as a tax collector. The city council's arts office is located here, making it a good place to find information about theatre, music, and flamenco performances.

Across the square from the Posada, the **Museo de Julio Romero de Torres** (Pl. Potro 1, tel. 95/749-1909, 8:30 A.M.–2:30 P.M. Tues.–Sat., 9:30 A.M.–2:30 P.M. Sun., €4) profiles the life and work of one of Córdoba's most famous sons. Depending how you feel about black velvet paintings, Romero de Torres's artwork, which abound with guitars and women in various states of nudity, are either a profound exploration of Andalusian culture or a sexist embarrassment. Be warned that locals don't put up with criticism of their most famous painter.

The building also houses the **Museo de Bellas Artes** (tel. 95/747-3345, 2:30–8:30 P.M. Tues., 9:30 A.M.–8:30 P.M. Wed.–Sat., €1.50). The museum is home to the works of various prominent Spanish painters and focuses on artists from the Córdoba area.

Museo Arqueológico

Close to Plaza del Potro is the Museo Arqueológico (Pl. Jerónimo Paéz 7, tel. 95/747-4011, 3–8 P.M. Tues., 9 A.M.–8 P.M. Wed.–Sat., 9 A.M.–3 P.M. Sun., €1.50), housed in a Renaissance mansion that turned up some unexpected surprises when it was being renovated years ago. Workers discovered a Roman patio in the basement as they were renovating the floor. Archaeologists from the Junta de Andalucía were called in, the basement was excavated, and the building eventually became the home of a remarkable collection of artifacts from around the region, including some priceless pieces from the nearby site of Medina Azahara.

Plaza de la Corredera

Reminiscent of the Plaza Mayors of cities like Madrid and Salamanca, Plaza de la Corredera looks like it belongs in Castille rather than in

Andalucía. The area surrounding the plaza is undergoing something of a rebirth, with trendy cafés and upscale restaurants taking over the storefronts. Given that it is so far away from the main tourist beat, it has been a haunt for local vagabonds. However, the city council has made an effort to clean the place up, and the streets leading to the plaza offer some of the prettiest displays during the annual Cruces festival.

Plaza de la Corredera sits on the site of the former Roman amphitheatre, whose pillars are not to be confused with those in the plaza on Calle Marín, which originally belonged to the **Templo Romano.** As is the case with a lot of areas around the city, Roman ruins have the habit of popping up in sometimes inconvenient places. By law, the Junta de Andalucía has the right to protect any property which is considered archaeologically important, meaning that no matter where you go, the past is always lurking nearby to surprise you.

ENTERTAINMENT AND EVENTS
Flamenco

Córdoba is a hotbed of **flamenco** and has produced many outstanding guitarists, dancers, and singers. Still, seeing good flamenco here often requires a bit of work. The tourist office usually directs most tourists to the **Tablao Cardenal** (C/ Torrijos 10, tel. 95/748-3320, closed Sun. P.M., €18), a fairly standard show with decent performers. It will definitely please the casual observer. If you want something more authentic and don't mind schlepping out to the suburbs, the arts office located in the Posada del Potro can put you in touch with the different *peñas* (flamenco societies). *Peñas* generally operate out of very small premises and are obliged to admit members before strangers. That said, they generally welcome anyone who's got a genuine interest in the art. Big-name flamenco artists (and touring theatre groups, performing in Spanish and sometimes English) perform at the **Gran Teatro de Córdoba** (Av. Gran Capitán 3, tel. 95/748-0237, www.teatrocordoba.com).

Festivals and Events

If you've never experienced an Andalusian festival such as **Semana Santa** (Holy Week), Córdoba provides a good alternative to the larger cities. Events are open to visitors, and though the city gets its fair share of tourists, it doesn't get overwhelmingly crowded the way Granada and Sevilla do. Be sure not to miss the procession of processions on Good Friday, when six of the 12 *cofradías* (Catholic brotherhoods) in the city pass along the main route through Plaza de las Tendillas. (See sidebar, *All About Semana Santa.*)

The first weekends of May are devoted to the celebration of **Cruces de Mayo,** when huge crosses constructed of wire and red carnations and decorated with embroidered shawls are paraded through the city. Following Cruces is the **Concurso y Festival de Patios Cordobeses** (the patio competition), during which owners and residents of traditional homes with Andalusian patios pull out all the stops and decorate almost every surface with geraniums galore and any other kind of plant life that will fit. There's no charge to visit the patios, and during slow times, owners may even offer a drink and a chat, but jars are often set out for donations to offset the costs of the decorations.

Córdoba's **Feria de Mayo** is one of the best places to experience a down-home Andalusian fair. Held in the fairgrounds on the east side of town, the spectacle has to be seen to be believed. The estimated 250,000 light bulbs used to illuminate the replica of the Mezquita throw so much heat that ladies in flamenco dresses will often stand under the structure to warm up. Drinks don't cost much more than €3 in most places, and if you get fed up with the endless stream of *sevillanas* (a popular strand of flamenco), head to the *casetas* (booths) of the main political parties, which usually have pop, rock, or folk concerts. Leave your vehicle at the hotel and take advantage of the free shuttle bus service leaving from the center of town.

Next up, June and July bring the **Festival Internacional de la Guitarra** (tel. 95/748-0237, www.guitarracordoba.com). The guitar festival brings hundreds of students from all over the world—including British Prime Minister Tony Blair—to study with the best. Additionally, various music venues around town hold concerts by internationally renowned guitarists like Pat Metheny and B. B. King.

SPORTS AND RECREATION
Arabic Baths
Slip into one of Córdoba's oldest forms of relaxation at the **Medina Califal Hammam** (C/ Corregidor Luis de la Cerda 51, tel. 95/748-4746, www.hammamspain.com, 10 A.M.–midnight daily, €20). In this spectacularly designed Arabic bathhouse, guests can move from hot to warm to cool pools. The main pool is situated in a room that is a near mirror reflection of the red-and-white arched room of the Mezquita. For €7, add a massage and aromatherapy to your visit (though the massage tends to be tepid, taking away from the whole experience). There is also an Arabic tearoom on the premises.

Bullfighting
Córdoba's bullfighting season takes place mostly in the spring months, when heat is less of a problem, and peaks during the Feria in May. Tickets are difficult—but not impossible—to come by. The bullring is located in the western suburb of Ciudad Jardín (Av. Gran Vía del Parquetel, tel. 95/723-2507), near the train and bus stations. The local tourist office can also provide information on guided tours (Spanish only) of the bullring.

ACCOMMODATIONS
Since most visitors to Córdoba often just stop by on their way to another Andalusian city, there's usually no need to book in advance. However, as with most rules, there are a few exceptions: the youth hostel, which ranks as the best in Spain, and during the spring and summer festivals.

Under €50
The **Albergue Juvenil de Córdoba** (Pl. Judá Levi 1, tel. 95/729-0166, www.inturjoven.com, €14.50 for a dorm bed) is a youth hostel with upscale hotel allusions. In addition to being centrally located, this modern, bright facility boasts air-conditioned double, triple, and dorm rooms, Internet access, parking, a swimming pool, and a small restaurant. Prices go up to €19 if you are over 26.

The immensely popular **Hotel Seneca** (C/ Conde y Luque 7, tel. 95/747-3234, €40) has a dozen cozy rooms located around a flower-filled patio. Breakfast is included. If you're traveling solo, **Hostal Los Arcos** (C/ Romero Barros 7, tel. 95/748-5643, €35) and **Hostal Plaza Corredera** (C/ Rodríguez Marín, 15, tel. 95/748-4570, €38) offer clean, affordable accommodations that are central to all the major city sights, as well as the bus and train stations.

€50-100
◖ **Hotel Mezquita** (Pl. Santa Catalina 1, tel. 95/747-5585, €69) is a lovely family-run hotel in a pair of converted 16th-century houses. Its atmospheric tiled courtyard and column-filled public spaces are crammed with local art and antiques. Rooms are comfortable, with a refined Victorian feel, and those with a view over the Mezquita are hot property—book early. For a real treat, upgrade to the Capilla suite, located in the old chapel of the house. The bed sits beneath the angel-festooned former altar. Kitty-corner is the **Hotel Marisa** (C/ Cardinal Herrero 6, tel. 95/747-3142, www.hotel marisacordoba.com, €70). While it lacks Hotel Mezquita's charm, it does offer clean, modern rooms, a few with spectacular views over the Patio de los Naranjos. **Hotel Los Omeyas** (C/ San Fernando 24, tel. 957/472-716, www.hotel losomeyas.com, €53) is nestled right in the heart of the Judería and features a lovely colonnaded courtyard that allows light to flood into the building. Rooms are simple but comfortable with dramatic carved headboards and if you snag one on the top floor you'll have a view of the tower of the Mezquita. Opt for the €3.50 breakfast in the courtyard. **Hotel Maestre** (C/ Romero Barros 4, tel. 957 472 410, www.hotel maestre.com, €65), near the Plaza del Potro, is another Andalusian charmer with an arcaded

inner courtyard boasting a magnificent tiled fountain, gleaming marble floors throughout, and classically styled rooms. For about €15 less you can stay in their *hostal,* which offers simpler rooms; for the same amount more, you can choose an apartment with a kitchen, sitting room, and terrace. **Casa de los Azulejos** (C/ Fernando Colón 5, tel. 95/470-0000, info@ casadelosazulejos.com, www.casadelosazulejos .com, €90) means "house of tiles," and that is just what you will find in this charming 17th-century Cordovan house. The courtyard is a joyous riot of color and plants and houses a Mexican cantina. Most of the rooms open up onto it. There is also an attached restaurant that offers a fusion of Andalusian and Latin American fare. **Hotel Plateros** (Pl. Séneca 4, tel. www.hotelplateros.com, €60) is not far from the Museo Arqueológico on a lovely little square. While not as lovely as some of the other hotels in this category, it offers clean grandmotherly rooms, a central courtyard, and even an atmospheric old bodega in the cellar. The attached tapas bar is excellent.

Over €100

Maimónides (C/ Torrijos 4, tel. 95/748-3803, info@hotelmaimonides.com, www.hotelmaimonides.com, €105) will make you feel like you are staying in La Mezquita from its mouth-dropping carved wood ceiling in the lobby to its red-and-white arches throughout. The lovely inner patio is laid with wrought-iron tables perfect for having a tea or filling out postcards. Request a room with a view over La Mezquita. **Hotel Amistad de Córdoba** (Pl. Maimónides 3, tel. 95/742-0335, nhamistad cordoba@nh-hotels.com, www.nh-hotels.com, €140), located in two 18th-century mansions that back onto the Moorish wall near the Puerta de Almodóvar. The mansions are connected by a fine Mudejar courtyard and the Moorish theme is carried throughout the hotel. A more modern extension offers sleeker rooms in deep blue and blonde wood. Run by the apt NH chain, the amenities are up-to-date—excellent baths with good water pressure, comfortable mattresses, Wi-Fi. The hotel can be

hard to find, so work out a map before going. **Hotel Lola** (C/ Romero 3, tel. 95/720-0305, hotel@hotelconencantolola.com, www.hotel conencantolola.com, €140) is a fancy little hotel run by the affable Lola. Public areas and rooms are done up in the style of an old-moneyed Andalusian home—antiques, floral fabrics, heavy drapes, classic wall hangings and art, and lots of Spanish knickknacks. Though it is just moments from La Mezquita, it is located on a quiet street and boasts a rooftop terrace with views of the Mezquita's tower.

The **Parador de Córdoba** (Av. Arruzafa, tel. 95/727-5900, cordoba@parador.es, www .parador.es, €135), about five kilometers (three miles) north of town, is perfect for those who are driving (though a taxi will run you less than €10). Unlike most paradors, which are housed in historic monuments, Córdoba's parador is a large modern hotel surrounded by tranquil, leafy gardens and a fantastic swimming pool. It also boasts spacious, sunny rooms. However, the balconied rooms looking out over the city are the real treat. Be sure to request one. Another option if you want convenience and amenities over rambling charm is the **Hesperia Córdoba** (Av. de la Constitución, s/n, tel. 957/421-042, www.hesperia-cordoba.com, €110), located on the south bank of the Guadalquivir. It is a member of Spain's fastest-growing upscale hotel chain. Rooms are clean, modern, and new yet have charming Andalusian touches. Bathrooms are spacious and stocked with goodies. Service is professional and apt, and the amenities include on-site parking, a pool in a lovely tiled Andalusian courtyard, Internet access, a decent restaurant serving local fare, and a bar with a view over the city. Definitely request a room overlooking the city view. Old Córdoba lit up at night is simply magical.

FOOD

Córdoba's native cuisine draws heavily on its Roman and Muslim roots, utilizing lots of olive oil, dried fruits and nuts, Moroccan spices, and fresh produce. Of course, as in the rest of Andalucía, fresh seafood and hearty meats are an addiction here. Local dishes to try are *salmorejo* (a thick savory type of gazpacho), *boquerones en vinagre* (fresh anchovies marinated in vinegar and garlic), and the hearty *rabo de toro* (bull's tail stew). For dessert, have the *pastel cordobés,* a puff pastry round stuffed with "angel's hair," a sticky sweet confection made from pumpkin. The cake is topped with almonds, powdered sugar, and cinnamon.

Tapas

Welcome to tapas heaven. Cordobeses take their tapas-crawling very seriously—it would take you a month to eat your way through all of the tapas bars in town! To give it a go, check with the tourist office; they distribute several publications detailing different tapas routes. Locals wash snacks down with *montilla,* a type of sherry endemic to this region. Tapas bars in Córdoba tend to open early and stay open through lunch (about 10 A.M.–4 P.M.) and then open again around 7 P.M. until the last customer leaves, about 11 P.M. Many tapas bars also close on Sunday and Monday evenings. The best-loved clutch of tapas bars is the **Sociedad de Plateros** (Pl. Séneca 4, tel. 95/749-6785), which was established as a charitable society for silversmiths in 1868. The chain publishes a map of all nine Plateros establishments in the city and they are famed for their wonderful anchovies—either stuffed in artichokes or deep-fried. The **Taberna El Pisto** (Pl. San Miguel 1, tel. 95/747-8328), an atmospheric old tavern with ham legs hanging above, old black-and-white photos of Córdoba on the wall, and a creaky checkerboard floor underfoot, is famed for its *montilla* sherry. Pair it with a plate of *jamón jabugo.* **Taberna El Gallo** (C/ María Cristina 6, tel. 95/747-1780) has over a century's worth of charm to attract diners, as well as its own house-brewed *montilla,* said to be among the finest produced in the region. It offers a wealth of classic tapas. **Casa Salinas** (Puerta de Almodóvar, s/n, tel. 95/729-0846) has an unmatched flamenco atmosphere, as well as a great selection of wines and homey tapas. **Bar Santos** (C/ Magistral González Francés 3) is a beloved Spanish-style dive. Under fluorescent lights, walls

with faded bullfighting posters, and flamenco on the stereo, this standing room only joint serves simple tapas that start at just €3 each. **La Cazuela de la Espartería** (C/ Rodríguez Marín 16, tel. 95/748-8952) is a typical old-style Cordovan house with a tapas menu that marries tradition with innovation. Try their smoked salmon. **Bodegas Guzmán** (C/ Judíos 7, tel. 957/290-960) is the place where *aficionados* (serious bullfighting fans) go to drink *montilla* and shoot bull.

Local Cuisine

If you like your meal with pomp and circumstance, head to **El Caballo Rojo** (C/ Cardenal Herrero 28, tel. 95/747-5375, www.elcaballo rojo.com, 1–4:30 P.M. and 8–11:30 P.M. daily, €42). It has been the top choice for Córdoba's high-flyers since it opened. Amid a typically lush Andalusian setting—tiles, plants, stained glass, marble, high-arched ceilings—the highly rated kitchen turns out sophisticated dishes that blend Spanish, Arabic, and Jewish cuisine. Try *cordero al miel* (lamb in honey) or *rape mozarabe* (monkfish with Moroccan spices). If your budget doesn't stretch to a full meal, there's a tapas bar at the front. **El Churrasco** (C/ Romero 16, tel. 95/729-0819, 1–4 P.M. and 8 P.M.–midnight daily, closed Aug., €36) is the place to go for a dose of protein. It is also more favored by locals than Caballo Rojo. The house specialty is *churrasco,* a massive grilled pork chop served with spicy sauces that will have you licking your fingers. However, the kitchen also excels with its fresh seafood and vegetable dishes. Another top-rated local favorite is **Bodegas Campos** (C/ Los Lineros, 32, tel. 95/749-7500, www.bodegascampos .com, 1–4 P.M. and 8:30 –11:30 P.M. Mon.–Sat., 1–4 P.M. Sun., €40). Located in a clutch of old houses including an ancient bodega, the dining rooms are an Andalusian refuge of elegance and sophistication. The menu takes Andalusian standards and raises them to its sublime heights. Highly recommended are the *ajoblanco* (a cold soup of almonds and grapes), *trigueros con langostinos* (young asparagus and shrimp), and *solomillo con crema de coliflor* (filet steak with a cauliflower sauce). It has an extensive, well-priced wine list.

◖ **Casa Pepe de la Judería** (C/ Romero 1, tel. 95/720-0744, 1–4 P.M. and 8:30 P.M.– midnight daily, €35) located in a typical Cordovan house offers traditional Sephardic (Spanish-Jewish) recipes with modern touches. Try the *berenjena con miel* (eggplant with honey). The restaurant has a separate bar for tapas that is very popular with locals. **Los Marqueses** (C/ Tomás Conde 8, tel. 95/720-2094, 1–4 P.M. and 8:30–11:30 P.M. Mon.–Sat., 1–4 P.M. Sun., closed Sun. in summer, €26) is located in a lovingly restored 18th-century palace in the Judería. The menu is a nice balance of classic Andalucía and creative touches. Try the praline foam for dessert. **Federación de Peñas** (C/ Conde y Luque 8, tel. 95/747-5427, 12:30–4 P.M. and 8:30–11 P.M. Thurs.–Tues., closed Wed., €15) is housed in a typical blue-tiled courtyard and features classic Cordovan specialties at surprisingly reasonable prices.

INFORMATION

Both the regional Andalusian **Oficina de Turismo** (C/ Torrijos 10, tel. 95/747-8956, 9:30A.M.–6:30 P.M. Mon.–Fri., 10 A.M.–2 P.M. and 4–6 P.M. Sat., 10 A.M.–2 P.M. Sun.) and the **Oficina Municipal de Turismo** (tel. 90/220-1774) offer up-to-date information on Córdoba city and province. The municipal office has three public access points: in front of the Alcázar (C/ Campos Santo de los Mártires, s/n, 9:30 A.M.–7 P.M. daily); in the Plaza de las Tendillas (10 A.M.–2 P.M. and 4:30–7:30 P.M. daily); and in the train station (9:30 A.M.– 2 P.M. and 4:30–7:30 P.M. daily). Additionally, tourist information can be found on the departure platform of the train station.

The local tourist office runs the excellent www.turismodecordoba.org, while Andalucía offers Córdoba information at www.andalucia .org and www.andalucia.com.

GETTING THERE AND AROUND
Train

Córdoba's central location in Andalucía makes it an easy city to get in and out of. All trains operate out of the **Estación de Tren** (Av. América, tel. 95/740-0202) and are run by **Renfe** (tel. 90/224-0202, www.renfe.es). Córdoba is part of the AVE high-speed trains, which run to Sevilla in 40 minutes (over 20 daily, €21.90) and Madrid in 1 hour and 40 minutes (over 20 daily, €52.50). Take note, the Alta Velocidad train from Córdoba to Sevilla takes only 10 minutes more than the AVE and costs only €13.

Bus

As in the rest of Andalucía, buses are the most economical way to get around. Córdoba's **Estación de Autobuses** (Pl. Tres Culturas, tel. 95/740-4040) is home to **Alsina Graells** (tel. 957/278-100, www.alsinagraells.es), which runs most intercity bus services throughout western Andalucía, including services to Granada (six daily, €11.40), Málaga (five daily, €11.60) and Seville (six daily, €9.50). **Socibus** (www .socibus.es) also operates out of the same station and runs buses to Madrid (six daily, €13.50).

Car

Córdoba sits on the national highway A-4, which goes through Sevilla and Jerez de la Frontera and terminates in Madrid. Via this road you can get anywhere in Spain from Córdoba. The A-45 connects it to Málaga. The A-92 leads east through Almería into Levante.

VICINITY OF CÓRDOBA
Medina Al-Zahra

Located just eight kilometers (five miles) west of Córdoba on the A-431 highway, the archaeological ruins of Medina Al-Zahra (tel. 95/732-9130, 10:30 A.M.–8:30 P.M. Tues.–Sat., 10 A.M.–2 P.M. Sun. May–mid-Sept., 10 A.M.– 2 P.M. Tues.–Sun. mid-Sept.–Apr.) are a worthwhile excursion from the city. Conceived and executed by Caliph Abd ar-Rahman, who reportedly spent a third of the annual state budget on its construction between 936 and 961, the sumptuous palace-city flourished for nearly a century. In 1010, Islamic purists from North Africa destroyed the city. They believed that it represented a much too liberal interpretation of the Koran. It was not heard of again until 1911 when Spanish archaeologists uncovered it. They have working on it ever since, but due to its enormous size and complex structure, they refuse to offer a timeline for its completion and only 10 percent of the area has been uncovered since work began. Bit by laborious bit, they're trying to re-construct the city, a task not made any easier by centuries of looting.

Upon entering the complex, you walk through the reconstructed **Dar al-Wuzara** (House of the Viziers), where most of the day-to-day governing of the city would have taken place. From there, the route turns eastward to a gallery of red-and-white arches, much like the ones in Córdoba's Mezquita, and then turn southwards to pass by Medina Azahara's *mezquita* (mosque) and head towards the **Salón de Abd ar-Rahman.** It wasn't until 1944 that archaeologists uncovered the building materials—including stucco carvings and fabulous tile work—which, interestingly enough, show signs of representations of animal and human life, a distinct no-no in Islamic art.

By car, take the A-431 towards Almodóvar del Río and watch for signs for the turnoff to the right. **Córdoba Vision** (tel. 957/760-241; www.cordobavision.com) organizes day trips to the site leaving from the center of town. The **tourism office** also runs a bus for €5 with an erratic schedule. See their website or visit their offices for details. As a last resort, a taxi will take you there and back and give you an hour to see the ruins for less than €30. Córdoba's tourist offices have information on this option.

Sierra Subbética

An hour south of Córdoba lies the Sierra Subbética mountain range (www.subbetica.org). Although it's not one of the biggest or highest in Andalucía, it is definitely one of the prettiest for walking and biking. The area's greatest attraction, aside from scenic walking country, is the **Cueva de los Murciélagos** (Cave of the Bats). After a brisk uphill walk from the town of Zuheros, local guides conduct hourly tours of the stalactite- and stalagmite-filled cave. Be sure to bring a sweater as even in summer it doesn't get above 13°C (55°F).

Running along the northern side of the Subbética is the **Vía Verde de la Subbética,** a rail trail that stretches for 113 kilometers (70 miles) between the towns of Jaén and Lucena. Formerly used to transport olive oil to market, the tracks were ripped up and resurfaced in the late 1990s and are now designed to be accessible to all, including wheelchair users. The town of Cabra has an interesting museum dedicated to telling the story of the local olive oil industry.

Subbética towns are connected by four buses a day (two on Sat. and Sun.) run by **Carrera** (tel. 95/740-4414) bus line, which leaves from Córdoba's bus station. By far the best hotel in the region is the **Hotel Zuhayra** (C/ Mirador 10, tel. 97/769-4693, www.zercahoteles.com, €70) in Zuheros. The friendly owners know the area well and can recommend routes for hiking and mountain biking.

Écija

Situated halfway between Seville and Córdoba, Écija is known as the "City of the Towers" for the 11 ceramic-laden steeples that dot the town. After the earthquake of 1755 that devastated Lisbon and much of southwestern Andalucía, the local nobles stepped in and helped fund the reconstruction of the entire town. The result: a small provincial city with an astonishing array of Renaissance architecture, most of which has been immune to reconstruction. It's a good thing, too, as often when homeowners pull up a floorboard or go digging around in the basement they come across Roman or Visigothic ruins. That was just the case with the **Plaza Mayor.** No sooner had construction workers begun tearing up the pavement did they hit the remains of a Moorish cemetery and had to call in the archaeologists. Excavating the cemetery revealed a series of Roman homes that were filled with artifacts—the remains of the Roman city of Astigi, one of the most important for olive oil and minerals trading in the western part of the empire.

Most of these historic remains can now be

© PATRICIA DAWN SEVERENUK

a Roman mosaic in Museo Histórico Municipal de Écija

ANDALUCÍA

found in the **Museo Histórico Municipal de Écija** (C/ Canovas del Castillo 4, tel. 95/590-2919, museo@ecija.org, www.museo.ecija.org, 10 A.M.–1:30 P.M. and 4:30–6:30 P.M. Tues.–Fri., 10 A.M.–2 P.M. and 5:30–8 P.M. Sat., 10 A.M.–3 P.M. Sun.) located in the Palacio de Benamejí. The inner walls of the former palace are lined with huge recovered Roman mosaics. Displays outline the evolution of human settlement in the area and contain comprehensive explanations (Spanish only) of why the area has been so important to so many civilizations. Chief among the holdings is the "Amazona Herida" (Hurt Amazon), one of the few examples of painted Roman sculpture ever found. The artifacts in the museum represent a small fraction of the treasures that have recently been uncovered; visits to the warehouse can be arranged by calling in advance.

Écija is currently working to organize the schedule of visits to its most important churches and their towers; until then, the best way to experience them is during a twilight stroll through town. Check with the tourist office in the **Ayuntamiento** (Pl. España, tel. 95/590-2933, 9:30 A.M.–3:30 P.M. and 4–7 P.M. Mon.–Fri., 9:30 A.M.–3:30 P.M. Sat. and Sun.).

The churches that are regularly open to the public include **Iglesia Mayor de Santa Cruz,** four blocks north of Plaza de España, which still retains some of its Moorish and Visigothic arches, and **Iglesia de Santa María,** just off the same plaza. Unfortunately, you can't visit the **Palacio de Peñaflor** (C/ Caballeros 26) anymore, as it has been bought by a hotel chain. It will re-open in early 2008 as a luxury property that aims to re-create 17th-century life.

Accommodation options in Écija are getting better and more diverse. Top of the lot is the **(Palacio de los Granados** (C/ Emilio Castelar 42, tel. 95/590-5344, info@palaciogranados.com, www.palaciogranados.com, €135), a dreamy Moorish palace full of blue-tiled courtyards, reflecting pools, chandeliers, and ornate wrought-iron detailing. It is run by a charming, English-speaking Puerto Rican couple. **Hotel Platería** (C/ Garcilópez 1, tel. 95/590-2754, hotelplateria@retemail.es, www.hotelplateria .net, €56) is a nearby, economical alternative that features its own restaurant.

Tapas bars abound in the streets in and around Plaza de España. **Bisturí** (Pl. España), which translates as "scalpel," has a good assortment of tapas as well as the added attrac-tion of being open later than other places, until 11 P.M. most nights.

Both the **Linesur** (www.linesur.com) and **Alsina Graells** (www.alsinagraells) bus companies run regular services to and from Seville (leaving from the Prado de San Sebastián bus station, 1.5 hours) and Córdoba (1 hour). The closest train station is at Palma del Río, 24 kilometers (15 miles) north of Écija.

Málaga

Boasting Andalucía's biggest airport, Málaga gets a lot of traffic from tourists going elsewhere. Those who decide to stop are nearly dissuaded by the almost intentionally ugly ring of 1970s high-rises that surround the city. Like a shy *señorita*, Málaga hides her beauty behind a shawl of concrete. Get past it and you'll find a charming central district dotted with palm trees, blue-and-white An-

dalusian tiles, and colorful old buildings all against the backdrop of the sun dappled deep blue sea. The sun shines over 300 days of the year and, except for the sticky mire of August, the temperature is vacation-resort perfect all year long. Málaga offers something that is often missing from the sun-and-sand resorts that line the coast—Spaniards. This is a uniquely Spanish town and the Malagueños (as locals are called) are proud of it. You'll run into more of them during a Sunday afternoon tapas-crawl than in a week anywhere else on the Costa del Sol. Over Easter, they throw one of Andalucía's largest Semana Santa (native son Antonio Banderas brings wife Melanie Griffith and their family to participate each year) and have made a cultural phenomena out of the *chiringuito* (beachside bar). These little shacks line the beaches serving local wine and smoked sardines called *espeto* (see sidebar, *Fish Sticks*). The town also offers a few sights worth seeing, including the museum and birthplace of another famous native—Pablo Picasso.

Initially settled by the Phoenicians, who named it Malaka, the city came under Roman control in the 3rd century B.C. When the Moors conquered Spain in the 8th century, they turned the city into a vibrant trading port. In 1487, the Catholic monarchs took control of Málaga near the end of their advance through Andalucía. Each of these civilizations has left its mark on the city, as can be seen by the diversity of the architecture and monuments.

© SEVE PONCE DE LEON

only some of the beautiful arches that dot Málaga's Alcazaba

SIGHTS

The heart of Málaga is its historic downtown. It is bordered on the west by the Río Guadalmedina, beyond which lay commercial and residential areas. To the east is Mount Gibralfaro and to the south, running along the coast, are Málaga's seaport and beaches. Most of the monuments are condensed in the eastern part of the historic center and are within walking distance. Just keep in mind, as in the rest of Andalucía's big cities, petty crime is all too frequent. Look out for boys trying to induce you into shoe shines, old women pushing sprigs of rosemary, or anyone getting too close for no reason. Practice common-sense safety measures, and you'll find Málaga a safe, comfortable town, where in just a few days you could easily feel at home.

Centro Histórico

Bisected by the elegant pedestrian boulevard **Calle Marqués de Larios,** crammed with shops, boutiques, and cafés, the Centro Histórico unfurls in a mosaic of tiny streets perfect for happy wandering. They entice with a ramble shackle grace—the alleyways are a bit uneven, the carefully lettered signs over shops pleasingly yellowed. Some buildings boast simple Moorish arches, others elaborate Renaissance facades. Some of the quietest streets come boisterously to life after dark. Others fall into a deep slumber soon after midnight. Seek out **Pasaje Chinitas,** near Plaza de la Constitución, which hides several hole-in-the-wall bars lined with old wine barrels and legs of cured ham where locals young and old sip the local Málaga wines and while hours away. In the warren of streets leading to **Calle Nueva,** another main road, though decidedly downscale from than Marqués de Larios, you'll find more old shops, more time-tattered bars, and the local melting pot at its most cultural—old men in berets, African immigrants, gypsy guitarists, map-toting tourist, and giggling young locals.

Sitting on the eastern edge of the barrio under the rising hulk of Mount Gibralfaro is **La Catedral de la Encarnación** (C/ Molina

Málaga's Calle Marqués de Larios makes for a pleasant stroll day or night.

Lario 9, 10 A.M.–5 P.M. Mon.–Sat., Sun. for worshippers only, €3.50), Málaga's main cathedral. It was begun in the 16th century on the site of a former Muslim mosque. Over two centuries it was built in fits and starts and eventually money gave out leaving the church with only one of its two planned towers. Malgueños promptly nicknamed the building La Manquita, (the "one-armed woman"). A persistent rumor purports that the money was re-routed to help the United States fight its War of Independence against the British. Across the street from the cathedral stands **Palacio Episcopal** (Pl. Obispo, s/n). Composed of two buildings—a stunning 16th-century civil building with an impressive facade, and a bishop's residence from the 18th century—this complex now houses a lovely interior patio and serves as a venue for exhibitions.

South of the cathedral, the lovely **Paseo del Parque** stretches east along the port. This lovely promenade runs through a lush slice of land thick with palm and other tropical trees and peppered with benches and statues. At Christmastime, the city dresses it up in lights that could rival Rockefeller Center. Running from the paseo's west end, **Alameda Principal,** another pleasant tree-lined boulevard, stretches to the river. To the south, the **Centro de Arte Contemporáneo** (C/ Alemania, s/n, tel. 95/212-0055, www.cacmalaga .org, 10 A.M.–8 P.M. Tues.–Sun., closed Mon., free) is a vast, gleaming hangar-sized building dedicated to hosting the most cutting-edge mixed-media artwork of our times. It is a good place to take the pulse of modern Spanish art, though the exhibitions are not limited by national boundaries.

Picasso's Málaga

Between the historical center and Mount Gibralfaro, you'll find a pair of Picasso monuments that are essential touring for anyone interested in modern art, specifically the mark this 20th-century genius left. **Museo Picasso** (C/ San Augustín 8, tel. 90/244-3377, www .museopicassomalaga.org, 10 A.M.–8 P.M. Tues.–Sun., closed Mon., €6) houses 200-plus works that cover every stage of Picasso's career.

Consisting mainly of pieces from Picasso's private collection, the collection is refreshingly intimate. They were donated by Christine and Bernard Ruiz–Picasso, the artist's daughter-in-law and grandson, who wanted to be sure that Málaga had a world-class venue for its most famous son. Inaugurated in 2003 in the 16th-century Palacio Buenavista, the museum offers an archaeological bonus. In the process of refurbishing the palace, 2,000 years' worth of ruins were uncovered. The museum has incorporated the archaeological site and here you can view the remains of the Phoenician, Roman, Moorish, and Christian empires that once inhabited Málaga.

A few blocks away, the delightful Plaza de la Merced is home to the **Fundación Pablo Ruiz-Picasso: Museo Casa Natal** (C/ Plaza de la Merced 15, tel. 95/206-0215, www.fundacion picasso.es, 10 A.M.–8 P.M. Tues.–Thurs., 10 A.M.–9 P.M. Fri.–Sat., 10 A.M.–8 P.M. Sun., closed Mon., free). It is the house where Picasso was born and spent his early years before moving to Barcelona. It houses a collection of his early sketches as well as personal items such as his christening robe. The museum also exhibits works by nearly 200 other artists.

Mount Gibralfaro

Rising from the web of Málaga's old city center, Mount Gibralfaro offers not only the best views of the city and its enviable position on the Mediterranean but also a trio of important monuments. At its base is the **Teatro Romano** (C/ Alacazabilla, s/n, tel. 68/613-0978, closed Mon. and Tues., free). The remains of this original theater, dating from the 1st century A.D., were discovered in the 1950s. By day, explore and sit where the Romans once did. By night, enjoy a picture-perfect view as both amphitheater and the Alcazaba fortress are illuminated against the dark sky.

Above the ruins, the fortified walls of **La Alcazaba** (C/ Alacazabilla, s/n, tel. 95/221-6005, 9:30 A.M.–8 P.M. Tues.–Sun. summer, 8:30 A.M.–7 P.M. Tues.–Sun. winter, closed Mon., €1.95) is one of Málaga's major landmarks. This Moorish fortress dates back to the

ANDALUCÍA

700s, however the bulk of what you see today is from the mid-11th century. One of the largest Moorish military structures preserved in the country, the fortress features a double wall and rectangular towers. Within the walls, bougainvillea, jasmine, and a sprinkling of palm and orange trees are a lush contrast to the fortress' sun-baked brick walls and provide shelter for an 11th-century palace. Originally housing Moorish military leaders and dignitaries, it was later occupied by the Catholic Kings Fernando and Isabel after the town had fallen into their hands. The Puerta del Cristo (Christ's Gate) is so named because it was here that the Christian rulers held the first Catholic mass after capturing the city. Ascend to the tower via a zig-zagging entrance off of Calle Alcazabilla or take the elevator from Calle Guillén Sotelo. Once on top, you'll be rewarded with lovely views over the fortress's walls.

For even better views, head to **Castillo Gibralfaro** (Camino de Gibralfaro, s/n, 9 A.M.–7:45 P.M. daily summer, 9 A.M.–5:45 P.M. daily winter, €1.90). Built in the 14th century by a Moorish leader from Granada, this majestic castle derives its name from the Phoenician lighthouse that once stood here. The Moors called this mount *yabal faruk* (rock of the lighthouse). The castle was used for protection and defense and during the 1487 Reconquest battle, the Muslim citizens of Málaga survived a three-month siege. They only gave up once starvation forced them to. Ascend to the castle by car along Calle Victoria or catch the shuttle that leaves several times a day from the park near Plaza de la Marina.

ENTERTAINMENT AND EVENTS
Nightlife
The bulk of Málaga's nightlife happens in the historic quarter. A classic night out should start at **Antigua Casa de la Guardia** (Alameda Principal 18, tel. 95/221-4680). Málaga's oldest bar looks pretty much the same today as it did back in 1840 when it opened. Lined with ancient wine casks, locals pile two deep at the bar to drink tiny glasses of cold *malagueño* (sweet local wine) and down boiled shrimp, tossing the shells right on the floor. Another good place to ease into night is **Bodega Bar El Pimpi** (C/ Granada 62, 95/222-8990, noon–2 A.M. Tues.–Sun.) a cavernous warren of bars tucked into a former convent. Pay heed to the Virgin in her shrine before you down your first glass of sweet wine. If it gets too crowded, head for the barrel-lined tavern out back or the leafy indoor courtyard. **Terraza Larios** (C/ Marqués de Larios 2, tel. 95/222-2200, summer only), a swanky club located on the roof of Hotel Larios, is the "it" bar of summer. Come for the beautiful views of the old quarter and stay for the beautiful people. A DJ spinning low-key house comes on after the sunset. For flamenco music and performances, head to **Vista Andalucía** (Av. Guindos 29, tel. 95/223-1157, reservations suggested). Heat it up a bit at nearby **Sala Möet** (Pl. Mártires, www.moet malaga.com), a massive club popular with Málaga's wild young things. Serving more than just champagne, this place rocks with a mix of techno, house, and old Spanish favorites that keep the crowd hopping until wee hours. Popular Spanish DJs spin Thursday nights.

The under-25 set congregates in Plaza de la Merced, usually with a massive *botellón* (bring-your-own street party). When that breaks up, they stream into dozens of bars in the vicinity. **Picasso Bar** (Pl. Merced 20, Wed.–Sat.) is very popular with party-minded international students. On the weekends it often stays open until 6 A.M. Their two-for-one *chupitos* (shots) special on Friday nights comes with the promise that "after your fifth shot your Spanish will be better!" **Onda Passadena** (C/ Gómez Pallete 5, tel. 95/260-0984, closed Sun. and Mon.) may look closed with its tight shutters, but this place is hot. On Tuesday nights they feature live jazz and Thursday nights a flamenco performance. Both shows begin around 12:30 AM and are free, though you'll have to buy a drink. On the weekends, this place hops until 6 A.M. **La Botellita** (C/ Álamos 36, tel. 95/277-1404, 11:30 P.M.–4:30 A.M. Thurs.–Sat.) is just what its name (The Little Bottle) implies. Drinks are served via the tiny liquor bottles you normally get on airplanes. The pure Spanish pop draws a young, local crowd. Set in a grand old mansion, **Liceo** (C/ Beatas 21, 11 P.M.–6 A.M. Thurs.–Sat.) offers two floors of fun and four ways to have it with different music being pumped into different dance rooms. The young crowd is full of students, tourists, and some party-hearty locals.

Along the beaches, *chiringuitos* (beachside bars) provide a laid-back vibe under the stars. Because of the many Spanish-language schools in this area, the crowd is international and young. One of the most popular is **La Chancla** (Playa Pedregalejo), where all you need is a pair of flip-flops to kick off so you can dance in the sand until the wee hours.

Festivals and Events

Semana Santa is practiced in Málaga with what seems like a holy vengeance. Only Sevilla has the participation of more brotherhoods, but Málaga has the biggest *tronos* (floats) to bear the statues of their Virgins and Christs. Weighing up to 5,440 kilograms (six tons) and featuring distinctive velvet and golden drapes to cover the statues, the floats have to be moved through the city's streets laboriously by over 100 *costaleros* (the members of the brotherhood who carry the float on their backs). (See sidebar, *All About Semana Santa*.)

Málaga's **Festival de Cine** (www.festcine malaga.com) was launched in 1998 to promote Spanish cinema. It is held in the spring, but check the website for specifics.

The third week of August brings the **Feria de Málaga.** Originally begun as a celebration of the arrival of the Spanish Monarchy in 1487, Today, this nine-day fest, is best known for its bullfights, wine tastings, outdoor concerts, fireworks, and non-stop partying. On the first Saturday of the festival, there is horse-drawn pilgrimage along the Paseo del Parque. The remaining festivities are celebrated on the streets of the historic district.

SPORTS AND RECREATION
Arabic Baths

Andalucía is dotted with the ruins of hundreds of 1,000-year-old Arabic baths. **El Hammam** (C/ Tomás de Cózar 13, tel. 95/221-2327, www.elhammam.com, 10 A.M.–10 P.M. daily), located in an elegant 18th-century building, offers a very traditional experience. Rather than floating in pools as in many of the modern *hammams,* here you move from hot to cool marble rooms. You are given a towel, special soaps, a scrubbing cloth, and a bowl. In the rooms you can collect water from gurgling fountains and pour it over your body. There are various massage options that can be added to your experience, including an ancient method using olive oil and salt. Prices start at €23 and reservations are a must.

Beaches

Malaga has over 15 medium-grained beaches stretching along 16 kilometers (10 miles) of the Mediterranean Sea. Most offer services including children's playgrounds, restaurants, and changing areas. As in the rest of Spain, topless bathing is legal and common. Most beach services (except the *chiringuitos)* close around 8 P.M., but you can stick around for fishing (or low-key merry-making) from 9 P.M.–10 A.M. Beaches are best reached by cab or bus from Alameda Principal. **Playa de la Malagueta,** about 1.5 kilometers (nearly a mile) long and 45 meters (150 feet) wide, is the most popular because of its proximity to the city center. To the east is the popular **Playa Acacias** and **Playa del Chanquete** and to the southwest, **Playa Misericordia.**

ACCOMMODATIONS
Under €50

In this price range, you are looking at youth hostels, including **Picasso's Corner Hostel** (C/ San Juan de Letrán 9, tel. 95/221-2287, www.picassoscorner.com, €19 for a dorm bed), "ranked number two in the world." Right near the Plaza de la Merced party zone (and the Picasso museum), this cheery hostel offers free Internet and Wi-Fi, breakfast, an Arabic teahouse, a BBQ area, bike hire, and themed dinners and parties—fun, fun, fun! Rooms hold 4–6 beds and there is an "Arabic Double" for €45. With less style but more Spanish guests, **Residencia**

Universitaria Santa Paula (C/ Especeria 5, tel. 95/221-4148, www.rsantapaula.com, €15 for a dorm bed) offers a lot more than you'd expect for the price: a clean common area, free Internet access, bright rooms, and a great location. Their "student-only" policy is not strictly enforced, but most guests are young.

€50-€100

Barely edging into the over-€50 category, **Hostal Larios** (C/ Marqués de Larios 9, tel. 95/222-5490, info@hostallarios.com, www.hostallarios.com, €53) is a decent little place offering great views of swanky Calle Marqués de Larios. Rooms are clean and bright, if a bit dully decorated. **Kris Tribuna** (C/ Carretería 6–10, tel. 95/212-2230, kristribuna@kris hoteles.com, www.krishoteles.com, €80) is a smart-looking hotel in the western part of the historic quarter. Rooms are bright and airy and come with free Internet. The hotel also offers a full menu of amenities. The ground-floor restaurant, La Barbacana, serves traditional Málaga fare. **Hotel Atarazanas** (C/ Atarazanas 19, tel. 95/212-1910, www.balboahoteles.com, €95), across the street from the bustling market Mercado de Atarazana, has a romantically aged exterior hiding an updated, modern interior. Rooms feature Wi-Fi and excellent showers. The only downside: nightly street noise as partygoers make their way home. Opened in 2005, **Hotel del Pintor** (C/ Álamos 27, tel. 95/206-0980, info@hoteldelpintor.com, www.hoteldelpintor.com, €85) is a modern-art lover's dream. Black, white, and red all over, this hotel/art gallery combines technology, design, and paintings by owner Pepe Bornoy to provide a comfortable stay just off Plaza de la Merced.

◖ **Hotel Monte Victoria** (C/ Conde de Ureña 58, tel. 95/265-6525, info@hotelmonte victoria.com, www.hotelmontevictoria.com, €73), situated on the hill leading to Castillo Gibralfaro, is a lovely family-run villa. It is a 20-minute walk to the center but a world away, with a tranquil garden boasting excellent views over the city. Escape a little further to the beach at **Hostal Domus** (C/ Juan Valera 20, tel. 95/229-7164, www.hostaldomus

.com, €58), a delightful inn just minutes from the Playa del Pedregalejos. Painted bright blue and surrounded by flowers, this is a cozy retreat. Bus 11 runs near here from the Parque del Paseo and cabs run to the center cheaply and efficiently.

Over €100

Hotel MS Maestranza (Av. Canovas del Castillo 1, tel. 95/221-3610, maestranza@ms hoteles.com, www.mshoteles.com, €120) is about midway between Malagueta beach and the Picasso museum—a perfect location! The rooms are a decent size and most boast balconies. Request one on the upper floors to minimize sounds from the busy road below and to maximize views. There is also a spa and solarium for guests. **Hotel Larios** (C/ Marqués de Larios 2, tel. 95/222-2200, info@hotel-larios .com, www.hotel-larios.com, €120) is a boutique hotel with a bright color scheme that the hotel boasts as being art deco. Heavy velvet curtains and zebra-striped bed coverings are defiantly decadent and a lot of fun compared to Málaga's somewhat staid hotel scene. The rooftop bar, open only in summer, is one of the hottest spots in town. The location is also excellent, smack on the historic district's pedestrian shopping street. **AC Málaga Palacio** (Cortina del Muelle 1, tel. 95/221-5185, mpalacio@ ac-hotels.com, www.hotelacmalagapalacio .com, €130), right off the Parque del Paseo, boasts spacious rooms, most with great views over the port and the old city (make a request when booking). Nice perks include Wi-Fi, free mini bar with water, soft drinks, and beer, and a 15th-floor pool in the summer. As part of the stylish Spanish chain AC, decor is modern and service attentive.

Málaga has two paradors. **Parador Gibralfaro** (Castillo de Gibralfaro s/n, tel. 95/222-1902, gibralfaro@parador.es, www .parador.es, €150) shares Málaga's famed hilltop with the Castillo Gibralfaro. Set in a rambling stone mansion surrounded by palm, pine, and orange trees and lots of pink bougainvillea, the hotel boasts a gorgeous view over the city and sea plus a refreshing rooftop pool. **Parador**

del Golf (tel. 95/238-1255, málaga@parador.
es, www.parador.es, €135), located about 16
kilometers (10 miles) outside of Málaga, has
a country-club atmosphere with an Andalusian twist. It is located right in the middle of
a sprawling 18-hole golf course, which in turn
sits right on the sea.

FOOD

Málaga's culinary claim to fame is *fritura
de pescaítos a la malagueña* (small fried fish
Málaga-style). It is so famous that you can't
tell a Spaniard you are going to Málaga, without him immediately insisting that you try
this plate of mixed fish—sardines, red mullet,
and small squid. When you do you'll be happily surprised—the batter is so light and crispy
and the fish so fresh you'd swear that it just
swam right into the oil. Another fish specialty
is *espeto* (fresh sardines grilled on spears). (See
the sidebar *Fish Sticks* for more on this seaside
treat.) A local soup, now popular throughout
Andalucía, is *ajoblanco*, a white gazpacho made
of grapes and ground almonds. Málaga is also
famed for its sweet wines made from muscatel
grapes. They can range from cloyingly sweet
to velvety rich. Most of the tapas bars in town
serve their own brand, straight from the cask
into your glass.

Cafés and Desserts

Lepanto (C/ Marqués de Larios 7, tel. 95/244-
7012) is a cute little gourmet bakery perfect for
breakfast (tea, coffee, croissants, muffins), but
sweet temptation may lead you back for their
desserts (homemade ice cream, elaborate pas
tries, decadent chocolates). They also offer a
varied menu of light lunches from salads to sandwiches to pizzas. **Café con Libros** (Pl. Merced
19, tel. 65/634-8024, 11 A.M.–midnight) offers
an array of coffees, teas, milkshakes, and even
a few cocktails. Sip away while perusing a book
or just people watching in the plaza. **Comoloco**
(C/ Denis Belgrado 17, 1 P.M.–1 A.M.) can be a
lifesaver (or at least a hunger-sater) during the
infamous Spanish siesta 4–8 P.M. While the
other cafés doze, this one serves up heaping salads and tasty pita sandwiches.

Like many Andalusian towns, Málaga em-
braces its Moorish roots with a plethora of
teterías (Arabic tea houses). Two of the best are
Tetería La Manquita (C/ Duque de la Victoria 8, tel. 95/260-8783), where you can sip
teas, juices, and milkshakes while leaning back
into a bed of pillows, and **La Tetería** (C/ San
Augustín 9, tel. 67/683-9097, 9 A.M.–1 A.M.
daily), which also serves sublime crepes, savory or sweet.

Gourmet

Café de París (C/ Vélez Málaga 8, tel. 95/222-
5043, www.rcafedeparis.com, 1:30–4:30 P.M.
and 8:30–11 P.M. Tues.–Sat., 1:30–4:30 P.M.
Mon., closed Sun., €50) is one of Málaga's
most-beloved top-end restaurants. Chef José
Carlos García's sophisticated Andalusian dishes
have earned the restaurant great acclaim. Any
of his fish dishes are sublime. The sexy mahogany dining room makes this a perfect romantic
date destination. **Trayamar** (Pl. Uncibay 9, tel.
95/221-5459, 2–4 P.M. and 9 P.M.–midnight
Mon.–Sat., closed Sun., €30), a slickly modern
dining room, offers a culinary adventure that
mixes tradition with modernity.

Local Cuisine

Málaga naturally has hundreds of seafood restaurants. You'll find many clustered around
the Paseo Marítimo along Malagueta beach
and around the port, but they are all over the
city. Here are a couple favorites. At **La Casa
del Piyayo** (C/ Granada 33, 96/222-0096,
1–4 P.M. and 8 P.M.–midnight Tues.–Sun.,
closed Mon., €15, cash only) you'll feel at sea
at this *freiduría* (fried-fish restaurant). The bar
resembles an old fishing boat and the menu
consists of shellfish, fried-fish, and salads with
shellfish. **El Tintero** (Ctra. Almería 99, tel.
95/220-6826, 1 P.M.–1 A.M. daily) is as famed
for its service as it is for its amazing seafood.
Make a cheat sheet from your Spanish food
glossary. You'll need it. There are no menus,
instead waiters circle the rooms with plates
straight from the kitchen. *Boquerones* (fresh
anchovies), *gambas* (shrimp), and *sepia* (cuttlefish) are just a few of the things that might go

ANDALUCÍA

FISH STICKS

It would be a culinary crime to travel to Málaga and not take a walk along the beach for a late-afternoon snack of *sardinas en espeto,* a local specialty. Sardines fresh from the fishing net are skewered on a stick, which is then stuck directly into the sand or into an old, sand-filled fishing skiff. The stick is angled so that the fish dangle over the heat from the embers of a long-burning fire. Olive wood is traditionally used for the fire because it burns slowly. The trick to a perfect *espeto,* as any good *espetero* (traditional *espeto* chef) will tell you, is that the fish must never be licked by the flames. Using just the heat rising off the fire ensures that the fish turn out juicy and tender and full of flavor.

Though many restaurants offer *sardinas al espeto,* they are best at the many *chiringuitos* (beachside bars) located right on the sand. Enjoy them with nothing more than a squeeze of lemon and a chunk of bread. Fish sticks never tasted so good.

© SEVE PONCE DE LEON

by. Take what you want. Everything costs the same and you'll be charged by the number of plates on your table. It is a very tasty display of organized chaos located just off the Playa del Dedo promenade in El Palo.

La Ménsula (C/ Trinidad Grund 28, tel. 95/222-1314, 1–5 P.M. and 9 P.M.–midnight Mon.–Sat., closed Sun., 12–20) has a classic Spanish look and traditional Andalusian food and wines from the region. **Restaurante Mariano** (Pl. Carbón 3, tel. 95/222-9050, 1–5 P.M. and 8 P.M.–12:30 A.M. Mon.–Sat., 1–5 P.M. Sun., €20) serves modern Mediterranean and Malagueñan food on the plates and Sinatra on the stereo in their elegant dining room in the heart of the historic quarter. **El Chinitas** (C/ Moreno Monroy 4–6, tel. 95/221-0972, 1–4 P.M. and 8 P.M.–midnight daily, €25) is a long-time favorite. Oozing Andalusian style—cured ham legs hanging over the bar and Spanish tiles adorning the walls— you'll have to jostle with locals for a table, but it's worth it. Try the *solomillo,* an exquisite

cut of filet sizzling in a sweet Málaga wine sauce. **Antonio Martí** (Pl. Malagueta, s/n, tel. 95/222-7398, 1–4 P.M. and 8 P.M.–midnight Tues.–Sat., 1–4 P.M. Sun., closed Mon., €35) has a serious turf-and-surf theme going on. One dining room overlooks the sea, the other is swimming in bullfighting memorabilia. The menu is chock-full of seafood and fish, as well as hearty steaks and pork dishes. If you are really feeling adventurous, try the surprisingly tender *rabo del toro* (bull's tail).

Tapas

To a true-tapas lover, Málaga's historic town resembles a giant food market and all the tiny tapas bars are the stalls. You'll find a big concentration around Calle Nueva and Pasaje Chinitas, but all you have to do is pick a street, any street, and walk until you see the tiny spot with the locals bursting out the doors, tiny plates and tinier glasses clutched in their hands. Málaga's tapas bars are generally open from noon until midnight, though a few do close during mid-day (4–7 P.M.). **Bar Orellana** (C/ Moreno Monroy 5, tel. 95/222-3012, closed Sun. and Mon.), run by the folks at El Chinitas, offers great Málaga-style tapas including *rosada empanada* (deep-fried pink fish)—it looks far from appetizing, but is quite tasty. Around the corner, **Taberna Rincon Chinitas** (Pasaje Chinitas 9, tel. 95/221-0972) is an old-time bar with a certain bohemian grace—possibly because it was once a hang-out for Federico García Lorca. Try the *berenjenas con miel* (eggplant in honey), a local favorite that dates back to the Moors. At the very popular wine bar **Gorki** (C/ Strachan 6, tel. 95/222-1466, closed Sun.), try the *erizos naturales en su concha* (fried sea urchin) presented in its spiky shell. **Mesón Lo Güeno** (C/ Marín García 9, tel. 95/222-3048) has been a Málaga fixture for over 30 years. They are famous for their extensive list of traditional tapas with a twist.

INFORMATION

There are several **tourist offices** in Málaga, including: the Aeropuerto de Málaga (tel. 95/204-8484, ext. 58617), Estación de Autobuses (Po. Tilos 21, tel. 95/235-0061), Plaza de la Marina (tel. 95/220-9603), and in front of the Alcazaba (no phone). Offices are generally open 9 A.M.–6 P.M. daily, with extended hours in summer. On the Internet, try the official site of Málaga at www.malagaturismo .com. The two regional sites, www.andalucia .com and www.andalucia.org also offer excellent city information.

GETTING THERE AND AROUND
Air
El Aeropuerto de Málaga (tel. 95/204-8804) is about eight kilometers (five miles) outside the city center. With over 118 airlines arriving from some 30 countries worldwide, it is the largest in Andalucía and boasts several car rental agencies. Within Spain, air travel to Málaga is often the cheapest way to go from cities like Madrid, Barcelona, Santiago, and Bilbao. To get from the airport to Málaga,

take bus number 19 to Alameda Principal or take local train C1 to Centro Alameda. Buses and trains run every half-hour approximately 6 A.M.–midnight.

Taxis (tel. 95/204-0804 or 95/233-3333) are available just outside the arrivals hall. Fares are not metered, so be sure to negotiate a price before getting in the cab, but expect to pay €12–15 .

Train
Renfe (tel. 90/224-0202, www.renfe.com) offers direct train service between Málaga and a number of Spanish cities, including Barcelona, Madrid, Valencia, Cordoba, and Seville. However, Málaga is not located on the AVE, so from Madrid, this is not a favorable option. The Málaga train terminal is located on the Explanada de la Estación, just west of the city center —a taxi will cost roughly €5 or catch local bus 72 to Alameda Principal for less than €1.

Bus
If you are traveling by bus into Málaga, you will arrive at the city's **Estación de Autobuses** (Po. Tilos 21, tel. 95/235-0061, www.estabus .emtsam.es). You can purchase tickets to destinations throughout Spain, and even to other countries, at the station's ticket counters. Schedules and fares vary by bus company. To reach Málaga's city center, take local bus 19 from the bus station to Alameda Principal.

Car
Málaga is just off the E-15/N-340 highway, which runs parallel to the coast and the N–331, which runs north–south.

VICINITY OF MÁLAGA
Antequera
Just 40 kilometers (25 miles) north of Málaga, in the heart of Andalucía, lies the provincial town of Antequera, a quiet escape from the hustle and bustle along the coast. Its medieval towers rise over a rambling town of whitewashed buildings surrounded by mottled fields. Come in spring and maybe you'll catch the full bloom of the acres of sunflowers

planted here. Antequera is famous for its olive oil production and if you are in town on a Friday, you'll see the sleepy streets come alive as farmers from neighboring villages come to the market at Antequera for supplies. It is also famous for 5,000-year-old history, represented by Bronze Age ruins, Roman architecture, a Moorish castle, and a smattering of medieval churches. Over 50 nationally recognized monuments are located within its boundaries.

As you enter Antequera, you cannot miss **La Peña de los Enamorados** (Lover's Leap), a nearly one-kilometer-high (0.5-mile-high) limestone rock that overlooks the town. Legend has it that a pair of star-crossed lovers—a Moorish girl and a Christian man—were driven to the top of the cliff by soldiers. Rather than surrender, the two lovers leapt off the rock together. A more accommodating spot for nature lovers and hikers is **Torcal de Antequera** (15 kilometers/nine miles south of Antequera), a small national park with beautiful limestone formations.

On the edge of town, Antequera's most spectacular monuments are the prehistoric **dolmens** (9 A.M.–3:30 P.M. Tues., 9 A.M.–6 P.M. Wed.–Sat., 9:30 A.M.–2:30 P.M. Sun., free), a set of three megalithic stone burial sites attributed to the Iberian tribes who lived in this region 5,000 years ago. The **Cueva de la Menga** is the most spectacular. In town, visit the Roman era at the recently excavated *baños romanos* (Roman baths) or the **Museo Municipal** (Palacio de Nájera, tel. 95/270-4051, 10 A.M.–1:30 and 4:30–6:30 Tues.–Fri., 10 A.M.–1:30 Sat., 11 A.M.–1:30 Sun., €3), which houses *Efebo,* a perfectly preserved bronze sculpture of a boy that dates to the Roman era.

The Moors left their mark in the rambling stone **castillo fortress** that sits above the town. When they pulled out of the city in 1410 under pressure from the Christian Reconquista troops, the Christians used the fort as a base from which to attack Granada.

See a bit of the Christian's legacy in a clutch of medieval churches. The 16th-century **Iglesia de Santa María** now houses an exhibition center. **Iglesia San Sebastián** is distinguished by its soaring Mudejar tower topped by an angel, nicknamed *angelote* ("big angel") by the locals. The baroque **Nuestra Señora del Carmen** boasts a soaring altar.

Outside of Antequera, the **Laguna de Fuente de Piedra,** a vast salty lagoon, is nicknamed "the pink lagoon" because of the thousands of ping flamingoes that spend their summers grazing on seaweed and crustaceans.

For complete details on all the sights, within and outside of Antequera, visit the **tourist office** (Pl. San Sebastián, tel. 95/270-2505).

Though Antequera can be seen in a morning, if you would like to stay the night, you have some very enticing options. **Hotel Antequera Golf** (Santa Catalina, s/n, tel. 95/270-4531, info@hotelantequera.com, www.hotelantequera.com, €65) has it all—from a spa and a golf course to two in-house restaurants and a night club. Rooms are classically styled and comfortable—not to mention cheap! However, you can upgrade to a luxury suite for €150. The hotel will also arrange golf packages. **Pensió Colon** (C/ Infante Don Fernando 29, tel. www.castelcolon.com, €40) is a cute little hotel suited for any traveler's budget and is situated right in the center of town.

For traditional Andalusian fare, dine at **La Espuela** (Pl. Toros, s/n, tel. 95/270-5104, noon–10 P.M. Mon.–Sat., noon–4 P.M. Sun., €30) and try the *porra,* a local take on gazpacho that is thickened with olive oil and bread and topped with chopped boiled egg and *jamón.* **El Angelote** (Pl. Coso Viejo, tel. 95/270-3465, 1:30–4 P.M. and 9–10:30 P.M. Tues.–Sat., 1:30–4 P.M. Sun., closed Mon., €34), a rustic, two-room dining room popular with both locals and day-trippers, also features excellent local Andalusian fare, particularly game from the nearby mountains.

If traveling by car from Málaga, follow the N-331 north and then take the A-354 west into Antequera. Buses also run between both cities and tickets can be purchased at Málaga's Estación de Autobuses.

Ronda

One of the oldest cities in Spain, Ronda sits on top of a towering plateau. The commanding views are one of its greatest charms. The most dramatic feature of the town is El Tajo—a dramatic gorge famous throughout Spain—that divides the plateau in two. At its rocky base flows the Río Guadalevín. The gorge is traversed by the magnificent 17th-century bridge, Puente Nuevo, which connects the new part of town, El Mercadillo (home to the historic bullring and the lovely Alameda del Tajo park), with the old Moorish Casco Antiguo, often called "La Ciudad" by the locals.

Given its strategic location nestled between five different mountain ranges, it's hardly surprising that Ronda's ancient history is full of battles and invasions. Whoever controlled the valley leading up from modern-day Algeciras effectively controlled fertile southern Andalucía. Today's invaders are more likely to be wielding backpacks and cameras. The town received over three million visitors in 2003, but a relatively small percentage stays past sunset. Although good transportation links to Seville, Cádiz, and Málaga make Ronda an excellent destination for a day trip, it's worth staying the night to discover the charm that day-trippers miss.

Ronda comes alive with festive spirit in late August and September during the wild carnival known as **Feria de Ronda.** Usually held the last week of August or the first week of September, the festival is a typical display of Andalusian exuberance with fun fairs, food booths, and dancing in the streets. The **Festival Goyesca** is held consecutively. It is named for the great Spanish painter Francisco de Goya who created etchings and paintings of Ronda's bullring in the 18th century. The entire town participates, decked out in white tights, velvet corsets, and tassled hair nets. Bullfights are

Ronda's breathtaking view

also held in 18th-century costume, including the very popular *rejoneo,* a bullfight performed on horseback.

HISTORY

Though archaeologists have found remains of settlements at Cueva de la Pileta that they believe go back 20,000 years, the first full-scale colonization of the area came with the Romans, who founded Acinipo 19 kilometers (12 miles) northwest of modern-day Ronda. Regional government archaeologists regularly get calls from homeowners asking them to take a look at walls, pottery, and relics from the basements of houses located along Calle Armiñán. After the Romans lost control of the area in the 2nd century A.D., the Visigoths took over. They were, in turn, booted out by the Moors during their invasions in 711. The Moors managed to hold onto the settlement of Medina Runda until 1485, when the Christian Reconquest swept in from western Andalucía towards Granada. Fernando and Isabel used the city as their base for reclaiming most of the area north of Gibraltar. Their logo, the yoke-and-arrow, is still used on the town's coat of arms.

SIGHTS
Plaza de Toros

No visit to Ronda would be complete without visiting La Plaza de Toros de Ronda (C/ Virgen de la Paz 15, tel. 95/287-4132, www.rmcr .org). Inaugurated in 1785, it is considered the spiritual home of *la corrida* (bullfight). Bullfighting, which was originally performed on horseback using a spear, didn't become a pedestrian sport until the early 18th century. Three generations of the legendary Romero family helped transform bullfighting into the sport we know today. Grandfather Francisco Romero (born in 1698) was the first to bring the action off the horse and onto the ground and formalize the use of the cape. Father Juan Romero incorporated the use of the support team, called *la cuadrilla.* And son Pedro Romero formalized the current rules.

In its heyday, the ring was home to not only the Romeros, but also to another bullfighting

dynasty, Cayetano Ordóñez and his son Antonio Ordóñez. Their skill, as well as the town's bullfighting legacy, lured famed aficionados such as Orson Welles and Ernest Hemingway to Ronda's bullring. Despite its history, the bullring sees little action outside of the Festival Goyesca, held every September. (Unless you've got excellent local connections or big bucks, tickets are almost impossible to get, given the small capacity of the bullring.)

The monument, currently managed by Patrimonio Nacional, is open daily for visits (10 A.M.–8 P.M., €5, €3 under age 16). Even if you're not likely to become a fan of bullfighting, the museum contains a good selection of bullfighting memorabilia from the past 150 years, and decent English translations to explain the intricacies of *la corrida.*

Alameda del Tajo

The area between the bullring and the edge of the River Tajo has been converted into a long, rambling park. This is the place to see and be seen, especially during the hour before sunset, when it seems like every local is out with dogs, kids, and grandparents in tow having their evening paseo (stroll). The park stretches northward past the back of the Reina Victoria Hotel for nearly a kilometer (a half-mile or so). Walking southward through the park, you reach the **Paseo de Blas Infante,** just behind the bullring. The area around the band shell is a favorite place for visitors and residents alike to take in the sunset. At the end of the gardens, step out onto the vertigo-inducing balcony that juts right out over the gorge.

Following the edge of the Tajo takes you around the periphery of the parador. It was formerly the home of Ronda's municipal market and boasts the best views in town. Beyond that, lies the **Puente Nuevo,** a 100-foot-long architectural marvel built in 1616. The elongated body of the bridge wasn't designed just for structure strength; the halls under the bridge also housed the municipal jail. The bridge spans **El Tajo,** a spectacular gorge 110 meters (360 feet) deep and 64 meters (210 feet) across. The view down is dizzying and has been deadly. The architect of the bridge fell to his death here. During the Civil War, hundreds of people were hurled to their deaths from the bridge. Climb the parapet to get a better view of just how dramatic the gorge beneath the bridge is. Crossing the bridge, you encounter the **Monasterio de San Francisco,** which was reopened in 2005 and is currently being used as an exhibition space by a Málaga savings bank.

🄲 La Ciudad

The most logical tour of Ronda's historic old town would begin by the Puente Nuevo. Once over the river, take the first right onto Calle Tenorio and follow it down to the **Plaza María Auxiliadora,** a charming square filled with rose bushes and neighborhood cats. (If you'd like to descend to the Tajo to get a better view of the Puente Nuevo, look for the footpath on the right-hand side at the end of the garden.)

Turning left on Calle Ruedo Garnedo will take you to the **Palacio de Mondragón** (Pl. Mondragón, 10 A.M.–7 P.M. Mon.–Fri., 10 A.M.–3 P.M. Sat. and Sun, €2). Built in the early 14th century, it's worth the price of admission to see the original wood carvings on the doors and ceiling beams. There's also a fascinating display (in English and Spanish) on the burial rites of the Islamic tribes who inhabited the area.

As you come out of the Palacio, turn right and follow the plaza to the end, where it becomes Calle Manuel Moreno; the street opens up into the **Plaza de Duquesa de Parcent,** where the **Iglesia de Santa María la Mayor** (10 A.M.–7 P.M. daily Apr.–Sept., until 6 P.M. Oct.–Mar., €2) sits on the north side of the square. Built on the site of a former mosque, you can still see the minaret upon which the bell tower was built.

Coming out of the square, turn left on Calle Armiñán and walk for another couple of yards until you see the 14th-century **Minarete de San Sebastian,** the site of a former mosque converted into a church. Continue walking down Calle Marqués de Salvatierra, past the **Palacio de los Marqueses de Salvatierra,** which is currently not open to the public.

After a bend in the street, you will reach the **Puerta de Carlos V,** a ceremonial gate built to honor a visit by the Habsburg king. Turning right down the stone walkway leads you to the **Baños Árabes** (C/ San Miguel, 10 A.M.–6 P.M. Mon.–Fri., 10 A.M.–1:45 P.M. and 3–6 P.M. Sat., 10 A.M.–3 P.M. Sun., €2), one of the best-preserved examples of an original Moorish *hammam* (bath) in the region.

Crossing the Guadalevín River, the medieval **Puente de San Miguel** will lead you to the **Fuente de Ocho Cañones,** which stands in front of the Gothic-turned-Renaissance **Iglesia de Nuestro Padre Jesús.**

If you're not in the mood for the steep walk up Calle Remedios to get back into town, turn up Calle Escolleras towards the **Jardines de Cuenca,** which has benches to let you rest as you work your way uphill.

SPORTS AND RECREATION

As Ronda is located between two important nature parks **(Parque Natural Sierra de las Nieves** and **Parque Natural Los Alcornocales),** outdoor sports fans are rather privileged. You could spend weeks here doing nothing but mountain biking, caving, hiking, parasailing, bungee jumping, rock climbing, and hang-gliding. Based in the neighboring town of Grazalema, **Horizon Grazalema** (C/ Corrales Terceros 29, tel. 95/613-2363, grazalema@horizonaventura.com, www.horizonaventura.com) offers half-day and full-day activities in the nearby Sierra de Grazalema and the Alcornocales park. If you can't settle on just one activity, they offer a half-day multi-adventure package that gives you the chance to try four different activities, plus paintball, for €34 per person. The guides speak English. For those who like their fun on two wheels, **Cycle Ronda** (C/ Serrato 3, tel. 95/287-7814, www.cycleronda.com), run by a pair of multi-lingual Dutch guys, rents mountain bikes and touring hybrids by the day or by the week.

ACCOMMODATIONS

Provided your visit to Ronda is not during the *feria* season or July (when the University of

Málaga runs summer-school sessions in town), you shouldn't have any trouble finding a bed.

Under €50

Located close to the Plaza del Socorro, the **Hostal Ronda Sol** (C/ Almendra 11, tel. 95/387-4497) is bare-bones basic, but immaculately clean and run by an extremely pleasant woman who speaks French and can make herself understood in English and German. This is a great deal for solo travelers, but pass on the singles (€13) and go for a double, which is only €20, even in high season.

Active sports fans will love the **Hotel Morales** (C/ Sevilla 51, tel. 95/287-1538, reservas@hotelmorales.com, www.hotelmorales.com, €45). Juan and his staff welcome hikers and bikers with open arms and are great sources of information about routes in the Sierra de las Nieves.

€50-100

Ever wonder what happens to those people who drop out of the rat race and swear that they're going to open a bed-and-breakfast somewhere? If they're persistent and creative, they end up opening a place like (**Hotel Enfrente Arte** (C/ Real 40, tel. 95/287-9088, reservations@enfrentearte.com, www.enfrentearte.com, €99). This delightful 14-room hotel has unparalleled views south towards the Sierra de las Nieves. Bohemian, funky, and friendly just begins to describe the place. To get to the Gaudí-inspired pool, walk over a goldfish-filled reflecting pool and through the billiards hall. Along the way, you'll pass a barely tamed bamboo garden with an old scooter sprouting flowers. Rooms are colorful and atmospheric with unique lighting and kitschy posters of pin-up girls. Guests have unlimited use of the self-service bar, which is always stocked with beer, wine, and soft drinks. A breakfast/brunch buffet is included in the price and consists of a glorious spread of fruit kebobs, melons, cereals, and pastries.

Another enchanting option is **Baraka Bed & Breakfast** (C/ Ruedo Doña Elvira 16, tel. 95/287-2843, www.barakaronda.com, closed Nov.–Jan., €70, no credit cards). Located on a cobbled pedestrian street in the Casco Antiguo, this rambling inn boasts colorful tiled common areas, including a bright yellow Andalusian patio, and soothing, tranquil rooms all decorated by the gracious owner Anahid. She is a world traveler and lover of Spain and can offer tips not only about Ronda, but the rest of Andalucía as well. If you're looking for something that's more Moorish, check into **Alavera de los Baños** (C/ San Miguel, s/n, tel. 95/287-9143, alavera@telefonica.net, www.andalucia.com/alavera, €85), located right beside the Baños Árabes. There's a daily traditional tapas tasting 1:30–3 P.M. and the hotel's restaurant (8–10:30 P.M.) features Andalusian and Moroccan specialties. Full breakfasts are included in the price. A quirky bit of trivia—the hotel was used as a backdrop during filming of the operatic favorite *Carmen*.

Over €100

Though other paradors in the system are more ancient and atmospheric, none can compete with **Parador de Ronda** (Pl. España, s/n, tel. 95/287-7500, ronda@parador.es, www.parador.es, €120) for its stunning view down into the Tajo and stretching across towards the Sierra de Grazalema. The spacious, modern rooms are soothing in shades of cream and feature enormous bathrooms. However, if you want one with a gorge view, it will cost you €20 extra—it will be the best €20 you've ever spent. If your budget can't cover a room for the night, console yourself with the *menú del día* in the restaurant. At €30 (wine not included), it's worth every *céntimo*. Just around the corner from the bullring, the **Hotel Acinipo** (C/ José Aparicio 7, tel. 95/216-1002, hacipino@serraniaderonda.com, www.hotelacinipo.com, €130) is housed in a restored building that once served as a home for two artists—Ronda painter Téllez Loriguillo and Japanese watercolorist Miki Haruta. Their artistic legacy is evident throughout this modern hotel. Rooms are serene and classic and boast large mosaic-tiled bathrooms. Make sure you request a room with a view. It is also one of the few Ronda hotels that is wheelchair-accessible. **Hotel San Gabriel** (Marqués de Moctezuma 19, tel. 95/219-0392, info@ hotelsangabriel.com, www.hotelsangabriel.com, €100) is a charming hotel with the feel of a family-owned inn—in fact the family lives in part of the hotel. Housed in a building that dates to 1736, rooms have a wealthy Spanish villa feel with terra-cotta flooring, carved wood headboards, and heavy drapes. The staff is very helpful and the location is excellent. If you've had enough of walking and want a quiet night in, take advantage of the hotel's home cinema stocked with Hollywood classics from the 1940s and 1950s.

FOOD
Local Cuisine
The minimalist **Restaurante Tragabuches** (C/ José Aparicio 1, tel. 95/219 0291, closed Sun. P.M. and Mon., €55) is one Andalucía's top restaurants, drawing foodies from all over the region and beyond. Chef Benito Goméz from nearby Málaga offers a very creative take on traditional Andalusian fare. Lamb is drenched in fresh herbs, pork gets a sauce of clams and lemongrass, and ice cream gets a touch of garlic and pine nuts. **Restaurante de Escudero** (Po. Blás Infante 1, tel. 95/287-1367, www.del escudero.com, closed Sun. P.M., €30) is run by an ex-chef from Tragabuches—Sergio Lopéz, who has won awards for his culinary skill. He offers sublime renditions of classic Andalusian dishes in this colonial house with lovely views over the Tajo gorge. If you prefer a basic meal local-style, head to the Casco Antiguo and **Bar Luciano** (C/ Arminá 42, tel. 95/287-0428, 9 A.M.–5 P.M. Mon. –Fri., closed Sun.), which offers a delicious *menú* for just €9.

Tapas
While you could try some of the more tourist-oriented spots around the Plaza de Socorro and Calle Virgen de la Paz, walking a block away gets you into places that are more authentic and affordable. **Café-Bar Faustino** (C/ Santa Cecilia 4, tel. 95/287-6777) gets packed on Saturday and Sunday afternoons but is worth it for its good *raciones* (portions) of *jamón*

ibérico (Iberian ham) and *tortillitas de camarones* (baby shrimp fritters). **Bar La Farola** (Pl. Carmen Abela 9, tel. 95/287-8466) serves great breakfasts on the terrace in addition to excellent tapas. The best bet for low prices and local color is **La Lechuguita** (C/ Los Remedios 31), where happy locals lap up €0.50 tapas all day long. **Vinoteca La Gota del 13** (C/ Sevilla 13, tel. 95/287-8076) specializes in local wine vintages and the tapas that complement them best. **Café de Ronda** (C/ Tenorio 1) makes a good stop for snacks and ice cream, with lovely views from the terrace.

INFORMATION
Ronda has two separate tourist offices that are located within steps of each other. The better—and more helpful of the two—is the local **Oficina de Turismo de Ronda** (Po. Blas Infante, tel. 95/218-7175, 9:30 A.M.–6:30 P.M. Mon.–Fri., 10 A.M.–2 P.M. and 3–6:30 P.M. Sat. and Sun.). The regional Andalucía office, **Junta de Andalucía** (Pl. España 9, tel. 95/287-1272, 9 A.M.–8 P.M. Mon.–Fri., 10 A.M.–2 P.M. Sat. and Sun.), has more in-depth information about the surrounding region, including every town in Andalucía.

On the Internet, the official tourism website of Ronda, www.turismoderonda.es, is excellent and easy to use. The regional sites, www.andalucia.org and www.andalucia.com, have comprehensive Ronda sections.

GETTING THERE AND AROUND
Train
The **Estación de Tren de Ronda** (Av. de La Victoria 31, tel. 95/287-1673) does not offer the best connections. **Renfe** (tel. 90/224-0202, www.renfe.com) offers direct destinations out of the station to Algeciras in the south (1.75 hours, four daily) and Granada in the west (2.25 hours, three daily). The Granada line also stops in Antequera, where connections can be made to Málaga, Córdoba, and Madrid. To get to Sevilla, you have to transfer at Antequera to La Roda, and catch the train to Sevilla from there.

ANDALUCÍA

Bus

Ronda practically sits at the junction of Cádiz, Sevilla, and Málaga provinces, and bus service is frequent to the respective capital cities. Five bus companies operate out of the **Estación de Autobuses de Ronda** (Pl. Concepción García Redondo 2). **Los Amarillos** (tel. 95/218-7061, www.losamarillos.es) has several connections daily to Sevilla and Málaga. **Transportes Comes** (tel. 95/287-1992, www.tgcomes.es) goes to Jerez de la Frontera (three hours, four daily) and Cádiz (three hours, five daily). Both provide sporadic service to the Pueblos Blancos in northern Cádiz province. **Portillo** (tel. 95/287-2262, www.ctsa-portillo.com) operates to the Costa del Sol, including Marbella, Fuengirola, Torremolinos, and Málaga. Also check **Alsina Graells** (www.alsinagraells.es) for more connections in Andalucía.

Car

The A-376 highway runs from Sevilla to Ronda in 137 kilometers (85 miles), about two hours. From there, A-376 continues on to San Pedro de Alcántara, on the Mediterranean coast, where travelers can catch the AP-7 toll road that runs along the coast from Algeciras to Málaga.

VICINITY OF RONDA

Acinipo

The Roman ruins of Acinipo (9 A.M.–5 P.M. Wed.–Sat., 10 A.M.–2 P.M. Sun., free), known locally as Ronda la Vieja (Old Ronda), are miraculously intact. They show that, in its time, Acinipo was an important center for trade and commerce, even possessing the right to mint its own coinage. The ruins are located 19 kilometers (12 miles) northwest of Ronda, just off the A-376 highway.

Cueva de la Pileta

To the southwest, the Cueva de la Pileta (tel. 95/216-7343, www.cuevadelapileta.org, 10 A.M.–1 P.M. and 4–6 P.M. daily, €6.50) is the home of Andalucía's most important cave paintings. Archaeologists estimate that the caves were inhabited some 25,000 years ago, and the various paintings of cattle, deer, and magic symbols predate those of the more famous Altamira caves in Cantabria. Bring a flashlight and a sweater, and make sure all your valuables are out of the car; theft has been a problem in the past. The caves are located on the MA-501 local road. From Ronda, take the A-376 to the MA-555.

Costa del Sol

Up until the 1950s, the Costa del Sol was a rugged stretch of coast as sleepy as could be. It was nothing more than a string of battered fishing villages and tumble-down towns. Even the coast, lapped by some 320 kilometers (nearly 200 miles) of warm, turquoise Mediterranean Sea, was nothing special. The sand is not particularly fine, and in many spots it is rocky. The landscape inland is barren, a dull palette of khaki, tan, and mottled green. So how did this unlikely spot become Spain's busiest, most notorious vacation land? Simple. Cheap land. After the visionary German/Spanish Prince Alfonso de Hohenlohe built the Marbella Club, turning that town into the preferred resort of the jet set, developers moved in all over the coast, building massive tourist towns all along on the sea. High-rise after high-rise went up. The building continued unabated in the 1960s and 1970s, with little to no government intervention. After all, Spain was still in the throes of Franco's dictatorship. Poverty was still the norm. Tourism was barely a drop in the olive jar. As the resorts went up, tourists duly followed, drawn not only by the convenience of the all-inclusive vacation package that was practically born on the Costa del Sol, but also to the sun and the sea. With over 300 days of sunshine and 365 days of silky smooth Mediterranean Sea, the Costa del Sol does have the makings of a perfect beach vacation. Over the years, thousands of those tourists decided to stay and the Costa del Sol is now home to a 300,000-strong expat community, comprised mainly of Brits and Germans. It is possible to spend a week on the Costa del Sol and not hear Spanish spoken at all. In fact, if you are looking for the "real" Spain, this is not it. This is the real Costa, where sun and sand are complemented by Irish bars, strip clubs, theme parks, golf courses, glittering neon casinos, all-you-can-eat Chinese buffets, and kilometers of concrete. If you are seeking a vacation where you can really tune out and turn off, try Torremolinos, the original resort town (and one of the best examples of unchecked development in Western Europe). Type "Torremolinos" and "vacation" into your search engine and you'll get thousands of options.

However, there are a few jewels along the Costa de Sol. Málaga, the province's capital and covered earlier in this chapter, is one of them. Very Spanish, very atmospheric, and very affordable, it is a great base for a sun, sand, and sangria vacation. Nerja, just east of Málaga, is also a good option. Its development has been kept in check (partly because its beaches are pebbly) and the result is a charming Andalusian town with resort amenities. Marbella is where to go if you've got cash and like flash. It is still the most exclusive and expensive stretch on the Costa del Sol. If you want a little resort action but still want to feel like you are in Spain, head to Fuengirola or Benalmádena, where you can crash in a big hotel but still tapas-hop with the locals in town.

NERJA

Of all the Costa del Sol resort towns, Nerja seems to have borne the brunt of its tourist development the best. The old town, sitting above the Mediterranean, offers slow-moving Andalusian grace with whitewashed buildings, pocket-sized gardens, and a handful of old-fashioned tapas bars.

Sights

The town's top sight is the lofty **Balcón de Europa** (the balcony of Europe). Built over the ruins of a 9th-century castle, this elegant balcony offers brilliant vistas over the sea and the beaches and coves on its shore. Stretching in either direction from the balcony are long, wide promenades, perfect for a paseo (stroll).

Nerja offers several fine **beaches,** though they tend to be rockier than others along the Costa del Sol. **Playa del Salón,** lying practically at the foot of the balcony, is the sandiest— and the most popular. Continue west from this beach to arrive at **Playa de Torrecilla.** It begins about where the promenade ends in **Plaza de los Cangrejos,** a delightful jumble of cafés, terraces, and greenery. To the immediate east of the balcony is the pebbly **Playa Calahonda,** dotted with coves and craggy formations. Follow that to **Playa Burriana,** Nerja's top beach.

Just east of Nerja, **Las Cuevas de Nerja** (Crta. Maro, s/n, tel. 95/252-9520, www.cuevadenerja.es, 10 A.M.–2 P.M. and 4–6:30 P.M. daily, all day in summer, €7) are Nerja's top attraction. These caves are a geological wonder created over hundreds of millions of years by underground water flow. The caves have more than five halls of rock and crystal formations including the world's largest stalactite column. In July, the caves host a dance and music festival. To reach the caves, take the 10-minute bus ride from the **Nerja Bus Station** (C/ Avenida de Pescia, tel. 95/252-1504) for less than €1. If you are driving, take the N-340/E-5 to exit 295.

Visit the **tourist office** (Puerta del Mar 2, tel. 95/252-1531, www.nerja.org) for information on the caves, the beaches, and the town, as well activities such as scuba diving, Jet Skiing, mountain biking, and scooter rentals.

Accomodations and Food

Just at the steps of the Balcón and nestled in the rocks along the sea, **Hotel Balcón de Europa** (Po. Balcón de Europa 1, tel. 95/252-0800, www.hotelbalconeuropa.com, €125) offers 110 rooms—many suites—boasting fine sea views. Expect all the standard resort amenities, including an elevator right down to the beach. **Hostal Miguel** (C/ Almirante Ferrándiz 31, tel. 95/252-1523, hostalmiguel@gmail.com, www.hostalmiguel.com, €50) is an adorable little whitewashed guesthouse. Run by an English-speaking expat couple, the *hostal* boasts a homey atmosphere and a wonderful roof terrace with great views over the town and the mountains. Another cheap charmer is the rustic **Hostal Lorca** (C/ Mendez Nuñez 20, tel. 95/252-3426, hostallorca@teleline.es, www.hostallorca.com, €49). Run by a lovely Dutch couple, it boasts a private backyard and swimming pool.

Most of the beaches of Nerja have a few *chiringuitos* (beachside bars) where you can snack on traditional Spanish cuisines in your bathing suit. **El Chiringuito de Ayo** (Playa Burriana, tel. 95/252-2289) is the place for paella, which is prepared in large pans over open flames. For something to put your clothes on for, any of the restaurants around Balcón de Europa will offer excellent seafood. Up in the old village, you'll find neighborhood bars that make up for in authentic goodness what they lack in views. Seek out the top-rated **Casa Luque** (Pl. Cavana 2, tel. 95/252-1004, closed Sun. A.M., Wed., and Jan., €36) offering beautifully rendered Andalusian food accented with creative twists. For a break from seafood, try their *cochinillo,* suckling lamb basted with honey and brown sugar. There is also a great tapas bar if you want a lighter meal.

Getting There and Around

From Málaga's airport you will need to take a bus to Málaga's bus station and transfer to a bus to Nerja's city center. The bus stop is just that, a stop, on Avenida de Pescia. An information booth is open 6 A.M.–9 P.M. and schedules are clearly posted on the stop. Buses to/from Málaga travel once an hour. The trip lasts 1.5 hours and costs under €5. If you are driving, take the A-7 East. In Nerja, everything you could want is within walking distance.

FUENGIROLA

Once a local fishing village, this Costa del Sol resort has unfortunately succumbed to high-rise development and package-tour mania. Downtown feels like any nameless resort town. Menus come in four languages, beers come in steins, and everyone speaks English. However, just inland from the beach, the local Spanish population is as Andalusian and traditional as anywhere else in the region. The contrast makes for a vacation that appeals to all.

Sights

The town's draw has always been its lovely beaches. **Playa Gaviotas,** where young, good-looking windsurfers come to play, is lined by the busy promenade **Paseo Marítimo Rey de España.** Farther from the center of town is the popular **Playa Torreblanca** and at **Playa Fuengirola,** near the port, you can watch the local fishermen at work.

For a Spanish cultural experience, visit the lively **Mercadillo** (street market) at the fairgrounds near Los Boliches (9 A.M.–2 P.M. Tues. and Sat.). It is the largest on the Costa del Sol and draws local residents in by the thousands.

Without doubt, the best time to visit Fuengirola is October 6–12 during **Feria del Rosario,** which honors El Virgen del Rosario (Virgen of the Rosary). Religious worship aside, this is a typically exuberant Andalusian festival which brings out the local *señoritas* dressed in their finest flouncy skirts, carnations tucked behind their ears. Their men folk don short-waisted coats and broad-brimmed hats. After parading around on horseback, all-night parties ensue with dancing and drinking until dawn. There are also bullfights and equestrian performances.

Visit the **tourist office** (Av. Jesús Santos Rein 6, tel. 95/246-7457, closed Sun.) for details on the beaches and events in Fuengirola and around.

Accomodations and Food

Hostal Marbella (C/ Marbella 34, tel. 95/266-4503, info@hostalmarbella.info, www.hostalmarbella.info, €60) offers newly renovated—though smallish—rooms with free Wi-Fi. The fun-loving Swedish staff are your best resource for restaurants, bars, and activities. **Hotel Yaramar** (Po. Marítimo Rey de España 64, tel.95/292-1100, www.yaramar.com, €210) is a high-rise hotel offering spacious, light rooms, many with balconies overlooking the sea. The location, right on the main promenade, is perfect.

Hermanos Blancos (Po. Marítimo Rey de España 7, tel. 95/211-9299, 10 A.M.–11 P.M. daily Apr.–Oct., closed Nov.–Mar.) is a long-standing *chiringuito* (beachside bar) on Playa de Santa Amalia offering the most delicious *espeto* (sardine skewers) and cold beer. It is extremely popular with locals—both Spanish and expat. **Casa Lozano** (C/ Larga 6, tel. 95/266-4980, closed Mon.), a quaint little restaurant near the Plaza de la Constitución, is known for their fish and paella.

Getting There and Around

Fuengirola is located on the coastal road A-7 (at times it is AP-7, a toll road). It is located just about midway between Málaga and Marbella. You can access the town via train from Málaga on the local C1 (www.renfe.es/cercanias). Fuengirola's train station is located on Avenida Jesús Santos Rein. You can easily walk around Fuengirola or catch very inexpensive cabs, however there is also a trolley that does a circuit on the main routes for under €3.

BENALMÁDENA

Benalmádena is made up of three parts. **Benalmádena Pueblo** and **Arroyo de la Miel** (which translates evocatively into "stream of honey") are both inland along a mountainside almost five kilometers (about three miles) from the coast. Benalmádena Pueblo is a hilly, whitewashed town with a beautiful church, **La Iglesia del Santo Domingo** and a garden, **Jardines Muro.** The family-friendly Arroyo de la Miel has an amusement park, **Tivoli** (Av. Tivoli, tel. 95/257-7016, www.tivoli.es, €16), for kids of all ages. This is also where the Renfe train from Malaga stops.

On the beach is **Benalmádena Costa.** It's package-tourist central and you'll be lucky to meet even one Spaniard here. In addition to lovely beaches stretching out from the city in both directions, the town boasts a fabulous wharf, **Puerto Marino,** and a casino at **Torrequebrada Hotel** (Av. Sol, s/n, tel.

95/244-6000, www.torrequebrada.com). A Moorish castle, **Castillo de Bil Bil,** is situated on the beach of the same name. With its rich color, decorated tiles, and exhilarating views, this castle is worth a peek. The **tourist office** (C/ Antonio Machado 10, tel. 95/244-2494, www.benalmadena.com) is located in this district of Benalmádena.

Accomodations and Food

The bulk of the housing and food options are in Benalmádena Costa. **Flatotel Internacional** (Av. Sol, s/n, tel., 95/244-5800, www.flatotel costadelsol.com, €115) offers a high-rise building with hotel rooms or one-, two-, and three-bedroom apartments. There is a lovely pool and all the usual resort amenities. It is located near the top-rated Torrequebrada Golf Club. **El Mero** (Puerto Deportivo, s/n, tel. 95/244-0752) is a great place for surf-and-turf, Andalucía-style. A bit more upscale, **Mar de Alborán** (Av. Alay 5, tel. 95/244-6427, closed Sun. P.M. and Mon., €35), next to the yacht harbor, offers Basque-influenced seafood dishes and an excellent wine list.

In the pueblo, stay at ☾ **La Fonda Hotel** (C/ Santo Domingo 7, tel. 95/256-8324, lafonda@ fondahotel.com, www.fondahotel.com, €85), a delightful small hotel built into an old whitewashed building. Rooms are brightly decorated and many open up onto the inner courtyard that boasts a pool. This is where you want to eat, too. The building houses a cooking school and the school-run restaurant, **El Balcón,** is excellent, though it is closed on weekends.

Getting There and Around

From Málaga's airport, take train C1 (www .renfe.es/cercanias for fares and schedules) to the Arroyo de la Miel station (Avenida Jesús Santos Rein). Drivers should take A-7—it should not take more than 20 minutes.

MARBELLA

In the years after the Civil War, Marbella was nothing more than a sleeping fishing village, bristling with lazy charm, cheap land, a warm year-round climate, and amazing sea views.

ANDALUCÍA

In the 1950s and 1960s, spurred on by Prince Alfonso de Hohenlohe-Langenbur, a visionary businessman of royal descent, the town transformed into the playground of choice for Europe's rich and famous. Before long, it was crammed with Hollywood starlets, sheiks, and dispossessed royals from around the world. Today, it is still a hot spot for Spain's *famosillos* (second-tier celebrities), Saudi royalty, and a handful of Hollywood hotshots—Antonio Banderas, Bruce Willis, and Michael Douglas all own mansions here. Their yachts clog the harbor and the country's top gossip rags cover their parties and social events in glossy spreads. However, unless you are packing some serious buying power and the elusive Spanish clout known as *enchufe* (contacts), you probably won't get access to their world. Stretching for kilometers on either side of the city are the private resorts, members-only restaurants, and guarded compounds where the Marbella aristocrats do their gossip-making.

Mere mortals can divide their time in the two worlds of everyday Marbella. **Casco Antiguo** (Old Village) is a labyrinth of pedestrian, cobblestone streets shimmering with laid-back Andalusian charm. On the waterfront, **Puerto Banus** feels like Miami Beach—fancy cars, fancy people, and fancy restaurants vie to be the fanciest. When the celebrities do come out to play, it is here—though more often than not, it is clogged with rich tourists—mainly Spanish and European—hoping for glimpse of the glittering high life.

Sights

The Casco Antiguo, still partially enclosed by Moorish walls, is small enough to stroll through in one day. While you do be sure to stop and smell the oranges in **Plaza de los Naranjos**, which is also home to the city's **tourist office** (tel. 95/282-3550). These narrow streets offer a wide range of shopping and dining options.

Once you've seen the old quarter, the beach should be your next stop. The best route is Avenida del Mar. As you stroll to **Playa El Fuerte** you will find a few bronze sculptures by Salvador Dalí and a number of outdoor seafood eateries

Marbella's Casco Antiguo

© SEVE PONCE DE LEON

off Paseo Maritimo. You can also catch a cab to **Playa Fontanilla,** another good sunbathing location. Once at the beach you will see a few *chiringuitos* (beachside bars) where you can grab a snack or cocktail. The sand is bit rocky, so the beach chairs (€4) are nice investment for the day.

To get to **Puerto Banus,** take a 30-minute bus ride (number 6 direct or 7 local from Avenida Ramón y Cajal or Avenida Ricardo Soriano, €1). If you really want to fit in, rent a convertible sports car and make the drive on your own—straight down Boulevard Príncipe Alfonso de Hohenlohe.

The Puerto Banus harbor is the perfect place to watch yachts and sports cars roll by while having an afternoon snack. It is a shopper's paradise with the likes of Fendi, Versace, Burberry, Dolce & Gabbana, Roberto Cavalli, Dior, Lacoste, Louis Vuitton, and Jimmy Choo all within walking distance of one another. Once you are shopped out, head to either **Playa Levante** or **Playa de Poniente** to indulge in some serious eye candy as impossibly beautiful Europeans cavort on the sand.

© SEVE PONCE DE LEON

Puerto Banus boasts sunny beaches, a vibrant nightlife, a wealth of fashion, and an unrivaled marina.

ANDALUCÍA

Nightlife

Hidden on a narrow street of Casco Antiguo is **Bambina** (C/ Pasaje 5), a wine bar with comfy black leather couches and funky lighting. You'll find a few other bars in the old quarter, but, for serious partying, you need to head to Puerto Banus. Dozens of trendy bar/lounge/restaurants line this harbor. Grab a table at the entrance and enjoy watching the masses of fashionable tourists go by. Just behind the waterfront is **Calle Ribera,** where you will find more than 20 flashy nightclubs, lounges, and bars, from Irish pubs to chic spaces. The prime bar-hopping time is between 11 P.M. and 2 A.M. Some bars open earlier, and the bigger clubs stay open until dawn on the weekends. In Plaza Antonio Banderas (yes, the actor—he was born in Málaga) you will find a few up-market hot spots where you can be sure to have a good time—as long as you are dressed to impress.

Dreamer's (Crta. Cádiz km. 175, Puerto Banus, tel. 95/281-2080, www.dreamers-disco .com) is one of Costa del Sol's most famed dance clubs. Hot DJs spin techno-tinged elec-tronica to a young crowd. The club is open nightly during the summer with parties last-ing until dawn. During the winter, days are reduced. Check their website for upcoming events. In the summer, **Nikki Beach** (Playa Hotel Don Carlos, Ctra. Cádiz, km. 192, tel. 95/283-6329, www.nikkibeach.com, 11 A.M.–2 A.M. daily June–Aug., 11 A.M.–8 P.M. Apr., May, and Sept., cover varies) is the playground of choice for jet-setters. Sprawling over a beach-side terrace, Nikki's offers cushy bed-sized seat-ing, tropical cocktails, go-go dancers, a roster of world-famous DJs, and a light menu of cre-ative Mediterranean fare.

Accommodations

Despite its glitzy sheen, Marbella does offer cheap accommodations, mainly in the Casco Antiguo. The liveliest is **Hostal del Pilar** (C/ Mesoncillo 4, Casco Antiguo, tel. 95/282-9936, www.marbella-scene.com, €40). Run by some fun-loving Scots, this is a budget traveler's delight with a pool table and a roof-top terrace. Rooms come in singles, doubles, or triples. **Hostal Berlin** (C/ San Ramón 21, tel. 95/282-1310, info@hostalberlin.com, www.hostalberlin.com, €60) is a modern, friendly facility offering small but comfortable rooms, Internet, and the use of a lovely tiled courtyard. **Hotel Don Alfredo** (C/ Portada 11, tel. 95/276-6978, info@hoteldonalfredo.com, www.hoteldonalfredo.com, €65) has clean, bright rooms and beautiful night-time views of the remains of a nearby 9th-century Moorish castle. This hotel also has a sister property, **Hostal Aduar** (C/ Aduar 7, tel. 95/277-3578, €60) near the Plaza de los Naranjos. Moving up the price scale, **◖ La Villa Marbella** (C/ Principe 10, tel. 95/276-6220, www.lavillamarbella.com, €150), a lovingly restored centuries-old building in the Casco Antiguo, offers a handful of individually decorated suites complete with all amenities and luxurious beds.

Moving towards Puerto Banus, the massive **Gran Meliá Don Pepe** (Avenida José Meliá, s/n, tel. 95/277-0300, gran.melia.don.pepe@solmelia.com, www.solmelia.com, €250) is located right on the beach and offers two enormous pools, updated rooms with grand vistas, and top-hotel services. Check online, as you can often get cut-rate prices at this Sol Meliá property. And unless they are included in your package, avoid the tired meal buffets. **Park Plaza Suites** (Paseo Marítimo de Benabola, s/n, tel. 95/290-9000, www.parkplazasuiteshotel.com, €250), located in the heart of Puerto Banus right above the harbor, offers spectacular sea views. The rooms are spacious, however the design is uninspired. **Gran Hotel Guadalpín Marbella and Spa** (Blvd. Príncipe Alfonso de Hohenlohe, tel. 95/289-9400, reservas@granhotelguadalpin.com, www.granhotelguadalpin.com, €270), located on the golden mile that connects downtown Marbella to Puerto Banus, offers pampered luxury and classic style along with a top-notch day spa. Nearby, **Marbella Club Hotel** (Blvd. Príncipe Alfonso de Hohenlohe, tel. 95/282-2211, reservas@marbellaclub.com, www.marbellaclub.com, €400 and up) is where it all started. This is the luxury hotel that Prince Hohenlohe built, begetting a resort that created Marbella the legend. Set in a lush, rambling grove of flowers and tropical trees, the resort boasts secluded villas, a world-class spa, swimming pools, exclusive bars, top-rated restaurants, and impeccable service.

Food

The majority of the restaurants in the Casco Antiguo are typical Andalusian. Along the beach, seafood restaurants abound. **Bodega la Venencia** (C/ Miguel Cano 15, tel. 95/285-7913, 1 P.M.–1 A.M. daily) offers a long roster of traditional Mediterranean tapas. Across the street, **El Burlaero** (C/ Miguel Cano 10, tel. 95/286-6112, noon–11:30 P.M. Mon.– Sat., closed Sun.) offers homey Spanish meals amid bullfighting memorabilia. **Bar Altamirano** (Pl. Altamirano 3, tel. 95/282-4932, 1–4 P.M. and 8–11 P.M. Thurs.–Tues., closed Wed.) offer 33 different seafood-based *raciones* (tapas sized for two)—it is considered by locals to be the best seafood joint in town. **Marisquería La Pesquera** (Pl. Victoria, s/n, tel. 95/276-5170, noon–11 P.M. daily) lets you choose your seafood right from their aquarium and serves it simply prepared to you on their lovely outdoor terrace. They also do a nice paella. **La Fonda de Marbella** (C/ Los Caballeros 4–6, tel. 95/290-3288, 1 P.M.–1 A.M. Mon.–Thurs., 7 P.M.–1 A.M. Fri.–Sat., closed Sun., €25) offers sophisticated local fare in their romantic open-air patio. Reservations suggested. **La Veranda** (C/ San Lázaro, tel. 95/285-7686, 8 P.M.–11 P.M. Mon.–Sat., €30) offers light French/Mediterranean fare. They also have a lounge area where you can enjoy a flavored hookah pipe as you chill out to smooth Spanish vibes. **The Orange Tree** (Pl. General Chinchilla 1, tel. 95/292-4613) offers modern takes on traditional fare with Asian and Arabic touches.

Restaurants in Puerto Banus include some of the best—and priciest in the country. The current darling is **Calima** (tel. 95/276-4252, dinner only, closed Sun. and Mon., €85), located in the Hotel Gran Meliá Don Pepe, has garnered praise from the world's culinary press. Chef Dani García starts with impeccable local ingredients, draws inspiration from traditional Andalusian fare, and then injects it with mad scientist techniques. Liquid nitrogen turns olive oil into popcorn-like morsels, perfect for garnishing seafood salads. His famed *sopa fría* (cold soup) menu offers a nuanced, textured, refreshing taste of Andalucía brimming with tastes of the sea and land.

Getting There and Around

Marbella is just 56 kilometers (35 miles) away from Málaga's airport. To arrive by car, take the A-7 from Málaga and follow the signs. There is a bus that runs directly from the airport to Marbella for under €5. From the Marbella bus station (Av. Trapiche, tel. 95/276-4400) take local bus 8 or 9 to Casco Antiguo for just €1.

Granada

More than anywhere else in the country, Granada remains proud of its ties with Islam, Judaism, and Christianity, and—unlike many other parts of the country—suffered greatly when the first two were torn from its social fabric. These days, most visitors come to the city to see the Alhambra Palace, one of the world's most dazzling buildings. But Granada is dotted with so many architectural jewels and culturally important monuments that it would be a shame to limit yourself to the Alhambra alone. From the evocative old Moorish quarter of the Albaicín to the gypsy caves of Sacromonte to the hundreds of bustling tapas bars spread deliciously all over the city, Granada entices all the senses. A local saying concludes, "there is no worse fate than to be blind in Granada." Take a walk around, get lost in its winding streets and in its delicious blend of cultures, drink from its ancient fountains gurgling along 900-year-old lanes, awe at the great brush of burnished copper that paints the Alhambra at each sunset, and you'll understand why. Granada, more than any other city in Spain, is a feast for the eyes.

HISTORY

Granada has been inhabited for millennia. Iberian tribes had camps here. The Greeks landed around 500 B.C. and named the town Elibyrge. Romans arrived late in the 3rd century B.C. and settled in the area around the El Albaicín. They called the town Illiberis. When the Visigoths pushed the Romans out, they turned the town into a military stronghold. A large Jewish community, named Gárnata, eventually built up the town. When the Moors arrived in 711, the Jews gave them their support and by 713, the city was in Muslim hands. It grew in fits and spurts, beleaguered by wars with Christians and infighting among the Muslim factions. However, by the early 11th century, Granada had secured its present name and was fast becoming a powerhouse in Al-Andalus, fueled by large-scale agriculture and trade. Eventually, settlements became concentrated on the northern hill rising on the slopes of the Río Darro, and by the 12th century, both military and mercantile strength had become concentrated in what we know today as the El Albaicín neighborhood. Under the control of the Nasrid sultanate, one of the most powerful of the Islamic dynasties in Al-Andalus, the city thrived and grew. The Alhambra was built during their reign. When the Cordoban caliphate lost their grip on the area after the Battle of Navas de Tolosa in 1212, the Christian armies began in earnest to chip away at the Muslim hold on power. By 1492, Granada was the only Muslim city that had yet to fall. That changed on January 2, 1492, when King Fernando and Queen Isabel's Reconquista troops captured the city. They gave its Muslim residents an ultimatum: Convert, or leave. Jews were expelled outright.

The conquest of Granada is considered the birth of modern Spain. It ended 800 years of Muslim rule and freed the Christians from the stress of constant warfare. They turned their energies to building a united nation. It was not

ANDALUCÍA

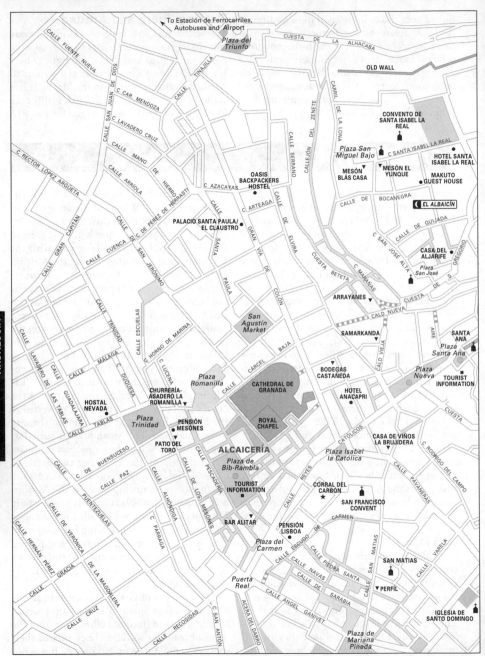

To Estación de Ferrocarriles, Autobuses and Airport

Plaza del Triunfo

CUESTA DE LA ALHACABA

OLD WALL

CALLE FUENTE NUEVA

C CAR. MENDOZA

C LAVADERO CRUZ

CALLE SAN JUAN DE DIOS

CALLE

TINAJILLA

CALLE SERRANO

CALLEJÓN DEL ZENETE

CARRIL DE LA LONA

CONVENTO DE SANTA ISABEL LA REAL

Plaza San Miguel Bajo

C SANTA ISABEL LA REAL

HOTEL SANTA ISABEL LA REAL

MESÓN BLÁS CASA

MESÓN EL YUNQUE

MAKUTO GUEST HOUSE

C. RECTOR LÓPEZ ARGÜETA

CALLE GRAN CAPITÁN

CALLE MANO DE HIERRO

CALLE ARRIOLA

C. AZACAYAS

C. ARTEAGA

OASIS BACKPACKERS HOSTEL

CALLE SANTA PAULA

GRAN VÍA DE COLÓN

CALLE DE ELVIRA

CALLE DE BOCANEGRA

EL ALBAICÍN

C SAN JOSÉ ALTA

C. SANTA

CALLE DE QUIJADA

CASA DEL ALJARIFE

GREGORIO

PALACIO SANTA PAULA/ EL CLAUSTRO

C DE PÉREZ DE HERRASTY

CALLE CUENCA

CALLE DE C. DE

SAN JERÓNIMO

CUESTA BETETA

C MARAÑAS

Plaza San José

DE S

CALLE TRINIDAD

CALLE MÁLAGA

C. DUQUESA

C. LUCENA

CALLE ESCUELAS

C HORNO DE MARINA

San Agustín Market

CARCEL BAJA

ARRAYANES

CALD NUEVA

CUESTA

CALD VIEJA

AIRE

SANTA ANA

Plaza Santa Ana

SAMARKANDA

CALLE LAVADERO DE LAS TABLAS

CALLE GUADALAJARA

CALLE

CALLE TABLAS

HOSTAL NEVADA

CHURRERÍA-ASADERO LA ROMANILLA

Plaza Romanilla

CALLE

SEVILLA

BODEGAS CASTAÑEDA

CATHEDRAL DE GRANADA

HOTEL ANACAPRI

Plaza Nueva

TOURIST INFORMATION

C. DE BUENSUCESO

CALLE PAZ

Plaza Trinidad

PENSIÓN MESONES

PATIO DEL TORO

CALLE PESCADERÍA

ALCAICERÍA

ROYAL CHAPEL

Plaza Isabel la Católica

CATÓLICOS

CASA DE VIÑOS LA BRUJIDERA

C RODRIGO DEL CAMPO

CALLE PUENTEZUELAS

CALLE DE LOS MESONES

CALLE REYES

CALLE PAVANERAS

CALLE HERNÁN PÉREZ

CALLE DE VERÓNICA

GRACIA

DE LA MAGDALENA

C PARRAGA

C. ALHÓNDIGA

Plaza de Bib-Rambla

TOURIST INFORMATION

BAR ALITAR

PENSIÓN LISBOA

Plaza del Carmen

CORRAL DEL CARBÓN

SAN FRANCISCO CONVENT

CARMEN

CALLE ESCUDO

CALLE PIEDRA SANTA

CALLE SAN MATIAS

SAN MATIAS

CALLE VARELA

CALLE CRUZ

C. SAN ANTÓN

ACERA DEL DARRO

Puerta Real

CALLE ANGEL GANIVET

CALLE NAVAS

CALLE DE SARABIA

PERFÍL

Plaza de Mariana Pineda

IGLESIA DE SANTO DOMINGO

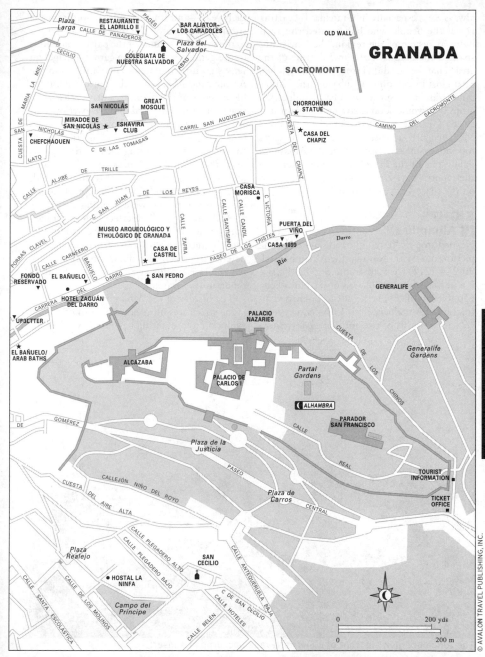

GRANADA

SACROMONTE

Plaza Larga
RESTAURANTE EL LADRILLO II
CALLE DE PANADEROS
PAGES
BAR ALIATOR-LOS CARACOLES
Plaza del Salvador
OLD WALL
CECILIO
COLEGIATA DE NUESTRA SALVADOR
ABAD
SAN NICOLÁS
GREAT MOSQUE
CHORROHUMO STATUE
MARIA LA MIEL
MIRADOE DE SAN NICOLÁS
ESHAVIRA CLUB
CAMINO DEL SACROMONTE
SAN NICHOLAS
CHEFCHAOUEN
CARRIL SAN AGUSTÍN
CUESTA DEL CHAPIZ
CASA DEL CHAPIZ
CUESTA
GATO
C DE LAS TOMASAS
ALJIBE
DE
TRILLE
DE LOS REYES
CALLE
CASA MORISCA
C. VICTORIA
PORRAS CLAVEL
C SAN JUAN
CALLE SANTISIMO
CALLE CANDIL
PUERTA DEL VIÑO
MUSEO ARQUEOLÓGICO Y ETNOLÓGICO DE GRANADA
CALLE ZAFRA
CASA DE CASTRIL
PASEO DE LOS TRISTES
CASA 1899
Darro
FONDO RESERVADO
EL BAÑUELO
CALLE CARNEERO
BAÑUELO
DARRO
SAN PEDRO
Rio
GENERALIFE
CARRERA
DEL
HOTEL ZAGUÁN DEL DARRO
UPSETTER
PALACIO NAZARIES
Generalife Gardens
EL BAÑUELO/ ARAB BATHS
ALCAZABA
CUESTA
DE
LOS
CHINOS
PALACIO DE CARLOS I
Partal Gardens
DE
GOMÉREZ
ALHAMBRA
PARADOR SAN FRANCISCO
Plaza de la Justicia
CALLE
REAL
CALLEJÓN NIÑO DEL ROYO
CUESTA
DEL
AIRE
ALTA
PASEO
Plaza de Carros
CENTRAL
TOURIST INFORMATION
TICKET OFFICE
CALLE PLEGADERO ALTO
CALLE PLEGADERO BAJO
SAN CECILIO
Plaza Realejo
CALLE ANTEQUERUELA BAJA
HOSTAL LA NINFA
Campo del Príncipe
C DE SAN CECILIO
CALLE HOTELES
CALLE BELEN
CALLE DE LOS MOLINOS
CALLE SANTA ESCOLASTICA

0   200 yds
0   200 m

always easy, especially in Granada. By getting rid of the people who had created the agricultural system of the region, the Christians sparked the gradual economic decline of the area. That decline didn't stop until 1898, when Spain lost its colonies in Cuba and the Philippines—and their sugar and tobacco industries, crops that would soon thrive on the plains between Granada and San Francisco de Loja. More recently, tourism has become the city's top money-maker: Not only is the Alhambra Palace one of the most-visited monuments in the country, but over 100,000 students descend on the city every year to study.

SIGHTS
◖ Alhambra

Nestled atop a forested hill and flanked by the picturesque Sierra Nevada, the Alhambra (tel. 90/244-1212, www.alhambra.org, 8:30 A.M.– 8 P.M. Mar.–Oct., 8:30 A.M.–6 P.M. Nov.–Feb., €10, Generalife €5) is the not-to-be-missed attraction of Andalucía. This 13th-century marvel sees upwards of two million eager visitors

each year—and understandably so. From the stunning views atop the fortress watchtowers, to the soothing sounds of the palace fountains, to the gentle aromas of the garden foliage, no senses go unstimulated. The name, from the Arabic *calat al-hambra* (the red castle), most likely refers to the plain, repetitive brick walls that create the heavy and massive exterior. This seemingly humble facade, however, only serves to contrast with the lively and mystical world that it conceals. Recalling the first time he entered the Alhambra, American author Washington Irving wrote, "we were transported, as if by magic wand, into other times and an Oriental realm, and were treading the scenes of Arabian story." The effect is pretty much the same today. With its seductive patios, delicate filigreed stucco, acres of marble, and ornately carved ceilings, doors, and arches, the Alhambra is worlds away from busy, bustling modern-day Granada.

The history of the Alhambra, like many Islamic structures of its era, is one of continual evolution, representing a dynamic work of art

The Alhambra glows in front of a Sierra Nevada backdrop at sunset.

rather than a static creation. Although a fortress had existed here since the 9th century, the Alhambra first began to take shape in 1238 thanks to the original emir of the Nasrid dynasty, Mohammed Al-Ahmar. It wasn't until the 14th century that the cherished Palacio Nazaríes was built by Yusuf I and his son Mohammed V. The structure then evolved to include the medina, fortress, and garden. As Granada was conquered in 1492, the site hosted the Christian court of Isabel and Fernando. After the Reconquista was complete, the Alhambra suffered a similar fate to that of Cordoba's Mezquita—modifications. Most notably, sections of the palace were destroyed during the reign of Carlos I to make room for his Renaissance-style palace (which was never completed). Such arguable blemishes would interrupt forever the original mystique and unity that the Islamic structure exuded.

By the 17th and 18th centuries, the Alhambra was neglected and became a refuge for the homeless. In 1808, it gave shelter to Napoleon's troops as the French attempted to sack Spain. Wreaking havoc, they proceeded to blow up various sections of the building. Were it not for a visionary defector who defused the explosives, the entire complex might have been destroyed. Hope for the beleaguered monument came some 20 years later when Washington Irving took up residence in the palace. His famous book, *Tales of the Alhambra,* published in 1832, reintroduced the abandoned wonder to the Western world. In 1870, Spain named the Alhambra a national monument and over the century extensive restoration was done to reclaim the building's original beauty. In 1984, UNESCO designated it a World Heritage Site.

The complex can be divided into four sections: the medina; the military fortress, Alcazaba; the palace, Palacio Nazaríes; and the gardens, better know as the Generalife. A typical tour begins with a walk through the **medina,** the ancient town that once provided homes for craftspeople, government officials, and servants. Although almost none of the original construction remains, the foundations and ruins of many typical Islamic-style houses and baths can be seen along the main street, Calle Real.

The **Alcazaba** fortress is the oldest and least well-preserved structure of the Alhambra. Though it once served as both a barracks and a center for military operations, all that remains are the main walls and several watchtowers. The latter afford panoramic views of the city and mountains. The undisputed attraction here—particularly for Spanish visitors and history buffs—is the **Torre de la Vela,** the site from which the Castilian flag was raised in 1492 after Isabel and Fernando's troops captured Granada.

The undisputed highlight of the Alhambra is the **Palacio Nazaríes,** an exemplary Islamic palace that has the habit of seducing visitors into lingering longer than they had anticipated. Originally housing the emirs of Granada, the interior would have been concealed from public view, kindling a flame of speculation surrounding the treasures that lay inside. Today, visitors enjoy its labyrinth of magnificent hallways and rooms, descending upon central courtyards and fountains. The wonderfully symmetrical patios are lined with myriad pillars and arches, made from exquisite marble and stucco, and decorated with colorful patterns and tiles—arguably the finest preserved Islamic architecture in the world.

The original palace was divided into three sections. The entrance, or **mexuar,** was a public hall where citizens would go to voice their requests to administrative officials. Later, the room was used as a residence by members of Carlos I's court. During that time, a baroque chapel was install in the room. It was later removed. What is left today is bland in comparison with the rest of the building, yet it does help prepare the visitor for what is about to come.

Next is the **serallo,** the main reception hall that used to welcome visitors. The jewel of this section, built for Yusuf I, is the **Palacio de Comares** and its central **Patio de los Arrayanes.** While taking in refreshing views of the graceful central pool, notice the unusual lack of symmetry rising above the southern end

© SEVE PONCE DE LEON

the reflecting pool of the Patio de los Arrayanes

of the palace. This was created by the imprudent destruction inflicted on the building to make room for the Palacio de Carlos I. Across the pool, the **Torre de Comares**—a prominent tower distinguishable from the neighboring Albayzín district—houses the finely decorated wooden ceiling of the **Sala de la Barca** (Boat Room). Although the ceiling resembles a boat, the name more than likely stems from its phonetic similarity to the original Arabic designation *barakah,* a term denoting spiritual wisdom or blessing.

The third and final section of the palace, the **harem,** was the private living quarters built for the successor and son of Yusuf I, Mohammed V. Here, linger in the precious **Patio de los Leones** and witness Islamic architecture at its finest. A forest of over 100 beautifully crafted marble pillars creates a truly magical world. If you can, arrive in the morning when the sunlight streams through in a fantastical dance of light. If you arrive later in the day—along with hundreds of other tourists—try to block out the sounds of cameras and mum-

bling and focus on the chorus of water as it flows from the four channels to the central fountain. Originally, the 12 lions were said to keep time, with water configured to flow from each successive lion on the hour. Unfortunately, when the Christian court did their remodeling, they sent the timekeeping secrets flowing right down the drain.

The three main rooms surrounding the patio—the **Sala de los Reyes,** the **Sala de los Abencerrajes,** and the **Sala de Dos Hermanas**—all beg to be explored as well.

Deriving from the Arabic phrase *jannat al-'arif* (Architect's Garden), the **Generalife** is the name given to the large complex of gardens dating from the 14th century. The name is most likely a reference to the Creator as the architect. Today, the complex includes flowerbeds, orchards, the summer palace, and a modern-day amphitheater. Strolling through the splendid aromas from the garden's flowers and herbs is a perfect way to end a visit to the Alhambra—in tranquility.

Straddling the Palacio Nazaríes is the

TICKETS TO THE ALHAMBRA

Only about 9,000 Alhambra entry tickets are sold per day, which means that anyone planning to visit the monument in high tourist season would do well to secure a ticket in advance. Only 2,000 tickets are reserved for same-day sales, so between Semana Santa (Easter week) and October visitors must be in line before 7 A.M. to get a place.

The easiest way to guarantee your ticket is to buy one online at **www.alhambra tickets.com.** The website, run by the Spanish BBVA bank, permits users to buy up to five individual tickets at once, with a commission charge of €0.88 per ticket. Tickets can also be purchased at any BBVA branch in Spain; the most centrally located one in Granada is in the Plaza Isabel la Católica, just west of the Plaza Nueva.

Additionally, tickets are available by **phone** (tel. 90/222-4460, 8 A.M.-6 P.M., VISA or MasterCard only). Same-day tickets must be purchased from the Alhambra ticket office itself. Conversely, you can't buy tickets in advance from the ticket office – that can only be done by phone, Internet, or visiting a BBVA branch directly.

When purchasing your ticket, you'll be of-fered a selection of times during either the morning or afternoon sessions when you can enter the Alhambra. Only 300 people are permitted to enter the Palacio Nazaríes during any given half-hour slot; pay special attention to this time, which will be printed on the ticket. You will not be allowed to enter the Palacio Nazaríes before or after this time.

When you buy your tickets over the phone or online, you'll be given a reference number for your purchase. Don't lose this number. You must present it, along with a passport or EU identification card, to collect your tickets at the ticket office.

If the thought of 8,000 people in a small place gives you the willies, consider a night-time visit. Not only is it less crowded (only 600 people can enter after dark), but the effect is magical, and made even better by a post-visit drink at the parador's bar.

Tickets to the Alhambra cost €10 for adults (for both day and night visits) and €7 for retirees. Children under eight can enter free, but require a ticket.

Get more information on tickets and the palace in general at www.alhambra.org or by calling 90/244-1212.

Palacio de Carlos I. Whereas the former demonstrates the light and organic style characteristic of Islamic architecture, the latter is a strictly heavy and imposing Renaissance-style palace. This sudden contrast makes the otherwise impressive structure appear obtrusive and simplistic. It houses the **Museo de la Alhambra** and the **Museo de Bellas Artes,** both of which contain interesting artifacts and paintings from the Alhambra and Granada.

For the best overall view of the building, you have to ascend into the Albaicín and head to the Mirador de San Nicólas, a lookout point that allows you to take in the Alhambra in all its glory.

To get to the Alhambra by bus, catch numbers 30 and 32, which run every few minutes and costs €0.90. **CitySightseeing** (tel. 90/210-1081, €10), Granada's hop-on, hop-off touristic bus also runs to the Alhambra. The best place to catch either their main bus or their mini-bus is on Calle Gran Vía de Colón, in front of the Cathedral. **By car,** it is recommended to take the Ronda Sur road in the direction of the Sierra Nevada and park in one of the two lots on the east side of the complex. **By foot,** begin in Plaza Nueva and walk up Cuesta de Gomérez. After arriving at the Puerta de Las Granadas, continue almost a kilometer (another half-mile or so) to the ticket office and entrance at the Puerta de La Justicia on the left. To get the most out of your visit, consider renting the audio guide (€3). It provides a comprehensive commentary on all the sights in the Alhambra.

If seeing the Alhambra with thousands of

ANDALUCÍA

other tourists doesn't suit your tastes, consider arriving first thing in the morning and proceeding directly to the Palacio Nazaríes to enjoy people-free photos and a relatively unhurried atmosphere, even during high season. (For more information on visiting, see sidebar, *Tickets to the Alhambra*.)

El Centro

The best place to start a foot tour of the center is the **Catedral de Granada** (Gran Vía de Colón 5, tel. 95/822-2959, 10:45 A.M.–1:30 P.M. and 4 P.M.–8 P.M. Mon.–Sat., 10:45 A.M.–1:30 P.M. Sun., €3). Designed by Diego de Siloé in the early 16th century and built in fits and starts as the money came in, the Cathedral features several interesting chapels, but the overall effect is slightly choppy. The most magnificent of the chapels is **Capilla Real** (C/ Oficios s/n, tel. 95/822-9239, www.capillarealgranada.com, 10:30 A.M.–1 P.M. and 4–7 P.M. Mon.–Sat., 11 A.M.–1 P.M.and 4–7 P.M. Sun., €3). Built between 1505 and 1517, the ornate Gothic chapel is the final resting place of Isabel and Fernando, the Catholic Monarchs. The simple lead coffins that you see in the crypt belong to (left to right) Felipe el Hermoso, the son-in-law of the monarchs; Fernando; Isabel; Juana la Loca (Joanna the Mad), their daughter; and Miguel, their eldest grandchild. It's easy to see that Isabella's tomb is slightly lower than Fernando's. The official reason is because Fernando, grandson of a Holy Roman Emperor, was "more royal" than his wife. Royal jokers, however, claim that, as the more intelligent of the two, Isabel's head weighed down more heavily into the lead casket. The really historic treasures are located in the chapel's sacristy: Fernando's sword and Isabel's scepter and personal art collection, which is heavy on Flemish works, but also has some outstanding Italian pieces.

Directly across Calle Oficios from the entrance to the chapel is the **Madraza,** which is the current home of the University of Granada's Translation and Interpretation faculty, but started out as an Islamic religious school when it was built in the early 15th century. The facade has been altered significantly since it was

first built, but the original prayer room, complete with domed ceiling, can still be visited when school's in session. At the far end of Calle Oficios lies the **Alcaicería,** located on the site of the former silk market. The buildings in the current configuration aren't original (the area was rebuilt in the 19th century) but the narrow streets are charming when they're not choked with people. Look carefully beyond the Moroccan sandals and windsocks and you'll be able to find some of the city's more traditional merchants, such as **Feliciano Foronda** (C/ Zacatín 22, tel. 95/821-5125, 10 A.M.–2 P.M. and 5–7 P.M. Mon.–Fri., 10 A.M.–2 P.M. Sat., closed Sun., selling embroidered *mantones de Manila,* traditional Spanish silk shawls.

On the other side of Calle Reyes Católicos, the **Corral del Carbón** can easily be seen from the street. Its keyhole arch once marked the entrance to the *caravanserai* (lodgings for traveling merchants). There's not much to be seen once you get through the arch. The city council hasn't quite decided what to do with the property, but in the summer flamenco concerts are held in this space.

Heading back up to Plaza Isabel la Católica and then down to the end of Calle Pavanes (and its continuation, Calle Santa Escolástica), you reach the **Realejo** neighborhood. This was the location of the lively Jewish quarter, **Garnata al Yahud,** established even before the Moors arrived and not dismantled until the Christians arrived in 1492. It is a charming tangle of streets, perfect for wondering, however the **Campo del Príncipe** is the place you'll want to end up. This "Field of the Prince" was originally built by the Catholic Monarchs to celebrate the wedding of their short-lived son Juan. Later it was used as a parade ground for Carlos V. Today, the entire south side of the square is lined with a dozen different tapas bars and restaurants, frequented more by Granada residents than tourists.

South of the Plaza del Realejo sits the **Iglesia de Santo Domingo** (tel. 95/722-7331), currently open only during services. Not long after the Catholic Kings rode triumphantly into the city of Granada, the land (which had previously belonged to Aixa, the mother of King Boabdil, the last Moorish emperor of Al-Andalus) was given to the Dominican brothers so they could construct a monastery and chapel. The Dominicans were kicked a political uprising in the mid-1830s, but the church was returned to their control in 1951.

◖ El Albaicín

Sloping up the hillside in a jumble of white-washed buildings is the atmospheric Albaicín, the center of old Moorish Granada. Described by a 17th-century poet as "a paradise closed to many," the barrio is honeycombed with narrow cobblestone streets, secluded plazas bursting with bright flowers, mosques rebuilt as churches, and horseshoe-shaped arches so distinctive in Islamic art. The barrio faces the Alhambra on the opposite of the Darro valley.

Plaza Nueva, with its clutch of impressive buildings, is the natural starting place. On the north side rises the imposing facade of **Real Chancillería.** This was the building from which the Catholic Monarchs ruled over the newly established Kingdom of Granada. Now it is home to the city's main courthouse. On the other side is the **Iglesia de Santa Ana,** a former mosque. Soon after the plaza was first built in the early 1500s, tens of thousands of books were pulled out from the Muslim library and torched in front of this church. The name "Plaza Nueva" (New Plaza) refers to the fact that the Christians didn't build this plaza until the 16th century, hence it was newer than the surrounding city. Originally, it consisted of a series of bridges crossing the Río Darro. Eventually, they were paved together and now the river flows beneath the plaza.

Be sure and stop at the tourist office in the plaza to get maps and up-to-date information on the Albaicín. Also, if you are not the hiking-uphill type, there is a local bus 31, which leaves from the plaza and does a loop through the barrio. Sit on the right for the best views. The fare is less than €1. A word of caution, as one of the busiest squares in Granada, Plaza Nueva draws quite a few unsavory types, drug users, and petty thieves. Exercise personal safety here

and be on full alert if you are in this neighborhood at night. Remember these thieves are looking for easy victims. Don't be one.

Moving up and eastward, the street known as the **Carrera del Darro** contains a number of noteworthy sights. **El Bañuelo** (C/ Darro 31, tel. 95/802-7800) houses a marvelously preserved set of Arab baths. Built in the 11th century, the various rooms of the complex are illuminated with star-shaped skylights, and the capitals (the top stones in the columns) were salvaged from Roman and Visigothic remains. After the Moors were forced out of Granada, the rooms were used for various different purposes, among them a wash house. El Bañuelo will be closed until mid-2007 for renovations. After that time, check with the tourist office for visiting hours. The Renaissance **Casa de Castril** (C/ Darro 43) features an exuberant facade. The interior boasts a large courtyard from which you can see the towers of the Alhambra. Today, it houses the **Museo Arqueológico y Etnológico de Granada** (tel. 95/822-5603, 2:30–8:30 P.M. Tues. 9 A.M.– 8:30 P.M. Wed.–Sat., 9 A.M.–2:30 P.M. Sun., €1.50), an impressive collection of artifacts that reveals Granada's history from prehistoric times through the Moors to the Christians.

Unfortunately, many of the churches along this road—such as the **Iglesia de San Pedro y San Pablo**, hanging picturesquely over the river gorge across from Calle Zafra—aren't open on a regular basis (though no one seems to mind if you poke your nose in before or just after religious services). Keep in mind that all of these churches were once mosques. Strolling further up, the Carrera del Duero turns into **Paseo de los Tristes,** the "road of the sad ones," so named because before the advent of the automobile, locals had to carry their dead up this road to get to the cemetery at the top of the hill.

At the end of the paseo, the **Cuesta del Chapiz** turns left and proceeds to take you up a leg-burning ascent into the heart of the Albaicín. The stately-yet-abandoned home that you see on your right is the **Casa de Chapiz.** Built in the style of the Alhambra in the 16th century, it was reclaimed and renovated as the local university's School of Arabic Studies, but has since fallen on hard times and been closed.

Throughout the Albaicín, you'll see that the streets are dotted with waist-high arches of sand-color brick that have been boarded up. These are *aljilbes,* the former water wells of the Moorish El Albaicín. In the 14th century, residents drew water from over 30 of these reservoirs scattered throughout the neighborhood. Some have run dry, while others have been fitted with faucets and the fresh, cold water is perfectly safe to drink. Have a drink of history!

Further up, the street opens up into the **Plaza del Salvador** home to the **Colegiata de Nuestra Salvador.** It is called *colegiata* rather than *iglesia* because its original, 16th-century purpose was to teach Christianity to the Moors. Before that it was a mosque and the courtyard of ablutions, where the Muslims washed their feet before entering the mosque, remains intact in the cloister of the church. A few years back, Salvador was nearly converted back into a mosque at the request of local Muslims. The Christian community balked. Salvador had become one of their most emblematic churches (the processions for the local **Fiestas de San Miguel del El Albaicín** begin from here). Instead, a grand mosque, the **Mezquita Mayor de Granada** (tel. 95/820-1903, info@ granadamosque.com, www.granadamosque .com) was eventually built nearby on Plaza de San Nicolás.

From Colegiata Salvador, **Calle de Panaderos** (Bakers' Street) leads past a clutch of food shops, butchers, vegetable markets, and yes, bakeries. At its end is **Plaza Larga,** the pulsating heart of Albaicín. In Moorish times, it was the location of the market. Today, most mornings bring in a modern market where you can by everything from cheap ceramics to tie-dyed sarongs to pirated DVDs. Be sure to visit a fruit stand for a *chumbo,* a prickly pear fresh-picked in nearby Sacromonte. The vendor will gladly peel it for you for a few *centímos* tip. The tree-lined square is lined with cafés and come evening their tables and chairs replace the market.

At the end of the plaza stands the **Puerta Nueva.** This "New Gate" was built in the 11th century, making it older than the Alhambra. It leads through the 8th-century city walls. Wind along the lane (following the crowds!) to the **Plaza Mirador de San Nicolás.** This tree-lined plaza sits on one of the most picturesque overlooks in the world. From here you can see over the Alhambra and into the Sierra Nevada mountains beyond. At sunset, the falling rays paint the Alhambra an unforgettable shade of coppery red. The name Alhambra comes from the Arabic *calat al-hambra,* "the red castle." From here it is easy see why. This will be a view you won't forget for the rest of your life. And maybe, like President Clinton who first witnessed it as a college student, you'll be impelled to return years later, your family in tow.

Unfortunately, the Albaicín (and Granada in general) requires a few words of caution. Granada has a bigger problem with petty crime and drugs than it would like to admit. The police are ineffectual and the city seems under no desire to do something about the problem. It is up to you, the visitor, to be alert and be smart. The thieves go after people they think are easy prey and loaded down with goodies. Always be aware of your surroundings. Enjoy the views and wander about, but if you feel uncomfortable or notice someone standing too close to you, walk away or duck into a shop or bar quickly. There are several main scams on the Albaicín. First, watch out for young teens talking on cell phones or pay phones but not speaking. They are often casing out the crowd, looking for victims who seem easy to rob. Second, avoid at all costs older women who try to push a sprig of rosemary on you. It seems sweet enough, but in the transaction, someone else will be picking your pocket. Say no and walk away. Second, be wary of diversions. At Mirador de San Nicolás, groups of thieves often work together to create a distraction; it could be as amusing as an impromptu flamenco performance or something as ugly as a violent fight. While the crowd is distracted, thieves mingle in picking pockets. So how to not look like a victim? Keep your possessions to a minimum and firmly attached to your body at all times. Backpacks in front, purses small and worn across the body, cameras and video cams tightly strapped to your wrist. Try to avoid walking down deserted roads, but if you must, keep your senses on full alert, know exactly where you are heading, and do it fast. (See sidebar, *Don't Be a Victim,* in the *Barcelona* chapter.)

Other Barrios

The university area slightly northwest of the Cathedral has two very remarkable buildings. The 16th-century **Monasterio de San Jerónimo** (C/ Rector López Argueta 9, tel. 95/827-9337, 10 A.M.–1:30 P.M. and 4–7:30 P.M. Mon.–Sat., 11 A.M.–1 P.M. and 4–7:30 P.M. Sun., €3) should not be missed. Like the Cathedral, this building features a number of important features designed by Diego de Siloé, but the overall effect—especially the two evocative Renaissance patios—is much warmer and welcoming. Check out the church, which was painstakingly restored after having been used as military barracks. The Monastery is also the final resting place of Gonzalo de Córdoba, *El Gran Capitán,* one of the great liberators of Spain from the Muslims. If you're looking for a deliciously unique souvenir, you can buy cakes and marmalade from the nuns who currently reside in the Monastery.

One block northeast, heading towards Gran Vía, is the **Hospital de San Juan de Dios** (C/ San Juan de Dios 23) founded in 1552 as a hospital for orphans and currently used as a local health center. The attractions here are the two Renaissance patios, both of which retain their original frescoes; the hallway linking the two has a sadly disintegrating fresco depicting the saint's miracles. Though there's no charge to enter the complex, it is technically only open to patients and their visitors. However, if you pass by on the weekend, there is usually no problem entering as the nurses and doctors are much more amenable to peering eyes than the porters who stand guard during the week.

West of the center of town, the Huerta de San Vicente park houses the **Casa-Museo Federico García Lorca** (C/ Virgen Blanca, s/n, tel. 95/825-8466, www.huertadesan vicente.com, 10 A.M.–1 P.M. and 5–8 P.M. Tues.–Sun. Apr.–June and Sept., 10 A.M.–1 P.M. and 4–7 P.M. Tues.–Sun. Oct.–Mar., 10 A.M.–3 P.M. Tues.–Sun. July and Aug., closed Mon. year-round, €1.80). This museum transports visitors back to the early 1900s and the world of Federico García Lorca, Spain's most international playwright and unofficial gay martyr. The house (which still contains the original image of Saint Vincent purchased by the playwright's father) recreates the atmosphere as it would have been when García Lorca spent summers there as a young man. His bedroom contains one of the few surviving posters printed for his traveling theater company, La Barraca, and his piano still rests in the downstairs salon—the tour guides are only too happy to give you a list of the notable musicians who have since played it. It is a must for fans of this esteemed writer. For others, it is nice, but not much more.

Sightseeing Tours

Cicerone Walking Tours (tel. 62/041-2051 or 67/054-1669, info@ciceronegranada.com, www.ciceronegranada.com) offers interesting—and very informative—walking tours of the center of the city. The 2.5-hour walks are guaranteed every day, rain or shine, and depart from the Plaza del Carmen at 10 A.M. in the summer, 11 A.M. the rest of the year. The cost is €10.

By bus, **City Sightseeing Granada** (www.sevillacomercio.com/cityss, €12.40 adult, €6.40 kids) offer hop-on, hop-off tours on two different routes. The "Monumental Tour" winds through the city, making 10 stops that include the Capilla Real and the Alhambra. The "Romantic Tour" uses a mini-bus to get up into the Albaicín. It makes five stops. Buy tickets at the tourist office or on one of the buses. Plaza Nueva is a stop and transfer point between the two lines. However, if you are considering the bus, it might make more sense

© SEVE PONCE DE LEON

With 124 slender marble columns, the Alhambra's Patio de los Leones is one of Spain's jewels.

to purchase the **City Pass** (www.granadatur .org). Created by the tourism board of the city, the City Pass includes a 24-hour ticket for the City Sightseeing bus, entrance to several monuments (including the Alhambra, Generalife, and the Capilla Real), a pass for nine trips on the city bus system, and discounts at a host of restaurants, bars, and shops. You can buy it at the ticket offices at the Alhambra or the Capilla Real or at the Caja General de Ahorros bank on Plaza Isabel la Católica 6. However, if you are jetting into Granada for just a day or two in peak summer season, you may find that there are no available spots open for the Alhambra. In that case, order it in advance at www.caja-granada.es. Then click Entradas, and Bono Turístico. At this point, you will finally be given an "English" option. You can also order by phone at 90/210-0095. When you purchase your pass you will be required to schedule your Alhambra visit. Finally, if you prefer a private guide, contact the **Granada Tourist Guides Association** (Pl. Nueva 2, tel. 95/822-9936).

ENTERTAINMENT AND EVENTS
Nightlife

Given the number of Spanish and foreign students who study in the city, it's kind of surprising to see that Granada's nightlife doesn't match the *marcha* seen in Seville or Málaga. It exists—just on a much lower key. One surefire way to keep on top of the latest offerings for both bars and clubs is to check out the sides of the pay phones in the Plaza Bib-Rambla and the Plaza Nueva. They'll be plastered in posters announcing the latest gigs.

No self-respecting jazz or flamenco fan would ever dream of visiting Granada and not going to the **Eshavira Club** (C/ Postigo de la Cuna 1, just off C/ Azacayas). Owner Juan functions as a kind of godfather figure to musicians of all ages and experience, and part of the fun is seeing just who drops in. Drinks cost €5 and the cover for live concerts is just €8 (including your first drink). Newer, but with similar offerings, is **Upsetter** (Carrera del Darro 7). Steps from the Plaza Nueva it offers jazz, flamenco, salsa, reggae, and all kinds of world music performances. If you need a little late-night action of the booty-shaking kind, head to a dance club **Fondo Reservado** (Cuesta de Santa Inés 4, tel. 95/822-2375) bills itself coyly as a "night-time pub." However, it is a full-on funhouse with a crowded dance floor, thumping house music, drag shows, and theme parties. It draws a diverse crowd of, well, every-one—locals, tourists, gay, straight, students. If you're in town in February, their Carnival party is not to be missed. **Perfíl** (C/ Rosario, at C/ Navas) in Realejo is probably the most clas-sic club a la Ibiza. Dress up and slap on the atti-tude. The music is a mix of techno, house, and a bit of Spanish pop. **La Sal** (C/ Santa Paula 11, near San Agustín market) is Granada's old-est gay bar. Once you are past the imposing she-bouncer from Galicia, you'll find a tiny, crowded dance bar and a boisterous crowd of attractive young, preppy types. A lot of women (lesbian and not) come here.

Flamenco

While bars like the Eshavira often host fla-menco nights, seeing a full-on flamenco show in Granada requires a trip to Sacromonte, the traditional *gitano* (Andalusian gypsy) barrio. For decades the *gitanos* lived in caves called *zambras* all along the barrio's main strip, Camino de Sacromonte. After a torrential rain-fall flooded the caves in the 1950s, most of the *gitanos* were moved out to low-income housing on the outskirts of town. Since then, the caves have been restored and now host flamenco shows and restaurants. The tourist office can provide a complete list and can even arrange transport from your hotel if you'd rather not go on your own. Purists will haughtily decry the-ses places, but they are an enjoyable, even mov-ing, introduction to flamenco. Also, while it's easy for the self-proclaimed flamenco expert to trash the quality of the performances, keep in mind that the majority of Granada's most famous artists earn their crust performing in places like these. One charming *zambra* that always puts on a good show is **Venta el Gallo** (Barranco de los Negros 5, just off the Camino

de Sacromonte, tel. 95/822-2492 or 95/822-8476, ventaelgallo@hotmail.com, www .ventaelgallo.com). They are partnered with another solid venue, **Los Tarantos** (Camino de Sacromonte 9, www.cuevas-los-tarantos .com). Shows at both usually run 9 P.M. and 10 P.M. and cost upwards of €35 per person (prices vary widely). Los Tarantos will pick you up from your hotel and also offer a walking tour of Sacromonte.

For something closer to pleasing a purist, **Bar el Flamenco** (C/ Vereda del Enmedio at Camino de Sacromonte) is worth checking out, if only to see who shows up there after they finish their show for tourists. It gets started 1 A.M. or later, if at all. If you do luck upon a performance, it will be skin-tinglingly, heart-clutchingly good. Another option, out-side of the summer months, is to pay a visit to one of the two *peñas* (private social clubs) operating in the city. The **Peña Flamenca la Platería** (Patio de los Aljives, 13, near San Miguel Bajo, 10 P.M.–close, Fri. and Sat. only) in the Albaicín has been going for nearly 100 years. Many of the city's biggest names got their start here. The only downside is the ad-missions policy, which sometimes allows non-members and sometimes doesn't (though one or two people can usually get in with a smile and some charm). **El Niño de los Almendras** (corner of C/ Muladar de Doña Sancha and C/ Tiña, look for "Peña de Socios" on the wall) is a semi-private *peña* run by the first non-*Gitano* vocalist in the city to make a living at sing-ing. El Niño only opens on Friday nights (and things don't get started until at least midnight) but when you get in there, it's hard to know which is the more incredible—the "Alice-in-the-Rabbit-Hole" feeling of the place, or the quality of the artists who come to blow off steam. The host is more than happy to give you a tour of all the rooms of his house, and his collection of flamenco memorabilia.

In the summer, there are various flamenco shows scheduled by the city. One of the best is **Los Veranos del Corral,** held in the atmo-spheric Corral de Carbón in August and Sep-tember. Also look out for performances by

ALL ABOUT SEMANA SANTA

Though Semana Santa (Easter Week) is celebrated throughout Spain, in few places does it reach such passionate heights as it does in Andalucía. The most spectacular and solemn of events occur in cities such as Sevilla, Córdoba, Granada, and Málaga, but even the smallest towns throughout the region hold elaborate Semana Santa processions. Every night, from Domingo de Ramos (Palm Sunday) through to Domingo de Resurrección (Easter Sunday), ornate flower-bedecked floats bearing life-sized figures from the Passion of Christ are paraded through the streets borne on the backs of up to 100 men. They are accompanied by hooded figures, bearing crosses, candles, and incense burners. It is an astonishing, moving sight whether you understand it or not. However, a little bit of information will increase your awe of and respect for this most venerated of Spanish and Roman Catholic events.

HISTORY

The origins of Semana Santa processions go back at least to the 14th century, though many of the current groups were formed in the 17th century – which is also when the bulk of the dramatic figures that are carried through the streets were created. For centuries, a philosophy of penance was part of the processions and those accompanying the parade would practice acts of self-mutilation. In the 18th century, a royal decree outlawed this behavior, yet it still exists to some degree. A group of Semana Santa penitents in San Vicente de la Sonsierra in La Rioja indulge in self-flagellation with spike-covered belts. In Andalucía, you'll most likely notice penitents walking barefoot as a mild form of self-abasement.

Though the processions have traditionally been limited to Roman Catholic groups, in 2005 with the support of the city council of Torrevieja in Alicante, a group of British expats formed the first foreign brotherhood. Their first procession was warmly greeted by locals, who were generally honored that the foreigners wanted to support their sacred traditions.

Today, Semana Santa in Andalucía is one of the most important events of the calendar. Many of the processions have been designated national cultural treasures and thousands of tourists and locals pour into the cities to see the processions each year. Crowd estimates at some of Sevilla's more famous processions regularly top one million. Be sure to make reservations well ahead of time if you want to witness this evocative spectacle.

WHO

The processions are carried out by brotherhoods called *cofradías*. These groups have long, illustrious names and are associated with particular neighborhood churches. Sevilla has nearly 60 brotherhoods with hundreds of members each. Members of the brotherhoods play different roles during the procession. The *nazarenos* are the most distinctive. Dressed in colorful, silky robes, they wear tall, pointy hoods that cover their faces completely with only two slits for their eyes. This costume has led many spectators to comment that the outfits are reminiscent of the Ku Klux Klan. This is a highly disgraceful comparison. The centuries-old traditions of Semana Santa have nothing to do with the idiotic and shameful racism of some very ugly Americans.

Penitentes (penitents) also march with the procession. They are dressed as the *nazarenos* but they do not have the inner cardboard cone in their hood (called a *capirote*), therefore their hoods hang down on their backs. These are the figures who will most likely be barefoot – not a pleasant experience as the thousands of spectators who line the streets awaiting the procession traditionally eat sunflower seeds, littering the ground with the sharp-edged, sticky shells. Many of the penitents also carry heavy crosses.

Perhaps the most important group within the brotherhood is the *costaleros*, which roughly translates as the "bearers." These hearty men lift the heavy floats onto their backs and carry them on their route to and from the cathedral. Often they are under the float, hidden from view of the spectators except for their espadrille-clad feet.

WHAT

The main focus of the processions are the *pasos*, the floats that bear the images of Christ and the Virgin Mary. In some regions these floats are called *tronos* (thrones). The floats are extremely elaborate, often covered in flowers and featuring hundreds of electric candles, silver candelabras, palm trees, hanging plants, and religious decoration of all manner.

Most brotherhoods will carry two floats. The *Paso del Cristo* features a life-sized statue of Christ in a scene from the Passion. The images can be very gory, graphically displaying the bloody wounds that Christ suffered. The second float is called *El Paso Palio* and it bears a luminous statue of *La Virgen*, also called *La Dolorosa* (the pained Virgin), *La Amargura* (the bitter Virgin), or more optimistically, *La Esperanza* (the hopeful Virgin). The life-sized statue is set under an elaborate canopy of velvet fabric and dressed in *El Manto*, a long-flowing, delicately embroidered cape that hangs over the back of the float.

The statues, many of which date back several centuries, are carved of solid wood. Some feature silver or gold plating. Along with all the decorations, plus a few car batteries to power the lights, a typical *paso* can weigh over 450 kilograms (1,000 pounds), and in the truly intricate floats typical in Málaga and Sevilla, over 1,000 kilograms (more than a ton). The *costaleros* who carry the float train for months and many spots on the "*costalero* team" are passed down through the generations from grandfather to father to son. Though the heavy weight of the float demands that the *costaleros* be in shape, it is not unusual to see middle-aged men among the bearers.

The *costaleros* carry the float through the narrow streets using a very hypnotic swaying motion. As many of them are in the dark beneath the float, they take their cues from the *capataz*, the pace-keeper who calls out orders to guide the float correctly through the streets.

Many processions are accompanied by a marching band of drums and horns. They provide a steady beat to help the *costaleros*. The procession has several scheduled stops during the route, at which point the band performs a mournful song called the *saeta*, literally an "arrow to the heart."

The routes of the processions were established by royal decree in the 17th century and basically follow a path from the local church to the cathedral and back. Most processions begin after sunset and may continue until the wee hours of the morning.

THE CROWD

The crowd that gathers to watch the event is called *la bulla*. It is heavily peppered with little old *señoras* dressed in black and clutching rosaries. Entire families with kids propped up on shoulders are also very common. Of course, there are also many camera-wielding tourists, both Spanish and foreign. Unlike those of so many Spanish festivals, Semana Santa crowds are solemn and silent. The procession is a serious, sacred affair. Loud talking, drinking, and general revelry is frowned upon. The one time *la bulla* does get rowdy is when the Virgin's float passes by. Many people call out "*Guapa!*" ("Beautiful!"), while others are reduced to tears. Occasionally, clapping breaks out. You may be surprised to find that you are moved as well.

MORE INFORMATION

The Internet teems with information on Semana Santa, but one of the best resources comes from the Sevilla tourism board, www.guiasemanasanta.com. The site recently added an English version. Also, always visit the tourist office in the town where you are attending Semana Santa. You will be able to pick up a local guide that will offer background information on each of the brotherhoods as well as practical information on the routes and times of the processions.

ANDALUCÍA

the **Ballet Flamenco de Andalucía,** a world-renowned ensemble. They've been known to mount shows in the gardens of the Generalife.

Festivals and Events

Although it doesn't reach the same intensity (or have the same number of brotherhoods) as Sevilla or Málaga, **Semana Santa** is played out with just as much passion and dedication in Granada as anywhere else in Andalucía. The main processions to watch out for are the **Virgen de la Aurora,** whose float leaves the Santa Isabel church in the Albaicín on Calle San Miguel Bajo and can be subjected to much football-style cheering by the local teenage girls. Visit the tourist office for complete details. Also check out www.granadamap.com/santa.

Several weeks later, during the week of May 3, Granada hosts the colorful **Feria de las Cruces** (Crosses Festival). In most of the major plazas in town, immense carnation-covered crosses are erected. There are also fun fairs and food booths in the various neighborhoods. Don't be surprised if local children, bearing crudely built and decorated crosses, hit you up for a donation to defray the costs of their *cruz* (cross).

In late June and early July, the city bustles with creative activity during the **Granada Festival of Music and Dance** (www.granada festival.org), which features all kinds of musical performances, from opera to ballet to whirling dervishes.

ACCOMMODATIONS
Under €50

Just steps from the Plaza de la Trinidad and the Plaza Bib-Rambla, **Pensión Mesónes** (C/ Mesónes 44, tel. 95/826 3244, Mesónes44@ hotmail.com, €38) has 12 rooms plus one suite that sleeps three or four. Rafael and Filo, the husband-and-wife team in charge, run a spick-and-span establishment that's decked out in cheery yellow and blue plaid. Nearby, the **Hostal Nevada** (C/ Tablas 8, tel. 95/825 9223, info@hostalnevada.com, www.hostal nevada.com, €48) has clean, comfy rooms plus a cute Andalusian-tiled garden. Unlike a lot of establishments in this category, they also offer

parking (€11 per day). **Pensión Lisboa** (Pl. Carmen 27, tel. 95/822-1413, www.lisboaweb .com, €48) overlooks the Plaza Carmen and offers simple but clean rooms and a very unintentionally kitsch wood-panelled lobby.

In recent years, budget accommodations—especially youth hostels—have been popping up in the cracks and corners of El Albaicín. **Makuto Guest House** (C/ Tiña 18, tel. 95/880 5876, info@makutoguesthouse.com, www.makuto guesthouse.com, €15 for a dorm bed) is located steps from the Plaza San Miguel Bajo. This converted home is decked out in Moroccan style full of trippy colors, floor pillows, and a flowering garden laden with hammocks. Breakfast is included and guests have access to a kitchen and the Internet, plus the option to take half-a-dozen courses—including flamenco and wine-tasting lessons. The hostel also has two double rooms with private kitchen and bath (€45) in the same fun, funky style. **Oasis Backpackers Hostel** (C/ Placeta Correo Viejo 3, tel. 95/821-5848, www.oasisgranada.com, €15 for a dorm bed) is part of a mini-chain of Spanish youth hostels that offer a hip style and fun atmosphere in a traditional setting. In Granada, the setting is a refurbished Albaicín house with an plant-filled inner courtyard, a large private terrace, an outdoor grill, plus backpacker amenities like free Internet, free breakfast, sponsored theme parties, walking tours, and events. One double is available for €36, but you'll have to share facilities with the rest of the hostel.

€50-100

Hotel Anacapri (C/ Joaquín Costa 7, tel. 95/822-7477, reservas@hotelanacapri.com, www.hotelanacapri.com, €90) remains a perennial travelers' favorite for its central location and its friendly service. The courtyard lounge is a spectacular retreat of marble and sunshine. Didn't book those Alhambra tickets before arriving? Beat the crowds by staying at **Hotel Guadalupe** (Po. Sabica, s/n, tel. 95/822 3423, guadalupeh@infonegocio.com, www .hotelguadalupe.es, €95), located directly across from the Alhambra's parking lot. This classically styled hotel features big, colorful rooms and a great terrace overlooking the Alhambra. If your idea of a good time is to *tapa* yourself silly and collapse into bed, you can't do much better than the whimsical ◖ **Hostal La Ninfa** (C/ Campo del Príncipe, s/n, tel. 95/822-7985 or 95/822-7985, reservaslaninfa@hotmail .com, www.hostallaninfa.net, €55), located on *the* street for tapas in Granada. Covered with painted ceramic stars and flowers, the Ninfa has 16 singles, doubles, and triples—all with en-suite bathrooms, television, and air-conditioning. The same owners run the Ninfa pizzeria on the other side of the square. Remember, this is an old building in a busy zone, so if you are light sleeper, bring earplugs.

In El Albaicín, **Casa del Aljarife** (C/ Placeta de la Cruz Verde 2, tel. 95/822-2425, most@ wanadoo.es, www.casadelaljarife.com, €95) has charming 17th-century rooms facing out onto one of the barrio's quieter *plazuelas*. Christian, the affable German owner, will come pick you up from the Plaza Nueva to save you getting lost. **Hotel Zaguán del Darro** (Carrera del Darro 23, tel. 95/821-5730, info@hotelzaguan.com, www .hotelzaguan.com, €75) is a precious little hotel on one of the Albaicín's most evocative streets. Built in 1563, the restored house has rooms full of antiques, thick floral drapes, Andalusian tiles, and heavy shutters to block out the sun. Open them up in the evening to get a wonderful view of the Alhambra. Be aware, though, that rooms facing the street are exposed to day-and-night traffic going up into the El Albaicín. Bring earplugs if you are a light sleeper. If you like the thought of going native in your hotel choice and want to be away from the crowds in the center of town, consider the **Cuevas del Abánico** (C/ Vereda del Enmedio 89, tel. 95/822-6199) in Sacromonte. All five caves have been kitted out with all mod cons, including full kitchens. There's a minimum two-night stay but at €60 for a double or €80 for a triple, it's a picturesque (and in summer, cooler) alternative to a *hostal*.

Over €100

Over the past several years, investors have been opening upscale hotels using the traditional courtyard-based architecture as the structure for modern lodgings with a 16th-century touch. The oldest of these is the ◖ **Casa Morisca** (C/ Cuesta de la Victoria 9, tel. 95/822-1100, info@hotelcasamorisca.com, www.hotelcasa morisca.com, €144) in El Albaicín, not far from the river and the Cuesta del Chapiz. Built at the end of the 15th century, Casa Morisca retains the original woodwork and stucco design from the building's earliest days. You'll truly feel like you've landed back in medieval Granada—only with extra-fine linens, air-conditioning, Internet, and a very accommodating staff—perfect! Near the Cathedral, **Hotel Santa Isabel la Real** (C/ Santa Isabel la Real 19, tel. 95/829 4658, info@hotelsantaisabel lareal.com, www.hotelsantaisabellareal.com, €105) is another lovely retreat, also centered on a magnificent inner courtyard. The comfortable rooms are accented in deep reds with Moroccan details. Parking is available for an extra €12 per night.

The jewel in the crown of the national parador chain is Granada's **Parador San Francisco** (tel. 95/822-1440, granada@parador.es, www .parador.es, €265). Located within the walls of the Alhambra Palace, this former monastery, built on royal decree of Fernando and Isabel, once held the bodies of the Catholic Kings in state. It is by far the most popular hotel in the parador system, and one of the most evocative in Spain, if not the world. Though the rooms are lovely, they are not spectacular; you come here for the chance to sleep in the Alhambra and the opportunity to walk its gardens at night, free from the maddening crowds. Dinner on the terrace is a very romantic must-do, and at only €27 for three courses, it is good value, too. Staying here requires some planning; rooms must be booked at least six months in advance, longer for peak times like Semana Santa and summer. If you want the luxury of the parador but prefer to be closer to the center of town, the **Palacio Santa Paula** (Gran Vía de Colón 31, tel. 95/880-5740, psantapaula@ ac-hotels.com, www.ac-hotels.com, €200) is a fashionable alternative. The 16th-century building housed a convent before being turned into a private residence in the early 19th century. Run by the swish Spanish AC chain, the amenities are top-notch and include Arabic baths and an excellent restaurant, El Claustro, that specializes in game and seafood.

FOOD

Granada's Moorish past shows up on the plate in the use of almonds, fruits, and spices. Tasty cases in point are *el remojón granadino de bacalao y naranja* (cod with oranges), *bastela* (a puff pastry filled with spiced meat, pine nuts, and almonds), and *crema de almendras* (a thick almond soup). The Alpujarra mountains contribute an earthy touch with fresh game, hearty peasant dishes, and the region's best *jamón*. The latter is paired with broad beans to make the local favorite *habas con jamón*. The nearby Mediterranean brings glistening seafood to the table, while the surrounding farmlands offer fresh produce. Vegetarians (and meat-eaters, too) will love *albornía,* a medley of vegetables, spices, and olive oil. In fact, most everything you point out on a menu will be delicious, but you should know one more thing about Granada's gastronomy. It hails from a long past marred by poverty. Some of the most traditional dishes come from the days when the rule was to use every bit of the animal. *Tortilla de Sacromonte,* offered on menus everywhere, is an omelet made of pigs' brains and testicles. *Olla de San Antón* is a stew of broad beans, pigs' head and ears, bacon, and blood sausage. Locals lap it up. Join them if you dare. For something more palatable, and a whole lot sweeter, the Moors come to the rescue with a variety of pastries and sweets using pine nuts, almonds, sweetened pumpkin, honey, and more. Find a yummy array at any pastry shop, or better yet, a convent where otherwise reserved nuns exercise a divine exuberance for making sweets.

Cafés and Desserts

One of Granada's most historic cafés, **Casa Pasteles** (Pl. Larga 1, tel. 95/827-8997, 8 A.M.–9 P.M. daily) is located in Albaicín's main square, making it a good place to stop for a breather if you're tired from wandering around the maze of the ancient Arabic quarter. For a bit of old Moorish café culture—it has to be tea. All along and around Calle Caldería Nueva are wonderful *teterías* (Arabic tea houses) where you can sip sweet mint tea, smoke a pipe of apple tobacco, and have a sticky sweet pastry or three. Ice cream is an addiction and considering the licking that the summer sun unleashes on the city, it's understandable. *Heladerías* abound in the center of the city, the best of them being **Los Italianos** (Gran Vía 4, tel. 95/822-4034) with a mouthwatering rainbow of flavors. Also try both outlets of **La Perla** (Pl. Nueva 16 and Av. Reyes Católicos 2), where a cone of handmade heaven will set you back €2.

Local Cuisine

In El Albaicín, **El Ladrillo II** (C/ Panaderos 35, tel. 95/828-6123, noon–5 P.M. and 8–midnight Thurs.–Tues., €20) offers great fried fish and paella. It's decked out like a Sacromonte *tablao* cave—curvaceous whitewashed walls, lots of copper doodads, and a seven-foot tile mural of the Virgin Mary. **Mesón El Yunque** (Pl. San Miguel Bajo 3, tel. 95/880-0090, €25) is renowned for its grilled fish platters and savory local dishes like chicken stewed in almonds. Locals clamor for a spot on its terrace in the center of the plaza, but inside is much more charming with a ceramic bar and tiled walls cluttered in flamenco memorabilia. The owner, Antonio Sotomayor, is a renowned local flamenco singer. The word *yunque* means "anvil" and refers to the chanting of gypsy blacksmiths. Across the way, **Mesón Blás Casa** (Pl. San Miguel Bajo 15, tel. 95/827-3111, noon–5 P.M. and 8 P.M.–midnight Tues.–Sun., closed Mon., €15) is another option offering traditional local fare. Though it lacks the flamenco flair, it boasts a nice fireplace perfect for chilly nights.

Granada shows its hard-working, good-eating roots in cozy, inexpensive restaurants all over town—most offering cheap and yummy *menus del día*. **Restaurante Boabdil** (C/ Hospital Peregrinos 9, tel. 95/822-8136, 9 A.M.–

midnight daily, €10) is a comfy neighborhood place run by a family from Murcia who does great fried fish platters.

Granada goes gourmet at a handful of top-rated places. In the Palacio Santa Paula hotel, **El Claustro** (Gran Vía de Colón 31, tel. 95/880-5740, 1:30–4 P.M. 8:30–11:30 P.M. daily, €50) serves up modern Andalusian fare in the atmospheric refectory of a 16th-century convent. Try the artichoke salad with *cigalitas* (a cross between a shrimp and a crayfish). **Cunini** (Pl. Pescadería 14, tel. 95/825-0777, 1–4 P.M. and 8:30–11 P.M. Tues.–Sat., 1–4 P.M. Sun., closed Mon., €35) offers the most exquisite fish in town—appropriate as it is located on a square whose name translates to "fishmonger." The fish, laid out on the bar in a Gaudí-esque display of silver and green scales, comes straight from the sea every morning. Try it *a la plancha* (grilled), *frito* (fried), or served up in fragrant stews. **Mirador de Morayma** (C/ Pianista García Carrillo 2, tel. 95/822-8290, closed Sun. evenings, €30) is hidden deep within the Albaicín behind a closed door. Knock to gain entrance. When you do, you'll enter a charming old Granada home with a fantastic terrace overlooking the green gorge of the Darro with the Alhambra soaring beyond. The menu is laden with classic *granadina* dishes such as *remojón* (cod with oranges) plus rustic fare like roasted lamb chops and smoked fish.

If you love Arabic food, you'll be in heaven in Granada. Many of the roots of Andalusian cuisine come from North Africa and **Chefchaouen** (C/ Nueva San Nicolás 1, tel. 95/820-2633, €15) features Moroccan cooking just like your mom would make it… had your mom been raised among North African Berber tribesmen. Members of the local Moroccan community rave about the *tajines* (stews of meat, fruit, and almonds), couscous (especially the chicken with peaches), and the delicious pastries. It's rumored to be a favorite of Granada's Arabic-speaking mayor. **Samarkanda** (C/ Caldería Vieja 3, tel. 95/821-0004, €12) bills itself as a Lebanese restaurant, though their menu leans a little farther west as well, including a sublime Moroccan *harissa* (spiced tomato soup). Nearby **Arrayanes** (C/ Cuesta Marañas 4, tel. 95/822-8401, €15) serves authentic North African cuisine. They are so, uh, kosher, that they refuse to serve alcohol, however a yummy selection of house-made soft drinks is available.

Tapas

In Granada, the concept of tapa has two meanings. When you order a drink, any drink—Coke to *caña*—you get a free snack on the side. Locals call it *tapichuela*. This "tapa" can be as simple as a few olives in garlic oil or a good-sized portion of a savory stew. Two or three drinks down and you could find yourself stuffed. And now is not the time to be picky. You get what they give—remember, it's free. Tapa also means *racion,* a larger portion of something you order off the menu. Locals love their *raciones* and a night of tapas-hopping usually involves traipsing around town after their favorites. Do like they do. Try one dish here, one dish there, and keep going until your tummy can't keep up anymore.

Good "tapas zones" include Calle Navas, off the Plaza del Carmen, and Campo del Príncipe, where dozens of tapas bars are lined up like a tasty brigade. Paseo de los Tristes offers loads of tapas bars under the evening glow of the Alhambra. Further up in the Albaicín, good tapas bars are spread around like "olés!" at a bullfight. The normal operating hours for tapas bars in Granada is 1–3 P.M. and 8–11 P.M., with bars reaching peak capacity around 9 P.M.

In the Albaicín, **El Ají** (C/ San Miguel Bajo 9, tel. 95/829 2930, 12–4 P.M. and 7 P.M.–midnight daily) offers classic Spanish tapas with fun, modern touches. Their outdoor terrace is lovely, but be aware of the 10 percent surcharge for sitting there. **Bar Aliator-Los Caracoles** (Pl. Aliatar, s/n) specializes in snails served in a piquant sauce that will leave you begging for more bread to sop it up with. They also have a few heartier dishes including a fall-off-the-bone roasted leg of *cabrito* (young goat). **Casa 1899** (Po. Tristes 3, tel. 95/822-8306) is a dark and cozy wine bar with good vintages from all over Spain plus a large selection of deli products, which in Spain means *jamón, jamón, jamón!* Next door, **Puerta del Vino** (Po. Tristes 5, tel. 95/821-0026) offers great wine and a delicious *verbena ahumada* (smoked fish platter).

Down in town, **Bodegas Castañeda** (C/ Almiceros 1, tel. 95/821 5464) and **Bodega la Mancha** (C/ Joaquín Costa 10, 95/822-8968), practically next door and run by the same family, are rustic local bar/restaurants famous for taking the Granada tradition of serving free tapas with every drink to the extreme. Three beers and you'll be full! **Patio del Toro** (C/ Mesónes 52, tel. 95/852 3633) looks suspiciously corporate (who else could afford to put a bronze statue of a bull in the dining room?) but provides an oasis of quiet and shade away from the hustle and bustle of nearby Plaza de la Trinidad—the eating's fine, too. **Puerta del Carmen** (Pl. Carmen 1, tel. 95/822-3737) offers excellent cheese and a nice selection of salads (vegetarians, listen up!). It is also a little slicker than your average tapas bar. Another choice place for wine is **Casa de Vinos la Brujidera** (C/ Monjas del Carmen 2, tel. 95/822-2595). **Bar Alitar** (C/ San Sebastián,4), not to be confused with the snail bar, is lovable Spanish dive that has been serving traditional tapas since 1947, but now they are more known for their incredible *bocadillo* (sub sandwich) list which offers over 30 tasty types from bacon to grilled pork to artichoke! Unassuming as it is, this local favorite brings in everyone from factory workers to soccer stars.

INFORMATION

The **Tourist Office of Andalucía** (C/ Santa Ana, 4, tel. 95/822-5990, 9 A.M.–7:30 P.M. Mon.–Fri., 10 A.M.–7:30 P.M. Sat., and 10 A.M.–2 P.M. Sun.) moved digs a few years ago. The new location isn't as dark as the previous location in the Corral del Carbón, and the extra space allows them to carry a better selection of tourist-oriented publications, including their excellent city and regional maps. The service, however, remains as curt as ever. The **regional tourist office** (Pl. Mariana Pineda 10, tel. 95/824-7146) offers information on anything within Granada city and Granada province.

The tourist office runs the excellent www .turismodegranada.org and the city runs the very confusing, often dead-end www.granada tur.com. The two Andalucía sites, www .andalucia.org and www.andalucia.com, both offer good information on the city and region. Granada is also fortunate to have several sites run by Granada lovers, just do a search. The most informative and fun is www.vivagranada .com, run by Lorenzo Bohme. Passionate about his adopted hometown, he has authored *Granada, City of My Dreams,* available at book shops in Granada or by visiting his website. He also owns a charming set of rustic houses for rent in the village of Montefrio in the hills of Granada province. Before your trip, spend some time on his site; his love for Granada is infectious.

GETTING THERE AND AROUND
Air

Unless you are catching a cheapie flight within Spain, you probably won't need to visit **El Aeropuerto Federico García Lorca** (tel. 95/824-5200). It's located about eight miles outside of town on the A-92 highway in Chauchina. **Iberia** (www.iberia.es) flies here, as do a pair of cut-rate European airlines, **Ryanair** (www .ryanair.com) and **Vueling** (www.vueling .com). There is an **airport shuttle bus** that runs 8 A.M.–6 P.M. about every two hours during the week only. Unless you are seriously on a budget, take a cab.

Train

The **Estación de Ferrocarriles** (Av. Andaluces, s/n, tel. 95/824-0202), located less than 1.5 kilometers (less than a mile) west of the center, is operated by **Renfe** (tel. 90/224-0202, www.renfe.es), which runs three TALGO trains daily from Madrid to Granada (€36.90, six hours). However, it is cheaper and quicker to go to Madrid via bus. There are also three regional trains per day which go to Ronda (€12.55, three hours), four to Sevilla (€20.05, three hours), and four to Almería (€13.40).

Bus

Granada's bus station, **Estación de Autobuses** (Crta. Jaén s/n, tel. 95/818-5010) lies on the north end of the city. Within Andalucía, bus service is run by **Alsina Graells** (tel. 95/818-5480, www.alsinagraells.es), offering service to Sevilla (nine per day, €17.60, three hours), Málaga (10 per day, €8.90, 2.25 hours), Jaén (15 per day, €6.91, one hour) and Córdoba (seven per day, €11.40, 2.75 hours). Although the bus station is safe enough during the day, be especially wary of the bathrooms at night. Some backpackers have been jumped by local junkies. Bus station staff are either extremely uninterested or unwilling (or both) to help the victims. To get to the city center, catch the local bus 3, which runs along Gran Vía.

If you are traveling by public transport between Granada and Madrid, the bus is your best bet. Bus service, from Madrid's Avenida de América and Mendez Álvaro stations isn't just quicker (five hours) and more frequent (15 per day) than the train, at €14.80, it's less than half the price.

Car

Several highways transect Granada. A-92 connects it to Sevilla, Málaga, Murcia, and Almería. N-44 goes to Motril and Madrid. N-432 goes to Córdoba. It is highly suggested that you not attempt to drive into Granada unless you have your parking sussed out beforehand (ask your hotel). The Albaicín is closed off to all but local residents and the center is a confusing web of one-way streets and constant construction. If you must bring a car into town, park it until you are ready to leave.

City Transport

Granada's municipal **bus system** is cheap and efficient. One ride costs €1, a nine-ride *bono* (pass) is just €5.45 and 20 rides costs €10.80. Bear in mind that two or more users can use the rides on one card—great if you're traveling with family or a group. The large red buses traverse the center and **taxis** (tel. 95/828-0654) are available in the Plaza Nueva and all up and down the Gran Vía de Colón. A trip around the most central areas (including the Albaicín) shouldn't cost more than €7.50.

VICINITY OF GRANADA
Sierra Nevada

From Granada it is hard not to miss the snow-topped peaks of the Sierra Nevada mountains, and while serious skiers don't venture this far south to ski, there are obvious advantages to runs that remain well-packed until after Easter. Plus the idea of skiing in the morning and having tapas on a terrace in the Albaicín by night is so decadently enticing!

Most of the ski action is based out of the **Solynieve Ski Resort** in Monachil, only 25 minutes by car from Granada. Though it's possible to show up with your boards and wax, most Spanish travel agencies will sell you ski packages for a fraction of the cost of doing it yourself. If you'd like to head up for the day, you can get information about conditions and lift tickets from the **Sierra Nevada Activo** (tel. 90/270-8090, www.sierranevada.es), which runs the ski resort and also arranges trekking expeditions and mountain biking in the warmer months. Extensive English-language information is on www.turismodegranada.org, under Sierra Nevada.

Spaniards didn't really come here to ski until the 1970s. Before that, it was mostly hikers, who followed routes laid down by miners and *neveros* (icemen) who brought blocks of ice down from the mountains and sold them for use in refrigerators. That route can still be walked and biked up to the peak of **Veleta,** the second-highest mountain in peninsular Spain. Early in the 20th century, a group of engineers constructed a highway that traversed the mountains, linking Granada with the town of Capileira on the other side. While several sections of the road coming up from the resort remain intact, Sierra Nevada Park authorities have been agitating to have the road removed to minimize damage to the environment. Though the road is closed to motorized traffic above Solynieve, it's still possible to ride or walk to just below the peak of Veleta. On a clear day, you can see straight to Morocco, but be warned that weather is extremely changeable up here;

even in summer, make sure to bring adequate water- and windproof clothing.

For a complete list of hiking options with detailed routes, go to www.turismodegranada .org and click on "Excursions, hill walking, and climbing."

During ski season, there are three buses a day from Granada's Estación de Autobuses (four on weekends); there's one per day, leaving Granada at 9 A.M. (returning at 5 P.M.), when there's no ski action. By car, take the A-395 road out of the city and straight to the mountains.

Provincia de Almería

Sitting in the far southeastern corner of the Iberian peninsula, Almería is the sunniest, hottest, driest patch of Europe. Home to the continent's only desert, inland Almería is a lunar landscape of low, mostly barren mountains and dried up riverbeds. It is awash in a palette of sun-baked browns, occasionally streaked with a smudge of dark green scrub. If it looks familiar to fans of spaghetti westerns, that is because it is. This is where Clint Eastwood and his cowboy pals did much of their filming. In the 1960s, the film boom boosted Almería's economy. (See sidebar, *Starring Almería*.) Today, the movie sets have made way for the province's current industrial boom—agriculture. Vast areas of inland Almería and kilometers of its western coast are swathed in low-lying plastic greenhouses. This *mar de plastico* ("sea of plastic") as the locals call it, provides Spain and Northern Europe with most of their hothouse vegetables. It has also helped lift Almería from the economic despair that plagued it for decades after the Civil War.

If it all sounds rather dreary, and you are starting to wonder why bother visiting Almería at all, then consider the coast. Almería city and the province's eastern coast offer a charming, low-key Mediterranean escape from the crowds. With a summer that starts in May and finishes in November, the coast also offers some of Spain's balmiest waters, perfect for swimming year-round. However, the real jewel of this part of Almería—and indeed, of Spain—is the Parque Natural de Cabo de Gata-Níjar, a stunning swath of protected coastal land that offers wild beaches, secluded coves, and rugged landscape reminiscent of California's fa-

bled Big Sur. Because of its protected status, this area is unspoiled by development. You won't find big resorts or clutches of hotels and restaurants. You *will* find solitude and peace among kilometers of pristine beaches glistening under Almería's other natural resource—its pure, shimmering light. The sky is so clear in Almería that the European Union installed the continent's most powerful telescope here near the town of Gergál. While you can't visit the telescope, you can enjoy Almería's brilliant luminosity in the Moorish streets of old Almería city, on the deserted coves of Cabo de Gata, or in lovely coastal towns like Mojácar. You'll have to rent a car to really enjoy this part of the country, but it is worth it to enjoy a slice of authentic Andalucía.

ALMERÍA CAPITAL

Almería city, the capital of the Provincia de Almería, is a pleasant, modern town tucked between an ancient sun-parched mountain and the deep blue Mediterranean Sea. The clutch of old whitewashed houses at its center offer an old world Andalusian contrast to the bustling port all around. During the Moorish occupation of Iberia, Al-Meraya (as it was called) was one of the most important ports in the kingdom. To protect it, in 955, Abd ar-Rahman III, the Caliph of Córdoba, built the tremendous fortress Alcazaba, which towers over modern Almería to this day. The white buildings at its base were the busy medina, home to thousands of Moors, Jews, and early Christians. After the Catholic Kings captured the city in 1489, they added their own monumental structures, mainly churches and a few civil buildings. In 1522, an earthquake destroyed much of the city. Later, during the Civil War, Almería was one of the last holdouts against Franco's forces. The German navy shelled the city before it finally fell. From the war on, the city as well as the entire province of Almería experienced economic despair and poverty. It was not until the late 20th century and the onslaught of the *invernaderos* (greenhouses) throughout the region that the city began to rebound. Today, these remnants of the past, mingle seamlessly with a modern Almería that is distinguished by its wide, tree-lined avenues, upmarket shops, outdoor cafés, and a lively harborfront. While pleasant enough, a tourist might not find reason to stay here beyond a day, but it is a good base from which to begin exploring Cabo de Gata and the eastern coast.

Sights

The main sight of interest is the 10th-century **Alcazaba** (C/ Almanzor, s/n, tel. 95/027-1617, 9 A.M.– 6 P.M. Tues.–Sun., closed Mon., €1.50). This massive Moorish military fortification is one of the best examples of its kind. It has three walled enclosures; in one enclosure you can visit an old mosque that was later converted into a Christian chapel. When Almería was an independent Moorish kingdom, this citadel could hold over 20,000 troops and contained palaces and gardens so beautiful that it rivaled the Alhambra. You will have to use your imagination a lot today, because although the size is impressive, little of the grandeur has survived. The Christians who moved in modified or sold off much of its decor and the 1522 earthquake dismantled the rest. Still the walls and towers are a sight to behold and the views over the sea from the top are impressive. Looking almost directly down and slightly to the west, the picturesque jumble of white buildings called **Barrio de la Chanca** lay in plain view. This was the old Jewish quarter where many of the houses were built into caves.

Not far from the Alcazaba, deep in the tangle of old Moorish Almería, looms the 16th-century **Catedral de Almería** (Pl. Catedral,

s/n, 10 A.M.–4:30 P.M. Mon.–Fri., 10 A.M.–1 P.M. Sat., Sun. for worship only, €2). From the outside it looks more like a fortress, with its heaving battlement towers and stern facade. In fact, it once housed its own cannons. This is understandable, as the cathedral was built in dangerous times. The Mediterranean coast was rife with pirate bands from Turkey and North Africa who raided the city periodically throughout the 16th century. Inside, the cathedral is a flight of architectural fancy with heavy touches of both Gothic and baroque design. The altar contains a tabernacle designed by Spanish court architect Ventura Rodríguez who designed many of 18th-century Madrid's finest buildings.

Around the **Puerta de Purchena,** a 16th-century city gate, you'll find a lively barrio full of tapas bars and cafés. From there, stroll down the tree-lined **Paseo de Almería,** with its boutiques and shops, until you arrive at the bustling harbor. To the east are the city's beaches, **Playa Almadrabillas** is a tiny slip of grayish sand under the old 19th-century rail tracks called the **Cable Inglés** (English Cable). Beyond that, the **Paseo Marítimo** (Seaside Promenade) runs along the **Playa Ciudad Luminosa,** a long city beach that is nowhere near as nice as its name, "City of Light."

Accommodations

In the **under €50** range, **Hostal Americano** (Av. Estación 6, tel. 95/025-8011, €49) is a clean, cheap charmer near the bus station. **Hostal Maribel** (Av. Garcia Lorca 153, tel. 95/023-5173, €45) is a friendly place near bustling Puerta de Purchena.

At **€50-100, Hotel Costasol** (Po. Almería 58 tel. 95/023-4011, www.hotelcostasol .com, €80) is one of Almería's grand old hotels. The sweeping checkerboard lobby is impressive and the rooms are comfortable, if a bit old-fashioned. Upgrade to a suite for just under €100. **Hotel Torreluz III** (Plaza Flores 3, tel. 95/023-4399, www.torreluz.com, €80) is a very hotelesque property with clean, spacious rooms and all the classic amenities. Also in the plaza, the same group operates **Hotel Torreluz II,** a bit cheaper

STARRING ALMERÍA

Where did Clint Eastwood begin his rise to stardom? Where were *Lawrence of Arabia, Indiana Jones and the Last Crusade,* and *The Good, the Bad, and the Ugly* filmed? Which Spanish town got an airport thanks to the film industry? If you answered Almería to all of these questions – Congratulations!

In the 1950s, Almería was one of Spain's most backward provinces. The capital had no hotels, airports, or even a sewage system. Because this province was the last to fall to Franco in the Civil War, he later ignored it. The only feasible future for a young *almeriense* was to emigrate elsewhere – anywhere. Then Hollywood came along.

What first attracted Tinseltown was the low cost of labor (and lack of unions) and cheap lodging and transport. What hooked them was the landscape. Monotonous yet malleable, it had the ability to take on many personalities. Almería was the ultimate character actor. It could play Arabia, the American West, Mexico, and even Africa.

When the cameras and crews, directors and stars, first descended upon Almería, barely anyone spoke English. No one knew about film – much less American film. Men were simple laborers. Women nursed children and dressed in high-necked black dresses. Living under the reign of Franco's oppression, Almería was the polar opposite of Hollywood glitz.

Despite the differences, the seeds of stardom were quick to take root in Almería's crusty soil. Locals began adapting themselves to the call of the set. Young people learned the tech-

nical aspects of the profession, others became stuntmen, and whole families dedicated themselves to specific occupations like hospitality or transport.

Almería's first western, *The Savage Guns,* was a U.S./Spanish co-production shot in 1962. Almería next featured in a couple of Spanish films – *El sabor de la venganza* and *Antes llega la muerte* – directed by Joaquín Romero Marchent, who was cinematographically drawn to Almería for its unique light and hard beauty.

Soon, foreign directors began aiming their cameras at the province and an increasing number of scenes or entire films were shot there, including *King of Kings, Cleopatra,* and *Lawrence of Arabia,* the Academy Award-winning masterpiece starring Peter O'Toole.

Italian director Sergio Leone chose Almería for part of his 1964 western *For a Fistful of Dollars,* launching the career of the then-little-known actor Clint Eastwood. The following year, Leone and Eastwood returned to film *For a Few Dollars More* entirely in the province. The set is now a theme park where actors in period dress stage shoot-outs for tourists. The film marked the beginning of the spaghetti western genre. It made Eastwood a star and composer Alessandro Alessandroni's haunting whistle to the backdrop of a tumbleweed-strewn desert a familiar sound to moviegoers for generations. Leone and Eastwood's next Almería project, 1966's *The Good, the Bad and the Ugly,* is widely considered the best western ever filmed.

Almería also drew big-name superstars to its

than the III, and **Torreluz Apartmentos,** which feature self-catering apartments for around €80 per night.

Moving up to the **over €100** price range, Torrreluz also runs the four-star **AM Torreluz** (Pl. Flores 5, tel. 95/023-4999, www.amhoteles.com, €120), which features a lovely pool and posh rooms. **⬛ Hotel Catedral** (Pl. Catedral 8, tel. 95/027-8178, www.hotelcatedral.net, €100) is Almería's first and only boutique

hotel. Housed in a historic building facing the cathedral, this 16-room charmer is rich in stylish details from the Moorish arches in the lobby to the modern furniture in the bedrooms to the rooftop whirlpool overlooking the cathedral and the Alcazaba up above. Breakfast is included. **Gran Hotel Almería** (Av. Reina Regente 8 tel. 95/023-8011, www.granhotelalmeria.com, €135) is the city's long-standing hotel of choice for visiting movers and shak-

environs. In 1966, the satirical comedy *How I Won the War* starring John Lennon was filmed here. It was on set in Almería that Lennon wrote one of rock's greatest songs – "Strawberry Fields Forever." In 1970, Oscar-winning *Patton* starring George C. Scott brought World War II to Almería. Two years later, Almería's dull desert became *The Treasure Island*, starring Orson Welles.

Between 1965 and 1973, over 150 films were made in Almería. With money pouring in, the construction industry boomed, creating homes, hotels, restaurants, schools, and roads. When film producers complained about the long journey from the Málaga airport over bad roads that entire crews endured, Almería built an airport. Before long, there weren't enough workers to cover the demand in the service industry. Technicians and secondary actors worked on several films at a time. Films were sometimes shot within yards of each another. There were often mix-ups where actors were dropped off at the wrong location, only discovering the mistake after they were already in costume.

Big stars accustomed to the Hollywood high life found Almería's conditions appalling, and the cultures clashed. Brigitte Bardot insisted on being chauffeured in her Rolls Royce through Almería's poverty-stricken streets. While shooting *The Ruthless Four*, a drunken Klaus Kinski was incarcerated after throwing his pay packet to a group of gypsies (they often played the roles of Mexicans). The French star Alain Delon beat up a Civil Guard officer. Charles Bronson demanded to be driven to a mountain location in a Cadillac, with a second one following behind as a backup in case the first one broke down.

By 1973, the western was on the wane and the cost of filming in Almería was rising. Penny-pinching directors began heading for places like Morocco and Yugoslavia. Only a few big Hollywood productions were filmed here over the next two decades – *The Wind and the Lion* in 1975, Schwarzenegger's *Conan, the Barbarian* in 1982, and the James Bond film *Never Say Never Again* in 1985. Steven Spielberg's epic *Indiana Jones and the Last Crusade*, filmed in 1989, was the last major shoot in the province.

Hollywood may have gone, but the stories remain and locals love to reminisce about Almería's glory days. One of them, Juan Fernández, comes from three generations of production drivers. He grew up listening to stories about how Eastwood used to give his great-uncle Diego a big tip every weekend or how Lee Van Cleef (Eastwood's co-star) bought his driver a taxi so he could start his own business. Today, Almería is still a shooting locale for Spanish productions, as well as a handful of international projects. It is enough to keep Juan and his family still working in the movie biz.

Every June, Almería celebrates its cinematographic past with the Festival Internacional de Almería en Corto, a short-film competition. The awards include a cowboy statuette. It is held in conjunction with a retrospective of a film professional who has worked in the province.

(*Contributed by Anita Haas, a Madrid-based writer who frequently writes about film and Spain.*)

ers. It offers classic rooms, classic service, and a classic view over the harbor, as well as a lovely pool surrounded by palm trees.

Food

Around Puerta Purchena there are a lot of options for tasty tapas. Be sure and try *cherican,* a thick piece of toast slathered with aioli and topped with just about anything. Along the Paseo de Almería, there are dozens of classy cafés and bars, most with tables on the sidewalks. Inside, many boast lovely glass enclosed dining rooms. Try the **Marisqueria Baviera** (C/ Tenor Iribarne 10, tel. 95/023-9658, 11 A.M.–4:30 P.M. and 7 P.M.–midnight Mon.–Sat., closed Sun.) for wonderful shellfish. **Bodega Las Botas** (C/ Fructuoso Pérez 3, tel. 95/023-4239, 11 A.M.–4 P.M. and 7:30 P.M.–1 A.M. Mon.–Sat., closed Sun.) pairs great local fare with excellent wine. Try their *tinto de*

ANDALUCÍA

verano (a red wine spritzer) with a plate of the local cheeses.

For casual local fare, you can't do better than the row of restaurants lined up on the Paseo Marítimo. At any of them you can have a delicious plate of grilled fish and a glass of wine for under €10. In the historic center, try the top-rated **La Encina "Plaza Vieja"** (C/ Marín 16, tel. 95/027-3429, noon–4 P.M. and 8 P.M.–1 A.M. Tues.–Sat., noon–4 P.M. Mon., closed Sun., €35) for an eclectic take on Andalusian dishes in a charming 19th-century mansion. **El Asador Torreluz** (C/ Fructuoso Pérez 14, tel. 95/023-4545, 1:30–3:30 P.M. and 8:30–11:30 P.M. Tues.–Sat., 1:30–3:30 P.M. Mon., closed Sun., €25) is where to go when you need a break from seafood; it specializes in roast lamb and suckling pig. **Club de Mar** (Playa de Las Almadrabillas 1, tel. 95/023-5048, 10 A.M.–4 P.M. and 9 P.M.–midnight Wed.–Mon., €30) is one of Almería's most popular, posh dining rooms. The view of the harbor is magnificent and the perfectly prepared seafood impeccable.

Information

The regional **Andalucía tourist office** (Pl. Bendicho, s/n, tel. 95/062-1117, , 8 A.M.–3 P.M. Mon.–Fri., closed Sat. and Sun.) is located in a charming square just around the corner from the cathedral. The **local tourist office** (Parque San Nicolás Salmeron, s/n, tel. 95/027-4355, 9 A.M.–7:30 P.M. Mon.–Fri., 10 A.M.–2 P.M. Sat.–Sun.) is located within a pretty park, just outside the old center of town. Online, check out www.almeriaturismo.org, as well as the regional sites, www.andalucia.com and www.andalucia.org.

Getting There

Almería is well connected by train. The **Estación Intermodal** (Pl. Estación, s/n) is serviced by **Renfe** (tel. 90/224-0202, www.renfe.es), which runs daily trains to Barcelona, Madrid, Sevilla, and Granada.

By bus, Almería is serviced by several companies that travel throughout Spain. The bus terminal is at the train station, **Estación Intermodal** (Pl. Estación, s/n, tel. 95/026-2098).

If you are traveling from Madrid, Barcelona, or any point in Northern Spain, you might consider flying to save time. Both **Spanair** (www.spanair.es) and **Iberia** (www.iberia.es) operate low-cost flights between Almería and major cities in Spain. The Aeropuerto de Almería is located eight kilometers (five miles) outside of the city in Nijar. Shuttle buses leave the airport every half-hour for the city center.

By car, Almería city is located on the old N-340, slowly being replaced by the new multilane E-15, also called the A-7. You might see any of these signs on the same road.

◖ CABO DE GATA

The Parque Natural de Cabo de Gata-Níjar, known simply as Cabo de Gata, is a protected park that comprises some 38,850 hectares (150 square miles), including arguably the most beautiful coasts on the Iberian Peninsula. The protected zone also reaches about 1.5 kilometers (a mile or so) out to sea. The triangular park, stretching between the coastal cities of Almería and Carboneras and inland to Níjar, is of volcanic origin. The soil is spiked white and along the coast it forms dramatic crags and sheer cliffs that plunge straight down to the sea. Declared a Biosphere Reserve in 1997, the area is home to numerous species of flora, fauna, and marine life. Its great salt marshes are also a stopping point for migratory birds, garnering the park status as a Special Bird Protection Area under the international Ramsar Agreement. For the conservationist, ecologist, and marine biologist, this is all great news. The park is the largest protected area in the western Mediterranean and looks to remain that way. For the tourist, this means that Cabo de Gata offers an unspoiled vacation paradise. Oh, there are a handful of tiny villages and several salt beds in operation, but for the most part you'll find nearly deserted beaches, dime-sized secluded *calas* (coves), and panoramic vistas where the land meets the sea in a theatrical display of natural beauty.

The only time you might feel the slightest crunch in Cabo de Gata is in July and August when Spanish holiday-makers flock here.

However, because of its protected nature and strict limits on development, there are just not a lot of services such as hotels, restaurants, even gas stations are scarce. If you go in summer, book well ahead, or plan on staying in Almería or Carboneras (a rather unpleasant largish town, surrounded by Cabo de Gata, but not part of the park). Also, give charming San José a try. It has the most lodgings of the Cabo de Gata villages.

The only feasible way to travel through Cabo de Gata is by renting a car and driving. From Almería, the E-15/A-7 arcs through Cabo de Gata several kilometers inland. Along the length of the road are signs pointing the turn-offs to the various villages on the coast. Take a good map with you or visit an online mapping site to plan your route. And do expect to get lost. Roads are small, windy, and can change names three times in the span of half a kilometer.

Traveling by bus is tricky and limited.

From the Almería's **Estación Intermodal** (Pl. Estación, s/n, tel. 95/026-2098), **Autobus Becerra** (tel. 95/022-4403) has twice daily connections to the village of Cabo de Gata. **Autobus Bernardo** (tel. 95/025-0422) has two buses to San José, one to Aguamarga, and one to Isleta del Moro.

Before you go, learn more about the park at www.degata.com, which has a decent English-language section.

San Miguel de Cabo de Gata

The first village in the park after leaving Almería is San Miguel de Cabo de Gata, also shortened to Cabo de Gata—and yes, the names can lead to some confusion. When making reservations or getting directions, be sure to make it clear that you are speaking about Cabo de Gata, *el pueblo*. This tiny fishing village is a bit ramshackle but it offers a pleasant little boardwalk with a handful of excellent seafood restaurants. If you are really hungry, order the local specialty *migas*, a rustic dish made with chunky breadcrumbs, sausage, and lots of seafood.

The beach is long and a bit rocky, but it stretches for kilometers and there is nothing to see but the sea itself. About midway to the salt flats is a *chiringuito* (beachside bar) where you can sip a cocktail while you watch the sun sink to a soundtrack of Spanish pop.

South of the village, stretch **Las Salinas,** a series of lagoons for extracting salt. In spring, when the lagoons are full, they are a natural draw for migratory birds. Over 160 species have been spotted, but it is the flamingoes that everyone remembers. Many stick around to breed, and by the end of summer, the sight of hundreds of flamingos flapping their broad pink wings is a spectacular experience.

Beyond Las Salinas is the **Faro de Cabo de Gata,** a lighthouse perched on a promontory offering beautiful views over the sea and the rocky cliffs below.

There are a handful of decent accommodations in the village. **La Brisa** (C/ Las Joricas 49, tel. 95/037-0001, www.blancabrisa.com, €70) is a majestic building with spacious, clean rooms and an excellent in-house restaurant. **Hostal Las Dunas** (C/ Barrio Nuevo, tel. 95/037-0072, €50), just 30 meters (100 feet) from the beach, offers nice, clean rooms with views to the sea.

San José

Substantially bigger than Cabo de Gata, but still very much a sleepy village 10 months out of the year, San José sits on a shallow bay of the same name. Along its sandy main strip, **Calle Correos,** you'll find a clutch of restaurants and tapas bar, dive shops, and bike and kayak rental shops.

The town also boasts three fantastic beaches. **Playa San José** stretches for a nearly a kilometer (a half-mile) right from the pueblo. **Playa de los Genoveses,** is a 1.2-kilometer (0.75-mile) crescent surrounded by brush-covered hills and bordered by rocky headlands on each end. The water is shallow and very clear. While not a designated *playa nudista* (nude beach), don't be surprised to see folks baring all. **Playa de Mónsul** is a beach of fine gray sand surrounding by soaring chunks of lunar-looking volcanic rock.

San José offers quite a few accommodations, from simple to sumptuous. **Albergue San José** (C/ Montemar, s/n, tel. 95/038-0353, info@alberguesanjose.com, www.albergue sanjose.com, €12 per person) is a youth hostel open to all. Rooms sleep two, four, or six, and the ancient whitewashed building has two great terraces for hanging out with new friends. **Hotel Atalaya** (C/ Correo, s/n, tel. 95/038-0085, €85) offers spacious yet simple rooms in a lovely whitewashed building boasting a quaint inner courtyard and a good in-house restaurant. **Cortijo El Sotillo** (tel. 95/061-1100, www.hotelsotillo.com, €145) is an 18th-century *finca* (country estate) located right at the entrance to San José. It offers romantic rooms and a full range of activities from horseback-riding to archery.

Find complete tourist information for San José and all of Cabo de Gata at the village's **tourist office** (C/ Correos, s/n, tel. 95/038-0299, 10 A.M.–2 P.M. and 5–8 P.M. daily).

Los Escullos

Teeny tiny Los Escullos makes San José seem like New York. Principally a fishing village, it offers a one of the least crowded beaches in Cabo de Gata, **Playa El Arco.** The beach—and the village—are surrounded by dramatic outcroppings of fossilized rock, creating an eerie moonscape. **Cala Granda** is a tiny cove where nudism is allowed, though it is a good 1.5-kilometer (about a mile) hike off the nearest road. Los Escullos also has a restored 18th-century fort, **Castillo de San Felipe,** that once warded off pirates.

Stay at **Hotel Los Escullos** (tel. 95/038-9733, www.hotellosescullos.com, €75), which also a nice restaurant. There are two other restaurants in town, **La Ola** and **Casa Emilio.** All three will run you about €20 per person for lunch and fare is about the same in each—fish, seafood, grilled meats, and simple salads.

La Isleta del Moro

Another speck of a fishing village, La Isleta del Moro offers not much more than its lovely cove beaches. **El Peñón Blanco** is a wide gray-sand beach popular with camper-trailers because of its easy road access. **Cala de los Toros** is a wonderful black-sand beach surrounded by cliffs and palm trees. Nudism is accepted here. In town, accommodations and food are limited to **Hostal Isleta del Moro** (C/ Mohamed Arraez 28, tel. 95/038-9713), which offers 11 simple rooms and a restaurant whose stated philosophy is "from the sea to the table." The paellas are especially delicious.

Las Negras

Las Negras is a clutch of tiny whitewashed houses tucked between the sea and the majestic black volcanic mountain that lends the town its name. Fronting the town, **Playa Las Negras** is a broad, pebbly beach with somewhat rough waters that are popular with divers. **Cala San Pedro,** located about five kilometers (three miles) down a narrow path leading away from the town along the sea, is a tiny cove dotted with ruins of ancient houses and a fort. Nudism is practiced.

Stay at the **Hotel Cala Chica** (www.cala chica.com, €105), a charming hotel with terra-cotta-floored rooms, many with their own terraces overlooking the beach. It also has a small pool and a café. Many people in Las Negras rent out private apartments and rooms in their own homes. Check www.las negras.com and www.degata.com (click the orange icon of the house) for extensive listings. Prices have to be negotiated with the landlord, but expect to pay €50–100 per night, less off-season.

If you are a certified diver or would like to be, **Buceo Las Negras** (C/ Playa, s/n, tel. 95/038-8217, www.buccolasnegras.com) offers classes and rental equipment, as well as a range of activities from kayak rentals to boat tours. They even have Internet service at their offices.

Agua Amarga

Agua Amarga, which translates to "bitter water," is anything but. Sitting on a sheltered bay in the midst of some of the hilliest coasts of the park, Agua Amarga (sometimes written Aguamarga) is one of the larger villages in Cabo de Gata. Along its shores, it boasts a long, sandy beach with full amenities including showers and *chiringuitos* (beachside bars). The length of the beach is pockmarked with cozy little coves. In town are a several bars and restaurants, as well as outfitters offering trekking, horseback riding, and boat rides.

The town boasts two of the most luxurious stays in Cabo de Gata. **La Almendra y El Gitano** (Camino de Cala Plomo, s/n, tel. 61/506-1587 or 67/850-2911, www.laalmendra yelgitano.com, €120) is a whitewashed wonderland of romance and sophistication located in the hills outside of Agua Amarga. Run by the creative couple that go by the nicknames of "la almendra" (her, the almond) and "el gitano" (him, the gypsy), this boutique property features a handful of rooms and suites each individually decorated with themes including romance, rustic, Arabic, and modern. In town, **El Tío Kiko** (C/ Embarque, s/n, tel. 95/013-8080, www.eltiokiko.com, €180) takes a traditional whitewashed Andalusian home and infuses it with very modern style somewhere between Polynesian cool and rustic chic. Each of its rooms comes with a private terrace, whirlpool bath, and large picture windows overlooking the sea. Service is impeccable and the pool lovely.

◖ MOJÁCAR

After leaving Cabo de Gata, you'll soon come to one of the most beautiful white villages in all of Andalucía—and that is saying a lot. Sitting high above the sea, the town of Mojácar wraps itself around a spur of mountain in a tight weave of bright white houses. From the beach below, the town looks like a stack of sugar cubes glinting sweetly in the sun. Up top, the town reveals itself as a honeycomb of tiny alleyways and pin-sized plazas, all washed in brilliant white, trimmed in Mediterranean blue, and draped in kilometers and kilometers of pink and red bougainvillea. Mojácar's labyrinth layout is a legacy of its Moorish past. Its bohemian charm is more recent. In the 1960s, facing a crippling loss of population, the mayor offered free land to anyone who would build and stay in Mojácar. Artists responded in droves, turning the town into a melting pot of Andalusian charm and bubbling creativity. For nearly every bar, there is an art gallery. Meanwhile, the beaches that stretch out in the new town below, gave birth to a low-level resort boom—yet, thankfully, nothing like the high-rise horror on the Costa del Sol.

Sights

There is only one way to truly soak in the spirit of Mojácar—get lost in it. Each corner turned brings new delights—a blood red peony against an ancient blue windowsill, a sun-wizened artist painting abstract watercolors in a postage-stamp-sized patio, a tiny bar offering vegetarian couscous, or one of those sudden alleys bursting out through the whitewash to reveal an achingly beautiful view over the sea and land. Have your camera handy. During your wanderings, look out for the *indalo*. A stick figure with an arc connecting its two outstretched arms, this symbol of Almería is estimated to date back to 3000 B.C.

On the lower side of the town, facing the sea is **El Fuente,** the lovely 12-font public fountain. It dates back to Moorish days, though it has been refurbished as recently as the 1980s. In the past, it supplied the water to the town and was the main sight where women washed laundry using their feet. The **Puerta de la Ciudad,** standing between Plaza Fores and Plaza del Caño, is the original 16th-century entrance to the city. The white arch, which features the city's seal, sits on the foundation of the original Moorish gateway to the city. **La Casa del Torreón** (C/ Jazmín) was once the toll house for goods entering the city. Today, clad in a blanket of bright bougainvillea, it is a pretty, picturesque spot. It also houses a tiny *pensión*. The desert-colored **Iglesia de Santa María de Mojácar** (Pl. Parterre) church was built in the 16th century as both a house of worship and a fortress, hence its blocky, austere facade. **Plaza Nueva** is the thumping center of town. The broad mosaic-tiled plaza is lined with cafés on one side and on the other, an expansive view over the sun-mottled land beyond the town. Finally, at the top of the hill, **El Mirador del Castillo Belvedere** is a beautiful lookout point offering panoramic views of the sea. It was once home to a fort and castle, both destroyed in a 16th-century earthquake. All that remains is the cistern, which is now an arts center.

Below charming Moorish Mojácar, runs modern Mediterranean Mojácar, with some 21 kilometers (13 miles) of golden **beaches** unfurling in each direction along the sea. The urban beaches run just below the city along the lively **Paseo del Mediterraneo,** a road and promenade lined with cafés, restaurants, shops, and hotels. From the upper town, go straight down Avenida de Andalucía and you are there.

Accommodations

In the pueblo on the hill, there are a couple of charming lodging options. **Mamabel's**

(C/ Embajadores 3, tel. 95/047-2448, www
.mamabels.com, €80) is the most famous. This
family-run house features nine lovingly decorated rooms, all with sea views and romantic
ambience. The inn is decorated throughout
with antiques and art as well as dolls and other
crafts created by Mamabel herself, owner Isabel Aznar. **Pensión El Torreón** (C/ Jazmín
4, tel. 95/047-5259, €65) is another sweetly
decorated old house, located in the original
tollbooth of the town. It is also the locus of the
town's most peculiar rumor. Locals claim that
Walt Disney was born in this house in 1901
as one José Guirao Zamora. His mother gave
him up for adoption in Chicago to one Elias
Disney, and the rest is history. Though no one
in the Disney camp gives this story any credence, the rumor persists. **La Esquinica** (C/
Cano, s/n, tel. 95/047-5009, €55) offers simple rooms right in the heart of the charming
old quarter. **Vista Natalia** (C/ Cuesta de la
Fuente 22, tel. 95/047-2089, visnata@cajamar
.es, €85) are mini-apartments for daily rent on
the hillside sloping up into town. They come
complete with kitchen, laundry, a pool, and
weekly maid service.

Down on the beach, you can have your
choice of anything from cheap charmer to
luxe lodgings. At the top of the latter category is the **Parador de Mojácar** (Po. Mediterráneo 339, tel. 95/047-8250, mojacar@
parador.es, www.parador.es, €120). It is a new
parador with spacious rooms, lovely pools,
excellent views, wonderful local food, and
the beach at your doorstep. **Puerto Marina
Mojácar** (Po. Mediterráneo, s/n, tel. 95/047-
5811, www.hotelpuertomarinamojacar.es,
€130) is a sprawling resort complex that you
never have to leave. Activities from archery
to salsa dancing go on round the clock, the
food is hearty and plentiful, and the staff is
extremely accommodating. It is a perfect hotel
for families with kids. The only drawback is
the bland, uninspired (yet spacious) rooms.
Hotel Continental (Po. Mediterráneo 78, tel.
95/047-8225, www.continental-mojacar.com,
€100) is much more manageable. A bit past
its design prime, this hotel nonetheless offers

clean rooms, most with sea views (book one!),
and all the amenities including a climatized
pool and a beachside bar. **El Puntazo** (Po.
Mediterráneo 257, tel. 95/047-8265, info@
hotelelpuntazo.com, www.hotelelpuntazo
.com, €80) is a modern hotel in a sprawling
whitewashed complex on the sea. The pool
and gardens are meticulously manicured and
the entire place has a lot more charm than
some of the larger resorts.

Food
The old town is full of traditional bars and,
reflecting its artistic roots, a few interesting
ones as well. **Mamabel's** (C/ Embajadores 3,
tel. 95/047-2448) hotel offers some of the best
food in town with creative Mediterranean fare
including interesting salads, fresh seafood,
and Arabic-influenced dishes like couscous.
Opening hours are sporadic here. An upscale
local favorite is **Palacio** (Pl. Caño 3, tel.
95/047-2846, €30), which offers an internationally inspired menu. **Casa Minguito** (Pl.
Ayuntamiento, s/n, tel. 95/047-8614) specializes in traditional Spanish fare, particularly
grilled meats. Along the beach, you'll find the
usual assortment of seafood restaurants, piz-
zerias, and fast-food joints. During the high
season (spring and early summer), most eating
establishments are open daily from 1–4 P.M.
and 8–11 P.M. However, in winter and other
slow times, hours are drastically reduced.

Information and Services
The **tourist office** (C/ Glorieta, s/n, tel.
95/061-5163) is in the old town, close to the
Plaza Nueva. There is also an office on the
beach, at the intersection of Avenida de Andalucía with the Paseo del Mediterráneo.

Getting There and Around
Mojácar is located just off the E-15/A-7, which
runs between Almería to the south and Murcia to then. Coming from Almería, take the
exit 530 towards Los Gallardos/Turre/Mojácar.
From Murcia, follow exit 534 towards Antas/
Vera/Garrucha/Mojácar and then switch to
exit 525 into Mojácar.

ANDALUCÍA

By bus, **Alsa** (tel. 90/242-2242, www.alsa.es) runs daily routes from Almería, Murcia, and Madrid. The closest train service is in Almería, which is to say, it's not close at all.

Within Mojácar, you can move between the hilltop pueblo and the beach via local bus. It originates near the tourist office in the pueblo and goes down Avenida de Andalucía, and then makes a loop around the city's beaches. It runs about every half-hour in summer with service stopping around midnight. In winter, it is less frequent and service stops at 10 P.M.

VALENCIA AND MURCIA

Comprising one of the most fertile swathes of the Iberian Peninsula, Valencia and Murcia make up the area called Levante. The name comes from the phrase *"se levanta"* ("it rises"), referring to the sun. The sun is a vital part of the region. It bathes the 800 kilometers (500 miles) of glittering coast in year-round balmy temperatures and it nourishes the thousands of hectares of crops—orange orchards, vegetable farms, olive trees, almond trees, vineyards, rice paddies—that have given this land its nickname, Huerta de Europa (Europe's Garden). This garden has been watered since time immemorial by the main rivers of Turia in Valencia and Segura in Murcia and, since the Moorish times, helped considerably by an ingenious irrigation method involving water wheels and canals.

Levante lies on the Mediterranean coast just below Cataluña and Aragón. Castilla-La Mancha and Andalucía form its western border. The region of Valencia (Comunidad Valenciana) sits on top. It has three provinces—Castellón, Valencia, and Alicante. Valencia city is its capital. The region of Murcia (officially called the Comunidad Autónoma de la Región de Murcia) is comprised of just one province—itself, and Murcia city is its capital. This Spanish habit of naming capital cities after their corresponding regions can be confusing to a tourist. Just be aware of the difference should it come up in your travels. Another difference may crop up, too—the language. In the 13th century, after the Christians re-took the region from the Moors, many people moved in from Cataluña, introducing their Catalan tongue. Over

HIGHLIGHTS

◖ Barrio del Carmen: This lively barrio of Valencia, nicknamed "El Carme," is a medieval mecca of arty boutiques, creative cuisine, and bars, bars, bars (page 705).

◖ La Ciutat: Officially called the Ciudad de las Artes y las Ciencias, this cultural city includes a science center, a planetarium, an opera house, and Europe's largest aquarium. The all-white complex, designed by Spanish architect Santiago Calatrava, is stunning (page 706).

◖ Albufera: Just miles from downtown Valencia, this misty lagoon is a haven for hundreds of species of birdlife. It is also the best place in the region for paella (page 718).

◖ Sagunto: The ancient city of Saguntum where the Second Punic War got its bloody start, this town is a treasure trove of well-preserved, little-visited Roman ruins (page 719).

◖ Isla de Tabarca: Escape the 21st century on an island with no cars. Tiny Tabarca offers miles of glittering beaches, an old historic core surrounded by medieval walls, and charming fishermen's cottages that have been turned into peaceful inns (page 732).

◖ Elche: This charming town has an archaeological heritage going back nearly 2,500 years and a fascinating date-palm forest that was planted by the town's Moorish rulers in the 10th century (page 732).

◖ Dénia: If you are craving a Costa Blanca resort with a little bit of Spanish culture thrown in, you can't go wrong in this bustling port town with excellent beaches, a wealth of water sports, and some of Spain's liveliest traditional festivals (page 734).

◖ Altea: Right in the middle of some of the most over-exploited real estate on the Costa Blanca, tiny Altea offers a charming alternative of winding cobblestone streets, whitewashed buildings, gourmet restaurants, and art galleries (page 738).

◖ Cartagena: With a wealth of Carthaginian and Roman ruins, this bustling maritime town offers ancient history, a romantically tattered medieval center, a lively fishing quarter lined with seafood restaurants – and easy access to the wild Mediterranean coast to the south and the beautiful resort of Mar Menor and La Manga (page 745).

LOOK FOR **◖** TO FIND RECOMMENDED SIGHTS, ACTIVITIES, DINING, AND LODGING.

VALENCIA AND MURCIA

© AVALON TRAVEL PUBLISHING, INC.

the centuries, it evolved into the regional language of Valenciano. Though not as prevalent as Catalan is in Cataluña, you will encounter it especially on street signs, public transportation, and restaurant menus—in short all the tourist spots. To complicate things further, Murcia has its own version called, not surprisingly, Murciano. But don't fret: Levante, particularly along the coast, survives on the bread and butter of tourism, so Spanish translations will always be available—and in very touristy areas, such as the Costa Blanca, everything will be in English.

Levante is famous in Spain for two reasons—its festivals and its food. Throughout the region, the wild fire-fest known as **Las Fallas** takes place. Giant, elaborate effigies are dotted around town and then torched at midnight on March 19. Nowhere is this party more celebrated than in the city of Valencia. (See sidebar, *Burn, Baby, Burn.*) Also characteristic of this region are the, **Moros y Cristianos festivals** that take place in April. Locals dress as warring bands of Moors and Christians to reenact thousand-year-old battles. These festivities are famed for the brilliance and beauty of the costumes. (See sidebar, *A 500-Year Losing Streak.*) In June, the region celebrates Saint John with the **Hogueras de San Juan.** The culmination of this fiesta is giant bonfires on the beach. One thing that all three of these festivals (and their many small-town variants) have in common is noise. The people of Valencia and Murcia love noise. Leading up to Las Fallas and extending past San Juan, the international sale of fireworks peaks as every man, woman, and child invests a lot of euros in *petardos* (firecrackers). They are strung from trees, piled in plazas, and flung randomly on the streets. The noise is deafening and non-stop. Even though you'll be jumping in your shoes each time one goes off, you'll soon notice that neither dogs nor babies seem fazed. Bring earplugs (and a long-sleeve shirt to ward off burns) and you'll be fine, too.

The food of Levante is a gastronomic feast. It's based on the freshest of produce; the bounties of the sea; game, fowl, and meat from in-land ranches; and legumes and rice from the paddies in the region. Of course, this culminates in the one Spanish dish that is famous throughout the world—paella. Though all paellas have as their base rice, saffron, and olive oil, the classic *paella valenciana* consists of rabbit and broad beans—no seafood at all! In fact, hard-liner locals will tell you that a true paella never mixes meat and seafood. (See sidebar, *All About Paella,* for more information on this local dish.)

Everywhere you go in the region, you will see signs and booths hawking *horchata* (*orxata* in Valenciano). This milky, nutty drink has neither milk nor nuts. Rather it is crushed *chufas.* The closest English translation is "tiger nuts" and the easiest explanation is that it is a soft, sweetish tuber. One of the oldest plants to be cultivated, sacks of them were found in the tomb of Tutankhamen. Chufa has been cultivated in Levante for millennia and the resultant *horchata,* tasting sweetish and vaguely of almonds, is an absolute addiction throughout Spain.

PLANNING YOUR TIME

You could do like the Spaniards and easily while away an entire month's worth of vacation here, but if you are coming from the United States determined to see Spain in all its fabled glory, you might just skip the whole region. That'd be a shame though. At an absolute minimum, give the interesting city of Valencia two days. It is just a few hours away by train from either Madrid or Barcelona, and cheap in-country flights will have you in the capital of oranges and paella in less time than that. In two days you can see La Ciutat (the arts and science center), explore the old town and Barrio del Carmen, plus have time to spend on the city's excellent beaches. With another day, you can travel to charming Alicante. One more, and you'll be able to add a train ride up the Costa Blanca with a stop in atmospheric Altea.

When to go depends on your schedule. Sun shines much of the year, but the only really hot time is summer. Fall and spring can be chilly and winter downright cold—though it rarely drops below freezing and the sun still throws its Mediterranean glow most days. Festivals might also sway your agenda. If you are in Spain in March, you should definitely head to Valencia city for the magnificent Las Fallas, one of the country's most exuberant festivals. If you can't make it for an overnight, many travel agents in Madrid and Barcelona run one-day trips. Finally, consider the tourist season. Summer along the Costa Blanca is hopping. A year round refuge for Northern European travelers, the area picks up considerably as Spaniards descend in droves on their summer holidays—July and August being the busiest. In these months, you might consider heading a bit out of the way, maybe to the coasts of Murcia, which are much less developed. In any case, don't consider traveling in summer without first making reservations.

Valencia

Bustling Valencia is often overlooked when dreams of a Spanish vacation are conjured. Third in size behind Madrid and Barcelona, more reserved than sloe-eyed Andalucía, and more urban than the vast resorts lining Iberian's coasts, Valencia just doesn't stir the imagination. It should. Along with all of the amenities of big-city life—museums, cutting-edge cuisine, rollicking nightlife, good shopping—Valencia offers an evocative Gothic quarter, kilometers of sandy beaches, and arguably the most spectacular aquarium and science center in the world, La Ciutat. Throw in beautiful parks, architecture from medieval to ultra-modern, and a mild climate year-round and you have a nearly perfect vacation city. The feeling is only enhanced by what Valencia lacks—big tourist crowds. There are tourists, of course, but nothing like you will encounter in Barcelona, Sevilla, or Granada. There is still breathing room and the local-to-tourist ratio always tilts in favor of the former. However, the tide is changing and Valencia is fast emerging as a destination of choice for travelers in the know. Part of the push has come from the wind-blown sails of the 32nd America's Cup. Valencia is hosting this world-class event (only the Olympics and soccer's World Cup draw larger television audiences) in 2007 and preparations have included a complete revamping of the city's once down-and-dreary port. With sponsors like Prada and Louis Vuitton, the Port America's Cup (the official name of the new port) has been decked out in stylish restaurants, flashy high-end clubs, and trendy boutiques. Full yachting and pleasure boat services have also been added. The result is a city bristling with the new but still rooted in the past. Visit in March when the dizziness of Las Fallas takes over and you'll see the Spanish love of fiesta at its most fiery. Have a glass of the ancient drink *horchata* while gazing upon the city's magnificent cathedral—rumored to hold the Holy Grail. Enjoy a *paella valenciana* on the beach in the town where the world-famous dish was born. The delicious possibilities are endless.

HISTORY

Iberian tribes, the Greeks, and later the Carthaginians each set roots along the Río Turia, but the city didn't start to take shape until the Romans founded Valentia in 137 B.C. and began the cultivation of the region's famed *huertas* (vegetable farms). After being captured by the Moors in the 8th century, Valencia flourished as a powerful agricultural center thanks to extensive improvements to the irrigation systems. Many of the Moorish techniques are still in use today (though, obviously, the equipment has been updated). As the Christian Reconquista waged throughout the Iberian Peninsula, many military leaders and minor noblemen fought for their own piece of the action, including the legendary soldier El Cid. (See sidebar, *El Cid: Fact and Fiction,* in

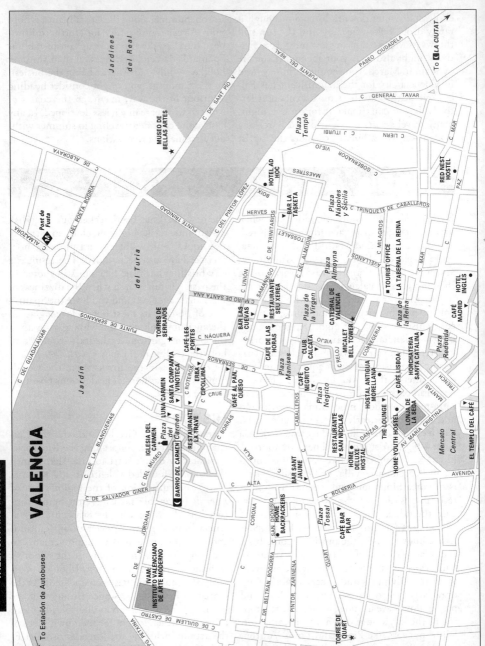

VALENCIA

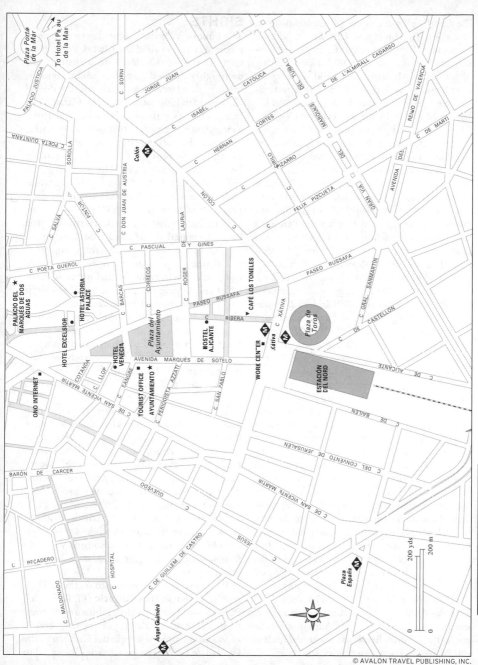

VALENCIA AND MURCIA

the *Castilla y León* chapter.) Commanding an army of both Moors and Christians, he took Valencia in 1094 and ruled the city as his own kingdom until he died in1099. Upon hearing of his death, Moorish forces laid siege to the city. Legend has it that El Cid's wily wife Jimena propped the dead leader's body on his horse and sent it to the gates of the city. The Moors, terrified of the powerful leader, retreated. The rouse didn't hold for long and the siege began again in earnest. Alfonso VI intervened, but faced with a major loss, he torched the city rather than hand it over. The Moorish Almoravids took over and ruled Valencia until Jaume I captured it definitively for the Spanish crown in 1238. However, rather than annex it to the Kingdom of Aragón or Cataluña, it was made its own self-governing state. The 15th and 16th centuries—Spain's Golden Age—were good to the city and it prospered economically and culturally. However, warfare marred the city throughout the 18th and 19th centuries. In the early 1700s, Valencia sided with Austrian King Charles in the War of Spanish Succession. The city was a major site of battle and English forces in support of the Austrians held it for over a year. When the Bourbons won and King Felipe ascended to the throne, he punished the city by taking away most of its legislative powers. During the Peninsular War (the Napoleonic war that attempted to take Spain for the French), Valencia suffered a months-long siege. Shell marks are still visible on the Torres de Quart. In the Spanish Civil War, Valencia served for a time as the capital of the Republican forces. As a result, Franco's nationalists unleashed a heavy siege and blockade on the city. Following the war, the Valenciano language was outlawed (as were all the regional tongues). In 1957, the Río Turia spilled from its banks putting Valencia under up to two meters (six feet) of water in places. The government responded by re-routing the river and created a lovely park in its place. After Franco's death and the institutionalization of democracy, Valencia received Autonomous status in 1982. Since then it has reasserted itself as one of Spain's most dynamic cities.

SIGHTS

The bulk of Valencia's sights lay in a circle of medieval streets called the **Ciutat Vella,** (Old City) in the local Valenciano dialect. It can be roughly divided into four zones: Ayuntamiento, El Mercat, Catedral, and Barrio del Carmen. Snaking away from the Ciutat Vella in a rambling swathe of green is the Río Turia, a long-dammed riverbed that now boasts parks, playgrounds, walking paths, and museums. At the end of Turia is the Ciudad de las Artes y las Ciencias, locally called "La Ciutat," an architectural wonderland housing an aquarium and science museum. Beyond that are the city's beaches and Port America's Cup.

Valencia's tourist bureau (www.turisvalencia .es) has created the **Museu Obert,** or open-air museum. It is a series of walking itineraries to Valencia's top sights. Each sight has a code listed on a sign in front. By dialing tel. 65/080-0200 and keying in the number of the sight and your language preference, you can get a complete introduction to the sight. However, you must have a cell phone and be ready to pay for the charges (with an American phone, fees could be astronomical). Alternatively, you can purchase the €1 *Tourist Guide Valencia* at the tourist office and follow the several itineraries it lays out.

To get a quick overview of the city from someone who really knows it, contact **Valencia Guias** (Po. Pechina 32, tel. 96/385-1740, www .valenciaguias.com). Part of the Valencia Tourism Commission, this group of professional guides can arrange private and group tours. They also give regularly scheduled tours leaving from the main tourist office in the Plaza de la Reina at 10 A.M. every Saturday with extended days in summer (two hours, €12, children €6). The same group also runs **Valencia Bikes,** which offers guided tours on bike and bike rentals.

If you prefer someone else to do the driving, try the **Valencia Bus Turistic** (Pl. Reina, tel. 96/341-4400, www.valenciabusturistic.com, €13). The one-hour route offers an overview of Valencia from the Barrio del Carmen to the Ciudad de las Artes y las Ciencias. No need to book ahead, just show up to the bus stop in the Plaza de la Reina (you can't miss the big red bus) and pay on boarding. Headphones give an overview of the sights in eight languages, though the static can be annoying. The company also offers excellent bus trips to the sights outside of Valencia city. Check their bilingual website for detailed information.

Ayuntamiento

Anchored by the train station to the south, this bustling barrio comprises Valencia's commercial zone. It also houses the city's most expansive square, the **Plaza del Ayuntamiento,** composed of the Renaissance town hall building on one side and the opulent Correos (main post office) on the other. The plaza is ringed with palm trees and a dozen delightful art deco flower stalls. Next to the train station—an exuberant display of modernist architecture—you'll find the **Plaza de Toros** (C/ Xátiva 28, tel. 96/351-9315, closed Mon.). Built in 1850, it hosts the city's most important bullfighting events during Las Fallas and in July. There is an interesting museum attached.

The most intriguing sight in this barrio is the baroque **Palacio del Marqués de Dos Aguas** (C/ Rinconada García Sanchís, s/n, tel. 96/351-6392, 10 A.M.–2 P.M. and 4–8 P.M. Tues.–Sat., 10 A.M.–2 P.M. Sun., closed Mon., €2.40). The alabaster doorway is nothing short of astonishing with its life-sized carved figures. The inside is given over to Spain's national ceramics museum. It is interesting enough, but after the opulence of the doorway, a bit of let down. Only go if you are really into ceramics. If not, enjoy the exterior of the building from the Café de Dos Aguas just across the alleyway.

El Mercat

This colorful barrio stretches out around the central market in a web of streets lined with laid-back cafés, neighborhood bars, flea markets, and grimy sex shops. One of its most peculiar squares is actually round. The ancient **Plaza Redonda** is a completely encircled plaza featuring a ring of tiled booths mostly selling

© CANDY LEE LABALLE

detail of the doorway of the Palacio del Marqués de Dos Aguas

sewing supplies. It makes for some interesting photos, however the real star of this barrio is the **Mercado Central** (Pl. Mercado, s/n, 7 A.M.–2 P.M. Mon.–Sat., closed Sun.). One of the largest covered markets in Europe, it has a delightful modernist exterior of red brick, colorful tiles, and iron-grated windows. The slate-roofed cupola is topped by a fanciful weathervane. Inside, over 900 stalls are laden with vibrant displays of fruit, vegetables, candies, spices, and meats. The fishmonger area lies right under the spectacular cupola and is a riot of activity in the early morning when the city's chefs descend to pick out the day's specials. There are also cozy, open-air bars tucked along the outside of the market, most specializing in fried fish and sandwiches.

Kitty-corner from the market is the **Lonja de la Seda** (Pl. Mercado, s/n, tel. 96/352-5478, 10 A.M.–2 P.M. and 4:30–8:30 P.M. Mon.–Sat., 10 A.M.–2 P.M. Sun., closed Mon., €2), the "Silk Exchange." One of Europe's most impressive Gothic structures, this UNESCO World Heritage Site was begun in 1483 and finished in 1498. Its 20,000 square meters (five acres)

© CANDY LEE LABALLE

Try the counters around El Mercat for fresh fried seafood and sandwiches.

of marble and stone served as Valencia's medieval trading center and is evidence of the city's wealth during that time. The main salon is both austere and soothing, with inlaid floors and impossibly high ceilings with heavy iron chandeliers. Wandering through, try to evoke the bustle of the merchants who did business here almost 600 years ago.

Catedral

The central portion of the Ciutat Vella is anchored by two majestic plazas flanking the city's imposing cathedral. **Plaza de la Reina** is the locus of all tourism. The main tourist office is here and this is where most tour groups and the tour busses take off from. As such, it is lined with souvenir stalls, cheap bars, and snack shops. By night, nearly every seat on the sidewalk is full with holiday-makers. At the northern tip of the Plaza, the Gothic bell tower of **Micalet** (10 A.M.– 12:30 P.M. and 4:30–6:30 P.M. Mon.–Fri., 10 A.M.–1:30 P.M. and 5–6:30 P.M. Sat. and Sun., €2.20) rises 51 meters (167 feet) above

the bustle in centuries-old stoic glory. It is home to 14 medieval bells, including its namesake, Micalet, a nearly 11,000-kilogram (24,000-pound) monster built in 1539. For a spectacular 360° panoramic view of Valencia, climb the tower's 207 steps to the top. The winding staircase is not for the weak of thighs or faint of heart—it is a long way up, but the view does compensate and the rooftop benches give you time to catch your breath for the dizzying way down.

Built between the 13th and 15th centuries, the **Catedral** (tel. 96/391-8127, 10 A.M.– 6:30 P.M. daily, reduced hours in winter, €3) is a wonderful mesh of styles with three grand doors representing different architectural epochs. The **Puerta de los Apóstoles** (Apostle's door) is Gothic, the **Puerta del Palau** is Romanesque, and the iron **Puerta de los Hierros** is baroque. Enter through the latter, off the Plaza de la Reina. The gaping interior is decidedly Gothic in its moody austerity. After some respectful ogling of the altar and its rather grotesque display of the mummified left arm of the long-

one of the cathedral's three doors on the Plaza de la Virgen

dead San Vicente (Saint Vincent), head straight for the **Capillo del Santo Cáliz** (Chapel of the Holy Grail). Yes, the same one that has kept fans of Indiana Jones and Dan Brown intrigued by the millions. Supposedly the chalice from which Jesus drank at the Last Supper, this red agate and gold cup is said to have arrived in Spain around A.D. 258. It bounced around from church to church until finally landing in Valencia in 1437. Whether or not it is the real Holy Grail is debatable and considering the astounding lack of interest in the cup's potential touristic value, it is also doubtable. The cathedral also houses a small museum with a few lovely works by Goya. Get your best view of the cathedral from the elegant, marble-floored **Plaza de la Virgen.** Here, each Thursday at noon, seven elected wise men gather to hold the Tribunal de las Aguas in front of the Apostle's door. This water tribunal has been meeting to mediate disputes over water usage in the surrounding farms for over 1,000 years. The tribunal is quite a tourist attraction, so get there early if you want to see the legal action.

Barrio del Carmen

The lovely Barrio del Carmen, locally called "El Carme," is the most atmospheric in all of Valencia. What it lacks in major sights, it more than makes up for in charm, color, and style. Walking its streets by day leads you through enchanting alleyways, past colorful buildings sporting flower-laden iron balconies, and into quiet, tree-lined plazas. Long a mecca for Valencia's bohemian crowd, El Carme also boasts more than its fair share of modern boutiques, hip bars, and trendy restaurants. It more or less spreads out in a triangular arc west and north from the Plaza de la Virgen. Two of its liveliest streets are Calle Cabelleros, where most of the Ciutat Vella's nightlife is located, and Calle Roteros, jammed with tiny restaurants and bars. The barrio takes its name from the **Iglesia del Carmen** (Pl. Carmen 7), a rambling baroque complex that boasts an outstanding facade. The building attached to the main church now serves as an extension of the fine arts museum and offers free exhibits. At the end of Calle Serranos is the **Torres**

de Serranos (Pl. Fueros, s/n, 10 A.M.–2 P.M. and 4:30–8:30 P.M. Tues.–Sat., 10 A.M.–2 P.M. Sun., closed Mon., €2). Built from 1392 to 1398, this castle-like structure served as the northern gate into the city. A few blocks away, the eastern gate, **Torres de Quart** (Pl. Santa Úrsula, s/n, 10 A.M.–2 P.M. and 4:30–8:30 P.M. Tues.–Sat., 10 A.M.–2 P.M. Sun., closed Mon., €2) was completed in 1460. Its exterior bears the marks of cannon fire inflicted by the French during the Napoleonic wars.

Valencia's modern art museum, **Instituto Valenciano de Arte Moderno** (C/ Guillém de Castro 118, tel. 96/386-3000, 10 A.M.–8 P.M. Tues.–Sun., later hours in summer, €2), better known as IVAM, houses an excellent collection of 20th-century art from sculpture to photography, particularly from Spanish artists.

Río Turia

In the 1950s, after centuries of flooding by the unpredictable River Turia, the city had the river re-routed. At first the plan was to put a motorway in the dry riverbed, but public outcry led to the creation of one of Valencia's most distinctive features. Today, the once turbulent river is a lovely swathe of green coursing 6.5 kilometers (four miles) through the heart of the city. It boasts thousands of trees, hundreds of benches, dozens of pathways, playgrounds, soccer fields, basketball courts, and cultural centers. Check www.culturia.org for a complete overview of the river and its offerings. Cross the park over the **Puente de la Trinidad** to get to **Museo de Bellas Artes** (C/ San Pío V, s/n, tel. 96/387-0300, 10 A.M.–8 P.M. Tues.–Sun., closed Mon., free). One of Spain's most important fine arts museums, it houses works by Velázquez, Goya, Bosch, and several prominent Valencian artists. Alongside the museum is the lovely, manicured **Jardines del Real,** blooming with rose gardens, fountains, and even a small zoo.

Midway down the river towards the sea, the **Palau de la Música** (www.palauvalencia.com) bursts from the greenway like an oasis of white stone and glass. Built to look like a Victorian greenhouse, this is Valencia's premier classical music venue. During festivals and summers, there are often free concerts in the gardens surrounding the building. The last sight of note you'll come to on the river before arriving at the arts and science complex is the whimsical **Gulliver playground.** Lying on his back, much larger than life, the hero from Jonathan Swift's book *Gulliver's Travels* plays host to hordes of happy children who slide down his legs and climb through his ears.

◖ La Ciutat

One of the most ambitious cultural projects begun in Europe in decades, the **Ciudad de las Artes y las Ciències** (Av. Autopista del Saler, s/n, tel. 90/210-0031, www.cac.es, €29) dominates the lower beds of the Turia with a futuristic series of buildings that comprise a massive arts and science complex, called La Ciutat (The City) in Valenciano. The **Museu de les Ciències Príncipe Felipe** rises out of the earth like a giant, shiny white roto-tiller. Under its soaring, ribbed windows, it houses a science museum with a strict hands-on policy for its creative displays. Kids love it. Just next door, like a Ferris wheel half stuck in the earth, **L'Hemisferic** is a planetarium and IMAX theater. Next to that is La Ciutat's latest addition, the **Palau de les Arts Reina Sofía,** opened in late 2006. It is an eye-shaped, state-of-the-art performing arts center that serves as one of Spain's top opera venues.

The top draw to La Ciutat is the amazing **L'Oceanogràfic** (10 A.M.–9 P.M. daily). With more than 45,000 specimens from over 500 different species of marine and sea animals living in nine underground water towers, this is easily Europe's largest marine park and one of the most spectacular in the world. Displays cover the breadth of the world's marine habitats from tropical to artic. In the Oceans tower you can walk underwater as sharks swim over your head. There is also a crowd-pleasing dolphinarium with daily dolphin shows. Prices for La Ciutat are frequently adjusted, but L'Oceanogràfic is the most expensive venue at a minimum €22. You can buy a combined pass for the entire complex for under

the entrance to L'Oceanogràfic at Valencia's La Ciutat

€30. Also, if you travel to Valencia by train from another city in Spain, bring along your ticket, as there are frequent discount agreements between Renfe and La Ciutat.

ENTERTAINMENT AND EVENTS
Nightlife

Valencia's liveliest nightlife is clustered in the Barrio El Carmen. Bars get going around 9 P.M. and stay busy until about 1 A.M. during the week and 3 A.M. on the weekends. The partying goes on in the mega-discos that line Malvarrosa beach until dawn, with most of the clubs opening Thursday through Saturday from 11 P.M.–6 A.M. To find the best scene in El Carme, head straight to Calle Cabelleros, an elegant pedestrian street lined with old mansions and new bars from classy to questionable. **Taverna Cavellers** (C/ Cabelleros 23, tel. 96/391-2516) serves excellent wine in a cozy New Orleans–style bar complete with red walls, black-and-white photos, and jazz on the stereo. **Fox Congo** (C/ Cabelleros 35, tel.

96/392-5527) draws an older crowd with its animal-print decor and solid onyx bar. Despite the cheesy name, **Johnny Maracas** (C/ Cabelleros 39, tel. 96/391-5266) is a den of tropical cool with wacky touches like a fish tank-bar and television sets embedded in the urinals. Music is a mix of pop and Latin. On weekends it gets rowdy with an older, party-seeking crowd mixed in with letting-it-all-hang-loose tourists. **Sant Jaume** (C/ Cabelleros 51, tel. 96/391-2401) is a classic bar complete with dark wood and brass fittings. It is the place to go if you want to try the famed *agua de Valencia*, orange juice with *cava* (Spanish sparkling wine).

Why it is so popular, no one really knows, but the place to start the night is **Café Negrito** (Pl. Negrito 1, tel. 96/391-4233). The crowd—always a hearty mix of locals and tourists—bursts out onto the plaza during warmer months. **Bolseria Café** (C/ Bolseria 41, tel. 96/391-8903) is another longtime local favorite that pumps out a please-everyone mix of house, funk, Latin, and pop. Down the street, **Murrayfield** (C/ Bolseria 19, 96/391-9545) is a classic pub/dive. It boasts nonstop sports on the television sets and nonstop heavy guitar riffs on the sound system. **Radio City** (C/ Santa Teresa 19, tel. 96/391-4151) is a thoroughly modern bar/cultural center that offers a roster of events from flamenco to short films. Weekend nights are given over to heavy doses of Spanish disco. **Café de las Horas** (C/ Conde de Almodóvar 1, tel. 96/391-7336) is where to head if you just want to chill out. The over-the-top decor is equal parts baroque and kitsch, complete with fluttering angels, dozens of candles, and a marvelously worn mosaic tile floor. Mixed among the lovey-dovey couples are some of Valencia's most colorful characters. **Records de L'Avenir** (C/ Roteros 14, tel. 96/391-5260) is run by denizens of Valencia's film and music scene. As such, it is impossibly hip, yet surprisingly friendly. Music runs from reggae to funk to soul.

Closer to the Mercat, seek out the funky **Café Lisboa** (Pl. Doctor Collado 9, 96/391-9484), which draws an intellectual coffee crowd by day and a bohemian, punky group at night. **La Claca** (C/ San Vicente 3, www .laclaca.com) is a favorite among the expat crowd with a daily mix of music from Smashing Pumpkins to Aretha Franklin. They also host flamenco nights and live DJ sessions. **Café Madrid** (C/ Abadía de San Martín 10) is a classic belle epoque café that becomes a jam-packed dance spot at night. The music is solid Spanish pop and the crowd mostly local and early 30s. If you want to keep going late, but don't want to head out to the beach, El Carme has one consistent late-night player. **Calcata** (C/ Reloj Viejo, s/n) offers three floors of fun around a traditional courtyard in one of Valencia's old mansions. It is tricky to find, but the street is short—just follow the crowds, especially after 3 A.M. when the bar really picks up. Closing time is around 6 A.M.

For big clubs, bigger beats, and the biggest parties in Valencia, head to the beach. Along Malvarrosa beach and on the surrounding streets—especially Calle Eugenia Viñes—are dozens of mega-clubs offering a little bit of everything from chill-out cool to hard-rock grunge. Most places are open by 10 P.M., which means you can get there via metro (Metro: Eugenia Viñes). Once the metro shuts down at midnight, you'll have no choice but to take a cab back into the city center. The ride should run about €10. The best place to start the evening is **Luna Jardín** (C/ Isabel de Villena 59, 6 P.M.–3 A.M.), a sexy beachside club offering interesting tapas and meals alongside the latest in sophisticated techno. The majority of the nightclubs are generic super-discos complete with requisite burly bouncers, deafening Euro-trash techno, and laser light shows. The granddaddy of them all is **Akuarela** (C/ Eugenia Viñes 152, www.akuarela.es, Thurs.–Sun. June–Sept.), which lords over the beach with a glowing intensity and volume that is stunning. Packed to the gills all summer long, this is your spot if you just want to go wild on the dance floor. For a more chilled-out experience, head to **Gandhara** (C/ Eugenia Viñes 225, www.gandharaterraza .com). The front part of the complex is a standard dimly lit, brashly loud disco, but keep going back until you hit the spectacular open-air terrace. Lined with tiki torches and Moroccan-style mini-dens with cushy floor cushions and veiled curtains, this is the perfect place to unwind with excellent cocktails and low-key house music. The crowd scales demographics with everyone from 20-something girls in micro-minis to 40-something couples deep in conversation. If you want to keep going straight into daytime, head to the legendary all-day Saturday and Sunday parties at **Flamingo Club Social** (C/ Isabel de Villena 57), which doesn't even open its doors until 8 A.M.

Festivals and Events

Each March, Valencia hosts one of the world's most famous fiestas, **Las Fallas.** A boisterous celebration that combines tradition, art, bonfires, religion, and a whole lot of noise, Las Fallas takes place every year March 16–March 19. To enjoy it you only need to know three things. One, book your room at least six months early and be prepared to pay a large deposit. Two, bring very good earplugs. One of Las Fallas most distinctive characteristics is the noise and fireworks explode all day and night. Three, leave any fear of crowds or of fire back home. This is a typical, jam-packed Spanish festival that to an untrained foreign eyes seems to be teetering on the brink of catastrophe. Did I mention the fires? You have to let loose if you are going to enjoy this one. Finally, if you are in Barcelona, Madrid, or any other major city during Las Fallas, check the tourist offices and local travel agents. Most organize one-day trips to Las Fallas leaving on the morning of March 19 and returning in the wee hours of the 20th. Just enough time to get a taste of the fun. (See sidebar, *Burn, Baby, Burn.*)

On July 21, Valencia trades it flames and firecrackers for flowers and floats in the **Batalla de las Flores** (Battle of the Flowers). Rather than a floral competition, the flowers are actually used as missiles. As young ladies in costume ride down the streets on flower-covered floats, the crowds belt them with brightly colored marigolds. The battle goes on for about an hour, leaving the streets of Valencia carpeted in flowers. Valencia hosts dozens of other festivals from the solemn and religious to the raucous and colorful. For a complete listing, including dates and details in English, check www.turisvalencia.es.

SPORTS AND RECREATION
Beaches

The two city beaches are **Las Arenas,** running behind the hotel complex of the same name on the southern end of Valencia's Mediterranean coast, and **Malvarrosa,** which runs to the north. Despite reports that they are dirty and polluted, the contrary is true. The wide beaches are remarkably clean boasting kilometers of fine, white sand. The beaches both have lifeguards, umbrella and cot rentals, playgrounds, and dozens of restaurants and bars lining the beachside promenades. Both beaches are easily accessible from the city center by catching metro line 4 and taking it to the end where it loops around in a series of beach stops. (Metro: Ponte de Fusta is the closest stop to the Ciutat Vella.) Most of line 4 is actually above ground and is referred to locally as the "tram" rather than the underground metro. You can also catch bus 19 year round to the beach. During summer months, additional beach bus lines 20, 21, 22, and 23 are set up. Check with the tourist office or look for the bright yellow posters announcing the opening of the lines on bus stops. The one major drawback of these beaches is that they get extremely crowded in summer and on weekends.

For a more low-key beach, fronting lovely protected lands rather than city lights, you'll have to head out of town. South along the coast is **El Saler,** a pristine stretch of white beach that is less than half an hour away by bus. Head to the Estación de Autobuses and catch any one of the Autocares Herca lines towards Perelló. Any piece of coast from El Perelló south towards Cullera is worth going to.

Biking

Valencia is a bike-friendly city, especially the paths through the lovely Turia park and the promenades along Malvarrosa beach. Take a guided tour or rent your own at **Orange Bikes** (C/ Santa Teresa 8, tel. 96/391-7551, www .orangebikes.net), a full-service bike shop near the Mercado Central. They are also the first in the city to rent electric bicycles. Another good choice is **Do You Bike** (Pl. Horno San Nicolas, tel. 96/315-5551 or 67/573-0217) in Barrio del Carmen. **Valencia Bikes** (Po. Pechina 32, tel. 96/385-1740, www.valenciabikes.com) is run by Valencia Guia and offers several short introductory tours of the city.

Boating

The America's Cup changed the face of Valencia's port and has created opportunities for tour operators to offer boat excursions. The **Tourist-Info Valencia** (Pl. Reina 19) reserves two of the best. The **Sailing Boat Crossing** (€15) includes an explanation of sailing technique, while the **Sunset Sail** (€18) is a lovely evening tour that takes in the sunset while listening to jazz and enjoying a glass of *cava*. Personalized excursions can be arranged by contacting www.americascup.com or calling 96/381 6066 or 62/556-5067.

ACCOMMODATIONS

When deciding upon a hotel in Valencia, you need to decide if you'd rather be in town or on the beach. Easily traversed by tram, bus, and inexpensive taxis, the distance between the two areas is not feasibly walkable. Both areas boast wonderful restaurants, but for shopping, tapas-hopping, and lively plazas, choose the city center. If your plan is sun, sand, and siesta, stick with the beach.

Under €50

Proving that cheap doesn't have to mean sketchy is the wonderful little **C Hostal Antigua Morellana** (C/ En Bou 2, tel. 96/391-5773, info@hostalam.com, www.hostalam .com, €48). Run by the four Martínez sisters, the hotel offers clean, airy rooms at youth hostel prices. Rooms facing the courtyard are silent despite the location right near the central market. No breakfast is available, but just up the road, the sisters run a wonderful little

BURN, BABY, BURN: LAS FALLAS IN VALENCIA

An elaborate papier-mâché statue awaits a fiery fate at Las Fallas.

March 19. Valencia. Midnight. The night air is charred. Smoke hangs heavily over every street. The skyline has a nuclear orange glow. Over 500 massive works of art have been torched. Within the popping flames you can glimpse the still-smiling statues, some reaching as high as 15 meters (50 feet). As the crowd looks on, the smiles peel away, gaily painted clothes fade black, and then finally, the figure falls. A mad wave of applause surges through the city. As drinks and hugs are passed out freely, Valencianos gear up for a farewell blowout because Las Fallas has come to an end.

Las Fallas is a uniquely Valencian celebration that dates back as far as the 16th century. It started humbly enough when local carpenters decided to celebrate the beginning of spring by burning their *parots*, a type of wooden candelabra used to work by during dark winter evenings. Being fun-loving guys, they started dressing the *parots* to mimic the gentry class. A few centuries later, an artists guild was born

whose sole job was to build the figures now called *fallas*. Today, the *fallas* are masterful pieces of art composed of wood, plaster, fabric, and any other material that will burn. They can reach as high as a five-story building and take nearly a year to complete. (The building of a new *falla* traditionally begins the day after the old one has burned.) True to their origins, they still mock the government, the famous, and just about anyone else who has somehow drawn attention over the previous year.

In the pre-dawn hours of March 16, the hundreds of *fallas* are set up in an act called *la planta*. Each *falla* is sponsored by a neighborhood group that takes its name from the street or plaza where the *falla* is to be installed. The groups, also generally called *fallas*, raise money year-round to pay for the expensive statues. Most neighborhoods also sponsor a much smaller *falla* called a *ninot*, which the children of the barrio adopt as their own. After an 8 A.M. visit by a city judging committee, the *falleros* (as celebrants of the fiesta are called) take to the street. For the next four days, the city hosts a non-stop party. As Valencianos love to boast, ain't no sleeping going on.

Each barrio starts the day at 8 A.M. sharp with an ear shattering *desperta* – a heavy round of *petardas* (firecrackers). Then it's off for a breakfast of chocolate and *buñuelos*, a typical Valencian fritter. By noon, locals have gotten decked out in their *trajes de huertana de lujo* – elaborate baroque-style costumes. The women's dress is particularly lovely with full-bustled skirts and long-flowing veils. They parade around their barrios followed by a marching band belting out traditional music. At 2 P.M., the city explodes when the *mascleta* (a massive firecracker display) is unleashed in the Plaza del Ayuntamiento. It can last up to half an hour and the only rule is, the louder the better. Windows rattle, streets seem to shake, booming echoes whip around corners and hit your chest like an anvil. Earplugs – a brisk seller among street vendors – barely blunt the noise. Expect ringing ears for a few days. Afterwards, everyone makes their way to Plaza de la Virgen to offer flowers to a statue of the Virgen de los Desamparados (Our Lady of the Forsaken). Over the days of the festival, the flowers form a massive, flowing skirt for the virgin. The rest of the day and night is given over to frivolity. Lots of dancing and drinking in the streets goes on, especially in the bar-lined Barrio del Carmen. Meanwhile, social clubs prepare giant paellas in the streets and alleys. Normally, these are private affairs, not open to the public, though if you ask nicely, you might get a taste.

A tour of the *fallas* is a must and you'll find one on nearly every street. On the can't-be-missed list are those in Convento de Jerusalén, Plaza del Pilar, Na Jordana, and Plaza de la Merced. These regular blue-ribbon winners, standing head-to-head with surrounding buildings, will have you swooning like an Alejandro Sanz fan. Then just as soon as you recover from the realization that these gorgeous creations are slated for the pyre you'll notice that they are situated just scant meters from buildings that date back to pre-Fire Marshall days. Don't dwell on this. Valencia has been ritually setting itself on fire for centuries. No problem.

After a few evening glasses of *agua de Valencia* (a glorious combo of fresh OJ, brandy, and Spanish sparkling wine), check out the midnight fireworks. Each night, the display is bigger, culminating in the sky-scorching *nit de foc* (night of fire) extravaganza held on March 18.

Finally, the night of March 19, the day of San José, patron saint of Valencia and of carpenters, *la crema* (the burning) commences. First up, at 10 P.M., are the *ninots*. As they burn, teary-eyed children clasp hands and dance around the fire until it's gone. Of all the magnificent structures built for Las Fallas, only the *ninot* voted the best will be spared from the flames.

As midnight approaches, the crowd around each *falla* grows thicker. Shiny-suited firemen begin hosing down those worrisome historic/fire hazard buildings around 11 P.M. Then, as the clock strokes midnight, the first in a chain of firecrackers is lit. A few rapid-fire whiz-bangs later and the *falla* bursts into flame. For the first time in a week, the city is almost quiet. Except for the low swish of the fire hoses and the crackling pops of the fire, Valencia is holding its breath. When the *falla* falls, the noise rushes up again with locals and tourists alike cheering and hugging. The crowds then rush to the Plaza del Ayuntamiento to see the burning of the city *falla* – the largest one of all, often several stories tall. When it finally falls in a cracking, sizzling blaze, Las Fallas is officially over. However, the all-night party is just beginning. Drinking, dancing, and more firecrackers will go on until, like the *fallas* themselves, the last body falls – exhausted, ears buzzing – into bed.

If you want to attend Las Fallas, be sure to book well in advance. If you are in town any other time of year and would like a glimpse into this colorful fiesta, visit the **Museo Fallero** (C/ Monteolivete 4, tel. 96/352-5478, www.fallas .com, 10 A.M.-2 P.M. and 4:30-8:30 P.M. Tues.-Sat., 10 A.M.-2 P.M. Sun., closed Mon., €2), where all the winning *ninots* since 1934 are kept.

bakery, **Horno y Pastelería Alfonso Martínez** (C/ Ercilla 17). **Hostal Alicante** (C/ Ribera 8, tel. 96/351-2296, €45) is located on a lively pedestrian street, barely a block from the train station. Don't let the opulent staircase fool you, the rooms are basic and simple, but for price and location, you can't complain. At **Home Deluxe Hostel** (C/ Cadirers 11, tel. 96/391-4691, www.likeathome.net, €42) you can enjoy the laid-back, international vibe of a youth hostel but with private double rooms, each decorated in fun shabby-chic fashion. If you are after a youth hostel atmosphere, Home has two good choices in town: **Home Backpackers** (Pl. Vicente Iborra, s/n, tel. 96/391-3797, €12) in Barrio El Carmen and **Home Youth Hostel** (C/ La Lonja 4, tel. 96/391-6229, €15), which boasts a cool rooftop terrace. All three Home properties have Internet and sponsor parties and excursions for party-loving 20-somethings. Another popular hostel is the funky **Red Nest** (C/ La Paz 36, tel. 96/342-7168, www.nest-hostels.com, €14), which offers a central location, communal kitchen and laundry, a fun international staff, and wildly colored rooms and dorms. Also try their sister property, **Purple Nest** (Pl. Tetuan 5, tel. 96/353-2561, www.nest-hostels.com, €14).

€50-100

Hotel Venecia (C/ En Llop 5, tel. 96/352-4267, reservas@hotelvenecia.com, www.hotelvenecia.com, €85) is located on Plaza Ayuntamiento and offers modern, spotless rooms and an efficient staff. The location is ideal, but to make your stay extraordinary request a room looking over the lively plaza. **Hotel Excelsior** (C/ Barcelonina 5, tel. 96/351-4612, www.hoteles-catalonia.com, €85) is an exceptional hotel for the price, with art deco touches, an excellent location, and spacious rooms. Beds and baths both well exceed the hotel's three-star rating. Just outside of the old center, **Hotel Villarreal** (C/ Ángel Guimerá 58, tel. 96/385-3937, www.hotel-villarreal.com, €79) is a friendly little hotel offering good double rooms not far from the train station. The decor is a bit on the confectionary side, but everything is new and well maintained.

On the beach, **Hotel Sol Playa** (Po. Neptuno 56, tel. 96/356-1920, reservas@hotelsolplaya.com, www.hotelsolplaya.com, €85) offers just what its name implies—sun and sand—and not much more. The room decor is firmly entrenched in the 1970s and the hotel itself is a bit worn around the edges, but if you snag a room with a beachside terrace, the view more than makes up for the lack of style. The rooms next door at **Hostal El Globo** (Po. Neptuno 42, tel. 96/372-7777, reservas@hostalelglobo.com, www.hostalelglobo.com, €65) are a bit more updated and many offer sea views. If budget is a concern, both hotels offer rooms without a view for much cheaper.

Over €100

Ad Hoc (C/ Boix 4, tel. 96/391-9140, adhoc@adhochoteles.com, www.adhochoteles.com, €195) is a lovely boutique hotel tucked into an 19th-century townhouse. The owner collects antiques and his eye for exquisite detail is obvious throughout. Rooms feature high-beamed ceilings and exposed brick walls as well as luxurious linens. Breakfast is not included and at €9 you'd be better off joining the locals for a coffee at a sidewalk café in the bordering historic quarter. The hotel restaurant is a good bet for an excellent paella and draws as many locals as it does hotel guests. **Hotel Inglés** (C/ Marqués de Dos Aguas 6, tel. 96/351-6426, melia.ingles@solmelia.com, www.solmelia.com, €125), located in a turn-of-the-20th-century mansion, has long been a favorite for classic bedrooms, elegant public rooms, and attentive service. Since the Meliá chain took over, standards have only gone up. This is a great choice for those who like their hotel experience to feel grand. Be sure and have a coffee on the sidewalk café, which overlooks the astonishing alabaster doorway of the Palacio de Marqués de Dos Aguas. If you want luxury and don't mind paying for it, Valencia complies. **Hotel Astoria Palace** (Pl. Rodrigo 5, tel. 96/352-6737, www.hotelastoriapalace.com, €250) offers plush, well-appointed rooms that have drawn the admiration of Spanish opera stars and bullfighters, as well as a host of other highbrow movers and shakers. Every amenity is provided and the rooms are refreshingly spacious by European standards. The **Palau de la Mar** (Av. Navarro Reverter 14, tel. 96/316-2884, www.hospes. es, €140) is a lush cosmopolitan refuge. Stylish rooms boast dark-wood floors, soothing off-white walls, and cushy bed linen. It is quite a surprise after entering through the stately 19th-century mansion facade to find the hotel's tranquil Japanese style garden.

On the beach, the best (or at least most over-the-top) hotel is the luxury mega-resort **Las Arenas** (C/ Eugenia Viñes 22, tel. 96/312-0600, www.hotel-balneariolasarenas.com, €150). Opened in summer 2006, just in time for Valencia's hosting of the America's Cup, the 254-room hotel arcs around an 1898 historic bathhouse. All the usual five-star amenities are available, as well as personable, English-speaking staff. It is worth the extra money to splurge for a seaside room for the view and private balcony. The deluxe spa is expected to open by 2007. Skip the overpriced hotel dining room. Just around the corner, lining Paseo Neptuno, are several restaurants serving excellent local specialties at half the price, including favorite Casa Chimo.

FOOD
Like the rest of Levante, Valencia is known for its rice dishes (including world-famous paella), the freshness of its seafood, and the earthy goodness of its abundant vegetables. There are amazing restaurants and bars in all price ranges tucked all over town. For variety, head to El Carme—especially Calle Roteros—and browse the menus in the windows until you find something you fancy.

Cafés and Desserts
Tiled to the hilt, the charming **Horchateria Santa Catalina** (Pl. Santa Catalina 6, tel. 96/391-2379, 8 A.M.–9:30 P.M. daily) has been serving *horchatas* and pastries to Valencianos for nearly two centuries. It stays packed all day with locals of all ages tucking into excellent coffee drinks, ice-cream concoctions, and milkshakes. On weekends, clubbers on their last stop before heading home stop off for a sweet last call. With

less lineage, but better vistas, **El Micalet** (Pl, Virgen 4, 9 A.M.–10 P.M. daily) is a tiny corner spot offering *horchatas,* ice creams, frozen drinks, and cocktails on a massive terrace right in front of the cathedral. Do not be tempted to eat here—food is frozen and bleck. However, the cold, liquid offerings, all homemade by owner María Angeles, are just perfect.

For something more hearty than ice cream and pastries try one of Valencia's many bar/cafés—neighborhood places that segue from breakfast to lunch to cocktails in a single day. **Café Boatella** (Pl. Mercado 34, tel. 96/391-1314, 8 A.M.–10 P.M. daily) is a raucous little bar with a lively lunch scene. Clientele is as local as it is tourist and the food is basic Spanish from *tortilla* to fried fish. The trendy **El Templo del Café** (Av. María Cristina 12, tel. 96/315-2080, 8 A.M.–midnight daily) is open all day serving breakfasts, sandwiches, coffees, and cocktails in a modern dining room encircled by a wall of windows. It is the perfect perch to watch the buzzy street leading to the nearby Mercado Central. Just a few blocks from Plaza de la Reina, **The Lounge** (C/ Estamiñería Vieja 2, tel. 96/391-8094, 10 A.M.–1:30 A.M. Mon.–Fri., 6 P.M.–2:30 A.M. Sat. and Sun., €10) is a laid-back café by day with cheap, simple food from salads to stuffed pitas. The €7 daily menu is a steal for both the quantity and quality. By evening The Lounge takes on a neighborhood bar feel with a large English-speaking clientele. Wi-Fi is free, and so are the Spanish language exchanges on Monday nights.

Fusion Cuisine
In El Carme, there is no shortage of hip little restaurants offering exciting new takes on local products. One of the best is ◖ **Santa Companya Vinoteca** (C/ Roteros 21, tel. 96/392-2259, 7 P.M.–1 A.M. daily), famed both for its creative dishes and for its lack of a kitchen. The staff is long-haired hippy, the floors hardwood, the ceiling an undulating wave of weathered plaster, and the walls papered in old black and white photos. The menu is a luscious feast of non-cooked items—raw carpaccios, meal-sized salads, artisan

ALL ABOUT PAELLA

Without question, paella is Spain's most famous contribution to the world's table – edging out even tapas. Unfortunately, the uninitiated think paella is nothing more than glorified pilaf with a little yellow coloring. Even worse, outside of Spain – and, shamefully, within as well – what is served as paella is just glorified yellow pilaf. To enjoy this ubiquitous dish at its most delicious, fragrant, savory best, it will help to know a few facts.

Let's start with the name. It is pronounced "pie-AY-ya" and the word is actually Valenciano for "pan." As the dish has become synonymous with the name, the broad, flat-handled pan used to cook paella is now called the *paellera*. Paella's origin goes back to the rice-field workers of Valencia. They created paella as a simple one-pot lunch dish cooked over an open fire using whatever local products were close at hand. Today, it is one of the most versatile, emblematic dishes in Spain and a worldwide favorite for festive dinner parties.

Paella always starts with rice and the rice from Valencia's Albufera region is the most acclaimed in the country. It is so special that it even has its own *denominación de origen* (appellation), which carefully monitors the harvesting and processing of the rice. The favored type of rice is *bomba*, a short, low-starch grain. Albufera rice forms the basis of much of Valencia's *arroces* (rice dishes), including

paella. In fact, let's debunk the name paella right now. The correct name, and what you will see on menus, is *arroces*. Paella is only one of many different rice-based dishes.

The two main ingredients of paella are rice and olive oil, with saffron being a close third. After that, ingredients vary widely depending on the region, the season, and the chef's whim. The dish that started it all is simply called *paella valenciana* and it is traditionally made of rabbit, *ferraduras* (a broad green bean), and a handful of snails. Paellas are usually served "dry," that is, without any type of sauce or liquids. Many other rice dishes are "wet," or *caldoso* (served with stock).

The best place to guarantee a good rice dish is at an *arrocería*, or rice restaurant. Nearly every town in Spain will have at least one. The guaranteed way to insure a bad rice dish is to order one in a place that has a giant full-color sign out front advertising several different "paellas." This means the restaurant doesn't make their own paella, but rather uses a mass-producer of frozen paella, such as the company Paellador.

Paella and other rice dishes are often only offered for a minimum of two people (a good sign that the paella is being made to order). In other restaurants, particularly at lunchtime, restaurants prepare a large paella and serve it in individual portions as a starter course. When you order a paella as a meal, it will be

cheeses, and cured meats. Desserts are wild inventions such as whole sweet cherries sealed in cubes of martini jelly. The food is balanced by a reporter's notebook of wines from every Spanish D.O. (appellation) in the country, priced €7–35 the bottle. At least 20 by the glass are chalked on the wall. **Luna Carmen** (C/ Padre Huerfanos 2, 11 A.M.–4:30P.M. and 7P.M.–midnight daily) is a crisp modern bar with above average snacking. Their short menu features local favorites like cod and wild mushrooms amped up with worldly flavors like Korean kimchi sauce or dried plums. The location, right on the Plaza del Carmen, is

perfect for watching the locals—both trendy and crazy—rushing by. Less than a block from the Torres de Serranos, **Erba Cipollina** (C/ Padre Tosca 7, tel. 96/392-0496, 9 P.M.–midnight Mon.–Fri., 2–4 P.M. Sun., closed Sat.) is a crisp, clean, green and yellow temple to all things vegetarian—though this being Spain, there are a few carnivorous plates available. The salads are ample and intriguing and the *sushi de verdura* (vegetable sushi) is refreshing. The owners also sell jars of their own marmalades. (Note: Carrer Padre Tosca's original street name was Viriato and many maps still reflect this.)

brought to your table and set in the center. Traditionally, Spaniards eat directly from the pan, though restaurants now almost exclusively place plates down for individual servings. You may notice the waiter or your Spanish dining companions scraping up the bits stuck to the bottom of the pan. This caramelized rice is considered the highlight of the dish and even has its own name, *socarat* (so-KA-raht). If you want to show you are really in the Spanish rice know, be sure to ask for a bit of *socarat* with your serving.

For more information about paella and rice dishes, check out the official tourism site of the Valencian community, www.comunitat valenciana.com. You can also look for specialized books such as *Paella! Spectacular Rice Dishes From Spain* by Penelope Casas. If you want to make your own once you are back home, consider buying a *paellera* in Spain. A pan large enough to serve eight costs under €10, an incredible bargain compared to the exorbitant amount you'd have to pay stateside, where paella pans are usually only available in high-end gourmet shops.

As they say in Valencia, *Bon Profit!* (Enjoy your meal!)

PAELLA AND RICE GLOSSARY

paella valenciana	with rabbit (or chicken) and broad beans
paella de marisco	with seafood, usually a variety plus monkfish
paella de peix	with fish only
paella mixta	a meat and seafood combination
arroz a banda	cooked with seafood and stock and served *a banda* (apart) in two courses
arroz negro	black rice with squid ink and calamari, often served with aioli
fideuà	"paella" made with short, fat noodles instead of rice, common in Cataluña
arroz al horno	cooked in the oven in a terra-cotta pot, often with sausages and meats
caldero	served in a soupy base, common in Murcia
arroz con costra	baked in an oven with a variety of meats, chickpeas, and an egg crust, the recipe dates to the 16th century

Gourmet

Acclaimed by foodies worldwide, (**Ca Sento** (C/ Méndez Núñez 17, tel. 96/330-1775, 2–4 P.M. and 9–11 P.M. Tues.–Sat., 2–4 P.M. Sun.–Mon., €70) is a family-owned establishment that takes fine fish and seafood dining seriously. Son Raul handles the creative dishes while mother Mari focuses on traditional rice dishes. Father Sento adds personality and charm to the classy dining room. There are just nine tables surrounding the open kitchen, so reservations are required. The best way to get an overview of the capabilities of this gastronomic clan is by ordering the tasting menu.

El Surcursal (C/ Guillem de Castro 118, tel. 96/374-6665, 2–4 P.M. and 9–11 P.M. Mon.–Fri., 9–11 A.M. Sat., closed Sun., €55), located in the IVAM modern art museum, offers an appropriately minimalist backdrop for some of the most innovative cuisine in town. The house specialty is creamy rice with razor clams and octopus. **Seu Xerea** (C/ Conde de Almodóvar 4, tel. 96/392-4000, 1:30–3:30 P.M. and 8:30–11:30 P.M. Mon.–Fri., 8:30–11:30 A.M. Sat., closed Sun., €40) offers an elegant, affordable approach to high-end cuisine in a minimalist dining room. Drawing on Mediterranean and Asian influences, English expat chef Stephen

Anderson offers sublime dishes such as octopus and mango carpaccio with seaweed and soy, oxtail ravioli with foie gras, and roasted duck with blackberries. The lunch menu is an amazing value at €15.

Local Cuisine

Despite having given rise to Spain's most famous dish—paella—there are surprisingly few places in town that do it well. By all means, avoid paella from big pots laid out on bar tops and never, ever order it from anyplace that features it photographed on a slick, colored menu—more than likely it will be frozen. In town, locals point to the beach for a few good restaurants. **Casa Chimo** (Po. Neptuno 40, tel. 96/371-2048, 1:30–4 P.M. and 8:30–11 P.M. Thurs.–Tues., closed Wed., €20) is a blue-and-white-tiled rice house fronting Las Arenas beach and boasting a very loyal clientele. Along the boardwalk, **El Bobo** (Po. Marítimo 3, tel. 96/355-0292, 10 A.M.–5 P.M. daily, open for dinner 8–11 P.M. in summer only, €25) is a classic favorite with an elegant linen-tablecloth dining room and sublime rice dishes. **La Murciana** (Po. Maritimo 10, tel. 96/355-0076, 1–5 P.M. and 8:30–11 P.M. Tues.–Sun., closed Mon., €35) is another excellent, elegant choice. Go for their set menu at €20, not including wine. **La Pepica** (Po. Neptuno 6, tel. 96/371-0366, 1–3:45 P.M. and 8:30–10:45 P.M. daily) is the most famous of the seaside spots. Many locals shrug it off as a tourist trap, but it was good enough for Ernest Hemingway, whose photo hangs on the walls alongside the mugs of other famous patrons.

In Barrio del Carmen, you can't go wrong at long-time local favorite, **San Nicolas** (Pl. Horno de San Nicolas 8, tel. 96/391-5984, 1:30–4 P.M. and 9–11:30 P.M. daily, €35). This intimate dining room is simply furnished and decorated with walls of photos and signed memorabilia from its illustrious clientele. The charming Elisa Martínez handles the dining room with a Mona Lisa grace, while husband Felipe Bru turns out excellent paellas, rice, and fish dishes. He is famed for his *papillote*—the freshest fish brushed with saffron and lemon, then steamed in vegetable paper.

Quick Bites

Al Pan, Queso (C/ Serranos 19, tel. 96/392-4841, noon–midnight daily) is a bright and tiny café offering fresh squeezed juices, salads, homemade croquetas, and *pan relleno,* fresh-baked bread stuffed with everything from cheese to olives. There are a few terrace tables on the quiet plaza out front. Down the street, right in the shadow of the Torres Serranos, is the laid-back little café **Les Portes** (Pl. Fueros 6, closed Mon.), which offers a tasty variety of homemade *tortas* (a type of pizza) on their sprawling chunk of sidewalk. **Trafico de Bocatas** (C/ Roteros 16, tel. 65/433-3108, 7 P.M.–12:30 A.M. daily, €10) is a sandwich shop with gourmet illusions. The house specialty sandwich *rueda* (wheel) is served on round bread and comes stuffed with everything form mozzarella and tomato to wild mushrooms and cherries. The scrumptious selections are complemented by a nice wine list, local art on the walls, and low-key lighting. Though fast-food chains rarely garner a mention in guidebooks, the beachside branch of **Pans and Company** (Playa Malvarrosa, 10 A.M.–10 P.M. daily, €5) is worth pointing out for its excellent location and large, cheap, tasty sandwiches. Eat on the large terrace on the boardwalk or take it to go for a beach picnic. A bonus is that they serve food all day long.

Romantic

Under an oversized replica of Velásquez' ode to debauchery, *Los Borachos,* **La Trave** (C/ Juan de Juanes 2, tel. 96/392-3116, 2–4 P.M. and 9–11 P.M. daily) offers a singular dining experience in Barrio del Carmen. The dining room, set in a 500-year-old stable, is beyond seductive with low lighting, brick archways, mismatched antique chairs, and a flea market collection of old bottles and Renaissance paintings. Antonio, who hails from Italy and has a penchant for breaking into opera mid-shift, commands the kitchen. Using the wood-burning oven he had built to his specifications, he roasts vegetables and meats to sublime perfection. His roasted artichokes will make you weep while his *chuleton de buey* (ox chop) will entice you to gluttony. Meanwhile, wife Carla lovingly caters to your every need in the dining room, including advice on the extensive wine list. Finish dinner with a shot of their homemade *limoncello* (Italian lemon liqueur).

Tapas

Valencia's tapas bars are sprinkled around the city. Hours are pretty standard from 1–4 P.M. and 8–11 P.M., with many bars closing on Sunday or Monday. A long-time local favorite is **Las Cuevas** (C/ Samaniego 9, tel. 96/391-7196, closed Sun.). The bar is covered in tapas, the best being vegetable based. Point to what you want and the barmen will heat it up for you. Stick to the tapas-laden front room as the cave-like backrooms are tiny and very smoky. The bohemian **La Tasketa** (Pl. Santa Margarita 1, tel. 96/392-3591) specializes in homemade rustic fare and they are famed citywide for their way with snails. **La Tasca de Ángel** (Pl. Negrita, s/n) is a hole-in-the-wall that is wildly popular with those who manage to find it. Tapas are beyond cheap and the best to try are the fresh sardines. **Café Bar Pilar** (C/ Moro Zeit 73, tel. 96/391-0497) is one of the oldest bars in Valencia and appears in almost every guidebook about the city. The acclaim is called for. This fun spot draws a lively crowd of locals and tourists who gorge on piquant steamed mussels. When done, just toss your shells in the trough along the floor. If you are near the train station and hankering for the best fried calamari sandwich you'll ever eat, head to **Los Toneles** (C/ Ribera 17, tel. 96/394-0181, daily, €10). This place gets manic with a great mix of both locals and tourists. Plaza de la Reina is lined with tourist trap bars and cafés. A happy exception is **La Taberna de la Reina** (Pl. Reina 1, tel. 96/315-2214, daily, €12). This classic tavern features dozens of elaborate *pinchos* (bite-sized snacks on toast) for €1–1.30. Take what you like and save your toothpicks, you'll be charged at the end.

INFORMATION AND SERVICES
Tourist Offices

The most complete tourist office in town is the spacious **Tourist-Info Valencia** (Pl. Reina 19, tel. 96/153-0229, 8:30 A.M.–8:30 P.M. Mon.–Fri., 9:30 A.M.–5:30 P.M. Sat.–Sun.) in the middle of the Plaza de la Reina, in front of the cathedral. Their free maps and guides are good, but for the best intro to the city, purchase the €2 *Tourist Guide Valencia*. Also, they may recommend the **Tourist Card,** which allows for unlimited travel on the trains, buses, and trams as well as discounted entrances to some museums and discounts at some bars. Only the most gung-ho traveler could make good use of the one-day €6 card, but €10 for two days is a reasonable option, especially if you will tram back and forth to the beach and the La Ciutat arts and science center. There are also mini-tourist offices at the train station and in the airport.

The tourist office runs the excellent www .turisvalencia.es. You can also get amazing panoramic views of the city prior to arriving there by visiting www.arounder.com, an advertising firm that posts wonderful 360-degree panoramic shots of major cities. Check out www.24-7valencia.com, the website of *24/7 Valencia,* an English-language guide to what's happening. Look for the print version at hotels and bars all over town. If your Spanish is up to par, check out the online tourism warehouse www.gtlvalencia.com, run by the Valencia Chamber of Commerce.

Internet Access

As Spain's third-largest city, Valencia has many options for Internet service. A good place to check your email is **Work Center** (C/ Xátiva 19), a 24-hour, full-service copy and office center across the street from the train station. Thirty minutes runs €1. **Ono** (C/ San Vicente 22, tel. 96/328-1902, 10 A.M.–10 P.M. daily) is a dedicated Internet center with dozens of terminals and a snack bar. Prices vary depending on the time of day and the amount of time you want to spend, but they are at their lowest before 2 P.M. and after 10 P.M. Of course, several hotels, restaurants, and bars offer Internet or Wi-Fi, just keep your eyes open as you tour. Finally, it bears repeating that cybercafés attract thieves who prey on distracted Internet surfers. Keep your belongings on your lap and one eye on your surroundings.

GETTING THERE
Air
The **Aeropuerto de Valencia** (tel. 96/159-8500) is located in Manises, about eight kilometesr (five miles) outside of the city. It has flights to and from major cities in Spain as well as to other European destinations. A cab from the airport to the city center runs €16–18. The efficient **Aero-Bus** (tel. 96/316-0707, www.etmvalencia.es, €2.50) runs every 20 minutes 6 A.M.–10 P.M. and takes about half an hour depending on traffic.

Train
The **Estación del Nord** (C/ Xátiva 24) is located just south of the Ciutat Vella and right on the metro line. **Renfe** (tel. 90/224-0202, www.renfe.es) runs several speedy Euromed trains to Barcelona as well as regular trains to Madrid, Alicante, Murcia, and beyond. When buying your ticket, be sure to go to the glass-walled room to the left of the main entrance. The charming, wooden booths are strictly for local *cercanías* trains. The train station has all the services you could need, including a tourist office, luggage storage (change only!), and a cafeteria. Even if you don't take the train into Valencia, if you are a fan of modernist architecture—think fanciful tiles and bright colors—be sure to visit the lobby, which is an homage to the area's favorite citrus fruit, the orange. There are plans to build an AVE high-speed train between Madrid and Valencia, which will cut the current time of 3.5 hours considerably. Also, keep in mind that the Madrid–Valencia route is very popular on weekends; buy your tickets in advance.

Bus
Valencia's **Estación de Autobuses** (C/ Mené-ndez Pidal 13, tel. 96/346-6266) is located just out of the city center on the other side of the Turia river. It has service throughout Spain and as far afield as London. Especially on weekends, trains to and from Madrid can be completely booked. If that is the case, the bus is your best bet with hourly departures to/from Valencia. **Alsa** (www.alsa.es) also runs daily buses along the Costa Blanca south to Alicante.

Car
Valencia is located on AP-7, which connects it easily to any major town in Spain. It is just about equidistant from Madrid (350 kilometers/218 miles to the northwest) and Barcelona (360 kilometers/224 miles straight north). If you'd like to rent a car in Valencia, try **Hertz** (www.hertz.es) in the airport, **Avis** (C/ Isabel la Católica 17, www.avis.es), or **Europcar** (www.europcar.es) at the train station.

GETTING AROUND
Valencia has an excellent system of public transport that includes buses, subways, trams, and commuter trains. The bus system crawls all over the city and you'll most likely use it to go to the beach or La Ciutat. Maps are available from the tourist offices, or just consult one of the maps posted on the bus stops. Cost is €1 and you pay upon boarding. The metro is easily identifiable by the lowercase red "m" that marks the stops. Cost is €1.20 and you must buy your ticket from either an automated machine or an attendant before boarding. Line 4 of the metro is above ground to the beach and is locally called the tram. Taxis are white and cruise around the city nearly non-stop. If you need to call one, try **Radio Taxi** (tel. 96/370-3333) or **Tele-Taxi** (tel. 96/357-1313).

VICINITY OF VALENCIA
◖ Albufera
In stark contrast to the big-city bustle of Valencia, Albufera is an oasis of calm waters, migratory birds, and rolling rice paddies-just 16 kilometers (10 miles) south of the city. A protected national park, Albufera is Spain's third-most important wetland. Its abundance of fresh

water also makes it one of the world's most productive ecosystems, supporting a rich abundance of flora and fauna. Albufera is a major stop for migratory birds on their way to winter nests in Africa. Over 200 species touch down annually in the park and dozens of those use the wetlands as breeding grounds. The parkland consists of a 2,425-hectare (6,000-acre) freshwater lagoon separated from the Mediterranean Sea by a wide sandbar that supports a pine forest called **Devesa del Saler.** To the north, closer to Valencia, are the crystal white beaches of El Saler. On its opposite side, the lagoon is surrounded by nearly 15,000 hectares (35,000 acres) of rice fields.

It is estimated that during the Middle Ages, Albufera's lagoon stretched over 20,000 hectares (49,000 acres). Over the centuries, land reclaim and the conversion of the lagoon into rice fields and orange orchards resulted in the lagoon measuring just over 14,000 hectares (35,000 acres) by the 18th century and 8,000 hectares (20,000 acres) by the 19th. By the mid-20th century, it had reached its current size and had gained the notice of conservation groups. It was named a protected Spanish wetland in 1986. In 1994, it was named a Damp Zone of International Importance by the world-governing Ramsar Convention. Since then, conversation steps have been enacted and the loss of the wetlands slowed. Despite these measures, Albufera continues to suffer great ecological damage. It is not an isolated zone and what happens in the areas surrounding it has a great affect on its ecosystem. The main culprits are pesticide run-off from nearby farmlands and inadequate sewage for the dozens of towns that border the Albufera. The result has been the decimation of several native species of bird and fish.

While ecologists struggle to maintain the area, Albufera's gorgeous allure draws admirers and visitors. The word *albufera* comes from the age of Moorish rule and means "the sun's mirror." A trip in an *albuferenc* (traditional, flat-bottomed wooden boat) across its placid, silver waters is a soothing experience not soon forgotten. If you happen to visit at sunset, you'll be treated to one of the most intensely colored displays of nature you'll ever witness as the skies and water turn a fiery shade of red and orange.

The only town in Albufera is the sleepy fishing village of **El Palmar,** home to a few dozen fishing families and several excellent paella restaurants. This is where Valencia's residents go when they want good rice. One of the best places to eat in El Palmar is the acclaimed **Racó de l'Olla** (Ctra. El Palmar 21, tel. 96/162-0172, 1:30–4:30 P.M. Tues.–Sun. Sept.–June, 1:30–4:30 P.M. and 9 P.M.–midnight Mon.–Sat., July and Aug., €40). Any of their dozen or so rice dishes will be exquisite, but for a real treat, try the traditional recipe of *all i pebre,* baby eels sautéed in garlic and sweet pepper sauce.

Get to Albufera by bus on from the Estación de Autobuses on any Autocares Herca line heading towards Perelló. They run about every hour 7 A.M.–9 P.M. If you prefer a more structured trip, the **Albufera Bus Turistic** (daily, Mar.–Dec., €12) leaves from Valencia's Plaza de la Reina and includes a boat ride across the lagoon. The trip lasts about 2.5 hours and leaves no time to enjoy one of El Palmar's restaurants. By car, take the CV-500 south about 29 kilometers (18 miles) to reach Albufera from Valencia.

🄲 Sagunto

The Roman enclave of Saguntum was where the Second Punic War started. In 219 B.C., Hannibal and his Carthaginian forces laid siege to the town. The Roman citizens held out for eight months expecting relief from the Roman army. When it finally dawned on them that Caesar's troops weren't coming to their rescue, the citizens burned the town and committed mass suicide rather than submit to the enemy. Today, Sagunto's Roman ruins are being excavated and tourists can visit the **Teatro Romano,** a well-restored amphitheater dating from the 1st century A.D., as well as the **Antiquarium Epigráfico,** a collection of Roman inscriptions and funeral stones. (Hours for both are 10 A.M.–8 P.M. Tues.–Sat., 10 A.M.–2 P.M. Sun. May–Sept., 10 A.M.–6 P.M. Tues.–Sat., 10 A.M.–2 P.M. Sun. Oct.–Apr.)

TOMATINA

On the last Wednesday of August, at the peak of the Spanish tomato season, the village of Buñol stages the world's largest food fight. For over an hour, 40,000 people merrily pelt each other with over 90,000 kilograms (100 tons) of overripe tomatoes, turning the cobbled streets of this tiny town into rivers of tomato juice. Thanks to heavy American press coverage among the MTV generation, this once very local event has become the "new" Pamplona, attracting thousands of backpacking college students every year.

The origins of the festival are pretty murky but some say it started in 1945 when disgruntled citizens pelted a local politician with tomatoes during the annual festival in honor of Buñol's patron saint. It was so much fun, they decided to keep it up. Fast-forward 60 years and Tomatina has become one of the most infamous festivals in a country full of infamous festivals.

The tomato battle is just one event in a week-long celebration. Both before and after smash Wednesday, the tiny village of less than 10,000 permanent residents throws a typically boisterous Spanish bash with live music, dancing in the streets, and fireworks. However, the big day is Tomatina. It opens with a pole-climb in the town's main square, Plaza del Pueblo. At the top of the pole dangles a leg of *jamón*. All you have to do to get it is climb to the top. The pole, however, is greased down with soap. It takes quite a few tries before someone manages to get to the top. When the ham is finally claimed, usually around 11 A.M., a starting gun is shot to announce the beginning of the tomato fight.

The streets are jammed with people who somehow manage to part just enough for the heavy trucks that roll through loaded with tomatoes. From the bed of the truck, a rowdy group of locals dumps bucketfuls of tomatoes on the crowd, who almost immediately begin

© DAMIAN CORRIGAN

pelting each other with fistfuls of squashed, dripping, wet tomatoes. For the next hour, the tomato flinging is furious. Tomato pulp reaches up to the ankles. Everyone is slipping and sliding about. Tomatoes end up in the hair, the ears, down pants, between toes, and yes – in mouths. It is pure unleashed tomato mania. Around noon, a second gunshot signals the end of the tomato fight.

If you decide to go, you need to keep a few practicalities in mind:

Lodging: There are very few accommodations in Buñol itself. It is much more practical to stay in Valencia and catch an early-morning train into Buñol. Some Buñol locals offer private rooms in their homes during the event. To snag one, show up on Tuesday at

Buñol's train station and you'll either see flyers or run into someone hawking their room. Prices and quality vary widely. Many folks opt to stay up all night – after all, a pretty wild fiesta is going on – but since the event doesn't start until 11 A.M., this could be tough.

Getting There: There are regional trains and buses from everywhere in Spain to Valencia. From Valencia's train station, the regional train C3 makes regular trips to Buñol. The ride is an hour long, so get to the train station no later than 8 A.M. to arrive in Buñol with enough time to enjoy the festive pre-fight atmosphere. If the trains are booked or you oversleep, you can also take a taxi, as it is only 22 miles away. Many organizations in Valencia, Madrid, Barcelona, and other cities offer one-day Tomatina trips. These are great options, as they handle your transportation, offer you a place to secure your stuff, and take care of all the logistics. Prices start as cheaply as €50. Youth hostels are the best place to find such trips.

What to Wear: Don't wear anything you don't want stained tomato-red. Many people wear bathing suits, which is a great idea, as are sports bras for women. Do bring a change of clothes – safely wrapped up in plastic. There is no place to secure goods, so you'll have to hold onto your change of clothes during the battle – so pack something light. Do not bring anything of value that can get destroyed by tomato juice – including mobile phones, jewelry, or your passport. Pack your money and train/bus ticket in a waterproof bag. Do bring a cheap pair of goggles as tomato juice in the eye can be quite painful.

Rules: Though it may seem out of control to a casual onlooker, there are actually a few rules to the Tomatina that not only control the chaos, but make the event relatively safe. One, only throw tomatoes – nothing else. If a local sees you throwing something besides tomatoes, you will be yelled at, reprimanded, and possibly physically restrained. That said, in recent years, it has become tradition for participants to throw their wet t-shirts in the air as the fight begins. Two, never throw a tomato without squishing it in your hands first. A whole tomato can be painful when launched, a smashed tomato is just delightfully messy. Three, don't throw tomatoes at the locals on the balconies above. They are up there because they don't want to participate – respect those wishes. Four, do not attempt to climb into the tomato-laden trucks. You will be pushed off – and not gently. Five, stop fighting when the second gun goes off. The city needs to clean up and get on with the rest of their celebrations. Again, this is a matter of respect for the locals who so generously sponsor the event.

Warning: You might get hurt. Between the pushing and shoving, tomato throwing and shirt flinging, this is not a benign event. If this isn't for you, stay on the outskirts of the main square and stick to side streets where the crowds are not as intense. Tomatina is not a place for kids.

Aftermath: Be ready to shower after the battle. Public trains and buses will not allow tomato-drenched passengers on board. Rows of free showers are set up near the train station. Locals also aim hoses down on the participants. Try to take advantage of this, as the shower lines can be long. Also, if you lost your shirt during the festivities, you'll need to find another one – trains and buses practice the no-shirt, no-service policy.

Information: The Internet is loaded with tons of Tomatina information. As you browse, be sure and go through the official site, www .tomatina.es.

The town is also dotted with the remains of Moorish fortifications. Visit the **tourist office** (Pl. Cronista Chabret, tel. 96/266-2213, 8 A.M.–3 P.M. and 4–6:30 P.M. Mon.–Fri., 9 A.M.–3 P.M. Sat., 9 A.M.–2 A.M. Sun.) for complete information on the history of this fascinating town.

If you have a morning free, it is definitely worthwhile making the trip from Valencia. You could easily sightsee yourself back into the past as you clamber over the evocative ruins. The liveliest time to visit this sleepy town is

August when the Roman ruins set the stage for the **Sagunto a Escena,** an open-air music, dance, and theater festival.

Sagunto is located 23 kilometers (14 miles) north of Valencia and can be easily accessed by car on the N-221. There are also frequent buses from Valencia's Estación de Autobuses and trains from the Estación de Nord. The no-hassle way to visit is by **Sagunto Bus Turistic** (Pl. Reina, Thurs.–Sun., Apr.–Nov., €15), which leaves from Valencia's Plaza de la Reina a few times per day.

Alicante

The cosmopolitan harbor town of Alicante is a refreshing contrast to the cement-block mega-resorts that soil so much of the Costa Blanca. The Romans called it Alicante Lucentum, "city of light," and when you see the purity of the blue sky and the ethereal haze of one of the city's nearly 360 days of sun, you'll understand why. With its marvelous seaside esplanade, charming medieval quarter, bustling city center, and easy access to gorgeous white-sand beaches, Alicante is the perfect base for a sun, sand, and sangria vacation—with a little bit of big-city culture thrown in for fun.

Alicante is the capital of the Spanish province of Alicante—Spain loves to name cities after provinces; it makes visitors crazy. Alicante province is the southernmost of the three provinces that make up the autonomous region of Valencia. The two cities share a lot in common, but Alicante is slower-paced, more laid-back, and as the major city on the Costa Blanca—the coast of the Alicante region—it is a city with a decidedly touristic slant.

SIGHTS
Castillo de Santa Bárbara
High above the Alicante seashore on top of rugged Mount Benacantil sits the rambling medieval castle, **Castillo de Santa Bárbara** (10 A.M.–8 P.M. daily summer, 9 A.M.–7 P.M. daily winter, free). Originally used as a defen-

sive fortress by the Moors in the 10th century, it took on its current name under the rule of Christian King Alfonso X el Sabio. Over the centuries it was both heavily damaged and heavily restored so that today it reflects 14th-, 15th-, and 16th-century design ele-

view of the Mediterranean Sea from Castillo de Santa Bárbara

© CANDY LEE LABALLE

VALENCIA AND MURCIA

ments. Today, it is home to a rotating modern art series called SEA, Simposium Escultura Alicante. Throughout the ancient structure you'll find the newest in sculpture, painting, and photography. It is an odd juxtaposition, but it works.

You can get to the castle in three ways. Pedestrians can take either the elevator from Postiguet beach (€2.40, change only) or make the long climb uphill along the city's medieval walls starting in the Casco Antiguo on Calle Teniente Daoiz. Drivers drive to the top via Avenida Alfonso X el Sabio. Note, once you get to the castle, you'll still have to do some serious uphill walking to see everything. Take your time and in the summer, bring water.

Next to the castle is the **Parque La Ereta,** which boasts sweeping vistas over Alicante and the Mediterranean Sea. It is reached either by climbing the medieval walls or descending from the castle.

El Barrio

Making up the oldest part of Alicante, sometimes called **Casco Antiguo,** is the grid of narrow medieval streets called El Barrio. They are lined with restaurants and bars, lively plazas, and ornate churches. The most magnificent church is **Basílica de Santa María** (Pl. Santa María, s/n, tel. 96/521-6026, 10 A.M.–noon and 6–7:30 P.M. daily), which was built in the 14th century on top of a mosque. Its main doorway is a feast of baroque stonework full of angels and saints. Inside, don't miss the golden rococo altar.

On the plaza across from the church is one of Alicante's best museums. **Museo de Asegurada** (Pl. Santa María 3, tel. 96/514-0768, 10 A.M.–2 P.M. and 5–9 P.M. Tues.–Sat. summer, 10 A.M.–2 P.M. and 4–8 P.M. Tues.–Sat. winter, free), also called the Muse de Arte Contemporáneo, represents the best in Spanish 20th-century art with works by Picasso, Miró, Tàpies, Gris, Dali, and Chillida.

As El Barrio climbs towards the base of Mount Benacantil, it takes on the name of Barrio Santa Cruz. A mostly residential area, Santa Cruz is a charming old neighborhood of

© CANDY LEE LABALLE

The elegant Explanada de España is Alicante's best strolling spot.

narrow, cobbled streets lined with whitewashed buildings laden with flower-filled iron balconies. It is worth a few hours of wandering.

Explanada de España

The fanciful tiled seaside promenade of Explanada de España is the main artery of Alicante's social life. It seems that everyone in town takes a stroll under its palm trees at least once a day. The esplanade is paved in red, white, and blue mosaic tiles that form a wave pattern. At its center is a bandstand where the local orchestra performs free Sunday concerts. The length of it is lined with ice-cream shops, cafés, and restaurants offering scary versions of paella under fluorescent lights. Do have a coffee or quick sandwich at one of them. Do not eat a full meal unless you really have a hankering for frozen, microwaved rice. At the eastern end of the Explanada, the **Plaza Puerto del Mar** houses a tram station and serves as the entrance to the *muelle* (port). All along the port are big restaurants and even bigger discos. If you follow the port to its end you'll pass the

VALENCIA AND MURCIA

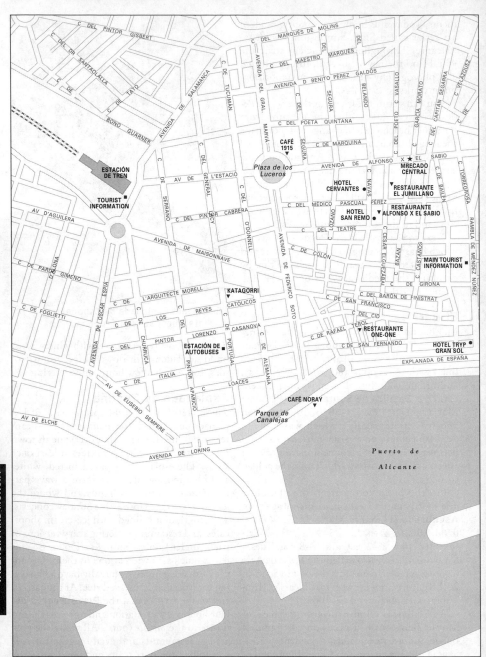

C. DEL PINTOR GISBERT
C. DEL DR. SANTAOLALLA
C. DE
C. DE TAYO
BONO GUARNER
AVENIDA DE SALAMANCA
C. DE TUCUMAN
AVENIDA DEL GRAL.
AVENIDA DEL MARVA
C. DEL MARQUÉS DE MOLINS
AVENIDA DEL MAESTRO MARQUÉS
C. DEL MARQUÉS
C. DEL
AVENIDA D BENITO PÉREZ GALDÓS
C. DEL SEGURA
BELANDO
C. DEL POETA VASALLO
GARCÍA MORATO
C. DEL CAPITÁN SEGARRA
C. VELAZQUEZ

C. DEL POETA QUINTANA
C. DE MARQUINA

CAFÉ 1915 ▼

Plaza de los Luceros

AVENIDA DE ALFONSO
X ★ EL SABIO
MRECADO CENTRAL

C. DE MÉDICO PASCUAL PÉREZ

ESTACIÓN DE TREN

TOURIST INFORMATION ■

AV D'AGUILERA

AV DE GENERAL L'ESTACIÓ
C. DE SERRANO
C. DEL PINTOR CABRERA
C. DEL O'DONNELL

AVENIDA DE MAISONNAVE

C. DE PARDO GIMENO
D. PAMPLONA

C. DE FOGLIETTI

AVENIDA DE L'OSCAR ESPLÁ

C. DE
C. DE LOS REYES
DEL PINTOR
C. DE CHURRUCA
C. DEL

C. DE ITALIA

AV. DE EUSEBIO SEMPERE

AV DE ELCHE

C. DEL PINTOR APARICIÓ

L'ARQUITECTE MORELL

KATAGORRI ▼
CATÓLICOS
C. DE CASANOVA
LORENZO
C. DE PORTUGAL
C. DE ALEMANIA

ESTACIÓN DE AUTOBUSES ■

LOACES

AVENIDA DE LORING

AVENIDA DE FEDERICO SOTO

C. DE COLON

HOTEL CERVANTES ●
C. NAVAS
RESTAURANTE EL JUMILLANO ▼
HOTEL SAN REMO ●
RESTAURANTE ALFONSO X EL SABIO ▼
C. DEL TEATRE
C. DEL LOZANO

C. CESAR ELGUEZABAL
C. BAZAN
C. DE CASTAÑOS
MAIN TOURIST INFORMATION ■

C. DE GIRONA

C. DEL BARÓN DE FINISTRAT
C. DE SAN FRANCISCO
C. DEL CID
TEROL
RESTAURANTE ONE-ONE ▼
C. DE RAFAEL
C. DE SAN FERNANDO

HOTEL TRYP GRAN SOL ●

EXPLANADA DE ESPAÑA

CAFÉ NORAY ▼

Parque de Canalejas

C. DE BAILEN
C. DE TORREGROSA
RAMBLA DE MÉNDEZ NÚÑEZ

Puerto de Alicante

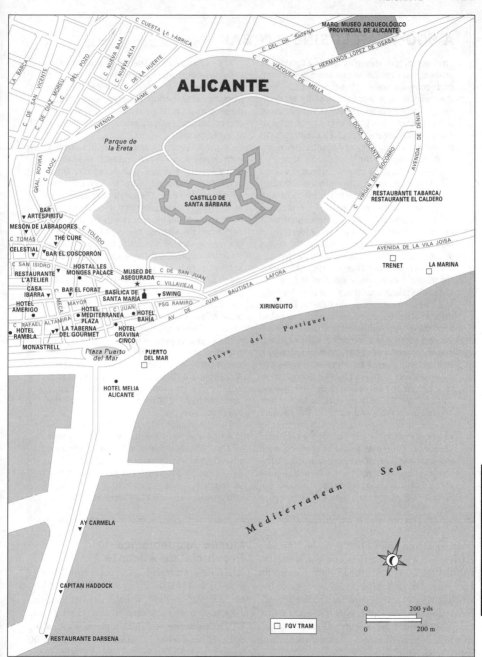

ALICANTE

MARQ: MUSEO ARQUEOLÓGICO PROVINCIAL DE ALICANTE

C. CUESTA LA FÁBRICA
C. DEL DR. SAPENA
C. DE VÁZQUEZ DE MELLA
C. HERMANOS LÓPEZ DE OSABA
LA BARCA
C. DE DIAZ MOREU
C. DE SAN VICENTE
DEL POZO
C. NUEVA BAJA
C. NUEVA ALTA
C. DE LA HUERTE
AVENIDA DE JAIME II
GRAL. ROVIRA
C. DAOIZ
C. DOÑA VIOLANTE
AVENIDA DE DENIA
C. VIRGEN DEL SOCORRO

Parque de la Ereta

CASTILLO DE SANTA BÁRBARA

▼ BAR ARTESPIRITU
MESÓN DE LABRADORES   C. TOLEDO
C. TOMAS
THÉ CURE ▼
CELESTIAL ▼ ▼ BAR EL COSCORRÓN
C. SAN ISIDRO
RESTAURANTE L'ATELIER ▼
HOSTAL LES MONGES PALACE
MUSEO DE ASEGURADA ★
C. DE SAN JUAN
CASA IBARRA ▼
MECA
▼ BAR EL FORAT
BASÍLICA DE SANTA MARÍA
C. VILLAVIEJA
LAFORA
▼ SWING
HOTEL AMERIGO
MAYOR
HOTEL ● MEDITERRANEA ●
C. JUAN
PSG RAMIRO
AV. DE JUAN BAUTISTA
HOTEL ● BAHÍA
C. RAFAEL ALTAMIRA
● HOTEL RAMBLA
▼ LA TABERNA DEL GOURMET
PLAZA
HOTEL GRAVINA CINCO
MONASTRELL
Plaza Puerto del Mar
□ PUERTO DEL MAR

RESTAURANTE TABARCA/ RESTAURANTE EL CALDERO
AVENIDA DE LA VILA JOISA
□ TRENET
LA MARINA □
▼ XIRINGUITO

Playa   del   Postiguet

● HOTEL MELIA ALICANTE

Mediterranean   Sea

▼ AY CARMELA

▼ CAPITAN HADDOCK

▼ RESTAURANTE DARSENA

0   200 yds
0   200 m

□ FGV TRAM

VALENCIA AND MURCIA

A 500-YEAR LOSING STREAK

The mock battles known as **Moros y Cristianos** are held in the provinces of Alicante and Valencia to commemorate a 13th-century battle that the Christians won thanks to the holy intervention of Saint George. The most distinctive of all the fiestas takes place in the small town of Alcoy (Alcoi), located about 29 kilometers (18 miles) north of the city of Alicante. There, according to legend, the young saint appeared during a particularly dismal battle and helped the Cristians to victory. In return the faithful of Alcoy promised to forever honor the saint with a commemorative celebration. Thus, Moros y Cristianos was born. Though the outcome is always the same – Christians win, Moors lose – many participants prefer to dress as the Moors as their costumes are the most elaborate.

The current festival takes place April 22-24. On the first day, processions of Moors and Christians take place throughout the city. Their costumes are simply stunning. Extravagance is the rule of the day as each group tries to outdo each other with feathered headpieces, jewel-encrusted turbans, studded leather chest plates, bright silk robes, hammered metal arm and shin guards, heavy swords, and silver shields. Every detail is covered, from gloves to shoes, as the outfits must be as authentic as possible. The only exceptions for modernity are eyeglasses and watches. The soldiers also chomp on oversized cigars. No one really knows why, but it is just part of the tradition. Throughout the day, bands of soldiers, both Moorish and Christian, parade through the streets showing off for the crowds and camera crews. They have to do it now because tradition holds it that no costume can be worn twice.

The second day of the festival has heavy religious overtones with masses held in the city's churches. The day's highlight is the appearance of St. George incarnate – a local boy dressed as a Christian soldier. At night there are more processions and a festive atmosphere ensues.

On the final day the battle is fought. Armed with gunpowder-loaded muskets, the Moors and Christians, some on horseback, fight each other in the old center of Alcoy. Smoke envelopes the city. The deafening gunshots echo off the buildings. At first it looks grim for the Christians as the Moors win the morning battle and the Moorish crescent is hung from the wooden fortress that has been erected in the main square. In the evening, the bands of soldiers square off again. During the fiercest stage of the battle, the boy Saint George appears on the rampart at the top of the fortress. The tide turns and the Christians are victorious – again. The symbol of Saint George, a red cross on a white background, is hung from the fortress and dozens of balconies throughout the city. The rest of the night is a raucous street party with fireworks and revelry. Many Alcoyanos are visibly sad to see the event end, but if you prod them they will optimistically point out that there are only 361 days until the next battle begins.

The sheer pageantry of the fiesta of Alcoy makes it worthy of a visit. If you can't make it in April, check with the Valencia or Alicante tourist office as there are over 150 Moros y Cristianos fiestas held throughout the region all year long. More about the Alcoy celebration can be found at www.associaciosantjordi.org.

boat departure point for Algeria in Northern Africa. Go a little further and you'll see the funniest vending machine in town. Set up for fishermen, the machine serves up cups of live worms. Choose your species from the full-colored photos on front, plunk in your coins, and boom, you have worms! There is a snack machine next to it in case you want something more appetizing.

Museo Arqueológico Provincial de Alicante

Alicante's archaeological museum, better known as **MARQ** (Pl. Doctor Gómez Ulla, s/n, tel. 96/514-9000, www.marqalicante.com, 10 A.M.–7 P.M. Tues.–Sat.,10 A.M.–2 P.M. Sun., €3), is one of the best in Europe. In a sprawling space of nearly 10,000 square meters (100,000 square feet), MARQ offers cutting-edge interactive displays and dioramas that take the visitor from prehistory through the Romans, and straight to contemporary civilizations. Full of activities for children, MARQ is a must if you have kids.

Beaches

Located right in the city center, **Playa del Postiguet** is an excellent beach with almost a kilometer of fine, golden sand hugging the Mediterranean. The beach stretches north from the end of the Explanada and runs under the watchful peak of the Santa Bárbara castle. It features lifeguards, a first-aid shack, a tourist office, and a couple of cafés and bars. You can also rent umbrellas and lounge chairs (€3.50 each). For ease of access, it can't be beat, though it does get very, very crowded in summer.

The best beach in the area is **Playa de San Juan,** located a few kilometers north of the city in residential area. At three kilometers (two miles) long and nearly a football field wide, it is a gorgeous stretch of very fine golden sand dotted with palm trees. There are several bars and restaurants located along the boardwalk and the beach features the lifeguards and umbrella rental. It is easily accessible from Alicante on the tram. Catch it at either the Puerta del Mar (near the Plaza Puerta del Mar) or La Marina (at the far end of the Postiguet beach). Exit at any of the stops from Costa Blanca to Fabraquer. Cost is €1.20 and the tram runs 6 A.M.–10:30 P.M. During summer, there are night buses (21N) that run between Alicante and San Juan 11 P.M.–6 A.M.

If you like to lie in the sun with nothing at all between you and the sand, head to the **Playa de la Almadraba.** Stretching along this part of the coast are several *cabos* (coves) where bathing suits are optional. Bus 22 from Alicante center will take you there.

ENTERTAINMENT AND EVENTS
Nightlife

Alicante's nightlife has two distinct *la marcha* zones. El Barrio is where the night begins with a crawl through several bars from grungy rock to ultra hip. After they close at 3 A.M., follow the crowds to El Puerto (the port). The dock that loops around the sailboats and yachts is jammed with discos that stay open until 6 A.M., later on weekends. There are also quirky neighborhood bars and *chiringuitos* (beach bars) offering low-key alternatives to the *marcha* madness.

Bars in El Barrio cater to all tastes. The favorite of all ages and persuasions is the gritty little dive **El Coscorrón** (C/ Tarifa 3). The name means a "knock on the head" and refers to the low door that you have to stoop through to enter. There is a pillow tacked up there now to preserve the noggins of those not prone to stooping. The walls are covered in graffiti, flyers, and postcards from around the world. Clientele runs the gamut from weathered old men to tanned and toned college students, all sipping on the bar's famed *mojitos.* **Artespiritu** (Pl. San Cristobal, s/n) offers a funky mix of reggae, techno, and ambient beats. It draws an equally eclectic crowd of artists and bohemians. **The Cure** (C/ Virgen de Belen 8) is nicknamed "The Ramones Pub" for all the autographed memorabilia from the band. The soundtrack, as you might guess, is early punk. **El Forat** (Pl. Santisima Faz 4) is a temple to all things kitsch with a lively gay, lesbian, and straight crowd to match. The music is pure 1980s disco and the ambience is pure fun. If you want to dance, swing by **Swing** (C/ Jorge Juan 18) to see what's on. During the week, this ballroom caters to middle-aged couples who slow dance to orchestral music. Most weekends, it draws a younger crowd with a roster of top DJs and house music. Look for their bright pink flyers all over town. **Celestial** (C/ San Pascual 1) has an over-the-top faux-baroque decor full of cherubs and chandeliers. Music is solid Spanish pop that draws an attractive 30-and-up crowd.

For a cocktail with a view, head to the Parque de Canalejas along the waterfront. Just on the other side of the Kontiki boat mooring, **Noray** (C/ Julio Guillen Tato, s/n) sits in a minimalist blonde wood, glass, and steel building that seems to floats over the harbor. Cocktails are classic and the music is laid-back from bossa nova to acid jazz. Just far enough off the beaten path, Noray draws a decidedly upscale, local crowd on weekends. On the absolute opposite end of the Explanada, midway up the Postiguet beach, look for **Xiringuito** (Playa Postiguet, s/n), the best beach bar in town. Have a drink under the stars, your feet in the sand, low-key electronica in the background, tiki torches for light. This is a great place to while away the early evening into night.

If you are after late-night discos with their requisite sweaty crowds, burly bouncers, and chest-thumping music, head to El Puerto. They are all pretty generic but two local favorites are **Ay Carmela,** which pumps out louder-than-life Spanish pop and Latin music and **Capitan Haddock,** which sticks to mainstream pop. If your tastes are more diverse, look for the free magazine *Üala,* which covers the nightlife scene in-depth, though it is available only in Spanish.

Festivals and Events

The last two weeks of June, Alicante celebrates **Les Foderes de Sant Joan** (the bonfires of Saint John) with an enthusiastic combination of music, gunpowder, art, and fire. As in Valencia's Las Fallas, neighborhood groups sponsor elaborate papier-mâché statues that are set up throughout the city at the start of the festivities. There are daily *mascletas* (deafening firecracker displays) and nightly partying in the streets. On the last day of the fiesta, all but one of the statues are burned and the masses head to the Postiguet beach for a truly spectacular fireworks display over the sea. The statue that is saved by popular vote is then moved to the **Museu de Fogueres** (Rambla 29, tel. 96/514-6828, 10 A.M.–2 P.M. and 6–9 P.M. Mon.–Sat., 10 A.M.–2 P.M. Sun., free).

From March to December, barrios throughout Alicante celebrate **Moros y Cristianos.** These spectacular processions reenact—with a great degree of poetic license—the 13th-century battle between Christians and Moors that led to the domination of Levante for the Christian King Jaume I. The best local celebrations are held in the barrio of San Blas in June

and the barrio of San Nicolás de Bari in December. (See sidebar, *A 500-Year Losing Streak.*)

ACCOMMODATIONS
Under €50

Hostal Les Monges Palace (C/ San Agustin 4, tel. 96/521-5046, info@lesmonges.net, www.lesmonges.net, €50) will have you wondering, "Is it a *hostal* or a palace?" The answer is a bit of both. Prices are rock-bottom, while details like antique-laden hallways, tapestry-covered walls, and whimsical tile work throughout scream luxe. Rooms are a bit of a let-down after the entryway, but are still unbelievable at these prices. There is also a delightful shabby-chic suite with a whirlpool and sauna (€95). Breakfast is included and Internet and parking are available. **Hotel Cervantes** (C/ Navas 39, tel. 96/520-9822, €45) is no-frills, but the price and the location—in the quiet central zone next to the main police station and five minutes walking to the Explanada—can't be beat. Just down the street, **Hotel San Remo** (C/ Navas 30, tel. 96/520-9500, info@hotel sanremo.net, www.hotelsanremo.net, €42) is another decent, cheap option with straightforward rooms, some with a balcony.

€50-100

Just minutes from the Explanada and El Barrio, **Hotel Rambla** (C/ Rambla 9, tel. 96/514-4580, reservas@hotelrambla.com, www.hotel rambla.com, €75) could not be better located. The lobby has a boutique-hotel look that doesn't extend to the run-of-the-mill rooms. Still, all the basic amenities are done right and if you get an upper room on the street, the view is lovely. **Hotel Bahía** (C/ Gravina 16, tel. 96/520-6522, info@hotelbahia.es, www .hotelbahia.es, €66) is located across from the Postiguet beach and features decent, updated rooms. Be sure to request one with a view of the sea. **Hotel Gravina Cinco** (C/ Gravina 5, tel. 96/514-7317, www.gravinacinco.com, €80) is a classy downtown hotel with sleek, modern touches and an excellent location at the midway point between El Barrio and Postiguet beach. **Hotel Tryp Gran Sol** (Rambla 3, tel.

96/520-3000, www.tryp.es, €80) is located in Alicante's first skyscraper and views from the upper floors are panoramic. As a member of the upscale Tryp chain, rooms and service are apt and professional, if a bit cold. The 27th-floor restaurant is a classic, white tablecloth affair with decent seafood and rices and amazing views. Their €18 lunch is a good value for the quality.

Over €100

The sleek, new **Amerigo** (C/ Rafael Altamira 7, tel. 96/514-6570, amerigo@hospes.es, www .hospes.es, €180) is an oasis of luxe comfort in the middle of El Barrio. Housed in an elegant former monastery, the rooms are all white with dark wooden floors and just a touch of red accents. Beds are plush and comfortable and amenities include hydro-massage showers. The best part is the rooftop garden and pool with spectacular views over the city and out to sea. The hotel boasts a very upscale restaurant with international food, a trendy cocktail bar, and a surprisingly good valued tapas bar. **Hotel Mediterranea Plaza** (Pl. Ayuntamiento 6, tel. 96/521-0188, www.hotelmediterraneaplaza .com, €100) is a classically detailed hotel with an attentive staff and a spectacular rooftop terrace. **Hotel Meliá Alicante** (Pl. Puerta del Mar 3, tel. 96/520-5000, www.solmelia.es, €120) was one of the first mega-hotels built on Alicante's port. It has over 500 rooms, all vaguely modern if a bit tattered. Most rooms feature a balcony overlooking either the sea and beach or the city and port. Check their website before booking as there are often cut-rate specials.

FOOD
Cafés and Desserts

In Alicante, you are spoiled for choice for basic, laid-back cafés offering breakfast, sandwiches, coffee, and desserts throughout the day. Along the Explanada there are dozens—some sketchy, some fine. For a decent continental breakfast or a quick sandwich, you can't go wrong at any of them—but if you order the paella in the picture, you are on your own. Moving into El Barrio, try **Alquimista** (C/ Munoz 3, tel.

96/514-2302, 8 A.M.–midnight daily, closed Sun.) for a decent €2 breakfast or a fresh, pasta-based €9 lunch menu. Their crepes are also great at any time of day. Around the corner, **Casa Ibarra** (C/ Mayor 22, tel. 96/514-5625, closed Sun.) is a local favorite for breakfast or lunch. If you need a snack at the beach try the **Mar de Seda Café** (Pl. del Mar 3, tel. 96/514-2140, 8 A.M.–10 P.M. daily) on the ground level of the Hotel Melia. Vaguely modern with a great view over Postiguet, the bar plays low-key techno and serves up decent breakfasts, sandwiches, and drinks.

For a sweet fix that you can take home with you, try some of Alicante's world-famous *turrón,* a nougat-like confection made with almonds. There are shops all along Calle Mayor offering dozens of varieties of this gooey treat, however the local favorite is **Helados y Turrones Espi** (Av. Alfonso el Sabio 4, 96/520-4865), just to the north of the Barrio. Their ice creams are also outstanding.

Tapas

For gourmet tapas, try **Katagorri** (C/ Portugal 29, tel. 96/592-6008, 9:30 A.M.–midnight Mon.–Fri., 11 A.M.–midnight Sat., closed Sun.) near the train station. Their Basque-style *pinchos* are sumptuous works of art at €2.50–5. The long wood striped bar fills up by 9 P.M. with a local crowd of young up-and-comers. The sleek back-room dining area serves full meals with an emphasis on impeccably fresh fish. Expect to pay about €40 per person. **Senzone** (C/ Rafael Altamira 7, tel. 96/514-6570, 12:30–4:30 and 8:30 P.M.–midnight daily) is the stylish tapas bar of Hotel Amerigo. The bar is long and high with a distinct Japanese feel, but the tapas are pure Spanish. Go for the *pinchos,* displayed along the bar like miniature works of culinary art. If you want less flash and more trash (on the floor that is), head to **Mesón de Labradores** (C/ Labradores 19, tel. 96/520-4846, closed Mon., €15), a typical Spanish tavern with a very jolly staff. There is no bar to eat at, but you can have a selection of tapas at your table. The house favorite is *patatas a lo pobre,* fried potatoes with green peppers and onion. For a cheap and easy tapa experience, try the chain **Lizarran** (Rambla 18, tel. 96/520-6830, daily). The bar is laden with bite-sized snacks on toast. Take what you want, conserve your toothpicks, and you'll be charged at the end for the number of toothpicks. And please don't think about ruining this honor system tradition by cheating!

Local Cuisine

Despite the dubious enticement of gorging, sunburned tourists, hawking waiters, and full-color posters of paella, avoid at all costs eating a lunch or dinner on the Explanada. The one good restaurant among the lot closed down years back and the rest specialize in frozen paellas and deep-fried fish bits. For superb rice and seafood, try **Darsena** (Muelle de Levante 6, tel. 96/520-7399, daily, €40). Jutting off the port like an ocean liner, the glass-walled dining room is an elegant setting for the restaurant's refined local dishes, including over 30 types of rice. Ask for the special of the day for the best the seasonal market has to offer or try the always-delicious rice with cod. The chef also whips up some very creative seafood-based dishes. A local favorite is **Tabarca** (C/ Virgen del Socorro 68, tel. 96/526-4963, 2–4 P.M. Wed.–Mon., 8–11 P.M. Fri.–Sat., €25), which has amazing *arroz a banda* (a type of paella served in two stages, fish stew and then rice) and to-die-for aioli. In the same building, **El Caldero** (tel. 96/516-3812, €25) specializes in its namesake dish, seafood and vegetables stewed in a cast-iron pot.

Founded in 1941, **El Jumillano** (C/ Cesar Elguezaba, 62, tel. 96/521-2964, closed Sun. P.M., €40) is an Alicante classic with traditional Spanish decor of bullfighting posters and colorful ceramics. The menu focuses on hearty fare like *olleta alicantina* (a chickpea stew seasoned with pork and sausages) and *rabo de toro* (oxtail). There is also *jamón*, manchego, and other typical Spanish dishes. It is also just far enough off the beaten path to be decidedly local. Just down the street, and lower in price, is neighborhood **Restaurant Alfonso X el Sabio** (C/ Cesar Elguezabal 54, tel. 96/521-7246, closed Sun., €15). Decorated with but-

terflies, this cozy place serves classically grilled fish and meats as well as excellent takes on all the Spanish favorites from *croquetas* to *tortilla*. The best bet is the €9.50 lunch menu.

For a bit of tradition in a thoroughly modern locale, head to **La Taberna del Gourmet** (C/ San Fernando 10, tel. 96/520-4233, noon–4 P.M. and 8 P.M.–1 A.M. daily, €20). Behind a wall of caged rocks, the bar/restaurant unfolds like something straight out of Soho—aluminum-topped bar, chalkboard walls, rusted steel floors. It is given warmth by the rustic deli behind the bar complete with baskets of fruit and hanging sausages and cheeses. Run by Genni, daughter of María José of Monastrell fame (see *Gourmet*), La Taberna offers a variety of excellent rice and paella, all made with only the freshest ingredients. There is also a daily ample selection of impeccable fish and fresh oysters. Round out your meal with excellent renditions of Spanish favorites like *gambas al ajillo* (garlic shrimp) and gazpacho. Wash it all down with an excellent selection of Spanish wines including some surprising reds from Alicante.

Gourmet

The most coveted tables in Alicante are at the tiny 🜨 **One-One** (C/ Valdés 9, tel. 96/520-6399, 8–11 P.M. Wed.–Sat., closed Sun.–Tues., €50). If you manage to get a reservation, owner Bartolo will sing the menu to you in a charming off-key French patois. Dishes are based on the market specials of the day, but recurring stars include lobster salad, rack of lamb, and duck. The wine-colored dining room, housing just half a dozen tables, is a cozy clutter of art, antiques, and colorful posters. If you prefer minimal decor and modern cuisine, head to **Monastrell** (C/ San Fernando 10, tel. 96/520-0363, www .monstrell.com, 1–4 P.M. and 8 P.M.–midnight Tues.–Sat., closed Sun. and Mon., €70), run by acclaimed chef María José Sanroman. Her sensuous takes on local ingredients result in dishes like caramelized artichokes with scallops and black truffles or calamari with garlic mousse. The menu changes regularly to take advantage of seasonal products. Be sure to ask for a local wine. Though many are barely drinkable, Monastrell stocks the best—including a wonderful shiraz from Bodega Enrique Mendoza. For a top-end meal that doesn't require an expense-account budget, head to the cool yet cozy dining room of **L'Atelier** (C/ San Nicolás 12, tel. 96/520-6287, 1–4 P.M. and 8 P.M.–midnight Tues.–Sat., 1–4 P.M. Mon., closed Sun., €25). The Argentinean chef whips up creative takes on the freshest local products, which he selects daily at the market. Try the tuna with a port sauce or the confit of cod.

INFORMATION

There are mini-tourist offices at both the train and bus stations, but the best-equipped is the **Tourist Office** (Rambla 23, tel. 96/520-0000, www.alicanteturismo.com, 10 A.M.–8 P.M. daily) on the Rambla halfway to the Explanada. They offer information and maps on the city as well as surrounding towns throughout the province of Valencia. Ask for their very helpful booklet "Alicante" for a complete rundown of sights, beaches, hotels, and leisure activities.

GETTING THERE AND AROUND
Air

Alicante is connected to the rest of the world via its **El Altet International Airport** (tel. 96/691-9000), which is about 13 kilometers (eight miles) outside of town. If you are pressed for time, catch a €20 cab ride into town. If not, go for local public bus C6, which runs every 40 minutes and takes about 20 minutes. To catch it, you have to exit the arrivals lounge, cross the street, and head left. Look for stop number 30 and you are there. The bus continues on to either Murcia or Benidorm. At the airport you can rent a car if you want to do a coastal drive vacation.

Train

Spain's national rail service Renfe has its Alicante base at **Estación de Tren** (Av. Salamanca, s/n, tel. 90/224-0202, www.renfe.es). There are several daily trains to Barcelona, Madrid, Valencia, and Murcia, as well as numerous other cities throughout Spain.

There is also a narrow-gauge train that runs along the coast from Alicante to Dénia. Famously creaky and inexplicably charming, **Trenet**, run by **FGV Tram** (www.fgvalicante .com), is actually a series of two trains. The first is the regular city tram that will take you to Campello, with stops all along Playa de San Juan. In Campello, exit the tram, cross the tracks and catch the well-worn, creaky train that rattles up the coast. The **FGV tram station** (Av. Villajoyosa 2), located at the end of the Postiguet beach, is given over to offices and does not issue tickets. Instead, you must buy tickets from the bar located in front of the station, which is at the eastern end of the Postiguet beach. The tram stop is La Marina. Any of the tourist offices in town can give you the time schedule. Prices run up to €6 one-way, depending on how far you are going. A word of advice about the Trenet—the trains are old, the tracks are narrow, and delays are not uncommon. Be prepared for at least an hour delay, especially if you are rushing back to Alicante to catch a plane or train.

Bus

Alicante's **Estación de Autobuses** (C/ Portugal 17, tel. 96/513-0700) connects the city to local, national, and international destinations. The local bus system **TAM** (www.subus.es) has buses crisscrossing the city and the region. The tourist office can help you find the right route for your destination or ask at your hotel. Playa de San Juan, the single most popular destination for visitors from Alicante, is accessed via lines 21 and 22.

Tram

There is a tram service called **Tranvía** (tel. 90/072-0472, www.fgvalicante.com) that runs from the Plaza de la Puerta del Mar to Campello, up the Alicante coast. It is being expanded to run to further points through the city and region. Check with the tourist office or your hotel for the latest. If you are taking the Trenet further north, you'll first take the tram to Campello to switch lines.

Car

Alicante sits on the major national highway A-31, which runs from Madrid. AP-7 and E-15, run south to Murcia and north to Barcelona. If you want to rent a car in town, there are several agencies at the airport, including **Avis** (tel. 96/528-6579, www.avis.es) and **Hertz** (tel. 96/691-9125, www.hertz.es), and a **Europcar** (www.europcar.es) in the Hotel Melia Alicante on Postiguet beach.

VICINITY OF ALICANTE
◖ Isla de Tabarca

The tiny island of Tabarca is the Valencia region's only inhabited island. Situated 20 kilometers (11 nautical miles) from Alicante, it makes for an excellent day trip. Rumor has it that Greek sage Ptolemy and Saint Paul of Tarsus once rested their philosophical heads on the isle's gentle shores. Years later, Barbary pirates supposedly used the isle as a base for plundering the Valencian coast. The first official record of the island dates from 1768 when Carlos III declared it a settlement for 600 Genovese fishermen who had been ousted from their home of Tabarka, an island near Tunisia.

The figure eight–shaped island has a low-key fishing port tucked in its waist. On the opposite side is the marvelous **Playa Grande** with its blinding wash of golden sand. The western half of the island is dominated by the medieval walled old town. It is a lazy maze of narrow streets dotted with local restaurants offering the local specialty, *caldero,* a seafood stew made with rice in an iron pot. One delightful surprise you'll find as you amble about the island is absolute silence. Motorized vehicles are forbidden on Tabarca, except for the occasional fork lift and a small truck that ferries deliveries from the port to the island's few full-time residents. The waters surrounding Tabarca have been declared a Mediterranean Marine Reserve because of their incredible biodiversity.

The majority of the visitors per day (up to 3,000) leave well before sunset, so if you want a truly unique off-the-beaten path experience, stay the night. The lovely **La Trancada** (C/ Del Motxo 12, tel. 63/050-3500, www.latrancada

.com, €100) is a traditional fisherman's cottage that has been outfitted with luxurious touches like fine linens and modern furnishings. The lower floor is a private studio (€140) for four that has a lovely garden. The rooftop boasts a romantic terrace with great views out to sea. There are only two double rooms, so book early. Another good option is the **Casa del Gobernador** (C/ Arzola 2, tel. 96/596-9886, www.casadelgobernador.com, €85), situated in the elegant 18th-century former governor's mansion. For a decent low-cost taste of the local rices, head to **Casa Gloria** (C/ Bernardo, tel. 96/597-0584, €15). On the beach, try **Rincón Ramos** (tel. 96/597-0581, €30).

Get to Tabarca via the ferry **Kontiki** (C/ Julio Guillen Tato, s/n, tel. 96/521-6396, €16 round-trip). Ferries leave Alicante at 11 A.M. and return at 5 P.M. The ride lasts about 45 minutes.

◖ Elche

The inland town of Elche (Elx in the local dialect) has two grand claims to fame. The first, *La Dama de Elche (The Lady of Elche),* is a magnificent stone bust that has been dated to the 4th century B.C. and is attributed to the ancient Iberian culture. The lady in question is a solemn-faced figure with an elaborate headdress that features two large coils, one over each ear. Archaeologists suspect that it may have been some sort of funerary urn. The controversy stems from the *Dama*'s current home. After it was unearthed in 1897, a French collector bought it and shipped it Paris, where it was displayed at the Louvre. After World War II, the French government returned it to Spain and Franco had it installed at the Prado in Madrid. It eventually moved to that city's archeological museum. For years, the people of Elche have demanded it be returned to its rightful home in Elche. In 2006, they got their wish—temporarily. After a six-month stint in town, the bust went back to Madrid. The controversy continues. See a copy of the bust as well as a fascinating overview of the nine successive civilizations that have been uncovered at Elche at the **Museo Arqueológico y** de **Historia** (Vía del Palau, tel. 96/545-3603, 10 A.M.–1:30 P.M. and 4:30–8 P.M. Tues.–Sat., 10 A.M.–1:30 P.M. Sun., closed Mon., free) which is housed in the spectacular medieval fortress, **Palacio de Altamira.**

Elche's second draw is not so easily removed. The **Palmerar d'Elx** (Palmeral of Elche) is a grove of over 200,000 date-palm trees first planted by the Muslim founders of Elche at the end of the 10th century. The elaborate irrigation system developed by the Muslims is still in use today, keeping this UNESCO World Heritage Site alive and bristling. Though it actually produces dates, the forest's palm fronds are the real value for Spaniards. Bundles are shipped all over Spain each year for Palm Sunday. If you are wandering through a village just about anywhere in the country and spot a yellowing palm still tied to balcony long after Easter, it is not because the homeowner is lazy, but rather a believer in the legend that says a palm frond from Elche will ward off lightning bolts. Visit the grove at the park **Huerto del Cura** (C/ Porta de la Morera 49, tel. 96/545-2747, 9 A.M.–6 P.M. daily, later in summer, €4.10). Seek out its weirdly branched Imperial Palm, which is 150 years old.

Elche boasts a second World Heritage tag for its annual production, *Misteri Play d'Elx.* This lyrical drama details the life of the Virgin Mary. What drew UNESCO's approval—as well as fans worldwide—was the fact that the play has been performed almost non-stop since the Middle Ages, when it was first created. It conserves not only medieval music and vocal performances, but also production styles, so that what you see on the stage today is also what Spaniards who lived 500 years ago saw.

See it every August 14 and 15 at the **Basílica de Santa María** (Pl. Congreso Eucarístico, s/n, tel. 96/545-1540), but book way ahead.

Elche can be visited in a day trip, but if you choose to stay overnight, consider **Huerto del Cura** (Porta de la Morera 14, tel. 96/661-0011, www.huertodelcura.com, €90), which boasts charming cabins right in the palm grove. The pool surrounded by palm trees is a true delight. Also taking advantage of the palm trees as a backdrop is the modern **Milenio** (C/ Prolongación de Curtidores, s/n, tel. 96/661-2033, www.hotelmilenio.com, €75). For a cheap sleep, you can't go wrong at the new **Hostal Madruga** (Pl. Jardí d'Asp 5, tel. 96/667-4794, €42) in an apartment block on the edge of town. The town also extends in suburbs out to the sea, where cheap *hostals* are clustered near Elche's three small beaches.

For good food, try **Mesón de Granaíno** (C/ José María Buck 40, tel. 96/666-4080, closed Sun. and Mon. P.M., €35), which offers excellent rice dishes and stews in a very traditional Spanish dining room. Don't forget to try the homemade date ice cream for dessert. For a cheaper meal, stick to the bar and their extensive tapas list. If you are looking for gourmet, Elche complies with the acclaimed **La Finca** (C/ Partida Perleta 1, tel. 96/545-6007, closed Sun. P.M. and Mon., €50), where local ingredients are given avant-garde touches in an elegantly converted farmhouse located just out of town.

Elche is easily accessed from Alicante (21 kilometers/13 miles to the east) or Murcia (50 kilometers/31 miles to the south) by bus or train. If driving, Elche is located on the A-7, which links the town to the rest of the Mediterranean coast.

VALENCIA AND MURCIA

Costa Blanca

This is the Spain where the "S" stands for stereotype. It is the imagined Spain of winter-weary tourists worldwide—endless sun, long stretches of white beach, wine cheaper than water. It draws hordes from Great Britain, which sends dozens of daily dirt-cheap flights to the region. Germany and the Nordic countries also send masses of tourists here. In the 1960s and 1970s, much of the coast's loveliest beachside towns experienced severe over-development due to the combination of gorgeous scenery, perfect weather, and Spain's financial slump. Developers snapped up the land and built entire cement cities on the waterfront. Benidorm has probably had the worst of it and the city, with its stunning beaches and lovely sea views, is now a jungle of skyscrapers, mega-discos, and a distinctive neon glow visible for kilometers out to sea. Rising real-estate prices and conservationist outcry has somewhat stemmed the tide of overbuilding, but the Costa Blanca still remains the land of the package tour—rock-bottom, all-inclusive deals that more often than not include ridiculous quantities of booze. You've heard about the ugly, drunken, loud, sunburned tourist? This is their Spanish ground zero.

Nonetheless, the Costa Blanca still has a few charms—including the gorgeous whitewashed town of Altea. And the upside of the development boom has been convenience. Whatever you want, you can find in the Costa Blanca, from gourmet restaurants to all-night bars, English-language television to Thai food. If you are looking for an easy escape, the stereotypical Spanish vacation of sun, sand, and sangria, with a bit of hedonism thrown in, you've come to the right place. And, if you venture just a little off the beaten path, you'll find bits of the Costa Blanca that are still rustic and remote. Also, know that Alicante city, the capital of Provincia de Alicante, lies smack in the middle of the Costa Blanca, but in this book we cover Alicante city on its own.

A note about transportation: The Costa Blanca runs along the coast of the province of Alicante from Dénia in the north, through Alicante city, and on to Torrevieja in the south. By car, it is easily accessed as the new AP-7/E-15 highway (toll in parts) runs along the coast the entire way. At times the highway merges with the old, two-lane road N-332. During your travels and when you stop for directions, you'll notice people using the three names interchangeably. If you are traveling by public transportation, the northern portion of the Costa Blanca is all yours. **Alsa** (www.alsa.es) runs daily buses from Valencia to Alicante with stops in Dénia, Calpe, Altea, and Benidorm. In addition, running along the coast between Dénia and Alicante is the narrow-gauge train called **Trenet,** operated by **FGV Tram** (tel. 90/072-0472, www.fgvalicante.com). See *Alicante* for more on this train. Getting to the southern portion of Costa Blanca is less feasible without public transport. There are a few buses heading out of Alicante, but no trains. No worries, it is the least attractive part of the coast and we'll not be covering it here.

◖ DÉNIA

Sprawled beneath a castle-topped mount, Dénia is one of the Costa Blanca's more popular resort towns. It is home to a bustling harbor full of leisure boats and boasts a lively resort scene. Despite this, the town has managed to retain a distinctive Spanish charm. This is best witnessed during the city's annual festivals, which involve bonfires, bulls, and lots of boisterous fun. Originally founded by the Romans and named Dianium in honor of the goddess Diana, Dénia was later ruled by the Moors and for a while was the capital of the *taifa* (kingdom) of Valencia and Ibiza. Today, Dénia is a perfect compromise between a coastal resort vacation and a Spanish beach vacation.

Sights

Looming above Dénia and its coast, the **Castillo de Dénia** (Av. del Cid, s/n, tel. 96/642-

one of Dénia's many *chiringuitos* (beachside bars)

© KELLY O'DONNELL

0656, 10 A.M.–1 P.M. and 3–6 P.M. daily, until 8:30 P.M. in July and Aug., €2.15) has seen over 800 years of changing tides, both natural and man-made. Built by the Moors in the 11th and 12th centuries, the castle sits on remains that date even further back to the days of Roman Dianium. In the 16th and 17th centuries, the **Palau del Governador** (Governor's Palace) was built within the castle's walls. Today the palace houses an interesting archaeological museum detailing Dénia's colorful and ancient past.

Down in town, there a couple of interesting churches, including the 18th-century baroque **Iglesia de la Asunción** (Pl. Constitución, s/n), but the real joy of the place is the town itself. **Baix la Mar** is Dénia's old fishing quarter, centered around the charming Explanada Bellavista road. This area is also known as the Puerto Pesquero. **Les Roques,** just below the castle, was the town's original Moorish medina and is a lovely old warren of whitewashed houses.

Just beyond the city is the **Montgó Parque Natural,** an impressive natural park where mountain meets sea in a turbulent landscape of stony mesas, verdant hillsides, thick forests, and dramatic coves. The tourist office offers hiking routes and the names of companies leading treks.

The other must-see in Dénia is the **Paseo Marítimo** (beachside promenade) that runs from the fishermen's quarter along the beaches south of the city. The beaches and the area are collectively known as **Les Rotes.** The promenade is long and lively, full of bars, restaurants, shops, and services. Running north, the coastal area is called **Les Marines.** There are quite a few top-end restaurants and rollicking nightclubs along this stretch.

Festivals and Events

Dénia is famous throughout Spain for both the number and the ferocity of its festivals. Mid-February, locals don spectacular costumes as warring factions of Christians and Moors for the **Moros y Cristianos** festivals. During **Las Fallas,** held March 16–19, giant paper and plaster figures are raised in the streets and burned in a frenzy of festivity. Expect lots

VALENCIA AND MURCIA

of firecrackers and noise. June 20–24 brings more fire and noise as the **Hogueras de San Juan** are celebrated with grand bonfires on the beach. **Bous a la Mar** (Toros de Agua in Spanish) takes the wild bull runs typical in Pamplona's Sanfermines and adds water, with both man and beast running into the sea. It takes place as part of the city's patron festivals in July. If you'd like to attend any of these very popular events, be sure to book your room in advance.

Sports and Recreation

Dénia has 19 kilometers (12 miles) of coastline and beaches. To the north, there are several lovely, long sandy beaches. To the south, the coast becomes rockier, and the beaches are tucked into small *calas* (coves). All along the beach, and in the town itself, you'll find dozens of outfits offering scuba diving (*buceo*), Jet Skis, sailing, kite-surfing, and other water activities. Most will speak English and the tourist office can set you up with a detailed list.

If you are a sailor, or just want to take to the seas, consider a **boat rental** with the friendly folks at **Golfiño Yates** (Marina de Denia, tel. 96/642-3111, info@golfinoyates .com, www.golfinoyates.com). They rent all sizes of boats and sailboats, with or without a skipper. They also run daily sea-taxis to Ibiza and Formentera. In addition, they can handle all your land bookings, from hotels to activities. Just ask for Juan, the English-speaking owner. Not only is he extremely accommodating, but he's also very enthusiastic about sailing and the Mediterranean.

Accommodations

At the lower end of the price categories, try **Hostal Loreto** (C/ Loreto 12, tel. 96/643-5419, www.hostalloreto.com, €60), right in the center of town. It's located in a former convent and there are lovely architectural details throughout. The rooms are comfortable and updated, if a bit bland. However, the owners, a Scottish/Dutch couple, are divine and extremely attentive. **Hotel Chamarel** (C/ Cavallers 13, tel. 96/643-5007, www.hotel chamarel.com, €90), set in a 19th-century mansion, is a charming inn with spacious rooms, each individually decorated with antique furnishings and modern art. The attic rooms, with exposed beam ceilings, are especially quaint. Located right on the beach, **Hostal El Oasis** (Les Marines, C/ Boga 5, tel. 96/642-4398, €65) offers rooms that will make you feel like you are staying at a friend's house. The beachside terrace is a great place to dine, especially during one of the *hostal*'s barbecue nights.

Moving into the **over €100** range, you can't do better than the **La Posada del Mar** (Pl. Drassanes 2, tel. 96/643-2966, www.laposada delmar.com, €150). Set in a lovely 13th-century building right beneath the castle, the hotel features lots of stonework and heavy wood details, yet the rooms are modern and light and many boast floor-to-ceiling windows overlooking the bay. If you've got the cash and are looking for a romantic retreat, **Hotel Buenavista** (C/ Partida Tossalet 82, La Xara, tel. 96/578-7995, www.hotel-buenavista.com, €200) is a gorgeously appointed chalet turned boutique hotel just minutes outside of the city, close to Montgó park. The 17 rooms are rustic-chic while the 1.6-hectare (four-acre) garden is natural elegance bristling with orange trees, jasmine, and rosemary bushes.

Food

Dénia has some of the best restaurants on the Costa Blanca. Of course, the sea's bounty takes pride of place in the local cuisine. Dishes to savor include *suquet de rape* (stewed monkfish), *llandet* (a simmering pot of local red shrimp with various types of fish and spices), and *arròs a banda* (a two-course seafood and rice dish).

For traditional tapas in a rustic Spanish atmosphere, head to **Tasca Eulalia** (C/ Marqués de Campo 47, tel. 96/642-1652). For excellent local fare (read: seafood), try any of the places along Les Rotes. A local favorite is **Trampolí** (Les Rotes, tel. 96/578-1296, €20); there's no address but you'll see the signs. The seafood is impeccable. For the most atmosphere with your meal, head to **Drassanes** (C/ Puerto 15, tel. 96/578-1118, closed Mon. and Nov., €30), located within the city's original medieval shipyards (*drassanes* in Spanish). **El Mosset** (C/ Sertorio 24. tel. 96/642-5416, €20) offers classic Spanish fare in addition to simply prepared seafood. They also have an excellent wine list. If you're a little seafood-ed out, try **Asador del Puerto** (Pl. Raset 10, tel. 96/642-3482, €30) for succulent grilled meats and hearty Castilian fare.

Information

Dénia's **tourist office** (Pl. Oculista Buigues 9, tel. 96/642-2367, 9:30 a.m.–2 p.m. and 5–8 p.m. daily summer; 9:30 a.m.–1 p.m. and 4–7 p.m. Mon.–Sat., 9:30 a.m.–1:30 p.m. Sun. winter) is located in a plaza in the old center of town, just off the Les Rotes promenade. The official website, www.denia.net, is excellent. You can also find good general information at www.costablanca.org.

Getting There and Around

Dénia lies on exit 62 of the AP-7/E-15 highway, and is just about equidistant between Valencia and Alicante. For a dramatic seaside drive, take the N-332. By train from Alicante, catch **El Trenet** (www.fgvalicante.com). By bus **Alsa** (www.alsa.es) has several coastal buses originating in Valencia.

Dénia is also a port for the ferry to the Balearic Islands. **Balearia** (Estación Marítima, tel. 90/216-0180, www.balearia.com) operates ferries to Ibiza, Formentera, and Palma de Mallorca.

CALPE

Calpe is another delightful surprise on the coast. A popular family resort, it is laid-back enough and charming enough to please even the most anti-resort vacationer. The city has a particularly long history, having once been a Phoenician outpost. Romans later took up residence, setting up a fishing community. Later came the Moors, and, finally, the Christians in the 15th century. Each culture left an imprint on this tiny seaside town.

Sights

Calpe's most distinctive feature is **Peñon de Ifach,** a monolith of rock that soars from the coast to a height of over 300 meters (1,000 feet). *Ifach* means "north" in the ancient Phoenician tongue. Visitors with rough-treaded shoes and strong thighs can ascend to the top in about 30 minutes. The path takes you through a tunnel that opens out on the top to reveal a magnificent bird's-eye view. On a clear day, it is possible to see all the way to the island of Ibiza. The rock, which juts down into the sea nearly a kilometer, is a haven for hundreds of species of flora and fauna, both terrestrial and marine. As a result, it has been declared a national park, which is what has helped Calpe resist growing into another version of Benidorm. Though do be aware, the town does draw a hefty, and very loyal, tourist following, particularly among English and other European families. It is probably not the best choice if you are partying your way around Spain.

Near the base of Ifach are the ruins of **Baños de la Reina** (Queen's Bath). In reality, they are the remains of a Roman hatchery and fish-drying shed built right into the sea. The fanciful name comes from their resemblance to Moorish bath houses. Also at the base of the rock is the **Puerto** (harbor). Take a place on the walkway in front of the **Lonja de Calpe** (fish exchange) to watch the lively action as the fishermen unload and sell off the day's catch. Many buyers are chefs at the local seafood restaurants, but to be sure you get the same fish you watch get hauled in, eat only at establishments with the round *Peix de Calp* (fish from Calpe) symbol.

On either side of the rock stretch beaches. **Playa Arenal,** running south, fronts the old town (it is sometimes called Playa del Puerto). **Playa Levante,** going north, is dotted with new housing and a handful of resorts. Both are lined with amenities including lifeguards, showers, umbrella rentals, bars, and restaurants. Calpe's **tourist office** (Av. Ejercitos Españoles 44, tel. 96/583-6920) is located inland, on the edge of the old town and can help arrange activities such as scuba diving and hiking.

The old town offers typical Spanish charm in whitewashed buildings, narrow streets, and the only Mudejar/Gothic church in the region, the 15th-century **Iglesia de las Nieves.** There are also some remains of the medieval walls. They were installed in the 15th century when the town was under constant attack from Barbary pirates. The best preserved bit is the **Torreón de la Peça.**

Accommodations and Food

Roca Esmeralda (C/ Ponent 1, tel. 96/583-6101, www.rocaesmeralda.com, €120) is as big and brash as it gets. The "emerald rock" really does glow emerald green come nightfall. Rooms are comfy oases of sea colors and the hotel offers all the amenities, from an in-house spa to in-house entertainment. **Pensión Centrica** (Pl. Ifach 5, tel. 96/583-5528, €50) is right in the old town and offers cheap and cheerful rooms as well as friendly, English-speaking service. **Venta La Chata** (Ctra. Valencia, km. 172, tel. 96/583-0308, €60) is a bit out of town, but worth it for its downscale size and rustic Spanish rooms, many boasting balconies opening onto the sea.

For traditional Spanish fare and tasty tapas, head to the old town. For seafood, go to the fishing port. For anything else, from Chinese to fish-and-chips, hit the myriad of places all along the beaches. One of the best restaurants in town is **Los Zapatos** (C/ Santa María 7, tel. 96/583-1507, closed Wed., €35), an elegant dining room offering a delicious blend of Mediterranean and Arabic foods. **El Santo** (C/ Torreones 3, tel. 96/583-2034) is a boisterous Argentinean steak house with exquisite meats.

Getting There and Around

Calpe lies just off the picturesque coastal road of N-332. Get there faster via the new AP-7/E-15. Just follow the exit to Calpe/Calp. By train catch the **El Trenet** (www.fgvalicante.com) from Alicante. By bus, **Alsa** (www.alsa.es) has several coastal buses originating in Valencia.

◖ ALTEA

Spanish poet Gabriel Miró once called Altea "a village roasted by the sun." Situated on a steep slope on a picturesque bay of the Levante coast, Altea does seem to bask in its particular wash of sunshine. Both bright and ethereal, Altea's light has long made it an artists' retreat and the Casco Antiguo (old town) is crammed with galleries and art studios.

Sights

The **Casco Antiguo** sits atop a steep hill threaded with medieval alleyways that climb past whitewashed houses draped in pink bougainvillea. It is simply beautiful. At the very top is the elegant bulk of **Iglesia Nuestra Señora del Consuelo.** Its blue-tiled roof looks almost edible with a confectioner's trim of white. It is the town's emblematic calling card, featured on all postcards and visible for kilometers. The church sits on Plaza L'Esglesia, which is rimmed with sidewalk cafés. In July and August, the plaza hosts a nightly **Feria de Artesanía** (8 P.M.–1 A.M.) featuring arts and crafts from local and national artists. Leading off in all directions from the plaza are tiny streets curling down the hill. They regularly bust out into postage-sized gardens lush with flowers and broad-leafed trees. At almost every turn, you'll find an expansive view over the deep blue of the Mediterranean, Altea's fishing harbor down below, or the craggy shadows of mountains all around.

If you walk down from the Casco Antiguo towards the sea, you'll end up on the **Paseo Mediterráneo,** Altea's seaside boardwalk. It faces the rocky shores of the sea and stretches out to the Malecón pier to the left and Calle Sant Pere to the right. The Paseo is lined with mostly tacky restaurants serving forgettable food to tourists drawn in by the neon glaze and rock-bottom prices. There are also quite a few bars and English pubs. Along Sant Pere runs the **Playa de la Roda,** Altea's main beach and the reason why this impossibly lovely village has withstood the building scourge that has consumed neighboring towns. The beach starts out as pebbles and gets progressively rocky on

Charming Altea offers a maze of whitewashed buildings and art galleries.

into the sea. This lack of fine golden sands has kept tourism at bay and helped preserve the sleepy charm of Altea. You can still get a tan by slapping on some heavy-soled flip-flops and renting a lounge chair (€3), but if you are after long walks in the tide, you'll have to hop the train to either Benidorm or Calpe. If you want some quiet contemplation with the Mediterranean, you've come to the right place—and if you've got a special someone, even better. With its unabashed charm and gorgeous vistas, Altea exudes romance and attracts many in-love couples. This is not the place to come with your kids, nor your party-loving mates. It is also not for the weak of heart or thigh, as its steep hills can be taxing.

Accommodations

For a cheap sleep with a priceless view, check into **Hotel San Miguel** (C/ Sant Pere 7, 96/584-0400, €48). One of the oldest hotels in Altea, its simple rooms are equipped with very basic amenities and a very extraordinary view over the Mediterranean Sea. The hotel is situated so close to the sea that you will see nothing but deep blue ocean from your bed and be lulled to sleep by the waves. Reception is in the dining room and if you arrive during lunch, you'll have to wait until the waiter can give you a key. (Their rice dishes are excellent, by the way.) The staff is very friendly, but if you can't get a room with a view, don't bother. Head instead uphill to **Hostal El Fornet** (C/ Beniarda 1, tel. 96/584-3005, €45), a cheap charmer with lovely views over the town and the blue dome of the church. Moving upscale, enjoy a bit of very stylish luxury at **Hotel La Serena** (C/ Alba 10, tel. 96/688-5849, www.hotellaserena.com, €150). This boutique hotel is all slate flooring, flowing silk curtains, muted tones, soft fabrics, modern art, and peaceful comfort. There are no televisions in the rooms, but the views are intoxicating and there is an intimate pool on the private terrace. The austere restaurant features healthy takes on local fare with an emphasis on seafood (€40). There is also a basement *hammam* (Turkish bath), where you can sweat and scrub away your cares.

VALENCIA AND MURCIA

For less cool and more cozy, head to **Abaco Inn** (C/ Salva 13, tel. 96/688-2500, reservas@abacoinnaltea.com, www.abacoinnaltea.com, €110). Rooms are lovingly decorated according to theme—Provence is all French country, America's Cup is a nautical blue-and-white suite. The most romantic of the rooms is Old Habana, with its four-poster bed, hardwood floors, and beamed ceilings. Down on the seashore, try **Hotel Atlaya** (C/ Sant Pere 28, tel. 96/584-0800, www.hotelaltaya.com, €93), a classic mid-priced hotel with a big-hotel feel. Request a room looking over the sea.

Food

As a romantic seaside destination, Altea boasts several intimate restaurants. The best is **Oustau** (C/ Mayor 5, tel. 96/584-2078, closed Mon. in winter and Feb., €35) run by the charming Olivier Burri, a Swiss expat. The food, created by chef Pascual Robles, is creative Mediterranean that draws playful inspiration from the world of cinema. Try a Sophia Loren mozzarella salad or a sirloin "Love Story" with a fresh strawberry glaze. The dining rooms are chic and warm, with sunset-colored tablecloths and modern, local art on the walls. **La Claudia** (C/ Santa Bárbara 4, tel. 96/584-0816, €30) offers dishes like prawn carpaccio with balsamic foam, confit of duck with cinnamon pears, and warm cheesecake with a sweet tomato glaze. The dining room is dark and modern, but the place to sit is on the terrace, which overlooks the city and the sea. For a more classic meal, head to the rustically elegant **La Capella** (C/ San Pablo 1, tel. 96/584-1763, €36), which prepares excellent rice dishes (the best is *arroz al horno)* and *salazones,* cured fishes that are typical to the region.

For more casual dining, head down to the sea and **Pizzeria Claudio** (C/ Sant Pere 4, tel. 96/584-2873, closed Wed., €20), which uses local produce and seafood in its pizzas. The dough is handmade by the Italian chef daily and pasta is freshly made to order. Try the roasted vegetable salad to start. This place is popular with locals and limited on tables, so expect to wait, especially on weekends. There are several English pubs along the water offering regrettable, greasy food, but one café stands above the rest. **Café Bar Med** (Po. Mediterráneo 20, tel. 96/584-1226, 10 A.M.–10 P.M. daily, €15) offers an excellent selection of fresh salads, sandwiches, and very hearty English breakfasts. English-speaking owner Jamie is a charmer. If you prefer a lighter breakfast, try the very Spanish **L'Alteana** (C/ Filarmonica 1, tel. 96/584-3136, closed Wed.), a café/pastry shop with excellent coffee that is open all day.

When dining out in Altea, note that most restaurants are open daily in the summer. The rest of the year, most places close at least one day per week, more often than not on Wednesday.

Information

Altea's well-equipped **tourist office** (C/ Sant Pere 9, tel. 96/584-4114, 10 A.M.–2 P.M. and 5–7:30 P.M. Mon.–Fri., 10 A.M.–2 P.M. Sat., closed Sun.) offers excellent information on Altea and the surrounding villages. The city's website, www.ayuntamientoaltea.es, is in Spanish only, but you can get good information in English at www.comunitatvalenciana.com and www.costablanca.org.

Getting There and Around

N-332 runs right through Altea, separating the seaside from the Casco Antiguo. You can also catch the speedier AP-7/E-15 and exit 64. By train, it is a €5 ride on the **Trenet** (www.fgvalicante.com) from Alicante. **Alsa** (www.alsa.es) runs buses through Altea and along the coast.

BENIDORM

Benidorm is a town of extremes. In the obvious ways—turquoise blue seas versus concrete gray skyscrapers, star-dappled sand versus neon-lit strip clubs—but also in the reaction this seaside Las Vegas evokes: People either love it or hate it. Approaching Benidorm by rail or road, the sudden sight of its Lego-like skyscrapers plunged into the mottled landscape is a shock. There are hundreds of them and more always under construction. This is the bane of Benidorm, and why the purists complain. As recently as the 1950s, this was little more than a ramshackle seaside village. It also boasted eight kilometers (five miles) of pristine sand beaches and an average of 315 sunny days per year. Those natural luxuries led to a very unnatural evolution. From the 1960s onwards, Benidorm underwent a massive building boom. Soon after, hordes of tourists from colder climes, particularly Great Britain, started pouring in. By the 1980s, Benidorm was synonymous with sunburned Brits jam-packed into too-short shorts, drinking, puking, and brawling their way through their vacations. Today, that has changed. Benidorm has cleaned up its act and alongside the package-tour mayhem stands a pearl of a city with a thriving cultural scene, excellent restaurants, and a population—that contrary to popular myth—is actually more Spanish than foreign. Don't be misled. It is still a major destination for tourists with nothing more than beach and beer on their mind, but it is by no means as horrid as the general press would make it out to be. In fact, if you are looking for a mid-priced vacation resort with all the amenities, Benidorm might just be your thing.

Sights

The main sight in Benidorm is its golden coastline. The **Playa de la Levante** is the loveliest beach, with over 1.5 kilometers (over a mile) of fine sand. It is also the most popular and can get insanely crowded. Just south of the harbor, the **Playa de Poniente** is slightly less busy, though equally as beautiful. Both beaches sport long promenades dotted with cafés and snack bars. Between the two beaches, located on a promontory overlooking the sea is the **Casco Antiguo.** The Old Town is in stark contrast to the skyscrapers surrounding it. Its blue-domed **Iglesia de San Jaime** was built in the 18th century and looms over a network of cobbled streets and alleyways. From here, walk up and up to a white set of vaguely Greek steps. These lead to **Balcón del Mediterráneo,** a lookout point offering panoramic views of Benidorm, the sea, and beyond.

Benidorm caters to kids with several supersized theme parks. **Terra Natura** (www.terra natura.com, €21, kids 4–12 €14) offers a glimpse into the far-flung corners of the world

© GREGORY MORLEY

Benidorm's beaches are lined with skyscrapers.

VALENCIA AND MURCIA

with environments that show off local animals, art, architecture, and cultures in themed areas of Asia, Europe, and the Americas. There is also a water park where you can swim with sharks. **Terra Mítica** (www.terramiticapark.com, €33, kids 4–10 €25) offers rides and activities in areas named for Rome, Greece, Egypt, Iberia, and the Mediterranean isles. **Aqualandia** (www.aqualandia.net, €23, kids 3–12 €18) is Europe's largest water park with massive pools, slides, and watery fun for all ages. Just next door is **Mundomar** (www.mundomar.es, €20, kids 3–12 €14), a park/zoo full of marine life and exotic animals and birds.

Nightlife

Benidorm's nightlife offers a little bit of everything from Atlantic City–style shows for the blue-haired set to all-you-can-drink discos for the young and drunk at heart. There are also flamenco shows, techno clubs, and English pubs galore. Almost all the big hotels in town offer shows, from stale comedians to stunning singers—it is all the luck of the draw. The website www.benidorm-spotlight.com offers extensive reviews, though all you really have to do is follow the crowds in Casco Antiguo or anywhere along the beach. Be on the lookout for free drink coupons being passed out, especially in British Square, at the corner of Avenida de Mallorca and Calle Gerona. While in the square, you may notice flyers for "Sticky Vicky." She is a Benidorm legend who has been performing a raunchy comedy routine for decades. She is rumored to be in her 70s and married to a local policeman. If you do see a flyer for her, make an effort to see her show—that is if she really exists, no one seems to know! Benidorm also draws a huge international gay crowd and there are dozens of bars from the laid-back to the raunchy catering to the gay and lesbian scene. Check www.gaybenidorm.com for details.

Accommodations

Massive hotel buildings abound in Benidorm and they are all pretty similar. Most offer the choice of full- or half-board. However, don't

forget you are in Spain, not some deserted island where all-inclusive meals make sense. If you go for the meals, more than likely you'll find big buffets heavy on the English specialties and light on the quality. At the most, go for breakfast and then dine out in the Casco Antiguo or at any of the hundreds of restaurants all around town. Average room prices hover around €75 and include air-conditioning, swimming pools, and all the standard amenities. Cut-rate places are usually clustered in the Casco Antiguo or inland, far from the beach. If you go anytime but summer, you can usually score excellent prices. In August, don't bother showing up without a reservation.

In a town jammed with over-the-top megahotels, **Gran Hotel Bali** (C/ Luis Prendes, s/n, La Cala, tel. 96/681-5200, www.granhotelbali.com, €90) stands above rest. Literally. At 56 floors, it is the highest building in Spain. As a grande dame of the Benidorm hotel scene, it offers all the perks and more, including spacious rooms (request a view), good service, pools, whirlpools, gardens, bars, and restaurants. It is located on the beach in La Cala, the southernmost portion of the city, about 20 minutes walking to the Casco Antiguo. Closer to town, **Sol Pelícanos Ocas** (C/ Gerona 45–47, tel. 96/585-5058, sol.pelicanos.ocas@solmelia.com, €85) is a 700-room hotel with all the super-sized hotel amenities. Though these types of places are a dime a dozen, Pelícanos outdoes its competition with its over-the-top cloverleaf-shaped pool surrounded by palm trees and faux-Roman columns. This is also the perfect place for children with the hotel's "Flintstones" theme geared towards kids throughout. Also in the center of action, **Hotel Orange** (C/ Mallorca 11, tel. 96/585-1720, orange@servigroup.es, www.servigroup.es, €60) is a long-time holiday-maker's favorite, with 247 recently remodeled rooms and a lovely pool just steps from the beach.

Food

If you want English pub food or cheap Chinese, just follow the masses, as these types of joints abound in Benidorm. However, if you are after some good Spanish fare, tapas-style, head to the Casco Antiguo. Locals refer to the streets running from Plaza de la Constitución and along Calle Santo Domingo as "tapas alley." Pay a visit and you'll see why. The most popular spot for both Spanish and expat locals is **La Cava Aragonesa** (Pl. Constitución 2, tel. 96/680-1206, 9 A.M.–11 P.M. daily). This place offers España on a plate with excellent cured ham, *croquetas, tortilla,* and more. Rumor has it that if you lined up all their tapas plate by plate it would stretch for nearly half a football field. The wine list is impressive too with over 500 Spanish vintages. But be aware, this place is elbow-to-back crowded, just the way the Spaniards like it. Work your way in and you won't be sorry. A lot less crowded, but just as good is **Aurrera El Bodegon** (C/ Santo Doming, 12, tel. 96/585-6372, 11 A.M.–2 P.M. and 8–11 P.M. daily). It is Spanish all over with wine barrels for tables and cured ham legs hanging over the bar. One of the best restaurants in town is **Ulía** (Av. Vicente Llorca Alós 15, tel. 96/585-6828, closed Sun. P.M. and Mon., €45) in La Cala. It is famed for the quality of its seafood and its impeccable presentation.

Information

Be sure to hit the **tourist information office** (Av. Martínez Alejos, 16, tel. 90/210-0581, 9 A.M.–8 P.M. Mon.–Fri., 10 A.M.–1 P.M. and 4–7 P.M. Sat., 10 A.M.–1:30 P.M. Sun.) for maps, information, and flyers about local events. An Internet search will also reveal tons of information and forums in English, catering to the large English-speaking population. The city's website is a good place to start at www.benidorm.org.

Getting There and Around

Benidorm is located off the AP-7/E-15 highway and the N-332 coastal road. Just follow the neon glow. From Alicante, take the **Trenet** (www.fgvalicante.com) The ride lasts an hour. If you are flying into Alicante specifically to head to Benidrom, you can catch an **Alsa** bus (www.alsa.es, €7 one-way) right from the airport. There is also the slower local C-6 bus. A taxi should offer you a fixed rate of about €58 for up to four people. The rate is posted in the cab and if the driver attempts to use the meter, just firmly refuse and point at the posted rate. Going by bus from Valencia, or anywhere else on the coast, means Alsa.

Comunidad de Murcia

Lying in Spain's southeast corner, Comunidad de Murcia is hemmed in by Andalucía, Castilla-La Mancha, and Valencia and lapped by about 170 kilometers (105 miles) of turquoise blue Mediterranean Sea. Despite being one of the driest regions in Spain, Murcia has traditionally been the one of Spain's top *huertas* (vegetable farms), providing thousands of tons of produce for the country yearly. The crops have been helped by an irrigation system first devised by the Moors, who called the area Mursiya. The major source of water is the Río Segura, once deemed the filthiest river in Spain. Though its levels are notoriously low, since the 1970s water has been diverted from the Río Tajo in Castilla-La Mancha in a controversial project that still has the Manchegos seething.

Other than its capital city of Murcia, the inland areas hold little interest for the casual tourist. It is lovely enough, with dusty one-road towns dominated by medieval castles and churches. The landscape unfurls in a mosaic of desert, mountain, and kilometers of farmland that is refreshing in its rural calm. Locals speak their own dialect called Murciano, a version of Valenciano (which derives from Catalan). Some rural villages even speak a language called Panocho, an ancient patois that is incomprehensible to Spanish speakers. Around the northern-lying towns of Yecla and Jumilla lie hectares of vineyards that recently have begun producing amazing award-winning wines. Look for **Bodegas Castaño** from Yecla and **Finca Luzon** from Jumilla. Another small town of note is **Lorca,** with its looming Moorish castle and spectacular baroque palace. If you are driving along the coast from Valencia or Alicante to Granada, it is worth the detour. Along the lower part of the Mediterranean coast, there are untamed beaches where the rocky cliffs fall straight off into the sea, forming perfect little coves.

The region's main points of touristic interest are the evocative seaside city of **Cartagena,** a naval base since the Carthaginians founded it nearly 2,500 years ago, and the **Mar Menor,** a large saltwater lagoon sitting just in from Murcia's Costa Cálida (warm coast). The lagoon is Murcia's largest resort, full of large-scale hotels and bristling with water-based activities. Yet, for whatever reason, it has failed to attract the tourist masses in the same way that nearby Costa Blanca and Costa del Sol have. In fact, the region as a whole has been mostly immune to tourism. With its coast jutting out to sea, bypassed by the A-7/E-15 highway, it has just been easier to skip the region, speeding through it on the way to see the big sights of Granada and Valencia. The result is a much slower pace inland, of course, but also on the barely developed coast stretching west from Cartagena to Almería. That should be changing in the next decade. Since the early 2000s, expat emigration has slowed in Alicante and Costa del Sol, and slowly increased in Murcia. By 2006, the region of Murcia had the fourth-highest number of British residents behind Alicante, Málaga, and the Balearic Islands.

MURCIA CAPITAL

Inland just 84 kilometers (52 miles) southwest of Alicante, the capital of the Provincia de Murcia is also called Murcia. A bustling city of 400,000, its center is a throwback to Spain's 19th-century heyday, full of ornate sienna-colored buildings. Though Murcia was a thriving town under the Moors from the 9th to the 12th centuries, and later one of the wealthiest of the early Christian cities, little of Murcia's

distant past remains. The town was devastated by vicious flooding from the Río Segura in the 17th, 19th, and early 20th centuries. Dams and levees have since been built. The popular **Paseo de Malécon** runs atop one of the levees. Today, the city has a vibrant feel, fueled in part by its university. Like any good Spanish capital, its streets are lined with tapas bars and cafés, boutiques and markets. First time visitors to Murcia always have the same reaction—surprise. They are surprised at just how lovely the town is and also at how untouched by tourism it seems. Despite its charms, this probably won't change as the temptation to stay at a beachside resort is very strong and Murcia, set inland, just can't compete.

Sights

The top sight is the **Catedral de Murcia** (Pl. Cardenal Belluga, tel. 96/821-6344), located in the lively Plaza del Cardenal Belluga. The building dates from a 14th-century church built on top of a Moorish mosque, though the present structure, with its baroque facade and over-the-top Gothic interior, was built in the 18th century. Edging out the cathedral in terms of sheer exuberance is the **Casino de Murcia** (C/ Trapería 18, tel. 96/821-5399). Having nothing to with gambling, "casino" once referred to private clubs for upper-crust men. Built in 1847, this mansion features several expansive rooms designed to look like famous buildings—the glass-roofed patio recreates the Alhambra, the dance hall evokes the chandeliered halls of Versailles. **Calle Trapería** and nearby **Calle La Platería** are the two oldest streets in the city. Both boast buildings that date back to the 14th century.

Accommodations

Refreshingly, Murcia's hotels are inexpensive and attentive. At the rock-bottom end of the lodging options, **Pensión Segura** (P. Camachos 14, tel. 96/821-1281, €42) is the best. A cheap charmer with updated rooms, it is located just steps from the cathedral. **Hotel Hispano I** (C/ Trapería 8, tel. 96/821-6152, www.hotelhispano.net, €70), located on one of the town's most emblematic streets, offers old-fashioned rooms with updated amenities. The in-house restaurant is elegant and good, specializing in Murcia's two best resources—fresh vegetables and fresh seafood. The hotel has a sister property around the corner, **Hotel Hispano II** (€85), which is a bit more upscale. Both can be booked at the same number. The thoroughly modern **Hotel Zenit Murcia** (Pl. San Pedro 5, tel. 96/821-4742, murcia@zenit hoteles.com, www.zenithoteles.com, €70) has a great location on the corner of the lovely Plaza de las Flores. **Hotel Casa Emilio** (C/ Alameda de Colón 9, tel. 96/822-0631, www.hotelcasa emilio.com, €60) sits across from the lovely gardens, Jardín de Floridablanca, and offers basic, comfortable rooms and a friendly staff.

Food

Tapas can be found throughout the old town; the best are in the Plazas of San Juan, Santa Catalina, Las Flores, and Romea. Expect local takes on traditional tapas such as *matrimonio*, a marriage of a salty cured anchovy with a freshly marinated one, or *marineros,* a cold vegetable salad served on a round bread studded with anchovies. For an excellent local restaurant, go no further than the top-rated **Rincón de Pepe** (C/ Apósteles 34, tel. 96/821-2239, 1:30–4 P.M. and 8 P.M.–midnight daily, €20), where local seafood specialties get a haute touch from the creative chef. **El Churra** (C/ Obispo Sancho Davila 13, tel. 96/827-1522, 1–4 P.M. and 8 P.M.–midnight daily, €35) is a local classic serving impeccable Murciano fare, including delicious *calderos,* stews of seafood and rice. It is Murcia's answer to paella.

Information

Murcia's **tourist office** (Pl. Cardenal Belluga, s/n, tel. 96/835-8749, 10 A.M.–2 P.M. and 4:30–8 P.M. Mon.–Sat., 10 A.M.–2 P.M. Sun.) is located in the town hall building across from the cathedral. It offers both city and regional information. The city website, www.murcia ciudad.com, is not bad, while the regional site, www.murciaturistica.es, is excellent.

Getting There and Around

Murcia is connected to Castilla-La Mancha and on to Madrid via the A-30. The E-15/A-7 connects to Valencia in the north and Andalucía in the southwest. By train, Murcia's **Estación el Carmen** (Pl. Industria, s/n) is serviced by **Renfe** (tel. 90/224-0202, www.renfe.es) with several daily trains to Valencia, Cartagena, Almería, Madrid, and beyond. Other major cities, including Barcelona, can be reached via Valencia. By bus, Murcia's **Estación de Autobuses** (C/ Bolos, s/n, tel. 96/829-2211) has several bus companies connecting throughout Spain.

◖ CARTAGENA

Home to the Spanish Navy since the 18th century, bustling little Cartagena has an enviable position on a lovely, wide harbor opening onto the Mediterranean Sea. The harbor is so well suited to seafaring notions that is has been used as such for millennia. The Carthaginians founded the town as Qart Hadast around 230 B.C. and made it the capital of their Iberian kingdom. The Romans seized control of the city in 209 B.C. and renamed it Cartago Nova during the Second Punic War (one of three between the empires of Rome and Carthage). Cartagena has the only remaining piece of a Punic defensive wall in the world. The Romans built up the city extensively and many of Cartagena's most impressive sights are from this era. Following Rome's fall, Cartagena faded into oblivion until the 18th century when Carlos I made it the headquarters of Spain's naval operations. The city's fate turned around as money poured in and many of Cartagena's loveliest buildings date from this golden era.

Today, Cartagena seems like an archaeological site posing as a city. You can't turn a corner without running into a thousand-year-old monument. Add to that the bustling seaport with all its military pomp and purpose, a vibrant university, and some very lovely beaches, and you have a perfect little Spanish vacation spot, refreshingly free of the heavy tourism that mars much of the Mediterranean coast.

Sights

Get your historical bearings with a visit to the **Puerto de Culturas** (C/ Gisbert 10, tel. 96/850-0093, www.puertoculturas.com). This initiative has drawn together all of Cartagena's historic monuments under one umbrella and offers self-guided maps, tours, and a tourist bus. Their offices are in the **Refugio-Museo de la Guerra Civil,** a Civil War museum built in the caves where locals hid from Franco's frequent and vicious bombing raids. On the Puerto de Culturas itinerary is the not-to-be-missed **Castillo Concepción** (€3.50), the remains of a 14th-century fortress built on top of the city's highest hill. Reach it via the panoramic glass elevator (C/ Gispert 10, €1). The views up top are inspiring. There is also an enjoyable interpretation center explaining Caratagena's long history. The hilltop is also home to a nice open-air bar, and having a drink here while watching the sunset is one of the nicest things you can do in town.

The **Muralla Púnica** (C/ San Diego 25, €2.50) gets you up close and personal with this 2,200-year-old piece of punic wall. It too has a dynamic interpretation center. Next, experience a bit of Rome at the **Casa de la Fortuna** (Pl. Risueño 14, €2.50), a wonderfully preserved Roman home where you can witness a bit of domestic life from 2,100 years ago. The mosaic-tiled floors and the intricately painted walls are simply beautiful. The nearby **Augusteum** (C/ Caballero 2, €2.50) contains the remains of two Roman buildings as well as a host of Roman artifacts. Close to the harbor, the **Teatro Romano** (Pl. Condesa Peralta, s/n, tel. 96/852-5326) is the fourth-largest Roman theater in Spain. Dating from the 1st century B.C., it is particularly impressive when you learn that the large seating area was sculpted out of solid rock.

Cartagena also offers a handful of sights related to its naval history. Near the port on Paseo de Alfonso XII, the **Submarino Peral** sits like a beached whale in a patch of grass. This is the original 1884 submarine built by Spanish scientist Isaac Peral. It was the world's first U-boat designed specifically for military use. The **Museo Naval de Cartagena** (C/ Menéndez Pelayo 8 tel. 96/812-7138, free) documents the naval history of both Cartagena and Spain.

Despite its seafront local, there are no good beaches of note within city limits. Locals and visitors alike usually travel to the gorgeous stretches of sand leading to and around La Manga del Mar Menor. There is a small nudist beach, **Playa El Portus,** to the west of town.

Accommodations

On the lower end of the accommodations options, consider **Hotel Peninsular** (C/ Cuatro Santos 3, tel. 96/850-0033, www.verial.es/hotelpeninsular, €45), located smack in the center of all the best sights. Moving up, the **Hotel Carlos III** (C/ Carlos III 49, tel. 96/852-0032, www.carlosiiihotel.com, €78) is a lovely mid-sized hotel with spacious, if bland, rooms. **NH Cartagena** (C/ Real 2, tel. 96/812-0908, www.nh-hotels.com, €85) offers modern, stylish rooms at a surprisingly good price. As a member of the NH chain, service is top-notch. **Hotel Cartagonova** (C/ Marcos Redondo 3, tel. 96/850-4200, www.hotelcartagonova.com, €130) offers very spacious, sophisticated rooms as well as the city's only luxury spa. For €15, you can enjoy the modern facility with sauna, whirlpool, and optional massages.

Food

For good seafood tapas, particularly mussels, try **La Mejillonera** (C/ Mayor 4, tel. 96/852-1179). Ask for *el grillo,* a savory blend of fresh anchovies and tomatoes. **Azafrán** (C/ La Palma 3, tel. 96/852-3172) is a wonderful place to try Murcia's famed rice dishes, especially *caldero.* In the fishing quarter of Santa Lucia, there are quite a few exquisite seafood restaurants. However, do not go on a Monday. There is no fish market on Sunday, so that means no fresh fish on Monday. **El Varadero** (Puerto Pesquero, s/n, tel. 96/850-5848) is one of the local favorites. A few doors down is **Los Techos Bajos** (tel. 96/850-5020), a fun little place where the specialty is fried fish. For a little meat variety, **La Tartana** (Puerta de Murcia 14, tel. 96/850-0011) specializes in game and grilled meats.

Their house dish is *conejo al ajillo* (rabbit in garlic), but the tapas spread is also wonderful.

Information

Cartagena's **tourist office** (Pl. Bastarreche, s/n, tel. 96/850-6483, 10 A.M.–2 P.M. and 4–6 P.M. Mon.–Fri., 10 A.M.–1 P.M. Sat.) is located in the old walls, Muralla Carlos III. There is also a **tourist kiosk** on the Paseo del Muelle (10 A.M.–1:30 P.M. and 4–6 P.M. Mon.–Sat., 10:30 A.M.–1:30 P.M. Sun.). The offices can arrange bus or boat tours of the city and harbor.

Getting There

Cartagena lies about 32 kilometers (20 miles) off the A-7/E-15 towards the coast. From Murcia, you can take the A-30 straight into Cartagena. Coming from the Andalucía coast, Cartagena lies on the N-332. By bus, Cartagena is well connected with several companies operating out of **Estación de Autobuses** (Av. Trovero Marín, s/n, tel. 96/850-5656). By train, Cartagena is served at **Estación de Renfe** (Pl. México 2, tel. 90/224-0202, www .renfe.es) with direct routes to Murcia, Alicante, Valencia, Madrid, and Barcelona.

VICINITY OF CARTAGENA
Mar Menor and La Manga

About 23 kilometers (14 miles) northeast of Cartagena lies one of Spain's jewels—the saltwater lagoon of Mar Menor. The name means "small sea" and at about 170 square kilometers (65 square miles), it does indeed feel like a sea. Up to six meters (20 feet) deep and filled with a very still, tranquil body of warm, salty water, Mar Menor has drawn health-seekers to its curative waters for centuries. The waters are said to be especially good for arthritis and rheumatism. On the northern tip of the lagoon, near La Puntica, natural pits produce clay that promises to rejuvenate your skin.

The lagoon is separated from the Mediterranean Sea by a long narrow strip of land called La Manga, which means "sleeve." It is 24 kilometers (15 miles) long and varies in width from less than three meters (10 feet) to over 200 meters (650 feet). Several *golas* (narrow channels) allow the Mediterranean to continually feed the Mar Menor.

For centuries, Mar Menor and La Manga del Menor were sleepy areas given over to small-scale fishing. All that changed in the 1960s when Spaniards took notice of this great natural resource and began vacationing here in droves. Sprawling resorts and hotels went up and with them all the vacation resort amenities—golf courses, tennis courts, nautical outfitters, restaurants, and bars. Yet, it is still low-key compared to the other resort towns on the Mediterranean coast. And it is very family-oriented. Not only is the calm water perfect for young swimmers, but most of the hotels offer activities with the youngsters in mind. Though it can get crowded in summer, if you go off-season, you'll enjoy reduced prices and fewer people. However, with an average daily temperature of 18°C (65°F) and 315 days of sunshine per year, you'll still have a wonderful time.

There are hundreds of hotels and resorts. The biggest, most luxurious, and most expensive is the **Hyatt Regency La Manga** (tel. 96/833-1234, www.lamanga.hyatt.com, €300 and up), but you can find anything to fit your budget at the Mar Menor section of www.murcia turistica.com.

Getting to Mar Menor via car is easy. It is 80 kilometers (50 miles) south of Alicante on the AP-7, which originates in Barcelona. Cartagena, to the south, is also on the AP-7. From Madrid, take the A-3. By bus, you can get to the area from Cartagena's **Estación de Autobuses** (Av. Trovero Marín, s/n, tel. 96/850-5656) via **Alsa** (www.alsa.es).

ISLAS BALEARES

Sitting in the Mediterranean Sea less than 160 kilometers (100 miles) off the coast of Valencia, the Islas Baleares glisten gold, green, and white in the always-shining sun. Mallorca, Ibiza, Formentera, and Menorca share stunning scenery and an almost mythical status as a paradise. The beaches are fine as powder and almost as white. The turquoise waters are crystal clear and gentle. Coasts, dramatically carved by millennia of wind and water, offer cozy coves and spectacular caverns.

Despite these picture-perfect sentiments, the Baleares don't fit quite so neatly on a simple postcard. Mallorca offers the kind of big-city sophistication you'd expect on the mainland. With its art galleries, yacht clubs, and glistening resorts, it dispels any notion of a sleepy little island in the sun. Ibiza goes further, blasting that image with a deep bass beat that has reverberated out to the entire club-going world. Alongside some of the most spectacular scenery in the Baleares, Ibiza has emerged as the glitziest, most stylish, and most decadent of the islands. Tiny Formentera, shimmering just below Ibiza's radar, has emerged as the green island—and not just for its deep emerald foliage. It offers Balearic beauty unsullied by resorts, clubs, parties, and shops—confidently beautiful and silent. Menorca, the furthest away and the least developed, seems oblivious to all the fuss. Battered for eons by the *tramontana* wind, Menorca boasts the most secluded coves, the most unspoiled land, and the most mysterious charm of all the Islas Baleares. Like the ancient megaliths that dot its mottled surface high above the sea, Menorca is timeless and enduring.

HIGHLIGHTS

❰ Palma de Mallorca: On an island known for white beaches and deep blue seas, the urban buzz of Palma is a lovely surprise with its atmospheric medieval core, monumental Gothic church, and gorgeous Renaissance patios (page 753).

❰ Western Mallorca: With the Serra de Tramuntana carving the western coast into a series of cliffs and coves, this is Mallorca at its most spectacular. All along the coast are charming towns worth exploring, including the artist's colony of Deià (page 762).

❰ Cap de Formentor: At the tip of a peninsula reached via a long winding road, eastern Mallorca's Cap de Formentor offers views that are nothing short of intoxicating (page 766).

❰ Artà: This dusty inland Mallorcan town offers an impressive roster of sights that have nothing to do with sun and sand – including 3,000-year-old megaliths and a massive network of underground caves (page 768).

❰ Sant Antoni de Portmany: Surrounded by some of the most beautiful scenery in the Mediterranean, this town on the western coast

of Ibiza is the most notorious party spot in the world. Watch the sun set to a trance beat, then dance to world-famous DJs until it rises again (page 776).

❰ Es Trucadors: Tiny Formentera is a jewel of glistening white sands, deep-green landscapes, and the shimmering turquoise of the Mediterranean Sea. Nowhere on the island is this natural beauty more mesmerizing than in Es Trucadors, a narrow slip of sand jutting into the sea (page 779).

❰ Northeastern Menorca: In addition to truly spectacular beaches, this area is home to prehistoric ruins, an artisan cheese factory, the best scenic overlook in the islands, and the King of Spain's favorite place to eat lobster (page 785).

❰ Cala Macarella: Surrounded by pine trees and soaring cliffs, the cove beaches of Macarella and nearby Macarelleta are two of the most beautiful in all of Spain. Hard to get to and way off the beaten Menorcan path, these are beaches where you can almost feel like you are on a deserted island (page 787).

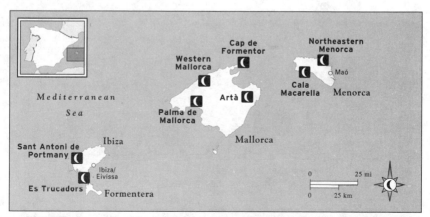

LOOK FOR **❰** TO FIND RECOMMENDED SIGHTS, ACTIVITIES, DINING, AND LODGING.

ISLAS BALEARES

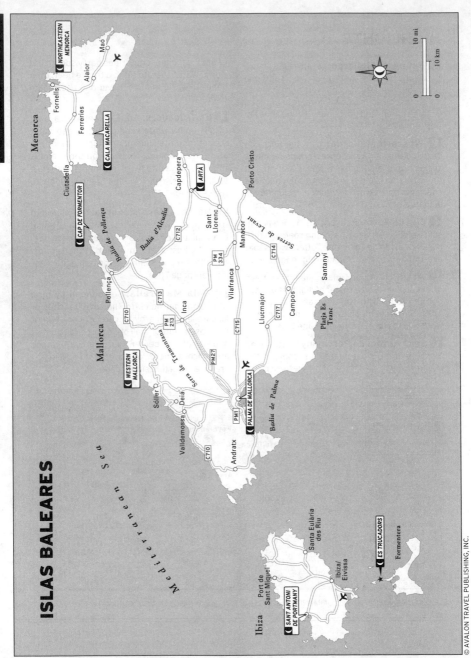

NORTHEASTERN MENORCA

Menorca

Maó

Alaior

Ferreries

Fornells

Ciutadella

CALA MACARELLA

CAP DE FORMENTOR

Badia de Pollença

Pollença

Badia d'Alcúdia

Capdepera

ARTÀ

Porto Cristo

Sant Llorenç

Serres de Levant

Manacor

C712

PM 334

Vilafranca

C714

Santanyí

Mallorca

C710

C713

Inca

PM 213

C715

PM27

Llucmajor

Campos

C717

Platja Es Tranc

Serra de Tramuntana

WESTERN MALLORCA

Sóller

Deià

PM1

PALMA DE MALLORCA

Badia de Palma

Valldemossa

C710

Andratx

Mediterranean Sea

Santa Eulària des Riu

Port de Sant Miquel

Ibiza

Ibiza/Eivissa

SANT ANTONI DE PORTMANY

ES TRUCADORS

Formentera

10 mi

10 km

Catalan is the official language of the Baleares, but Spanish is also widely spoken (and English, German, and French can also be heard). Signs and maps can get confusing, but most are easy enough to decipher. Ibiza's Catalan name is Eivissa and it is used almost exclusively, even defiantly, on the island and in the city.

PLANNING YOUR TIME

Each of the islands offer the main plate of pristine beaches and seductive blue waters; only you can decide what you want on the side. If time is short and money tight, Mallorca is your best bet. Dirt-cheap flights from the mainland can put you into Palma for less than €100 in less then two hours. Once there, base yourself in Palma the city, not the bay. In two days' time you can see the main sights and have your fill of fun in the sun. One more day and you can take in the northwestern coastal towns of Deià and Sóller and maybe have a hike in the hills.

If you have three days minimum, head to Ibiza. Stay in Ibiza City and partake in the nightlife as little or as much as you'd like. Devote at least one day to Formentera. Menorca is best enjoyed slowly, like a good meal. You have to rent a car to see it best and though it only takes two hours to go from coast to rocky coast, there are so many enticing turn-offs—hidden beaches, famed rural restaurants, prehistoric relics—that you could easily spend two days traversing the island.

From mid-June to mid-September, the Baleares swell with tourists. Prices can double or triple, hotels book solid, and space on the sand becomes scarce. The plus side is the sizzling vibe as streets, restaurants, bars, and nightclubs burst to full. There is always a party and it is usually wherever you happen to be standing. Some people love this, others loathe it. A nice compromise is the shoulder time of May and October. Waters are still warm, the sun still mostly shines, and prices take their first dive. It is still a buzzing time, just a lot more manageable. Many people find the silent, slow-moving off-season months of November to March irresistible. Though it might be a bit too chilly for the water, there is still enough sunshine to make lunch on a sidewalk terrace a possibility—you'll just have to plan ahead carefully as many hotels, bars, restaurants, and shops shut down during winter. Cities like Palma, Ibiza, and Ciutadella will still be functioning, just at a much slower metabolic rate.

Mallorca

The largest of the Balearic Islands, Mallorca (my-YOR-ka), often called Majorca in English, is both beautiful and brash. An almost excessive wealth of the former is exactly what led to the latter. In a spate of unrestrained resort development in the late 1960s, the loveliest coasts on the Bay of Palma were converted from a natural state of grace to a crass statement of commercialism. Of course, tourists flocked in. The result is some of the foulest little strip mall resorts marring some of the best beaches on the island. That is the bad news. The good is that the blight is restricted to the Bay of Palma. The further you get from it, the lovelier and less crowded the beaches become. It is still quite possible to find a pristine Mallorcan spot of sand to call your own—at least for a blissful bit of time.

But Mallorca is not all sand and sun and deep blue sea—Palma de Mallorca offers a charming medieval core. The Serra de Tramuntana winds seductively along the western edge of the island, creating a natural paradise for bikers and hikers. The eastern coast is pockmarked with massive, magical caves and caverns. Inland, prehistoric remnants of the millennia-old Talaiot culture sit stoically in ancient groves of olive and lemon trees. Back to the sea—but far from the resorts—beaches like the rocky exuberance of Formentor in the north and the peaceful sweep of Es Trenc in

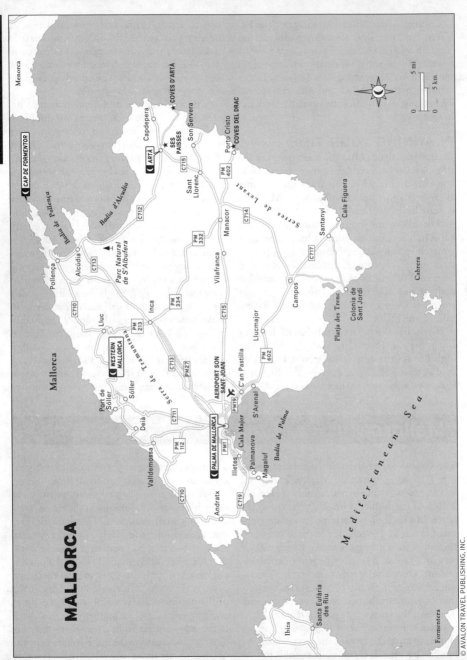

MALLORCA

Menorca

Mallorca

Ibiza

Santa Eulària
des Riu

Formentera

Cabrera

《 CAP DE FORMENTOR

Pollença

Badia de Pollença

Alcúdia

Badia d'Alcúdia

Capdepera

★ COVES D'ARTÀ

Son Servera

《 ARTÀ

★ SES PAÏSES

Sant
Llorenç

Porto Cristo

★ COVES DEL DRAC

Cala Figuera

C715

PM
402

Serres de Llevant

Parc Natural
de S'Albufera

C712

PM
332

Manacor

C714

Santanyí

Lluc

C710

Inca

PM
213

Vilafranca

PM
334

C717

C715

Campos

Colonia de
Sant Jordi

Serra de Tramuntana

**《 WESTERN
MALLORCA**

C713

PM 27

Llucmajor

Platja des Trenc

Port de
Sóller

Sóller

PM
602

Deià

C711

AEROPORT SON
SANT JOAN ✈

C'an Pastilla

S'Arenal

PM 19

Valldemossa

PM
112

《 PALMA DE MALLORCA

PM1

Cala Major

Illetes

Palmanova

Magaluf

Badia de Palma

Andratx

C710

C719

Mediterranean Sea

5 mi

0

5 km

0

the south still have the power to stun even the most finicky traveler.

In short, whatever your idea of a Mediterranean vacation is, Mallorca delivers, boldly and beautifully.

C PALMA DE MALLORCA

The buzzing city of Palma de Mallorca is the only real urban spot in the islands. With a population of over 300,000, it is as vibrant as any capital city on the mainland. Many sun and sand seekers stop here only long enough to catch a cab from the airport to the resorts on the Bay of Palma, but those who stick around find a charming medieval center lined with elegant 18th-century mansions, a handful of impressive Gothic structures (including the monumental cathedral), and every luxury a traveler could want—from upscale boutiques and art galleries to world-class cuisine and sizzling nightlife.

Sights

The **Catedral de Palma de Mallorca** (Pl. Almoina, s/n, tel. 97/172-3130, 10 A.M.–5:15 P.M. Mon.–Fri. April, May, and Oct., 10 A.M.–6:15 P.M. Mon.–Fri. June–Sept., 10 A.M.–3:15 P.M. Mon.–Fri. Nov.–Mar., 10 A.M.–2:15 P.M. Sat. year-round, Sun. worship only, €3.50) is not only Mallorca's greatest structure, it is one of Spain's most magnificent cathedrals. Built over the course of four centuries, Sa Seu, as it is affectionately known, was begun in 1230 under the auspices of Jaume I of Aragón. During a harrowing sea battle the previous year, the king pledged to build a shrine to the Virgin Mary if his troops successfully defeated the Moors. They did and, true to his word, Jaume had his architects begin Sa Seu right on top of the Moorish mosque that previously stood here.

The dimensions of the cathedral are staggering. Start with a walk along the **Parc de la Mar** promenade to get an idea of just how massive this Gothic structure is. Rising up above the old city walls, it is an imposing sight, covered in an officious row of buttresses and topped with rocket-shaped spires. Inside, with your back to the majestic **Portal Major,** you are struck by

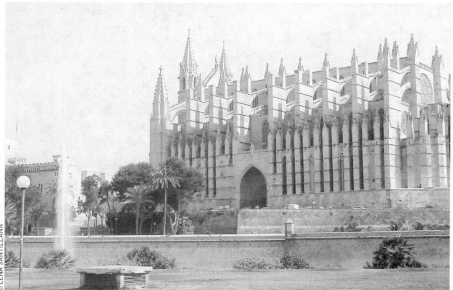

© LENA SANTILLANA

Palma de Mallorca's imposing Gothic cathedral

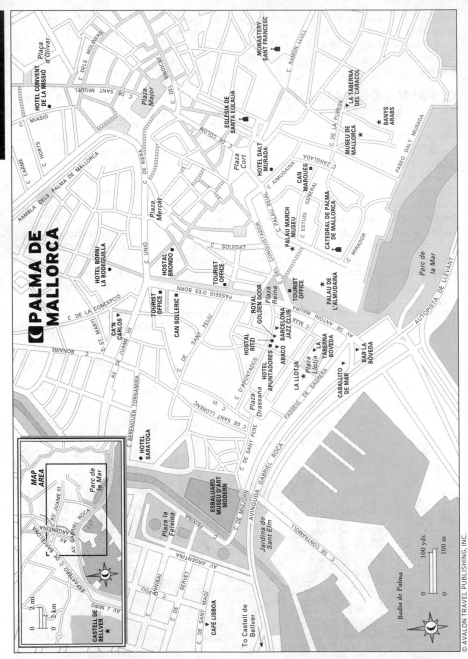

PALMA DE MALLORCA

- HOTEL CONVENT DE LA MISSIÓ
- Plaça d'Olivar
- C. DELS MOLINERS
- C. DE SANT MIQUEL
- C. MIASIÓ
- C. CARME
- C. HORTS
- Plaza Major
- C. DEL SINDICAT
- C. DE COLOM
- MONASTERY SANT FRANCESC
- C. RAMON LLULL
- EGLÉSIA DE SANTA EULÀLIA
- LA TABERNA DEL CARACOL
- C. DE LA PURESA
- BANYS ARABS
- MUSEU DE MALLORCA
- C. AIMUDAINA
- PASEO DALT MURADA
- RAMBLA DELS PALMA DE MALLORCA
- C. DE RIERA
- HOTEL DALT MURADA
- Plaza Cort
- CAN MARQUÉS
- C. GENERAL
- C. ESTUDI
- Plaza Mercat
- C. SOLEDAT
- C. UNIÓ
- PALAU MARCH MUSEU
- C. PALAU REIAL
- CATEDRAL DE PALMA DE MALLORCA
- C. MIRADOR
- HOTEL BORN/ LA BODEGUILLA
- HOSTAL BRONDO
- TOURIST OFFICE
- PASSEIG D'ES BORN
- Plaza Reina
- TOURIST OFFICE
- PALAU DE L'ALMUDAINA
- Parc de la Mar
- C. DE LA CONCEPCIÓ
- C. ST. MARTI
- TOURIST OFFICE
- CAN SOLLERIC
- CAN CARLOS
- C. DE SANT FELIU
- ROYAL GOLDEN DOOR
- C. DE ANTONI MAURA
- AUTOPISTA DE LLEVANT
- BONAIRE
- AV. DE JUANE III
- HOSTAL RITZI
- ABACO
- BARCELONA JAZZ CLUB
- C. MAR
- LA TABERNA BÓVEDA
- BAR LA BÓVEDA
- C. BERENGUER TORNAMIRA
- HOTEL APUNTADORES
- C. D'APUNTADORS
- Plaza Llotja
- LA LLOTJA
- PASSEIG DE SAGRERA
- CABALLITO DE MAR
- HOTEL SARATOGA
- C. DE SANT PERE
- Plaza Drassana
- C. V
- C. DE SANT LLORENÇ
- C. DE MIGJORN
- ESBALUARD MUSEU D'ART MODERN
- AVINGUDA GABRIEL ROCA
- Jardins de Sant Elm
- C. DE CONTRAMOLL
- Plaza la Feixina
- Badia de Palma
- FEIXINA
- AV. ARGENTINA
- POU
- C. DE SANT MAGÍ
- C. DE SANT MAGÍ
- ANNIBAL
- SERVET
- AV. J. MIRÓ
- CAFÉ LISBOA
- To Castell de Bellver

Inset map:

- MAP AREA
- Parc de la Mar
- AV. J. JUANE III
- AV. GABRIEL ROCA
- ESPARTERO C. DE BARCELONA
- AV. ARGENTINA
- CASTELL DE BELLVER
- 0 2 mi
- 0 2 km

- 0 100 yds
- 0 100 m

MALLORCA'S SWEET BUNS

Wherever you go in Mallorca, you'll find bakeries, cafés, and even souvenir shops hawking *ensaimadas*. A spiral-shaped pastry liberally sprinkled with powdered sugar, the *ensaimada* is Mallorca's most popular sweet. Yeast-based, the *ensaimada* is made impossibly light through repeated risings and baked in portions from palm- to pizza-sized. Traditionally, it is stuffed with *cabello de angel*, strands of pumpkin in sweet syrup, but it might also come with whipped cream or nothing at all. Be sure and treat yourself to a breakfast of *ensaimada* and *café con leche* at least once during your Mallorcan vacation. In Palma, try **Ca'n Joan de S'aigo** (C/ Sant Sanc 10, tel. 97/171-0759, 8 A.M.–9:15 P.M. daily), an elegant belle epoque café that has been serving *ensaimadas* since 1700. Joan Miró was a regular. If you will be visiting Spanish friends on the mainland after leaving Mallorca, be sure and pick up a large *ensaimada* from the airport. Mallorcan *ensaimadas* are famed throughout Spain and your friends will be thrilled that you brought them one.

the unexpected loftiness of the building. The nave spans some 19 meters (63 feet) held aloft by 14 palm tree–thin columns that spread out at the top like elegant stone fronds to support the 21-meter-high (70-foot) roof. A glorious rose window spanning 12 meters (40 feet) in diameter floods the 122-meter-long (400-foot) nave with a kaleidoscope of color. It is both breathtaking and appropriately solemn.

Antoni Gaudí worked on cathedral restorations here in the early 1900s and his imprint is clear in the **Capilla Real** (Royal Chapel), which sits under a Gaudí-designed iron canopy/chandelier that is supposed to represent Christ's crown of thorns. It wasn't much appreciated when built and Gaudí was fired from the restoration project before he could do more "damage" to the original structure. Art and architectural history has proven that to be a bad move on the part of Palma's leaders. Gaudí's crowning chandelier is definitely a highlight of the cathedral.

The cathedral's bell tower holds nine bells, including the massive N'Eloi bell built in 1389. Some two meters (six feet) across and weighing 4,517 kilograms (nearly 10,000 pounds), it is rumored to shatter glass windows when it tolls. The cathedral is also home to the **Museu de la Catedral,** a collection of religious art and antiquities— King Jaume I's curious silver and wooden portable altar, some impressive 14th- and 15th-century Gothic paintings, and

Christian mementos, including three supposed "thorns" from Christ's crown.

Sharing the plaza with the cathedral is the **Palau de l'Almudaina** (Pl. Almoina, s/n, tel. 97/171-9145, www.patrimonionacional.es, 10 A.M.–5:45 P.M. Mon.–Fri. summer, 10 A.M.–1:15 P.M. and 4–5:15 P.M. Mon.–Fri. winter, 10 A.M.–1:15 P.M. Sat. year-round, closed Sun., €3.50), a splendid palace built on the site of a long-gone Moorish citadel. In the 13th century, it was outfitted as the seat of the medieval court of the independent kingdom of Mallorca and King Jaume I lived the last of his years here. Though the palace is ornate and full of lovely tapestries and medieval art work, it is a bit boring. However, it is exciting to be present when it is half cordoned-off, indicating a member of the current Spanish royal family is about.

Just north is the evocative modern art museum **Palau March Museu** (C/ Palau Reial 18, tel. 97/171-1122, www.fundbmarch.es, 10 A.M.–6:30 P.M. Mon.–Fri. summer, 10 A.M.–6 P.M. Mon.–Fri. winter, 10 A.M.–2 P.M. Sat. year-round, closed Sun., €4.50). The collection is heavy on sculpture by some heavy-hitters—Rodin, Eduardo Chillida, and Henry Moore among them. The location, in a palatial mansion with a regal courtyard, is a treat in itself.

Behind the museum, a tangled web of atmospheric streets and squares brimming with historic buildings, trendy shops, and inviting cafés. This is Palma's old historical core and while it is full of worthy sights, the real pleasure is just getting lost here. As you wander, keep an eye out for the the the charming Plaça Sant Francesc, home to the beautiful 13th-century monastery **Sant Francesc** (€1). Built on the grounds of a Moorish soap factory, it was originally founded for Jaume I's oldest son who shunned the crown in favor of life as a monk. The cloisters are worth a visit.

This area was also home to Mallorca's medieval Jewish quarter. The **Església de Santa Eulàlia** (Pl. Santa Eulalia, s/n, free) was the sight of a mass forced conversion of Jews to Christianity in 1435. The tourist office leads a very interesting **Jewish Quarter Tour** (tel. 97/172-0720, €10) through the barrio.

On the southern edge of this barrio stands one of the few remaining monuments from Moorish rule of Mallorca, the public baths known as **Banys Arabs** (C/ Can Serra 7, tel. 97/172-1459, 9 A.M.–8 P.M. daily summer, 9 A.M.–6 P.M. daily winter, €1.50). Standing in a lovely lemon grove, the baths date to the 10th century and consist of a simple, yet moody, domed bathhouse with circular skylights to let out the accumulated steam.

Around the corner, the **Museu de Mallorca** (C/ Portella 5, tel. 97/171-7540, 10 A.M.–7 P.M. Tues.–Sat., 10 A.M.–2 P.M. Sun., closed Mon., €3) contains an impressive archaeological collection dating back to prehistory. The 17th-century Renaissance mansion in which it is housed is a lovely example of Mallorcan architecture and features an exemplary inner courtyard.

After a devasting fire, much of this area was rebuilt in the 17th and 18th centuries according to the Renaissance style popular at the time—including majestic inner courtyards with great arched arcades around which the home was built. These patios served as the public space of the house and a retreat from the bustle of the town. The majority of these homes are privately owned, but the tourist office has cajoled a few dozen owners into opening the patios to the public completely—or by

at least leaving the split-level doors half-open. The *Ruta dels Patis de Palma,* a walking map of these buildings, is available at any tourist office or in the free tourist magazine *Palma 365.*

At **Can Marqués** (C/ Zanglada, 2, tel. 97/171-6247, www.casasconhistoria.net) you can see a lot more than just the patio. A majestic Palma house dating to the 14th century, it has been outfitted in the style of a typical bourgeoisie home from the turn-of-the-20th century. Visiting it feels like stumbling on a private home just moments after the family stepped out—laundry is piled in a basket, a shawl is draped on a chair, the table is set. The atmospheric kitchen, complete with soot-stained wall, is a highlight.

The buzzing **Passeig d'es Born** runs along the eastern edge of the historic district and has been Palma's see-and-be-seen strolling promenade since the 15th century. Today, there are more horns screaming than preening, but it is still a vibrant place to be. **Can Solleric** (Pg. Born 27, free) is an 18th-century mansion that has been refitted as a public art space.

South of here is Palma's busy harbor, home to a few more worthy sights. **La Llotja** (Pl. Llotja, s/n, tel. 97/171-1705, 11 A.M.–2 P.M. and 5–9 P.M. Tues.–Sat., 11 A.M.–2 P.M. Sun., closed Mon., free) is one of the best examples of civil Gothic architecture in the world. Built in the 15th century as a trade exchange, it rose to become the most important maritime exchange in the medieval Mediterranean. Today, it houses a roving selection of art and cultural exhibits.

Es Baluard Museu d'Art Modern (Pl. Porta Santa Catalina 10, tel. 97/190-8200, www .esbaluard.org, 10 A.M.–11 P.M. Tues.–Sun. summer, 10 A.M.–8 P.M. Tues.–Sun. winter, closed Mon., €6) is Palma's very minimalist modern art museum. Creatively lodged in a stone bastion of the old city walls, the museum has a surprisingly small collection of work considering the price. The highlight is the room dedicated to Joan Miró. However, if you are really a fan of his work, head to the **Fundació Pilar i Joan Miró** in nearby Cala Major (see *Bay of Palma*).

Just across the river from the museum is **Santa Catalina,** a working-class barrio that has recently undergone a bohemian makeover. Located just west of the historic center around the Plaça Porta de Santa Catalina, this area teems with hip boutiques, Italian coffee shops, sushi bars, and even American-style diners. It is the perfect place to let an afternoon of shopping segue into an evening of wine and tapas.

On the western edge of the harbor rises the pink-tinged turrets of the **Castell de Bellver** (C/ Camilo José Cela, tel. 97/173-0657, 8 A.M.– 7 P.M. Mon.–Sat., 10 A.M.–5 P.M. Sun. winter, 8 A.M.–8:30 P.M. Mon.–Sat., 10 A.M.–7 P.M. Sun. summer, €2). Built in the 14th century for King Jaume II, the remarkably well-preserved fortress is notable for its circular inner construction. Surrounded by three imposing towers and a deep moat, it is easily one of the most evocative Gothic castles in Europe. It is a haul from the center. Your best bet is a cab or local bus 6 from Plaça de la Reina to Plaça Gomila, which still leaves you with an uphill jaunt of nearly a kilometer.

Nightlife

With hundreds of bars and discos and a very well-deserved reputation as a party town, Palma has a thumping nightlife. It reaches its peak from mid-June to September, but you can find a party pretty much any time of year. Of course, the resorts stretching out from Palma around the bay have their own wild scenes from English pubs to glitzy clubs, but if you want something with a little more Palma personality, stick to the city. Bars teem in the streets all around Passeig d'es Born and its Southern extension Avinguda d'Antoni Maura. Check out Carrer Apuntadores in particular. The area around La Llotja is also sizzling, as is the harbor front along Avinguda Gabriel Roca as far west as the Castell de Bellver.

Abaco (C/ Sant Joan 1, tel. 97/171-4939, 9 P.M.–2 A.M. daily) is must-see. Somewhere between kitsch and baroque, this genteel bar located in an old manor house features fruit cascading down stairwells, mammoth flower arrangements, birds in gilded cages, cande-labras, and Renaissance statues, all set to a classical music soundtrack. The courtyard is equally lush with the added bonus of a tinkling fountain. All this atmosphere does not come cheap—drinks run around €14 and up, but a fresh-squeezed juice with a swirl of Cuban rum was never sipped in a lovelier surrounds. **Royal Golden Door** (C/ Apuntadores 5, tel. 97/172-0817) offers chic cocktails in a sexy candle-lit, red-velvet setting. Next door, **Barcelona Jazz Club** (C/ Apuntadores 3, Sun.–Mon.) is cozy and tight the way a good jazz joint should be. It stays packed with local 30-somethings. **Café Lisboa** (C/ Sant Magí 33, tel. 97/145-3859, 10 P.M.–4 A.M. daily) is a popular live music venue with an ongoing mix of jazz, bossa nova, Latin, and local bands every night.

For late-night, high-energy carousing, head to the harbor. **Pacha Mallorca** (Av. Gabriel Roca 42, www.pachamallorca.com, 10 P.M.–6 A.M. daily) is a crowd-pleaser with a rambling club that includes a massive dance room, the ever-important VIP zone, and a stylish terrace overlooking the luxe yachts moored in the harbor below. Music is infectious house and very loud. There is a different party every night. During the week, the parties last to about 3 A.M.; on the weekend until 6 A.M. Check the website for the current offerings. The cover starts around €15. **Tito's** (Pl. Gomila 3, tel. 97/173-0017) is a legend on the clubbing scene in Mallorca. Since 1937, it has rocked the likes of Ray Charles and Marlene Dietrich; it will surely do the same for you. Situated some 46 meters (150 feet) above street level, it is reached via a swish glass elevator on Avinguda Gabriel Roca. Up top, thousands of international partiers, including a large gay and lesbian crowd, shake it until dawn to a mix of Euro-techno, bass-heavy house, and Spanish pop. **Black Cat** (Av. Joan Miró 75, 11 P.M.– 5 A.M. Thurs.–Sun.) is Palma's most famous gay and lesbian club, with a nightly drag show and lots of very poppy music and pretty boys and girls to keep the crowd happy all night.

Festivals and Events

The last two weeks of January bring the **Revetlla de Santa Sebastía,** Palma's most jubilant festival. The calendar is jammed with events large and small—including free concerts, street parties, fireworks demonstrations, and a spectacular bonfire display called **La Nit dels Foguerons** held on the January 19. With the summering hordes gone and the weather a bit chilly, this raucous party is a delightfully local affair.

In February, Palma celebrates **Carnaval** with a colorful and boisterous parade along the Platja de Palma. Unlike the decadence of Ibiza, this carnival still has a very strong family atmosphere with lots of activities for kids.

In June, as part of the **Corpus Cristi,** many of Palma's citizens open up their lovely courtyard patios to host free music concerts. Musical styles range from opera to flamenco to jazz, but the highlight is listening from within these normally private, privileged patios with the stars overhead and the rustle of plants brushing against the privileged visitors.

Accommodations

When looking for lodging in Palma, keep in mind that mid-June–September is peak time—prices rise and rooms go fast. Book ahead! **Under €50,** you can't go wrong with **Hostal Apuntadores** (C/ Apuntadores 8, tel. 97/171-3491, www.palma-hostales.com). Located on one of the liveliest streets in town, this no-fuss, no-frills *hostal* offers bright, clean rooms at rock-bottom prices. If you are willing to share a bath, the price for a double is €45. A private bath puts you up to €60. A bed in their five-bed dorm is just €20 per night. The staff is particularly helpful and friendly and there is a ground floor café that serves as a meeting point for guests from around the world. The best part is the rooftop terrace, which offers some of the best views of the cathedral in town. Sister hotel **Terramar** (Pl. Mediterraneo 8, tel. 97/173-9931, www.palma-hostales.com), just steps off the harbor, is owned by the same family and offers similar accommodations and prices. The lovely terrace (and many of the rooms) boasts excellent views over the harbor and Castell de Bellver. In addition to doubles (€52, €40 with shared bath), there are dorms (€20), and rooms with fully equipped kitchens (€60). **Hostal Ritzi** (C/ Apuntadores 6, tel. 97/171-4610, www.hostal ritzi.com, €45) is a classic Palma *hostal*. Located in a lovely old building in the heart of old Mallorca, the Ritzi offers personable charm, lots of rustic antiques, and a very friendly staff. Rooms, however, are a bit sparse—but at these prices, you really can't complain.

In the **€50-100** range, **Hotel Born** (C/ Sant Jaume 3, tel. 97/171-2942, www.hotel born.com, €75) is your best bet. This is an unassuming two-star hotel set in five-star surroundings—a 15th-century mansion with a gorgeous 18th-century courtyard. There are several over-the-top details, such as the dramatic red and yellow chandeliered dining room. Some rooms share baths—check before you book. **Hostal Brondo** (C/ Ca'n Brondo 1, tel. 97/171-9043, www.hostalbrondo.net, €60) is located in a building that dates back to the Roman Empire. Suitably atmospheric, the hotel features updated, modern rooms and a very attentive staff.

The sky is the limit in the **over €100** category. At the lower end, try the **Hotel Saratoga** (Pg. Mallorca 6, tel. 97/172-7240, www.hotel saratoga.es, €140), an old Palma favorite in a big, brash building near the harbor. Rooms have been recently updated and are a pleasing blend of classic and contemporary. Wi-Fi has been installed, which makes a perfect compliment to the lovely rooftop café and swimming pool. **Hotel Convent de la Missió** (C/ Missió 7, tel. 97/122-7347, www.conventdelamissio.com, €240) has the sort of sparseness you'd expect of a former convent, but that is where the similarities end. Minimal, stylish, and very lush, this boutique hotel is owned by a very creative, very attentive pair of architects who have seen to every detail from the luxury linens to the well-stocked wine cellar to the modern art gallery. The in-house restaurant **Refectori** (€50) is making culinary waves for its adventurous, international cuisine. **Hotel Dalt Murada** (C/ Almudaina 6, tel. 97/142-5300, www.daltmurada.com, €140) has an austere medieval look with heavy wood antiques, soaring ceilings, oil paintings of long-dead counts, and tapestries. It is one of the few of the mansion hotels that has really managed to retain an old-world feel. Breakfast is served in the flower-festooned inner courtyard.

Food

Palma's historic town is teeming with tapas bars. Generally, from May to April, they are open daily from 11 A.M. until midnight. Off-season, hours are drastically reduced, with many places closing between 4 and 8 P.M. One of the best is **La Bóveda** (Pg. Sagrera 3, daily), which manages to be both classy and boisterous. The walls are stacked high with wine bottles, the bar is tiled, and the local crowd that pours in tends to be ravenous. Tapas are exquisite renditions of Spanish favorites. Its sister property, **La Taberna Bóveda** (C/ Botería 3, tel. 97/171-4863, closed Sun., €22), has more of a sit-down feel but is astonishingly more popular. Get there before 9 P.M. if you want a seat and a chance to try their delicious *revuelto* (scrambled eggs with shrimp) or *bacalao al pil-pil* (Basque-style cod). **La Taberna del Caracol** (C/ Sant Alonso 2, tel. 97/171-4908, closed Sun.) is hidden deep in the historic quarter behind a postcard-perfect red and gold sign. The narrow arched bar is crammed with old wine barrels and rustic wooden tables and chairs. The simple things are best here—*pimientos al Padrón* (fried tiny green peppers), a plate of *jamón Jabugo* (exquisite cured ham), and the bar's namesake dish: *caracoles* (snails sautéed in olive oil and garlic).

Considering Palma's cosmopolitan flair, it is not surprising that fusion and international cuisine are both readily available and extremely good. **Baisakhi** (Pg. Marítim 8, tel. 97/173-6806, closed Mon. P.M., €20) offers excellent Indian food in a very romantic dining room across from the busy port. The floors are strewn with rose petals, the bathroom is hung with *Kamasutra* prints, candles flicker on the tables. The kitchen offers set menus that change daily and include classic Indian curries, rice dishes, and tandooris. There is a vegetarian option. **La Bodeguilla** (C/ Sant Jaume 3, tel. 97/171-8274, 1–11:30 P.M. Mon.–Sat.,

closed Sun., €35) is a sexy little dining room of red velvet seats, dark wooden floors, and walls of wine bottles. The chef finds inspiration in the varied cuisines of Spain to which he adds his own bold touches. There is also a selection of very stylish tapas for €15 per person. The wine list features over 200 wines on any given day and the staff is very well versed in Spanish wine.

For classic Mallorcan cuisine, head to **⬛ Cellar Sa Premsa** (Pl. Obispo Berenqer de Palon 8, tel. 97/172-3529, closed Sun., €25). Just north of the historic district, this boisterous dining hall is jammed with heaving wooden tables, old wine vats, and loads of laughing locals and delighted tourists. It is one of those places that is just fun. It helps that the hearty Mallorcan food is also tasty and, considering island prices, quite affordable. For equally hearty island fare in a more low-key setting, try **Ca'n Carlos** (C/ Aigua 5, tel. 97/171-3869, closed Sun. €30). The deceptively simple menu is surprisingly long on substance and the chef's daily special is guaranteed to please. **Caballito de Mar** (Pg. Sagrera 5, tel. 97/172-1074, closed Mon., €35) is one of Palma's favorite seafood restaurants. Casual yet chic, this bustling dining rooms serves up savory dishes like *caldereta de bogavante* (lobster stew) and *dorada a la sal* (sea bream cooked in a salt crust). Seats on the lively terrace are highly sought after—arrive early or make reservations.

Information

The **regional tourist office** (Pl. Reina 2, tel. 97/171-2216, 9 A.M.–8 P.M. daily, closed Sun.) is just off Passeig d'es Born and has all the information you could want on Mallorca and the other islands. The main **municipal tourist office** (Pg. Born 27, tel. 90/210-2365) is located in the Can Solleric. **Ajuntament de Palma** (tel.97/172-0720) offers walking tours of Palma that take in everything from the port to the convents (€10).

On the Internet, you are spoiled for choice. The official regional site www.illesbalears.es is chock-full of tourist information, as is the municipal site, www.palmademallorca.es, and the regional government site, www.infomallorca .net. Privately run sites include www.mallorca online.com and www.mallorcaweb.com.

Getting There

The easiest and best access to Mallorca is by air into Palma de Mallorca's **Aeroport Son Sant Joan** (97/178-9099, www.aena.es). Flights from mainland Spain can run as low as €30 with companies including **Iberia** (www.iberia. es), **Spanair** (www.spanair.es), and **Air Europa** (www.aireuropa.com). A dozen other airlines provide flights to Northern Europe, but there are no direct flights to the United States or Canada—you have to transfer in mainland Spain. The airport is 11 kilometers (seven miles) east of the city. Get into the center via public bus 1, which leaves every 15 minutes and costs less than €2 (have change on hand). A taxi will run under €20.

Mallorca is also served by three ferry companies: **Trasmediterranea** (tel. 90/245-4645, www.trasmediterranea.es), **Balearia** (tel. 90/216-0180, www.balearia.net), and **Iscomar** (tel. 90/211-9128, www.iscomar.com). Tickets cost €60 and up (one-way), depending on the time you travel, number of passengers, and various other factors. You can also try Palma's ferry terminal, located about three kilometers (just under two miles) from the center of Palma. Catch local bus 1 (€2) or take a taxi for about €10.

Getting Around

The city of Palma is compact enough to maneuver by foot, but for some of the beaches and sights, you might want to take the local buses, most of which stop in Plaça Espanya and Plaça de la Reina. Your hotel or the tourist office can help you find the right bus or you can visit the website www.emtplaca.es.

To get around the island, you have the option of car, bus, or limited train. Renting a car is hands down the best option for seeing the island. There are dozens of companies based in Palma, many at the airport. Despite this surplus, cars can be hard to come by June–September. You should always book ahead with

the company directly or with a broker such as www.holidayautos.com.

An efficient and inexpensive bus system links Palma to all the main towns, yet it can be mindboggling as there are dozens of companies with their own policies and hours. However, they all operate from the **main bus station** (Parc de Ses Estacions, C/ Eusebi Estada, s/n, tel. 97/117-7777), which is located just behind Plaça Espanya. It has an excellent information booth with all the details on the buses and their routes. You can also consult their website, http://tib.caib.es. Because the island is so small, no single bus trip will cost more than €8.

Mallorca has a small rail system that is based out of Palma. One track travels over the mountains north to Sóller (www.trendesoller.com), while the other goes inland to the towns of Inca and Sa Pobla. The train stations are located next to each other behind Plaça Espanya, alongside the bus station.

BAY OF PALMA

Though the city holds pride of place on the bay (Badia de Palma), the beaches arching out on either side of the city are package-holiday heaven (or hell, depending on your tastes). If you book a Palma trip through an agent you'll probably end up somewhere on this 30-kilometer (19-mile) stretch of glistening sand backed with high-rises. There are no less than a dozen resorts jammed all along the bay and it is pretty hard to tell where one starts and another ends. Going east and north towards Palma, the most interesting and notorious are: Magaluf, Palma Nova, Illetes, and Cala Major. East and south of Palma are C'an Pastilla and S'Arenal. A very good online analysis of these resorts can be found at the British website www.majorca-mallorca.co.uk.

Magaluf

The infamous Magaluf is the favored spot of young Brits looking for a cheap package vacation of sun, sand, and sex—fueled by lots of booze. Its naturally lovely beach is rimmed by an unsightly glut of holiday hotels, neon signs, and way too much cement. In the late

© ZIVILE VITEIKAITE

an elaborate sand castle on the Bay of Palma

1990s, the local government tried to curb the uglier aspects of this type of tourism by bulldozing several of the cheaper, more decrepit hotels in the area. It has done little to stem the tide and this retains a Brits-gone-wild feel, complete with English pubs and fish-and-chips shops. If any of this sounds even remotely appealing, an Internet search will reveal lots of package tours—don't try to go on your own as most hotels are booked outright by agencies.

Palmanova

Palmanova (also spelled Palma Nova) is similar in size and scope to Magaluf, but the crowds tend to be a bit older and just a tad more subdued. With its wide shallow bay rimmed by fine sandy beaches, it is easy to see why this became one of Mallorca's first resort developments. The beach here is a little quieter than Magaluf, mainly due to the fact that there are fewer hotels. Of course that is a relative assessment—the coast here teems with bulky, brash properties, though there are two delightful seaside boardwalks—Palmanova and Es Carregador—which boast tree-shaded areas and wonderful views. Again, most are booked solely to package tour agencies.

Illetes

Just about 10 kilometers (six miles) from Palma, Illetes (also spelled Illetas) is more upscale than Magaluf and Palma Nova. It comprises a string of upscale hotels, exclusive restaurants, and fine boutiques tucked between a steeply rising cliff covered in foliage and a golden ribbon of beach. Just off the coast lie three little isles that give the resort its name. The hotels and resorts are also considerably pricier, which helps ensure that the guests are well heeled, professional, and more likely to bring their families along. In the past they included figures like Rita Hayworth, Errol Flynn, and the King of Saudi Arabia. To the south of the resort is **Cala Comtesa,** a gorgeous stretch of coast punctuated by coves. It borders a military zone, which has kept the development here refreshingly minimal.

Cala Major

Practically a suburb of sprawling Palma, Cala Major is a must-see thanks to the spectacular **Fundació Pilar i Joan Miró** (C/ Joan de Saridakis 29, tel. 97/170-1420, http://miro .palmademallorca.es, 10 A.M.–7 P.M. Tues.– Sat. summer, 10 A.M.–6 P.M. Tues.–Sat. winter, 10 A.M.–3 P.M. Sun. year-round, closed Mon., €5), a gift to the people of Palma by the renowned artist Joan Miró and his wife Pilar. Miró had four workshops on these grounds and lived in Cala Major until his death in 1983. The complex contains his workshops, looking as if the great artist might have just stepped out for a breath of fresh air, and a modern gallery that shows a rotating selection of Miró's work. The gift shop is especially charming with a wide option of stylish, unique souvenirs. From Palma, catch public bus 3 or 6. It is about three kilometers (less than two miles) from the center, so a taxi is another inexpensive option.

Outside of the museum, Cala Major is a bustling resort with loads of hotels, restaurants, bars, shops, and people. Its beach is long, lovely, and, thanks to its proximity to the capital, bustling. Though there is still a resort vibe, the big resort players left a long time ago. However, the biggest player of them all, King Juan Carlos, still keeps a palace here, the Palacio de Marivent.

C'an Pastilla

One of the first mega-resorts on the bay, C'an Pastilla is big, bold, and bland. Hotel after heaving hotel blend into a hypnotic blur of cement, glass, and neon. It is the resort of choice for German couples and families as well as a smattering of Brits. Again, the hotels here are almost exclusively rented to agencies. At the resort's eastern edge, the best beach in the bay unfolds. **Platja de Palma** is four kilometers (2.5 miles) of ultra-fine sand backed by a lively promenade full of cafés and bars. During peak season, it gets a bit tough to find space to roll out your towel, but when you do, you'll be rewarded with some of the best people-watching in the islands (Ibiza excepted).

S'Arenal

The Platja de Palma ends at the S'Arenal resort; it is pretty similar to C'an Pastilla, but a whole lot younger. Call it the German version of Magaluf—though thankfully a bit more restrained. It is also the gateway to nearby **Aquacity** (Ctra. Palma-S'Arenal, km. 15, tel. 97/144-0000, 10 A.M.–6 P.M. daily, €20), a family-friendly water park jammed with super slides, wading pools, and children's water activities.

Information

Palma's tourist offices and websites offer lots of information and maps for the entire bay region. Also, www.majorca-mallorca.co.uk has detailed information on each of the resorts. For booking hotels, try www.playadepalma .net. Run by the local hotel association, it is full of resorts—big, bigger, and biggest.

Getting There and Around

By bus, any of the main resorts on the bay are easily accessed from Palma (and vice versa). From the Plaça Espanya bus terminal, public bus 15 travels east to C'an Pastilla and S'Arenal. There is also a pokey little tram connecting these two resorts. Public bus 20 leaves Plaça Espanya heading west to Palma Nova, while 3 and 6 go to Cala Major. There is also a "Playa-Sol" (beach-sun) bus run by **Transabús** (tel. 97/117-7777) that runs a route all along the coast. It is based at Plaça Espanya.

There is a speedy *autopista* encircling the bay. On the western side it is called PM-1, around Palma it is PM-20, and on the east it is PM-19.

◖ WESTERN MALLORCA

The western portion of Mallorca is notable for the **Serra de Tramuntana,** a rugged rise of mountains that follows the coast of the island from d'Andratx in the south to Pollença in the north. Billed by the local government as La Otra Mallorca (the other Mallorca), this coast is a land of jagged cliffs tumbling down to tiny, nearly inaccessible coves. It is the kind of natural beauty that will silence even the most jaded of nature lovers. Green brush, black rock, turquoise sea, and baby-blue sky paint the landscape as far as you can see. While you can bus or train into some of these villages for day trips from Palma, if you really want to get off the beaten path and see a Mallorca lightly tread by tourist's boots, rent a car and drive. Another possibility is to base yourself in either of the lovely villages of Deià or Sóller. Finally, if you are a biker, and fairly fit, you can bike the region.

Valldemossa

A lovely mountain town, Valldemossa offers shady streets lined with earth-colored stone houses boasting brightly painted doors, surprisingly lush gardens, and a glorious Gothic monastery. The **Reial Cartuja** (Pl. Cartuja, s/n, tel. 97/161-2106, 9:30 A.M.–1 P.M. and 3–6:30 P.M. Mon.–Sat. summer, 9:30 A.M.– 1 P.M. and 3–5:30 P.M. Mon.–Sat. winter, closed Sun., €8) was built in the early 14th century as a palace-away-from-palace for King Sancho. In 1399, it was donated to the Carthusian monks. In the early 19th century, the monks were expelled and the monastery became a lodging house. The most famous residents were composer Frédéric Chopin and his lover, the French writer George Sand (the prolific female writer who used a male pseudonym). Sand immortalized their three months in Valldemossa in the 1855 book *Winter in Mallorca,* which portrays the village and Mallorca as anything but charming.

Highlights of the monastery include a church with colorful frescoes painted by a brother-in-law of Goya, cloisters that house an intriguing pharmacy dating from 1723, the apartment where Chopin and Sand stayed (featuring Chopin's original piano, laboriously imported from France), and the original palace rooms of King Sancho.

Eight kilometers (five miles) down a heart-clutching, winding mountain road, the **Port of Valldemossa** offers a sheltered bay and some truly beautiful scenery. It also offers the excellent **Restaurant Es Port** (tel. 97/161-6194, €20), famed for its seafood and paellas. There

is little in the way of accommodations and what is here is very expensive, but also very memorable. **Hotel Valldemossa** (Ctra. Vieja de Valldemossa, s/n, tel. 97/161-2626, www .valldemossahotelrural.com, €250) is set in a centuries-old stone mansion and boasts stunning views over the sea and the mountains. Rooms are sumptuous retreats decorated in white linens, stylish furnishings, and rich tapestries. There is an acclaimed in-house restaurant and a luxurious spa.

Deià

A combination of extraordinary beauty and soul-soothing tranquility has made Deià a long-time favorite of artists and poets. Tucked on a cleft of hill above the sea and about midway between Sóller and Valdemossa, this cozy village of stone houses and achingly lovely views is most famously the home of writer and poet Robert Graves (1895–1985). Graves' children still live in Deià (son Tómas is author of award-winnng *Bread and Oil,* a celebration of Mallorcan cooking). The town is a jumble of cobblestone streets curling up to an old stone church. Tucked all around are pricey art galleries–cum–souvenir shops, laid-back bars, and expensive restaurants. Below town the **Cala de Deià** offers a lovely beach lining a cliff-backed cove. The sand is pretty stony, but the water is very clear and calm. The steep trail down takes about 30 minutes. Driving is an option, but in peak season, the ride could take even longer.

Avoid some of the day-tripping crowds by spending the night. The most atmospheric lodging in town is **La Residencia** (Son Canals, s/n, tel. 97/163-9011, www.hotel laresidencia.com, €500) run by the posh Orient Express group. Built within a 16th-century mansion, the hotel boasts an impressive art collection and has a lively art gallery. It hosts shows every few months that draw art collectors from throughout Spain and beyond. Every luxury you can imagine is provided. For mortal budgets, **Hostal Miramar** (C/ C'an Oliver, s/n, tel. 97/163-9084, www.pensionmiramar .com, €80) is situated in a romantic stone cottage tucked into a stand of trees on the edge of town. Rooms are monastic but comfortable. Those that share a bath cost €60. Dine at either of the hotel's restaurants or any of the charming spots in town. For excellent seafood, try **Sa Dorada** (C/ Arxiduc Lluís Salvador 24, tel. 97/163-9509, 1:30–3:30 P.M. and 6–11:30 P.M. daily, €20).

Sóller

Sóller is a tiny little delight of a town nestled in the upper hills of Tramuntana. There really isn't much to it besides a cluster of old cobbled lanes, some atmospheric stone buildings, the quaint **Plaça Constitució,** and the ramshackle Gothic church of **Sant Bartomeu.** But it has a laid-back attitude that is immensely enjoyable. Part of this pleasure comes in arriving. Sóller is reached via a rickety old train originally built in 1911 to transport fruit to Palma. It lumbers through some of the loveliest landscapes in the Baleares. Learn more about the train, including schedules, at www.trendesoller.com.

© LENA SANTILLANA

The charming village of Sóller is typical of western Mallorca.

The only drawback to the town are the crowds that descend upon Sóller in throbbing hordes during the summer season. One way to get around them is to stay the night at **Hotel El Guía** (C/ Castanyer 3, tel. 97/163-0227, www.sollernet.com, €80). This long-time favorite is a classic Mallorcan house set around a lovely courtyard. Rooms are simple but comfortable, and many have spectacular views on the other side of the lacy white curtains. If you can't spend the night, at least try to eat at El Guía's restaurant. The dinning room is beyond charming with tiled walls, beamed ceilings, and a ceramic fireplace and the food is island hearty and refreshingly affordable at around €20 per person. If you prefer boutique B&B luxury, head into the hills above Sóller and **(Ca's Xorc** (Crta. Deià, tel. 97/163-8280, www.casxorc.com, €190). This mountain retreat features stone floors, canopied beds, luxe linens, dramatic details like a medusa chandeliers, great views all around, a picturesque pool and garden, and a restaurant that drew the acclaim of no less than *Food & Wine* magazine for its excellent Mallorcan fare and extensive wine list.

Port de Sóller

From Sóller, you can catch a shivering tram down the steep slope of the mountains to the cozy little harbor town of Port de Sóller. A resort built on top of a fishing village, the port is one of the most picturesque spots on the northwestern coast, surrounded by rocky cliffs and hugging a shimmering blue expanse of the Mediterranean. Mountain bikers and hikers will enjoy the panoramic path leading up to the **Cap Gros far** (lighthouse), while those in pursuit of sedentary pleasures will savor the port's two sandy beaches and promenade dotted with excellent restaurants.

Stay the night at **Hotel Es Port** (C/ Antoni Montis, s/n, tel. 97/163-1650, €90), a rambling 17th-century fortified manor with antique-filled rooms (request to stay in the old house), lush gardens, elegant terraces, a spa, and a massive pool. The restaurant is a treat, located in an old mill and oozing rustic time-gone-by charm.

Lluc

Tucked into a remote valley some 35 kilometers (22 miles) northeast of Sóller, the dusty village of Lluc is famed for its monastery. The austere **Monestir de Lluc** (tel. 97/187-1525, www.lluc.net, 10 A.M.–1:15 P.M. and 2:30–5:15 daily, €2.50) was built in the 18th century, though there has been a shrine on this site at least since the 7th century, when a local shepherd is said to have seen an image of the Virgin Mary hovering in the sky above here. The massive building is Mallorca's most important religious shrine and thousands make a pilgrimage here yearly. At the center of the complex is a small chapel holding the much-venerated *La Moreneta* (little dark-skinned one), a 14th-century statue of the Virgin holding baby Jesus in her arms. During the daily 11 A.M. and 7 P.M. masses, a boys' choir performs a haunting melody of hymns.

Many who venture here do so to stay overnight in the monastery. The **Santuari de Lluc** (tel. 97/187-1525) rents out former monks' cells for €11–25 per person, depending on the number of people the room can accommodate. The complex features a bar and three restaurants, but by 11 P.M. you have to be back in your room and silence is requested—this is a monastery, after all.

Sports and Recreation

The Serra de Tramuntana offers nearly unlimited outdoor activities from hiking to biking, climbing to kayaking. A really good outfitter is **Tramuntana Pursuits** (tel. 97/140-4222, www.tramuntana-pursuits .com), run by Ruth and Peter Evans. She handles bookings and logistics, he oversees the adventures. Any tourist office in Palma can give you a list of bike rental agencies and the website www.illesbalears.es has downloadable maps and routes.

Information

In addition to the tourist offices in Palma, www .illesbalears.es and www.theothermallorca .com offer extensive information for planning a trip in the Serra de Tramuntana.

pleasure boats in Port de Sóller

Getting There and Around

If you are day-tripping from Palma, check with the bus station at Plaça Espanya for connections to these towns. You can also consult their website http://tib.caib.es. By car, you have many options depending on where you want to travel. The C-710 snakes the length of the coast from Andratx to Pollença, connecting most of these towns. You can also take the C-711 straight to Sóller or the PM-111 to Valdemossa. All three of these narrow roads wind through truly breath-catching scenery. Look for *miradores* (scenic viewpoints) along the way.

EASTERN MALLORCA

From the twin bays of Pollença and Alcúdia, Mallorca's coast loops back down towards Palma with some of the most spectacular beaches on the island. The bays themselves are slowly catching up with the resort-ism that has swept the coasts around Palma, and there is at least one mega-resort on the southeastern flank of the island (Cala Millor). Despite this, if you have

wheels, you can escape to some truly spectacular, refreshingly remote, beaches and coves—above all the magical Cap de Formentor and the windswept beach of Es Trenc.

❰ Cap de Formentor

At the northern tip of the island, a 21-kilometer (13-mile) peninsula of ashen-colored earth fingers its way into the sea. This peninsula of wild, mostly barren ridge ends at the Cap de Formentor, which offers some of the most spectacular scenery you'll see anywhere. Craggy, molten-looking rocks soar nearly 400 meters (1,300 feet) up from the sea, creating an almost lunar landscape that will take your breath away. There are several *miradores* (lookout points) and you should stop at them all. The peninsula also boasts one of the island's best beaches, the sugary fine arc of sand called **Platja de Formentor.** Backed by a canopy of shady green evergreens, the beach is also home to **Hotel Formentor** (tel. 97/189-9100, www .hotelformentor.net, €250). Built in 1930, it was Mallorca's first luxury hotel. It is still one of

The coast of Mallorca is a dramatic mesh of sea, sky, and land.

© ZIVILE VITEIKAITE

the island's finest, with a sweet air of elegance permeating everything from the formally appointed rooms to the gardened dining terrace.

If you are not driving, you can access the Cap de Formentor via boat from nearby Port Pollença's **Estació Marítima** (tel. 97/186-4014). During summer, there are hourly boats 10 A.M.–4 P.M.

Pollença

Just inland from the coast, the historic town of Pollença (Pollensa in Spanish) rests in the bumpy foothills of the very end of the Serra de Tramuntana mountains. A maze of dusky cobbled streets twist their way to the **Plaça Major,** which bristles with lively cafés under the austere facade of the **Nostra Senyora dels Àngels** church. Grab a seat at the buzzing **Café-Bar Juma** (Pl. Major 9) for excellent tapas. North of town are the 365 stone steps of **El Calvari,** which the faithful climb in order to pray at the tiny hilltop chapel that houses a Gothic wooden cross. The impressive steps are lined with equally impressive cypress trees, many centuries old. At the top, pilgrims are rewarded for their effort with spectacular views over the coast.

Pollença's harbor, **Port de Pollença,** is located a few kilometers downhill from the town. As in the rest of the island this pattern of separating the town from the port was a way of protecting the town from the pirate raids that were a common feature of medieval Mediterranean life. The low-key port sits on the sweeping horseshoe-shaped **Badia de Pollença,** which boasts shallow, calm, clear waters perfect for swimming. The beach arcing around the bay is long, wide, and very fine. Resorts and hotels have clustered here but so far the area is practically a ghost town compared to the Bay of Palma's resorts.

If you want to stay in this area, there are oodles of options, mainly in the mid-to-high price range. A good mid-ranged choice is **Hostal Bahía** (Pg. Voramar 31, tel. 97/186-6562, closed Nov.–Mar., €100), which offers 30 spic-and-span rooms in a simple little hotel located right on the picturesque prom-

enade overlooking the bay. Find more choices at www.enjoypollensa.com. Tuck into some exquisite seafood at the port's best restaurant, **Restaurant Stay** (Moll Nou, s/n, tel. 97/186-4013, noon–4 P.M. and 7:30–10:30 P.M. daily, €35), which offers sleek style with a very romantic location on the pier.

The bay of Pollença and the adjoining bay of Alcúdia are nestled next to each other and offer ample opportunities for biking, both on asphalt paths and off-road. Rent a bike and get trail maps at **María's Bicycles** (C/ Roger de Flor 12, tel. 97/186 4336).

Alcúdia

Encircled by an impressive set of (much-restored) Moorish walls, tiny Alcúdia is an enticing alternative from the sun and sand sameness of the coast. Enter through the **Plaça Carles V** and get lost. Once a thriving Moorish town, the town still has the feel of an Arabic medina with its narrow streets, many lined with romantically tattered 17th- and 18th-century mansions. Be sure and visit the **tourist office** (C/ Major 17, tel. 97/189-7100, www.alcudiamallorca.com) if you want to visit the nearby **Parc Natural de S'Albufera,** a lovely wetland preserve on the Bay of Alcúdia. The tourist office can provide you with hiking and biking routes for the park. Their website offers similar information.

Finally, make your way to the **Museu Monografic** (C/ Sant Jaume 2, €2), a small museum exhibiting a big past. Centuries before the Moors arrived, Alcúdia was Roman settlement called Pollentia. Here you can see everything from an actual gladiator's helmet to oil lamps. Your entrance fee allows you to access the nearby **Roman ruins,** which include the remains of houses and a well-preserved theater.

North of town, the **Port d'Alcúdia** sits on the massive blue arc of the **Badia de Alcúdia,** northern Mallorca's most built-up resort area. The beaches are fine, the water clear, but the glut of resorts is disconcerting. Unless you do a package tour, you'd be better off in the Port de Pollença.

(Artà

Inland and east of the Badia d'Alcúdia, the ancient town of Artà sits on top of a hill surrounded by the spectacular peaks of the Serra de Llevant mountains. Clustered beneath the 14th-century fortified church of **Santuari de Sant Salvador,** the town is a web of tattered old streets thick with slow-moving charm. Things pick up on Tuesdays when a very lively market rolls into town. Climb up to the church for an expansive view of the surrounding countryside.

Just under a kilometer south of town, **Ses Paisses** (tel. 97/183-5017, 10 A.M.–1 P.M. and 2:30–6:30 P.M. Mon.–Sat. summer, 9 A.M.–1 P.M. and 2–5 P.M. Mon.–Fri. winter, closed Sat. in winter and Sun. year-round, €2) is a Bronze Age settlement dating somewhere between 1000 and 800 B.C. Its prominent features are the **Talaiotic** (stone megaliths) that are unique to the islands of Mallorca and Menorca.

On the coast are the **Coves d'Artà** (10 A.M.–7 P.M. daily summer, 10 A.M.–5 P.M. daily winter, €8), a fascinating network of underground caverns bristling with massive, eerie stalactites and stalagmites that burrow back into the earth nearly 457 meters (1,500 feet). First mention of the caves comes from the Reconquista when Jaume I found 2,000 Moors hiding here with their cattle. Over the centuries, the caves have sheltered hermits, pirates, and smugglers. Rumor has it that Jules Verne was inspired to write *Journey to the End of the Earth* after visiting the caves.

There is little in the way of worthwhile accommodation in Artà. However, if you are looking for a romantic experience and money is no object, about halfway between Artà and Son Servera is the sensual retreat of **Finca Son Gener** (Son Gener, tel. 97/118-3591, hotel@songener.com, www.songener.com, €255). Delightfully refurbished by the same group behind the gorgeous Hotel Convent de la Missió in Palma, the Finca Son Gener offers romantic rustic lodging with sophisticated, sexy style. The white rooms are both minimal and lush while the details such as limestone floors, modern art, organic gardens, and a pampering spa are pure luxury.

Porto Cristo

Porto Cristo was one of the earlier spots to be built up on the eastern coast, but it was soon eclipsed by mega-resorts such as nearby **Cala Millor** (www.calamillor-mallorca.com). The result is a port town that is much more low-key than surrounding towns. The harbor still bustles with working fishing boats and the sheltered beach is fine for sunbathing. Swimming is poor due to its location between two rocky ridges, but you are within an easy drive to many finer beaches. During the day, Porto Cristo sees heavy tourist traffic all headed towards the **Coves del Drac** (tel. 97/182-0753, www.cuevasdrach.com, 10 A.M.–5 P.M. daily summer, 10:45 A.M.–4:30 P.M. daily winter, €10), located across the Es Rivet, about a 15-minute walk from town. Also known by the Spanish name Cuevas del Drach, the caves wind back into the earth for about 1.5 kilometers (almost a mile) and culminate in one of the largest subterranean lakes in the world—nearly 185 meters (600 feet) long and 30 meters (100 feet) deep. Don't go expecting to commune with the marvels of nature. The caves have been thoroughly kitted out with tourist-friendly gardened entrances, mood lighting to enhance the mammoth stalactites and stalagmites, and a quartet of classical musicians adrift upon the lake performing appropriate cave music on the hour. Kitschy, yes—but in a very enchanting way. The tour lasts an hour and on summer weekends, expect long lines to get in. A couple kilometers to the west is a third set of Mallorca's caves. **Coves d'es Hams** (tel. 97/182-0988, 10 A.M.–6 P.M. daily summer, 10:30 A.M.–5 P.M. daily winter, €10) are not as impressive as those of Drac and Artà, but they are still intriguing—and have the bonus of less visitors. The tour follows an underground river that winds past stalactites and stalagmites.

In Porto Cristo, if you not on a package tour, stay in the quaint **Hotel Felip** (C/ Bordils 61, tel. 97/182-0750, www.thbhotels.com, €110), located right on the town beach. Rooms are sedate but spacious and updated. The best have a balcony overlooking the harbor. The hotel has a lovely portside terrace restaurant and a nice pool **Flamingo** (C/ Bordils, s/n, tel 97/182-2259, €25) offers excellent seafood and paella at a lovely terrace overlooking the sea.

If you are not driving, **AUMASA** (tel.97/155-0730) runs buses from Palma to Porto Cristo. Check with the station in Palma at Plaça Espanya for details.

Cala Figuera

On the coast just a few kilometers east of the buzzing town of Santanyi, Cala Figuera is a cozy port surrounded by billowing trees and terra-cotta-roofed houses on the water's edge. There is no beach here to speak of, but there are fishing boats unloading their wares in the tiny port and wonderful restaurants all around serving up the catch. It also offers some of the most affordable housing on the island. There is also a little tourist train that travels to the nearby beaches.

Simple little **Hostal Oliver** (C/ Bernareggi 37, tel. 97/164-5127, €50) has a friendly staff and a decent restaurant. **C Casa María** (C/ Marina 26, tel. 97/164-5178, www.aparta mentoscasamaría.com, €50) offers homey yet stylish rooms with great terraces. The staff is very accommodating and will help arrange all sorts of activities in the area. The owners also run the quaint little **Restaurant L'Arcada** (C/ Virgen del Carmen 80, tel. 97/164-5032, €20), which specializes in Mediterranean fare including wonderful seafood. It is also open all day with café fare such as sandwiches, salads, and sweets.

Platja Es Trenc

On the southern coast of Mallorca, about 48 kilometers (30 miles) east of Palma, Es Trenc is Mallorca's best beach. About three kilometers (nearly two miles) of wide, ultra-fine sand arcs around a stretch of the Mediterranean that is achingly beautiful. The beach backs up on a fairly undeveloped stretch of coast—thanks to Mallorcan activists. Afraid of ruining this beach with resort sprawl, some pressured the government to limit construction here. Though the beach is well known, it is large enough, and just far enough off the resort track that it rarely feels crowded. Even in the peak times of July and August, Es Trenc still feels refreshingly remote. In fact it is so comfortable that nudism is both practiced and legal here. Many consider this the premier nude beach in Spain.

Stay near the beach at the **C Finca Ses Arenes** (Crta. Campos, Colonia de Sant Jordi, tel. 97/165-5400, www.sesarenes.com, €115), a rambling farmhouse set in a protected pine grove just a few kilometers from Es Trenc. The six double rooms are rustic-chic and feature private terraces with views over the pine forest and the sea. There are a couple of simple bar/restaurants on the beach, but your best bet is to head to the lively harbor in the nearby resort of **Colonia de Sant Jordi.**

Of course, having a car is the best way to get around here, but you can access the beach via the Palma-Colonia de Sant Jordi. You'll then have to hoof it or take a taxi the 1.5 kilometers (about a mile) north to the beach.

Information

In addition to the tourist offices in Palma, www.illesbalears.es and www.theothermallorca.com offer extensive information for planning a trip in the eastern portion of Mallorca.

Getting There and Around

If you are day-tripping from Palma, check with the bus station at Plaça Espanya for connections to any of these towns. Trains go from Palma to Sa Pobla, just a few kilometers from the Bay of Alcúdia. From there you can catch a local bus or a taxi. Consult the website http://tib.caib.es.

By car, you have many options depending on where you want to travel. From Palma, motorways lead to the main towns from which you can then travel in any direction. Going around the eastern coast from north to south, roads tend to duck and dip inland as the terrain dictates. Always map your route before departing, as the maps provided by rental companies are often flaky. Also, keep in mind that rental cars may book out in July and August, so always reserve in advance.

Ibiza

At just 570 square kilometers (220 square miles), the island of Ibiza (Eivissa) has managed to send shockwaves around the world emanating directly from its dance-clubbing heart. The most notorious super-clubs in the world are based here—Space, Pacha, Amnesia, Privilege—and the DJs who changed dance music got their start here. Each year between May and October, everyone who is anybody in the club scene—DJs, promoters, musicians, label owners, music-video producers, dancers, fashionistas, and thousands of club-loving people of all ages—descend upon Ibiza for summer after summer of loving the music. The Rolling Stones famously partied here in the 1970s, Bono is still a regular. Director Roman Polanski owns a villa, as do hardy partier Jade Jagger, Kate Moss, Monica Bellucci, Jean Paul Gaultier, and Sean "Diddy" Combs. Models, racecar drivers, hair dressers, beautiful gay boys, aging playboys (and girls), college kids toting daddy's credit card, party-loving Brits on package tours, and jaw-droppingly outrageous drag queens round out the annual crowd. They all have the same thing on their mind—music, dance, party, repeat.

In spite of this (or maybe to spite it), recent fashion for magazines and newspapers is to tout the "other side" of Ibiza beyond the turntable. Visit Spain's official websites and you'll rarely see a peep about Ibiza's club scene. However, the bass-thumping, head-banging, deliciously delirious reality is that Ibiza *is* the club capital of the world, and if you are even remotely interested in club culture and music, you must visit at least once in your life. If you aren't into the scene, it can be avoided. Go off-season when the luxuriant beauties of natural Ibiza—turquoise waters, sugary white beaches, dramatic wind-carved landscape, and soul-soothing sunsets—shimmer in silence. Yet, it is somehow more satisfying to do like the fine folks at

the medieval quarter of Ibiza City, Dalt Vila

© KELLY O'DONNELL

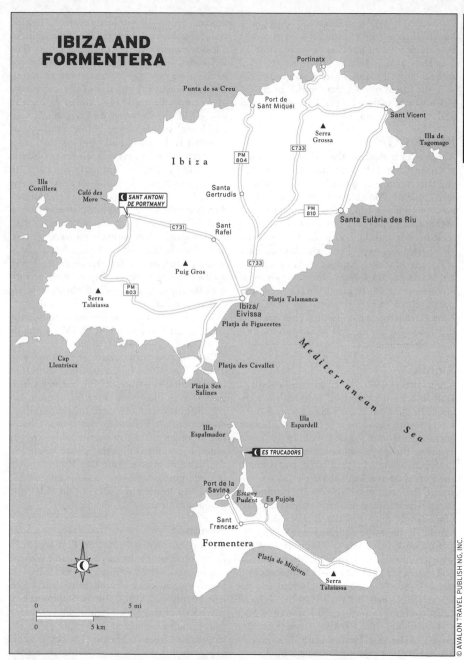

IBIZA AND FORMENTERA

Portinatx

Punta de sa Creu

Port de Sant Miquel

Sant Vicent

Serra Grossa

Illa de Tagomago

C733

PM 804

Illa Conillera

Caló des Moro

I b i z a

SANT ANTONI DE PORTMANY

Santa Gertrudis

PM 810

Santa Eulària des Riu

C731

Sant Rafel

C733

Puig Gros

PM 803

Serra Talaiassa

Platja Talamanca

Ibiza/ Eivissa

Platja de Figueretes

Cap Llentrisca

Platja des Cavallet

Platja Ses Salines

M e d i t e r r a n e a n   S e a

Illa Espardell

Illa Espalmador

ES TRUCADORS

Port de la Savina

Estany Pudent

Es Pujols

Sant Francesc

Formentera

Platja de Migjorn

Serra Talaiassa

0   5 mi

0   5 km

Café del Mar did decades ago and add a lovely backbeat to nature's beautiful ways. Lounge by a quiet cove all day (better yet, get lost on Formentera) then luxuriate in transcendental techno bliss all night. There is no need to divide the island into separate worlds of club v. nature—not when you can have your beach and dance on it, too.

IBIZA CITY

A haven for hedonism, Ibiza City is a thriving town with one of the most picturesque ports in the Baleares. Beneath the imposing medieval walls of **Dalt Vila** (High Town) and the harbor, two fonts of fun unfurl. To the west, **La Marina,** aka "the port," is a web of tiny streets seething with funky boutiques, trendy cafés, and bars, bars, bars. The main thoroughfare is Passeig Marítim. Nudged right up against La Marina is **Sa Penya,** another cluster of old streets that is home to Ibiza's prancing, preening, and very, very pretty gay scene. The **New Harbor** on the opposite side of the Port d'Eivissa is where some of Ibiza's most notorious clubs pulse and throb until dawn.

Sights

Completed in 1585, the 12-foot-thick walls of **Dalt Vila** rise 25 meters (82 feet) high and encircle the old town in a 2.5-kilometer (1.5-mile) loop boasting seven massive bastions. The best entrance is from Plaça de la Font in Sa Penya. Head up the mighty stone ramp, over a drawbridge spanning an ancient moat, and through the **Portal de ses Taules,** a triple gateway designed to withstand 16th-century cannon attacks. The entire structure is an amazing feat of medieval engineering that earned UNESCO World Heritage Site designation in 1999.

Just inside the gate is **Plaça de la Vila,** which is rimmed with stylish cafés, boutiques, and galleries. The **Museu d'Art Contemporani** (tel. 97/130-2723, 10 A.M.–1:30 P.M. and 5–8 P.M. Tues.–Fri., 10 A.M.–1:30 Sat., closed Mon. and Sun. summer; 10 A.M.–1 P.M. and 4–6 P.M. Tues.–Fri., 10 A.M.–1 P.M. Sat. winter, €3) is also here. Housed in an 18th-century arsenal, it offers an ever-changing exhibition of modern art, much of it by Ibiza artists. Behind the plaza, you can access the top of the walls for a lovely panoramic view of Ibiza's harbor. The well-worn cobbled streets leading up and out of the plaza give way to an atmospheric tangle of streets lined with still more cafés, more bars, and some very grand old houses. At the top of the hill, the **Catedral de Eivissa** (Pl. Catedral, s/n) stands on old holy ground—Carthaginians, Romans, and Moors all had their respective temples here. The current cathedral was built in Catalan Gothic style in the 14th century but got a baroque makeover in the 18th. Next door to the cathedral, the **Museu Arqueológic** (tel. 97/130-1231, 10 A.M.–2 P.M. and 5–7:30 P.M. Tues.–Sat., 10 A.M.–2 P.M. Sun., closed Mon. summer; 10 A.M.–1 P.M. and 4–6 P.M. Tues.–Sat., 10 A.M.–2 P.M. Sun. winter, €3) houses a fascinating collection of artifacts going back to the prehistory of Pitiuses (as the isles of Ibiza and Formentera are called together).

Below Dalt Vila, on the west side of the city, lie the **Puig des Molins** (Vía Romana 31, 10 A.M.–2 P.M. and 6–8 P.M. Tues.– Sat., 10 A.M.–2 P.M. Sun. summer; 9 A.M.–3 P.M. Tues.– Sat., 10 A.M.–2 P.M. Sun. winter), a Punic burial site from the 7th century B.C. It doesn't look like much from the outside, but this hilltop necropolis contains thousands of ancient burials. Follow the walkway to Chamber 3, which has 13 stone sarcophagi. Many remains excavated on this hill are housed in the adjacent **Museu Puig des Molins,** but it is undergoing long-term renovations and is scheduled to remain closed for an indefinite amount of time.

Beaches

Closest to town is **Platja de Figueretes,** a fairly urban beach with a pebble-sand mixture encircling a swatch of murky water. While it's fine for a quick day of sunbathing (and excellent people-watching), **Platja Talamanca** to the north of the New Harbor is much nicer. Make the half-hour walk there or catch the shuttle boat from La Marina. The best beaches are a few kilometers down the coast on the southern tip of the island. **Platja Ses Salines** and adjacent **Platja d'es Cavallet** each sport long arcs of glistening sand backed by scrub-covered hills. Es Cavallet is considered Ibiza's main nude beach and it is also the unofficial gay beach (cruising behind the dunes is very popular). The beaches are separated by a slip of land dotted with several lively *chiringuitos* (beachside bars) that are a natural extension of the nightclubs with DJs and thumping music. There are also a few restaurants and a small grocery. If you are not driving, take a cab for around €15 or catch local bus 11 from Ibiza City to Salines. From there you can easily walk to Es Cavallet.

Nightlife

Before embarking on Ibiza City's famous nightlife, get the facts at the excellent website, www.ibiza-spotlight.com. Click "clubbing" for all the basics. For gay nightlife, head to www.gayibiza.net.

In general, the night starts around sunset with tapas or dinner. Around 11 P.M., the smaller bars and terraces get going, particularly in La Marina or Sa Penya where most bars are open from around 9 P.M. until 4 A.M. Around 3 A.M., start heading to the clubs. There are two (Pacha and El Divino) in Ibiza City. The rest are spread between the capital and Sant Antoni to the west. A very convenient **Discobus** makes the route. Around 8 A.M., the after-hour parties kick off— the most infamous is at Space, some three kilometers (two miles) south of Ibiza City on the beach. Keep in mind that the clubbing season is summer. Many bars, clubs, restaurants, and even hotels shut down November–March. Nevertheless, if you plan ahead, you can have a good time off-season at cut-rate prices. Summer clubbing is expensive with top nightclubs charging up to €40 just to get in. Drinks can run €20. During your daytime wanderings, be on the lookout for discount coupons and flyers. Also, many smaller bars sell discounted entrance to the clubs. Do not buy such tickets from folks on the street, as you will get scammed.

In Ibiza City, start the night at **Bar Zuka**

(C/ Verge 75, daily Apr.–Oct.) which has a sophisticated charm with massive antique mirrors and a fireplace full of candles. Resident DJs keep the crowd happy with an eclectic low-key house vibe, but when you least expect it a big-name DJ slips behind the decks for a surprise spin. Always fun, always packed, Zuka is a must. **Base Bar** (C/ Garijo 15, daily May–Oct.) is a buzzing bar that attracts the kind of crowd that somehow manages to be infinitely cool without trying. Music is a mix of sexy Ibiza vibes that has spawned a few CDs. **Mao Rooms** (C/ Emili Pou 6, Thurs.–Sun. Nov.–April) is all flowing curtains, floor cushions, and stylish Buddha touches. The crowd is equally as laid-back and glamorous. **Bling Bling** (Pl. Drassaneta 13, daily Apr.–Oct.) is intimate and low-key with cushy black sofas where beautiful people relax to a soundtrack of funk and hip-hop.

Ibiza's gay nightlife is famous and during the summer Sa Penya is where it all gets started. Carrer de la Verge, which quite ironically translates as "street of the virgin," is ground zero for a nightly parade of drag queens, shirtless and chisel-chested boys, and sexy girls looking for fun—it is wild, crowded, and a whole lot of fun. On nearby Carrer d'Alfons XII, the parading continues. **Bar JJ** (C/ Verge 79, daily Apr.–Oct.) is a good place to start the night—and score passes for the late-night clubs. **Sunrise** (C/ Verge 44, daily Apr.–Oct.) is one of Ibiza's handful of lesbian bars, though the crowd is very mixed. The DJ/owner Monica runs a very friendly house that you'll want to return to a few times during your trip—it is that comfy. **Anfora** (C/ San Carlos 7, 11:30 P.M.–6 A.M. daily May–Oct.) is one of the few gay dance clubs in town. Tucked into Dalt Vila, the club looks unassuming from the outside, but inside it stretches off into a deep cavern that includes a massive dance floor, four bars, a Moroccan lounge, and a dark room where anything goes—and women are strictly forbidden from entering.

Ibiza City's New Harbor is home to the infamous **Pacha Ibiza** (Av. 8 d'Agost, s/n, www.pacha.com, daily Apr.–Oct., weekends Nov.–Mar.). Opened in 1973 on the grounds of a rambling old farmhouse, Pacha has gone on to spawn a nightclub empire with dozens of clubs around the world. Elegant and massive, this club houses a main dance floor as well as several smaller rooms focusing on anything from funk to experimental techno. The sprawling terrace is a delight, overlooking the harbor and the lit-up walls of Dalt Vila. Also in the New Harbor, **El Divino** (www.eldivino-ibiza.com, Apr.–Oct.) gives Pacha a run for its money with a glitzier space, better views, and a free shuttle boat from the Passeig Marítim. **Space** (Platja d'en Bossa, www.space-ibiza.es, June–Oct.) is another legendary Ibiza club that has led to the Space club brand all over the mainland. This rambling venue can hold 3,000 people in either its cavernous, laser-lit dance room or on its surprisingly elegant terrace. Space normally runs daytime parties that start around 8 A.M. and go until the late evening. They also host the infamous gay party **La Troya.** Keep in mind that parties such as La Troya can change venues suddenly. Always check current flyers for the latest. Most of the other big clubs are in Sant Antoni.

Shopping

Ibiza's shopping scene is a colorful clash of Rodeo Drive meets Moroccan medina meets SoHo funk. Streets are crammed with designer boutiques, high-end art galleries, imported furnishing stores, custom jewelry designers, nightclub gear, gourmet bakeries, sex shops, luxe pet-supply stores, flea markets, artists markets, and farmers markets. Those without storefront real estate set up stalls in alleys and plaza. Even more plop their wares of dubious origin on worn-edge blankets or makeshift cardboard tables. Wherever you go in Ibiza City there will be a dozen people looking to sell you something. It is a shopper's paradise—though it really does help if said shopper has deep pockets. In summer, most shops in town are open seven days a week and those in the old town and by the port stay open until 11 P.M.

Sa Penya is home to the unofficially nick-named **Mercat dels Hippies** along Carrer d'Enmig, a collection of some 80 stalls selling colorful everything from batik-print skirts to crocheted bikinis to oversized sunglasses. Also in Sa Penya, Carrer de la Verge is the street for gay clubbing clothes, fetish-wear shops, and piercing salons. Passeig Vara de Rey and around is home to very trendy, very expensive designer boutiques.

Accommodations

Lodging in Ibiza City tends to be mid- and high-range unless you are willing to share baths. In that category, try **Casa de Huéspedes** (Pg. Vara de Rey 7, tel. 97/130-1376, www.hibiza .com, €60), a friendly little place that puts the fun in funky with colorful rooms and a youthful vibe. Each room has its own wash-basin, while showers and toilets are down the tiled hall. **Hostal Bimbi** (C/ Ramón Muntaner 55, tel. 97/130-5396, http://hostalbimbi.com, closed winter, €45) is located a block from the Figueretes beach and features simple rooms, many with balconies offering a glimpse of the sea. A private bath raises the price to €65.

Mid-priced options include **Hostal Mar Blau** (Puig des Molins, s/n, tel. 97/130-1284, closed Winter, €85), which sits above the Ne-cropolis. Rooms are a bit ragged around the edges, but most offer lofty views over the sea. **La Marina** (C/ Barcelona 7, tel. 97/131-0172, www.hostal-lamarina.com, €85) offers bright and cheery rooms right on the port in the lively La Marina barrio. **Hotel Montesol** (Pg. Vara de Rey 2, tel. 97/131-0161, www.hotelmonte sol.com, €95) is a classic favorite. Rooms are a bit dowdy but the location is excellent and just downstairs is one of Ibiza's most classic meeting spots—the elegant Café Montesol.

Over €100, Ibiza City offers a world of lodging options from rustic-quaint to über-chic. **La Ventana** (C/ Sa Carrossa 13, tel. 97/139-0857, www.laventanaibiza.com, €175) is located in a romantically tattered mansion and features rooms with lovely touches such as can-opied beds, antique furnishings, and original art. The Moroccan-style rooftop terrace is a welcome retreat and the in-house restaurant is top-notch. For a splurge, upgrade to a room with a balcony overlooking the harbor. Open year-round, prices drop to €90 off-season. **Los Molinos** (C/ Ramón Muntaner 60, tel. 97/130-2250, www.thbhotels.com, €120), looming above Figueretes beach, offers resort-style lodging just minutes form the old town. Rooms are basic and modern, but the combination of location and price can't be beat. Splurge on a sea view for just €10 more. Open all year, prices drop to €70 in winter. **El Canónigo** (C/ Major 8, tel. 97/130-3884, www.elcanonigo.com, €180–420) is the most atmospheric hotel in town. Built into a 14th-century tower in the old city walls, high up near the cathedral, this charmer offers it all—great views, quiet luxury, and a very central location. Rooms are lushly decorated and the more expensive ones feature gorgeous balconies. Prices drop as low as €120 off-season.

Food

As with everything else in Ibiza City, eating has seasonal rhythms. From April to May, expect everything to be open daily from noon –4 P.M. and 8 P.M.–midnight. Tapas bars, cafés, and sandwich shops operate from 9 A.M.–11 P.M. or later. In winter, hours are reduced and many places close outright.

Cheap and easy eats abound in Ibiza City. **Pasajeros** (C/ Vicent Soler, s/n, closed winter, €15) is a grubby little diner with excellent inexpensive salads and sandwiches. **Eat Me** (C/ Enmig 22, tel. 61/682-7545, daily) offers upscale picnic food to go—from creative sandwiches to homemade chocolate cake. **El Pirata** (C/ Garijo 10, tel. 97/119-2630, €20) is a wildly popular bar/Italian bistro that serves thin-crust pizza and homemade pasta to a ready-for-action crowd. **Comidas Bar San Juan** (C/ Montgri 8, €20) is an old-time favorite that has stuck to its traditional roots for generations. Forget fusion, this is Spanish cooking good and simple and the locals love it. Get there early if you want a table and don't be surprised if the owners ask you to share your spare seats with a stranger.

Upscale dining is another Ibiza City pastime. **La Brasa** (C/ Pere Sala 3, tel. 97/130-1202, €30) has the most romantic terrace in town and a Mediterranean menu with exquisite grilled meats and fish. **El Portalón** (Plaça Desamparats 1, tel. 97/130-3901, €25) is famous for its seafood paella, which you can enjoy on the lovely terrace or in the classy red-walled dining room. **La Oliva** (C/ Sant Cruz, 2, tel. 91/730-5752, closed winter, €30) offers classic Mediterranean fare with French touches. Try their *hojaldre de queso de cabra* (goat cheese pastry). Their sidewalk terrace is a major people-watching perch.

Foodies should plot a course for **Cana Joana** (Crta. Eivissa-Sant Josep, km. 10, tel. 97/180-0158, closed Nov.–mid-Jan. and Mon. year-round, €50), which serves earthy French-Catalan food in a rustically refurbished old farmhouse about 13 kilometers (eight miles) west of Ibiza City. Run by well-known former journalist Joana Biarnes and her husband Michel, the restaurant has a cozy, welcoming atmosphere that is a perfect complement to the food. House specialties include potatoes with black truffles, cod with raisins, and rack of lamb.

Information

There are several **tourist offices** in Ibiza City including the port (C/ Antoni Riquer 2, tel. 97/130-1900), the new town (Pg. Vara de Rey, s/n, tel. 97/119-4393), and at the airport. They do not follow Ibiza's going-strong all day attitude. The hours are 10 A.M.–1 P.M. and 5–7:30 P.M. Monday–Friday, 10 A.M.–1 P.M. Saturday, and closed on Sunday. The city website is www.eivissa.org. Other websites include www.ibiza-spotlight.com for general holiday information, www.ibiza-voice.com for clubbing gossip and hype, www.digitalibiiza.com for more clubbing info, and www.ibz-style.com for lifestyle and gossip.

The number of English-language magazines published on the island is staggering. You can pick them up all over Ibiza City. Some are free, others cost, and almost all focus on style, celebrity, and Ibiza's over-the-top version of island glamour. Look for freebie *Amnesia* printed by the mega-club of the same name for general tourist info. The English-language paper *Ibiza Sun* is less useful for the tourist, but highly entertaining.

Getting There

Ibiza's **airport** (tel. 97/180-9000, www.aena .es) is about eight kilometers (five miles) south of Ibiza City and receives both domestic and international flights, though the latter are mainly from Northern Europe. If you are on the Spanish mainland, flying into Ibiza is often cheaper than taking a ferry. Check prices with **Iberia** (www.iberia.es), **Spanair** (www.spanair .es), and **Air Europa** (www.aireuropa.com) or visit any *agencia de viajes* (travel agent). An airport bus (€1) heads to Ibiza town on the hour. A taxi will run about €12.

By ferry, **Trasmediterranea** (tel. 90/245-4645, www.trasmediterranea.es), **Balearia** (tel. 90/216-0180, www.balearia.net), and **Iscomar** (tel. 90/211-9128, www.iscomar.com) offer passage from Barcelona, Valencia, and Mallorca. Tickets cost €60 and up (one-way), depending on your departure city, the time you travel, and the number of passengers in your group.

Getting Around

Ibiza has an inexpensive, efficient **bus system** (www.ibizabus.com) that runs year-round, connecting the major cities and beaches. The schedule is on the website and any tourist office can provide maps. During summer, the **Discobus** (tel. 97/119-2456, €2) travels between the main clubs in the towns of Ibiza, Sant Antoni, and Santa Eulària.

If you are just sunning and clubbing, you can get by easily without a car. If you want to get off the beaten path and explore some of Ibiza's wild inner landscape, remote northern beaches, or lesser-known villages, hire a car at the airport. In summer, always book ahead directly with your preferred company or with a broker such as www.holidayautos.com.

◖ SANT ANTONI DE PORTMANY

On the western coast of Ibiza, Sant Antoni de Portmany becomes European clubbing central every summer as thousands of party people from around the globe descend upon the resorts and mega-clubs that cluster around the sprawling beach of this once-sleepy port town. All the infamous Ibiza stories you have heard happened here. San An, as it's called, is a den of decadence fueled by beautiful beaches, bountiful booze, and booming beats—it is Spring Break a million times over. The crowds tend to be younger, rowdier, and less image-conscious than in Ibiza City. A huge portion of them are on package holidays from Britain— British tour operators offer an endless array of cut-rate, all-inclusive stays in the cement block hotels that clog San An's streets. They tend to congregate in the West End, an area known for massive discos, English pubs, fast-food restaurants, and lots of street brawling. Locals shrug and conclude that even soccer hooligans need a vacation.

Sights

Rather than any key sights, San An is made up of "party zones" that you should get to know in order to make wise party choices. The **Harbor** runs from the giant Egg sculpture at the end of Avinguda de Portmany. Along Passeig de Ses Fonts is a pleasant promenade lined with benches. Stretching north into the city behind the Club Nàutic is the notorious **West End.** It is centered mainly on Carrer Santa Agnés and is a warren of narrow streets that is a little slice of Britain (young, boozing, brawling Britain). Cheap eats and even cheaper drinks are the norm here. The dozens of discos offer uninspired, but very loud and infectious, Euro-pop, hip-hop, and dance music. Many do not charge a cover, insuring they stay packed with the budget crowd. Love it or hate it, you can't visit San An without talking a walk through this barrio of bars.

To the west, **Sunset Strip** is a stretch of rocky shoreline more or less centered between Carrer General Balanzat and Carrer Vara de Rey. It is exactly what the name promises—a place to watch the sunset, along with a few thousand like-minded people. This strip got its fame in the 1990s when world-famous club **Café del Mar** (see *Nightlife*) started holding chill-out music sessions at sunset. Then house DJ José Padilla turned his soundtracks into a few wildly popular CD compilations that helped bring lounge and chilled house music to the masses. See www.cafedelmarmusic.com for more. Today, the exclusive hipness of the original scene is dampened and Café del Mar has quite a few neighbors offering about the same experience. Nonetheless, Sunset Strip is still the place to be on summer evenings. The music is still good, the ambience still enticing, and the sunsets still gorgeous.

North of Sunset Strip, the **Caló des Moro** is a tidy little cove encircling a sandy beach lapped by a clear, shallow slick of clear Mediterranean Sea. It boasts a few trendy hotels and stylish bars and has become an upscale bohemian alternative to the crowded strip.

S'Arenal is San An's main beach. It stretches from the Egg south in a swooping arc around the Badia de Portmany (bay) to the **Punta del Molí,** a rocky outcrop of land topped by an ancient windmill. The beach is lined with a promenade featuring a few big bars, restaurants, and hotels.

Nightlife

The West End needs no guidance. Just follow your ears to the music you like best. All the clubs and bars listed here operate daily, unless otherwise noted. On the Sunset Strip, the famous **Café del Mar** (www.clubdelmarmusic .com, 5 P.M.–1 A.M. daily Apr.–Oct.) is really nothing more than a somewhat stylish café by the sea, but the CdelM legend draws legions from around the world—Ibiza's very own chill-out mecca. The in-house shop stocks all the CdelM compilations as well as groovy T-shirts and accessories. **Mambo Café** (www.cafe mamboibiza.com, 11 A.M.–4 A.M. May–Oct.) is where pre-clubbers go for their own sunset fix with world-famous DJs popping in for a quick spin before heading off to the big clubs. Open all day, it offers food from breakfast to sandwiches to dinner (€25).

In the Caló des Moro, always expect the hippest and hottest trends. If something new is going to happen in San An, it will happen here. **Sunsea Bar** (10 A.M.–2 A.M. Apr.–Oct.) is located on the grounds of a lovely modernist apartment building. Guests enjoy pools, posh patio furnishings, light eats, good beats, and lots of very pretty people-watching. **Coastline** (10 A.M.–2 A.M. Apr.–Oct.), next door, is almost exactly the same but music and crowds tend to be more upbeat. Both bars host pre-parties for big nights out at the mega-clubs. **Kanya** (10 A.M.– 4 A.M. Apr.–Oct.) is more of the same, but the crowd is younger, wilder, and on the prowl.

On the S'Arenal strip, the place to be is **Bar M** (10 A.M.–3 A.M. Apr.–Oct.). Simmering with style, this bar is a pre-club requisite with hot DJs and an even hotter crowd—including not a few famous faces. There are regular concerts and a riotous "Rockaoke" night where you can sing your favorite tune to a live band. The upper deck is great for sunning and there is a sweet little menu as well.

Ibiza's infamous big clubs are located in San An. DJs are world-famous, cover charges exorbitant, dancing furious, and good times guaranteed. **Amnesia** (Crta. Sant Antoni, km. 5, www.amnesia.es, 11 P.M.–6 A.M. June–Sept.) is the grand-daddy of them all. Going strong since the 1970s, this club has launched legendary DJs and is in many ways responsible for the clubbing phenomenon that thrives worldwide today. Amnesia packs in thousands with a roster of parties like "Cocoon" by DJ Sven Vath and "Espuma," the notorious foam parties where the crowd is doused in a mini-sea of bubbles. **Privilege** (Crta. Sant Antoni, km. 6, www.privilege.es, 11 P.M.–6 A.M. June–Sept.) is massive, holding 10,000 frenzied folks on any given night. On Fridays it hosts "Manumission" (www.manumission.com), the infamous club night that combines eroticism, performance art, and sex in a wild night of techno-fueled bacchanalia. **Es Paradis** (C/ Salvador Espiriu, s/n, www.esparadis.com, 11 P.M.–6 A.M. May–Oct.) is another famous club with a stunning setting that includes faux-Grecian arches, a pyramid-shaped glass roof, and a giant tropical fish tank. Music is a bit more varied with a few nights dedicated to soul, funk, and hip-hop.

Accommodations

Cheap lodging is clustered in the old town around the West End, and, of course, in many of the squat cement hotels around town (often booked only to agents). You can try to get in through the booking service at www .ibiza-spotlight.com. **Hostal Roca** (C/ San Mateo 11, tel. 97/134-0067, €50) is located on a pedestrian street in the old town and has simple but adequate room in a building popular with young Brits. Save money by sharing a bath. **Hostal Flores** (C/ Rossell 26, tel. 97/134-1129, closed winter, €40) features comfy little rooms in an old-fashioned hotel that boasts a hopping bar. **Hostal Florencio** (C/ Soledad 38, tel. 97/134-0723, www.hostalflorencio .com, €75) has recently refurbished rooms that are surprisingly spacious and modern considering the price. There is also a pool and sunning deck. Note, air-conditioned rooms cost €6 extra per day.

Pike's Ibiza Hotel (Camí de Sa Vorera, s/n, tel. 97/134-2222, reservas@pikeshotel .com, www.pikeshotel.com, €230) is Ibiza's most legendary lodging. Located on the grounds of a 15th-century farmhouse about three kilometers (two miles) east of San An, Pike's has a celebrated guest list that has included George Michael, Freddie Mercury, and Grace Jones. The grounds have a lush tropical garden with a tiled pool and expansive views over the Ibiza countryside. The rooms are decorated in a shabby-chic style with lots of color, flowing fabrics, and gently battered antiques. **Club Paraiso Mediterraneo** (C/ Cervantes 27, tel. 97/134-7774, €95) is one of the most notorious hotels in town. If you are 20-something and looking for a raging wild party that continues long after even the clubs have shut down, this is your place. Rooms are fine enough (air-conditioning costs extra), public spaces are very hotel-esque (except for the clubbers who are often passed out in them), and service is very laid-back (breakfast is served until 12:30 P.M. for hungover late-risers). The palm-lined pool is a hot spot for re-hashing the previous night's events and planning the next one. It is located in the old town, just north of the West End.

Food

Tuck into inexpensive pizzas and pastas at

David's (C/ Madrid, tel. 97/134-0470, €15), located in the old town with very vibrant terrace seating. **Casa Thai** (Av. Dr. Fleming 34, tel. 97/134-4038, €12) brings Thai noodles and Indian curries to the raving masses in a no-nonsense little place a bit inland from the Egg. **El Rincón de Pepe** (C/ Sant Mateu 6, tel. 97/134-0697, €15) is where to go when you want to remember that Ibiza is in Spain. With a tiled bar beneath hanging hocks of *jamón*, this friendly bar serves the best tapas in town.

Can Pujol (C/ Caló, s/n, tel. 97/134-1407, closed Dec. and Jan., €45), located in an unassuming seaside shack near Port Torrent, is one of Ibiza's top-rated seafood restaurants. The sunset views are spectacular, so arrive early. **L'Elephant** (C/ San Rafael, tel. 97/119-8056, €30) is a very self-consciously stylish restaurant serving Mediterranean fare with French touches in a warehouse-like dining room with giant Hindu statues, modern art, and low-lighting. On their upstairs terrace, they run Elephant VIP, an extremely exclusive club (Paris Hilton has partied here) that not even money can buy your way into. Look good, look rich, or hope it is a slow night and the celebs are away.

Information

San An's multi-lingual **tourist office** (Pg. Fonts, s/n, tel. 97/134-3363, 10 A.M.–1 P.M. and 5–7:30 P.M. Mon.–Fri., 10 A.M.–1 P.M. Sat., closed Sun.), on the harborfront near the Egg, has lots of information on Sant Antoni, including a good beach guide. For club information, pop into any of the bars or restaurants and check the fliers near the doors. Online, the aforementioned www.ibiza-spotlight.com is a goldmine.

Getting There and Around

If you are flying into Ibiza, a taxi to San An will run around €18, possibly more. Buses run between Ibiza City and Sant Antoni year-round, with increased service in summer. See www.ibizabus.com for schedules. If you are driving from Ibiza City, it is less than 16 kilometers (10 miles) via C-731.

Formentera

The smallest of the Balearic islands, Formentera is just 20 kilometers (11 nautical miles) south of Ibiza. Despite this proximity to the buzzing isle, Formentera is a barely developed paradise of ultra-fine white beaches and crystal jade waters. Even in the height of summer, it is possible to take a sandy path less traveled and find yourself nearly alone in Mediterranean paradise. Just 80 square kilometers (31 square miles), it offers a wealth of natural beauty. Inland, there are a pair of pristine salty lakes and flat rolling landscapes thick with green foliage and riddled with lazy biking and hiking trails.

If you decide to stay in Formentera, you can get pretty much anything you need from ATMs to groceries in one of the island's three small towns. One thing you might want to pack along is bug spray; mosquitoes can get bad here, particularly in the evenings.

Formentera's main **tourist office** (tel. 97/132-2057, www.turismoformentera.com, 10 A.M.–2 P.M. and 5 –7 P.M. Mon.–Fri., 10 A.M.–2 P.M. Tues., closed Sun.) is located on the port in La Savina. Their website is excellent, as is that of tour operator **Formentera Freetime** (www.formenterafreetime.com).

LA SAVINA

The tidy little Port de la Savina is where the ferry from Ibiza will drop you off. The tourist office is here, as are several bike rental agencies and a few cafés. Just south of the port are two saltwater *estanys* (lakes), the large Pudent and the smaller Peix. While not the loveliest of sights, the lakes form a natural wetland that attracts a diverse birdlife—and many dedicated birdwatchers. Northwest of the port are the salt beds of **Ses Salines** with their whimsical flamingo sculptures.

From La Savina you can catch a local bus to either the capital of the island, sleepy little **Sant Francesc** or **Es Pujols,** the closest thing Formentera has to a resort. If you decide to stay in Formentera, your cheapest lodging will be in one of these two towns.

◖ ES TRUCADORS

North of the salt beds, the long, wispy Trucador peninsula juts provocatively into the sea. A protected natural park, the peninsula is lined on all sides with some of the most inviting beaches of the islands. The longest and most attractive (and popular) is **Platja de ses Illetes.** In the summer, you can go parasailing or rent a flat-bottomed boat here. On the opposite side of the peninsula and over a sandy dune, the **Platja Llevant** is one of the most dazzling beaches in Spain. Backed by dunes, this beach is very popular with nudists. Continuing north (by foot only), the peninsula shrinks to less than a 30 meters (100 feet) wide and offers even more spectacular crystal white sand and clear waters. At the very tip of the peninsula, a sandbar connects Formentera to the islet **Es Pas.** The water running over it can be surprisingly rough, but if the seas are calm you can wade across.

PLATJA DE MIGJORN

On the south of the island, the nearly 6.5-kilometer (four-mile) Migjorn (Midday) beach is easily as stunning as those on Es Trocadors and usually a lot less crowded. Arcing in a blinding wash of white sand, Migjorn is mostly undeveloped—with the exception of its furthermost eastern and western points, which each host a small clutch of hotels. There are a few seasonal operators here who rent snorkeling and diving equipment as well as a couple of excellent *chiringuitos* (beachside bars).

SPORTS AND RECREATION
Biking

The tourist office has a handy book called *Circuits Verds* which details 20 biking and hiking paths throughout the island. In La Savina **Autos Ca Mari** (tel. 97/132-2921) and **Moto Rent Mitjorn** (tel. 97/132-2306) are both established rental companies, but there are many more lining the dock when you get off the ferry. You can also bring a bike over from Ibiza on

boats off of Formentera with Ibiza in the background

© KELLY O'DONNELL

the ferry, but it will pad your fare a bit. If you stay in Formentera, most of the hotels also rent bikes. The cost runs around €8 per day.

Diving

Formentera is well-known for its excellent diving. The crystal clear waters bathing its coasts reveal a staggering variety of underwater flora and fauna as well as shipwrecks and caves waiting to be explored. Warm most of the year and regularly boasting visibility of up to 40 meters, Formentera's waters are a paradise for both novice and experienced divers. To rent diving or snorkeling equipment or to schedule a course try **Blue Adventure** (C/ Almadrava 67, La Savina, tel. 97/132-1168, www.blue-adventure.com) or **Vellmarí** (Av. Mediterráneo 90, La Savina, tel. 97/132-2105, www.vellmari.com), which is PADI-certified.

ACCOMMODATIONS

If you haven't booked ahead or are having trouble finding lodging on your own, try Formentera's **reservation office** (tel. 97/132-1207, www.formenterareservations.com). They have an office in La Savina, near the tourist office.

Hostal Maysi (Els Arenals, tel. 97/132-8547, €75) offers spacious, sparse rooms in a low-rise building just off Migjorn beach. It has a pool and restaurant. **Roca Bella** (Es Pujols, tel. 97/132-8130, €140) is another simple little hotel with decent rooms, a pool, and a beachside bar. It is located close enough to Pujols to walk there, but far enough from it to feel secluded. **Hostal Ca Marí** (Es Ca Marí, tel. 97/132-8180, www.guiaformentera.com/camari, €80) is a cute little complex tucked into a lovely garden within walking distance of Migjorn beach. Grounds feature a pool, a small shop, a bar, and a restaurant. There are also cozy little bungalows available with terraces.

Hotel Riu La Mola (Pl. Migjorn, s/n, tel. 97/132-7000, www.riuhotels.com, €140), located right on Platja Migjorn is a big-time resort that still manages to have a laid-back Mediterranean feel. Rooms are airy and spacious, many with stunning sea views. Public areas are inviting and spacious and the pool is luxurious.

© KELLY O'DONNELL

The Formentera beach, Platja de ses Illetes, is surrounded on two sides by the sea.

FOOD

Dining in Formentera follows the same hours as in Ibiza. Restaurants hold daily, uninterrupted hours in the summer and reduced hours in the winter. Many of the beachside operations shut down completely in the off-season. If you are in Formentera during this time, check with the tourist office for a list of open establishments. In addition to the restaurants in the hotels, seek out **Le Cyrano** (Es Pujols, Pg. Marítim, s/n, tel. 97/132-8386, €25). On the waterfront in Formentera's bustling little resort, it is known for its Mediterranean fare with French flair. Try the *caracoles* (sautéed snails). **Pascual** (Caló de Sant Agustí, tel. 97/132-7014, €30) is a long-time local favorite serving excellent seafood paella on a lovely tree-shaded patio. **Lucky** (Platja Migjorn) is a funky little *chiringuito* (beachside bar) run by Andrea and Claudio, two Italian expats who serve exquisite pastas and salads right on the beach. Later on, the stoves are turned off and the drinks flow until the very wee hours. **El Mirador** (Crta. La Savina-La Mola, km. 14, tel. 97/132-7037, €25) offers simply grilled fish and meat along with one of the most spectacular views on the island. Make reservations if you want a front-row table for sunset. **Tanga Bar**

(Pl. Llevant, tel. 97/118-7905), located on the gorgeous Llevant beach, is a spacious bungalow serving tapas and excellent seafood—try their *caldereta de langosta* (lobster stew), a specialty of the Balearic Islands.

GETTING THERE AND AROUND

The only way to get to Formentera is via ferry from Ibiza. The **ferry terminal** is located in Ibiza on Avinguda Santa Eulària, on the west side of the harbor. There are several companies providing service. Highly recommended is **Balearia** (tel. 90/216-0180, www.balearia .net), which runs the most ferries. Prices range €18–35. Normally the trip is 30 minutes, but strong currents can make the passage rough and slow.

Getting around the island is a breeze with a bike. If not, you can take the handy public bus (tel. 97/132-3181) which runs around the island daily from 9:45 A.M.–8 P.M., connecting to La Savina, Es Pujos, Sant Ferran, and Sant Francesc as well as the beaches Illetes and Migjorn. During the summer, the buses run every 30 minutes or so. The tourist office can provide a detailed schedule. Off season, you'd be better off calling **Radio Taxi** (tel. 97/132-2342).

Menorca

The second largest of the Balearic Islands, Menorca (also spelled Minorca) is also the least visited. Less packaged than Mallorca, more laid-back than Ibiza, and much bigger than Formentera, it makes for an amazing Mediterranean vacation and a place where it is very easy to get off the beaten path. Offering two charming cities, over 100 pristine beaches, even more secluded coves, and a wealth of prehistoric ruins, there is much to keep you busy here, but the real joy of Menorca is its absolutely shimmering beauty. Rent a car and follow a dusty road anywhere and you are sure to be stunned silent by the craggy cliffs falling off into the crystal clear sea and the long, white beaches etching along the coast like fine lace. If it feels like a world treasure, that is because it is. In 1993, the entire island was declared a UNESCO Biosphere Reserve.

When planning your travels through the island, pay attention to the *tramontana*. This legendary wind buffets the island off and on throughout the year (though it is at its most furious in the winter). One day it can be on the north, the next in the south. Check with your hotel or the tourist office to find out where the wind is blowing and then head in the opposite direction.

MAÓ

The town of Maó (Mahón in Spanish) is a natural starting point for a Menorcan adventure. Boasting a bustling port and a clutch of tidy Georgian townhouses—a legacy from when the British ruled the island in the 18th century—Maó is lovely, refined, and a little bland. Take in the few sights, stock up on information at the tourist office, rent a car, and then head elsewhere.

Sights

Maó the town is wrapped neatly around Maó the port, one of the finest natural ports in the Mediterranean. Deep and long, it has been sought after and fought over for millennia.

Today, it makes a fine place to begin exploring Maó. Lined with a stately promenade, this is where locals go for their evening see-and-be-seen stroll. At the far end of the port is the **Xoriguer Gin Distillery** (Moll de Ponent 93, tel. 97/136-2197, www.xoriguer.es). Another legacy of British rule, Menorcan gin has a unique aroma and taste quite unlike that of standard gin. You can try several flavors at the shop in front of the distillery.

Above the port, **Església de Santa María** looms up from the charming Plaça de la Constitució. Originally built in the 13th century, the church was massively reconstructed in the 18th. Within is an impressive 3,200-pipe baroque organ dating from 1810. The streets around the plaza house some of the town's finest examples of 18th-century English architecture. Seek out Plaça d'Espanya, home to the **Mercat Claustre del Carme** (7 A.M.–2 P.M. Mon.–Sat., closed Sun.), a lively farmers market located within the atmospheric cloisters of the adjoining **La Verge del Carme** church. This is the perfect place to stock up on picnic fare, including some of Maó's famed artisan cheeses, Queso Mahón. Boasting their own *denominación de origen* (appellation), these hand-crafted cow's milk cheeses are exquisite, particularly the *curado* (cured) cheese.

Menorca has a remarkably rich archaeological heritage. As you tour the island, you'll come across the stone remains of the Talaiot culture, a Bronze Age civilization that lived on Menorca and Mallorca in the second millennium B.C. Maó's **Museu de Menorca** (C/ Doctor Guardia, s/n, tel. 97/135-0955, closed Mon., €2.50) provides more information about these remains. The museum has an extensive collection of artifacts from these remains with explanations. There are also displays about every other culture that occupied the island from the Romans through the Moors.

Accommodations

If you need a cheap sleep, you can't go wrong at

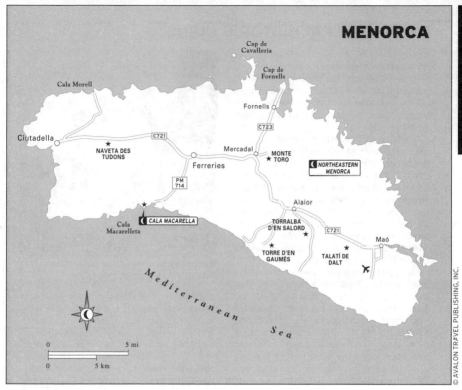

MENORCA

Cap de Cavalleria

Cap de Fornells

Cala Morell

Fornells

C723

Ciutadella

C721

★ NAVETA DES TUDONS

Mercadal

MONTE ★ TORO

Ferreries

◖ NORTHEASTERN MENORCA

PM 714

Alaior

★ ◖ CALA MACARELLA

Cala Macarelleta

TORRALBA D'EN SALORD ★

C721

Maó

TORRE D'EN GAUMÉS

★ TALATÍ DE DALT

Mediterranean Sea

0   5 mi
0   5 km

Hostal Orsi (C/ Infanta 19, tel. 97/136-4751, €45), a cheery little *hostal* with a friendly staff. Rooms are simple but clean and well maintained. If you choose to share a bath, the price drops to €35. **Hostal La Isla** (C/ Santa Catalina 4, tel. 97/136-6492, €45) is more of the same, but no option to share baths. The friendly family that runs the place also has a bustling little bar/restaurant on the ground floor.

A bit out of town but still on the port, ◖ **Hotel del Almirante** (Ctra. Es Castell, tel. 97/136-2700, www.hoteldelalmirante .com, €96) is a charming red-and-white, 18th-century manor. Formerly the home of Admiral Collingwood, the house offers 40 antique-y rooms, many with views of the port. Guests can enjoy the lovely sitting room, a swimming pool, a billiards rooms, and, just maybe,

a visit from Collingwood's ghost, rumored to still hang around. Back in town, **Hotel Port Mahón** (C/ Fort de l'Eau 13, tel. 97/136-2600, www.sethotels.com, €98) offers sea-view rooms with classic, if a bit staid, furnishings. It is located about 15 minutes walking from the center of town.

Food

For excellent Menorcan fare, exquisite seafood, stylish cafés, and even fast food—head right to the port. Cheap eats, including the laid-back sandwich and salad place **The American Bar** (Pl. Reial, s/n, tel. 97/136-1822, €12) can be found in the tangle of streets above the port.

La Minerva (Moll de Llevant 87, tel. 97/135-1995, €30) boasts a floating terrace and an anchored old boat that serves as a lively bar. The

MENORCA'S PREHISTORIC RUINS

Menorca has one of the richest collections of prehistoric monuments in the Mediterranean, with over 200 sites and thousands of ruins, the oldest dating to 2500 B.C. Archaeologists usually divide the prehistory of Menorca into three epochs: pre-Talayotic, Talayotic, and post-Talayotic.

Pre-Talayotic culture is the oldest. Some of the most important remains from this era are the burial monuments called *navetas*, mass tombs that resemble upturned boats. The Naveta des Tudons is the best known of these structures. Around 1400 B.C., Talayotic culture took root. This period is characterized by the building of stone towers or *talaiots*. The word *talaiot* derives from the Arabic *atalaya*, which means "watchtower." Also dating from this era are the *taulas*, megalithic stone "Ts" made by hoisting a massive granite base into a vertical beam and topping it with a large stone slab laid horizontally. The Talatì de Dalt, just outside of Maó, has one of the most impressive examples, rising to three meters (10 feet). The Talaiots also left behind thousands of remains, from houses to cisterns. The most important Talayotic sites on the island include Trepuco and Talati de Dalt near Maó, and Torretrencada and Torre Llafuda near Ciutadella. The most extensive sites, having produced the most re-

© BRIDGET O'TOOLE/DAVID FINCH

Menorca has a wealth of prehistoric Talaiot ruins such as this *taula*.

mains and clues into this prehistoric world, are on the western side of the island and include Torre d'en Gaumes and Torralba d'en Salord. The island of Mallorca also has several Talaiot sites. The post-Talayotic period occurred after other cultures entered the islands and the Talaiots adopted outside building techniques. By the time the Romans arrived, the Talayotic era had ended.

---

food is perfect Menorcan simplicity with excellent fish and shellfish. **Es Fosquet** (Moll de Llevant 256, tel. 97/135-0058, €25) is built in an old fisherman's cottage and bristles with romantic charm. Seafood and the savory *caldereta de langosta* (lobster stew) are the best choices. For something lighter, try **El Cachito** (Moll de Llevant 278, tel. 97/136-9792), a lively tapas bar with excellent cured hams and local cheeses.

Information

Maó's **tourist office** (tel. 97/135-5952, 10 A.M.–1 P.M. and 5–7:30 P.M. Mon.–Fri., 10 A.M.–1 P.M. Sat., closed Sun.) is located on the waterfront at the port. There is also a tourist information booth at the airport. Online, consult the city website, www.ajmao.org, as well as the island site, www.emenorca.org. The Baleares site, www.illesbalears.es, also has good basic information, and the commercial site www.webmenorca.com is excellent.

Getting There

Menorca's **Aeroport Maó** (tel. 97/115-7115, www.aena.es) receives flights from the Spanish mainland via **Iberia** (www.iberia.es) and **Air Europa** (www.aireuropa.com). There is also limited service to Northern Europe in the summer. The airport is about eight kilometers (five miles) outside of Maó and is connected to the city via an **airport bus** that goes to the bus station at Plaça de S'Esplanada every 30 minutes. A taxi will run less than €15.

By ferry, Maó is serviced by **Transmediterranea** (tel. 90/245-4645, www.trasmediterranea.es), **Balearia** (tel. 90/216-0180, www.balearia.net), and **Iscomar** (tel. 90/211-9128, www.iscomar.com). Prices vary on whether you are leaving from Barcelona, Valencia, Dénia, or Mallorca.

Getting Around

The Maó **Estación de Autobuses** is located on the Plaça de S'Esplanada. The main bus line is **Transportes Menorca** (tel. 97/136-0475, www.transportesmenorca.net), which handles most intercity transfers on the island. The tourist office has complete information.

Bus service is limited to the main cities and some of the bigger beaches. If you really want to have freedom of movement, rent a car. There are several car rental agencies at the airport including **Hertz** (www.hertz.es) and **Europcar** (www.europcar.es).

◖ NORTHEASTERN MENORCA

Menorca is traversed by a long, winding highway that ambles along for nearly 50 kilometers (30 miles) connecting Maó with the island's other major city, Ciutadella. Along the road are several spectacular prehistoric sights, the island's highest mountain, and dozens of roads leading to stunning beaches. At Monte Toro, swinging north brings you to the resort of Fornells. All of the Talaiot sites are clearly marked on the roads. The major ruins listed below are generally open in the summer from 9 A.M.–7 P.M. daily. In the winter those hours are normally limited to 10 A.M.–2 P.M. Tuesday through Sunday. However, the hours vary drastically month to month and from site to site. Even the tourist office seems baffled about exactly what the hours are. Your best bet is to visit the sites within the above-mentioned time frames and cross your fingers.

Talatí de Dalt

Just about five kilometers (three miles) out-

side of Maó, you reach the impressive Talatí de Dalt, a prehistoric Talaiot settlement dominated by a large T-shaped *taula*. This is considered one of the more significant sites on the island and is the focus of ongoing archaeological research assisted by archaeology students from around the world every summer.

Torralba d'en Salord

Another magnificent example of Talaiot culture, the site Torralba d'en Salord has structures dating to 1300 B.C. Most impressive is the massive *taula* at the center of a horseshoe-shaped sanctuary. Among the items excavated from this sanctuary was an extraordinary bronze bull, which is on display at the museum in Maó. All around the *taula* are the remains of houses and storage facilities.

Alaior

The town of Alaior is Menorca's third-largest and makes for a nice stopover—particularly if you like cheese. The Coinga factory, which makes some of the island's most sought-after Queso Mahón, is located here. Visit the **factory shop** (C/ Mercadal 8, tel. 97/137-1227) for tastings and to buy a bit for the road.

Monte Toro

After leaving Alaior, swing up to the town of Mercadal and follow the signs to the **Mare de Déu del Toro,** a pretty standard 16th-century church with a monumental 360° view. Located on the top of Monte Toro, Menorca's highest point at 357 meters (1,175 feet) above sea level, the church offers a spectacular panoramic vista of the entire island and the great blue sea beyond.

Fornells

Located on a stunning bay that swoops deeply into the northern coast of Menorca, Fornells is lovely little village of whitewashed houses with bright blue windowsills lining well-worn cobbled streets. In the 17th century, this was a favorite entrance point for pirates so a massive sand-colored castle was erected on the hill above the bay. All that remains is the **Torre de Fornells,** a squat watchtower.

When the *tramontana* wind is not furiously whipping, it adds just enough life to the water to keep windsurfers and sailors happy. In fact, one of the keenest sailors attracted to this port is King Juan Carlos. He steers his boat in here regularly to enjoy Fornells' other claim to fame—its *caldereta de langosta.* This savory lobster stew is a staple throughout Menorca, but the key ingredient—spiny lobster—comes from these waters. All along the port are excellent restaurants that draw day-trippers in by the hundreds.

Fornell is also home to the **Playas de Fornells,** a very glitzy, upscale resort of big seafront hotels beneath which big yachts dock. There are excellent beaches all around here. Look for **Son Parc,** a long, wide, blindingly white stretch of very fine sand along a shallow shelf of crystal clear water. There is a bar and other facilities on the beach. Nearby, **Arenal d'en Castell** is a large circular cove surrounded by a beautiful arc of white sand. The beach features a couple of lively bars with food. To the west of the lovely Cap de Cavalleria, **Agaiarens-La Vall** is a gorgeous swoop of beach backed by brush-covered dunes. Part of a protected area, the beach has very little development besides a few picnic tables.

Accommodations and Food

If you would like to stay the night in Fornells, try the charming **Hostal La Palma** (Pl. S'Algaret 3, tel. 97/137-6487, www.hostalla palma.com, €80), which feels more like a B&B than an inexpensive *hostal.* Rooms are cozily decorated and have views of the surrounding countryside. There is also a pristine pool if you don't want to trudge down to the beach. The in-house bar and restaurant are both very popular with locals and tourists.

If you'd rather dine where the king does, head to **Restaurante Es Plá** (Pasaje Es Pla, tel. 97/137-6655, €40). In addition to his highness's favorite *caldereta de langosta,* the restaurant does amazing things with local fish such as grouper and red mullet. If Es Plá doesn't

entice, you can do just as well at any of the restaurants on the port, but don't expect prices to drop too much—food fit for a king does not come cheap. Back in Mercadal, head to legendary Menorcan restaurant **Moli d'es Reco** (C/ Major 53, tel. 137-5392, €85). Located in an old mill, this rustic dining room serves hearty favorites like steamed snails with homemade *mahonesa* (mayonnaise); the world's favorite condiment was created a few centuries ago in Maó.

Getting There

From Maó, the C-721 rambles west to Mercadal. The Talaiot sights are just off the road. From Mercadal, the C-723 leads to Fornells.

WESTERN MENORCA

The western half of Menorca is anchored by the seaside city of Ciutadella, the capital of the island until the British arrived and set up headquarters on the strategically important bay in Maó. The city itself is worth a look, but the real jewels of this area lay on Menorca's coasts and countryside—its beaches and its prehistoric culture.

Ciutadella

Nicknamed Vella i Bella ("Old and Beautiful"), Ciutadella is a pleasant city with a charming historic district and a lovely port. **Plaça des Born** is the old military parade ground of the medieval city and a good place to begin a walking tour. Just next to it is **Plaça de S'Esplanada,** an elegant tree-filled plaza that also serves as a bus transfer point.

On the corner of Carrer Major des Born stands the **Palau Torresaura,** an expansive, ornate 19th-century palace. Note the very eerie veiled women carved above the doorway of the palace. Across the street, **Palau Salort,** also from the 19th century, boasts intricate serpentine door knockers. The building is occasionally open to the public.

Ciutadella's massive **Catedral** (Pl. Catedral, s/n) is an excellent example of the Catalan Gothic style. It was built on top of a Moorish mosque in the 14th century. The only remaining part of the once mighty mosque is its minaret, now the cathedral's belltower. The cobbled lanes leading from the cathedral west towards Plaça d'Alfons III are an inviting place to get lost in—full of tapas bars, trendy shops, and attractive buildings. **Ses Voltes** (also known as Carrer Josep M. Quadrado) is the city's pedestrian shopping street.

Naveta des Tudons

Sitting along the C-721 just a few kilometers east of Ciutadella, the archaeological site of Naveta des Tudons is one of Menorca's most unique megalithic structures. Dating to around 1400 B.C., this funerary structure pre-dates Talaiot culture and has given proof to archaeologists of the importance of ritual in prehistoric society. (*Naveta* specifically refers to a funeral construction with this peculiar upside-down vessel shape). This massive chamber was built to hold over 100 bodies. Visitors are allowed to enter the chamber.

◖ Cala Macarella

On an island boasting dozens of stunning beaches, it is very hard to say which is the best. Nonetheless, many visitors swear that Cala Macarella is the most beautiful. On a lovely stretch of flat coast about 16 kilometers (10 miles) southeast of Ciutadella, this *cala* (cove) seems more like an artist's rendition of what a perfect beach should be—a large wash of emerald-hued sea is embraced by a shimmering gold arc of sand that's fringed by a deep tuft of pine trees, which are protected by chalk-colored cliffs. It is quite simply paradise. Around the cliff is an even tinier, more perfectly rendered cove—**Macarelleta,** popular with nudists.

Fortunately paradise has been updated with a cozy little beachside bar tucked very discreetly in a tuft of pine trees at the end of the beach.

Accommodations

In Ciutadella, get a good, cheap sleep at **Hostal Residencia Ciutadella** (C/ Sant Eloi 10, tel. 97/138-3462, €60), a recently refurbished *hostal* with shiny new rooms, a friendly English-speaking staff, and a thumping little bar on the 1st floor. **Hesperia Patricia** (Pg. Nicolau 90, tel. 97/148-1120, www.hoteles-hesperia.es, €100), located near the lively port, offers modern, spacious rooms. Catering mainly to the business trade, prices drop on the weekend.

Find rural luxury a few kilometers outside of the city at **Hotel Rural Sant Ignasi** (Ctra. Cala Morell, s/n, tel. 97/138-5585, www.sant ignasi.com, €220). This 18th-century chalet was once the home of a Menorcan aristocrat. Today, its antique-filled rooms, chandeliered hallways, large pool, and lush gardens host visitors who appreciate aristocratic treatment. The hotel's restaurant, **El Lloc,** run by Barcelona-trained chef, Oscar Riera, is one of the best in the islands. Try the *escupinyas de la isla,* a tasty mollusk that is similar to an oyster. Room prices drop by a third off-season.

Food

Tapas bars and traditional restaurants are all over the old center and around the cathedral. **Cas Quintu** (Pl. d'Alfons III) is a good example of the former with a buzzing little bar and lots of inexpensive Spanish tapas. **Ca'n Nito** (Pl. Born, 11, tel. 97/148-0768, €25) is a longtime favorite for quality local food including paellas, grilled meats, and tapas. **Cas Ferrer de sa Font** (C/ Portal de la Font, tel. 97/148-0784, €35) also offers excellent Menorcan fare in an 18th-century mansion with a stunning interior patio. Try their *cochinillo* (roasted suckling pig).

Ciutadella's port is lined with great restaurants, from cheap eats to haute spots. The best of the latter is **Café Balear** (Pl. Sant Joan 15, tel. 97/138-0005, €33), Ciutadella's top-rated restaurant. Boasting the most romantic seaside terrace in the city, the dining room serves exquisite seafood including their famous *arroz caldosa de langosta,* a creamy rice and lobster dish.

Information

The Ciutadella **tourist office** (Pl. Catedral 5, tel. 97/138-2693, 9 A.M.–1 P.M. and 5–7 P.M. Mon.–Fri., 9 A.M.–1 P.M. Sat., closed Sun.) can offer extensive information on the city as well as the surrounding beaches and Talaiot remains. On the Internet, try the island site, www.emenorca.org; the Baleares site, www.illesbalears.es; and the commercial site, www.webmenorca.com.

Getting There and Around

The ferry company **Iscomar** (tel. 90/211-9128, www.iscomar.com) offers direct service into Ciutadella from Alcúdia on the isle of Mallorca. If you are arriving into Menorca via Maó, you can get to Ciutadella via **Transportes Menorca** (tel. 97/136-0475, www.transportesmenorca.net).

By car, Ciutadella is on the western end of C-721. Get to the southern beaches by following the road to Ferrerias and then swinging south on the road toward Cala Galdana.

BACKGROUND

The Land

Located in southwestern Europe on the Iberian Peninsula, Spain and Portugal are separated from the rest of Europe by the Pyrenees mountain range. Spain is bordered by France and Andorra in the northeast, the Bay of Biscay in the northwest, the Mediterranean on the east and southeast, and the Atlantic Ocean on the western border that is not shared with Portugal. At the southern tip of Spain, Gibraltar, which is controlled by Great Britain, soars above the narrow Strait of Gibraltar that separates Spain from Northern Africa.

GEOGRAPHY

Spain comprises nearly 500,000 square kilometers (192,874 square miles) of wildly varied land.

In the center of the country is the dry, elevated Meseta where Madrid is located. To the north and east rise the soaring peaks of the Picos de Europa and Pyrenees mountain ranges respectively. From Cataluña south to Murcia, the coast harbors pristine beaches and nearly inaccessible coves while the inlands shelter fertile farmlands. The lowlands of Andalucía stretch from deserts in Almería through mountains in Granada to wetlands in Huelva. Galicia houses deciduous forests and dramatic coastlines. Pais Vasco, Navarra, and La Rioja are deeply green with fertile valleys fed by the Duero River. The Duero is joined on its horizontal path across Spain by two more major rivers, the Tajo and the Guadalquivir.

© J. ALBERTOS/WWW.VIGOENFOTOS.COM

© MEGAN CYTRON

Interior Asturias is a dramatic mesh of green scenery, mountains, and rivers.

The Meseta

The central elevated plateau called the Meseta makes up nearly half of Spain's total landmass. Sitting in the middle of it, Madrid is Europe's highest capital located 646 meters (2,120 feet) above sea level. Several mountain ranges carve natural divisions in the Meseta. The Sistema Central range borders Madrid, creating the north–south division of the Meseta. Some of those mountains, including Madrid's weekend playground, the Sierra de Guadarrama, remains snow-capped for most of the year. The southern portion of the Meseta, in Castilla-La Mancha, is split further by the Sierra de Guadalupe in the west and the Montes de Toledo in the east. The Meseta is also home to the Tajo River, the longest river in Spain, which empties into the Atlantic in Portugal.

The Mountains

The Meseta as a whole is enclosed by mountains on almost all sides. Marking the southern border, the rugged and long Sierra Morena extends to Southern Portugal. To the north,

the Cordillera Cantabrica is a limestone formation running parallel to the northern coastline and boasting some of the country's most dramatic sights, especially in the area of Picos de Europa where rocky cliffs soar majestically beyond a carpet of deep green pastures filled with grazing cows and Romanesque ruins. Finally, the Sistema Iberico follows the eastern coast of Spain down from La Rioja to Aragon along the Ebro River.

Spain's most famous mountain range is the Pyrenees, which lumbers for 450 kilometers (280 miles) from the Bay of Biscay to the Mediterranean. The range is shared with Southern France. It is a wonderland of soaring peaks, woven through with fast-flowing water, thick forests, and deep, green valleys. It goes through the Spanish regions of Navarra, Aragón, and Cataluña. In Aragón, the Pyrenees offer its highest peaks including Aneto (3,404 meters/11,168 feet), Monte Perdido (3,355 meters/11,007 feet), and Maladeta (3,308 meters/10,853 feet). Historically, these imposing peaks isolated the Iberian Peninsula from the rest of Europe but rhanks to modern roads, today the mountains are easily passable and accessible. Outdoor enthusiasts from skiers to hikers head to the Pyrenees in search of adventure all year long.

The Lowlands

The southern expanse of Spain rolls out in stark contrast to the dramatic mountains of the north as much of the area is covered in lowlands. The Andalucía region in the south is a large river valley kept fertile by the Río Guadalquivir, the main river of the region. Rolling green pastures and olive orchards mark the lowlands, despite the overwhelmingly hot temperatures, which can reach 32°C (90°F) on a daily basis in the summer. The area is not all flat, however, as the Sierra Morena runs along northern Andalucía and the Sistema Penibetico wanders along the southern coast by Granada and Malaga. The system gives rise to the Sierra Nevada range near Granada and the Sierra de Grazalema near Cadíz. The entire southern coastline makes up 4,962 square kilometers (1,916 square miles) of both rocky shores and sandy beaches.

Desert

Spain's only desert region is in the province of Almeria in Andalucía, on the southeastern coast. It exists despite the higher latitude because of warm winds from Africa's northern coast that are brought to Spain over the Mediterranean Sea. The landscape of parched earth and tumbleweed will look familiar to fans of old spaghetti westerns, as many were filmed here, including the Clint Eastwood classic *The Good, the Bad, and the Ugly.* (See sidebar, *Starring Almería,* in the *Andalucía* chapter for more on the region's cinematic past.)

Islands

Two groups of islands, the Balearic and the Canary, are also part of the geography of Spain. Four islands make up the Balearic Islands, which are situated off the eastern coast of Spain and exist as an extension of the Sistema Penibetico from the mainland. The northwest part of the main island of Mallorca consists of mountainous regions that are per-

fect for hiking, while the rest of the island is mostly low-lying plains. The Canary Islands, located off the west coast of Africa, formed as a result of volcanic activity and boast black volcanic soil and intriguing, almost lunar landscapes. The Canaries also have some impressive mountains, with the highest on the island of Tenerife reaching up to 3,700 meters (12,140 feet). Both archipelagos are popular tourist spots for their gorgeous beaches.

CLIMATE

Given the varied geography of Spain, the country has a number of different climates. Generally, Spain is characterized by long, intensely hot summers and cold, blustery winters. Fall and spring are delightful with sunny days and cool nights. Rainfall is irregular and unreliable; the Meseta receives an average of 43 centimeters (17 inches) of rain each year but that has been decreasing over the last decade. Summers in Andalucía are much hotter than in the other regions. July temperatures in Sevilla regularly break 38°C (100°F). Relief comes at wintertime, when the temperatures can be quite pleasant. All coastal regions, including the islands, have milder temperatures given the coastal breezes. In general, the coast can be split into the Mediterranean side, east of Gibraltar, and the Atlantic side to the west. The Atlantic waters are colder and remain cold well into summer. In winter they are downright frigid. If you are thinking of going swimming in Cádiz in February, forget it unless you are a lover of ice-cold water. The Mediterranean waters are warmer, though winter also finds them cold.

The northern mountains and coasts of Spain have a much more temperate climate. The four seasons are more distinct there with warm summers and cold winters. A main feature is the abundance of precipitation compared to the rest of the country. Here there is an average precipitation of 89 centimeters (35 inches) a year. Trendy hotels in Bilbao and San Sebastián now feature umbrellas as part of their room perks. The north is also more humid than the rest of Spain, leading to fog, especially in the mountains.

Flora and Fauna

Thanks to its geographic and climatic diversity, Spain has a wide variety of flora—greater than that of any other European nation. There are some 8,000 known species, and at least 25 percent of these are native to the Iberian Peninsula. There is less diversity in fauna, due mainly to decreasing habitat and pressure from humans. This overview briefly covers what you can expect if you step off the urban path, but for extensive information visit www.iberianature.com, run by British expat Nick Lloyd. Look also for Lloyd's forthcoming book, *Wildlife in Spain.* Another good source, particularly for planning outdoors-focused travel and bird-watching excursions, is www.wild-spain.com.

FLORA
Trees

Though only about 25 percent of the Iberian Peninsula is now covered in forests, it is es-timated that over 90 percent of the land was once forested. The majority of today's forests are in the northwest mountainous regions, and more than half of those are made up of pine trees. The mountains are also home to firs, juniper, oak, and beech. The Selva de Irati forest in Navarra has Europe's second-largest beech forest. In general, it is estimated that there are over 100 species of trees native to Spain. The most populous is the holm oak (*encina* in Spanish), an evergreen that grows over much of the peninsula, especially in the central Meseta and in the scrubland in the west and south. Also called ilex oak, this tree litters the grounds with acorns *(bellotas)* that provide the principal diet for the Spanish black pig, *cerdo ibérico,* which becomes the country's most prized food product—*jamón ibérico.* Another common tree is the cork oak (*alcornoque);* it is harvested for its outer bark, which is turned into *corcho* (cork). The chestnut tree *(castaño)* is also common,

La Rioja is perfectly suited for growing grapes.

© WWW.THEWINELOVE.COM/ GONZALO GONZALO

and stalls pop up on city corners throughout Spain selling roasted chestnuts from around October to February.

Throughout the country, though mainly in the scrubland of Andalucía, olive trees *(olivos)* are extensively cultivated. They fuel Spain's olive oil production the largest in the world. Spain is also one of the world's biggest producers of almonds, cultivated from almond trees *(almendra)* along the Mediterranean coasts. Palm trees *(palmera)* are also common throughout the Mediterranean regions. In the town of Elche in Valencia province, there is an amazing forest of some 200,000 date palms that were planted in the 10th century by the Moors. The forest has a UNESCO World Heritage designation.

Other Vegetation

Wildflowers grow in abundance throughout Spain. The valleys of the Pyrenees are particularly colorful in springtime, attracting an active butterfly population. The Vall d'Aran is one of the best places to see this display of nature's exuberance. Mountain soil also gives rise to a wide variety of orchids, particularly in the Picos de Europa where dozens of orchid species have been documented.

Shrubs and herbs are endemic throughout the central Meseta. Fragrant herbs such as lavender *(lavanda)*, rosemary *(romero)*, and thyme *(tomillo)* grow wild even in urban centers.

Much of the Iberian Peninsula is well suited for grape cultivation. Vineyards cover wide expanses of land in La Rioja, Castilla y León, around Jerez in Andalucía, along the Río Miño in Galicia, and in the foothills of the Pyrenees in Huesca and Cataluña. Spain is the world's second-largest wine producer.

FAUNA
Mammals

Spain has over 110 species of indigenous mammals, including wolves, fox, lynx, boar, wild goats, deer, and rabbits. The country's endangered brown bear *(oso pardo)* population is much in the press as conservationists are engaged in a full-on battle to bring this majestic animal back from the brink of extinction. Once populous throughout Spain—in fact, the shield of Madrid features a bear—the animal reached a low of just 80 individuals in the early 1990s. Various methods, including species protection and reintroduction of bears from outside of Spain, have spurred population growth, and in 2005, 160 bears were documented in the Cantabrian mountains.

The Pyrenean ibex was not so lucky. A type of mountain goat that once ranged widely throughout the Pyrenees, the ibex became extinct in 2000 when a tree fell on the last living individual—a female. In a case straight out of science fiction, the Spanish government has teamed with a genetics company to clone the fallen animal. It is a dubious prospect at best because even if the operation is successful, one female alone cannot regenerate a species. Scientists are researching the prospect of manipulating the DNA to also create a male clone as well.

The Iberian lynx *(lince)* is a big cat species native to Spain. Covered with leopard-like spots, the lynx is fairly small and hunts mainly small prey such as rabbits. Once common throughout the Iberian Peninsula, it is currently confined to just two breeding zones in Andalucía. Despite years of effort by conservationists, the Spanish government, and international organizations, the lynx is heading steadily towards extinction. In fact, it is considered one of the most endangered species in the world. In 2005, just 100 individuals were documented, compared to over 1,000 a decade ago. The reasons for the decimation of the species include the usual suspects—poaching, loss of habitat, and most dramatically, a drastic decrease in the lynx's natural prey. In the 1980s and 1990s, disease swept through the rabbit population of Spain, killing up to 80 percent of adult rabbits—the lynx's main food source. Despite the dire outlook, conservationists have had some success in 2005 and 2006 with breeding lynx cubs in captivity.

Another Spanish mammal species that gets loads of press is the wolf *(lobo)*. Spain is a refuge for the European wolf, and the Iberian wolf population is growing steadily. Once considered a pest and killed indiscriminately, attitudes have changed and since the 1990s wolves have enjoyed greater protection. However, wild wolves regularly inflict damage upon livestock, killing sheep, donkeys, and even cows and causing large financial losses. This has created a conflict between the conservationists and the afflicted herders. The result has been decreased protection for wolves in some areas and even a return to hunting the animals in others. The topic of wolf management in Spain remains volatile and the future of the wolf uncertain.

Birds

Spain has Europe's most wildly diverse bird population and the country is a major destination for bird-watchers. There are nearly 400 species documented throughout the country, though distribution varies with geography and climate. Seasonal migrations and a yearly influx of wintering birds also provide opportunities for sightings. If you are a serious birder, check with the sites mentioned at the start of this chapter, as well as with the **Association for Spanish Bird Watching** (www.apgoa.org), which is developing the English-language portion of its website.

Even the most casual tourist can appreciate Spain's birdlife, if for no other reason than many of Spain's birds are huge. Throughout La Rioja, Castilla y León, Castilla La Mancha, Madrid, and Extremadura, churches, turrets, castles, and almost every available perch are topped by massive stork nests. The white stork *(cigüeña)* is one of Spain's most populous birds, with nearly 33,000 individuals counted in 2004. Other large species readily sighted include birds of prey such as eagles, hawks, and kites. The Griffon vulture *(buitre leonado)* and the black vulture *(buitre negro)* are common in mountain regions and are often seen soaring between ridges. In the wetlands of Andalucía, large birds include the flamingo *(flamenco)*. The greater flamingo, distinctive for its long neck and pink-tipped feathers, descends every summer by the tens of thousands to breed in the Laguna de Fuente de Piedra, a lagoon near Antequera in Málaga province. If you are in Málaga around that time, check with the tourist office. This is a sight of natural beauty you don't want to miss.

Some of Spain's birds are endangered, mainly due to development and the loss of natural habitat. There are 15 species, including two types of duck, in critical danger (which means possible extinction within 50 years). Listed as "in danger" are 39 species, including some larger birds such as the Egyptian vulture and the lammergeier. The latter is one of the most spectacular birds in the country. Sporting a wingspan of over six feet, this bird of prey is one of Europe's rarest vultures. In Spanish, lammergeiers are called *quebrantahuesos* ("bone-breakers") for their method of dropping bones from great heights onto rocks to expose the marrow within. Their numbers are slowly increasing, with 80 breeding pairs counted in 2004. Though they live mainly in the Aragón section of the Pyrenees, there have been recent sightings in the Picos de Europa, which is a good sign. Another 45 species classified as "vulnerable" include different species of vultures, gulls, storks, and partridges.

Environmental Issues

The major environmental concern for Spain is lack of water. The Mediterranean climate leads to irregular rainfall, which raises the threat of droughts throughout the country. In 2005, Spain experienced its harshest drought in al-most 60 years. Since then, the Spanish government has set aside €300 million to handle the water-shortage crisis.

In addition to immediate concerns like a lack of drinking water, droughts wreak havoc

PRESTIGE OIL SPILL

Environmental devastation hit Spain in 2002 when the *Prestige* oil tanker sank in the Atlantic Ocean, wreaking havoc on the Galician and Cantabrian coasts, the fishing industry, and Spain's economy as a whole.

In November 2002, the Greek oil tanker *Prestige* sunk 250 kilometers (155 miles) off the coast of Galicia in northwestern Spain. One of the ship's tanks had burst in a storm and was awaiting permission to dock in a port. The Spanish, French, and Portuguese governments had diverted the dangerous ship from their own waters to protect their coastlines. While waiting for permission to port, the ship broke in two and sank, spilling 4.5 million kilograms (5,000 tons) of oil into the ocean.

Each day after the *Prestige* sunk, an additional 115,000 kilograms (125 tons) continued to leak into the sea. The oil invaded the Spanish coastline, affecting coral reefs, marine animals, birds, and the fishing industry. As a result of the spill, fishing in that region came to a complete stop for six months. In the end, over 54.5 million kilograms (60,000 tons) of oil, 80 percent of the ship's total, leaked into the ocean, affecting more than 3,215 kilometers (2,000 miles) of coastline. The spill, which has had a monumental effect on Spain's environment and economy, has been compared to Alaska's 1989 Exxon *Valdez* crisis in scope.

The clean-up efforts for the spill were massive, costing more than €2.8 billion. Thousands of volunteers joined in, cleaning the muck from the beaches with their hands. These efforts made considerable progress but nothing could repair the harm already done to the environment. Significant damage was also inflicted on the national Spanish budget as well. The

government was unable to balance its budget for several years after the crisis. The fishing and tourism industries took large hits as well. Meanwhile, the environmental effects continue to haunt the coast five years on and experts say it will be another half a decade before the environment makes a solid recovery.

The catastrophe also sparked a major environmental movement in Spain, Nunca Mais (Never Again). Environmentalists from all around the country joined together in confronting the Spanish government on its failure to address the problem when it first arose in the waters off northwestern Spain. Nunca Mais wants the Spanish and local governments to accept the blame for letting the obviously old and ailing ship linger out at sea and not allowing it to dock. Nunca Mais continues its search for accountability with an annual demonstration in Santiago de Compostela in Galicia.

Environmentalists are not the only ones asking questions. Investigations into the spill found that the ship left the port in St. Petersburg, Russia, without being inspected properly and it had structural deficiencies that went undetected. The failure to fix the ship has been blamed on the owner, but that is also a topic of controversy as the question of who exactly owns the tank is unclear. *Prestige* flew under a Bahamian flag, was operated by a Greek crew, and was chartered by a Swiss-based Russian oil company. On paper, the owner is reputed to be a company from Liberia, but as of yet, no one has been identified. Greenpeace has collected over 150,000 signatures pushing for the owner to come forward and take responsibility for the catastrophe and the ongoing clean-up efforts.

in Spain's biggest industries—agriculture and tourism. Combined with searing summer temperatures, the lack of rainfall causes fields to dry out, leaving no grass for cows and other grazing animals to feed on. All crops reliant on irrigation systems suffer as well. On top of it all, Spain worries that tourists, a major source of economic revenue, will be scared off by the drought problems. The luxury mega-resorts of the southeast, with their plush golf courses and pristine pools, are completely dependent on pumped-in water.

Local regions of Spain take action against drought by actively promoting conservation of water to both residents and tourists. Water has been rationed, public fountains turned off, and lawn sprinkler use limited. The national government has invested significant time, money and resources into solving the problem, including the creation of over 1,300 reservoirs. It has also invested heavily in water diversion systems that can transfer water from river valleys to drier areas such as Extremadura, Valencia, and Murcia. These systems are controversial, not only because of their high costs, but also because of the environmental toll they extract, including the devastation of important wetlands. Water scarcity has been and will continue to be a raging issue in Spain marked by fear, high costs, and endless political debates.

While water tops the national agenda, Spain also deals with problems common to the rest of Europe, such as pollution in the Mediterranean Sea, deforestation, and air pollution. Noise pollution is also a hot topic, especially in ear-shattering cities like Madrid where screeching car horns, near-constant construction, and booming nightclubs create a daily acoustic assault. A "noise law" was passed in 2003, but it is still a raging battle.

History

While Spaniards of the past and present have prided themselves on their uniquely Spanish identity, the truth of the matter is that over the generations, these Iberian people have been formed from many different peoples. From ancient Romans and Phoenicians to Iberians and Berbers, from Muslims and Jews to Visigoths and French, Spain has had it all. These many diverse cultures have shaped what Spain and its people are today.

ANCIENT CIVILIZATIONS

Over the course of the millennia, Spain has played host to countless peoples and it is here on the Iberian Peninsula where the beginnings of European civilization have been traced. The archaeological site of Atapuerca in the province of Burgos, is home to 800,000-year-old human remains. Studies suggest that these descendents of Neanderthals most likely entered the European continent via Africa. The excavations continue to uncover ever-older civilizations, and the site has led to the building of a world-class natural history museum in Burgos. (See sidebar, *The Old, Old Bones of Burgos*, in the *Castilla y León* chapter.)

The successive generations have also left behind clues about Spain's long-ago ancestors. The Altamira caves in Cantabria house paintings from the Magdelenian people, Paleolithic hunter-gatherers that lived around 15,000 B.C. The New Stone Age, which arrived from Egypt and Mesopotamia around 6000 B.C. brought with it both simplistic farming techniques and pottery and textiles. Post–Ice Age cave drawings have been found in eastern Spain, and remnants in Almería indicate the rise of a metal-working culture around 3000 B.C.

The civilizations extant on the Iberian Peninsula during the millennium prior to the arrival of the Romans in 218 B.C. were named Iberians, or "dwellers on the River Ebro," by the ancient Greeks. These peoples most likely arrived in Spain around the third millennium B.C. from the eastern shores of the Mediterranean, and the distinct groups that they formed are infamous for their continuous intertribal warfare. However, they later began mixing with other inhabitants to form diverse, new peoples. When the Central European Celts crossed the Pyrenees (between the 9th and 7th centuries B.C.), bringing with them their iron technology, they settled in Northern Spain and soon merged with the people of the central plain to become the Celtiberians.

Another notable civilization, which predates the Iberians and remains an extant ethnic group today, are the Basques. Little is known about their origins and their unique, pre-Indo-European language, which is unlike any other. Their name derives from Vascones, the title assigned to them by the Romans.

PHOENICIANS, GREEKS, CARTHAGINIANS, ROMANS, AND VISIGOTHS

By 1100 B.C., Phoenician culture was thriving in the western part of Andalucía in the cities of Gadir (now Cádiz), Baria, Adra, Almunecar and Málaga. The Phoenicians, a Semitic people originating from Lebanon, established permanent trading colonies along the coast and have been accredited with founding the oldest city in Western Europe, Cádiz, which is even older than Carthage in North Africa.

The Greeks arrived on the Iberian Peninsula in the 8th century B.C., introducing writing, coinage, the potter's wheel, the grapevine and, most importantly, the olive tree to the region. This last item later proved to be a great source of Spanish wealth.

Beginning with the 6th century B.C., the Phoenicians, Greeks, and Carthaginians began competing with the Iberians for control of the Peninsula's vast coastline and rich interior resources. The Carthaginians eventually pushed the Phoenicians and Greeks out of the western Mediterranean. However, the Carthaginians did not hold control of Spain for very long. After being defeated by Rome in the First Punic War (264–241 B.C.), to compensate for their loss of Sicily, Carthage rebounded by rebuilding their commercial

Roman tombs sit in the middle of Barcelona's Plaça Villa de Madrid.

© CANDY LEE LABALLE

empire in Spain. When, in the Second Punic War (218–201 B.C.), Hannibal's epic invasion of Italy was foiled by the Romans, the former Carthaginian Spain fell under the control of the Roman Empire. The territory, known to the Romans as Hispania, was divided into Hispania Citerior and Hispania Ulterior.

The Romans made fast work of conquering the rest of Spain. Though the Iberian tribes fiercely resisted their rule, by 19 B.C. the entire Peninsula (except for the País Vasco, Basque Country) had been subdued and Romanized by the Emperor Augustus. By the 1st century A.D., Hispania had become a highly cosmopolitan extension of the Roman Empire. The land was divided into three separately governed provinces: Baetica (Andalucía, southern Extremadura, and Castilla-La Mancha), Lusitania (Portugal and northern Extremadura), and Tarraconesis (the rest of Spain).

Rome had just as much to offer Hispania as Hispania had to offer it. The Romans brought with them their roads, aqueducts, theatres and amphitheatres, baths and temples. Some of the world's finest Roman ruins are found in Spain, such as the aqueduct of Segovia and the amphitheatre in Tarragona. The ancient Romans also introduced irrigation projects for improved agriculture, a legal system, early Christianity, and Latin, which later formed the basis for Spanish. They gave full Roman citizenship to all Hispano-Romans (Romanized Iberians and Iberian-born descendants of Romans) and admitted former Iberian tribal leaders into their aristocracy, allowing them to participate in the governing of Spain. In exchange, Hispania gave Rome gold, silver, wool, wine, olive oil, grain, soldiers and even emperors. Trajan (ruled 98–117), Hadrian (ruled 117–138), and Marcus Aurelius (ruled 161–180) were all born in Spain.

In the late 3rd century A.D., Germanic tribes marched over the Pyrenees, wreaking havoc in their path, and a century later, when the Huns arrived in Eastern Europe from Asia, the Germanic peoples that they displaced headed westward towards Hispania. In 405, Germanic tribes of the Suevi and the Vandals devastated Gaul until they were driven onto the Iberian Peninsula by the Visigoths. Turmoil ensued.

Around 410, the Visigoths seized the opportunity of Rome's turmoil to conquer much of Hispania, founding their capital in Toledo in 484. Life under Visigothic rule was not easy. These Germanic people were cruel leaders prone to infighting and not nearly as culturally refined as the Hispano-Romans, who consequently remained in charge of the civil administration, maintaining Latin as the language of both government and commerce. Above all was religious tension. The Roman Catholic Hispano-Romans considered their Aryan Visigoth rulers heretical and open rebellions were commonplace. Finally, in 587 the Visigoth king Reccared converted from Aryan to Orthodox Christianity, thus assuring his alliance with the Hispano-Romans. This would be the first of several times in Spanish history that political unity would be sought through religious uniformity.

Within no time, the Church became Spanish society's uniting factor. However, aside from the Church, all was not well in the Visigothic state. The Visigoths had inherited the legacy of Rome but had not known how to make it work for them. With ongoing civil war, assassinations, and usurpation, it wasn't long before other peoples began to intervene in internal disputes and royal elections: first the Greeks, then the Franks, and finally, the Muslims.

MOORS

Muslim rule in Spain, which lasted almost 800 years, is divided into three periods: the Emirate (711–756), the Caliphate (756–1031), and the Reinos de Taifas, or small independent kingdoms (1031–1492).

The Conquest

Islam arrived in North Africa in the mid-7th century, following the death of its founder, Mohammed, in 632; it rapidly took root. The decline of Visigothic kingdom gave the Muslims the opportunity they needed to expand their realm of power onto the Iberian Peninsula. In 711, the governor of Tangier, Tariq ibn Ziyad, assembled some 10,000 troops of Berbers (indigenous North Africans) and Moors (Muslims) and invaded Andalucía via Gibraltar.

It didn't take the Moors long to gain control of the entire Peninsula; in just three years they had conquered the entire territory and renamed it Al-Andalus. The Moors attempted to extend their empire across the Pyrenees but were pushed back by the Franks.

The Emirate

Al-Andalus was originally an extension of the Syrian Caliphate of Damascus, ruler of the Muslim world. In 750, the Abbasids, a rival clan, ousted the Omayyad dynasty and moved the caliphate to Baghdad. However, the Omayyad Abd ar- Rahman I established himself in Córdoba in 756 as the independent emir of Al-Andalus. Abd ar- Rahman I is remembered fondly today not only for founding the first capital city of the Moors but also for constructing Córdoba's Mezquita (mosque), one of Islam's greatest monuments, known for its tall pillars and arches of red and white limestone.

After several centuries of harsh Visigothic rule, the Moors were welcomed by many on the Peninsula, particularly by Jews and slaves, who had been the most badly mistreated. The Moors were tolerant rulers, and they allowed Jews and Christians alike to continue practicing their religion under Islamic rule, though they had to pay higher taxes. The 9th century saw the rise of the golden age of Muslim Spain. While the rest of medieval Europe wallowed in the Dark Ages, Spain was alight with new forms of architecture, mathematics and astronomy, philosophy, literature, and agricultural techniques and products, like sugar and oranges. Many words in modern Spanish, particularly ones beginning in "al" like *almohada* (pillow), *alfombra* (rug), and *alcachofa* (artichoke) originate from the Arabic of the Moors. The Muslims also built palaces, mosques, public baths, lush gardens, universities, markets, and libraries. Caliph Al-Hakam II, who ruled 961–976, founded by far the largest library in Europe at that time, consisting of hundreds of thousands of volumes. Muslim Spain was prosperous both for the Moors and their Iberian subjects.

The Caliphate

The era of prosperity didn't last forever. After several hundred years of glory, the caliphate of Córdoba was dissolved by civil war and financial difficulties, which resulted in the fragmentation of Al-Andalus in 1031 into the first 39 *taifas* (petty kingdoms), the most powerful of which was Sevilla, which became the new center of Muslim Spain around the year 1040.

Throughout Muslim rule, the Christians steadily gained force in their Reconquista (reconquest) efforts to regain control of the Peninsula. By the beginning of the 11th century, the Moor's grip on Spain was starting to slip. They called upon the Almoravids, a strict Muslim sect of North African nomads, to help ward off the Christian armies in the North. Though the Almoravids did soundly defeat the Christian forces, in 1091 they also invaded the Peninsula. The Almoravid occupation of Al-Andalus ushered in the beginning of the end of Al-Andalus.

In 1146, the Berber tribe of Almohads marched onto the Iberian Peninsula, and in 1224, the Banu Marins followed them. The Moors were left weakened and open to Christian attack.

The Nasrid Emirate of Granada

After Sevilla fell to the Christians in 1248, Muslim Spain was reduced to the Nasrid Emirate of Granada, located between the Strait of Gibraltar and Cape Gata (in modernday Almería). The Nasrids ruled their tiny kingdom from their extravagant Alhambra palace, which was constructed between 1248 and 1354. This site has since become one of the most popular tourist destinations in Spain as it offers an intact example of the intricate forms of art and architecture from Muslim Spain.

The Nasrid Emirate of Granada withheld against the ever-growing Christian forces for more than 200 years. In 1492, they finally succumbed, and the 800-year-long chapter in Spanish history that was Muslim Spain came to a close.

THE CHRISTIAN RECONQUEST

Shortly after the Moors invaded the Iberian Peninsula in 711, the Christians began their Reconquista efforts, which lasted from the battle at Covadonga (Asturias) in 718 to the fall of Granada in 1492. Though initially weak and small in number, the pockets of Christian resistance in the north and center of the territory gradually gained both followers and power. They managed to found the kingdoms of Asturias, León, Navarra, Castile, and Aragón, continually pushing the Muslims further and further south. By the 15th century, Catholicism was firmly entrenched on the Peninsula, thus giving rise to the reign of the Catholic Monarchs and their religious Inquisition.

One of the key elements of the Reconquista was the mythical battle fought in Clavijo in 811, where Santiago (Saint James), one of the 12 apostles, is said to have appeared on a white horse and slain 70,000 Moors in one fell swoop, earning him the epithet of Matamoros (Moor-slayer). When his tomb was discovered in Galicia in 813, the town of Santiago de Compostela was founded, and it soon became the third-most holy site, after Rome and Jerusalem, for medieval Christian pilgrims. Santiago later became the patron saint of Spain for the inspiration he provided to the soldiers and generals of the Reconquista.

The Rise of Castile

The Reconquista proceeded slowly but surely over the next several hundred years. They fought many battles against the Muslims along the way but nearly always came out victorious, increasingly so as Al-Andalus splintered into smaller and smaller individual kingdoms. One important exception to their winning streak occurred in 981 at Rueda when Ramiro III was defeated by Almansur and was forced to pay tribute to the Caliph of Córdoba.

Bit by bit, the Christians regained the land they considered to be rightfully theirs. At the turn of the 9th century, Alfonso II conquered various Moorish strongholds just south of the Duero River and settled them with Christians. A century later, Sancho I established the kingdom of Navarra. The original Christian territory, the kingdom of Asturias, was eventually moved to León, which, in turn, gave rise to Castile, "land of castles," in 950 with the help of Count Fernán Gonzalez. Though Castile's beginnings as a mere principality of the kingdom of León are humble, in time it grew to become the center of Reconquista power.

Of the many brave warriors of the Spanish Reconquista, one in particular stands out from the rest: El Cid. (See sidebar, *El Cid: Fact and Fiction,* in the *Castilla y León* chapter.) This mythical figure fought alongside Sancho II, García, King of Galicia, and Alfonso VI, King of León, in epic battles across the Peninsula against the Moors.

In 1085, when Alfonso VI of Castile captured Toledo, he and his Christian forces were so greatly feared by the Moors that they called upon the Almoravids for back-up. The Almoravids helped the Moors in their battles, but then decided to invade Iberia for themselves. Soon they held territories from Zaragoza to Valencia.

Though the Almoravids were strong, they only managed to hold on to Zaragzoa until 1118, at which point Alfonso I of Aragón came storming in with his troops and conquered the land. Upon his death, Aragón was united through royal marriage to Cataluña, thereby forming the fearsome Christian powerhouse of the Kingdom of Aragón.

Little by little the Iberian Peninsula was taking on the form it now has today. By 1200, Portugal had secured the borders of its independent Christian kingdom. Meanwhile, in what was to become Spain, the Christians suffered a few setbacks here and there, most notably their defeat by the Almohads at Alarcos (south of Toledo) in 1195. However, in 1212, the combined Christian forces from Castile, Aragón, and Navarra reached the culmination of their Reconquista at the battle of Las Navas de Tolosa in Andalucía. This victory marked the beginning of the end of Muslim Spain. Shortly thereafter, the Christians regained Extremadura and Mallorca (1229), Valencia (1230s), Córdoba (1236), and Sevilla (1248). By 1248, all that remained in the hands of the Moors was Granada.

Of the many things that Alfonso X El Sabio (the Wise) did during his rule over Castile from 1252 to 1284, the most significant was his declaration of Castilian (Spanish) as the official language of the people. He also proceeded with the Reconquista and was forced to face the Mudejar revolts in Andalucía and Murcia. He must have thought highly of himself, because in 1257, he sought election as emperor of the Holy Roman Empire. Alfonso X's reign was characterized by uprisings and revolts, some even coming from within his own family. Castilian nobility continued to challenge the throne until well into the 15th century.

Throughout this era, religious intolerance began to fester. The Christians and Muslims were already enemies, but by the turn of the 14th century, negative sentiment towards the Jews, known as Sephardim, had greatly increased. Under Christian rule, the only trade the Sephardim were allowed to practice was money-lending, as it was forbidden by the

Catholic Church. However, due to the constant inter-nobility warring and the Reconquista efforts against the Muslims, money-lenders were in high demand. The Jews prospered, inciting jealousy and hatred amongst their not-so-wealthy Christian counterparts, and eventually, a series of pogroms were unleashed in the 1390s. (See sidebar, *Jews in Spain*.)

Several generations of ineffectual monarchs throughout the land came to a halt in 1469 when Isabel I of Castile and Fernando II of Aragón wed, thus uniting two powerful kingdoms and consolidating their power into one nation: Spain, one of the first modern states of Renaissance Europe. The *Reyes Católicos* (Catholic Monarchs), whose reign officially began when Fernando II succeeded to the throne of Aragón in 1479, lived to become the most significant rulers in the history of Spain. León soon joined Castile and Aragón, and a formidable Spanish Christian force was formed.

The Fall of Granada

Isabel and Fernando wasted no time in redoubling the Reconquista efforts. They launched their final crusade against the Muslims in 1482. Though they had a mighty army funded by Jewish loans and the Catholic Church, it didn't take much to defeat the Moors in Granada, the last stronghold of Al-Andalus. Riddled with internal feuds, Granada soon erupted into civil war, which offered the Christians the perfect opportunity for victory. On January 2, 1492, Granada succumbed to the Christian forces. The Moors were ousted once and for all, giving rise to Spain as we know it today.

The Catholic Monarchs were surprisingly generous with the terms on surrender offered to Boabdil, the last emir of Muslim Spain. They gave him the Alpujarras valleys that lay just south of Granada and 30,000 gold coins. To the rest of the Muslims, religious tolerance was promised, but as it later turned out, Isabel and Fernando were not always true to their word.

The Inquisition

Founded in 1478 by the Catholic Monarchs, the purpose of the Inquisition was to root out all religious heresy and purify the land from the "infidels" that did not practice Catholicism—this meant Jews and Muslims. The Inquisition used brutal methods of torture to determine people's true religious loyalties. Although initially aimed at the Jews, eventually all Christians were potential suspects and traitors and could be called upon by the Inquisition, have their property seized by the state, and even murdered.

By 1492—the biggest year in Spanish history—Isabel and Fernando, with the help of their right-hand man, Tomás de Torquemada, head of the Inquisition, had succeeded in expelling some 200,000 Jews and countless Muslims from newly united Christian Spanish territory. Some went to North Africa, others to the New World on Columbus' ships, but 400,000 or so chose to stay behind and convert to Catholicism. Although some turned their back on their religion and assimilated into the Catholic tradition, many continued to uphold their age-old practices in secret. Regardless all *conversos* (Jewish converts) and *moriscos* (Muslim converts) were labeled *marranos* (pigs). In the eyes of the Catholic Monarchs, no ex-Jew or ex-Muslim would ever be worthy of equal status with the rest of Spain's citizens.

Over the 300 years in which the Spanish Inquisition was in full effect, it was responsible for the deaths of about 12,000 people. Although its power eventually waned, the establishment itself was not abolished until 1834 by Isabel II, and it was only in 1968 that Isabel and Fernando's Edict of Expulsion was officially revoked, at which point the first synagogue in almost half a millennia was established in Madrid.

THE NEW WORLD

By the late 1400s, Europeans were getting curious about what lay beyond the edges of their very incomplete map. Some maintained that the world was flat. Other believed there were monsters out there in the unknown. Italian explorer Christopher Columbus (Cristóbal Colón to Spaniards) was itching to find out.

Though Isabel and Fernando had funded

his crossing of the Atlantic in order to search for new trade routes to the Orient, he and his three ships that set sail from the Andalusian town of Palos de la Frontera in early August of 1492 never made it to Asia. After more than two months of sailing and near mutiny, crew-member Rodrigo de Triana cried land-ho! On October 12, 1492, the *Niña,* the *Pinta,* and the *Santa María* landed on the Bahamian island of Guanahaní, which Columbus renamed San Salvador.

Though Columbus and his 120 men were not the first Europeans to set foot in the New World (Viking Leif Eriksson arrived centuries before him), they were, indeed, the first to impact history with their contact with the Americas. They went on to discover Cuba and the island of Hispaniola before returning to Spain, where Columbus was received as a hero.

Columbus went on to make three more voyages to the New World. He found, among many other Caribbean islands, Jamaica and Trinidad, and established the city of Santo Domingo on Hispaniola (the modern day capital of the Dominican Republic). Finally, on his third and final voyage, he reached the mainland, on the Atlantic coast of Central and South America. Despite his hero status, Columbus died penniless in Valladolid in 1506.

After centuries of the Reconquista, Spain was well prepared to conquer, colonize, and exploit the new lands and their people. The Americas soon became the new frontier, and by the mid 1500s, Spain had occupied two key viceroyalties: Mayan Mexico and Incan Peru.

THE GOLDEN AGE

The Golden Age (1492–1570)—marked by what historian J. H. Elliot describes as "a ruthless… self-defeating quest for an unattainable purity"—was a busy time for Spain. Soon after the discovery of the New World, Spain began to colonize the lands. The native Incan, Aztec, and Mayan tribes were quickly conquered and converted to Catholicism. In return for the "priceless" gift of religion, Spanish conquistadors like Hernán Cortés and Vasco Nuñez de Balboa hoarded their gold and silver, and

it wasn't long before Spain had become the world's wealthiest nation.

Meanwhile, back on the Iberian Peninsula, Isabel and Fernando had occupied themselves with securing the rise of Spain to European glory by intermarrying their children with other European royalty such as the Austrian Hapsburgs. Certainly the endless flood of precious metals and agricultural products from Central and South America helped make their children—especially the mentally unstable ones—more attractive potential spouses. Their daughter, Juana la Loca (Joanna the Mad) and her German husband Felipe El Hermoso (Philip the Fair) inherited the Spanish throne upon the death of Isabel in 1504. However, Juana was deemed unfit to rule the fledgling Spain, and so Fernando resumed control until his own death in 1516. However, he did not die before annexing Navarra, thereby bringing all of Spain under one rule for the first time since Visigothic rule.

Shortly following Fernando's death, the

Madrid's Plaza de Oriente is lined with statues of Spain's long lineage of kings.

© CANDY LEE LABALLE

throne was turned over to Carlos I of Flanders, Juana La Loca's son. He ruled the country for 40 years, although he only lived 16 of them in Spain and didn't even speak any Spanish. During his reign, Spain expanded to include not only Castile and Aragón, but also the Italian and German dominions of the Hapsburgs. Eventually, it became the seat of the Holy Roman Empire when, in 1519, Carlos I was crowned Emperador Carlos V.

Throughout 16th-century Europe, it was generally accepted that religious unity was a necessary element of political unity—but only in Spain was the search for *pureza de sangre* (purity of blood) taken to the extreme. By 1525, all residents were officially Christian, but to ensure that no former Muslims and Jews secured governmental and other top positions, regulations were imposed on all candidates, thereby barring anyone whose ancestors had once been of another religion, no matter how far in the distant past.

The 16th century, commonly referred to as Spain's Golden Age, was a good time in Spanish history. The Catholic Monarchs had succeeded in "cleansing" the land of all religious traitors, the Americas were proving to be profitable investments, and Spain was emerging as one of Europe's foremost powers. Its naval fleet, the Spanish Armada, was the most advanced of the era and considered to be invincible.

In retrospect, the Golden Age actually marks the beginning of Spain's decay. Despite the plethora of goods and treasures streaming into the Iberian Peninsula from Mexico and Peru, most of the wealth went towards Carlos V's incessant wars throughout the Mediterranean. In 1556, Carlos V abdicated the throne and entered the monastery of Yuste. By the time his son, Felipe II, took over in 1558, Spain was hopelessly in debt.

When Felipe II came to power, the Spanish Empire had grown to cover the entire Iberian Peninsula, Central Europe, much of the Americas, and for a time, even England, during his brief stint as husband of Mary Tudor (Mary I). There was simply too much land for one king alone to control. Though he did move Spain's capital to Madrid and had the massive monastery-palace known as El Escorial constructed outside the city, Felipe II did Spain much more harm than good. While the homefront was riddled with widespread insurgency and revolt, the Catholic Felipe II was busy spending Spanish fortunes on Counter-Reformation efforts. In 1588, he sent his allegedly unshakable Spanish Armada to conquer England and its religious "heretics," the Protestants. The 125 ships were soundly defeated by Sir Francis Drake and his men. This loss marked the beginning of the rise of English power and the end of Spanish glory, a decline into darkness from which Spain did not fully recover until the establishment of a post-Franco democracy in the 1980s.

The so-called Spanish Golden Age is a rather contradictory notion. Spanish power reached its peak through conquest of the Americas and intermarriage with other European dynasties. Wealth flooded the country, and culture flourished. It was a time celebrated for its explosion of art, music, theater, and literature—styles that were imitated across Europe. However, it was also a time of great decadence, warfare, and waste. In essence, Spain suffered from itself.

With the death of Carlos II in 1700, the mighty Hapsburg dynasty came to a close, and shortly thereafter, the War of the Spanish Succession broke out between Spain, France, England, and Austria. When the war ended 14 years later, Spain lost Belgium, Luxemburg, Milan, Naples, Sardinia, Minorca, and Gibraltar. France declared Philip of Anjou (Felipe V) to be king and Spain fell under foreign dominion. Portugal, which had been united with Spain for 60 years under Felipe II, was returned to the Portuguese, the British gained control of Gibraltar in accordance with the Treaty of Utrecht of 1713, and the French occupied the rest of the Peninsula. Spain had now lost almost all its territories, a good portion of its population, and most of its wealth.

BOURBON DYNASTY

The French Felipe V was the first in a long line of foreign royalty to rule Spain. Over the course of his rule, Spain passed through three distinct phases: guidance from France, independence, and finally, equilibrium with their mighty neighboring country. Though he ruled Spain from abroad for over 40 years, he did contribute significantly to the development of the country. He is remembered for building the Palacio Real in Madrid and La Granja in Segovia and for ushering in the Enlightenment, a period of great reform, advances in interior development, and congruous foreign relations.

Upon the death of Felipe V in 1759, Carlos III was named to the throne. Unlike past rulers, this leader actually sought to keep Spain out of conflict rather than in the line of fire. He reorganized the nation's infrastructure, reformed its agriculture, and improved upon modern urban planning. He gave Spanish citizenship and equal status to the Gypsies and enforced early childhood education. By all accounts, Carlos III was a noble ruler.

Though he is commemorated throughout Spain, no city celebrates Carlos III more than Madrid, where a university (Universidad Carlos III) and various statues have been erected in his honor, most notably in the Puerta del Sol. Madrid is right to remember Carlos III so fondly: single-handedly, he transformed Spain's capital from just another *pueblo* of Castilla-La Mancha into the elegant capital that it is today.

During the reign of Carlos III, which lasted until 1788, the Enlightenment flourished on Spanish soil. Despite characteristic initial resistance to new ideas and thinking, eventually the nation's intellectuals became receptive to these innovations, and Spain began pumping out top architects, geographers, engineers and naturalists. Although they never penetrated the ruling and political classes, democratic ideas drawn from the nearby French Revolution even managed to worm their way into 18th-century Spanish culture.

THE PENINSULAR WAR

France's revolutionary ideas weren't the only thing to spill over into Spain. At the turn of the 19th century, the Revolution itself made its way into Spain. After a short-lived alliance with the French, which peaked with the British defeat of a Franco-Spanish fleet at Trafalgar, Napoleon and his troops marched onto the Iberian Peninsula. He declared his younger brother, Joseph, ruler of Spain, thereby replacing the Bourbons with the Bonapartes. Once again, Spain found itself in the hands of foreign dominion.

Few Spaniards were willing to accept the new French monarchy, as they considered it to be both illegitimate and a product of treason. On May 2, 1808, they rose up in revolt, initiating the brutal, six-year Peninsula War—known in Spain as the Guerra de Independencia. Painter Francisco Goya chronicled the two bloodiest days of the war in his famous paintings *Dos de mayo* and *Tres de mayo,* both of which hang on the walls of the Prado museum in Madrid.

The Peninsular War was a landmark event for Spain in that it solidified the concept of Spanish nationality. With the enforcement of Spain's first constitution in the city Cádiz on March 12, 1812, Spain entered a new phase in its long history, one that has endured into the present day: constitutionalism. Since 1812, an additional 69 constitutions have been drawn up, including the most recent one from 1978.

In 1813, with the help of the English, Spain finally succeeded in wresting control from the French. However, six years of war had taken their toll on the land, leaving it poor and ravaged. From there on out, it was all downhill for Spain. By 1833, the majority of Spanish American colonies had gained their independence from the weakening "mother country," reducing the territories of the formerly vast Spanish Empire to just Cuba, Puerto Rico, and the Philippines.

CARLIST WARS

If losing land weren't enough to trouble the Spanish, constant internal warfare was. Upon the death of Fernando VII without a male heir, the crown was passed to his daughter Isabel II, an event that marked the revocation of the prohibition on female succession. However, Isabel II's legendary uncle Don Carlos contested Isabel's claim to the throne and won the fanatical support of traditionalists who maintained that female succession was illegitimate. Carlos and his mighty military forces thus proceeded to embroil the Peninsula in a series of petty wars known as the Guerras Carlistas, the Carlist Wars. Over the course of several decades, these wars shook the entire nation as noble families struggled for power.

THE MID-19TH CENTURY

While Spain was preoccupied with their ever-diminishing national and international power, the rest of Europe and the United States entered the Industrial Revolution. The technological, socio-economical, and cultural changes that Spain missed out on during this era left it floundering in the dust, hopelessly isolated from the modern world.

Mid-19th century Spain is characterized by rapid turnover in the seat of power. In 1843, General Narvaez deposed General Espatero, who served as regent of the kingdom for a grand total of two years. Shortly thereafter, in 1854, Leopoldo O'Donnell rebelled against Narvaez and got a shot at being Prime Minister of Spain. Although O'Donnell's 12 years in power saw only modest economic gains, mainly in the already-industrialized Cataluña and País Vasco, foreign investors were encouraged to provide Spain with a railroad, and some overseas expansion in Africa was sponsored. In 1866, O'Donnell was ousted by a military coup. Two years later, Queen Isabel was successfully overthrown by an army revolt headed by Generals Serrano and Prim. Upon the assassination of General Prim in 1870, Amadeo of Savoy, the Duke of Aosta, became king of Spain. However, just three years later, Amadeo I was forced to abdicate the throne, at which point a republic was proclaimed.

THE FIRST REPUBLIC

Spain's First Republic, which lasted just eight months, was built on the principle of internally self-governing provinces bound to the federal government by voluntary agreement. This style of government, which is similar to the one in place in modern Spain, was an excellent idea. However, in its short existence, the First Republic was faced with more problems than any single political entity could reasonably handle. Between 1873 and 1874, Spain dealt with the war in Cuba, the third Carlist War, and uprisings in the south and southeast of the country. After four shaky presidencies, a military *pronunciamiento* (declaration of principles) restored the Bourbon monarchy with Alfonso XII at the head as king. However, the guise of this constitutional monarchy barely covered its true purpose as an interim military dictatorship.

Alfonso XII's rule came as somewhat of a relief, even to republic supporters. He cultivated good relations with the army and brought Carlism to an end. He also brokered an end to the 10-year struggle in Cuba by signing the Peace of Zanjon treaty promising the island more autonomy, and enabled Spain to establish a relatively stable government. When he died in 1885, his son Alfonso XIII assumed control of the land. However, his mother, Queen María Cristina de Hapsburgo y Lorena, acted as regent until 1902, whereupon Alfonso XIII came of age and was crowned King of Spain. But his glory days were numbered.

SPANISH-AMERICAN WAR

Emigration from Spain to Cuba was heavy in the 19th century and the emergence of a sizable middle and upper class on the island with very strong ties to Spain meant it was in Spain's interest to keep the Caribbean island Spanish. Minor insurgencies occurred periodically beginning in 1868, but Spain always managed to keep the Cuban revolutionaries from breaking away. However in 1895, the Cuban fight for independence began in earnest. Hostilities—clandestinely supported by the U.S.—escalated, and in less than three years, the U.S. declared war on Spain.

The fighting did not last long. Although the Spanish had pledged to defend Cuba "to the last peseta," without aid from the rest of Europe (Germany excluded), the Peninsula was hopeless at the hands of the Americans, the rising world power. Within a matter of months, the U.S. managed to destroy the remains of the once mighty Spanish empire. Cuba, Puerto Rico, and the Philippines, the last of Spain's colonies, were turned over to the victors.

THE EARLY 20TH CENTURY

Though 1898 was a year of big loss for Spain, it did gain one thing: Morocco. In the same year that it lost its last territories, Spain—along with France—took on this North African country as a protectorate, a move that would soon prove a source of internal friction. Although warring against the Berber tribes went unabated until 1926, the Spanish government refused to supply its troops with adequate supplies. Spain sustained heavy losses, as their opponents were both stronger and better equipped.

Spain never fully recovered from the Spanish-American War. The delicate state of both its economy and society led to great internal tension and instability, which was expressed throughout the Peninsula in a number of ways. The most pacifistic was the formation of the intellectual group called La generación del '98 (The Generation of '98), which maintained that Spain had long ago ceased to be of any worldly importance. These harsh but true accusations wounded the pride of this once noble nation.

A second outgrowth of the Spanish-American War were nationalist movements within Spain itself. That the Spanish colonies could succeed in breaking away from the mother country motivated the more progressive regions of Calaluña, País Vasco, and Galicia to begin their own campaigns for freedom from the dying Castilian government.

One of the more aggressive ways that Spaniards demonstrated their state of turmoil was through anarchical uprisings. Riots against conscription for the unjust war in Morocco—which often were characterized by church burnings— were commonplace throughout Spain. However, the most volatile region of all was Barcelona, where street fighting erupted in 1909 in what is known as the Semana Trágica (Tragic Week). With so many problems back at home, it's no wonder that Spain chose to remain neutral when World War I broke out in 1914.

General Primo de Rivera

While the rest of Europe and the U.S. were busy fighting each other, Spain was preoccupied with rapidly rising prices and a diminishing European market, which produced an even greater measure of instability. In 1917, the General Parliamentary Assembly held in Barcelona introduced both constitutional reforms and a general strike in August of that year. Spain's high levels of anarchical and communist terrorism, failing economy, and war in Morocco provided General Primo de Rivera with the perfect opportunity to seize control.

On September 13, 1923, a coup d'etat brought Primo de Rivera into office. Supported by the masses, Primo de Rivera also held the confidence of the king and the loyalty of the army. During his seven-year rule over Spain in a mild authoritarian regime through a Military Directory, he actually managed to significantly improve the country's conditions. He ended the war in Morocco, curbed unemployment rates through public works, and boosted the economy. However, General Primo de Rivera fell short on numerous accounts: having abolished Parliament, not only did he fail in restoring the former constitutional government of the 19th century, but he didn't succeed in creating a replacement political system at all. Over time, support—civilian, royal, and military— for Primo de Rivera plummeted. In 1930, he resigned and died shortly thereafter in exile.

THE SECOND REPUBLIC

The municipal elections of 1931 favored the anti-monarchist parties. King Alfonso XIII was wise to interpret the elections and subsequent riots as a premonition of a future civil war, and thus, he packed up his family and belongings and attempted to rule the kingdom from abroad with military aid. However, upon learning that that the army would not back the throne this time, Alfonso XIII was forced to abdicate and was exiled to Italy. On April 14, the Segunda República (Second Republic) was proclaimed.

The goals of the Second Republic were lofty, including everything from social and economic reform to the granting of regional autonomy and the separation of church and state. The former revolutionary committee formed the new provisional government, with Niceto Alcala Zamora as president. Elections were called for in June of that year.

Spain's first general election gave the seat of power to the Izquierda Republicana (IR, Leftist Republicans) coalition leader Manuel Azaña and the Partido Socialista Obrero Español (PSOE, Spanish Socialist Worker's Party) labor leader Francisco Largo Caballero. The mission of this new government would be to gradually introduce socialism through the democratic process. However, this unique form of government backfired, as the gradualism alienated the political left and the socialism the right.

Azaña shocked the world with his progressive social values, which at that time were revolutionary not only for Spain but for the rest of the world as well. The new constitution, drawn up in December 1931, gave women the vote, legalized abortion and divorce, abolished Catholicism as the nation's official religion, separated religion from education, and gave Cataluña a measure of autonomy by granting it the right to have its own parliament. For a country that for hundreds of years had lived a life of repression and uniformity, the Second Republic, which lasted just five short years, provided the people with a much-needed breath of fresh air.

When the next elections rolled around in 1933, the right received the majority of the votes due to lack of unity on the left, anarchist disruption, and an economic slump. The new group in power was a Catholic party known as Confederación Española de Derechas Autónomas (CEDA, Spanish Confederation of Autonomous Rights). Along with CEDA, other political entities formed around this time, most significantly the fascist Falange, backed by the Church and military and led by José Antonio Primo de Rivera, the former dictator's son. Far from a pacifistic bunch, members of the Falange made a name for themselves in street violence.

Despite the advanced society that Azaña's government built, the Second Republic was doomed even before it began and ultimately served only to further polarize the Spanish populace. In 1934, the state of general chaos increased. In protest of CEDA's participation in the government, mini-revolutions swept over highly industrialized regions, particularly Cataluña and Asturias. Labor strikes were the labor unions' choice of political weapon. When Asturian miners went on strike that year—openly supported by Azaña—rising General Francisco Franco and his cohort General José Millán Astray, crushed the rebellion, thereby confirming to each political extreme that the other could not be trusted. The nation had been sliced in two and was on the brink of civil war.

The miners' strike had definitively divided Spain into the left-wing IR and the right-wing Partido Comunista de España (PCE, Communist Party of Spain), with the radical left of PSOE and the radical right of Falange thrown into the bag along with a few additional parties. A new general election was called for February 1936 and the left-wing Popular Front defeated the rightist National Front by a narrow margin and Azaña became President of the Republic. However, the Popular Front's mission was not to form a stable government but rather to defeat the right. The violence continued, with a growing number of extremist and revolutionary groups on both sides. Church burnings, street riots, and politically motivated assassinations were becoming commonplace.

SPANISH CIVIL WAR

Following the assassination on July 12, 1936 of prominent right-wing leader Calvo Sotelo, the Spanish North African military garrison in Melilla rose up on July 17 against the left-wing government and the Spanish Civil War began. The next day, many more garrisons throughout Spain followed suit, led by five generals including Francisco Franco. On July 19, Franco flew to Melilla to take control of the troops. In September, Franco was named head of the Nationalist government and commander of the armed forces with the rank of *generalísimo* (most high general) and title of *el caudillo* (leader). By the end of the year, the Nationalists—supported by Italian and German troops—had taken a large part of Andalucía, Extremadura, many important cities in Castilla la Vieja, Galicia, País Vasco, Navarra, Aragón, and the Canary and Balearic Islands. By this time, all that remained in the hands of the Republicans—backed by the International Brigades (made up of foreign volunteers, including 2,000 Americans)—was Castilla la Nueva, Cataluña, Valencia, Murcia, Almería, and a few cities in País Vasco and Asturias. However, among these territories were the very strategic cities of Barcelona and Madrid.

Franco and his compatriot, General Emilio Mola, established the seat of their government at Burgos, a northern Castilian city. Franco, a well-trained, first-rate army professional, easily gained the confidence and respect of his subordinates. At 33, he was Europe's youngest general since Napoleon Bonaparte.

Franco was a man with a mission, and his number one goal was to separate the Republican Cataluña, Valencia and Murcia from Madrid. However, the Republicans were unwilling to go out without a fight and managed to fend of the Nationalists for three years. In 1937, the Nationalists secured Asturias, Cantabria, and the rest of País Vasco. Some of the most vicious fighting occurred in the desolate regions of Aragón. The Nationalists firmly held Zaragoza, and the Republicans wanted it to solidify a position in the north. In July of 1938, the area broke out into the Battle of the Ebro. Though the Republicans began strong, they were no match for the Nationalists' air support. When it ended four months later, nearly 37,000 men were dead. It is considered one of the decisive battles in the war and the start of the downfall of the Republican forces.

The Civil War was not a fair fight. While the Republicans managed to industrialized areas, most notably Madrid, for the entirety of the war, the Nationalists held all the food-producing areas and willingly used food embargoes and starvation tactics against Nationalist strongholds. Moreover, the Republicans did not have a regular trained army and relied upon the forces of the workers' militia and independently organized armed political units, such as the Partido Obrero de Unificación Marxista (Trotskyite Worker's Party of Marxist Unification). As the name suggests, this group was backed by Soviet communists, who supplied arms and munitions to the republic from day one of the war until Stalin lost interest in the ailing republic in 1938, one year short of the Nationalist victory.

While the Republicans had to rely upon faulty Soviet military aid, the Nationalists were able to form their own regular army and enjoyed the support of foreign troop. Some 91,000 Italians were sent over by the fascist dictator Benito Mussolini and 20,000 troops arrived from Nazi Germany. The German Condor Legion later became known for the infamous bombing of the tiny Basque town of Gernika (Guernica) in April 1937, commemorated by Pablo Picasso in his masterpiece *Guernica*.

With the start of 1938, the remains of the Republic crumbled rapidly. Barcelona fell in January and Valencia, the Republic's temporary capital, in March. Though Madrid, the only Republican city still standing, managed to resist the enemy for a bit longer, on March 28, 1939, the Nationalists prevailed. They entered the city unchallenged and victorious. Three days later, on April 1, the war was over.

Though the Spanish Civil War lasted only three years, it managed to devastate the once mighty nation, dissolving villages, friendships, and even families along the way. Both sides were equally guilty of bloody atrocities, employing death squads and mass shootings and hangings to eliminate the "enemy." By the time the fighting came to a halt estimated 350,000 people—the majority of them civilians—had died. Yet, that figure is hotly debated, with some scholars suggesting the deaths reached nearly a million.

FRANCO'S RULE

The end of the Civil War marked the beginning of the rule of General Francisco Franco. For four decades, Franco ruled over Spain in a strict military dictatorship that stifled all opposition and alienated the outside world. It is not easy for one man to take control of an entire nation, particularly one as volatile as Spain. Thus, Franco's dictatorship was turned to the most powerful institution in the country—the Catholic Church. With the support of the Church, Franco created what Pope Pius XII declared as the model Catholic State, an example to the rest of the world. In reality, Catholicism served as a form of governmental repression.

When Franco became absolute dictator of Spain, he inherited a broken nation. Military force and repression on a massive scale was the only method he had for dominating a bitter and divided people. Countless Spaniards were taken captive as political prisoners, thousands were executed as enemies of the state, and so many more were thrown into exile. Franco relied upon the idea of uniformity to help build his nation. Under his rule, all political parties were illegal except for the National Movement, and the only legal trade union was the government-run Sindicato Vertical. He set an early example for what would happen to anyone who dared to contradict his regime with the 1940 shooting of Lluís Companys, the president of the Catalán government. The independently minded Catalans, Basques, and Galicians were targeted. Spanish was declared the one and only language of Spain and all regional languages—Catalán, Euskera (Basque), and Gallego (Galician)—were banned under severe penalty. Ironically, Franco himself was born in Galicia.

Regional identities weren't the only thing Franco stifled in his years as dictator. As a staunch Nationalist, he hunted all leftists, from the moderate, democratic left to communists and anarchists. His alliance with the Church encouraged him to declare Catholicism the official religion of Spain and all its people. Under Franco, no other religions were practiced, and atheists and gypsies, in particular, were persecuted. All of the progressive rights granted to the people under the Second Republic—civil union, divorce, female suffrage—were revoked. Women were no longer allowed to hold jobs once they were married and were forced to live at home and serve their husbands and families. So severely did the dictatorship fall upon women that they did not even have the right to choose how they dressed; by law, women could only wear dresses and skirts. Under Franco, a self-professed anti-academic, hundreds of intellectuals, scientists, writers, educators, and artists were forced to take refuge in neighboring countries or risk death by firing squad. Their absence rendered Spain devoid of life and culture.

Spain and World War II

While General Franco was busy establishing his new government, war broke out in Europe in September 1939. The other European fascists, Hitler and Mussolini, had both provided Franco with military aid during the Spanish Civil War and expected Franco to join on their side. Franco infuriated them when he chose to keep Spain out of the war.

Though Spain did not actively fight in World War II, it did play an important role, as it offered refuge to roughly 50,000 Jews fleeing Nazi persecution. However, once the war was over, most of the world turned its back on Spain and its dictatorship. The nation was denied entry to NATO and the United Nations, which actually sponsored a trade boycott that led to what was later known as *los años de hambre* (the years of hunger) of the 1940s, an intense period of starvation and poverty.

Economic Recovery

The post-war years did not treat Spain well. In addition to economic crisis, Franco was constantly fighting off small, leftist guerilla units in the north, Andalucía, and Extremadura. However, in the early 1950s, U.S. President Eisenhower took an interest in Spain. With the onset of the Cold War, Spain provided a key geographical location. In exchange for large sums of financial aid, the U.S. was permitted to establish four military bases on Spanish soil. The deal was sealed with Pact of Madrid, signed on Eisenhower's visit to Spain in 1953. Two years later, Spain was admitted to the United Nations.

Life in Spain began to improve. In 1959, under the new Stabilization Plan of the Catholic group Opus Dei, the peseta (then Spain's currency) was devalued in order to decrease the rate of inflation. This resulted in a great improvement in the Spanish economy. Modern technology and techniques were introduced to Spain, and economic aid continued to pour in from the U.S., either in the form of actual capital or by allowing over a million Spaniards to get jobs overseas.

However, the real source of Spain's recovery came not from abroad but from within: tourism. Whereas during the previous two decades hardly any foreigners had visited Spain, by 1965, the number had soared to over 14 million a year, most of which took advantage of Spain's excellent climate on the Mediterranean coast.

The 1950s is remembered as a time of great economic growth in Spain. However, other important events occurred simultaneously, most notably, Spain's retreat from Morocco. In 1956, Franco reached an agreement with Moroccan sultan Sidi Mohamed ben Yusef to end the Spanish protectorate over Morocco, and in 1958, Spain handed over control of Tarfaya (in Southern Morocco) to the Moroccan government. However, Spain held on to the Western Sahara region until the 1970s and to this day maintains two Spanish cities, Ceuta and Melilla, on the North African coast. Spain's other African colony, Equatorial Guinea, did not gain its independence until 1968.

Franco's Last Decade

By the 1960s, Franco had relaxed considerably in his policy making. Spaniards were subjected to far less cultural censorship than before. However, military presence—Franco's main means of controlling the people—was ever noticeable, with Guardia Civil (military police force) officers on every street corner with submachine guns, just waiting for someone to act out against the regime.

Although Franco restored the Spanish monarchy in 1947, he never bothered to designate a monarch. However, in 1969, Juan Carlos de Borbón was officially invested with the title of Crown Prince and Franco named him as his successor with the title of King.

As Franco's years in power wore on, tensions in the country resurfaced. Unemployment rates began to climb. Regional issues arose once more, this time in the form of the Basque separatist terrorist group called Euskadi Ta Azkatasuna (ETA, Basque Homeland and Liberty). With every terrorist attack, it became clearer that Franco was slipping.

By 1973, Franco had forfeited his position as prime minister of Spain, keeping only his positions as official head of the country and commander-in-chief of the military forces. The seat of the prime ministry was turned over to Luís Carrero Blanco, who, through cautious reforms provoked a violent reaction from right-wing extremists. On December 20, 1973, he was assassinated by a strategically placed car bomb, the culmination of ETA's activity. When Franco died on November 20, 1975, the state of the nation was not looking good.

Franco's Legacy

For a man who ruled the nation for four decades, few physical traces remain of Franco today. Many places named in his honor (every town had a main street called "Calle del Generalísimo") have since changed their names, and nearly all the monuments dedicated to him have been torn down. However, Franco did succeed in leaving a lasting impression on Spanish culture. Like his predecessors, Franco encouraged Spain to follow a path of exclusion. Having spent so many decades and centuries in isolation, Spain had a difficult time opening itself up to new ideas and people after Franco, a challenge it has struggled with into the present day.

DEMOCRATIC TRANSITION

Two days after the death of Spain's dictator, 37-year-old King Juan Carlos I took the throne. The Spain that was so eager for democracy had little hopes from Franco's former ally. However, Juan Carlos I shocked the nation when he declared a democracy. In 1976, he deposed prime minister Arias Navarro, replacing him with Adolfo Suárez. Political parties, trade unions, and strikes were all legalized, the Nationalist Movement was all but eliminated per royal decree, and the first general national election in 41 years was called for June 15, 1977.

Constitutional Democracy

Suárez's centrist Unión de Centro Democrático (UCD) party won almost half of the seats in the new Cortes (congress), formed as a result of the 1977 elections. Coming in at a close second was the left-of-center PSOE, led by Felipe Gonzalez. The Cortes began a constituent process with the end result being a new Constitution, ratified by universal suffrage on December 6, 1978. Spain was well on its way to becoming a stable democracy.

During Suárez's time as prime minister, Cataluña, País Vasco, Galicia, and Andalucía were all approved for statutes for self-government, something that would have been unheard of just five years earlier. By 1983, Spain had been divided into its present-day 17 autonomous communities with individual regional governments with elected parliament representatives.

The fledgling democracy floundered for a moment in 1981. In January, Suárez resigned and Leopoldo Calvo Sotelo was elected. On the day of his inauguration, February 23, Antonio Tejero, a lieutenant-colonel of the Guardia Civil, led a coup d'etat, storming the Cortes with troops and taking the prime minister and several parliamentary leaders hostage. That evening, King Juan Carlos I, dressed in full military regalia, appeared on television, commanded the Spanish military to step down, and promised the people that democracy would proceed. The coup ended and to this day King Juan Carlos is revered in Spain.

Freedom of Expression

After so many years of repression, the 1980s served as an outlet for creative personal and social growth in Spain. Homosexuality, divorce, and contraceptives were all legalized. The once forbidden artistic and intellectual life came alive. Spain underwent a sexual and creative revolution. This was the era of *la movida,* the all-night party scene that began in Madrid as an excuse to do everything that hadn't been allowed under Franco; in other words, sex, drugs, and rock and roll. Pedro Almodóvar, the multi-Oscar-winning film director, was a key figure in this movement and made his first films in Madrid during this time.

The PSOE

In the elections of 1982, PSOE secretary general Felipe Gonzaléz won the vote. In his 14 years as Prime Minister, Spain flourished. Although unemployment levels rose significantly, the middle class grew exponentially and women moved out of the home and into the universities and work force. A national health system was created, and state education was drastically improved, increasing university enrollment to over a million students by the early 1990s.

The PSOE was in power during some of modern Spain's most important events. In the mid 1980s, Spain joined NATO and then later, in 1986, it entered the European Union, which brought on an economic upswing that carried Spain into the 1990s. In the subsequent elections in 1986, 1989, and 1993, the PSOE also triumphed. Meanwhile, the Partido Popular (PP, Popular Party), a more conservative, right-wing party whose roots were firmly Francoist, emerged as the second-most influential political power.

MODERN SPAIN

1992—the 500th anniversary of the most important year in Spanish history—was a big one. Spain did what it does best—celebrate. The Expo '92 World Fair was held in Sevilla and the summer Olympics took over Barcelona. Meanwhile, the PSOE's economy hit an all-time low, with unemployment at nearly 23 percent and the government entangled in a web of scandals. The slump bottomed out in 1993, but the scandals only multiplied. Luis Roldán, the head of the Guardia Civil from 1986 to 1993, disappeared in 1994 following charges with embezzlement and bribery. The following year he was arrested in Thailand and jailed for

28 years in Spain. Similar stories were all too common in the early and mid-1990s.

The scandals eventually proved to be the downfall of the PSOE's hold on the government. The biggest outrage of all involved the Grupos Antiterroristas de Liberación (GAL, Antiterrorist Groups of Liberation), a government-sponsored group that systematically murdered 28 suspected ETA terrorists, several of whom were later found innocent. When the elections rolled around again in 1996, the PSOE was defeated by the PP.

PP Rule

Headed by Aznar, the PP led Spain through eight years of solid economic progress. They liberalized the telecommunications sector, which ended the monopoly of the one and only Spanish phone company, Telefónica. However, the most important reformation made was employment. While severance pay was reduced, it became easier for the young, the middle-aged, and the long-term unemployed to get jobs. Thus, the unemployment rate began to drop rapidly. The economy was further bolstered by the abandonment of the peseta and adoption of the euro currency in January 1999. By the year 2000, Spain had successfully created the fastest growing economy in the EU.

Aznar and the PP won again in the 2000 elections. At the time, the PSOE was led by Joaquín Almunia, who was shortly thereafter replaced by José Luis Rodríguez Zapatero, who immediately swept out all past PSOE influences to start anew.

Aznar continued his previous trend of economic progress, lowering unemployment to just 11 percent and was only slightly deterred by the *Prestige* oil spill off the coast of Galicia. He took a hard approach towards ETA, which by this point was responsible for 800 deaths and countless kidnappings, robberies, and bombings. ETA's political wing, Batasuna, was outlawed in 2002 and Aznar refused to negotiate with ETA unless they renounced all forms of violence.

One of Aznar's important policies came into effect after the September 11, 2001 attacks on the United States. Standing firmly behind the U.S. and Great Britain, Aznar shipped 1,300 troops to Iraq. However, the war in Iraq was extremely unpopular back in Spain, with polls showing 90 percent of the population opposed. Aznar's time as prime minister was nearly up.

Madrid Bombings

On March 11, 2004, several bombs exploded on the Madrid commuter trains during the morning rush hour just days before the election. Deaths totaled 192 and injuries topped 1,800. Everyone's first thought was that it must be ETA. However, it was soon discovered that ETA, in fact, had nothing to do with the bombings and that an Islamic extremist group linked to Al-Qaida was the responsible party.

Many believed that the terrorist attack would directly influence the upcoming elections, but no such connection was ever able to be proven. Zapatero and the socialist PSOE came away from the election victorious.

Upon entering office as the Spanish Prime Minister, Zapatero pulled the troops out of Iraq and then set about instituting a host of social changes, including granting full marriage and adoption rights to homosexual couples. He also worked to further the process of the Statute for Cataluña's autonomy and has initiated a peace process with ETA and discussions with the País Vasco for their own autonomy goals. Meanwhile, the opposition PP, under the leadership of Mariano Rajoy, has unleashed a full attack on the PSOE government, going so far as to accuse them of orchestrating the March 11 attacks. The disputes between the two parties, as well as the continual, passionate debates over questions of autonomy, increasing unemployment, and a soaring cost of living, has brought Spain back to a time of political uncertainty. The next elections are scheduled for 2008. Expect even more changes.

Government

The present government of Spain was established in the 1978 constitution as a parliamentary monarchy. The democratically elected government handles the day-to-day affairs of the country while a monarchial king has political power that is rarely evoked. The prime minister, currently José Luis Rodriquez Zapatero (elected on April 17, 2004), is responsible to the Cortes Generales, a national assembly or parliament made up of two chambers. The current king is Juan Carlos I, who has held that position since 1975 and is expected to continue in that role until his death and succession by his son, Prince Felipe.

ORGANIZATION

Spain's national government is organized into three bodies according to function: executive, legislative, and judicial. The executive branch, led by the prime minister, consists of the Consejo de Ministros (Council of Ministers), whose members are appointed by the prime minister usually from within his or her own political party. The position of deputy prime minister, or vice president, is a non-mandatory position that can be filled at the discretion of the prime minister. The legislative branch consists of two houses, Congreso de los Diputados (Congress of Deputies) and Senado (Senate), each of which is composed of elected members who serve four-year terms. Together, they make up the Cortes Generales and their main job is to create laws, produce budgets, and generally manage the government. The most significant difference between the two houses is in their respective legislative abilities. The power to create and approve laws rests firmly with the Congreso. The Senado can ratify or even oppose various laws, but the Congreso has the final say. At the top of the judicial branch is the Tribunal Supremo (Supreme Court). The rest of the judiciary system consists of an array of professional judges and magistrates. The king is officially the head of state and commander in chief of the military. In practice,

however, the monarchs do not exercise this power; rather they function as diplomats. In addition to these national bodies, Spain consists of 17 autonomous communities similar in structure to state-level governments in the United States. These communities also have their own executive, legislative, and judicial institutions. This duplication of offices and functions contributes to much of Spain's infamous bureaucratic red tape.

POLITICAL PARTIES

On a surface level, Spain has a fairly straightforward political system with two dominant parties—the Partido Socialista Obrero Español (Socialist Workers' Party), or PSOE, and the Partido Popular (People's Party), or PP. In practice, however, Spain has a very diverse group of national political parties, many with strong regional affiliations, due

© CANDY LEE LABALLE

Spain's Congreso de los Diputados is located in Madrid.

to the country's complicated makeup of autonomous regions and communities.

The PSOE, which took control of the government in 2004, is generally considered left of center and liberal. The PP is a moderate right-wing group; it firmly held power until 2004, when dissatisfaction with former Prime Minister José María Aznar's political tactics and his handling of the war in Iraq led to an upset in the elections and a shift in power. The PP still holds a majority in parliament, and its leader, Mariano Rajoy, is a major figure in Spanish politics and is expected to make a run for prime minister in the next elections.

Izquierda Unida, the United Left, is the third most-powerful party. Though it has little hope of ever winning the majority in Parliament, its presence is significant enough to draw attention—and votes—from the more dominant parties.

The most significant regional parties are the Convergence and Union (CIU) in Cataluña and the Basque Nationalist Party (PNV) in the Basque Country. Both regions are vehemently seeking increased independence and are very active on the national scene. The Basque situation is complicated by the terrorist group Euskadi Ta Askatasuna (Basque Homeland and Freedom), more commonly known as ETA. It has claimed responsibility for dozens of bombings that have caused over 800 deaths. In March 2006, ETA declared a permanent ceasefire and its political wing Batsuna began seeking representation at the negotiations on Basque autonomy. This has driven a divisive and volatile wedge between the PSOE and the PP, with the former advocating prudence and the latter refusing to negotiate with any group related to ETA. This confrontation has colored all aspects of Spanish politics and effectively stifled the government's ability to get anything done.

POLITICAL FUTURE

The future of Spanish politics is unclear. The divisions in modern Spanish politics have allowed a number of separatist-driven states to evolve into highly represented bodies. By the end of 2006, Cataluña was deep in the process of obtaining far-reaching autonomy from the central Spanish government. Meanwhile, the Basque movement for regional autonomy is embroiled in the controversy over whether to allow Batsuna to participate in talks. Though outcomes are still hazy, a dynamic restructuring of Spain in the next few years is entirely possible.

On an international level, Spaniards are ever aware of the changing global community. Issues such as the "war on terror" have recently stirred up political debate. It is acknowledged that the change in power and the appointment of Zapatero as prime minister was aided, if not directly caused, by the Madrid bombings in March 2004. The elections took place just two days after the attack. Continuing problems with immigration—Spanish coastal towns in the south and in the Canary Islands are inundated by African immigrants—are also sure to affect the future of Spanish politics. Meanwhile, Spanish politics and government are also affected by the European Union. As more nations are accepted into the Union and the body continues to grow, Spain's EU representatives and political leaders will have their hands full ushering the new Spain into an even newer Europe.

JUDICIAL AND PENAL SYSTEMS

The Spanish judicial system is divided based on the severity of crimes. Minor violations are dealt with and decided locally, while all other violations are decided within courts composed of professional judges. Major offenses that carry a maximum six-year prison sentence are decided in single magistrate penal courts. The remaining major offenses are resolved by three-member penal chambers, which are present in all of Spain's provinces. Finally, the Penal Chamber of the Supreme Court deals with offenses that merit review above the provincial level. As in the United States, all of the higher courts also have the responsibility to review and decide on appeals from the lower levels. Spain's constitution has little or no recognition for special courts outside of civil, family courts, and juvenile courts.

Citizens can be charged with two classifications of offenses—*delitos* (serious) and *faltas* (less serious). Often the choice between the two is made solely on the grounds of which is more likely to be indictable. The age of criminal responsibility in Spain is 16 years.

Spain's penal system overall is more lenient than that of the United States. The death penalty is non-existent and a murder conviction is normally punished by 20–30 years of imprisonment. Drug offenses are considered serious, depending on quantity and intentions, but on an average, carry far less serious sentences than in the United States.

Economy

Currently the fifth-largest in Western Europe, Spain's economy has been growing steadily for the last three decades. The Spanish GDP hovers at just over US$1 trillion. Though tourism is the main source of revenue, a housing and building boom in the early 2000s has sparked unprecedented growth and made Spain an economic model for the rest of Europe. However, there is also fear of backlash as the inflated housing market, lingering unemployment, and increasing interest rates threaten to harm the economy.

Agriculture

Agriculture has long been one of Spain's most important industries. Though agriculture as a whole has been declining in importance to the overall economy, the two main agricultural products—grapes and olives—are still highly in demand and fuel the country's large wine and olive oil industries. Other important agricultural products include oranges, tomatoes, onions, grains, and almonds.

Tourism and Other Industries

The biggest industries in the country are tourism, textiles, apparel (including footwear), food and beverages, metals, and machinery. Of these, tourism is the most important. Spain is the second-most popular country for tourism in the world and welcomes over 50 million visitors per year. Visitors pumped US$45.2 billion into the Spanish economy in 2004. That figure is poised only to increase.

Building

Since the late 1990s, Spain has undergone an explosive building boom. In 2004, it provided for nearly 10 percent of the Spanish GDP. New housing construction that year exceeded that of Germany, France, and Italy combined. Despite this huge construction boom, the cost of housing has skyrocketed over the last eight years by nearly 200 percent. Salaries have not kept pace and Spaniards are mortgaging themselves into lifelong debt to afford even the smallest of homes—a 50-year mortgage is not uncommon. It is estimated that homeowners now pay over 55 percent of their salaries towards their mortgage. Meanwhile, inflation rates have been climbing slowly. If they continue to do so, many mortgage holders will not be able to meet their payments. Many economists have labeled the housing boom a real estate bubble and are predicting that it will burst.

Economic Future

Spain's economic policymakers have no small obstacle in front of them. The future of Spain's economy is far from certain. Despite economic growth rates predicted at nearly 3 percent for 2006, economists warn that Spain could be due for an economic crisis. The import/export balance has been tipped dangerously in favor of imports for several years. On the industrial front, there has been little investment in research and development, advanced technologies, and high-tech industries. Unemployment has steadily held at around 10 percent for several years. Meanwhile, Spanish salaries have continuously lagged

the headquarters of Spain's stock exchange, La Bolsa de Madrid

behind those of other EU countries. Additionally, Spain has been a recipient of European Union subsidies since it joined the EU in 1986. These funds have helped build infrastructure, spark investment, and contribute to overall growth. They are due to end in 2008—a loss of some €8 billon per year. All of this, combined with the threat of a housing bubble and rising inflation, means that sunny Spain could well be facing a bleak and gray future.

People

DEMOGRAPHICS

In 2006, the Spanish population hovered around 44 million people. The gender makeup of that number is 49.4 percent men and 50.6 percent women. Madrid is the most populous city with over three million inhabitants (a number that nearly doubles if you include the suburbs). Barcelona is second with 1.6 million inhabitants. All Spaniards enjoy a life expectancy of 77.2 years for men, 83.7 years for women. Spanish women have one of the highest life expectancies in all of Europe. However, Spain also has one of the lowest birth rates. In fact, the United Nations reported in 2000 that Spain had the lowest birth rate in the world, with an average of 1.07 children born to each woman. An average of 2.1 is needed for a population to replace itself over a generation. However, the birth rate is greatly increasing, mainly due to the country's booming immigration population.

IMMIGRATION

As of mid-2006, over 3.5 million, or approximately eight percent, of Spain's 44 million inhabitants were foreigners—a number that has risen sharply in recent years thanks to the influx of immigrants from Northern Africa and

Latin America, the majority fleeing economic hardship in their home countries. This phenomenon has grown at an extraordinary rate: In 1999, for example, the number of immigrants represented only 1.9 percent of the population. As a result, the literal "face" of Spain has changed in recent years, as Moroccans, Ecuadorians, Colombians, Senegalese, Chinese, and many other nationalities have set roots in Spanish soil, preferentially in the regions of Madrid, Catalonia, Valencia, and Andalucía.

Overall, the integration of the immigrant population has been smooth, without the marginalization that has arisen in some other European countries. Spaniards' attitudes towards immigrants are generally positive and sympathetic— something that historians and sociologists attribute partly to the fact that Spaniards themselves fled as economic immigrants to other countries in the difficult years following the Spanish Civil War, a trend that kept up even through the 1980s.

Nevertheless, as the arrival of immigrants continues at a rapid pace, some of this Spanish openness has given way to a certain amount of unease. In Madrid, for example, where nearly a quarter of the workforce and over 10 percent of school-age children are of foreign origin, some sectors have expressed apprehension about the effects of immigration, citing "declining salaries," "fewer jobs," and "poorer health care and education" among their fears. Studies have proven, however, that such fears are by and large groundless, and the effects of immigration are overwhelmingly positive for Spain, helping boost Spain's low birth rate and creating growth in the Spanish economy.

One final aspect of immigration worth mentioning is the large number of European citizens, particularly retired people, who have taken advantage of the comparatively low prices in Spain to buy a second home and escape the cold winters in their homelands. In particular, British and German immigrants have been drawn to the mild climate of the Spanish islands and the Mediterranean coasts, and indeed make up more than a quarter of the population of many towns, making it a common experience to hear barely a word of Spanish spoken while touring the Spanish coast.

YOUNG SPANIARDS TODAY

One thing that may surprise visitors to Spain is Spaniards' very frequent use of the word *jóven* (young) to describe people up until their late 30s. Listening to them, you might assume Spaniards go straight from their "youth" to a mid-life crisis.

Unfortunately, the stark reality is that many of Spain's *jovenes* are indeed caught in a sort of arrested development. Within the European Union, Spain has the highest proportion of adults over 25 still living with their parents. In fact, nearly half of Spaniards aged 30–34 still live at home, and the average age at which "young" Spaniards leave their family household is 29.

Certain cultural aspects play a part in creating this situation. One cultural fact is that marriage has traditionally been considered the "proper" moment to leave home, and young people are increasingly delaying marriage until their early 30s. The root of the problem, however, can be found elsewhere—in the poor employment prospects and high housing costs that have conspired to keep Spaniards living at home at an age when most other Europeans have long since fled the nest.

The employment situation of Spain's young people is not very favorable. Two-thirds of workers under age 25 are on temporary work contracts, often successive short-term contracts in the same company. Indeed, only a small fraction of contracts offered to people under 35 are permanent. As a result, the level of job rotation is high, and younger workers are unable to make plans regarding their career or future. Those who are lucky enough to land permanent jobs, moreover, often find themselves subsisting on paltry wages that do not match the education, experience, and skills they provide. So common is this situation that a term has even been coined to describe such highly educated, low-paid young workers: *mileuristas*—that is, workers who earn no more than €1,000 per month despite holding professional jobs. With employment prospects like this, it is no wonder that Spanish youth face difficulties achieving professional stability, and, consequently, leaving their parents' homes.

Housing is the second obstacle blocking the way to young Spaniards' economic independence. Recently, property prices in Spain have taken a sharp upturn, coinciding with a spectacular surge in the construction of housing. In 2004 and 2005, for example, Spain built more dwellings than France, Germany, and the United Kingdom combined. Meanwhile, since the late 1990s the price of housing has risen by nearly 150 percent. As a result, only young people with high incomes are able to buy property on 30- or 40-year mortgages, while a young couple may spend up to 65 percent of their combined income on their home. Young Spaniards quite simply can't afford to leave home. The only upside to this is that there is no social stigma attached with living at home until well into your 30s. It is a perfectly acceptable and understandable situation.

Although the present situation may seem bleak, things are looking up for Spain's youth, as more and more voices are heard, demanding that the government take measures to promote stable employment and healthy housing policies. If all goes well, the age of Spain's dependent "youth" will gradually retreat from the limits of middle age.

SPANISH WOMEN TODAY

Machismo, or male chauvinism, forms part of a stereotype about Spanish society that evokes a bygone era when women were generally expected to work at home, men wielded the economic power, and divorce was not only unthinkable but illegal. But how much truth is there to the *machismo* stereotype today?

In the past few decades, enormous progress has been made in the path towards gender equality. Women have entered the workforce and higher education in droves. More women occupy highly skilled jobs, particularly technical and professional jobs, in which they make up more than 50 percent of the workforce.

Much progress remains to be made, however. The pay gap between men and women continues to hover between 15 and 30 percent due in part to gender-based discrimination in salaries. Men and women work in different sectors, and men tend to hold more senior positions, a fact that leads to gender-based differences in employment conditions. Unemployment is higher among women than men, and women are more likely to have temporary contracts. Finally, women are also being kept out of the highest echelons of management, and today hold only about four percent of the directorships at Spain's largest companies.

As if the slightly skewed conditions in the labor market weren't enough, women still do three times more housework, even if they have a full-time job. A recent study by the Center for Sociological Investigation revealed that Spanish fathers spent an average of only 13 minutes a day caring for children, and only one in five Spanish men thought mothers of school-age children should have a full-time job. Women, indeed, are still mainly responsible for family issues and often are faced with a choice between their careers and family life.

Change is in the air, however, and Spanish women are claiming their place in society, with an attitude. Like the tide of change that swept through Spain during the transition to democracy, women are storming into areas formerly reserved to men. Witness, for example, Cristina Sánchez's debut in 1996 in the definitively macho profession of bullfighting, or Prime Minister Zapatero's move in 2004 to appoint a cabinet with 50 percent female members, including Spain's first-ever female deputy prime minister (a post equivalent to Vice President in the United States). New legislation is also underway to curb domestic violence, promote life-work compatibility measures, and increase the number of women in corporate boardrooms. All in all, a healthy outlook for equality in Spain and another blow to the old idea of *machismo.*

Culture

RELIGION

For centuries Catholicism has been a key element of Spain's national identity. The Reconquista, the forced conversion or expulsion of Muslims and Jews, the Inquisition, and the triumph of Christianity throughout the peninsula have made the terms "Spaniard" and "Catholic" nearly inseparable. Today, however, more than exerting influence over souls, the Catholic faith provides a set of traditions defining essential aspects of Spanish life.

Spaniards' lives are marked by festivities and rites of passage born of Catholic rituals. Baptisms, first communions, weddings, and funerals are traditionally held in the Catholic Church. Meanwhile, almost every fiesta is a celebration of a religious event: The fire and fireworks of Las Fallas in Valencia commemorate the feast day of Saint Joseph; the bull runs and high frivolity of San Fermín are dedicated to Saint Fermín; the solemn, drum-beating processions of Semana Santa (Easter Week) act both as a social event and a public demonstration of faith; and local festivities—every town in Spain has its own official fiestas, marked by fun-fair attractions, music, drinking, and even bullfights—are normally celebrated on the feast day of the local patron saint. Spain enjoys several national holidays thanks to Catholic events, Epiphany (January 6), Holy Thursday and Good Friday, the Assumption of the Virgin (August 15), All Saints' Day (November 1), and the Immaculate Conception (December 8), as well as Christmas day. Near Christmastime, city halls set up elaborate nativity scenes for the public to admire, and many children at public schools create figurines during the school day to depict the scene of baby Jesus' birth. Religion even reaches so far as Spain's pastry shops and kitchens, giving rise to the marzipan "Saints' Bones" sold at the time of All Saints Day, the Roscón de Reyes (Three Kings' Pastry), a sweet pastry circle with a prize hidden inside, sold during the Christmas holidays, or the almond-based *torta de Santiago*

Semana Santa processions are rooted in Catholicism and practiced with fervor throughout Spain.

© ZIVILE VITEIKAITE

(Saint James' Cake), whose powdered-sugar top is marked with a cross. Erase Catholicism, it would seem, and you would erase a good many of the most visible and delightful traditions of Spain.

It may come as a surprise, then, that the Catholic faith in Spain is experiencing a steady decline, giving way to increasing secularism among the population. Church attendance is falling. According to recent Spanish demographics, over 77 percent of Spanish citizens currently describe themselves as Catholic, nearly half of those persons stated that they never attended Mass. In addition, 13 percent of Spaniards defined themselves as agnostics, 6 percent as atheists, and approximately 2 percent were of another religious faith. Additionally, a recent survey of Spain's young population revealed that, for the first time, less than half of Spaniards aged 15–24

JEWS IN SPAIN

If you're looking for Jewish culture, modern-day Spain will be an extreme disappointment. Only about 30,000-40,000 Jews live in the country today. Since the days of the Inquisition, Spain has upheld a tradition of exclusion to such an extent that even today, more than 500 years later, many Spaniards have never even met a Jew. The absence of Jews becomes obvious if you look at the menu at any Spanish restaurant: heavy on the ham, light on the bagels and lox. The ubiquity of pork dates back to the 15th century. When Isabel and Fernando kicked out the Jewish and Muslim "infidels" in 1492, Spaniards began to hang hams in their doorways and include it in every dish to prove their loyalty to Catholicism, as pork is prohibited in both Judaism and Islam.

Spain wasn't always so unfriendly towards Jews. Once upon a medieval time, Jews were prominent and prosperous on the Iberian Peninsula. They held official posts, served in the military, and worked as artisans, doctors, and philosophers. All that remains today of their great legacy are some old Jewish neighborhoods, known as juderías, and a few synagogues, most of which have been transformed into Catholic churches.

The most significant period of time for Sephardim (Spanish Jews) was under Moorish rule. In 711, the Jews aided Moorish invaders in wresting control of Spain from the oppressive Christian Visigoths who had been ruling the county for several centuries. The change in rulers ushered in an era of relative peace for the Sephardim and for the next few centuries, Jewish, Moorish, and Christian cultures flourished side-by-side and members of each faith rose through the ranks of society. Toledo was one of the most notable examples of a town enriched by this Middle Ages multi-culturism.

As Christian forces began to assume power throughout Spain, a wave of anti-Jewish sentiment took root. In Christian-ruled towns, Jews were forced to live within the boundaries of their juderías and in towns where Jews and Christians had once lived peaceably together schisms and intolerance arose. In 1391, a series of bloody pogroms were carried out on Jewish communities in Sevilla, Barcelona, Valencia, and Córdoba. Thousands of Jews were killed and synagogues were destroyed. One reaction to this violent intolerance was the massive conversion of Jews to Christianity. From the 15th century on, a new social group of conversos, or converted Jews, began to rise through the ranks of Spanish society, obtaining powerful positions in the government and in the church – often by becoming very vocal, very severe, detractors of Judaism.

In 1478, Isabel and Fernando instituted the Inquisition with the goal of enforcing Catholic orthodoxy throughout their kingdoms. Jews, Moors, and conversos were frequent targets of Inquisition courts and were often killed during the course of their trials. With the 1492 fall of La Alhambra, the last Moorish stronghold on the peninsula, the Christians rose to absolute power. That same year, remaining Jews were given an ultimatum – convert or get out. An estimated 200,000 Jews were driven out of the country by this edict. Those who remained converted to Catholicism, began eating jamón, and attempted to integrate into Catholic

described themselves as Catholic, either practicing or non-practicing.

Another sign of the Church's declining role in Spanish life is the decreasing number of people choosing to celebrate religious ceremonies such as weddings or communions. Civil ceremonies now account for nearly 40 percent of all weddings nationwide, and the number

of children celebrating their first communion has been decreasing slowly but steadily every year. Of those who do choose to celebrate these religious ceremonies, a certain number admit to being drawn mainly to the festive quality of the event. This is the case, for example, for many of the families organizing a party to celebrate a child's first communion, a ceremony

Spanish society. It was difficult. They were called *marranos* (pigs), suffered discrimination, and were continually under threat of the Inquisition's tribunals. The Inquisition was not abolished until 1834 and the edict of expulsion wasn't officially repealed until 1968, but by the mid-1800s, Jews had begun to trickle back into Spain. By the 20th century, the atmosphere, despite an overwhelming Catholic majority, was fairly benign.

Today, Jews in Spain are a welcome but still very small fraction of the population. Visitors can discover the historical impact the Sephardim have had on the Iberian Peninsula by visiting heritage sites across the country.

Toledo is home to two of Spain's three remaining synagogues, the **Sinagoga del Tránsito,** built in 1203, and the **Sinagoga de Santa Maria la Blanca,** built in 1366. The latter houses the Spanish Museum of Sephardic Jewish History.

In **Córdoba,** the Jewish quarter was once known for its gold- and silversmiths. It is home to the third of Spain's original synagogues. Built in 1315, this simple structure was converted into a church, used as a hospital, a shoemakers' guild, and finally a 19th-century primary school. However, Córdoba's greatest contribution to Sephardic heritage was Maimonides, who was born there in 1135. A Jewish philosopher whose influence reached even his Christian and Muslim neighbors, Maimonides helped form the foundation for the Jewish Orthodox belief. A commemorative statue of him stands in Tiberiadus Square.

Sevilla boasts an ancient Jewish history, as it was one of the first Spanish cities to be inhabited by Jews before the time of Christ. The Jews lived and prospered in the city while enduring hostilities. In 1391, Sevilla's Jewish quarter suffered one of the bloodiest pogroms in the country. The entire barrio was closed off and murderous mobs swept through killing entire families. The synagogues were converted to churches, and the *judería* transformed into the Christian parish Santa Cruz, still the most atmospheric and tranquil of Sevilla's barrios.

Granada also has a long history of Sephardim and it was home to Samuel Ha-Nagid, who became the chief minister of Spain in the 11th century. Unfortunately, Jewish rule ended with his death, and in 1492, Isabel and Fernando signed the edict of expulsion right in this former "City of the Jews."

Barcelona also had a very lively *judería* until the 14th century. Today, it is being resurrected thanks to a committed group of conservationists who have formed the **Associació Call** on the grounds of the recently uncovered main synagogue. "Call" is a Hebrew word for community and much of Barcelona's *judería* is on and around the street of this name.

Girona, Just outside of Barcelona, is even richer in Jewish history and the atmospheric *judería* is home to the **Museum of the History of the Jews,** which focuses on the Jews of Cataluña. The cobbled streets of the neighborhood remain unchanged from the age of Jewish prosperity.

Madrid has very little to offer in terms of Jewish history, though the city did become a point of settlement for many of the 19th-century Jews who immigrated back to Spain. A new synagogue was opened in 1968 to mark the official revocation of the 1492 edict of expulsion.

that costs, on average, about €2,500. This money pays for the special communion outfit (billowy white dress for girls and navy costume for boys), catered meal for family and friends, small souvenirs for guests, and, of course, gifts for the child. More than a religious sacrament, a child's first communion can often, in practice, turn into a celebration marked by extravagant materialism. Similar trends can be seen among those who opt for sumptuous baptism or wedding celebrations.

Finally, the Church is also losing ground in the Spanish school system, where religious classes are offered throughout primary and secondary school. Over the past decade, the number of students enrolled in these optional

BULLFIGHTING

For many, bullfighting is as intrinsically linked with Spain as is flamenco, sangria, and tapas. Though in recent years many Spaniards – especially young urban-dwellers – have decried it as little more than animal cruelty, bullfighting is still popular, matadors are celebrities, and *corridas* (bullfights) are covered both on television and in the daily papers – in the arts, not the sports, section. With the exception of Cataluña, where bullfighting is technically banned, even the tiniest of villages hold bullfights.

Visitors to Spain who attend a bullfight should be prepared: It is indeed a bloody event and six bulls will die. Yet, *la corrida* is much more than a spectacle of man versus beast. Like a good opera, a bullfight encapsulates history, culture, drama, nature, bravery, honor, and, of course, death. Though it may be difficult for a tourist to see beyond the final bloody outcome, knowing a little about what is going on can open the way to also seeing the art in the afternoon.

THE SEASON

The bullfighting season runs from March to October with bullfights held every Sunday. During major *ferias taurinas* (bullfighting festivals), they are held nightly. Two of the most important festivals in Spain are Sevilla's Feria de Abril, held in April, and Madrid's San Isidro, held in May and June.

IN THE RING

A *corrida* lasts under two hours and consists of six bullfights fought by three matadors (also called *toreros*). The *toros* (bulls) are at least four years old and weigh a minimum of 460 kilograms (1,015 lbs). The matador works with a team called a *cuadrilla*, which usually consists of two *picadores* mounted on horseback and three *banderilleros* who work on foot. The entire team is dressed in elaborately embroidered outfits called *trajes de luces* (suits of light). They are so named because they are often trimmed in gold and when the sun hits just right, they seem to glow.

The bullfight begins with a *paseo* when the three matadors and their teams enter the *plaza de toros* (bullring) and greet the crowd and the president who oversees the event. Next, the bull is released into the ring and the matador and his team perform a series of passes with the bull using their *capotes*, large pink and yellow capes. Upon entering the ring, a bull is evaluated by *aficionados* (hard-core fans) for its bravery and strength. A weak, cowardly, or lame bull will be booed (expressed with whistling) and subsequently pulled from the ring by the president.

When the horns sound, the first bullfight begins. It consists of three parts called *tercios*. In the first, the *picadores* enter on horseback. Their job is to cause the bull to charge the horse. When it does, the *picador* pierces the bull's powerful neck muscle with a long lance. In the second *tercio*, the *banderilleros* enter. Armed with two colorful 75-centimeter-long (28-inch) darts called *banderillas*, they take turns running directly at the bull and plunging the darts between the animal's shoulders.

The final *tercio* is known as *la faena* and is the moment of truth for the matador. Alone with

Catholic classes has slowly declined, especially among older students. Less than half of secondary and upper high school students now opt to take religious classes.

In addition to Catholicism, many other faiths are also practiced on Spanish soil, thanks in part to the upswing in immigration in recent years. There are, for example, about 400,000 evangelical Christians and other Protestants, of whom about 30 percent are immigrants from Latin America and Africa. The size of the Muslim community, meanwhile, is estimated at more than one million, including both legal and illegal immigrants. Some 30,000–40,000 Jews live in the country, as well as approximately 9,000 Buddhists. The Mormons and Jehovah's Witnesses are present as well, and even the Church of Scientology has opened glitzy

the bull, he performs a series of passes using a *muleta*, a small red cape. There is a long artistic legacy to *la faena* and each of the matador's moves has a specific name. To the tourist, it may all look spectacular, but *aficionados* are carefully watching the types of passes the matador makes, looking to see that he is using both his left and right hands, and judging his moves based on both the grace in which they are executed and the level of courage they display. Most matadors prove their bravery by getting as close as possible to the bull. If all goes well, the crowd will begin to emit the famous cry of approval – *Olé!*

Finally, the matador will walk to the side of the ring where he receives a sword for the final act of the bullfight – the kill. The matador lines himself in front of the bull, aims the sword, and makes a running advance to thrust it into the beast. Correctly executed, the kill should be clean and quick, with the sword going right into the heart. If this happens, the crowd goes wild and the matador is assured adulation. If the sword is not properly inserted and the bull is not killed – too often the case – the crowd will express disapproval with whistling and *broncas* (verbal abuse).

Once the bull is dead, the crowd heartily expresses its opinion of the bullfight. If impressed with the matador's skill, spectators wave white handkerchiefs (a tissue suffices). This is a symbol to the president that they want the matador to be awarded with the bull's ear. If the matador was especially brave, two ears may be awarded. For a spectacular bullfight, both ears and the tail are given. If the matador receives any of these, he takes a triumphant walk around the ring as the crowd throws down flowers or – more often – hats to be picked up by the matador and thrown back to the crowd.

The entire bullfight takes about 15 minutes. Once the first is done, there is a slight break in action before the next begins. Each of the three matadors will fight twice.

OTHER BULLFIGHTS

Novilladas are bullfights fought by apprentice matadors called *novilleros*. True *aficionados* may note many differences between these events and *corridas*, but tourists will be thrilled with either. *Novillada* tickets are also cheaper and easier to get than those for *corridas*. Also look out for *rejoneos*, bullfights that are held on horseback.

MORE INFORMATION

This is only a brief overview of what to expect at a bullfight. There is a world of culture and history behind the event and everything from the matador's socks to the specific songs played in the bullring are governed by ritual. If you want to learn more, hit the books. The classic is Ernest Hemingway's *Death in the Afternoon*. A big fan of *la corrida*, Hemingway attended hundreds of bullfights; this monumental work, first published in 1932, is still considered the best introduction. A modern overview is found in 2005's *Death and the Sun: A Matador's Season in the Heart of Spain*. Written by Edward Levine, a *New York Times* correspondent and bullfighting fan, the book chronicles a year in the life of matador Francisco Rivera Ordoñez.

centers in recent years (Tom Cruise's visit to the Madrid center was a huge event), although this last group has been denied official status as a religion by Spanish authorities.

The practice of other faiths is protected by the Spanish constitution. Article 16 provides for religious freedom and states, "No faith shall have the character of a state religion." Nevertheless, the Catholic Church enjoys certain benefits from the Government that other religions do not. For example, taxpayers are allowed to check a box on their income tax forms to contribute a small percentage of their taxes to the Catholic Church, a practice that provides the Church with over a hundred million euros each year. The Church also receives state funding for religion teachers in public schools and other indirect support. This "favoritism" can be understood only in a historical context, as a remnant of the many privileges enjoyed by the Church before the advent of democracy following the Franco regime.

For the time being, Spain continues to be a nation marked by its deep Catholic roots. And while its Catholic traditions and religious festivities will undoubtedly continue to thrive in years to come, the increasing secularization of the population and the expansion of alternative faiths will also slowly change the nature of the country's religious practices.

LANGUAGE

Spain's cultural diversity is no more clearly seen than its languages. Spanish—or, more correctly, Castellano (Castilian Spanish)—is the official language of the nation and constitutes the mother tongue of the vast majority of Spain's 44 million inhabitants. However, there are several regions where Castilian Spanish is not the dominant tongue, and the local languages hold co-official status. The most widely spoken of these other languages are Gallego (Galician), Euskara (Basque), and Català (Catalan), though there are also many others to be found throughout the country. Generally speaking, about 35 percent of the Spanish population speaks at least one of these regional tongues.

During Franco's dictatorship in the 20th century, Castilian Spanish was the sole official language of the nation and use of regional languages was confined to the home—yet, speakers had to be very careful lest authorities overhear. The regional tongues were banned from public use in all forms, including the media, schools, street signs, and art. In fact, even foreign languages were all but banned. Hollywood films were all dubbed into Spanish. In fact, until this day, Spaniards prefer to watch films in Spanish and popular English-speaking celebrities such as Meg Ryan, George Clooney, and even Homer Simpson have distinctive Spanish voices used to dub them.

Ever since Franco's death in 1975 and the subsequent restoration of democracy, great efforts have been made to re-establish the use of the minority tongues. Thousands of books and dozens of local newspapers are published in these languages every year, and numerous TV channels and radio stations broadcast programs geared to non-Spanish-speaking or bilingual audiences. Likewise, the regional languages with co-official status are widely used as languages of instruction in schools, as well as in governmental proceedings, not to mention the shops, bars, street signs, and streets in general.

Gallego

Galician is a language spoken by about three million people in the in the northwest corner of Spain, where it is the co-official language in the autonomous region of Galicia. The language is extremely similar to the neighboring language of Portuguese. In fact, whether Galician and Portuguese are two separate languages or dialects of a single language is still in question.

Euskara

Basque, meanwhile, is a truly unique tongue. Unlike all other languages in Western Europe, Basque is not part of the Indo-European language family and cannot be linked to any other known language. It stands alone as the sole relic of an ancient tongue used by pre-Roman tribes. As such, Basque is considered one of the oldest documented languages in use in the world today. Today it is the co-official regional language spoken by more than half a million people in the Basque Country in northwestern Spain and parts of southwestern France.

Català

Catalan is spoken by approximately 10 million people, mainly in the east of Spain. It is the co-official language in the autonomous communities of Cataluña and the Balearic Islands. A variety of Catalan is also spoken in Valencia, where it is called Valenciano. However, the differences between the Valencian language and Catalan are minimal, and—much to the dismay of Valencians with nationalist sentiments—linguists generally treat them as two varieties of the same tongue.

Art and Architecture

Over the span of its history, Spain has been a constant center of artistic activity, churning out painter after famous painter, as well as some of the most well-known works in the history of art. Fine national and international art is ubiquitous throughout the country, but its nucleus is Madrid, thanks to its trio of world-class museums. Every major movement in painting is reflected in the pieces hanging on walls of the Museo del Prado and the Museo Thyssen-Bornemisza, while the Museo de la Reina Sofía boasts hall after hall of some of the world's finest modern art. The world's two most famous paintings also reside in Madrid—Velázquez's *Las Meninas* and Picasso's *Guernica.*

MAJOR ART EPOCHS
Mannerism
The chaos of Europe's mid-16th-century religious and political upheaval translated onto Spanish canvases in the form of oddly elongated bodies, dark themes and color schemes, and unusual perspectives. This style is somewhat hard to categorize and it is best seen in the work of the Greek-turned-Spanish painter El Greco, who adopted the style in the later years of his career. Toledo, where he lived and worked, pays homage to this artist by holding his art in its cathedral and museum. (See sidebar, *The Greek in Toledo,* in the *Castilla-La Mancha* chapter.)

Baroque
After the mid-16th-century Reformation split the church into two factions: Catholics and Protestants, the Catholic Church launched an aggressive Counter-Reformation movement. Catholic leaders needed a vehicle to convince the largely illiterate masses of the Church's purity. Art was the chosen method. Various artists, such as Caravaggio in Italy, were enlisted to restore the faith. They ushered in the period of baroque painting (late 16th century to 17th century).

Baroque, which literally means "irregular

pearl," tends to depict moments of high drama, with rich colors and deep contrasts between light and shadows. The intention is to evoke profound emotions, especially in works with religious themes.

Spain was a vibrant center of baroque art, giving rise to many famous painters. The most renowned of whom was Diego Velázquez, the leading artist in the court of Felipe IV. Other notable Spanish artists who painted in this style include José de Ribera, Francisco de Zurbarán, and Bartolome Estéban Murillo—all of whom have works hanging throughout Spain.

Rococo
Rococo (18th century) arose as an offspring of the baroque period. Shifting its focus from religion to more frivolous portraiture and landscapes, rococo art has a more suave feel with delicate colors, curves, and less-sharp lines. Francisco Goya, also a court painter, was trained in this style and is often considered a Spanish rococo painter, however his work transcended boundaries. Every church, museum, or civil building possessing a Goya—and there are legions—will proudly proclaim that fact on their tourism literature. However, the best collection of his work is in Madrid's Prado.

Romanticism
Smoothly transitioning from the emotional appeal of baroque and rococo art, romantic paintings packed the same sentimental punch while focusing on lighter subject matter. Romantic art typically took on the form of portraits and landscapes. The most noteworthy paintings are Goya's, which cross the very blurry line between the art epochs of romanticism (19th century) and rococo. Goya helped establish some of the distinguishing characteristics of romanticism with his personal portraits and historically relevant paintings. His paintings *Dos de mayo* and *Tres de mayo* reflect the turmoil of Napoleon's invasion of Spain.

Impressionism

Marked by a concern for light and atmosphere, landscape and frivolity, impressionism (late 19th century to early 20th century) did not take root in Spain the way it did in France. One Spanish master of the form was Joaquín Sorolla (1863–1923), who painted many a light-filled, happy image of his hometown of Valencia. He spent his later life painting in Madrid. Upon his death, Sorolla's widow converted their home into the charming Museo Sorolla in Madrid's Chamartín district. Here you can get a glimpse into the inner workings of an artist, as Sorolla's personal studio has been kept in tact. Mariano Fortuny is another noteworthy Spanish impressionist.

Cubism

Developed from the partnership of Pablo Picasso and Georges Braque in Paris around 1908, cubism (early 20th century) sought to reflect objects and figures by painting them from multiple points of view and angles. Picasso's famous dog, which appears in many of his paintings, is at once a front view and a profile. Though it was the most important of the avant-garde art movements of the 20th century, it only lasted until the end of WWI. Despite this short reign, it helped influence subsequent art movements including expressionism and surrealism. The most famous cubist of them all is, of course, Málaga-born Pablo Picasso, whose must-see masterpiece *Guernica* is displayed in Madrid's Reina Sofía. Many of his early works, including his cubist reinterpretation of Velázquez's *Las Meninas,* are housed in the Museu Picasso in Barcelona.

Surrealism

In the 1920s, the nihilist and slightly irrational Dada art movement developed into surrealism. Surrealism blurred the boundaries of consciousness and dreams in a manner that reflected the new psychological theories of Sigmund Freud. The most famous surrealist (though he joined the movement quite a few years after it had started) was Salvador Dalí. His paintings featuring melting clocks and shifting shapes are well known throughout the world.

There are two places in Spain where the surrealist movement can be seen at its peak. The first, the Teatro-Museo Dalí in Figueres, was founded by Dalí himself in 1974, and even the museum walls themselves reflect Dalí's Surrealist sentiments. The second is the Reina Sofía, where some of Dalí's greatest works are displayed.

Catalan painter Joan Miró, who is often described as a surrealist, is also exhibited in this museum.

MAJOR ARTISTS

Bosch

Though Hieronymus Bosch (1450–1516) was a Dutch painter, he was revered in Spain where he worked for the Spanish courts and is known as "El Bosco." Specializing in allegorical paintings usually done on wood as triptychs (three-paneled works), his work combined icons, symbols, and religious lore to make pointed criticisms of the Catholic Church. The paintings, which were far ahead of his time in their mix of reality and fantasy, helped inspire the surrealist movement of the 1900s. El Bosco's most well-known triptych is *The Garden of Earthly Delights,* which traces the way from the paradise of the Garden of Eden to the torture of hell. It hangs in the Prado.

Titian

A painter of the Venetian school, Titian (1485–1576) is certainly more of a fixture in Italy than Spain. However, his work as a court painter during the reign of Carlos V puts him on the Spanish map. Renowned mostly for his portraits, Titian created some masterpieces, including *El Emperor Carlos V en Mühlberg* and several portraits of King Felipe II. He is also known for his paintings on mythology.

El Greco

Born in Crete, Domenikos Theotokopoulos (1541–1614), spent most of his life and career in Spain, where he was renamed "El Greco" ("The Greek"). Some of his first—and most famous—commissions came from the churches of Toledo, such as *El entierro del Conde de*

Orgaz, which hangs in the Iglesia de Santo Tomé in Toledo. His style developed under the teaching of Titian and later progressed to mannerism. El Greco's paintings became darker and the figures in them increasingly exaggerated and uncomfortably posed.

Velázquez

Diego Velázquez (1599–1660) is widely exalted as the greatest painter who ever lived and his *Las Meninas,* a study in perspective, is widely considered the greatest painting ever painted. Born in Sevilla, Velázquez was apprenticed to the painter Francisco Pacheco and later married Pacheco's daughter. Eventually, Velázquez moved to Madrid and quickly climbed the ranks of Felipe IV's court, rising to become the court curator. Over the course of his life, Velázquez produced more work than any other artist. Some of his most famous are portraits, especially of the unfortunate court buffoons. The Prado in Madrid holds the world's most important collection of his work.

Goya

Francisco Goya (1746–1828) headed down a road quite similar to the one Velázquez took. He painted portraits and became an influential court painter. However, the style of his paintings and the life he lead diverged from the calm path of his mentor. Goya, a renaissance man of art, was famous for paintings, drawings, and engravings. He painted the family of Carlos IV, as well as aristocrats. He was a master at using his portraits to dig beneath the surface of appearance and hit at the essence of his subjects.

In 1792, he was rendered deaf after a serious illness. After this, his work became increasingly dark and disturbing. Goya projects the despair and turmoil caused by France's invasion of Spain in his paintings *El Dos de mayo* and *El Tres de mayo.* His *Saturno devorando a su hijo (Saturn Devouring His Son),* a truly gruesome scene of mythology, was once a mere decoration in Goya's dining room.

His life from court painter, to historical commentator, to somewhat batty old man is documented in all its glory throughout several rooms of the Prado. His death is commemorated in the Ermita de San Antonio de la Florida in Madrid, where his tomb is located amidst his own murals and frescoes.

Picasso

A child prodigy, Pablo Picasso (1881–1973) began painting at a very early age, churning out semi-masterpieces as early as his teens. The most famous painter of the 20th century, Picasso's work can be split into three aptly named periods. During his Blue Period, Picasso worked with shades of blue and painted melancholy portraits of the poor and marginalized people such as prostitutes. In the cheerier Rose Period, Picasso used a rose-tinted palate on his canvasses to convey his happy personal life. The third of Picasso's painting stages is his most recognized contribution to the art world: cubism. The Museu Picasso in Barcelona is a virtual timeline of Picasso's painting periods. The museum also holds many of his unknown sketches and lewd works. Málaga, the city of his birth, also has an excellent Museo de Picasso.

Miró

Joan Miró (1893–1983) refused to be pegged into any artistic hole. He is typically classified as a surrealist, but in reality he is part surrealist, part subist, part abstract. Born in Barcelona, he lived and painted for most of his life in Palma de Mallorca, producing many great works that mixed shapes and colors. Since he was opposed to art critics and definition, Miró worked outside of the system both style and material-wise.

Barcelona and Mallorca are both home to Fundació Joan Miró museums, each reflecting different aspects of the artist's work. The one in Mallorca houses Miró's sketches, paintings, sculptures, and etchings, while Barcelona provides an overview of his work and includes works by many artists who influenced him.

Dalí

Salvador Dalí (1904–1989) rivals Picasso in terms of his 20th-century influence. The star of the surrealist movement, Dalí's vivid images warp the line between reality and dream and have formed a lasting impression on modern art. An admirer of Picasso, Dalí spent some time nailing down his own style, finally becoming an official member of the Surrealist group in 1929. He also met his muse and love, Gala, that year.

Dalí eventually split with the surrealists over politics but continued with his style of painting. His also experimented in film and photography. A few lasting testaments of his work remain in Spain. Dalí's hometown of Figueres is home to the Teatro-Museo Dalí, which in itself is a work of art. This museum is one of the most popular in Spain and has the most extensive collection of his work.

Tàpies

Antoni Tàpies (born in 1923) was the great Spanish talent to emerge after WWII. His paintings are a blend of surrealism, Dadaism, and expressionism. Nowadays, he is best known for works of mixed media. His works often incorporate everyday objects like string, wire, or even furniture. The best retrospective of his life and work can be found at Barcelona's Fundació Antoni Tàpies.

Eduardo Chillida

Born in the Basque region of Spain, Eduardo Chillida (1924–2002) became one of the world's most important—and famed—20th-century sculptors. Although he preferred the label of realist, the bulk of his work can be labeled abstract. Earlier works focused on human form, but in his later life, Chillida experimented more with shape and material. His monumental, moving works—often rendered in steel and stone—have a living, emotional quality. They reside in museums and landscapes all over the world, but the best are found in Spain, including the famed series of sculptures *El peine del viente (Comb of the Wind)*, which looms over the city of San Sebastián. On the outskirts of the city, the Museo Chillida-Leku gives the best overview of this master's work and life.

ARCHITECTURE

Spain's architecture, in all of its varied glory, is a fairly accurate metaphor for Spain itself, at times austere and conservative and at others astonishingly modern. Although the country's modern architectural revolution is dominating international press these days, Spain has been a constant innovator in building for well over 1,000 years.

Architecture reflects history and that is nowhere more evident than in Spain. From B.C. Roman amphitheaters through 8th-century Moorish *alcazars* (fortresses) to the contemporary, highly original array of 20th-century museums, civil buildings, and housing complexes found in urban centers. Naturally, Spain's largest cities—Madrid, Barcelona, Bilbao, and Valencia—are the go-to spots for viewing the breadth of Spanish architecture, but almost anywhere in Spain can serve up its own fascinating architectural timeline.

Caliphal/Mozarabic

Before the beginning of Spain's lapse into Catholic fervor (9th–11th century), the Iberian Peninsula—especially Andalucía—was quite the Muslim stronghold. Smatterings of Christian populations lived and built side-by-side with the Muslim majority, and as a result, the Christians developed a new kind of architectural style that was highly influenced by Arab culture. There are dozens of these structures scattered throughout Spain. The most impressive ones are the Alhambra in Granada and the Mezquita in Córdoba.

Mudejar

The Spanish Reconquista, which spanned the entirety of Muslim rule from the 8th to the 15th centuries, made a minority of the once Muslim majority. Master builders, the Muslims who remained among the newly empowered Christian populations elaborated upon Mozarabic to create the distinctly Islamic style of Mudejar (12th–17th century). Churches were constructed in the midst of Arabic *mezquitas* (mosques) and then promptly decorated with Muslim arches and mosaics, creating a unique new style. You can find this style throughout Spain, including the palace complex of the Alcázar Real in Sevilla and the towers of Teruel in Aragón.

Romanesque

A homage to the monuments of the Roman and Byzantine times, Romanesque architecture (11th and 12th centuries) used the then new method of stone vaulting to create buildings that would last. The goal was accomplished, and dozens of these brooding stone churches with rounded arches remain intact today. The most impressive are the Catedral Vieja in Salamanca, the Real Basílica San Isidoro in León, and the Catedral de Santiago de Compostela in the town of the same name in Galicia, which contains a wonderfully preserved Romanesque interior and doors, despite extensive baroque features added in the 18th century. The town of Oviedo, Asturias has World Heritage status for its large clutch of such buildings.

Toledo's cathedral is one of the largest Gothic structures in the world.

© CANDY LEE LABALLE

Gothic

Incubated in France in the 12th century, the Gothic architectural style (13th–15th century) took hold of Spanish churches about 100 years later. One of the earliest Gothic cathedrals constructed was the magnificent Catedral de Burgos, begun in 1221, followed very closely by the Catedral de León. The style, at once ornate and imposing, utilized technical innovations that allowed Spanish churches to become bigger and better—clearly evidenced in the aforementioned cathedrals. With peaked arches, ribbed ceilings, and flying buttresses, these churches were built to last. Thousands of Gothic structures remain throughout Spain. The Barri Gòtic of Barcelona is an entire neighborhood composed of such structures.

Over the centuries of its popularity, Gothic Spanish architecture evolved into distinctive periods, most notably Isabelline Gothic, named for Queen Isabel the Catholic. It foreshadowed Renaissance architecture and incorporated details such as basket-handled arches, Royal shield decoration, and the inscription

of commemorative text in the structure. The Monasterio de San Juan de los Reyes in Toledo is a gorgeous example of this style.

Plateresque

In Spain, the Renaissance hit with a chisel. In the 16th century in other European countries, Renaissance architecture manifested itself with classically inspired columns, but Spain's architectural revolution consisted of sprucing up old styles. Buildings were still constructed in heavy stone like in the earlier Romanesque and Gothic periods, but they were ornamented with delicate detail and sculpture, most often around doorways and windows. The elaborate details echoed the intricately detailed work of *plateros* (silversmiths), hence the name Plateresque. Salamanca is the capital of Plateresque architecture with its ornate university and magnificent Plaza Mayor.

Spanish Baroque

Baroque style (early 17th–late 18th century) developed as the architectural counterpart to the Catholic Church's Counter-Reformation. Characteristics of baroque include dramatic use of light, opulent ornamentation, ceiling frescoes, and spacious, circular naves. The Spanish King Felipe II, while not the first to show ardent religious devotion via incredibly massive buildings, perhaps did it best with his monumental monastery complex, El Escorial. It was designed by Juan de Herrera, who planned various buildings and monuments around Madrid as well. Though inspired by baroque, the austere, moody, gray-stoned style was such a unique accomplishment that it subsequently was given its very own architectural category: Herrera.

Not everyone equated religious fervor with contemplative, dark constructions and soon other Spanish architects arose up in contrast to Herrera's sober style. The Churrigueresque style of Spain's later baroque period signaled a return to the celebratory and ornamental styles that had marked Plateresque architecture. In the hands of the Churriguera family of architects, stone facades began to curve, dipped, and flourish once more. Churrigueresque highlights include the Catedral de Toledo, the Palacio del Marqués de Dos Aguas in Valencia, and the Catedral de Cádiz.

Neoclassical

Neoclassical architecture (18th–early 19th century) provided a change of pace from the over-the-top decorations of Plateresque and Churrigueresque monuments. A favorite of reform-minded King Carlos III, the style features simple geometric shapes, blank walls, and tall columns, all based on classic Greek architecture. Madrid became the center of neoclassical Spain, as the king's team of architects remodeled the city. Contemporary hotshots Juan de Villanueva and Ventura Rodriguez were responsible for such important additions to Madrid as the Museo del Prado, the Plaza de Cibeles, and the monumental Palacio Real.

Modernisme

The late 1800s brought a great revolution in the architectural world: *modernisme*. Not to be confused with modernism, *modernisme* with an "e" was inspired by art nouveau—the eclectic, florid, nature-based architectural that emanated from Paris. In Spain, particularly Cataluña, it was adopted and morphed into surrealist reinterpretations of Gothic architecture, creating what is sometimes called Catalan art nouveau or *modernisme*.

Important Catalan architects of this epoch included Lluís Domènech i Montaner and Josep Puig i Cadafalch, and Josep María Jujol. However, it was Antoni Gaudí who became world famous for his radical, visionary works. Over the course of four decades, Gaudí erected ethereal buildings all over Cataluña and Spain. Of note are Barcelona's La Sagrada Família church and the hilltop hideaway of Parc Güell. These magical structures caused the world to rethink its assumptions about architecture and helped make Barcelona the tourist destination it is today. (See sidebar, *Architectural Madman, Monumental Genius*, in the *Barcelona* chapter.)

21st-Century Architecture

Upon its admittance to the European Union in 1986, Spain received over 100 billion euros, which it wisely invested in epic works of architectural wonder that have permanently changed the Spanish landscape. This Spanish architectural revolution provided a much-needed breakaway from the oppressive, nationalistic style enforced under Franco (all the ugly, monotonous buildings you see blighting Spanish cities are legacies of Franco). The buildings have also given Spain the opportunity to boost its once severely lagging economy.

While Gaudí may have been one the father of trippy design, Barcelona's creative architectural output has hardly slowed. Its Mercat de Santa Caterina food market was recently topped with a curvy, colorful roof that looks like a patchwork blanket thrown over its surrounding Gothic neighbors. Barcelona is also home to the phallic skyscraper Torre Agbar, designed by French architect Jean Nouvel, which is covered in colorful LCD filaments and lit up on weekend nights. American Richard Meir designed the futuristic-looking Museu d'Art

Contemporani de Barcelona (MACBA), with sloping curved walls and lots of glass.

The most famous example of 21st-century architecture in Spain is Bilbao's Guggenheim museum, designed by Frank Gehry. With its multi-layered, swooping titanium exterior, it made Bilbao an overnight tourist hot spot and has inspired lesser-known Spanish towns to use architectural tourism as a means of boosting their economy.

In Valencia, Santiago Calatrava's Cuitat de las Artes y les Ciencias (Arts and Science Complex), housing one of Europe's most important aquariums, is a futuristic city of dazzling, jagged, mechanical white forums situated around clear blue pools.

In Madrid, the Museo de la Reina Sofía was recently renovated by Jean Nouvel, who added some striking glass structures and a red-roofed restaurant to the back of the building. Bara-jas airport got a much-needed expansion when British architect Richard Rogers built Terminal 4, a massive structure made light with an undulating bamboo roof, natural lighting, and rows of canary yellow supports.

The Museo de Cantabria, set to open in Santander in 2008, will look like a mountain range, complete with jagged peaks. Its unique hybrid form will be adaptable to both traditional and unorthodox installations.

With prestigious architectural contests, major funding, and a sense of adventure being thrown at new building projects, Spain's architectural revolution only stands to become even more stunning, as once glum neighborhoods, museums, and city buildings get inspired facelifts. The movement has received some hefty publicity worldwide, including an unprecedented 2006 show at New York's Museum of Modern Art called "On Site: New Architecture in Spain."

ESSENTIALS

Getting There

BY AIR

There are many international airports in Spain, the most important being Barajas in Madrid, which is where most North American carriers land after crossing the Atlantic. A couple of carriers also land in Barcelona. Other cities with international airports include Alicante, Málaga, and Sevilla. All of Spain's airports are run by **AENA** (www.aena.es). On their homepage, choose English and then the city you will land in from the drop-down menu. You'll find everything from flight times to rental car agencies to the location of services in the selected airport.

Carriers

From the East Coast of the **United States,** the flight to Spain lasts a bit over eight hours. If you have a layover or plane change in Europe, expect to add a minimum of three more hours. To avoid this, seek a non-stop flight on one of the following carriers. **Delta** (www.delta.com): New York (JFK) to Madrid and Barcelona, and Atlanta to Madrid and Barcelona. **Continental** (www.continental.com): Newark and Houston to Madrid. **American Airlines** (www.aa.com): New York (JFK) and Miami to Madrid. **U.S. Airways** (www.usairways.com): Philadelphia to Madrid and Barcelona.

From the **United Kingdom,** many carriers offer daily flights into airports all over Spain. **British Airways** (www.britishairways.com) is the granddaddy of U.K. airlines with top service and matching prices (though with increasing competition from cut-rate airlines, BA has started offering deals, particularly online). The budget carriers are numerous and include **BMI Baby** (www.bmibaby.com), **easyJet** (www.easyjet.com), which is scheduled to make Madrid its new hub in 2007, **Ryanair** (www.ryanair.com), and **Virgin Express** (www.virginexpress.com).

Spanish carriers, including **Iberia** (www.iberia.com) and **Spanair** (www.spanair.com), also provide flights from North America and the United Kingdom to Spain.

Costs and Booking

As of fall 2006, a round-trip ticket from North America to Spain cost $500–1,000. Several factors affect prices, including when you fly, your city of departure, how early you book your trip, and whether your ticket is restricted or not. The easiest solution is to work directly with a travel agent who will sift through the flights for you. You can also find great deals and book yourself by using an online agent such as www.travelocity.com, www.expedia.com, and www.cheaptickets.com. Finally, if you are loyal to a particular airline for points or other reasons, it is best to book with that airline directly through their website.

To cut costs, peruse websites such as www.johnnyjet.com, which is a mother lode of travel deal information. Basic cost-cutting tips include purchasing your ticket in advance and choosing a round-trip. Try several dates when searching for your flight. Try booking your ticket out of various airports, as the price can be dramatically different. Request a flight before 7 A.M. or after 7 P.M., thus avoiding peak travel time and prices. The cheapest days of the week to fly are Tuesday, Wednesday, and Thursday.

If your main concern is the cheapest flight possible, flight couriers and air-hitching might be for you. As a courier, you accompany a package to Spain on a deeply discounted ticket. The catch is that you must give up your luggage allowance in order to accommodate the package. With restrictions on carry-on items greatly increasing, these means you can bring very little with you on your journey. Air-hitching involves taking advantage of otherwise empty seats on airlines. The website www.airhitch.org explains the concept in exhaustive detail.

Finally, many cost-cutters try flying into London and then catching a cheap flight to Spain—prices can be as low as €30 round-trip. There are also often rock-bottom flights from New York into London. If you are a savvy booker, you can indeed save money, but you need to keep in mind that ground transfer in London is very expensive. Many of the cheapest carriers, such as easyJet, fly from Gatwick, not Heathrow. The two airports are about an hour apart with train and subway transfers. The costs can exceed £20(about $40). You will need to use pounds, not euros or dollars, so that means exchanging money if you want to buy a bottle of water or other item. Finally, you'll have to collect and transfer your luggage between your two flights. Do careful research to determine if all this hassle is worth the amount you will save.

Checking In

For international flights, always confirm your flight with your airline and then plan to arrive at the airport at least three hours early, possibly more if you are flying from a busy airport on a busy day of the week. In the case that your airline has overbooked the flight, the earlier you check in, the less likely you are to be bumped.

Security check-ins have greatly slowed down the checking in process. You can speed things up by checking into your flight online if possible; reducing the metal worn on your body (watches, jewelry, hairclips, underwire bras, zippered boots); having all your documents in order and ready to present to the check-in counter including your passport and flight confirmations or ticket.

Restrictions on carry-on luggage have been greatly increased and are still being modified.

Check before you go, either with your airline's website or at the travelers' section of the Federal Aviation Administration (www.faa.gov). Once you know the regulations, pack accordingly or you will have to re-pack at the security gate.

Insurance

A travel insurance policy can cover anything from lost or missed flights to stolen goods and medical emergencies. The types of coverage and attendant costs vary widely. Your first step should be to check your existing insurance policies to see if you are already covered for traveling. For car rentals, often a gold card will come with rental car insurance automatically—check with your card provider. If you decide to purchase insurance, your own insurance company may offer you a trip supplement package to your regular policy. You can also consult a travel agency, but keep in mind, agents make commission off of insurance packages and are inclined to sell whether you need it or not. Find basic information at sites like www.insuremytrip.com or tripinsurancestore.com.

There are dozens of companies specializing in travel insurance, but you should stick with an established company such as **Betin** (www.betins.com), which specializes in emergencies, **Access America** (www.accessamerica.com), **Travel Insured** (www.travelinsured.com), or **Travelex** (www.travelex-insurance.com). **World Nomads** (www.worldnomads.com) specializes in backpackers and budget travelers and offers excellent prices.

BY LAND

If you are already traveling through Europe, you can take trains or buses into Spain. By train, the main hub to Spain is Paris (11 hours to Barcelona). If you want to travel Europe by railpass and include Spain, be sure to check your options before you buy. Try **Eurail Pass** (www.eurail.com) and **Rail Europe** (www.raileurope.com).

By bus, you are looking at a very long ride, but the price is often right. Check with the bus station of the town you are in or try the main European bus company **Eurolines** (www.eurolines-pass.com). If you are young (in age or spirit), consider a bus-hop across Europe with the hop-on, hop-off bus company **Busabout** (www.busabout.com).

BY SEA

Many cruise ships dock in Spanish cities, including Barcelona and Cádiz. If you are traveling via cruise ship, the onboard crew will provide you with all the information you need to disembark in those cities and get around.

Many people traveling from the United Kingdom—usually with their cars—choose ferry transport into Spain. The major companies are **Brittany Ferries** (www.brittany-ferries.com), which sails to Santander, and **P&O Ferries** (www.poferries.com), which lands in Bilbao.

Getting Around

BY AIR

The combination of low-cost air travel and increased airports means that often the best way to travel within Spain is by plane. This is especially attractive if your time is limited and you need to make a long distance transfer such as from Bilbao to Valencia or Barcelona to Sevilla. All the Spanish carriers offer domestic flights including **Iberia** (www.iberia.com), **Spanair** (www.spanair.com), **Air Europa** (www.aireuropa.com), **Click Air** (www.clickair.com), and **Vueling** (www.vueling.com). Spanair and Air Europa tend to have the most flights at the cheapest prices. If your Spanish is up to snuff, the online booker **eDreams** (www.edreams.es) consistently has the best prices.

The same rules that apply to your international flight are valid here. Show up early for your flight, two hours is usually more than sufficient. Bring your passport and other travel documents and pack your luggage and carry-on items to international standards.

BY TRAIN

Spain has one of the most efficient, timely rail systems in the world—a point they are very proud of. The rail system is overseen by **Renfe** (tel. 90/224-0202, www.renfe.es). Their AVE (Alta-Velocidad, pronounced AH-vay) high-speed trains are excellent ways to get around the country. Madrid to Sevilla is just 2.5 hours, making the flamenco-fueled city a feasible day trip if you are short on time. AVE is currently being extended with the next major connection, Madrid to Barcelona, expected to be up and running sometime in 2007. Check with www.renfe.es/ave for details.

Be aware that AVE routes book up quickly, especially those to Sevilla and Toledo. Buy your ticket upon arriving in Spain. You can use www.renfe.es to buy or, if you find the site intimidating, pop into any travel agency such as **El Corte Inglés,** which will book your ticket for a fee of a few euros. Do not just show up to the train station in Madrid. You will have to wait in a line that can be up to an hour long and often the tickets will sell out while you are waiting.

When purchasing tickets, be aware that buying round-trip comes with a substantial savings. If you don't buy a round-trip ticket, but then decide to make the return trip anyway, show the stub of your original ticket to the ticketing agent to get the discount.

Travel Passes

There are rail passes available for travel on the Renfe system, but they must be purchased outside of the country. Check **Eurail Pass** (www.eurail.com) and **Rail Europe** (www.raileurope.com) for options. Keep in mind that train passes such as these come with lots of rules and regulations and often flying or taking a bus can be more convenient and/or cheaper for various legs of your route. Plan your trip out carefully and research the details before investing in a pass.

Local Trains and Subways

Major cities are connected to their satellites and suburbs via local **commuter trains.** The bulk of these trains are operated by **Renfe/Cercanías** (www.renfe.es/cercanias). Tickets usually cost less than €10 as the distances are short. These trains tend to be hard-seated and make frequent stops. Not all come equipped with bathrooms.

Many cities, including Barcelona, Bilbao, Madrid, and Valencia are served by excellent **subway** systems called "metros." Each offers inexpensive, fast transport around the city. Check the appropriate destination chapters for information on passes and fares. When you arrive in each city, be sure and get a free *mapa de metro* from the nearest tourist booth or a metro station. In cities like Barcelona and Madrid, before embarking on a metro trip, read up on the system so you know what to expect. The easiest way to find your way around is to locate where you are on the metro map, then located where you want to go. You'll have to devise a connection route between the two points. Metro

the Gran Vía Metro stop in Madrid

© CANDY LEE LABALLE

lines are always named by a color, a number, and their end points. So Madrid's line 3 is yellow and is also called Moncloa–Legazpi. To determine which train you need to catch, find your destination and then look where that line ends. As you figure all this out in the metro station, be especially wary of your surroundings. Pickpockets thrive on the confusion that metro systems create. Consult your map with your back up against the wall.

BY BUS

Spain is covered by a very extensive network of buses connecting every town, big and small. Unlike the scary tin-can coaches that crisscross the back roads of America, Spanish buses are clean and comfortable. Seating is assigned, air-conditioning is assured, and there is usually a movie (albeit in Spanish). Not all buses have bathrooms, however, so if you need to go frequently, be sure and book a bus with an *aseo*. Most buses do stop every two hours at a rest stop. For a luxury bus trip, upgrade to *gran clase* if it is available. Often for less than €10 more, you'll enjoy a supersized seat, an on-bus hostess, magazines, plus free snacks and drinks. The only time you will find bus travel difficult is on Sundays and *festivos* (holidays) when schedules are dramatically reduced.

Companies

The main problem with Spanish bus travel is that there are dozens of companies in operation. Unless you are at the bus station, where destination information is posted, you'll need to know what bus company goes where in order to book your trip. The destination chapters in this books list the relevant bus companies for each area. You can also check with the official tourism website for the town you want to travel to. Using a travel agent is not always helpful as different companies have different contracts with different agents. The largest cross-country carrier is **Alsa** (www.alsa.es), which allows you to buy and print your tickets online. When you do buy a ticket, if you have to transfer, make sure you board the bus from the company whose ticket you hold as many companies may very well go to the same destination.

Local Buses

All major cities are served by bus systems. However, as with the national buses, the bus system can be very confusing. Part of the problem is that stops and end points are named for various places in the city. If you don't know the city, it is hard to figure out the routes. Your best bet is to get the information you need from your hotel or a local. Again, the destination chapters have some bus information, particularly for getting into town from the airport or train station.

BY TAXI

Though they once suffered a bad reputation for rudeness and overcharging, Spanish taxi drivers have improved greatly—thanks in part to the government and tourist boards who have pushed through extensive reforms. If your Spanish is non-existent, don't try telling the driver the address since he won't understand you. Have the address of your destination written on a piece of paper that you can give him. If you have a map, you can point it out on the map as well—though most taxis come GPS-equipped these days.

Fares

Official fares are posted in the back seat of the taxi in Spanish and English. There are almost always surcharges for airport pick-up/drop-off, luggage, and traveling at night or on holidays. In some cities, set airport rates apply.

In-city trips rarely top €10, making taxi travel in Spain a bargain compared to New York City, London, or Paris. Be sure and have small bills available. Though bound by law to break anything up to a €20 bill, drivers often ask you to pay with small bills especially if the fare is under €5. Drivers are not obligated to break a €50 bill and if you present one, the driver may insist that you get out and find change while he/she keeps the meter running.

Tipping is not a required or expected custom in Spain. That said, it is usual to round the fare up to the nearest euro, or to give the driver a €1 tip. Anything more and you just look like a sucker. Of course, if the driver went out of his way to help you, feel free to leave €2.

Unscrupulous Drivers

Occasionally you will encounter an unscrupulous driver who will attempt to rip you off. The most common way is by not turning on the meter—a serious offence, punishable by a fine against the driver. If this happens to you, point to the meter and insist. If the driver refuses, get out of the cab. He cannot force you to pay as there is no record of the charge. If a police officer is called over, he will side with you and fine the driver for not turning on the meter. Another way to insure proper service is to ask for a *factura,* or bill.

The reality is that most taxi drivers are honest and hard-working. That said, you can't live in the country long without getting ripped off at least once. Figure that it will happen. If it is only a matter of a few euros, it is easier to just let it slide. If it is a larger amount, you may flag over a police officer or refuse to pay, in which case, the taxi driver will flag the police officer if he/she is in the right, or curse you out if he/she is in the wrong.

BY CAR

Traveling by car is the best way to see off-the-beaten path Spain. You'll need a car to tour the coasts of Galicia and País Vasco, to get into the mountains, to see the white villages of Andalucía, to explore natural parks, to tour the bodegas of La Rioja, or to follow Don Quixote's footsteps through La Mancha.

Rental Agencies

It is usually cheapest to arrange your rental car before arriving to Spain. The major companies (Avis, Budget, Hertz, National) all have extensive networks in Spain. The biggest European agency is **Europcar** (www.europcar.es). You can also use online bookers such as Travelocity and Expedia. Finally, there are car rental agencies in all major cities if you decide to book at the last minute. **Pepe Car** (www.pepecar.com)

and **Easy Car** (www.easycar.com) are two cut-rate bookers. Make sure to rent for unlimited mileage and to have car insurance.

When renting a car in Spain, be aware that almost all cars are manual shift. You can consult with your rental agency to reserve an automatic, but even if your agency guarantees you will have one, you probably will not. Customer service just ain't what it should be in these matters. If you cannot drive a manual shift, learn before you arrive in Spain.

Costs and Insurance

A rental car will cost around €200 for the week, depending on a myriad of factors. Reduce the costs by renting early, shopping around, and renting for a week or more.

It is a good idea to get Collision Damage Waiver insurance, or CDW. It costs €10-20 per day depending on various factors. The rental agency can provide it or you can purchase it independently through a broker such as **Travel Guard** (www.travelguard.com). If you rent the car on your gold card, CDW is often provided by the credit card company. Be sure and research this before taking off on your trip.

Legal Requirements

You must be 18 years old to rent a car and have a valid driving license from your home country. In addition, it is a good idea to have an International Driving License. Technically, it is not required, but rules change depending on who is interpreting them and you do not want to try explaining to a small town police officer why you don't have one. The cost is less than $20 and you can get one instantly at any AAA office.

Road Rules

Speed limits are in kilometers, as are speedometers. The upper limit is 120 km/h (about 75 mph) on highways and 50 km/h (30 mph) in towns. Seat belts are required for everyone in the car, both front- and back-seat passengers. The **alcohol limit** is 0.05 percent blood alcohol level or about two glasses of wine, less if you are small-framed. Children under 12 are not allowed to travel in the front seat. You are not allowed to stop on the shoulder of a highway except in the case of an emergency. If so, you must place the emergency triangle that came with your rental about 30 meters (100 feet) behind the car and you must don the yellow safety vests that are also in your car. Both of these items are required by law to be in a car.

Breaking any of these above laws can result in an on-the-spot fine (starting around €90) or in the case of drunk driving, possible arrest. For more details on driving in Spain, visit (www.drive-alive.co.uk). Click on "Driving Tips," then "Spain" to see the rules and regulations plus details on roads, trip planning, and more.

Gas Stations

Gasolineras (gas stations) are plentiful on the national highways and in big cities and are usually open 24 hours. In smaller towns and back roads, gas stations will be open 7 A.M.–11 P.M. Newer cars all use *gasolina sin plomo,* or unleaded gas. Prices are set by the government and are the same for full- or self-service. In Spain, gas is sold by the liter (there are about 3.75 liters to the gallon). The costs in fall 2006 for one liter was around €1 (just under €4 for a gallon). If you have a diesel car, you will need to fuel up with *diesel.*

Parking

Parking in the major cities can be a real nightmare. If your driving itinerary takes you into Madrid, Barcelona, or Sevilla, consider turning your car in at the beginning of your stay and renting a new one as you leave town. If you must keep the car, chooses a hotel with a parking garage or use a secured public lot. Parking fees (even in hotels) run around €15 per day. See the destination chapters for Madrid and Barcelona for specific parking information for those cities.

Safety

Be sure you have rental insurance that will cover damage caused by break-ins, as rental cars are often targets for thieves. Ward off break-ins by not leaving anything of value visible in the car. While on the road, all of your goods should be secured in the trunk. At night, leave nothing in the car. If you have a hatchback car, remove the cover at night so the thieves can see that there is nothing of value inside. While driving, keep your purse and other valuables on the floor, away from the windows. Thieves on motorcycles are known to pull up, punch out the window, grab the bag, and be gone before you even register what is happening.

On the roads into and out of major cities, particularly Barcelona, thieves on motorcycles or scooters have begun targeting tourists in rental cars. The scam is as follows: They puncture your rear tire, either while you are stopped in traffic or at a gas station. As you are on your way out of town, your tire deflates and you pull over. Within moments, a "friendly" motorcyclist arrives offering help and claiming to be a mechanic—often in English. Do not engage with him (or her). Call out *No!* and turn your attention immediately to the car. While the thief is distracting you, another motorcyclist has often pulled up to your car. They can be off with your suitcase in less than 20 seconds, so do not leave your bags unlocked for even a second. The way to avoid the robbery is by continuing to drive until you reach a crowded gas station or until you see a police officer. If you must stop, make sure you lock up everything in your car. If you have to remove your luggage from the trunk to get to the spare tire, do so one piece at a time, moving the luggage into the locked backseat. Do not set the bags on the ground. If you are traveling with two or more people, have someone look out for all approaching motorcyclists and keep eyes on the car. If the cyclist won't leave, get back in the car and drive away regardless of the damage caused to the wheel.

Maps and GPS

Detailed road maps are readily available all over Spain at newsstands, bookstores, and department stores. The most comprehensive and easiest-to-use maps are the road atlases by **Campsa** and **Michelin.** If you plan your driving trip while still in the United States, consider printing your maps before you go from www.viamichelin.es or www.mappy.com.

Luxury cars may come with a GPS system, but it is by no means standard. You can rent a GPS from www.onspanishtime.com, run by an American expat. Costs begin around €100 for the week, with discounts for longer rentals.

Roads and Highways

The Spanish highway system is wonderfully maintained with an extensive network of new, wide highways covering nearly 8,050 kilometers (5,000 miles). That said, some of the secondary roads and old highways are in a dreadful, even dangerous state.

A tourist driving in Spain may be confused by roads with multiple names, such as A-7/E-15. Additionally, locals, restaurants, and hotels may call a road by its end points such as the Madrid–La Coruña road. Here is a run down of the basic names and what they mean:

National highways: *Carreteras nacionales* are indicated by an "N" and the number in white lettering on a red background. They radiate from Madrid across the country. The principal roads are indicated by Roman numerals (though some maps use the numerical equivalent) and often called by their end points, so the N-I is locally called the road to San Sebastián, N-II is the road to Barcelona, N-III is Valencia, N-IV is Cádiz, N-V is Badajoz, and N-VI is La Coruña.

Toll roads: *Autopistas* are toll (*peaje*) roads and are indicated by the abbreviation "AP."

They are among the nicest, best-maintained, fastest roads in Europe. They are also relatively free of traffic as the tolls are fairly high—a distance as short as Valencia to Alicante costs over €12. Spaniards either can't or won't pay the fees and therefore jam the secondary roads instead.

Highways: Non-toll highways are called *autovías* and are indicated by the letter "A."

European highways: Some Spanish highways are also European roadways and therefore have an "E" name as well, such as the E-5, which runs from France down to Andalucía.

Regional roads: They roads often begin with the letter "C" or the first two initials of the province through which the road runs.

Traffic

As in any major city in North America, traffic in Spain's cities can be a horrendous mix of backed up cars, irate, defensive drivers, and an incredible amount of roadwork. Try to avoid driving in cities unless you absolutely have to. If you are heading to a hotel's parking lot, make sure you have the directions clearly printed out and someone on board guiding you. At all costs, avoid entering areas called *casco viejo, ciutat vela,* or *parte vieja,* as these names refer to the old, medieval city centers where roads are often one-way, dead-end, and/or extremely narrow.

Outside of big cities, you should have no problems except for Friday evenings when everyone in Spain is heading somewhere away from the city and Sunday afternoons when they are all returning.

Visas and Officialdom

Upon arrival into Spain, you will be greeted by an immigration officer—and potentially a customs agent—at the airport. Depending on your home country, you could be subject to visa regulations. The immigration officer will verify that you have your paperwork (valid passport and/or current visa) in order. The customs officer may check your luggage to

ensure you aren't smuggling in too many cigarettes or any live animals. Follow the guidelines below to ensure that your entry into Spain goes smoothly.

VISAS AND PASSPORTS

Spain is a party to the Schengen Agreement in which most European Union nations (Great

Britain and Ireland excluded) agreed to abolish checks at internal borders. Moreover, a visa from one Schengen member country is valid in all other member countries. However, there may be some exceptions to this rule so be sure to check with the consulates of all the countries you plan to visit well before your trip.

All persons entering Spain must hold a passport valid for at least six months from the date of arrival in Spain. European Union nationals do not need a visa to enter Spain, regardless of the length of their stay or purpose of their visit. They are, however, required to register with the police if they plan to stay longer than 90 days to obtain a *tarjeta de residencia* (residence card).

Passport holders from Australia, Canada, Israel, Japan, New Zealand, Switzerland, and the United States do not need a visa to enter Spain for tourist or business purposes for a maximum of 90 days. If you are from any other country, you will most likely have to apply for a tourist visa at your Spanish consulate. You will need a valid passport and a day off from work to wait in line, as a visa must be applied for in person. The time limit on these visas will vary depending on your country of origin, but will not exceed a 90-day maximum. Also note that visa regulations around the world can alter with changes in the political climate, so check with your embassy and the embassy of the nation you are visiting well in advance of your trip to be sure you conform to the most current rules.

STUDENT AND WORK VISAS

Non-EU students who wish to study abroad in Spain for more than three months must obtain a student visa. Student visas must be solicited in person at the Spanish embassy or consulate in your jurisdiction at least 60 days before you expect to travel to Spain and a prior appointment is necessary in order to be attended. As with studying abroad, those who wish to work in Spain will need to apply for a residence visa and work permit.

American citizens can find the documentation requirements for student and work visas

at www.spainemb.org/ingles/indexing.htm (click "consular services," then click the link for the consulate governing your area). If this link doesn't work, do an independent search as the embassy's site is extremely jumbled and difficult to navigate. You may have to search around to find the correct information. Canadians can visit www.cgspaintoronto.com. Australian and British citizens can refer to *Spanish Embassies and Consulates* for their embassy contact information (with links to visa requirements).

SPANISH EMBASSIES AND CONSULATES

In the United States the Spanish Embassy (tel. 202/452-0100, www.spainemb.com) is located in Washington, D.C. There are nine Spanish consulates in the United States, located in Boston, Chicago, Houston, Los Angeles, Miami, New Orleans, New York, San Francisco, and Washington, D.C. For contact information for these consulates visit www.spainemb.org/ingles/indexing.htm (click "consular services"). For Spanish embassies in other countries, visit www.maec.es.

FOREIGN EMBASSIES IN SPAIN

Embassies and consulates in Spain are your home away from home. If you need emergency medical attention, have lost your passport, have been arrested, or have experienced another type of emergency, contact your embassy or your closest consulate immediately. Embassies are located in the host country's capital, which for Spain is Madrid. Consulates are located in larger cities around the country. To contact your embassy or consulate in Spain call or visit the following websites: **American Embassy** (C/ Serrano 75, Madrid, tel. 91/587-2240, http://madrid.usembassy.gov/cons/offices.html); **Australian Embassy** (C/ Santa Engracia 120, tel. 91/353-6600, www.spain.embassy.gov.au); **British Embassy** (C/ Fernando El Santo, 16, tel. 91/700-8200, www.ukinspain.com); **Canadian Embassy** (C/ Núñez de Balboa 35, tel. 91/423-3250, www.canada-es.org).

CUSTOMS

Customs regulations determine what you are allowed to bring into and out of a country. These rules differ by individual nation. In Spain, a customs agent may determine if the items you are bringing in are for personal or commercial use. Taxes may be imposed on the items designated as resale merchandise. You are also expected to declare if you are carrying more than €6,010.12 in cash. You are not allowed to bring animal food products into Spain. Other foodstuffs are limited to one kilogram.

Travelers from outside the European Union are allowed to make the following duty-free purchases: one liter of liquor, two liters of wine, 200 cigarettes, 50 cigars, and 50 milliliters of perfume. You must be at least 18 years old to purchase alcohol and cigarettes.

Upon returning home, you will be subject to the customs regulations of your country. For U.S. citizens, $800 worth of goods purchased for personal use is allowable as duty-free. Items above the $800 threshold or items for commercial use will be taxed. Fresh fruits and vegetables, as well as animal food products, are not allowed into the United States. This means no *jamón* for your loved ones back home.

As of 1999, there are no duty-free restrictions for travel between EU nations, so long as the items of purchase are for personal use only.

BORDER CROSSINGS

The Schengen agreement, which removed border controls from travel within member nations, has made it easy to travel from Spain to other Schengen countries. One visa usually works in all member nations. In addition to Spain, the nations are: Belgium, France, Germany, Luxembourg, Netherlands, Italy, Portugal, Greece, Austria, Denmark, Finland, Iceland, Norway, Sweden, Cyprus, Czech Republic, Estonia, Hungary, Latvia, Lithuania, Malta, Poland, and Slovakia. This list is added to every few years, so check with your consulate before traveling.

For travel to Andorra, Gibraltar (a U.K. territory), and Morocco, a visa is not required for American citizens, but be sure to carry your passport. For requirements for travelers from other nations, contact your country's department of travel/consular affairs. Everyone should be aware that crossing borders by car may be both expensive and time-consuming, as your car may be searched, and the lines to cross may be long depending on the time of day.

POLICE

Spain is a relatively safe country, but as a tourist, you could be a target for petty theft. Be aware of your surroundings and be conscious of your belongings. Should you need help, the emergency number throughout the European Union is **112.** Calling from Spain, operators on this line are available in Spanish, English, French, and German.

There are three branches of police in Spain. The Guardia Civil wear green uniforms and are a remnant of Franco's dictatorship. These officers serve as Spain's highway patrol and customs agents. The Policía Nacional are responsible for public safety and crime scene investigations (including theft) within their cities. Their uniforms are dark blue, decorated with a badge of the Spanish flag or white shirts and black trousers. The Policía Municipal wear blue and white, operate on a local level, and deal with local traffic and parking violations.

If you are approached by a member of one of these Spanish police forces, be respectful. Should you be pulled over for a traffic violation, provide your driver's license, passport (or copy), and rental car contract. Spanish police are authorized to collect fines of up to €300, and non-residents are expected to pay on the spot. It is possible that in smaller cities, the police may not speak English. To report a crime, go to the nearest police station or call 90/210-2112 to request an English-speaking operator.

Accommodations

Housing options abound in Spain. During the low season, which varies from region to region, it is not necessary to book ahead. However, when tourism picks up, it can be extremely difficult to find last-minute lodging. In general, **high season** is July, August, and Easter Week. **Low season** is everything else, but many towns have festivals and events that qualify as high season sprinkled throughout the year, so be sure and do your research ahead of time to ensure that you have a room. Remember when booking that *habitación sencilla* is a single room and *habitación doble* is a double one (but be sure to ask for *cama matrimonial*, a double bed, if you want one large bed as opposed to two singles).

Hostales, Pensiones, and Fondas

Hostales are small, locally owned and operated budget hotels, similar in quality to motels in the United States. They follow a three-star rating system and offer few amenities or services. They come in many varieties ranging from dormitory-style with shared room and bathroom to private rooms with full en-suite bathrooms. Notice that the word is spelled with an "a." Hostel with an "e" almost always refers to a youth hostel (*albergue* in Spanish).

Pensiones and *fondas* are similar to *hostales* in that they are privately owned guest houses offering little more than a place to sleep. *Pensiones* are a step up from *hostales,* and *fondas* typically have a restaurant or small dining room. All three of these types of accommodation cost considerably less than conventional hotels (€25–50, depending on the location and type of rooming) and have a very informal atmosphere. For a decent list of Spain's budget accommodations or to make reservations visit www.hostelworld.com.

Albergues Juveniles

There are about 200 *albergues juveniles* (youth

Hostales often advertise their presence with signs above the street – look up!

© CANDY LEE LABALLE

hostels) in Spain. This accommodation category was designed for the under-26 crowd, although many properties do not have an age policy. *Albergues* offer dorm rooms with bunk beds, shared baths, a common kitchen/living space, and no privacy. Sheets and linens are not always included though are always available for rent, and you will most likely be assigned a locker to safeguard your belongings. *Albergues* are the cheapest housing option, typically costing less than €20 per night per person. This is the way to go if you are a college student backpacking through Europe or on a tight budget. However, in many larger towns, if you are a couple traveling, it can cost the same or less to rent a double room in a *hostal*. One major advantage of *albergues* for young travelers is the opportunity to meet fellow travelers. In larger cities such as Barcelona, Madrid, and Valencia, *albergues* run events for international visitors such as bar and tapas crawls, parties, flamenco shows, and excursions. In smaller towns and villages, *albergues* tend to cater more to Spanish travelers and focus on outdoors activities. Get the best prices on youth hostels by booking through a website like www.gomio.com, which is a portal for European youth hostels.

Hotels

Hotels run from as cheap at €50 to over €300. Style and service also varies wildly from simple and sparse to creative and luxurious. However, every accommodation bearing the "hotel" title will have private rooms and bathrooms, and often a restaurant as well. Hotels observe the following five-star rating system:

- one-star: low budget, may not have maid service
- two-star: budget, daily maid service
- three-star: moderate pricing with basic amenities
- four-star: expensive, all the basic facilities and limited luxury services (business center, gym)

- five-star: luxury hotel with luxury services (golf courses, spas, etc.)

Take note: Five-star service in Spain may fall short of expectations, especially when compared with five-star service in the United States. Most hotels in this category should have 24-hour English-speaking staff to help you with all your needs from travel tips to medical emergencies, but in practice it doesn't always happen. In the four-star category, there are several reliable Spanish chains with hotels throughout the country. They include **NH** (www.nh-hotels.com), **Husa** (www.husa .es), **Abba** (www.abbahhoteles.com), and **AC** (www.ac-hotels.com).

Hotel reservations can easily be made online, though some websites are Spanish-only. You can also book through American-based websites, though prices tend to be a bit higher.

Spain has very recently undergone a boom in luxury and boutique hotels. Find good listings at www.notodohotels.com (Spanish only). The site www.rusticae.es specializes in unique, stylish, luxury properties, often in private converted chalets.

Paradors and *Casas Rurales*

For a classic Spanish feel, and something off-the-beaten path, try booking a night or two at a parador (www.parador.es), a state-run luxury hotel built inside a castle, mansion, monastery, or other historical building. Many are centuries old and were in various states of disuse before the government stepped in to revive them as luxury accommodations. A stay in one of these ancient buildings lets you experience life as it was in the Middle Ages with all the amenities of our modern age. Paradors have good restaurants attached where the food is local and hearty. A double room costs approximately €130.

A *casa rural* is a family-operated country house, often with a very rustic feel. Found in smaller Spanish towns and throughout the countryside, *casas rurales* start at about €45 for a double though many have minimum stays of a weekend or a week. The best website is www .toprural.com, which is partially in English.

Food

In Spain, it is said, *"la geografía manda"* ("geography dictates"). Nowhere is this saying better exemplified than on the plate. The País Vasco, with its ample coastline, does wonders with fish— especially the classic *bacalao al pil-pil,* cod cooked in olive oil and garlic over a low fire. The name comes from the popping sound the fish makes as it cooks. Andalucía offers its own take on the bounties of the sea—*pescaíto frito,* a mixed platter of seafood dusted with flour and fried lightly in olive oil. The central plateau of Spain, including Castilla-La Mancha, Castilla y León, and Madrid, suffers long, cold winters and the food is hearty. Roasted meat and game are specialties. In Segovia, dishes like *cochinillo asado* (roasted suckling pig), are so tender the waiter will serve it by cutting it into pieces with the edge of a plate. In Burgos, it's *lechazo* (roasted suckling lamb) that takes pride of place on the table. Extremadura and western Andalucía are prime grazing areas for the *cerdo ibérico,* the Iberian pig that gives rise to the exquisite *jamón ibérico,* the cured ham that is so revered throughout the country. Navarra and La Rioja are rich with fertile lands yielding a wealth of vegetables that become local specialties including the fat, white asparagus that Navarra is famed for. In La Rioja, where wine production is a region-wide activity, it is not surprising that a local specialty is *chuletillas al sarmiento,* lamb chops grilled over vine twigs. Valencia and Murcia are known for their vast rice paddies, produce, game, and seafood—all of which come together deliciously in Spain's most famous dish: paella. Cataluña, wedged between the Mediterranean Sea, the Pyrenees mountains, and France, brings each of these regions to the tables in unique dishes that combine seafood and meat such as *andonguilles amb sepia* (meatballs with squid) or *conill amb cargol* (rabbit with snails). Of course, both Cataluña and País Vasco have been at the forefront of the Spanish culinary revolution, led by famed chefs such as Ferran Adrià and Juan Mari Arzak.

Typically Spanish

Yet despite these regional differences, you will find certain Spanish dishes—often offered as tapas—nearly everywhere in Spain. These include: *tortilla española* (potato and egg omelet), *croquetas* (croquettes made with béchamel sauce and often bits of ham), gazpacho (a cold tomato soup), *patatas bravas* (fried potatoes with a spicy tomato sauce), *ensaladilla rusa* (a mayonnaise-based potato and vegetable salad), *calamares fritos* (battered and fried calamari rings), *pimientos de Padrón* (bite-sized green peppers fried in olive oil and salted—some are very hot), *patatas ali-oli* (cold potato salad with garlicky mayonnaise), *gambas al ajillo* (shrimp cooked in olive oil and garlic), and *boquerones* (fresh, white anchovies marinated in olive oil, vinegar, and garlic).

Embutidos (cured sausages and meats) are also very popular. Common items you'll encounter all over the country include chorizo (sausage seasoned with paprika), *morcilla* (blood sausage often thickened with rice), and, of course, *jamón.* Almost every tapas bar in the country will have at least one leg of *jamón* hanging, hoof and all, over the bar.

Quesos (cheeses) are also an important part of the Spanish gastronomic landscape with *manchego* from Castilla-La Mancha being the most famous. Other cheeses to look out for include Cabrales, a very potent blue cheese from Asturias; *torta del casar,* a strongly flavored, very soft cheese from Extremadura; and *idiazábal,* a hard, smoky cheese from País Vasco.

Tapas

Tapas are Spain's culinary jewels. They can be as simple as fat, green olives glistening in a slick of vinegar or as elaborate as a miniature work of art involving several ingredients. In Spain, it is common to forego an evening meal for a night of tapas-hopping. It is such a part of life that it has entered the vocabulary—the noun is *tapeo* and the verb is *tapear.* Though explanations of the origins of tapas vary widely, most

© CANDY LEE LABALLE

a typical Spanish breakfast of *café con leche* and churros

agree that the tradition descends from Spain's medieval days when a piece of bread was often placed atop a drink as a sort of cover (*tapa* also translates as "cover" or "top") to keep out fruit flies. Soon bartenders began to add a little something to the bread—a slice of *jamón,* a fried sardine—and the tradition was born.

The visitor should keep a few rules in mind when enjoying these tasty tidbits. In Madrid and much of the center of the country, a small tapa—often called a *pincho* (pinch or bite)—is served on the side of your drink for free. It can simply be a bowl of potato chips or maybe a small portion of a pork stew the chef prepared that day. In Córdoba and much of Andalucía, free tapas are larger in size, but slightly higher drink prices reflect that. Occasionally, you will be allowed to choose your tapa from the dishes on display under the glass case on the bar, but usually the bartender does the choosing for you. In most other places in the country, tapas cost €1.50–5 for the most elaborate dishes.

One thing to keep in mind as you *tapear* is that you will rarely see a "tapas list." Instead, tapas are often advertised on menus—or more than likely on a sign above the bar—by size. A *ración* is a tapa big enough to share between two or three people. If you are dining alone, or not that hungry, ask for a *media-ración,* which is half-sized. A *pincho* (spelled *pintxo* in País Vasco) is bite-sized, often served with a toothpick. In the País Vasco, especially San Sebastián, *pintxos* have been elevated to an art form, with bar after bar specializes in these tasty treats. *Montaditos* are tiny rolls stuffed with anything from *jamón* to *tortilla. Tostas* are tapas served on top of a thick slice of rustic bread.

Culinary Homework

If you are even remotely interested in gastronomy and food, do your research before arriving in Spain. The Internet is loaded with information about Spanish food. A good place for a basic introduction is Spain's official tourism site, www.spain.info. True foodies should peruse the Spain boards at www.egullet.com, which is packed with solid recommendations from Spanish food lovers who

A NIGHTLIFE SURVIVAL GUIDE

Going out in Spain is a ritual practiced throughout the country. Even the tiniest village will have a few bars and at least one late-night place. Going out is so common it even has its own verb, *marchar*. Wherever you go in Spain, reserve at least one night to join *la marcha* yourself. Here are a few details on how to participate.

WHAT IS A NIGHTLIFE SPOT?

The line separating a tapas bar from a bar from a café is very flexible, and it is quite possible that the same café where you have your 9 A.M. coffee will be the place where you end up dancing until dawn. In general, a café is more known for eating than for drinking. For a bar, it's the reverse. However, many bars begin as tapas bars and morph into club mode once the clock swings into single digits. Throughout Spain, cafés, bars, and tapas bars will be the first to close down, usually by 2 A.M.

Clubs, discos, and *discoclubs* are up next. The variety is astounding – from heavy-metal dives to trendy VIP clubs to anything-goes gay discos. However, there are a few things they have in common. Most will charge an *entrada* (cover charge) of €5-20. In exchange you'll receive a slip of paper. Don't toss it out! It is valid for your first drink, whether you choose a cheap beer or a pricey cocktail.

WHAT DOES IT COST?

After your first drink, you'll have to pay for your drinks. Prices depend on the club, what you drink, the town, and the time of year, but expect to pay €4-18, with €8 being the average. Unlike in tapas bars or cafés, in clubs you have to pay as you order. Tipping is not required. Bartenders in clubs are notorious for being inefficient and rude. Tipping them will not much improve things; in fact, it will probably just earn you a "pathetic sucker" look. Also, remember to bring cash. Few bars will accept credit cards.

WHAT TO DRINK?

Keeping in mind that this is your vacation and you should enjoy yourself in anyway you want, there are some social drinking norms followed by the Spaniards. Beer and wine are drunk until about midnight or until you hit the first club. *Copas* (cocktails or mixed drinks) are usually only consumed at clubs. *Chupitos* (shots) are not usually ordered and there is no concept of a "beer and a shot." One exception is at a *chupitería*, a shot bar that specializes in sweet, low-alcohol shots. Fancy cocktails – Cosmo-

can tell you exactly what to eat, where. Also, check the introductions for each of the chapters in this book for more on the regional foods. Finally, if you want to eat at one of Spain's many temples of haute cuisine, you will need to reserve ahead.

Conduct and Customs

SOCIAL BEHAVIOR
Daily Conduct

One of the most delightful aspects of Spanish culture is the sense of civility that permeates even the most mundane of tasks. Young people jump up to offer their seats to the elderly on buses and subways. Upon entering shops, restaurants, tapas bars, and even elevators, Spaniards always say *"Buenos días!"* ("Good day") and upon leaving, *"Hasta luego"* ("See you later!"). In crowded places, bars, clubs, festivals, no one takes offense at being bustled about. If you accidentally spill a drink on someone, they are more likely to end up buying you a drink than getting angry. There is definitely a live-and-let-live attitude (though

politans, White Russians, Manhattans – are not readily available. One exception is *mojitos*, Cuban concoctions with rum and mint that are wildly popular all over Spain. Most cocktails are of the single mix variety – *ron y coca-cola* (rum and Coke), *gin-tonic* (gin and tonic), *vodka y zumo de naranja* (vodka with orange juice). Note that in Spain, *whisky* is always Scotch whisky. If you want bourbon, it is best to ask for a brand name such as Jack Daniels, as bourbon is not a popular drink. Be aware that Spanish pours are heavy. Three to four shots of alcohol are poured into a tall glass and the mixer (juice, soda, etc.) is served in a bottle on the side. If you are not used to such heavy pours, pace yourself carefully.

ARE THERE FIRE CODES IN SPAIN?

Technically, bars and clubs are limited as to the number of people they can allow in. In practice, few follow the rules. If you are out on a Friday or Saturday night, expect to be jam-packed in a bar or club to sometimes-scary proportions. Wear lots of deodorant and be ready to be jostled about. Definitely keep your personal belongings to a minimum and take advantage of the coat check if available. If you don't do well in crowds, go early or stay as close to the door as possible. Spaniards are more than accustomed to these types of crowds and generally show respect, allowing people to pass through to the bar and not getting angry when pushed by the crowd. In fact, if you go out regularly in the States or the U.K., you'll be delighted to learn that the concept of a "bar brawl" just doesn't exist in Spain. At night, the general attitude is we are all out to have a good time, why fight? Go with the flow, relax, and you too will soon be a *la marcha* expert.

WHAT ABOUT THE SMOKE?

Spain has been slow to ban smoking in public places. Though sweeping public smoking laws were enacted in 2006, enforcement is sporadic at best. Smaller bars are allowed to choose to be smoking or non-, and most go with the former. Larger bars must provide for smoking and non-smoking sections, however the smoking section is often just a part of the bar that has been roped off. Suffice it to say, if you are allergic to smoke, you won't enjoy going out in Spain very much. Try to choose an open-air bar or stay close to the door. Your clothes will reek of smoke once the night is done. If you can't wash them (typically the case with coats or jackets), a trick to get the smoke out is to hang your items outside overnight on a windowsill or balcony.

it all but disappears in the country's frequent traffic jams).

The Spanish are extremely social, gregarious, and love to be out and about. Workers gather in cafés a few times throughout the day, and entire families take to the streets in the evenings for a paseo (stroll). Parties, group dinners, and of course, fiestas, fiestas, fiestas, are a way of life. Spaniards also love to talk, giving lots of advice and opinions on everything. After a dinner party, this tendency is expressed in the tradition of *sobremesa* (literally "table covering"), an animated, drawn-out post-meal conversation.

However, this energetic outgoingness is tempered by an inclination towards politeness and formality. Spaniards are particularly reserved with people whom they don't know well. They'll commonly use the formal form of the word "you," *usted,* in such situations. They will also refrain from personal questions and will be taken aback if you ask them personal questions. They also monitor their public behavior, taking care to not be socially unacceptable. Much more so than in the United States, Spaniards actually do care what others think of them.

Though foreigners may find it difficult at first to make friends, once you've made a Spanish friend, you'll have them for life. Spaniards are extremely loyal, not only to their friends but to their family, their favorite soccer team, their native village, their country, and their customs.

ETHICAL TRAVEL IN SPAIN

When planning an overseas trip – or even out of your own hometown – you can enrich your travel experience by adopting the tenets of ecotourism. Ecotourism means travel and tourism that aids in the conservation of not only the environment, but also local traditions, peoples, and economies. It is such an integral concept that the United Nations declared 2002 the "International Year of Ecotourism." The following tips will help you not only travel responsibly, but to also increase the pleasure of your stay in Spain.

Plan ahead and prepare: Arriving with a sense of the social, political, and environmental issues in Spain will make your travels more meaningful. Educate yourself about the geography, customs, manners, and cultures, and remember to respect local traditions and taboos. This book is a good start, but if you want more, check online for the basics. For current events, try searching your favorite online newspaper. Be sure also to check out www.expatica.com and click on "Spain" for the local news of the day in English.

Learn the language: Taking the time to learn basic courtesy phrases cultivates goodwill and enhances your knowledge of local culture. Unlike many European countries, where English is commonly spoken, Spain still very much speaks only *español*. One way to turn off locals and create a feeling of ill will with everyone from shopkeepers to subway attendants is by assuming they will speak English. The best thing you can do to both show your respect for the language as well as indicate you can't speak it is to learn the simple phrase, *No hablo castellano. Habla usted inglés?* (no ah-BLO kahs-TAY-yano, ah-BLA oo-STED in-GLAYS?), or "I don't speak Castilian Spanish, do you speak English?"

Travel with an open mind: Spain truly is different, from greetings (a kiss on each cheek) to eating hours (dinner at 10 P.M.). Learning about these cultural quirks and going with the flow for the duration of your trip can make the difference between an enjoyable visit and a frustrating one.

Minimize your environmental impact: If you visit one of Spain's beautiful natural parks, please follow basic tenets of environmental respect and ecological responsibility. Each natural park you visit will provide you with a set of guidelines, however many will be in Spanish only. To be sure you don't impact the environment negatively, review the principles of **Leave No Trace** (www.lnt.org). In brief: Always travel and camp on durable surfaces; dispose of waste properly; minimize campfire impacts; respect wildlife; travel in small, low-impact groups; always follow designated trails; and do not disturb animals, plants, or their natural habitats. Learn about and support local conservation programs and organizations working to preserve the environment. A good place to start is the excellent website run by British expat and conservationist Nick Lloyd, www.iberianature.com.

Leave what you find: Follow the mantra of "take only photographs, leave only footprints." The impact of one person may seem minimal, but the global effect of removing items from their native place can be decimating.

Support the local economy: Be aware of where your money is going by supporting locally owned businesses and buying locally produced artisan products. Consider knives from Albacete, pottery and ceramics from Talavera and Toledo, wool blankets woven in Grazalema, kitchen linens from the País Vasco, paella pans, esparto grass baskets, bowls made from olive wood, and hand-painted fans. Food products to look for include olive oils, sherry from Andalucía, wines from throughout Spain, *pimentón* (smoky paprika) from Extremadura, and *mazapán* from throughout Castilla-La Mancha. To avoid buying products made from endangered plants or animals or products not allowed into the United States, go to www.cbp.gov, click "Travel," and then "Know Before You Go" for the U.S. Customs list of restricted items.

Bargain fairly: Bargaining is rarely practiced in Spain. The price you are given is what you are expected to pay.

Respect the privacy and dignity of others: Inquire before photographing people or private property. Always ask for permission of the parents before photographing children.

Etiquette

General etiquette as practiced in North America will suffice here, though there are a few behavioral taboos worth noting. The following acts are considered rude in public: yawning without covering your mouth, stretching strenuously, and any sort of hygienic act such as brushing your hair or putting on makeup, even lipstick. Though burping is rude in North American as well, in Spain it is considered extremely rude and a sign of very bad upbringing.

There are also several social rules associated with eating. While dining at a table, keep both hands on the tabletop, as a hand in the lap is considered bad manners. You should not eat foods with your hands, except those specifically meant to be eaten that way (olives, chicken wings, canapés). For almost everything else, a fork and knife is used. Breakfast croissants, grilled sandwiches, even fruit, are eaten with cutlery. Of course, on the other extreme, it is perfectly acceptable to throw trash on the floor of tapas bars including napkins, sugar packets, and olive pits. If you dine with Spaniards, particularly for tapas or dinner, you'll find that they often eat directly out of one big serving platter. If a first course, including a salad, is ordered, side serving plates are almost never asked for nor used—everyone just sticks their fork in. Another big surprise for North Americans comes with the arrival of the check. It is always divided evenly among the guests, regardless of what each person consumed. Protesting or complaining is considered not only rude, but extremely cheap. If there is change left over, it is put into the *bote*, or "pot" and used towards the first round of drinks at the bar—for there is always a stop at a bar (or three) after a dinner out.

Greetings

Upon being introduced, Spaniards exchange two kisses, on each cheek—women to women, men to women, but not men to men (though in the gay culture and among good friends and family, it is common). The only time the *besos* (kisses) are withheld is during business introductions where handshakes are the accepted greetings. A handshake offered in a social context is seen as cold and foreign.

Public Displays of Affection

In general, Spaniards are affectionate in public, and hand-holding, hugging, and kissing are common behavior for couples of all ages. However, the young take it to extremes in parks, public squares, bars, and restaurants. No one minds. You shouldn't either.

Not My Problem

Spaniards have a reputation for shrugging off problems and complaints. Visitors will most likely encounter this with hotel staff. Even in four- and five-star hotels, it is not uncommon for staff to be cold, rude, and genuinely uninterested in you and your need for a hypoallergenic pillow. Some people claim this attitude is a hold over from the days of Franco's dictatorship when complaining got you nowhere. Whatever the reason, don't try to fight it. Yes, you'll find yourself completely flummoxed as to why your confirmed reservation was lost, why you can't have a corner table in an otherwise empty restaurant, why the cashier needs to finish her cell phone conversation before ringing you up, but no amount of frustration nor anger will do anything more than add frustration and anger to the situation. You'll need a sense of humor, adaptability, and a bit of patience if you find yourself confronted with the "not my problem" attitude.

SOCIAL CUSTOMS
Meals

Breakfast *(desayuno)* may be taken anytime from 8 A.M. to 11 A.M., depending upon whether you are on a working or vacationing schedule. It is usually a light meal and most typically consists of coffee, fresh-squeezed orange juice, and a pastry or toasted bread. Churros (thin, fried strips of dough) are a common choice as is the decadent *croissant a la plancha,* a buttery croissant, sliced lengthwise, buttered and grilled, then served with still more butter and marmalade. The cost of a typical *desayuno* rarely exceeds €3. If you want a more elaborate meal, some hotels offer English-style breakfast buffets. You can also order a *sandwich mixto,* a grilled ham and cheese sandwich served with a sunny-side-up egg.

Lunch *(comida* or *almuerzo)* is usually eaten between 2 and 4 P.M. and is the largest meal of the day. It normally consists of a first course *(primera),* an entrée *(segunda),* and dessert *(postre).* Most restaurants throughout Spain offer a *menú del día* that includes these three dishes plus a drink (soft drink, beer, or wine) and bread. The cost depends upon the restaurant, but €10 is about average.

Dinner is often lighter than lunch, though it really depends on the occasion and the diners. Often, a sit-down meal is forgone for an evening of tapas-hopping instead. Spaniards usually have dinner around 10 P.M. or later. It is not unusual for a dinner party to sit down at midnight. However, most restaurants open up by 8:30 P.M. and they are perfectly accustomed to the earlier dining habits of tourists. You will have no problem getting a table, but you will end up eating without boisterous Spanish dining companions.

To ward off hunger between meals, Spaniards indulge in a snack *(merienda),* usually mid-morning and again around 5 P.M. If you'd like to eat during the non-meal hours, look for an open tapas bar or try a sandwich shop or delicatessen. You will not be able to find an open restaurant, except in a few cases in major cities such as Barcelona or Madrid or in towns with a large expat population.

Siesta

Though fast-paced, modern Spain left behind the mid-day siesta years ago, most family-owned shops and smaller chains, as well as offices, travel agents, hairdressers, pastry shops, newsstands, museums, and monuments, still close for at least two hours mid-afternoon. The siesta coincides with the lunch hour and can start as early as 1:30 P.M. and finish as late as 5 P.M. Keep this closing time in mind as you plan your day. Also, it is highly recommended that you indulge in siesta during your travels. Spain is as vibrant at night as it is by day; trying to see it all the way through is physically draining. If you don't want to end up in bed by sundown, take a few hours to nap (or at least rest) mid-afternoon.

Tips for Travelers

ACCESS FOR TRAVELERS WITH DISABILITIES
Facilities

Though facilities for physically challenged or special needs visitors in Spain have improved quite a bit over the past decade, accessibility remains woefully inept. Part of the problem is that so much of the older parts of town were constructed in medieval times. Buildings are narrow, flooring cobbled and crooked, and bathrooms often up or down very narrow stairways. Airports, newer hotels, top-end hotels, and most major sights almost always have elevators, wide hallways, and adapted bathrooms. That said, it can be difficult to try and plan a trip without a little guidance. Your first step should to visit the site of organizations like the **Society for Accessible Travel and Hospitality** (www.sath.org), a group that promotes accessible travel through advocacy and activism. Their "travel tips" section is useful, though there is no specific information on Spain. There are also several websites that offer collected information and links about accessible hotels and vacations. These include www.access-able.com and www.accessatlast.com.

Tour Operators

The easiest option is to contract a tour provider that runs accessible vacation packages in Spain. **Accessible Barcelona** (tel. 93/476-6343, info@accessiblebarcelona.com, www.accessiblebarcelona.com) is run by Craig Grimes, a long-time British expat living in Barcelona and a wheelchair user himself. He arranges tours, transport, accessible hotels, and wheelchair/electric chair rental for trips to Barcelona. In Andalucía, **Las Piedras** (tel.

95/203-3100, info@laspiedras.co.uk, www
.laspiedras.co.uk) is a resort in the mountains
just outside of Málaga that specializes in vacation packages for people with physical disabilities. Run by British expats Adrian and
Hannah Stone, who worked for years in the
accessible tourism industry, the resort offers
airport pickup (from Málaga), fully accessible
facilities that include a lovely pool with a view
over the mountains, and escorted excursions
to nearby Granada to see the Alhambra. They
can also arrange overnight trips to many places
throughout Andalucía. There are also several
American tour agencies specializing in travel
for people with disabilities. One of the best is
the award-winning Minnesota-based company
Flying Wheels Travel (tel. 507/451-5005,
www.flyingwheelstravel.com).

TRAVELING WITH CHILDREN

If you like to travel with your children, you will
love Spain. Spaniards adore children and the little ones are welcome at almost any event—weddings, late dinners, evening strolls, museums,
shops, even bars. It is not unusual during the
summer and on weekends to see kids playing
in the squares at midnight while their parents
enjoy tapas with their friends at nearby sidewalk
café. Children are not considered a burden or
something to check in with a babysitter, rather
they are an essential part of the social fabric.

Sightseeing

All monuments and sights are open to children,
often with discounted entrance fees. One way
to get your child involved in the trip is to let
them choose some of the sights for the family
to see. They will feel more involved in the trip
and you may end up visiting a place you hadn't
thought of before (such as the Chocolate Museum in Barcelona!). Also do an Internet search
for kid-friendly ideas and activities. A good
starting point is www.travelforkids.com.

Restaurants

Even in the finest of restaurants, you'll find staff
and other diners more than accepting of your
children. It is not uncommon for parents to let
their children run around freely. The waiters
and staff don't mind (though they may repri-
mand them if they get in the way of hot plates)
and the other guests aren't bothered, in fact
most Spaniards will take warmly to any child,
engaging him/her into conversation. You will
not find a special child's menu, high chairs, or
booster seats. Children are expected to eat what
their parents eat and it is perfectly acceptable to
request a plate for your child to share your food.
You can also always order something simple
such as *macarrones* (pasta with tomato sauce) or
patatas (fried potatoes) for the truly picky eater.
Most Spanish towns also have their share of fast
food including McDonald's, Burger King, and
KFC. A good thing about these chains is that
they are open all day long.

Transport, Accommodations, and Supplies

If you are moving about the country with your
children, car travel, train, or plane are your
best options. Long bus rides are much too con-
fining for a fidgeting child. Keep in mind, by
law a children under 12 must travel in the back
seat of the car—buckled up of course. Trains
and planes usually offer a discounted children's
fare. Most hotels will also offer a discounted
price for children and will provide a *cuna* (cradle) upon request. Larger, more expensive hotels, especially in resort areas, also offer *canguro*
(babysitter) services. If you know you will be
in a certain city at a specific time, it is useful
to peruse the expat websites for that region, as
many English-speaking expats offer babysit-
ting services.

Pharmacies and grocery stores will sell anything you may need for your baby including
pañales (diapers) and *leche maternizada* (for-
mula), though you may want to bring your baby's favorite foods from home.

WOMEN TRAVELING ALONE
Going Out

Spain does not impose any special problems
or threats to women traveling alone. The only
time you may feel uncomfortable is if you go
to a club or a disco, but not because you will

FIESTA!

Spain loves a good day off and the Spanish calendar is liberally sprinkled with national holidays. If any of the following days correspond with your visit to Spain, expect shuttered shops, restaurants, and businesses. Only in the most touristic of areas will establishments remain open. However, on Christmas Eve, Christmas, New Year's Eve, and Los Reyes Magos (Three Kings' Day), even monuments and musuems will shut down. In addition, most towns have their own roster of local holidays called *fiestas* or *días festivos*. Again, businesses not directly related to tourism will close on these days.

January 1	Año Nuevo (New Year's Day)
January 6	Los Reyes Magos (Three Kings' Day)
March 19	San José (Spanish Fathers' Day)
March or April	Jueves Santo (Holy Thursday)
March or April	Viernes Santo (Good Friday)
March or April	Domingo de Resurrección (Easter Sunday)
May 1	Día del Trabajo (Workers' Day)
August 15	Asunción (Day of Assumption)
October 12	Día de la Hispanidad (Columbus Day)
November 1	Todos los Santos (All Saints' Day)
December 6	Día de la Constitución (Constitution Day)
December 8	Concepción (Day of Immaculate Conception)
December 24	Noche Buena (Christmas Eve)
December 25	Navidad (Christmas)
December 31	Noche Vieja (New Year's Eve)

be threatened, rather it is still quite unusual to find a woman alone in such a place. If you do want to go out, you might seek companions from your hotel—quite easy to do if you are staying in a youth hostel. You can also join wine, tapas, or pub tours.

Common Sense and Safety

The best advice for a woman traveling alone is to use common sense and take basic safety precautions. These include not walking on dark streets alone, not getting drunk or otherwise incapacitated alone or with an unknown man, avoiding empty train compartments when traveling, and not dressing overly sexy or in a way that may draw unwanted attention. Try to reduce your "tourist look" by planning your walking route before setting out for the day, walking confidently in the streets, and ducking against a wall or into a café to consult your maps. If you have stored money or credit cards in a money belt or your bra, go into a restroom stall to retrieve it—never reveal in public where your money is stashed.

Staying in Touch

Keep in frequent contact with friends and family back home, making sure they know your itinerary and what hotels you are staying at. Renting a cell phone is probably the best investment you can make for peace of mind. Contact www.onspanishtime.com before you leave on your trip. They will email you your cell phone number before you even leave home.

For a fee, they will also meet you at the Madrid airport, phone in hand.

Harassment and Violence

Verbal and sexual harassment is minimal in Spain. However, women who are traveling alone should be aware that European men—yes, construction workers—are known for their catcalls. Most of the time the catcalls are innocent and designed more to impress their co-workers than to intimidate you. Be sure and not respond unless you want to get involved in a stressful verbal brawl. The best response is no response, and to keep moving. If you feel uncomfortable, head into a shop or restaurant or towards the nearest crowd.

In major tourist areas, single men will often try to latch onto you by speaking in English, offering to show you around, and asking simple questions about where you are from. You can assume correctly that they are up to no good, looking to either rob you or end up in bed with you or both. Trust your instincts and get away. The easiest thing is to just shake your head, say "no," pick up your pace, and move towards the closest open bar or shop. They often will take advantage of your unwillingness to be rude. Be rude if it comes to it, though never aggressive. Do not use verbal barbs or physical contact. Say "no" loudly and firmly again, and get away. They don't want to raise the attention of authorities, so they will most likely back off.

Rape and violent attacks are rare, but not unknown. Exercise the same kind of caution you would back home. Whether you are on a budget or not, if you need to return to your hotel late at night, invest in a taxi. If you truly feel threatened at any time, by anyone, run and call out "*Socorro!*" (sew-KOH-ro, "Help!").

GAY AND LESBIAN TRAVELERS

In 2005, Spain became the third European nation to legalize gay marriage, putting gay and lesbian couples on the same legal footing as heterosexual couples, including the right to adopt children. Gay and lesbians are definitely out of the closet of oppression created by Franco's long dictatorship when being gay was a crime. In large cities, it is not uncommon to see gay and lesbian couples holding hands or walking arm-in-arm. However, most continue to refrain from stronger public displays of affection simply out of a sense of decorum. There are many areas of Spain that are completely gay and lesbian friendly—Madrid's Chueca barrio, "Gayxample" in Barcelona, Sitges on the Costa Brava, Benidorm, and Ibiza—where couples are free to be as affectionate and overt as they want. In smaller regions of Spain and in the back roads, public displays of affection between gay and lesbian couples are less common and often frowned upon. Sadly, in some of the rough-and-tumble working-class barrios of major cities, violence against gays and lesbians occasionally flares up.

The Internet is full of information for gay and lesbian travelers to Spain and most major cities have websites devoted to the subject, including www.gaymadrid.com, www.staygay barcelona.net, www.gayibiza.net, and www .gaybenidorm.com. If you are a lover of wild parties, you must schedule your visit to Spain around Gay Pride (called Orgullo Gay in Spanish), held the last weekend in June, first weekend of July. Madrid has the most notorious festival with the entire barrio of Chueca turning into a massive outdoor party with DJs, drag queens, lots of dancing in the streets, and an anything-goes mentality.

Health and Safety

As in any modern, developed country, Spain offers up-to-date medical facilities and professional police and emergency services. The general help number to call for police or emergencies is **112**. If you need an ambulance, call **061** or take a cab to the nearest *urgencias* (emergency room) of any major hospital. For non-emergency health needs, visit the local *farmacia*. Most hotels are extremely helpful with any type of emergency and you'll find Spaniards on the street more than willing to direct you to a pharmacy or hospital.

BEFORE YOU GO

Before leaving for Spain, make sure all your medical information is up-to-date. Carry prescribed medications (including birth control pills) in their original containers. This will not only make it easier to pass through Customs, but if you need a refill while in Spain, the Spanish pharmacist can read the label and cross-reference it to find the European equivalent. If you have a serious condition, it is helpful to carry a letter from your doctor describing your medical condition, particularly if you have to carry syringes. If you have allergies, be sure to list them with their Spanish translations to show to waiters for prevention or doctors for treatment.

Health Insurance

Dozens of companies offer health insurance to travelers, including **Travel Guard** (www.travelguard.com), the student agency **STA Travel** (www.statravel.com), and **World Travel Center** (www.worldtravelcenter.com). Also be sure to check with your regular provider to determine if your policy will cover you while you are out of the country—and exactly what that coverage entails. Also inquire about emergency medical evacuation back home. It is a common mistake to assume that the U.S. embassy will provide emergency medical evacuation. They can help you arrange it, but you are on your own for payment. Most American policies require you

to pay up front for services in Spain and then request a refund once you arrive home. Spanish hospitals, doctors, and pharmacies will not honor your U.S. policy and you will have to pay out of pocket for medical attention and medications. However, such services can be as much as 75 percent cheaper than in the United States. Also note that public hospitals will treat you free of charge in the case of an emergency. However, if they give you stitches (*puntos),* you'll be on your own to see a private doctor and have them removed for a fee.

Vaccinations

When traveling to Spain you don't need any specific inoculations, but it is a good idea to be up-to-date on tetanus and polio vaccinations regardless. If you plan to make a side trip into Morocco, consider getting typhoid, hepatitis A, hepatitis B, diphtheria, tuberculosis, and rabies booster shots. More information on vaccinations for travel can be found on the World Health Organization's website (www.who.int/en).

HEALTH MAINTENANCE
Pharmacies

Minor health issues from headaches to cuts to travelers' diarrhea can be taken care of at the *farmacia*. Spanish pharmacists are also able to help with many problems that would require a doctor's visits in the States—from strep throat to a twisted ankle. Be sure to go equipped with your English-Spanish dictionary in order to be able to explain what ails you—many pharmacists, especially in small towns, don't speak English. Pharmacies are listed in local papers, but it is easier to find one on the street. Just look for the flashing green cross. Pharmacies sell basic over-the-counter medications but their names will be different from U.S. brands. Pharmacies can also refill your prescription medications if needed. Just be sure to show the pharmacist the original container. A welcome side effect

Look for the green cross indicating a pharmacy.

of refilling your prescription in Spain is that the cost of medications is much lower than in the United States, often even lower than your stateside co-pay. Be aware that pharmacies keep Spanish store hours (9 A.M.–1 P.M. and 4–7 P.M.), but pharmacies take turns staying open 24 hours. The open pharmacy is called the *farmacia de guardia* and the address of the nearest one will be listed on the door of all pharmacies in town.

Medical Kit

Anything you need to treat a minor medical condition is easily and readily available at any pharmacy, but carrying a small medical kit is a good idea. It should contain aspirin (or a similar pain-reliever), Imodium (or a similar product) for upset stomach and/or diarrhea, Band-Aids or other adhesive bandages, insect repellent, sunscreen, and tweezers. If you have space, you can also carry an antibiotic cream for cuts, calamine lotion (or similar) for relieving bug bites, and any other creams or lotions for your specific health needs.

HEALTH ISSUES
Bug Bites

Insects are not a major problem in Spain and insect-borne illnesses are virtually unheard of. The worst you'll encounter are the same pests as back home—bees *(abejas)*, wasps *(avispas)*, and mosquitoes *(mosquitos)*. In urban areas, you'll have almost no problems. However, if you are allergic to bees or wasps then make sure you always have a syringe of epinephrine, which blocks anaphylactic or allergic reactions. Mosquitoes are just as annoying in Spain as back home, particularly in wet, humid areas and woodlands. Traveling with a DEET-based insect repellent is your best bet for warding off these pests. Treat bug bites with calamine lotion and, above all, remember what your mother always told you—don't scratch!

Dehydration, Heat Exhaustion, and Heat Stroke

Traveling in Spain during summer carries with it a risk of dehydration. It is imperative to stay hydrated. Always carry a bottle of water and do not wait until you are thirsty to drink water. Thirst is one of the first signs of dehydration. Other signs include a dry, sticky mouth, low or no urine output, dark-colored urine, lethargy, and headache. Treat dehydration with lots of fluids, especially water and electrolyte solutions such as Aquarius, a soft drink that is readily available in Spain.

Heat exhaustion is also a threat in Spain's hot summers. Symptoms include heavy sweating, paleness, muscle cramps, tiredness, weakness, dizziness, headache, nausea, vomiting, and fainting. The treatment is to cool down immediately. Get out of the sun, take a cool shower or bath, rest, and drink lots of water.

If untreated, heat exhaustion can become heat stroke, a potentially life-threatening illness. Symptoms are headache, dizziness and disorientation, fatigue, hot skin with no sweating, high temperature, and rapid heartbeat. The victim may also have seizures, hallucinations, or lose consciousness. If heat stroke is suspected, medical attention should be sought. In the meantime, it is imperative to reduce the victim's temperature. Get the person indoors and have them lie down in a cool area with feet elevated. Remove clothing and apply cool water to the skin followed by fanning. Apply ice packs to the groin and armpits. Intravenous fluids will probably be administered at the hospital. Bed rest for a week or two may also be prescribed.

Everyone is susceptible to heat-related conditions, but children, people over 60, those with heart conditions, and the obese are more susceptible. Again, avoid these problems by staying hydrated, drinking water throughout the day, and avoiding strenuous activity during the height of the daily sun. Instead, take a hint from the Spaniards, who often retreat behind doors for a long, extended lunch break at the height of the day's heat. Particularly in Andalucía, you'll find the streets virtually deserted 2–6 P.M. as the masses avoid the heat with indoor activities. Do the same by visiting an air-conditioned museum or taking a nap in a cool hotel room.

Hypothermia

On the polar opposite of heatstroke is hypothermia, which is a lowering of the body's core temperature. This is a threat in Spain's mountainous regions, even in warmer months. Every year, at least a few climbers die of exposure while hiking in the Pyrenees or Picos de Europa. As you spend the day hiking, the temperature can plunge. Be prepared by always having a waterproof jacket and several layers of clothing on hand. Shivering is the first sign of hypothermia. Once you begin to shiver, make an effort to warm yourself. Be aware that symptoms of hypothermia begin slowly. As it progresses, the victim experiences drowsiness, weakness, loss of coordination, confusion, uncontrolled shivering (though it often stops if the body reaches extremely low temperatures), and slowed breathing and/or heart rate. If hypothermia is not treated, shock, cardiac arrest, and coma can occur. Death is a possibility.

If hypothermia is suspected, medical attention must be sought. In the meantime, seek warm shelter immediately. Change the victim out of any wet clothes. Be sure to cover the victim's neck and head, as about 50 percent of heat loss happens here. Apply warm rocks or warm bottles of water to the armpits and groin area. If the victim is conscious, administer warm, sweetened, non-alcoholic fluids. However, if the victim is severely hypothermic, with a body temperature of 26.6–32.2°C (80–89.9°F), only medical professionals should attempt to warm the victim. If the body heats too quickly, shock and cardiac arrest are possibilities. While waiting for medical attention, the best treatment is to have two or three people get under blankets with the victim and apply skin-to-skin contact, preferably on the torso, with one person on each side of the victim. Be gentle with the victim, and do not rub the extremities or move any joints. Unnecessary movement on their part can cause cold blood in the extremities to move to the body's core, leading to shock.

Again, the best treatment is prevention. Do not go into cold or mountainous areas without proper preparation, equipment, and clothing.

If you are planning on hiking or camping in extreme environments, you should be completely aware of the dangers of hypothermia as well as other health threats.

Sexually Transmitted Diseases

The only sure way to prevent catching a sexually transmitted disease (STD) is through abstinence. In lieu of that, using a condom is the best option. Condoms (*condones*) are readily available at pharmacies, grocery stores, and in bigger towns, through vending machines on the streets and in public restrooms. Prices are comparable to those in the United States. Be sure to look for the European CE logo, which means that the product has been properly tested.

New cases of AIDS (SIDA in Spanish) in Spain reached a peak in 1994 and have steadily declined since then. An intensive public-awareness campaign is one of the main reasons for the decline. Nonetheless, it is estimated that some 155,000 Spaniards are living with AIDS. Use the same prevention methods you practice back home—safe sex and common sense. For more information on STDs and AIDS, including prevention, symptoms, and treatment, visit the CDC's website (www.cdc.gov/std).

Skin Care

The Spanish sun can be harsh, especially during the warmer months and on the coast. You should wear a high-level sunscreen every day, regardless of whether you are at the beach or sightseeing in Sevilla. Sunscreens are widely available in Spain. The best brands are ISDIN and Eucerin, both available at any pharmacy, as well as perfume shops such as the chain Juteco. However, sunscreens and skin products (including lotions and make-up) are much more expensive in Spain than in the United States. Your best bet is to stock up before leaving home. You might want to take smaller bottles so you can carry one in your backpack or purse for regular re-applications.

Travelers' Diarrhea

The up-all-night, stomach-cramping misery that is travelers' diarrhea is most likely caused by consuming contaminated food or water. Using common sense can help you avoid this discomfort. Especially in the summer months, food can spoil quickly. If you stumble into a seedy-looking bar and their tapas look a week old, stick with chips. If you are eating something and it tastes or smells bad, stop eating it right away. Always choose bottled water and thoroughly wash any raw fruit you purchase.

If you come down with travelers' diarrhea, the remedy is to drink a lot of water or soft drinks with added electrolytes, such as Aquarius. Most cases respond to an *antidiarreico,* (anti-diarrhea medicine), available at any pharmacy. If you have a severe case that lasts for more than three days, or if diarrhea is accompanied by fever and/or bloody stool, you should seek medical attention.

Spain's tap water is perfectly safe to drink, but in some places, such as Valencia, it has a disagreeable smell and taste. Bottled water is widely available and is very cheap. If you are in a park or natural area and find a public fountain, be sure to see that it is marked *potable,* which means you can drink it. If it is marked *agua no potable,* steer away.

CRIME

Overall, Spain is a very safe country. Violent crime rates are low and muggings and gun hold-ups virtually unknown. However, petty crime is rampant, especially in busy cities like Barcelona, Madrid, and Sevilla. There is an entire class of thieves that makes a living off hapless tourists. Being aware of their tactics and mindful of your behavior will help prevent you from becoming a victim. (See sidebar, *Don't Be a Victim,* in the *Barcelona* chapter.)

Theft

Pickpocketing and purse-snatching are by far the most common crimes inflicted on tourists. Your first step in self-protection is to leave most of your valuables in your hotel room, so even if you fall victim to a pickpocket you won't lose everything. However, the lower down on the price chain your hotel, the more chance for robbery by a hotel worker. Use the room safe if available and if you have a laptop bag, put a lock on it. In the street, both men and woman should carry the bulk of their money in the front pockets of their pants. If carrying a purse with long straps, ensure that the straps lie across the body, shoulder to hip. Keep the purse hanging in front and keep one hand on it all times when moving through crowds.

Always keep in mind that the criminals are waiting for the moment that you are distracted. At cafés, sitting on park benches, and while wandering museums, make sure that you are aware of your surroundings and the location of your goods at all times. Never leave anything unattended, even for a second.

In crowded spots, such as the metro or on tightly packed buses, thieves working in pairs might try to distract you. Hold onto your valuables because while you're being distracted, the partner in crime is trying to dip into your pocket.

If you are robbed, seek out the closest po-lice officer or call 012. It is unlikely that you will ever regain your belongings, but a police report can help if you have travel insurance. If your passport was among the items stolen, you'll have to report to your nearest embassy. If credit cards were among your losses, contact the credit card company and/or your bank im-mediately.

Drugs

Marijuana is legal in Spain in very small amounts intended for personal consumption. The catch-22 is that it is illegal to sell it, so, in essence, if you are buying it you are risking il-legal behavior. You will see people on the street and even in bars rolling hash (called *costo* on the street) cigarettes. For the most part, the po-lice turn a blind eye to this practice, but it is il-legal and you can be arrested if you are caught. Other drugs, such as ecstasy and cocaine, are regularly proffered in clubs and discos. These are illegal, unregulated, and dangerous.

Information and Services

MONEY
Currency

Spain is part of the European Union and ad-opted the euro in January 2002. The bills are denominated in 5, 10, 20, 50, 100, 200, and 500 euros. Coins are available in 1, 2, 5, 10, 20, and 50 cents, as well in 1 and 2 euros. Be careful, a €1 coin may look like a quarter, but it is worth five times as much! The biggest ad-vantage for the traveler is that as you are mov-ing between European countries that share the euro, you don't need to convert money at each border crossing.

Many older Spaniards still think in terms of pesetas, the old Spanish currency. In smaller bars you may still see menus printed with pe-setas listed alongside euros. The changeover rate from peseta to euro was 166 pesetas to the euro. A major gripe, still commonly voiced, is that when the conversion occurred, shops, res-taurants, and bars made the much easier cal-culation of 100 pesetas to the euro, therefore a 100-peseta coffee became €1, or 166 pese-tas—a more than 50 percent increase. Unfor-tunately, salaries and mortgages stuck to the strict rates, so while the daily cost of living jumped, people's bank accounts did not.

When traveling through Spain, always carry small bills and coins. Taxis are not obliged to accept anything over a €20 bill and often do not have change. It is a good idea when arriv-ing at the airport to take out an odd amount of money, such as €180, in order to have a few €20 bills to use for getting into town. Metros and buses are easier to board using change, rather than bills, and sundries such as luggage storage or soda machines often only take coins.

Exchange Rates

Exchange rates are in constant fluctuation, but the main thing to remember is that the euro is both a strong and a stable currency. It is easy to think of the value of €1 as more or less comparable to that of $1, but for the last several years €1 has maintained a value of about $1.25. For current exchange rates, visit www.oanda.com or www.xe.com. Rates listed at bank tellers or in exchange shops tend to be skewed in favor of the exchanger. You are always guaranteed the best rate at ATMs.

ATMs

Cajeros automáticos (ATMs) are widely available throughout Spain and in major city centers you'll see them every few meters. The two most common networks are Servired and 4B. ATMs accept most major debit and credit cards and are the easiest and most convenient way to get access to cold, hard cash. They also use the official market-set exchange rate, so you end up getting the best rate for your dollars. Usually, Spanish ATMs do not charge the user of a foreign card for the transaction. If they do, you will be informed before you make your transaction. However, your own bank will probably charge a foreign withdrawal fee of a few dollars. Be sure to confirm the fee with your bank before traveling. Most ATMs can dispense a maximum of €300 per account per day; again, check with your bank. In general, the La Caixa (KAI-sha) allows for the largest withdrawals.

Spanish ATMs will detect that your card is foreign and offer you the option of English for your transaction. If not, the two words you need to know are *sacar* (withdraw) and *cuenta corriente* (checking account). Finally, you might want to bring two cards with you in case the primary card becomes damaged. Be sure to have your bank's number for lost or stolen cards and your account number tucked safely away in case you should need it (emailing them to yourself is a good idea). Of course, you should practice the same precautions at Spanish ATMs as you would at home. Cover the keypad as you key in your PIN, be aware of your surroundings, and try not to take money out while alone on a deserted street. Finally, if you are nervous that your card won't work, your best back up is to bring travelers checks that you can keep hidden away should you need them.

Three important tips to keep in mind—one, inform your bank that you will be using the card in Spain before you leave the United States. Because of the threat of fraud, American banks often have a built-in protection that will deny unusual charges to your card. If you have been banking in Iowa for years and suddenly go to Spain and withdraw money or try to pay for a hotel, it could raise alarms at your bank. Avoid this by calling customer service and letting them know. Two, if you have memorized your PIN with letters, learn the corresponding numbers before you leave home. ATM machines in Spain almost never have the letters printed on them. Neither do most phones. Three, if the first machine you try doesn't work, don't panic. Try a few different ATMs before you resort to calling your bank.

Changing Money

In major cities, most of the major banks in the tourist zones provide foreign-exchange services (*cambio* in Spanish). Usually one teller will be dedicated to this service. You must show your passport to make the exchange, as a photocopy will not suffice. Throughout the tourist areas you'll see gaudily colored currency-exchange shops. These shops often advertise the best rates, but in smaller print, you'll see that they charge a commission that overcompensates for the difference. Bottom line? Only use these shops if you are absolutely desperate for euros after banking hours. Also, be aware that thieves are known to hang about these spots posing as tourists. Make your transaction at the counter, count your money at the counter, and put your money safely away on your person at the counter.

Banks

Spanish banking hours are generally 9 A.M.–2 P.M. Monday–Saturday. During the summer, banks are usually closed on Saturdays. Banks provide currency-exchange services as well as access to ATMs. Some of the bigger banks in Spain include are **La Caixa** (www.lacaixa .es), **Santander Central Hispano** (www.grupo santander.es), **BBVA** (www.grupobbva.com),

Sabadell Atlántico (www.sabadellatlantico .com), and **Banesto** (www.banesto.es). You will find them all over Spain and in major city centers, and most will have a customer-service attendant who speaks English. There are also branches of Citibank in major cities, but they are their own entities separate from their U.S. counterparts.

Bank Transfers and Wiring Money
Bank transfers and wiring money are the best options to get cash if you need more money than an ATM can handle, particularly if some emergency has arisen. For more information on bank transfers, check with your bank at home. There will probably be a fee of up to $50 and you'll need an active account in Spain to make the transfer to. For information on wire transfers, visit www.westernunion.com. To find the authorized agent nearest your location, click on "agentes."

Travelers Checks
Travelers checks are on the verge of extinction, but are still accepted at banks and currency exchange offices. To exchange travelers checks for cash, you will need a valid passport. A commission fee may be charged for the transaction and you often won't get the best exchange rates. Skip the hassle and stick with cash and credit cards. If you prefer the security and safety of travelers checks, opt for an **American Express Travelers Cheque Card** (www.americanexpress.com) or get a prepaid debit card from your own bank.

Credit Cards
Visa and MasterCard are universally accepted in Spain, and American Express to a lesser extent. Cards such as Diners Club and Discover are rarely, if ever, accepted. Be aware that independent, local shops may not accept credit cards. The same goes for many small bars and restaurants. Be sure to ask before running up a bill. Also, be aware that your credit card company may charge you a foreign currency transaction fee. Check with them before leaving home. Finally, you should always advise your credit card company that you will be using your card abroad.

Sales Tax
Value-added tax, sometimes called VAT (IVA in Spanish) is typically 16 percent for products and services and 7 percent for food, drinks, and hotel rooms. IVA is included in the price, unless specifically stated.

Non-residents of the European Union can request a sales tax refund on individual store purchases over €90. When shopping, ask for a tax-refund receipt *(cheque)* at participating shops. You will need to show proof of non-EU residency, such as a valid passport. At the airport before your departure from Spain, show your tax-refund *cheques* (and possibly your purchases) to a customs agent for a stamp of approval. Next, take this validated tax-refund documents to an IVA refund office such as **Global Refund** (www.globalrefund.com). Madrid's airport has a Global Refund office in Terminal 1, in departures. In Barcelona, the office is within the airport bank branches of BBVA and La Caixa, both in departures. These offices will charge a small fee for refunding your money. Refunds can be made immediately in cash or can be applied to your credit card account. Alternatively, you can request your refund via the mail, which could take several weeks. To be safe, arrive at least three hours ahead of your departure in order to take care of refund procedures.

For some, the IVA refund is just not worth all the paperwork and trouble. For big shoppers, it is like winning the lottery. Just remember, you have only three months from the time of purchase to claim your tax rebate. If you are wandering through Europe for a summer, you could miss your window of opportunity to get your money back.

Bargaining
Haggling for a deal in Spain is just not done, even at flea markets or with street vendors. If you try, it will be considered very strange and even rude. Prices are already very competitive at flea markets. The price you see is the price to pay.

When shopping, know that Spain has two major sale seasons—in January after the holidays and again in August as the summer is ending. Red signs proclaiming *rebajas* will appear in all the shop windows, but don't expect the kind of American super 80 percent–off sales you are used to. A Spanish sale might only be 20–30 percent off.

If you are a student, under 18, over 65, or are a teacher, be sure and always carry around identification proving such. Many museums and cultural events offer discounts to these groups.

Tipping

Unlike in the United States, menu prices include service. Service staff are paid regular competitive wages, not tips. Tipping in Spain is totally optional and rarely practiced by Spaniards in daily visits to coffees shops and bars. However, if you dine at a fine restaurant or your service at a cheaper restaurant is especially attentive, a 5 percent tip is a nice gesture. Rounding up to the nearest euro is recommended for taxi drivers. In nightclubs and discos, no tipping whatsoever is expected or encouraged. Most bartenders working here are fill-ins with little experience and even less personality. Leaving a tip will not get you better service, or a bigger drink.

COMMUNICATIONS AND MEDIA
Mail

Stamps can be purchased at one of the Spain's surplus of *estancos* (tobacco shops). They are easily identified by their maroon signs with *Tabacos* written in yellow. You can also visit any *correo* (post office). Check www.correos .es or the local yellow pages or ask at your hotel or the tourist office for the nearest location. At of the end of 2006, it cost €0.78 to send a postcard or letter to the United States, €0.57 to locations in Europe, and €0.29 within Spain. Deposit your mail in any of the bright yellow mailboxes that line city streets.

Since it is extremely expensive to ship across the Atlantic, it's best to buy what you can in Spain rather than have it sent to you. Likewise,

Look for the yellow mailboxes all over Spain.

© CANDY LEE LABALLE

try to fit all your souvenirs into your suitcase on the return trip rather than mail them. The regular Spanish mail system is slow (delivery and pick-up only Mon.–Fri.) and somewhat unreliable. If you must ship something important home, be sure to send it *certificado* (registered), which costs an additional few euros. For a bit more you can have something sent *urgente* (rush). Shipping options outside of *correos* include **FedEx** (www.fedex.com) and **DHL** (www.dhl.es).

Telephone

Calling home from Spain is easy and ironically, it's often cheaper than making a call within Spain to a Spanish cell phone. The most economical and easiest option is to visit a *locutorio* (private call center), which offers low-rate overseas calls that you pay for immediately upon finishing your call. Bring coins and small bills.

Another option is to use calling cards, which can be bought at *tiendas de alimentación* (small variety stores) or at *estancos*. You can also purchase calling card codes on various websites. Depending on the card and how you call (landline to landline is cheapest), you can get up to 4,500 minutes for just €6. One of the best value calling cards is **Eurodirect,** which you can purchase online at www.euro phonecards.com even before you depart for your trip to Spain in order to save time when you arrive.

To call the United States, dial 001 + area code + number. To call Spain from the United States, dial 011 + 34 + number. To make a local call within Spain, use your spare change at the blue payphones on the street or a slot-in *tarjeta telefónica* (phone card) that is sold at kiosks and *estancos*. Note that since cell phones have absolutely swept Spain, payphones have fallen into disuse and, in many cases, disrepair, so you may have to check a few before finding one that works.

All Spanish landline numbers begin with a 9 and cell phones with a 6. Remember, 900 numbers are toll-free, whereas 901 and 902 numbers charge a fee. Unfortunately, most of the customer service numbers for big companies like Renfe, some hotels, and airlines are 902 numbers.

Area codes are always written with the number. Some common codes are: Barcelona: 93; Bilbao: 94; Cadiz: 956; Granada: 958; Leon: 987; Madrid: 91; Malaga: 952; Palma De Mallorca: 971; Pamplona: 948; Santander: 942; Sevilla: 95; Valencia: 96; and Vigo: 986.

Cell Phones

Cell phone calls are not cheap in Spain (a mobile-to-mobile call can cost more than €0.50 a minute), but the convenience of having a cell phone while traveling makes this option worth looking into. As with landline calls, the person making the call assumes all charges. For Spanish cell phones, there is no charge to receive a call on your cell phone. If your American phone is of the tri-band variety, then it should work in Spain, though the roaming fees will be extremely high. A more cost-effective solution is to buy a Spanish SIM card for your American cell by visiting the all-English www

.spainSIM.com. You can also purchase *tarjetas de SIM pre-pago* (prepaid SIM cards) at any El Corte Inglés department store (www.elcorte ingles.es) or FNAC (www.fnac.es). If you have an American SIM card you will have to get it *liberado* (unlocked) before you can use it. A *locutorio* (a small mobile phone store) will do it for around €10.

One way to avoid all the hassle is to go straight to the experts at **Onspanishtime** (C/ Correos 4, Madrid, tel. 65/626-6844, U.S. toll-free 800/240-6993, www.onspanish time.com). Run by American expat Jeremy Reines, this complete mobile service can help you rent a phone. It will cost around €35 a week. There are various payment calling options available. The rental service is geared towards Americans and allows you to call back to any phone in the United States from their rental cell phones for as little as €0.40 for a full hour. One of the biggest bonuses of using this company is that you can arrange everything in English from the United States, and have your cell phone number before you even get on the plane. Simply visit the website or call the U.S./Canada toll-free number. Jeremy will also deliver the phone to the airport or to any location in Spain for a fee. He is also an expert in all calling matters from SIM cards to phone cards.

If you will be in Spain for a month or more, you best bet is to just buy a cell phone (prices can be as low as €40) with a *tarjeta SIM de pre-pago*. Any electronics shop will sell them, but to ensure quality of service and product, try El Corte Inglés, FNAC, or specialty shops like The Phone House, which sells phones and pre-paid plans with Spain's three biggest providers—Orange, MoviStar, and Vodafone. **Vodafone** is the most popular company in Spain, with the most users and an extremely large network. Their bright red shops are all over the country. If you wish to buy a phone and SIM package before leaving for Spain, it will cost a bit more but you can do so at www.spain SIM.com and have your phone number before you leave home.

Fax

You can send faxes from various places throughout Spain. Its easiest, but most expensive, from your hotel. Other locations include the aforementioned *locutorios,* post offices, and copying centers such as **Work Center** (www .workcenter.es), which has locations in most major cities including Madrid, Barcelona, Sevilla, and Valencia. Prices for a fax from Spain to the United States generally run around €14 with about €4 for each additional page.

Internet Access

The Internet is easily accessible in Spain. Major cities have an abundance of cybercafés where you pay by the hour, and even small towns have at least one or two Internet facilities. Most hotels, even cheap ones, now offer some sort of Internet service to their clients, be it terminals, DSL connections, or Wi-Fi. Prices run from free to exorbitant, depending on the owners. When using public cybercafés, be aware that they are notorious breeding grounds for thieves who take advantage of their victim's online distraction to make off with their goods. On the upside, cybercafés are great places to meet fellow travelers and usually they have some sort of bulletin board posting all kinds of events and activities.

Wi-Fi is still not as available in Spain as in the United States. You may find a network in the area of your hotel, but it will more than likely be locked. Many cafés in bigger towns now offer Wi-Fi free to their clients. Be on the lookout for places as you do your sightseeing or ask at the tourist office. Some places such as the ultra-luxe ice-cream shops **Giangrossi** (Madrid, Barcelona, and Marbella, www .giangrossi.es) offer free, unlimited Wi-Fi with the purchase of any food or beverage. The Spanish-owned coffee house **Faborit** (Madrid and Barcelona) also offers Wi-Fi for its customers, and its fare is more varied and cheaper than Giangrossi. The ubiquitous **Starbucks** that has sprouted up all over the country charges customers €4.50 an hour to use their Wi-Fi and then only if you first purchase a beverage.

If you are going to be in the back roads with your laptop, far from a Wi-Fi network or even a cybercafé, **Onspanishtime** also rents a special Internet card that has a data SIM in it to provide your laptop with Internet access throughout Spain.

English-Language Press

If you are feeling a bit nostalgic for English-language newspapers and magazines, fear not. The kiosks in major cities and tourist areas of Spain (mainly the coasts) sell current international press alongside the Spanish. You'll often find the daily papers *USA Today* and *International Herald Tribune,* which regularly pairs up with Spanish paper *El País* to offer an English version of the Spanish news. Magazines readily available include *Time* and *Newsweek.* In less-traveled regions of Spain it is often hard to find English-language press, much less up-to-date publications.

Most of the major cities, especially those with large expat populations, have local papers and magazines in English. You'll find copies at tourist offices, in hotels and youth hostels, and in Irish pubs. One nationwide publication that offers some interesting travel articles on off-the-beaten path destinations as well as a rundown of Spanish cultural events is *TBS: The Broadsheet,* which can be found at bigger kiosks. You can also check www.tbs.com.es for distribution points.

Spanish Press

The Spanish press is readily available in kiosks on nearly every city street corner and free daily newspapers litter the subways throughout the day. The main national newspapers are *El País* (www.elpais.es), *El Mundo* (www.elmundo .es), and *ABC* (www.abc.es). For a complete guide to leisure activities, pick up the *Guía del Ocio* (€1), which covers everything from where to eat to what is playing at the cinema.

Websites

Dozens of expats across the country have set up online guides to getting the most out of Spain. You can track down info anything from sushi restaurants in Alicante to an English-speaking dentist in Santiago. These are also the best places to get insider information on what to do, where to go, when, and how. Some general Spanish sights worth perusing prior to your trip are www.spainexpat.com, www.justlanded .com, and www.idealspain.com. More locally based information can be found at sites such as Madrid's www.multimadrid.com or www .madaboutmadrid.com and Barcelona's www .barcelonaconnect.com. A quick Internet search will reveal many more. For news and views on Spanish life, try www.expatica.com and click on "Spain."

MAPS AND TOURIST INFORMATION
Tourist Offices and Websites

Planning ahead gives you the knowledge you need to make your experience in Spain unforgettable. All you need to know about Spain is at your fingertips thanks to the Internet. The official tourism site is **Spain Tourism** (www .spain.info). It offers advice on when to visit and what to see in Spanish, English, and a variety of other languages. It includes almost any sight you could imagine visiting plus a wealth of restaurant, hotel, and cultural information. **The Tourist Office of Spain** (www.okspain .org) offers a concise summary of the regions of Spain. The site also has a listing of tourist offices worldwide. Contact the office nearest you for a free travel kit.

Maps

The maps in this guidebook are designed to be user-friendly, but may be limited to specific areas within a town or city. Tourist information centers offer maps free of charge that cover the entire area. You can also purchase maps at most souvenir shops. With **Google Maps** (www.maps.google.com), you can search for any address (be sure to include city and/or zip code) and it will generate a street-specific map. Other good map-generating sites are www .mappy.com and www.viamichelin.es. For bigger cities, these maps will even show subway stops. Additionally, there is the **Google Earth** software (www.earth.google.com), where you can get a satellite image of the actual street.

You will know what you are looking for before you even leave home.

For driving in Spain, the best maps are the orange, fold-out maps by Michelin or road atlases by Michelin or Campsa. You can pick these up in most large department stores in Spain including El Corte Inglés and FNAC. If you want to get your maps before leaving your home country, try www.amazon.com or a local travel shop in your town.

Listings

Search the national leisure guide **Guía del Ocio** (www.guiadelocio.com) by Spanish province and type of activity to find out what the locals are up to. From art exhibits, theater, and festivals to hotels, restaurants, and nightlife, this magazine and online guide has every day of the week planned for you. It is partially in English. Get suggestions from fellow travelers at **TripAdvisor** (www.tripadvisor.com). You can post specific questions to veteran Spain travelers as well as search archived discussions to get advice on where to go and what to do,

There are also tons of expat-run message boards and online forums throughout Spain. In Madrid try www.multimadrid.com, www.mad aboutmadrid.com, and www.madridconnect .com. In Barcelona, try www.barcelonaconnect .com, www.absolutebarcelona.com, and www .barcelona-metropolitan.com. (See the *Resources* section for more sites.)

WEIGHTS AND MEASURES

Spain uses the **metric system.** See the conversion chart at the back of this book.

The **electrical system** is 220 volts. In North America, the voltage is 110. This means if you plug an American product into a Spanish system it will overheat, burn out, or even start a fire. If you need to bring electrical items such as hair dryers or electric shavers, consider buying travel versions that switch between 110 and 220. Re-chargers and power units for laptops, cameras, video cameras, and other items often convert automatically to changes in voltages. Check the manufacturer's information, look right on the charger, or call customer service to be sure. Unless you are coming to Spain for an extended period of time, there is no reason at all that you would need to buy a voltage converter. These small, but very heavy, items convert any 110 product into 220 and you will have to choose one of appropriate voltage capacity—a hair dryer needs more capacity than a battery re-charger. Finally, for your items that do convert automatically, you'll need a plug adapter that turns the American slot-prong plug into the European two-hole plug. They can be hard to find and expensive in North America (try a travel store) but are readily available and cheap (around €1) throughout Spain.

Spain is in the **Central European Time Zone,** six hours ahead of the American East Coast, nine hours ahead of the American West Coast. This means that at 9 P.M. in Spain, it is 3 P.M. in New York, and noon in Los Angeles. Spain also uses the **military or 24-hour clock,** especially for transportation. Be familiar with it to ensure that you don't miss your train, plane, or bus. Starting with 0000 (which equals midnight), add one hour for each hour of the day. 0100 is 1 A.M., 0800 is 8 A.M., 1200 is noon, 1300 is 1 P.M., 1400 is 2 P.M. and so on through 2300, which is 11 P.M. If you get confused with the numbers above 1300, always remember to subtract 12 to get back to your tried-and-true 12-hour clock.

A note about numbers. In Spain, prices are written with a comma, not a period, such as 19,95 or 8,50. However, decimal points in numbers are the reverse. Spaniards use periods not commas, so one thousand is 1.000, and eighty thousand is 80.000.

RESOURCES

Glossary

abierto open
abono pass, coupon book
aceituna olive
aguacate avocado
ajo garlic
albahaca basil
alcachofa artichoke
almeja clam
almendras almonds
anchoa anchovies
aquí here
atún tuna
Av. Avenida, Avenue
aves poultry
ayuntamiento town hall
bacalao salt or regular cod
berenjena eggplant
besugo red sea bream
bien well
bogavante clawed lobster
bonito tuna
boquerones white anchovies
bueno good
butifarra white fresh sausage
butifarra negra fresh blood sausage
C/ Calle, Carrer, Street
cabra goat
cada each
café coffee, coffee shop
café americano espresso with water added
café bombon espresso with condensed milk
café con hielo iced espresso
café con leche coffee with milk
café cortado shot of espresso with a bit of milk
café solo shot of espresso

calabacín zucchini
calabaza squash
calamar squid
calor hot
caña small draft beer
cangrejo crab
caracol land snail
carne meat
casi almost
cazón dogfish
cebolla onion
cecina dry cured beef
cerdo pork
cereza cherry
cerrado closed
cerveza beer, bottle or tap
champiñón button mushroom
chiringuito beachside bar
chopitos tiny squid (usually fried)
chorizo sausage (cured, smoked or fresh)
chuleta chop
churros fried dough
ciervo deer
ciruela plum
cochinillo suckling pig
codorniz quail
conejo rabbit
copa cocktail, mixed drink
cordero lamb
cordero lechal suckling lamb
costillas ribs
croqueta croquette
Ctra. Carretera
D.O. appellation (for wine, food)
día day

doble double
donde where
dorada gilthead sea bream
empanada/empanadilla pastry with (usually) savory fillings
emperador swordfish
entrada entrance, cover charge
espárrago asparagus
espinaca spinach
este this
estos these
FCG: Ferrocarrils de la Generalitat
frambuesa raspberry
fresa strawberry
frío cold
fruta fruit
gambas shrimp or prawns
gente people
gobierno government
gran great
guisante pea
hammam Arabic bath
hecho made, done, fact
higo fig
hoy today
iglesia church
jabalí wild boar
jamón cured ham
jerez sherry
lacón cooked ham or shoulder
langosta spiny lobster
lechazo suckling lamb
lechuga lettuce
limón lemon
maíz corn
mañana morning, tomorrow
mantequilla butter
manzanas apple
marchar to go out at night
mariscos shellfish and crustaceans
mejillón mussels
melocotón peach
membrillo quince
merluza hake
metro subway
morcilla blood sausage
mundo world
nada nothing

naranja orange
noche night
nombre name
nuez walnut/nut
nunca never
oreja ear
ostras oysters
otro other, another
país country
pan bread
parador state-run luxury hotel
pasas raisins
pastel pastry/pie
patata potato
pato duck
pavo turkey
pensíon motel
pepino cucumber
pera pear
perdiz partridge
pescado fish
pez espada swordfish
Pg. Passeig
pimienta black pepper
pimiento pepper
pimientos de Padrón green peppers, some spicy
pimientos del piquillo red roasted peppers
piña pineapple
Pl. Plaza, Plaça, Placeta
plátano banana
playa beach
Po. Paseo
poco little, not much
pollo chicken
Pr. Praza
Ptge. Passatge
pulpo octopus
qué what
rabo (de toro) (ox/bull) tail
rape monkfish
sal salt
salchichas sausage links
salmón salmon
sandía watermelon
sepia cuttlefish
seta wild mushroom
sobrasada soft, spreadable sausage

solomillo tenderloin/filet
sopas y cocidos soups and stews
tablao bar with a stage for performances
tapear to go out for tapas
tarde afternoon
tarta/torta cake
tiempo weather
todo all
todos everyone
tomate tomato
tortilla potato omelette
trucha trout
trufa truffle

uva grape
vamos let's go
verduras vegetables and greens
vermut (de grifo) vermouth (on tap)
vida life
vieira scallop
vino wine
vino blanco white wine
vino rosado rosé
vino tinto red wine
yogur yogurt
zanahoria carrot
zumo juice

Spanish Phrasebook

Too many travelers make the mistake of thinking that everyone in Spain will speak English. In reality, the lack of English spoken in the country makes it a great place for both English teachers looking to earn euros and students of Spanish seeking language immersion. Part of the problem stems from the rule of the dictator Franco, who prohibited languages other than Castilian Spanish from being used. All films and television shows were dubbed into Spanish – a practice still in use today – meaning that few people got to hear other languages spoken. Another problem is the school system. English (and other language) teachers were rarely native speakers of the language themselves and thus lessons were grammar-focused rather than based on actual usage. Finally, Spaniards are a proud people and are reticent to embarrass themselves by speaking poorly. Even the most fluent speakers of English will swear up and down that they don't speak a word. What this all comes down to is one thing – you'll need some basic Spanish to enjoy your trip. A word of advice: Attempting to speak even a little Spanish will be appreciated and can make the difference between a cold reception or a warm welcome. The best phrase you can learn is, *lo siento, no hablo castellano* (low SEE-en-toe, no a-BLO kas-TEE-ya-no), "I'm sorry, I don't speak Castilian Spanish." It lets the listener know

that you can't speak their language, but you are respectful enough to acknowledge it. The worst thing you can do is just approach someone and start speaking English, it comes off as rude and insensitive.

Spanish commonly uses 30 letters – the familiar English 26, plus four straightforward additions: ch, ll, ñ, and rr. (See *Consonants*.)

PRONUNCIATION

Once you learn them, Spanish pronunciation rules – in contrast to English – don't change. Spanish vowels generally sound softer than in English. (Note: The capitalized syllables shown here receive stronger accents.)

Vowels

a like ah, as in "hah": *agua* AH-gooah (water), *pan* PAHN (bread), and *casa* CAH-sah (house)

e like ay, as in "may": *mesa* MAY-sah (table), *tela* TAY-lah (cloth), and *de* DAY (of, from)

i like ee, as in "need": *diez* dee-AYZ (ten), *comida* ko-MEE-dah (meal), and *fin* FEEN (end)

o like oh, as in "go": *peso* PAY-soh (weight), *ocho* OH-choh (eight), and *poco* POH-koh (a bit)

u like oo, as in "cool": *uno* OO-noh (one), *cuarto* KOOAHR-toh (room), and *usted* oos-

TAYD (formal form of you); when it follows a "q" the **u** is silent: *que* kay (what); when it follows an "h" or has an umlaut, it's pronounced like "w": *Argüelles* are-GWAY-yez (neighborhood in Madrid)

Consonants

b, d, f, k, l, m, n, p, q, s, t, v, w, x, y, z, and ch
pronounced almost as in English; **h** occurs, but is silent – not pronounced at all.

c like k as in "keep": *cuarto* KOOAR-toh (room); when it precedes "e" or "i," pronounce **c** like th, as in "this": *cerveza* thair-VAY-sah (beer), *encima* ayn-THEE-mah (atop). Note that this lisping "th" is unique to Spanish in Spain and is not used by other speakers of Spanish

g like g as in "gift" when it precedes "a," "o," "u," or a consonant: *gato* GAH-toh (cat), *hago* AH-goh (I do, make); otherwise, pronounce **g** like h as in "hat": *giro* HEE-roh (money order), *gente* HAYN-tay (people)

j like h, as in "has": *Jueves* HOOAY-vays (Thursday), *mejor* may-HOR (better)

ll like y, as in "yes": *toalla* toh-AH-yah (towel), *ellos* AY-yohs (they, them)

ñ like ny, as in "canyon": *año* AH-nyo (year), *señor* SAY-nyor (Mr., sir)

r is lightly trilled, with tongue at the roof of your mouth like a very light English d, as in "ready": *pero* PAY-doh (but), *tres* TDAYS (three), *cuatro* KOOAH-tdoh (four).

rr like a Spanish r, but with much more emphasis and trill. Let your tongue flap. Practice with *perro* pay RROH (dog), *carretera* ka-rray-TAY-ra (highway), and *Carrillo* (proper name), then really let go with *ferrocarril* fay-rroh-CA-rreel (railroad).

y sounds like the English y except when being used as the Spanish word for "and," as in "Alfonso y Susana." In such case, pronounce it like the English ee, as in "keep": Alfonso "ee" Susana

z is pronounced like a soft th as in "pith": *zapato* tha-PAH-toe (shoe), *Zaragoza* tha-ra-GO-tha (capital of Aragón).

Accent

The rule for accent, the relative stress given to syllables within a given word, is straightforward. If a word ends in a vowel, an "n," or an "s," accent the next-to-last syllable; if not, accent the last syllable.

Pronounce *gracias* GRAH-theahs (thank you), *orden* OHR-dayn (order), and *carretera* kah-ray-TAY-rah (highway) with stress on the next-to-last syllable.

Otherwise, accent the last syllable: *venir* vay-NEER (to come), *ferrocarril* fay-roh-cah-REEL (railroad), and *edad* ay-DAHD (age).

Exceptions to the accent rule are always marked with an accent sign: (á, é, í, ó, or ú), such as *teléfono* tay-LAY-foh-noh (telephone), *jabón* hah-BON (soap), and *rápido* RAH-pee-doh (rapid).

BASIC AND COURTEOUS EXPRESSIONS

Most Spanish-speaking people consider formalities important. Whenever approaching anyone for information or some other reason, do not forget the appropriate salutation – good morning, good evening, etc. Standing alone, the greeting *hola* (hello) can sound brusque.

Hello. *Hola.*
Good morning. *Buenos días.*
Good afternoon. *Buenas tardes.*
Good evening. *Buenas noches.*
How are you? *¿Cómo está usted?*
Very well, thank you. *Muy bien, gracias.*
Okay; good. *Bien.*
Not okay; bad. *Mal.*
So-so. *Más o menos.*
And you? *¿Y usted?*
Thank you. *Gracias.*
Thank you very much. *Muchas gracias.*
You're very kind. *Muy amable.*
You're welcome. *De nada.*
Goodbye. *Adios.*
See you later. *Hasta luego.*
please *por favor*
yes *sí*
no *no*
I don't know. *No sé.*

Just a moment, please. *Momentito, por favor.*

Excuse me, please (when you're trying to get attention). *Disculpe or Con permiso.*

Excuse me (when you've done something wrong). *Lo siento.*

Pleased to meet you. *Mucho gusto or Encantado/a.*

What is your name? *¿Cómo se llama usted?*

Do you speak English? *¿Habla usted inglés?*

Is English spoken here? (Does anyone here speak English?) *¿Se habla inglés?*

I don't speak Spanish well. *No hablo bien el español.*

I don't understand. *No entiendo.*

How do you say... in Spanish? *¿Cómo se dice... en español?*

My name is... *Me llamo...*

Would you like... *¿Quisiera usted...*

Let's go to... *Vamos a...*

TERMS OF ADDRESS

When in doubt, use the formal *usted* (you) as a form of address, though Spaniards under the age of 40 normally use the familiar *tu*.

I *yo*
you (formal) *usted*
you (familiar) *tu*
he/him *él*
she/her *ella*
we/us *nosotros*
you (plural) *ustedes*
they/them *ellos* (all males or mixed gender); *ellas* (all females)
Mr., sir *señor*
Mrs., madam *señora*
miss, young lady *señorita*
wife *mujer*
husband *marido*
friend *amigo* (male); *amiga* (female)
boyfriend; girlfriend *novio; novia*
son; daughter *hijo; hija*
brother; sister *hermano; hermana*
father; mother *padre; madre*
grandfather; grandmother *abuelo; abuela*

TRANSPORTATION

Where is...? *¿Dónde está...?*

How far is it to...? *¿A cuánto está...?*
from... to... *de... a...*
Where (Which) is the way to...? *¿Dónde está el camino a...?*
the bus station *la terminal de autobuses*
the bus stop *la parada de autobuses*
Where is this bus going? *¿Adónde va este autobús?*
the taxi stand *la parada de taxis*
the train station *la estación de ferrocarril, la estación de trenes, or Renfe*
the boat *el barco*
the airport *el aeropuerto*
I'd like a ticket to... *Quisiera un billete a...*
first (second) class *primera (segunda) clase*
round-trip *ida y vuelta*
reservation *reservación*
baggage *equipaje*
Stop here, please. *Pare aquí, por favor.*
the entrance *la entrada*
the exit *la salida*
the ticket office *la oficina de billetes*
(very) near; far *(muy) cerca; lejos*
to; toward *a*
by; through *por*
from *de*
the right *la derecha*
the left *la izquierda*
straight ahead *derecho; directo*
in front *en frente*
beside *al lado*
behind *atrás*
the corner *la esquina*
the stoplight *la semáforo*
a turn *una vuelta*
right here *aquí*
somewhere around here *por acá*
right there *allí*
somewhere around there *por allá*
street; boulevard *calle; bulevar*
highway *carretera*
bridge; toll *puente; peaje*
address *dirección*
north; south *norte; sur*
east; west *oriente (este); poniente (oeste)*

ACCOMMODATIONS

hotel *hotel*

Is there a room? *¿Hay cuarto?*
May I (may we) see it? *¿Puedo (podemos) verlo?*
What is the rate? *¿Cuál es el precio?*
Is that your best rate? *¿Es su mejor precio?*
Is there something cheaper? *¿Hay algo más económico?*
a single room *un cuarto sencillo*
a double room *un cuarto doble*
double bed *cama matrimonial*
twin beds *camas gemelas*
with private bath *con baño*
hot water *agua caliente*
shower *ducha*
towels *toallas*
soap *jabón*
toilet paper *papel higiénico*
blanket *manta*
sheets *sábanas*
air-conditioned *aire acondicionado*
fan *ventilador*
key *llave*
manager *gerente*

FOOD

I'm hungry *Tengo hambre.*
I'm thirsty. *Tengo sed.*
menu *carta*
order *pedir*
glass *vaso*
fork *tenedor*
knife *cuchillo*
spoon *cuchara*
napkin *servilleta*
soft drink *refresco*
coffee *café*
tea *té*
bottled water *agua de botella*
tap water *agua de grifo*
bottled carbonated water *agua mineral*
bottled uncarbonated water *agua sin gas*
beer *cerveza*
wine *vino*
milk *leche*
juice *zumo*
cream *crema*
sugar *azúcar*
cheese *queso*

snack *merienda*
breakfast *desayuno*
lunch *almuerzo, comida*
daily lunch special *el menú del día*
dinner *cena*
the check *la cuenta*
eggs *huevos*
bread *pan*
salad *ensalada*
fruit *fruta*
mango *mango*
watermelon *sandía*
papaya *papaya*
banana *plátano*
apple *manzana*
orange *naranja*
lime *limón*
fish *pescado*
shellfish *mariscos*
shrimp *gambas*
(without) meat *(sin) carne*
chicken *pollo*
pork *cerdo*
beef; steak *carne; bistec*
bacon; ham *tocino; jamón*
fried *frito*
roasted *asada*
barbecue; barbecued *barbacoa; al carbón*

SHOPPING

money *dinero*
money-exchange bureau *cambio*
I would like to exchange travelers checks. *Quisiera cambiar cheques de viajero.*
What is the exchange rate? *¿Cuál es el tipo de cambio?*
How much is the commission? *¿Cuánto cuesta la comisión?*
Do you accept credit cards? *¿Aceptan tarjetas de crédito?*
money order *giro*
How much does it cost? *¿Cuánto cuesta?*
expensive *caro*
cheap *barato; económico*
more *más*
less *menos*
a little *un poco*
too much *demasiado*

HEALTH

Help me please. *Ayúdeme por favor.*
I am ill. *Estoy enfermo.*
Call a doctor. *Llame un doctor.*
Take me to... *Lléveme a...*
hospital *hospital; sanatorio*
drugstore *farmacia*
pain *dolor*
fever *fiebre*
headache *dolor de cabeza*
stomachache *dolor de estómago*
burn *quemadura*
cramp *calambre*
nausea *náusea*
vomiting *vomitando*
medicine *medicina*
antibiotic *antibiótico*
pill; tablet *pastilla*
aspirin *aspirina*
ointment; cream *pomada; crema*
cotton *algodón*
sanitary napkins *use brand name, e.g.,*
  Kotex
birth control pills *pastillas anticonceptivas*
contraceptive foam *espuma anticonceptiva*
condoms *preservativos; condones*
toothbrush *cepilla dental*
toothpaste *pasta de dientes*
dentist *dentista*
toothache *dolor de muelas*

POST OFFICE AND COMMUNICATIONS

long-distance telephone *teléfono larga distancia*
I would like to call... *Quisiera llamar a...*
collect *por cobrar*
station to station *a quien contesta*
person to person *persona a persona*
credit card *tarjeta de crédito*
post office *correo*
general delivery *lista de correo*
letter *carta*
stamp *estampilla*
postcard *tarjeta*
air mail *correo aereo*
registered/certified *certificado*
money order *giro*

package; box *paquete; caja*
string; tape *cuerda; cinta*

AT THE BORDER

border *frontera*
customs *aduana*
immigration *migración*
tourist card *tarjeta de turista*
inspection *inspección; revisión*
passport *pasaporte*
profession *profesión*
marital status *estado civil*
single *soltero*
married; divorced *casado; divorciado*
widowed *viudado*
insurance *seguros*
title *título*
driver's license *carnet de conducir*

AT THE GAS STATION

gas station *gasolinera*
gasoline *gasolina*
unleaded *sin plomo*
full, please *lleno, por favor*
tire *rueda*
air *aire*
water *agua*
oil (change) *aceite (cambio)*
grease *grasa*
My... doesn't work. *Mi... no sirve.*
battery *batería*
radiator *radiador*
alternator *alternador*
generator *generador*
tow truck *grúa*
repair shop *taller mecánico*

VERBS

Verbs are the key to getting along in Spanish. They employ mostly predictable forms and come in three classes, which end in *ar, er,* and *ir,* respectively:
to buy *comprar*
I buy, you, he (she, it) buys *compro, compras, compra*
we, you, they buy *compramos, comprais, compran*
to eat *comer*

I buy, you, he (she, it) eats *como, comes, come*
we, you, they eat *comemos, comeis, comen*
to climb *subir*
I climb, you, he (she, it) climbs *subo, subes, sube*
we climb, you, they climb *subimos, subeis, suben*
to do or make *hacer*
I do or make, you, he (she, it) does or makes *hago, haces, hace*
we do or make, you, they do or make *hacemos, haceis, hacen*
to go *ir*
I go, you, he (she, it) goes *voy, vas, va*
we go, you, they go *vamos, vais, van*
to go (walk) *andar*
to love *amar*
to work *trabajar*
to want *querer*
to need *necesitar*
to read *leer*
to write *escribir*
to repair *reparar*
to stop *parar*
to get off (the bus) *bajar*
to arrive *llegar*
to stay (remain) *quedar*
to stay (lodge) *hospedar*
to leave *salir* (regular except for *salgo*, I leave)
to look at *mirar*
to look for *buscar*
to give *dar* (regular except for *doy*, I give)
to carry *llevar*
to have *tener* (irregular but important: *tengo, tienes, tiene, tenemos, teneis, tienen*)
to come *venir* (similarly irregular: *vengo, vienes, viene, venimos, veneis, vienen*)

Spanish has two forms of "to be." Use *estar* when speaking of location or a temporary state of being: "I am at home." "*Estoy en casa.*" "I'm sick." "*Estoy enfermo.*" Use *ser* for a permanent state of being: "I am a doctor." "*Soy medico.*" *Estar* is regular except for *estoy*, I am. *Ser* is very irregular:
to be *ser*
I am, you, he (she, it) is *soy, eres, es*
we are, you, they are *somos, sois, son*

NUMBERS

zero *cero*
one *uno*
two *dos*
three *tres*
four *cuatro*
five *cinco*
six *seis*
seven *siete*
eight *ocho*
nine *nueve*
10 *diez*
11 *once*
12 *doce*
13 *trece*
14 *catorce*
15 *quince*
16 *dieciseis*
17 *diecisiete*
18 *dieciocho*
19 *diecinueve*
20 *veinte*
21 *veinte y uno* or *veintiuno*
30 *treinta*
40 *cuarenta*
50 *cincuenta*
60 *sesenta*
70 *setenta*
80 *ochenta*
90 *noventa*
100 *ciento*
101 *ciento y uno* or *cientiuno*
200 *doscientos*
500 *quinientos*
1,000 *mil*
10,000 *diez mil*
100,000 *cien mil*
1,000,000 *millón*
one half *medio*
one third *un tercio*
one fourth *un cuarto*

TIME

What time is it? *¿Qué hora es?*
It's one o'clock. *Es la una.*
It's three in the afternoon. *Son las tres de la tarde.*
It's 4 A.M. *Son las cuatro de la mañana.*

six-thirty *seis y media*
a quarter till eleven *un cuarto para las once*
a quarter past five *las cinco y cuarto*
an hour *una hora*

DAYS AND MONTHS
Monday *lunes*
Tuesday *martes*
Wednesday *miércoles*
Thursday *jueves*
Friday *viernes*
Saturday *sábado*
Sunday *domingo*
today *hoy*
tomorrow *mañana*
yesterday *ayer*
January *enero*

February *febrero*
March *marzo*
April *abril*
May *mayo*
June *junio*
July *julio*
August *agosto*
September *septiembre*
October *octubre*
November *noviembre*
December *diciembre*
a week *una semana*
a month *un mes*
after *después*
before *antes*

Suggested Reading

ARTS AND CULTURE

Gibson, Ian. *Federico García Lorca: A Life.* Faber and Faber, UK/Pantheon US, 1999. Written by a long-time resident of Spain and an acute chronicler of Spanish culture and society, this award-winning book is a fascinating insight into this emblematic Spanish poet who was killed by Nationalist forces at the beginning of the Spanish Civil War. Look also for Gibson's *The Shameful Life of Salvador Dalí* (W. W. Norton, 1998), an ambitious and fascinating biography of the Spanish surrealist.

Hemingway, Ernest. *Death in the Afternoon.* Since first being published in 1930, this book has been hailed as the best English-language introduction to bullfighting. Hemingway examines the *corrida de toros* with wonderful detail, history, anecdotes, and photographs, revealing both the pageantry and the art of this quintessentially Spanish spectator sport.

Moffitt, John F. *The Arts in Spain.* Thames and Hudson, 1999. From cave paintings to Picasso, this book provides an essential and highly accessible introduction to Spain's artistic trends and treasures.

Riley, Terence. *On Site: New Architecture in Spain.* Museum of Modern Art, 2006. Ever since Frank Gehry's Guggenheim Museum in Bilbao put Spain on the map of modern architecture, ambitious Spanish developers have commissioned dozens of cutting-edge buildings. This handy paperback details the best of them.

Totton, Robin. *Song of the Outcasts: An Introduction to Flamenco.* Amadeus Press, 2003. Written by a British correspondent for a Spanish flamenco magazine, this wonderful book offers an easy-to-read introduction to this passionate art form. Be sure and pick up the version that comes with a bonus flamenco CD.

von Bremzen, Anya. *The New Spanish Table.* Workman Publishing Company, 2005. There are hundreds of Spanish cookbooks on the market but this one is destined to be a classic. Alongside recipes from simple peasant dishes to traditional tapas to new Catalan cuisine, von Bremzen, a long-time resident of Spain, offers engaging cultural and social commentary.

HISTORY

Brenan, Gerald. *The Spanish Labyrinth.* Cambridge University Press, 1990. Brenan lived in Southern Spain for years before the outbreak of the Spanish Civil War and this book is a fascinating account of the social and political climate that led to the conflict.

Carr, Raymond, ed. *Spain: A History.* Oxford University Press, USA, 2001. Compiled, edited, and written by an acknowledged expert in the field, this new history takes the whole of Spain's fractious, complicated past—from prehistory through the 16th-century Spanish empire to the fall of dictatorship and the rise of democracy—and makes it both readable and enjoyable. Look also for Carr's books *Modern Spain 1808–1975, Phoenix: The Spanish Tragedy, the Civil War in Perspective,* and *From Dictatorship to Democracy.*

Fletcher, Richard. *Moorish Spain.* University of California Press, 1993. This excellent introduction to the culture and history of Spain under the rule of the Moors uses examples from Arabic poetry, architecture, and politics to recreate Moorish Spain. He also makes a convincing argument that Moorish Spain served as a conduit for Islamic philosophy into European consciousness during the Middle Ages.

Fraser, Ronald. *Blood of Spain: An Oral History of the Spanish Civil War.* Pantheon, 1986. Weaving together memories and stories from hundreds of Spaniards from all political allegiances and social backgrounds—Nationalist and Republican, soldiers and civilians, rich and poor—this book presents a fascinating insight into what it was like to live through the Spanish Civil War.

Hooper, John. *The New Spaniards.* Penguin, 1995. First published in 1986, this book vividly describes Spanish society from the death of Franco to the end of the 20th century. Hooper was a correspondent for a prominent British paper during the 1980s and this book is an excellent sociological and culturally study of that fascinating time. A classic if you want to understand contemporary Spain.

Menocal, María Rosa. *The Ornament of the World.* Back Bay Books, 2003. This very readable history book documents the era when Christians, Jews, and Muslims lived side by side. Though often contentious, the overall theme from 786 to 1492 was of peaceful coexistence where culture, philosophy, and poetry flourished. Death, genocide, and horror only arose when one culture decided it was better than the others—a scenario tragically played out again and again in the history of the world.

Orwell, George. *Homage to Catalonia.* Harvest Books, 1969. In 1936, Orwell traded his pen for a rifle and joined a Catalan brigade of militia soldiers fighting against Franco's Nationalist forces. This book vividly describes his experiences in the trenches and gives a thoughtful analysis of why the war ended as it did. Though by no means a traditional history, it is one of the most fascinating reads of this horrible time in Spanish history.

Tremlett, Giles. *Ghosts of Spain: Travels Through a Country's Hidden Past.* Faber and Faber, 2006. Mixing the genres of history, travel, and journalism, this engaging book provides insight into how Spain's past continues to influence its present. Written by a journalist and long-time resident of Spain, the book shines an eloquent light on topics, facts, and memories that many Spaniards would prefer not to discuss. In doing so, it offers a fascinating analysis of modern Spanish culture.

Williams, Mark R. *The Story of Spain: The Dramatic History of Europe's Most Fascinating Country.* Golden Era Books, 2004. A highly readable and comprehensive overview of Spain's history and culture up to the turn of the millennium.

LITERATURE

Cervantes, Miguel de. *Don Quijote*. First published in 1605, Cervantes's tale of the bumbling knight Don Quixote de la Mancha and his faithful sidekick Sancho Panza is quite arguably the most famous novel ever published. If you only read it in high school, it deserves a re-read. Look for the excellent translation by Edith Grossman (Harper Perennial, 2005) or grab one of the dozens of other translations at your local library.

Gordon, Noah. *The Last Jew*. St. Martin's Griffin, 2002. Set during the 15th century at the height of the Spanish Inquisition, this historical novel tells the story of Yonah Helkias, a 16-year-old who is left behind in Spain when his Jewish family is forced to flee the country. His brother and father wind up dead and Yonah sets out on a life of wandering and waiting for vengeance.

Hemingway, Ernest. *For Whom the Bell Tolls*. This classic novel, first published in 1940, tells of a young American soldier with the International Brigades who joins an antifascist Republican unit during the Spanish Civil War. Hemingway's earlier book, the 1926 *The Sun Also Rises*, recounts the antics of a group of expatriates in Europe in the 1920s. Originally titled *Fiesta!* by Hemingway, the book made the running of the bulls in Pamplona an international phenomenon.

Marías, Javier. *A Heart So White*. New Directions, 2002. This award-winning novel by one of Spain's most popular contemporary writers tells the tale of a Spanish son unearthing the murky past of his twice-widowed father. The writing is at turns quirky, intelligent, engaging, and unforgettable.

Michener, James. *The Drifters*. Fawcett, 1986. Though a bit dated, this novel by one of the greatest travel writers of all time follows six young Americans as they navigate their lives through 1960s Spain and North Africa.

Ruiz Zafón, Carlos. *The Shadow of the Wind*. Penguin, 2005. A bestseller in Europe, this intriguing novel tells the story of the son of a bookshop owner who becomes obsessed with a book and its mysterious author. Equal parts thriller, historical fiction, mystery, and love story, this book has garnered comparisons to Umberto Eco, Paul Auster, and Gabriel García Márquez. Set in 1950s Barcelona, it offers a fascinating glimpse into a city still very much in mourning after the tragedies of the Civil War.

Vázquez Montalban, Manuel. *Southern Seas*. Serpent's Tail, 2000. Pepe Carvalho is a hard-drinking detective with a penchant for fine food and frequent women. He is the starring character in a series of novels by the late Spanish writer, Vázquez Montalban. In this tale, the hunt for the killers of a wealthy businessman takes him through the streets of Barcelona, providing an enthralling look at the city's cultural identity from its seedy underside to its bourgeoisie upper crust.

TRAVEL AND IMPRESSIONS

Brenan, Gerald. *South to Granada*. Kodansha Globe Series, 1998. First published in the 1920s, this travel memoir describing the author's experiences in a small Spanish village near Granada still resonates with truth and clarity despite the passing of decades, a Civil War, a dictatorship, and a return to democracy. It is a classic well worth seeking out.

Cela, Camilo José. *Journey to the Alcarria*. University of Wisconsin Press, 1990. Written by a Nobel prize–winner, this book deftly details the author's experiences in rural Castile in 1946.

Irving, Washington. *Tales of the Alhambra*. Kessinger Publishing, 2004. The author of *The Legend of Sleepy Hollow* served as a diplomat in Spain and in 1829 actually lived in the then-abandoned Alhambra Palace in Granada. This collection of stories and impressions of the palace captured audiences on both sides of the Atlantic and sparked efforts to restore the magnificent Moorish palace.

Lee, Laurie. *As I Walked Out One Midsummer Morning*. Viking, 1979. This classic of travel writing details the adventures of a young Englishman who left his home in 1934 to walk across Spain. He had never been away from his hometown before and his only travel companion was his violin. Though a bit outdated, Lee's sense of wonder and lyrical prose make this a good read.

Lewis, Norman. *Voices of the Old Sea*. Caroll & Graf, 2006. This engaging book captures both the delights and hardships of life in a tiny fishing village on the Costa Brava. It is a fascinating account of a world—and people—long-gone. Soon after Lewis arrived on the Costa Brava, the touristic hordes did too, forever changing the region from a string of sleepy fishing villages into a concrete swath of vacation resorts. In *The Day of the Fox*, Lewis tells of a soldier mistakenly decorated for heroism by Franco's Nationalist government and the fallout of those accolades upon returning to his small village after the Civil War. It is a good account of the bitter post-war clash between those on opposite sides of the battle. Sadly, that bitterness simmers even today.

Michener, John. *Iberia*. Random House, 1989. Don't let the mammoth proportions of this book scare you off. Michener's passionate account of his travels in the Spain of the 1960s vividly brings to life a country on the brink of massive change. This is a classic, not only of Spanish travel, but of the genre in general.

Nooteboom, Cees. *Roads to Santiago: A Modern-Day Pilgrimage Through Spain*. Harcourt, 2000. Among the hundreds of books about the Camino de Santiago, this one stands out specifically because the Camino takes a back seat. Less about a spiritual quest than a Spanish odyssey, Nooteboom explores Spain by always taking the road less traveled. His observations on Spanish art, architecture, and culture are wonderfully written and shimmer with a love and respect for Spain that is infectious.

Richardson, Paul. *Our Lady of the Sewers*. Abacus, 2001. This entertaining book details the author's journeys way, way off the beaten path in search of Spain's quirkiest festivals and most obscure traditions. At turns hilarious and intriguing, this book details a fascinating side of Spanish culture that few outsiders get to see.

Stewart, Chris. *Driving over Lemons*. Vintage, 2001. One-time drummer of the rock band Genesis and professional sheep-shearer, Stewart weaves an engaging and funny tale of moving his family to a remote farm in Andalucía and setting down roots among a hilarious cast of local characters. His follow-up, *A Parrot in a Pepper Tree* (Sort of Books, 2002), details the family's ongoing Andalusian adventures from enrolling his daughter in the local school to accepting the presence of a rogue parrot into the household.

Webster, Jason. *Duende: A Journey in Search of Flamenco*. Broadway, 2003. In this lighthearted and highly entertaining travel memoir, the author tells of his attempts to become part of the flamenco world. Less about flamenco than about the author's decision to abandon his life of academia in search of his flamenco soul and all the cultural clashes that ensued, this book is an engaging read for those with wanderlust in their hearts.

Internet Resources

No trip to Spain (or anywhere for that matter) should be undertaken without at least a perusal of the resources available on the Internet. From hotel reviews to directions to museums to social groups, the quantity of information is staggering. Unfortunately, the quality varies from excellent to dismal. The following brief list comprises the most useful sites we've come across. Obviously there are hundreds more. The best advice for wading through it all is to never stick with just one site on a topic, read a few to find the least biased information. You may want to also do a search for your hobby or personality. A hiker might search for "hiking in Spain" and a gay or lesbian traveler could search for "gay Spain." Finally, do take time to search the travel sections of the online archives of major newspapers. All of the major American papers regularly do stories on Spain. Because flights from Great Britain to Spain are so cheap, the British papers offer heavy coverage of Spain for all budgets. One of the best sources is the *Guardian UK* (www.guardian.co.uk). For websites on specific regions within Spain, please refer to that region's travel chapter within this book.

TRAVEL INFORMATION

Spain Tourism
www.spain.info

This is the official website of the Spanish tourism industry and it is a mother lode of information on Spanish cities small and large, cultural sights, routes, museums, food, transportation, and more. Though a bit dry in tone, the information is solid and comes in English. They will offer links to the main tourism sites for regions throughout Spain, but unfortunately not all of those are in English. Check the destination chapters of this book for specific addresses.

All About Spain
www.red2000.com

This simple site gives solid introductory advice on all regions of Spain as well as basic information on culture, traditions, and customs.

Spanish Fiestas
www.spanish-fiestas.com

Run by an expat couple who offer cultural tours to Spanish fiestas, this site is incredibly comprehensive, useful, and friendly.

Spain and Portugal for Visitors
www.spainforvisitors.com

Run by travel writer John Gordon Ross, this comprehensive site touches on all sorts of topics related to Spain from "food and drink" to "what's on." It is definitely a good place to browse for a while. He also offers extensive links to other sites of interest.

TRIP PRACTICALITIES

State Department
www.state.gov

For basic statistics and the latest U.S. government statements about Spain as well as all the legalities of visiting Spain, you can't go wrong with the State Department's site.

Spanish Airports
www.aena.es

The group Aeropuertos Españoles y Navagación Aérea runs the majority of Spain's airports and their website offers a review of each airport in the system, including flight information.

CURRENT AFFAIRS

Expatica
www.expatica.com

Aimed at the European expatriate community, this website offers the current news of Spain in English, plus a wealth of articles aimed at Spain-based expats and visitors.

Index

MAP SYMBOLS

≡≡≡	Expressway	**【**	Highlight	✕	Airfield	⚓	Golf Course
—	Primary Road	○	City/Town	✈	Airport	**P**	Parking Area
—	Secondary Road	⊕	State Capital	▲	Mountain	▲	Archaeological Site
- - - -	Unpaved Road	⊛	National Capital	✦	Unique Natural Feature	♠	Church
- - - -	Trail	★	Point of Interest			▣	Gas Station
··········	Ferry	•	Accommodation	⋰	Waterfall	◌	Glacier
-••-••-	Railroad	▼	Restaurant/Bar	▲	Park		Mangrove
	Pedestrian Walkway	■	Other Location	**T**	Trailhead		Reef
▥▥▥▥	Stairs	▲	Campground	⛷	Skiing Area		Swamp

CONVERSION TABLES

$°C = (°F - 32) / 1.8$
$°F = (°C \times 1.8) + 32$
1 inch = 2.54 centimeters (cm)
1 foot = 0.304 meters (m)
1 yard = 0.914 meters
1 mile = 1.6093 kilometers (km)
1 km = 0.6214 miles
1 fathom = 1.8288 m
1 chain = 20.1168 m
1 furlong = 201.168 m
1 acre = 0.4047 hectares
1 sq km = 100 hectares
1 sq mile = 2.59 square km
1 ounce = 28.35 grams
1 pound = 0.4536 kilograms
1 short ton = 0.90718 metric ton
1 short ton = 2,000 pounds
1 long ton = 1.016 metric tons
1 long ton = 2,240 pounds
1 metric ton = 1,000 kilograms
1 quart = 0.94635 liters
1 US gallon = 3.7854 liters
1 Imperial gallon = 4.5459 liters
1 nautical mile = 1.852 km

MOON SPAIN

Avalon Travel Publishing
1400 65th Street, Suite 250
Emeryville, CA 94608, USA
www.moon.com

Editor: Erin Raber
Series Manager: Kathryn Ettinger
Acquisitions Manager: Rebecca K. Browning
Copy Editor: Ellie Behrstock
Graphics Coordinator: Stefano Boni
Cover Designer: Stefano Boni
Production Coordinator: Darren Alessi
Map Editor: Kevin Anglin
Cartographers: Kat Bennett, Chris Markiewicz,
    Kat Smith, Suzanne Service
Cartography Director: Mike Morgenfeld
Proofreader: Amy Scott
Indexer: Judy Hunt

ISBN-10: 1-59880-045-0
ISBN-13: 978-1-59880-045-6
ISSN: 1936-4938

Printing History
1st Edition – May 2007
5 4 3 2 1

Some photos and illustrations are used by permission
and are the property of the original copyright
owners.

Front cover photo: © jupiterimages / Workbook Stock /
    P. Shane O'Donnell
Title page photo: Sevilla's Barrio Santa Cruz
    © Seve Ponce de Leon
Interior photos: pg. 23, © Cellar Tours/www.cellar
tours.com; pg. 24, © www.thewinelove.com/
Gonzalo Gonzalo; pg. 25, © Francesc Guillamet;
pg. 26, © Candy Lee LaBalle; pg. 29, © Jeremy Reines/
www.multimadrid.com; pg. 29, © Seve Ponce de Leon;
pg. 30, © Candy Lee LaBalle; pg. 32, © Candy Lee
LaBalle; pg. 35, © Candy Lee LaBalle; pg. 38,
© C. Bolton; pg. 40, © Patricia Dawn Severenuk

Printed in the United States by Worzalla

KEEPING CURRENT

If you have a favorite gem you'd like to see included in the next edition, or see anything
that needs updating, clarification, or correction, please drop us a line. Send your
comments via email to feedback@moon.com, or use the address above.